Handbook of Human Rights

In mapping out the field of human rights for those studying and researching within both humanities and social science disciplines, the *Handbook of Human Rights* not only provides a solid foundation for the reader who wants to learn the basic parameters of the field, but also promotes new thinking and frameworks for the study of human rights in the twenty-first century.

The *Handbook* comprises over sixty individual contributions from key figures around the world, which are grouped according to eight key areas of discussion:

- foundations and critiques;
- new frameworks for understanding human rights;
- world religious traditions and human rights;
- social, economic, group, and collective rights;
- critical perspectives on human rights organizations, institutions, and practices;
- law and human rights;
- narrative and aesthetic dimensions of human rights;
- geographies of rights.

In its presentation and analysis of the traditional core history and topics, critical perspectives, human rights culture, and current practice, this *Handbook* proves a valuable resource for all students and researchers with an interest in human rights.

Thomas Cushman is Deffenbaugh de Hoyos Carlson Professor in the Social Sciences and Professor of Sociology at Wellesley College, USA. He is the Founding Editor and former Editor-in-Chief of *Human Rights Review*, and Founding Editor, former Editor-in-Chief, and Editor-at-Large for the *Journal of Human Rights*. He is a Faculty Associate of the Center for Cultural Sociology at Yale University and an Honorary Professor in the Social Sciences at the University of the Witwatersrand in Johannesburg, South Africa.

Handbook of Human Rights

Edited by Thomas Cushman

Routledge
Taylor & Francis Group
LONDON AND NEW YORK

First published 2014
by Routledge
2 Park Square, Milton Park, Abingdon, Oxon OX14 4RN

and by Routledge
711 Third Avenue, New York, NY 10017

Routledge is an imprint of the Taylor & Francis Group, an informa business

British Library Cataloguing in Publication Data
A catalogue record for this book is available from the British Library

Library of Congress Cataloging in Publication Data
Handbook of human rights / edited by Thomas Cushman.
p. cm.
1. Human rights–Handbooks, manuals, etc. I. Cushman, Thomas.
JC571.H34755 2011
323–dc22
2010048560

ISBN: 978-0-415-48023-9 (hbk)
ISBN: 978-1-138-01947-8 (pbk)
ISBN: 978-0-203-88703-5 (ebk)

Typeset in Bembo
by Cenveo Publisher Services

Printed and bound in the United States of America by
Edwards Brothers Malloy

This book is dedicated to the spirits of my mother, Dolores Cushman,
and my father, Orton Adelbert Cushman, III

Contents

Contributors

M. Rodwan Abouharb, Ph.D., Binghamton University, 2005, is a Lecturer in International Relations at University College London. His research examines human rights, World Bank and IMF structural adjustment, and civil and international conflict. His 2007 book *Human Rights and Structural Adjustment*, co-authored with David Cingranelli, won the *Choice* Outstanding Academic Title 2009. He has published widely in *International Studies Quarterly*, *Journal of Politics*, *Journal of Peace Research*, and *Review of International Organizations*.

Raquel Aldana, a Law Professor at Pacific McGeorge, is a prolific scholar who is an internationally recognized expert on matters of immigration law and human rights in the Americas. She is the founder and director of the Pacific McGeorge Inter-American Program, an innovative project committed to educating bilingual and bicultural lawyers who wish to pursue a domestic or transnational career with a focus on Latinos or U.S.–Latin American relations.

Clair Apodaca is an Associate Professor in the Department of Politics and International Relations at Florida International University. Dr. Apodaca has published extensively in the areas of the international protection of human rights, women's rights, and refugee studies. Her latest book, *Child Hunger and Human Rights: International Governance,* investigates the effects of national and international governmental policies on the incidence of chronic hunger in children. Currently she serves as Vice-Chair of the Human Rights section of the International Studies Association.

David Archard is Professor of Philosophy and Public Policy at Lancaster University, having previously taught at the universities of Ulster and of St. Andrews. He has published extensively in social, political, legal, and applied moral philosophy, particularly on the topics of children, family and state, and of sexual morality and the law. He is Chairman of the Society for Applied Philosophy and a Member of the United Kingdom's Human Fertilization and Embryology Authority.

Ariella Azoulay is the author *of Civil Imagination: The Political Ontology of Photography* (2011*)*, *Constituent Violence 1947–1950* (in Hebrew), *Act of State 1967–2007 – Photographic History of the Occupation* (2008, in Hebrew; 2009, in Italian), and *The Civil Contract of Photography* (2008). She is Curator of Untaken Photographs (2010, The Moderna Galerija, Lubliana, Zochrot, Tel Aviv), Architecture of Destruction (Zochrot, Tel Aviv), and Everything Could Be Seen. She is also the director of the documentary *I Also Dwell Among Your Own People: Conversations with Azmi Bishara* (2004), and *The Chain Food* (2004).

Mirko Bagaric is a Professor of Law at Deakin University, Australia. He is the author of over twenty books and 100 articles in major journals. He is also a lawyer practicing in human rights.

Florian Becker has taught as an Assistant Professor of German at Bard College since 2005. He studied philosophy, politics, and economics at Magdalen College, Oxford University, before earning his Ph.D. in German Literature at Princeton University. Recent articles have appeared in *Modern Drama* and the *Brecht Yearbook*. He is currently completing a book on Bertolt Brecht, Peter Weiss, and Heiner Müller, *How Theater Works: Realism as Critique in 20th-Century German Drama*.

Daniel A. Bell is Professor of Ethics and Political Philosophy at Tsinghua University (Beijing). His books include *The Spirit of Cities* (2011) and *China's New Confucianism* (2010) as well as the co-edited volumes *Ethics in Action: The Ethical Challenges of International NGOs* (2007) and *The East Asian Challenge for Human Rights* (1999).

Roger Berkowitz is an interdisciplinary scholar exploring the philosophical and ethical foundations of law and politics. He is Professor of Political Studies and Human Rights at Bard College where he is Academic Director of the Hannah Arendt Center for Ethical and Political Thinking. His first book, *The Gift of Science: Leibniz and the Modern Legal Tradition*, offers a genealogy of positive law through the history of science. He is co-editor of *Thinking in Dark Times: Hannah Arendt on Ethics and Politics*.

Gerald J. Beyer, Ph.D., is Associate Professor of Christian Social Ethics at Saint Joseph's University (Philadelphia, PA). His areas of expertise are economic justice, human rights, solidarity, Catholic social thought, and contemporary Polish society. His publications include *Recovering Solidarity: Lessons from Poland's Unfinished Revolution* (2010) and articles in *Journal of Catholic Social Thought, Journal of Religious Ethics, Notre Dame Journal of Law, Ethics, and Public Policy*, and *Human Rights Review*.

Lorenz Blume, Ph.D., born 1971 in Germany, has been a member of the Economics Department at the Philipps-University of Marburg since 2008. He started his academic career as a Research Associate and Associate Professor at the University of Kassel. His areas of research are Institutional Economics, Regional Economics, and Economic Policy.

Graeme Bristol, a Canadian architect, is the founder and executive director of the Centre for Architecture and Human Rights, an international foundation advancing a rights-based approach to development in the practice of architecture through ongoing demonstration projects, research, and education programmes. He holds a master's in Architecture from the University of British Columbia and a master's in Human Rights Law from Queen's University Belfast.

Kerry Bystrom is Assistant Professor of English and Associate Director of the Foundations of Humanitarianism Program of the Human Rights Institute at the University of Connecticut, Storrs. She is also Research Associate at the School of Languages and Literatures at the University of the Witwatersrand and lecturer in the International Human Rights Exchange Program. She has published a variety of articles and book chapters on literature and visual culture, human rights, and humanitarianism.

Luigi Caranti (Ph.D. Boston University) is Associate Professor of Political Philosophy at the Università di Catania (Italy). His research interests are modern and contemporary philosophy (in particular Kant), human rights, and democratic peace theory. Publications include: *Kant and the Scandal of Philosophy* (2007); and "Perpetual War for Perpetual Peace? Reflections on the Realist Critique of Kant's Project" (*Journal of Human Rights*, 2006). He has been Visiting Professor at Columbia, ANU, and Marburg University.

Henry F. Carey is Associate Professor of Political Science at Georgia State University in Atlanta. His forthcoming books are: *Reaping What You Sow: Torture Reform in the United States, France, Argentina, and Israel* (2011) and *Privatizing the Democratic Peace: Policy Dilemmas of NGO Peacebuilding* (2011). He is editor of *What Difference Does the European Union Make for Human Rights and Democratization?* (2011) and was co-editor of the international law section's essays of the *International Studies Compendium*, published in 2010 by the International Studies Association.

Thomas Cushman is Deffenbaugh de Hoyos Carlson Professor in the Social Sciences and Professor of Sociology at Wellesley College, USA. He is the Founding Editor and former Editor-in-Chief of *Human Rights Review*, and Founding Editor, former Editor-in-Chief, and Editor-at-Large for the *Journal of Human Rights*. He is a Faculty Associate of the Center for Cultural Sociology at Yale University and an Honorary Professor in the Social Sciences at the University of the Witwatersrand in Johannesburg, South Africa.

Robert J. Delahunty is an Associate Professor of Law at the University of St. Thomas School of Law in Minneapolis, MN. He was previously the Deputy General Counsel in the White House Office of Homeland Security and a Special Counsel in the Office of Legal Counsel of the U.S. Department of Justice.

Marie-Bénédicte Dembour is Professor of Law and Anthropology at the University of Sussex. She is the author of *Who Believes in Human Rights? Reflections on the European Convention* (2003). She has co-edited *Culture and Rights: Anthropological Perspectives* (2001), *Paths to International Justice: Social and Legal Perspectives* (2007), and *Are Human Rights for Migrants? Critical Reflections on the Status of the Irregular Migrant in Europe and the United States* (Routledge, forthcoming).

Amitai Etzioni is a University Professor at the George Washington University. He has taught at the universities of Columbia, Harvard, and Berkeley and served as a Senior Advisor to the Carter White House and as a President of the American Sociological Association. He founded the Communitarian Network. His books include *The Active Society*, *The New Golden Rule*, *The Monochrome Society*, *New Common Ground*, and *Security First*.

Andrew Fagan, Ph.D., is Deputy Director and Director of Academic Programmes of the University of Essex, Human Rights Centre. He has lectured on human rights across the world and has a particular interest in the teaching of human rights in Central and East Asia. His research interests focus upon the philosophical foundations of human rights law, the relationship between cultural diversity and human rights, and that between religion and a respect for human rights principles. He is the author of *The State of Human Rights Atlas* (2010) and *Human Rights: Confronting Myths and Misunderstandings* (2009). He is the author of many journal articles and contributions to scholarly volumes.

Edward Feser is Associate Professor of Philosophy at Pasadena City College in Pasadena, CA. He has been a Visiting Assistant Professor at Loyola Marymount University in Los Angeles and a Visiting Scholar at the Social Philosophy and Policy Center at Bowling Green State University in Ohio. He is the author of *On Nozick, Philosophy of Mind, Locke, The Last Superstition: A Refutation of the New Atheism,* and *Aquinas,* and editor of *The Cambridge Companion to Hayek.*

Robert Fine is Professor of Sociology at the University of Warwick. His books include *Cosmopolitanism* (Routledge, 2007); *Democracy and the Rule of Law: Marx's Critique of the Legal Form* (2002; 1984 and 1985); *Political Investigations: Hegel, Marx, Arendt* (Routledge, 2001); *Being Stalked: A Memoir* (1997); and *Beyond Apartheid: Labour and Liberation in South Africa* (with Dennis Davis, 1990). His edited collections include: "Cosmopolitanism: Past and Future," with Vivienne Boon, Special issue of the *European Journal of Social Theory* April 2007; *Social Theory after the Holocaust* (with Charles Turner, 2000); *People, Nation and State* (with Edward Mortimer, 1999); *Civil Society: Democratic Perspectives* (with Shirin Rai, 1997); *Policing the Miners' Strike* (with Robert Millar, 1985); and *Capitalism and the Rule of Law* (with Richard Kinsey, John Lea, and Jock Young, 1979).

Doris Zames Fleischer, together with her late sister, disability rights activist Frieda Zames, is the author of *The Disability Rights Movement: From Charity to Confrontation* (2001). Dr Fleischer is now completing an updated version of this book. A full-time member of the Humanities Department at New Jersey Institute of Technology since 1988, she has published articles on disability issues and lectured on this subject at universities and other venues in the United States and abroad.

Michael Galchinsky is the author of *Jews and Human Rights: Dancing at Three Weddings* (2008) and "The Jewish Settlements in the West Bank: International Law and Israeli Jurisprudence" (2004). His current work is on two tracks: human rights law and counterterrorism, and problems in the study of human rights culture. He is a Professor of English at Georgia State University and a fellow of the Yale Center for Cultural Sociology.

Mark Goodale is Associate Professor of Conflict Analysis and Anthropology at George Mason University and series editor of Stanford Studies in Human Rights. He is the author, most recently, of *Surrendering to Utopia: An Anthropology of Human Rights* (2009), editor of *Human Rights: An Anthropological Reader* (2009), and co-editor of *Mirrors of Justice: Law and Power in the Post-Cold War Era* (2010) and *The Practice of Human Rights: Tracking Law Between the Global and the Local* (2007).

Michael Goodhart is Associate Professor of Political Science and Women's Studies at the University of Pittsburgh. His research focuses on global injustice and on the theory and practice of democracy and human rights in the context of globalization. Recent publications include *Democracy as Human Rights: Freedom and Equality in the Age of Globalization, Human Rights: Politics and Practice,* and *Human Rights in the 21st Century: Continuity and Change since 9/11.*

Don A. Habibi is Professor of Philosophy at the University of North Carolina Wilmington. He received his B.A. from UCLA and his M.A. and Ph.D. at Cornell University. His research interests focus on moral, legal, social, and political philosophy. At UNCW he is the recipient of the Chancellor's Teaching Excellence Award and the Distinguished Teaching Professorship Award.

Richard P. Hiskes is Professor of Political Science at the University of Connecticut with a specialty in political theory. He is also editor of the *Journal of Human Rights* and Associate Director of the Connecticut Human Rights Institute. He has published widely in the field of political theory and is the author of five books and numerous articles. His most recent book, *The Human Right to a Green Future: Environmental Rights and Intergenerational Justice* (2009), was selected co-winner of the American Political Science Association 2010 Award for Best Book in Human Rights Scholarship.

Bonny Ibhawoh is an Associate Professor of History and Director of the Centre for Peace Studies at McMaster University, Canada. His research interests include human rights history and peace and conflict studies. He was previously a Research Fellow at the Carnegie Council for Ethics and International Affairs, New York, and at the Danish Institute for Human Rights, Copenhagen. His book *Imperialism and Human Rights* was named *Choice* Outstanding Academic Title in 2007.

Jonathan B. Imber is Jean Glasscock Professor of Sociology at Wellesley College, where he has taught for the past thirty years. He is author and editor of ten books, including *Abortion and the Private Practice of Medicine* (1986) and *Trusting Doctors: The Decline of Moral Authority in American Medicine* (2008). He has been editor-in-chief of *Society* since 1998.

David Ingram is Professor of Philosophy at Loyola University of Chicago. He has taught courses on Continental as well as Anglo-American social philosophy and philosophy of law. His research interests include critical race theory, human rights, philosophy of social science, democratic theory, globalization, and immigration. His most recent books include *Group Rights* (2000), *Rights, Democracy and Fulfillment* (2004), *Law* (2006), and *Habermas* (2010); he is also the editor of several anthologies on critical theory and European social philosophy, including most recently *From Critical Theory to Structuralism* (2010).

Damien Keown is Professor of Buddhist Ethics in the History Department at Goldsmiths College, University of London. His research interests center on theoretical and applied issues in Buddhist ethics. He is founding co-editor of the *Journal of Buddhist Ethics*, the Routledge Critical Studies in Buddhism Series, and co-editor of the Routledge *Encyclopedia of Buddhism*. He is the author of many books on Buddhism including *The Nature of Buddhist Ethics, Buddhism and Bioethics*, and *Buddhism: A Very Short Introduction*.

Ari Kohen is Schlesinger Associate Professor of Political Science and Director of the Human Rights and Humanitarian Affairs Program at the University of Nebraska–Lincoln. His first book was *In Defense of Human Rights: A Non-Religious Grounding in a Pluralistic World* (Routledge, 2007). Recent articles have appeared in *Human Rights Review, Journal of Human Rights, Critical Review of International Social and Political Philosophy*, and *Polis*.

Jenny Kuper has worked for many years as a lawyer on issues involving children. Initially qualified as a UK solicitor, she then obtained a Ph.D. in international law and has written two books: *International Law Concerning Child Civilians in Armed Conflict* (1997) and *Military Training and Children in Armed Conflict: Law, Policy and Practice* (2005) and numerous articles. Since 1999 she has been employed as a Research Fellow at the London School of Economics and Political Science (LSE), where she is doing research on law and HIV/AIDS.

Fuyuki Kurasawa is Associate Professor of Sociology at York University in Toronto and Faculty Fellow of the Center for Cultural Sociology at Yale University. Kurasawa is the author of *The Ethnological Imagination: A Cross-Cultural Critique of Modernity* (2004) and *The Work of Global Justice: Human Rights as Practices* (2007). He is currently researching the history of the visual representation of humanitarian crises, as well as the use of social media by human rights campaigns.

Brian D. Lepard is Law Alumni Professor of Law at the University of Nebraska College of Law, where he teaches international human rights law, among other subjects. He worked for three years as a human rights specialist at the United Nations Office of the Bahá'í International Community. Professor Lepard has written numerous books and articles on international law, human rights, world religions, and ethics.

Daniel Levy is Associate Professor in the Department of Sociology at Stony Brook University in New York. As a political sociologist he is interested in issues of globalization, collective memory studies, and comparative-historical sociology. Among his books related to memory studies are: *The Holocaust and Memory in the Global Age* (2006) and *Human Rights and Memory* (2010), both with Natan Sznaider. He is co-editor, with Jeffrey Olick and Vered Vinitzky-Seroussi, of *The Collective Memory Reader* (2011).

Tibor R. Machan holds the R. C. Hoiles endowed chair in Business Ethics and Free Enterprise at the Argyros School of Business & Economics at Chapman University, Orange, CA. He has published some thirty books, edited another twenty plus, most of them focused on political philosophy, ethics, and business ethics as well as circa 200 papers in academic journals such as the *American Philosophical Quarterly*, *Review of Metaphysics*, *Philosophy of Social Science* and *Philosophy of Science*. His latest books are *The Morality of Business, A Profession of Human Wealth Care* (2009) and *The Promise of Liberty, A Non-Utopian Vision* (2009). His memoir is entitled *The Man Without a Hobby, Adventures of a Gregarious Egoist* (2006). His main work in political philosophy is entitled *Individuals and Their Rights* (1989).

Stephen May is Professor of Education in the School of Critical Studies in Education, Faculty of Education, University of Auckland, New Zealand. He is a leading international authority on language rights. Among his key books is *Language and Minority Rights* (Routledge, 2008), which has been recognized as one of the American Library Association *Choice*'s Outstanding Academic titles. Stephen is editor of the interdisciplinary journal, *Ethnicities* and associate editor of *Language Policy*.

Frédéric Mégret, Ph.D., is an Assistant Professor at the Faculty of Law, McGill University. He also holds the Canada Research Chair in the Law of Human Rights and Legal Pluralism and is affiliated with the McGill Centre of the same name. He is co-editor with Philip Alston of the forthcoming second edition of *The United Nations and Human Rights*. His work focuses on the theoretical dimensions of international human rights law.

Murray Milner, Jr. is Professor Emeritus of Sociology and Senior Fellow at the Institute for Advanced Studies in Culture at the University of Virginia. His books include *Freaks, Geeks, and Cool Kids,* and *Status and Sacredness*, which won the American Sociological Association's distinguished book award. Much of his work provides theoretical explanations of various status systems including Indian castes, American teenagers, religious rituals and doctrines, celebrities – and human rights.

Richard Mullender studied law in the universities of Exeter and Oxford before becoming a Lecturer in Exeter. He now works in Newcastle Law School and holds the post of Reader in Law and Legal Theory. He researches in the fields of human rights law, legal theory, and tort law. He has recently written on intimations of utopianism in British human rights law and is currently undertaking research on Holocaust denial and the well-ordered society.

Ereshnee Naidu is a Ph.D. student in the Sociology Department at the City University of New York, Graduate Center. She completed her master's degree at the University of the Witwatersrand in South Africa and was previously employed as a project manager and senior researcher at the Centre for the Study ofViolence and Reconciliation in South Africa and as the Programme Director for Africa and Asia at the International Coalition of Sites of Conscience in New York. Her research interests lie in the areas of reparations, memorialization, and transitional justice. In this regard she has conducted extensive research around the role of memorialization as a form of symbolic reparations in post-conflict contexts including South Africa, Sierra Leone, Kenya, Rwanda, and Liberia.

Irene Oh is Assistant Professor of Religion and Director of Peace Studies at the George Washington University. She is the author of *The Rights of God: Islam, Human Rights, and Comparative Ethics* (2007). She serves on the board for the Society of Christian Ethics, is a founding member of the Society for the Study of Muslim Ethics, and sits on Comparative Religious Ethics Group Steering Committee for the American Academy of Religion.

Elena Pariotti, Ph.D. in legal philosophy, is Professor at the University of Padua (Italy), Department of Comparative Law, Faculty of Political Sciences. She teaches human rights and legal theory. Her main research interests have been dealing with legal interpretation, theory of regulation and emerging technologies, multiculturalism, theory of international law, human rights, and international justice.

Esther D. Reed is Associate Professor of Theological Ethics, University of Exeter, UK. She is author of *The Ethics of Human Rights: Contested Doctrinal and Moral Problems* (2007) and *Good Work: Christian Ethics in the Workplace* (2010). She is currently working on issues of theology and international law including territorial borders and the militarization of humanitarian intervention, and she is co-editing *Civil Liberties, National Security and Prospects for Consensus: Legal, Philosophical and Religious Perspectives.*

Luis Roniger is a comparative political sociologist and Reynolds Professor of Latin American Studies at Wake Forest University. His publications include numerous articles in English, Spanish, Portuguese, Italian, Hebrew, Russian, and German, and fourteen books, among them: *Patrons, Clients and Friends*; *Clientelism, Democracy and Civil Society*; *The Legacy of Human-Rights Violations in the Southern Cone*; and *Globality and Multiple Modernities.* His most recent books are *The Politics of Exile in Latin America* (with Mario Sznajder, 2009) and *Transnational Politics in Central America* (2011).

Dan Saxon is the Leverhulme Visiting Professor of International Humanitarian Law and International Criminal Law at the University of Cambridge. For twelve years, Saxon was a prosecutor at the United Nations International Criminal Tribunal for the Former Yugoslavia, the last five years as a Senior Prosecutor. Saxon is the author of *To Save Her Life: Disappearance, Deliverance and the United States in Guatemala* (2007), as well as articles and book chapters about international justice.

Fabrizio Sciacca, B.A. in law, Ph.D. in legal philosophy, is Full Professor in Political Philosophy at the University of Catania, Italy. He has been Jean Monnet Professor of Human Rights. He is a key staff member of the Arts and Humanities Research Council (AHRC) (UK) International Research Network "Institutionalising Values: Beyond Human Rights?" at the University of Stirling, Scotland, UK. Sciacca's research has concentrated on political concepts and fundamental normative concepts in modern and contemporary philosophy. His current research concerns political liberalism, the idea of equality, and the theories of rights. These lines of research are mostly presented in the books *Ingiustizia politica* (2003) and *Filosofia dei diritti* (2010). He has edited four books on rights.

Roger Scruton is a Visiting Scholar at the American Enterprise Institute, Visiting Professor in the Philosophy department at Oxford University and Visiting Research Professor in Philosophy, St. Andrews University, Scotland. He is the author of 40 books, including works of philosophy, essays, fiction, and political theory. His latest publication is *The Uses of Pessimism* (2010). His writings have been translated into over 20 languages, and he is a Fellow of the British Academy, of the Royal Society of Literature, and of the European Academy of Arts and Sciences.

Irene Bruna Seu is a psychodynamic psychotherapist and senior lecturer in psychosocial studies at Birkbeck, University of London. For over ten years she has investigated moral apathy in response to information about human rights abuses through research grants from the Leverhulme Trust and the Nuffield Foundation. She has published widely on the topic and is currently running a multidisciplinary research project on how audiences respond to mediated humanitarian knowledge with colleagues from the London School of Economics and Political Sciences.

Hakan G. Sicakkan is Associate Professor of Comparative Politics at the University of Bergen, Norway. In addition to teaching European politics, he leads the EU-funded international project EUROSPHERE, focusing on the conditions for the emergence of a European public sphere. He is co-editor of the *Nordic Journal of Migration Research* and has authored the book *Do Our Citizenship Requirements Impede the Protection of Political Asylum Seekers? A Comparative Analysis of European Practices* (2008).

Sidonie Smith is Martha Guernsey Colby Collegiate Professor of English and Women's Studies and 2010 President of the Modern Language Association of America. Her fields of interest include human rights and personal narrative, autobiography studies, women's studies in literature, feminist and postcolonial theory. Recent publications include *Human Rights and Narrated Lives: The Ethics of Recognition* (with Kay Schaffer, 2004); the second edition of *Reading Autobiography: A Guide for Interpreting Life Narratives* (with Julia Watson, 2010); and numerous articles.

Marina Svensson is an Associate Professor at the Centre for East and Southeast Asia Studies, Lund University, Sweden. Her research focuses on legal, social, and media developments in China. Among her major works are *Debating Human Rights in China: A Conceptual and Political History* (2002). She is also a co-editor of *The Chinese Human Rights Reader* (2001) with Stephen Angle; *Gender Equality, Citizenship and Human Rights: Controversies and Challenges in China and the*

Nordic Countries (2010) with Pauline Stoltz, Zhongshan Sun, and Wang Qi; and *Making Law Work: Chinese Laws in Context* (2010) with Mattias Burell.

Natan Sznaider is Professor of Sociology in the School of Behavioral Sciences at the Academic College of Tel-Aviv-Yaffo in Israel. His recent publications include (together with Daniel Levy), *Human Rights and Memory* (2010).

Mario Sznajder occupies the Leon Blum Chair and is a Professor of Political Science at the Department of Political Science of the Hebrew University of Jerusalem, and he is a Research Fellow at the Truman Institute for the Advancement of Peace. His most recent book, with Luis Roniger, is *The Politics of Exile in Latin America* (2009). He has published a large number of scientific articles on human rights and democracy, democratization, Latin American politics, Fascism, and other subjects. He is Chair of the Research Committee on Democratization of IPSA – RC 13.

Justin Tiwald is Assistant Professor of Philosophy at San Francisco State University. He has published several articles on Confucian ethics and political philosophy, including "A Right of Rebellion in the *Mengzi*?" He has been Visiting Assistant Professor of Philosophy at the University of California, Berkeley.

John Torpey is Professor of Sociology at the Graduate Center, City University of New York. Among other works, he is the author of *Making Whole What Has Been Smashed: On Reparations Politics* (2006) and editor of *Politics and the Past: On Repairing Historical Injustices* (2004).

Nancy Tuana is DuPont/Class of 1949 Professor of Ethics and Director of the Rock Ethics Institute at Penn State University. Her current research focuses on climate change and human rights, as well as coupled epistemological–ethical issues regarding climate science. She is author of *Global Climate Change and Human Rights*, a forthcoming volume in the Penn State Press Essays on Human Rights series. She is a founding member of the Collaborative Program on the Ethical Dimensions of Climate Change and Co-Director of the Worldwide Universities Network Gender and Climate Change initiative.

Bryan S. Turner is the Presidential Professor of Sociology at the Graduate Center, the City University of New York. He was previously the Alona Evans Distinguished Visiting Professor at Wellesley College, USA. He recently published *Vulnerability and Human Rights* (2006) and *Rights and Virtues* (2008). With Engin Isin he edits the journal *Citizenship Studies*. He was awarded a Doctor of Letters by Cambridge University in 2009.

Margaret Urban Walker is Professor of Philosophy at Arizona State University. She is author of several books, including *Moral Understandings: A Feminist Study in Ethics*; *Moral Contexts*; *Moral Repair: Reconstructing Moral Relations After Wrongdoing*; and *What is Reparative Justice?* She has contributed to projects with the International Center for Transitional Justice on gender and reparations and on truth-telling as a transitional justice measure. She continues to work on an expressive conception of reparative justice and on the moral significance of post-conflict truth-telling.

Brenda Werth is Assistant Professor of Spanish and Latin American Studies at American University in Washington, D.C. Her research focuses on Latin American theater, performance, memory studies, and human rights. She is author of the book *Theater, Performance, and Memory Politics in Argentina* (2010). Her future project explores urban imaginaries in twenty-first century theater and performance in the Americas.

Iain Wilkinson is a Senior Lecturer in Sociology at the University of Kent, UK. His publications include *Anxiety in a Risk Society* (2001), *Suffering: A Sociological Introduction* (2005), and *Risk Vulnerability and Everyday Life* (2009).

Morton Winston is Professor of Philosophy and Chairman of the Department of Philosophy and Religion at the College of New Jersey. His areas of specialization include human rights, ethics, political philosophy, and philosophy of technology. Professor Winston served as chairman of Amnesty International USA's national board of directors from 1995 to 1997. In 2007 he held the Danish Distinguished Chair of Human Rights and International Relations at the Danish Institute of Human Rights in Copenhagen, Denmark.

Joshua J. Yates is Research Assistant Professor of Sociology at the University of Virginia and Director of the Program on Culture, Capitalism, and Global Change at the Institute of Advanced Studies in Culture. He is a cultural sociologist focusing on three overlapping themes: the changing moral foundations of economic life, the development and institutionalization of a rudimentary global culture, and the conflicts and dilemmas such processes are generating both at home and across the world.

John Yoo is a Professor of Law at the University of California at Berkeley. His new book is *Crisis and Command: A History of Executive Power from George Washington to George W. Bush* (2010). He has contributed to the editorial pages of the *Wall Street Journal, New York Times, Washington Post, Los Angeles Times, Philadelphia Inquirer,* and *Chicago Tribune.*

Acknowledgments

First, I would like to thank all of the contributors in this volume, who graciously accepted my offers to write for it and were fabulous at meeting deadlines, as well as patient with delays and my special editing requests. This volume is the fruit of a global network of outstanding scholars, who have contributed to a work that is truly expansive, powerful, and unique. It is an exciting collective vision of the field of human rights, and the authors deserve the lion's share of the credit for making the *Handbook of Human Rights* a reality.

I owe special thanks to the Wellesley College Committee on Faculty Awards for generous funding of the expenses related to the production of this scholarly effort, and my other research endeavors over the years. I would also like to offer special thanks to my editorial assistant, Norah Piehl, who did exceptional service editing and proofing the manuscript in the last stages of its production.

Specific individuals who assisted in many things personal and professional during the compilation of this volume deserve special attention: Jonathan Imber, Adriana Mihal, Bryan S. Turner, Peter Baehr, Jeffrey Grady, Laura DuBois, Simon Cottee, Carol Hartigan, Sophie Cushman, Eliza Cushman, and Elizabeth Cushman Brandjes. I owe a special debt to many members of the staff of Wellesley College, too numerous to mention, who have given selflessly of themselves in assisting my teaching and research at Wellesley College. They will know who they are. Gerhard Boomgaarden, my editor at Routledge, who helped me conceive of this project and did me the honor of selecting me as Editor-in-Chief. He is the consummate editor: brilliant, expansive, patient, and effective.

Introduction

Thomas Cushman

The *Handbook of Human Rights* is the product of several years of collaboration among some sixty-six authors who agreed to write original essays on topics within the field of human rights, broadly defined. The distinguishing characteristic of the *Handbook* is its theoretical, empirical, and epistemological pluralism. It represents an effort to reconfigure and redefine the study of human rights in the twenty-first century by expanding significantly the range and scope of what falls under the rubric of "human rights." The present effort is radical, in an intellectual sense, since it breaks from a number of traditional approaches to the study of human rights.

First, it is widely interdisciplinary in scope, perhaps more so than any existing compendium of this nature. In making this move, the *Handbook* offers perspectives from disciplines that have traditionally had little to say about human rights, but which are now moving to the forefront of human rights scholarship. Since the foundation of the Universal Declaration of Human Rights (1948), the theory of human rights has burgeoned into a major field of study and a powerful form of political practice. Up until relatively recently, scholarly contributions to the field of human rights have mainly come from philosophy, political science, and law. This intuitively makes sense, since human rights are inescapably about ethics, power and powerlessness, and the legal mechanisms by which human rights have been put into practice. Yet in the last decade or so, the discourse on human rights has become remarkably more pluralistic, moving beyond the confines of philosophical, legalistic, and political theoretical interpretive frameworks. This movement itself is an interesting question for the sociology of knowledge: how did it happen that perspectives on human rights began to emerge from scholarly fields such as anthropology, sociology, literary and cultural studies, and art history?

In some cases, as with anthropology, the very idea of universal human rights was treated with hostility from the very start, with a strong statement of condemnation of such rights put forth by the American Anthropological Association after the writing of the Universal Declaration of Human Rights. In sociology, questions regarding rights seemed normative, and the domination of positivism and scientism in sociology precluded serious examination of human rights issues. These disciplines have changed, partly as a result that scholars have realized that they have important empirical and theoretical insights to offer, insights that overcome the limitations of legalism and traditional political theory in terms of understanding basic questions such as: what are human rights? Where do they come from? Why do some people have them and some people do not? How are they realized through new institutional and organizational forms which have emerged in modernity? Traditional approaches offer answers to these questions, but we are now in the midst of a new interpretive and epistemological revolution in the study of human rights. The central task of this *Handbook* is to offer some of the most original new voices of this revolution.

Scholars in the traditional disciplines that have addressed human rights provided deep understandings of these questions, but they were not sufficient to answer the questions and problems and issues that have emerged as a result of the globalization of human rights discourse or the new social changes brought on by what Anthony Giddens (2002) has referred to as the "juggernaut" of modernity. The cultural discourse of human rights has become a permanent part of the landscape of global modernity. Not only are traditional liberal ideas of individual rights now diffused across the globe, but also newer ideas of social, economic, group, and cultural rights. And with that diffusion, we see new intersections between these new global cultural models and the particular cultures of specific times and places. The very processes of modernity facilitated new perspectives from across the range of scholarly disciplines in order to make sense of this new human rights diffusion and to understand that diffusion in all of its complexity.

Rather than explain exactly how it is that this theoretical and epistemological pluralism has emerged, this collection presents it in its various forms. It begins with some traditional approaches from philosophy and political theory, in homage to the important and enduring contributions of these fields to the foundations of understanding human rights. There is always the danger in the rise of the new – and the emergent interpretive frameworks on human rights are decidedly new – that the contributions of classical foundations are lost. In this respect, Part I of the *Handbook* presents chapters on the historical and philosophical underpinnings of the study of human rights, which are the firm bedrock upon which new understandings must proceed.

In Part II, new perspectives, in particular from anthropology and sociology, are presented as examples of new thinking about human rights that serve as models for how the very idea of human rights might be re-conceptualized and re-envisioned. Anthropologists, for instance, having long resisted the ideas of human rights universalism, have abandoned the pure form of that critique, as well as an untenable critique of relativism, for a new approach which focuses not on the vexing question of whether or not there are any rights outside of particular cultures, but simply how supposed universalistic human rights ideas intersect with local and particular cultures (see, for instance, Cowan et al. 2001). Anthropologists have abandoned the interminable debate between universalism and relativism by making the turn toward ethnography to see exactly how it is and with what consequences universalistic cultural ideas intersect with local cultural practices in various times and places. Similarly, sociologists are beginning to look at human rights not so much in terms of the traditional ideas of social constructivism, which to date have been the most useful contribution, but in terms of how human rights operate in various social fields as cultural practices in the formation of systems of status and prestige or the formation of social movements. Thinking, for instance, as Murray Milner, Jr. does in Chapter 16, that human rights have become part of a system of status relations on a global scale is precisely an example of this new kind of sociological thinking about rights and allows us to ask a whole host of questions about the operation and meaning of human rights in modernity.

Part III includes chapters by scholars of religion who seek to understand the important relations between the major world religions and human rights. Some scholars have offered the view that human rights themselves are a new kind of what Auguste Comte once referred to as the "religion of humanity." Michael Perry (2000) has argued that human rights are "ineliminably religious" in their origins. A foundational approach to human rights must include a section on human rights and religion, especially since human rights are often offered as a secular replacement for more age-old and still quite salient religious belief systems. Religious belief systems are enduring facets of global culture and quite often new ideas of human rights run up against them, or, in some cases, complement some of the most elementary ideas of the major world religions. While much of religious thinking emphasizes duties that human beings have toward each other, human rights also imply duties and so it is interesting to see the intersections between religions and the various constructions of human rights (and not to forget that early rights struggles and movements were grounded and legitimated in very powerful religious language and beliefs, such as, for instance, the Digger movement in England in the seventeenth century).

The reader will immediately recognize that the focus of the *Handbook* is a non-geographical one, which favors a conception of rights as being related to specific categories of vulnerable populations rather than populations wholly contained within nation-states. Traditionally, it has been common for scholars to write about human rights in particular countries or continents. This makes sense historically, and even in the present, given the fact that it is still citizenship in a particular nation-state that is the principal means by which human beings realize their rights (or, lacking citizenship, do not enjoy the protection of rights). Yet, given the idea that human rights have become a widely diffused form of culture, it makes sense to move away from a purely geographical focus on human rights, since such a focus "contains" human rights in nation-states, the boundaries of which have become much more porous in a globalized world. Three chapters on human rights in China, Latin America, and Africa are included in Part VIII of the *Handbook* in order to show that nation-state and continental boundaries are still relevant to human rights. Yet, by the same token, the future study of human rights lies in recognizing the most fundamental categories of human vulnerability that transcend time and place and exist as something more general than citizenship status in this or that country.

Part IV focuses on these forms of vulnerability. The chapters in this part are grounded in the work of Bryan S. Turner, whose seminal work, *Vulnerability and Human Rights* (2006) attempts to steer clear of the Scylla and Charybdis of universalism and relativism. Turner argues that the one cultural universal that cannot be denied is that human beings are embodied and vulnerable creatures. Social institutions, in Turner's view, are structural attempts to alleviate this vulnerability, and human rights, as social constructs, emerge to alleviate the natural vulnerabilities of human beings. Following Turner, Part IV of the *Handbook* offers discussions of social, economic, group, and collective rights that seek to protect the various categories of human vulnerability. This part offers something like a "cradle to the grave" approach, looking at vulnerability as deeply structured in the biological life course – the fetus, the child, and the elderly are examples of vulnerable populations with special rights. The part also includes socially constructed categories of vulnerability – those who are vulnerable not by virtue of biology, but by social and historical contingency, such as refugees and other displaced persons; those people who, in relation to those who are privileged with resources and rights, are referred to by Zygmunt Bauman (2004) as "wasted lives."

Part V presents critical perspectives on human rights, although several chapters in other parts are also critical of human rights, especially those by Roger Scruton (Chapter 11) and Amitai Etzioni (Chapter 12). The *Handbook* is specifically designed to be critical, meaning that it problematizes and resists the usual idea of human rights as an ideal that is outside of history and of necessity worth valuing. Indeed, most of the authors in this volume would, if asked, value the idea of human rights, regardless of the complexities of just what is meant by the term "human rights" (for instance, which human rights do we value or are there any worth valuing above others and why?). It is quite uncommon to find students and scholars of human rights who are, so to speak, "against" human rights. Yet, there are very good arguments against human rights, and there are those who find the very idea of human rights to be dangerously utopian, or particular types of rights – particularly social and economic rights – to be a violation of more classical libertarian ideas of rights such as the right to private property. There is a general tendency in modern human rights discourse and policy to favor more social democratic economic rights. This makes sense since the emergence of so much human rights theory and practice emanates from Europe, which has taken the social welfare state as its model.

Yet, in a book of this sort, it is important to present dissenting ideas, that is, ideas which challenge the very idea of human rights as some kind of "absolute value." This is necessary in the first instance since the conservative, Marxian, and utilitarian critiques (in the form of Burke's, Marx's, and Bentham's attacks on the French Revolution) were such an elementary part of the history of human rights (Waldron 1987). The strident critiques of rights have not been a staple of human rights discourse and activism because there has been little question, especially for activists, that human rights are anything but valuable. Yet there is still a need to present criticisms of human rights, both in theory and practice. These appear across a range from mild critiques to shrill attacks reminiscent of Burke's and Bentham's onslaughts against the French Revolution. The utilitarian Peter Singer (2004), for instance, shares many of the dreams and aspirations of those who call themselves human rights activists, but proceeds from the assumption that one does not have to invoke any language of rights whatsoever to work toward the utilitarian good of fostering the well-being of the many. Others, like the conservative Roger Scruton, in Chapter 11, see rights in much the same way as Burke, as utopian constructions that are the new basis of power for an undemocratic and unelected elite and which throw societies into turmoil with their "anarchical fallacies," as Bentham would put it. Similar ideas have been put forth in quite powerful critiques of non-governmental organization (NGO) activism and "global civil society" by Kenneth Anderson and David Rieff (2004). Still others, as Tibor R. Machan does here in Chapter 10, problematize the social democratic, welfare state assumption that it is legitimate to violate the more fundamental rights of some by expropriating their property (in the form of taxes) to give to others in the name of socially constructed and politically driven positive, social, and economic rights.

Ordinarily, the voice of critics of human rights, or advocates of more traditional liberal rights, would not find a place in a collection such as this. Yet they are included here because the understanding of human rights proceeds best in dialectical relationship to arguments against them. This kind of dialectical interplay is often lacking in collections where there is one ideologically acceptable line about the value of human rights and such collections often become occasions for hagiographies of human rights and uncritical and politicized advocacy of human rights. There is, of course, a strong place for advocacy in what is generally called "human rights practice," but this must always take place in dialogue with critics. Human rights, as an intellectual field, must resist the usual tendency of advocates to politicize the field and introduce human rights as a closed system of ideological orthodoxies. This *Handbook* is an example of human rights as a heterodox field, both ideologically and in terms of theoretical and epistemological perspectives. As such, the chapters in Part V include probing and critical analyses of problems and prospects of reparations, ethics and the corporation, memory and truth commissions, humanitarianism, the problem of bystanding, and the proportionality problem in human rights reporting. Mirko Bagaric, in Chapter 50, asks the provocative question of whether human rights have failed humans, in a world with so much economic prosperity.

Part VI, on the law and human rights, must appear anomalous, given the fact that so many works on human rights are legalistic in orientation. The inclusion of only three chapters on the law and human rights is intentional, and not meant to disparage the contributions of legal theory to the study and practice of human rights. Indeed, it is important to stress that the major advancements in the provision and protection of rights have taken place through the mechanisms of the law. There exists a voluminous amount of material on human rights and the law, and the present *Handbook* is meant to offer a new approach that is centered around emergent perspectives primarily from the social sciences and the humanities. Nonetheless, three chapters on the historical development of international law, the prosecution of human rights violations, and international law and the war on terror are included to give readers a sense of some of the most basic perspectives on law and human rights in the modern world.

Part VII presents new and exciting perspectives from the humanities. Perhaps more than any other field, scholars in literature, art history, architecture, theater, and photography have made major contributions to the expansion of new perspectives in human rights. The chapters in this part include scholars and practitioners, who show how aesthetic forms embody in material form some of the more abstract and conceptual understandings that have been the traditional approach to human rights. The introduction of aesthetics to the understanding of human rights represents one of the more interesting and radical departures in the current refiguration of the study of human rights.

This *Handbook*, though expansive and ecumenical, by no means covers the entire range of topics in the study of human rights. No doubt, it also reflects the interests and networks of the editor. It ought to be read as an attempt – by no means definitive or complete – to expand the theoretical, conceptual, epistemological, and substantive range of the study of human rights to reflect new generations of thinking in this area. It is, in this respect, a first step in broadening the range of study in human rights as a field; it is by no means a definitive cartography of what has become a huge area of inquiry. It is a work that is meant to be built on, rather than completed in any definitive sense: it is, in other words, an ongoing production, just as human rights are as a project.

References

Anderson, Kenneth and David Rieff. 2004. "'Global Civil Society': A Skeptical View," pp. 28–39 in Helmut Anheier, Marlies Glasius, and Mary Kaldor, eds., *Global Civil Society 2004/2005* (London: Sage).

Bauman, Zygmunt. 2004. *Wasted Lives: Modernity and Its Outcasts* (London: Polity).

Cowan, Jane K., Marie Bénédicte Dembour, and Richard Wilson. 2001. *Culture and Rights: Anthropological Perspectives* (London and New York: Cambridge University Press).

Giddens, Anthony. 2002. *Runaway World: How Globalization is Shaping Our Lives* (London: Routledge).

Perry, Michael. 2000. *The Idea of Human Rights: Four Inquiries* (New York and London: Oxford University Press).

Singer, Peter. 2004. "Outsiders: Our Obligations to Those Outside Our Borders," pp. 11–32 in Deen K. Chaterjee, ed., *The Ethics of Assistance: Morality and the Distant Needy* (Cambridge: Cambridge University Press).

Turner, Bryan S. 2006. *Vulnerability and Human Rights* (College Station: Pennsylvania State University Press).

Waldron, Jeremy. 1987. *Nonsense Upon Stilts: Bentham, Burke and Marx on the Rights of Man* (New York: Methuen).

Part I

Foundations and critiques

1

Philosophical foundations of human rights

Andrew Fagan

Introduction

This chapter presents and analyzes philosophical contributions to the theory and practice of human rights. More specifically, I will focus on attempts to justify human rights as a universally valid moral doctrine in a culturally and politically diverse and complex world. The task of seeking to identify and formulate an ultimate justification for a commitment to human rights is complex and has attracted consistent criticism. Many supporters of human rights have argued that institutionally established human rights require no ultimate justification: the very fact that they have been legally recognized and implemented is sufficient evidence in support of human rights claims. Others have also declined an appeal to philosophical reasoning and argumentation in their commitment to human rights and have argued that we have human rights simply by virtue of being human. As Jack Donnelly has stated, human rights "*are the rights one has because one is a human*" (2002, p. 7). Many advocates of human rights base their belief in the moral authority of human rights on such apparently self-evidently or intuitively true proclamations and rarely, if ever, subject these assumptions to critical scrutiny. Basing one's belief in the moral authority of a doctrine as potentially controversial and revolutionary as human rights upon mere assumption provides a poor basis for defending one's commitments in the face of skepticism or systematic opposition. There are many people in the world who simply do not believe in human rights. One of the major criticisms of human rights is that the ideals of individual liberty and equality, which are central elements of the foundations of human rights, simply do not apply to the cultural or religious traditions and practices to which they adhere. It is rare that such opponents reject all human rights to the same degree in such instances, but restrictions are commonly applied to the human rights of members of such societies that entail imposing severe restrictions upon the human rights of many. An inability to offer sound justification for one's commitments to protecting and promoting the individual liberty and equality of all human beings will further compound the human rights violations of many human beings, including, for example, many women across the globe, as well as those belonging to ethnic, religious, and sexual minorities.

In addition to disputes over *who* is entitled to possess human rights, there are also serious disputes and controversies surrounding *which* human rights should be considered as such: disputes reign over what may legitimately be included in the category of human rights. Thus, some have long held to the view that civil and political rights are somehow more important and legitimate than their economic, social, and cultural counterparts. It has been argued that in cases where the protection of a civil and political right may come into conflict with an economic, social, and cultural counterpart, priority should generally be accorded to the former over the latter on the grounds that civil and political rights are somehow more incontestably human rights than their economic, social, and cultural counterparts (Cranston 1973). A separate position holds that human rights can only be said to exist meaningfully as legally recognized elements by a legally sovereign authority (Kelsen 1978). So-called legal positivists have long argued that a belief in the universal and pre-legal existence of human rights is intellectually incoherent and, in some cases, politically dangerous. On this view, rights gain their authority over us only through the process of becoming legally codified. Until that point, they are better understood as mere moral aspirations or prejudices. Both of these positions warrant serious consideration by supporters of human rights as defensible elements of a universally and generally valid moral doctrine. Simply relying upon a position that imagines that genuine human rights are self-evidently recognizable or intuitively identifiable is of no use in settling such disputes and offering a defense of human rights that have yet to be legally recognized within specific jurisdictions. It is important to note that such issues have life-and-death implications and consequences for many; these concerns are not mere artifacts or philosophical language games. Many of these disputes and conflicts are settled not by appeal to an assumption of the universal validity of human rights but by the use of power and force, which results in countless incidences of systematic human rights violations.

Thus, disputes over the ultimate basis and scope of human rights remain. It is manifestly not the case that all societies recognize the moral authority of human rights. Many remain to be persuaded by the arguments offered in support of human rights as a universally valid doctrine. There remains a normative challenge that confronts supporters of human rights and consists of the need to establish genuinely compelling and rationally acceptable arguments in support of human rights. How is this challenge being addressed and how successful have these responses been?

Philosophical arguments for human rights

There have been many attempts by philosophers to offer compelling arguments in support of human rights. Existing attempts to justify human rights may be classified into two somewhat different perspectives or approaches: the *interest theory approach* and the *choice theory approach*. The latter is more complex and detailed than the former, so I shall begin by analyzing the interest theory approach before analyzing the choice theory approach in greater detail.

It is impossible to begin to engage with the foundational questions of human rights without delving into the theoretical questions on the nature of being human. Typically, attempts to answer these questions and thereby provide a justification for human rights as a distinct moral doctrine seek to identify the fundamental elements or prerequisites for human agency. Theoretical justifications of human rights invariably begin and end with an attempt to identify what it is that ultimately constitutes us as human agents. All such attempts aim to identify what we all commonly share by virtue of being human and then construct from this commonality an account of the scope and application of human rights. Both the interest theory and the choice theory approaches attempt to identify the essential attributes of humankind. They differ in respect of what they consider to be the fundamental basis for the possession of human rights.

The interest theory approach is a label that has been applied to the work of John Finnis, Bryan S. Turner, Martha Nussbaum, and Amartya Sen, among others. The common basis for the interest theory approach consists of the appeal each theorist makes to the existence of fundamental human interests. Human beings are viewed as physiological and social agents who require the sufficient protection and promotion of certain interests in order to be human. These interests pre-exist, so to speak, the institution of human rights and social institutions more generally. That is to say, human rights are viewed as grounded in our very nature and exist in order to promote and protect those interests that constitute us: human rights are viewed as the mechanism through which these interests are best identified and secured. Historically and analytically, the concept of human interests precedes that of human rights. However, it would also be accurate to say that the language of human rights is fast replacing and superseding that of human interests, to the extent that the two are viewed in many quarters as simply synonymous. This can be unfortunate to the extent that it may obscure how some interest theorists conceive of human rights: as instrumental means for securing those "goods" and interests that (purportedly) make us what we are. On this view, human rights are considered to be instrumentally valuable to realizing our fundamental interests, rather than the form those interests must necessarily take.

Few interest theories foreground the concept of human nature in their formulations of the basis and scope of human rights, which is understandable, given the deeply controversial character of any such appeal. Many theorists, for example, have rejected the very notion of some essence or first nature to humankind. Over the past fifty years or so, the discussion of what our nature may be has been completely transformed by the contributions of historians, social anthropologists, and sociologists who have empirically challenged a conception of human "nature" as timeless and unchanging. Appeals to human nature or essential human interests have increasingly provoked disagreement and dissensus rather than agreement and consensus. This is also apparent within the interest theory approach, insofar as different interest theorists present different accounts of our fundamental interests.

Drawing upon a tradition of natural law, John Finnis (1980) argues that there are seven basic forms of human flourishing, which are universal and encompass social and physical attributes of the human condition, ranging from a capacity for practical reason, to play and recreation, and culminating in a capacity for spiritual experience. He argues that this account is not beholden to some overly physiological conception of human nature and is comprehensive and robust enough to encompass the empirical diversity of human life. According to Finnis, the function of human rights is to secure our access to and enjoyment of these seven basic forms of human flourishing and they are justified to the extent that they are successful in providing for this end. By contrast, the neo-Aristotelian philosopher Martha Nussbaum (2002) identifies ten basic goods, ranging from "life"; bodily health and bodily integrity; to emotions; affiliation, which comprises friendship and respect; and finally, control over one's environment. Some may be inclined to dismiss the differences between Finnis and Nussbaum as mostly irrelevant to the underlying vision of humankind they seek to express. The differences, however, are apparent enough and reveal the extent to which the two authors are influenced by different normative principles: visions of what humankind ought to be, rather than what it is. In this respect, they do share a somewhat "idealized" account of humanity that largely excludes human beings' capacity for inhumanity. It seems somewhat counterintuitive to suggest that each and every one of us has a fundamental interest in our capacity for inhumanity, but perfectly reasonable to insist that an account of human rights takes this capacity into account, given that the very need for many human rights is most apparent in their being violated, rather than respected.

The interest theory approach may be analyzed through what I shall refer to as the motivational question: which motives are identified as securing individuals' and states' respect for human rights generally? The motivational question aims to account for why each and every human being has a fundamental interest in respecting human rights as a general institution. This is not a question for interest theories alone and it will also be applied to the latter discussion of the choice theory approach. Both Finnis and Nussbaum imply that this question can be answered adequately by an accurate understanding of our nature and of human reason as a constituent of that nature: the realization of our common attributes will entail the establishment of an institutional commonality. Both Finnis and Nussbaum, however, fail to adequately address those less worthy and salubrious aspects of our condition. One might say that both accounts fail to accord sufficient weight to the Holocaust and genocide as human facts; both neglect the phenomenon of systematically induced human suffering as an essential feature of any account of humankind and correlative rights.

The same cannot be said of another interest theorist, the sociologist Bryan S. Turner. Like other interest theorists, Turner (2002) ultimately appeals to central features of the human condition as providing the basis and scope for the social institution of human rights. Unlike some other sociological contributions to the study of human rights, however, he does attempt to identify some mostly asocial and trans-historical elements of the human condition out of which and in response to which our concern for human rights should be directed. Put succinctly, Turner argues that the institution of human rights exists to protect human beings from one another, as much as to provide for a more flourishing human life. The ultimate feature of the human condition, Turner argues, is that we are physically frail and potentially vulnerable to one another. Turner insists that this is a universal condition; by virtue of being physically embodied beings we are frail and vulnerable to one another. The function of human rights is to provide protection and security for all of us to a broadly equal degree. All must return to dust eventually, but in the meantime, we all have a similar capacity for suffering. To the extent that this suffering has man-made causes, we all have an interest in avoiding and preventing human suffering as much as possible. Human rights aims not at achieving some perfect humanistic utopia but rather is motivated by our physical and social frailty and a desire to avoid or reduce our exposure to this.

How might the interest theory approach be criticized? Its most apparent weakness would appear to lie in the necessary role played by the concept of human nature as the foundation for purportedly essential interests. Placing to one side those who challenge the very notion of a human essence, it is clear that even those who do appeal to human nature harbor different conceptions of what constitutes our nature. All accounts of human nature appear to be unduly partial and insufficiently comprehensive to provide a fully objective and accurate menu of essential human interests. While important, this is not the most important criticism of the interest theory approach. It would be foolish to deny that our physiological and social functioning is adversely affected by a lack of access to certain goods or attributes. The most obvious of these are, perhaps, food and water. I do not personally think that the identification of certain fundamental human interests, that is, interests that positively promote our individual well-being, is an exercise doomed to failure. Interest theories should be commended precisely to the extent that they do place the fact of our embodiment at the very center of any attempt to define the basis and scope of human rights. The interest theory approach, however, suffers from at least one fundamental weakness, and this consists of what I earlier referred to as the motivational question.

Human rights address humankind but are ultimately possessed by separate individuals; individual moral sovereignty is central to the human rights doctrine. Thus, in identifying the human rights that any individual may legitimately possess, we would appear to be bound to apply these to all human agents. Such neat conclusions can be easily drawn in the comfort of a theorist's study. In the real world, however, things are rather different. Put bluntly, it is easier to see why I should take a self-interested reason in having my human rights secured than why I should simultaneously act to ensure that some distant other's human rights should also be secured. This would not matter if my actions and inactions had no bearing at all upon others' conditions. Unfortunately, however, they do. The unequal distribution of essential resources across the globe is an obvious case in point. Human rights exist against the backdrop of haves and have-nots, where the immediate self-interest of the former may positively require the continuing deprivation of the latter. This has significant consequences for an evaluation of the interest theory approach, which can be illustrated by critically analyzing Turner's argument.

Turner has been criticized on many grounds, including for not being sufficiently "sociological" in his approach to human rights. This claim harbors a number of rather different issues and concerns, but one of these is particularly important for present purposes. One may discern a distinct Hobbesian influence upon Turner's approach to human rights, grounded, as it is, upon our capacity to harm one another. Hobbes famously sought to identify a political means by which self-interested individuals may nevertheless prudentially live under the same political roof. Although few go so far as to endorse his account of the Leviathan as the ultimate guarantor of prudential self-interest, his approach has profoundly influenced modern political theorists who have similarly appealed to prudential self-interest as the basis for securing reciprocal respect for fundamental human rights (Gauthier 1986).

For some, drawing a comparison between Turner and Hobbes will serve to reinforce the validity of the former's claims. Turner's argument, however, shares with Hobbes's (and other such theorists) a fundamental weakness. The weakness is of a more empirical than purely normative character. I term this weakness a "false political economy of harm." What do I mean by this? Like all contractarian accounts of the basis and scope of political authority, Turner's is vulnerable to an empirical falsification of one of his argument's central assumptions; namely, that all of these agents addressed by the theory are in fact similarly situated in respect of their capacity to harm or aid one another, or can be hypothetically represented as so situated. Turner's approach shares with other interest-theory-based accounts of human rights a desire to avoid appealing to unduly hypothetical or metaphysical visions of the nature of humankind and aims to restrict the vision to that which is empirically demonstrable or credible. Put simply, his account assumes the existence of a relatively level playing field, inhabited by each and every frail and vulnerable human being. This assumption is manifestly false, and its falsity has devastating effects upon his claims concerning each agent's motives for respecting others' human rights.

This criticism applies, of course, even within the nation-state context of much contemporary political theory. The theory of human rights, however, must necessarily extend its boundaries well beyond national frontiers to embrace humankind in its entirety. When viewed from this perspective, the criticism is even more damning. It simply is not true to claim that the peoples of the world are similarly or equally vulnerable to one another. The so-called South, for example, has been far more vulnerable to the economic and political conditions of the North than the other way around. We may be increasingly occupying a single global space, but the distribution of a capacity for harming others is anything but equal. This is important insofar as it potentially undermines a motivation for the relatively invulnerable peoples of the world to recognize the human rights of the vulnerable. A more "rational" approach might be to erect barriers and secure borders, literally and figuratively, between communities: the establishment of so-called "gated communities" on a grandiose scale, if you will. This criticism applies with most force to the more overtly contractarian approach of Turner, but its logic also extends to affect other interest theory accounts. Thus, one can similarly argue that Finnis's or Nussbaum's accounts may provide a set of reasons why I should enjoy access to the conditions for basic flourishing or basic goods, but they do not similarly explain why I should act to ensure these conditions are enjoyed by everyone. They lack an account of justice sufficient for justifying the distribution of resources in a currently deeply unequal world.

As an account of human rights, the interest theory approach generally has to extend its application beyond the parameters of more parochially conceived contractarian political theories and must aim to identify both a set of fundamental interests we all share and the means by which these may be adequately secured for all. Interest theorists cannot be blamed for the existence of tangible obstacles to the realization of their principal ends. However, it is reasonable to demand from them some account for how these might be overcome. This is largely absent from the interest theory approach. The interest theory approach rightly stresses the fact of our embodiment as an essential feature of being human. Its focus upon physiological and social attributes generates a relatively robust account of essential interests. The interest theory approach, when taken all together, does a relatively good job at defining what constitutes being human. The central weakness, however, lies in generating a realizable and politically effective reciprocal commitment to all peoples' human rights out of a vision of what any single individual must have access to if he or she is to be human in the first place. This will require not just a means by which the geopolitical barriers between the haves and the have-nots may be overcome but also a determination of the scope of human rights so that one individual's human right does not become another's mere social privilege. Does the choice theory approach fare any better in determining the basis and scope of human rights?

The pursuit of human rights is driven by a profound ambition: the establishment of a set of material conditions by which each and every human being may enjoy the fundamental protection offered by the gamut of human rights. Fully realizing the ambition of human rights can only be achieved once the human rights of all human beings are adequately secured and free from systematic abuse and restriction. So far, I have argued that the interest theory approach provides a substantive account of what constitutes being human but fails to satisfactorily confront the challenge presented by a world that falls very far short of securing the fundamental interests of all. The ambition of human rights places very heavy demands upon any normative attempt to justify the doctrine. Essentially it requires identifying the basis upon which any individual's legitimate claims to the enjoyment of human rights secures the legitimacy of all individuals' claims to their human rights. It also requires delineating the scope of any individual's exercise of human rights consistent with all other individuals' potential for exercising their human rights. This challenge may be understood as an attempt to square the circle of two normative ideals that have been essential to the development of human rights and are also central to the choice theory approach: individual liberty and equality.

Within the theory of human rights the ideals of individual liberty and equality effectively complement one another. The two ideals, however, have separate historical developments and separate conceptual structures. Equality has become predominantly understood as non-discrimination so that all individuals are accorded an equal moral and legal standing within the principal legal and political institutions of modern states. From a human rights perspective, individuals' claim to equal standing is not based upon merit or accomplishment: we do not earn our equality, we possess it inalienably. Nor should any individual's standing be determined by features such as race, gender, ethnicity, physical capabilities, religious or ideological commitments. Although a commitment to securing human rights does not, necessarily, require political authorities being "blind" to such distinctions, it does require the eradication of disadvantage and discrimination on these grounds. The ideal of equality is central to many modern societies. However, it would be fair to say that individual liberty enjoys a somewhat higher profile. Thus, appeals and references to liberty are ubiquitous in modern societies, from the pronouncements of politicians to the marketing of mass consumer commodities. The very ubiquity of the ideal threatens to obscure understanding the nature of individual liberty. This is not a purely theoretical concern. The ideal of individual liberty figures prominently in the constitutions of many countries with otherwise very poor human rights records. Identifying the abuse of an ideal entails the possession of a clear understanding of its genuine character and form.

Theoretical understandings of individual liberty owe much to the distinction drawn by the political philosopher Isaiah Berlin (1969). Berlin distinguishes between two conceptions of liberty, which he refers to as negative liberty and positive liberty. Negative liberty consists primarily in non-interference in an individual's private sphere. Berlin writes, "I am normally said to be free to the degree to which no man or body of men interferes with my activity. Political liberty in this sense is simply the area within which a man can act unobstructed by others" (1969, p. 122): we are negatively free to the extent that our actions and thoughts are not directed or unduly coerced by some external agent or institution. Negative liberty expresses what we can call the condition of liberty. That is to say, to enjoy negative liberty is to possess the untrammelled capacity for being free. By contrast, positive liberty expresses and refers to the exercise or actualization of this condition. Logically speaking, negative liberty's focus upon restricting the interference of others says nothing about what we actually do (or do not do) with this condition. One can, in this sense, enjoy negative liberty and never lift a solitary finger. This is a manifestly incomplete account of human agency, lacking as it does agency's distinctly "active" element. Thus, positive liberty is evidenced by an agent formulating and pursuing goals and projects, the formation and the pursuit of which have not been unduly determined or influenced by externally coercive forces. Individual liberty then consists of these two essential elements: the condition of non-interference and the ability to exercise liberty through the active formulation and pursuit of goals and projects. Having established the very broad features of both equality and individual liberty, it is now time to turn directly to that theory of human rights that places greatest emphasis upon these two ideals as determining both the basis and the scope of human rights: the choice theory approach.

The choice theory approach differs from the interest theory approach primarily by the emphasis placed upon the free exercise of choice as the foundational stone for human rights. Choice theorists refrain from speculating on the substantive constitution of our nature and focus instead on the capacity for individual liberty as the distinguishing feature of humankind. On this account, to be a human agent is to possess both the condition of liberty and sufficient opportunities for exercising that liberty. If we have a fundamental essence, it is a capacity for individual liberty: the value of all other interests is determined by this end. The purpose of human rights is to secure and promote the exercise of free choice. There is no question that the ideal of liberty is central to the human rights doctrine. A concern for human rights, however, is not merely for individual liberty per se, but for *equal* individual liberty. Choice theorists aim to identify the basis of this condition and to determine the scope of its application. The most sophisticated and detailed formulation of choice theory is to be found in the work of the American philosopher Alan Gewirth.

Gewirth's contributions to human rights theory are profound and far-reaching. He presents, arguably, one of the most ambitious accounts of the status and importance of human rights. He states, unequivocally, that "human rights are derived from the necessary conditions of human action" (1982, p. x). He continues, "human rights are of supreme importance and are central to all other moral considerations, because they are the rights of every human being to the necessary conditions of human action; i.e. those conditions that must be fulfilled if human action is to be possible either at all or with general chances of success in achieving the purposes for which humans act" (1982, p. 3). In effect, he argues that being human entails the possession of human rights.

Gewirth argues that we are all moral agents. We all possess certain purposes and goals, which we wish to see realized. This is an inherent feature of human agency, something we all share. He proceeds to argue that reason demands that we are committed to the view that we must accept the necessity of access to the basic means for satisfying the realization of our purposes and that we are logically bound to accept that all such agents must similarly enjoy access to the means for satisfying their basic goals and purposes. Gewirth formulates the details of this argument in what he refers to as "the principle of generic consistency" (PGC). He identifies what he considers to be four logically necessary steps to a conclusion that holds that we are bound to accept the necessity of human rights by virtue of being rationally purposive agents (1982, p. 20). These four steps are as follows:

1. Every agent holds that the purposes for which he or she acts are good.
2. Every agent must logically accept the legitimacy of freedom and well-being as necessary conditions for purposive action.
3. Every agent must hold that he or she has rights to freedom and well-being, since denying this is to accept the legitimacy of others interfering in one's actions.
4. Every agent is a purposive agent, and rights to freedom and well-being are prerequisite to this condition.

Gewirth concludes this formulation with what he considers to be a dialectically necessary claim (as opposed to a merely assertoric one) by stating that "my argument for the existence of human rights is that every agent logically must hold or accept that he and all other agents have these rights because their objects are the necessary conditions of human action" (1982, p. 20).

He argues then that human rights are the essential means for securing the realization of our goals and that having and realizing goals is what makes us human agents in the first place. Having claimed that we are rationally bound to accept that all agents enjoy access to these means, Gewirth argues that this claim demonstrates that all rational agents are logically bound to accept that all rational agents should possess fundamental human rights. In this respect, he insists that we are all both respondents and subjects of rights. Being a moral agent entails enjoying access to the necessary conditions of human agency and a simultaneous obligation to respect (and if necessary to provide for) other agents' possession of these fundamental prerequisites of agency. Ultimately, he claims that for any individual to see themselves as a rational agent is to necessarily acknowledge that one shares a basic character with all other rational agents and that this recognition entails a necessary acceptance of human rights for all such agents as the very means for being an agent. One may deny human rights to others, but, in so doing, one is acting irrationally in the deepest sense. Thus, he states that a denial by any agent that any or all other agents possess human rights is "a failure of rationality" (1982, p. 21). Although he accepts that this happens all the time in the real world, Gewirth claims to have provided a definitively logical and rational justification for human rights that precedes considerations of politics, feelings, or religion.

This appeal to the apparent force of logic is also present in many of the central elements and concepts of his argument. Thus, he views freedom and well-being as constituents of action, rather than as particular normatively attributed consequences or results of action. He defines freedom as "controlling one's behavior by one's unforced choice while having knowledge of relevant circumstances, with a view to achieving some purpose for which one acts" (1982, p. 15). Similarly, in respect of his concept of well-being, Gewirth distinguishes between three levels of goods that are constitutive of well-being: basic, non-subtractive, and additive (1982, pp. 55–56). The first consists of the essential preconditions of action, the second to abilities and conditions for maintaining one's level of purposive action, and the third to abilities and conditions for increasing one's level of purposive action. He insists that these are all inherent and necessary aspects of human agency and owe nothing to the particular or partial outlook or commitments of any single agent, including, of course, himself as author of this account.

The style and the general orientation of Gewirth's account of the basis and scope of human rights has its origins in the rationalist moral philosophy of the eighteenth-century German philosopher, Immanuel Kant (1993). Like Kant, Gewirth claims to have identified a set of principles that apply to all rational agents as such and are thus binding upon all such agents, at least in theory. This represents an attempt to identify the grounds upon which I, you, and every other such rational agent may claim to possess human rights: the grounds for my possession of human rights logically commit me to accept that all other such agents also possess human rights. The theory aims to combine individual liberty and equality as fundamentally reciprocal ideals, while purporting to have identified the grounds upon which all moral agency everywhere is constituted. Finally, like Kant's moral philosophy, it is also a version of philosophical foundationalism. Indeed, one might describe Gewirth as the definitive rights foundationalist of the contemporary age.

Gewirth's theory of human rights and his account of rational moral agency have attracted significant criticism from various quarters. Some have objected more broadly to any foundationalist moral philosophies. On this view, foundationalism represents a refusal to engage with the social and historical origins of morality. The anti-foundationalist critique ultimately denies that there are any trans-historical human truths and asserts that no conceptual foundation is ever truly secure. Gewirth has also been criticized more directly on the grounds that his focus upon purposive agency as the ground for possessing human rights effectively serves to deny human rights to all those human beings who have permanently lost the capacity for purposive deliberation and action: the so-called marginal cases. My critical focus, however, takes a slightly different angle to both of these.

Taken at face value, Gewirth's theory of human rights appears to satisfy the ambition of human rights: to identify the basis for all human beings' possession of fundamental rights, while also indicating the grounds upon which the scope of their application may be determined through the combination of liberty and equality. If human rights exist at all, they must adhere to essential features of humankind. Focusing upon the attributes of human agency is a perfectly reasonable place to construct an account capable of expressing the primacy of human rights. If human rights are to legitimately exist at all they must not be based upon and consist of what might be termed value-added extras of human life but must be fundamental to, if not constitutive of, being human in the first place. Gewirth's account of human rights appears to have grasped and assimilated this aspect of human rights.

Gewirth's theory would also appear to have dealt more effectively with the so-called motivational question than his interest theory counterparts. For him, the exercise of choice is essential to human agency, but is limited to the extent that any agent's exercise of choice is consistent with every other agent's opportunity to also enjoy their liberty. On his highly rationalist reading of the human condition, Gewirth insists that reason itself serves to identify the grounds for supporting the rights of self and other. For him, to be an agent entails necessarily accepting that all agents enjoy access to that which constitutes agency in the first place: fundamental human rights. He states, "what for any agent are necessarily goods of action, namely freedom and well-being, are equally necessary goods for his recipients, and he logically must admit that they have as much right to these goods as he does, since the ground or reason for which he rationally claims them for himself also pertains to his recipients"'(1982, p. 53). He presents a very neat, and in places a quite beautifully consistent, account of human rights, but it is ultimately an account that is undermined by concerns which he does not satisfactorily address. Two are particularly problematic: his formulation of reason in the contemporary age and his premise concerning the centrality of human rights to human agency. I shall consider each in turn.

A failure by a human rights theorist to place sufficient importance upon reason as a human faculty would be worthy of criticism, but that does not, of course, apply to the rationalism of Gewirth. Despite his appeals to the authority of logic, however, Gewirth's account of the rationality of human rights is inadequate to the modern world in which human rights must secure their existence. If it is a failure of rationality to accept and respect the rights of all other moral agents, then countless millions of human agents must be condemned as irrational. We presently live in a world in which the principal motive for human rights is the very fact that such rights are being systemically abused in sometimes highly planned and complex ways; human rights possess a distinctly reactionary character in environments where they are systematically abused. Understanding how this occurs requires knowledge of many things, foremost of which is the role that power plays in determining the fate of people's lives. Gewirth's rationalism owes much to the systematic character of his thought, but largely appears to ignore the social, political, and economic realities of the modern world. Representing those realities as significantly irrational is ultimately unhelpful to understanding them better in the aim of overcoming them in order to secure human rights more effectively.

One might conceivably defend Gewirth's strategy here by arguing that he is ultimately concerned to identify the definitive justifications for the very existence of human rights. On this view, the counterpart to transcending the debased character of material reality is to succumb to it, so that the grounds and parameters of one's proposed rational remedy are themselves unduly infected by the very condition they purport to diagnose and overcome. This line of criticism has been levelled at all those theorists who view reason and rationality as a manifestation of power, principal among which are the so-called Nietzscheans and Foucauldians. For many defenders of human rights, the essential purpose of the doctrine is to impose constraints and limits upon the exercise of power. Identifying a rational basis and purpose to human rights in this context will serve only to contradict its presumed *raison d'être*. If securing the conditions for equal liberty is central to the very purpose of human rights, then the doctrine must not become a mere manifestation of power in a world beset by deep divisions and inequalities. To this extent, justifications of the basis and scope of human rights must extend to include a formulation of reason as a central element of human agency. If it is to retain its critical purchase, this account of reason must be sufficiently robust and detailed to confront existing realities without either simply reducing to those realities or avoiding engagement with them through an appeal to logic, which lacks a worldly realization. This is a daunting task and remains a deep challenge for theorists of human rights. An account of reason that effectively dismisses as irrational all thought and action that is not supportive of human rights is not particularly helpful in this regard.

The second area of criticism concerns Gewirth's claims regarding the centrality of human rights to human agency. This line of criticism raises concerns for how human rights may be justifiably extended to cover human beings who have lost the capacity for purposive agency and concerns both the purported logical character of his claims and the recognition that all human life is not based upon the satisfactory establishment of human rights.

Gewirth insists that his claims are not assertoric. He insists that his account is not simply yet another purely normative depiction of how things ought to be according to the prejudices or moral wish list of the author. He describes his defense of human rights as a form of metaethics that transcends separate substantive and more partial ethical perspectives (1982, pp. 45–46). Indeed, he argues that the logical basis of his central claims derives its origin from the very basis and structure of morality itself. He appeals to what he considers to be, in effect, the very DNA of morality: the necessary conditions for freedom and well-being. Unlike other accounts of human rights, Gewirth views his own account as having overcome the partiality and perspectival limitations of mere ethics. When he cracks open the core of human morality he finds human rights. To appreciate the basis and force of this second line of criticism it is imperative to recognize the extent of Gewirth's claims and ambition in this regard.

Put simply, it is manifestly wrong to claim that human rights are prerequisites for human agency per se: they are not. It might seem normatively desirable to attempt to extend their importance in this way but it is not empirically sustainable. Human life has proceeded and continues to proceed in many places without the protection and enjoyment of human rights. Too much of human life comprises the abuse of human rights, but if one takes away the fundamental rights, human life does not thereby simply dissolve into some purportedly logical contradiction. One might be intellectually charitable to Gewirth and assume he means that a right to life is fundamental to human life; this seems far less controversial, if a little unduly self-evident. However, his account of human rights extends to include conditions for freedom and for well-being. His account thus extends far beyond a mere right to life. The relevance of this particular line of criticism is not so much that Gewirth falsely represents human empirical reality: he cannot genuinely think that wherever one finds human agency one will also find secure human rights. I do not base this criticism of his work on this claim, but rather on what he indicates about the nature of his attempt to justify human rights. The defense of human rights is based not upon identifying the conditions for human life, but upon identifying the conditions for a certain quality of life. The human rights doctrine is inherently and necessarily evaluative in its approach toward both the basis and the scope of human rights. This is crucial to understanding human rights and essential to any attempt to justify human rights claims. One cannot escape this, despite its attractions at times, by appealing to logic or to "life" without thereby dissolving the capacity of human rights to hold certain forms of life to critical account. Gewirth provides a highly ambitious and intellectually complex account of human rights. His argument, however, is subject to significant criticism, which serves to undermine the theory's ability to adequately gauge the role human rights has to play in securing human agency. Like its interest theory counterpart, choice theory leaves us begging a number of important questions.

To this point I have discussed how the normative challenge of human rights has been addressed by the interest and choice theory approaches. Readers may be concerned by how apparently successful these approaches have been in offering a defensible normative justification for a commitment to human rights as a universally valid moral doctrine: both approaches have been shown to suffer from some significant shortcomings. What conclusions might be drawn from this? Should the Pandora's box of intellectual inquiry never have been opened in the first place? Does philosophy, as some of its critics claim, truly have little to offer human rights? These are important considerations, and any account of the philosophical foundations of human rights ought to address them.

A commitment to human rights is a commitment to a moral vision of how the world should be regulated. A commitment to human rights entails the drawing of a moral line in the sand between what is permissible and impermissible in respect of how human beings are to be treated by those who hold authority over them. Where one seeks to draw the line ultimately rests upon assumptions about morality. Against this, we have seen that human rights is confronted by a normative challenge; some might even say that a normative deficit lies at the core of human rights. The task of philosophy is to address this challenge or remedy the deficit by providing rationally coherent arguments in support of a commitment to human rights. It is important to appreciate the general context in which this task is undertaken. As a moral doctrine, human rights owes much to the spirit of the European Enlightenment and its focus upon the ideals of individual liberty, equality, and an attempt to subordinate political power to the will and interests of those subject to its jurisdiction. What is also typically considered to be a central element of the Enlightenment is a spirit of critical inquiry and an aversion to dogma and mere assertion masquerading as rational argument. This spirit of critical inquiry extends to affect ongoing philosophical attempts to justify human rights to the extent that any such account is almost inevitably met with counter-claims and critique, which, for some, appear only to frustrate and obstruct securing the degree of moral certainty apparently required in order to definitively justify human rights. The effects of the Enlightenment, or what I prefer to call modernity, are also apparent in the interest and choice theory approaches' avoidance of any overt appeal to metaphysical or transcendental arguments or concepts in their attempts to support human rights. Both approaches express a central tenet of modernity to the extent that the sources of their respective moral claims are restricted to "this-worldly" claims about the attributes of human agency or fundamental and demonstrable needs. The refusal to appeal to metaphysical, transcendental, or even divine sources of moral argumentation has attracted criticism from some who claim that humankind is simply too fragmented and fallible to offer secure moral foundations for a universal morality (Perry 1998). In general terms, this is the intellectual context in which contemporary philosophical foundations of human rights should be understood. What implication does this hold for our desire to justify human rights?

A reasonable and fundamental basis for the establishment of human rights is available. Picture, if you will, the devastating effects of global poverty and the countless millions of human beings who die prematurely or must endure lives of abject misery as a consequence of lack of basic resources. Include in this picture all those who are subject to authoritarian and totalitarian regimes and how the desire to retain power by the few affects the lives of the many. One may extend this vision of a this-worldly hell by including all those whose ethnic, racial, religious, or sexual identities expose them to persecution and violence. Very few, if any, moral philosophies have sought to celebrate or espouse these conditions. Hence, it may be reasonably argued that human rights are justified on the basis and to the extent to which they serve to prevent human beings from being exposed to the effects of significant and systematic suffering (Fagan 2009). Given the spirit of modernity, questions will and should still be raised in respect of how one precisely identifies and measures "suffering." In the meantime, the lives of sufficient numbers of human beings are daily blighted and prematurely ended by unequivocal and unmistakable suffering. In a world as absolutely rich in resources as ours, such conditions are truly indefensible. Beyond addressing the moral urgency of significant and systematic suffering, a reasonable justification for human rights can be found in a concern for what the philosopher James Nickel refers to as the conditions for a "*minimally good life*" (1987, p. 51).

Nickel defends the human rights doctrine as a form of minimal moral perfectionism. Human rights are thereby presented as encompassing a conception of what a minimally desirable human life must comprise. This extends to include physiological, social, and rationally deliberative elements. However, as a form of minimal moral perfectionism, human rights do not extend to determine everything that may be considered good and desirable for fully active agents. Rather, the doctrine aims to establish a minimal threshold below which a minimally good life is not possible. Given the global perspective of human rights, this threshold must necessarily be universalized and will require the setting of standards that, while sensitive to "local" conditions, do not serve ultimately to exacerbate discrepancies between human rights' haves and have-nots. It does recognize the importance and value of individual liberty and personal equality to the extent that severe restrictions upon the former or violations of the latter may result in denying individuals' opportunity for leading a minimally good life.

Conclusion

Philosophical justifications of human rights are developed against the context of intellectual, cultural, ideological, and political diversity, which may often serve to frustrate attempts to identify the moral grounds for human commonality. The very exercise of human rights to such things as freedom of conscience and thought contributes to the creation of conditions that some consider to be antithetical to securing fundamental and universal moral consensus. The exercise of human rights under conditions free of extreme material scarcity provides an opportunity for pursuing the emancipatory promise of modernity. However, much of the world is yet to achieve such secure material conditions. The essential role of human rights is to condemn and seek to overcome forms of systematic and significant human suffering. This is a matter of utmost moral urgency. Beyond and in conjunction with this ambition, the justification for human rights rests upon a concern for establishing the conditions for all human beings' opportunity to lead a minimally good life. Human life and human societies cannot be morally perfected. Bad luck and bad decisions will continue to blight many people's lives. Even in a world where every human being lived in a society which genuinely did provide opportunities for leading a minimally good life, free from systematic and significant suffering, many will continue to lead unfulfilled and frustrating lives: the purpose of human rights is not to make people "happy." The current global order falls very far short of ensuring such opportunities for all. Significant progress is still to be made in the normative analysis of human rights. For the moment, philosophy provides us with the means for continuing to condemn justifiably the current global order while retaining a positive conception of what a sufficiently moral global human community must be founded upon.

References

Berlin, Isaiah. 1969. "Two Concepts of Liberty." pp. 118–172 in *Four Essays on Liberty* (Oxford: Oxford University Press).

Cranston, Maurice. 1973. *What Are Human Rights?* (London: Bodley Head).

Donnelly, Jack. 2002. *Universal Rights in Theory and Practice* (Ithaca, NY: Cornell University Press).

Fagan, Andrew. 2009. *Human Rights: Confronting Myths and Misunderstandings* (Cheltenham: Edward Elgar).

Finnis, John. 1980. *Natural Law and Natural Rights* (Oxford: Clarendon Press).

Gauthier, David. 1986. *Morals by Agreement* (Oxford: Clarendon Press).

Gewirth, Alan. 1982. *Human Rights: Essays on Justification and Applications* (Chicago: University of Chicago Press).

Kant, Immanuel. 1993. *Critique of Practical Reason*. Trans. Lewis White Beck. 3rd edn (New York: Macmillan).

Kelsen, Hans. 1978. *The Pure Theory of Law*. Trans. Max Knight (Berkeley: University of California Press).

Nickel, James. 1987. *Making Sense of Human Rights: Philosophical Reflections on the Universal Declaration of Human Rights* (Berkeley: University of California Press).

Nussbaum, Martha. 2002. *Women and Human Development: The Capabilities Approach* (Cambridge: Cambridge University Press).

Perry, Michael J. 1998. *The Idea of Human Rights: Four Inquiries* (New York: Oxford University Press).

Turner, Bryan S. 2002. "Outline of a Theory of Human Rights." *Sociology*, Vol. 27, No. 3, pp. 489–512.

2

The metaphysical foundations of natural rights

Edward Feser

Apart from "the" and "of," every word in the title of this chapter is bound to raise eyebrows. Many contemporary moral and political theorists would deny that there are any such things as "rights," at least apart from (what they would consider) the purely legal fictions created by framers of constitutions and legislators. Of those who do affirm their existence, many would deny that rights can be given a theoretical "foundation." And among those who would allow for such a foundation, few would hold that it can be found in "nature" and fewer still that it could be in any sense "metaphysical." All the same, my position is that there are such things as rights, and that their foundation lies not in convention but in the metaphysics of human nature. If this view sounds reactionary, the case I would make in its defense is bound to sound even more so, resting as it does on a broadly Aristotelian–Thomistic–Scholastic approach to moral philosophy. What follows is an outline of that case. In the course of making it, I will indicate how certain modern, alternative defenses of natural rights have failed to do the job, and thus why the more traditional approach I advocate is necessary as well as sufficient to do it.

Classical natural law theory

Here is one way to look at the history of Western philosophy. There is the classical tradition, and there is the modern one. The former tracks an upward trajectory from the Pre-Socratics through Plato, Aristotle, and Augustine on up to Thomas Aquinas, whose synthesis of the best elements of the thought of his predecessors marks the tradition's high point. The latter constitutes a decline whose origins can be discerned in late medieval writers such as William of Ockham, begins in earnest with the likes of Hobbes and Descartes, is massively accelerated by Hume and Kant, and may be reaching its nadir in the moral and metaphysical *bizarreries* of contemporary writers such as Derek Parfit and Peter Singer. Needless to say, the story is far more complicated than that. But (so this account goes) definite white hats and black hats can nevertheless be clearly made out on the heads of the key players. Something like this view has been defended in recent decades by thinkers such as Richard Weaver, Mortimer Adler, Henry Veatch, Alasdair MacIntyre, and many neo-Scholastics and neo-Thomists. And as we will see presently, a far larger number of writers who would not go so far as to pit classical against modern philosophy in such a wholesale fashion would still endorse the view that the moderns' critique of the classical tradition was seriously deficient, and that certain aspects of the classical tradition long thought to have been definitively refuted ought to be reconsidered.

Suppose one accepts this (admittedly highly contentious) thumbnail history, at least for the sake of argument. What exactly marks the difference between the classical and modern traditions? How does the transition from the one to the other constitute the beginning of a decline (if it does)? And how is this relevant to the topic of natural rights? Let's take the first question first. Obviously there are many differences between the classical tradition and the modern one; equally obviously, there are many differences among classical philosophers themselves, and also among modern ones. Still, some clear, general tendencies can be identified, and the most important are these: classical philosophy tends toward *essentialism*, while modern philosophy tends toward *nominalism* and related views; that is to say, classical philosophers tended to take the view that things have essences or natures as a matter of objective fact, while modern philosophers have tended to hold either that things have no essences or that their essences are conventional, made by humankind rather than found in nature. Classical philosophy also tends toward a *teleological* view of nature, while modern philosophy tends toward a *mechanistic* one. In other words, classical philosophers generally held that things are naturally oriented toward the realization of certain ends or goals ("final causes," as followers of Aristotle famously call them), while modern philosophers generally deny this.

These differences over metaphysics entail differences over morality. For the classical tradition, the essence or nature of a thing determines an objective standard of goodness. To take a simple example, the fact that the essence of a triangle is to be a closed plane figure with three straight sides entails that a triangle drawn slowly and carefully on art paper with a fine-tip pen and a straight edge is a *good* triangle and one drawn hastily in crayon on the cracked plastic seat of a moving bus a *bad* one, because the former will at least closely approximate the essence while the latter (with its inevitable broken and wavy lines) will fall far short of doing so. Similarly, there is an obvious sense in which a whole and healthy squirrel, which likes to scamper up trees and gather nuts for the winter, is a *good* squirrel while a sickly squirrel, missing a tail or a leg, which prefers to stay in a cage eating toothpaste on Ritz crackers, is a *bad* squirrel. For the former more closely approximates the normal anatomy and pattern of life that nature has set for squirrels, as defined in part by the ends, goals, or tendencies (such as scampering about and gathering nuts) that are typical of the species.

Obviously the examples given so far are not examples of *moral* goodness per se. (It would make no sense to accuse a badly drawn triangle or an injured squirrel of an ethical lapse!) But for the classical tradition in philosophy they illustrate a general concept of goodness of which the moral kind is a species. As the contemporary neo-Aristotelian ethicist Philippa Foot (2001) has emphasized (and as the squirrel example indicates), with living things especially, their "natural goodness" or lack thereof is to be defined in largely *teleological* terms. The lioness who nurtures her cubs is a *good* lioness because she fulfills (to that extent anyway) the ends set for her by nature, while the lioness who allows her cubs to starve is to that extent *defective*, just as a three-legged squirrel or badly drawn triangle is defective. Unlike the goodness or defectiveness of triangles and the like, that of a living thing has to do not only with the static realization of some archetypical shape or structure, but also with the development over time of certain paradigmatic behavioral patterns. In human beings, this standard of goodness or defectiveness takes on a moral character to the extent that our realization of, or failure to realize, the ends set for us by nature results from our freely chosen actions. Hence, to take a simple example, the human intellect is according to the classical tradition naturally oriented toward the pursuit of truth; that is its *purpose*, its *final cause*, even if it does not always realize that purpose (just as it is the natural end or purpose of the heart to pump blood, even if it sometimes fails to do so because of genetic defect or injury, or because Hannibal Lecter decides to make of it a meal instead). For us to fulfill this end or purpose is for us to flourish as the kind of beings we are, while to fail to do so is to that extent to atrophy as a human being. It follows that to pursue truth is good for us and to fail to do so is bad, and that those who pursue it are to that extent good or virtuous while those who do not are to that extent bad or vicious.

Now practical reason, on this view, has as its own natural end the pursuit of what the intellect perceives to be good for us and the avoidance of what it takes to be bad. Hence Aquinas's famous claim that the self-evident first principle of natural law is that *good is to be done and pursued and evil is to be avoided.* Aquinas was not suggesting that it is self-evident that we are bound by the moral law. What he means is that it is self-evident that whenever we choose to do something, we do so because we regard it as good *in some way or other,* and that when we avoid doing something we do so because we regard it as bad *in some way or other.* This is true even of someone who is convinced that what he is doing is morally wrong. The mugger who admits that robbery is evil nevertheless takes his victim's wallet because he thinks it would be good to have some money to pay for his drugs; the drug addict who knows that his habit is wrong and degrading nevertheless thinks it would be bad to suffer the unpleasantness of withdrawal; and so forth. We are simply built to pursue good and avoid evil in this thin sense. But suppose that the intellect comes to perceive that what is *in fact* good for us is to realize the ends that nature has set for us and to avoid anything that frustrates the realization of those ends. Then to the extent that we are rational we will strive to realize those ends. In short, reason is built to pursue what it takes to be good; what is in fact good is the realization of the ends set for us by nature; and thus a rational person apprised of the facts will seek to realize those ends. In this sense to be moral is simply to act rationally, and to be immoral is to be irrational. The obligatory force of morality thus follows from the natural end or final cause of reason, just as the content of morality follows from the natural ends or final causes of our various capacities more generally. Morality, for the classical philosophical tradition, is thus doubly dependent on an essentialist and teleological conception of nature.

Suppose, though, that things do not really have essences or ends set for them by nature, and that what common sense takes to be the objective essences and natural ends of things are really just projections of the human mind or artifacts of human convention. Then the moral conclusions associated with the classical essentialist-cum-teleological metaphysical picture of the world will come to seem little more than the expression of subjective sentiments (as Hume would have it) or reflective of contingent historical and cultural prejudices (as moral relativism implies). Indeed, *any* possible system of morality might come to seem ultimately subjective and relative. To forestall such a consequence and provide morality with a new objective basis, thinkers such as Kant sought to ground it in the nature of reason itself. But if, like everything else, reason too lacks any essence or natural end, then this strategy seems doomed from the start. What we take to be paradigmatically "rational" will, like what we take to be the nature or purpose of a thing, be merely the expression of some ultimately subjective and relative standard. Nor could a trendy appeal to evolutionary psychology or some other Darwinian *deus ex machina* help if the concepts and standards of argument underlying contemporary biological theory are as subjective or conventional as any other. The nominalism and mechanism of the moderns seems inevitably to undermine the foundations of morality, indeed of reason itself.

Where do natural rights come in? Writers such as Leo Strauss (1953) have suggested that the point of the idea of "natural rights" was to replace the classical "natural law" picture of morality that I have been describing. For if there is no human essence or natural end to human action, then, as I have suggested, there can be no *objective, rational* foundation for morality. To redefine "nature" in a nominalist-cum-mechanistic fashion, as the moderns did, is accordingly to make our "natural" condition out to be a complete liberty, and thus a "right," to do anything we wish. The result is not a hedonistic paradise, however, but Hobbes's state of nature, that war of all against all between combatants whose lives are inevitably solitary, poor, nasty, brutish, and short. To escape this sorry condition we agree to abide by a social contract, a non-aggression pact between parties who, out of self-interest, agree to put some limits on their "natural right" to do as they will. "Keep your knife out of my back and I'll keep mine out of yours." This is not morality so much as a replacement for morality, and natural rights theory comes to seem the antithesis of natural law.

But that is hardly the only possible construal of "natural rights," and as scholars such as Brian Tierney (2001) have shown, the concept long predates Hobbes, having its origins in medieval canon law – that is to say, in a context permeated by the classical metaphysical picture described above. (Though it is also, admittedly, to be found in Ockham; the ambiguity of "rights" language between nominalist and essentialist readings seems long-standing indeed.) While the idea of natural rights is not explicitly found in Aristotle or Aquinas, late Scholastic writers argued that it was implicit in the Aristotelian–Thomistic conception of human nature. Most famously, Francisco de Vitoria and Bartolomeo de Las Casas developed a Thomistic theory of natural rights for use in critiquing Spanish treatment of the American Indians. By the time of the neo-Scholasticism of the late nineteenth and early twentieth centuries, the existence of natural rights was commonly argued for in Thomistic manuals of moral philosophy, and precisely on traditional Aristotelian–Thomistic grounds.

The basic argument is this. We are rationally obliged to pursue what is good for us and to avoid what is bad, where "good" and "bad" are to be understood in terms of the classical metaphysical picture described above. Hence we are obliged (for example) to pursue truth and avoid error, to sustain our lives and health and avoid what is damaging to them, and so forth (ignoring for present purposes the various qualifications and complications a fully developed natural law theory would have to spell out). The force and content of these obligations derive from our nature as human beings. Now it is part of that nature that we are *social* animals, as Aristotle famously noted. That is to say, we naturally live in communities with other human beings and depend on them for our well-being in various ways, both negative (such as our need not to be harmed by others) and positive (such as our need for various kinds of assistance from them). Most obviously, we are related to others by virtue of being parents or children, siblings, grandparents or grandchildren, cousins, and so on. Within the larger societies that collections of families give rise to, other kinds of relationships form, such as that of being a friend, an employee or employer, a citizen, and so forth. To the extent that some of these relationships are natural to us, their flourishing is part of what is naturally good for us.

For example, as Foot (2001, p.15) has noted, "like lionesses, human parents are defective if they do not teach their young the skills that they need to survive." It is part of our nature to become parents, and part of our nature that while we are children we depend on our own parents. Accordingly, it is as a matter of objective fact good for us to be good parents to our children and bad for us to be bad parents, just as it is (even more obviously) an objective fact that it is good for children to be taken care of by their parents. Now if it is good for a parent to provide for his or her children, then given that we are obliged to do what is good for us, it follows that a parent has an obligation to provide for them. Similarly, since given their need for instruction, discipline, and the like, it is good for children to obey and respect their parents, it follows that they have an obligation to obey and respect them. But an obligation on the part of a person A toward another person B entails a right on the part of B against A. It follows in turn, then, that children have a *right* to be provided for by their parents, and parents have a *right* to be obeyed and respected by their children. And since the obligations that generate the rights in question are obligations under *natural* law (rather than positive law) it follows that they are *natural* rights, grounded not in human convention but in human nature.

Other obligations we have under natural law toward various other human beings will similarly generate various other natural rights. At the most general level, we are all obliged to refrain from interfering with others' attempts to fulfill the various moral obligations placed on them by the natural law; the most *basic* natural right is the right to do what is good and not to be coerced into doing evil. Individual talents and circumstances inevitably leave open several possible equally legitimate ways in which one might concretely pursue the goods set for him by nature, so that the natural law also entails a right to a significant measure of personal liberty (e.g., with respect to choice of spouse, career path, where to live, and so forth). And of course we cannot pursue any good or fulfill any obligation at all if our very lives could be taken from us by others as they saw fit, so that the natural law entails that every human being (or at least every innocent human being) has a right not to be killed. Yet other rights would follow from various other aspects of the ends set for us by nature.

This gives us some idea of how rights are generated under classical natural law theory, though it is, of course, very general, and natural law theorists would add a great many further details, complications, and qualifications to this basic account. It is particularly important to emphasize that the classical natural law approach to rights theory puts definite limits on what we can be said to have a natural right to. While the very concept of a right entails a certain measure of liberty, that liberty cannot be absolute; for since the point of natural rights is to enable us to realize the ends set for us by nature, there cannot, even in principle, be a natural right to do what is contrary to the realization of those ends. In short, there cannot be a natural right to do wrong. That does *not* mean that classical natural law theory entails a paternalistic nanny state or the institution of a morality police. There might be all sorts of reasons, including moral ones, why that would be a bad idea even from a natural law point of view. The point is just that there can be no question of a *natural right* to indulge in vice, even if there might be pragmatic grounds, or moral grounds apart from rights-based ones, to tolerate such indulgence.

The key point to note for our purposes here is that both the grounds and the limits of natural rights stem from the same essentialist-cum-teleological metaphysical picture of the world. Given the ends set for us by our nature, we cannot fail to have certain natural rights, even if there also cannot fail to be certain limits to those rights. That, in any event, is what adherents of the classical tradition in Western philosophy have tended to hold when they have addressed the question of natural rights. If representatives of the modern philosophical tradition have increasingly tended to put less emphasis on the limits to our rights, that is, unsurprisingly, precisely because they have rejected the essentialist and teleological metaphysics definitive of the classical tradition, and thus abandoned the idea that there are any natural human ends or purposes that rights are intended to further. But it is also precisely because of this rejection that they have found it increasingly difficult to give a rational foundation for the claim that there are any natural rights in the first place.

Modern natural rights theory

This difficulty is already evident in the work of John Locke, the preeminent modern theorist of natural rights. Horrified by Hobbes's conception of our natural state, Locke argued that a moral law governs human beings even in the state of nature, prior to any social contract. In particular, he held that parties to a social contract already possess a right of self-ownership, so that they cannot justifiably be harmed by others with respect to their lives, health, liberty, or possessions. This right puts severe constraints on the sort of government that could be set up by those who agree together to leave the state of nature and establish civil society, and thus it rules out Hobbesian absolutism. At the same time, like Hobbes, Locke rejects the classical metaphysical picture that underlay the Aristotelian–Thomistic–Scholastic theory of natural law. So what foundation for natural law and natural rights can he put in its place?

It is one of the great ironies of intellectual history that the modern philosopher Locke here needed to do something that his supposedly more "faith-based" Scholastic predecessors did not need to do: appeal directly to God as the source of our natural rights. As the careful reader will have noticed, no reference was made to any theological premises in the exposition of classical natural law theory given above. For though any Thomist or Scholastic will of course regard God as the ultimate explanation of the natural world, the essences and final causes of things can from the point of view of the classical philosophical tradition be known just by investigating the natural world itself, without raising the question of where it came from; and the moral implications of these essences and final causes can at least to a significant extent be known in the same way. Indeed, though he was a philosophical theist of sorts, Aristotle himself did not consider essences and teleology to be something especially in need of a theological explanation, being in his view just irreducible features of the natural world. But Locke, who rejected Aristotelian essentialism and teleology, can find no basis for morality in nature per se. He appeals instead to the idea that since we are God's "workmanship" or creatures, we belong to him, so that to harm another human being in his life, health, liberty, or possessions is in effect to damage God's property. Despite Locke's talk of our right to self-ownership, strictly speaking it is in his view not we who own ourselves, but God; we "own" ourselves only in the loose sense that we are as it were *on lease* to ourselves from God and granted authority to direct our lives for ourselves rather than have some absolutist despot try to do it for us. Still, we are answerable to God for how we direct them, and talk of our "natural rights" is thus a kind of shorthand for our duty not to violate what are really *God's* rights over us as his property.

Given that it is God rather than us who in the strict sense has all the rights, Locke's position already amounts to a massive backpedaling away from the "rights" element of the idea of natural human rights. The "natural" element is also severely attenuated given Locke's endorsement of a mechanistic conception of nature devoid of inherent purpose, and thus of moral import. Still, Locke took his position to be a "natural law" approach at least insofar as he thought that the existence of God as creator of the world (and thus as the ultimate rights-holder) could be known through pure reason rather than divine revelation. But here Locke's account still faces three severe difficulties. First, his empiricist theory of knowledge notoriously tends to undermine the sort of cosmological argument for God's existence that he favored. Second, his rejection of Aristotle's idea of final causes makes his appeal to our duty to respect God's purposes for us practically useless. For how are we to know what those purposes are? It is hard to see how we could know them through observation of the natural world, for if Locke's mechanistic conception of nature is followed out consistently, there *are no* purposes there to observe in the first place. And if we appeal to divine revelation to know what God intends for us (the only remaining alternative, it seems), then we no longer have a natural law theory at all (and into the bargain embroil ourselves in the very theological controversies that Locke, with his famous emphasis on religious toleration, wanted his political theory to enable us to avoid). Third, and as Jeremy Waldron (2002) has emphasized, Locke's view that the essences of things are man-made rather than (as the classical tradition holds) discovered in nature also practically undermines his appeal to God's will for us. For to know how to apply Locke's dictum that we must never harm another human being in his life, health, liberty, and possessions, we must first know what a human being *is*. Do fetuses count? People of races other than or own? People with severe brain damage? Whatever answer we give, Locke's metaphysics implies that it will ultimately be a matter of convention. "Every human being has natural rights that no one can take away." Hooray! "But we get to decide who counts as a human being and who doesn't." Oh. What Locke gives us with one hand he inadvertently takes back with the other.

When the Lockean appeal to God goes the way of the classical appeal to essences and final causes, natural rights unsurprisingly come to seem without any foundation at all. Hence Robert Nozick (1974), who was probably the most prominent contemporary defender of the idea of natural rights, was also notoriously sketchy at best about where exactly they come from. Though he makes a powerful case that a fairly radical libertarianism follows from a consistent application of the thesis of self-ownership (a more thoroughgoing conception of self-ownership than Locke would have accepted given his theism, to which Nozick is not committed), the basis of the right of self-ownership itself is left unclear. Nozick implies that it derives from Kant's principle of respect for persons as ends in themselves, though he never spells out how exactly, and few have been persuaded that such a derivation can be made out. The more fundamental problem, though, is explaining *why* we should regard persons as ends in themselves in the first place (a claim that seems if anything to *presuppose* that people have rights rather than to provide grounds for the claim that they do). As indicated earlier, Kant's own appeal to reason seems hopeless if reason itself is as devoid of an essence or natural end as (given a mechanistic conception of the world) everything else is.

Forward into the past

Suppose one agrees that belief in natural rights does indeed become indefensible apart from the essentialist and teleological metaphysical assumptions of the classical tradition in philosophy. Obviously, it does not follow that those assumptions are correct after all. One might very well say instead "So much for natural rights, then."

Well, to paraphrase H. R. Haldeman paraphrasing Richard Nixon, we could do that, but it would be wrong. For it is not just natural rights that go when classical metaphysics goes, but morality in general, science, and reason itself, or so I would argue. Certainly it would be naive in the extreme to think that essentialism and teleology can be neatly carved off from the rest of common sense and set aside, leaving our conception of ourselves as rational and moral agents otherwise more or less intact – albeit that such *naivete* seems par for the course among contemporary philosophers.

It was not always so. In an article in the *Atlantic Monthly* in 1948, the then-eminent (if now largely forgotten) philosopher W. T. Stace – an empiricist who was not himself in sympathy with the Aristotelian–Scholastic philosophy I have been describing – said this about the moderns' decision to abandon that philosophy:

> The real turning point between the medieval age of faith and the modern age of unfaith came when the scientists of the seventeenth century turned their backs upon what used to be called "final causes" ... [belief in which] *was not the invention of Christianity [but] was basic to the whole of Western civilization, whether in the ancient pagan world or in Christendom, from the time of Socrates to the rise of science in the seventeenth century ... They did this on the ground that inquiry into purposes is useless for what science aims at: namely, the prediction and control of events ... The conception of purpose in the world was ignored and frowned upon. This, though silent and almost unnoticed, was the greatest revolution in human history, far outweighing in importance any of the political revolutions whose thunder has reverberated through the world* ... The world, according to this new picture, is purposeless, senseless, meaningless. Nature is nothing but matter in motion. The motions of matter are governed, not by any purpose, but by blind forces and

> laws ... [But] if the scheme of things is purposeless and meaningless, then the life of man is purposeless and meaningless too. Everything is futile, all effort is in the end worthless. A man may, of course, still pursue disconnected ends, money, fame, art, science, and may gain pleasure from them. But his life is hollow at the center. Hence, the dissatisfied, disillusioned, restless, spirit of modern man ... Along with the ruin of the religious vision there went the ruin of moral principles and indeed of all values ... If our moral rules do not proceed from something outside us in the nature of the universe – whether we say it is God or simply the universe itself – then they must be our own inventions. Thus it came to be believed that moral rules must be merely an expression of our own likes and dislikes. But likes and dislikes are notoriously variable. What pleases one man, people or culture, displeases another. Therefore, morals are wholly relative.
>
> *(Stace 1948, pp. 53–55; emphasis added)*

There are three points from Stace's remarks that are worth emphasizing. First, the moral significance of the moderns' abandonment of the classical metaphysical picture of the world cannot be overstated. The French Revolution, Communism, National Socialism, the "Great Disruption" in traditional morality (as Francis Fukuyama (1999) has called it) that came to a head in the 1960s – all have their roots in the notion that there is nothing in the nature of things, no fixed human essence or natural end, that could provide a rational basis for objecting *in principle* to even the most radical schemes of social transformation (even if *practical* limitations are sometimes acknowledged). Dramatic as these political and social revolutions have been, they are but manifestations of the far deeper if "silent and unnoticed" revolution in *thought* that began in the seventeenth century. That morality is an entirely artificial construct that we may redesign at will – even to the point of making what has always been considered evil out to be good, and vice versa – seems inescapable given the abandonment of final causes.

Second, despite a widespread assumption to the contrary, this intellectual revolution was not *of itself* a rebellion against some system of revealed theology, but rather the rejection of a purely philosophical doctrine that had always been understood to be grounded in reason. To be sure, that the philosophical doctrine in question was thought to give intellectual support to traditional Christian theology was a key motivation for its abandonment. But the philosophical doctrine and the theology are nevertheless distinct, whether or not one thinks the former can be used to uphold the latter. It would be a mistake, then, to think that the dispute between modern and classical philosophy can be identified with the so-called "war between science and religion."

Third, and also contrary to the conventional wisdom, this intellectual revolution was *not* justified by any discovery of modern science. It was instead an arbitrary redefinition of what would be allowed to *count* as science. The classical tradition had regarded intellectual life as concerned with wisdom, understood as knowledge of the ultimate causes and purposes of things. It was, accordingly, somewhat otherworldly in its orientation; contemplation of the eternal verities and improvement of one's soul were its goals. The moderns wanted to redirect intellectual efforts in a practical and this-worldly direction, toward increasing "human utility and power" (as Bacon put it) so as to make us "masters and possessors of nature" (in the words of Descartes). Dramatic advances in what Bacon called the "mechanical arts" or technology were the intended payoff. Hence, as Stace observes, the "prediction and control of events" became the *sine qua non* of the new science, and whatever is "useless" for this purpose – such as the search for final causes – came to be "ignored and frowned upon." Now to ignore and frown upon something is not to prove that it does not exist. Nevertheless, what has never been anything more than a mere methodological stipulation imperceptibly took on the status of a settled metaphysical result, as if the stubborn refusal to look for final causes constituted a demonstration of their unreality. As the historian and philosopher of science E. A. Burtt (1952, pp. 305–306) concluded in his classic *The Metaphysical Foundations of Modern Physical Science*, the early modern philosophers and scientists were as guilty of "wishful thinking" and "uncritical confidence" in promoting their new mechanistic conception of the natural world as they accused their medieval forebears of being.

Now there are many reasons to think that the classical commitment to essentialism and teleology has not only not been refuted by modern science, but is unavoidable if we are going to make sense of science, and indeed of reason itself. Needless to say, this is a large claim. I have defended it at length in my books *The Last Superstition* (2008) and *Aquinas* (2009); what follows is a brief summary of just some of the key points.

It is important to emphasize in the first place that a key obstacle to acknowledging the reality of final causes is the prevalence of certain crude misunderstandings. For example, it is often assumed that to attribute a final cause or natural end to something is necessarily to attribute to it something like conscious awareness and/or something like a biological function. It is then concluded that anyone committed to the reality of final causes must believe such absurdities as that asteroids and balls of lint (or whatever) somehow play a role within the larger universe that is analogous to the role an eye or a kidney plays in an organism, and that they are at least dimly conscious of doing so. But this is a travesty. In fact the Aristotelian view has always been that most final causality is not associated with consciousness at all and that biological functions constitute only one, relatively rare kind of final causality among others.

The heart of the idea of final causality is rather that "every agent acts for an end," as Aquinas put it. What this means is that anything that serves as an efficient cause (i.e., as that which brings about a certain effect) is directed towards production of that effect as its natural end or goal. The cause "points to" that effect specifically, rather than to some other effect or to no effect at all; or in other words, when A is the efficient cause of B, that is only because B is the final cause of A. To take a simple example, a match "points to" or is "directed at" the generation of flame and heat specifically, rather than frost and cold, or the smell of roses, or the sound of thunder. That is the effect it will naturally bring about when struck unless prevented in some way from doing so, and even if it is never in fact struck it remains true that it is that specific effect that it always "aimed at." As Aquinas argued, unless we acknowledge the reality of final causes in this sense, we have no way of explaining *why* it is that efficient causes have exactly the effects they do; efficient causality is unintelligible without final causality.

That there is something to what Aquinas is saying here should be obvious to anyone familiar with the history of philosophical debate over causation since Hume. Famously, Hume argued that the necessity with which we think some cause A will bring about some effect B reflects only the subjective tendency of the human mind to expect B on the occurrence of A, rather than anything objectively true of A and B themselves. As far as the objective facts are concerned, A might be followed instead by C, D, E, or indeed by no effect at all, rather than by B. The fact that we find this possibility hard to take seriously reflects only our psychological makeup, not physical reality. Hence, if science is in the business of discovering objective necessary connections between physical events, it seems there can be no science. Moreover, our confidence in the inductive reasoning upon which science depends becomes rationally unjustifiable insofar as, given that there are no objective necessary connections between causes and effects, we have no grounds for believing that the future will be like the past or in general that those parts of the world that we have not observed are like the parts we have observed. All of these long-standing philosophical difficulties (and many more) follow from abandoning the idea that things have final causes, ends toward which they inherently point by virtue of their essence or nature. They disappear when we acknowledge that teleology is real.

It is by no means only old-fashioned Aristotelians who would defend essences and teleology today. John Hawthorne (Hawthorne and Nolan 2006) is one prominent contemporary philosopher who has advocated at least a reconsideration of final causes. One finds a hint of final causality even in the work of the prominent materialist philosopher D. M. Armstrong (1999, pp. 138–140), who suggests that in order to explain intentionality– the mind's capacity to represent the world beyond itself – we ought to consider the dispositions physical objects possess (such as the disposition glass has to break even if it never in fact shatters) as instances of a kind of "proto-intentionality" or "pointing beyond themselves" toward certain specific outcomes. Similarly, the late metaphysician George Molnar (2003) held that the causal powers inherent in physical objects manifest a kind of "physical intentionality" insofar as, like thoughts and other mental states, they point to something beyond themselves, even though they are unlike thoughts in being unconscious. Molnar was representative of a movement toward what the philosopher of science Brian Ellis (2002) has called a "new essentialism," the view that the usual mechanistic, empiricist interpretation of science simply does not hold up in light of actual scientific discoveries and the facts of scientific practice. Ellis and Nancy Cartwright, another prominent "new essentialist," are forthright about the neo-Aristotelian character of their position. Actual experimental practice, Cartwright argues (1992), shows that the hard sciences are in the business of discovering the hidden essences universal to, and the causal powers inherent in, things of a certain type. Contrary to popular presentations of scientific procedure, physicists do not embrace a regularity as a law of nature only after many observed trials. Rather, they draw their conclusions from a few highly specialized experiments conducted under artificial conditions, on the basis of an abstract and idealized theoretical description of the object of study whose features are rarely if ever directly observed at all. That is to say, they give every appearance of trying to determine what the *inner tendencies* are that a physical thing will manifest *of its nature* when the interfering conditions usually present in real-world circumstances are removed – just the features one would expect there to be if an essentialist-cum-teleological account of the natural world is true.

Several mainstream contemporary thinkers are also prepared to acknowledge the continuing applicability of Aristotelian concepts in biology no less than in physics. For example, the philosopher of biology André Ariew (2007) has noted that even if natural selection suffices to explain the adaptation of an organism to its environment, there is also the question of the internal development of an organism, and in particular of what accounts for the fact that certain growth patterns count as aberrations and others as normal. Here Aristotle would say that there is no way to make this distinction apart from the notion of an end toward which the growth pattern naturally points: normal growth patterns are those that reach this end, aberrations (clubfoot, polydactyly, and other birth defects, for example) are failures to reach it. Ariew seems to allow that there is nothing in Darwinism that undermines this sort of argument for final causes. The biologist J. Scott Turner (2007) is even more explicit that accounting for such phenomena requires attributing an unconscious "intentionality" to biological processes.

The persistence of teleological thinking within biology is perhaps most clearly evident from the way in which biologists describe DNA. Accounts of this famous molecule regularly make use of concepts like "information," "instructions," "data," "blueprint," "software," "code," "program," and the like, and there is no way to convey what DNA does without something like them. But all of these concepts are suffused with intentionality, a thing's pointing beyond itself in the way our thoughts do – in this case to an organism's physiological and behavioral traits, including those determining the species it belongs to. Of course, no one would claim that DNA molecules can be said to think. But the notion of something pointing to an end or goal beyond itself despite being totally unconscious is just the Aristotelian notion of final causality. In his book *The Fifth Miracle* (1999), the physicist Paul Davies has complained of the contradiction implicit in biologists' use of informational concepts that entail meaning or purpose while purporting at the same time to be committed to a completely mechanistic or non-teleological picture of the world. Recognizing that such concepts are indispensible, he at least tentatively raises the question of whether purpose might after all be a genuine property of nature "right down to the cellular or even the subcellular level" (1999, p. 122).

It should go without saying that human action, which is inherently goal-directed, is perhaps the most obvious example of a phenomenon that seems in principle impossible to account for in non-teleological terms (as many philosophers have argued, Scott Sehon and G. F. Schueler most recently). Then there is human thought, which, even apart from the actions it sometimes gives rise to, manifests intentionality or "directedness" toward something beyond itself and is thus as problematic for a mechanistic picture of the natural world as teleology is. Indeed, this is the reason that modern philosophers have (unlike their classical forebears) been obsessed with the so-called "mind–body problem." Having adopted a characterization of the physical world that strips it entirely of goal-directedness, purpose, or meaning, they seem thereby committed to the view that the human mind, which is of its very nature purposive and goal-directed, must *necessarily* be non-physical. In this sense, Cartesian dualism, far from being a pre-scientific holdover, is an *inevitable byproduct* of the mechanistic revolution heralded by modern science – as early modern thinkers like Descartes and Locke realized, even if their materialistic successors often do not. Of course, the latter would complain, and rightly, that the mind's relationship to the physical world becomes mysterious on such a dualist account. But since the mechanistic picture of nature that they share with their Cartesian rivals generates the mystery, this shows (or so I would argue) that it was a mistake to adopt that picture in the first place.

The alternative, if one is to avoid dualism, would seem to be to deny the very existence of intentionality, and thus the existence of the human mind itself. This, in the view even of some prominent non-dualists such as John Searle, is what every extant form of materialism implicitly does. An extreme form of materialism known as "eliminative materialism" does so explicitly, claiming as it does that there are *no such things* as thoughts, beliefs, desires, and other mental states, and that a truly scientific account of human nature would have to re-describe us *entirely* in terms of neuronal wiring patterns, electrochemical signals, muscular contractions, and other concepts drawn from neuroscience and physiology, completely eliminating any reference to purposes, meanings, and the like. Bizarre as this sounds, it is the inevitable final stop on the train leading away from final causes, or so I would argue. It is also utterly incoherent, amounting to the denial of the existence of human reason, and thus of the very possibility of science, in the name of reason and science.

Much more could be said in support of the classical teleological and essentialist picture of the natural world. Again, I have said much more elsewhere. But to forestall irrelevant objections, I should perhaps emphasize in closing that I am by no means criticizing modern science. What is at issue is a certain *philosophical interpretation* of the findings of modern science, not the findings themselves (albeit it is an interpretation that many modern scientists have unfortunately tended to adopt in their philosophical moments). Furthermore, the view I am defending has nothing to do with "intelligent design" theory, creationism, or other such bogeymen. It is not William Paley, but Aristotle, whose rehabilitation I am recommending. If I am right, there is a powerful case to be made for the view that ends or goals toward which things are directed by nature pervade the natural order from top to bottom, from the level of human thought down to that of basic physical particles. It follows that defectiveness or failure to realize a natural end also pervades the natural order – as does the opposite circumstance, the manifestation in things of their "natural goodness." And in that case, the metaphysical foundations the classical philosophical tradition would give natural rights theory are secure.

I will be accused of wanting to turn the clock back. I plead guilty. But the antiquity of an idea is hardly evidence of its falsehood; quite the opposite, I would say. Nor is novelty an infallible mark of truth, progress, or beneficence. If there is a lesson to be drawn from the twentieth century, it is that to deny the existence of natural human rights is to invite a level of inhumanity that is nothing if not modern.

References

Ariew, André. 2007. "Teleology." In David L. Hull and Michael Ruse, eds., *The Cambridge Companion to the Philosophy of Biology* (Cambridge: Cambridge University Press).

Armstrong, D. M. 1999. *The Mind–Body Problem: An Opinionated Introduction* (Boulder, CO: Westview).

Brett, Annabel S. 1997. *Liberty, Right, and Nature: Individual Rights in Later Scholastic Thought* (Cambridge: Cambridge University Press).

Burtt, E.A. 1952. *The Metaphysical Foundations of Modern Physical Science* (Atlantic Highlands, NJ: Humanities Press).

Cartwright, Nancy. 1992. "Aristotelian Natures and Modern Experimental Method." In John Earman, ed., *Inference, Explanation, and Other Frustrations: Essays in the Philosophy Of Science* (Berkeley: University of California Press).

Davies, Paul. 1999. *The Fifth Miracle: The Search for the Origin and Meaning of Life* (New York: Simon & Schuster).

Ellis, Brian. 2002. *The Philosophy of Nature: A Guide to the New Essentialism* (Chesham, UK: Acumen).

Feser, Edward. 2007. *Locke* (Oxford: Oneworld Publications).

Feser, Edward. 2008. *The Last Superstition: A Refutation of the New Atheism* (South Bend, IN: St. Augustine's Press).

Feser, Edward. 2009. *Aquinas* (Oxford: Oneworld Publications).

Foot, Philippa. 2001. *Natural Goodness* (Oxford: Oxford University Press).

Fukuyama, Francis. 1999. *The Great Disruption: Human Nature and the Reconstitution of Social Order* (New York: Simon & Schuster).

Hawthorne, John and Daniel Nolan. 2006. "What Would Teleological Causation Be?" In John Hawthorne, *Metaphysical Essays* (Oxford: Oxford University Press).

Molnar, George. 2003. *Powers: A Study in Metaphysics* (Oxford: Oxford University Press).

Nozick, Robert. 1974. *Anarchy, State, and Utopia* (New York: Basic Books).

Oderberg, David S. 2000. *Moral Theory: A Non-Consequentialist Approach* (Oxford: Blackwell).

Schueler, G. F. 2003. *Reasons and Purposes: Human Rationality and the Teleological Explanation of Action* (Oxford: Oxford University Press).

Sehon, Scott. 2005. *Teleological Realism: Mind, Agency, and Explanation* (Cambridge, MA: MIT Press).

Stace, W.T. 1948. "Man against Darkness." *Atlantic Monthly*, September.

Strauss, Leo. 1953. *Natural Right and History* (Chicago: University of Chicago Press).

Tierney, Brian. 2001. *The Idea of Natural Rights* (Grand Rapids, MI: Eerdmans).

Turner, J. Scott. 2007. *The Tinkerer's Accomplice: How Design Emerges from Life Itself* (Cambridge, MA: Harvard University Press).

Veatch, Henry B. 1985. *Human Rights: Fact or Fancy?* (Baton Rouge: Louisiana State University Press).

Waldron, Jeremy. 2002. *God, Locke, and Equality: Christian Foundations in Locke's Political Thought* (Cambridge: Cambridge University Press).

3

Kant's theory of human rights

Luigi Caranti

Many philosophical accounts of human rights are currently presented as Kantian or strongly based on Kant's assertion of human beings' inherent worth. Many more are fashionably announced as anti-Kantian, or at least post-Kantian, for their firm refusal of adopting tentatively universal yet ultimately parochial standards of normativity. Despite this vast array of positive and negative references, it is surprising that no commentator has ever attempted to reconstruct what would be an authentically Kantian theory of human rights. To be sure, we have at our disposal sophisticated interpretations of Kant's theory of justice (*Recht*), of rights in general, of cosmopolitan law, of humanity (Sciacca 2000) and of many other concepts that are clearly relevant for any theory of human rights. Yet, with the exception of few remarks scattered here and there, and a recent attempt by Gunnar Beck (2006), no one has ever read Kant's moral and political thought to find in it what we would call today a philosophical theory of human rights.

There are at least two motives for this gap in the literature. To begin with, Kant seldom uses the expression "human rights." The only occurrences I found are in *Perpetual Peace*. In the context of the discussion on the relation between morality and politics, Kant claims, "The rights of man must be held sacred. However great a sacrifice the ruling power may have to make" (Reiss 1970, p. 125). Moreover, when he comes closest to it, in his account of humans' innate right to freedom, it is not clear whether such right can be safely considered as equivalent to a "human right." More precisely, it is not clear whether Kant's idea that humans have an innate right to freedom "by virtue of their humanity" is sufficiently similar to the central intuition behind the culture of human rights, i.e., that certain rights are bestowed on humans independently of their belonging to political groups, cultural traditions, religious loyalties, or races, but merely by virtue of their membership in the human species. In fact, "humanity" is a technical notion in Kant's system and is rightly viewed as potentially divisive once the metaphysical apparatus on which it rests (our alleged membership in a noumenal world) is brought to light. Let us call this "the terminological motive."

On a more profound level, Kant's ethics is perceived as diametrically opposed to the effort, recommended by virtually *any* expert of human rights, to find some intercultural, non-parochial, possibly a-metaphysical, basis on which representatives of profoundly different cultures and traditions can give their assent. There are at least two features of Kant's account of basic rights that seem to run counter to this pluralism-sensitive approach. To begin with, Kant's notion of humans' inherent worth depends on a controversial belief in our peculiar characteristic of being transcendentally free. Moreover, Kant's implicit assumption that the individual is the sole legitimate subject of ethics is questioned by alternative, non-Western approaches that are told to give priority to the group, exemplified by the so-called East Asian challenge to human rights. As a result, there are very few thinkers who venture to use Kant's practical philosophy as an explicit intellectual basis for establishing a philosophical foundation of human rights. In this regard, Alan Gewirth (1984) is probably the last, controversial exception. Let us call this "the philosophical motive."

Notwithstanding the terminological and philosophical motives, and their strong plausibility, the absence of a truly Kantian theory of human rights in the literature remains problematic. On close consideration, Kant interestingly manages to combine rigidity on certain universal standards (in particular freedom and equality) with a surprising flexibility concerning the implementation of these standards *vis-à-vis* the moral pluralities of our world. Kant would condemn the tendency to water down the universals of justice and consider the worldwide violations of the right to freedom and formal equality as inexcusable for cultural or religious reasons (a position that virtually no theoretician today would dare to embrace). At the same time, he would also condemn the contemporary tendency to impose violently these *minima moralia* – a prudence that many think incompatible with a commitment to universal standards. Kant does not deflect from considering maximum liberty for each individual and perfect formal equality as rights inherently human, but he allows great flexibility to each society in its progress toward the implementation of these standards. This combination of rigidity about the principles and flexibility about the times and manners of their implementation deserves more attention than is usually conceded.

This chapter offers only the first step toward a Kantian foundation of human rights. The main goal is to identify the material from which such a theory could be developed. The analysis consists of three parts. First, I analyze Kant's idea that we have an innate right to freedom by virtue of our humanity. Second, I examine our "capacity to set ourselves ends" that Kant considers determinative of our "humanity." In particular, I will deal with the question whether this "capacity" is best understood as a form of practical freedom or rather of autonomy, two kinds of freedom that are quite different for Kant. Third, I will argue that Kant identifies our ability to be *moral* agents – i.e., our autonomy – as the ultimate ground on which the innate rights to external freedom and formal equality rest. In the attempt to spell out precisely how autonomy grounds these rights, I conclude by proposing an argument that mediates between two opposed hermeneutical schools.

"There is only one innate right"

Probably the text where Kant comes closest to expressing a theory of human rights, as we would understand it today, is the *Metaphysics of Morals*, in particular the section devoted to the General Division of Rights. There Kant claims that, "There is Only One Innate Right" (Gregor 1996, p. 30; AA VI 237), i.e., freedom, understood as "independence from being constrained by another's choice" (Gregor 1996, p. 30; AA VI 237). From our right to external freedom Kant infers analytically our right to (formal) equality. He claims:

> This principle of innate freedom already involves the following authorizations, which are not really distinct from it (as if they were members of the division of some higher concept

of right): innate equality, that is, independence from being bound by others to more than one can in turn bind them.

(Gregor 1996, p. 50; AA VI 237)

Kant's reasoning here is quite simple. Since each individual has a right to a sphere of freedom whose extension is limited only by the condition that such freedom be compatible with that of all others, it follows that these spheres must be all equal. Otherwise we would be adding some extra condition besides that of compatibility. Before the autonomous decision of the members of the society to limit their freedom through, say, obligations, promises (legal or moral), contracts, and so forth, the sphere of freedom I enjoy should be of a size identical with that of all others. And again, this seems to be a right that precedes the establishment of the commonwealth. A state is merely supposed to enforce and secure a right to equality whose ground precedes any societal compact. Our "sole" innate right has actually given birth to another crucial entitlement: perfect equality before the law, or, formal equality.

But what is the ground on which our right to freedom, and therefore to equality, rests? Kant argues that each individual has a right to external freedom "by virtue of his humanity." In the *Metaphysics of Morals* and elsewhere, Kant construes humanity as the capacity "by which he [the human being] alone is capable of setting himself ends" (Gregor 1996, p. 151; AA VI 387). More explicitly, "the capacity to set oneself an end – any end whatsoever – is what characterizes humanity [as distinguished from animality]" (Gregor 1996, p. 154; AA VI 392). We have an innate right to freedom (and to equality) because we are capable of setting ourselves ends. What does that mean? How is it that the alleged possession of a mere ability to set ends entitles me to anything? If I am capable of killing in cold blood, this certainly does not entitle me to any right, moral claim, or the like. Why, then, does Kant believe that the capacity to set ends for themselves entitles humans to a right to external freedom? The answer to this question presupposes clarity on humans' capacity to set ends for themselves. Since the expression, as it stands, evokes at least two kinds of freedom, practical freedom and autonomy, both present in Kant's system, it is incumbent on us to introduce them in their bare essentials in order to decide then which of the two Kant means in this context.

Two kinds of freedom

Notoriously, for Kant human actions are not fully determined by the sensuous inclinations that normally motivate us. Rather, given any inclinations, no matter how strong, it is always up to the individual to "endorse" them or to resist them. With the rather obvious exception of nonvoluntary responses to stimuli (such as the familiar knee coming up on a hammer strike), Kant thinks that human behavior as a whole is subject to free rational deliberation. This means that all voluntary actions stem from the individual's free evaluation of a certain maxim, understood as a subjective rule of action. Thus humans scrutinize through the use of their reason the opportunity (moral or prudential) of a certain maxim and are free to adopt it or reject it. Kant at times expresses this crucial point with reference to the notion of an *arbitrium liberum*, distinguished from the *arbitrium brutum* typical of animals (A533–534/B561–562). Humans, on this theory, set for themselves the ends of their life without being driven or fully determined by desires and needs. At most, desires and needs *suggest* a certain path of action. A free decision on the part of the actor to endorse or reject such a path, thereby making it one's own end, is, however, always necessary. This explains the force of the reflexive clause ("capable of setting *himself* ends") that appears in the formula above. Humans set *for themselves* ends. These ends are in no way imposed on them by external forces or internal passions. Humans enjoy what Kant at times calls "freedom in the practical sense" (A534/B562).

The Kantian notion of practical freedom comes very close to what one would call rational agency. This can be captured by two essential characteristics: (a) independence from pathological necessitation and (b) capacity to act on the basis of imperatives (rules of action) in the pursuit of a given goal. Thus humans are rational agents for Kant because they select the rule that guides their behavior (they do not act randomly), and they are free to select such a rule. To give an obvious example: if I am thirsty, and I see no reasons why I should resist or delay the satisfaction arising from the extinguishing of my thirst, I can freely select the maxim "any time an agent X is thirsty, she should drink." As emphasized by Henry Allison (1990), although apparently plain, this account of rational agency is already highly controversial in that it expresses an incompatible account of human freedom. In fact, for Kant the decision to drink is not fully determined by my inclination, nor is it determined by a more sophisticated pleasure calculus or the like. The decision to endorse the maxim in question is irreducible to one of the many natural causes we experience in the sensible world. The decision is a radically free act on the part of the subject. As Kant sometimes puts it, it is only on this condition that I can say that *I* perform any action, as opposed to "something in me led me to act" or "that particular objective state of affairs evolved in a certain direction."

As a historical point, this is in a nutshell the theory of freedom Kant presents in the first critique and that circa 1781 he thought to be sufficient for the sake of morality. Although many commentators are inclined to identify practical freedom with autonomy, and the hermeneutical issue would deserve a long discussion, there are good reasons (historical, systematic, textual) to resist this tendency. The historical reason is that Kant introduced the notion of autonomy relatively late in his career, i.e., after 1781. Until the first critique, in fact, Kant believes that all morality requires is practical freedom. And since practical freedom presupposes that some empirical end determines (without necessitating) my path of action, by Kant's own later standards, this moral theory would count as heteronomous. The systematic reason is that the distinction makes room for free (hence imputable) immoral behavior, thus salvaging Kant from the usual charge of embracing the grotesque view that on his account only moral behavior counts as free. The textual reasons are, quite simply, the definitions of autonomy from the *Groundwork* on, that insist on the human will's capacity to be a law to itself independently of *any* sensuous stimuli (i.e., without those empirical motives that determine practically free behavior) as the hallmark of autonomous agency. In the *Groundwork* (1785), however, we assist to the grand *entrée* of the concept of autonomy that makes Kant's theory of freedom even more problematic for the contemporary philosopher's sensitivity. Autonomy, as defined in the *Groundwork* and in the *Critique of Practical Reason*, entails more than independence of pathological necessitation, a feature underlying all kinds of rational behavior and equivalent to the notion of *arbitrium liberum*. It entails more than the ability to take distance from our contingent inclinations in view of some distant, yet still empirically motivated, end (I resist my desire to smoke in view of the higher goal of avoiding cancer). For the mature Kant, an agent whose freedom is limited to this ability is free but irremediably heteronomous. The agent is free because her inclinations (no matter how strong) do not exhaust the causal story behind her actions (it always takes a free rational act of endorsement), yet the agent is heteronomous because inclinations are necessary components of the motivational story behind the action.

To the contrary, being autonomous for Kant entails the ability to act in *complete* independence from inclinations. Positively expressed, this means to be able to find a sufficiently strong motivation in a very special kind of non-empirical interest, that is, obviously the respect for the moral law, or ability to be determined by the authoritative force of morality. As Henry Allison (1990, p. 97) puts it, a "will with the property of autonomy is one for which there are (or can be) reasons to act that are logically independent of the agent's needs as a sensuous being."

An autonomous agent does not merely give herself the rule of her action (this is spontaneity or practical freedom). She does so independently of *any* inclination. This is what Kant expresses with a slightly different language in one of the official definitions of autonomy in the *Groundwork*, where this form of freedom is presented as "the property the will has of being a law to itself (independently of every property belonging to the objects of volition)" (Kant 1781, p. 44; AA IV 440). While the human will is always a law to itself, because even heteronomous behavior presupposes that one makes a certain sensuously motivated maxim *one's* maxim, i.e., that one gives a law to oneself, it is only in autonomous agency that this law is self-imposed without sensuous influences. This is the force of the parenthetical clause in the definition of autonomy.

Thus, for Kant, humans display two kinds of freedom. Through practical freedom, they set ends for themselves and do it without being fully determined by inclinations, even if the motivational package that leads to action is sensibly influenced. Through autonomy, they set ends for themselves independently of any empirical motive. Since for Kant any form of agency, including moral agency, presupposes that the agent is moved by some interest, so that the question regarding the *principium executionis* be answered, this means that moral/autonomous agency will be motivated by the only form of *pure* (i.e., non-empirical) interest open to humans, i.e., respect of the moral law. On this reconstruction, autonomous behavior is equivalent to moral behavior, although, obviously, moral behavior is only a subset of free behavior (that includes heteronomous actions). Now, the crucial question for us is: which of these two forms of freedom is alluded to in the definition of "humanity" as "the capacity to set oneself an end – any end whatsoever"?

Autonomy as the basis of the right to external freedom

Both practical freedom and autonomy appear as respectable candidates for the role of the basis of our innate right to freedom because both are peculiar to human beings and satisfy Kant's definition of humanity. As explained, both practical freedom and autonomy share this feature. The difference is that autonomy adds to this ability the mark of complete independence from sensuous motivation. The reference to "*any* end whatsoever" suggests that Kant means practical freedom, because even immoral ends seem to be contemplated. Other considerations, however, of systematic and textual nature, lead us much more convincingly in the opposite direction. Starting from the systematic reasons, the fact that a certain capacity is peculiar of a species hardly grounds any right of that species. As we said above, the human species is arguably the sole capable of killing in cold blood or even for amusement, but this hardly grounds a human right to kill in this mood. Thus, the nerve of the argument cannot be the exclusive possession of an ability, but its intrinsic worth. Kant's argument must be that freedom, as a property of our will, displays something intrinsically good about humans, something that grounds human dignity and a fortiori lays the foundation for our right to external freedom. This something, as any student of Kant knows, is precisely autonomy, understood as a property necessary for a will to become a good will, i.e., the only thing in the world that is "good without qualification" and that, like a jewel, shines "by its own light as something which has its full value in itself" (Kant 1781, p. 8; AA IV 394). Practical freedom at most displays our nature of rational beings, a feature that in a sense already positions us above the natural world. Practical freedom, however, does not establish our greater worth compared to other entities of the sensible world. For this, the ability to follow the moral law even at the detriment of any empirical interest (including our survival) is required. To put it another way: while practical freedom makes us kings and queens of the sensible world, autonomy makes us demi-gods, inhabitants of this world, but at the same time qualified members, or, perhaps more modestly, qualified applicants to another kingdom.

Moving to the textual reasons, we find confirmation of the insufficiency of practical freedom when Kant affirms that the sheer capacity to set ends for themselves makes humans extrinsically more valuable than animals or things, but not superior to them as for their intrinsic, unconditioned value. He writes:

> In the system of nature, a human being (*homo phenomenon, animal rationale*) is a being of slight importance and shares with the rest of animals, as offspring of the earth, an ordinary value (*pretium vulgare*). Although a human being has, in his understanding, something more than they and can set himself ends, even this gives him only extrinsic value for his usefulness (*pretium usus*); that is to say, it gives one man a higher value than another, that is a *price* as of a commodity in exchange with these animals as things, though he still has lower value than the universal medium of exchange, money, the value of which can therefore be called preeminent (*pretium eminens*).
>
> But a human being regarded as a *person*, that is, as the subject of morally practical reason, is exalted above any price; for as a person (*homo noumenon*) he is not to be valued merely as a means to the ends of others or even to his own ends, but as an end in himself, that is, he possesses a *dignity* (an absolute inner worth) by which he *exacts* respect for himself from all other rational beings in the world. He can measure himself with every other being of this kind and value himself on a footing of equality with them.
>
> *(Gregor 1996, p. 186; AA VI 434–435)*

Kant denies explicitly that practical freedom confers an unconditioned value to humans. At most, understanding and practical freedom make humans particularly efficient and functional entities, goods more valuable than any other in the world, yet inescapably mere goods. To the contrary, considered as subjects of a morally practical reason, as autonomous beings, humans elevate themselves above any price, become ends in themselves, and legitimately demand respect from similar creatures. Kant re-emphasizes the point when he claims: "Humanity in his person is the object of the respect which he [man] can demand from every other human being" (Gregor 1996, p. 186; AA VI 434–435). Humanity as the basis for the only innate right to external freedom is ultimately our being subject to the moral law, our being autonomous.

To be sure, Kant is not consistent in the use of the term "humanity," especially in its distinction from personality. At times, as in the passages above, "humanity" refers not only to the capacity to set ends, but also the capacity to be ends in themselves, namely both to practical freedom and to autonomy. Other times, for example in *Religion* (AK VI 26–27), this latter capacity, i.e., the capacity of moral agency, is attributed to personality. Likewise, at times Kant claims that humanity "is a dignity" (Gregor 1996, p. 209; AK VI 462) and only a few lines later, as well as in many other passages, he claims that our dignity lies in our personality. This has led some commentators to believe that "humanity," understood as mere rational capacity (practical freedom), is for Kant the source of our absolute objective worth, which in turn is the ground of morality (Wood 2008, p. 88). But despite appearances, this view is highly problematic. As the passage quoted above shows beyond doubt, for Kant (or at least the mature Kant) the source of our absolute worth is autonomy, or, which is the same, our capacity for moral agency. Practical freedom makes us at best free, intelligent means for bringing about heteronomous ends. But it does not even make ends in ourselves, because we remain "things among things," objects, perhaps particularly efficient if compared with other animals, but even less valuable than the thing that can buy all things, i.e., money. It follows that when Kant claims that humanity can be the basis of our dignity, he clearly takes the term in the broad sense that encompasses not only rational capacity (practical freedom), but also autonomy.

If we are right in this reading, this leads to a series of sub-results. To begin with, there is no such thing as a *Kantian* foundation of human rights that can do without autonomy and therefore without Kant's arguments meant to prove that we are autonomous. Second, Kant links the innate rights we have on something that raises humans above the natural world. Third, we have these rights neither because we have a skill – understanding, or practical freedom – that no other animal has (something true but irrelevant for Kant), nor because we have yet another, even more sophisticated skill (autonomy), but because the latter reveals that we all are at least capable of something extraordinary: truly moral behavior. This and only this raises us above the natural world and makes us invaluable and inviolable. It is this view of humans as points of inalienable worth that Kant proposes for his foundation of human rights. It follows, fourth, that the ambiguous view of human nature that we find in *Religion* where Kant notoriously depicts humanity as "naturally" prone to prioritize self-love over morality cannot become a surrender to a fully pessimistic view of human nature on pain of inconsistency with, among other things, his theory of innate rights.

Is autonomy really necessary?

At this point, it remains to be explained how *precisely* our autonomy – an inner faculty – leads to the protection of the external freedom and inviolability we usually associate with human rights. The inference is less direct and clear than one may think, and we must face a crucial difficulty. Some interpreters, who by and large share the idea of making autonomy necessary for human rights, argue that one can infer almost analytically our right to external freedom from autonomy. Mary Gregor, for example, claims that external freedom is presupposed in the very concept of autonomy. For humans to be autonomous, Gregor thinks, it is required they be given the possibility to choose among alternative courses of action (Gregor 1963, p. 27). Recently this interpretation has been endorsed by a number of commentators who insist on the necessary link between autonomy and external freedom, the latter explicitly construed as a condition of the possibility of the former (Molholland 1990, p. 402n; Weinrib 1992, p. 27; Carr 1989; Bielefeldt 1997; Doppelt 1981).

There is, however, a second group of scholars who reject altogether our interpretation and hold that one can ground within Kant's system the right to external freedom without any reference to autonomy and that this was in fact Kant's intention. Thomas Pogge (2002), for example, argues in favor of the possibility and opportunity to separate ethics from politics in Kant, and a fortiori, to keep the right to external freedom (as expressed in the universal principle of right) as logically independent of autonomy. As textual evidence in favor of this heterodox reading, Pogge cites a passage from the "Introduction to the Doctrine of Right," in which Kant affirms that the normative force of the universal principle of right is independent on my endorsement of the moral basis of this principle. As Kant puts it: "reason says only that freedom *is* limited in its idea to those conditions [the universal principle of rights] and that it may be actively limited by others; and it says it as a postulate that is incapable of further proof" (Gregor 1996, pp. 24–25; AA VI 231). Kant would be here severing the bonds between the categorical imperative and the universal principle of right by stating that the "bindingness" of the latter does not depend on that of the former. To the contrary, the obligation to conform our actions to the universal principle of right follows *from the very idea of freedom* ("in its idea"), because this idea already contains the restriction that the freedom of one be compatible with that of all others. The main task of the *Rechtslehre* would thus be to come up with a set of rules enabling the "co-existence game," under the specified restriction. Such restriction – and this is the crucial point – is already contained in the definition of the game and is not imported from external sources.

Recently, and more closely to our discussion, Gunnar Beck has reached a similar conclusion. Beck raises two fundamental objections to our interpretation. On the one hand, he claims that this reading has scant textual evidence (2006, p. 381). On the other hand, he claims that since one remains autonomous even if his/her human rights are all violated, it follows that autonomy is at best irrelevant for human rights. To make his point more vivid Beck invites us to imagine the case of a slave. As he puts it:

> As long as the agent possesses a morally good will, no external force can obstruct his internal state of autonomy, even though restrictions on his external liberty may prevent the agent from exercising or acting upon his autonomy, i.e., to act in accordance with what he nevertheless accepts as his duty and wills to act on.
>
> *(Beck 2006, p. 383)*

Thus we have on one side interpreters who claim that autonomy and human rights are barely distinguishable (the analytic inference) and on the other side scholars who deny any relevance of autonomy for human rights. I conclude by proposing a middle ground interpretation.

The general impression is that there are pieces of truth scattered in the two hermeneutical schools, although the first group of interpreters seems closer to Kant's spirit and, *pace* Beck, Kant's text. To begin with, although Kant does not justify humans' right to external freedom through an *explicit* reference to autonomy, it is sufficient to investigate in his notion of "humanity" to find autonomy around the corner. As we saw, humanity is the explicit ground Kant offers for our right to external freedom. Man has that right "by virtue of his humanity," says Kant. If our reconstruction of Kant's argument is correct, however, the essence and worth of our humanity consists of our capacity to conform to the moral law. That is: it consists of our autonomy. Analogously, Pogge's sterilized reading of the *Rechtslehre* and of Kant's liberalism shows at most that if we all decided to play the coexistence game (say, for prudential reasons), then this game would obviously have its rules. In other words, if it is assumed from the beginning that free rational agents must coexist in such a way that their freedoms be compatible, then of course the rule that will best organize this coexistence is the universal principle of right. As pointed out by Bernd Ludwig (2002), however, Pogge cannot give an authentically Kantian reason why these free individuals should play the *Rechtslehre* game, as opposed to, say, *bellum omnium contra omnes* game.

The bit of truth to be found in the second orientation, and in particular in Beck's reading, is that external freedom does not really seem to be a presupposition, let alone a condition of the possibility, of autonomy. Here is precisely the problem with the first group of interpreters. Although they rightly view external freedom as *somehow* dependent on our autonomy, they exaggerate when they construe this logical dependence as if the latter were a condition of possibility of the former. As in the case of the slave, one can remain an autonomous individual even if deprived of external freedom (Danto 1984). Autonomy, as a property of our will, can always be exercised, even when our external freedom is most compressed. (It is something, so to speak, "nobody – individual or state – can take away from you.") Incidentally, this is one of the features of autonomy that makes it attractive as a candidate for the foundation of human rights. These in fact are universally considered as pertaining to humans independently of the circumstances in which they happen to live. Autonomy grounds a dignity for the individuals that even they could not alienate, remove, or compromise through immoral behavior. This is another advantage of having the dignity defended by human rights rest on autonomy.

Human rights should in fact protect even the most heinous criminals, dictators, abusers; in other words, those who have done their best to remove any trace of decency from their lives. Few human rights advocates, in fact, would deny that Saddam Hussein's execution was a violation of his inalienable entitlements.

This does not mean, however, that autonomy does not play any role in the foundation of our right to external freedom. It means merely that we have to abandon the hope of finding a transcendental argument that moves from autonomy to external freedom as its condition of possibility. More modestly one can investigate into the presuppositions not directly of autonomy but of the peculiar respect we are entitled to by virtue of being autonomous. The argument would be this:

1. humans are autonomous (in the Kantian sense);
2. this property bestows on them a status which entitles them to respect, understood as a guarantee not to be treated as mere means;
3. any arbitrary limitation of the freedom of some members of the society amounts to treating them as mere means, i.e., as a failure to respect them in the required manner;
4. the only a priori limitation of external freedom permitted is that necessary to make the external freedom of one compatible with that of all others;
5. any individual has a pre-political, inborn right to the maximum amount of freedom compatible with the same freedom of all others; and
6. all humans have a pre-political, inborn right to external freedom and formal equality.

Respect here bridges the logical gap, which has by and large gone unnoticed by the first group of interpreters, namely between autonomy and external freedom. From respect originates the prohibition to limit arbitrarily not autonomy itself, which is, strictly speaking, immune from restriction, but humans' external freedom. Without a reference to respect, however (and this is the problem with the second group) at best humans can be said to have an ability to be externally free, but not a *right* to external freedom.

Even if this reading appears closer to Kant's spirit and text, one needs to realize that our foundation of human rights faces two main defects. On the one hand, it renders this foundation of human rights dependent on Kant's proof of the reality (from the practical point of view) of our autonomy. Since both the arguments offered in the *Groundwork* and those of the second critique are controversial, to say the least, the price to pay is considerable. On the other hand, even granting that these or other similar arguments succeed, the problem of the significance of autonomy in non-Western cultures remains untouched. If we are proven to be autonomous, but being autonomous is not seen as the sole, or even as the main, source of human worth, then Kant's arguments will be ineffective as a first step toward an intercultural consensus on human rights. Replying to these worries would be the next step in considering a Kantian approach to human rights.

References

Allison, H. 1990. *Kant's Theory of Freedom* (Cambridge: Cambridge University Press).

Beck, G. 2006. "Immanuel Kant's Theory of Rights." *Ratio Juris*, Vol. 19, No. 4, pp. 371–401.

Bielefeldt, H. 1997. "Autonomy and Republicanism: Immanuel Kant's Philosophy of Freedom." *Political Theory*, Vol. 25, pp. 524–558.

Caranti, L. 2002. "Moralità Senza L'imperativo Categorico? Risposta a Philippa Foot." pp. 63–95 in H. Allison and L. Caranti, *Libertà Trascendentale ed Autorità Della Morale in Kant* (Roma: Luiss Edizioni).

Carr, C. 1989. "Kant's Theory of Political Authority." *History of Political Thought*, Vol. 10, pp. 719–731.
Danto, A. 1984. "Comment on Gewirth Constructing an Epistemology of Human Rights: A Pseudo Problem?" *Social Philosophy and Policy*, Vol. 1, pp. 25–30.
Doppelt, G. 1981. "Rawls' System of Justice: A Criticism from the Left." *Nous*, Vol. XV, No. 3, pp. 259–307.
Gewirth, A. 1984. *"The Epistemology of Human Rights."* pp. 1–24 in E. F. Paul, F. D. Miller, Jr., and J. Paul, eds., *Human Rights* (Oxford: Blackwell).
Gregor, M. 1963. *Laws of Freedom* (Oxford: Blackwell).
Gregor, M., ed. 1996. *The Metaphysics of Morals* (Cambridge: Cambridge University Press).
Kant, I. 1781. *Grounding for the Metaphysics of Morals* (Indianapolis, IN: Hackett).
Ludwig, B. 2002. "Whence Public Right? The Role of Theoretical and Practical Reasoning in Kant's Doctrine of Right." pp. 159–183 in M. Timmons, ed., *Kant's Metaphysics of Morals. Interpretative Essays* (Oxford: Oxford University Press).
Molholland, L. S. 1990. *Kant's System of Rights* (New York: Columbia University Press).
Pogge, T. 2002. "Is Kant's *Rechtslehre* a 'Comprehensive Liberalism'?" pp. 133–158 in M. Timmons, ed., *Kant's Metaphysics of Morals: Interpretative Essays* (Oxford: Oxford University Press).
Reiss, H., ed. 1970. *Kant: Political Writings* (Cambridge: Cambridge University Press).
Sciacca, F. 2000. *Il Concetto di Persona in Kant. Normatività e Politica* (Milano: Giuffré).
Weinrib, E. J. 1992 "Law as Idea of Reason." In *Essays on Kant's Political Philosophy* (Cardiff: University of Wales Press).
Wood, A. 2008. *Kantian Ethics* (Cambridge: Cambridge University Press).

4

Hate speech, human rights, and G. W. F. Hegel

Richard Mullender

Introduction

Humans have expressed feelings of hatred (including detestation and ill-will) toward others for millennia. For example, in AD 83–84, the Caledonian chieftain, Calcagus, described the Romans as arrogant "robbers of the world" who "make a desolation" (by plundering, butchering, and stealing) and, then, call it "peace" (Schama 2000, p. 34). But it was (according to the *Oxford English Dictionary*) only in the 1980s that the noun "hate speech" entered political discourse. It did so in the context of the so-called "culture wars" that became a prominent feature of politico-legal life in the USA at that time (Hughes 1993, pp. 18–26). We can also, however, place hate speech in a global context: the human rights revolution that began at the end of World War II and places emphasis on "recognition of the inherent dignity ... of all members of the human family" (Universal Declaration of Human Rights, Preamble, 1948). Moreover, it is a topic that we can theorize by reference to the egalitarian philosophy of government that has informed developments in the field of human rights in the last half-century. To this end, in this chapter, I draw on a prominent contributor to this philosophy of government, G. W. F. Hegel, who, among other things, identified "the imperative of right" as: "*be a person and respect others as persons*" (Hegel 1991a, p. 60). Hegel's thinking throws light on the three legal responses to hate speech that we will examine in this chapter. But before turning to hate speech, we must look at Hegel's political philosophy in some detail. Likewise, we must examine the law in the three countries under scrutiny: the USA, Canada, and Germany.

Hegel

G. W. F. Hegel (1770–1831) is a controversial political philosopher. Some commentators characterize him as a state-worshipping authoritarian (Popper 1962, p. 31; Berlin 2003, pp. 74–104). However, others, including John Rawls, regard him as a bearer of the progressive, Enlightenment tradition into which he was born and as a proponent of "the liberalism of freedom" (Rawls 2000, p. 330). Certainly, Hegel argues that, in a just social order, "universal freedom and equality ... will reign" (Harris 1972, p. 512). Moreover, prominent strands in Hegel's political philosophy reveal the strength of his commitment to this view. Like his compatriot Immanuel Kant, he set out a universal history. This history traces a rational process of development that culminates in egalitarian practical arrangements (Beiser 2005, p. 263). Hegel's history begins in "the Oriental world," where relations of lordship and bondage exist. He tells us that this is a context where only one person, the lord, is free (Beiser 2005, p. 266). Hegel then turns his attention to ancient Greece and Rome and declares that they were contexts in which the consciousness of freedom spread. His narrative ends in the Western world of his day. On his account, this is an egalitarian context in which people have grasped that humanity as such enjoys freedom (Hegel 1991b, pp. 456–457; Beiser 2005, p. 266).

Hegel identifies the state as central to the process of development he traces (Rawls 2000, pp. 352–353). For the state gives expression to an ideal that underwrites the idea that all people (with the capacity to do so) should enjoy freedom. This is the ideal of abstract right (*Recht*), according to which societies should accommodate the interests of all their members defensibly (Hegel 1991a, pp. 59–72). But as Hegel's historical narrative makes plain, humankind has struggled to grasp, let alone act in accordance with, this ideal. For while we may find in any actually existing community (*Sittlichkeit*) intimations of abstract right, those who live within it are apt to privilege their own interests in ways that impede the pursuit of justice (Pippin 2008, p. 222; Williams 1997, p. 232). For this reason, Hegel describes history as a "slaughter bench" (*Schlachtbank*) on which humankind has struggled to approximate (more and more adequately) the ideal of abstract right (Hegel 1991b, p. 21; Hampsher-Monk 1992, pp. 476–479). Alongside these stands in Hegel's political philosophy, we must set a theme that has great relevance to hate speech. Hegel argues that humans seek to secure adequate recognition (*Anerkennung*) from others (Wood 1990, pp. 77–93).

Hegel on recognition

In the *Phenomenology of Spirit* Hegel argues that adequate recognition from others is the foundation of just social relations (Williams 1997, p. 2). In staking out this position, Hegel developed a theme that his compatriot, Fichte, had pursued (Williams 1997, p. 1). However, Hegel, unlike Fichte, made the practical significance of recognition apparent to his readers by unfolding a dramatic narrative concerning the roots of ethical life or community (Fukuyama 1992, p. 148; Williams 1997, p. 2). Hegel imagines a primitive "first man" who lives at the beginning of history. Like other animals, this man desires, *inter alia*, food, shelter, and sleep. But, unlike other animals, he seeks the recognition of other men (Fukuyama 1992, p. 146). This desire is, on Hegel's analysis, entirely understandable. For individuals cannot become self-conscious (aware of their separateness from others and their capacity for freedom) without the recognition of those around them (Hegel 1977, p. 111; Fukuyama 1992, p. 146).

This explains why Hegel is highly specific on the nature of the recognition sought by the first man. This individual does not merely want to be recognized; rather, he wants others to recognize him as a person: i.e., as one who possesses the capacity to live freely (Fukuyama 1992, p. 147; Wood 1990, p. 85). With this point in place, Hegel imagines an encounter between his "first man" and another who shares the same desire for recognition. The upshot is "a life-and-death struggle" (Hegel 1977, p. 114). This battle can have one of three outcomes. The participants may kill one another. One of the two may perish, with the result that the survivor will not enjoy the recognition he desires. Both may, however, survive as a result of one submitting to the other. In such circumstances, an unequal relationship of lordship and bondage or master and servant comes into existence. On Hegel's analysis, this relationship is unsatisfactory not just for the one in bondage but also for the one who exercises power over him. This is because the one who has prevailed in the struggle has denied himself the recognition of an equal (Hegel 1977,

p. 115; Williams 1997, p. 56). For the slave is no longer in a position to bestow authentic recognition on those around him (Hegel 1977, p. 115; Williams 1997, p. 63). In light of these points, Hegel concludes that the only way to avoid this unsatisfactory state of affairs is for individuals to renounce coercion and recognize one another on a reciprocal basis (Williams 1997, p. 56; Wood 1990, p. 89).

The renunciation of coercion is a theme that Hegel continued to pursue in a later work, his *Encyclopaedia*. This text gives even greater emphasis than *The Phenomenology of Spirit* to "affirmative relationships based on reciprocal recognition" and thus pursues a theme later developed by Martin Buber (Williams 1997, p. 69; Buber 1947, pp. 249–264). We find Hegel arguing that, in order to enjoy adequate recognition, master and slave must achieve liberation together. To this end, they have to fashion inclusive institutions in which the "I" (prone, as it is, to egoistic self-affirmation) becomes a "We" (in which the interest in freedom shared by all is recognized) (Williams 1997, pp. 6, 25–26, 63, 78). In light of these points, Hegel has been read as giving expression to the view that freedom or, at least, the possibility of living freely, becomes actual through the process of recognition (Williams 1997, p. 80).

The concept of freedom that features in Hegel's argument for reciprocal recognition has, on the analysis offered by Ludwig Siep, four main features (Siep 1992, pp. 159–171). They are autonomy (*Autonomie*), union (*Vereinigung*), self-overcoming (*Selbstüberwindung*), and release (*Freigabe*). We will look at each of them in some detail since they are relevant to the legal responses to hate speech that we will examine below.

Autonomy: Hegel follows Kant in treating autonomy as the self-originating capacity of the will that makes it independent from everything else. Moreover, he identifies autonomy both negatively and positively. Autonomy in the negative sense has to do with freedom from external influences (e.g., those that exist in actually existing communities). Independence, self-determination, and spontaneity each give expression to autonomy in the positive sense.

Union: By "union," Hegel means relationship. In circumstances where a group of people establish relations of reciprocal recognition, the other ceases to be a hindrance or limit to freedom. Hegel puts the point thus: "[s]ince freedom consists in my identity with the other, I am truly free when the other is free and recognized as such by me" (Williams 1997, p. 82; cf. Abraham Lincoln's declaration that: "[i]n giving freedom to the *slave* we *assure* freedom to the *free*" [Keneally 2003, p. 139]).

Self-overcoming: On Seip's analysis, self-overcoming follows from union. This is because the impact of union on individuals is transformative. For the other decenters the self and provides the occasion for it to overcome its narrow, parochial individualism (Williams 1997, pp. 82–83). Moreover, the self – once free from parochialism – renounces domination and allows the other to be (or, to put the same point another way, behaves tolerantly) (Williams 1997, p. 83). In such circumstances, reciprocal recognition becomes a reality. Hegel describes this as a "condition" of "universal freedom" (Williams 1997, p. 83).

Release: This feature of freedom has both negative and positive connotations. Negatively, it has to do with the renunciation of attempts to dominate the other. Positively, it signifies openness to the other and affirming the other as she determines herself. Release is the consummation of reciprocal recognition. On one analysis, the presence of this concept in Hegel's political philosophy makes it plain that he is "after a community of freedom that does not absorb or reduce individuals to some homogeneity" (Williams 1997, p. 84). Since release marks the culmination of the process in which humans adequately meet their shared need for recognition, it is central to Hegel's account of human history (Williams 1997, p. 84; Rawls 2000, pp. 370–371).

If Hegel is correct in claiming that humans have a need for recognition, then the form of expressive activity to which we now turn (hate speech) is a matter of great practical concern.

Hate speech

Hate speech: conceptual analysis

"Hate speech" is an intensely controversial topic. Those eager to protect free expression will argue for a narrow definition. By contrast, those who seek to advance the agenda of equality are likely to argue for a more expansive definition (see Table 4.1 at the end of this chapter). I seek, in what follows, to describe a central case of hate speech (on which Hegel – as we will see – throws light). This central case exhibits the following features:

Hate

"Hate," the *Oxford English Dictionary* tells us, is both a noun (hate as emotion) and a verb (hate as activity). "Hate" in each of these senses is highly relevant to hate speech. According to Robert Post, the emotions that find expression in hate speech are "extreme" (in Hare and Weinstein 2009, p. 125). Another commentator states that hate-as-emotion is "inspired by beliefs which stimulate a set of ... emotions in the hater, chief among them fear, ignorance, jealousy, anger and disgust" (Grayling 2002, p. 86). This goes some way towards capturing the young Adolf Hitler's response to Jews on encountering them in Vienna (on moving from Linz to the Austrian capital). The future leader of the Third Reich records that he "suddenly encountered a phenomenon in a long caftan and wearing black side-locks ... I watched the man stealthily and ... the question shaped itself in my brain: Is this a German?" (Jetzinger 1976, p. 74). As Hitler dwelt on this question, his feelings assumed the shape of hate as emotion. The anti-Semitic outpourings that were central to Hitler's later political career gave expression to this emotion and instantiated hate as activity. But "hate" has to do with more than a noun and verb. It is also relevant to a disposition central to which is the activity (and positive valuation) of hating. This activity provides a basis on which to identify a second feature – intention – that gives central cases of hate speech their distinctive shape. Moreover, we might identify the formation of this intention as part of a process that can lead from beliefs to invidious discrimination and, on occasion, the infliction of harm.

Intention

In circumstances where individuals such as Hitler seek to cultivate in themselves and others hatred towards a particular group of people, we can describe them as acting intentionally. Although this point applies to central cases of hate speech, some commentators go further and identify intention as a feature common to all instances of this form of expressive activity. Jerome Neu, for example, states that "[h]ate speech ... is designed to make individuals feel demeaned, despised, and rejected" (Neu 2008, pp. 153–154). On this view, we have to accept that hate speech does not include, *inter alia*, the views of males who unreflectively describe females in misogynistic terms (hooks 1994, pp. 65 and 69 [on the use of "ho" (for woman) by some African-American males]). However, expression of this sort may, nonetheless, "[i]ntensify ... stereotypical representations of women" (D. Kennedy 2002, p. 105).

An invidious ground

Those who engage in hate speech denigrate or vilify others on invidious grounds such as race, sex, sexual orientation, and religion (Waldron 2009, pp. 1597–1598). Although invidious expression of this sort has become a hot topic in the USA and other Western countries in recent decades, examples of it are legion in human history. When, for example, Germanic warrior tribes began to displace Celts from the country we now call England, they identified those they displaced as their inferiors. The word they chose to indicate this rank-ordering was "Wealas" (slave) – which has echoed through the centuries in the word "Wales," the name of one of the constituent nations of the United Kingdom (Bragg 2003, p. 5).

The decision to denigrate others on an invidious ground brings us back to the topic of intention. As the "Wealas" example illustrates, those who engage in this type of expressive activity seek to identify others as inferiors and, to this end, use denigratory language. The Nazis, for example, applied the term "amphibians" to people whose ethnic identity was ambiguous (Mazower 2008, p. 187). Moreover, those who endure the type of denigration we are contemplating typically experience it as insulting. For it gives expression to "an attitude of disrespect, an attitude of insufficient regard" (Neu 2008, pp. 18–19, 139).

Inflicting or attempting to inflict harm

Those who engage in hate speech do so with the aim of causing harm (more or less directly) to those they target. This is true of a white man who describes an African-American as a "nigger" so as to undercut his sense of self-esteem and diminish his capacity to flourish (R. Kennedy 2002; Rawls 1971, pp. 440–446). Likewise, it is true of one who incites others to act violently towards a particular ethnic group, for example, the leader of the British Union of Fascists, Sir Oswald Mosley, who incited violence against Jews in the 1930s (Dorril 2006, pp. 295–315, 369–397).

Assuming that hate speech does cause harm, this yields a widely accepted ground for prohibiting or, at least, restricting it (Waldron 2009, p. 1604). This is the harm principle according to which: "the only purpose for which power can rightfully be exercised over any member of a civilized community, against his will, is to prevent harm to others" (Mill 1977, p. 223). But while this principle has (since its enunciation by John Stuart Mill) won wide approval (as a liberal liberty-limiting principle), it raises the large and difficult question as to how we should define "harm" (Feinberg 1984, pp. 26, 31–64). Should we, for example, identify loss of self-esteem (resulting from racist abuse) as harm? This is a question to which W. E. B. Du Bois's account of "double-consciousness" (which may be induced or reinforced by hate speech) is relevant: "It is a peculiar sensation, this double-consciousness, this sense of always looking at one's self through the eyes of others, of measuring one's soul by the tape of a world that looks on in amused contempt ... One ever feels this two-ness, – an American, a Negro, two souls, two thoughts, two unreconciled strivings" (Du Bois 2007, p. 8).

Just as Du Bois's analysis is relevant to the question as to whether a loss of self-esteem is harmful, so too is that of James Griffin. Griffin argues that "[s]imply to be a member of a hated ... group would be likely to undermine one's life as an agent. A member of a hated minority would be inhibited from speaking out on unpopular issues, and from acting in a way that would attract the majority's attention" (Griffin 2008, p. 42). Some feminist commentators offer a robust variation on this theme when they argue that pornography is harmful since it silences and works to subordinate women (MacKinnon 1994). But others argue that such material is offensive and, hence, a less acute threat to the interests of individuals (Sumner 2004). However, offense can have "measurable and even serious effects," among which we may number the "inward agonies" of those who wrestle with feelings of humiliation and a "diminish[ed] ... ability to lead a[n] ... autonomous life" (Neu 2008, p. 139; Raz 1986, p. 421; Roth 2001, p. 109).

Political expression

Central cases of hate speech are political in the sense specified by Carl Schmitt. They have the effect of carving the world up into "friends" and "foes" (Schmitt [1927], 1996). We see this when, for example, Nazis in Hitler's Germany spoke of their "boundless and unalterable loyalty towards one's own race" while describing members of other races as, *inter alia*, "maggots" (Mazower 2008, pp. 26, 45). Expression of this sort is a matter of great practical concern. For it may prompt those who are influenced by it to act in invidiously discriminatory ways towards the relevant "foe." In extreme cases, the upshot may be violence. Thus cross-burning by members of the Ku Klux Klan has often been the prelude to violence against African-Americans (Neu 2008, p. 141). Likewise, it is true of *Reichskristallnacht*, the anti-Jewish pogrom that unfolded in Nazi Germany on November 9–10, 1938. After "five years of incessant anti-Semitic propaganda," which was intensified by Propaganda Minister Joseph Goebbels immediately before the pogrom, there followed "a massive outbreak of unbridled destructive fury" (Evans 2005, p. 589). This resulted in at least 91 (and, in all probability, many more) Jewish deaths, the destruction of at least 520 synagogues, and the destruction of 7,500 Jewish shops (Evans 2005, pp. 584–585, 590). Moreover, at least 300 Jews subsequently committed suicide (Evans 2005, p. 590).

These examples throw light not just on the Schmittian character of the political expression engaged in by the Ku Klux Klan and the Nazis; they also lead us back to the concept of hate. For hate (on the analyses of Erich Fromm and Karl Lorenz) is strongly associated with "militant enthusiasm" (Fromm 1974, pp. 52–53; Lorenz 1966). Those in the grip of militant enthusiasm draw a sharp distinction between their own group and a common enemy. Moreover, they grow increasingly insensitive to "moral inhibitions" on "communal aggression" (Fromm 1974, pp. 52–53; Sunstein 2009, pp. 105, 119–120). This is apparent in, for example, a statement made by Oliver Cromwell (when in the role of Lord Protector of Protestant England in the 1650s). While at war with (Catholic) Spain, he identified "[t]he Spaniard" as "the providential enemy" (deserving only of extirpation) (Meier 1998, p. 59).

Although we can identify central cases of hate speech as exhibiting the five features noted here, the type of expressive activity with which we are dealing gives rise to definitional difficulties.

A definitional difficulty

If we make the large assumption that hate speech is harmful, this leads immediately to a definitional difficulty. Where those who engage in hate speech seek to inflict harm on others, we might draw a distinction between speech and conduct. C. S. Lewis draws just such a distinction when writing on "the vocabulary of abuse." He argues that words may pass out of "the realm of language (properly so called)" and become "the equivalent of actions ... of growls, blows" (Lewis 1990, p. 321; Lawrence 1990, p. 455). A broadly similar view appears to inform the thinking of the US Supreme Court in *Black v. Virginia* (2003). For it concluded that the state of Virginia could apply criminal sanctions to members of the Ku Klux Klan in circumstances where they seek to intimidate African-Americans by burning crosses near their homes. But although the Supreme Court employed the distinction between expression and conduct to justify this decision, some analyses raise doubts about its use. Laurence Tribe, a commentator on American constitutional law, argues that "[e]xpression and conduct ... are inextricably tied together in all communicative behavior" (Tribe 1988, p. 827; see also Wittgenstein 1968, p. 546, who notes that "words are also deeds").

Seeking to offer clear answers to definitional questions such as those raised by the speech–conduct distinction is a matter of great practical importance. If we fail to provide clear answers, we may fashion a body of law that, due to its lack of clarity, exerts a chilling effect on freedom of expression. This brings us to a dilemma that is of central importance.

A dilemma: liberty v equality

Conceptual analysis does not have to proceed far before it becomes clear that central cases of hate speech are an assault on the egalitarian assumptions associated with human rights law and liberal political philosophy (see Kymlicka 2002, p. 4, who argues from the standpoint of liberal political philosophy, that all humans inhabit an "egalitarian plateau"). Hate speech, however, presents the proponents of human rights with a dilemma. This is because it is political expression. This point is important since courts and commentators have consistently identified political expression as falling squarely within and enjoying (at least, presumptively) strong protection from the qualified right to free expression (Fenwick and Phillipson 2006, pp. 39–40). But hate speech is, as we have noted, Schmittian in character and, for this reason, sometimes poses an urgent threat to the constellation of egalitarian values that find expression in human rights law. Among these values we may, according to Chief Justice Dickson of the Canadian Supreme Court, number: "respect for the inherent dignity of the human person, commitment to social justice, and equality, accommodation of a wide variety of beliefs, respect for culture and group identity, and faith in social and political institutions which enhance the participation of individuals and groups in society" (*R v Oakes* 1986, p. 736). Thus the question arises as to whether legislators and judges should give priority to those norms that underwrite equality or to those that protect free expression (Post 1995, pp. 291–331; Sumner 2004, p. 52). Those who address this question often do so in discussions that also embrace the vexing topic of political correctness. Examination of this topic is useful in the context of this discussion since it throws light on assumptions that inform the thinking of many of those who call for prohibitions on hate speech.

Political correctness and egalitarianism

Critics of political correctness present an account of a political agenda that is or threatens to become oppressive on account of its association with restrictions on free expression. Criticism of this sort is typically uncharitable (e.g., Browne 2006, p. 30). For political correctness gives expression to an egalitarian philosophy of government (concerned with securing the interests of all those who live within, for example, a particular nation-state) (Fish 1994, p. 91). The proponents of political correctness make ambitious contributions to this body of thought. Among other things, they seek to secure equality in particular social contexts by placing restrictions on expressive activity (Stourton 2008, p. 9).

This is an agenda that Hegel would immediately recognize. Restrictions on expressive activity that serve to secure the equal status of, for example, a religious or ethnic minority are not merely the witness and external deposit of a particular society's moral life. They bespeak a commitment to the ideal of abstract right. Moreover, we might detect in them a commitment to the pursuit of a realistic utopia. This involves probing the limits of practicable political possibility with the aim of establishing ever more adequate sets of practical arrangements (Rawls 2001, p. 16).

While debate on the topic of political correctness is rarely edifying, we might see it as having to do, among other things, with two understandings of freedom that feature in Hegel's political philosophy. The first of these understandings is negative (and finds expression in Hegel's account of autonomy): freedom is simply the absence of interference from government or other individuals. The second view is positive and is apparent in Hegel's account of "release" (involving, *inter alia*, the [freedom-enhancing] affirmation of others). Individuals are free in this sense when they enjoy those conditions that enable them to exercise their capacity for autonomy. The critics of political correctness see this body of thought as a threat to freedom in the negative sense, while its proponents see themselves as championing the cause of positive freedom. As we will see in a moment, freedom in the negative sense features prominently in US law, while the positive variant informs Canadian responses to hate speech.

Legal responses to hate speech

The United States of America

In the USA, the First Amendment (which establishes a qualified right to free expression) gives strong protection to free expression (Dworkin 1977, pp. 191–192). Judges and commentators have offered a wide range of rationales for this right. They include democracy (which cannot exist in the absence of free expression), the pursuit of truth (through the operation of a marketplace of ideas), and self-realization (through acts of self-expression) (Greenawalt 1989, pp. 9–39). As a consequence of the importance attached to free expression in the USA, judges exhibit little enthusiasm for offense-based restrictions on the rights set out in the First Amendment. Indeed, in *Texas v Johnson*, Justice Brennan stated that, "[i]f there is a bedrock principle underlying the First Amendment, it is that government may not prohibit the expression of an idea simply because society finds the idea itself offensive or disagreeable" (*Texas v Johnson* 1989, p. 414).

Those wishing to restrict forms of expression that fall within the category of hate speech have to meet the requirements of the clear and present danger doctrine (as elaborated by the US Supreme Court in *Brandenburg v Ohio* 1969). This doctrine specifies that expressive activity must pose a threat of "imminent lawless action" in order to lose the First Amendment's protection. The case of *Collin v Smith* (1978) points up some of the hurdles that those seeking protection from hate speech must surmount. In *Collin*, a group of neo-Nazis planned to march through Skokie, Illinois. Their aim was to cause emotional distress to the large numbers of Holocaust survivors residing in the town. When local lawmakers sought to ban the march, the leader of the neo-Nazi group invoked the First Amendment in the Federal courts. The Court of Appeals concluded (by a majority) that the march did not pose a clear and present danger and identified the ban as unconstitutional. Commentators often use *Collin* to illustrate the lack of protection given to the victims of hate speech in the USA (e.g., Fish 2001, pp. 79–92; Waldron 2009, p. 1599). However, *Collin* and other such decisions should be set alongside a body of private law that has afforded the victims of hate speech some measure of protection. Many plaintiffs have successfully used the tort of intentional infliction of emotional distress as a means by which to seek redress for hate speech (R. Kennedy 2002, p. 64).

There can, however, be no gainsaying the fact that US constitutional law places many barriers in front of those seeking redress for hate speech. Two such barriers are the overbreadth and vagueness doctrines. The overbreadth doctrine applies to prohibitions that curtail or exert a chilling effect on legitimate expressive activity (Tribe 1988, pp. 1024–1029, 1034–1035). The vagueness doctrine identifies as unconstitutional prohibitions that lawmakers have specified so loosely that people of "common intelligence" must necessarily guess at their meaning (*Connally v General Construction Co* 1926). The case of *Doe v University of Michigan* (1989) illustrates the relevance of these doctrines to hate speech. *Doe* concerned a campus speech code, the purpose of which was to maintain a supportive learning environment by prohibiting hate speech in a wide variety of forms. District Judge Cohn recognized that those responsible for the speech code were pursuing a laudable egalitarian end. However, he identified the code as unconstitutional on, *inter alia*, the ground that it would exert a chilling effect on expressive activity protected by the First Amendment.

Canada

Like US law, Canadian law gives strong protection to freedom of expression (in the form of the qualified right set out in section 2(b) of the Canadian Charter of Rights and Freedoms). However, lawmakers and judges have exhibited greater receptivity to egalitarian arguments in favor of providing protection against hate speech. For example, in *R v Keegstra* (1990) the defendant faced prosecution under section 319(2) of the Canadian Criminal Code, which prohibits the willful promotion of hatred against an "identifiable group." In the course of his work as a teacher, Keegstra had described Jews as "money-loving," "power-hungry," "child-killers." At trial, the prosecution secured a conviction. Following a successful appeal, the Supreme Court of Canada reinstated the lower court's verdict. By a majority of 4–3, the Court decided that section 319(2) was compatible with the right to free expression. In support of this decision, the majority relied on, among other things, the sections of the Charter that enshrine Canada's commitment to equality (section 15) and multiculturalism (section 27) (Mullender 2007, pp. 243, 250–252).

Germany

As in the USA and Canada, the constitution (the Basic Law or *Grundgesetz*) establishes (in Article 5[1]) a qualified right to free expression. German law (like Canadian law) is more receptive to arguments that countervail against free expression than is the case in the USA. Consequently, the victims of group defamation (e.g., "Jews use the Holocaust to extort money from Germany") enjoy the protection of the Criminal Law (Brugger 2002, paragraph 31). The Basic Law also affords a form of protection against hate speech far more powerful than anything on offer in the USA or Canada. Article 18 contains an abuse of rights provision according to which those who seek to undermine the egalitarian assumptions that find expression in Germany's constitution may forfeit their rights. In having woven this measure into the fabric of their Basic Law, the Germans have made it plain that they will not tolerate forms of intolerance that strike at the egalitarian foundations of their society (Thiel 2009, p. 117). This is unsurprising. They do not want to repeat the unhappy history of the inter-war years during which the leaders of the Weimar Republic failed to counter the threat posed to its liberal–democratic values by Hitler and his acolytes (Stein 1986, pp. 278–279).

In what follows, I examine some of the ways in which Hegel's thinking deepens our understanding of hate speech and the responses made to it in the USA, Canada, and Germany.

Applying Hegelian political philosophy to hate speech

While the law in the USA, Canada, and Germany exhibits distinctive features, we find lawmakers and judges in each of these countries seeking to underwrite a strong right to free expression. Likewise, we find them seeking to provide adequate protection against hate speech. To put the same point more generally, they strive to fashion a framework that defensibly accommodates two sets of competing interests. This is a daunting task. The goods that compete with one another have high value. Moreover, those who must rank them wrestle with a problem that lacks an obvious solution. Little wonder then that we find significant differences between the bodies of law we have surveyed. Americans typically take pride in their strong commitment to free expression and the associated ideal of toleration (Bollinger 1990, p. 979). Canadians regularly place emphasis on a multicultural ideal that they regard themselves as having played a significant part in fashioning (Kymlicka 2001, pp. 211–212; and Kymlicka 2007, pp. 106–107). Germans, while strongly committed to free expression, are determined not to forget a past that is a source of shame (Judgment of September 18, 1979 (German Federal Supreme Court); see also Stein 1986, p. 319). But in each case, the relevant law gives expression to *Sittlichkeit*. It is, to put the same point another way, the "witness and external deposit" of a community's "moral life" (Holmes 1897, p. 459). This, moreover, is a moral life that has, in each case, to do with the pursuit of the same egalitarian ideal: abstract right.

In light of these points, we can draw the conclusion that Hegel's universal history throws light on an ideal, abstract right that informs human rights law. However, this is not the most significant contribution that Hegelian political philosophy makes to our understanding of hate speech. This insight emerges when we apply Hegel's account of the practical significance of adequate recognition, as pursued in the historical process, to central cases of hate speech. As we have noted, those who engage in such expressive activity identify others as inferiors. Expression of this sort works to identify the targeted individual or group as unfit for inclusion in a community of equals (Waldron 2009, p. 1601). From the standpoint of Hegelian philosophy such expression is not merely an assault on a particular individual or group. It also involves the repudiation of abstract right and the efforts of those who have sought, as the historical process has unfolded, to fashion institutions that give expression to that ideal.

The application of Hegel's political philosophy to hate speech affords an opportunity to point up some large assumptions that inform his thinking. These assumptions are deontological in character. They give expression to the view that certain states of affairs, goods, and interests are intrinsically valuable, as are modes of behavior that serve to secure or sustain them (Hondereich 1995, p. 187). The deontological dimension of Hegelian political philosophy is plain to see in his account of abstract right: he identifies this ideal as something utterly sacred (Rawls 2000, p. 339). This feature of Hegel's thinking has an important corollary. Social relations that give expression to this ideal, likewise, have intrinsic value. This becomes clear when Hegel identifies the state as an end in itself (Rawls 2000, p. 368). In light of this point, it surely follows that those who seek to deny or undercut the equal standing of those with a capacity for freedom act in a way that is intrinsically objectionable. Moreover, these points may provide a basis on which to pin down the central concern in the debates that rage on the subject of hate speech. While these debates embrace urgent consequentialist considerations (most obviously the harmful effects of hate speech), they have to do with the (egalitarian) assumption that all addressees of the law have intrinsic (and equal) significance.

As well as pointing up the relevance of deontology to debate on and legal responses to hate speech, Hegel also prompts us to consider more concrete matters. Siep's analysis of Hegel serves to illustrate this point. As I have noted, Siep identifies "freedom" as described by Hegel as exhibiting four distinct features (autonomy, union, self-overcoming, and release), each of which throws light on the bodies of law we have examined. While the ideal of autonomy looms prominent in US, Canadian, and German law, we find in each of these countries a distinct approach to the problem of hate speech. As we have noted, US law sharply circumscribes the circumstances in which those subjected to hate speech may secure protection or redress. As well as making plain a strong commitment to free expression, this feature of US law also bespeaks a strong commitment to toleration. For individuals and groups must endure the expressive activity of others, save where it threatens imminent lawless action or issues in significant harm (e.g., actionable emotional distress). Some commentators identify this feature of US law as revealing insensitivity to the "victim-perspective": the standpoint of those who have to endure hate speech (Matsuda 1989, p. 2320). However, we should set views of this sort alongside Siep's account of "self-overcoming." In circumstances where people are ready, in the absence of a clear and present danger or harm, "to allow others to be," they act in a way that recognizes the importance of this dimension of freedom. This would not be the case where they take steps to silence, among others, those who give expression to views that, while they may be offensive, do not give rise to harm.

This analysis is, however, unlikely to convince those who argue from the perspective of hate speech's victims. They may find in the emphasis placed on multiculturalism in Canadian law a more adequate basis on which to address the problems posed by hate speech. This is a view for which they could find support in the notion of "release" (*Freigabe*) as described by Siep. As we have noted, "release" has to do with affirming, rather than merely tolerating, the other. However, some may place emphasis on a less utopian sounding concern: the need to maintain "union." Thus they may find in German law an eligible basis on which to address the problem of hate speech.

Conclusions

Hate speech presents those who seek to uphold human rights with a dilemma. They recognize the centrality of free expression to any society that values, *inter alia*, individuality and a democratic form of life. But they also want to protect people – particularly the victims of historical disadvantage – from invidious expressive activity. Those who wrestle with this dilemma seek to identify ways in which to accommodate all relevant interests defensibly. This being so, their approach to political philosophy bears obvious similarities to that of Hegel. Moreover, they will find in Hegel resources that will enable them to gain analytic purchase on debates concerning hate speech. For Hegel identifies the pursuit of reciprocal recognition as the motive force in human history. The desire for adequate recognition has led humans to move (on the slaughter bench of history) in the direction of institutions that recognize the moral equality of persons. As they have made this journey, some (determined to privilege their own interests) have denigrated others on invidious grounds.

Impediments to the pursuit of justice such as this remain a feature of practical life in all societies. But Hegel-the-universal-historian (or, some might say, prophet) tells us that humankind will ultimately arrive at an end-state in which the interests of all enjoy adequate protection. In this there is an obvious strand of utopianism (as there is in human rights law and the egalitarian philosophy of government that informs it). But we should pause before assuming that Hegel points the way to an optimal end-state. Those who argue that a strong right to free expression entails a strong commitment to toleration make a point that we must accept. So too do those who argue that a strong right to free expression means that the victims of invidious expressive activity may (particularly when the matter is viewed from their perspective) suffer injustice. If we cannot rank these (or other egalitarian) responses to hate speech relative to one another, we cannot progress to an optimal end-state. In a further respect, moving to this end-state seems to be fraught with difficulty. For it would appear to be a state of affairs in which "everyone's attitudes [and conduct] are utterly just" (Waldron 2009, p. 1622). On one analysis, such a state of affairs is a "utopian fantasy" (Waldron 2009, p. 1622). Hegel's fellow historian, Kant, lends support to this view. According to Kant, "the arbitrary play of human freedom" is a standing

Table 4.1 A central case of hate speech (and counter-arguments)

Central case of hate speech (specified with the aim of countering the threat of chilling effects on free expression)	*Arguments for a more expansive understanding of hate speech (advanced with the aim of protecting those who are or who may be vulnerable)*
Hate: hate as (extreme) emotion and hate as activity.	Expression not informed by strong emotions may nonetheless have an adverse impact on those that it, for example, stereotypes.
Intention: perpetrators act with the desire, aim, or purpose (direct intention) of treating others in invidiously discriminatory and harmful ways.	The scope of prohibitions on invidious expression may be broadened by including statements, etc., that are the result of carelessness.
Invidious grounds: these grounds include race, sex, sexual orientation, and religion.	Just as invidious expression may have to do with, *inter alia*, race and sex, so too it may relate to, for example, social class.
Harm or attempted harm: this requirement means that hate speech does not embrace the broad notion of offense (which, if applied as a criterion of liability, seems likely [on account of its vagueness] to exert a chilling effect on expressive activity).	The protective scope of prohibitions would be broadened if they were to embrace not just harm but also offense (caused by, for example, blasphemous attacks on the tenets of a particular religious faith).
Political expression: being directly discriminatory, hate speech concerns the basic terms of social life and is, thus, political. Since political expression typically enjoys strong rights-based protection in democratic societies, restrictions on it should be used sparingly (e.g., where there is a clear and present danger of imminent lawless action).	Hate speech is political in a distinct (Schmittian) sense: i.e., it carves the world into (superior) "friends" and (inferior) "foes" (and is thus anti-egalitarian). This being so, we can prohibit expression of this sort without undercutting political discourse in a democratic society.

threat to just social relations (Reiss 1991, p. 52). Where this threat manifests itself in the form of hate speech, it is proof of the fact that we do not inhabit an optimal end-state. However, we do (as the Preamble to the Universal Declaration of Human Rights makes clear) live in a context where the impulse to bestow adequate recognition on all members of the human family is a feature of our practical life. This would not come as a surprise to Hegel for whom "The imperative of right" is: "*be a person and respect others as persons*" (Hegel 1991a, p. 60).

References

Beiser, F. 2005. *Hegel* (Abingdon, UK: Routledge).

Berlin, I. 2003. *Freedom and Its Betrayal: Six Enemies of Human Liberty*. Ed. H. Hardy (London: Pimlico).

Black v Virginia 2003, 538 US 343.

Bollinger, L. 1990. "The Tolerant Society: A Response to Critics." *Columbia Law Review*, Vol. 90.

Bragg, M. 2003. *The Adventure of English: 500AD to 2000, The Biography of a Language* (London: Hodder & Stoughton).

Brandenburg v Ohio 1969, 395 US 444.

Browne, A. 2006. *The Retreat of Reason: Political Correctness and the Corruption of Public Debate in Modern Britain* (London: Civitas).

Brugger, W. 2002. "The Treatment of Hate Speech in German Law (Part 1)." *German Law Journal*, Vol. 3.

Buber, M. 1947. *Between Man and Man* (Abingdon: Routledge).

Collin v Smith 1978, 578 F 2d 1197 (Court of Appeals for the Seventh Circuit); 447 F Supp 676 (Federal District Court).

Connally v General Construction Co 1926, 269 US 385, 391.

Doe v University of Michigan 1989, 721 F Supp 852.

Dorril, S. 2006. *Blackshirt: Sir Oswald Mosley and British Fascism* (London: Penguin Books).

Du Bois, W. E. B. 2007. *The Souls of Black Folk*. Ed. B. Hayes Edwards (Oxford: Oxford University Press).

Dworkin, R. 1977. *Taking Rights Seriously* (London: Duckworth).

Evans, R. 2005. *The Third Reich in Power 1933–1939* (London: Allen Lane).

Feinberg, J. 1984. *Harm to Others* (New York: Oxford University Press).

Fenwick, H. and G. Phillipson. 2006. *Media Freedom under the Human Rights Act* (Oxford: Oxford University Press).

Fish, S. E. 1994. *There's No Such Thing As Free Speech and It's a Good Thing, Too* (Oxford: Oxford University Press).

Fish, S.E. 2001. *The Trouble with Principle* (Cambridge, MA: Harvard University Press).

Fromm, E. 1974. *The Anatomy of Human Destructiveness* (Middlesex, UK: Penguin Books).

Fukuyama, F. 1992. *The End of History and the Last Man* (London: Penguin Books).

Grayling, A. C. 2002. *The Meaning of Things: Applying Philosophy to Life* (London: Phoenix).

Greenawalt, K. 1989. *Speech, Crime, and the Uses of Language* (New York: Oxford University Press).

Griffin, J. 2008. *On Human Rights* (Oxford: Oxford University Press).

Hampsher-Monk, I. 1992. *Modern Political Thought: Major Political Thinkers from Hobbes to Marx* (Oxford: Blackwell).

Hare, I. and J. Weinstein, eds. 2009. *Extreme Speech and Democracy* (Oxford: Oxford University Press).

Harris, H. S. 1972. *Hegel's Development: Toward the Sunlight 1770–1801* (Oxford: Clarendon Press).

Hegel, G.W. F. 1977. *The Phenomenology of Spirit*. Trans. A.V. Miller (Oxford: Oxford University Press).

Hegel, G. W. F. 1991a. *The Philosophy of Right*. Ed. A. W. Wood (Cambridge: Cambridge University Press).

Hegel, G.W. F. 1991b. *The Philosophy of History*. Trans. J. Sibtree (Amherst, NY: Prometheus Books).

Holmes, O.W. 1897. "The Path of the Law." *Harvard Law Review*, Vol. 10.

Hondereich, T., ed. 1995. *The Oxford Companion to Philosophy* (Oxford: Oxford University Press).

hooks, b. 1994. *Outlaw Culture: Resisting Representations* (New York: Routledge).

Hughes, R. 1993. *Culture of Complaint: The Fraying of America* (New York: Oxford University Press).

Jetzinger, F. 1976. *Hitler's Youth* (Westport, CT: Greenwood Press).

Judgment of September 18, 1979, BGHZ 75, 160 = NJW 1980, 45 (German Federal Supreme Court).

Keneally, T. 2003. *Lincoln* (London: Phoenix).

Kennedy, D. 2002. "The International Human Rights Movement: Part of the Problem?" *Harvard Human Rights Journal*, Vol. 15.

Kennedy, R. 2002. *Nigger: The Strange Career of a Troublesome Word* (New York: Vintage Books).

Kymlicka, W. 2001. *Politics in the Vernacular: Nationalism, Multiculturalism, and Citizenship* (Oxford: Oxford University Press).

Kymlicka, W. 2002. *Contemporary Political Philosophy: An Introduction*. 2nd edn (Oxford: Oxford University Press).

Kymlicka, W. 2007. *Multicultural Odysseys: Navigating the New International Politics of Diversity* (Oxford: Oxford University Press).

Lawrence, C. R. III. 1990. "If He Hollers Let Him Go: Regulating Racist Speech on Campus." *Duke Law Journal*, Vol. 431.

Lewis, C. S. 1990. *Studies in Words*. 2nd edn. (Cambridge: Cambridge University Press).

Lorenz, K. 1966. *On Aggression* (New York: Harcourt Brace Jovanovich).

MacKinnon, C. 1994. *Only Words* (London: HarperCollins).

Matsuda, M. 1989. "Public Response to Racist Speech: Considering the Victim's Story." *Michigan Law Review*, Vol. 87.

Mazower, M. 2008. *Hitler's Empire: Nazi Rule in Occupied Europe* (London: Allen Lane).

Meier, H. 1998. *The Lesson of Carl Schmitt: Four Chapters on the Distinction between Political Theology and Political Philosophy* (Chicago: University of Chicago Press).

Mill, J. S. 1977. *Collected Works of John Stuart Mill*. Vol. 18. Ed. J. M. Robson (Toronto: University of Toronto Press).

Mullender, R. 2007. "Hate Speech and Pornography in Canada: A Qualified Deontological Response to a Consequentialist Argument." *Canadian Journal of Law and Jurisprudence*, Vol. 20.
Neu, J. 2008. *Sticks and Stones: The Philosophy of Insults* (New York: Oxford University Press).
Pippin, R. B. 2008. *Hegel's Practical Philosophy: Rational Agency as Ethical Life* (Cambridge: Cambridge University Press).
Popper, K. R. 1962. *The Open Society and its Enemies*, Vol. II, *The High Tide of Prophecy: Hegel, Marx, and the Aftermath*. 4th edn. (London: Routledge).
Post, R. C. 1995. *Constitutional Domains: Democracy, Community, Management* (Cambridge, MA: Harvard University Press).
R v Keegstra 1990, 3 SCR 697.
R v Oakes 1986, 1 SCR 103.
Rawls, J. 1971. *A Theory of Justice* (Oxford: Oxford University Press).
Rawls, J. 2000. *Lectures on the History of Moral Philosophy* (Cambridge, MA: Harvard University Press).
Rawls, J. 2001. *The Law of Peoples* (Cambridge, MA: Harvard University Press).
Raz, J. 1986. *The Morality of Freedom* (Oxford: Clarendon Press).
Reiss, H., ed. 1991. *Kant: Political Writings*. 2nd edn. Trans. H. B. Nisbet (Cambridge: Cambridge University Press).
Rorty, R. 2007. *Philosophy as Cultural Politics: Philosophical Papers*. Vol. 4 (Cambridge: Cambridge University Press).
Roth, P. 2001. *The Human Stain* (London: Vintage Books).
Schama, S. 2000. *A History of Britain*, Volume I, *At the Edge of the World? 3000BC–AD1603* (London: BBC).
Schmitt, Carl. [1927] 1996. *The Concept of the Political*. Ed. George Schwab (Cambridge: Cambridge University Press).
Siep, L. 1992. *Praktische Philosophie im Deutschen Idealismus* (Frankfurt: Suhrkamp).
Stein, E. 1986. "History against Free Speech: The New German Law against the 'Auschwitz' Lie." *Michigan Law Review*, Vol. 85.
Stern, J. P. 1990. *Hitler: The Führer and the People*. Rev. edn. (London: Fontana Press).
Stourton, E. 2008. *It's a PC World: What It Means to Live in a Land Gone Politically Correct* (London: Hodder & Stoughton).
Sumner, L. W. 2004. *The Hateful and the Obscene: Studies in the Limits of Free Expression* (Toronto: University of Toronto Press).
Sunstein, C. R. 2009. *Going to Extremes: How Like Minds Unite and Divide* (New York: Oxford University Press).
Texas v Johnson 1989, 491 US 397.
Thiel, M. 2009. *The Militant Democracy Principle in Modern Democracies* (Farnham, UK: Ashgate).
Tribe, L. H. 1988. *American Constitutional Law*. 2nd edn. (Mineola, NY: Foundation Press).
Waldron, J. 2009. "Dignity and Defamation: The Visibility of Hate." *Harvard Law Review*, Vol. 123.
Williams, R. R. 1997. *Hegel's Ethics of Recognition* (Berkeley: University of California Press).
Wittgenstein, L. 1968. *Philosophical Investigations*. 3rd edn. Ed. G. E. M. Anscombe (New York: Macmillan).
Wood, A. W. 1990. *Hegel's Ethical Thought* (Cambridge: Cambridge University Press).

5
Hannah Arendt on human rights

Roger Berkowitz

Hannah Arendt approaches human rights as someone who lived through their failure in the first half of the twentieth century. A German Jew, Arendt understood anti-Semitism, experienced the denationalization of Jews in Germany, and witnessed how the world and even the diaspora Jewish community largely ignored the plight of European Jewry. Arendt also saw how other minority peoples in Europe – Germans in Russia, Slovaks in Czechoslovakia, Muslims in Yugoslavia, Gypsies, and many others – were systematically denaturalized, persecuted, and killed – all, as she emphasized, within the strictures of national and international law. For Arendt, the failure of human rights is a fundamental fact of modern times.

Not only did human rights fail to stop the atrocities of the twentieth century; more provocatively Arendt suggests that the rise and failure of the human rights discourse is itself part of the reason for the Holocaust, concentration camps, and refugee camps that mark our era. These disasters, she writes, are made possible, at least in part, "because the Rights of Man, which had never been philosophically established but merely formulated, which had never been politically secured but merely proclaimed, have, in their traditional form, lost all validity" (Arendt 1973, p. 447). It is not that human rights in some simple way cause the very abuses they are meant to protect against. Rather, Arendt argues that the failure and vapidity of human rights claims both reflect and deepen the incontrovertible fact that human rights are mere phantoms. To advocate for human rights in the face of their obvious invalidity is, she insists, to risk bringing attention to their powerlessness and therefore unintentionally to further their abuse.

Even as she fearlessly explores the paradoxes, weaknesses, and dangers of human rights, Arendt works to reformulate human rights on a more stable and meaningful foundation. In *The Origins of Totalitarianism*, first published in 1951, Arendt is clear that the "subterranean stream of Western history has finally come to the surface and usurped the dignity of our tradition." She is equally determined, however, to discover "a new political principle," what she calls "a new law on earth," that will replace Kantian dignity as the ground of human rights (1973, p. ix). A skeptic regarding the Rights of Man, Arendt is also deeply committed to elaborating and defending a meaningful and effective idea of human rights.

Arendt's charge that the dignified foundations of the Rights of Man have been usurped and her effort to offer a new foundation for human rights are developed throughout her works, but most directly in her first published work, *The Origins of Totalitarianism*. Arendt furthers her reformulation of human rights in *The Human Condition*, *Eichmann in Jerusalem*, and *Men in Dark Times*, as well as in numerous essays. Taken together, Arendt's writings form the most coherent and critical appraisal of human rights since Immanuel Kant's philosophical grounding of human dignity. As Seyla Benhabib (2004, p. 49) has argued, "After Kant, it was Hannah Arendt who turned to the ambiguous legacy of cosmopolitan law, and who dissected the paradoxes at the heart of the territorially based sovereign state system." In the *South Atlantic Quarterly*'s special issue titled "And Justice for All? The Claims of Human Rights," (Balfour and Cadava 2004), Arendt's approach to human rights dominates throughout; three of the fourteen essays (by Jacques Rancière, Werner Hamacher, and Etienne Balibar) focus specifically on Arendt's critical and reconstructive accounts. And for Peg Birmingham (2006, p. 3), in her book *Hannah Arendt and Human Rights*, Arendt's overriding life's work is the "working out of a theoretical foundation for a reformulation of the modern notion of human rights." No other twentieth-century thinker has thought so deeply, so critically, and so powerfully about the limits and possibilities for human rights.

This chapter explores Arendt's critique and reformulation of human rights in three sections. Section I offers a summary of Arendt's critique of human rights as she develops it in the central chapter of *The Origins of Totalitarianism*, "The Decline of the Nation-State and the End of the Rights of Man." Section II explores the intellectual foundations of Arendt's reconstruction of human rights as the "the right to have rights" in her concept of natality, the core condition of human being. Finally, Section III engages Arendt's effort in *Eichmann in Jerusalem* to think clearly about how international law might meaningfully understand the concept of "crimes against humanity."

Section I

Hannah Arendt's critical account of human rights is concentrated in "The Decline of the Nation-State and the End of the Rights of Man," the final chapter of "Imperialism," the second part of *The Origins of Totalitarianism*. Arendt's chapter is divided into two parts. Part one, "The 'Nation of Minorities' and the Stateless People," connects the breakdown of the nation-state system and the failure of human rights. The basic problem was that Europe was peopled by dozens of national, religious, and ethnic groups. In creating the nation-state system, the European powers divided these peoples into three groups: first, state peoples; second, other nationalities like the Slovaks in Czechoslovakia who were said to be equal partners in the state, "which of course they were not"; and third, a group of nationalities called simply minorities who were provided by a Minority Treaty with specific protections and rights (1973, p. 270).

Arendt saw the "real significance of the Minority Treaties" was that now "millions of people" were legally recognized by international law to live "outside normal legal protection and [in need of] an additional guarantee of their elementary rights from an outside body" (1973, p. 274). The Minority Treaties made plain that minorities within nation-states needed special extra-legal protection because those nation-states could and at times would strip citizens of citizenship en route to expelling them or worse. The treaties framed the issue of minorities as a choice between assimilation or liquidation. Since nation-states possess "the sovereign right of denaturalization," the creation of stateless peoples and refugees deprived of national and civil rights are not exceptions, but are problems inherent to the regime of nation-states.

Arendt argues that the refugee introduces into the nation-state a class of persons who are denied the equal rights of citizenship, the very rights upon which the legitimacy of the nation-state depends. Further, she insists that there is no solution to the refugee problem. On the contrary, the centrality of stateless refugees to nation-states unveils the tragic flaw of the modern system of nation-state, what Arendt calls the paradox of sovereignty.

The paradox of sovereignty refers to the Janus-faced nature of self-determination. On the one hand, sovereignty, the right of a rational people to control its own destiny, is the Enlightenment's gift to the modern political order. At the same time, however, sovereignty, the right of a people to live according to its singular idea and to pursue its own collective interests, is also the Enlightenment's dangerous empowering of nations to pursue their ends by whatever means necessary. The liberty of self-determination blends seamlessly with the dangers of ethnic cleansing and genocide.

Part two of Arendt's chapter "The Decline of the Nation-State and the End of the Rights of Man" – titled "The Perplexities of the Rights of Man" – is Arendt's most concentrated critique of human rights. The overarching claim of "The Perplexities of the Rights of Man" is that human rights – at least as traditionally understood – have not succeeded and will not succeed in doing what they aspire to do: guaranteeing the protection of human dignity. To understand why this is so, Arendt presents a number of perplexities that attach to human rights, perplexities that show the limits, weaknesses, and incoherence of human rights. What follows is an attempt to explore ten of the perplexities she identifies.

First, human rights claim to express something in man worthy of absolute protection, and yet they only emerge at a time in history when man's dignity and freedom could only be understood as relative values. The relativity of our modern age is importantly defined by both Darwinism and liberalism. Darwinism sees humanity as one species among many. Since evolution does not stop, there will be higher species. Darwinism thus kicks out one crutch supporting the idea of an absolute and inviolable human dignity. Similarly, liberalism is the political thinking of man governed by power rather than reason. Since power is unlimited, there can be no absolute values; the idea of an inviolable and sacrosanct humanity must fall amidst liberalism's rationalist determination to employ any means necessary to achieve desirable ends. Together, Darwinism and liberalism expose the contingency of all contemporary claims to absolute human rights. Far from absolute, human rights arise only once it is seen that "Man, and not God's command or the customs of history, should be the source of Law" (1973, p. 290). To declare that men have human rights is to put in mortal hands the absolute guarantees that were the traditional provenance of gods, ancestral traditions, and timeless customs.

Second, human rights are hailed as a sign of man's progress and also a symptom of a particularly frightening and specifically modern form of rightlessness. Building on Alexis de Tocqueville's and Baron von Montesquieu's insights into the need for intermediary institutions that balance the power of sovereignty, Arendt argues that individual and emancipated men – men freed from those all-encompassing religious, social, spiritual, and traditional orders that for millennia had limited and moderated the evils that man might do to man – stand naked before the power of sovereign states. Instead of viewing human rights as a progressive advance, she understands the rights of man as a rearguard action necessitated once men had lost their traditional rights. Only when men were "no longer secure in the estates to which they were born or sure of their equality before God as Christians," did they seek abstract human rights to protect them from the newly empowered sovereignty of nation-states and the unlimited arbitrariness of self-determining sovereign nations (1973, p. 291). Human rights, for Arendt, are less a solution to the problem of oppression and rather a symptom of a specifically modern form of rightlessness.

Third, the Rights of Man are indistinguishable from and incompatible with the rights of peoples. Emancipation meant that not only individuals, but also peoples, were free to determine their own fate. "The whole question of human rights, therefore, quickly and inextricably blended with the question of national emancipation; only the emancipated sovereignty of the people, of one's own people, seemed to be able to insure them" (1973, p. 291). The realization and import of this identification of the rights of man with the rights of people came to light only with the rise of rightless peoples, comprising those who were *en masse* deprived of human rights. All men prior to the twentieth century belonged to some kind of organized political community such that "what we must call a 'human right' today would have been thought of as a general characteristic of the human condition which no tyrant could take away" (1973, p. 297). Today, when the United Nations counts more than 42 million refugees, at least 15 million of whom are stateless, tens of millions of people are deprived of this general human condition. For these stateless persons, there is no home except an internment camp, the "only 'country' the world had to offer the stateless" (1973, p. 284). And for the states of the world, the presence of refugees within and without is a curse that gives the lie to the principle of equality before the law on which nation-states are built. The rights of man were supposed to be absolute and independent of government; but when emancipation meant also national self-determination, the absence of a government left certain human beings with no authority to protect their individual human rights.

Fourth, the recourse to human rights had the perverse effect of turning the beneficiaries of those rights into animals. Arendt is alert to the ways that human rights organizations and the declarations they issued "showed an uncanny similarity in language and composition to that of societies for the prevention of cruelty to animals" (1973, p. 292). Human rights speaks the language of victimization, "a right of exception necessary for those who had nothing better to fall back upon" (1973, p. 293). To seek the protection of human rights is to portray oneself as a helpless victim, a being, like a speechless animal, whose only claim to assistance is an appeal to our pity.

Fifth, human rights are actually second-class rights, fundamentally less meaningful than civil rights. What political liberals and defenders of rights want are civil rights, rights that are spelled out in tangible and enforceable laws. It is no accident, therefore, that when activists in the United States and other constitutional states advocate for the rights comprised by the eternal Rights of Man, they seek civil rights, whether by "legislation in democratic countries or through revolutionary action in despotisms" (1973, p. 293). Only those who have no confidence in the civil and legal institutions of their state abandon the concrete protections of civil liberties for the abstract hope of human rights. Human rights emerge only as a desperate plea once the claim for civil rights has failed.

Sixth, human rights were embraced for being inalienable, and yet, in fact, they were unenforceable. "Whenever people appeared who were no longer citizens of any sovereign state," these stateless refugees might appeal for the protection of their human rights, but those rights were guaranteed by no institution with the power to enforce them (1973, p. 293). Although human rights were to attach to humans simply in their being human, the truth was that without membership as citizens of a polity, human rights proved to be powerless.

Seventh, the rights typically thought to be basic human rights – like the right to life or the right to be equal or the right to property – are not actually human rights. The soldier during war is deprived of his right to life; the criminal of his right to freedom; minors of the right to vote; citizens during an emergency of the right to happiness (1973, p. 295). In none of these instances, Arendt argues, does a violation of human rights take place. On the contrary, these same civil rights can be granted by a totalitarian government even under conditions of fundamental rightlessness.

Eighth, the rights of man, the most fundamental of all rights, are without foundation. The age of human rights, the eighteenth century, sought to ground human rights in nature. "The very language of the Declaration of Independence as well as the *Déclaration des Droits de l'Homme* – 'inalienable,' 'given with birth,' 'self-evident truths' – implies the belief in a kind of human 'nature' which would be subject to the same laws of growth as that of the individual and from which rights and laws could be deduced" (1973, p. 298). Arendt sees, however, that we have become suspicious of and alienated from nature. In the age of human fabrication and the advance of automation and technologies of government, men have "become just as emancipated from nature as eighteenth-century man was from history" (1973, p. 298). History and nature, she writes, have become equally alien to us. Just as the thinkers of the eighteenth century denied the foundation of human rights in history, we today no longer accept the claim that human rights can be founded in nature.

Ninth, absent history and nature, the only possible foundation of human rights is that the right of every individual to belong to humanity be grounded by humanity itself. How humanity itself can ground human rights, however, is not clear. Moreover, "it is by no means certain whether this is possible" (1973, p. 298). The sphere of humanity, unlike the nation-state, does not yet exist. Further, the evolution of a world government would not inaugurate such a government of humanity; it is more than likely, Arendt sees, that a world government would be just as liable to justify the extermination of some for the benefit of the whole as it would to embody the ideals of humanity promoted by its idealistic proponents.

Tenth, and finally, it should be the case that when a human being loses his political status and becomes "nothing but human," he would be protected by the very human rights that human rights discourse advances. For Arendt, however, "the opposite is the case. It seems that a man who is nothing but a man has lost the very qualities which make it possible for other people to treat him as a fellow-man" (1973, p. 300). The final paradox of human rights is that human rights, both their existence and their loss, "coincides with the instant when a person becomes a human being in general – without profession, without a citizenship, without an opinion, without a deed by which to identify and specify himself" (1973, p. 302). Human rights, in other words, imagines and thus paves the way for the emergence of men so deprived of what makes them human that they are nothing more than barbarians and savages.

The paradoxes that Arendt exposes in the idea of human rights do not lead her to any simple rejection of human rights. What is needed, instead, is a rethinking of human rights, an effort to think what human rights might actually exist and how they might be philosophically founded independent from their grounding in sovereignty. This requires, first, that we abandon the traditional discourse of human rights as it has emerged since the eighteenth century. This discourse itself, Arendt worries, helped make possible, through its failure, the very outrages of the twentieth century. Second, and more speculatively, Arendt calls for a new thinking of human rights, what she renames "the right to have rights."

Section II: The right to have rights

Arendt seeks her bearings in reformulating human rights from her experiences of the Jews and other minority peoples during and preceding the Holocaust. The true "calamity of the rightless" in the middle of the twentieth century, Arendt writes, is "not that they are deprived of life, liberty, and the pursuit of happiness, or of equality before the law and freedom of opinion … but that they no longer belong to any community whatsoever" (1973, p. 295). Human rights reflect the legalized exclusion of human beings from civilized communities, and these human rights are "much more fundamental than freedom and justice, which are the rights of citizens" (1973, p. 296). The rights of man, in other words, are not revealed by the deprivation of specific rights, but by the plight of those who are expelled from all rights; the truly rightless are those who are so oppressed that they are deprived of legal status so that no one will even oppress them. It is this total deprivation of rights that makes manifest the one truly human right, what Arendt calls the "right to have rights." As she writes: "We became aware of the existence of a right to have rights (and that means to live in a framework where one is judged by one's actions and opinions) and a right to belong to some kind of organized community, only when millions of people emerged who had lost and could not regain these rights because of the new global political situation" (1973, pp. 296–297).

The right to have rights has proven an enigmatic formulation. Seyla Benhabib (2003, p. 82) has worried that Arendt simply does not offer a full and philosophical elucidation of the right to have rights: "by withholding a philosophical engagement with the justification of human rights, by leaving ungrounded her own ingenious formulation of the 'right to have rights,' Arendt also leaves us with a disquiet about the normative foundations of her own political philosophy." At the same time, Benhabib tries to read a founding moment back into Arendt's formulation. She divides the formula the "right to have rights" into two parts and argues that the two uses of "rights" are substantively distinguished. The first use of "right," Benhabib argues, "evokes a moral imperative." It is a moral demand to "treat all human beings as persons belonging to some human group and entitled to the protection of the same" (2004, p. 56). On the basis of this first moral demand to belong, the second use of rights means, "I have a claim to do or not to do A, and you have an obligation not to hinder me from doing or not doing A." Among those who are in a community, these rights are the civil and political rights of citizens. Taken together, Benhabib reads Arendt's formula as providing first the moral demand for, and second, the rights of citizenship and civil rights (2004, p. 57).

As appealing as Benhabib's interpretation is, it complicates Arendt's hard-minded characterization of the right to have rights as "a right to belong to some kind of community." Arendt means the right "to live in a framework where one is judged by one's actions and opinions." In doing so, Arendt excludes the traditional civil rights of life and liberty that Benhabib wants to read into Arendt's formula. For reasons at the core of Arendt's thinking, she clearly limits the right to have rights and thus human rights to only two rights, the right to act and the right to speak.

The only truly human rights, for Arendt, are the rights to act and speak in public. The roots for this Arendtian claim were only fully developed several years later with the publication of *The Human Condition* (1958). Acting and speaking, she argues, are essential attributes of being human. The human right to speak has, since Aristotle defined man as a being with the capacity to speak and think, been seen to be a "general characteristic of the human condition which no tyrant could take away" (1973, p. 297). Similarly, the human right to act in public has been at the essence of human being since Aristotle defined man as a political animal who lives, by definition, in a community with others. It is these rights to speak and act – to be effectual and meaningful in a public world – that, when taken away, threaten the humanity of persons.

When human rights are properly limited to those activities that concern the humanity of persons, they should not be invoked to protect people's freedom or even their lives. There will be times when one's humanity demands that one die, especially in those situations in which one must fight for freedom, even to the death. It is human to fight for and die for freedom, Arendt insists, but these are not rights had simply by being human. "Man," Arendt writes, "can lose all so-called Rights of Man without losing his essential quality as man, his human dignity. Only the loss of a polity itself expels him from humanity" (1973, p. 297).

Human rights, in other words, are only those rights to speak and act amidst a people such that one's words and deeds are seen and heard in such a way that they matter. At bottom, the only truly human right – the right to have rights – is the right to speak and act as a member of a people. Confusion over this point – and thus the efforts of human rights advocates to extend human rights to life and liberty (and also to second and third generation rights like economic prosperity) – cleaves human rights from its foundation in the human condition and risks, therefore, exposing the entire edifice of human rights as nonsense upon stilts.

Arendt names the human condition of acting and speaking that underlies the right to have rights natality. Natality, the capacity to be born, is, as Peg Birmingham has seen, a double principle. On the one hand, natality reflects the fact that man can – by acting and speaking – start something new. In this sense, natality refers to man's freedom in the sense of his spontaneity, the ability to begin and initiate something new. On the other hand, natality says also that a human being is born and, having been born, is given the gift of existence. This givenness – this "mere existence" that is "mysteriously given us at birth" – is an "anarchic" principle that is "cut off and adrift from any sovereign constituting power or foundation" (2006, p. 86). Since human existence, as *physis*, is cut off from any prior reason or ground, man is unjustifiable and thus vulnerable. Man stands alone as alien and strange. And this radical singularity that attaches to man's natality both underlies Arendt's defense of plurality and her insistence that the right to have rights includes the right to be as you are. It is the obligation in the face of the alien that must be respected as part of the human that, *pace* Birmingham, underlies Arendt's guarantee of the right to have rights to every human being.

Section III

One important consequence of her reformulation of human rights upon the human condition of natality is that Arendt offers a critique and reconstruction of the emerging international law offense of crimes against humanity. In her book *Eichmann in Jerusalem* (1963), Arendt insists that one of the principal flaws of the Israeli Court's judgment is its mistaken conception of what a crime against humanity is. For Arendt, neither a breach of the peace nor war crimes are meaningful crimes that might be prosecuted by international law. Instead, the only crime for which someone like Eichmann ought to be punished is the crime against humanity, by which she understands a very specific activity, an attack upon the human condition of plurality itself.

Since the Nuremberg trials, international human rights trials like the Eichmann trial have focused on three crimes: "crimes against the peace" (the crime of aggressive war itself); "war crimes" (the illegal prosecution of war); and "crimes against humanity" (inhuman acts against civilians before or after war). For Arendt, neither of the first two crimes are meaningful today. Crimes against the peace – the crime of initiating war – has never been officially recognized as a crime and, moreover, it is rarely the case that only one side is responsible for initiating war. Few countries who might prosecute another for crimes against the peace have not themselves attacked others, thus leaving them open to the *tu-quoque* argument – and what about you?

War crimes, too, are subject to the *tu-quoque* argument since it is impossible to fight a war under modern conditions without committing war crimes. The truth of the matter, Arendt writes, is that "by the end of the Second World War everybody knew that technical developments in the instruments of violence had made the adoption of criminal warfare inevitable" (1963, p. 256). Given modern modes of war, the "distinction between soldier and civilian" upon which the definition of war crimes rests "had become obsolete." War crimes, today, cannot be understood except to address those crimes that are simply inhuman, those acts done from mere cruelty "outside all military necessities, where a deliberate inhuman purpose could be demonstrated" – crimes that are better addressed by the category of "crimes against humanity" (1963, p. 256). The problem is that in war, almost any attack on civilian populations can be militarily justified. From suicide bombers who justify their acts as necessary given the asymmetry of power to the dropping of the atomic bomb on Hiroshima and Nagasaki to expedite Japanese capitulation and save American lives and from Shock and Awe in Iraq to Predator Drone attacks in Pakistan, there are almost no military acts today that, as Arendt understands it, can legitimately constitute a war crime. Provocatively, therefore, she suggests that we might need to abandon war crimes as a crime of international law.

If neither crimes against the peace nor war crimes are meaningful today, Arendt does believe that the charge of crimes against humanity is an important, albeit misunderstood, crime. A crime against humanity, as Arendt understands it, is a fully new, modern, and unprecedented crime. Although it was formulated already in the Nuremberg Charter, the Tribunal largely refused to use what seemed such an unprecedented crime; Arendt cites the French Judge at Nuremberg, Donnedieu de Vabres, who writes: "the category of crimes against humanity which the Charter had let enter by a very small door evaporated by virtue of the Tribunal's judgement" (1963, p. 257).

Article 6-c of the Nuremberg Charter defined a Crime Against Humanity as "Murder, extermination, enslavement, deportation, and other inhumane acts committed against any civilian population, before or during the war." Against this formulation, Arendt disavows folding murder, extermination, enslavement, and deportation – all of which are existing and very different crimes – into the crime of crimes against humanity. Neither the Slavic pogroms nor even the Nuremberg laws that legalized discrimination against German Jews were, she insists, crimes against humanity. Also the crime of expulsion, the "enforced emigration" that the Germans practiced officially after 1938, was a well-recognized crime of the international order, and not an unprecedented crime against humanity. Even genocide, to the extent that "massacres of whole peoples are not unprecedented" is inadequate in itself to constitute a crime against humanity (1963, p. 288).

Only when genocide – the effort to eliminate a race of people from the earth – is combined with the non-responsibility of bureaucratic administration does it become a crime against humanity, what Arendt terms "administrative massacres" (1963, p. 288). What makes a crime a crime against humanity is that it is "an attack upon human diversity as such, that is, upon a characteristic of the 'human status' without which the very words 'mankind' or 'humanity' would be devoid of meaning" (1963, pp. 268–269). Properly understand, there is an important distinction between discrimination, murder, expulsion, and even massacre, on the one side, and the administrative effort to systematically eliminate from the earth a race of people. For Arendt, only the latter rises to the level of a crime against humanity.

References

Arendt, Hannah. 1958. *The Human Condition* (Chicago: University of Chicago Press).

Arendt, Hannah. 1963. *Eichmann in Jerusalem* (New York: Penguin Books).

Arendt, Hannah. 1973. *The Origins of Totalitarianism* (New York: Harvest Books).

Balfour, I. and E. Cadava, eds. 2004. *South Atlantic Quarterly*, special issue, "And Justice for All? The Claims of Human Rights." Vol. 103.

Balibar, Etienne. 2004. "Is a Philosophy of Human Civic Rights Possible? New Reflections on Equaliberty." Trans. James Swenson. *South Atlantic Quarterly*, Vol. 103.

Benhabib, Seyla. 2003. *The Reluctant Modernism of Hannah Arendt* (Lanham, MD: Rowman & Littlefield).
Benhabib, Seyla. 2004. *The Rights of Others* (Cambridge: Cambridge University Press).
Birmingham, Peg. 2006. *Hannah Arendt and Human Rights* (Bloomington: Indiana University Press).
Hamacher, Werner. 2004. "The Right to Have Rights (Four-and-a-Half Remarks)." Trans. Kirk Wetters. *South Atlantic Quarterly*, Vol. 103.
Rancière, Jacques. 2004. "Who Is the Subject of the Rights of Man?" *South Atlantic Quarterly*, Vol. 103.

6
Democracy as human rights

Michael Goodhart

Democracy as human rights is an interpretation of democracy as a set of emancipatory rights anchored in the political principles of freedom and equality. In this chapter I provide a brief historical and conceptual overview of this idea and offer a broad normative defense of it (for a fuller account see Goodhart 2005). Although most of my previous work on this subject has emphasized and defended the democratic character of *democracy as human rights*, my primary focus here will be on what the idea suggests about the way we typically understand human rights.

Political modernity arguably began with the articulation of the political principles of freedom and equality in the seventeenth century. Thomas Hobbes was the first to base a political theory on human freedom and equality, which to him were empirical propositions that roughly characterized the condition of people in a hypothetical state of nature. From these propositions Hobbes inferred that life without political society would be a brutal war of all against all, and this inference led him to the conclusion – which he viewed as logically inescapable – that people would agree jointly to authorize an absolute sovereign to provide them with protection in exchange for obedience. Some of Hobbes's royalist associates were anxious about basing authority in consent, and with good reason: a generation later John Locke reformulated natural freedom and equality into a revolutionary creed that justified resistance to tyrants and upended the established social and political order. These principles have defined the modern political idiom ever since.

Locke asserted that people were free and equal in their *rights*. Crucially, for him, this made freedom and equality *moral* rather than logical or empirical propositions. These normative claims allowed him, in his *Two Treatises of Government*, to justify a transfer of sovereignty from the king to the people, arguing that free and equal persons could only be legitimately subordinated to political authority by their own consent. He nonetheless defended the subordination of women to men and of laborers to masters, by arguing that only people who were free, equal, and independent – literally, not dependent upon others – could be citizens. In Locke's view this excluded wives, who consented to subordination in marriage, and workers, who consented to subordination through employment contracts. This position relied on highly tendentious arguments about the natural inferiority of women and laborers, arguments that were incompatible with his premises and inconsistent with his reasoning. Still, Locke's insight into the radical potential of freedom and equality to level social hierarchies let the genie of democracy out of its bottle; he became the first democratic theorist rather in spite of himself. All subsequent normative accounts of democracy and democratization begin with the principles of freedom and equality for the same reason that Locke began with them: together, they delegitimate all bases for natural subordination (Pateman 1988, p. 39).

Locke treated independence as an additional prerequisite for citizenship, smuggling many of the old hierarchies back in under the cover of consent. But others saw freedom and equality as *requiring* independence – that is, they saw independence as one of the normative aims of citizenship rather than as a precondition of it. For these theorists, freedom and equality were closely associated with emancipation or liberation from all forms of legal, political, social, and economic dependence. This emancipation was to be achieved by securing human rights. By the end of the eighteenth century, Thomas Paine and Mary Wollstonecraft were advocating a thoroughgoing democratization of society, to be realized through a much more expansive understanding of natural or human rights than the one Locke had articulated. These thinkers stand at the forefront of what I have called the "emancipatory tradition" of democratic theory. Theorists in this tradition see emancipation as the aim of democratization and invoke human rights as the language of democratic empowerment. In addition to Paine and Wollstonecraft it comprises many nineteenth-century feminists (Stanton), abolitionists (Phillips, Douglass), and radicals (the Chartists, some in the labor movement), and it has contemporary echoes in the work of theorists such as Carole Pateman, Iris Marion Young, and Ian Shapiro.

It has become commonplace today to identify democracy with the political method usually associated with it. But such an identification conflates particular democratic mechanisms and procedures with the democratic ideals that animate them (Beetham 1999). The reigning "electoral" consensus – democracy equals periodic elections and representative government – ignores that questions about the specific form a democratic polity and society should take have been quite contentious historically and remain the subject of debate and deep disagreement today (Markoff 2004). Emancipatory democracy recognizes the importance of political participation; it also acknowledges, however, that "democracy is as much about opposition to the arbitrary exercise of power as it is about collective self-government," even though this oppositional aspect of democracy is not frequently mentioned in the academic literature (Shapiro 1999, p. 30). Indeed, in the emancipatory tradition, elections and representative government are valued less for the equal (even infinitesimal) degree of control over decisions that they afford to citizens than for the mechanisms they provide to check power, to counteract domination and oppression.

Democracy as human rights (DHR) picks up this emancipatory strand of democratic theorizing, revivifying its emphasis on achieving emancipation through human rights. DHR conceives democracy as a political commitment to universal emancipation through securing the equal enjoyment of fundamental human rights for everyone (Goodhart 2005, p. 135). A democratic political system, on this view, is one designed to respect, protect, and fulfill human rights. This means that a democracy must provide secure guarantees – institutionalized forms of social protection – for human rights (Shue 1996, p. 13; Pogge 2000). These include rights that constrain power and limit its abuse as well as rights that enable meaningful political participation. These rights fall roughly into four groups or clusters: fairness rights (to due process, equal treatment, etc.), liberty and personal integrity rights (against unwarranted imprisonment or detention, bodily or psychological abuse or torture, etc.), social and economic rights (including rights like health care, education, and a guaranteed income), and civil and political rights (rights to expression, assembly, to vote, stand for office, etc.).

As this brief overview indicates, linking democracy with human rights through the aim of emancipation opens up a much broader understanding of democracy's purpose and promise than do conventional treatments of democracy as a political method. This view therefore also requires a much broader set of social (institutional) arrangements for its realization. Meaningful political agency remains essential: institutionalized opportunities to deliberate, shape, and contest collectively binding political decisions are all central to achieving emancipation; as Shue (1996, p. 84) has argued, we have no basis for believing that it is possible to design non-participatory institutions that will ensure that basic rights are protected. In addition to the familiar political mechanisms associated with democracy, protections for rights outside the traditional "political" sphere are also indispensable – including a guaranteed subsistence or basic income, without which a person might become economically dependent upon employers, family members, bureaucrats, or others (Goodhart 2007).

Democracy as human rights clearly marks a significant departure from conventional conceptions of democracy. I have defended its democratic pedigree and credentials extensively elsewhere. I want to devote the remainder of this chapter to a discussion of how it illuminates various issues about the theory of human rights and about the frequently misunderstood relationship between human rights and democracy.

A good place to begin is with the meaning of emancipation and its relationship to human rights. In the emancipatory democratic tradition, emancipation has a specific and, in some respects, rather narrow meaning. It refers to the absence of domination and oppression. Domination describes a relationship in which some person is dependent upon another actor (a person or corporate entity) for her survival or well-being. The dominated person is subject to the dominating actor, who enjoys the privilege of arbitrary interference in the dominated person's life – regardless of whether or not that privilege is exercised (Skinner 1998, p. 84; Pettit 1997). Oppression refers to unwarranted interference in a person's life or affairs. As Young (1990, p. 38) argues, there is significant overlap between these two concepts: "Oppression usually includes or entails domination." Still, the concepts are distinct: the mere threat or possibility of interference constitutes domination, while some forms of interference that are not arbitrary might nonetheless be unwarranted (and thus oppressive without being dominating) (Wall 2001). The absence of domination and oppression characterizes the state or condition I am calling emancipation, a condition in which the dignity, autonomy, and inviolability of the person are protected (Wall 2001).

Emancipation, then, does not mean "all good things." Theories of human rights (and of democracy) are often criticized on just this ground. The conception of human rights offered here, while expansive, properly reserves the label *human* rights for those rights of the highest moral and political importance – those necessary for achieving emancipation, that is, for eliminating domination and oppression. Still, this conception remains minimal or "thin" in that it does not specify a complete or robust idea of the good life. Emancipation, as defined through human rights, is the starting point from which diverse ideas of the good life can take shape and flourish. Yet it is not too thin: achieving emancipation would, for many people around the world, mark an almost unimaginable improvement in their lives.

Crucially, in DHR the condition of emancipation is created through secure guarantees of human rights for everyone. Human rights enable emancipation. This relationship can be further clarified by thinking about the work that human rights do in counteracting domination and oppression. Domination and oppression are relationships of power. The work of human rights – their function or purpose – is to limit power and prevent its abuse, to eliminate domination and oppression. As just described, both direct constraints on power and meaningful political agency are needed to achieve this objective, and democratic institutions to secure human rights ultimately have this aim in view. One way to understand democratization, then, is as the progressive dismantling of structures of domination and oppression in society through extending secure guarantees of fundamental human rights. This way of conceptualizing democratization encompasses historical struggles for rights and inclusion as well as contemporary projects for global democracy. Both represent efforts to use the logic of emancipation to critique and ultimately dismantle structures of domination and oppression; both rely on democracy's global appeal as a promise of emancipation for all to push it beyond its traditional limits.

This understanding suggests a much broader and more thoroughgoing approach to democratization than that entailed by electoral conceptions of democracy. The latter interpret democracy as a set of institutions or procedures and democratization merely as the proliferation of these forms, with the implication that countries already possessed of such institutions are fully democratic. DHR conceives a democratic political system as one that provides secure guarantees of all of the human rights necessary for emancipation. Thinking about social organization from this perspective makes it possible to re-envision schools, police forces, social welfare agencies, and a range of other governmental agencies as *democratic* institutions, that is, as institutions intended to respect, protect, and fulfill human rights. This way of understanding the relationship between human rights and democracy demonstrates the relevance of both in relatively rich and stable countries. Human rights in particular are often associated, consciously or inadvertently, with abuse, suffering, and powerlessness in faraway places. DHR provides a critical framework for thinking about the further democratization of all societies in terms of progressive realization of emancipation through creating secure guarantees for human rights.

This critical framework can be utilized in addressing difficult problems concerning the horizontal and vertical extension of democracy – its extension outside of a given society and into the transnational domain. Since democracy means achieving emancipation for everyone, there is no difference conceptually between democracy in the family, the economy, and in global governance – although institutionally the differences will be quite significant. The goal of emancipation requires democratization of all of these domains, as the sources of domination and oppression are not confined to the political as it has traditionally been understood. This conceptual consistency helps to clarify the close connection between securing fundamental human rights and dismantling structures of subjection across the various contexts that give shape and meaning to human life.

As the foregoing discussion indicates, DHR treats human rights as interdependent and indivisible. These two terms are employed frequently by human rights advocates insistent that all human rights should be treated as equally important and as part of a "package deal." They are even included in legal documents and political declarations on human rights. Yet to date the precise meaning of interdependence and indivisibility remains under-theorized, more a confession of faith than a rigorous analytic claim. Of the two notions, interdependence has received more, and more comprehensive, attention. The definitive work is that of Henry Shue (1996), who has argued that there are some rights, which he calls basic rights, that are mutually presupposing. Each is a necessary condition for the secure enjoyment of the others. Unfortunately, many people have interpreted Shue as arguing that the basic rights are few in number and quite limited in their scope. There is no reason to assume that this should be so, however: in DHR, the key rights (which I have called fundamental or emancipatory human rights) include the four clusters of fairness rights, liberty and personal integrity rights, social and economic rights, and civil and political rights. It can be demonstrated that each of these clusters of rights is necessary for the secure enjoyment of the others, that the rights are interdependent in precisely Shue's sense.

The question of indivisibility has received much less attention in the human rights literature. Indivisibility often seems to be invoked simply to reinforce and add emphasis to interdependence, stressing the idea that it is impossible to secure the enjoyment of some fundamental rights without also securing enjoyment of the others. I think it makes more sense, however, to interpret indivisibility as a normative rather than an empirical or analytic claim. (It is, after all, possible to protect some rights without protecting others – even if, on the view proposed here, the former would not be secure in the full sense.) In DHR, indivisibility underscores the point that human rights, clearly valuable in themselves, are also jointly constitutive of emancipation. All of the fundamental rights, together, describe the condition of freedom and equality without subjection achieved when domination and oppression are eliminated. Indivisibility can thus be interpreted as a normative claim that all of the fundamental rights should be conceived and pursued together. Put differently, it expresses the conviction that, in light of the purpose or function of human rights (achieving emancipation), and in light of conceptual interdependence among them, all of the rights should be regarded as equally vital and should be understood as jointly necessary for achieving a moral and political aim of the highest importance. This too is an expression of conviction, but it replaces the vague hope that there is coherence among the human rights with a substantive, principled account of that coherence.

It is unusual to discuss human rights, as I have been doing here, in terms of their function or purpose, the work that they do (though they are sometimes justified in terms of fundamental human needs or interests). But this distinctly political understanding of human rights recognizes that historically they were invented precisely to do political work (Minogue 1979). If one considers abolition, labor movements, struggles for women's rights, anti-monarchical rebellion and anti-colonial resistance, opposition to authoritarian and tyrannical governments, resistance to the massive social and economic dislocation triggered by capitalism, and other historical challenges to power in which human rights claims have figured prominently, the nature of this political work becomes clear enough.

A political account of human rights like this one contrasts markedly with the standard moral accounts ubiquitous in the literature. The distinction matters most in the realm of justification. Moral accounts require grounding, universal and irrefutable foundations on which the argument for human rights can rest. This problem of justifying human rights morally has so far defied solution (though not for lack of brilliant attempts), with the result that human rights can often appear to be on shaky normative ground and seem to remain vulnerable to skeptical and relativist objections. Yet the search for moral foundations of the indicated kind continues, seemingly without regard to how the diversity of moral viewpoints and traditions of moral reasoning in our world assures that it will be in vain.

Treating human rights as political claims does not deny their normative character; they represent an unequivocal rejection of domination and oppression, a clarion call for emancipation. It does, however, change the way we think about their justification. Conceiving human rights as political rather than moral claims signals a turn away from the search for moral foundations and towards a political justification. That justification, I contend, lies precisely in the promise of a better life expressed in human rights. That promise explains their global appeal directly as a function of the political work that human rights are designed and well suited to do. DHR is my attempt to articulate that promise and appeal in an explicitly political justification of human rights, one that makes clear the centrality of human rights to a democratic conception of emancipation.

This understanding of human rights as (normative) political claims helps to resolve several thorny issues that result from treating them as moral concepts in need of grounding. That approach has, as anyone familiar with the debates on human rights knows well, led to vociferous disagreements about the universality of human rights. A good deal of that debate reflects confusion over what exactly the "universality" of human rights means (see Donnelly 2007; Goodhart 2008). Still, defenders of human rights are often nonplussed by objections that the principles they extol do not reflect the values or worldviews of many people in the world, as many people suppose moral truths should do. This lack of complete consensus proves much less problematic, however, to a political conception of human rights. A political view, one informed by a historical and conceptual understanding of what human rights are for, leads us to expect human rights to be contentious. They will necessarily be so because they seek to dismantle and delegitimize structures of domination and oppression that privilege some and subjugate others.

One advantage of a political conception is that it does not demand moral uniformity among supporters of human rights. People will have various reasons for finding the promise of human rights appealing, and they will frame and articulate those reasons in divergent ways. A political conception opens up space for the kind of overlapping moral consensus on human rights that many scholars have hoped for and that some have recently seen emerging globally (see, for example, Donnelly 2007). The more different reasons we can find for supporting the political commitment to emancipation for everyone, the better. There is no need, and from what I can tell no benefit, in finding a moral foundation for human rights in the traditional sense. The point is, after all, to eradicate domination and oppression, not to win a scholarly debate.

Another problem resolved by the political view is the controversy over whether, and in what sense, human rights are really rights. There is an extensive literature insisting that rights must assign clear duties or obligations to specific agents, with some positivists also claiming that rights must be legally enacted and enforceable. Clear, legally enforceable rights certainly play an important role in securing human rights within a society. But human rights are first and foremost political demands, demands that challenge the existing state of affairs and demand change. Ignoring this jeopardizes our understanding of their historic role in democratization. As Jack Donnelly has argued in his discussion of the "possession paradox," human rights are often invoked in urging the creation or enforcement of legally enacted rights. People often need human rights most precisely in those contexts where the positivist or even strict moral interpretations would deny they have them (Donnelly 2003, pp. 10–13).

Of course, not everything people demand politically is therefore a human right. By defining human rights in terms of what they aim to achieve, DHR helps to resolve another ongoing problem in the theory of human rights: the question of which rights, exactly, there are. DHR simultaneously limits the content of human rights and embraces a protean and open-ended understanding of them. They must include all of those rights necessary for achieving emancipation, yet their precise content can never be fixed. It is possible – as in the account of the clusters of rights just mentioned – to work out analytically many of the rights that are necessary for emancipation, but this list should always be treated as provisional, for several reasons. First, new threats of domination and oppression will arise; for example, although sixty years ago the authors of the Universal Declaration of Human Rights were not concerned with the threat of control over genetic information, today this threat seems much more concrete.

Second, it is crucial to ensure that people experiencing domination and oppression can articulate their experiences and grievances through human rights claims. On the account defended here, all instances of domination and oppression must be human rights violations (this is true by definition). In some instances, present understandings of human rights will be inadequate to articulate or to combat the subjection that some people experience. For example, international human rights law is presently silent on the rights of gay, lesbian, bisexual, transsexual, intersexual, and queer people. Although some human rights can be interpreted in ways that address some of the forms of domination and oppression they experience – e.g., rights to fair treatment, to personal integrity, protection against torture, etc. – new rights (and ultimately, laws and institutions) that explicitly address these wrongs should be formulated. Similarly, as has been achieved in part through the feminist critique of human rights, traditional understandings of rights like the right to security must be constantly challenged and revised to ensure that they provide meaningful security for everyone. This means subjecting human rights to an ongoing critique, informed by experience, of the standard threats that differently positioned people experience – here, for example, the threats posed by husbands, bosses, occupying forces, etc. It is therefore also essential to DHR that the processes of defining rights and designing institutional guarantees for them be open to deliberation, influence, and contestation. Otherwise, as critics have pointed out, human rights norms and institutions themselves become sources of domination or oppression. It is an epistemological requirement of human rights on this view that this process of reflexivity about the meaning and application of rights be institutionalized, so that the emancipatory promise of democracy can be realized for everyone. Again, this is not to say that human rights are simply whatever (a majority of) people say they are. The point is rather that participation is a crucial epistemological and procedural tool for combating domination and oppression.

Defining human rights in terms of their purpose also helps to resolve longstanding worries about different cultural interpretations of rights. If we accept, as many scholars now do, that different cultural or contextual interpretations of rights are legitimate and appropriate, we need some way to assess how far that legitimacy extends. The problem has been to determine those criteria with some rigor but without simply falling back on the thicker – and necessarily more controversial – understandings of rights whose specificity generated the need for greater flexibility in the first place. DHR has a simple solution: if the interpretation of some right undermines its role in helping to secure the others, it goes too far. So a right to education that did not include literacy for everyone would clearly be insufficient. Similarly, a society that limited important offices and positions to members of its dominant faith would be suspect. But an educational system that included some religious training, or state backing of the dominant religion (say in the form of legal recognition) might pass the test, presuming that the education was not indoctrination and that the offices and positions in society were coupled with careful protections for members of religious minorities that made them genuinely, and not just formally, open to all. The key point here is that rights, at the level of concepts and conceptions, are too general to give guidance on specific interpretations. DHR can assess different conceptions of rights and differing interpretations of them with reference to its aim (emancipation) and in light of the conceptual and practical interdependence that aim captures. Variations in interpretation are thus judged not in light of irresolvable debates about what some right does or does not require but rather in light of what rights as a whole aspire to achieve.

In concluding this discussion, I want to consider a few ways in which the conception of human rights articulated here illuminates the complex yet crucially important relationship between human rights and democracy. Often democracy and human rights are seen as distinct concepts at least potentially in tension with one another. The electoral conception of democracy, with its emphasis on majority rule, either threatens (in the view of liberals) or is constrained by (in the view of communitarians) human rights. Liberals worry that parliamentary or social majorities will dominate and oppress minorities. Communitarians see human rights as a form of domination limiting the community's ability to express its own conception of the good.

In answer to liberals, it is true that majorities do sometimes lord it over minorities. When democracy and human rights are seen as distinct concepts, this possibility appears as a tension or conflict between them. The existence of a genuine conflict, however, would presume that a democratic majority (normally) has a right to act in an unconstrained fashion, that its power is unlimited. Few democrats in fact hold this position, but no matter. The presumption shows why, from the perspective of DHR, no such conflicts can arise. Democracy is not defined as a political method but rather as a commitment to emancipation. The familiar political method of democracy has an instrumental justification on this view, one oriented toward this commitment: participatory government is an important mechanism for preventing domination and oppression. So "democratically" enacted laws or policies (the scare quotes indicate democracy in the minimalist, electoral sense) that violate human rights are axiomatically undemocratic. Critics will complain that such theoretical niceties do not butter bread, that in practice majorities can and do tyrannize minorities with disturbing frequency. I do not deny this; my point is not that we should ignore the realities of politics but that we should assess them properly. The problem is not a conflict between democracy and human rights but rather an abuse of power. This change in perspective matters in practice: the conflict view requires trade-offs and fuels suspicion about the aims and methods of democracy. The abuse of power view shows just the opposite, that any use of "democratic" power to dominate or oppress a minority is really an abuse of democratic power.

In answer to communitarians, it is true that human rights constitute (minimally) substantive constraints on the political community. If the objection is that policy should be decided by democratic deliberation, the response would be to point out that human rights delimit the range of democratically acceptable policy options without imposing specific political programs. (The right to an education does not dictate how the education should be delivered, paid for, does not specify its content, etc.) The point is, the minimal constraints that human rights impose on policy are best understood as setting the parameters for what counts as democratically acceptable policy, not as setting policy. If the objection is that these standards were not set by the community itself, the response would be that they are nonetheless the standards that democratic community requires. We can only properly call a community democratic when it adheres to them. A more robust communitarian position might maintain, in response to this argument, that the community's right to self-determination is prior to and supersedes the rights of its individual members. Such a community might reject the human rights of some of its members, or reject some human rights as contrary to the moral understandings of the community. But then the issue is not whether there is a tension between human rights and democracy but whether the community is democratic in the first place – regardless of the decision-making procedures it follows.

In sum – and this seems an appropriate way to conclude – DHR views democracy and human rights as mutually constitutive, conceptually and empirically. Each defines the other in part, and each supports the other practically and institutionally. This way of understanding democracy as human rights *for emancipation* provides powerful insights into many of the central problems in the theory and practice of democracy and human rights today.

References

Beetham, David. 1999. *Democracy and Human Rights* (Cambridge: Polity Press).

Donnelly, Jack. 2003. *Universal Human Rights in Theory and Practice*. 2nd edn (Ithaca, NY: Cornell University Press).

Donnelly, Jack. 2007. "The Relative Universality of Human Rights." *Human Rights Quarterly*, Vol. 29, No. 2, pp. 281–306.

Goodhart, Michael. 2005. *Democracy as Human Rights: Freedom and Equality in the Age of Globalization* (New York: Routledge).

Goodhart, Michael. 2007. "'None So Poor That He Is Compelled to Sell Himself': Democracy, Subsistence, and Basic Income." In S. Hertel, A. Minkler, and R. A. Wilson, eds. *Economic Rights: Conceptual, Measurement and Policy Issues* (Cambridge: Cambridge University Press).

Goodhart, Michael. 2008. "Neither Relative Nor Universal: A Response to Donnelly." *Human Rights Quarterly*, Vol. 30, No. 1, pp. 183–193.

Markoff, John. 2004. "Who Will Construct the Global Order?" In B. Morrison, *Transnational Democracy in Critical and Comparative Perspective* (London: Ashgate).

Minogue, Kenneth. 1979. "The History of the Idea of Human Rights." In W. Laquer and B. Rubin, *The Human Rights Reader* (New York: New Amsterdam Library).
Pateman, Carole. 1988. *The Sexual Contract* (Stanford, CA: Stanford University Press).
Pettit, Philip. 1997. *Republicanism: A Theory of Freedom and Government* (Oxford: Oxford University Press).
Pogge, Thomas W. 2000. "The International Significance of Human Rights." *Journal of Ethics*, Vol. 4, No. 1, pp. 45–69.
Shapiro, Ian. 1999. *Democratic Justice* (New Haven, CT: Yale University Press).
Shue, Henry. 1996. *Basic Rights: Subsistence, Affluence, and U.S. Foreign Policy* (Princeton, NJ: Princeton University Press).
Skinner, Quentin. 1998. *Liberty before Liberalism* (Cambridge: Cambridge University Press).
Wall, Steven. 2001. "Freedom, Interference, and Domination." *Political Studies*, Vol. 49, No. 2, pp. 216–230.
Young, Iris Marion. 1990. *Justice and the Politics of Difference* (Princeton, NJ: Princeton University Press).

7

Human rights, justice, and pluralism

Fabrizio Sciacca

An analysis of the nature of human rights may be carried out by using the tools of normative political philosophy and legal theory, following an established tradition in contemporary thought. More specifically, its object mainly concerns two issues.

(1) The issue of the *foundation* of rights: what are human rights? The search for a linguistic use of "human rights" entails the question of why human rights are human? In this sense, founding rights implies defining rights. If rights come in a variety of types, I refer here to human rights as the rights that everyone holds.
(2) The issue of the *justification* of rights: *human rights* are justified by good reasons that cannot be defeated by competing reasons. Good reasons are powerful reasons based on the importance of features of the individual right-holder or some relationship. *Other* rights are not justified by powerful reasons but on the basis of the relevance of other interests, perhaps the public interest or the collective interest (legally created rights).

In this perspective, the philosophically significant aspects of the nature of human rights entail the political relation between human rights, justice and pluralism.

1. The issue of human rights is centered on the concept of *modernity*. Some political philosophers go back to the "European juridical morality" as the origin of human rights as *rights* . The Western world is very proud of human rights. In European culture, human rights have undoubtedly become an iconographical presence (Weiler 2001). This, however, does not mean that a similar concept did not exist previously and elsewhere: in Greek philosophy, Hebraism, and Christianity, previously (in the Western world); in Africa; in Islamic culture. The problem is that human rights are modern, because before there were no legal foundations for rights. The idea of equality among mankind is certainly neither European nor modern; what is new, however, is the juridical formalization of rights. The problem of the modernity of human rights is, in any case, less important than its modernization. If this idea is considered as being good, human rights implicate the problem of *extension*. John Rawls and Jürgen Habermas, from different methodological perspectives, are willing to accept this preparatory assumption. The underlying question is cultural integration. Habermas expresses his concern for this problem

(1994, pp. 661–680). The main focus is on the formal (legal) bindingness of rights and, therefore, on the fact of modernization: on the process of universalization of historically given cultural contexts (Skirbekk 1994, p. 216). Modernizing is not conforming: it deals with taking seriously the fact that global enters everywhere in relations with local.

The Habermasian perspective is *discursive*: it entails an instrumental vision of the legal process as a means to create the extension of rights and, hence, a hermeneutical reflection on the "starting-point situation" (1998). Human rights are a condition for political autonomy and are based upon the communicative faculty of the members of the political community and on the law as a structure for safeguarding political autonomy, in a perspective in which acting communicatively is opposed to acting politically as a strategy oriented towards success. "The discrepancy between the universally human content of the classic rights to freedom, on the one hand, and the statutorily limited validity by their legal positivity, on the other hand, makes us aware of the fact that a discursively founded 'system of rights' always looks beyond a single democratic state, aiming at the globalisation of rights" (Habermas 1994, p. 672).

The Rawlsian perspective is *normative* and is based on the idea of the justification of the scopes of extension. The problem is substantially the same: it deals with different methods of realizing "the reasons for a choice of principles that has a definite place within a fixed context of the reference to our identity but that aims at being worth something beyond their context" (Veca 2002, p. 108).

At this stage, it seems advisable to support a concept of *inclusive* "human rights": congruent in part with the Habermasian idea of safeguarding political autonomy and, above all, the idea suggested by Hampshire, of a *minimal procedural justice*, that is to say, with a theory aimed at the foundation of a normativity in which the inclusion contemplates *all* of those affected and in which the parties adopt a principle of justice able to universally guarantee equal rights and basic liberties. This is a *thin* and universal notion of justice, coherent with plural visions of the good (Hampshire 1989, pp. 77, 140). The minimum procedural justice is a method to exemplify the concept (more than the conceptions) of justice, which is "unvaried with respect to the variations of the historical contexts and circumstances," a sort of "filter mechanism between the interpretations of law, generated by different regulations between values that contingently live in the space which for us is ethically valuable" (Veca 2002, p. 108). The test of injustice, hence, will give rise to a positive outcome when *any* deliberation process is carried out in a non-inclusive manner.

I want to shed light on the underlying situation in which the discussion of human rights is to be placed. Before proceeding to the enunciation of the linguistic use, which is here considered preferable, for now it is enough to point out various aspects inherent in the problems of definition. When we speak of "human rights," we often tend to reduce them, at least in a terminological manner, to "fundamental rights." "Human rights" do not coincide with "fundamental rights"; the latter in fact have a more open and relative dimension, which can refer to a single individual or the whole of society. Therefore, we may not necessarily be able to preach universality (given that "fundamental" is herein *formally* referred to for its being a priority regulation for the law and functional to the same, that is to say, not incompatible with the pursuit of public ends). In this sense, one should not speak of the human rights of a specific legal system, even if every legal system has a set of *legal universals* (without any references to particular entities such as individuals or times or places: Kramer 2007: 145) as "ought," "may," "shall," "is authorised," "is required," and so on (Finnis 2008, p. 2).

Therefore, the idea appears to be acceptable that human rights cover a global space, where fundamental rights seem to register themselves more on a local dimension, given that they are also expressions of the values, culture, and concepts of a specific legal system. Fundamental rights are in that sense constitutional rights: legal regulations upon which the legal system turns. They deal with rights having *moral strength*, given that they are upheld by different doctrines and morals. Another aspect in the spotlight is that of guarantees. Do rights have guarantees? If it should be so, by *what* are they guaranteed? The problem, more than pointing out the subject of guarantees *stricto sensu*, regards the adoption of the laws that provide fundamental rights as criteria for the recognition of the validity of a legal system. If the key to understanding fundamental rights, as suggested, is not so much democracy as the rule of law, we find ourselves obligated to "rights in a legal sense" even when corresponding "primary guarantees" (duties) and "secondary guarantees" (sanctions) do not exist.

Still, "human rights" actually concern mankind, taken from every context and specification: here the problem of universality and extension become urgent, as they are *urgent* requirements of political morality (Cohen 2006, p. 230). The principle of universality is the cornerstone of human rights and the characterizing feature of that which Robert Alexy calls *kantische Grundposition*; according to this principle, all mankind has fixed rights. Alexy distinguishes between "*absolute* human rights" and "*relative* human rights." We could even accept this distinction – it is only a problem of terminology, not a semantic question. The first are the rights that everybody could claim for everybody, the second refers to rights of the individuals as members of a political community, valid within the same (Alexy 1995, p. 128). It is advisable to move on from this ambivalence of rights in order to pick out human rights and fundamental rights for the purposes of their conceptual and special separation, also because fundamental rights are founded as a rational product of the tension between constitutionalism and democracy, originally conceived as an instrument of political control of power, yet certainly interpretable as an expression of the political *modus* of power. Their positive confirmation is geared towards considering the idea that some legal principles do not have to be considered as mere *reason without force*, and that the force must be rationalized through the criteria of priorities that are therefore also moral priorities. From this point of view, the problems of legal protection and ethical justification of rights (*internally* within a political society for fundamental rights; *externally* from the same for human rights) converge into the objective of the promotion of their efficacy. Such an identification of "fundamental" and "human" rights occurs in the term *Zweizüngigkeit* well described in Kant's work on perpetual peace. In the argumentation of Kant, this denotes the relation of politics to morality (Kant 1795, p. 138). This Kantian argument conveys the double relation of *rights* to morality (Sciacca 2000, p. 104).

What do fundamental and human rights have in common? Kant speaks of politics in relation to morality and observes that the first assumes a double relation to the latter if it is intended as a doctrine of *virtue* or a doctrine of *right*. In the first case, morality is intended as *ethics*, which finds an immediate agreement with politics, to "surrender men's rights to their rulers" (Kant 1795, p. 139); in the latter case, morality is intended as a doctrine of right and, therefore, acquires a theoretic supremacy over politics, becoming a doctrine of right as the applicative moment of politics. With reference to ethics, morality corresponds to the duty of love of mankind; to morals as law, the duty to respect their rights. It seems that these duties assume that individuals are reasonable and rational in exercising those capacities that John Rawls expresses as two *moral powers* for a basis of equality: the "capacity for a sense of right and justice" and the "capacity for a conception of the good" (Rawls 1982, p. 4), the capacity to understand and apply the principles of justice (Rawls 1971) as correct cooperative social conditions, and the capacity to conceive stable ends and aims, something like a worthy life. I consider that within the two moral powers presented by Rawls the traits can be found that make up the double declination represented by Kant. The conception of a human life worthy of value is close to morality as a doctrine of virtue (all is worthy of value in everyone's life as an individual system of final ends in a well ordered society: the perspective of the rational); the sense of right and justice is close to morality as a doctrine of right (the intersubjectiveness of acting *cooperatively* in view of a public and regulatory concept of justice: the perspective of the reasonable). Therefore, a doubleness of conduct exists as much in "fundamental rights" as in "human rights," a cohabitation of the two aspects that make compatible the relational conduct of moral agents and the priority claims for safeguarding rights. In both modalities, the tension remains between ethics and right in the light of the relationship between morality and politics. This double modality of rights with reference to the moral expectations refers directly to the Kantian concept of autonomy of the moral individual, as much as in the private sphere, regarding the choices concerning the *personal* conception of good, as in the public sphere, concerning the choices on the *political* views of good (of right and justice).

The application to human rights of the Kantian double relation of politics to morality allows us now to move to the problem of their definition, accepting the proposal of Bernard Williams, according to which the notion is founded on the *common humanity*. As Williams writes, "there are ... definable characteristics universal to humanity, which may all the more be neglected in political and social arrangements. For instance, there seems to be a characteristic which might be called 'a desire for self-respect' ... Kant's view not only carries to the limit the notion that moral worth cannot depend on contingencies, but also emphasises, in its picture of the Kingdom of Ends, the idea of *respect* which is owed to each person as a rational moral agent" (Williams 2005 (1962), pp. 100–101).

It seems that the point of difference between human rights and fundamental rights lies in the fact that the first pose the problem of their universality on a global scale. Considering this as *the* primary problem is neither trivial nor taken for granted. Therefore, the idea of a double relation (ethical and legal) of human rights in a national dimension, as much as in a global dimension, should be maintained.

To consider human rights as "legal rights with a moral content" (or as "moral rights with a legal content"), is, however, not sufficient. Our sense of "shared humanity" may not be shared by others; and the sense of humanity of others may not be shared by us: "claims of global justice encounter considerable resistance among the members of affluent societies, whose way of life and standard of living they appear to threaten" (Scheffler 2001, p. 82). This has to do with the non-neglectable feature of the modern origin of human rights as a formalizing process of the idea of human rights: the fact that their modernization (or extension) is, however, rooted in their definition. Moreover, a coherent linguistic use of human rights could benefit from the following: human rights should be endowed with morality and universality, not insofar as being transcendent rights or "natural rights" but as subjective legal rights and bearing in mind that their formalization is the *cause*, not the effect, of their universality. In this way it should be said that human rights are the rights that everyone holds.

2. The denaturalization of human rights, therefore, automatically gives rise to the problem of their justification. Every individual expectation has to reckon with others: therefore, it is necessary to justify the expectations with moments that lead to the requisites of human beings as persons, through good reasons. Therefore, it should be clear that the selection of human rights doesn't depend on things like a *modus vivendi*, interest groups, or *lato sensu* forms of life. Perhaps human rights can have an instrumental value because they serve important interests, but their value is not entirely instrumental (Cruft 2008, p. 93). This is exactly why the forms of life could contain very different social policies, and a sensitive and sensible theory of a "planetary" justice could demonstrate itself as being neutral with respect to the fact of pluralism and to different cultures.

It could be reasonable to be universalist in order to "listen to the other side" in the regulation of conflicts, but not to defend the particular results of particular conflicts between moral opinions (Hampshire 2000). It could be pointed out that in regards to human rights there exists a moral obligation of the universal type, proposing the idea of their implementation by the entire international community in terms of law and legal enforceability (Gearty 2006, p. 63). Anyway, what appears attractive about this perspective is not so much the orientation toward a possible neutral interpretation of human rights, but the attempt, through this, to overcome the dilemma between a complete noninterference with forms of life and a unilateral manipulation of the same. The problem of the so-called humanitarian intervention hence becomes crucial in matters of *injustice* and shows the difference between philosophy and international law, that is between the question of foundation and the problem of application of human rights (Buchanan 2004; Griffin 2008, pp. 191–211; Miller 2007, pp. 168–172; Shue and Rodin 2007). Promoting an authorization to interfere in the affairs of the entire international community means taking seriously the possibility of assigning the obligation to make human rights valid for everybody and anybody, regardless of the contexts of validity of international organisms. Nobody can make justice for themselves because justice is not a person but a value; nevertheless, identifying a violation of human rights is a very delicate issue because it involves political equilibriums, moral considerations related to the definition of "moral status" (Kamm 2007, pp. 227–236) and often tragic choices come into play. Humanitarian intervention implicates the consideration of the existence of human rights as "absolute human rights" and of limits to what may be done in the pursuit of their protection (Finnis 1980, pp. 223–224).

Consider this passage: "Government must not only treat people with concern and respect, but with equal concern and respect" (Dworkin 1977, p. 272). The problem of intervention regards the plan of values and also the plan of rights. Three points are relevant here.

(1) Human rights are not equivalent to fundamental values (the latter being "cultural values").
(2) Not all fundamental values become human rights. If certain values are shared in a certain culture, it would appear incongruent and perhaps unjust to impose (or export) them onto other cultures in which such values are absent or foreign, due to tradition or other reasons.
(3) If only some fundamental values, regardless of the context of sharing and cultural pertinence, can become human rights, identifying them is the problem that should lead to the legitimization (and to the compulsoriness) of any ques the intervention.

The scheme presented herein does not adopt an extensive interpretation of cases of intervention, but suggests a *restrictive* theory according to which only *some* fundamental rights become human rights and, therefore, justify intervention. Our ethical–political intuitions lead us to favor the restrictive hypothesis not so much for reasons of a prudential nature (the complication in operational terms and the immense cost that application of this thesis would give rise to), than for that which is structural: what comes into play is the safeguarding of pluralism and the necessity not to impose a style of life on those who do not have the same values for various cultural reasons. It is due to this, and only for this, that very few values are transformed into rights. Different ideals of a good life can and must persevere in distinct forms of life, but what should really be shared is a restricted core of rights. It is for this reason that the theory of international justice presented by Rawls (1999) can be considered a useful model on which to base reasonable pluralism and, above all, the foundation for a legal order of peoples that must be able to accept the diversity of the contexts to which it refers, made up of reasonable (those who are worried about the fate of other peoples) and rational (those who are worried about themselves) peoples.

Yet what value should be attributed to a case of a government's violation of human rights? It is necessary to make two points in regard to the problem of justification:

(1) The first is a pragmatic point: a necessary and sufficient condition for humanitarian intervention to prevent serious violations of human rights should be based on a *continuist* assumption. Unlike what Rawls claims, it is not necessary to adopt an originalist political justification but just to extend the ethical theory to different contexts.
(2) The second is a methodological point: the problem regards the identification of the techniques of interference from armed intervention, to be utilized as *extrema ratio*, to commercial instruments, as for example the freezing of transactions, or diplomatic negotiations or legal-institutional ones.

Furthermore, it should not be ignored that the core problem of the justification of human rights is constituted by the concept of freedom, in the *legal-political* sense, which Kant dealt with in the *Metaphysics of Morals* to be precise, the sense of *fundamental liberty* being the "independence from being constrained by another's choice." He writes that liberty is the only condition of coexistence "with the freedom of every other in accordance with a universal law," that is to say, "the only original right belonging to everyman by virtue in his humanity" (Kant 1797, p. 30). This category, in turn, conditions the political exercising of equality in terms of equal respect: even in this light Kant speaks of independence and precisely of that independence that configures "a human being's quality of being his own master (sui iuris)" (Kant 1797, p. 30).

The idea of basic liberties is rooted in Rawls's conviction that rational and reasonable individuals are inclined to share a common project based on the equal distribution of the rights of freedom (indeed, justice consists in part in a distribution of freedom. [Carter 1999, p. 4]). This idea is confirmed by Rawls (1993; 1999) also with consideration for the extension of a theory of local justice to a theory of global justice. With that "riddle of extension" (Veca 1998, p. 108) the identifying question of the subject is still strong: important matters at a local level, such as those regarding conflicts between citizenship and residence, are succeeded by central and similar questions regarding identity problems like the following: "What do we share with political individuals in a dimension of global justice?" Any attempt to reply cannot come from an idea of "shared humanity" as stated by Amartya Sen (1999) but from the Rawlsian project of a set of specifying basic liberties as a constituent element of human rights.

Notwithstanding this, the language of human rights as a common world language remains deeply rooted in the Western world. The question of the universalization of rights clashes with other non-Western conceptions of "rights," and with the fact that moral pluralism does not exclude the existence of a multitude of incompatible but morally valuable forms of life (Raz 1986, p. 133); moral pluralism seems to turn its face into a competitive pluralism (Raz 1994, pp. 178–179). In Europe, the increase of the non-EU migrants makes the shape of the European countries even more multicultural. Possibly, this point implies the need to rethink the philosophical question of the definition of human rights and renders the question of universalization quite serious for public institutions. Theories of liberal equality afford a comparison among individuals without discriminating on grounds of race, age, creed, disabilities, ethnic cultures, and economic background. Nevertheless, even in European countries, inequalities among individuals are increasing. The point here is how it should be possible to attenuate inequalities (first of all, cultural inequalities), by enforcing the mutual sharing of an overlapping, comprehensive sense of citizenship. The main theories of justice in contemporary western philosophy (utilitarianism, egalitarianism, welfare theories) show how these theories of justice reflect, in different ways, the importance of rights as sets of basic values deeply embodied in European culture. In these terms, rights can be considered as "the elementary particles of justice," as "the items which are created and parcelled by justice principles" (Steiner 1994, p. 2). Equality is the goal of egalitarianism and of all other liberal theories of justice. The relevant question here remains: *how* can institutions reduce the individual claims of in equality in the public sphere of politics. This question is strictly related to the problem of the relationship between human rights and social rights. It is enough to observe that among some of the so-called assistance rights, even in the light of important provisions of the law, there are surely human rights.

The discussion concerning "social rights" intended as "human rights" is certainly not self-evident. It can be said that the problem of the equalization between social rights and patrimonial rights did not lead either to narrow distinctions or to acceptable solutions. In fact, if social rights, as many affirm, are rights entailing duties of assistance from others, the second point should also be self-evident, that is to say, every assistance right would determine the equal distribution regarding the relation between social services and patrimonial rights. However, this is not the case. There are various unresolved points: (a) social rights, unlike liberty-rights (rights entailing duties of noninterference from others), could be negotiable and/or derogable, given that they are assistance rights (rights to specific welfare services); (b) how do we resolve the problem of the identification of the asset to be safeguarded? Probably in a positive sense, and, hence, social rights safeguard some sort of asset in relation to individual expectations like minimum income, housing, healthcare, and education (Fabre 2000, p. 4); (c) how are social rights effectively guaranteed, being that at a local level services are not typically clarified? It cannot be expected that private services are not protection agencies could/should register themselves completely on a public dimension. It is this *private* dimension of allocation of rights that could give rise to new problems for the definition of the concept of "citizenship"; if, therefore, the "social right" is something that is non-derogable, public and private assistance become the same thing; (d) lastly, it is necessary also to reflect on how much, on a *global* level, it could be considered as harmful, if guaranteeing a set of social rights were to equal the ratification of a paternalistic assistance policy aimed at the allocation of to rights some people, without bearing in mind the urgent necessity of others. Therefore, it is necessary to safeguard the principle that the *entire* subject of human rights, including social rights, cannot set aside the consideration of the right of every individual to live in an acceptable manner, that is to say, decently.

References

Alexy, R. 1995. *Recht, Vernunft, Diskurs: Studien zur Rechtsphilosophie* (Frankfurt am Main: Suhrkamp).

Buchanan, A. 2004. *Justice, Legitimacy, and Self-Determination: Moral Foundations for International Law* (Oxford: Oxford University Press).

Carter, I. 1999. *A Measure of Freedom* (Oxford: Oxford University Press).

Cohen, G. A. 2006. "Is There a Human Right to Democracy?" pp. 226–248 in C. Sypnowich, *The Egalitarian Conscience. Essays in Honour of G.A. Cohen* (Oxford: Oxford University Press).

Cruft, R. 2008. "Diritti umani e comunità umana: Sul valore non strumentale dei diritti umani." pp. 93–109 in F. Sciacca, ed., *Struttura e senso dei diritti: L'Europa tra identità e giustizia politica* (Milano: Bruno Mondadori).

Dworkin, R. 1977. *Taking Rights Seriously* (London: Duckworth).

Fabre, C. 2000. *Social Rights under the Constitution: Government and Decent Life* (Oxford: Clarendon).

Finnis, J. 1980. *Natural Law and Natural Rights* (Oxford: Clarendon).

Finnis, J. 2008. "Universality, Personal and Social Identity, and Law." *University of Oxford Legal Research Paper Series*,Vol. 5, pp. 1–27.

Gearty, C. 2006. *Can Human Rights Survive?* (Cambridge: Cambridge University Press).

Griffin, J. 2008. *On Human Rights* (Oxford: Oxford University Press).

Habermas, J. 1994. Nachwort. In J. Habermas, *Faktizität und Geltung. Beiträge zur Diskurstheorie des Rechts und des demokratischen Rechtsstaats* (Frankfurt am Main: Suhrkamp).

Habermas, J. 1998. "Zur Legitimation durch Menschenrechte." pp. 170–192 in *Die postnationale Konstellation: Politische Essays* (Frankfurt am Main: Suhrkamp).

Hampshire, S. 1989. *Innocence and Experience* (Cambridge: Cambridge University Press).

Kamm, F. M. 2007. *Intricate Ethics: Rights, Responsibilities, and Permissible Harm* (Oxford: Oxford University Press).

Kant, I. 1795. *Zum Ewigen Frieden: Ein philosophischer Entwurf* (Königsberg: bey Friedrich Nicolovius). English translation: "To Perpetual Peace: A Philosophical Sketch." pp. 107–143 in *Perpetual Peace and Other Essays on Politics, History, and Morals*, trans. T. Humprey (Indianapolis: Hackett) 1983.

Kant, I. 1797. *Die Metaphysik der Sitten* (Königsberg: bey Friedrich Nicolovius). English translation: *The Metaphysics of Morals*, ed. Mary Gregor (Cambridge: Cambridge University Press), 1996.

Kramer, M. H. 2007. *Objectivity and the Rule of Law* (Cambridge: Cambridge University Press).

Miller, D. 2007. *National Responsibility and Global Justice* (Oxford: Oxford University Press).

Rawls, J. 1971. *A Theory of Justice* (Cambridge, MA: The Belknap Press of Harvard University Press).

Rawls, J. 1982. *The Basic Liberties and their Priority*. pp. in S. M. McMurrin, ed., *The Tanner Lectures on Human Values III* (Salt Lake City: University of Utah Press).

Rawls, J. 1993. *Political Liberalism* (New York: Columbia University Press).

Rawls, John. 1999. *The Law of the Peoples* (Cambridge, MA: Harvard University Press).

Raz, J. 1986. *The Morality of Freedom* (Oxford: Oxford University Press).

Raz, J. 1994. *Ethics in the Public Domain* (Oxford: Clarendon).

Scheffler, S. 2001. *Boundaries and Allegiances: Problems of Justice and Responsibility in Liberal Thought* (Oxford: Oxford University Press).

Sciacca, F. 2000. *Il concetto di persona in Kant: Normatività e politica* (Milano: Giuffrè).

Sen, A. K. 1999. *Development as Freedom* (New York: Knopf).

Shue, H. and D. Rodin, eds. 2007. *Preemption. Military Action and Moral Justification* (Oxford: Oxford University Press).

Skirbekk, G. 1994. *Rationality and Modernity: Essays in Philosophical Pragmatics* (Oslo: Scandinavian University Press).

Steiner, H. 1994. *An Essay on Rights* (Oxford: Blackwell).

Veca, S. 1998. *La filosofia politica* (Roma-Bari: Laterza).

Veca, S. 2002. *La bellezza e gli oppressi: Dieci lezioni sull'idea di giustizia* (Milano: Feltrinelli).

Weiler, J. H. H. 2001. "Human Rights, Constitutionalism and Integration: Iconography and Fetishism." *International Law Forum du Droit International*,Vol. 3, pp. 227–238.

Williams, B. 2005 (1962). "The Idea of Equality.," pp. 97–114 in *In the Beginning was the Deed: Realism and Moralism in Political Argument* (Princeton, NJ: Princeton University Press).

8

Human rights and democracy

Luigi Caranti

Contemporary discussions of human rights are characterized by a widespread tendency toward normative prudence. While the drafters of the 1948 Universal Declaration felt it natural to reaffirm, in Article 1, the two leading ideals of the American and French revolutions – freedom and equality of all humans – sixty years later theoreticians seem to think that the founding fathers of the human rights culture were simply too ambitious. The ideal of perfect (formal) equality, and the consequent refusal of all forms of arbitrary discrimination, is currently set aside to make room for different ethical sensitivities in a world characterized by the fact of a more or less reasonable pluralism. The cultural challenge to human rights is taken more and more seriously, and one can safely affirm that the "cultural/moral skeptic" has won a significant battle. At least since Rawls's (1999) work on global justice, theoreticians have generally moved toward a compromise between liberal justice and the standards set by human rights ideals. This compromise entails tolerating discriminatory practices carried out by governments on religious or ethnic grounds, as long as these leave room for some degree of individual freedom and do not cause and are not accompanied by serious harm such as genocide, ethnic cleansing, and mass deportation. Very few today hold onto the idea that if a person is discriminated against – independently of how serious the damage is – because of her belonging to a religious or ethnic minority group, or merely to a gender, her human rights are violated.

This tendency toward compromise, not only political but also philosophical, started with Rawls but undoubtedly increased after the war in Afghanistan and significantly more after the second war in Iraq. The reason is quite easy to grasp. Many observers thought that the neoconservative ideology that fuelled the Iraq war was close to, and perhaps even made possible by, a conception of human rights capable of limiting too strongly national sovereignty. After all, the Wilsonian, left–liberal, or even Trotskian origins of neoconservatism appeared to many as sufficient evidence of another perverse *coup de théâtre* in the history of ideas. The ideals of the Enlightenment had become the main justificatory source for "wars on terrorism" or "wars for freedom." More and more people came to think that those ideals, especially if considered as the main source of inspiration for the list of human rights, i.e., a universal code of conduct for all nations and all individuals, had to be seriously mitigated if not abandoned completely.

One significant and particularly lucid representative of this prudent attitude is Joshua Cohen. In a recent article that expands Rawls's sketchy theory of human rights, Cohen (2006) argues that there is no human right to democracy. Democracy is here understood not merely as a form of institutional organization based on widespread suffrage and periodic elections, but also as a political system committed to considering citizens as free and equal. The characterization of citizens as equal is particularly important. Cohen argues, "an idea of equality plays a central role in any reasonable normative conception of democracy" (2006, p. 239). He also cites Tocqueville's interpretation of American democracy as based not so much on widespread suffrage, but on the overcoming of the aristocratic regime through the revolutionary idea of "equality of condition." Finally, Cohen identifies two components that characterize a society as democratic: (1) each member is understood as entitled to be treated with equal respect and (2) the basis of equality lies in the capacity to be part of a system of cooperation, by understanding the requirements of a mutually beneficial and fair cooperation (2006, p. 240). Another way to put Cohen's insistence on the indissoluble connection between democracy and equality is to say that, at a very minimum level, equality in a democratic society means non-discrimination. Inequalities of status, opportunities, and wealth cannot be the result of privileges arbitrarily bestowed on a certain group of citizens but denied to others. This refusal of a priori discriminations marks the overcoming of the *ancien régime* and seems to be both the common feature of any modern democratic regime and the threshold below which the government can no longer be considered democratic.

Although very minimal, this position is not universally accepted in the contemporary world, or so the majority of observers believes. The ethical sensitivities of certain polities seem to be far from endorsing the democratic form of government and the underpinning notion of equality/ non-discrimination of all citizens. Partly for this reason, Cohen suggests considering something less demanding than democracy, namely membership, as the normative threshold below which the human rights of citizens should be considered as violated. A political system respects the standards of membership if the basic institutions and political decisions are oriented to the common good and the interests of each person are taken into consideration in the issuing of laws and policies. In addition, the rights to dissent and appeal, freedom of expression and consciousness, and the obligation of the government to justify publicly its decisions to citizens and non-citizens living within the boundaries of the country must be part of the country's "constitutional essentials." If a government is not democratic but nonetheless organized around the idea that each individual is a member of the society and as such entitled to *some* recognition and respect of her interests in the shaping of societal laws, the polity is to be considered beyond reproach regarding its human rights record. It is acceptable that the interests of some may be given less weight than those of others, but it is unacceptable that some be given no consideration at all in the public life.

This chapter argues against this prudent attitude. The first section contains a critical reconstruction of Joshua Cohen's approach to human rights *via* global public reason. The second contains a critical analysis of the three political values – self-determination, toleration, and obligation – that Cohen uses in the foundation of his normative position. In the third, I offer my replies to the arguments based on these values. The fourth section discusses two further arguments one can identify in Cohen. In the concluding remarks, I sketch how the relationship between human rights and limits of toleration could be construed in a manner that appears more flexible and promising than the one advocated by Rawlsians.

The human rights finder: global public reason

Like Rawls, Josh Cohen is evidently no enemy of democracy. Liberal democratic institutions, oriented towards economic redistribution, are for Rawls and his students the requirements of justice. This holds, however, only for the theory of justice within national borders and, in particular, is valid only if applied to states already characterized by a liberal democratic public culture. But what about the part of the world that does not share our liberal democratic public values? Cohen points out that, while there are both consequentialist and deontological reasons for welcoming the diffusion of democratic ideals beyond present boundaries, these do not suffice (or are not relevant) to consider democracy as a human right, i.e., as a right that by definition overrides local traditions and practices. As we saw, instead of democracy, respect for the ideal of membership should be considered as the moral threshold below which a political system forfeits its sovereignty and lends itself to the possibility of some degree of interference by the international community, ranging from light forms of "naming and shaming" to more robust political, economic, and even military sanctions.

How do we obtain this new normative threshold? Cohen relies on a new methodological tool and on a number of arguments largely based on it. Questions of global justice, including new definitions of human rights, should be addressed for Cohen through the device of "global public reason." Although public reason, in Rawls's *Political Liberalism*, was the authorized speaker, as it were, of the public culture of a standard liberal democratic society, global public reason is thought of as "a shared basis for political argument that expresses a *common reason* that adherents of conflicting religious, philosophical, and ethical traditions can reasonably be expected to share" (Cohen 2006, p. 226). As in the case of public reason within national borders, it is not necessary that global public reason capture the set of moral principles commonly held by otherwise conflicting cultural and religious realities present in today's world. In fact, there might be little or perhaps no overlapping consensus among the comprehensive doctrines held by these traditions. For global public reason to serve as the legitimate speaker of a perhaps not fully developed, yet latent global public culture, only two things are required: (1) representatives of conflicting traditions must be ready to step outside their *Weltanschauungen* and (2) they must adopt a distanced standpoint from which agreement with other representatives becomes possible. In other words, although global public reason can be considered as a sort of common denominator among the various moral sensibilities represented in today's world, it need not be conceptualized as such to perform the functions Cohen assigns to it. Global public reason can also, and I think preferably, be considered as a common *disposition* which human beings divided by conflicting religious, philosophical, and ethical traditions can use to generate universal norms of conduct. This disposition entails a willingness to take distance from one's position, to negotiate, to conduct dialogue in good faith for the sake of the collective *discovery* (as opposed to a mere expression) of a common denominator. On this interpretation, global public reason is not the authorized speaker of an already defined and predetermined global morality, but a widely shared commitment to find one. Be it a general disposition or a common denominator, or some combination of these two things, global public reason ensures the universal validity of human rights, and is thus meant to avoid any parochial, imperialist, discriminatory interpretation of our global normative language.

What global public reason dictates in the realm of human rights, argues Cohen, is more than a minimalist conception defended by others, including Michael Ignatieff and Jean Cohen, centered mainly on the protection of bodily security, yet less than the maximalist conception that includes democracy. Instead of democracy, global public reason, properly applied, suggests to construe human rights around the ideal of *membership*. To show that membership is the right threshold for human rights Cohen offers two sets of arguments, each of which contains three main ideas.

Three anti-maximalist arguments

Cohen first focuses on three values to which we all grant authority and that, properly interpreted, serve as reasons to prefer membership over democracy as the gist of global public ethics.

The values are collective self-determination, the priority of political obligation over justice, and global toleration. The arguments based on these values become particularly convincing if one keeps in mind that any theory of human rights has to take into account, beside justice and the fact of moral pluralism, what Cohen calls the *urgency* condition: one may have to abandon certain requirements of justice, even if they are *not* parochial or limited in their validity, because they take too long to be satisfied. For example, a reasonable theory of global justice may hold that holidays with restitution is a right of all workers in the world, independently of the arrangements of justice in a specific socio-economic context. It may thus hold that the right of having holidays with pay is normatively prior over local practices. Yet it may consistently resist the transformation of such right into a *human* right, because it knows as a fact that the goods human rights are supposed to protect are usually more urgent than having paid leisure time. In a context of limited resources and realistically utopian political plans, the theory may therefore conclude that this right does not pass the test of urgency that would make it into a human right.

With this qualification in mind, let's approach Cohen's three anti-maximalist arguments.

Self-determination

A society determines itself if it can decide autonomously the political structure of the state and the principles of justice on which it will act as a collective body. Collective self-determination, in Cohen's view, is a standard of political decency more general than democracy – a society can determine itself toward non-democratic forms – and therefore less ambitious, yet urgent enough to qualify as a minimum below which human rights of citizens are violated. In collective self-determination one finds roughly the same requirements Rawls set for the political decency of a people and that in turn Cohen borrows for his ideal of membership. Self-determination so defined sets a minimum that many governments today are unable to meet and yet is compatible with polities not willing or unable to implement the right of *perfect* equality of citizens concerning rights. Self-determination has thus two related virtues: (1) it is a standard of political morality that combines moderation and utopia. It steers away from any charge of homologation to Western ideals and yet does not merely overlap on the status quo of numerous polities that are still far from decency. (2) In describing a minimum below which individuals are hopelessly and arbitrarily dominated by their government, it meets the condition of urgency.

The reasons why Cohen prefers this standard over democracy, however, are not merely based on political moderation/realism and sensitivity to the condition of urgency. There is also a purely normative component. Cohen alerts us that if the ideals of democracy and perfect equality do not have wide resonance among citizens of a country, "the value of collective self-determination itself recommends resistance to the idea that the political society should be required to meet the standards expressed in a principle of equal basic liberties, even if we think that the standards represent the truth about justice" (Cohen 2006, p. 234). Cohen relies here on a deeply rooted intuition for which each social group has a right to decide "autonomously" the institutional structure of the state. If there are peoples that authentically prefer to be ruled by non-democratic governments, one can hardly argue that they do not have a right to live in these conditions or that some moral wrong happens in these polities. The value of self-determination overrides any consideration inspired by external normative standards, and human rights should be construed in the light of this priority relation. Self-determination, however, cannot mean a decision to forfeit freely all individual liberties (a sort of spontaneous alienation of one's fundamental rights). Rather, individuals belonging to a people that freely decides to be ruled by a less than democratic regime are interested or, on this interpretation, have an objective interest in the institutional features that guarantee their status as *members* of the society as opposed to mere subjects.

Obligation

Cohen focuses here on a feature common to all polities politically organized around the idea of the *rule of law* and a fortiori common to all liberal democratic polities. Citizens living under these regimes at times obey rules and laws that they judge as ineffective, inconsistent, or even morally dubious. Consider the case of the recent anti-terrorism laws passed by the Bush administration. Until the Supreme Court considered the imprisonment (without trial) of "enemy combatants" at Guantánamo incompatible with constitutional principles, US citizens were asked to respect the Patriot Act, even if its moral stance appeared to many as largely questionable. And even after that ruling, many thought that times and manners of compliance with it remained in the government's power to decide. To give another example: many European citizens think that the very idea of a "crime of opinion," sanctioned by the recent sentence against the negationist historian David Irving in Austria, is inconsistent with the fundamental and overarching principle of free speech. Yet few Europeans inferred from the alleged moral wrongness of these sentences an authorization to disobey the court's ruling or to disregard the authority of those legislative bodies that issued the laws on which those sentences were based. It follows that political obligation is partially independent from the perceived moral rightness of the government's decisions. Put simply, we must obey all laws our governments pass, quite independently of whether we consider them just or unjust.

Political obligation, of course, has its limits, as exemplified by the Eichmann case, in which the Nazi criminal Karl Adolf Eichmann defended himself from the accusations of mass extermination by saying that he was ordered to carry out the "final solution." If our legislation is inconsistent even with the minimalist conception of human rights turning on the protection of bodily integrity of individuals, not only are we authorized to disobey our government, but we are morally obliged to do so. Similarly, the cases of civil disobedience, more or less of Ghandian inspiration, show that we are authorized to disobey a government that, as with colonial rule, is clearly detached from the will of the subjects. Besides these extreme cases, however, the possibility of a temporary discrepancy between political obligation and citizens' moral judgment is a normal and essential feature of any well-ordered polity, and obedience to state laws relatively independent of the citizens' moral convictions is a sort of precondition for the right functioning of the state. Now, if even insiders (i.e., citizens of the state under consideration) are obliged to respect laws that they perceive as unjust, isn't it the case that outsiders (the international community) should respect these laws even if they clash with their considered moral judgment? As long as the globally perceived moral wrongness of a government remains within certain limits, external observers seem even more bound to respect the state's political authority than the citizens who live under that regime.

Toleration

Since any reasonable account of human rights must be compatible with the value of toleration among different polities and cultures, we must conceptualize human rights in such a way as to be as tolerant as we can, perhaps even more tolerant than we are ready to be with illiberal groups within our liberal democratic polities. An important difference, in fact, is to be noticed between the toleration that, following Rawls's *Political Liberalism*, we should implement within our borders and the amount of toleration required at the international level. For example, patriarchal communities are, given the standards of *Political Liberalism*, to be permitted as long as the patriarchal group does not attempt to impose its way of living on outsiders and as long as a "right to exit" from that group is guaranteed to its members. In other words, patriarchy is fine as long as it remains the freely chosen way of living of certain citizens and as long as the members of the patriarchal group do not challenge *politically* the principle of individual freedom and equal opportunity around which the state is organized. Moreover, illiberal "private" practices are permitted as long as they recognize the overarching authority of the liberal state in case of an unavoidable conflict between the implementation of these traditional, illiberal values and the fundamental rights of the citizens (including those who currently belong to that group).

At the global level, however, the limits of toleration extend to encompass practices that would not be tolerated within the liberal state. In fact, even if illiberal practices (say the exclusion of women or of minorities from political power) are part and parcel of the body of laws (or of some unwritten code), for Cohen (as well as for Rawls) we have to tolerate them as long as they do not degenerate into sheer political oppression or threats to physical security. What in a liberal polity counts as non-reasonable, at the global level can very well become reasonable. After all, it would be quite strange if toleration among peoples coincided with what the liberal portion of the world intends as toleration. To put it with a slogan, global toleration cannot be identical with liberal toleration. There must be room for a theory of global justice (and the theory of human rights is just that) that accepts forms of discrimination that would be considered intolerable (un-reasonable) within a liberal polity.

Three replies

Cohen's points are powerful and well taken. Moreover, they enjoy a sort of intuitive appeal rooted in their proximity to some form of commonsensical "moderate relativism" or "weak universalism" that seem to be the most accepted currency among contemporary global ethicists. Yet there are reasons to doubt that a weak universalism of this kind should be the last word on the matter.

Self-determination answered

As a matter of historical truth, the principle of self-determination after the Second World War has been vindicated by countries that wanted to overcome the burden of a colonizing power, not by elites or common citizens of peoples protesting against the ideological tyranny of the West. To be sure, this vindication has been later used by corrupted elites of third world governments to divert the people's attention from their misdeeds and inefficiency. Blaming the persistence of the white man's influence on the country has often allowed corrupted leaders to hide their responsibilities. Nonetheless, the first and original vindication of the right to self-determination was motivated by a genuine thirst for freedom. This by itself casts some doubts on the purely normative component of Cohen's argument. As announced, that component turned on the lack of resonance that democratic ideals may have in certain polities. Certain peoples – this is the line of reasoning – exploit the principle of self-determination by choosing non-democratic political institutions. But one could ask quite straightforwardly: Who is the "self," in this perspective? Charles Beitz (1979) famously noted that the frequently invoked principle of self-determination contains three levels of ambiguity, one of which is particularly relevant for us. When people appeal to the principle of self-determination, points out Beitz, "it is not clear whether the 'self' in 'self-determination' refers to the government or to the population of a group. Does the principle simply require the creation of an independent government among a previously dependent group, or does it require, in addition, that the new government be 'self-government,' i.e., institutionally responsible to its people?"(1979, p. 93). Clearly, Cohen would like his position to fall neatly in the second category. But does it really?

If the polity is not democratic, which is our working hypothesis, the risk that self-determination be nothing but a wonderful tool in the hands of the elites in power is very concrete. As we saw, Cohen would insist that we are considering non-democratic societies in which "democratic ideas lack substantial resonance in the political culture, or the history of tradition of the country" (Cohen 2006, p. 234), namely polities in which a hierarchical form of government is authentically preferred over a democratic one. Yet, even if the preference to live under a hierarchical society is authentic, in the sense that a vast majority endorses a non-democratic form of government, there is no guarantee that elites' decisions will take into due consideration the interests of all, in particular of those minorities that would see their rights better defended by liberal institutions. If this is the case, the "self" in the self-determination would be a rather oppressive majority. Cohen says that we must "suppose" that the process of political decision based on self-determination does not end up in a de facto exclusion of the minorities' interests from the political agenda (2006, p. 234). But what if it does? In this case, we would have (1) the majority of a people that accepts the hierarchical organization of the society (quite understandably given their interests), (2) a minority or more minorities that do not and that, severely diminished in their rights, protest against this situation (remember, they keep their right to dissent and appeal), and (3) a government that is deaf to the protesters' voices because it claims that in its view the interests of *all* have been taken into consideration. Since it would be hard to say that in this case the polity is not based on self-determination, it would follow that, from an external (read: the international community's) viewpoint, we could utter no word of critique against the hypocritical reassurance by the government and no word of support for the oppressed minorities. If we did, we would be violating the overarching normative force of the principle of self-determination, thus interfering illegitimately in the internal affairs of the state.

But let us imagine, to be as fair as possible to Cohen's intentions, that the rulers are benevolent enough to let minorities' voices be heard and count *something* in the political process. In this case, the government would *not* be hypocritical in claiming that "the interests of all have been taken into consideration" in the production of societal laws and public decisions. Let us imagine also that a minority of radicals in that polity insist that "something" is not enough and that it wants an *equal* consideration of its rights. How would or could the international community react to this radical, yet quite sharable, request? If Cohen's standards of global ethics were accepted, the international community would again be reduced to some form of embarrassed silence. Clearly, speaking as representative of her own country, the foreign minister, say, of Canada could stigmatize the discrimination against our radicals. Yet, if she were to speak as a representative of the United Nations, any word of reprobation would be out of place given the fact that the polity is organized politically around the ideal of self-determination and such an ideal is largely (yet not universally) accepted by the citizens.

Finally, something must be said on the empirical soundness of Cohen's operating assumption that there are polities in which "democratic ideals" do not have wide resonance. Translated in clearer terms, this means that in certain polities there would be significant sectors of the population that, happily and consciously, give up some of their rights on the basis of some deeply rooted moral tradition. One thinks immediately of the often-cited cases of "Asian Values," namely an alleged disposition of most Asians to sacrifice some of their individual rights for the sake of the group (be it the family, the village, or the country), or of the Islamic challenge to human rights based on the supposedly wide rejection of perfect equality between men and women on certain issues (partner choice, political power, property and inheritance rights, and so on).

After decades of reflection on these "challenges" to human rights universalism, one point seems to be clear and relatively non-controversial. Non-Western cultures are far from monolithic and unchangeable blocks. Rather they are composed of many different and often conflicting self-interpretations of the same culture. Often the interpretation that is selected in the discussion is the most conservative and least compatible with the human rights culture. There is no necessity, however, to select *that* interpretation as representative of entire "civilizations," assuming that there are such things. Amartya Sen (2006) has famously and convincingly vindicated the non-Western roots of democracy. Many authoritative scholars of the Islamic tradition (An-Na'im 2001; Al-Azm 1970; Talbi 1998) have argued that some illegitimate (and interested) radicalization of the Islamic juridical tradition has led to the identification of political Islam with Shari'a and therefore to a gross underestimation of the tolerant and democratic potential of the "Islamic world" (if there is such a thing). Why should drafters of human rights lists be oblivious to the logical and historical complexities that make up a "civilization" and give into the most conservative self-interpretation of traditions "other than ours"? Or should we consider President Yew's praise of Asian Values and the Saudi Arabian delegate's famous rejection of the 1948 UDHR as not respectful of the "wisdom" of their patriarchal tradition as truly representative of their "civilizations"? (Johnson and Symonides 1998, pp. 52–53).

Political obligation answered

Cohen is certainly right in pointing out that in a liberal democratic polity citizens are asked to obey laws that some of them or even most of them consider either ineffective and/or morally unjust. He is not right, though, when he infers that this precludes external criticism of unjust laws passed within non-democratic polities. To begin with, there is a crucial difference between unjust laws generated through a procedure in which each affected individual has a say, and unjust laws generated unjustly, i.e., through a procedure in which some have been arbitrarily excluded from the process of law making. In the first case, the injustice of the laws is ascribable to human imperfection, contingencies, limited information, and the like. Citizens are willing to obey because they know that even the best political setting is not immune to error. In fact, obedience cannot reasonably be conditioned on the rulers' infallibility. In the second case, though, the injustice is less acceptable (or not acceptable at all) because the unjust laws were, at least to a certain extent, imposed on the citizens as opposed to generated – with all possible imperfection and indirect distortion – from their collective will. After all, this is one of the reasons why democracies are generally more solid than autocracies. The civic attachment to institutions is facilitated by the guarantee that laws and decisions, no matter how imperfect or even unjust, are ultimately generated from a procedure widely accepted and considered as fair. Under this condition, although obviously within limits, citizens are ready to bear the negative consequences of their rulers' imperfect or even immoral political judgment. While the justice of the procedure that generated an unjust law in a liberal democracy elicits respect from the citizens of that polity and a fortiori from outsiders, the injustice of the procedure that generated an unjust law in a hierarchical society allows different degrees of civic disobedience from the subjects and different levels of criticism from outsiders. Briefly put, political obligation over and above morality is a function of the justice of the procedure through which laws are generated. Cohen's failure to appreciate this point leads him to a dubious analogy between political obligation in a liberal democracy and political obligation in a hierarchical society, and from this to an equally dubious prohibition of external interference within autocratic polities.

Toleration answered

While the previous argument based on political obligation seems to be based on a conceptual mistake (it treats unlike cases as alike), the argument on toleration is free from such a failure and tackles a real problem for any theorization of global justice. As far as it goes, the slogan "tolerance at the global level cannot be identical with *liberal* tolerance" enjoys a clear attractiveness. If we want to take toleration seriously, setting the limits of toleration precisely as a liberal democratic public culture would have them does not seem a promising starting point. Yet Cohen's redrawing of the limits of toleration is not convincing.

To begin with, he does not want to be a relativist on the fundamentals of global justice, but if he defines, as he does, democracy not merely in terms of political institutions but also as the political regime in which individuals are treated as equal (no *default* discriminations against individuals or groups), by removing it from the list of human rights Cohen is also denying rather minimal accounts of *formal* equality. Forms of discrimination as serious as the exclusion from political office of entire groups (perhaps a group as large as that including all women) become acceptable. If these forms of discrimination are allowed, one wonders what distance remains from relativism. More importantly, one wonders whether, in allowing this moral flexibility, Cohen is not betraying a common-sense notion of justice that is already part of a rising global public conscience. After all, the idea of a fundamental entitlement to equal respect is grounded in general moral rules considered as common to all "civilizations." Think of the Golden Rule portrayed in Norman Rockwell's famous painting, not accidentally elected by the UN as a picture that represents what all moralities in the world share. More importantly, consider how existing declarations and treaties insist on this fundamental idea. Article 1 of the UDHR reads: "All human beings are born free and equal in dignity and rights." But also texts more legally binding such as the 1966 International Covenant on Civil and Political Rights and the 1966 International Covenant on Economic, Social, and Cultural Rights recognize in their Preamble "the inherent dignity and ... the *equal* and inalienable rights of all members of the human family."

Interestingly, Cohen imposes on any conception of human rights (including his own) the condition of *fidelity*. Any conception of human rights, argues Cohen, "must be broadly faithful to the content of the rights as laid out in the standard statements, in particular the Universal Declaration" (2006, p. 238; see also p. 230). Notoriously, the first articles of any declaration or constitution are the most important, those that define the moral essence of the entire text. Now the above-cited Article 1 of the of UDHR affirms that all humans are *equal* in dignity and rights. It is hard to see how this article could be interpreted in such a way to leave room for the kind of default discriminations that Cohen's principle of "membership without perfect equality" allows. Therefore, Cohen's view of human rights seems to violate the condition of fidelity he himself advocates. To be sure, one could say that the fidelity condition requires a *broad* faithfulness to the UDHR, as opposed to a narrow or rigid one. But is there even a broad faithfulness to UDHR if its *first* article is so evidently contradicted?

It could be objected at this point that the endorsement of UDHR and of the ensuing treaties by many countries did not reflect their authentic preferences. Many developing countries signed the UDHR and the following documents either as a sign of alignment to one of the two hegemons of the Cold War period or as a piece of political opportunism, in the hope of avoiding an overt and dangerous confrontation with the ideological wave of reform and idealism that dominated the period after the Second World War. Hence, so the objection continues, there has never been a broad consensus on the essentials of human rights, and a stripped-down list of them is nothing but an approximation to the minimal consensus one can reasonably expect.

Even if true, this reconstruction pays no attention to the logic of what Michael Ignatieff (2001, pp. 5–7) has called the "Juridical Revolution" initiated by the UDHR. Not only satellite states but even America and the European states signed the UDHR with a considerable degree of hypocrisy. In 1948 the USA still had serious forms of slavery in the Southern states, and many European countries were still exercising the yoke of colonizing power on a vast number of developing countries. Nonetheless, as Ignatieff (2001, p. 6) succinctly puts it, "once articulated as international norms, rights language ignited both the colonial revolutions abroad and the civil rights revolution at home." In other words, individuals across the universe used this language to express their legitimate demands, proving that a fertile terrain of moral consensus on certain basic issues already existed among individuals, if not among elites. Building on that initial moment, and independently of the original intentions of the signers of the UDHR, the culture of human rights – the original one, not that offered by the cautious Rawlsian – has now reached a level of acceptance that is widely considered a common normative language in international relations. If a government discriminates against the female members of the community, it takes upon its shoulders the burden of proving that this serious deviation from the accepted standards, this exception to the normative language commonly spoken in the world, is not what it seems – i.e., a sheer violation of some individuals' human rights – but something that can and should be conceptualized otherwise. Were Cohen's reforms of the human rights culture to be implemented, however, this government would be alleviated from the burden of offering an explanation for its discriminatory policies. A sixty-year long, partly non-intentional, slow progress of the human rights culture would be undone for a sort of mistaken normative prudence.

If philosophy is about what can be reasonably hoped for (the Rawlsian "realistic utopia"), why should it be even less ambitious than what humanity has already achieved, i.e., trans-cultural agreement on the value of equality/non-discrimination? Why should we tolerate what history has already considered no longer tolerable? Were we really too ambitious in 1948 and in 1966? Isn't it the case, perhaps, that the move from metaphysical to political conceptions of justice, combined with a simplistic interpretation of the link between human rights violations and limits of national sovereignty, has reduced what can be reasonably hoped for to the current status quo, or to something very close to it? Aren't those who misused the ideals of the Enlightenment for their military enterprises winning the war of ideas if the standards of justice are made so sensitive to these adventures and to their disasters?

Two more reasons not to consider democracy as a human right

Cohen does not ground his prudence merely on the three values just discussed – self-determination, obligation, toleration – but also offers extra reasons for expunging democracy from the list of human rights. Two of them are particularly revealing of how the Rawlsian strategy is at the same time appealing and plausible, but ultimately problematic.

Truth

Cohen concedes that there is a sense in which the claim that that all men are equal is *true*. He holds onto the idea that democracy, understood as equality of all humans in dignity and rights combined with widespread suffrage, is not just "a good idea" for the world, an efficient way of organizing public life. The principle of equality is rather a moral truth, something with intrinsic validity. The principle perhaps does not mirror some ontological property (clearly, we expect a Rawlsian to be a constructivist, not a realist in meta-ethics). Nonetheless, equality is for him as true as the categorical imperative is for a Kantian. Even if the principle does not pinpoint an objective feature of the world, a denial of it would be as false as the denial of a solid empirical fact. Nonetheless, argues Cohen, *right now* this truth is not part of global public reason. And since a theory of human rights is not a textbook of metaphysics, but something that ultimately we all have to agree to, this lack of universal acceptance has its weight.

Reply. Although the resistance to transforming a theory of human rights into some form of metaphysics is clearly plausible, one can doubt the effectiveness of the instrument – global public reason – called to replace practical reason (or other traditional philosophical tools) in this enterprise. We touch here perhaps the deepest problem of Cohen's approach. It should be recalled that global public reason is nothing but an extension of the instrument – public reason – that Rawls uses to identify the principles of political liberalism within a polity already imbued with the ideal of persons as free and equal. Is such an extension legitimate?

We face four main problems. To begin with, assuming the point of view of *public* reason presupposes a willingness, and, I would say, a habituation to establish a degree of detachment from our deepest convictions in favor of a negotiation with other individuals who are radically different from us. Not accidentally, Rawls confines the idea of public reason "to a conception of a well-ordered constitutional *democratic* society" and clarifies that "[t]he form and content of this reason are part of the idea of democracy itself" (1999, p. 131; my emphasis). In other words, public reason presupposes a *liberal* attitude toward difference shared by all reasonable citizens, liberal and non-liberal. Non-liberal citizens living in a liberal democratic society are expected to share an ability to adopt, when discussing public and political issues, a viewpoint detached from their comprehensive doctrines. This expectation is well grounded because they are socialized within a society whose institutions are mainly based on liberal values and on neutrality toward comprehensive doctrines. One cannot expect the same, though, of non-liberal citizens socialized within non-liberal institutions. Why should they discuss justice (national or global) by adopting a detached viewpoint? Public reason can hardly be generalized to non-liberal peoples in such a way as to become a *global* public reason. Obviously, non-liberal peoples may arrive at the same normative conclusions concerning human rights dictated by Cohen's global public reason. In all likelihood, however, they will do so not because they use this instrument, but because of some overlapping with parts of their comprehensive doctrines. Religious believers in a hierarchical society, for example, may be ready to negotiate on some deep convictions – say the concession of a right to active, but not passive, electorate to members of minority religious communities – not because they adopt the point of view of global public reason, but simply because the value of tolerance is part of their comprehensive doctrine, or, more precisely, of a progressive interpretation thereof (think of an updated implementation of the tolerance practiced within the Ottoman empire). When one concedes that minorities will be no longer merely "consulted" in the process of law making, but actually given weight through the right to active electorate, representatives of the religious majority will be appealing to an innovative interpretation of their comprehensive doctrine as opposed to global public reason. If the detachment from one's own deepest convictions is, as it seems, a typically liberal attitude, why should we rely on global public reason in the process of defining human rights?

It could be objected that global public reason is only *our* instrument to define human rights, and that it is not necessary for the theory that it be also *theirs*. In this case, Cohen's normative effort would be a particular application of the perspective adopted by *The Law of Peoples* (1999) in which Rawls defines the guidelines for the foreign policy of liberal peoples, as opposed to defining "from nowhere" principles of global justice. Unfortunately, if this is Cohen's perspective, things become even more complicated. To begin with, human rights are standards that nobody should impose on anyone. No one is entitled to think for other individuals in the process of defining what norms and principles we share or we should share. Nowhere more than in a theory of human rights is the suspicion that normative standards have been parochially defined more disastrous. Moreover, and more importantly, even if *liberals'* global public reason and "other" worldviews were to reach agreement on a list of human rights, this would be a mere de facto agreement, completely contingent and as such deprived of obligatory force. Instead of agreeing on certain normative standards *for good reasons*, whatever these are, we would have a mere *modus vivendi*.

Second, while public reason is a promising tool to become "as tolerant as we can" inside a liberal democratic state, namely to respect the fact of pluralism of our societies, one should never forget that the main reason we can afford to be tolerant toward illiberal forms of life is that citizens preserve the "right to exit" any illiberal context in which either they simply find themselves or they have previously chosen but no longer endorse. This right to exit, however, is not guaranteed in polities based on membership, simply because it is the basic structure itself that promotes discriminations. For an adult woman to forfeit freely her right to vote as long as she decides to do so in virtue of her, say, religious beliefs, is one thing. To live in a country in which there is no way out from this condition of discrimination is quite another. Global public reason cannot capture this crucial difference because it has an intrinsic tendency to identify as legitimate representatives of a people only the voice of the cultural or religious majority.

This problem arises from a general difficulty of *The Law of Peoples* already noticed by careful critics (Maffettone 2001, pp. xxi–xxii). Rawls's preference of peoples over individuals as authorized speakers in the ideal assembly defining the moral code of international affairs, combined with his toleration towards decent illiberal peoples that by definition mirror the prevailing illiberal values of the majority, entails that liberal minorities or liberal individuals living inside a decent polity have no legitimate demand to make to the international community to redress possible discrimination. Actually, they have no voice at all because the international community is supposed to accept decent polities as members *bona fide* of the well-ordered society of peoples. Human rights, however, are tools to be used mainly by victims of the government's (i.e., the majority's) oppression. Therefore any source of normativity, like global public reason, that deprives the victims of their voice looks suspicious.

Third, a global public reason constituted by representatives of "peoples" runs contrary to the point made by Amartya Sen (2006) regarding the dangers – intellectual and political – of grouping human beings according to one criterion of classification. The selection of representatives of different "civilizations" or even of smaller entities (peoples) that collectively constitute global public reason is ultimately the outcome of a previous, morally far from neutral, grouping of human beings according to *one* preferred criterion. If rights in general and human rights in particular are intrinsically biased in favor of individualism, why should we abandon this perspective if it has not even sufficiently solid objective ground – Sen's point – and when and where such bias would be most beneficial, namely where the need of defending individuals from all possible forms of a majority's oppression is particularly urgent?

Fourth, even if one concedes that global public reason does *not* over-represent the views of the majority, one still has to check how *informed* and free is individuals' alleged consent (in the former example, women) to practices that undermine their equal dignity and rights. Sometimes ethicists put this point by talking about adaptive preferences. It may be instructive here to recall Xiarong Li's interesting position on female genital mutilation. She argues that this practice should be allowed in a liberal democratic country and banned in non-democratic countries, even if arguably the practice is rooted in the traditions of the latter and nearly absent in the former (2001). This paradoxical "double standard" that turns upside down the commonsensical idea that a morally dubious practice is to be allowed where it is culturally rooted, and banned where it is not, rests on the powerful consideration that only in a free country can one be relatively confident that the practice is authentically chosen by the individual and not an adaptive preference. To the contrary, the suspicion that the alienation of one's rights is not freely chosen or informed enough is unavoidable in authoritarian societies. The case of female genital mutilation shows that a preference is authentic not merely when alternative models are available, but also when one is free to abandon the practices imposed by the tradition to endorse alternative identities. Of course, if there are reasons to believe that some of the preferences influencing global public reason are merely adaptive, it follows that this methodological instrument is hardly reliable for defining global justice or for identifying the "proper" list of human rights.

Bootstrapping

Cohen argues that today global public reason does not already contain the conception of persons as free and equal. The often-cited cases of Islamic and Confucian cultures prove this allegedly evident truth. It follows that such a conception should not shape the standards we all are supposed to share, i.e., human rights. Two considerations are relevant here.

To begin with, as already recalled, Article 1 of the UDHR affirms precisely what Cohen's global public reason denies, namely that all human beings are equal in dignity and rights. Wasn't this crucial principle recognized by a vast majority of states in 1948? What happened since then that suggests the desirability of lowering our standards? More importantly, even if we were too optimistic in 1948, the fact remains that moral and religious traditions need to reinterpret themselves on certain issues and often do so. This is already going on. Many non-Western contemporary theoreticians insist on how one-sided (and often simply interested) is the view of those who read the Islamic and Confucian tradition as incompatible with the gist of the human rights culture. We have already mentioned a few examples. Sadik Al-Azm (1970), Abdullahi Ahmed An-Na'im (2001), Mohammed Talbi (1998) – just to name some scholars coming from different regions of the "Islamic world" – argue that one can reinterpret the Muslim tradition and make it coherent with human rights by discarding Shari'a as a late and unnecessary addition to the core of the Islamic faith. Insisting that Islam is incompatible with the human rights culture is no different from considering Christianity to be at odds with the same culture because of the submissive role assigned by the Bible to women. Regarding the Confucian tradition, which is becoming the new official ideology of post-Marxist China, most scholars, both Asian and Western, emphasize that a marriage between Confucianism and human rights/democracy is possible, and nobody mentions in this context the desirability of introducing limitations on the principle of non-discrimination (Angle 2002; Chan 2007). Moreover, it is not without significance that China recently signed the International Covenant on Civil and Political Rights, which, as we saw, contains an unmistakable commitment to equality/non-discrimination. Finally, the point is not whether compatibility is hermeneutically plausible, but whether there is the political will to *make* it so. Traditions, cultures, and revealed religions are constantly reinterpreted. They do "bootstrap" themselves toward new outcomes depending on what we want to make of them. If we think that the principle of non-discrimination is something more than the cunning of Western reason to subject non-Western civilizations, we shouldn't hesitate in encouraging a particular "bootstrapping" of traditions, i.e., one that leads them closer to human rights, as opposed to other reinterpretations that are possible, but less desirable. Violations of human rights around the world are primarily a political problem, not a cultural one. The interests of the elites holding power, often combined with the perverse influence of wealthy countries allied with them, are far more dangerous enemies of human rights than are alleged cultural barriers. We do not want an overcautious attitude toward cultural difference to end up slowing down the evolution toward less discriminatory interpretations of local traditions.

This concludes our criticisms of the arguments Cohen offers and that, I suspect, most human rights theoreticians today would endorse in one version or another. More could be said against the idea of removing democracy from the list of human rights. One could further question: (a) the vagueness of the membership criterion of "taking into account the interests of all citizens" (who decides whether the interests of all have been taken into account?); (b) the empirical vacuity of a theory whose truth seems to depend both on the existence of rather mythical "decent peoples" (it is instructive how difficult it is to find an example of decent people in the real world) and on the existence of "happy victims" who accept their discriminated condition more than as a *modus vivendi*; (c) the illiberal conception of rights (rights conceived as instruments of social inclusion – membership – rather than as instruments of individual defense against all forms of majority oppression). Instead of expanding these suggestions, however, we prefer to conclude with a suggestion on how most of the worries that motivate the Rawlsian overcautious normative attitude could be met without impoverishing the traditional list of human rights.

Human rights and global tolerance

We have already noticed that one unpalatable consequence of Cohen's approach is that even rather soft and non-violent forms of interference (e.g., naming and shaming) would be prohibited to the international community even in the face of discrimination against entire groups in terms of political rights. This consequence is in turn the result of too quick and too rigid an equation between human rights and the limits of toleration. The Rawlsian is right in making non-tolerance dependent on the most serious violations of human rights. He is wrong though in limiting the list of human rights to those things that would justify non-tolerance and intervention. Why can't we consider certain things as human rights simply because we would not be ready to support an intervention on grounds of their violation? As James Nickel (2003) puts it:

> Leaving out any protection for equality and democracy is a high price to pay for assigning human rights the role of setting the bounds of tolerance, and we can accommodate Rawls' underlying intuition without paying it. The underlying intuition is that countries with massive violations of the most important human rights are not to be tolerated … But to use this idea we don't need to follow Rawls in equating human rights with some radically stripped down list of human rights. Instead we can develop a doctrine – which is needed for other purposes anyway – of which human rights are the most important.

To be more precise, we need a doctrine, not of which human rights are more important, but of which of them are more *urgent*. While human beings can survive if their political rights are momentarily suspended or even denied permanently, they cannot if their bodily security is put at risk by a governmental program of mass extermination. But this is no reason to consider, like Cohen does with his criterion of urgency, only the rights protecting the latter good as human rights. It is rather a reason to consider the violation of the latter as grounds for more serious and more timely forms of intervention by the international community. In other words, the relation between human rights and interference in national affairs may and should be made more flexible and articulated than what the Rawlsian scheme suggests. We need to identify those human rights whose violation (on a sufficient scale) would justify the most serious form of interference, i.e., military intervention. This is in fact what the UN document *The Responsibility to Protect* has already done. Then we need a second set of human rights whose violation would license less serious forms of intervention – say economic and/or diplomatic sanctions – in a descending order of seriousness of human rights violations and corresponding forms of international sanctions. To be as sympathetic as possible to Cohen's intuitions, we can concede that the least serious form of interference, the practice of naming and shaming, would be reserved to those polities based on the normative ideal of membership (assuming that they exist or will ever exist). By so doing, we would be able to accommodate Rawls's underlying idea of being as open as possible to pluralism, as well as to ease the worries of liberal thinkers that their ideals become instruments of dubious wars for freedom, while avoiding stripping down the list of human rights. Accommodating tolerance, self-determination, political prudence, and moral universalism fortunately does not require us to backdate the evolution of the human rights culture to the pre-1948 era.

References

Al-Azm, Sadik. 1970. *Critique of Religious Thought* (Beirut: Naqd al-Fikr al-Dini).

An-Na'im, Abdullahi Ahmed. 2001. "Human Rights in the Muslim World." In P. Hayden, ed., *The Philosophy of Human Rights* (St. Paul, MN: Paragon House).

Angle, Stephen C. 2002. *Human Rights and Chinese Thought: A Cross-Cultural Inquiry* (New York: Cambridge University Press).

Beitz, Charles. 1979. *Political Theory and International Relations* (Princeton, NJ: Princeton University Press).

Chan, Joseph. 2007. "Democracy and Meritocracy: Toward a Confucian Perspective." *Journal of Chinese Philosophy*, Vol. 34.

Cohen, Jean. 2008. "Rethinking Human Rights, Democracy and Sovereignty in the Age of Globalization." *Political Theory*, Vol. 36.

Cohen, Joshua. 2006. "Is There a Human Right to Democracy?" In C. Sypnowich, ed., *The Egalitarian Conscience. Essays in Honour of G. A. Cohen* (Oxford: Oxford University Press).

Ignatieff, Michael. 2001. *Human Rights as Politics and Idolatry* (Princeton, NJ: Princeton University Press).

Johnson M. Glen and Janusz Symonides. 1998. *The Universal Declaration of Human Rights: A History of its Creation and Implementation, 1948–1998* (Paris: UNESCO).

Li, Xiarong. 2001. "Tolerating the Intolerable: The Case of Female Genital Mutilation." *Philosophy and Public Policy Quarterly*, Vol. 21.

Maffettone, Sebastiano. 2001. "Premessa." In John Rawls, *Il diritto dei popoli* (Milano: Edizioni di comunit).

Nickel, James. 2003. "Human Rights." In Edward N. Zalta, *The Stanford Encyclopedia of Philosophy* <http://plato.stanford.edu/entries/rights-human/#GenIdeHumRig>.

Rawls, John. 1999. *The Law of Peoples* (Cambridge, MA: Harvard University Press).

Sen, Amartya. 2006. *Identity and Violence* (New York: Norton).

Talbi, Mohammed. 1998. "Religious Liberty." In C. Kurzman, ed., *Liberal Islam* (Oxford: Oxford University Press).

9

Cosmopolitanism and human rights

Robert Fine

Introduction

My topic is the relation between cosmopolitanism and human rights. Let me begin with a rough-and-ready formulation of this relationship. Cosmopolitanism imagines a world order in which the idea of human rights is a basic principle of justice and mechanisms of global governance are established specifically for their protection. The cosmopolitan imagination is not restricted to this agenda. It incorporates wider issues concerning social solidarity across borders, the legitimacy of international law, the effectiveness of global governance, the role of global civil society, and the establishment of peaceful relations between and within states. It also envisages the reformation of political community at national and transnational levels to render them compatible with and supportive of cosmopolitan values. However, it would be implausible to think of the cosmopolitan imagination apart from some notion of human rights, that is, of rights that belong to all people by virtue of their human status. If the closeness of the relationship between cosmopolitanism and human rights is straightforward enough, it still begs the question of what we mean both by the idea of human rights and by the idea of cosmopolitanism. To explore further this question I shall focus first on the human rights side of this relationship and then on the cosmopolitan.

Human rights

I begin this section by outlining in a condensed form some of the key propositions I wish to make concerning the idea of human rights.

First, the idea of human rights is an *achievement of the modern age* – albeit an achievement that is under threat, may be rolled back, and can never be taken for granted. This broad statement about the modernity of human rights obviously needs further specification, but it underlines the historicity of the concept.

Second, the existence of human rights is, for better or worse, now part of the *social world* we inhabit. It is the task of sociology to understand human rights as a social phenomenon that is external to our own subjective feelings and opinions about it.

Third, the idea of human rights has a legal status within *international law*. There has now arisen a body of law known as "human rights law" that has its own (more or less coercive) means of adjudication and enforcement. This body of law has percolated into other areas of international law (such as international criminal law and humanitarian law) and domestic law (including criminal, welfare, immigration, and family law).

Fourth, the idea of human rights is endowed with a *normative* force that prescribes that human rights ought to be respected by states, corporations, and individuals. It is implicit in the idea of human rights that human rights ought to be made actual in the world, that violations of human rights matter, and that they ought to be prevented by those with the capacity so to do.

Fifth, in a world in which sovereign states have hidden even their most heinous crimes behind national boundaries or insulated them from criticism on the grounds of non-intervention in their internal affairs, the idea of human rights creates a *political* wedge that allows an external standard of justice to enter into what was previously the exclusive terrain of state sovereignty.

Sixth, the idea of human rights means that rulers who commit serious crimes even against their own people should be punished for the crimes they have committed. It *removes the impunity* that rulers once held and exposes them to the same kind of criminal sanctions ordinary people face for the ordinary crimes they commit. This holds whether or not rulers have acted within the bounds of their own domestic laws.

Seventh, the idea of human rights contains within itself a *promise of civil repair* (Alexander 2006) for wrongs committed by the state or more boldly of transforming the existing order of injustice. This promise flows from the conflicts that emerge between the idea of human rights and their violation in practice and can be pushed towards ever more dramatic ways of reimagining self and society.

Eighth, the idea of human rights can be imagined as a transcendent norm or in the Kantian sense as a regulative idea that can never be fully realized either in practice or in principle but that nonetheless provides a necessarily elusive standard against which to measure worldly affairs (Douzinas 2007).

Ninth, the development of human rights is the result both of the struggles of social movements from below and of initiatives of states and groups of states from above. Legal activists and non-governmental organizations have played a crucial role in both kinds of initiative and in mediating between them (Stammers 1999).

Tenth, the idea of human rights is at once a form of freedom, one of the various forms of freedom that human subjects enjoy in the modern age, and a form of coercion that places limits on the ways we human beings can treat one another.

These propositions are neither self-contained nor mutually incompatible. My claim here is that the idea of human rights is *at once* a historical product of the modern age, a social phenomenon external to our knowledge of it, a component part of our current legal order, a source of moral obligation, a political challenge to the sovereignty of states, a means of breaking down the impunity of rulers, a way of being with others, a resource for civil repair, a transcendent norm of resistance, an effect of power and resistance, and a form of freedom and discipline. The complexity of the idea of human rights is that it can play all these roles.

In speaking of the *idea* of human rights I do not mean to say that it is a "mere idea" in the heads of philosophers with no external existence in the world. I have in mind something more like what Hegel called "objective spirit," that is, something that is both spirit and objective (Fine 2001). The idea of human rights, as I see it, contains both the *category* or *concept* of human rights and its legal and institutional *existence* in the world. The idea of human rights is, as it were, both ideal and material. Our world contains both the category and the social reality the category refers to but can never quite capture. The shadow that falls between the *concept* of human rights and the *reality* of human beings actually entering into social relations as bearers of rights (though not exclusively as bearers of rights) is an integral aspect of the idea of human rights itself.

The relation between the category and the reality of human rights is, as I see it, dialectical. On the one hand, the category of human rights cannot be understood in isolation from its social existence; on the other, the social existence of human rights cannot be understood independently of the concept. Dialectical thinking is the attempt to hold these two aspects together. Both concept and existence are equally one-sided and false when abstracted from the other. In seeking to understand the idea of human rights we are like a tightrope walker: we can fall one way into what I call conceptual thinking, the other into realism.

The conceptual way of thinking dissolves the laws, institutions, and judgments through which the idea of human rights is actualized into the concept itself. In a conservative mode it endows existing institutions, say the office of the UN High Commissioner for Human Rights, with the authority of the concept of human rights itself. Missing from this framework is the *differentia specifica* that allow us to address the adequacy of this particular form of existence or of the judgments made. It reifies the concept of human rights before deducing from it the mundane institutional forms of international law. It might offer a more or less accurate empirical description of how the idea of human rights currently functions, but its aim is simply to rediscover the concept in every sphere of human rights practice it finds – to fasten on what lies nearest at hand and prove that it is an actual moment of the concept. In this mode it has an affinity with a basically uncritical positivism.

In its more critical mode the conceptual way of thinking strives to elevate laws and institutions up to the level of the concept of human rights. In its wish to evaporate the shadow between the category of human rights and the actuality of human violence, it looks to the construction, say, of an ideal cosmopolitan state in which human rights are for the first time properly legislated (e.g., through a global parliament), properly adjudicated (e.g., through a network of world courts), and properly enforced (e.g., through a UN army and police). It endorses the vision of a wholly legalized international order in which human rights are hegemonic over power. It resolves the political instrumentalization of existing human rights – and the consequent "dressing up of strategic power-plays in a universalistic garb" (Cohen 2004, p. 10) – by accelerating the transition from traditional international law based on state sovereignty to a cosmopolitan legal order based on human rights. The politics of human rights is here conceived as an anticipation of a world in which human rights are firmly embedded within an international legal framework and serious human rights violations are prosecuted as criminal acts within a legal order (Smith 2007).

Realism offers a counterpoint to both these conceptual approaches. The realist way of thinking discounts the concept of human rights as mere froth on the surface of what is real and addresses laws, institutions, and practices from an exclusively non-conceptual point of view. Its focus is on the political and economic interests concealed behind the concept of human rights and on its rhetorical uses and ideological appropriation. It constructs a hermeneutics of suspicion in which human rights are devalued either as a tool for understanding the world or as a standard for judging what goes on in the world. Its instinct is to treat the appeal to human rights as a ploy designed to stigmatize those accused of violating human rights and to put on a pedestal their accusers. It is not to be faulted for addressing the uses and abuses of the idea of human rights, which includes processes of denial on one side and demonization on the other, but for imagining that these uses and abuses exhaust the significance and validity of the concept itself (Zolo 2002).

Both conceptual and realist ways of thinking about human rights are one-sided. As a specific legal form of right, the idea of human rights should be understood developmentally, that is, as part of the dynamics of modern capitalist society. T. H. Marshall (1950) wrote famously of a movement from civil rights to political rights to social rights that has characterized modern constitutional states. Hegel (1991) wrote of a complex movement from rights of personality to rights of property, moral conscience, civil association, political participation, and national self-determination. Based on either way of thinking we can represent the emergence of the idea of *human* rights as a stage in the development of the idea of right itself – one that Hegel and Marshall prefigured but remained at the margins of their thinking. In this sense, the idea of human rights may be viewed as an emergent property of the system of rights as a whole. It should not be viewed, however, as the telos of an evolutionary process.

Most legal textbooks link the idea of human rights to major changes that have occurred in international law since the Second World War: the creation of the Nuremberg Tribunal and "crimes against humanity" (1945), an all-inclusive United Nations (1945), the International Court of Justice (1946), the Universal Declaration of Human Rights (1948), Convention on the Prevention and Punishment of the Crime of Genocide (1948), the European Convention on Human Rights (1950), the International Covenant on Civil and Political Rights and the International Covenant on Economic, Social and Cultural Rights (created 1966, came into force 1976), a variety of other human rights conventions, declarations, and instruments at regional and global levels, the Vienna Convention on the Law of Treaties (1969), the United Nations Convention against Torture and Other Cruel, Inhuman or Degrading Treatment or Punishment (1987, adopted by the UN Assembly 2002), ad hoc tribunals to try war crimes in the former Yugoslavia (1993) and Rwanda (1994), the International Criminal Court (excluding the USA, China, and India, 2002), and so on. We might also refer to the development of *ius cogens* (the idea of a higher and compelling law) in international law, the transition from the sovereignty of states to sovereign equality under international law, the inclusion of individual human beings as subjects of international law, and the transformation of human rights from a moral declaration to an enforceable legal system.

If it no longer sounds completely hyperbolic to speak of an international human rights revolution since 1945, the strength of cosmopolitanism is to recognize its existence. If it is recognized that all the legal norms associated with the idea of human rights are frequently violated, what is new is that they exist as legal norms. From 1989 onwards the idea of human rights has also become increasingly central to political argument in contrast to its relative invisibility in the post-1945 period when human rights "law" was widely regarded as ineffective and both states and citizens were inclined to rely on the resources of domestic legal systems. Today, appeal is often made to the idea of human rights to decide on the legitimacy of acts of state: whether, for example, such acts constitute disproportionate responses or collective punishment or ethnic cleansing or even genocide. The enhanced role of the idea of human rights in political argument is reflected in legal theory, where from a surprising number of different theoretical and political perspectives the idea of human rights in determining the legitimacy of state action is invoked – so much so that it has almost come to function like a universal law of nature against which the positive actions of nation-states should be critically assessed.

The emergence and development of the idea of human rights should not be understood as making obsolescent older or less-developed legal forms. The idea of human rights does not supplant the civil, political, and social rights associated with the nation-state; rather, it supplements them. When Marshall analyzed the development of citizenship as a development of *civil*, then *political*, then *social* rights, he assigned them broadly to the eighteenth, nineteenth, and twentieth centuries respectively. His distinctive contribution, however, was to argue that modern citizens are only full citizens if they possess all three kinds of right and that this possession of full rights is linked to *social class*. Analogously, the idea of human rights should be understood as a finite achievement alongside other rights – be they rights of property, conscience, association, participation, welfare, sovereignty, etc.

In legal terms some human rights are considered "absolute." These include the prohibition on torture in the UN Convention Against Torture and the European Convention of Human Rights. In reality, states can circumvent this absolute prohibition by redefining either what counts as torture or what their responsibilities are in cases of torture. The existence of absolute human rights should not be confused with the doctrine that treats the idea of human rights itself as absolute in the same way some neoliberal thinkers have considered as absolute rights of private property or some *étatist* thinkers have made absolute the sovereignty of the state. Human rights do not substitute for civil, political, and social rights; they exist alongside them, they depend on them, and they impact upon them. If we can speak of there being a *system* of rights in the modern world, human rights are not the *telos* of this system, not the final result of the idea of right. However, they can deeply affect the civil, political, and social rights that arise in the context of the nation-state. This is evident in the fact that nearly all national constitutions now nominally guarantee basic human rights – even if many do so more in word than deed.

Cosmopolitanism

In its modern guise, cosmopolitanism was born out of the endeavor to realize the universalistic potential inherent in the idea of the "rights of man." This product of eighteenth-century revolutions announced that every man should be conceived as a bearer of rights simply by virtue of the fact that he is a man. It contrasted the modern notion of subjectivity to ancient societies in which the possession of rights – personality in the language of Roman law – was a privileged status distinct from the mass of slaves and other dependants. Although the idea of the rights of man was for the most part restricted to certain sections of the male adult citizen population and undercut by the growth of regressive nationalisms (Kristeva 1991), the universality implicit in this idea provided the framework in which struggles for the rights of women, slaves, servants, wage laborers, the colonized, and the racialized were added to the original conception of bourgeois man (cf. Dubois 2000). Class struggles from below combined with state-formation from above to construct a power able to guarantee civil rights, extend political participation, and provide access to social welfare and mass education. The success of the modern state was to yield rights of religious freedom while keeping religious fervor and fanaticism under strict control, rights of political participation while transforming political resistance into agonistic competition between political parties, and rights of social inclusion that tempered the destructive force of free markets as well as the revolutionary momentum of class struggle (Brunkhorst 2008).

The expansion of the rights of man, however, came at a price. No sooner were the rights of man articulated than they entered into conflict with the organization of political community that underwrote their existence. The revolutions that declared the rights of man and citizen also designated that nation-states are the power that grants these rights and in its radical form declared there could be no rights the nation did not grant. The contradiction between the universalism of the concept and its particular national existence was expressed in the lawlessness apparent in relations between states, the colonization of non-European states, and the stigmatization of foreigners within nation-states. It was under the heading of the cosmopolitan point of view that Kant (1991) addressed these contradictions.

Kant argued first that republican government had to be extended across all political communities if the rights of man were to belong to all men in practice and not merely in theory; second, a League or Federation of Nations had to be conceived and established with the capacity to enforce genuinely legal relations between states and put an end to aggressive wars, military conquests, and the barbarities of colonization; third, cosmopolitan rights in the strict sense of the term had to be recognized so as to guarantee *inter alia* the right to hospitality for strangers landing on foreign shores. For Kant, this visionary agenda – the extension of republicanism to all states, the formation of an international legal authority, and the endorsement of cosmopolitan rights – provided the foundations on which to translate the formal universality implicit in the concept of the rights of man into a concrete universal (Chernilo 2007).

These moves proved more problematic, even in conception, than Kant envisaged. The idea of the rights of man was inverted into a duty of unconditional obedience to the state, which grants these rights, and an internal dynamic was set in motion toward legal authoritarianism on the part of the state and militant patriotism on the part of citizens. The extension of republicanism across Europe and the globe was undertaken through wars of liberation and conquest, the brutalities of which run roughshod over the rights of everyone (we might think, for example, of Goya's representations of the "disasters of war" consequent upon the French effort to make Spain into a republic). The establishment of a League of Nations could not provide the alchemy Kant envisaged: that of turning perpetual war into perpetual peace. An alliance of powerful states, committed to republicanism, could find itself in a stronger position than individual states to destroy their enemies, subdue their subjects, and acquire new territories. The idea of cosmopolitan rights, though restrictive in scope, was to be sure a harbinger of human rights to come, but it also continued to serve powerful states as a pretext for the conquest of "barbarous" peoples who declined to provide the required hospitality (Fine 2007, p. 25).

Kant's observation that every right is a right of coercion was a reminder that every *expansion* of rights is also a *re-invention* of new forms of coercion. This was apparent not least in the imperialist presuppositions of the European division of the world. From the first European divisions of the world in the Treaties of Tordesillas (1494) and Saragossa (1529) between Spain and Portugal, from the Christian missionaries and inquisitors of the sixteenth century, through expansionist ideologies of "civilizing the heart of darkness" in the nineteenth century (Koskenniemi 2001), to movements for decolonization and nation-building in the twentieth, and finally to the "war on terror" and the exclusion of outlaw states in our own times, imperialism has not ceased to appear and reappear under various guises – some of them "anti-imperialist" (Brunkhorst 2008; Anghie 2004).

For all its conceptual shortcomings, Kant's cosmopolitan vision of generalizing the "rights of man" through a reformation of the system of nation-states provides a continuing resource in the face of the escalating violence of the modern world. Let me offer two examples. In his study of *The Germans* (1998), the sociologist Norbert Elias identified the absence of external legal authority at the international level as a key source of violence in the modern age:

> There is no monopoly of force on the international level. On this level we are basically still living exactly as our forefathers did in the period of their so-called "barbarism" ... In inter-state relations people today do not find themselves on a lower rung of the civilising process because they are naturally evil or because they have inborn aggressive urges, but rather because specific social institutions have been formed which can more or less effectively impose a check on every state-authorised act of violence in relations within the state, while such institutions are completely lacking in relations between states.
>
> *(Elias 1998, pp. 176–177)*

The political theorist Hannah Arendt argued along similar lines in her analysis of the lesson to be drawn from her study *The Origins of Totalitarianism*:

> Anti-Semitism, imperialism and totalitarianism … demonstrated that human dignity needs a *new guarantee* which can be found only in a *new political principle*, a *new law on earth*, whose validity this time must comprehend the whole of humanity, while its power must remain strictly limited, rooted in and controlled by newly defined territorial entities.
>
> *(Arendt 1979, p. ix; my emphasis)*

What was needed, she argued, was not world government, which could still act on the basis of "the essentially barbaric idea that 'right' is what is good for the whole," but a *philosophy of right* whose principle was that "the right to have rights, or the right of every individual to belong to humanity, should be guaranteed by humanity itself" (Arendt 1979, p. 298). The Kantian inspiration behind these words is palpable.

At the time of Arendt's writing, norms of international law still operated largely in terms of treaties and agreements between sovereign states. New declarations of human rights lacked means of enforcement. The modern nation-state was still largely restricted to Europe, America, Russia, and Japan while the rest of the world was either under their imperialist control or outside world society. Equality still meant internal equality for citizens of a state and external inequality for those who did not belong. And the UN claim to universal authority at the global level still had the vulnerability of an infant faced with heavily armed parents: the Western and Eastern blocs.

Between Arendt, Elias, and the present day much has changed. Classical imperialism has vanished, Eurocentrism has been radically fractured, equal sovereignty under law has become a universal principle, individuals have become subjects of international law, and human rights have become a subdiscipline within the study of international law. Social exclusion and social inequalities are no longer perceived exclusively as "our own" problems, not only because we need each other to solve our particular problems (Beck 2006) but also because we now have various legally binding claims in relation to others. To be sure, these legal norms are frequently broken by nation-states, but what is new is that they exist.

In response to restraints imposed by international law, nation-states respond with a variety of strategies: they instrumentalize existing international law to suit their own interests, reshape the rules of international law to exempt themselves from its provisions, create zones of exclusion where the norms of international law have no purchase (as in Guantánamo Bay), substitute domestic law over which they retain control for the less certain authority of international law, or simply withdraw from international law and bring their military superiority to bear. However, nation-states have their own interests in supporting international law for reasons to do with regulation (it sets rules), pacification (it reduces resistance), stabilization (it preserves the current order), and legitimation (it justifies power). Even the most hegemonic of states may have a long-term rational interest in "binding emerging major powers to the rules of a politically constituted international community" (Habermas 2006, p. 150).

Hauke Brunkhorst (2008) has argued in a very compelling way that the current legitimacy crisis of nation-states may be understood to derive from their relatively recent incapacity to harmonize positive with negative freedoms – freedom of markets with freedom from the negative effects of markets, freedom of religion with freedom from the negative effects of religion, freedom of identity with freedom from the negative effects of identity. We may think of growing social inequalities even within the privileged Organization for Economic

Cooperation and Development (OECD) world, the expansion of religious communities beyond controls exercised by nation-states (as in the case of American Evangelists or Islamic fundamentalists), and the rebirth of ethnic forms of nationalism. In the face of such societal changes the expansion has occurred of regional and global institutions from the European Union (EU) to the World Trade Organization (WTO), associations of global civil society from Amnesty International to the International Chamber of Commerce, and the global public sphere where matters as far apart as the Iraq war and Princess Diana's death are debated all over the world.

The legitimacy of this global sphere lies in supplementing the declining functional capacities of nation-states. However, the normative equivocations of this development in the system of right are also visible. On the one hand, the constitutionalization of international law has given new impetus to the Kantian project of constructing a cosmopolitan condition. On the other hand, it is creating its own distinctive legitimacy problems (Sands 2006). They are apparent, for example, in the incapacity of supranational institutions and laws to address social inequalities, or apply human rights impartially, or match the democratic requirements of the modern nation-state. These legitimacy problems give rise to the perception that the idea of human rights functions to obscure global inequalities or is used as a political rhetoric to vilify one's enemies (Habibi 2007).

Within the cosmopolitan literature much effort has gone into confronting such legitimacy problems. For example, in relation to the democratic shortfall apparent in international law, Jürgen Habermas has argued that supranational constitutions receive backing from processes of democratic legitimation institutionalized within nation-states, the normative substance of human rights rests on legal principles tried and tested within democratic constitutions, and global civil society confers a supplementary level of democratic legitimacy on the decisions of global organizations. Habermas in any event justifies the restricted democratic legitimacy of international institutions by virtue of the relatively limited functions they serve compared with nation-states. Nonetheless, the political costs are involved in the evolution of postnational regimes and the mediations involved in the interpretation and application of human rights. Hauke Brunkhorst (2008) writes of the "latent legitimation crisis of world society" brought about by the coexistence at the global level of the abstract idea of human rights and concrete norms of social and legal exclusion.

If a crisis of the idea of human rights is in the air, it does not bode well for democratic thought. Hatred of the idea of human rights remains what hatred of law was for Hegel, "the shibboleth whereby fanaticism, imbecility and hypocritical good intentions manifestly and infallibly reveal themselves for what they are, no matter what disguise they may adopt" (1991, p. 258n). Sheer negativity opens the way for unholy political alliances.

Conclusion

Cosmopolitanism offers a generally critical outlook on human rights. It embraces the idea of human rights – not just in the juridical sense but in the wider political sense of the right of all human beings to have rights – and at the same time recognizes that the human rights revolution has taken off in a radically asymmetrical political–economic order (Toscano 2008, p. 134). Recognizing the equivocations present in the human rights revolution, cosmopolitans link to another Kantian thematic: not just the constitutional law of his political writings but also the role of judgment as "the faculty for thinking the particular" (Kant 1987, p. 18; Ferrara 2007).

Hannah Arendt picks up this dimension of the issue when in her lectures on Kant's *Philosophy of Judgment* she comments:

> One judges always as a member of a community, guided by one's community sense, one's *sensus communis*. But in the last analysis, one is a member of a world community by the sheer fact of being human; this is one's "cosmopolitan existence." When one judges and when one acts in political matters, one is supposed to take one's bearings from the idea, not the actuality, of being a world citizen.
>
> *(Arendt 1992, pp. 75–76)*

Arendt's call to fashion a space for cosmopolitan judgment out of the equivocation of human rights is the note on which I end. For as of now it is safe to say that the development of what we might call a "human rights culture" lags behind the institutionalization of human rights, and this is one of the most important observations on which to proceed in the future study of human rights (Fine 2009).

References

Alexander, Jeffrey. 2006. *The Civil Sphere* (Oxford: Oxford University Press).

Anghie, Antony. 2004. *Imperialism, Sovereignty and the Making of International Law* (Cambridge, MA: Harvard University Press).

Arendt, Hannah. 1979. *The Origins of Totalitarianism* (New York: Harcourt Brace).

Arendt, Hannah. 1992. *Lectures on Kant's Political Philosophy*, ed. Ronald Beiner (Chicago: University of Chicago Press).

Beck, Ulrich. 2006. *Cosmopolitan Vision* (Cambridge: Polity Press).

Brunkhorst, Hauke. 2008. "Cosmopolitanism and Democratic Freedom." Paper presented at Onati (Spain) Institute for Sociology of Law, Conference on Normative and Sociological Approaches to Legality and Legitimacy, 24–25 April.

Chernilo, Daniel. 2007. "A Quest for Universalism: Re-Assessing the Nature of Classical Social Theory's Cosmopolitanism." *European Journal of Social Theory*, Vol. 10, No. 1, pp. 17–35.

Cohen, Jean. 2004. "Whose Sovereignty? Empire versus International Law." *Ethics and International Affairs*, Vol. 18, No. 3, pp. 1–24.

Douzinas, Costas. 2007. *Human Rights and Empire: The Political Philosophy of Cosmopolitanism* (London: Routledge-Cavendish).

Dubois, Laurent. 2000. "La Republique Métissée: Citizenship, Colonialism and the Borders of French History." *Cultural Studies*, Vol. 14, No. 1, pp. 15–34.

Elias, Norbert. 1998. *The Germans* (New York: Columbia University Press).

Ferrara, Alessandro. 2007. "Political Cosmopolitanism and Judgment." In Vivienne Boon and Robert Fine, eds., "Cosmopolitanism: Between Past and Future." Special issue *European Journal of Social Theory*, Vol. 10, No. 1, pp. 53–66.

Fine, Robert. 2001. *Political Investigations: Hegel, Marx, Arendt* (London: Routledge).

Fine, Robert. 2007. *Cosmopolitanism* (London: Routledge).

Fine, Robert. 2009. "Cosmopolitanism and Human Rights: Radicalism for a Global Age." *Metaphilosophy*, Vol. 40, No. 1, pp. 8–23.

Habermas, Jürgen. 2006. *The Divided West*. Ed. and trans. Ciaran Cronin (Cambridge: Polity Press).

Habibi, Don. 2007. "Human Rights and Politicised Human Rights: A Utilitarian Critique." *Journal of Human Rights*, Vol. 6, pp. 3–35.

Hegel, Georg. 1991. *Philosophy of Right*. Ed. Allen W. Wood, trans. H. B. Nisbet (Cambridge: Cambridge University Press).

Kant, Immanuel. 1987. *Critique of Judgment*. Trans. Werner S. Pluhar (Cambridge: Hackett).

Kant, Immanuel. 1991. *Kant: Political Writings*. Ed. Hans Reiss (Cambridge: Cambridge University Press).

Koskenniemi, Martti. 2001. *The Gentle Civilizer of Nations: The Rise and Fall of International Law 1870–1960*, Hersch Lauterpacht Memorial Lectures (Cambridge: Cambridge University Press).

Kristeva, Julia. 1991. *Strangers to Ourselves* (New York: Columbia University Press).
Marshall, T. H. 1950. *Citizenship and Social Class and Other Essays* (Cambridge: Cambridge University Press).
Sands, Philippe. 2006. *Lawless World: Making and Breaking Global Rules* (Harmondsworth: Penguin).
Smith, William. 2007. "Anticipating a Cosmopolitan Future: The Case of Humanitarian Military Intervention." *International Politics*, Vol. 44, No. 1, pp. 72–89.
Stammers, Neil. 1999. "Social Movements and the Social Construction of Human Rights." *Human Rights Quarterly*, Vol. 21, No. 4, pp. 980–1008.
Toscano, Alberto. 2008. "Sovereign Impunity: Review of Danilo Zolo, *La Giustizia Dei Vincitori: Da Norimberga a Baghdad*." *New Left Review*, No. 50, March–April, pp. 128–135.
Zolo, Danilo. 2002. "A Cosmopolitan Philosophy of International Law? A Realist Approach." *Ratio Juris*, Vol. 12, No. 4, pp. 429–444.

10

A critique of positive rights

Tibor R. Machan

Introduction: concept distortion

A very powerful and influential idea that has been in circulation for nearly two centuries and that challenges fully free society, the kind envisioned by John Locke and the American Founders, is what political philosophers call "positive rights." The idea of positive rights has challenged the traditional meaning of liberalism. Whereas in earlier times to be a liberal meant to champion limited government, civil liberties, economic freedom, and a restrained role for the military, the meaning has changed so that it now means a system in which government takes on a more expansive role in a society, where markets are highly regulated, where more and more social problems are addressed by public policies instead of the private sector, and where the emphasis is on the entitlements of the citizenry and less about their basic negative or freedom rights, rights not to be interfered with in their persons and property.

So in today's political parlance, "liberalism" means mostly the opposite of what it used to. To put it plainly, it means a political position prescribing the systematic violation of the liberty of individuals for the sake of redistributing wealth and otherwise engineering society. Proponents of this new liberalism often insist that they are the authentic champions of human liberty because having a positive right to liberty means enabling people to do what they would otherwise be unable or unfree to do.

To be sure, modern liberalism includes a sub-clause stipulating that people may at least enjoy the sexual and other non-economic freedoms distinctive to one's chosen "lifestyle." But even these allowances are more and more falling victim to the logic of this liberalism's command-and-control statism – as when "liberals" and conservatives team up to urge censorship of sexually explicit fiction or insulting labels on the basis of a shared determination of politically incorrect language. In certain cultures, of course, it is routine to censor such language, but in Western liberal societies words have traditionally been legally protected from official censure. Nonetheless, there are very serious scholars, working in prominent institutions, who do not embrace even this central tradition of classical liberalism. Catherine MacKinnon (1983), for example, argues that demeaning language about and depiction of women should be construed as injurious and therefore banned. And when it comes to conduct on the economic front, the command-and-control style public policy is now routine both on the Left and the Right – minimum wage mandates exemplifying the former's proclivities, protectionism the latter's.

Just as critics have argued, I believe convincingly, that the new liberalism is fake liberalism, so I will argue that "positive rights" are fake rights. They are means by which to secure for those who have no right to them certain governmentally guaranteed benefits – "entitlements" or "enablements." Especially in the United States, where the Founders held that governments are instituted so as to secure basic rights, once one achieves this transformation of sought-after values into rights, governments can be enlisted to secure them.

In each case, a valid principle has been replaced with one that is fundamentally flawed. Exactly for reasons why unappealing, insulting language and art require legal protection, so wealth deemed excessive by some (e.g., populists) may not be used without the consent of those who own it regardless of how needy some people may be. To take wealth from people without their consent is, itself, a violation of a fundamental right in classical liberal thought. Acceptance of this idea justifies the rejection of the notion of basic positive rights. I will here explain why.

Bona fide basic rights are negative

The classical liberal idea of basic, natural rights – or, as they have been un-euphoniously dubbed, "negative rights" – pertains to everyone's freedom from the uninvited and unwelcome interventions of others. It secures the sovereignty of adult human individuals, sovereignty that in more statist systems has been claimed exclusively for rulers, men and women who oppressed their fellows in the name of their allegedly innate superior birth, membership in superior classes, and similar dubious notions. Respect for negative rights requires that all individuals abstain from invading one another's sphere of authority – or, as the late Harvard political philosopher Robert Nozick (1974, p. 39) so very aptly dubbed it, our "moral space." These rights are founded on the idea that human beings are free and independent, meaning capable of initiating their own conduct, and do not belong to others, certainly in their adulthood. And they are responsible to act ethically (in John Locke's terms, to obey the law of nature) of their own volition. For this they all require liberty in their community lives, so they have it *by right*. Though, of course, complications do arise and laws are necessary to apply this idea in a complex society. Yet the basic notion is clear – in just a society no one may expropriate someone else's property under threat of coercion.

A brief history of the idea

Positive rights require that all who are defined as being in need be provided with goods or services at the expense of other persons and that this can only be accomplished by systematic coercion. This idea is also known as the doctrine of entitlements; that is, some people are said to be entitled to that which is earned by other people. Some of the earliest prominent advocates of positive rights include Auguste Comte and Thomas Hill Green. Here is what Comte says that implies such rights:

> Everything we have belongs then to Humanity ... Positivism never admits anything but duties, of all to all. For its social point of view cannot tolerate the notion of [negative] *right*, constantly based on individualism. We are born loaded with obligations of every kind, to our predecessors, to our successors, to our contemporaries ... Whatever may be our efforts,

> the longest life well employed will never enable us to pay back but an imperceptible part of what we have received. And yet it would only be after a complete return that we should be justly authorized to require reciprocity for the new services. All [negative, Lockean] human rights then are as absurd as they are immoral. This ["to live for others"], the definitive formula of human morality, gives a direct sanction exclusively to our instincts of benevolence, the common source of happiness and duty. [Man must serve] Humanity, whose we are entirely.
>
> *(Comte 1973, pp. 212–230)*

Comte implies, surely, that everyone has positive rights claims against everyone else, rights to have services performed for him or her at the expense of the immense benefits others have reaped. And as with rights in general, such rights, too, must be secured by means of legal force.

Green's language is more directly supportive of positive rights by way of his explanation of positive freedom. The two ideas are closely related – when one's positive rights are secure, one enjoys positive freedom:

> We shall probably all agree that freedom, rightly understood, is the greatest of blessings; that its attainment is the true end of all our efforts as citizens. But when we thus speak of freedom, we should consider carefully what we mean by it. We do not mean merely freedom from restraint or compulsion. We do not mean merely freedom to do as we like irrespective of what it is that we like. We do not mean a freedom that can be enjoyed by one man or one set of men at the cost of a loss of freedom to others. When we speak of freedom as something to be so highly prized, we mean a positive power or capacity of doing or enjoying something worth doing or enjoying, and that, too, something that we do or enjoy in common with others. We mean by it a power which each man exercises through the help or security given him by his fellow-men, and which he in turn helps to secure for them. When we measure the progress of a society by its growth in freedom, we measure it by the increasing development and exercise on the whole of those powers of contributing to social good with which we believe the members of the society to be endowed; in short, by the greater power on the part of the citizens as a body to make the most and best of themselves.
>
> *(Green 1861)*

The freedom Green champions is the kind we refer to when we say such things as, "Well, finally I am free to buy myself health insurance, now that I've received that raise" or "I am finally free to seek the help of a physician for what ails me, now that the government provides us with health insurance." The other type of freedom, the type Green thinks is a "mere" freedom, is referred to when we lament the lack of freedom of political dissidents or of slaves or of women in countries where they are forbidden to live as they choose.

The main problem with "positive rights" is that as basic principles of community life they void the right to individual liberty essential to a just legal order. According to the positive rights doctrine, human beings by nature owe, *as a matter of enforceable obligation*, part or even all of their lives to other persons. Generosity and charity thus cannot be left to individual conscience. If people have such positive rights, no one can be justified in refusing service to others; one may be conscripted to serve others regardless of one's own choices and goals. If basic positive rights are valid, then basic negative rights cannot be, for the two are mutually contradictory. In the present discourse of human rights, the default mode has placed emphasis on positive rights. How did this occur, and what are the ramifications of this development?

America's political system was founded on a theory of human rights outlined in the Declaration of Independence. The theory had been most fully developed by the seventeenth-century English philosopher John Locke. It held that every human being possesses the inalienable right to, among other things, life, liberty, and property. (Jefferson cast the triumvirate as "life, liberty, and the pursuit of happiness.")

The rights Locke identified – following several centuries of political and legal thinking – are "negative" insofar as they require only that human beings refrain from forcibly intruding on one another. Their existence means that no one ought to enslave another, coerce another, or deprive another of his property; and that each of us may properly resist such conduct when others engage in it. Ordinary criminal law implicitly rests on such a theory of individual rights. On a commonsense basis, murder, assault, kidnapping, robbery, burglary, trespassing, and the like are all easily understood as violations of negative rights.

The integrity of law would be seriously endangered if the government entered areas that required it to make very particular judgments and depart from serving the interest of the public as such. We have already noted that the idea of "satisfying basic needs" can involve the difficulty of distinguishing those whose actions are properly to be so characterized. Whatever else people think about them, rich persons are indeed satisfying their basic needs as they protect and preserve their property rights. In a Lockean view, private property rights are necessary for a morally decent society. The Lockean libertarian argues that private property rights are morally justified in part because they are the concrete requirement for delineating the sphere of jurisdiction of each person's moral authority, where his or her own judgment is decisive. This is a crucial basis for the right to property. And so is the contention that we live in a metaphysically hospitable universe wherein people normally need not suffer innocent misery and deprivation – so that such a condition is usually the result of negligence or the violation of Lockean rights, a violation that has made self-development and commerce impossible. If exceptional emergencies set the agenda for the law, the law itself will disintegrate. A just legal system makes provision for coping with emergencies that are brought to the attention of the authorities, for example, by way of judicial discretion, without allowing such cases to determine the direction of the system. If legislators and judges do not uphold the integrity of the system, disintegration ensues. This can itself encourage the emergence of strong leaders, demagogues who promise to do what the law has not been permitted to do, namely, satisfy people's sense of justice.

Even if we grant that some helpless, physically or mentally handicapped or destitute persons could offer nothing to anyone that would merit wages enabling them to carry on with their lives and perhaps even flourish, we are left with the problem of those who seek help as a result of their own bad choices: people who drop out of school, have children they cannot afford, who find that their personal choices leave them relatively poorly off. "'Ought' implies 'can'" must not be treated ahistorically – some people's lack of current options results from their failure to exercise previous options prudently. I refer here to the "truly needy," to use a shop-worn but still useful phrase – those who have never been able to help themselves and are not now helpless from their own neglect. Are such people being treated *unjustly* – rather than uncharitably, ungenerously, indecently, pitilessly, or in some other respect immorally – by those who, knowing of the plight of such persons, resist forcible efforts to take from them enough to provide the ill-fated with what they claim to need? Actually, if we pry the needed goods or money from the well-to-do, we cannot know whether or not without coercion they would act generously. Charity, generosity, kindness, and acts of compassion presuppose that those well enough off are not coerced to provide help. These virtues cannot flourish, nor can the corresponding vices, of course, without a clearly identified and well-protected right to private property for all.

In the Lockean tradition, a fundamental, irresolvable conflict of valid rights cannot exist. There may be disputes about boundary lines, the exact historical record determining the propriety of a rights claim, and similar practical details. But once the facts are unambiguously established, so is the specific right. And the justice of any specific claim to ownership (of a parcel of land, say) is grounded in more basic, universal rights (to life and freedom) that in turn are justified by a correct understanding of human nature and what that implies about how we ought to live and organize ourselves in communities.

Understanding human nature

Of course, that an understanding of human nature is even possible is, among some philosophers anyway, highly doubtful. Yet skepticism here, as in other cases, stems from an unrealistic conception of what it takes to know something – the idea that we must know everything perfectly before we can know anything at all. But if knowing something means to have the clearest, most self-consistent, most reality-grounded, and most complete conceptualization possible to date, then sweeping skepticism is unjustified. We need simply admit that we will amend our knowledge if later observation and thinking warrant it (Machan 2006).

What we know now is that human beings, uniquely among animals, survive by means of their reason, which is a faculty of choice and hence of morality. This moral and rational faculty does not function automatically: the social condition required to gain and retain the fruits of its unhindered exercise is freedom. If human beings are to survive and flourish in a social context, the rights to life and liberty must be recognized and protected.

From the rights to life and liberty there emerges the right to private property. It rests on two considerations: (a) that human beings require spheres of individual jurisdiction, in which they may carry out their moral responsibility to choose to do the right thing; and (b) that choosing to acquire valued items, from nature or through trade, is a moral responsibility, entailed by the exercise of the virtue of prudence. Acquisition of property is something everyone ought to engage in to some degree to survive – even a complete ascetic needs food and a loincloth. We are not ghosts.

A political system, the purpose of which is the fostering of human life and community, must be organized so as to protect the rights to life, liberty, and their implementation, private property. Thus any political rights must not violate the more basic rights from which political rights derive. Political rights include the right to vote, serve in government, take part in the organization of political campaigns, and so forth. Practically speaking, the exercise of one's political rights may have an impact on who may govern, various internal rules of government, and the organization of political processes. But under a regime erected to protect natural rights, there can be no political right to override anyone's right to life, liberty, or property. If the legal system of a community does override those rights in a systematic way, that is *ipso facto* evidence that the system has become corrupted. It is no longer a bona fide rights-protecting regime but one governed by arbitrary (even if majority) rule. Indeed, one of the deficits of contemporary conservative legal theory is its failure to appreciate the intimate connection between Lockean individualism and democracy. Because of this, many think democracy may trump our basic rights. It may not.

To secure our rights

The American Founders conceived of government as a means by which to secure individual rights because they believed, with Locke, that *justice requires communities to recognize our moral agency* for which our rights need to be protected. As already noted, we adults all – excepting those rare individuals who are crucially incapacitated – have the responsibility to run our own lives. (Such individuals would rely on support from their fellows, in what is somewhat misleadingly referred to as the "private sector.") Governments are established among us so as to procure, preserve, and protect a realm in which moral agency can be freely exercised. This is the unique classical liberal view of a just human community's legal system, one that places all citizens on an equal moral footing, with no one the master or the slave, serf or ruler, of anyone else.

Here, of course, is where the most controversial aspect of the natural (negative) rights doctrine must be faced. Do human beings have the natural capacity for self-direction by means of their freely chosen rational thinking and action? As already mentioned above, the very idea of "the nature of X" is in much dispute. And while ultimately the skeptical outlook is self-defeating – since even to express it requires the possibility of defining one's terms other than merely stipulating them – skeptics have some plausible reasons in support of their doubts. For example, throughout the world there are some groups of human beings who to all appearances live more like most animals than like familiar human beings. They make no advances in their way of living, but have remained in an ancient static state for centuries, engaging in barbaric practices such as cannibalism. Yet from an anthropological perspective they are human nonetheless.

Among modern members of the human species there are many damaged people whose constitution does not contain those elements that are part of the conception of human nature as Locke and other classical liberals have understood it. Certain scientists are contending that a new human nature has already emerged, or evolved, by means of technology and neurophysiology. For example, an article on the website of a well-funded project to revise our understanding of human nature states:

> The U.S. legal system incorporates assumptions about behavior that, in some cases, are centuries old and based on common sense and culture. For example, it tends to assume that people make deliberate choices and that those choices determine what they do. However, recent breakthroughs in neuroscience research indicate that such choices may sometimes be based upon electrical impulses and neuron activity that are not a part of conscious behavior. These actions can include not only criminal activity, but also decisions made by police, prosecutors, and jurors to arrest, prosecute, convict, or mandate treatment.
>
> *(MacArthur Foundation 2007)*

These are but a few of the more general sources of skepticism about human nature and, thus, any doctrine of natural rights that could in part rest on it. There are other, more technical sources laid out in the discipline of philosophy, particularly epistemology (Machan 1989). Without entering the debate in full here, it needs to be said that the central source of the skeptical concerns is a distorted notion of what it is for there to be a nature of something. This is a final, perfect understanding of the crucial, distinguishing attributes of some kind of thing instead of an up-to-date, comparatively more comprehensive one that is sound beyond a *reasonable* doubt.

Those who sought to retain some elements of the political outlook that Locke's theory had overthrown – namely, the view that people are subjects of the state (in fact, belong to the state) – found a way to utilize skepticism about human nature and thus the concept of individual natural (human) rights to advance what amounts, actually, to their reactionary position, just as they expropriated and exploited the concept of liberalism. Riding on purloined prestige, they perverted the concept of individual rights at its root so that it came to mean not liberty from others but the demand for service from others. Who needs the right to pursue happiness when one has the right to be made happy (even if the thus-extracted "happiness" should render the indentured providers of it miserable)?

This was a view of rights that wiped moral agency right out of existence. Positive rights are thus nothing more than mislabeled preferences, or values, that people want and have managed to get the government to satisfy or attain for them – by the exercise of political power, namely, by force. They are grounded in nothing that pertains to the fundamental requirements of human nature and human survival. The theorizers of such rights in fact go out of their way to ignore such requirements. Yes, man needs bread, as stipulated. But he does not live by bread alone. He is not an ant who can survive on whatever crumbs fate happens to strew in his path. He needs the freedom to make the bread and trade the bread.

And he needs consistent and objective governance. But when the conceptual confusion, maybe even subterfuge, known as positive rights becomes the guiding principle of a polity, the state cannot govern by anything like the consistent standards that emerge from the theory of negative rights. The alleged positive rights of the citizenry must clash constantly with negative rights. To the extent one person is conscripted to serve another, he can no longer serve his own purposes, nor, indeed, even the purposes of many others, given the scarcity of the time and skills to which others are supposedly naturally entitled. There is no principle implicit in the doctrine of positive rights that can resolve the conflicts, so this doctrine serves to support arbitrary power by government officials. Most importantly, however, the idea of positive rights conflicts with our basic negative rights to life, liberty, and property and empowers those who would rather not concern themselves with respecting these fundamental rights.

To appreciate this fact, consider that, guided by such a doctrine, governments cannot merely protect our rights. They must positively pit some rights against others. Instead of simply "securing these rights," they must scrounge for some additional standard to tell which and whose rights should get protection. Since no intelligible such standard is available, the situation collapses into one of rule not by objective law but by the subjective impressions of certain individuals – ones who will decide, based on their impressions, which rights need protection, and which do not, on a shifting case-by-case basis. Perhaps the ascendant pressure group of the moment will carry the day, or perhaps the latest opinion polls, or media hype, or voter panic. In practice, the working principle is: "You have a right to whatever you can get away with," the same consideration governing any plain criminal.

The theories defending positive rights are just as incoherent as the practice of them must be. Positive rights have even been defended on the grounds that negative rights – of the very poor, for example – entail positive ones. This is the position of the philosopher James P. Sterba (1991, 1995). Others argue that all rights are in fact positive insofar as they are all meaningless unless they are actively protected; and the right to the protection of one's right to freedom is a positive right, not a negative one. Both views suffer fatal flaws. The first generalizes into a principle of law an understandable but regrettable response to what amounts to a rare moral emergency – one that becomes more and more rare the longer a society is free and able to build its prosperity. In some rare cases, an innocent person might indeed be totally helpless and have no choice but to obtain resources by stealing them. Perhaps only filching that piece of fruit will stave off immediate starvation. But extraordinary circumstances cannot generate laws granting a permanent right to steal, not when stealing itself means taking by force what by right belongs to others. There is no need for a society to send the occasional Jean Valjean, as in *Les Misérables*, to prison for twenty years; he might well be forgiven the transgression. But on the other hand, if the general concern for the plight of such individuals is genuine, there is no reason private charity cannot suffice to meet the need either. Moreover, if the members of a society engage in theft as a regular way of life, it will only undermine the production of wealth that everyone's survival depends on, including that of the poorest.

As for those who believe that protection of negative rights requires positive rights, they fail to show that any such right to protection can exist unless there already exists the more fundamental – and "negative" – right to liberty. To gain protection for something presupposes that one has the right to act for that purpose, including the right to voluntarily combine with others to delegate authority, form the government, and gain protection. The services of government are something people must choose to obtain by their consent to be governed. They do not have a natural right to them prior to having freely established that institution. Indeed, for that reason taxation, which fits well those regimes that treat people as subjects, is anathema to the free society in which even the funding of the legal order must be secured voluntarily (Machan 1982).

Because it is itself arbitrary and incoherent, the doctrine of positive rights leaves government free to be arbitrary and incoherent. One of the main activities of government is to ensure that some people are getting resources that were earned by somebody else. One day it is subsidizing AIDS research that is a priority, the next it is fostering the arts by splurging on the National Endowment for the Arts and Public Broadcasting Service (PBS), and the day after that, it is curing everyone of smoking and plundering the tobacco companies. No principles, no logic, no standards of restraint, and no surefire way to know from day to day what one will be free to do and what one will be prohibited from doing. Whatever the leaders say goes, so long as they continue to mechanically genuflect before the altar of democracy. The latest of such developments is exhibited in the US Supreme Court's ruling in Kelo *v.* City of New London, Connecticut (July 2005) in which the originally highly restricted provision of eminent domain – confined to be used only to promote a public use – was expanded to include takings that serve any public purpose (by which is meant whatever goal or objective public officials wish to promote).

If we are to reverse course and achieve a more consistently free society we must tear up the counterfeit standard of positive "rights" and restore a gold standard: the Lockean natural rights doctrine, as developed and elaborated by later classical liberals and libertarians, one that enables us to actually pursue, and achieve, life and happiness.

References

Comte, Auguste. 1973. *The Catechism of Positive Religion* (Clifton, NJ: Augustus M. Kelley).

Green, Thomas Hill. 1861. *Liberal Legislation and the Freedom of Contact*, Hanover Historical Texts Project at: <http://history.hanover.edu/courses/excerpts/111green.html>.

MacArthur Foundation. 2007. *About the Law and Neuroscience Project*, at: <http://www.macfound.org/atf/cf/{B0386CE3-8B29-4162-8098-E466FB856794}/FINAL%20NEUROSCIENCE%20FACT%20SHEET.PDF>.

Machan, Tibor R. 1982. "Dissolving the Problem of Public Goods: Financing Government Without Coercive Measures." In T. R. Machan, ed., *The Libertarian Reader* (Lanham, MD: Rowman & Littlefield).

Machan, Tibor R. 1989. *Individuals and their Rights* (Chicago: Open Court Publishing).

Machan, Tibor R. 1998. *Generosity: Virtue in Civil Society* (Washington, DC: Cato Institute Press).

Machan, Tibor R. 2006. *Objectivity, Recovering Determinate Reality in Philosophy, Science, and Everyday Life* (Burlington, VT: Ashgate).

MacKinnon, Catherine. 1983. *Only Words* (Cambridge, MA: Harvard University Press).

Nozick, Robert. 1974. *Anarchy, State, and Utopia* (New York: Basic Books).

Sterba, James P. 1991. *Justice: Alternative Perspectives* (Belmont, CA: Wadsworth).

Sterba, James P. 1995. "Reconciling Conceptions of Justice." In *Morality and Social Justice* (Lanham, MD: Rowman & Littlefield).

11
Nonsense on stilts

Roger Scruton

The idea that there are universal human rights was expressed by its early defenders – notably by John Locke in his *Second Treatise of Government* – in another way. According to Locke there are "natural" rights – rights that attach to individuals by virtue of their "nature" as human beings, and independently of any man-made "convention." The distinction between nature and convention was a cornerstone of the Stoic philosophy of ancient Athens, and an important input into Roman jurisprudence. The Roman jurists distinguished the *ius naturale* or natural law, whose force derives from human nature and which is therefore recognized as binding by all people everywhere, from the *ius civile* or civil law, which summarizes the rights and duties conferred by Roman jurisdiction on the citizen. The idea of a "natural law" thereafter entered the thinking of philosophers and theologians, to become a standing justification offered by bishops for ecclesiastical jurisdiction, and for the right of the Church to adjudicate conflicts between sovereigns.

Aquinas frequently refers to the natural law as the true foundation for every legitimate jurisdiction, but does not give a clear account of what it says. Nevertheless, it was one of the achievements of medieval Christendom to persuade people that laws exist that are not made by princes. These "natural" laws do not provide a complete legislative program, sufficient to govern a real human community in all the contingencies that generate the conflicts for which law courts are needed. But they set limits to the civil law. Natural law describes the boundaries that cannot be transgressed without forfeiting the legitimacy of the jurisdiction. It therefore provides the fulcrum outside the political system, whereby the system's claim to legitimacy can be overturned.

Modern discussions of natural law began with Grotius, the author of *De jure belli ac pacis*, the first comprehensive treatise on international law, and one to which we are all in the modern world indebted. Grotius argued that if there is such a thing as natural law it is not law because God so commands it; it is law because reason so discerns it. Even if God did not exist, Grotius argues, there would be a natural law, and rational beings would be equipped to recognize its claim on their behavior. Although Grotius famously qualifies his observation by condemning atheism as an intolerable sin, his thought has been endorsed by all defenders of the natural law in our tradition, and most notably by Kant, whose theory of the Categorical Imperative can be seen as providing metaphysical foundations for a natural-law theory of government.

There is an important contrast here with Islamic law. In no respect does Islam recognize the existence of natural law. Although the *shari'ah* stands in judgment above all human codes, it is, like them, simply another system of universalized commands – although a system issued by the highest authority. There is no requirement that the commands of God should correspond to anything other than the will of God; certainly no requirement that they should correspond to a law independently accessible to all rational beings (such, at least, is the interpretation of Islamic law that prevails today, thanks to the triumph of the Ash'arite school of theology in the eleventh century of our era. See Robert Reilly [2010]). Nonsensical commandments, such as the forbidding of foods arbitrarily pronounced unclean, stand side by side with laws forbidding murder, rape, and fraud, as though sharing the same authority. And the arbitrariness of the one command in time communicates itself to the other so that, as we have seen, Muslims who begin from the trembling sense that all is forbidden, can quickly end in the defiant belief that everything is permitted – including the mass murder of innocents. It is precisely our natural law tradition that prevents us from going in any such direction. The natural law is a system of *constraints* – rules that forbid things, even to God who, being rational, freely both commands these rules and conforms to them. These constraints form a wall around every individual – they are the sum of what *cannot be done* to him. How they are justified is a deep question of moral and legal philosophy; but unless they can be justified, the law becomes as much a threat to the individual as a shield. Laws that protect the individual from the community and from the state are, according to natural law theory, the *sine qua non* of legitimate government. Such laws are not imposed from the top down, by a system of sovereign commands. They are built up from below, by studying the freedoms and constraints that reside in rational nature itself and that must be respected if the law is to be accepted as legitimate by those subject to its demands. Not surprisingly, therefore, the idea of natural law tends to be stated in terms of the natural *rights* of the individual.

It is not only Islamic law that sees top-down commands, rather than bottom-up constraints, as the ultimate source of law. Jurists like Jeremy Bentham and John Austin saw law as a system of universalized commands, laid down by a sovereign power and enforced against transgressors. They recognized the existence of laws that define rights, powers, liabilities, and freedoms; but saw these as parasitic upon the commands that held the system in place. And they recognized a distinction between justified and unjustified laws; though it was one that they analyzed in utilitarian terms (Bentham 1789; Austin 1832). The idea of natural law seemed to them absurd. Either it meant a law laid down by God – and therefore another species of universalized command, not different in kind from that of any human legislator – or it referred to law without a legislator, without an enforcer, without an identifiable source in the world of written records, and without any court to decide its verdicts. At best the idea of such a law was a pious hope, at worst "nonsense on stilts," to use Bentham's famous phrase. Genuine law, for Bentham and Austin, was "positive" law, not natural law – law "posited" by convention and enforced by a sovereign power. And the dispute between this legal positivism and the legal naturalism of Grotius, Locke, and Kant continues in one form or another to this day.

Bentham was explicitly referring to the emerging philosophy of "natural rights." For he was writing in the period of the French Revolution, when the clamor for the "rights of man" was reaching fever pitch. Bentham's ridicule notwithstanding, the idea of natural or human rights has lost none of its appeal, and has even become the first legislative principle of international bodies, and indeed the sole rational ground for adjudication in at least one court of law – the European Court of Human Rights in Strasbourg. The pursuit of human rights is fundamental to the UN Charter, and the European Court of Justice, whose remit is to adjudicate disputes under the insane regime of regulations invented by the European Commission, is also under an obligation to align its judgments with those of the ECHR in Strasbourg. The UK has followed the example of other member states within the EU and incorporated the European Convention on Human Rights into its municipal law, and all attempts at international order are accompanied by the rhetorical demand for the protection of human rights, as the *sine qua non* of any lasting agreement. In an age of official skepticism, in which authoritative liberal thinkers, from Hart and Rawls to Dworkin and Nussbaum, assume that law is or ought to be neutral regarding the individual's "conception of the good," there seems nevertheless to be complete agreement about the underlying principles of morality and a desire to enforce them against all comers. These underlying principles are those enshrined in the doctrine of human rights. The stilts have gotten longer since Bentham's day, but the question remains whether the thing that sways on top of them is really nonsense.

The topic of natural rights was controversial in the years following Bentham's treatise on legislation, not only on account of the conflict between his utilitarianism and prevailing theories of natural law, like those of Locke and Samuel Pufendorf (1672). The experience of the French Revolution was fresh in people's memory; people recalled the paper constitution of the Revolutionaries – the *Déclaration des droits de l'homme et du citoyen* – which had been put forward as the fount of all revolutionary law, shortly after the storming of the Bastille. When the doors of the Bastille were thrown open, seven prisoners emerged, two of whom proved to be insane and had to be reincarcerated. Two years later 500,000 people were in the prisons of France, a great many of them dying, most of them imprisoned on trumped-up charges, and none of them with any hope that those rights announced in the Declaration could be demanded from the people who had so glibly declared them. The Revolutionary Tribunals denied to the accused a right of representation, even a right of self-defense, and judge and prosecutor were identical. This violation of natural *justice* was defended as the only way to ensure that the population as a whole could enjoy their natural *rights*. Nonsense on stilts, but nonsense with teeth.

Nowadays, of course, we think of human rights precisely as a shield against that kind of despotism – which Robespierre called the "despotism of liberty." And the construction of this shield has brought about the coexistence in the current legal orthodoxy of two seemingly incompatible views: first that all law is positive law, whose validity is established by convention, and second that all law must conform to human rights, which have a universal and overriding validity of their own. This seems like an uncomfortable amalgam of positivism and naturalism: it certainly calls out for an explanation. It seems as though, at the very moment when the law is being reshaped as an instrument of moral relativism, by which the freedom of the individual is exalted above all the virtues that might restrict it, the prevailing ideology is becoming ever more absolutist, insisting on a list – and a constantly growing list – of human rights as the sole and sufficient justification for all political action.

In fact, however, the two currents of opinion are connected. The emphasis on individual freedom and the desire to see the law as an instrument for maximizing that freedom arise from a profound distrust of government. From Mill to Robert Paul Wolff, the idea has been prevalent that all claims to authority are fraudulent, that no one really has authority over anyone else, and that the sole excuse for government is that it makes us more capable of exercising our freedom (Mill 1859; Wolff 1970). No one is entitled to dictate to anyone, and no moral judgment has a greater right to be enforced than any other: the law should remain neutral for the simple reason that it should not be there at all, and is necessary only because people have the intolerable habit of restricting each other's freedom – a habit that can be rectified only by coercive rules.

The emphasis on human rights comes from the same anti-authoritarian stance. All governments, and all claims to authority, are potential threats to the individual. He must be shielded from their worst effects by a wall of rights. These rights protect his ability to go about his business undisturbed. And the first concern of government must be to uphold those rights, since the legitimacy of government is determined (perhaps entirely) by the extent to which it protects the individual and his liberties from encroachment. Behind the doctrine of human rights, therefore, there lies the same deep suspicion of government and authority that animates the view that law should be morally neutral. Human rights have, as a result, been shaped as *moral absolutes that protect moral relativism.* They confer on us the absolute right to repudiate all absolute duties. And that is part of their point: they belong to a world beyond duty, in which nobody can tell us what to do.

That makes it look as though human rights are to be understood always as fundamental *liberties* – freedom rights which we respect by leaving people alone. The doctrine of human rights is there to set limits to government, and cannot be used to authorize any increase in government power that is not required by the fundamental task of protecting human freedom. The original text of the European Convention on Human Rights certainly suggests that this is so; and the rights there specified spell out implications of those rights – to life, liberty, and the pursuit of happiness – advocated in the American Declaration of Independence.

The search for liberty has gone hand in hand, however, with a countervailing search for "empowerment." The negative freedoms offered by traditional theories of natural right, such as Locke's, do not compensate for the inequalities of power and opportunity in human societies. Hence egalitarians, who dislike hierarchies of every kind, have begun to insert more positive rights into the list of negative freedoms. The liberty rights specified by the various international conventions have therefore been supplemented by certain claim rights – rights that do not merely demand non-encroachment from others, but also impose a positive duty on others. This is particularly apparent in the UN Declaration of Human Rights, which begins with a list of freedom rights and then suddenly, at article 22, begins making radical claims against the State – claims which can be satisfied only by positive action from government. Here is article 22:

> Everyone, as a member of society, has the right to social security and is entitled to realization, through national effort and international co-operation and in accordance with the organization and resources of each State, of the economic, social and cultural rights indispensable for his dignity and the free development of his personality.

There is a weight of political and social philosophy behind that article. Contained within this right is an unspecified list of other rights called "economic, social and cultural," which are held to be indispensable not for freedom but for "dignity" and the "free development of personality." Whatever this means in practice, it is quite clear that it is likely to involve a considerable extension of the field of human rights, beyond those basic liberties acknowledged in the American Declaration. Those basic liberties are arguably necessary for any kind of government by consent; the same is not true of the claims declared in section 22 of the UN Declaration.

The Declaration goes on in this vein, conjuring a right to work, to leisure, to a standard of living sufficient to guarantee health – and other rights that are, in effect, claims against the State rather than freedoms from its encroachments. I am not saying that these are *not* rights: but even if they are rights, they are not justified by the same philosophical arguments as justify the freedom rights granted earlier in the Declaration. Moreover, they open the door to the "rights inflation" that we have witnessed in recent decades, and to an interpretation of human rights that is prodigal of conflicts.

Here is an example that might help to focus the issue. Between the wars there was much concern in Britain over the growth of urban sprawl and the way in which the countryside was being invaded by "ribbon development," using the road network as a cheap substitute for proper urban infrastructure. Businesses were relocating to the edge of towns to take advantage of lower rents and rural amenities, town centers were decaying, and the countryside was being eaten up in a random and destructive way. The process – which we still witness in modern America, and which has been the subject there of radical and unanswered criticism from Jane Jacobs (1961) and James Howard Kunstler (1993), among others – was widely deplored, and the war-time government decided that, as soon as the emergency was over, the problem must be addressed. The aim was to find a policy that would reconcile as many of the interests as possible – interests of the towns in retaining businesses in the center, of urban residents in being shielded from pollution and noise, of rural residents in retaining their tranquility, of farmers in retaining undisturbed fields, and of all of us in maintaining a self-sufficient agriculture in a beautiful countryside. The result was the 1946 Town and Country Planning Acts, which have remained in force and which created the green belts around the towns, while strictly controlling building in the countryside. This legislation has met with widespread approval, and has helped to stabilize land use and land prices in the countryside. Planning controls mean that someone who buys a house in the countryside can be more or less certain that it will still be in the countryside when he sells it, since no building will be permitted in the vicinity, except according to strict guidelines, and he himself has a statutory right to raise objections and influence the course of any planning inquiry.

I do not deny that there are negative aspects to this legislation. But it illustrates an important point: namely that the law can aim at a compromise solution, that it can take many competing interests into consideration, and that it can provide a set of rules that achieve the most reliable way of reconciling the conflicts that are generic to the activities that stand to be regulated, in this case the conflict between the one who wishes to develop land and the neighbor who will thereby suffer a loss of amenity and a loss in the value of his property. All in all, it is one of the reasons for preferring legislation to adjudication, as a source of law, that a legislature can take the widest possible view of the many interests that need to be addressed and if possible reconciled.

All went reasonably well until Irish travelers, taking advantage of the EU's freedom of movement provisions, began to settle in the English countryside, buying fields from farmers at agricultural rates and then developing them as sites for mobile homes. The farmer cannot sell these fields for agricultural use, since agriculture is in a state of crisis. Nor can he obtain planning permission for any other use, and specifically for development as houses. So the deal offered by the travelers is the best he can get. Their practice is to scrape away the topsoil and replace it with concrete, then install mobile homes and gradually change the mobile homes to stationary prefabs. Why, you ask, is this permitted? Well, it is not. However, since the incorporation of the European Convention of Human Rights into UK law, the travelers have argued that they have a right to pursue their traditional way of life, a right to which they are entitled as an ethnic minority, to deny which would be tantamount to "discrimination" as forbidden by that very same law, and that this right entitles them to move freely about the country, settling where they will. Of course this is a piece of nonsense – nonsense on stilts, of a kind that makes one sympathize with Bentham. Nevertheless the courts have upheld the argument and therefore granted a right that effectively nullifies one of the most carefully considered and expensive pieces of UK legislation and one that represents an enormous investment on the part of the whole community.

The consequences of this are worth studying. In the village of Minety, near where I live, the development of farming land as a travelers' camp has led to the collapse of property values all around, causing enormous social tensions between residents in the camp and those whose savings they have wiped out. It has also led to anger among villagers who have had planning permission for this or that comparatively innocent addition refused, and who now refuse to obey the law, causing huge problems of enforcement. So far there have been no murders – which distinguishes the Minety case from a similar case in Cambridgeshire – but there is also no sign that people are or ever will be reconciled to the decision of the court.

The case illustrates four very important matters. The first is that, as Dworkin (1977) puts it, "rights are trumps." That is, in a court of law, if you can show that your interest in the matter is also protected by a right, then you win the case against anyone whose interests, however great, are not so protected. (Rights provide "exclusionary reasons," in Raz's (1979) plausible way of putting it.) The huge interest of the Minety residents in retaining the value and amenity of their properties (which represent, for most of them, their life's savings) counted for nothing in the case I am considering, since – although protected by planning law – those interests were not protected as a right, but only as an interest.

The second important point is that, unlike the solutions issued by a legislature, those issued by a court are not compromises: they are not attempts to reconcile the many interests involved in a situation, and even if you think that Dworkin is right that questions of policy can play a part in determining the outcome of adjudication, the court does not see itself as formulating a policy for the good government of a community – that is the task of a legislature, not a court. The court sees itself as resolving a conflict in favor of one or other of the parties. In normal circumstances, a case before a civil court is a zero-sum game, in which one party wins everything, and the other loses everything. There are no consolation prizes. Moreover, the doctrine of precedent ensures that the court's decision will punch a hole in any legislation designed to solve issues of the kind that come before it. The decision could do irreparable damage to a delicate piece of legislation, and destroy a process of conciliation and compromise that has issued in that legislation. This is what has happened with the Town and Country Planning Acts. And it is a very good illustration of the dangers inherent in "human rights" legislation – namely, that it places in the hands of the ordinary citizen a tool with which even the most vital piece of public policy can be overturned, and overturned in favor of the individual, regardless of the common interest and the common good.

The third important point is that the human rights declared by the various pieces of legislation and the various decisions of the courts are not obviously of the same philosophical, moral, or political standing. A doctrine of natural rights is entitled to the name only if the rights declared under it can be established a priori. The attempt to do this, in the case of basic freedom rights, has been made by various writers – by Nozick (1974), beginning from Kantian premises; by Finnis (1980) beginning from Thomist premises; and so on. I think we can all see the force of the idea that there are certain things that cannot be done to human beings – certain basic goods, including life itself, that cannot be taken away from them unless they in some way *forfeit* them. Life, limb, and the basic freedom to pursue our goals undisturbed (compatible with a similar freedom enjoyed by others) are plausible candidates. You can see how the entitlement to these things lies at the heart of political cooperation: for without some guarantee that, in these respects at least, people are protected from invasion, there really could not be a system of law that enjoyed the consent of those subject to it. And the rights in question correspond to basic deliverances, both of the Thomist argument concerning the fundamental goods that are the premises of practical reasoning and of the Kantian categorical imperative.

Furthermore we can understand those basic freedoms as rights partly because we can understand the reciprocal duty to respect them. My right to life is your duty not to kill me: and duties of non-encroachment and non-infliction are naturally upheld by morality and easily enforced by the law. Once we step outside this narrowly circumscribed area of basic freedoms, however, the freedoms presupposed in consent, we enter a much more shady and conflictual territory. The travelers' case depends upon the provision for "non-discrimination" – a provision that steps outside the area of basic freedoms and into that of justice. And the amazing thing is that this provision, meant to prevent one group of citizens from arbitrarily enjoying privileges denied to another, has been used precisely to claim minority privileges that are legally denied to the majority. Nonsense on stilts this may be; but it has an uncanny ability to survive the criticisms made in court.

Fourth, the case illustrates the increasing intrusion into the field of human rights law of the concept of a "group right." The original invocation of natural rights by Locke, Pufendorf, and others was designed to protect the individual from arbitrary power. You held your natural rights, according to those thinkers, as an individual, and regardless of what group or class you belonged to. These rights force people to treat you as a free being, with sovereignty over his life, who has an equal claim on your respect. But the new ideas of human rights allow rights to one group that they deny to another: you have rights as a gypsy, a woman, a homosexual, which you can claim only as a member of that group. To think in this way is to resurrect the abuses to which Locke and others were in search of a remedy – the abuses that led to people being arbitrarily discriminated against on account of their class, race, or occupation.

The case is one of many that have led to a certain disaffection toward the idea of human rights and a belief that it has been used illegitimately at both the legal and the political level, to dispense arbitrary justice in disputes that ought to be resolved by compromise and not by zero-sum solutions. One thing is certain, which is that those who announce human rights seldom if ever attempt to prove that there are any such things, or that the rights they propose are included among them. The increasingly arbitrary lists that form the substance of international declarations seem to be more the product of political orthodoxies or social aspirations than any well-founded intuition concerning the a priori grounds of law. So how should we proceed in winnowing out the plausible from the implausible candidates?

First we should do well to respect the classic analysis of W. N. Hohfeld (1946), whose typology of legal rights brought order into an increasingly disorderly discussion. Hohfeld was not dealing with natural rights, but with rights as defined by a legal system, and he distinguished claim rights from liberty rights, and both from powers on the one hand and immunities on the other. It is the first two of those, and the distinction between them, that is of principal concern to the discussion of human rights. A claim right typically arises from some past circumstance whereby one person becomes responsible to answer a claim made by another. For example, if I have transferred to you my house in accordance with a contract of sale, then I have a claim against you for the agreed price, and this is a claim right of mine – in other words, a right that would be upheld in a court of law, should any dispute arise. Claim rights also arise in tort. If your negligently allowing your cows onto my lawn causes £500 worth of damage, then I have a claim right against you for that sum.

In those straightforward cases of contract and tort, we easily see that every claim right in one person defines a duty in the other. Indeed, Hohfeld defines a claim right as a "directed duty" – a duty directed towards the particular person who has the claim. And this duty is a legal burden. Often it cannot be discharged: the person claimed against may not have the means to satisfy the claim. However, he ought to satisfy it, and the law will compel him to do so to the best of its power. Furthermore, the duty that the law imposes arises from a relationship of responsibility. In both contract and in tort – as well as in trust – the law holds someone *liable* for a claim made by another. And this liable person is identified, either as an individual, or a company, or a group, which has acted so as to *incur* the liability in question.

Hence claim rights, in the normal cases when they arise, are quite different from freedom rights. A freedom right imposes a general duty on others to observe it; but it may arise from no specific relationship, and may make no specific demands of any individual. It is a right that may be invaded by others; but by doing nothing they respect it, and the duty to observe it is neither onerous nor a special responsibility of any particular person. Such is my right to move freely from place to place, my right to life, limb, and property, and the other rights traditionally acknowledged as flowing from the natural law. You respect them by non-invasion, and the duty to respect them falls clearly and unambiguously on everyone.

This does not mean that there are not legal difficulties over enforcing freedom rights, or that special relations may not bear on them. For one thing, freedom rights can conflict, as when my freedom to grow vegetables in my garden conflicts with your freedom to plant a leylandi hedge next to it. The law takes the sensible view that freedoms of this kind are not unqualified and that the conflicts can be resolved by inserting the qualifications. Nevertheless, if you really have a right to do something, then you are wronged by any judgment that forbids you to do it. A conflict of rights that cannot be resolved by qualification is strictly analogous to a moral dilemma in which one is obliged to perform two incompatible courses of action. This absolute nature of rights should not be misunderstood. Rights define what Raz has called exclusionary reasons – i.e., reasons whose validity excludes countervailing arguments – not overriding reasons, i.e., reasons that must prevail. My right to close my door against you is breached by your decision to break it down. However, unknown to me, but observed by you, a fire has broken out on the second floor and you are breaking in to fight it. In such a case your moral duty to save my life overrides my right to exclude you. Nevertheless, your decision to break down my door is a violation of a right.

Claim rights arise in contract and tort – as Hohfeld recognizes. I doubt that in Hohfeld's day there was any legal recognition afforded to claims against everyone by anyone, regardless of the relation between the parties. However, this is the kind of right that has begun to creep into the lists of supposed "human rights" proposed by transnational legislatures. The switch from freedom rights to claim rights is made easier by the ambiguity of many formulations. Take the right to life. As proposed in the American Declaration of Independence this means the freedom to go about my business without threat to my life. It imposes on others the duty not to kill me, and since this is a duty under any moral understanding, and one that Kant, for example, held to be justifiable a priori, there is no intellectual difficulty in including the right to life among the list of natural rights. However, the phrase "right to life" can easily be inflected so as to acquire another meaning, as the right to be protected against anything that threatens to take my life away – disease, for example. A person with a life-threatening illness is, on this understanding, suffering a breach in his rights. And if we put it that way, we are immediately saddled with the question of duty: whose is the duty to help him, and how? Suppose there is a doctor somewhere who can cure the disease, but who is too tired, too far away, too fed up with unpaid demands on his time, and so on, and who therefore does not respond to the call for help. We might reproach this doctor. But do we want to go along with the claim-right understanding of the phrase, and say that he has violated another's "right to life"? At the very least we can see that this is controversial in a way that the freedom–right understanding of the phrase is not. We surely have other, and better ways, of describing the duties involved in cases like this, ways which do not place the kind of absolute claim on another's conduct that is implied in the language of rights.

Now it is easy to see why a libertarian might object to the expansion of the list of human rights to include claim rights – especially claims to non-specific benefits like health, education, a certain standard of living, and so on. For, in the absence of any relation of liability, specifying who is to satisfy these claims, they inevitably point to the state as the only possible provider. And large, vague claims require a massive expansion of state power, a surrender to the state of all kinds of responsibilities that previously vested in individuals, and the centralization of social life in the government machine. In other words, claim rights push us inevitably in a direction that, for many people, is not only economically disastrous but also morally and politically dangerous. Moreover it is a direction that is diametrically opposed to that for which the idea of a human (natural) right was originally introduced – a direction involving the increase, rather than the limitation, of the power of the state.

But there is another reason for disquiet over the idea that claim rights might also be human rights. Hohfeld argued that the concept of a right belongs in a family of concepts – liability, immunity, duty, permission, power, and so on – which are like modal concepts, such as possibility, necessity, and probability – in identifying interlocking operations of rational thought. The concept of a right belongs to a "circle of juridical terms," which are intricately interdefinable and which between them specify a systematic operation of the rational intellect. There is, as I would prefer to put it, a kind of "calculus of rights, responsibilities and duties," which rational beings use in order to settle their disputes and to reach agreement over matters of common or conflicting interest. The availability of this calculus is one of the things that distinguish us from the lower animals, and it would be available to us even if we did not attempt to back it up with a shared legal system. The concept of justice belongs to this calculus: injustice residing in the denial of rights or deserts, undeserved punishment, and so on.

There is an interesting philosophical question as to how this "rights talk," as it has been called, is grounded. And there is another question, partly philosophical, partly anthropological, as to the *function* of rights talk. Why do human beings make use of juridical terms? What do they gain from it, and why has it stabilized in so many different parts of the world, so as to be received as entirely natural? I would like to venture an answer to those questions. It seems to me that rights talk has the function of enabling people to claim a sphere of personal sovereignty: a sphere in which their choice is law. And spheres of personal sovereignty in turn have a function, namely that they give the advantage to consensual relations. They define the boundaries behind which people can retreat and which cannot be crossed without transgression. The primary function of the idea of a right is to identify something as within the boundary of me and mine. If I have a right to sit in a certain room then you cannot expel me from it without wronging me. By determining such rights we define the fixed points, the places of security, from which people can negotiate and agree. Without those fixed points negotiation and free agreement are unlikely to occur, and if they occur, their outcome is unlikely to be stable. If I have no rights, then the agreement between us provides no guarantee of performance; my sphere of action is liable to constant invasion by others, and there is nothing that I can do to define the position from which I am negotiating in a way that compels you to acknowledge it.

Rights, then, enable us to establish a society in which consensual relations are the norm, and they do this by defining for each of us the sphere of personal sovereignty from which others are excluded. This explains Dworkin's view, in *Taking Rights Seriously,* that "rights are trumps." A right belongs to the fence that defines my sovereign territory: by claiming it, I put an absolute veto on things that you might do. It also explains the direct connection between right and duty: the absoluteness of the right is tantamount to a duty to respect it. And it explains the zero-sum nature of disputes in a court of law, when rights are invoked to decide them.

If we look at rights in this way, as instruments that safeguard sovereignty and so make free deals between sovereign partners into the cement of society, then we see immediately why freedom rights have the best claim to universality and why claim rights – detached from any history of responsibility and agreement – present a threat to the consensual order. A claim against another, if expressed as a right, is an imposition of a duty. If this duty arises from no free action or chain of responsibility that would provide a cogent ground for the claim, then by expressing it as a right we override the other's sovereignty. We say to him: here is something you must do or provide, even though your duty to do so arises from nothing you have done or for which you are responsible. This is simply a demand that you must satisfy.

How different such a case is, at least, from that of freedom rights. For these are by their very nature "sovereignty protecting" devices. They are vetoes on what others can do to me or take from me, rather than demands that they do something or give something that I have an interest in their doing or giving. The duty that they define is one of non-interference, and the interest that they protect is the most fundamental interest that I have, namely my interest in retaining the power to make decisions for myself in those matters that most closely concern me.

If there are such things as "natural rights," therefore, they ought to have the essentially negative aspect of freedoms: rights not to be molested, rather than claims to be fulfilled. But no such limitation is acknowledged by the bodies that pretend to declare human rights in modern conditions. Bentham's view was the first conscious recognition of the danger represented by "rights inflation," the danger that people might claim as a right, and on no legal authority, what is merely an interest.

And that is what we have been seeing. The ordinary Italian wakes up one morning to discover that the crucifix on the wall of his child's classroom has been condemned as a violation of human rights. The ordinary Englishman wakes up to discover that the failed asylum-seeker who negligently ran over his daughter has a human right not to be deported to his home country and meanwhile to be maintained indefinitely at the taxpayer's expense. The ordinary Belgian has been told that saying the truth about radical Islam in public violates the human rights of his fellow citizens. The ordinary Pole has discovered that his country's abortion laws violate the human rights of women under the European Convention, which says nothing about the rights of the unborn child. The Catholic Church in Britain has been told that its policy of putting children for adoption only with heterosexual married couples is a violation of the human and legal rights of homosexuals. And so on. The cases (all recent) are controversial. But they have the accumulative effect of undermining the conception of human rights. That conception was supposed to provide a neutral standpoint *outside* legal and moral controversies, from which the legitimacy of any particular decision can be evaluated. In fact it is now used to *take sides* in political controversies – usually the side congenial to liberals and offensive to conservatives. And since nobody who makes use of the conception, so far as I can see, ever asks how a right can be justified, I cannot help feeling that they have no greater trust in the notion than I have. They do not seem to care about the nonsense, so long as they can make use of the stilts.

References

Austin, John. 1832. *The Province of Jurisprudence Determined* (London, n.p.).

Bentham, Jeremy. 1789. *Introduction to the Principles of Morals and Legislation* (London, n.p.).

Dworkin, Ronald. 1977. "Taking Rights Seriously." In *Taking Rights Seriously* (Cambridge, MA: Harvard University Press).

Finnis, John. 1980. *Natural Law and Natural Rights* (Oxford: Oxford University Press).

Hohfeld, W. N. 1946. *Fundamental Legal Conceptions as Applied in Judicial Reasoning* (New Haven, CT: Yale University Press).

Jacobs, Jane. 1961. *The Death and Life of Great American Cities* (New York: Random House).

Kunstler, James Howard. 1993. *The Geography of Nowhere* (New York: Free Press).

Mill, John Stuart. 1859. *On Liberty* (London: J.W. Parker and Son).
Nozick, Robert. 1974. *Anarchy, State and Utopia* (New York: Basic Books).
Pufendorf, Samuel. 1672. *De Jure Naturae et Genium.*
Raz, Joseph. 1979. *The Authority of Law* (Oxford: Oxford University Press).
Reilly, Robert. 2010. *The Closing of the Muslim Mind* (Wilmington, DE: ISI Books).
Wolff, Robert Paul. 1970. *In Defence of Anarchism* (New York: Harper & Row).

12

A communitarian critique of human rights

Amitai Etzioni

Communitarianism is a rather small philosophical school. Communitarians share the view that liberalism (in the political science sense of the term), especially its focus on individual freedoms and rights, is at best a partial philosophy that leaves out the important concept of the good as communally defined. Communitarians hold that the concept of the good should be at the core of a robust philosophy. Nevertheless, scholars and advocates that are considered communitarians differ a great deal from one another; indeed, some dismiss the concept of human or individual rights altogether.

The most extreme communitarian criticism of human rights has come from Alasdair MacIntyre, who argued that human rights are as real as unicorns. (Jeremy Bentham called human rights "nonsense on stilts.") According to MacIntyre (1979, p. 16), one can only understand ethical and moral precepts within the context of the tradition in which these concepts were developed. Without a shared vision of the good life in a given community, no consensus on ethics or morals can be reached. As such, "contemporary moral debates ... are unsettlable and interminable" as each "argument characteristically gives way to the mere and increasingly shrill battle of assertion with counterassertion" (MacIntyre 1979, p. 17). These community-based and historically bound conceptions of the good conflict with the core assumption of human rights that they are universal and a given rather than time-bound, that they are to be viewed as self-evident truths. (Note that although MacIntyre is often cited as a communitarian, he has stated that he does not consider himself one.) Other communitarian positions regarding rights tend to be more nuanced.

Authoritarian or East Asian communitarianism

Authoritarian or East Asian communitarians hold that maintaining social order and harmony requires that individual rights and political liberties be greatly limited. They view individuals as organic parts of a great whole – the society – just as human cells are in a human body. As such, individuals find their role and meaning in their service to the common good.

Some East Asian communitarians (for instance, former Singaporean Prime Minister Lee Kuan Yew and Malaysian head of state Mahathir Bin Mohammad) stress the importance of a strong state and robust social bonds, including those of the family and local communities, but above all, that of the nation. Authoritarian communitarians claim that the Western value of "liberty" results in social, political, and moral anarchy and that civil and political rights are a distinctively Western idea. The West is said to use the precepts to chastise other societies and to impose its own vision on other cultures with their own preferred values. Lee Kuan Yew (1991) has stated that Asians have "little doubt that a society with communitarian values where the interests of society take precedence over that of the individual suits them better than the individualism of America." A. M. Hussein writes that, "Any emphasis on individual human rights, apart from the rights of the community in which this individual lives, is sheer nonsense. In real history, human rights for the community come first, and human rights for any individual are conditioned by a healthy social environment and appropriate social institutions" (quoted in Donnelly 1999, p. 77).

Over the last few decades, East Asian communitarians have moderated many of these views and made more room for individual rights. However, they suggest that these rights are best introduced after economic development takes place. For example, Liu Huaqiu, the former Chinese vice minister of Foreign Affairs, has stated (2002, p. 737) that, "to respect and protect human rights is first and foremost to ensure the full realization of the rights to subsistence and development." East Asian communitarians have been increasingly eclipsed, at least in the West, by responsive communitarians (Bell 2000).

Academic communitarianism

In the 1980s, communitarian thinking was largely associated with the works of political philosophers such as Charles Taylor, Michael Sandel, and Michael Walzer. These scholars called attention to the mistaken assumptions about the nature of the self that liberal philosophy, especially as espoused by John Rawls, rested upon. These communitarian critics challenged the liberal view of the person as divorced from all his particularistic moral commitments and communal attachments. Instead, communitarians depicted the self as fundamentally "situated" or "contextualized" in a given culture, within a particular history and a set of values. Academic communitarians, and the sociologists who preceded them, such as Émile Durkheim and Ferdinand Tönnies, stressed that individuals in viable communities are more reasonable and productive than isolated individuals and that communities are essential for human flourishing. And they pointed out that communal pressures to conform must rise to high levels before they undermine the development and expression of the self.

Academic communitarians also demonstrated that liberalism misunderstands the nature of the political community. Liberal philosophers have described a neutral framework of rules within which a diversity of commitments to moral values can coexist, but communitarians showed that such a "thin" conception of political community was both empirically unavailable and normatively dangerous. Good societies, these authors showed, rested on much more than "neutral" rules and procedures; they relied on shared moral culture.

Several of the most often cited academic communitarians – such as Charles Taylor and Michael Walzer – have not directly addressed the status of human rights. Michael Sandel (2009, pp. 9, 19–20) has criticized the liberal position that each person should be free to choose his own conception of the good, and argued that society requires particularistic conceptions of virtue. This in turn entails curbing some freedoms and rights – for the sake of the common good.

Responsive communitarianism

A group of social philosophers, social scientists, and activists developed a communitarian position in the early 1990s that takes as its starting point that both individual rights and communal concepts of the good are two equally compelling sources for normativity and ought to be honored (the Communitarian Network). This view was developed by Mary Ann Glendon, William A. Galston, Philip Selznick, Daniel A. Bell, and Amitai Etzioni, among others.

For responsive communitarians, the common good is not determined by merely aggregating all of the private or personal goods in a society. Instead, it connotes those goods that serve all members and institutions of a given community. As such, it includes goods that serve no identifiable particularistic group and goods that serve members of unborn generations: for instance, basic research. Contributing to basic research is one of those social activities that often pays off only many decades after the initial investments were made, and the benefits often go to individuals and groups that could not be predetermined. Hence, those investing in it seek to promote the common good rather than their own good or that of those closest to them. (National defense, the preservation of national monuments, environmental protection, and climate improvements are also common goods. Other goods include at least some elements that serve the community as a whole, public health for instance.) Responsive communitarians seek to understand and to design society in light of the inevitable conflicts between individual rights, which privilege the person, and concerns for the common good, which privilege the community or society.

Moral dialogues provide an important way to proceed in the face of conflicting values. Liberal authors and proponents of deliberative democracy point to the exchange of information and weighing of evidence, reasoned arguments, impartiality, and enlightened understanding as the key ways in which citizens of a democracy come to change their judgments. They emphasize "cool" and rational processes while minimizing the role played by emotions and other such "hot" factors. The evidence strongly suggests, however, that such "cool," rational deliberations are almost impossible to achieve or even to approximate under most circumstances. The examination of actual processes of decision making, especially when they concern normative matters, shows that they are much more impassionate and proceed by different means than those depicted by the champions of deliberative democracy. More important, deliberative democracy is the "wrong" model for determining the normative bases of political acts. Instead, individual preferences and judgments are largely shaped through interactive communications about values, through moral dialogues that combine passion with normative arguments and rely on non-rational processes of persuasion, education, and leadership. I do not mean to suggest that in dialogues about which policies are legitimate, information and reason ought to play no role, but merely that they play a much smaller role than is often asserted. This is so both because they are much weaker tools than believed and because a much greater role is played by another factor: the appeal to values.

Moral dialogues often have no clear opening point or closing event. They are prolonged, heated, and seemingly meandering. However, they often lead to new or reformulated shared normative understandings. These dialogues take place by linking millions of local conversations (between couples, in neighborhood bars, in coffee- or teahouses, around water coolers at work) into society-wide networks and shared public focal points. They take place during regional and national meetings of many thousands of voluntary associations in which local representatives dialogue; in state, regional, and national party caucuses; in state assemblies and in Congress; and increasingly via electronic links (such as groups that meet on the Internet).

Responsive communitarianism also holds that the common good is best promoted by informal social controls, by social pressures generated by communities, rather than by the state. To the extent that people discharge their responsibilities to the common good because they have been persuaded, educated, or led to do so, rather than coerced by the state, the conflict between rights and the common good can be attenuated. To the extent that members of the community go far beyond what any law requires in attending to their children, helping their friends, volunteering, donating, voting, etc. because they seek the approbation of their fellow community members and wish to avoid their disapproval, rights are not engaged one way or the other.

Although this model of the good society is applicable to all societies, at different moments in history a given society is likely to miss the desired balance between rights and the common good, between particularistic loyalties and society-wide bonds – in its own direction. Hence, different societies may need to move in different directions in order to approximate the same balance. Thus, contemporary East Asian societies require moving towards much greater adherence to individual rights and much greater tolerance for individualism and pluralism, while in American society, as Robert Bellah and his colleagues showed in the 1980s, excessive individualism had to be reined in (Bellah et al. 1985).

Universalism and particularism

Some ethicists have directly (and some others implicitly) advocated a position that sees human obligations – especially to rights – on a strictly universal level. These scholars argue that we owe the same to someone halfway around the world that we owe to someone in our own community. Peter Singer has famously advocated this strict universalism and its corollary: the moral illegitimacy of communal or "particularistic" obligations. He writes: "if I am walking past a shallow pond and see a child drowning in it, I ought to wade in and pull the child out ... It makes no moral difference whether the person I can help is a neighbor's child ten yards from me or a Bengali whose name I shall never know ten thousand miles away" (1972, pp. 231–232).

At the other end of the spectrum, some have denied the very existence of universal moral values, rights included, and embraced a position that sees room for only particularistic values – i.e., moral relativism. Although he later changed his position, Michael Walzer (1983, p. 313) once held that the community itself is the ultimate arbiter of that which is good, arguing that a "given society is just if its substantive life is lived ... in a way faithful to the shared understandings of the members." M. E. S. van den Berg (1999, p. 195) critiques a communitarian perspective that conceives values as deriving from communal practices and sees the community as the "ultimate originator of values." He argues that this perspective does not address women's lack of rights and leaves social hierarchies unexamined (1999, pp. 208–209).

According to cultural relativism, culture is the only basis upon which one may judge the validity of morals or ethics. In other words, morals can only be understood in the context of the culture from which they originate. Rights are culturally determined and culturally specific; thus, there are no universal moral standards and no universal human rights.

Richard Rorty, a cultural relativist, states that "nothing relevant to moral choice separates human beings from animals except historically contingent facts of the world, cultural facts." And while he believes that our human rights culture "is morally superior ... [he does] not think this superiority counts in favor of the existence of a universal human nature" (1995).

Others adopt a less radical relativistic position, holding that one is entitled to judge the legitimacy of the policies of others but should make clear that one is merely expressing one's own culturally conditioned normative position, and that people of other cultures may readily justify rather different positions by drawing on their respective cultures. This approach has been developed, among others, by Stanley Fish (2002).

As I see it, the strict opposition between particularistic and universal values holds only if we assume that one's position on this matter must be all encompassing. There is no logical requirement to assume such comprehensiveness, and in social reality people often combine the two orientations. Thus, even if we owe certain obligations to all human beings, we still have additional obligations to members of our own communities, whether local, national, or regional.

The notion that we have the same obligations to all children as we have to our own is very difficult to entertain.

On the other hand, full-blown moral relativism greatly undermines the essence of moral claims – the call on the other to recognize the value for which one is appealing. Moral judgments become like expressions of taste. I like broccoli and recommend it to you, but I rush to declare that you may have strong reasons to prefer carrots, and I have no standing to complain about such a preference. Such conditional, contingent claims are pale ones, unlikely to sway anyone, or even foster serious deliberations, especially in the world in which many others pose strong, unhedged claims. In contrast, if one maintains that the moral truth of one's position is rooted in universal values – that one expects everyone to hear the voice which makes the position compelling and that those who do not hear it have not been properly subject to open dialogue – the potency of one's claim is sustained.

Like most stark dichotomies, the opposition between particularism and universalism is greatly overstated. Societal designs are not limited to either keeping one's community, identity, and culture and ignoring all universal values or rejecting community in order to ensure full-blown universalism. This kind of contrast is evident among those European and Japanese intellectuals and leaders who approach immigration as though the only options to dealing with it are either unbounded multiculturalism or full assimilation. Unfortunately, this philosophical monotheism – that either particularism *or* universalism must be the sole value – often has a considerable effect on public deliberations and policies. A case in point is a widely debated report issued by the Commission on the Future of Multi-Ethnic Britain, chaired by political theorist Lord Bhikhu Parekh. It concluded that the United Kingdom would best be viewed as a territory which English, Scottish, Welsh, West Indian, Pakistani and other such groups inhabit like tribes resting next to each other with little in common. Furthermore, because "people living in Britain cannot adhere to the values of one community," in order to avoid offending or injuring any of these groups, the government should avoid promoting any "fixed conception of national identity and culture" (2000).

Similarly, the conception that people's worldview is either that of villagers (of "locals") or cosmopolitan is clearly inaccurate. It is a serious sociological misunderstanding to assume that people follow *either* local, particularistic values *or* universal ones, such as those encased in the Universal Declaration of Human Rights.

If one accepts that both obligations to rights and the common good, to universal and particularistic values, are compelling, it follows that one cannot maximize either rights (and in their name destroy particularistic values and the communities on which they are based) nor maximize community and ignore our obligations to all human beings. Responsive communitarians see the tension between the two as a given, and hence, it is best to seek out how commitments to both core values can be combined. For example, banning torture and allowing each person to choose which authority will marry them can be combined with a commitment to communal values, such as expecting all members to learn a shared language, respect shared historical narratives, and take responsibility for past and future burdens. There is room for considerable difference as to which rights are to be universally respected and which particular values to hold essential, but the basic duality of community *and* rights seems incontestable.

References

Bell, Daniel A. 1993. *Communitarianism and Its Critics* (Oxford: Oxford University Press).

Bell, Daniel A. 2000. *East Meets West: Human Rights and Democracy in East Asia* (Princeton, NJ: Princeton University Press).

Bellah, Robert N., Richard Madsen, William M. Sullivan, Ann Swidler, and Steven M. Tipton 1985. *Habits of the Heart: Individualism and Commitment in American Life* (Berkeley: University of California Press).

The Communitarian Network. *The Responsive Communitarian Platform*, at: <http://www.gwu.edu/~icps/RCP%20text.html>.

Donnelly, Jack. 1999. "Human Rights and Asian Values: A Defense of 'Western Universalism.'" In Joanna R. Bauer and Daniel A. Bell, eds. *The East Asian Challenge for Human Rights* (Cambridge: Cambridge University Press).

Etzioni, Amitai. 1993. *The Spirit of Community: Rights, Responsibilities and the Communitarian Agenda* (New York: Crown Publishers).

Fish, Stanley. 2002. "Don't Blame Relativism." *Responsive Community: Rights and Responsibilities*, Vol. 12, No. 3, pp. 27–31.

Galston, William A. 1991. *Liberal Purposes: Goods, Virtues, and Diversity in the Liberal State* (Cambridge: Cambridge University Press).

Glendon, Mary Ann. 1991. *Rights Talk: The Impoverishment of Political Discourse* (New York: Free Press).

Huaqiu, Liu. 2002. "Statement at the World Conference on Human Rights in Vienna, 17 June 1993." *Chinese Journal of International Law*, Vol. 2, p. 737.

MacIntyre, Alasdair. 1979. "Why Is the Search for the Foundations of Ethics So Frustrating?" *Hastings Center Report*, Vol. 9, No. 4, pp. 16–22.

MacIntyre, Alasdair. 1991. "I'm Not a Communitarian, But ..." *Responsive Community*, Vol. 1, No. 3, pp. 91–92.

Parekh, Lord Bhikhu. 2000. *The Future of Multi-Ethnic Britain: Report of the Commission on the Future of Multi-Ethnic Britain* (London: Profile Books).

Rorty, Richard. 1995. "Human Rights, Rationality, and Sentimentality." *Belgrade Circle Journal*, Vol. 3–4, at: <http://www.usm.maine.edu/bcj/issues/three/rorty.html>.

Sandel, Michael. 1998. *Liberalism and the Limits of Justice*. 2nd edn. (Cambridge: Cambridge University Press).

Sandel, Michael. 2009. *Justice: What's the Right Thing to Do?* (New York: Farrar, Straus and Giroux).

Selznick, Philip. 2002. *The Communitarian Persuasion* (Washington, DC: Woodrow Wilson Press Center).

Singer, Peter. 1972. "Famine, Affluence, and Morality." *Philosophy and Public Affairs*, Vol. 1, No. 3, pp. 229–243.

Taylor, Charles. 1992. *The Ethics of Authenticity* (Cambridge, MA: Harvard University Press).

Van den Berg, M. E. S. 1999. "On a Communitarian Ethos, Equality and Human Rights in Africa," *Alternation*, Vol. 6, No. 1.

Walzer, Michael. 1983. *Spheres of Justice: A Defense of Pluralism and Equality* (New York: Basic Books).

Yew, Lee Kuan. 1991. *International Herald Tribune*, November 9–10.

Part II

New frameworks for understanding human rights

13

What are human rights?

Four schools of thought

Marie-Bénédicte Dembour

Introduction

Different people hold different concepts of human rights. This proposition might initially appear somewhat at odds with the commonly heard assertion that human rights are both universal and obvious (in the sense that they are derived from reason), which may suggest that human rights are unambiguous and uncontroversial. However, there is in practice a lack of agreement on what human rights are. Based on an analysis of the human rights academic literature (but without reproducing quotations here for reasons of space), this chapter identifies four schools of thought on human rights. It proposes that "natural scholars" conceive of human rights as *given*; "deliberative scholars" as *agreed*; "protest scholars" as *fought for*, and "discourse scholars" as *talked about*. It further proposes that these four schools act as ideal-types, which, arranged around two axes, potentially cover the whole conceptual field of human rights (see Figure 13.1). This mapping exercise is useful in that it clarifies positions from which various arguments about human rights are made, helping to understand where, why, and to what extent agreements are reached and disagreements persist in the human rights field. It also highlights the salience of a variety of positions, which are far less idiosyncratic than the received orthodoxy would suggest. (At the end of a presentation that I gave to the Danish Center for Human Rights, two members of the perhaps twenty-strong audience came to me [independently of each other] to say that my identification of four schools was a relief to them, lifting their sense of being almost a fraud in the Center due to their fear that their position on human rights was just too unorthodox to be acceptable.)

The schools in a nutshell

Introducing each school

The *natural school* embraces the most common and well-known definition of human rights: that which identifies human rights as those rights one possesses simply by being a human being. This definition, where human rights are viewed as given, can be considered the credo of the natural school. For most natural scholars, human rights are entitlements that, at their core, are negative in character and thus are absolute. The natural school tends to conceive of human rights as entailing negative obligations that can be expressed as an obligation (e.g., on the government) to refrain from doing something (e.g., torturing). Only negative obligations can be absolute, for positive obligations (e.g., to provide education) are never as clear-cut as a simple prohibition to do something. These entitlements are based on "nature," a short cut that can stand for God, the Universe, reason, or another transcendental source. The universality of human rights is derived from their natural character. Natural scholars believe that human rights exist independently of social recognition, even though recognition is preferable. They welcome the inscription of human rights in positive law. The natural school has traditionally represented the heart of the human rights orthodoxy.

The orthodoxy is increasingly moving, however, toward the *deliberative school* of thought, which conceives of human rights as political values that liberal societies *choose* to adopt. Deliberative scholars tend to reject the natural element on which the traditional orthodoxy bases human rights. For them, human rights come into existence through societal agreement. Deliberative scholars would like to see human rights become universal, but they also recognize that this will require time. In addition, they understand that this will happen only when and if everybody around the globe becomes convinced that human rights are the best possible legal and political standards that can rule society and therefore should be adopted. This school invariably stresses the limits of human rights, which are regarded as fit to govern exclusively the polity and not being relevant to the whole of moral and social human life. Deliberative scholars often hold constitutional law as one of the prime ways to express the human rights values that have been agreed upon.

The *protest school* is concerned first and foremost with redressing injustice. For protest scholars, human rights articulate rightful claims made by or on behalf of the poor, the unprivileged, and the oppressed. Protest scholars look at human rights as claims and aspirations that allow the status quo to be contested in favor of the oppressed. As such, they are not particularly interested in the premise that human rights are entitlements (though they do not reject it). Protest scholars advocate relentlessly fighting for human rights, as one victory never signals the end of all injustice. They accept that the ultimate source of human rights lies on a transcendental plane, but most of them are more concerned with the concrete source of human rights in social struggles, which are as necessary as they are perennial. If they sometimes regard the elaboration of human rights law as a goal, they nonetheless tend to view human rights law with suspicion as participating in a routinization process that tends to favor the elite and thus may be far from embodying the true human rights idea.

The *discourse school* is characterized by its lack of reverence towards human rights. In its perspective, human rights exist only because people talk about them. Discourse scholars are convinced neither that human rights are given nor that they constitute the right answer to the ills of the world, but they do recognize that the language surrounding human rights has become a powerful language with which to express political claims. Discourse scholars fear the imperialism of human rights imposition and stress the limitations of an ethic based on individualistic human rights. Nonetheless, some accept that the human rights discourse, as the prominent political ethical discourse of our time, occasionally yields positive results. But they do not *believe* in human rights, and often wish superior projects of emancipation could be imagined and put into practice.

Mapping the field

The four schools identified above should be approached as Weberian ideal-types rather than as fixed categories that neatly and perfectly describe single-track thought processes. The model does not assume or claim that social reality (here, academic writings on human rights) always

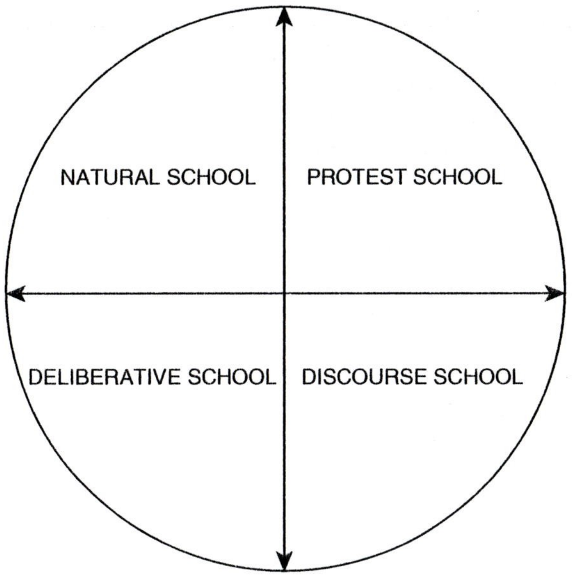

Figure 13.1 The human rights field

exactly conforms to its propositions. Moreover, for two people to belong to the same school does not mean that they conceive of human rights in precisely the same way – in many respects, they may fiercely disagree with each other. Nonetheless, the model is able to identify the connections among broad orientations, as the next section demonstrates by exploring the way each of the four schools approaches various issues, including human rights law, the foundation of human rights, their concrete realization, what it means to say they are universal, and whether one can/should believe in them.

The four-school model leads to a mapping of the entire human rights conceptual field, as Figure 13.1 suggests. In this figure, the top half of the field corresponds to an orientation that tends to ground human rights transcendentally and the bottom half to an orientation that tends to see human rights as a society/language-based reality; the left-hand side of the field corresponds to a liberal and individualistic orientation and the right-hand side to a more collective orientation of social justice.

The model was constructed abductively: while trying to make sense of academic writings, the author identified two, three, and then four schools. It is only when relationships among schools were examined that it suddenly appeared that the four schools could cover the whole conceptual human rights field. Empirically, so far, the model has not yet been found unable to accommodate existing views on human rights. However, its heuristic value will need to be confirmed over time, including by persistence in an ability to associate any human rights thinker with particular school(s).

The position of the schools

On human rights law

Natural scholars tend to celebrate human rights law. For the great majority of them, human rights law embodies the human rights concept: the law exists in direct continuation with the transcendental existence of human rights. Admittedly, a small minority is not convinced that human rights law, as it has been developed, corresponds to human rights. Nonetheless, most natural scholars regard the development of international human rights law in the last half-century as undeniable progress. For natural scholars, societies where human rights, by and large, are respected either already exist or can be created.

Deliberative scholars also have great faith in the potential of human rights law. All of their efforts are geared toward identifying, agreeing, and entrenching principles that allow for democratic decisions and fair adjudications. For them, there are no human rights beyond human rights law: the law, especially as it is embodied in constitutional principles of deliberation, is all there is to human rights. This law is more procedural than substantive in nature: it acts as a guide on how to do things in the political sphere.

By contrast, it would be hard to persuade protest scholars that conditions of effective human rights protection have been realized. In their perspective, there is always further injustice (human rights abuses) in need of redress. They tend to distrust human rights law: they fear that it may be hijacked by the elite and are wary of bureaucratization. They generally do not believe that institutions, including so-called human rights institutions, can be trusted to realize the human rights ideal. For them, human rights law is unlikely to be true to the human rights ideal. They regard human rights law as a mitigated progress at best and a sham at worst.

The discourse scholars, the nihilists on the concept of human rights, believe that human rights law is as good or as bad as any other law. It must be judged in each different situation on its merits.

On the foundation of human rights

Natural scholars believe human rights are founded in nature. However, they are aware that founding human rights on something akin to nature is unlikely to be universally compelling. Faced with this difficulty, many fall back on the legal consensus. As stated above, natural scholars tend to see human rights law in direct continuation with the human rights concept. From there, conflating transcendental human rights with human rights law is a step that some natural scholars are ready to take. This explains why a good number of them are happy to rely on the concrete manifestation of human rights in international law in order to dismiss the need to find a metaphysical basis for human rights. However, logically, in the natural school's perspective, a legal consensus can only ever be the *proof* of the existence of human rights, not a foundation of human rights. Presumably, natural scholars would still believe in human rights even in the absence of the so-called consensus that has developed since World War II. Indeed, occasionally, a natural scholar rejects the present form of human rights law as wrong. Not surprisingly, there are natural scholars who specifically refuse to rely on consensus to found human rights. The search for an ontological basis for human rights occupies some key natural scholars.

The protest scholars encounter the same problem as the natural scholars when it comes to identifying the ground on which they base their belief in human rights. Naturally suspicious of human rights law, they cannot adopt the route followed by some natural scholars of relying on the legal consensus. Instead, they rely on the less specific idea of the historical development of a tradition. Belgian philosopher and protest scholar Guy Haarscher (1993, pp. 124, 130) speaks of "*dressage*," a French word that connotes the training of animals and, thus, may provocatively suggest an internalization by the individual of a logic that is not entirely instinctive. The typical emphasis of this school on a learned tradition explains why protest scholars are generally very interested in human rights education. Although a long-established tradition may perhaps seem to offer more permanence than the mere legal consensus of a particular historical moment, it is still criticized by those who deny the existence of human rights. It is ultimately as dissatisfying for protest scholars as it is for natural scholars to shun completely a metaphysical foundation on which to base human rights. Not surprisingly, some protest scholars (e.g., Douzinas 2000) seek to ground human rights on a more metaphysical basis than a social discourse.

The foundation of human rights concerns the natural and protest schools only. It simply does not interest the discourse school, which believes that human rights exist only because they are talked about. Discourse scholars look at discussions of the foundation of human rights with disdain and as fundamentally flawed. As for deliberative scholars, who see human rights as emerging from agreement, the foundation of human rights is not an interesting issue. This does not detract them from being highly concerned with the issue of how to find, found, or reach agreement (where the emphasis shifts, expectedly given their general orientation, to process). They are more interested in justification than foundation (see, for example, Nickel 2007).

On the realization of human rights

Natural scholars conceive of human rights as entitlements: entitlements to specific objects that every individual should have respected. For them, human beings *have* human rights, and human rights are typically realized through individual enjoyment. A possession paradox arises, as noted by the natural scholar Jack Donnelly (1989, p. 14): "Where human rights are effectively protected, [the individual] continue[s] to *have* human rights, but there is no need or occasion to *use* them." Donnelly (2003, p. 9) rephrases this idea: "'[H]aving' a right is of most value precisely when one does not 'have' (the object of) the right ... [,] [leading to a situation of] 'having' (possessing) and 'not having' (not enjoying) a right at the same time." For the purpose of classification, the important point is that most natural scholars stress that the individual *has* human rights by virtue of being a human being.

Protest scholars would also accept that human beings have human rights. Though, instead of thinking of human rights as entitlements to particular objects that each individual as it were is selfishly at liberty to claim for herself, they think of the concept of human rights as a call to ensure that the rights of others be respected. In other words, when my rights are secured, I must ensure that the rights of my neighbor are secured as well as the rights of the neighbor of my neighbor and so on. In their perspective, the problem that arises out of the possession or enjoyment of human rights is that once individuals enjoy human rights, they often only use them for their own benefit. The loss of the sense of obligation to fight for the human rights of others is a betrayal of the human rights concept. For the protest school, human rights are realized through a perpetual fight for their realization. They conceive of human rights not so much as tangible, but as a utopia or a project always in the making (and reversible).

Having human rights does not enter the logic of the deliberative school. For deliberative scholars, human rights serve to guide action. As such, human rights are not and cannot be a matter of possession. They lay down the parameters of deliberation, the outcome of which is not presumed in advance. In the perspective of this school, human rights do not directly dictate how things should be substantively, therefore granting little sense to the idea that human rights could be possessed. What mark the realization of human rights are liberal, democratic, and fair processes that enable good political governance. Human rights are realized not through possession but through a particular mode of political action.

It makes no sense for discourse scholars to think about the realization of human rights, as they do not believe in human rights to begin with. Discourse scholars instead repeatedly point to the shortcomings of the human rights discourse that does not deliver what it promises, namely, equality between human beings. Discourse scholars are not surprised by the repeated failures of the human rights discourse to achieve its declared goals. Many of them intimate that a more solid project of emancipation is needed. Some simply refrain from making grand pronouncements on ethical issues and seek, from a resolutely empirical approach, to observe and describe the contradictory features of human rights discourse.

On the universality of human rights

For natural scholars, human rights derive from nature; their universality is therefore a given. Faced with the fact that human rights have taken different forms over time, they concede that human rights can, in practice, receive particular articulations. These are legitimate as long as they remain true to the principle of human rights, which, by contrast, is unique. The notion of "overlapping consensus" encapsulates this idea.

For protest scholars, the ubiquity of injustice points to the universal relevance of human rights. Less inclined than natural scholars to look at human rights as entitlements to specific objects, the different articulations of human rights over time is not a logical problem for their school of thought. Indeed, as the world evolves, so do the forms of suffering, potentially requiring new formulations of human rights.

For deliberative scholars, the universality of human rights is at best a project: it is certainly not a given. In their perspective, human rights will only become universal through the global adoption of the liberal values they express. Whether this will happen or not remains to be seen. While deliberative scholars would welcome the universalization of human rights principles, not all of them concern themselves deeply with what is happening in societies that they regard as geographically, politically, and culturally very different from their own.

Discourse scholars are extremely irritated by the claims of scholars in the other three schools about the universality of human rights. They find the natural school's perspective intellectually untenable in view of the diversity of moral forms in human society over time and space. They denounce its imperialism. Discourse scholars are also wary of the deliberative school and feel that the school's repeated invocation of consensus dangerously obscures power relations. They tend to be more sympathetic to the position of the protest school, which shares their commitment to denouncing injustice.

On their overall faith/position towards human rights

Natural scholars *believe* in human rights. Historically, they also are the ones who set up the parameters within which human rights came to be both conceived and debated, at least intellectually. They have traditionally represented the human rights orthodoxy.

Protest scholars also *believe* in the concept of human rights, though they deplore the fact that human rights have been institutionally hijacked. Thus, they call for a return to true human rights. Furthermore, they stress that human rights constitute an extremely demanding ethic (one can never do enough in the perpetual fight for the realization of human rights). They could be said to be to human rights what Liberation theologians are to Catholicism and, in that sense, they are dissidents from the Orthodoxy.

In keeping with the religion analogy, deliberative scholars would represent secularity in human rights thought. This label does not make any presumption about their lack or possession of religious faith. Rather, in this context, a secular label with respect to human rights (and human rights only) points to the fact that deliberative scholars do not *believe* in human rights, even though they are entirely committed to the idea of trying to enact and perhaps to spread the values they associate with human rights. In a somewhat ironic twist of language, they increasingly represent the current human rights orthodoxy.

Finally, discourse scholars are human rights nihilists. Philosophically, nihilism does not entail the rejection of all moral principles. Instead, following Nietzsche, it can signal the call for new values to be created through the reinterpretation of old values that have lost their original sense. Having to live with the supremacy of the language of human rights in contemporary political discourse, to the extent that discourse scholars accept this language, they call for its re-evaluation.

Summary in the form of a table

Table 13.1 lays out the propositions presented in this chapter in a systematic form. It can serve as a reference when attempting to place arguments made about human rights in one of the four sections of the human rights conceptual field. For example, the conflation of human rights with human rights law, whether expressed or implicit, can generally be considered a powerful clue for an affiliation with the natural school. However, this clue is not devoid of possible ambiguities: deliberative scholars tend to equate (rather than conflate) human rights law with human rights, making it potentially difficult to interpret a positive reference to human rights law. To complicate matters further, some identifying clues can be missing or expressed in a very different way than what is generally the case in that school. For example, Mark Goodale (2009, p. 37), a recognizable natural scholar, specifically rejects current human rights law as being unfaithful to the true human rights: "[The ethnography of human rights] calls into question many of the basic assumptions of postwar human rights theory and practice. Moreover, to the extent that the international human rights system is a reflection of these assumptions, then it too must be reconsidered." Moreover, the appearance of a key word can be misleading. For example, the fact that Jürgen Habermas is famous for his discourse theory on law and democracy does not make him a discourse scholar – Habermas is best classified as a deliberative scholar. Affiliation to a particular school, to be securely assessed, must always be confirmed on a number of issues. Even then, it is possible for an argument to straddle different schools.

Final observations

Avoiding boxing academic disciplines in particular corners

Elsewhere (Dembour 2006, 2010) I have systematically classified one philosopher, political/social theorist, lawyer, and anthropologist in each of the four schools. No doubt this exercise could be repeated with respect to further disciplines such as sociology, international relations, cultural studies, psychology, and history, as well as theoretical perspectives, such as feminism. In light of the oversimplified external renditions of disciplines current in human rights scholarship (of the type: "lawyers believe that ..." asserted by, say, an anthropologist – or vice versa), the fact that the model allows every academic discipline to be found anywhere in the human rights conceptual field should be welcomed, for it is simply wrong to assume that two scholars who are trained in the same discipline share the same conception of human rights.

The respective prevalence of the schools

The empirical investigation of the actual prevalence of the schools remains to be done. Some preliminary suggestions as to the respective influence of each school can nonetheless be

Table 13.1 Systematic comparison of the schools

Schools of thought (orientation)	*Natural school (HR old orthodoxy)*	*Deliberative school(HR secularism/new orthodoxy)*	*Protest school (HR dissidence)*	*Discourse school (HR nihilism)*
Human rights (HR)				
Are conceived, in short, as	A given	Agreed upon	Fought for	Talked about
Consist in	Entitlements (probably negative at their core)	Principles	Claims/aspirations	Whatever you put into them
Are for	Every single human being	Running the polity fairly	First and foremost those who suffer	Should be, but are not, for those who suffer
Can be embodied in law?	Definitely – this is the aim	Yes – law is their typical if not only mode of existence	Should be, but law too often betrays the HR idea	HR law exists but does not embody anything grand
See HR law since 1948 as definite progress	Yes*	Yes	No	No
Are based on	Nature/God/Universe/ Reason (with legal consensus acting as a fallback for many)	A consensus as to how the polity should be run (with reason in the background)	A tradition of social struggles (but with a yearning for the transcendental)	Language
Are realizable?	Yes, through individual enjoyment (and good substantive laws)	Yes, through political organization (and good procedural laws)	No, they require a perpetual struggle (and implementing laws risk being an abject deformation of their ideal)	No, unsurprisingly, they are a failure
Are universal?	Yes, definitely, they are part of the structure of the universe (even if they get translated in practice in slightly different forms)	Potentially, if the consensus broadens	At source, yes, if only because suffering is universal	No, their supposed universality is a pretence

Note: * Though exceptionally a natural scholar will reject the present form of human rights law as not embodying human rights.

tentatively offered. As hinted above, the natural school has long represented, in the Western world at least, the prevalent "common-sense" or human rights orthodoxy that defines human rights as the rights that everybody has by virtue of being a human being. In academic circles, however, a new orthodoxy, represented by the deliberative school, seems to be replacing this old orthodoxy. The protest school seems to host the most human rights activists (and thus perhaps also activist-scholars). The discourse school of thought, with its lack of faith in human rights, is probably the least prevalent, especially among human rights academics who most likely choose their field of research partly out of a commitment to furthering the concept of human rights: discourse scholars often do not explicitly share the non-transcendental commitment to human rights that characterizes the deliberative scholars. Interestingly, some empirical qualitative work, which is admittedly limited, suggests that a variety of positions are found among non-scholars in a way that echoes the model presented in this chapter.

For the sake of conceptual clarity, the model has been presented here in a clear-cut manner. However, it should be stressed that both multiple and ambiguous affiliations are possible (Dembour 2006, pp. 258–261). Each school of thought presents persuasive arguments – all have something of interest to offer. Not surprisingly then, many scholars waver in their orientations.

Acknowledgements

From Marie-Bénédicte Dembour. "What Are Human Rights? Four Schools of Thought." *Human Rights Quartely*, 32:1 (2010), pp. 1–20. The Johns Hopkins University Press. Abridged with permission of the Johns Hopkins University Press.

Research and writing of this chapter were made possible by a Standard Research Grant from the Social Sciences and Humanities Research Council of Canada.

References

Dembour, Marie-Bénédicte. 2006. *Who Believes in Human Rights? Reflections on the European Convention* (Cambridge: Cambridge University Press).

Dembour, Marie-Bénédicte. 2010. "What Are Human Rights? Four Schools of Thought." *Human Rights Quarterly*, Vol. 32, No. 1, pp. 1–20.

Donnelly, Jack. 1989. *Universal Human Rights in Theory and Practice* (Ithaca, NY: Cornell University Press).

Donnelly, Jack. 2003. *Universal Human Rights in Theory and Practice*. 2nd edn (Ithaca, NY: Cornell University Press).

Douzinas, Costas. 2000. *The End of Human Rights: Critical Legal Thought at the Turn of the Century* (Oxford: Hart Publishing).

Goodale, Mark. 2009. *Surrendering to Utopia: An Anthropology of Human Rights* (Stanford, CA: Stanford University Press).

Haarscher, Guy. 1993. *Philosophie des Droits de L'homme*. 4th edn (Brussels: Éditions de l'Université de Bruxelles).

Nickel, James W. 2007. *Making Sense of Human Rights*. 2nd edn (Oxford: Blackwell).

14

Social suffering and human rights

Iain Wilkinson

In recent years, the concept of "social suffering" has been widely adopted in social science as a means to refer us to lived experiences of pain, damage, injury, deprivation, and loss. Here it is generally understood that human afflictions are encountered in many different forms and that their deleterious effects are manifold; but a particular emphasis is brought to bear upon the extent to which social processes and cultural conditions both constitute and moderate the ways in which suffering is experienced and expressed. With reference to "social suffering," researchers aim to attend to the ways in which subjective components of distress are rooted in social situations and conditioned by cultural circumstance. It is held that social worlds comprise the embodied experience of pain and that there are often occasions where individual suffering is a manifestation of social structural oppression.

From the late eighteenth century onwards it is possible to find writers making occasional references to experiences and events of "social suffering" (Wordsworth 1793; Frothingham et al. 1862, p. 26; Blaickie 1865, p. 30; Schilder 1938; van Sickle 1946). For most of this time, the concept was used either as a means to label state policies as the primary cause of people's miseries or to comment in general terms upon the social hardships that result from physical disability or mental illness; but it was never identified as a pivotal matter for theory or research. It is only since the 1990s that "social suffering" has been formally incorporated within the language of social science. It is from this point onwards that problems of "social suffering" have been headlined as focal points of analytical concern.

In part it is due to the extent to which the French sociologist Pierre Bourdieu and the American anthropologist and psychiatrist Arthur Kleinman have placed this notion at the center of their attempts to document and explain the lived experience of pain and distress that it has acquired the status of a key concept. There are now distinct movements of social research that draw inspiration from the respective ways in which Bourdieu and Kleinman have fashioned "social suffering" as a term of analysis and critique. It is often with a mind to contribute to debates featured in either one or both of these writers' works that researchers explain their interests and practices in terms of a contribution to our understanding of "social suffering."

In *La Misère du Monde* (1993) (translated in 1999 into English with the title *The Weight of the World*), Bourdieu, working with a team of social researchers, documents the "ordinary suffering" of people living on the outskirts of Paris in areas of industrial decline. In this context, the focus on "social suffering" is intended to draw attention to the cumulative miseries of everyday life that contribute to people's overriding sense of alienation and attitudes of despairing ennui. Here it is assumed that, in addition to the more familiar hardships and traumatic circumstances through which suffering is visited upon society, there are also many less obvious and mostly hidden ways in which people suffer due to the mundane circumstances in which they are made to live. It essentially concerns the suffering that takes place within "the most intimate dramas" of everyday life; and as such, "social suffering" is largely unformulated as a matter of public discourse and remains beyond the purview of official surveys and opinion polls. (Bourdieu and Wacquant 1992, p. 102). It is apprehended through the stumbling language, awkward silences, and humiliated look of individuals living in poor housing conditions and working for low wages in the most demeaning circumstances. Although it is often the case that "social suffering" takes place in contexts of social and material deprivation, on this account, it more directly concerns the damage done to a person's sense of dignity and worth when the field of possibilities before them is heavily circumscribed by structural conditions that offer no means of respite or escape.

For Bourdieu, the attempt to bring public attention to the force and parameters of "social suffering" comprises a broader program of critical inquiry into the moral character of contemporary capitalism and the increasingly authoritarian forms of technocracy through which the government of populations takes place. Such work has drawn some to analyze the traditions of philosophical understanding and methodological practices in evidence in the move to make "social suffering" a matter for public sphere debate, but for the most part, commentators have viewed this as a component of Bourdieu's attempt to fashion sociology as a form of political engagement (Boyne 2002; Charlesworth 2000; Dejours 1998; McRobbie 2002; Renault 2008; Vitellone 2004). Accordingly the evidence of social suffering is taken as a moral register of political processes and economic conditions that create social conditions in which people experience themselves and others as alienated, superfluous, and without hope. It is also viewed as an instance of sociological writing being fashioned as a moral rebuke toward neo-liberal state policies that abandon welfarist principles so as to promote the market as a disciplinary force of regulation in matters pertaining to the maintenance of public housing and the quality of people's working environments.

While the interests featured in Bourdieu's work have a place within the programs of research associated with Kleinman, it is also the case that here they are located within a wider range of human problems. In this context we find the term "social suffering" being applied to any situation in which experiences of pain, trauma, and disorder take place as a result of "what political, economic and institutional power does to people and, reciprocally, from how these forms of power themselves influence responses to social problems" (Kleinman et al. 1997, p. ix). On this account, a focus on "social suffering" not only serves to highlight the "corrosion of character" that takes place in situations of material deprivation and social breakdown, but also the harms done to and pains borne by people in contexts of ill-health, interpersonal violence, large-scale social conflict, and cultural collapse. Notably, it is also the case that in the projects initiated by Kleinman and colleagues there is a marked concern to demarcate the historically specific and culturally situated factors that condition the ways in which individuals encounter, express, and respond to various forms of affliction. The suffering experienced in contexts of "advanced" industrial capitalism is set alongside ethnographically detailed accounts of the pains and hardships borne in "developing" and "under-developing" sectors of the globe. Efforts are made to have us recognize the global multiplicity of human conditions and the extent to which experiences of and responses to suffering are comprised by the many contingencies of social life in process.

For Kleinman, a focus on "social suffering" serves as a means to highlight the moral challenges faced by individuals set in, and moving through, particular socio-political spaces.

His interest lies in the extent to which "social suffering" always takes place within morally charged environments where individuals experience life in terms of "what really matters" (Kleinman 2006). "Social suffering" casts the existential plight of individuals in stark relief; but always with attention being drawn towards the moderating force of prevailing social structures and established cultural practices on people's moral sensibilities and ethical dispositions. In this regard, Kleinman presents his work as a contribution to a new "anthropology of subjectivity" that aims to expose the shifting social grounds of moral experience and its bearing upon the myriad ways in which individuals struggle to make sense of their lives while beset with the task of forging and maintaining relationships with others (Kleinman and Fitz-Henry 2007).

In a more critical vein, he seeks to alert us to a series of radical transformations that are taking place across the dynamic fields of local experience as forces of "rationalization," "mediatization," and "commodification" acquire a heightened technological and institutional capacity to intrude upon, and routinely discipline, the ways we relate to ourselves and other people (Kleinman 1999). A substantial component of his research focuses on the experience of social suffering in the context of health care. In this respect it is the ever-intensifying forces of rationalization experienced under the aegis of "medicalization" that occupy his critical attention; particularly in contexts where the possibility of attending to a person's illness experience is sacrificed to a drive for technical efficiency and the dictates of bureaucratic process (Kleinman 1988, 1995a). Kleinman highlights the socio-political and technological processes in which abstruse forms of measurement and analytical practice are used to gloss over the moral obstinacy and interpersonal turmoil of human experience. On the understanding that many social procedures and cultural conventions are being disciplined to operate "without regard for persons," he stands with Max Weber in decrying the dehumanizing force of rationalization.

Kleinman also raises troubling ethical questions in relation to the cumulative impacts of media representations of the suffering of distant others on the "moral–emotional processes" by which we acquire a capacity for empathy and compassion (Kleinman 1995b; Kleinman and Kleinman 1997). He shares in the concerns raised by Luc Boltanski in his thesis in *Distant Suffering* (1999); namely, that via the cultural appropriation of the imagery of suffering as commodified forms of "infotainment," we are involved in moral practices where the possibility of engagement or solidarity with sufferers is denied. Kleinman suggests that, when repeated over time, such experience serves to erode our capacities for moral feeling and thereby makes it all too easy for us to dissociate ourselves from ties of responsibility towards others. He goes so far as to claim that the mass dissemination of the imagery of suffering via commercial forms of cultural reproduction and exchange is effecting a major transformation in the experience of social subjectivity; for this "normalizes" a vivid awareness of others' suffering in contexts that foreclose possibilities for participation in public debate and withhold the option of a compassionate engagement with human needs.

As a field of study, "social suffering" not only provides insight into the social engagements and cultural practices that comprise our inner being, but also serves as a means to sound political alarms over the moral deficits of current modes of social organization and cultural reproduction. In both French and American contexts, research and writing on "social suffering" takes place at "the intersection of social science, politics and civic ethics" (Bourdieu and Wacquant 1992, p. 200). For those working in these fields, it is readily acknowledged that the task of understanding social life involves us in expressions of moral worth and political longing; and indeed, that it is via a thoroughgoing examination of such commitments that we uncover opportunities to catch glimpses of what really matters in people's lives. Empirical social research, and ethnography in particular, is valued both as a means to bring the evidence of lived experience to bear upon theoretical terms of analysis and public debate, and as a component of a "reflexive" process whereby practitioners are sensitized towards the moral values and political investments that shape their professional conduct and genres of writing. As fields of social practice and as spaces of knowledge production, the social sciences are placed under moral and political scrutiny. More often than not this also draws researchers into debate over the social meaning and worth of academic work and the formal processes whereby the problems of human life are adopted as scholarly concerns.

Social suffering and human rights

Problems of human rights and humanitarian social action are featured throughout research and writing on social suffering. In these contexts, an overt attempt is made to examine the ways in which social research can be applied to the task of building humane forms of society. On many accounts this involves the re-founding of social science as a humanitarian project that requires researchers to work at making explicit the form and quality of their moral and political commitments. Indeed, it is important to understand that here it is very much the case that social research is approached as a moral endeavor wedded to the furthering of human understanding and the practical realization of human rights. In what follows, this is examined in terms of its historical antecedents and critical praxis.

Critical humanism and the politics of sentimentality

"Critical humanism" tends to feature as a presiding concern within most research and writing on social suffering (Plummer 2001). This is manifested in the effort made to document a great variety of human conditions and possibilities and, more directly, in a careful attendance to the moral tensions and political frustrations borne by individuals in conditions of extreme hardship and adversity. It is also displayed in a commitment to understanding how the witness of suffering serves to establish social bonds and the political imperative to care for others. Social suffering is a field of inquiry that aims to make known the many ways in which suffering takes place and, most importantly, how it is met in human *experience*. In this context, a privileged position is given to the task of understanding how the cultural capacity to "feel for" the suffering of others can be nurtured as the common ground on which to establish principles of human rights (Turner 1993, 2006).

In order to grasp the sociological issues at stake here, it is important to attend to the late-eighteenth-century origins of the concept of "social suffering" and the cultural circumstances under which this was forged. It is now widely understood that the second half of the eighteenth century witnessed a revolution in social attitudes towards human suffering and that this in turn was heavily implicated within nascent conceptions of the "the social" as a domain constituted by bonds of "fellow-feeling" (Barker-Benfield 1992; Denby 1994; Ellis 1996; Vincent-Buffault 1991). Here the sociological imagination is understood to be animated as much by the force of moral sentiment as by the cognitive capacity to conceptualize structures of society (Smith 1759). Human emotions are taken up as pressing matters for sociological inquiry, both in terms of how they are used to express social experience and in their role as components of the attitudes and behaviors with which we respond to others.

When focusing on problems of "social suffering," researchers often *return* to a set of moral debates and political disputes that had their heyday in the late eighteenth and early nineteenth centuries. These not only concern conflicts of interpretation over the meaning of particular states of moral feeling such as "sympathy," "pity," and "compassion," but also bring dispute to the part these play within the constitution of civil society; and indeed, whether they *should* have any part to play at all in legal and political affairs (Henderson 1987; Spelman 1998; Woodward 2002). The politics of sensibility have always courted controversy. There is no doubt that moral sentiment provided a vital spur to the development of modern discourse on human rights, but there has been a tendency to cast this as a matter of intellectual immaturity that has no serious part within a politics of principle (Hunt 2007). At its origins many were inclined to question the authenticity of expressions of fellow feeling and were worried by the possibility that this could be enjoyed as an end in itself or be used as a force for social manipulation (Ellis 1996, pp. 190–221). More often than not, within the history of Western political science, writers have been more concerned to expose the ideological cast of moral feeling than to explore the possible ways in which this might be cultivated as a means to further social understanding or pursue matters of social justice (Amato 1990, 1994; Arendt 1963; Barreto 2006; Reddy 2001). It is only in recent years that there has been a concerted movement to reappraise the cultural histories of sentiments such as "pity" and "compassion" so as to chart their wider social significance and contribution to public affairs (Boltanksi 1999; Halpern 2002; Nussbaum 1996, 2001; Sznaider 2001; Tester 2001).

It is important to note that although the larger part of debates on the politics of pity and compassion are concerned with matters of abstract principle, in the context of "social suffering" a privileged role is given to *lived experience* as a guide to moral values and political commitments. In this regard, those engaged with the study of "social suffering" tend to draw inspiration from traditions of pragmatism, though it would be a mistake to identify this as aligned to the standpoint of figures such as Richard Rorty. Where Rorty's (1998) critique of "human rights foundationalism" leads him to conclude that "sad stories" do more to advance the recognition of human rights than arguments that appeal to abstract philosophical principle, whether such stories are drawn from experience or not, does not appear to matter too much to him. By contrast, this matters a great deal to those with a commitment to studying problems of "social suffering." Here researchers tend to be acutely alert to the "sentimentalist fallacy" outlined by William James as a situation where individuals "shed tears over abstract justice and generosity and beauty, etc., and never know these qualities when (they) meet them in the street, because circumstances make them vulgar" (James 1907, p. 153). On these grounds Richard Rorty may be portrayed as "insufficiently pragmatic," for he is too narrowly focused on problems of language and not sufficiently engaged with the task of understanding the harms that are done to people *in experience* and how such *experience* might be made to change (Kloppenberg 1996).

From "politics of recognition" to "sociodicy"

It is possible to characterize a great deal of research and writing on "social suffering" as a form of critical praxis that seeks to establish the right of people to have rights (Arendt 1973). Some are inclined to label what takes place here as a "politics of recognition." Axel Honneth argues that it is often the case that contexts of social suffering are discussed as part of a "disclosing critique" that aims to make known the "pathologies of the social" in which "the other of justice" is denied moral recognition and respect for their rights (Honneth 1995). For example, Paul Farmer contends that "a failure of imagination is one of the greatest failures in contemplating the fate of the world's poorest," and aims to use ethnographic texts and photography as a means to shock his readers into questioning the human values and responsibilities that bind them to the victims of suffering (Farmer 2006, p. 145). He uses whatever "rhetorical tools" are available to him to convey the experience of individuals dying from AIDS and seeks to offend readers' sensibilities with images of the physical torment suffered by people living in circumstances of extreme material deprivation. Farmer uses such methods to advocate an expanded notion of human rights that gives as much importance to the right to "freedom from want" as to civil and political rights.

Similarly, Veena Das explains her work as an attempt to devise "languages of pain" by which social sciences might be crafted as a textual body on which "pain is written" (1997a, p. 67). Her ethnographic practice is designed to fashion a re-entry to "scenes of devastation" and worlds "made strange through the desolating experience of violence and loss" (ibid.). Here the efforts made to convey the standpoint of women who have been subjected to brutal acts of violence in the internecine conflicts of India's civil wars are intended as a means to "convert" such experience into a script that can be used to establish ties of empathy and communal self-understanding. Das presents this as part of a "work of healing" that creates a social space for the recognition of human rights and possibilities for a retrieval of human dignity (Das et al. 2001).

While engaging with such struggles for recognition, writers such as Farmer and Das tend to present this as merely a point of beginning. Here the foregrounding of people's experiences as social suffering is intended not only as a plea for recognition but also as a means to initiate a wider set of inquiries into the institutional foundations of civil society and the grounds upon which it may be possible to realize people's social and economic rights. For example, Farmer writes:

> [R]ecognition is not enough ... We need another modern movement, a globalized movement that will use whatever stories and images it can to promote respect for human rights, especially the rights of the poor. For such a movement to come about, we need to rehabilitate a series of sentiments long out of fashion in academic and policy circles: indignation on behalf not of oneself but of the less fortunate; solidarity; empathy; and even pity, compassion, mercy, and remorse ... Stories and images need to be linked to the historically deeper and geographically wider analyses that can allow the listener or the observer to understand the ways in which AIDS, a new disease, is rooted in the historically defined conditions that promote its spread and deny its treatment; the ways in which genocide, like slavery before it, is a fundamentally "transnational" event; the reasons why breast cancer is inevitably fatal for the most affected women who live in poverty; the meaning of rights in an interconnected world riven by poverty and inequality. In short, serious social ills require in-depth analyses.
>
> *(Farmer 2006, p. 185)*

In this context, Das seeks to position problems of "theodicy" as a key matter for analysis and holds that there is much to be gained through the recovery of classical traditions of sociological inquiry into the ways in which populations are liable to come under a compulsive struggle to make the experience of suffering productive for thought and action (Das 1997b). Accordingly, Max Weber's studies of the impact of repeated attempts to solve problems of theodicy on wider processes of rationalization are set alongside Emile Durkheim's account of the social origins of moral individualism and Karl Marx's focus on the ways power is exercised through the toil of work, as indispensable components of a movement to expose how social forces condition the experience of suffering and set limits on the ways this is acknowledged and responded to in the political realm (Wilkinson 2005). She calls for the development of "secular theodicies" that bring a sociological frame of analysis to bear upon the ways in which harms are caused and distributed, and she holds that these should also work to account for the many different ways in which experiences of suffering might be "culturally appropriated" for competing moral and political ends (Das 1997b, p. 570).

While theodicies traditionally worked to establish a "higher" Divine purpose for suffering that was not immediately apparent to believers, a secular "sociodicy" proceeds in a more pragmatic vein that holds that it may always be the case that a substantial part of suffering will appear to be utterly "useless" and without meaning (Levinas 1988). In this respect, the experience of "useless suffering" may well be identified as the means by which "bare life" is brought into relief and we encounter the moral demand to be responsible for others (Agamben 1998); though of course, this is a demand that is all too often denied (Cohen 2001). In this context, the relevance of research and writing on social suffering for human rights might well lie in the extent to which the former can be used to open up avenues of inquiry into the ways in which the latter now serves as a primary means to address problems of "sociodicy" (Morgan and Wilkinson 2001).

As a field of inquiry, "social suffering" brings critical attention to the ways in which the social origins of the concern for human rights are rooted in the response to suffering as morally deplorable and unjust. It also aims to understand the historical and cultural conditions under which suffering is made to appear, and is open to be interpreted as such. It attends to the ways in which the political drive to expand and realize human rights is a product of a course of rationalization that is irretrievably bound to the attempt to provide solutions to the problem of human suffering. While there are many instances where this is set to be the cause of great social upheaval and political unrest, it is also where people work to forge civil and legal processes that move to convert our "sympathy for all that is human" into forms of society that uphold our dignity as human beings.

References

Agamben, G. 1998. *Homo Sacer: Sovereign Power and Bare Life* (Stanford, CA: Stanford University Press).

Amato, J. A. 1990. *Victims and Values: A History and a Theory of Suffering* (New York: Greenwood Press).

Amato, J. A. 1994. "Politics of Suffering." *International Social Science Review*, Vol. 69, No. 1–2, pp. 23–30.

Arendt, H. 1963. *On Revolution* (Harmondsworth: Penguin).

Arendt, H. 1973. *The Origins of Totalitarianism* (New York: Harcourt Brace Jovanovich).

Barker-Benfield, G. J. 1992. *The Culture of Sensibility: Sex and Society in Eighteenth-Century Britain* (Chicago: University of Chicago Press).

Barreto, J. M. 2006. "Ethics of Emotion as Ethics of Human Rights: A Jurisprudence of Sympathy in Adorno, Horkheimer and Rorty." *Law and Critique*, Vol. 17, No. 1, pp. 73–106.

Blaickie, W. G. 1865. *Heads and Hands in the World of Labour* (London: Alexander Strathern).

Boltanski, L. 1999. *Distant Suffering: Morality, Media and Politics* (Cambridge: Cambridge University Press).

Bourdieu, P. et al. 1999. *The Weight of the World: Social Suffering in Contemporary Life* (Cambridge: Polity Press).

Bourdieu, P. and L. Wacquant. 1992. *An Invitation to Reflexive Sociology* (Chicago: University of Chicago Press).

Boyne, R. 2002. "Bourdieu: From Class to Culture." *Theory, Culture & Society*, Vol. 19, No. 3, pp. 117–128.

Charlesworth, S. 2000. "Bourdieu, Social Suffering and Working-Class Life." In B. Fowler, ed., *Reading Bourdieu on Society and Culture* (Oxford: Blackwell).

Cohen, S. 2001. *States of Denial: Knowing about Atrocities and Suffering* (Cambridge: Polity Press).

Das, V. 1997a. "Language and Body: Transactions in the Construction of Pain." In A. Kleinman, V. Das, and M. Lock, eds., *Social Suffering* (Berkeley: University of California Press).

Das, V. 1997b. "Sufferings, Theodicies, Disciplinary Practices, Appropriations." *International Journal of Social Science*, Vol. 49, pp. 563–572.

Das, V., A. Kleinman, M. Ramphele, M. Lock, and P. Reynolds, eds., 2001. *Remaking a World: Violence, Social Suffering and Recovery* (Berkeley: University of California Press).

Dejours, C. 1998. *Souffrances en France: La Banalization de L'injustice Sociale* (Paris: Seuil).

Denby, D. 1994. *Sentimental Narrative and the Social Order in France, 1760–1820* (Cambridge: Cambridge University Press).

Ellis, M. 1996. *The Politics of Sensibility: Race, Gender and Commerce in the Sentimental Novel* (Cambridge: Cambridge University Press).

Farmer, P. 2006. "Never Again? Reflections on Human Values and Human Rights." In G. B. Peterson, ed., *The Tanner Lectures on Human Values* (Salt Lake City: University of Utah Press).

Frothingham, N.L. et al. 1862. *Society for the Relief of Aged and Destitute Clergymen: Extracts from Records Relating to Its History and Objects* (Boston: John Wilson & Son).

Halpern, C. 2002. *Suffering, Politics and Power: A Genealogy in Modern Political Theory* (Albany: State University of New York Press).

Henderson, L. 1987. "Legality and Empathy." *Michigan Law Review*, Vol. 85, No. 6, pp. 1574–1653.

Honneth, A. 1995. *The Struggle for Recognition: The Moral Grammar of Social Conflicts* (Cambridge: Polity Press).

Hunt, L. 2007. *Inventing Human Rights: A History* (New York: W.W. Norton).

James, W. 1907. "Pragmatism's Conception of Truth." *Journal of Philosophy and Scientific Methods*, Vol. 6, No. 4, pp. 141–155.

Kleinman, A. 1988. *The Illness Narratives: Suffering, Healing and the Human Condition* (New York: Basic Books).

Kleinman, A. 1995a. *Writing at the Margin: Discourse Between Anthropology and Medicine* (Berkeley: University of California Press).

Kleinman, A. 1995b. "Pitch, Picture, Power: The Globalization of Local Suffering and the Transformation of Social Experience." *Ethnos*, Vol. 60, Nos. 3–4, pp. 181–191.

Kleinman, A. 1999. "Experience and Its Moral Modes: Culture, Human Conditions and Disorder." In G.B. Peterson, ed., *The Tanner Lectures on Human Values* (Salt Lake City: University of Utah Press).

Kleinman, A. 2006. *What Really Matters: Living a Moral Life Amidst Uncertainty and Danger* (Oxford: Oxford University Press).

Kleinman, A. and E. Fitz-Henry. 2007. "The Experiential Basis of Subjectivity: How Individuals Change in the Context of Societal Transformation." In J. Biehl, B. Good, and A. Kleinman, eds., *Rethinking Subjectivity: Ethnographic Investigations* (Berkeley: University of California Press).

Kleinman, A. and J. Kleinman. 1997. "The Appeal of Experience; The Dismay of Images: Cultural Appropriations of Suffering in Our Times." In A. Kleinman, V. Das, and M. Lock, eds., *Social Suffering* (Berkeley: University of California Press).

Kleinman, A., V. Das, and M. Lock, eds., 1997. *Social Suffering* (Berkeley: University of California Press).

Kloppenberg, J. T. 1996. "Pragmatism: An Old Name For Some New Ways of Thinking?" *Journal of American History*, Vol. 83, No. 1, pp. 100–113.

Levinas, E. 1988. "Useless Suffering." In R. Bernasconi and David Wood, eds., *The Provocation of Levinas: Rethinking the Other* (London: Routledge).

McRobbie, A. 2002. "A Mixed Bag of Misfortunes? Bourdieu's *Weight of the World*." *Theory, Culture & Society*, Vol. 19, No. 3, pp. 129–138.

Morgan, D. G. and I. Wilkinson. 2001. "The Problem of Suffering and the Sociological Task of Theodicy." *European Journal of Social Theory*, Vol. 4, No. 2, pp. 199–214.

Nussbaum, M. C. 1996. "Compassion: The Basic Social Emotion." *Social Philosophy and Policy*, Vol. 13, No. 1, pp. 27–58.

Nussbaum, M.C. 2001. *Upheavals of Thought* (Cambridge: Cambridge University Press).

Plummer, K. 2001. *Documents of Life 2: An Invitation to Critical Humanism* (London: Sage).

Reddy, W. M. 2001. *The Navigation of Feeling: A Framework for the History of Emotions* (Cambridge: Cambridge University Press).

Renault, E. 2008. *Souffrances Sociales: Philosophie, Psychologie et Politique* (Paris: Éditions La Découverte).

Rorty, R. 1998. "Human Rights, Rationality, and Sentimentality." In *Truth and Progress: Philosophical Papers*, Vol. 3 (Cambridge: Cambridge University Press).

Schilder, P. 1938. "The Social Neurosis." *Psychoanalytic Review*, Vol. 25, pp. 1–19.

Smith, A. 1759. *The Theory of Moral Sentiments* (Oxford: Clarendon Press).

Spelman, E.V. 1998. *Fruits of Sorrow: Framing Our Attention to Suffering* (Boston: Beacon Press).

Sznaider, N. 2001. *The Compassionate Temperament: Care and Cruelty in Modern Society* (Lanham, MD: Rowman & Littlefield).

Tester, K. 2001. *Compassion, Morality and the Media* (Buckingham: Open University Press).

Turner, B. S. 1993. "Outline of a Theory of Human Rights." *Sociology*, Vol. 27, No. 3, pp. 489–512.

Turner, B. S. 2006. *Vulnerability and Human Rights* (University Park: Pennsylvania State University Press).
van Sickle, J. V. 1946. "Regional Aspects of the Problem of Full Employment at Low Wages." *Southern Economic Journal*, Vol. 13, No. 1, pp. 36–45.
Vincent-Buffault, A. 1991. *The History of Tears: Sensibility and Sentimentality in France* (Basingstoke: Macmillan).
Vitellone, N. 2004. "Habitus and Social Suffering: Culture Addiction and the Syringe." In L. Adkins and B. Skeggs, eds., *Feminism after Bourdieu* (Oxford: Blackwell).
Wilkinson, I. 2005. *Suffering: A Sociological Introduction* (Cambridge: Polity Press).
Woodward, K. 2002. "Calculating Compassion." *Indiana Law Journal*, Vol. 77, No. 2, pp. 223–246.
Wordsworth, W. 1793. "Descriptive Sketches." In E. de Selincourt, ed., *The Poetical Works of William Wordsworth* (Oxford: Clarendon Press).

15

Human rights as cultural practices

Fuyuki Kurasawa

Introduction

Discussions of human rights in the social sciences today are dominated by a formalist approach that understands these rights as legally institutionalized norms – as the implementation of abstract principles and the products of official institutions (namely, states and international organizations) prescribing and granting them from above to persons and groups. As a result, human rights are analytically juridified, the legal-institutional inscription of socio-economic and civil–political rights (in national and supranational constitutions, multilateral treaties, etc.) overshadowing their cultural grounding and enactment by subjects imbedded in concrete lifeworlds.

One of the most prominent versions of formalist thinking is normativism, which takes its cue from various philosophical sources (ancient Greco-Roman Stoicism, Enlightenment Kantianism, non-Western humanism, etc.) in order to undergird human rights in an ethic of universal moral equality. For normativists, all human beings are entitled to the realization of the same rights as well as to the enjoyment of the same freedoms and protections, regardless of their specific circumstances or socio-cultural location (normativist writings on human rights include Bohman and Lutz-Bachmann 1997; De Greiff and Cronin 2002; Derrida 2001; Habermas 2001; Pogge 2002; and Singer 2002). Moreover, normativism specifies moral principles, such as hospitality and egalitarian reciprocity, that can inform the creation of a peaceful, multilateral world order based on cultural pluralism and global distributive justice.

Formalism also manifests itself in institutionalist frameworks, which emphasize the realization of human rights through a reform or complete overhaul of the existing transnational legal infrastructure and set of multilateral political institutions (see, for instance, Archibugi 2008; Beck 2006; Falk 2000; and Held 2004). Proposals range from a world parliament to multi-scaled yet interconnected executive structures with overlapping jurisdictions, and from global citizenship to the enforcement of an international legal regime that would regulate domestic governments, interstate relations, and the conduct of powerful transnational private actors. Put succinctly, institutionalists believe that transforming the official system of planetary governance produces the clearest path to implementing human rights.

Although essential to the study of human rights, normativism and institutionalism neglect what can be termed the socio-cultural substance of these rights, that is to say, how they are put into practice by persons and groups engaged in performing collective rituals and beliefs that cannot be reduced to normative principles and may not seek official institutional recognition or juridical inscription. Hence, formalism poorly grasps the cultural processes and forms of social interaction that are at the core of human rights, which become meaningful realities for ordinary persons through what are frequently non-legal, extra-institutional discourses, claims, and actions.

Therefore, what is needed as an alternative to formalism is a socio-cultural pragmatist framework, which draws upon three distinctive bodies of literature: a sociology of conventions (Boltanski and Thévenot 2006; Thévenot 2006); the paradigm of contentious politics within comparative political sociology (McAdam, Tarrow, and Tilly 2001; Tilly 2006); and the sociology of human rights and cosmopolitanism (Beck 2006; Calhoun 2003; Gilroy 2005; Kendall, Woodward, and Skrbis 2009; Woodiwiss 2005). All three of these perspectives enable us to focus on how human rights are put into practice and how their manifestations take shape in specific social and political settings; specifically, a pragmatist approach studies the conventions and repertoires of enacting human rights by performing tasks and encountering various obstacles. It is this process of attempting to realize such tasks and overcome difficulties that constitutes the social and cultural labor of human rights, or what I have termed elsewhere the work of global justice (Kurasawa 2007). Accordingly, from a pragmatist vantage point, human rights are not simply legal entitlements that trickle down to citizens after being legislated by states, courts, or international organizations. Rights are, equally and just as importantly, dependent upon the symbolic and material capacities of individual and collective subjects performing conventionalized modes of practice, and upon the cultural meanings that such subjects give to their conventionalized forms of social action.

Shifting from formalism to pragmatism requires conceptually anchoring the study of human rights in the notion of practice, which is neither the structuralist following of a pre-existing code nor the cognitivist adherence to a rule (Bourdieu 1990; Taylor 1995). Instead, a practice represents a public "regime of engagement" (Thévenot 2006), requiring subjects to tackle the problem of coordination of their actions in relation to others and to their surroundings. A human rights practice confronts specific perils and, in working through them, enacts a certain repertoire of tasks. However, to interpret human rights as cultural practices involving creativity in resolving the problem of coordination of action and the encountering of difficulties does not signify that such practices are improvisational or spontaneous acts that are invented anew in each situational context. On the contrary, the idea of regime is designed to conceive of human rights practices as involving patterns or repertoires of socio-political discourses and action, which are defined by their "modularity" (Tarrow 2005) or isomorphism across different historical and cultural settings; modes of practice are transposable among various human rights campaigns and can be diffused from one situation to another as actors learn from and seek to borrow certain approaches and tactics from one another. Foundational human rights struggles establish a set of cultural and socio-political conventions that set templates guiding persons and groups facing similar injustices – templates that are modified in accordance with variations in local and global conditions, yet retain analogous features across cases (Tilly 2006). The most striking instance of this is the manner in which eyewitness accounts by Holocaust survivors have created a repertoire of testimonial practices for victims of subsequent genocides and crimes against humanity across the world. A regime of engagement, then, is composed of similar configurations of social relations in several periods and sites, which may significantly vary in their local manifestations while retaining their general isomorphic qualities.

Thinking of human rights as practices

Moving away from strictly normative or institutional dimensions, a pragmatist framework leads us to consider two oft-neglected features of human rights. First, human rights are concretized through intersubjective processes, that is, through forms of social interaction among various parties whose demands, strategies, and conduct are influenced by the expectations of other actors and their responses. Human rights carrier-groups (such as non-governmental organizations and social movements) perform rituals of political action in order to involve key institutions in their campaigns (the media, governments, etc.), counter the claims of the perpetrators of human rights violations and their allies, and convince public opinion. In turn, how these institutions and groups react to such rituals guides the kinds of strategies pursued by carrier-groups and the discourses they advance. Thus, pragmatism draws attention to the socially interactive nature of human rights practices. Second, it insists upon the fact that, in specific situations or campaigns (frequently referred to as "case studies"), human rights should be examined in concrete "worksites" (Balibar 2004, p. 156), namely, varied spaces and arenas of public debate in which injustices and human rights violations are discussed. This means that – aside from courts, parliaments, multilateral organizations, and other conventionally studied formal institutions – scholars should take seriously everyday cultural worksites in which human rights may be centrally present: film festivals, popular music, art exhibits, novels, protest marches, and so on. These sorts of spaces are important to the extent that they facilitate the "informalization" of human rights, which can stand down from their seemingly rarified or remote standing to touch more directly the experiential lifeworlds of ordinary persons; as such, we should examine how human rights are encountered in informal or banal settings, in daily culturally or aesthetically oriented activities.

Taking these features into account, we can identify five practices that define contemporary human rights campaigns: bearing witness (testimonial acts and responses); forgiveness (asking to be forgiven and the granting of it); foresight (preventing human rights violations); aid (assisting victims of humanitarian crises); and solidarity (cultivating bonds of responsibility for others). The cultural and socio-political substance of these practices is found in the repertoire of tasks performed by actors and of obstacles that they try to overcome in the process of campaigning for human rights (see Table 15.1).

Each of these cultural practices should be discussed in turn. Because of the widespread use of testimonial activities as a means for eyewitnesses of human rights abuses to document what they experienced or saw first-hand, the practice of bearing witness is pivotal in our day and age. It gives voice to these eyewitnesses, whose oral and visual accounts aim to parry the possibility that injustices and crimes against humanity will remain unknown or silenced by perpetrators. At the same time, the fact that such accounts can be incomprehensible to national and transnational publics due to the scale and intensity of the suffering that they describe transforms testimonial practices into interpretive exercises, whereby eyewitnesses translate their experiences and their audiences use their moral imaginations to transpose themselves in the shoes of the abused party. Yet interpretive labor is inadequate to the task of countering the prospects of generalized indifference toward the suffering of victims, which explains the tendency of human rights campaigners to present testimonies in ways that generate public empathy by appealing to citizens' moral beliefs (in human dignity, equality of treatment, etc.) or sentiments (pity, compassion, outrage, etc.). Moreover, since instances of injustice and crimes against humanity can be forgotten over time, testimonial practices are geared toward the creation and reproduction of rituals of collective remembrance as well as the preservation of evidentiary artifacts. To guard against and prevent grave violations of human rights being repeated over time, bearing witness

Table 15.1 The five practices of human rights

Practices	*Tasks*	*Obstacles*
Bearing witness	• voice • interpretation • empathy • remembrance • prevention	• silence • incomprehensibility • indifference • forgetting • repetition
Forgiveness	• remembrance • responsibility • exercise of justice • reconciliation	• forgetting • "deresponsibilization" • impunity • vengeance
Foresight	• capacity for anticipation • far-sightedness • public judgment	• inscrutability of the future • presentism • alarmism
Aid	• egalitarian reciprocity • collaboration • new world order	• status asymmetries • domination • global segregation
Solidarity	• recognition of pluralism • networked affinities • creativity of action	• cultural homogeneity • political fragmentation • social thinness

works to educate and warn present and future generations (a task captured by the motto "never again").

Forgiveness is a second noteworthy cultural practice of human rights, since its institutionalization through truth and reconciliation commissions has become the focal point of collective endeavors in numerous transitional societies (following a period of authoritarian rule or civil war, for instance) and in certain "New World" societies (to begin to confront the mistreatment of indigenous peoples). Lest this point be misunderstood, two provisos should be mentioned. In the first instance, keeping with a pragmatist outlook, forgiveness is not an intrinsically desirable ideal, but rather a form of social action whose effectiveness is conditional upon the performance of specific tasks and the overcoming of corresponding perils. Second, what should be considered is less the strictly formal modes of forgiveness (granted or requested by governments, for instance) than the relations between such official processes and the sorts of public debate and deliberation that they generate within civil societies and among ordinary citizens. Accordingly, rather than being premised on societal amnesia toward past wrongs and human rights violations, the practice of forgiveness has often required the investigation of mass violence and the reconstruction of historical injustices. Forgiveness has also been facilitated by perpetrators of human rights violations acknowledging responsibility for their actions and asking to be forgiven, or by their responsibility being established through formal means. Nonetheless, the possibility of what might be called "deresponsibilization" exists in cases where perpetrators refuse to accept responsibility and in societies operating with a conception of collective guilt (according to which all citizens are responsible, and thus, ultimately, no one is). This is why human rights campaigns can insist on forgiveness being preceded by the public establishment of different degrees of responsibility: criminal responsibility for direct perpetrators of abuses, moral responsibility for those who abetted perpetrators or remained bystanders, and political responsibility for groups within the general population that benefited from such abuses. Yet even if responsibility is assigned to various social actors, impunity remains a peril that human rights advocates aim to address by demanding and participating in formal processes of exercising a combination of retributive and restorative justice at national and international levels, including the prosecution of perpetrators and the redress of structural gains acquired during a period where mass violations of human rights occurred. Likewise, the prospect of formerly victimized groups taking revenge upon their erstwhile perpetrators is commonly mitigated by civil societies developing various mechanisms and discourses of reconciliation between parties, which themselves foster forgiveness.

Over the last decade or so, human rights campaigns have acquired a precautionary orientation based on the conviction that it is no longer sufficient to react to past or ongoing abuses, since anticipating and preventing them is increasingly important. Rather than accepting the commonplace idea that the future remains unknowable, a number of non-governmental organizations have devoted considerable resources to acquire the capacity for early detection of possible human rights violations. In this way, such organizations are opposing the presentist values suffusing Euro-American societies, in which the emphasis on immediacy and "living in the moment" takes the form of a short-sighted disregard for the future. Hence, the practice of foresight supports the idea that we have a responsibility to protect others from eventual harm, as well as an intergenerational duty to ensure the well-being of those who follow in our wake. On the other hand, since the practice of foresight can be manipulated by states or civil society actors to foster alarmism about certain situations (e.g., to urge armed intervention to suit a country's geopolitical interests), human rights campaigns and organizations engaging in the practice of foresight are subjecting their claims to anticipate future abuses to public scrutiny, in order to enable both their evidence and proposals for prevention and protection of vulnerable populations to be examined and debated within public spheres.

Human rights actors are performing an ensemble of tasks and confronting obstacles that form a fourth cultural practice, that of aid. In the past few years, these same actors have come to view projects of rescue and assistance to vulnerable or victimized populations in poorer regions of the world less in terms of charity or benevolence than political and socio-economic justice. As such, they have begun to address status asymmetries conventionally appearing between the donors of aid and the recipients of it, whether at the level of symbolic or material resources. Increasingly, then, rescue operations and aid projects are guided by a commitment to egalitarian reciprocity, whereby participatory decision-making is applied to empower groups receiving assistance to determine how such assistance can be used and to adapt it to their existing ways of life and beliefs. However, given the long history of aid to the Global South serving as an instrument of Euro-American domination, many human rights-based organizations are seeking to foster symmetrical relations of collaboration between donor agencies and recipient communities, which are treated as full-fledged partners through mutual learning and joint involvement in project management and implementation. Similarly, the renewed insistence on aid as justice has meant that many North–South partnerships are advocating for structural transformations of the current world order, supported by the contention that the realization of the rights of all human beings is conditional upon ending global, spatially based socio-economic segregation and the unequal distribution of resources globally.

The last of the five practices to be proposed here consists of the creation of global solidarity, since discourses about the universality of human rights simultaneously advance and are sustained by a sense of common purpose and shared responsibility among all human beings. Whereas some believe that this sense of human togetherness can only be generated once socio-cultural differences are overcome to produce a homogenous planet, several civil society groups argue that assimilationist notions of humanity are, in fact, sources of division between peoples. By contrast, these groups are advocating for versions of human rights that, without compromising the latter's core principles, recognize cultural diversity and the variety of understandings of human dignity across the world. But rather than concluding that the recognition of cultural pluralism necessarily leads to a fracturing or dilution of a universal commitment to human rights, we can observe that transnational solidarity around such a commitment is made possible by the gradual construction of networks of affinity among persons concerned about human rights, who publicly debate about the precise shape of these rights in different socio-cultural settings. Moreover, whereas this kind of discussion about the universal applicability of human rights risks yielding a socially thin consensus – that is to say, one that remains formal or abstract and thus without much capacity to bind human beings to each other – it need not do so. Indeed, a sense of borderless solidarity is cultivated by what can be termed "the creativity of action" (Joas 1996), as the performance of human rights campaigns can itself forge socially thick and experientially rich ties between persons and groups who, together, join political struggles to resist injustices, contribute to public discourse about human rights, and participate in aesthetically themed human rights events (such as musical concerts or art exhibitions).

The implications of a pragmatist reworking of human rights

Without claiming that the practice-based model described in this chapter incorporates the entire range of issues around human rights, I believe that its merits lie in shifting the analytical scope toward understanding how groups and persons enact rights by performing cultural and socio-political labor. The model captures the incredible assortment of human rights struggles and campaigns in the world today, which, far from being random or infinite in their variety, can be regrouped into a defined set of tasks and obstacles organized around practices of bearing witness, forgiving, foresight, aid, and solidarity. Furthermore, the framework proposed here is designed to include a greater array of participants involved in human rights questions than formalism allows, and to recalibrate the latter's focus on official institutions by insisting upon the significance of seemingly minor civil society actors for a notion of human rights that is meaningful in everyday life; to this extent, diasporic ethno-cultural communities, artists, media outlets, and public health advocates, among others, are as important as courts, parliaments, and international organizations.

This pragmatist model espouses a "perspectival dualism" (Fraser 1997; Fraser and Honneth 2003) that cuts across the traditional distinction between civil–political rights, on the one hand, and socio-economic rights, on the other, for both categories are relevant for all five cultural practices. For instance, action to prevent a forthcoming famine is directed toward ensuring that a population's fundamental right to food is respected, but also toward addressing the sources of political conflict that often underlie it (such as civil war or ethnic cleansing). Because these five modes of social action are mutually constitutive, they demonstrate the indivisibility of the two categories of human rights when they are enacted. To take but one illustration, forgiveness for past violations of the civil or political rights is required for the construction of solidaristic bonds between people, bonds that are themselves necessary for the legitimacy and effectiveness of calls for economic justice underpinning the practice of aid.

Taken together, these practices are made up of repertoires of tasks involving patterns of discourse, rituals, and belief systems, which represent nothing less than the social and cultural substance of human rights. To insist that human rights are either ontological attributes of persons (as per natural law theory) or institutionally derived entitlements is to miss their existence as forms of social labor that agents invest with meaning through their performance and capacities that they exercise when confronted with structural obstacles that compromise human dignity and equality. Aside from devising normative ideals and organizational configurations, human rights scholars should examine how these rights take shape provisionally and situationally, as well as how social and political actors acquit themselves in putting them into practice. Modes of practice constitute processes of permanent invention and reconfiguration of human rights claims, including the interrogation of laws, institutions, and norms, as well as the identification of previously unknown or unrecognized violations of human rights.

Put strongly, a pragmatist approach asserts that human rights matter to the extent that the social and cultural labor undergirding them has tangible and beneficial effects upon the circumstances of vulnerable groups in the world, either by protecting them from forms of situational and structural violence or, more affirmatively, by contributing to the meeting of their needs and the advancement of their capabilities. Human rights are devices, valuable in that they can be effectively employed to denounce abuses of power and transform relations of domination, as well as to create a more just and equitable world order for all human beings.

For its part, the notion of labor is important to a pragmatist framing of human rights because it stresses the fact that the five cultural practices are not norms whose worth should be determined by their abstract design, but rather patterns of social action implemented under particular circumstances by individual and collective subjects arduously struggling against obstacles and, consequently, often imperfectly or partially performing certain tasks advancing human rights. Additionally, the term "labor" is intended as an alternative to the belief that human rights are simply static principles or objectives to which is attached an endpoint. By contrast, I want to suggest that we analyze the *processual dimensions* of human rights, their being composed of sociocultural dynamics and rituals that are repeated and modified, as well as belief systems that are reaffirmed or reinvented, over time and in different settings. Universal human rights cannot be permanently secured; they can only be advanced by remaining constantly vigilant about instances where they are being transgressed and by acknowledging the prevalence of such instances in the world today: crimes against humanity, genocides, extreme poverty, gender-based violence, pandemics, and so on. The unrelenting existence of these realities means that actors involved in human rights campaigns must continually engage in the labor of bearing witness, forgiveness, foresight, aid, and solidarity, without a horizon of finality in sight.

Treating human rights pragmatically allows us to evaluate whether and how their enactment is assisting vulnerable groups and persons in specific situations, and how it is affecting existing configurations of relations of power in such situations. Thus, as practices, human rights can be located on the terrain of cultural invention and political struggle, without carrying any essentialized attributes or guaranteed outcomes; it is the manner in which social actors employ them that establishes what they do. Increasingly and in various parts of the globe, these social actors are harnessing the symbolic power of human rights (Lefort 1986, pp. 260–262); by positioning their experiences of injustice (or their demands for justice) "under the sign of the defence of human rights" (Lefort 1986, p. 242), they can symbolically invest their struggles with a publicly validated moral grammar. Consequently, once rhetorically invested in this manner, such experiences of injustice become violations of civil–political or socio-economic rights – symbolic categories to which is attached collective moral condemnation and circumstances that cannot be publicly tolerated because they pose an affront to the dignity to which all human beings are entitled. Social actors utilizing this symbolic dimension can gain political traction with states, international organizations, and civil societies, and thereby expand the discursive and cultural space to pursue forms of action concerned with upholding human rights by witnessing, forgiving, preventing, aiding, and generating solidarity.

Conclusion

Although scholarship about human rights remains beholden to a formalist paradigm of analysis, a more pragmatist approach enables us to focus on the regimes of engagement through which actors give these rights meaning in their lives and the repertoires of social action through which they take shape in different contexts. Fundamentally, it is in the work of pursuing specific tasks and trying to overcome difficulties in performing acts of testimony, forgiveness, prevention, assistance, and solidarity that human rights become experiential realities in social life; the cultural substance of rights is produced in and through their being put into practice situationally around the world.

Hence, one of the key questions for human rights research is to gauge in what measure are the forms taken by human rights performances – undertaken under a given set of circumstances, with the constraints and possibilities of actual political struggles – capable of transforming the normative ideals and institutional configurations that have conventionally given birth to the panoply of civil, political, social, and economic rights with which we are now familiar. How can human rights, as they are practiced on the terrain of the everyday filtered through ways of acting and belief systems, be reconciled with the universal moral principles on which their public legitimacy rests? If they are to answer this query, social scientists may not need to wholly abandon formalism, but at the very least take the pragmatist challenge seriously in order to reconsider how they understand the social and cultural existence of human rights in our age.

Acknowledgment

Research and writing of this chapter were made possible by a Standard Research Grant from the Social Sciences and Humanities Research Council of Canada.

References

Archibugi, D. 2008. *The Global Commonwealth of Citizens: Toward Cosmopolitan Democracy* (Princeton, NJ: Princeton University Press).

Balibar, E. 2004. *We, the People of Europe? Reflections on Transnational Citizenship* (Princeton, NJ: Princeton University Press).

Beck, U. 2006. *The Cosmopolitan Vision* (Cambridge: Polity).

Bohman, J. and M. Lutz-Bachmann, eds. 1997. *Perpetual Peace: Essays on Kant's Cosmopolitan Ideal* (Cambridge, MA: MIT Press).

Boltanski, L. and L. Thévenot. 2006. *On Justification: Economies of Worth* (Princeton, NJ: Princeton University Press).

Bourdieu, P. 1990. *The Logic of Practice* (Stanford, CA: Stanford University Press).

Calhoun, C. 2003. "The Class Consciousness of Frequent Travellers: Towards a Critique of Actually Existing Cosmopolitanism," pp. 86–116 in D. Archibugi, ed., *Debating Cosmopolitics* (London: Verso).

De Greiff, P. and C. Cronin, eds. 2002. *Global Justice and Transnational Politics* (Cambridge, MA: MIT Press).

Derrida, J. 2001. *On Cosmopolitanism and Forgiveness* (New York: Routledge).

Falk, R. A. 2000. *Human Rights Horizons: The Pursuit of Justice in a Globalizing World* (London: Routledge).

Fraser, N. 1997. *Justice Interruptus: Critical Reflections on the Postsocialist Condition* (New York: Routledge).

Fraser, N. and A. Honneth. 2003. *Redistribution or Recognition? A Political–Philosophical Exchange* (London: Verso).

Gilroy, P. 2005. *Postcolonial Melancholia* (New York: Columbia University Press).

Habermas, J. 2001. *The Postnational Constellation: Political Essays* (Cambridge, MA: MIT Press).

Held, D. 2004. *Global Covenant: The Social Democratic Alternative to the Washington Consensus* (Cambridge: Polity Press).

Joas, H. 1996. *The Creativity of Action* (Cambridge: Polity Press).

Kendall, G., I. Woodward, and Z. Skrbis. 2009. *The Sociology of Cosmopolitanism: Globalization, Identity, Culture, and Government* (New York: Palgrave Macmillan).

Kurasawa, F. 2007. *The Work of Global Justice: Human Rights as Practices* (Cambridge: Cambridge University Press).

Lefort, C. 1986. *The Political Forms of Modern Society: Bureaucracy, Democracy, Totalitarianism* (Cambridge, MA: MIT Press).
McAdam, D., S. Tarrow, and C. Tilly. 2001. *Dynamics of Contention* (Cambridge: Cambridge University Press).
Pogge, T.W. 2002. *World Poverty and Human Rights: Cosmopolitan Responsibilities and Reforms* (Malden, MA: Blackwell).
Singer, P. 2002. *One World: The Ethics of Globalization* (New Haven, CT: Yale University Press).
Tarrow, S. 2005. *The New Transnational Activism* (New York: Cambridge University Press).
Taylor, C. 1995. "To Follow a Rule," pp. 165–180 in *Philosophical Arguments* (Cambridge, MA: Harvard University Press).
Thévenot, L. 2006. *L'action au Pluriel: Sociologie des Régimes D'engagement* (Paris: La Découverte).
Tilly, C. 2006. *Regimes and Repertoires* (Chicago: University of Chicago Press).
Woodiwiss, A. 2005. *Human Rights* (New York: Routledge).

16

Human rights as status relations

A sociological approach to understanding human rights

Murray Milner, Jr.

Introduction

The development of the notion of human rights and the creation of social institutions to articulate and defend such rights is one of the most striking developments since World War II. An enormous amount has been written about this development, especially in the fields of law, politics, and philosophy. Sociologists have certainly discussed and analyzed human rights from several perspectives, including collective memories (Levy and Sznaider 2006) and new institutionalism (Hafner-Burton and Tsutsui 2005), as a means to address social inequalities (Blau and Moncada 2006), and some have attempted to empirically test the strength and weakness of these various approaches (Cole 2005). According to Turner (2009) the existing literature has not, however, theorized human rights to the same degree that it has notions of citizenship. This chapter will attempt to make a contribution to better theorizing human rights by looking at it through the lens of one particular sociological theory – the theory of status relations. The theory attempts to explain the patterns of behavior that emerge when status is not due solely to economic or political power; why, for example, people behave the way they do in teenage cliques or in the presence of celebrities. The details of the theory will be elaborated below.

The theory has been used to analyze several other phenomena that at first appearance seem far removed from the analysis of human rights. These include the Indian caste system (Milner 1994a), patterns of religious behavior (Milner 1993, 1994b), American teenagers (Milner 2004), celebrities (Milner 2005), and the interaction between relatively universal status processes and particular cultural traditions (Milner, in press). There is no claim that this theoretical approach can adequately explain all or even most of the interesting questions surrounding the development of human rights, but only that it can throw new light on some aspects of this phenomenon.

As a preliminary statement, it can be said that human rights insure that all persons are endowed with a minimum level of social status that protects them against certain kinds of penalties and entitles them to certain kinds of resources. Often a distinction is made between negative or individual rights that protect the individual from oppression (e.g., arbitrary arrest, torture, and religious persecution), and positive or social rights that give the individual some entitlement (e.g., guaranteed employment, educational opportunity, and health insurance). Sometimes distinctions are drawn between civil liberties (e.g., a fair and open trial), civil rights (e.g., protection against discrimination), and social rights (e.g., a minimum income). Although such distinctions can be useful, there is not a clear line between them. Implicit in the notion of minimal rights is that these are ascribed (i.e., they do not have to be earned by the individual), they are inalienable (i.e., they cannot legitimately be taken away from the individual), and they are universal (i.e., all people in all contexts should have these protections and entitlements). There are, of course, extensive disagreements about what protections and entitlements should be considered universal human rights.

Other types of minimal rights

For purposes of sociological analysis it is useful to keep in mind that there are other types of minimal levels of protections and privileges that are tied to the status of individuals and groups. In his poem "The Death of the Hired Man" Robert Frost writes:

> Home is the place where, when you have to go there,
> They have to take you in.
> I should have called it
> Something you somehow haven't to deserve.

In virtually all kinship systems members are entitled to at least minimum levels of assistance. Of course, sometimes such relationships break down, and whether one is considered a member or non-member can change, but these are exceptions and qualifications rather than the absence of such a principle.

Such minimal rights apply at other levels of social organization. In feudal societies freemen had certain minimal rights that were not available to slaves. In work organizations that have union contracts, workers are guaranteed minimum levels of pay, benefits, and job security. Nation-states offer citizens certain minimum rights that non-citizens are not automatically entitled to – starting with the right to live within the borders of the state.

The key analytical point is that human rights are the extension to a particular type of social arrangement that is quite old: the guarantee of some minimum level of protection and entitlement. But this is always contingent upon the individual having some minimum level of status and respect within the relevant social unit. It is also contingent on some third party to legitimate and defend the rights of the less powerful. Before spelling out the implications of the above points, the definition and nature of status needs to be clarified.

What is status?

Within the realm of sociological analysis the word "status" tends to have two related clusters of meaning. One focuses on difference and has such synonyms as position, category, class, "the other," and standing (e.g., legal standing). A key example of this usage is found in role theory. Such scholars as Ralph Linton (1936) and Robert K. Merton (1957) used status to refer to a social position: tinker, tailor, soldier, sailor ... doctor, lawyer, and Indian chief. The other cluster of meaning focuses more on rank and gradations and includes such synonyms as prestige, grade, rank, and level. This emphasis is associated with such notions as honor, esteem, disgrace, and degradation. Max Weber's well-known discussion of status groups (1978) and numerous kinds of prestige scales (Warner 1963; Blau and Duncan 1967; Marmot 2004) are examples of this emphasis. Of course there is not a hard-and-fast line between these two meanings, and often the word "status" simultaneously implies both meanings; for example military ranks refer to both a gradational hierarchy and to distinctive social positions that generally have different job responsibilities. The theory of status relations focuses primarily on the second meaning of status, though I will talk about how the gradational type of status is transformed into a more bounded social category.

Status in the gradational sense can be considered the accumulated expressions of approval and disapproval toward an actor, a group, or a cultural object (e.g., a picture, a piece of music, a religious doctrine, a law, a collective memory, etc.). Obviously, there can be disagreements between those expressing such opinions, but often there is a dominant consensus: doctors usually have a higher occupational status than garbage collectors; most people hold Rembrandt paintings in greater esteem than the art produced by amateurs.

Legitimacy as status: the role of third parties

The very notion of rights implies conflict or disagreement. If there is no contention there is no need to declare something a right. When there is conflict the parties can either fight it out themselves or they can appeal to third parties for support. This can take the form of seeking allies to continue and hopefully win the conflict. It can also take the form of asking a third party to serve as a mediator or arbitrator. In simple societies this role is often exercised by a group of elders or chieftains. An antagonist may or may not accept the legitimacy of the arbitrator's decision, but the crucial issue is whether most other third parties do. That is, do those who make up the social context of the antagonists think that the arbitrator's decision is more or less just? The antagonist who goes against such third-party judgments becomes the illegitimate deviant, the outsider, the criminal.

More generally for norms to be enforced effectively the role of third parties is crucial. The number of the third parties involved can vary considerably. For the tyrant the crucial third parties are his henchman; as long as they obey him and are strong enough to enforce his commands, his power is effective – even if he is hated and considered a despot. The ruler's position is much stronger, however, if the promulgation and enforcement of laws is seen as legitimate. Instead of arbitrary orders, he issues laws and commands generally considered to be reasonable. Instead of brutal henchmen, he needs a police force that is at least to a minimal degree even-handed and effective enforcing rules and laws.

But what is legitimacy? In large measure it means that a particular social pattern is widely approved of by those whom it affects. Widely expressed approval is the definition of high status. So stated in other terms, a rule or an order is legitimate if it has relatively high status. This does not mean that everyone necessarily abides by the rules or orders they consider legitimate. Most drivers have broken the speed limit; this does not mean they think there should be no speed limits – at least on the streets in front of their children's school or their home. In sum, the more third parties who approve an order, rule, or law, the more legitimate it is and the more likely it is to be effectively enforced.

The legitimacy of human rights – expanding the network of third parties

Another way to think about the problem of human rights is to ask how the relevant norms can be made more legitimate. That is, how can we raise the status of the norms that protect human rights and expand the network of third parties that will express disapproval of anyone who violates such norms? The focus here is not on changing the status of the relevant actors, but on changing the status of the relevant norms. To give an example of this difference, it is clear that the status of several of the Ten Commandments has declined. "You shall not make wrongful use of the name of your God" and "Remember the Sabbath and keep it holy" are routinely ignored by the majority of people in Western societies. This has occurred without a decline in the status of humans, and perhaps without a decline in the status of God. Rather, few people express approval of such norms and even fewer are willing to sanction others who violate them. On the other hand, more and more people condemn human rights violations. Even countries that routinely violate human rights try to keep such behaviors secret. No contemporary nation tortures people in public, though lynch mobs sometimes commit such atrocities with the collusion of officials, and a few regimes have publicly used brutal forms of punishment such as floggings and cutting off of limbs (Fathi 2008).

Sacredness as status

Just as it can be useful to see legitimacy as a form of status, it is useful to consider sacredness as a form of status – in some respects the ultimate form of status. Here the focus tends to be more on actors and objects rather than the norms, though these are usually correlated. One of the things that happen when beings, groups, or objects gain a very high status is that they take on an aura; they are held in awe; they may become "idols." This is true of all kinds of celebrities including movie stars, rock singers, popular politicians, and Nobel Prize winners. Often people want to see or be with them, but, at the same time, they fear being rejected or dismissed. The celebrity may take on an air of otherness and even holiness. Stated in other terms, social and cultural boundaries tend to emerge around very high status entities, and they develop a kind of sacredness; they are not just celebrities and "idols," but "gods." In the terms used above, status shifts from a gradational notion to a categorical notion; from variations in degree to a distinction between the sacred and the profane. Accordingly, great deference should be shown when approaching that which is sacred. Raucous, crude, and mundane behavior is considered inappropriate. Respectful attitudes and behavior are expected in most forms of religious worship. Even when forms of religious behavior involve expressions of emotion and enthusiasm, these are deferential toward the sacred deity. Parallel behaviors are used when approaching people of very high status, whether they are presidents, popes, or prima donnas. We see a similar pattern in museum exhibits: famous pictures are protected by guards and should never be touched; boisterous behavior can result in you being asked to leave. The same is true when visiting cemeteries and war memorials. Stated in other terms unwanted intrusion and intimacy are *verboten* and at least minimum levels of respect and decorum are expected. As with the case of legitimacy, sacredness is most significant when it involves networks of third parties. This is the reason that Durkheim (1995, pp. 41–43) emphasized the importance of there being a "church," i.e., a community of devotees who reinforce one another's expressions of approval and disapproval.

Human rights and sacredness

One thread running through much of human rights discourse is that all humans have a special kind of sacredness, and hence they have certain rights that should not be violated. A key motivation for attributing sacredness to humans is to give them a status that is rooted in something more than either the rules or whims of the political regime to which they are subject or the opinions of their immediate peers. The intent is to give them a minimum level of status that no one has the right to violate. Stated in other terms, human rights are supposedly rooted in something "higher than" the positive law of the immediate historical context or the opinions of neighbors. According to Hans Joas (2008) neither Beccaria's classic Enlightenment account, which sees the reform of prisons and the abolition of torture as a way of making punishment more rational and humane, nor Foucault's account, which sees these changes as due to the creation of more effective and insidious forms of social discipline, are adequate ways of understanding the emergence of human rights. Rather the abolition of torture and the development of human rights are seen to be, following Emile Durkheim's ideas, the result of the greater sacralization of humans.

The arguments used to justify the sacralization of humans vary considerably. The traditional religious argument is that humans are children of God created in her/his own image. Accordingly, all human beings, who are "little lower than the angels" (Psalm 8:6), should be honored by one another. This places limits on what people can legitimately do to one another. Michael J. Perry (1998) has argued that there is no meaningful notion of sacredness that is not derived from some kind of religious commitment. Others argue that there are adequate non-religious foundations for human rights. Ronald Dworkin (1994) observes that humans are self-creating and claims that this is a sufficient reason for them to be considered sacred. Ari Kohen (2006) suggests that a notion of the sacredness of human beings is not required, but that human rights can be rooted in a notion of human dignity. Bryan Turner (2001) argues that a basis for of human rights is the universality of the human body's frailty and vulnerability; all humans experience pain, illness, and death. Milner (2001), however, has argued that this is an inadequate foundation for human rights; the vulnerability of the body is recognized by all human societies. Since frailty is a constant, it cannot explain or provide a sufficient foundation for human rights, which are present in some societies and historical periods and not in others. My concern here is not to enter into the debate about the degree to which notions of sacredness are necessarily religious, but rather to point out that many advocates of human rights recognize the importance of having a foundation for human rights that is seen as more transcendent than the immediate social consensus. If the sacredness of human beings is an important foundation for human rights, then how do we make humans more sacred; in the terms of the theory of status relations how do we raise the status of all human beings?

In summary, social status, legitimacy, and sacredness are all essentially the same phenomenon: the accumulated expressions of approval (and/or disapproval), especially of networks of third parties. They all involve humans engaging in evaluative judgments and expressing these. The ways social status, legitimacy, and sacredness vary is in the intensity of the expressions of approval (and disapproval) and in the nature of the actor or object being evaluated.

If systems of status, legitimacy, and sacredness are in many respects the same phenomena, and if the establishment of human rights involves creating a social context in which elements of all of these are melded together, then a theory about how such systems operate should throw some light on the issues surrounding human rights. Hence, the next step is to outline the theory of status relations.

A strategy for explanation: the theory of status relations

The theory attempts to explain and understand the key features of social relationships when status is a central resource and is significantly insulated from, and hence not reducible to, economic and political power. This conditional assumption is important both analytically and substantively. If status is solely determined by how much money or political power you have, then no theory of status relations is needed; a theory explaining the sources of wealth or political power will explain who has status. Substantively the assumption is important because unless status is in some respects independent of wealth and political power, the poor and the powerless will have no status, and hence will be subject to the abuse of those who have wealth and political clout. One way to think of the expansion of human rights is to say that it involves insulating certain types of status from wealth and politics. In nearly all societies there are forms of status that are independent of wealth and politics, hence a theory of status relations should be of use in understanding some aspects of human rights.

The theory has four parts or elements and an addendum concerning pluralism. The first two elements focus on how status is different from other kinds of resources with respect to its inalienability and inexpansibility. The other two elements identify the sources of status as conformity to the group's norms and social associations (i.e., who and what one associates with). We will take up each of these elements in order, first dealing with how each affects status systems in general and then considering the implications for human rights.

Inalienability

Status is relatively inalienable. It is "located" primarily in other people's minds. Hence, in contrast to wealth or political position it cannot be simply appropriated. Robbers can take your property and usurpers may remove you from office. To change your status, however, they have to change the opinions of other people. This relative inalienability makes status a desirable resource. Those with new wealth or political power nearly always attempt to convert some of these into status to gain greater security and legitimacy. Conversely, even when people lose their political or economic standing, they often retain much of their status. Ex-governors and the not-so-rich children of old-money families retain some of their ancestor's status. Respected officials who are executed during a coup often come to be seen as heroic martyrs. Consequently, once status systems become institutionalized rankings are relatively stable. In the traditional Indian caste system individuals could not change their caste; American teenagers repeatedly report the difficulty of changing their status once it is established; those with a criminal record find it difficult to regain respect and employment. The ranking of social categories is also relatively stable; judges are not at the top of the occupational hierarchy one year only to be replaced by fireman or beauticians the next year.

Inalienable human rights

One of the reasons that it is useful and important to consider humans rights as a status relationship is because a well-established status is relatively inalienable; it is located in the minds of numerous third parties. The more that status is separated from economic and political power, the more status is inalienable; the war hero who has little money or political power is still a war hero; the admired religious or political leader who is imprisoned by a repressive regime often gains in status – and, at least in the modern period, is less likely to be tortured or executed than his unknown lieutenants. Some examples are Sheikh Mujibur Rahman of Bangladesh during their war for independence, Aung San Suu Kyi of Burma, Manuel Zelaya of Honduras, and Alexander Dubček of Czechoslovakia. This was also the case for the leaders of the Iranian opposition to the regime of Mahmoud Ahmadinejad in 2009; prominent figures such as Mir Hussein Moussavi, Mehdi Karroubi, and Mohammad Khatami were not arrested, but many of their assistants and followers were beaten, jailed, executed, and persecuted in various ways.

Status can be associated with ascribed social traits. For example, in Islam descendents of the Prophet (Sayyids, Syeds, Sharifs, etc.) receive a kind deference that other Muslims do not; the same tends to be true for Brahmins in Hinduism, as well as the descendents of Thomas Jefferson, the Rockefellers, the Kennedys, etc. This tends to be true even if these individuals have little wealth or political influence. Basic levels of status are not restricted to those from illustrious backgrounds. Respect and deference given old people is one example; "women and children first" is another; ascetics and mendicants are a third case. This is not to say that it is easy to institutionalize minimum levels of status for those without wealth or power, but there are a number of historical precedents.

The ascription of minimum levels of status was a characteristic of the two most famous modern revolutions. Following the French Revolution everyone was to be addressed as "citizen," and following the Russian Revolution "comrade" became the appropriate honorific form of address. People were "citizens" and "comrades" without regard for their wealth and political power. As Lynn Hunt notes in his historical account of the emergence of human rights following the French Revolution, "The convict was now a citizen, not a subject; therefore he or she … could not be made to endure torture, unnecessary cruel punishment, or excessively dishonoring penalties" (Hunt 2007, p. 141). Of course, in fact new forms of inequality quickly emerged and many "citizens" and "comrades" were persecuted. This was usually after being stripped of these forms of address and relabeled "counter revolutionaries," or "enemies of the people." In theoretical terms two points are relevant. First, their status had to be redefined to justify abusive treatment. Second, these status systems had not become sufficiently institutionalized and hence statuses were not yet inalienable. In contrast, in most modern nations individuals cannot be stripped of their citizenship, except in highly exceptional circumstances. Robbers, murders, rapists, and child molesters are still citizens and due the minimum rights held by all citizens, such as due process of law and immunity from torture and "cruel and unusual punishment." The aim of the human rights movement is to provide all people everywhere with a similar inalienable status that is seen as legitimate in the eyes of most other people, the governments of most nations, and the emerging international enforcement organizations, such as the International Criminal Court (ICC), International Criminal Tribunal for the former Yugoslavia (ICTY), International Criminal Tribunal for Rwanda (ICTR), and the Special Court for Sierra Leone.

Redeeming reification

As already noted, many think that such rights need to be defined not only as legitimate, but should be given the highest form of status, that is, become sacred and inviolate. One way to think about the sacralization of humans, and hence their right to certain basic protections and entitlements, is by means of the concept of reification. The dictionary definition of reification is, "The making of something abstract into something more concrete or real; the action of regarding or treating an idea, concept, etc., as if having material existence" (online *Oxford English Dictionary*, 2 August 2010). Generally the notion has had negative connotations suggesting "misplaced concreteness." Probably the best-known use of the concept comes out of Marx's discussions of alienation. Feuerbach, Marx, and others thought that treating gods as real, concrete actors with whom humans can interact is an illusory reification. The term was elaborately discussed by Georg Lukács in his essay, "Reification and the Consciousness of the Proletariat" (Lukács 1971). To simplify, what Lukács critiques is the ubiquity of the concept of commodity, which is taken to be an independent, real thing rather than a set of underlying social relationships. Supposedly, this false consciousness prevents the proletariat from seeing how they are being exploited and mobilizing to rectify this. Berger and Luckmann use the notion of objectivation to refer to "the products of human activity that are available both to their producers and to other men as elements of a common world" (1966, p. 34). According to them reification is when people "forget" that something they have produced is a human creation and attribute it to nature, the gods, or whatever (1966, p. 89).

I want to suggest that humans frequently engage in reifications to simplify their social lives; otherwise they would be overwhelmed with complexity. Some of these simplifications are certainly mystifications that disguise exploitation. It does not follow, however, that all forms of reification are socially harmful. Human rights are such a case. It is not difficult to deconstruct the notion and show that such ideals as natural rights and human rights were created by humans in particular historical contexts. A detailed knowledge of such a history is not only unnecessary for it to be a useful notion, but is probably detrimental to its effectiveness. Most people find it easier to become emotionally attached to a concrete entity than to an abstraction, to "my mother" rather than motherhood, to "our native soil" rather than nationhood, to Jesus, Krishna, or Allah rather than to divinity, to "our sacred rights" rather than the history of the human creation of rights. None of this is to deny the legitimacy of critique and deconstruction, nor is it a plea for ignorance. It is to suggest, however, that to "get through the day" most of us most of the time have to simplify the reality around us and that this often involves various forms of useful reification.

A caveat is required. I use the term "redeeming" because it implies both the recovery of something, but also that this rescue has a cost attached. Something has to be sacrificed for something else to be redeemed. Certainly, attempting to redeem the notion of reification creates dangers, risks, and costs, but I would argue that the failure to do so is both more costly and less honest.

In sum, political, economic, and legal safeguards are not enough; certain forms of status relations are also required. If poor people and political dissidents receive at least minimum levels of inalienable respect, this is much more likely to happen if aspects of their status are sacralized and reified. This is not to deny that those with political or economic power may be able to unjustly persecute people, but they cannot do so without risking the disapproval of numerous third parties.

Inexpansibility

Status is relatively inexpansible. Some societies have a per capita income that is a hundred times greater than other societies. In contrast, status is basically a relative ranking. If a thousand Nobel Prizes were awarded each year, they would be much less prestigious. Inexpansibility means that when someone moves up, someone moves down. Consequently, where status is the central resource, mobility tends to be highly regulated and restricted, as in the Indian caste system, the Jim Crow South, the Social Register, the National Academies of Science, and teenage cliques. Conversely, one way of staying on top or moving up is by pushing others down. This is apparent in the putdowns and gossip of teenagers, racism, negative campaigning, and intellectual critique.

Inexpansibility and human rights

What are some of the implications of the inexpansibility of status for human rights? If all are to have a minimum level of respect, this is more likely to occur when there are limits to how exalted and entrenched the ruler or elite can be. It is not accidental that the emergence of the rights of citizenship was accompanied not only by the abolition of torture, but by a decline in the significance of honor as a special characteristic of elites and by reductions in the public humiliation of criminals (Hunt 2007, pp. 142–143). Inexpansibility is also one of the reasons that well-established democracies, which limit the power of elites, have better records with respect to individual rights – though not necessarily social and economic rights. An absence of kings (much less god-kings), aristocrats, presidents-for-life, and one-party political systems means that there is less social distance between elites and non-elites. Moreover, if there is forced downward mobility of elites by such means as regular elections, term limits, progressive income and inheritance taxes, and mandatory retirement, then non-elites are likely to receive more respect.

One of the implications of these observations is that human rights are likely to be most secure when there are limits on most, if not all, forms of inequality. The classic pattern in liberal capitalist regimes is that individual or negative rights are in principle usually secure, but are in fact frequently compromised because of the lack of economic resources to defend the rights of the poor – in contrast to the substantial resources that are available to the rich to defend their rights. The classic pattern in communist societies is that minimum social or positive rights are relatively secure, but the highly unequal distribution of political power means that individual rights are frequently attenuated and violated.

A second important factor is the relative status of individuals versus collectivities. For example, in most military organizations the value and success of the collectivity is paramount; the success of the unit against enemy units is the primary value; the injury and death of some individuals is expected. This is in contrast to most voluntary organizations; if individual interests are regularly and openly sacrificed to those of the collectivity, membership usually declines rapidly. In very collectivist societies such as Sparta, Nazi Germany, Fascist Italy, Stalin's USSR, Mao's China, and Communist North Korea, individual rights are usually limited. The same is true of smaller kinds of collectivities such as warrior clans, kibbutzim, and communitarian religious sects. Where kinship and clan groups are especially strong, honor killings (e.g., the killing of women who have been seduced or raped) are not uncommon; the honor of the group is seen as more important than the rights of the individual. On the other hand, in societies that are highly individualistic, social and economic rights are usually weak. Of course, it is hard to separate the effects of collectivism from authoritarianism since many collectivist social units are also authoritarian, but it seems likely that each of these factors has an independent effect.

This is not to argue that high levels of individualism are necessarily good or bad, but to point out that individual human rights are more likely to be respected if the status of individuals and collectivities are relatively balanced. Of course, the relatively higher status of individuals and the demotion of collectivities occurred as a historical process. People developed a new sense of both the autonomy of the self and new forms of empathy with others and new ways of building solidarity (see Hunt 2007, pp. 26–34). This process could be reversed, especially if people perceive that the status and value of collective life need to be reinvigorated. This is one of the themes of communitarian thought. A crucial issue facing contemporary societies is how to best balance the status of individuals and collectivities – when status is an inherently limited and relatively inexpansible resource.

A third implication has to do with the status of third parties. The lower the status of third parties, the less effective are their expressions of disapproval in limiting governments or other powerful parties, such as vigilantes. At the institutional level a crucial third party is an independent judiciary that is not simply the tool of the executive or legislative branches. If the judiciary is structurally independent and has the respect of the general populace, it can be effective in limiting the violation of human rights. Analytically this is a matter of each branch of government having substantial levels of status, which make their authority effective in placing limits on the power of the other branches. On a broader level it can involve other institutional forms. Despotic kings were often kept in check by religious institutions that had an independent status. In contemporary societies there is often an emphasis on the importance of the civil society, that is, an array of voluntary organizations that are not primarily economic or political. The more developed and the higher the status of this sector, the more likely they are to serve as an effective third party in the protection of human rights.

At the individual level, the most important third party is a substantial middle class. This means that there are large numbers of people of at least moderate status who have the education and the means to resist violations of people's basic rights.

The key point is that because status is inherently limited, how it is distributed among institutions and individuals is likely to have a significant impact on whether there are meaningful human rights. Distributive justice and human rights are often closely linked.

Conformity

Conformity to the norms of the group is a key source of status within that group. This is an obvious point, but the consequences are somewhat less obvious: those with a valued status tend to elaborate and complicate the group's norms and rituals in order to make it easy to distinguish insiders and outsiders. Accent, demeanor, body language, and notions of taste and style are hard for outsiders to copy. Such elaboration is not limited to those with high status. Sometimes those with power elaborate the stigmas attached to those of low status; examples include branding slaves, making Jews wear a Star of David, forbidding Dalits to enter temples, and forcing women to cover their faces. Low-status groups may create their own insider norms, symbols, and rituals. This can result in counter or alternative subcultures. If there is little hope of conforming to the norms of upper strata, lowers create norms they can conform to. Sometimes these reverse old values and norms: "black is beautiful"; "blessed are the meek and poor"; "green is good." Lowers may create norms and rituals to hide behaviors that uppers see as deviant. Argots are often created to prevent superiors from understanding conversations.

Conformity and human rights

One of the key points of institutionalizing human rights is to give people an ascribed status that limits what can be done to them, even when they do not conform to laws and conventions. In the case of nation-states the ascribed status is citizenship; for those urging the international community to recognize and enforce human rights the relevant ascribed status is simply being a human. If punishments were supposed to fit the crime, some horrific crimes would seem to deserve the most gruesome of punishments. The logic of human rights denies this and notes that the only conformity required is that one be a member of the human species. All this is rather obvious.

What may be somewhat less obvious is that a key means of insuring such an ascribed status is the elaboration of the norms that are required to curtail such rights. This is the reverse of elites elaborating norms to exclude those of lower status; this is a matter of elaborating norms that exclude those with power from exercising it arbitrarily. Most commonly this involves elaborating the procedural rules of the due process of law. Such procedural due process laws require that a person charged with a crime or violation is entitled to be notified of such a charge and given sufficient time and resources to defend him or herself, that they be entitled to a hearing on such charges, and that the merits of the charges be decided by a neutral judge who has authority and privileges that are not dependent upon those who bring the charges. This is not to say that all procedural elaborations work to the benefit of the average person – for often they increase the cost of litigation. Elaboration is not limited to legal processes. As noted earlier, changes in modes of address were an important feature in the French and Russian revolutions. We see similar elaborations with respect to gender and racial inequality; women are addressed as Ms., not Mrs.; calling African-Americans "nigger" or "boy" is not just unacceptable, but highly deviant. These changes are not usually legal, but they do safeguard the levels of status and respect everyday people receive, which in turn tends to protect their human rights.

These are examples of rules and rituals being elaborated to protect the core rights and values and secure the status of members of the group. In this case, however, it is used to protect the dignity of all rather than the status and prestige of an elite or subgroup. Rules of procedural due process and forms of address are secondary norms and rituals that are used to insure and protect more primary norms and values. What is occurring in the contemporary globalized world is a long series of negotiations between nation-states about what the appropriate procedural rules are and who is empowered to enforce them. At the same time, a more informal process is elaborating rituals and norms of personal respect between those of different cultures. Both are crucial to the extension of human rights.

Another form of elaboration that occurs is the expansion of the content of human rights. In his classic discussion of citizenship T. H. Marshall (1950) argues that in Britain civil rights were first established, then political rights, and finally social rights. In formerly Communist societies the process seems to be occurring in a different order; the establishment of social rights came first; the establishment of political democracies came next; the elaboration and specification of civil rights is still underway. Of course, this pattern is by no means exactly the same in all these countries. Moreover, many of the social rights of earlier regimes are being eroded as individual rights are expanded.

The key theoretical point is that in most status systems the norms and rituals tend to be gradually elaborated to both expand and protect fundamental concerns. Just as traditional status groups elaborate norms to reduce competition and intrusion from outsiders, human rights tend to be elaborated to thicken the boundaries around such rights. Those without political rights are less likely to be able to protect their civil and social rights. Those without minimal levels of economic security are unlikely to be able to participate in politics to protect their civil liberties. Those without civil liberties are more economically and politically vulnerable.

Associations

If you associate with those of higher status, it improves your status, and if you associate with those of lower status, it decreases your status. This is especially so if the relationship is expressive and intimate rather than instrumental and impersonal. Intimate, expressive relationships that are consensual imply mutual approval. Sex and eating are the classic symbols of intimacy. Traditionally most Hindus would not marry or eat with those who were from a lower-status caste. American teenagers tend to be very concerned about who is going with whom, and who eats with whom in the lunchroom. But, as the theory would suggest, upper castes can supervise lower castes in the field, and students are much more relaxed about whom they associate with in the classroom because these activities involve instrumental activity. Outside the classroom, however, the same people who were friendly in class may ignore one another. When associations are non-consensual and unwanted they are more demeaning when they are intimate. Working with a colleague you do not like, but who is very good at her job, is much less demeaning than having to work with an incompetent colleague who sexually harasses you. In other words intimacy intensifies the effect of associations on status for both wanted and unwanted associations.

Associations and human rights

Since associations are one source of status, the more closely someone is associated with you, the more likely they will be treated as you are treated – both by yourself and others. Conversely, the less other people are thought of as associates, the more likely different norms are applied to them. In most societies at least some animals can be slaughtered for food; they are other than humans. When animals are kept primarily for expressive rather than instrumental reasons, they are pets, and much less likely to be considered appropriate food or abused in other ways.

Humans are most likely to mistreat and abuse others when they are seen as different, unlike, and dissimilar. This is especially the case where the other is thought to be associated with lesser status beings; where they are seen as "animals," "brutes," "hordes," "savages," "apes," that is, as less than fully human. This is one of the reasons that racism and ethnicity are so often a source of atrocities. Conversely, where the other is associated with a high status being (or beings) this improves their status. If all people are "children of God," they are our brothers and sisters. If, however, they are associated with the "wrong" god, they are not only "other" – heathens, infidels, kaffirs, gentiles, idolaters – but they also lower our status by dishonoring the "true" god who is a source of our status. So deities can be a great source of the solidarity needed for human rights and the fanaticism that violates such rights.

The nature of associations has been changing. Hunt (2007) argues that literacy and novels played an important role in both increasing the respect for the individual and in encouraging empathy with people one did not know personally. In more recent years many new forms of media have expanded people's associations beyond face-to-face interactions. People are much more familiar with others who are geographically distant from them. Movies, TV, phones, e-mail, and the World Wide Web have expanded exponentially. Often these include pictures of starving children or innocent civilians who have been killed or persecuted. In addition to the media, business and tourist travel have increased dramatically. Whereas pseudoscience was used to justify social differences, contemporary science has made clear that there are only minor biological differences in peoples of different races and ethnicities. None of this is to suggest that humans are one big happy family, but people from distant places in the world are no longer the strange barbarians and savages that they once were. All of this produces an important increase in social associations. This, in turn, has contributed to the tendency toward equalization of the status of people around the world. It is, of course, a set of limited and fragile associations, but it is nonetheless one of the bases of the human rights movement.

Another phenomenon the theory helps to understand is why nearly all nation-states, however much they might disagree on other matters, have officially rejected the legitimacy of torture – no matter how brutally they may in fact treat prisoners. Why is there such universal assent to this particular human right? Of course, it is in part because all humans have experienced pain and have the capacity to empathize with others. Humans' fear of pain is not a sufficient explanation, however, because there are situations in which pain is seen to be in the interest of the party undergoing it. This ranges from undergoing painful medical procedures to the "no pain, no gain" mantra of dedicated athletes. The near universal condemnation of torture is because it involves forced, unwanted, and deliberately prolonged intimacy. Shooting a non-combatant in the head is reprehensible, but it is not prolonged. Torture not only prolongs pain, but it deliberately demeans and humiliates. So although harsh regimes may shoot and beat people in public, in the modern context torture is always hidden. When torture is visible, the perpetrator, not the victim, is dishonored. In 2004 when reports and pictures made public the abuse and torture of Iraqi prisoners at the Abu Ghraib US military prison, the reaction was very negative; eleven soldiers were dishonorably discharged, two were sent to prison, the commanding officer was demoted, and American prestige around the world plummeted. Another quite different implication of associations is that status groups develop among nation-states, differentiating those who respect human rights and those who do not. Three cases illustrate this point. The first is the United Nations Commission on Human Rights and its successor the United Nations Human Rights Council. The former was frequently criticized because so many member states of the Commission had poor human rights records themselves. Eventually the Commission was dissolved and the new UN Council on Human Rights was created – supposedly made of representatives from nations truly committed to human rights. Several states, however, including the USA, initially refused to participate because they did not believe the criteria were rigorous enough in excluding human rights violators. In theoretical terms the issue that has been playing out is what nations should be allowed to join and participate in this particular status group. How high should your status as a human rights defender have to be to become a legitimate member of this status group? What norms does this elite status group affirm and attempt to enforce? To the degree that nations who violate human rights are admitted to the new Commission, both the status of the Commission itself and of the other member states will be degraded. A second case is Turkey's attempt to join the European Union. Many complicated issues are being negotiated, but some of the most visible matters have to do with Turkey's continuing denial of the Armenian genocide during World War I, the issue of Cyprus, the conflict with and treatment of Kurd separatists, the treatment of women, and more generally, respect for human rights. The point I am raising is not who is correct about the actual facts surrounding these issues, but that one of the key impediments to Turkey's admission is its status with respect to human rights broadly conceived. A third case is the considerable loss of prestige that the United States faced during the George W. Bush administration when it became known that as a matter of policy it engaged in waterboarding and other "enhanced interrogation techniques" that most people would define as torture. The US status was damaged even more when it became public that the administration had attempted to articulate a legal justification for their behavior. The key point is that within the community of nation-states status systems and status groups emerge. One important status system, and the groupings that occur from this, is based upon adherence to the norms of human rights. Nations vary in how concerned they are about their human rights reputation, but virtually none of them are completely indifferent to their standing in this status system.

Status systems and pluralism

There is a tendency for status systems to become pluralistic as they become larger. For example, when a professional association has a few hundred members it is relatively easy to have articles accepted by the association's premier journal. A high proportion of well-respected members will become association officers. When the same association expands to thousands, only a small percentage of the members can publish articles in the main journal, and an even smaller percentage can become association officers. Usually this leads to the development of subdisciplines with their own journals, officers, and status systems. The same tendencies occur in other status systems. As high schools grow in size, fewer and fewer students have any hope of becoming part of the "popular crowd" or even having any association with them. They are less inclined to copy their "superiors" in order to be accepted by them. Instead the excluded create alternative subcultures: brains, jocks, rappers, punks, skaters, etc. – each with their own norms, rituals, and symbols. The tendencies toward pluralism are further accentuated when the increase in the size of a group is accompanied by a greater diversity of cultural backgrounds. In high schools this often involves ethnic or class diversity. For a professional association greater methodological, theoretical, and political diversity has a similar effect. In sum, increases in size and cultural diversity tend to lead to more pluralistic status systems.

Pluralism and universalism

One way of conceiving of universal human rights is to think of it as the expansion of the network of third parties who see human rights norms as legitimate to the point of being sacred, that is, as having an extremely high status. The broader this legitimacy/sacredness/status network, the more universal the norms. But there is a paradox or dilemma associated with increasing universalism. The larger the status system and the more diverse the social and cultural backgrounds of the members, the more likely pluralism will emerge. That is, alternative and counter subcultures tend to develop. This was apparent in the debates between Communist and capitalist liberal democracies during the Cold War. Communist regimes pointed to their relatively egalitarian distribution of economic resources and their nearly universal access to health care and education. Liberal regimes emphasized freedom of speech, press, and due process of law, but did not always provide guaranteed levels of economic security. Such pluralism can also be seen in the debates in the 1990s over whether there is a distinctive set of "Asian Values," which supposedly draw on Confucian notions of hard work and loyalty to the family and the nation and which place less of an emphasis on personal freedom. Such values were especially advocated by the relatively authoritarian regimes in Southeast Asia. As the theory would predict, such regimes rated rather poorly with respect to traditional Western notions of human rights, but they were doing quite well economically. Their advocates attributed this to the lack of political conflict and the well-disciplined workforce, which in turn was seen as one of the benefits of their relatively authoritarian political system. That is, they emphasized norms and values that made them look relatively good. Other examples include the United States' refusal to join the International Court of Criminal Justice and the Bush administration's attempt to redefine torture as "enhanced interrogation techniques," so that they would not technically be violating human rights. The advocates of Asian Values, the leaders of Communist regimes, and the officials of liberal democracies, including the USA, all affirmed the notion of human rights. Failing to do so would have eroded their status and legitimacy as a modern nation-state. In this sense they were all part of an increasingly expanded status system. But as the scope of this network expanded in size and included societies of diverse cultural and political backgrounds, alternative definitions and measures of human rights emerged.

In part, some of this was simply cynical, deceptive propaganda used to justify brutality and self-interest. The matter is, however, more complicated than this. There were and are some genuine disagreements about what is important and legitimate. The person who is being subjected to torture is not primarily distressed because he is being made to miss lunch; he has a more immediate concern. But the person whose children have to miss meals may care about this much more than freedom of the press – or that someone she does not know is being tortured. The person who has a reasonable level of food security may be more concerned that his children have access to schools and hospitals than with the finer points of due process of law. All of this is to say that people in different situations do vary in what they see as their most urgent needs and rights. Hence, the precise content and emphasis they will give to human rights is likely to vary according to their historical and cultural context. Even those who share the same cultural background and socio-economic conditions may disagree about priorities. This is especially so when some are more willing or able to conform to the proposed norms than others. Stated another way, in status systems there is a built-in dialectic that tends to create alternative and counter subcultures. To recognize the structural sources of pluralism is not to dismiss the notion that there are some universal values. Much less is it to defend brutality and cruelty. It is to point out that the scope of the moral and political consensus may be rather limited.

Drawing on imagery that has been used in philosophical discourse in recent years, the moral, political, and metaphysical consensus may be "thin" rather than "thick" (Walzer 1994). At the same time it is likely that because of increased economic integration and cultural interchange, moral commonalities are increasing, that is, the global culture is thickening. The Helsinki Accords of 1975, the Kyoto Protocol of 1997, and the Copenhagen Climate Change Conference of 2009 are examples of expanding status systems – few nations wanted to be left out, and "thin" agreements about what constituted good and bad global citizenship emerged. The very process of expanding these systems, however, produced pressures for more pluralistic criteria of good and bad. This was so whether it had to do with the inviolability of political boundaries, the content of minimum civil liberties, the extent of global warming, or how to measure levels of pollution.

None of this means that the consensus cannot be thickened. Nor does is deny that many actors in varying degrees engage in the Machiavellian pursuit of self-interest. It does suggest, however, that beyond the cultural relativism rooted in different histories and traditions, the very process of expanding the scope of a value system produces structural sources of disagreement; reaching working agreements is seldom aided by ignoring this.

There are two implications of this for how we should proceed to deal with violations of human rights. On the one hand, it is probably useful to criminally prosecute the most egregious cases of human rights violations. This may give others pause about engaging in such activities as ethnic cleansing, genocide, and torture. Probably more important, it reaffirms human rights norms themselves and the international community's commitment to these norms. According to Emile Durkheim (1984, esp. chap. 2), it restores the collective conscience (i.e., the collective consensus and solidarity needed to enforce violations of the consensus). Another way of stating Durkheim's argument is that it reaffirms the low status of those who violate the norms of human rights. The second implication is that procedures that focus only on rigorously drawing the lines between conforming and deviant individuals, groups, societies, cultures, and governments are less likely to be successful in the long run; in virtually all status systems significant levels of inequality and segregation of those who conform and those who deviate produce multiple and often hostile subcultures. Instead, for many if not most cases of violations such mechanisms as truth commissions and efforts at healing will be more effective in the long run (see Cobban 2007 for examples of each approach). In sum, the theory suggests that both justice and reconciliations are needed – and that such a twofold approach will enhance the status and sacredness of international human rights norms.

References

Berger, P. L. and T. Luckmann. 1966. *The Social Construction of Reality* (Garden City, NY: Anchor Books).

Blau, J. and A. Moncada. 2006. *Justice in the United States: Human Rights and the U.S. Constitution* (Lanham, MD: Rowman & Littlefield).

Blau, P. M. and O. D. Duncan. 1967. *The American Occupational Structure* (New York: Wiley).

Cobban, H. 2007. *Amnesty after Atrocity: Healing Nations after Genocide and War Crimes* (Boulder, CO: Paradigm).

Cole, W. M. 2005. "Sovereignty Relinquished? Explaining Commitment to the International Human Rights Covenants, 1966–1999." *American Sociological Review*, Vol. 70, pp. 472–495.

Durkheim, E. 1984. *The Division of Labor in Society*. Trans. W. D. Halls (New York: The Free Press).

Durkheim, E. 1995. *The Elementary Forms of Religious Life*. Trans. K. E. Fields (New York: The Free Press).

Dworkin, R. 1994. *Life's Dominion: An Argument about Abortion, Euthanasia, and Individual Freedom* (New York: Vintage Books).

Fathi, N. 2008. "Spate of Executions and Amputations in Iran." *New York Times*, January 11.

Hafner-Burton, E. M. and K. Tsutsui. 2005. "Human Rights in a Globalizing World: The Paradox of Empty Promises." *American Journal of Sociology*, Vol. 110, pp. 1373–1411.

Hunt, L. A. 2007. *Inventing Human Rights: A History* (New York: W.W. Norton).

Joas, H. 2008. "Punishment and Respect: The Sacralization of the Person and Its Endangerment." *Journal of Classical Sociology*, Vol. 8, No. 2, pp. 159–177.

Kohen, A. 2006. "The Problem of Secular Sacredness: Ronald Dworkin, Michael Perry, and Human Rights Foundationalism." *Journal of Human Rights*, Vol. 5, pp. 235–256.
Levy, D. and N. Sznaider. 2006. "Sovereignty Transformed: A Sociology of Human Rights." *British Journal of Sociology*, Vol. 57, pp. 658–676.
Linton, R. 1936. *The Study of Man: An Introduction* (New York: Appleton-Century).
Lukács, G. 1971. *History and Class Consciousness* (London: Merlin).
Marmot, M. 2004. *The Status Syndrome: How Social Standing Affects Health and Longevity* (New York: Henry Holt).
Marshall, T. H. 1950. *Citizenship and Social Class and Other Essays* (Cambridge: Cambridge University Press).
Merton, R. K. 1957. *Social Theory and Social Structure*, rev. and enl. edn (Glencoe, IL: The Free Press).
Milner, M. 1993. "Hindu Eschatology and the Indian Caste System: An Example of Structural Reversal." *Journal of Asian Studies*, Vol. 52, pp. 298–319.
Milner, M. 1994a. *Status and Sacredness: A General Theory of Status Relations and an Analysis of Indian Culture* (New York: Oxford University Press).
Milner, M. 1994b. "Status and Sacredness: Worship and Salvation as Forms of Status Transformation." *Journal for the Scientific Study of Religion*, Vol. 33, pp. 99–109.
Milner, M. 2001. "Solidarity, the Sacred, and Human Rights: A Sociological Response [to Bryan Turner]." *Hedgehog Review*, Vol. 5, pp. 33–37.
Milner, M. 2004. *Freaks, Geeks, and Cool Kids: American Teenagers, Schools, and the Culture of Consumption* (New York: Routledge).
Milner, M. 2005. "Celebrity Culture as a Status System." *Hedgehog Review*, Vol. 9, pp. 66–76.
Milner, M. In press. "Status, Distinctions, and Boundaries." In J. R. Hall, L. Grindstaff, and M. Lo, eds., *Culture: A Sociological Handbook* (New York: Routledge).
Perry, M. J. 1998. *The Idea of Human Rights* (New York: Oxford University Press).
Turner, B. S. 2001. "The Ends of Humanity: Vulnerability and the Metaphor of Membership." *Hedgehog Review*, Vol. 5, pp. 7–32.
Turner, B. S. 2009. "A Sociology of Citizenship and Human Rights." In Rhiannon Morgan and Bryan S. Turner, eds., *Interpreting Human Rights* (New York: Routledge).
Walzer, M. 1994. *Thick and Thin: Moral Argument at Home and Abroad* (South Bend, IN: University of Notre Dame Press).
Warner, W. L. 1963. *Yankee City*, one volume abridged edn (New Haven, CT: Yale University Press).
Weber, M. 1978. Chapter IX. In Guenther Roth and Claus Wittich, eds., *Economy and Society: An Outline of Interpretive Sociology* (Berkeley: University of California Press).

17

Becoming irrelevant

The curious history of anthropology and human rights

Mark Goodale

It is necessary to examine the curious history of anthropology's ambivalent relationship to human rights for at least two reasons. First, this history illuminates certain basic dilemmas associated with the emergence of the postwar human rights project and the ways in which particular political and philosophical approaches to human rights became more powerful than other alternatives. Indeed, there is a distinct irony in the fact that a legal and ethical regime that was conceived in order to prevent or redress the violent assertion of illegitimate power within international relations itself came to be defined by subtle forms of power. The study of anthropology's exile from the early and formative development of human rights reveals how this shift in function was possible. Although this is not widely appreciated, either within the wider human rights community or in academia, the exclusion of anthropology from the critical moments in the emergence of the postwar human rights system would have lasting consequences. As we will see, at mid-twentieth century anthropology had established itself as the preeminent source of scientific expertise on many empirical facets of culture and society, from law to kinship, from religion to morality.

Yet it was at precisely this moment, when anthropology as a discipline was reaching the peak of its legitimacy and self-confidence, that it was blocked from contributing in any meaningful way to the development of understanding about what was – and still is – the most important putative cross-cultural fact: that human beings are essentially the same and that this essential sameness entails a specific normative framework. It was as if everything we know – or think we know – about the evolution of *Homo sapiens* included contributions from every discipline *except* biological anthropology, which, despite having been excluded, nevertheless continued to produce knowledge that spoke directly to the problem. In examining the history of anthropology's relationship to human rights, therefore, we will be able to better understand both how and why human rights developed as they did and, by extension, the ways in which they might have developed had the insights of anthropology played a role.

But the examination of this intellectual and political history is not only, or most importantly, retrospective. A basic assumption is that anthropological forms of knowledge and practical engagement can and should be used as part of a wider project of reconceptualizing the meaning and potential of human rights. The justifications for this assumption are to be found in both the historical absence of anthropology from the development of contemporary human rights, and the more recent attempts by individual anthropologists and the discipline's largest professional association to reengage with human rights as both an object of study and a vehicle for emancipatory political practice. Although some aspects of this history have already been related in different places (see e.g., Engle 2001; Goodale 2006a, 2006b; Messer 1993; Wilson and Mitchell 2003), this chapter provides a full and critical accounting.

If the wider engagement of anthropology is a necessary precondition for the transformation of contemporary human rights, this is in part because anthropology as a discipline is committed to the systematic and comparative investigation of social practices, including normative practices. The examination of human rights in terms of anthropology's troubled history is meant to reveal both profound potential and basic limitations – not within anthropology, but within a reconfigured human rights.

A curious history

In 1947 the United Nations Commission on Human Rights, which was chaired by Eleanor Roosevelt, sought statements on the draft version of what would become the 1948 Universal Declaration of Human Rights (UDHR). These statements were solicited in a variety of ways and through a variety of institutional channels, but perhaps the most important were the efforts of the United Nations Educational, Scientific, and Cultural Organization (UNESCO). UNESCO solicited statements on a proposed declaration of universal human rights from different academic, cultural, and artistic institutions and individuals. Although the essentially colonialist milieu within which the United Nations emerged after World War II made any attempt to achieve universal consensus through its working bodies utopian at best, the outreach efforts by UNESCO prior to the adoption of the UDHR were intended to gauge the diversity of world opinion about what Johannes Morsink describes as the "aggressive" push to forge an "international consensus about human rights" (1999, p. 12).

Within anthropology, it has become conventional wisdom to say that the American Anthropological Association (AAA) was one of those institutions that was solicited by UNESCO (see e.g., Messer 1993). This is because the *American Anthropologist*, the flagship journal of the AAA, published something called the "Statement on Human Rights" as the lead article in the October–December number of the journal (Vol. 49, No. 4, 1947). The Statement was prefaced by a note that indicated that it was submitted to the UN Commission on Human Rights by the Executive Board of the AAA. And it was not surprising that this Statement appeared in 1947, or that UNESCO had apparently turned to the AAA for an advisory opinion from anthropology on a proposed declaration of universal human rights.[1] By the mid-twentieth century, all three major anthropological traditions – "schools" is perhaps too strong a description – had, taken together, established themselves as an important source of scientific knowledge about the range of both diversity and unity in human culture and society.

But the evidence indicates that most of the conventional wisdom about the Statement on Human Rights is wrong. For example, there is the question of the actual relationship between UNESCO, the Commission for Human Rights, and the AAA. As I have said, the common understanding is that the AAA – as *the* representative of anthropology – was asked to write an advisory opinion on human rights, which it (through one or more of its members) did in 1947, after which this official AAA "Statement on Human Rights" was simultaneously published in the *American Anthropologist* and submitted to the Commission for Human Rights by the AAA Executive Board on behalf of its membership.

Yet according to documents in the US National Anthropological Archives,[2] there is no record of UNESCO making a request to the AAA for an advisory opinion on a declaration of human rights. Instead, it appears that one anthropologist, Melville Herskovits, was approached by UNESCO in his capacity as chairman of the Committee for International Cooperation in Anthropology of the National Research Council (NRC), a post which he assumed in 1945. Herskovits was a prominent American anthropologist, a member of the AAA's Executive Board during this time, and chairman of the Department of Anthropology at Northwestern University. Herskovits had been a student of Franz Boas at Columbia University, where he earned his PhD in Anthropology in 1923. Although his research and writings present a more complicated theoretical and political picture than has been supposed, there is no question that Herskovits's orientation to culture and society was shaped by his training in what is known as American historical particularism, an anthropological approach developed by Boas that placed the emphasis on studying the evolution of particular cultural traditions within their historical contexts (see Stocking 1989).

In focusing so intensely – and ethnographically – on particular cultures within what was believed to be their unique historical trajectories, American cultural anthropologists such as Herskovits became associated with a distinct outlook toward social phenomena. Two aspects of this outlook are relevant to the history of anthropology's relationship with human rights. First, the detailed study of cultures within history revealed the ways in which particular dimensions of culture – law, politics, religion, morality – were the result of a process of situated evolution, one that could not be understood in general terms or through the use of universal analytical categories. There might be "patterns of culture," as Ruth Benedict, another Boasian, described them; but these patterns were only rough outlines, ways of describing the fact that all cultures are in fact patterned in their own terms. The content of these patterns, however, the features that made a particular culture "Japanese," say, and not "Norwegian," was the result of the entire range of historical contingencies that could never be either reproduced again or predicted for other places and times. And it was only a short step from this essentially empirical approach to culture to something more normative: if each culture is unique, the result of a particular and contingent history, then it was not possible to evaluate or measure cultures in terms of some set of standards that could be justified in a way that was itself not part of a particular cultural tradition, or interplay between cultural traditions. This normative implication of American historical particularism is what is usually described as "cultural relativism."

Second, there was a political dimension to American historical particularism and the kind of anthropology pursued by the Boasians. Although Boas believed anthropology to be the "science of mankind," he also believed that it provided a valuable social function by documenting the richness of cultures that were either under threat of destruction, or tragically misunderstood, or both. American cultural anthropology at mid-century – less so British and French social anthropology – was concerned with the condition of what today would be described as marginalized or subaltern populations, and this concern was the result of both epistemological and political imperatives within American anthropology and of individual anthropologists. So when Melville Herskovits was approached by UNESCO through the National Research Council's Committee on International Cooperation in Anthropology, he also considered the ways in which a declaration of universal human rights would affect the cultural traditions and political standing of those populations that seemed to stand apart from the confluence of legal, political, and social forces that were behind the "aggressive" drive for an international human rights system.

Although Herskovits was contacted by UNESCO by virtue of his position as head of an influential NRC committee dedicated to fostering both international collaboration between anthropologists and other scientists, and the development of what today would be called "public anthropology" (i.e., the use of anthropological knowledge within consequential public debates), it is historiographically important to acknowledge that this NRC committee acted as a de facto committee of the American Anthropological Association, or at least coordinated its activities with the AAA Executive Board. Most of the members of the NRC committee during the mid-1940s were also members of the AAA, including (in 1946, the year before Herskovits drafted the Statement on Human Rights) one past and one future president of the AAA (Robert Lowie, 1935, and Frederica de Laguna, 1967).[3]

Nevertheless, the documentary record shows that the AAA was *not* first contacted by UNESCO; rather, Melville Herskovits's committee at the NRC was the entity solicited for a representative anthropological opinion on a declaration of human rights.[4] Herskovits worked on his Statement on Human Rights in early 1947 and began communicating with the AAA leadership about their intentions regarding it. By June 1947, Herskovits had already sent the Statement to UNESCO on behalf of both himself and the NRC anthropology committee. At the same time, Ralph Beals, an AAA Executive Board member, was writing to Clyde Kluckhohn, the AAA president, with a recommendation that Herskovits's "rights of man" statement be adopted by the Executive Board and published as the lead article in the forthcoming *American Anthropologist*.[5] To underscore the importance given to the Statement by the Executive Board, Beals recommended that the AAA order 1,000 reprints (with special covers) of the Statement for public relations purposes.

Although the Statement was published in *American Anthropologist* in late 1947 with a note indicating that the Statement was forwarded to UNESCO, this must be seen as a *post hoc* ratification of what Herskovits had already done some four to six months earlier. Although Herskovits was pleased that the AAA chose to *re-submit* the Statement on Human Rights on its behalf, there is very little evidence that the Statement was considered by the Commission for Human Rights during its deliberations. Further, despite the fact that the AAA was a much smaller and less representative organization at mid-century, it still functioned as a democratic association, in which major initiatives were voted on by the membership. With the Statement on Human Rights, however, no such vote took place and, except for correspondence between several high-ranking AAA members, there is no indication that association members had any knowledge of the Statement until its publication in *American Anthropologist*.

This brings me to a second way in which the relationship of American anthropology to human rights has been fundamentally misconstrued. In Morsink's otherwise excellent history of the "origins, drafting, and intent" behind the UDHR, he foregrounds the 1947 AAA Statement on Human Rights in a way that gives a distorted impression of its – and, by extension, anthropology's – impact on the emergence of human rights after World War II. In fact, he begins his history with a detailed discussion of the Statement's content; the implication is that the Commission on Human Rights went ahead with its work *despite* the objections and criticisms made in the Statement. As he says, in "1947 the UN Human Rights Commission that wrote the Declaration received a long memorandum from the American Anthropological Association (AAA)" (1999, p. ix). And then later, after reviewing different parts of the Statement, he observes that the "drafters of the Declaration … went ahead in spite of these warnings" (1999, p. x). But as Morsink's own comprehensive account of the drafting process makes clear, it is more likely that even if received in some technical sense – either on behalf of the NRC or, later, the AAA Executive Board – the Statement on Human Rights played almost no role whatsoever in the drafting of the UDHR.

If the Statement on Human Rights played a limited or (more likely) no role in the deliberations around the drafting of the UDHR, its status among anthropologists has also at times been misconstrued. With the exception of my own recent writings on the relationship between anthropology and human rights (see e.g., Goodale 2006a, 2006b), there were two earlier extended attempts to characterize this history, one by an anthropologist (Messer 1993) and the other by a law professor (Engle 2001). Both leave what I would suggest is the wrong impression about both the events surrounding the production of the Statement on Human Rights, and, more importantly, the impact of the Statement on anthropologists who might have participated more actively in the development of human rights theory and practice in the early post-UDHR period.

Although Messer and Engle have different agendas, and approach the issues from different vantage points, they both tend to read the early history of anthropology's relationship to human rights in terms of its much more recent history. So, for example, Engle says that anthropologists "have been embarrassed ever since" the publication of the Statement in 1947 (2001, p. 536). And she is even more direct in characterizing the impact of the Statement on the AAA itself. As she writes, "[f]or the past fifty years, the Statement has caused the AAA great shame. Indeed, the term 'embarrassment' is continually used in reference to the Statement" (p. 541). The problem is that with the exception of three brief comments on the Statement published soon after (Barnett 1948; Steward 1948; Bennett 1949), both the Statement, and, more important, human rights, vanish from the anthropological radar for almost forty years. It is difficult, in other words, to demonstrate that that Statement on Human Rights caused widespread shame or embarrassment after its publication. Indeed, there was very little reaction at all, either in the period immediately after its publication, or over the decades in which the international, and eventually transnational, human rights regimes emerged. Why and how this happened will be described in more detail below; but the fact remains that American anthropology, not to mention the wider discipline, played almost no role in the formal development of human rights theory or institutional practice in the important first decades of the postwar period.

Melville Herskovits's statement on human rights

I have said that the conventional wisdom about both the Statement on Human Rights and the early relationship between anthropology and human rights more generally has been largely wrong: in the details surrounding the origin of the Statement; in the impact of the Statement on both anthropology and key figures in the early postwar development of human rights; and in the supposed dark shadow that the Statement cast over anthropology in the decades since those early, formative, post-UDHR years. But what about the Statement itself? It too, perhaps more importantly, has been poorly understood. The most common way in which the Statement is construed – especially by scholars who have rewritten the early history of anthropology's relationship to human rights in order to make a clean break – is as an example of cultural relativism run amok, something made all the more unpardonable by the events that led to the founding of the United Nations and the "aggressive" push to create an international political and legal order based on universal human rights.

The intellectual historian Isaiah Berlin has written in several of his essays on the nineteenth-century Russian intelligentsia that what characterized the group of disaffected young people who would eventually become revolutionaries was their proclivity to borrow ideas from Western Europe and then take them to their logical, absurd, and violent extreme. This is how Herskovits's Statement on Human Rights is usually characterized: yes, he was well meaning; yes, cultural relativism was developed as an intellectual buffer against colonialism, racism, and all other universal systems that had the effect of oppressing some human populations while elevating others; yes, the principles of the Universal Declaration cannot be understood apart from the political and economic interests associated with its creation; *nevertheless*, what about the Nazis? How could anthropologists employ their services against the Nazis during the war (as they did in considerable numbers, in different capacities), yet lack a legitimate moral basis for doing so?

Shouldn't the contrarian Statement on Human Rights be simply dismissed as either the misapplication of certain ideas about cultural diversity, or as a piece of bad logic, or both?

But Herskovits's (and then the AAA's) Statement on Human Rights is much more complicated, and thus revealing, than the caricature of it would suggest. The Statement makes three distinct critiques of a proposed declaration of universal human rights. These can be divided into the epistemological, the empirical, and the ethical. First, Herskovits made the observation that because the Commission on Human Rights was interested in gathering opinions on human rights from different perspectives and approaches to knowledge, he was required to consider the idea of universal human rights *as a scientist*. And because the "sciences that deal with human culture" (AAA 1947, p. 539) had not developed methods for evaluating a proposed list of human rights in relation to the many other moral and legal systems that exist in the world, many of which would appear to conflict with the set of human rights emerging from the Commission, anthropology was unable to provide the tools necessary for proving – or disproving – their scientific validity.

Yet Herskovits also played both sides of the problem, assuming, for the sake of argument, that the anthropological evidence *could* be used to make claims about the validity (or not) of a proposed declaration of human rights. As he quite sensibly explained:

> Over the past fifty years, the many ways in which man resolves the problem of subsistence, of social living, of political regulation of group life, of reaching accord with the Universe and satisfying his aesthetic drives has been widely documented by the researches of anthropologists among peoples living in all parts of the world. All peoples do achieve these ends. No two of them, however, do so in exactly the same way, and some of them employ means that differ, often strikingly, from one another.
>
> *(AAA 1947, p. 540)*

This has been taken as a rigid and dogmatic expression of cultural relativism, which all but guaranteed that Herskovits would reject the idea of universal human rights. But what is ignored is what comes soon after. The real problem, he argues, is not with the idea of human rights itself; rather, the problem is that for political and economic reasons, proposals for human rights (so far) have always been conceived for the wrong purposes and based on the wrong set of assumptions. As he says, "definitions of freedom, concepts of the nature of human rights, and the like, have ... been narrowly drawn. Alternatives have been decried, and suppressed where controls have been established over non-European peoples. The hard core of *similarities* between cultures has been consistently overlooked" (AAA 1947, p. 540; emphasis in original). In other words, he seems to be suggesting here that the empirical question is still open: a declaration of universal human rights *might* be drafted that is legitimate across cultures, one that codifies and expresses this "hard core of similarities." But the Anglo-European proposals of 1947, which became the UDHR, did not speak to this "hard core of similarities" – whatever these might be, Herskovits does not elaborate – and so they should be rejected.

Finally, and arguably most importantly, Herskovits raised a number of ethical objections to the proposal for a declaration of human rights by the United Nations. This critique, more than any other, has been ignored in the subsequent rush to pigeonhole Herskovits as the anthropological equivalent of one of those Russian revolutionaries who could not wait to take abstract principles to their logical, if absurd, conclusions. Apart from the substance of the ethical critiques in the Statement on Human Rights, taken together they underscore a basic fact about the Statement that is rarely acknowledged: that it was, above all else, an act of moral and intellectual courage. Imagine the context: the horrors of the Holocaust and the violence of World War II were being fully exposed (through the ongoing Nuremberg trials, among other sources); there was broad consensus among the major powers around at least some kind of international legal and political order based on some version of human rights; and, behind all of this, scholars, experts, political leaders, and influential public figures across the range were hurrying to lend their services in order to bring this new legal and political order to fruition.

Despite all of this, Herskovits (and then the Executive Board of the AAA) forcefully dissented. Instead of serving as a bulwark against fascism and the oppression of the weak, a declaration of human rights would, eventually, no matter how well intentioned, tend toward the opposite: it would become a doctrine "employed to implement economic exploitation and ... deny the right to control their own affairs to millions of people over the world, where the expansion of Europe and America has not [already] meant the literal extermination of whole populations" (AAA 1947, p. 540). And this concern was not only, or most importantly, prospective; Herskovits drew from history in making the argument that declarations of human rights were often legal smokescreens for the oppression of one group of humans by another. For example, the "American Declaration of Independence, or the American Bill of Rights, could be written by men who themselves were slave-owners," and the revolutionary French embrace of the rights of man only became legitimate when extended "to the French slave-owning colonies" (p. 542). And regardless of the growing international consensus, regardless of the stated intentions of what claimed to be a diverse and representative Commission on Human Rights (and, more generally, United Nations), and regardless of the democratic nature of the UN Charter, Herskovits refused to see the proposed declaration of human rights as anything other than a set of aspirations "circumscribed by the standards of [a] single culture" (p. 543). Such a "limited Declaration," Herskovits argued, would exclude more people than it would include, *because of* – not despite – its claims of universality.

The wilderness years

After 1948 the international human rights system emerged only haltingly, in part because the imperatives of the bipolar Cold War world imposed a whole series of constraints – political, ideological, cultural – on the realization of what was clearly a competing vision for international affairs. So even though Eleanor Roosevelt had hoped that the idea of human rights would be carried along what she called a "curious grapevine" behind the walls of repressive states and ideologies, to reach those most in need of its protections, her dream would have to be deferred (see Korey 1998). In the meantime, anthropologists *were* participating in the development of postwar institutions and knowledge regimes, but not those that were framed in terms of human rights. A good example of this public anthropology during the 1950s and early 1960s was the formative role played by anthropologists – in particular Alfred Métraux, Ashley Montagu, and Claude Lévi-Strauss – in the series of UNESCO statements on race, which called into question the biological concept of race and described in some detail the ways in which race should instead be seen as a social construct (see UNESCO 1969). This was a provocative and progressive reframing of the race issue at a time when, in the United States for example, the traditional biological understanding of racial differences was still codified in law and reflected in patterns of political and social inequality.

Yet human rights did not frame this work on race, despite the fact that the basic idea of human rights assumes that human beings are essentially the same, both biological *and* morally. Even more telling, anthropologists were active in the civil rights movement in the United States throughout this period, including Melville Herskovits himself (see Gershenhorn 2004). But civil rights were understood in a quite different way from human rights, within a different system of political and legal legitimacy, and anchored in a different set of assumptions about human nature and the foundations of citizenship. And apart from the fact that anthropologists during the 1950s and 1960s did not frame their different *political* interventions in terms of human rights, the anthropological voice was equally absent from developments in the *philosophy* of human rights, especially to the extent that such evolving ideas influenced the content of the important instruments that followed the UDHR.

For anthropology, these were the wilderness years, the period in which the international human rights system was established as a set of ideas, practices, and documents, despite the fact that the actual protection or enforcement of human rights by nation-states and international institutions was often minimal throughout much of the world. The emergence and eventual transnationalization of human rights discourse after the end of the Cold War would not have been possible without these preexisting institutional and philosophical foundations, which were laid without contributions from anthropological forms of knowledge and methods of studying social practices.

Social justice and other universalist projects

The political and cultural climates changed dramatically during the mid- to late 1960s, and anthropologists were again active participants in these changes. But a major difference between the mid-1950s to early 1960s and the late 1960s through the 1970s was the fact that the anthropological contributions to the political and cultural movements of the latter period were fueled, in part, by correspondingly dramatic intellectual shifts within the wider discipline. Nevertheless, the idea of human rights was still not used by anthropologists in their writings to justify their participation in these political and cultural movements; rather, the most common intellectual (and political) rationale for the anthropological participation in anti-colonialism, or protests against the war in Vietnam, was some version of Marxism or neo-Marxism. What is important for my purposes here about the incorporation of the Marxist critique in anthropological writings on social justice issues is that it offered an alternative universalizing framework for addressing these pressing political and social problems, one that, at least theoretically, was as hostile to the cultural relativism of the 1947 Statement on Human Rights as the competing claims of the UDHR itself.

That is, during the 1960s and 1970s anthropology underwent a profound shift – one mirrored in other academic disciplines, both in the United States and elsewhere – that had the effect of creating formal *epistemological* links between scholarship and political activism. The Marxist (or neo-Marxist) emphasis on the inevitability of conflict, the role of intellectuals in political movements, and the importance of understanding structures of inequality within broad historical contexts, among others, made it an ideal source of inspiration for anthropologists desperately seeking a way out of the box created by the dominant theoretical approaches of earlier generations, which either ignored the dynamic interplay between cultures (American historical particularism), downplayed the wider historical, economic, and political forces that shaped particular cultures and societies (British functionalism and structural-functionalism), or denied the influence of history altogether (French structuralism). So although human rights did not figure into the profound shift in the way many anthropologists justified their participation in movements for social justice, an opening was inadvertently and ironically created by the influence of Marxism through which another (and essentially liberal) universalizing project could pass. By the end of the 1970s, anthropology was ready for human rights. But were human rights ready for anthropology?

The prodigal son returns

Although it would not be until the 1980s that anthropology as a discipline took a sustained interest in human rights for the first time, there was an earlier event that foreshadowed the shape this new interest would take. In 1972 the anthropologist David Maybury-Lewis and his wife Pia Maybury-Lewis co-founded Cultural Survival, Inc. Cultural Survival was not established as a research institution, but rather as a non-governmental organization dedicated to the survival of indigenous cultures through political advocacy, education, and public awareness programs. There is some question, however, about the extent to which Cultural Survival was founded initially as a human rights organization or an indigenous cultures organization that only later made indigenous rights a centerpiece for education and advocacy. Although Cultural Survival now makes "indigenous peoples' rights" the basic framework through which they work to ensure the survival of indigenous cultures in different parts of the world, this focus apparently did not emerge within the organization until the 1980s. Nevertheless, the plight of indigenous peoples eventually became *the* issue on which anthropology staked a claim within human rights; it was a small claim at the beginning, to be sure, but as an indigenous rights discourse took on greater importance later in the 1980s, anthropology's involvement suddenly became more noticeable and politically consequential.

The 1980s were turbulent times for anthropology. Especially in the United States, the epistemological shifts of the 1960s and 1970s, in which scholarship and political action were connected within one of several variations of Marxist/neo-Marxist social theory, came home to roost in the form of a period of intense disciplinary self-critique and eventual fragmentation. By the mid-1980s, anthropology as a discipline was in a state of crisis, with clear lines forming between anthropologists who wanted to reaffirm the scientific foundations of the discipline, and those who saw these same foundations as a symbol of a longer history of Western colonialism, Orientalism, and the assertion of technocratic power against vulnerable populations. The critics of scientific anthropology (see, e.g., Fox 1991; Marcus and Clifford 1986) came close to dismantling American cultural anthropology in particular; at the very least, they made a series of arguments about research methods, ethnographic writing, and the nature of anthropology as a neo-colonial encounter that had the effect of painting anthropology into a corner.

There were two major ways out of this corner, one theoretical and the other political. For some anthropologists, the period of intense critique was both revelatory and liberating. Finally, here was a public debate within anthropology about the basic questions of scientific legitimacy, the relationship between science and economic and political exploitation, and, even more abstractly, the questionable assumptions about the nature of social reality on which the "science of mankind" depended. But if this public debate was a revelation for many anthropologists, the path toward liberation quickly became highly theoretical and disconnected from the concerns with social practice that figured, at least symbolically, in some of the earlier critical writings. Instead, the earlier discussion of the problematic nature of the great object–subject divide within social science evolved into an extended debate about subjectivity itself (see Spiro 1986); the critique of ethnographic writing was transformed into a debate over the politics of writing genres (e.g., Sanjek 1990); and concerns over the way anthropologists chose places to conduct fieldwork evolved into an excursus into the definitions and implications of "space," "place," and "the field" (e.g., Amit 1999).

But there was another response to the disciplinary crisis within anthropology in the 1980s and early 1990s. Since much of the critique of anthropology focused on the ways in which anthropologists were unwitting actors in larger political and economic projects, some anthropologists reacted not by trying to eliminate the political from anthropology, but by making anthropology *more* political. The idea was to put anthropological knowledge to work at the service of specific groups of people struggling against specific forms of systematic oppression and violence. For anthropologists working with indigenous peoples this was an obvious move, since many indigenous groups found themselves suffering under a range of new or intensified constraints as the era of neoliberalism took root in places like Latin America. And parallel to the politicization of anthropology, and the increase in violence against indigenous peoples as a result of neoliberal political and economic restructuring during the mid- to late 1980s, there was another development during this time that made the anthropological embrace of human rights possible: the advent of "indigenous rights" as a distinct and recognized category within the broader human rights system.

For some anthropologists, indigenous rights discourse provided a means through which their understanding of an essentially political anthropology could be put into practice. What eventually became a transnational indigenous rights movement provided a way out of the human rights wilderness for anthropology. The discipline that embodied the most promise as a source of knowledge about the meanings and potential of human rights in 1948, but which had spent the intervening decades in exile as the idea of human rights was refined conceptually and elaborated institutionally, could now return home. The problem for anthropology was that this way home, while creating new openings for political and institutional action, had the effect of obscuring other possible ways in which anthropology might contribute to human rights theory and practice. But as we will see, this narrowness in anthropology's (re)engagement with human rights would prove to be only temporary.

The new orientation of anthropology toward human rights can be symbolized by major shifts within the American Anthropological Association. In 1990 the AAA established a Special Commission, chaired by Terence Turner, to investigate the encroachments on traditional Yanomami territory by the Brazilian state.[6] The creation of this commission and its subsequent report (1991) led to the establishment by the AAA Executive Board of a Commission on Human Rights (1992), which was charged "to develop a human rights conceptual framework and identify relevant human rights issues, to develop human rights education and networking, and to develop and implement mechanisms for organizational action on issues affecting the AAA, its members and the discipline" (AAA 2001). In 1995, the Commission on Human Rights was converted into a permanent standing committee of the Association – the Committee for Human Rights (CfHR). Among other activities, the members of the CfHR began working on a new statement of principles that would have the effect of definitively repudiating the 1947 Statement on Human Rights. These efforts culminated in the 1999 "Declaration on Anthropology and Human Rights." This declaration, unlike the Statement on Human Rights, *was* formally adopted by a majority vote of the general AAA membership.

The Declaration's most important assertion is that "[p]eople and groups have a generic right to realize their capacity for culture" (AAA 1999). Far from expressing any doubts about the cross-cultural validity of human rights instruments like the Universal Declaration, the 1999 Declaration locates a putative human right to realize a capacity for culture within a set of as-yet-to-be-articulated human rights that actually go well beyond the current rights recognized within international law. As the Declaration states, its new position "reflects a commitment to human rights consistent with international principles but not limited by them" (1999). The Declaration was thus a clear reversal by the AAA of its earlier position on human rights. But it also signaled something else: the conversion of – at least a subset of – the world's largest association of professional anthropologists into a human rights advocacy NGO focused on vulnerable populations and emerging rights categories.

Finally, in 2000 the Committee for Human Rights augmented its original set of guidelines and objectives and this list remains the current (as of 2008) set of operating principles for the Committee: (1) to promote and protect human rights; (2) to expand the definition of human rights within an anthropological perspective; (3) to work internally with the membership of the AAA to educate anthropologists, and to mobilize their support for human rights; (4) to work externally with foreign colleagues, the people and groups with whom anthropologists work, and other human rights organizations to develop an anthropological perspective on human rights and consult with them on human rights violations and the appropriate actions to be taken; (5) to influence and educate the media, policy makers, non-governmental organizations, and decision makers in the private sector; and (6) to encourage research on all aspects of human rights from conceptual to applied (AAA 2001).

Toward an ecumenical anthropology of human rights

After the ratification of the 1999 Declaration by the AAA, the Association continued to transform its orientation toward human rights. The Committee for Human Rights became one of the most visible and active of the Association's working bodies through a series of high-profile investigations and interventions, a website dedicated to human rights activism and education, and collaborations with other human rights bodies embedded within other professional associations.

The work of the Committee for Human Rights after 1995 was not simply political. Apart from the 1993 review essay by Ellen Messer that I have already mentioned – which was as much a programmatic call to action as a review of anthropology and human rights – several founding members of the Committee brought their arguments for a robust engagement with human rights together in a special issue of the *Journal of Anthropological Research* (1997). One of these articles, by Terence Turner, encapsulated both the importance and tone of this period in anthropology's relationship with human rights. Turner, whose own activist scholarship on behalf of the Kayapo has come to embody anthropology's rediscovery of human rights, and its repudiation of what are understood to be the mistakes of the 1947 generation, argued that anthropologists should contribute to an "emancipatory cultural politics." By this he meant that much of the emerging cultural rights discourse has been, and should continue to be, supported through a kind of anthropological research that is conducted *in terms of* specific projects for social change. And because human rights – for example, the "right to culture" that was described in the 1999 Declaration (which Turner played a major role in drafting) – had become essential to these projects, especially those involving indigenous people, anthropological knowledge could prove useful in making legal and political claims in the increasingly dominant language of rights. This emancipatory cultural politics approach to human rights through anthropology remains the primary orientation for anthropologists interested in human rights, including those who work outside academia in high-profile roles within the non-governmental and activist communities.

But beginning in about 1995, another anthropological approach to human rights emerged. Here anthropologists converted the practice of human rights into a topic for ethnographic research and analysis. Human rights were reconceptualized in part as a transnational discourse linked to the spread of neoliberal logics of legal and political control after the end of the Cold War. As such, anthropologists working in this analytical mode remained ambivalent, or even skeptical, about the use of human rights discourse by social actors in the course of struggles for social change. This research and analysis, which were made possible by the rapid rise in human rights talk and institutional development since the early 1990s, both documented the contradictions and contingencies that surround the practice of human rights, and led to the creation of a cross-cultural database on the meanings of human rights (see e.g, Clarke 2009; Cowan et al. 2001; Englund 2006; Goodale 2008, 2009; Goodale and Merry 2007; Merry 2006; Riles 2000; Slyomovics 2005; Speed 2008; Tate 2007; Wilson 2001; and Wilson and Mitchell 2003).

Finally, even more recently, yet a third approach to human rights through anthropology can be distinguished. To a certain extent, a critical anthropology of human rights synthesizes both the emancipatory cultural politics and ethnographic approaches: it is committed at some level to the idea of human rights, though in some cases a radically reconfigured idea, and it makes information derived from the practice of human rights the basis for analysis, critique, policy making, and political action (see e.g., Clarke 2009; Cowan 2006; Eriksen 2001; Goodale 2006b). There are profound implications to making the practice of human rights both the conceptual source for understanding what human rights *are* (and can be) and the source of legitimacy for claims based on human rights, not the least of which is the fact that it calls into question many of the basic assumptions of postwar human rights theory and practice. Moreover, to the extent that the international human rights system is a reflection of these assumptions, then it too must be reconsidered.

There can be no doubt about the important contributions by the range of legal scholars, philosophers, ethicists, and others who were instrumental in creating the modern human rights system (and the ideas that supported and then flowed from it). Nevertheless, the critical ethnography of human rights suggests both a different human rights ontology and grounds on which a potentially global normative project like human rights can be justified. In other words, there is still a tremendous reservoir of untapped potential in the idea of human rights, even if there are also certain basic limitations that must be acknowledged and institutionalized.

Acknowledgment

A previous version of this chapter appeared in Mark Goodale, *Surrendering to Utopia: An Anthropology of Human Rights*, Stanford University Press, 2009. Reprinted here with permission.

Notes

1 The Statement on Human Rights was published almost exactly one year before the UDHR was adopted by the UN Third General Assembly on December 10, 1948.
2 These are currently housed in a Smithsonian Museum Support Center in Suitland, Maryland. I thank the administrator of the NAA for allowing me to conduct research in the archives and for guiding me through the documentary sources of the AAA.
3 NAA, Box 23, General File, 1930–1949.
4 I have not been able to uncover any evidence that other professional anthropological associations were solicited by UNESCO during this time.
5 NAA, Box 192, AAA Executive Board Minutes, March 1946–May 1954.
6 The following is drawn from the *1995–2000 Cumulative 5-Year Report* published by the Committee for Human Rights, American Anthropological Association (AAA/CfHR 2001).

References

American Anthropological Association. 1947. "Statement on Human Rights." *American Anthropologist*, Vol. 49, No. 4, pp. 539–543.

American Anthropological Association, Committee on Human Rights. 1999. *Declaration on Anthropology and Human Rights*. At: http://www.aaanet.org/stmts/humanrts.htm.

American Anthropological Association, Committee for Human Rights. 2001. *1995–2000 Cumulative 5-Year Report*. At: http://www.aaanet.org/committees/cfhr/ar95-00.htm.

Amit, Vered, ed. 1999. *Constructing the Field: Ethnographic Fieldwork in the Contemporary World* (London: Routledge).

Barnett, H. G. 1948. "On Science and Human Rights." *American Anthropologist*, Vol. 50, pp. 352–355.

Bennett, John W. 1949. "Science and Human Rights: Reason and Action." *American Anthropologist*, Vol. 50, pp. 329–336.

Clarke, Kamari Maxine. 2009. *Fictions of Justice: The International Criminal Court and the Challenge of Legal Pluralism in Sub-Saharan Africa* (New York: Cambridge University Press).

Cowan, Jane. 2006. "Culture and Rights after *Culture and Rights*." *American Anthropologist*, Vol. 108, No. 1, pp. 9–24.

Cowan, Jane, Marie-Bénédicte Dembour, and Richard A. Wilson, eds. 2001. *Culture and Rights: Anthropological Perspectives* (Cambridge: Cambridge University Press).

Engle, Karen. 2001. "From Skepticism to Embrace: Human Rights and the American Anthropological Association from 1947–1999." *Human Rights Quarterly*, Vol. 23, pp. 536–559.

Englund, Harri. 2006. *Prisoners of Freedom: Human Rights and the African Poor* (Berkeley: University of California Press).

Eriksen, Thomas Hylland. 2001. "Between Universalism and Relativism: A Critique of the UNESCO Concept of Culture." In Jane Cowan, Marie-Bénédicte Dembour, and Richard A. Wilson, eds. *Culture and Rights: Anthropological Perspectives* (Cambridge: Cambridge University Press).

Fox, Richard G., ed. 1991. *Recapturing Anthropology: Working in the Present* (Santa Fe, NM: SAR Press).

Gershenhorn, Jerry. 2004. *Melville J. Herskovits and the Racial Politics of Knowledge* (Lincoln: University of Nebraska Press).

Goodale, Mark. 2006a. Introduction to "Anthropology and Human Rights in a New Key." *American Anthropologist*, Vol. 108, No. 1, pp. 1–8.

Goodale, Mark. 2006b. "Toward a Critical Anthropology of Human Rights." *Current Anthropology*, Vol. 47, No. 3, pp. 485–511.

Goodale, Mark. 2008. *Dilemmas of Modernity: Bolivian Encounters with Law and Liberalism* (Stanford, CA: Stanford University Press).

Goodale, Mark. 2009. *Surrendering to Utopia: An Anthropology of Human Rights* (Stanford, CA: Stanford University Press).

Goodale, Mark, ed. 2009. *Human Rights: An Anthropological Reader* (Oxford: Blackwell).

Goodale, Mark and Sally Engle Merry, eds. 2007. *The Practice of Human Rights: Tracking Law Between the Global and the Local* (Cambridge: Cambridge University Press).

Korey, William. 1998. *NGOs and the Universal Declaration on Human Rights: "A Curious Grapevine"* (New York: St. Martin's Press).

Marcus, George and James Clifford, eds. 1986. *Writing Culture: The Poetics and Politics of Ethnography* (Berkeley: University of California Press).

Merry, Sally Engle. 2006. *Human Rights and Gender Violence: Translating International Law into Local Justice* (Chicago: University of Chicago Press).

Messer, Ellen. 1993. "Anthropology and Human Rights." *Annual Review of Anthropology*, Vol. 22, pp. 221–249.

Morsink, Johannes. 1999. *The Universal Declaration of Human Rights: Origins, Drafting, Intent* (Philadelphia: University of Pennsylvania Press).

Riles, Annelise. 2000. *The Network Inside Out* (Ann Arbor: University of Michigan Press).

Sanjek, Roger, ed. 1990. *Fieldnotes: The Makings of Anthropology* (Ithaca, NY: Cornell University Press).

Slyomovics, Susan. 2005. *The Performance of Human Rights in Morocco* (Philadelphia: University of Pennsylvania Press).

Speed, Shannon. 2008. *Rights in Rebellion: Indigenous Struggle and Human Rights in Chiapas* (Stanford, CA: Stanford University Press).

Spiro, Melford. 1986. "Cultural Relativism and the Future of Anthropology." *Cultural Anthropology*, Vol. 1, No. 3, pp. 259–286.

Steward, Julian. 1948. "Comment on the Statement on Human Rights." *American Anthropologist*, Vol. 50, pp. 351–352.

Stocking, George, ed. 1989. *A Franz Boas Reader: The Shaping of American Anthropology, 1883–1911* (Chicago: University of Chicago Press).

Tate, Winifred. 2007. *Counting the Dead: The Culture and Politics of Human Rights Activism in Colombia* (Berkeley: University of California Press).
Turner, Terence. 1997. "Human Rights, Human Difference: Anthropology's Contribution to an Emancipatory Cultural Politics." *Journal of Anthropological Research*, Vol. 53, pp. 273–291.
United Nations Educational, Scientific, and Cultural Organization. 1969. *Four Statements on the Race Question* (Paris: UNESCO).
Wilson, Richard A. 2001. *The Politics of Truth and Reconciliation in South Africa* (Cambridge: Cambridge University Press).
Wilson, Richard Ashby and Jon P. Mitchell, eds. 2003. *Human Rights in Global Perspective: Anthropological Studies of Rights, Claims, and Entitlements* (London: Routledge).

18
Economics and human rights

Lorenz Blume

Introduction

Historically, economists have been rather reluctant to deal with human rights. Jeremy Bentham (1748–1832), as a leading proponent of utilitarianism, famously called them "nonsense on stilts." Representatives of the so-called classical or old institutionalism such as Gustav von Schmoller (1838–1917) from the German Historic School and John Commons (1862–1945), Thorstein Veblen (1857–1929), and Wesley Mitchell (1874–1948) from the American Institutionalist School criticized the neoclassical market model for completely ignoring interest conflicts, social relationships, and the importance of institutions, but their influence on the mainstream of economic research in the twentieth century is negligible.

It was only in the late twentieth century that the research on sets of rights (called institutions in economics) reached a new quality in the economic discipline, culminating in a research program commonly labeled as "New Institutional Economics." Principally, human rights have become part of the agenda of economists as part of this research program. Douglass North (1990, p. 3) – one of the pioneers of New Institutional Economics – defines institutions as "the rules of the game in a society or, more formally ... the humanly devised constraints that shape human interaction ... In consequence they structure incentives in human exchange, whether political, social, or economic." This encompasses human rights. Yet, when rights are explicitly analyzed, many economists hasten to add that their primary interest is in economic freedom rights. Economic publications with a focus on human rights are therefore still very rare in economics, in spite of the fact that they could have a prominent place in New Institutional Economics.

This chapter is organized as follows. In the next section, the origins of New Institutional Economics are described, followed by a section that deals with the central theoretical insights of this research program. These two parts shed light on the role of rights in economics in general. The fourth section deals with the economic literature on human rights in a more concrete manner. Three different lines of argumentation are separated. The final section is an outlook on open research questions for the future.

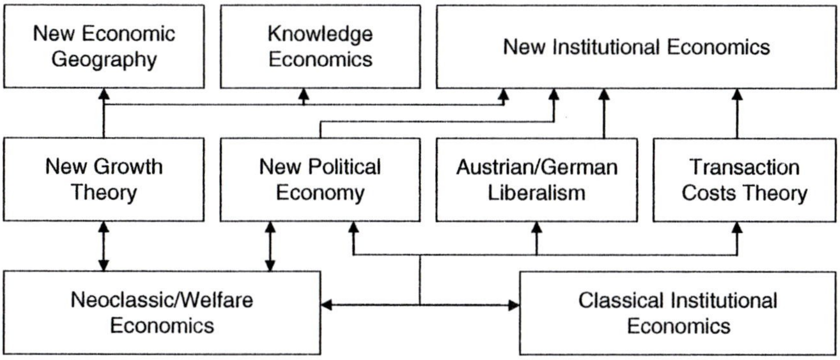

Figure 18.1 The origins of New Institutional Economics

The origins of New Institutional Economics

The increasing interest of economists in sets of rights since the beginning of the 1990s was motivated by the theoretical and empirical findings of the New Growth Theory on the one hand, and on the other hand the insights of pioneer works rooted in the history of thinking of the Transaction Costs Theory, New Political Economics (Public Choice), the Austrian School, and to some extent also the German Ordo school (Figure 18.1).

The central message of the New Growth Theory is that the neoclassical growth model (Solow 1956) tells us only a part of the story. Differences in the stock of physical and human capital only partially explain the differences in growth and welfare among countries (see for example Hall and Jones 1999; Easterly and Levine 2002a). The so-called Solow residual of cross-country studies – using a Solow production function based on constant or decreasing returns of the classical factor inputs capital and labor – has grown since the Second World War. Trade between countries is increasingly caused by external or internal economies of scale in production and less by comparative advantages in factor inputs, which explains the relative increase of trade among countries with similar factor endowments. These empirical findings led to the hypotheses of the pioneers of the New Growth Theory that there must be something like increasing returns of the classical factor inputs at least partially caused by additional environmental factors with a certain variation from country to country (Helpman and Krugman 1985; Romer 1987; Lucas 1987). With the purpose of identifying these growth-enhancing environmental factors, some of the literature concentrates on innovation and knowledge networks (Porter 1990; Grossman and Helpman 1991; Nelson 1993), some concentrate on agglomeration (Krugman 1991) and some on government policy actions (Barro 1991; Mankiw et al. 1992). While the latter studies directly influenced the research program of New Institutional Economics, the first line of thought laid the foundation for the actual research on innovation systems, network externalities and knowledge economies, and the second line of thought is now called New Economic Geography.

The history of thinking that makes New Institutional Economics more than integrating some policy variables into growth equations can be traced back to the so-called classical or old institutionalism of the early twentieth century already mentioned in the introduction. Because its influence on the analytical framework of New Institutional Economics is rather weak (and to keep this historical overview short) its ideas will not be dealt with in detail here (see instead Hutchison 1984; Langlois 1986; Hodgson 1988; or Rutherford 2001).

The first decisive impetus on the analytical framework of New Institutional Economics can be ascribed to the Transaction Costs Theory. Ronald Coase (1910–) challenges one of the central assumptions of the neoclassical market model, namely that market transactions (by specific contracts) are free of cost. In his "The Nature of the Firm," he points out that the "main reason why it is profitable to establish a firm would seem to be that there is a cost of using the price mechanism" (Coase 1937, p. 390). These costs referred to by Coase – later called transaction costs by others – are fundamentally linked to the division of labor in our developed economies. The costs of organizing a complex production process solely by market transactions (which means thousands of specific contracts between "one-person-firms") are anything but negligible (Furubotn and Richter 1997, p. 45). The key argument of the Transaction Costs Theorists interested in the theory of the firm (compare, e.g., Alchian and Demsetz 1972) is that the measurement, control, and information costs inside a hierarchical structure are much lower. If one entrepreneur at the top has the (property) right to subscribe all contracts, this on the one hand reduces the number of contracts and on the other hand opens the way for more general working contracts. Instead of a specific contract for each separate step in production (like in the case of market transactions), employee and employer agree to a general working contract that enables the employer to give orders and forces the employee to obey. If the contract also contains some rights for the employee that make it costly for the employer to hire and fire at will, both employer and employee have an incentive to undertake specific long-term investments. In production relations based on market transactions this sort of specific investment (in human or long-lasting physical capital) would not take place with the same intensity, because of the uncertainty regarding the duration of the relationship among the producers (Williamson 1975). From an economic point of view, hierarchies are therefore sometimes superior to markets in structuring social relations, so at least is the conclusion of the Transaction Costs Theory.

A second line of thought that contributed to the genesis of New Institutional Economics is rooted in Austrian and German Liberalism. In spite of the fact that the so-called Austrian School has a long-lasting tradition including several generations of well-known economists like Carl Menger (1840–1921), Eugen von Böhm-Bawerk (1851–1914), Ludwig von Mises (1881–1973), and Josef Schumpeter (1883–1950), we concentrate here on the work of Friedrich von Hayek (1899–1992). He in a way summarizes the work of the Austrian School especially with regard to the institutional question. While deeply affiliated with the methodological individualism and neoclassical rational choice approach, Hayek is at the same time strongly convinced that "institutions matter." He shows how intended individual behavior can result in unintended collective rules (1960, p. 1973). These sets of rules (in the form of constitutions, laws, norms, or concrete institutions), Hayek suggests, have a strong influence on the wealth of nations. When there is too much regulation and redistribution, the incentives for individuals to look out for new opportunities to increase their income (and, by extension, the national income) decline. From an evolutionary perspective competition helps overcome the problem of not knowing what is best for the future. Under unconstrained competition (which means hard budgetary constraints for each individual firm) only firms that implement superior technologies and have the better strategies and ideas will survive. This evolutionary perspective on competition as a discovery process separates Hayek from the general equilibrium theory of the neoclassic Walrasian market model. According to Hayek it would be a mistake to leave the search for new knowledge to the state. The cost of misdirected investments by the whole state would be much higher than the cost of failure by some private firms. In promoting a liberal market constituency as the key institution for development, Hayek is a representative of what is called normative institutionalism. In pointing out regularities in the evolution of institutions, he contributed to the positive literature on institutional change. Like Hayek, the German Ordo School (or Freiburg School) around Walter Eucken (1891–950) and Franz Böhm (1895–1977) also mainly contributed to normative institutionalism. Based on the principles of classical liberalism by Adam Smith, their writings were focused on the advantages of an institutional setting providing property rights, competition laws, price stability, and the rule of law. More clearly than Hayek they distinguish between the rules of the game (*Ordnungspolitik*) and the game itself (*Prozesspolitik*). According to their normative concept of a social market economy the state should abstain from playing the game itself and solely provide the framework for private economic activity (Eucken 1952).

The third line of thought that influenced the research program of New Institutional Economics is the New Political Economy (Public Choice) literature of authors such as Anthony Downs (1930–), William Niskanen (1933–), and Mancur Olson (1932–1998). New Political Economists have in common that they use the neoclassical *homo oeconomicus* behavioral model (sometimes in a modified way) to explain political decision making. This use of the rational choice approach is the methodological Rubicon that separates classical Political Economy from the New Political Economy. Like private households, politicians and bureaucrats are led by self-interest in Public Choice models. If citizens delegate power to politicians, they usually try to constrain the selfish behavior of politicians through institutional settings that ensure that the politicians represent citizen interests and not their own (principal–agent–problem). A democratic institutional setting with separation of power is one option here. Politicians are then forced to maximize votes to gain power, prestige, and income (Downs 1957), and to constrain the leeway of the selfish bureaucrats in the administration who permanently try to maximize their budget to gain power, prestige, and privileges (Niskanen 1971). While elections are an option to give the interests of citizens and taxpayers a voice, there are different channels to influence political decision making, even in democracies. Interest groups can organize themselves and begin to put pressure on politicians to act in their interest by lobbying. The probability that the cost of such rent-seeking activities is higher than the cost of organizing the activities decreases with the size of the group and increases with the homogeneity of the interests (Olson 1965).

Although the models mentioned are clearly part of positive research interested in how, for example, principal agent relations work, there is also a more normative line of thought in New Political Economy called Constitutional Economics. Constitutional Economics are strongly related to the work of James Buchanan (1919–). Like Hayek, Buchanan tries to answer the question of which institutional settings are best for a liberal society. He argues that it is rational for individuals to agree on a constitution with, for example, clear property rights, contract enforcement, and some social security because in the long run all individuals will be better off than in anarchy (Buchanan 1975). To overcome the problem of short-run interests (of, for example, rich individuals against each form of social security) in his heuristic model he introduces a so-called veil of uncertainty that prevents individuals from knowing whether they will be rich or poor in the future. The economic reasoning in his model leads Buchanan to a strong criticism of the status quo. From his point of view deregulation with regard to the market and stronger constraints on the behavior of politicians are necessary. He stresses the point that while the neoclassical Welfare Economics (Pigou 1920) only talk of market failure, the problem of state failure is often more dramatic.

The framework of New Institutional Economics

The decisive impetus for New Institutional Economics as a discrete research program must be dedicated to Douglass North (1920–). With regard to the question of the Solow growth residual he wrote: "I wish to assert a much more fundamental role for institutions in societies; they are the underlying determinant of the long-run performance of economies" (North 1990, p. 107). He was the first to come up with a clear distinction between institutions and policies on the one side and institutions and organizations on the other side. For him, institutions are the humanly devised constraints that shape human interaction. In making a distinction between constraints and preferences he clearly links his definition to the neoclassical rational choice approach. Each individual has certain preferences that only change very slowly over time; the choices the individual makes on the basis of these preferences are determined and limited by humanly devised constraints (i.e., institutions). Institutions can be formal rules like laws and informal rules like traditions. The rules can be "negative," i.e. they prevent people from doing something, or "positive," i.e. they set incentives to act in a certain way under certain circumstances. On a timescale, formal institutions are generally easier to change than informal rules that are often closely linked to social values and preferences. If formal and informal institutions do not fit together, problems of compliance can arise. People may oppose and ultimately not obey the law. On the other side of the coin, formal institutions can help change informal institutions at least in the long run. There is a whole strand of institutional economics literature concentrating on the question of "institutional change." La Porta et al. (1999) make a distinction between economic theories, which hold that institutions are created when it is efficient to create them, political theories, which hold that institutions are shaped by those in power to stay in power, and cultural theories, which hold that society's beliefs shape collective action and institutions.

The "institutions matter" assumption of New Institutional Economics is rooted in the basic insight that a society with formal and informal institutions is better off than a society in anarchy. Institutions reduce the uncertainty (and therefore transaction costs) in day-to-day social and economic life. If individuals know how other people that stick to the rules of the game behave under certain circumstances this will reduce information costs. In the case of formal institutions this is not hard to see. The costs for a person who lends money to another person are much lower in the case of clear and enforceable debtor laws than in a case of anarchy where a lot of information is needed on the trustworthiness of the debtor. With regard to informal institutions, the statement, however, includes the assumption that the rules are commonly known and accepted. And this is exactly the aspect of institutions that separates them from personal values and preferences. Values have to be shared at least by a certain part of the society to become social norms or conventions that constrain human behavior. Personal rules and "laws" not generally accepted by others are therefore not informal institutions, even if they may strongly determine the behavior of an individual.

This argument directly leads to another important aspect of institutions: the enforceability of the rules. Formal rules are normally enforced by state authority; informal rules are often self-enforcing. Breaking the rules leads to some form of sanctioning either by a court in the case of formal institutions or by other members of society in the case of informal institutions. The latter sanctions could take different forms (moral suasion, social exclusion, etc.). A social value that does not constrain the behavior of an individual with personal values different from the commonly shared values either in the form of social sanctions or in the form of incentives should not be called an institution. Institutions are widely known rules with the power to structure often repeated social or economic interactions. This enforcement component of institutions helps to overcome the free-rider problem in prisoners' dilemma situations. Rules that enhance social welfare in the long run (if everybody adheres to the rules) might not be stable when the gains from breaking the rules are higher for individuals in the short run. Sanctions that increase the costs for the individuals to break the rules help maximize welfare in the long run. The object of the so-called Comparative Institutional Analysis – a prominent research field in New Institutional Economics – is to identify these sorts of welfare-enhancing institutions by comparing existing social norms, constitutions, and institutional arrangements in their rule and enforcement components.

This economic definition of institutions is different from the concept of governance, more rooted in political science. The term "governance" refers to all sorts of policies that try to organize social, economic, or cultural life (often dominated by the interests of special interest groups). The decision making could take place in different governance regimes. A distinction between hierarchies, networks, and markets is common here. The concept of governance is used in modern political science as a counterpart to the classical concept of government that defines policy solely as decision making on public affairs by the state. All sorts of policies, whether they are infrastructure investments by the state or investments in an education program by a network of private initiatives, determine and constrain human behavior. So what is the difference from the concept of institutions? Above all else it is the stability in time. If economists refer to the term "institutions," they have long-lasting rules in mind and not discretionary decisions. To keep it simple, one might think of a cascade of rules and public choices ranked by their stability in time (Figure 18.2).

At the top of the cascade there are informal institutions that are rooted in long-lasting traditions, followed by constitutions usually implemented to transform important informal norms into formal rules. In the world of James Buchanan the veil of uncertainty in a constitutional assembly would help identify fair rules not dictated by vested interests of the makers of the constitution. The real world might tell another story, but constitutions are nevertheless in general made to last for decades if not for generations. The constitution usually defines rules to set up certain institutional arrangements like democracy, federalism, and the separation of power. These institutional arrangements are really close to what political science means by governance regimes. On the level of institutional arrangements societies choose how to choose. For example, they may use the price mechanism (i.e., the market) or democracy as the "decision-making procedure" for the allocation and distribution of a certain kind of good.

The day-to-day output of these institutional arrangements is some form of governance. The term "organizations" refers to the decision-makers (the political parties, the municipalities, private firms, trade unions, schools, and so on) responsible for these day-to-day policies. From the institutional economic point of view organizations are not themselves institutions; only the decision-making procedures are institutions (North 1990, pp. 5–6). To solely use the duration of institutions to separate them from policies is not enough. Many policy decisions like infrastructure investments are just as long-lasting, at least in a material sense. An additional aspect is the distinction between rules of the game and the choices within the rules. The choice of

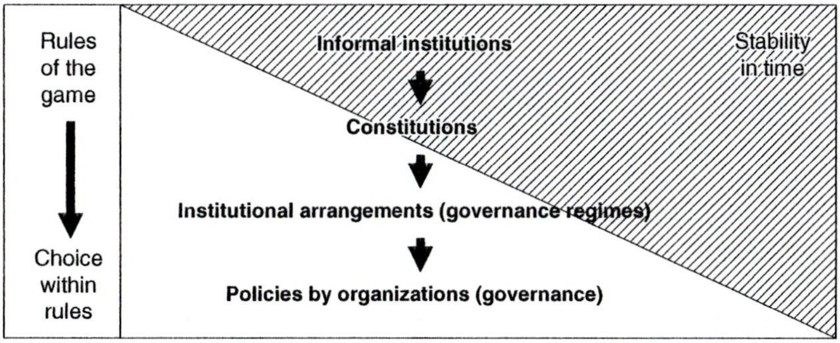

Figure 18.2 Institutions and governance

institutions has a certain distance from day-to-day bargaining between interest groups (organizations) and at least in the theoretical model should represent a broad social consensus on what rules are fair rules. An example often cited in literature to make the fundamental distinction between institutions and policies clear is that of taxation. The constitutional rule to finance public goods with taxes and the tax law that enforces the state to collect taxes from its citizens are both institutions. The determination of the tax tariff and the decision of which public goods will be financed is then up to policy.

Human rights and New Institutional Economics

In the last ten years comparative institutional economists conducted a great deal of empirical research to identify welfare-enhancing institutions. Until today the empirical studies have concentrated on cross-country differences in constitutional aspects and institutional arrangements, i.e., differences in formal institutions. There is strong and robust empirical evidence that the core institutions of Western-style market economies contributed to investment, growth, and income at least in the last four or five decades. Countries that efficiently secured property rights and contract enforcement grew faster on average than countries that failed to do so (Knack and Keefer 1995; Roll and Talbott 2001; Claessens and Laeven 2003; Saleh 2004). These findings strictly fit to the mainstream theory. Property rights and contract enforcement reduce the uncertainty and therefore the transaction costs of private business. An entrepreneur who faces the threat of expropriation will hold back or at least reduce future investment. If economic subjects have the right to subscribe contracts (free from too much state regulation) and can be sure that an impartial and incorrupt state will enforce the contracts, this will increase private economic activity. If the aggregate investment of a country is overwhelmingly based on private investment (as is the case in market economies) this sort of economic freedom is crucial for economic development. The so-called Economic Freedom Index (Gwartney et al. 1996), the most prominent index for the quality of economic institutions apart from business risk indicators, combines measures of legal security of ownership and contract rights with measures of state interference into private economic activities (by taxation, price controls, trade barriers, and so on). The Western-style rule of law assures that property and contract rights are protected with a certain procedural fairness and transparency. This again reduces transaction costs. The separation of power component enhances checks and balances and reduces corruption, binds state actors to the law, and empowers private investors vis-à-vis the state. According to empirical findings the rule of law (Barro 2000) and de facto judicial independence (Feld and Voigt 2003) help explain differences in per capita gross domestic product (GDP) growth across countries.

These three core institutions of the Western hemisphere (property rights, contract enforcement, and the rule of law) seem to have a greater impact on economic development than policy variables like trade openness, macroeconomic stability, or non-arbitrary taxation on the one hand and geographic characteristics like climate, natural resources, and access to open water on the other (Clague et al. 1997; Easterly and Levine 2002b; Rodrik et al. 2002). Findings of New Institutional Economists show that settler mortality and urbanization in 1500 are good instruments for the national quality of institutional arrangements and therefore economic development (Acemoglu et al. 2004); the same holds true for distance from the equator and the fraction of population speaking a European language (Hall and Jones 1999). In the period of colonialism European settlers spread to regions where settler mortality was low, overwhelmingly regions on a similar latitude to their home countries. In regions with low urbanization and population density (e.g., North America) it was easy for them to settle and implement their own European-style institutions. In regions with high urbanization and population density (e.g., Central and

South America) the European conquerors often chose a system that favored the exploitation of human and natural resources instead of sustainable settlement. In the following decades European investment was concentrated in the regions with sustainable settlement and more European-style institutions. Economic development in former colonies (e.g., the GDP per capita in 1995) is therefore negatively linked with population density and settler mortality in 1500 and positively linked with their distance from the equator. The legal origin of the settlers seems to have a certain impact too. Colonies under British influence developed *ceteris paribus* better than other colonies, at least partially because of the English common law tradition. According to La Porta et al. (1999), a French or German civil law tradition can be taken as a proxy for an intent to build institutions to further the power of the state and a common law tradition can be taken as a proxy for the intent to limit the state.

This reasoning about a strong state directly leads to the question of political institutions. According to Acemoglu et al. (2004), political institutions are those institutions that – together with the distribution of resources – determine the distribution of de jure and de facto political power in society. This distribution of power, in turn:

> affects the choice of economic institutions and influences the future evolution of political institutions. Economic institutions determine economic outcomes, including the aggregate growth rate of the economy and the distribution of resources at time t+1. Although economic institutions are the essential factor shaping economic outcomes, they are themselves endogenous and determined by political institutions and distribution of resources in society.
>
> *(Acemoglu et al. 2004, p. 6)*

While it is fairly obvious that in a world dominated by private investment, economic institutions like secure property rights are growth enhancing from a comparative perspective, the reasoning regarding political institutions is not that straightforward. New Institutional Economists discuss a phenomenon they call the dilemma of the strong state (Weingast 1993). On one hand the state favors economic development by correcting market failures (caused by externalities, asymmetric information, monopolistic competition) and providing public goods (e.g., economic institutions like secure property rights); on the other hand there might be problems of state failure (caused by an inefficient bureaucracy or rent-seeking activities of interest groups). A state that is strong enough to protect private property rights and enforce private contracts is also strong enough to expropriate private wealth (e.g., by taxation and redistribution). This dilemma of the strong state at least partially explains the empirical findings regarding political institutions. There seems to be a non-linear relationship between democracy and growth. Poor countries in an early stage of economic development can be developed either by an autocratic or a democratic regime. What influences growth at least on this stage of development is not so much the type of regime (dictatorship or democracy) but regime instability, that is, the propensity to coups and major changes of government (Barro 1991; Clague et al. 1997). Certain dictatorships that do not allow free elections, such as, for example, Taiwan and South Korea, have grown very fast in the last decades by creating the necessary environment for market activities to prosper (investment in education, secure property and contract rights); other dictatorships have performed very poorly. Strong income inequalities and a lack of civil liberties seem to be no growth barrier in the former countries; by contrast, "wealth inequality may be growth enhancing, because in this case at least someone will have enough resources to acquire education, generating positive externalities that will benefit other agents later" (Alesina and Perotti 1997, p. 26). At a certain stage of economic development the advantages of a democratic regime increase. Democratic institutions and civil liberties foster growth by improving the accumulation of human capital and lowering income inequality (Tavares and Wacziarg 2001). Income equality becomes more beneficial because even the middle class can start investing, e.g., in education. In systems with free elections, the higher the equilibrium tax rate, the poorer the median voter is relative to the voter with average income. A democratic political regime contains constraints on political leaders and reduces corruption through electoral, legislative, and judicial institutions. Bureaucratic efficiency is higher in such countries (Mauro 1995). Democracy, measured for example by the Gastil index of political rights (Gastil 1991), therefore leads to a strong state with the ability to provide a favorable business environment in middle- and high-income countries. "But in places that have already achieved a moderate amount of democracy, a further increase in political rights impairs growth and investment because the dominant effect comes from the intensified concern with income redistribution" (Barro 1998, p. 59). The relationship between democracy and economic development seems to have an inverse u-shape. In low-income countries other institutions and policies than political rights are important to enhance growth. Then, after a certain threshold in development is passed, democracy enhances growth. Too much democratization hinders growth by reducing the rate of physical capital accumulation and by raising the ratio of government consumption to GDP. These findings are sensitive to the concrete design of the democratic institutions. Presidential and majoritarian electoral systems have comparatively smaller governments than parliamentary and proportional systems, and they tend to have a lower factor productivity (Persson and Tabellini 2003). A certain fiscal decentralization seems to foster growth, especially in middle-income countries (Thießen 2003).

Simplifying, three positions concerning the economic effects of human rights discussed among economists can be distinguished. (i) The Hayek hypothesis, according to which basic human rights and property rights (negative rights) have a positive impact on welfare and growth, whereas a high degree of social rights (positive rights such as a right to employment or adequate housing) would be counterproductive. (ii) The Barro–Posner hypothesis argues that there is an important sequence to be observed: first, only property rights are important, which will lead to increases in income that will later allow societies higher levels in the other kinds of rights. (iii) The Sen hypothesis purports that freedom, fairness, and reciprocity are important and that social capital has a positive effect on welfare and growth, which is, however, not necessarily measured in terms of monetary income only. Figure 18.3 depicts these competing hypotheses graphically.

Hayek (e.g., 1976) takes up the traditional distinction between negative rights that create domains protected against trespassing and positive rights that endow their holders with a claim against the entire collective. Hayek only quarrels with the second kind of rights. He emphasizes that the creation of rights simultaneously means the creation of obligations. If people are given the right to work, to a paid holiday, to adequate housing, etc., this means that those who are now obliged to enforce the rights must be given the means to do so. Society must be – in Hayek's words – transformed into an organization with overarching collective goals that trump individual goals. This means that in order to enforce social rights, the classical liberal rights have to be at least attenuated. In short, Hayek believes that positive rights are incompatible with a market economy, but negative rights like basic human rights and property rights are welfare enhancing.

Authors such as Barro (2000) or Posner (1995) argue that the prerequisites for a well-functioning market economy are secure property rights and not human rights. They point to the fact that a regime may completely respect the property rights of foreign investors while simultaneously using violence against its own citizens. Autocratic regimes have proven that they are able to allocate substantial resources into research and development. Furthermore, democracies enable majorities to vote in favor of redistribution, which can, at least past some threshold, be interpreted as an attenuation of property rights. Representatives of this position

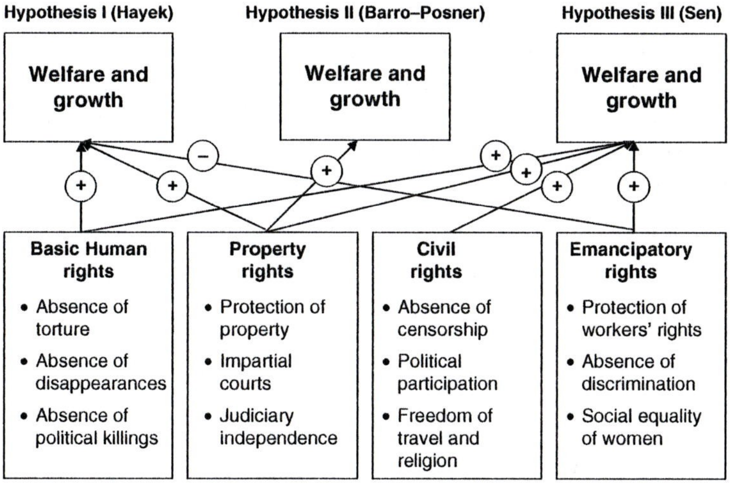

Figure 18.3 Prominent hypotheses on human rights and welfare

thus distinguish economic rights from civil and political rights. They are convinced that economic rights are crucial for economic development and that well-functioning market economies need not necessarily be democratic.

A third line of argumentation that is related to the work of Amartya Sen (1933–) purports that freedom, fairness, and reciprocity have positive effects on welfare and growth. Uncertainty regarding human rights makes the return on investment with regard to both human and other capital more uncertain, and government respect for human rights can be interpreted as a signal concerning the seriousness of government promises concerning other rights. The absence of basic protection could increase the probability of violent protest and thus lead to instability, and it could also lead to lower levels of innovation. According to this hypothesis the absence of human rights abuses is a crucial precondition that must be satisfied before talk of economic rights becomes meaningful. Like in a Leontief production function, basic human rights cannot be substituted by anything else. The right to one's own body is a crucial precondition for making productive use of one's other resources.

Outlook

As outlined in this chapter the relatively young theoretical framework of New Institutional Economics is a promising research program for dealing with the question of human rights in economics. But the research on human rights is still at its beginning, because in the past New Institutional Economists have concentrated on other sets of rights such as property rights and contract law. The competing hypotheses sketched out in Figure 18.3 dominate the current discussion on human rights in economics, and further research is strongly recommended in this field. Blume and Voigt (2007) is a first cross-country analysis that shows that none of the components of human rights have any significant negative impact on welfare and growth. The Hayek hypothesis, which implies that emancipatory rights might have a negative effect, is therefore not supported by this empirical study of a cross-section of more than one hundred countries. The study finds empirical evidence for both the Barro–Posner and the

Sen hypotheses, depending on the welfare indicator being looked at. With regard to economic growth, the Barro–Posner hypothesis is the most convincing one; with regard to investment, productivity, and happiness other human rights factors also have some positive impact, thus supporting the Sen hypothesis.

For future studies, three approaches seem to recommend themselves in order to shed further light on the debate: One could try to remain within the cross-country frame but give more attention to the transmission channels that relate human rights to different welfare indicators. Second, time-series or panel analysis might make sense. Before these tests can be actually carried out, some more time needs to pass in order to have time-series data on human rights available for a longer period. A third option would consist of having a closer look at the development of countries via case studies. Especially developing countries could be of a certain interest, since the fate of the poorest countries seems to be determined by slightly different regularities.

References

Acemoglu, D., S. Johnson and J. Robinson 2004. "Institutions as the Fundamental Cause of Long-Run Growth." NBER Working Paper No. 10481 (Cambridge: NBER).

Alchian, A. A. and H. Demsetz. 1972. "Production, Information Costs, and Economic Organization." *American Economic Review*, Vol. 62, pp. 777–795.

Alesina, A. and R. Perotti 1997. "The Politics of Growth: A Survey." In V. Bergström, *Government and Growth* (Oxford: Oxford University Press).

Barro, R. J. 1991. "Economic Growth in a Cross Section of Countries." *Quarterly Journal of Economics*, Vol. 106/2, pp. 407–433.

Barro, R. J. 1998. *Determinants of Economic Growth. A Cross-Country Empirical Study* (Cambridge, MA: MIT Press).

Barro, R. J. 2000. *Rule of Law, Democracy, and Economic Performance, Index of Economic Freedom* (Washington, DC: The Heritage Foundation), pp. 31–49.

Blume, L. and S. Voigt. 2007. "The Economic Effects of Human Rights." *Kyklos*, Vol. 60, No. 4, pp. 509–538.

Buchanan, J. M. 1975. *The Limits of Liberty: Between Anarchy and Leviathan* (Chicago: University of Chicago Press).

Claessens, S. and L. Laeven. 2003. "Financial Development, Property Rights, and Growth." *Journal of Finance*, Vol. 58, pp. 2401–2436.

Clague, C. Ph. Keefer, S. Knack, and M. Olson. 1997. "Democracy, Autocracy, and the Institutions Supportive of Economic Growth." pp. 91–120, in C. Clague, ed., *Institutions and Economic Development: Growth and Governance in Less-Developed and Post-Socialist Countries* (Baltimore, MD: Johns Hopkins University Press).

Coase, R. H. 1937. "The Nature of the Firm." *Economica*, Vol. 4, pp. 386–405.

Downs, A. 1957. *An Economic Theory of Democracy* (New York: Harper).

Easterly, W. and R. Levine. 2002a. "It's Not Factor Accumulation: Stylized Facts and Growth Models." Central Bank of Chile Working Papers No. 164.

Easterly, W. and R. Levine. 2002b. "Tropics, Germs, and Crops: How Endowments Influence Economic Development." NBER Working Paper No. 9106 (Cambridge: NBER).

Eucken, W. 1952. *Grundsätze der Wirtschaftspolitik* (Tübingen: J. C. B. Mohr).

Feld, L. P. and S. Voigt. 2003. "Economic Growth and Judicial Independence: Cross Country Evidence Using a New Set of Indicators." *European Journal of Political Economy*, Vol. 19, pp. 497–527.

Furubotn, E. and R. Richter. 1997. *Neue Institutionenökonomik, Eine Einführung und Kritische Würdigung* (Tübingen: Mohr Siebeck).

Gastil, R. D. 1991. "The Comparative Survey of Freedom: Experiences and Suggestions." In A. Inkeles, ed., *On Measuring Democracy* (New Brunswick, NJ: Transaction).

Grossman, G. M. and E. Helpman. 1991. *Innovation and Growth in the Global Economy* (Cambridge, MA: MIT Press).

Gwartney, J., R. Lawson, and W. Block. 1996. *Economic Freedom of the World: 1975–95* (Vancouver: Fraser Institute).

Hall, R. E. and C. I. Jones. 1999. "Why Do Some Countries Produce So Much More Output Per Worker Than Others?" *Quarterly Journal of Economics*, Vol. 20, pp. 83–116.
v. Hayek, F. A. 1960. *The Constitution of Liberty* (Chicago: University of Chicago Press).
v. Hayek, F. A. 1976. *Law, Legislation and Liberty*, Vol. I (Chicago: University of Chicago Press).
Helpman, E. and P. Krugman. 1985. *Increasing Returns, Imperfect Competition, and International Trade* (Cambridge, MA: Harvard Institute of Economic Research).
Hodgson, G. M. 1988. *Economics and Institutions* (Cambridge: Polity Press).
Hutchison, T. W. 1984. "Institutionalist Economics Old and New." *Journal of Institutional and Theoretical Economics*, Vol. 140, pp. 20–29.
Knack, S. and P. Keefer. 1995. "Institutions and Economic Performance: Cross Country Tests Using Alternative Institutional Measures." *Economics and Politics*, Vol. 7, pp. 207–227.
Krugman, P. 1991. *Geography and Trade* (Cambridge, MA: MIT Press).
Langlois, R. N. 1986. "The New Institutional Economics: An Introductory Essay." In R. N. Langlois, ed., *Economics as a Process, Essays in the New Institutional Economics* (New York: Cambridge University Press).
La Porta, R. F. Lopez-de-Silanes, A. Shleifer, and R. Vishny. 1999. "The Quality of Government." *Journal of Law, Economics, and Organization*, Vol. 15, pp. 222–279.
Lucas, R. 1987. "On the Mechanics of Economic Development." *Journal of Monetary Economics*, Vol. 22, pp. 43–70.
Mankiw, N. G., D. Romer, and D. N. Weill. 1992. "A Contribution to the Empirics of Economic Growth." *Quarterly Journal of Economics*, Vol. 107, pp. 407–437.
Mauro, P. 1995. "Corruption and Growth." *Quarterly Journal of Economics*, Vol. 110, pp. 681–712.
Nelson, R. R. 1993. *National Innovation Systems: A Comparative Analysis* (Oxford: Oxford University Press).
Niskanen, W. 1971. *Bureaucracy and Representative Government* (Chicago: Aldine).
North, D. C. 1990. *Institutions, Institutional Change and Economic Performance* (Cambridge: Cambridge University Press).
Olson, M. 1965. *The Logic of Collective Action: Public Goods and the Theory of Groups* (Cambridge, MA: Harvard University Press).
Persson, T. and G. Tabellini. 2003. *The Economic Effects of Constitutions* (Cambridge, MA: MIT Press).
Pigou, A. C. 1920. *The Economics of Welfare* (London: Macmillan).
Porter, M. E. 1990. *The Competitive Advantage of Nations* (London: Collier Macmillan).
Posner, R. A. 1995. "An Economic Perspective on Basic Rights: The Cost of Enforcing Legal Rights." *East European Constitutional Review*, Vol. 4, No. 3, pp. 71–83.
Rodrik, D., A. Subramanian, and F. Trebbi. 2002. "Institutions Rule: The Primacy of Institutions over Geography and Integration in Economic Development." NBER Working Paper No. 9305 (Cambridge: NBER).
Roll, R. and J. Talbott. 2001. "Why Many Developing Countries Just Aren't." Finance Working Paper No. 19-01 (Los Angeles: The Anderson School at UCLA).
Romer, P. R. 1987. "Growth Based on Increasing Returns Due to Specialization." *American Economic Review*, Vol. 77, pp. 56–62.
Rutherford, M. 2001. "Institutional Economics: Then and Now." *Journal of Economic Perspectives*, Vol. 15, No. 3, pp. 173–194.
Saleh, J. 2004. "Property Rights Institutions and Investment." World Bank Policy Research Working Paper 3311 (Washington, DC: World Bank).
Solow, R. M. 1956. "A Contribution to the Theory of Economic Growth." *Quarterly Journal of Economics*, Vol. 70, pp. 65–94.
Tavares, J. and R. Wacziarg. 2001. "How Democracy Affects Growth." *European Economic Review*, Vol. 45, pp. 1341–1378.
Thießen, U. 2003. "Fiscal Decentralization and Economic Growth in High Income OECD Countries." *Fiscal Studies*, Vol. 24, pp. 237–274.
Weingast, B. 1993. "Constitutions as Governance Structures: The Political Foundations of Secure Markets." *Journal of Institutional and Theoretical Economics*, Vol. 149, No. 1, pp. 286–311.
Williamson, O. E. 1975. *Markets and Hierarchies* (New York: Free Press).

19

Rights, reform, and resources

Malthusian reflections on scarcity and old age

Bryan S. Turner

Introduction: the right to life and the problem of scarcity

The Declaration of Human Rights and subsequent charters and legal elaborations embrace a range of rights relating to life itself, health and health care, protection from exploitation and slavery, and other rights that may be broadly construed as promoting well-being and the good life. Anybody who is committed in whatever way to the promotion and protection of human rights must welcome these developments. I have in *Vulnerability and Human Rights* (Turner 2006) argued that, because human beings are vulnerable, they require various legal and political institutions to protect themselves against the vagaries and perturbations of mere existence. Human rights provide us with some modicum of security against "bare life" (Agamben 1998). The implications of this argument are many and complex. Although the enjoyment of the rights that support life, health, and reproduction are basic to human rights as such, it is clearly difficult to deliver and enforce these rights. It is widely recognized that, without the support of nation-states, very few human rights could become effective. Furthermore, the institutions necessary for our survival are themselves precarious and often inadequate and inefficient. There is as a result a complex set of relationships among our vulnerability, institution-building, and state power. Current thinking about human rights in relation to the actual support of human life is weak in two fundamental respects. First, human rights declarations notoriously lack any parallel systematic development of the notion of human duties. In jurisprudential parlance, there is a lack of "correlativity." What are the specific duties that might correspond to a right to adequate health care? The absence of a discourse of human duties is partly connected to the fact that human rights are typically invoked *in extremis* when a population is faced with famine, degradation, civil disturbance, or extinction, namely when a population has become a community of victims. In such circumstances, it is bizarre and possibly immoral to start talking about duty. Nevertheless, human rights are typically invoked for individuals or communities who are incapable of undertaking any duties, because their entitlements are to some extent claims of last resort. Stateless people who may be exposed to genocide are people whose right to have a right has been called into question, and hence it is equally difficult, indeed morally objectionable, to raise the issue of correlativity in such cases.

Second, legislative and political instruments relating to the fundamental right to life contain little or nothing about the question of resources. Works on human rights characteristically lack any serious attention to political economy. There are at least two issues here. One is that, given social and economic inequality, the distribution of resources is necessarily unequal and therefore the majority of human beings are all too often condemned to live short and unpleasant lives. The obvious measure of this inequality is the variable nature of human life expectancy between rich and poor countries. While the lifespan of Japanese women continues to grow, showing little sign of curtailment, the lifespan of Congolese men continues to decline. The second problem is that many of the resources that are necessary to sustain life – most crucially water – are scarce. How then can human rights be enjoyed when resources are scarce and unequally distributed? These questions are most typically associated with Karl Marx's criticisms of capitalist society and the early doctrine of "the Rights of Man." Marx argued, for example in the so-called "Jewish Question," that the abstract rights of Man were empty claims in a society where property rights ensured that the working class would never enjoy true liberty without a revolutionary change in the very structure of capitalist society (Marx 1963). The condition of the working class in the manufacturing cities of England during the industrial revolution was sufficient evidence of this obvious fact, but this poverty, persisting into the early twentieth century, was famously explored by George Orwell (1937) in *The Road to Wigan Pier.*

These two issues are normally combined in arguments that suggest scarcity is a product of inequality. If resources were equally distributed, then people would not experience scarcity. The enjoyment of human rights would therefore require major social reforms to change the ways in which free markets, for example, operate. This view of scarcity is based ultimately on some notion that scarcity is *socially* produced. By contrast, the classical political economists, especially Thomas Malthus and David Ricardo, regarded scarcity as *naturally* produced. In this chapter I argue that resources, although socially mediated, are nevertheless finite, claiming along with Malthus that, given contemporary increases in population, technological change will not overcome, and may intensify, the (re)emerging resource crisis. Resources are finite, and there is an inevitable accumulation of waste with all forms of economic growth (Georgescu-Roegen 1971). The application of medical technology – stem-cell research applications, cryonics, and nanotechnology – in the modern quest for indefinite longevity and the quest to create a transhuman society, will only make this natural scarcity more profound and invasive. The quest to enhance longevity through exercise, vitamin supplements, cosmetic surgery, and regular medical surveillance may be available to Western elites, but these fashionable regimes will do little for the life-chances of the majority (Drexler 1986; Kirkwood 1999; Kurzweil and Grossman 2004). Medical technology will in the long run compound and deepen the problematic relationship among longevity, population growth, and scarcity. If this version of the Malthusian argument can be sustained, then there is an inevitable brake on the right to life. A universal right to life will sound increasingly hollow in a world short of water, arable land, and energy resources. By looking at the issue of scarcity, my intention is to suggest that human societies will need to support efforts to limit population growth, for example through a more positive ethical view of suicide and euthanasia. This debate inevitably raises the question: if there is a right to life, is there a duty to death?

Thomas Malthus: social reform versus demographic pessimism

Can life with the aid of modern medical technology and significant economic investment in health care be extended more or less indefinitely? This question can be formulated in at least two ways: namely, can we survive indefinitely, and ought we to live indefinitely? One is a factual question about what medical interventions would be necessary for human beings to extend their lives significantly. The second is an ethical issue about how the project of longevity could be justified. Medical arguments often presuppose that the extension of life needs no ethical justification since life itself is worth preserving. Medical ethics – along with most religious doctrines – commit doctors to preserving life, and hence in many societies euthanasia is thought, without further question, to be without any compelling moral grounding. The assumption is that to preserve life needs no justification. In practice of course doctors and nurses will often take into account situational factors, showing a concern for questions relating to the quality of life of the chronically sick. Such patients may simply be allowed to die rather than being subject to invasive medicine.

Can we live forever? This question asks whether the mere survival of the human body can be extended beyond the contemporary limit of around 115 years. Perhaps the obvious answer to the question is negative. In human history, despite rising life expectancy, very few humans live beyond average life expectancy and, although there are now many more centenarians, the final stages of life for the majority of people, even in developed societies, are typically punctuated by degrading and painful sickness and disability. But these common-sense responses to this question may, without further reflection, commit us prematurely to a pessimistic vision of life as inevitably and necessarily fixed and limited. Medical optimists want us at least to consider the possibility that not only can life be extended, but it can be dramatically improved (De Grey 2003, 2004, 2005).

The problem of longevity has been perfectly captured in Greek mythology (Appleyard 2007; Brown 2008). Tithonus, a mere mortal and brother of Priam, is loved by Eos, the beautiful dawn goddess. Realizing, however, that Tithonus will eventually die, she begs Zeus to grant her lover the gift of immortality, but omits to ask for his eternal youth. Being a jealous god, Zeus literally grants her wish, and Tithonus does indeed enjoy immortal life, but without the additional and crucial blessing of youthfulness. As Tithonus grows old, he also becomes decrepit, and Eos, finding her demented lover to be a disgusting and unbearable burden, is driven to despair by his senile and senseless babbling. Finally, Eos transforms the decaying Tithonus into a cicada whose ceaseless mechanical chirruping provides a parody of the babbling of the aging and decaying Tithonus. Alfred, Lord Tennyson's famous poem ("Tithonus"), published in the *Cornhill Magazine* of 1860, captures the sadness of this myth:

> Man comes and tills the field and lies beneath,
> And after many a summer dies the swan.
> Me only cruel immortality
> Consumes; I wither slowly in thine arms.

The claim of contemporary medical "immortalism" is that medical science and technology can solve the Tithonus puzzle by simultaneously granting us immortality and eternal youth. By contrast, critics of medical science argue that the project of longevity is not desirable, since senility cannot be overcome by technology and, although we might survive indefinitely, our troublesome physical discomforts and disabilities will inevitably accompany our longevity (Callahan 1987; Hayflick 2000, 2005). The pessimistic argument is that, while medicine may bring blessings to individuals, medical technology cannot overcome the collective problem of scarcity. In addition, these life-extension projects raise basic questions about employment, retirement, and pensions for which we have few adequate long-term policy solutions, and recent neo-liberal attempts to privatize pension funds may have compounded rather than solved existing institutional arrangements (Blackburn 2002).

Thus the contemporary debate, which involves an awareness that many developed societies are experiencing the rapid aging of their populations and the realization that there are medical interventions that could in principle significantly extend human longevity, divides people into optimists ("Immortalists") and pessimists ("Deathists"). More profoundly, it divides people into those with a utopian vision of what is technologically possible in modern societies and those with a dystopian vision who emphasize the negative economic, and possibly inhuman, consequences of any significant extension of human life.

After this preliminary consideration of the factual question, we can turn briefly to the second way in which we could formulate the question as an ethical issue: ought we to live forever? To this question I propose two possible responses – aesthetic and political. First, we can appeal to the idea of life as an aesthetic creation from the philosophy of Friedrich Nietzsche (1969) in, for example, *Thus Spake Zarathustra.* For Nietzsche, the only ultimate purpose to life (as opposed to mere existence) is to "become who we are." This goal involves an inner struggle to develop our selves as if we were a work of art (Nehamas 1985). To live creatively in this Nietzschean sense presupposes the acceptance of a heroic ethic. This struggle to govern the soul is corrupted by nihilistic drives such as resentment, the principal example of which is resentment against the passage of time itself. We should not resent the inevitable unfolding of time, but welcome each day as an opportunity for self-creation (Thiele 1990). Such an ethic might be a valuable counterforce to the purely medico-technological view of living forever as simply creating the conditions whereby people could survive with a tolerable level of health but with no purpose and no meaning. The justification for life that we might take from Nietzsche is simply in his terms to live life creatively and productively in order to contribute to the health of human society by creating strong individuals. There are problems, clearly, with this aesthetic justification because, as a heroic view of life as struggle, it sets a high standard on human beings to strive for excellence. It could be criticized as elitist – and of course in Nietzsche's case it is explicitly the aesthetic aim of the overman. Nevertheless Nietzsche provides a welcome challenge to the secular view that life could be lived with no ultimate purpose apart from life itself, and of course Nietzsche's personal fate – to live his final years in a vegetative state under the management of his sister – was an ironic negation of his quest to find value in life in a godless world.

The second type of justification is political by reference to a political notion of virtue in terms of some notion of contributory rights. As citizens we can be said to have certain rights – to education, to voting, to wealth, and to security – because in principle we can fulfill certain duties. These may be typically thought of as contributions to society through taxation, through public activity such as military service, and through our routine contributions to social life through, for example, raising children as the next generation of citizens. The medical care and attention that we receive, especially in old age, can be regarded as the outcome of the social rights we enjoy as retired citizens (Turner 2004). We could justify our longevity in terms of the rights we have as senior citizens on the basis of contributions, not necessarily lifelong, to the community. There are clearly problems with this contributory theory, because the balance between right and duty or between contribution and entitlement is never perfect. It also raises problems about the responsibility of society toward disabled persons, but a theory of contributory rights does offer some method, however inadequate, of assessing the reasonable claims of a citizen against the state. To argue that a person has full rights as a citizen regardless of contribution is to accept a view of the citizen as permanently passive and detached.

Resources

Neither the aesthetic nor the political justifications for life extension make any significant contribution to the political economy of resources, namely to the problem of scarcity. Recent accounts of citizenship have often ignored or denied that there is a scarcity issue. For example, in her *Genealogies of Citizenship* (2008), Margaret Somers argues that the notion of scarcity is part of the "market fundamentalism" that puts work and employment at the center of any notion of entitlement. For Somers, scarcity is an ideological notion of classical economics that is used to discipline labor. While her argument has considerable merit, it is implausible to argue that in general human society does not face any issue of scarcity. For example, because of overfishing, cod has become scarce in the North Sea, forcing prices up and resulting in the closure of many fishing enterprises as a result of European environmental legislation. Shortage of cod may be "man-made," but cod are as it happens scarce. With global warming, many other items that we take for granted today will disappear. The polar bear will become scarce. Is the opposite of a pessimistic view of scarcity an equally utopian view of the promise of abundance? But these examples may miss the point about the relationship between modernity and scarcity. I follow Nicholas Xenos (1989, p. 5) in believing that for the "denizens of this world, it is no longer a question of episodic insufficiency: out of affluence we have created a world of scarcity." Some aspects of scarcity may be socially constructed, but they are scarce nevertheless.

In this debate about scarcity, Malthus has received bad press, being accused by Thomas Carlyle of creating a "dismal science" and by Somers (2008, pp. 52–53) of "social naturalism" in subordinating the social world to the market via a theory of human desires. By contrast, we should treat Malthus's argument simply as an "if–then" account of the relationship among population, arable land, and the economy. Given a fixed amount of usable land, if population increases, then the price of corn will increase with negative consequences for the urban working class. Malthus at one level was a critic of urban society, arguing that the rustic condition of the agrarian working class was far superior to the misery suffered by workers in unhealthy, squalid, overcrowded cities. One could say that he anticipated Friedrich Engels's account of the working poor of Manchester, just as Ricardo's account of wages, profits, and rent anticipated Karl Marx's theory of social class. Apart from his theological views, some of the problems with Malthusian economics are purely technical, such as the comparison between potato and corn prices in England and Ireland (Staley 1989, p. 61).

I need therefore to provide a sketch of what I take to be the central resource problems of modern society, specifically from a Malthusian perspective, in order to highlight the gap between the discourse of rights and the stubborn facts of political economy. Therefore let us start with some consideration of the population issue. Scientific attempts to measure the world's population did not get underway until the 1940s and demography as a discipline did not emerge until nation-states sought to exercise greater surveillance of and control over the demographic characteristics of their populations. Estimates of human population growth before the twentieth century are consequently unreliable. We can reasonably claim, however, that around ten thousand years ago at the beginning of the agricultural revolution, the world population was around a few million, but with settled agriculture the human population began to rise steadily, if only slowly, and by AD1 it was between 200 and 300 million. By 1800 it was around one billion and it had reached two billion just before the outbreak of the Second World War. The global population was four billion by 1960 and around seven billion today (MacInnes and Pérez 2009a). The most significant social change of the twentieth century was the worldwide elimination, for the first time in human history, of premature death, especially infant deaths from infectious diseases. In 1950, seven out of ten of the world's women lived in countries where female life expectancy at birth was under 65 years. Life expectancy was well below this threshold throughout much of Africa and Asia, where it was generally in the low forties, and Latin America and the Caribbean, in the low fifties. Only in Europe, North America, Australia and New Zealand, Israel, Cyprus, Armenia, and Japan, could women expect to reach old age (MacInnes and Pérez 2009b).

Alongside the rise in life expectancy and the decline in the total fertility rate, there is a rapidly aging world population. Peter Laslett shattered many myths about family history and structure, particularly in his *The World We Have Lost* (1965). In his contribution to historical demography, he invented the term "secular shift" to describe rising life expectancy in the century after the 1880s (Kertzer and Laslett 1995). This secular change was dramatic (Fries 1980). If we take life expectancy at birth for men only in England and Wales, the increase was from 44.2 years in 1881 to 70.1 in 1991. Similar results for this period can be reported for other societies. For example in the United States, the increase was also from 42.5 to 71.3; in Canada, from 43.5 to 73.0; in France from 40.8 to 72; in Germany from 35.6 to 71.8; and in Japan, from 42.4 to 75.5. The proportion of the population over 60 years of age during the secular shift rose in England and Wales from 7.4 percent to 17.0 percent; in the United States, from around 5.4 to 15.9 percent; in Canada, from 5.4 to 11.3 percent; in France, from 12.3 to 16.6 percent; in Germany, from 7.9 to 16.7 percent; and in Japan there is no figure for the 1880s but it was 12.9 percent by the end of the twentieth century.

It is instructive to pause for a while to consider the Japanese case, because aging in Japanese society is often quoted as an example of extremely rapid change, but the figures from Japan are also used to support arguments for dramatic policy changes to counteract the negative consequences of an aging population. The population over the age of 65 will rise from its 1988 figure of 11.0 percent to 23.6 percent by 2021. Japanese women in particular are surviving in significant numbers into deep old age. In 2008, average life expectancy for Japanese women was 85 years and it is predicted to rise to 97 years by 2050. There are interesting regional variations, and it has been discovered that people in Okinawa have 600 people out of a population of 1.3 million who are centenarians – the highest density of centenarians in the world.

Similar outcomes have been found for the rate of aging in the United States, where the proportion of the population over 65 years rose from 12.4 percent in 2000 to a projected 19.6 percent in 2030. In absolute terms, the number of people over 80 years will rise from 35 million in 2000 to an estimated 71 million in 2030. There are, as in Japan, important regional and state differences. Florida had 19 percent of its population over 65 in 2003 and it is projected to rise to 26 percent by 2035. The percentage of the American population over 85 years was 0.1 percent in 1900, 1.5 percent in 2000 and an estimated 5 percent by 2050. In England and Wales, in 1948 7.2 percent of the population was between 65 and 74 years, and 2.9 percent were between 75 and 84 years. In 2006 these figures were 8.2 percent and 5.5 percent. In absolute numbers those over 80 years have increased from 1,572,160 in 1981 to 2,749,507 in 2007. This age group is the fastest growing sector of the population.

These demographic changes raise very large questions about the capacity of nation-states to provide adequately for their own citizens in a context of scarcity, but there is another aspect of this emerging Malthusian brake on the satisfaction of entitlements, namely the rising costs of basic commodities. In 2008, the international media were full of analyses of the end of the era of cheap food, the sudden increase in commodity prices generally, and the global increase in the number of people who now find themselves below the poverty line. Some of these problems are probably short term. They result from drought conditions in Australia and damaging floods in the American Midwest; they are also partly the outcome of market speculation, and finally a consequence of the increasing use of arable land to produce ethanol for fuel rather than food.

The price increase may be moderated by the fact that farmers will be encouraged to plant more wheat, soybeans, and rice in response to inflated commodity prices. However, the credit crunch and the resulting economic downturn in 2009 also suggest that the developed world will not invest in the underdeveloped world and that investment in green technology may shrink as governments attempt to secure energy supplies without close attention to environmental costs. If the decades of cheap money and easy credit have come to an end, then investment in longer-term projects to improve soil and agricultural production may be halted. The prospects for health programs and social development are bleak for the immediate future.

Increases in energy costs will have widespread negative consequences for many developing societies. For example, when there were steep increases in the price of oil – rising in July 2008 to $147 per barrel – truck drivers in Europe and fishermen in the Mediterranean went on strike, blocking roads and causing economic chaos. There were also food riots and urban crises in many societies from Haiti to Egypt to the Philippines over the price of rice, and Vietnam and Thailand stopped rice exports to guarantee a supply to their own people. Governments responded to these political pressures by measures that did not answer the long-term pollution problems caused by dependency on oil and the automobile. On the contrary, they were willing often to look for measures that were politically pragmatic to soften the blow of a spike in oil prices. We might imagine therefore that there is a continuum along which governments will select policies. At one end there is "short-termism," that is, subsidies on oil prices or reduction of existing taxes or handouts to those groups that are adversely affected such as taxi and truck drivers. At the other end is the option of authoritarianism; for example, in Singapore people who protested against rising commodity prices were arrested because they did not have the correct permits to organize a meeting. A crisis in commodity prices in societies with a weak tradition of democratic accountability will, in all probability, end in authoritarian measures to quell urban unrest among the discontented and resentful population. Oil prices fell back in 2009 because the slowdown in global economic growth undermined the demand for oil. Most analysts of oil argue, however, that the peak in oil production was reached in 2005 when world crude oil production came close to 75,000 barrels of oil per day and that as a result demand will continue to outpace supply, resulting in a significant increase in oil prices. As demand for oil in India and China continues to grow in a context where supply is stagnant, the prospect of "oil wars" alongside "water wars" is greatly increased. Both Japan and China have an acute historical scarcity of natural resources, and their foreign policies have been designed accordingly. In the Japanese case, that problem shaped the entire Greater East Asia Co-Prosperity Sphere.

Rights without reform?

One implication of this discussion so far is that one cannot have personal longevity without social reform. If the world population is aging, where will the resources come from to sustain the slow but apparently irresistible increase in life expectancy in the developed world? We can in fact regard these contemporary debates over human aging as simply the modern equivalent of the inquiry into human perfectability that was associated with the Enlightenment and the *philosophes* of the French Revolution, and hence with the philosophical origins of the idea of universal human rights. The modern argument that with the application of modern medical technology, people could in principle live indefinitely and in relatively good health implies quite clearly that the quality of human life can be subject to major improvement, indeed to medical perfectability. And perfectionism assumes abundance. Life extension requires determination to set new standards of health and considerable research funding, but above all it implies the systematic application of medical reason to life. In the past, the optimists who advocated both human and social perfection included William Godwin, Mary Wollstonecraft, and the Marquis de Condorcet. In the present, the optimistic camp includes the Methuselah Institute, the World Transhumanist Association, Aubrey de Grey and SENS (Strategies for Engineered Negligible Senesence), the Cryonics Institute, and enthusiasts such as Ray Kurzweil. The original pessimists were essentially a group of economists who followed the arguments of Malthus and Ricardo and who believed that basic economic principles relating to natural scarcity meant that human life for the majority could not be significantly improved. The most influential negative response to the idea of both "organic" and social perfectability was contained in Malthus's *An Essay on the Principle of Population* in 1798 (see Malthus 2004).

Malthus's arguments do not need to be repeated here in any great depth (Petersen 1979). In the first *Essay* he indemnified two "fixed laws of nature": that food is necessary for human existence and that sexual passion is more or less constant. Furthermore, the "power" of population to increase is greater than the "power" of earth to provide food. Population if unchecked will increase geometrically while subsistence can only increase arithmetically. Human beings will, other things being equal, always generate more offspring than the means to sustain them in the long run. We need therefore to understand the checks and balances whereby population and resources can be properly arranged to avoid such calamities as overpopulation, famine, and war. In more elegant terms, we might say that in traditional societies the relationship between resources (especially the food supply) and life expectancy was more or less regulated by a Malthusian logic. Given the sexual drive, the need for food, and the marginal utility of cultivated soil for settled agrarian societies, the increase in population would inevitably supersede the food supply. Population increase could either be controlled by "positive means" (such as famine, disease, and war) or by "preventive means" (such as vice, chastity, and late marriage). Malthus, who was all too aware of the problem of social class differences, noted that any attempt to improve the living conditions of the working class could not be sustained in the long term, because such social reforms would increase the population, thereby reducing living standards by reducing the food supply.

Malthusianism has become identified with an essentially pessimistic view of the human condition since it does not allow for much in the way of human improvement. In this pessimistic framework, technology will never solve the problem of the fixed quantity of land to provide food, and improvements in farming technology will never quite meet the needs of human population. The sexual drive can be moderated by human institutions – including both celibacy and prostitution – but it cannot be ultimately controlled. Overpopulation will be a more or less permanent cause of human misery. But what has this got to do with aging and longevity? Clearly the Malthusian model assumes that human life cannot be significantly extended, because otherwise the elderly would be an additional burden on the resources of younger cohorts. An aging population cannot be anything other than a demographic tax on the food supply, and therefore the Malthusian model raises important issues about intergenerational justice (Williamson, McNamara, and Howling 2003). For Malthusian pessimists, a short life expectancy must be one aspect of the preventive means by which the balance between land and population can be sustained.

Malthus's *Essay* was not, so to speak, a piece of naive demography. It was specifically addressed to those writers of his day – primarily his father Daniel Malthus – whom he thought were hopelessly optimistic about the future of human beings. As it happens, the late eighteenth century was a period of enormous optimism in which writers and political leaders such as Tom Paine and Thomas Jefferson welcomed revolutionary change, the fall of monarchies, and the prospects of a universal recognition of the "rights of Man." Paine (1995) in *Rights of Man* believed that with the fall of monarchy an age of peace and progress would begin. This political debate about revolutionary politics should be seen in the broader context of the Enlightenment in which Voltaire, Diderot, and Leibniz looked optimistically toward the radical improvement of human society through the application of human reason. In England, the political debate about human rights, constitutionalism, and human perfectability had initially been launched by the sermons and pamphlets of the Reverend Richard Price, who combined anti-Catholicism with an advocacy of basic political rights. These publications were the occasion for Edmund Burke's hostility to the French Revolution in his *Reflections*. Price had advocated the idea of citizenship of the world, universal benevolence, and the doctrine of perfectability. Burke, by contrast, had argued that the "rights of Man" would result in social chaos. For the conservatives, such human rights were merely "nonsense on stilts" (Waldron 1987). On the other side of the Atlantic, a similar division emerged between the Jeffersonians and Jacksonians who wanted to speed up the progress of America by releasing human energies from the artificial constraints of society and political leaders like John Adams who believed that the history of nations was like the life cycle of the individual, namely a story of rise and inevitable fall. For Adams, the speed of social change in the new nation would eventually unleash the negative vices of pride and avarice, leading to an inevitable collapse. Political wisdom was necessary to impede the rate of social change (Ellis 1993, pp. 238–239). The legacy of the Enlightenment debate about perfectability still haunts the modern debate about resources, population, and environmental damage and pollution. The debate can be posed in the question: can economic growth make us happy without at the same time depleting the environmental resources that are necessary to avoid collective famine and misery? Is the happiness of the long-living, rich communities of the northern hemisphere bought at the cost of the unhappiness of people in the Third World where life expectancy is now falling not rising? Is the notion of scarcity simply an ideological bogeyman to frighten the faint-hearted?

History of course does not appear to have entirely supported the argument of Malthus's *Essay*, and most standard textbooks on historical demography rehearse well-known criticisms of Malthusian political economy. For example, the invention of contraception in the 1820s, the enhancement of the food supply through colonial expansion, and technical improvements in agricultural cultivation and production controlled reproduction and expanded resources. The growth of colonies allowed Britain to export any surplus population threatening its food supply. With improvements in nutrition, food supply and distribution, water quality, public sanitation, and housing, the death rate fell through the nineteenth century, and at the same time, the increase in population was supported by technical improvements in agriculture and the increase in cultivated land. Eventually the birth rate also declined as life expectancy rose with the successful treatment of childhood illness such as whooping cough and as parents were able to regulate their fertility. Throughout most of the modern world, there has been a dramatic decline in fertility.

Malthus's arguments have typically been the target of critical, often emotional, responses. The romantic literati rejected Malthus without qualification. Lord Byron, Percy Bysshe Shelley, and Samuel Coleridge all dismissed Malthus's ideas as a cruel doctrine based on crude economic speculation about marriage in which men were advised not to marry without cash. Coleridge had, along with Robert Southey, devised a plan to create a utopia in America where twelve men and their wives would create a "pantisocracy" as an experiment in human perfectability. The standard criticisms of political economy were less emotional and more convincing. Marx and Engels condemned the doctrine of increasing human misery since they could not accept the possibility that under communism this degradation and suffering of the proletariat would continue. They too believed that through scientific management of the economy these so-called Malthusian "laws of nature" would no longer apply. Joseph Schumpeter, in his history of economic thought, condemned Malthus along with Ricardo as a pessimist, noting that, in the period when the classical economists developed their predictions of the tendency of the rate of profit to fall and the inevitability of low wages resulting from population pressures, Britain was in fact on the eve of an economic boom. In the modern debate about population pressures, Malthus and Malthusians continue to be characterized as right-wing ideologues employing the fear of overpopulation to convince people of the need for draconian measures to curb fertility. It is claimed that the scare about population pressures has been used by neo-liberal economists to promote economic and social policies to cut welfare provisions and to reduce pensions (Walker 1996).

However if scarcity remains an issue in modern societies, then there are many reasons for believing that Malthusianism is back on the agenda. The contemporary change that makes Malthus's argument increasingly relevant is global warming, which will result in the disappearance of many species that are important in sustaining life, especially among aboriginal peoples, as well as water shortages and loss of arable land. While some optimistic observers of global warming may argue that these climate changes will allow us to have vineyards in Greenland, there will be a significant decline in grain production, for example in Australia. Poor management of scarce resources will cause further diminution of basic foodstuffs. One classic example is the political mismanagement of the Murray River system in Australia, but more generally there is the argument presented in Jared Diamond's *Guns, Germs, and Steel* (1997) that human populations are prone to destroy the basis of their own livelihood – overfishing in the North Sea and the Pacific is a potent example. Rising food prices, water shortages, and famine will certainly constrain population growth in the developing Third World while new medical technology will increase life expectancy in the developed industrial world.

Following Malthus, we can think of some major negative ways in which population growth and resource scarcity might be solved. These could include, as a result in part of globalization, the return of many troublesome infectious diseases such as TB and malaria, along with the emergence of new diseases such as HIV/AIDS. Recent problems with SARS and H1N1 (swine flu) support the view by some epidemiologists that a pandemic might result in 300–500 million deaths (Kippax and Stephenson 2009). Global warfare would also put a disastrous brake on population growth. Tensions between China and its neighbors over control of the South China seas are likely to increase over time, raising the possibility of more conventional military crises. New wars will also contain population growth in many African and Central Asian societies.

These are global changes over which human beings might have little control, but there are other more positive interventions that are in principle available to human societies. With the expansion of rights discourse in the twentieth century, some philosophers called for a greater attention to the promotion of human duties. Alongside the right to indefinite life promoted by Aubrey de Grey, we need to think about some alternative rights to terminate life through suicide or euthanasia. We could conceptualize a range of complementary duties such as a duty of death for the deeply aged who have already enjoyed long and rich lives. With rapidly aging populations and in the absence of programs supporting the voluntary termination of life, one can imagine societies, such as Japan, developing strategies to store their elderly in geriatric gated communities (in Southeast Asia). In a dystopian mood, we could even imagine the growth of advanced geriatric storage systems, which would be the equivalent of hangers for the sick and the frail. One could equally imagine the need for the development of containment systems such as geriatric storage vats to manage the excess population of the deeply old. There might be other forms of medical storage, such as terminal storage containers, for the deceased who are waiting for the successful development and application of geriatric medicine such as cryonics and nanotechnology to restore them to the living.

The debate about scarcity is deep-seated and consequential. Pessimistic arguments such as Diamond's account of the propensity of human settlements to destroy the resources that sustain them have been attacked, for example from the evidence of indigenous peoples (Wilcox 2010) on the one hand and from advanced societies on the other (Somers 2008). Part of the problem is purely epistemological and concerns a distinction between natural and social scarcity. In my argument, both exist. The case against scarcity would have to demonstrate how a modern society like America could produce jobs in abundance, significantly reduce income inequality, and at the same time compete successfully against rising economic rivals such as India, China, and Brazil. We need to recognize in addition that societies rise and fall. By 2050 Korea will have moved into the "rich club" in terms of income per capita, while Italy will have moved down into the upper middle income group. By 2027, China will have overtaken the United States as the largest economy (Jacques 2009, p. 230). Scarcity exists within an international economic environment of competition in which the cost of labor plays an important part. This makes the task of achieving the morally and politically desirable outcome of full and effective social citizenship especially difficult. Western nations will have to sustain full employment, increase labor efficiency, and support an aging population in order to compete for scarce resources in a world economy where China will have significant advantages in terms of labor power.

Conclusion: ethics and scarcity

In this study of the problems of rights and resources, I have explored an aspect of the sociology of human rights through a discussion of the likely consequences of any significant enhancement of human longevity. In particular, I have sought to distinguish among several types of questions. These are (1) can we survive forever? (2) can we live forever? and finally (3) ought we to live forever? The answer to the first question would appear to be, at least in common-sense terms, negative, but it is the case that with medical technology the lifespan of human beings could be radically extended. Most scientists believe that the claims of gerontologists like Aubrey de Grey about rejuvenation have little support from modern science and the future applications of his project are impractical. In any case, survival or mere existence as such has no real significance in moral terms. It comes with no moral baggage. Mere survival is not in itself virtuous, but rather a matter of luck in terms of what genetic legacy people happen to inherit. The struggle for longevity may be merely a product of a competitive consumer society characterized by excessive greed and individualism.

The aesthetic justification to live well encourages us to live in a manner in which we can avoid personal stagnation. This notion implies that to live forever means to live in such a way that life remains a journey in which there is more or less continuous self-development. We can expand this idea by borrowing from Nietzsche, who argued that the only ultimate purpose to life is to become who we are, that is to develop our selves aesthetically into a work of art. To live creatively in the world presupposes a heroic ethic. To live successfully in these terms is to avoid resentment as the basic form of nihilism. Nietzsche argued that one aspect of resentment in modern society was resentment against time itself. Such an ethic might be a valuable counterforce to pessimism in terms of Nietzsche's "yes-saying" philosophy. The justification for life must include the notion of living life creatively and productively in order to contribute to human existence. To live life to the full in cultural terms is to leave a significant deposit that might add to human culture, making it richer and more diverse. Without such an ethic, it is difficult to see how life could be morally justified. It provides one possible criterion for departing this world not when we are corporeally and mentally rigid, but not culturally and spiritually so. In this ethic one's life as a work of art needs to be constantly refashioned if it is to be perpetually creative.

Given the resource problem, however, we need also to think about a right to death and therefore an ethic of dying to match an ethic of longevity. With limited health care resources, there needs to be some discussion of a duty of death (Battin 1987). If we have difficulty justifying life, what are the ethics of inter-generational relationships? How could one reasonably assume that one's use of resources did not reduce the chances of subsequent generations to live satisfactory lives? There are arguments to support the notion that human life should have a "fixed period" rather than an indefinite existence (Gruman 1979; Trollope 1990). At the very least, we need to take a more sympathetic and argued position as to the relevance of euthanasia (Warnock and MacDonald 2008). Given global warming, it seems likely that all future generations will experience serious natural depletion and hence will live lives that are less than optimal. In the new century it is already clear that the world is facing serious shortages of water, rice, and soybeans. It is very doubtful that an elderly population could be supported without some rapid changes in food production without confronting a Malthusian crisis. The relationship between rights and duties is becoming increasingly unbalanced. We cannot easily solve the resource problem without fundamental changes to and improvements in world governance, including the reduction of current overdependence on oil, the management of water supplies, and so forth. We can, however, start thinking seriously about developing what we might call the "ethic of longevity," namely a set of assumptions or values that might in principle offer some ethical justification not for existence but for life. We need to foster not some crass notions about the quantity of life (mere survival) but aesthetic arguments about the quality of life in a global context of limited resources. Such a debate would explore the real content of human rights. My discussion might be suitably summarized in terms of the sociological notion of life chances in the work of the sociologist Ralf Dahrendorf. He noted that while capitalist development tends to produce economic growth without redistribution, the dilemma for twentieth-century socialism was redistribution without economic growth. For Dahrendorf (1979), real social advancement had to involve the combination of both provision and entitlement. We should remain skeptical about the value of human rights where there is little prospect of raising the standard of living whereby the majority of the world's population could enjoy some modest amount of dignity and comfort. The basic lesson of this discussion of Malthus might simply be that rights without resources are merely talk, whereas resources without rights are a recipe for slavery. The unsolved dilemma is to combine, as Dahrendorf saw, provision and entitlement.

Acknowledgment

This chapter is based on arguments that were originally presented in Turner, Bryan S. 2009, *Can We Live Forever? A Sociological and Moral Inquiry* (London: Anthem).

References

Agamben, Giorgio. 1998. *Homo Sacer: Sovereign Power and Bare Life* (Stanford, CA: Stanford University Press).

Appleyard, Bryan. 2007. *How to Live Forever or Die Trying: On the New Immortality* (New York: Simon & Schuster).

Battin, M. P. 1987. "Age Rationing and the Just Distribution of Health Care: Is There a Duty to Die?" *Ethics*, Vol. 97, pp. 327–340.

Blackburn, Robin. 2002. *Banking on Death or Investing in Life: The History and Future of Pensions* (London: Verso).

Brown, Guy. 2008. *The Living End: The Future of Death, Aging and Immortality* (London: Macmillan).

Callahan, David. 1987. *Setting Limits: Medical Goals in an Aging Society* (New York: Simon & Schuster).

Dahrendorf, Ralf. 1979. *Life Chances: Approaches to Social and Political Theory* (Chicago: University of Chicago Press).

De Grey, A. D. N. J. 2003. "The Foreseeability of Real Anti-Aging Medicine: Focusing the Debate." *Experimental Gerontology*, Vol. 38, No. 9, pp. 927–934.

De Grey, A. D. N. J. 2004. "Three Self-Evident Life-Extension Truths." *Rejuvenation Research*, Vol. 7, No. 3, pp. 165–167.

De Grey, A. D. N. J. 2005. "The Ethical Status of Efforts to Postpone Aging: A Reply to Hurlbut." *Rejuvenation Research*, Vol. 8, No. 3, pp. 129–130.

Diamond, Jared. 1997. *Guns, Germs, and Steel: The Fates of Human Societies* (New York: W.W. Norton).

Drexler, Eric. 1986. *Engines of Creation: The Coming Era of Nanotechnology* (New York: Doubleday).

Ellis, Joseph J. 1993. *Passionate Sage: The Character and Legacy of John Adams* (New York: W.W. Norton).

Fries, James F. 1980. "Aging, Natural Death and the Compression of Morbidity." *New England Journal of Medicine*, Vol. 303, pp. 130–135.

Georgescu-Roegen, N. 1971. *The Entropy Law and the Economic Process* (Cambridge, MA: Harvard University Press).

Gruman, Gerald J., ed. 1979. *The "Fixed Period" Controversy* (New York: Arno Press).

Hayflick, L. 2000. "The Future of Ageing." *Nature*, Vol. 408, No. 9, pp. 267–269.

Hayflick, L. 2005. "Anti-Aging Medicine: Fallacies, Realities, Imperatives." *Journal of Gerontology: Biological Sciences*, Vol. 60A, No. 10, pp. 1228–1232.

Jacques, Martin. 2009. *When China Rules the World: The End of the Western World and the Birth of a New Global Order* (New York: Penguin).

Kertzer, David L. and Peter Laslett, eds. 1995. *Aging in the Past* (Berkeley: University of California Press).

Kippax, Susan and Niamh Stephenson. 2009. "Infectious Disease and Globalization." In Bryan S. Turner, ed., *The Handbook of Globalization Studies* (London: Routledge).

Kirkwood, Thomas. 1999. *Time of Our Lives: The Science of Human Aging* (Oxford: Oxford University Press).

Kurzweil, Ray and Terry Grossman. 2004. *Fantastic Voyage: Live Long Enough to Live Forever* (Emmaus, PA: Rodale).

Laslett, Peter. 1965. *The World We Have Lost: English Society Before the Coming of Industry* (New York: Macmillan).

MacInnes, J. and J. Pérez. 2009a. "Demography." In Bryan S. Turner, ed., *The New Blackwell Companion to Social Theory* (Oxford: Blackwell).

MacInnes, J. and J. Pérez. 2009b. "The Reproductive Revolution." *Sociological Review*, Vol. 57, No. 2, pp. 262–284.

Malthus, Thomas Robert. 2004. *An Essay on the Principle of Population* (Oxford: Oxford University Press).

Marx, Karl. 1963. *Early Writings* (London: C. A. Watts).

Nehamas, Alexander. 1985. *Nietzsche: Life as Literature* (Cambridge, MA: Harvard University Press).

Nietzsche, Friedrich. 1969. *Thus Spake Zarathustra* (New York: Penguin).

Orwell, George. 1937. *The Road to Wigan Pier* (London: Victor Gollancz).

Paine, Thomas. 1995. *Rights of Man* (New York: Literary Classics of the US).

Petersen, William. 1979. *Malthus*. (London: Heinemann).

Somers, Margaret R. 2008. *Genealogies of Citizenship: Markets, Statelessness and the Right to Have Rights* (Cambridge: Cambridge University Press).

Staley, Charles E. 1989. *A History of Economic Thought: From Aristotle to Arrow* (Oxford: Blackwell).

Thiele, L. P. 1990. *Friedrich Nietzsche and the Politics of the Soul* (Princeton, NJ: Princeton University Press).

Trollope, Anthony. 1990. *The Fixed Period* (Ann Arbor: University of Michigan Press).

Turner, Bryan S. 2004. *The New Medical Sociology: Social Forms of Health and Illness* (London: W.W. Norton).

Turner, Bryan S. 2006. *Vulnerability and Human Rights* (University Park: Pennsylvania State University Press).

Turner, Bryan S. 2009. *Can We Live Forever? A Sociological and Moral Inquiry* (London: Anthem).

Waldron, Jeremy, ed. 1987. *Nonsense upon Stilts: Bentham, Burke and Marx on the Rights of Man* (London: Methuen).

Walker, Alan. 1996. "Intergenerational Relations and the Provision of Welfare," pp. 10–36 in Alan Walker, ed., *The New Generational Contract: Intergenerational Relations, Old Age and Welfare* (London: UCL Press).

Warnock, Mary and Elisabeth MacDonald. 2008. *Easeful Death: Is There a Case for Assisted Dying?* (Oxford: Oxford University Press).

Wilcox, Michael. 2010. "Marketing Conquest and the Vanishing Indian." *Journal of Social Archaeology*, Vol. 10, No. 1, pp. 92–117.

Williamson, John B., Tay K. McNamara, and Stephanie A. Howling. 2003. "Generational Equity, Generational Interdependence and the Framing of the Debate over Social Security Reform." *Journal of Sociology and Social Welfare*, Vol. 30, No. 3, pp. 3–14.

Xenos, Nicholas. 1989. *Scarcity and Modernity* (London: Routledge).

Part III

World religious traditions and human rights

20
Buddhism and human rights

Damien Keown

Human rights issues in which Buddhism has a direct involvement feature regularly in the news. Global media coverage of the progress of the Olympic torch on its way to the opening ceremony of the Beijing Olympics in April of 2008 kept the issue of human rights in Tibet in the public eye, as did the accompanying violent riots in Lhasa. These scenes were soon followed by a reminder of the repression and denial of democracy in Burma in May of the same year as the military junta at first refused to allow aid relief into the country following the inundation of the delta region caused by Cyclone Nargis. In another Buddhist country, Sri Lanka, human rights violations have occurred constantly in the bitter and prolonged struggle between Sinhalese and Tamils in the northern part of the country, and became particularly severe as the civil war reached a climax before the government victory in May 2009. Examples could be multiplied, but my purpose here is not to catalog contemporary hotspots so much as to signal the importance of human rights in general for Buddhism in the world today. Leading Asian and Western Buddhists now routinely express their concern about social injustice in the Western vocabulary of human rights, but what I want to ask here is how appropriate is this language for an Asian tradition that historically seems to lack concepts of both rights and human rights? It seems some intellectual bridgework needs to be put in place to connect contemporary Western notions with traditional Buddhist teachings, and this is what I will attempt in this chapter. In speaking of "Buddhism" I should make clear that I am writing with reference to what might be termed "mainstream" Buddhism as opposed to the Buddhism of any particular school or region. It is hoped that the arguments and conclusions reached here are broad enough to apply to all major schools.

Buddhism and rights

The concept of a "right" has a long intellectual history in the West, and the contemporary notion of a right as an exercisable power vested in or held by an individual has its antecedents in a more impersonal understanding of what is objectively true or right. Etymologically, the English word "right" is derived from the Latin *rectus*, meaning straight. *Rectus*, in turn, can be traced to the Greek *orektos*, which means stretched out or upright. Both "right" and *rectus* themselves, however, have a more remote ancestor in the Sanskrit *ṛju* (straight or upright).

The equivalent form in Pali is *uju* (or *ujju*) meaning "straight, direct; straightforward, honest, upright." (Pali is an Indian language in which the earliest surviving complete set of Buddhist canonical scriptures is preserved; this corpus is known as the "Pali Canon". It would therefore appear that both the objective sense ("straight") and the metaphorical moral sense ("rectitude") of the word "right" occur in Buddhist as well as Western languages. Despite a common Indo-European etymology, however, there is no word in Sanskrit or Pali which conveys the idea of a "right" or "rights," understood as a subjective entitlement. (On the concept of rights in Hinduism and the meaning of *adhikāra*, see Bilimoria 1993; also Creel 1977, p. 19. In Buddhist languages the notion of rights may be distributed among a variety of terms, as perhaps, in Latin among the words *auctoritas, potestas, dominium, iurisdictio, proprietas, libertas* and *ius* [Dagger 1989, p. 291].) Does this absence of the necessary vocabulary mean that the concept of rights is alien to Buddhist thought? Not necessarily. Alan Gewirth has pointed out that cultures may possess the concept of rights without having a vocabulary that expresses it. He suggests that it is "important to distinguish between having or using a concept and the clear or explicit recognition and elucidation of it … Thus persons might have and use the concept of a right without explicitly having a single word for it" (quoted in Dagger 1989, p. 286. Gewirth claims that the concept of rights can be found in feudal thought, Roman law, Greek philosophy, the Old Testament, and in primitive societies. It seems, then, that the concept of a right may exist where a word for it does not. Could this be the case in Buddhism?

In Buddhism, the principle that determines both rights and duties is known as "Dharma." The word "Dharma" might best be translated as "natural law" in the sense of a universal principle of cosmic order that governs both natural phenomena and moral relationships. Dharma encompasses a cluster of moral concepts that in the West are labeled separately, such as justice, rights, and duty. It is Dharma, for example, that establishes the norms of a just and orderly society and governs the rights and obligations of citizens, as the Rev. Vajiragnana (1992) explains:

> Each one of us has a role to play in sustaining and promoting social justice and orderliness. The Buddha explained very clearly these roles as reciprocal duties existing between parents and children; teachers and pupils; husband and wife; friends, relatives and neighbors; employer and employee; clergy and laity … No one has been left out. The duties explained here are reciprocal and are considered as sacred duties, for – if observed – they can create a just, peaceful and harmonious society.

Since Dharma determines what is appropriate in relationships, such as the reciprocal duties of employers and employees (see, for example, the *Sigālovādasutta*), it seems we can say that the duties of one correspond to the entitlements or "rights" of the other. If the employee has a duty to do his or her job, the employer has a duty to pay wages, and so forth. If under Dharma it is the duty of a king (or political authority) to dispense justice impartially, then subjects (citizens) may be said to have a "right" to just and impartial treatment before the law. In this way it seems possible to build up a catalog of entitlements that correspond more or less to the Western notion of individual rights. Should it be concluded, then, that the concept of a right is, after all, present in classical Buddhism? The answer depends on the criteria adopted for "having" a concept. Dagger (1989, p. 297) sets out the options:

> If one is willing to look primarily for the idea or the notion, however it may be expressed, then one can confidently say that the concept of rights is virtually as old as civilization itself.

On the other hand:

> If one insists that the form of expression is crucial ... so that a concept cannot be said to exist unless there is a word or phrase that distinguishes it from other concepts, then one would have to say that the concept of rights has its origin in the middle ages.

In sum it might be said that in classical Buddhism the notion of rights is present in embryonic form although not yet born into history. Whether anything like the Western concept of rights has appeared, or would appear, in the course of the historical evolution of Buddhism is a question for specialists in the various Buddhist cultures to ponder. In many respects the omens for this development were never good. Buddhism originated in a caste society, and the Asian societies where it has flourished have for the most part been hierarchically structured. MacIntyre (1981, p. 69), citing Gewirth, mentions that the concept of a right lacks any means of expression in Japanese "even as late as the mid-nineteenth century." (See also de Bary 1988, p. 183, on the Chinese neologisms which have been coined to express these concepts). The preconditions for the emergence of the concept of rights would seem to be egalitarianism and democracy, neither of which has been a feature of Asian polity before the modern era. On the other hand, a justification for the rejection of hierarchical social structures is not hard to find in Buddhism – one need look only at the Buddha's critique of caste. Buddhism also holds, in the doctrine of no-self (*anattā*), that all individuals are equal in the most profound sense. Like the Christian doctrine that all men are created equal before God, this would appear to be fertile ground for a doctrine of natural rights.

Human rights

Granted that the Western concept of rights can be accommodated within the framework of Buddhist teachings, there would seem to be no conceptual barrier to elaborating a Buddhist doctrine of human rights. As an example of a modern charter of human rights we may take the Universal Declaration of Human Rights proclaimed by the General Assembly of the United Nations in December 1948. Since its promulgation this thirty-article code has been used as a model for many subsequent human rights charters. What is the Buddhist position with respect to declarations of this kind? It may be useful to begin by asking whether Buddhism would endorse the Universal Declaration of Human Rights. The repeated calls by the Dalai Lama for respect for human rights give some reason to think that it would. The signing of the *Global Ethic* (Kung and Kuschel 1993) by many Buddhists also suggests that Buddhism has no reservations about subscribing to charters or manifestos that seek to secure universal human rights. Moreover, there seems to be nothing in any of the thirty articles to which Buddhism would take exception. Perera's commentary on each of the thirty articles of the Universal Declaration shows them to be in harmony with early Buddhist teachings both in letter and in spirit. In his foreword to the commentary, Ananda Guruge (Perera 1991, p. xi) writes:

> Professor Perera demonstrates that every single Article of the Universal Declaration of Human Rights – even the labour rights to fair wages, leisure and welfare – has been adumbrated, cogently upheld and meaningfully incorporated in an overall view of life and society by the Buddha.

But how are these rights to be justified with reference to Buddhist teachings? In asking this question I am not seeking justification by reference to textual passages that seem to support the rights claimed. There are many passages in the Pali Canon, as Perera has ably demonstrated, which support the view that early Buddhist teachings were in harmony with the spirit of the Declaration. The justification required at this point has more to do with the philosophical presuppositions underlying these passages and the overall Buddhist vision of individual and social good.

The various declarations on human rights themselves rarely offer a justification for the rights they proclaim. MacIntyre (1981, p. 69) observes dryly how "In the United Nations declaration on human rights of 1948 what has since become the normal UN practice of not giving good reasons for any assertion whatsoever is followed with great rigor." A gesture toward justification is sometimes made in recital clauses by reference to the "inherent dignity ... of all members of the human family" or some similar form of words. The *Global Ethic*, which provides a fuller statement than most, echoes the Universal Declaration in its call for "the full realization of the intrinsic dignity of the human person" (Kung and Kuschel 1993, p. 14). It states: "We make a commitment to respect life and dignity, individuality and diversity, so that every person is treated humanely." This is amplified as follows:

> This means that every human being without distinction of age, sex, race, skin, color, physical or mental ability, language, religion, political view, or national or social origin possesses an inalienable and *untouchable dignity*. And everyone, the individual as well as the state, is therefore obliged to honor this dignity and protect it.
>
> *(Kung and Kuschel 1993, p. 23; original emphasis)*

It is by no means apparent, however, how human dignity is to be grounded in Buddhist doctrine. The very words "human dignity" sound as alien in a Buddhist context as talk of rights. One looks in vain to basic doctrines such as the Four Noble Truths for any explicit reference to human dignity, and doctrines such as no-self (*anattā*) and impermanence (*anicca*) may even be thought to undermine it. If human dignity is the basis of human rights Buddhism would seem to be in some difficulty when it comes to providing a justification for them. The theistic religions, on the other hand, seem much better equipped to provide an account of human dignity. Christians, Muslims, and Jews typically refer to the ultimate source of human dignity as divine. Article one (paragraph 1700) of the *Catechism of the Catholic Church*, for instance, states: "The dignity of the human person is rooted in his creation in the image and likeness of God." Buddhism, clearly, would not wish to make such a claim. Kung notes how leading Buddhists at the Parliament of the World's Religions felt called upon to protest at calls for "a unity of religions under God," and at references to "God the Almighty" and "God the Creator" in invocations during the proceedings. He suggests, however, that these differences are reconcilable since the Buddhist concepts of "Nirvana, Shunyata and Dharmakaya ... fulfil analogous functions to the concept of God" and can be regarded by Christians as "parallel terms for the Absolute" (Kung and Kuschel 1993, pp. 62ff.).

It may or may not be the case that Mahāyāna schools recognize a transcendent reality that resembles the Christian concept of God as the Absolute, and there are those better qualified than myself to address such a question. Here I will make only three brief points regarding the problems that arise in regarding these concepts as the source of human dignity. The first is that since these concepts are understood differently by the main Mahāyāna schools they are unlikely to provide the common ground required as a foundation for human rights. The second is that it is difficult to see how any of these concepts can be the source of human dignity in the way that God can, since no school of Buddhism believes that human beings are created by them. The third point is that even if some metaphysical ground of the above kind can be identified in

Mahāyāna Buddhism it still leaves the problem of how human dignity is to be grounded where Theravāda Buddhism is concerned. For the Theravāda, Nirvāṇa is not a transcendent Absolute, nor do the concepts of "Shunyata and Dharmakaya" have anything like the meaning or significance they attain later. No grounding for human rights can be truly satisfactory, I would suggest, unless it unambiguously forms part of the core teachings of classical Buddhism as a whole.

The approach adopted by Perera is rather different. Perera's main concern is to demonstrate that the articles of the Universal Declaration are adumbrated in early Buddhist teachings, rather than explore their philosophical foundations. He acknowledges (1991, p. 28, cf. p. 88) that "Buddhism credits the human personality with a dignity and moral responsibility," but does not explain fully whence this arises or how it provides a foundation for human rights. Perera comes closest to what in my view is the true source of human rights in Buddhism in his commentary on Article 1: "All human beings are born free and equal in dignity and rights. They are endowed with reason and conscience and should act towards one another in a spirit of brotherhood." In discussing the first sentence of the Article ("All human beings are born free and equal in dignity and rights"), he comments that "Buddhahood itself is within the reach of all human beings ... and if all could attain Buddhahood what greater equality in dignity and rights can there be?" To focus attention upon the goal, I believe, is the most promising approach. Perera seems to grasp its significance in a remark towards the end of his commentary on Article 1. He writes:

> It is from the point of view of its goal that Buddhism evaluates all action. Hence Buddhist thought is in accord with this and other Articles in the Universal Declaration of Human Rights to the extent to which they facilitate the advancement of human beings towards the Buddhist goal.
>
> *(Perera 1991, p. 24)*

Human rights and human dignity

I believe the above statement provides the key to understanding human rights from a Buddhist perspective. What is missing in Perera's commentary, however, is the explicit linkage between the goal and human dignity, and it is this that I will now try to establish. What I will suggest in general is that the source of human dignity should be sought not in the analysis of the human condition provided by the first and second noble truths, but in the evaluation of human good provided by the third and fourth. Human rights cannot be derived from any factual non-evaluative analysis of human nature, whether in terms of its psycho-physical constitution (the five "aggregates" which lack a self), its biological nature (needs, urges, drives), or the deep structure of interdependency (*paṭicca-samuppāda*). Instead, the most promising approach will be one that locates human rights and dignity within a comprehensive account of human goodness and that sees basic rights and freedoms as integrally related to human flourishing and self-realization. This is because the source of human dignity in Buddhism lies nowhere else than in the capacity of human nature for participation in goodness. A more familiar way of making the same point in Buddhist terminology would be to say that all beings are potential Buddhas or possess the "Buddha-nature."

The connection between human rights and human good can be illustrated by asking what the various declarations on human rights seem to secure. Documents that speak of human rights commonly announce a list of specific rights and freedoms and proclaim them to be inviolable. The rights proclaimed by the Universal Declaration include the right to life, liberty, security of person, equality before the law, privacy, marriage and protection of family life, social security, participation in government, work, protection against unemployment, rest and leisure, a minimum standard of living, and enjoyment of the arts. The exercise of these rights is subject only to such general limitations as are necessary to secure due recognition and respect for the rights and freedoms of others and the requirements of morality, public order, and general welfare (Article 29.2). Otherwise, the rights are expressed in categorical forms such as "Everyone has ... " and "No one shall ... " For example, Article 3: "Everyone has the right to life, liberty and security of person." And Article 4: "No one shall be held in slavery or servitude; slavery and the slave trade shall be prohibited in all their forms." The document thus understands the rights it proclaims as both "universal" and without exception.

What do these rights and freedoms amount to? It might be said that they map the parameters of human "good-in-community." In other words, these rights and freedoms are what is required if human beings are to lead fulfilled lives in society. Article 29.1 recognizes this when it observes, "Everyone has duties to the community *in which alone the free and full development of his personality is possible*" (emphasis added). In the absence of human rights the scope for human development and fulfillment through social interaction is drastically reduced. The rights specified define and facilitate aspects of human fulfillment. The right to life is clearly fundamental since it is the condition for the enjoyment of all other rights and freedoms. The right to "liberty and security of person" (Article 3) is also basic to any understanding of human good. Without these minimum conditions the scope and opportunity for human fulfillment would be intolerably restricted. The same would apply in the case of slavery (Article 4), torture (Article 5), and the denial of rights before the law (Article 6). It can also be seen that many of the detailed rights identified are actually derived from more fundamental ones. Article 3, for example, "No one shall be held in slavery," is clearly implied in Article 2, "Everyone has the right to ... liberty." It might thus be said that many of the thirty articles articulate the practical implications of a relatively small number of fundamental rights and freedoms, which are the basis of the common good.

It may be noted that the Universal Declaration itself and modern charters like it do not offer a *comprehensive* vision of human good. This is not intended as a criticism, for the purpose of such charters is to secure only what might be termed the "minimum conditions" for human flourishing in a pluralistic milieu. The task of articulating a comprehensive vision of what is ultimately valuable in human life and how it is to be attained falls to the competing theories of human good found in religions, philosophies, and ideologies such as Marxism. Buddhism provides one view of human nature and its fulfillment, Christianity another, secular philosophies a third. To pursue any of these different paths, however, requires the substructure known as "human rights," a complex of fundamental rights and liberties that are the preconditions for the realization of the particular opportunities made available by the competing ideologies.

If the aim of human rights declarations is understood in the way outlined above then human rights is fundamentally a moral issue. Where there is no right to life, liberty, and security of person, and where torture is routine, the opportunities for the realization of human good are greatly reduced. Freedom of religion (Article 18), for example, is vital to the Buddhist vision of individual and social good, and the consequences of the loss of these rights are all too obvious in places such as Tibet. Human rights is thus an area in which religions have a legitimate and vital stake, and there is every reason why it would be proper for Buddhism both to endorse the Universal Declaration and call upon others to respect and implement it. In the view of Perera:

> From the religious angle, it is possible to state that in this Declaration lie enshrined certain values and norms emphasized by the major religions of the world. Though not directly

> expressed, the basic principles of the Declaration are supported and reinforced by these religious traditions, and among them the contribution of the Buddhist tradition, to say the least, is quite outstanding.
>
> *(Perera 1991, p. xii)*

Though not wishing to deny that the early teachings support the principles of the Declaration, I do not agree that the historical contribution of the Buddhist tradition to the cause of human rights has been as distinguished as Perera claims.

If religions have a legitimate stake in human rights, we might expect to find many of the rights and liberties spelled out in human rights charters present in either an express or implied form in their moral teachings. These typically include commandments or precepts forbidding killing, stealing, adultery, and lying, as do the first four of the Five Precepts. These evils are prohibited because it is immediately apparent that they are antithetical to human flourishing-in-community. The rationale for these prohibitions, I suggest, coincides to a large extent with that of the various human rights manifestos. In certain areas (such as the prohibition on alcohol and matters of sexual morality), the precepts go beyond the more limited aims of human rights charters. This is because Buddhism provides a particular vision of human good and also defines the practices required for its fulfillment. These manifestos, indeed, may be regarded as a translation of religious precepts into the language of rights. The process of casuistry can be seen at work in both. Just as a limited number of moral precepts can be expanded to meet the needs of different social situations (many of the extensive Vinaya rules, for example, have their source in a handful of moral precepts [Keown 1992, p. 33]), so the many articles in human rights charters are extrapolated from a comparatively small number of basic rights and freedoms.

Conclusion

I suggest, then, that the apparent differences between the moral teachings of Buddhism and human rights charters is one of form rather than substance. Human rights can be extrapolated from Buddhist moral teachings in the manner described in this chapter using the logic of moral relationships to illumine what is due under Dharma. Many other human rights, such as the rights to liberty and security, can either be deduced from or are extant within the general corpus of Buddhist moral teachings. A right not to be held in slavery, for example, is implicit in the canonical prohibition on trade in living beings (*Aṅguttara Nikāya* ii.208).

If the foregoing is correct, it is legitimate to speak of both rights and human rights in Buddhism. Modern doctrines of human rights are in harmony with the moral values of classical Buddhism in that they are an explication of what is "due" under Dharma. The modern idea of human rights has a distinctive cultural origin, but its underlying preoccupation with human good makes it at bottom a moral issue in which Buddhism and other religions have a legitimate stake. The *Global Ethic* endorses the view that the principles it sets forth on human rights are neither new nor "Western" when it states: "We affirm that a common set of core values is found in the teachings of the religions, and that these form the basis of a global ethic" (Kung and Kuschel 1993, p. 14).

A final thought. Here I have spoken only of *human* rights, and in the context of Buddhism this perspective may be unduly narrow in that it seems to preclude the universe of sentient non-human beings from any entitlement to rights. Buddhists may feel, therefore, that it is less prejudicial in discussions of this kind to revert to the older terminology of "natural" rights. Whether or not animals have rights, and whether these are the same rights as human beings, is a matter requiring separate discussion. If human rights flow from human nature, as suggested, it may be that rights of different kinds flow from natures of different kinds. Such would seem to be the understanding of classical Buddhism.

Acknowledgment

Adapted from Keown, Damien. 1995. "Are There 'Human Rights' in Buddhism?" *Journal of Buddhist Ethics*, Vol. 2, pp. 3–27.

References

de Bary, W. Theodore. 1988. "Neo-Confucianism and Human Rights." pp. 183–198 in Leroy S. Rouner, ed., *Human Rights and the World's Religions* (South Bend, IN: University of Notre Dame Press).
Bilimoria, Purushottama. 1993. "Is 'Adhikāra' Good Enough for 'Rights'?" *Asian Philosophy*, Vol. 23, pp. 3–13.
Creel, A. B. 1977. *Dharma in Hindu Ethics* (Calcutta: Firma KLM Private Ltd).
Dagger, Richard. 1989. "Rights." pp. 292–308 in Terence Ball, James Farr, and Russell L. Hanson, eds., *Political Innovation and Conceptual Change* (Cambridge: Cambridge University Press).
Keown, Damien. 1992. *The Nature of Buddhist Ethics* (London: Macmillan).
Kung, Hans and Karl-Josef Kuschel, eds. 1993. *A Global Ethic: The Declaration of the Parliament of the World's Religions* (London: SCM Press).
MacIntyre, Alasdair. 1981. *After Virtue. A Study in Moral Theory* (London: Duckworth).
Perera, L. 1991. *Buddhism and Human Rights: A Buddhist Commentary on the Universal Declaration of Human Rights* (Colombo: Karunaratne and Sons).
Vajiragnana, Rev. 1992. "Justice in Buddhism." *Vesak Sirisara.*

21

Christianity and human rights

Esther D. Reed

"What we have is ours, and nobody can push us around. This is practically all we mean when we say we are free. Other rights derive from these, when we even bother with those other rights" (O'Rourke 2007, p. 42). The humorist P. J. O'Rourke represents familiar notions of rights as freedoms conceived in terms of individual autonomy and independence: "There is only one basic human right, the right to do as you damn well please. And with it comes the only basic human duty, the duty to take the consequences" (O'Rourke 1993). Forget "high-minded screeds" (O'Rourke 2007, p. 42) that promise nonsense comparable with unalienable rights to steak, beer, rest, and leisure. Property rights, rooted in the concept of self-ownership, are the only rights that really matter because these enforce at law the liberty of individuals to control their own lives unless the state has a compelling reason for denying them that control. Religions have no practical contribution to make to the politics of rights: "[e]veryone has an immortal soul and every soul is of identical value to God, maybe, but that doesn't take us far as a matter of practical political philosophy" (O'Rourke 2007, p. 40).

For our purposes, O'Rourke's satire points to difficult issues for many Christians: To what extent is modern rights-talk, including the language and conceptuality of human rights, tied up with modern notions of self-ownership, property rights, market exchange, and the unrestrained liberty of the individual? Can a Christian be faithful to biblical and traditional teaching and argue for a right to have rights? Have Christian convictions about the dignity of human nature, personal and social freedom, etc., been hijacked by a secularist human rights agenda in which God is denied? Mindful of these issues, I attempt to do three things in this chapter:

1. *Outline areas of unity and diversity among believers with respect to the compatibility of human rights with Christianity.* There is broad agreement in Christian tradition regarding the material aims of the international human rights movement. So, for instance, the Orthodox scholar Vigen Guroian who, as we shall see, rejects much modern rights theory, accepts "that the deepest inspiration of the doctrine of human rights has roots in Christian convictions. God is person, and so are human beings, who are created in God's image and likeness. Every human *hypostasis* has needs and makes legitimate claims to certain advantages necessary for human flourishing" (Guroian 2005, p. 14). Despite broad agreement with respect to

material aims, some Christians believe modern rights thinking to be alien to Christianity while others hold the concepts of natural rights and inherent rights to be thoroughly biblical. We investigate briefly the anxiety among many in the Christian community (myself included) that the idea of subjective, natural rights – which began arguably in the medieval era, notably with William Ockham – was to morph into the voluntarist, property-centered phenomenon described with laudable insight by O'Rourke as freedom from the exercise of arbitrary power so that we "can go to the mall and swipe our Visa cards until the magnetic strips are toasted crisp, if that's what we want" (2007, p. 43).

2. *Consider different ways in which Christians ground human rights theologically.* This involves historical awareness of how Roman Catholic social teaching (predominantly but not exclusively) has argued that human rights derive from the natural law while Protestants have tended to opt for grounds more immediately Christological. Today Roman Catholic and Protestant traditions enjoy an increasing degree of convergence with respect to human rights. As the Vatican has led the way in theological renewal, so Protestant scholars have been recovering the natural law in theological ethics and seeking Christologically focused ways of construing both "the natural" and rights-talk in relation to God's ordering of human affairs (Reed 2007). Protestants have also been finding grounds for human rights apart from the natural law. Bonhoeffer's eschatologically framed account of "the natural" in Christ requires believers to include questions of natural teleology and the norms of natural human flourishing because all human ontology is ordered by grace. To my mind, it is not surprising that different doctrinal routes converge upon agreed conceptions of human rights. Against a backdrop of concern that rights-talk does not properly have a home in Christian tradition but belongs to a secularizing agenda progressively at odds with older Christian traditions of political right, however, it is important to be clear about the different ways in which Christians approach human rights and conclude that subjective rights is a proper topic for Christian ethics.
3. *Comment on the implications of this kind of theological rooting of human rights in a religiously and otherwise plural world.* Drafters of the Universal Declaration of Human Rights (UDHR) were silent in the Declaration on matters of faith. More recently, theorists such as Michael Ignatieff urge those working with human rights to maintain this deliberate silence with respect to substantive beliefs. "Thin" (describing only the rights themselves) rather than "thick" (contextualizing rights in the religious, cultural, economic, and other complexes of a given society) theories of human rights are preferred because this tends to keep human rights instruments out of political debates about the relation of rights to traditional, religious, and authoritarian sources of power (Ignatieff 2001, p. 76). We consider briefly the choice between resisting questions about the religious or other foundations of human rights and recognizing the plurality of (perhaps incompatible) grounds. Can and/or should Christians welcome plural foundations for human rights in a religiously plural world? My answer is "yes!" Christians should reasonably expect persons and groups of different faiths, and none, to have different platforms from which they justify human rights claims. As the Muslim scholar Abdullahi An-Na'im has argued, a normative system cannot be culturally neutral; all normative systems are the product somehow of contextual specificities (An-Na'im 2000, pp. ix–xiv, 1–32). At the level of doctrinal commitment, there will be little or no agreement about the substance of belief between the religions. Of interest for our purposes is how a "thick" rooting of human rights in Christ's saving work and the promise of God's kingdom both allows Christians to affirm "thin" norms *and* seek colloquially pluralist, overlapping justifications for human rights. My thesis is that this kind of approach to the universality of human rights, i.e., not as a given, philosophical construct

but as a project to be undertaken, is the only sustainable way forward for human rights in the twenty-first century.

Christianity and the international human rights movement

Before getting started, it is worth recording the significant role played by diverse Christian influences before and during the 1940s as the institution of the United Nations was being created and the Universal Declaration of Human Rights (UDHR) drafted. Protestant and Roman Catholic Christians contributed enormously to the events that led up to the 1948 Universal Declaration of Human Rights. As early as the 1930s, ecumenical movements such as the World Alliance for the Promotion of International Friendship through the Churches provided networks of international allies in the fight against totalitarian ideology and were among the first to respond to condemn the violence against Jews (Barnett 1995). At the 1933 World YMCA conference in Sofia, Bulgaria, pastor Dietrich Bonhoeffer warned of the "growing persecution of minorities" under the Nazi regime. In the 1940s, organizations such as the US Federal Council of Churches and the World Council of Churches brought the thinking of the churches to bear in the corridors of power at crucial stages in the drafting process. Individuals such as the Dutch clergyman Visser t'Hooft and activist in the ecumenical movement Frederick Nolde contributed key ideas to the freedom of religion section of the UDHR (Nurser 2005, esp. ch. 5). The Roman Catholic thinker Jacques Maritain (1882–1973), whose influential book *Human Rights and Natural Law* (1943) held that the natural law entailed an account of human rights, was involved actively in drafting the UDHR.

Since 1948, Roman Catholic teaching has remained consistent in holding that the natural law has inspired and continues to give vitality to rights-talk, especially the UDHR, and has taken significant steps to link human rights to the core commitments of Christian faith (Migliore 2003). Pope John XXIII's *Pacem in Terris* (1963) exemplifies long-standing Catholic acceptance of the role of human rights in protecting individual freedom. It is self-evident to reason and stamped in human hearts, he claims, that rights and duties flow as a direct consequence of human nature and the power that humans have to avoid evil and choose good by free choice. Notes of concern have been sounded more recently about the excessive individualism that has increasingly characterized aspects of the human rights movement. On the occasion of the fifty-fifth anniversary of the Universal Declaration of Human Rights, Msgr. Celestino Migliore warned against the choice of "self-serving rights": "One of the greatest threats today to the integrity of the universal rights ... comes from exaggerated individualism" (Migliore 2003). Msgr. Migliore also affirmed, however, that human rights are "one of the highest expressions of the human conscience of our time" and "a real milestone on the path of the moral progress of humanity" (Migliore 2003).

Elsewhere, the World Council of Churches (WCC), a fellowship of more than 340 churches in 120 countries, has committed itself repeatedly to the principles of the UDHR, and to their promotion and defense, in the belief that they serve the whole of humanity (WCC 1999). Regarding positive rights and not merely negative rights, the WCC remains solidly with the United Nations in affirming that rights are universal, indivisible, and interdependent and interrelated (Paton 1976, pp. 40–45). "No rights are possible" says the WCC, "without the basic guarantees for life, including the right to work, to participate in decision-making, to adequate food, to health care, to decent housing, to education for the full development of the human potential, and to a safe environment and the conservation of the earth's resources" (WCC 1999). In other words, there is long-standing, broad consensus among Christians that human rights can be effective vehicles for the protection of human dignity and promotion of social justice. Anxieties persist, however, about the extent to which modern rights-talk is atomistic, inherently conflictual, and relates persons in terms of noninterference rather than shared interests or beliefs, and thus no basis for society (Hauerwas 1986, p. 130).

Theological concerns about modern rights-talk

Qualified unity among believers regarding the compatibility of the political objectives of human rights with Christianity has already been indicated. In this section, we look more closely at concerns regarding the naivety of some theological appropriations of rights-talk and the problematic nature of many modern and present-day treatments of rights. The issues are best explained by Joan Lockwood O'Donovan, who argues that the movement is tied historically and conceptually to liberal contractarian traditions associated with Hobbes, Locke, Rousseau, and Kant, and also detects "later utilitarian accretions" in the writings of contemporary contractarians such as John Rawls and Robert Nozick (2003, pp. 30–32). In particular, she identifies a major change in fourteenth-century Europe from older Christian traditions of political right in which justice (*iustitia*) was synonymous with objective right (*ius*) to the association of justice with an individual's claim-right to something. In defending the Franciscans' poverty as Christ-like against the Pope, William of Ockham birthed a notion of subjective natural right that broke with previous notions of right as an objective reality, e.g., that which is right according to the divine ordering of the universe.

The process began innocently enough with William of Ockham's defense of the Franciscans against Pope John XXII over whether their use of food, i.e., eating of it, amounted to property rights (as claimed by the Pope) or simple factual use or natural right (as claimed by Ockham). O'Donovan claims, however, that, in the hands of seventeenth-century philosophers, Ockham's theological model of natural right became the basis for another major shift to the effect that the first natural right is that of self-preservation. Hobbes, for instance, speaks in 1647 of the first foundation of natural right as "that *each man protect his life and limbs as much as he can*" (Hobbes 1997, p. 27, emphasis original). The theoretical construct of "the state of nature" has become his starting point for natural law teaching. "Right" is defined as "the liberty that each man has of using his natural faculties in accordance with right reason" from which it follows that, in the first instance, he has the right to use any means and to do any action by which he can preserve himself (Hobbes 1997, p. 27). Locke builds his ideas of political society on the basis of the "Rights and Privileges of the Law of Nature ... not only to preserve his Property, that is, his Life and Estate, against the Injuries and Attempts of other Men; but to judge of, and punish the breaches of that Law in others" (Locke 1960, § 87, p. 325). His arguments are theological to the extent that the argument in *The Second Treatise* starts from God's creation of Adam, the dominion that God gave Adam over the world at the time, and the analogous state of perfect freedom to order their actions that all persons have as a matter of natural right.

O'Donovan's account draws attention to the increasing assimilation of notions of subjective right to private property. The related concern is that modern rights-talk, with its notion of *inalienable* rights, is tied inextricably to the belief that individuals can do whatever they want to do with their own property including their own bodies: "The body is then a piece of property in a capitalist sense" (Hauerwas 1991). Such concepts of rights are fundamentally at variance with the Church, which recognizes no such assumptions about individual autonomy because they "oppose everything that Christians believe about what it means to be a creature" (Hauerwas 1991). The problem is rendered more complex by the mixed history of Roman Catholic teaching in this respect. At the turn of the nineteenth century, critics suggest with some justification that Roman Catholic social teaching drew as much from early modern philosophical as theological sources. Consider arguments in *Rerum Novarum* (*RN*) to the effect that the right to property belongs naturally to persons and is sanctioned by divine law: "For, every man has by nature the right to possess property as his own. This is one of the chief points of distinction between man and the animal creation" (*RN* § 6, see also §§ 11–13). Even while setting a new direction for papal teaching in addressing social issues directly, this encyclical betrays modern philosophical as well as theological influences in its claims that property rights flow from the nature of humanity itself within the purposes of God.

Skeptics who try to decode papal teaching remind us that this emphasis on the right to property belonging to humankind naturally is integral to Leo XIII's condemnation of socialism's attempt to do away with private property on the grounds that it would distort the functions of the state (§ 4), strike at the interests of every wage-earner (§ 5), and deny the natural right of private property (§ 6) (Curran 1988). It is also arguable that this association of rights with property persists into the mid-twentieth century, albeit in different form, as the move toward what is sometimes called Catholic personalism was bound up with Papal opposition to communism. By 1981, the focus was on the Marxists still functioning in Eastern Europe and the liberation theologians in Latin America. So, writes Charles Curran, John Paul II adopted just enough Marxist critique of capitalism to take away their moral initiative and to capture the moral high-ground of human rights and concern for the poor. Individual freedom and dignity are now the focus of attention rather than order and social cohesiveness (Keating and Keating 1998, p. 1796). Rights-talk in these documents still betrays an association with private property.

All this indicates concerns in Christian tradition about whether rights-talk cast in terms of an individual's claim-right to a form of *dominium* whereby the individual is a "moral proprietor (*dominus*)" not only of what they actually possess but also of what they demand as entitlement is antithetical to what Christians believe about the creaturely status of all humans before God, and likely to be destructive to the fellowship enjoyed by members of the body of Christ (O'Donovan 2003, p. 33). Supposing aspects of these concerns to be well founded, the challenge for Christian people is to think with and about human rights, and to conduct the politics of human rights, *differently* from approaches that focus on property or the powers and privileges attaching to quasi-ownership of one's body. Hence we look elsewhere in prominent Roman Catholic and also Protestant ways of grounding human rights theologically.

Natural law, revelation, and Christ: the measure of human rights

Pope John XXIII wrote in *Pacem in Terris* (1963) that "[e]very basic human right draws its authoritative force from the natural law, which confers it and attaches to it its respective duty" (§ 30) (*Catechism*, Pt. III, § I, ch. 3, art. 1.1). To the extent that the *jus gentium* or the Law of Nations and the UDHR are founded upon the objective moral order as given by God and discerned by right reason, they arise indestructibly from the natural law. "Thus, for example, the right to live involves the duty to preserve one's life; the right to a decent standard of living, the duty to live in a becoming fashion; the right to be free to seek out the truth, the duty to devote oneself to an ever deeper and wider search for it" (Pope John XXIII 1963, § 29). The natural law may be understood to mean humankind's participation in the Eternal Law, through reason and will; its first precept is that good is to be done and pursued, and evil is to be avoided (Aquinas 1947, I–II, *q*. 94 *a*. 1–2). It should *not* be understood to mean that God's law can be read off from what we identify as the successes, patterns, or features of this world's structure, events, and so on. Rather, the natural law reflects the divine reason and/or will of God that conserves the natural order and is a way of expressing God's relationship with creation. Natural law is a function of reason, "promulgated by the very fact that God instilled it into man's mind so as to be known by him naturally" (Aquinas 1947, I–II, *q*. 90, *a*. 4). *Pacem in Terris* – which serves for our purpose as representative of Roman Catholic teaching in this respect – makes no direct equation of natural law with human rights. Rather, human rights discourse is integrated into Roman Catholic social teaching to the extent that it facilitates the kind of order and relations between persons that are consistent with what we know of God's purposes for all creation.

Mindful that denominational differences are sometimes overblown, we note that *Pacem in Terris* appeals to the dignity of the human person not only via the natural law but also by means of reference to revelation and the incomparably increased estimate of this dignity because "[m]en have been ransomed by the blood of Jesus Christ" (§ 10). Later encyclicals, notably *Dignitatis Humanae Personae* and *Gaudium et Spes*, appeal jointly to the natural law and God's revelation in Christ as sources of human rights. The Christological focus of natural law teaching is expounded in *Veritatis Splendor* (1993) which finds the truth of natural law in Christ, and in *Ut Unum Sint* (1995) which talks about human rights in the service of the solidarity of humanity and defense especially of the poor, lowly, and defenseless (§ 43). These Christological arguments are remarkably close to those for human rights made in the 1930s and 1940s by the Protestant theologian Dietrich Bonhoeffer. *Ecce Homo!* "Behold the man!" (Jn 19:5) is his starting point for his discussion of natural rights (Bonhoeffer 2005, p. 82; also Westmoreland-White 1997, p. 69). Christ is the mediator through whom, and in whom, Christians believe they meet their neighbor: "There is no way from us to others than the path through Christ, his word, and our following him. Immediacy is a delusion" (Bonhoeffer 2003, p. 95). It is for Christ's sake, and the sake of his coming kingdom, that the rights of every person are to be recognized and respected; for his sake Christians affirm the human body has a claim to food and shelter. The human body has a claim to joy because God created and wills it for joy (Bonhoeffer 2005, pp. 186–187). The claim to joy, or to food and shelter, is not grounded in mutual obligation but in God's will and purpose. In Christ believers know that natural life has been formed and given by God, and is to be preserved and protected for God's sake; bodily life contains within itself the right to its own preservation because God has willed the continuation of life. These are positive, not merely negative, rights that do more than protect against interference.

There is at least one focus of debate, however, amid growing convergence regarding Christological justification for human rights. It concerns how appeal is made to the belief that humankind is created in the image and likeness of God (Gen. 1:26). Briefly, appeal to human creation *imago Dei* is the rationale behind many Catholic and Protestant attempts to forge links between human dignity and human rights (Ruston 2004). The benefits of this approach include ready emphasis on the equality and infinite value of all persons in God's sight, and as given in creation and revealed in Christ Jesus, who is the image of the invisible God from eternity (Col. 1:15–16). Thus the World Council of Churches Fifth Assembly, 1975, affirms: "All human beings are created in the image of God, equal, and infinitely precious in God's sight and ours. Jesus Christ has bound us to one another by his life, death and resurrection, so that what concerns one concerns us all" (WCC 1999). So far, so good. A problem arises, however, when belief in the creation of humans *imago Dei* is interpreted not in Christological terms but in terms of some kind of capacity given by God to humans, and when this capacity-related interpretation of the *imago Dei* then becomes the basis for human rights claims. So, for instance, the creation of humankind *imago Dei* has been understood variously to comprise the capacity to reason and speak, the kinship between the human mind and divine rationality, etc. This risks excluding those who lack the relevant capacity, e.g., those with particular types of intellectual disability. (This approach also restricts rights-talk unduly to humans, but that is a debate for another day. Suffice it to note that corrective moves are being made to interpret the creation of humans *imago Dei* with reference to Christ Jesus (Col. 1:15–16) in ways that are inclusive, not least by focusing on his incarnation as "flesh" rather than merely as a human being [Deane-Drummond and Clough 2009, esp. ch 5].)

Of itself, the doctrine of creation *imago Dei* cannot bear all the weight required to ground human rights theologically. This warning has been flagged recently by Reformed scholar Nicholas Wolterstorff, who picks up also on the concerns voiced by O'Donovan (see above). He argues vigorously in *Justice: Rights and Wrongs* (2008) that the conception of justice as inherent rights was not born in the twentieth century, or even fourteenth or seventeenth centuries, but goes back to the Hebrew scriptures and New Testament. Drawing upon the historical scholarship of Brian Tierney and Charles Reid to undermine the claim that natural rights was born of philosophical nominalism, he contends that the canon lawyers of the twelfth century employed a notion of natural subjective right that they had inherited from somewhere, notably biblical teaching about justice (Wolterstorff 2008, ch. 2). The anger of God over injustice is unmistakable in Israel's testimony, writes Wolterstorff. God is wronged by injustice and has the right to hold humans accountable for injustice. The wronging of a person is the source of rights because God's endowing of human beings with his image means that humans have worth. In Isaiah 1:17, Isaiah of Jerusalem says:

> Seek justice,
> rescue the oppressed,
> defend the orphan,
> plead for the widow.

Israel believes in God's salvation from poverty, alienation, and oppression, and was not satisfied with contemplation. The poor are wronged by their destitution. So too are those left helpless and abandoned. The language might be modern but there is a recipient-side to the moral order, a recognition of the worth of human beings, and an indication that this worth grounds how a person should be treated. If these elements are present, it does not matter whether the language of rights is used; it is not the word that matters but the shape of the reasoning. In Genesis 9:6, "all who bear God's image possess, on that account, an inherent right not to be murdered" (Wolterstorff 2008, p. 95).

Before concluding this section on theological justifications for human rights, the interdenominational group Evangelicals for Human Rights (EHR) warrants special comment. Its declaration issued in 2007 explains its commitment to human rights in relation to theological convictions – creation, God's law, the incarnation, Jesus's death and resurrection, etc.: "We ground our commitment to human rights," it states, "in the core Christian theological conviction that each and every human life is sacred.... The concept of human rights is not a 'secular' notion but instead finds expression in Christian sources long before the Enlightenment... Everyone bears an obligation to act in ways that recognize human rights" (Evangelicals for Human Rights n.d.). Part of the broader National Religious Campaign Against Torture, this association of evangelical Christians in conjunction with the preeminent evangelical associations, churches, and parachurch bodies, representing over 30,000,000 people, affirmed that a commitment to human rights was consistent with foundational Christian moral norms regarding the sanctity of life. All persons, they affirm, regardless of ethnicity, sex, nationality, ability/disability, social status, etc., "are to be perceived as sacred, as persons of equal and immeasurable worth and of inviolable dignity. Therefore they must be treated with the reverence and respect commensurate with this elevated moral status. This begins with a commitment to the preservation of their lives and protection of their basic rights."

Christianity and human rights in a religiously and otherwise plural world

Our question in this section is whether Christians should welcome plural foundations for human rights in a religiously and otherwise plural world, and, if so, on what theological grounds. Amid variations on the theme, we have seen so far that Christians affirm a right to have rights because of their conviction that the worth of every person is revealed preeminently in the incarnation, death, resurrection, and ascension of Christ Jesus. What are the implications, however, of this kind of theological rooting of human rights in a religiously and otherwise plural world? Does it open or close doors to conversation with those who ground human rights differently, and with what likely implications? Such questions mark a relatively new departure in Christian theological debate about human rights. No consensus has emerged yet among Christian people about either the need for a more radically pluralist approach than that conceived by drafters of the UDHR in 1948 or what such an approach might entail. Too often the options are seen as either an inability to talk across theological difference or freeform relativism. In what follows, I argue that these are not the only options. Rather, there are strong biblical and traditional reasons for *reasoning with other faith traditions* about the specifics of human rights, *reasoning over sacred texts*, and *reasoning pragmatically with extra-scriptural texts* such as the UDHR and related conventions.

The context of our question is a culture in which abstract appeals to universal reason no longer sound convincing. O'Rourke (2007, p. 40) captures this when he asks why we are all equal:

> We hold this truth to be self-evident, which on the face of it is so wildly untrue.... are we all equal because we all showed up?... Are we all equal because it says so in the American Declaration of Independence and the UN Universal Declaration of Human Rights? Each of these documents contains plenty of half-truths and nontruths as well.

Merely to appeal to a piece of paper, or even to the fact that lots of people have agreed to the words on it, is not ultimately a reason for believing these words to be true. In "Enlightenment's wake" (to borrow John Gray's phrase) the options are sometimes cast as either disenchantment at attempts by modern philosophers to ground human rights in universal human reason or acceptance that deep cultural diversity is an ineradicable feature of present-day existence, which means that we shall never agree about the universality of human rights. The tension between these two positions has historically been about not conceiving of human rights in terms of the values prevalent in Western Europe and North America. Today, the tension between the cosmopolitan norms of human rights and the need for legal rights that are universal and unconditional is yet more complex. A fundamental challenge for our times, writes Robert Post, is the construction of "a jurisprudential theory able to reconcile the universality of human rights with the partiality of positive law" (Post 2006, p. 3).

In this context, many religious people and others hold that the universality of human rights need no longer be assumed in terms of a Western philosophical construct based on the notion of "to each the same" (Aristotle), or a category derived from the faculty of judgment (Kant), or the product of consensus (*à la* discourse ethics), or even the reinvention or mythopoesis of natural law using the category of transcendence in a post-metaphysical world (Costas Douzinas). The justice of rights claims need not be treated merely as a branch of general utility (J. S. Mill) or determined solely by recognition in international law. In other words, the universality of human rights is not merely a philosophical or legal given but must be sought, identified, and instantiated at law. Rather, the faith traditions of the world have the scriptural resources and liturgical practices required for different, more relational, construals of universality. If, with

John Howard Yoder and Stanley Hauerwas, we suppose that the confusion of tongues at Babel was not a punishment or a tragedy but a benevolent act that brought blessing through dispersion and diversification, then constructed universalities such as that of human rights must be striven for, and sought, like the understanding between the peoples after the scattering. Like the "one language" spoken by the whole earth in Genesis 11:1, the ideology of modern human rights could become an attempt to resist God's will that there will be a diversity of cultures; this would be to conceive of human rights in absolute terms as a kind of foundationalist body of theory from which all uncertainty has been removed (Wolterstorff 1984, pp. 28–30). The struggle for overlapping justifications for human rights in a multicultured world is to be welcomed as preferable to what Hauerwas calls "imperially enforced uniformity."

While Christians and other faith communities have different ways of conceiving of the universality of human rights (for Christians the universality of rights is given by the creaturely status of all beings and their inclusion in the effects of incarnation and consequent hope of heaven), the point here is that universality across traditions may be sought via engagement with one another, in and through our deepest differences. Different faith traditions have different, and indeed incompatible, conceptions of universality. They have different conceptions of the nation-state and the nature of earthly governance within divine providence. Even so, believers can come together to read and reason with their scriptures, in the light of the wisdom of their traditions, and to read and reason with the UDHR, related conventions, and other texts. Witness the National Religious Campaign against Torture (NRCAT). A multifaith coalition against torture formed in 2006 as a campaigning coalition against USA-sponsored torture, the NRCAT comprises people of different faiths working together across points of theological incompatibility to take a stand against injustice among the most vulnerable, to create cultures of peace, etc. It presupposes that each faith tradition will grapple with its own sacred texts when asking whether and/or why torture is abhorrent. By reasoning both separately and together over sacred and other texts, faith traditions learn better to discern the ethical imperatives in their own traditions, not for the sake of reason per se (as if human reason could provide self-grounding justifications for action) but for the sake of practice; *tikkun olam*, to use the Jewish phrase for the moral labor of mending the world.

On the universality of human rights amid difference

At least amongst the Abrahamic faiths (and potentially among other traditions too), this approach to pursuing the universality of human rights across difference may be construed methodologically as an extension of the Scriptural Reasoning (SR) movement. By SR, I understand the movement as it has developed from conversations between Peter Ochs, a Jewish scholar based at the University of Virginia, David Ford of the University of Cambridge, and others (see the *Journal of Scriptural Reasoning* website, <http://etext.lib.virginia.edu/journals/jsrforum>). Scriptural Reasoners are typically Jews, Christians, and Muslims who meet, read, and reason together for the healing of our separate communities and repair of the world (Kepnes n.d.). We come together in tents of meeting, says Steven Kepnes, another founding figure of the SR movement, to read and reason with our scriptures: "We then return to our religious and academic institutions with renewed energy to bring criticism and healing to our institutions."

This extension of SR to the reading of shared extra-Scriptural texts is, in some respects, a re-posing of familiar Christian theological questions about natural law reasoning. To the extent that natural law reasoning is ethical thinking that supposes a divinely sanctioned morally lawful universe and has moral and political content, then multifaith practical reasoning is an exercise of this kind. The same biblical and traditional arguments by which Christians advocate natural law reasoning apply (e.g., the natural law is universal, i.e., "in all human persons"; despite the devastating effects of sin, the natural law still gives true knowledge of the moral law; humans have the ability to fulfill the natural law but this ability is seriously flawed by the effects of sin; the content of the natural law is the law of God for humankind and has often been identified with the Decalogue and/or with the Logos or reason present by the Spirit of God in humanity; the natural law is part of the natural endowment of all people and can reasonably be expected to be deduced; it is commonly associated with the claim that civil government is part of God's continuing care and a corrective for sin). The task is to hold together the reading of sacred texts – as, in some important ways, constitutive of moral reasoning in the various faith traditions – with moral reasoning about human rights. A potential challenge to this approach is the claim that the UDHR is a strong testament to the universality of human rights *precisely because* it floats free of any underlying justification: "The Declaration's vaunted 'universality' is as much a testament to what the drafters kept *out* of it," writes Ignatieff, "as to what they put *in*" (2001, p. 78). Ignatieff's challenge is not merely that religion should remain confined to the private spheres of life but that seeking religious justifications for human rights potentially undermines their currently established universality. "The universalism" of human rights (i.e., the contested interpretation and application of human rights in different contexts, often stirred up by the cultural relativist argument), has long been recognized as contentious, whereas the "universality of human rights" (i.e., the universal quality or global acceptance of human rights evidenced by the adoption of the UDHR around the globe), has held relatively firm (Baderin 2003, pp. 23–26). The implied warning is not only that the "inspirational rhetoric" of the world's religions in talking explicitly and in public about the "why?" that underlies their support for human rights lacks utility but that it puts "the universality" of human rights in question.

This challenge is to be taken seriously. There is an obvious sense in which the universality of human rights is achieved through political process and the implementation of standards agreed in international and national law and enforcement through various powers. Yet questions must be faced about why the rhetoric of human rights is often not matched by political action, or matched only selectively. Consider the so-called torture memos prepared by lawyers in the administration of President George W. Bush to the effect that the president had the legal authority to permit the use of torture during interrogation (O'Connell 2008, p. 1). This was not simply tinkering with the detail of human rights law but a comprehensive assault on the international regime in relation to torture. In the face of questions about state security, a fundamental human right was treated as a factor in a consequentialist-type calculus and weighed against other considerations. A fundamental human right was conceived as something to be balanced against security (Waldron 2003, pp. 194–195). Ignatieff's optimism is welcome to the extent that he supposes human rights will continue to protect human beings against cruelty, oppression, and degradation, on the strength of observations drawn from history and what we know is likely to happen when humans do not have the protection of rights (Ignatieff 2001, p. 80). Yet the Scriptural Reasoner is likely to be wary of saying "peace" so easily (Jer. 6:14). As the torture memos debacle exposes, human rights politics is embroiled continuously in trade-offs and compromises with the interests of nation-states.

In such contexts, it is at least arguable that one of the prophetic functions of the world religions today is to ask whether secularist minimalism, i.e., the refusal to ask the "Why?" question with respect to human rights and concentrate only on what they actually do, is enough to withstand selectivity on the part of nation-states with respect to which human rights they choose to protect. Christians, together with their fellow Scriptural Reasoners, are likely to be proactive in asking whether minimalist, propositionally derived human rights norms without roots in "thick" traditions of morality can withstand unilateral attention to state interests and have the resources to trump the hard-headed consequentialism of some politicians. Equally, Scriptural Reasoners will be quick to acknowledge that a "thick" conception of universality can issue in "thin" norms. For the Christian, the cross of Christ – i.e., the very heart of what Christians believe about the nature of God's love – is precisely what requires them to affirm that "everyone has the right to life, liberty and security of person" (Art. 3), "everyone has the right to freedom of thought, conscience and religion" (Art. 18), "everyone has the right to a standard of living adequate for the health and well-being of himself and of his family" (Art. 25), etc. Thus a Christian is likely to condemn torture because they have learned from Christ's crucified body and the eucharistic practice of the Church that the kind of reduction it effects in a person runs entirely contrary to the gospel. Theological reasoning moves between confession that what is truly universal for the Christian is the love of God for every creature as revealed pre-eminently in Christ, what this means in terms of the "thin" cosmopolitan norms of international human rights law, and how these norms might find homes in local, variously accountable legal structures.

Prioritizing social justice and the case for collective rights

In closing, I draw attention to the different priorities that theologically informed moral reasoning is likely to set as compared to some modern, secularist theorists – in particular, those who prioritize liberty, and especially economic liberty, over social and economic rights such as freedom of association and collective bargaining, equal pay at work, and minority rights. Consider O'Rourke's representation of the vision of society outlined by Adam Smith in *The Wealth of Nations* and, in particular, its undermining of Article 23 of the UDHR concerning the right to work, to just and free conditions of employment, to form and join trade unions, etc. "The UN proclaims, 'Everyone has the right to rest and leisure, including reasonable limitation of working hours,'" he writes. "I'll have my wife inform the baby" (O'Rourke 2007, p. 40). This mocking of the social dimension of human rights legislation and supposition that the purpose of laws is to ensure individual liberty, sits uneasily with established Jewish, Christian, and Muslim teaching about work and social responsibility. Consider briefly the following texts that are indicative of what might be studied at an SR session.

From the Tanakh:

> Justice, justice shalt thou follow, that thou mayest live, and inherit the land which HaShem thy G_d giveth thee. (Deuteronomy 16:20)
>
> Announce to my people their rebellion ... Look you serve your own interest on your fast day, and oppress all your workers. (Is. 58:1–3)

From the New Testament:

> When the Son of Man comes in his glory ... All the nations will be gathered before him, and he will separate people one from another as a shepherd separates sheep from goats. (Matt. 25:31–2 *NRSV*)

From the Qur'an:

> O you who believe! do not devour your property among yourselves falsely, except that it be trading by your mutual consent; and do not kill your people; surely Allah is Merciful to you. (4:29)

And We made your sleep to be rest (to you), And We made the night to be a covering, And We made the day for seeking livelihood. (78:9–11)

In contrast to the commonplace modern, liberal assumption that the purpose of laws is to maximize individual liberty and facilitate the free movement of money, goods, and services, members of the Abrahamic faiths are likely to prioritize human rights that provide for social justice, not least protection for workers, decent wages, effective and equitable social welfare provision, etc. Much work remains to be done among members of the Abrahamic faiths with respect to the differences and convergences between us regarding human rights. In the meantime, we agree that the struggle for social justice is broader than civil and political rights and that it converges around the cry of the oppressed. For this reason, human rights in the workplace remain, arguably, among the most urgent because work is "the key to the social question" (Pope John Paul II 1981).

References

An-Na'im, Abdullahi. 2000. "Human Rights, Religion, and the Contingency of Universalist Projects." Occasional Paper no. 2. PARC, Maxwell School of Citizenship and Public Affairs, Syracuse University, Syracuse, NY, September.

Aquinas, Thomas. 1947. *Summa Theologia*. Trans. Fathers of the English Dominican Province (New York: Benziger Bros.).

Baderin, Mashood. 2003. *International Human Rights and Islamic Law* (Oxford: Oxford University Press).

Barnett, Victoria J. 1995. "Dietrich Bonhoeffer's Ecumenical Vision." *Christian Century*, 26 April, pp. 454–457.

Bonhoeffer, Dietrich. 2003. *Discipleship: The Dietrich Bonhoeffer Works*. Trans. Barbara Green and Reinhard Krauss, from the German ed. Martin Kuske and Ilse Tödt (Minneapolis, MN: Augsburg Fortress).

Bonhoeffer, Dietrich. 2005. *Ethics: The Dietrich Bonhoeffer Works*. Vol. 6. Trans. Reinhard Krauss et al., from the German ed. Ilse Tödt et al. (Minneapolis, MN: Augsburg Fortress).

Catechism of the Catholic Church. At: http://www.vatican.va/archive/ENG0015/__P6U.HTM.

Curran, Charles E. 1988. "Catholic Social and Sexual Teaching: A Methodological Comparison." *Theology Today*, Vol. 44, No. 4. At: http://theologytoday.ptsem.edu/jan1988/v44-4-article1.htm.

Deane-Drummond, Celia and David Clough, eds. 2009. *Creaturely Theology* (London: SCM).

Evangelicals for Human Rights. N.d. *An Evangelical Declaration Against Torture: Protecting Human Rights in an Age of Terror*. At: http://www.evangelicalsforhumanrights.org/index.php?option=com_content&task=view&id=14&Itemid=42.

Guroian, Vigen. 2005. *Rallying the Really Human Things* (Wilmington, DE: ISI Books).

Hauerwas, Stanley. 1986. *Suffering Presence: Theological Reflections on Medicine, the Mentally Handicapped, and the Church* (South Bend, IN: University of Notre Dame Press).

Hauerwas, Stanley. 1991. "Abortion Theologically Understood." Taskforce of United Methodists on Abortion and Sexuality. At: http://lifewatch.org/abortion.html.

Hobbes, Thomas. 1997. *On the Citizen* (Cambridge: Cambridge University Press).

Ignatieff, Michael. 2001. *Human Rights as Politics and Idolatry* (Princeton, NJ: Princeton University Press).

Keating, Maryann O. and Barry P. Keating 1998. "Economics as a Discipline: The Crossroads Between John Paul II's Social Vision and Conservative Economic Thought." *International Journal of Social Sciences*, Vol. 25, Nos. 11/12.

Kepnes, Steven. N.d. "A Handbook of Scriptural Reasoning." At: http://etext.lib.virginia.edu/journals/jsrforum/writings/KepHand.html.

Locke, John. 1960. *Two Treatises of Government* (Cambridge: Cambridge University Press).

Migliore, Celestino. 2003. *Intervention By The Holy See at the 58th Session of the General Assembly of the United Nations Organization on the Occasion of the Fifty-Fifth Anniversary of the Universal Declaration of Human Rights*. 10 December. At: http://www.vatican.va/roman_curia/secretariat_state/2003/documents/rc_seg-st_20031210_human-rights_en.html.

Nurser, John. 2005. *For All Peoples and All Nations: The Ecumenical Church and Human Rights* (Washington, DC: Georgetown University Press).

O'Connell, Mary Ellen. 2008. *The Power and Purpose of International Law* (Oxford: Oxford University Press).
O'Donovan, Joan Lockwood. 2003. "Rights, Law and Political Community: A Theological and Historical Perspective." *Transformation*, Vol. 20, No. 1, January, pp. 30–38. At: http://www.ocms.ac.uk/transformation/free_articles/2001.030_odonovan.pdf.
O'Rourke, P. J. 1993. "The Liberty Manifesto." Cato Institute. At: http://www.cato.org/pub_display.php?pub_id=6857.
O'Rourke, P. J. 2007. *On the Wealth of Nations* (New York: Atlantic Monthly Press).
Paton, David M., ed. 1976. *Breaking Barriers, the Official Report of the Fifth Assembly of the World Council of Churches* (Grand Rapids, MI: William B. Eerdmans).
Pope John XXIII. 1963. *Pacem in Terris*. At: http://www.vatican.va.
Pope John Paul II. 1981. *Laborem Exercens* § 3. At: http://www.vatican.va/edocs/ENG0217/_INDEX.HTM.
Post, Robert. 2006. "Introduction." In Seyla Benhabib et al., *Another Cosmopolitanism* (Oxford: Oxford University Press).
Reed, Esther D. 2007. *The Ethics of Human Rights: Contested Doctrinal and Moral Issues* (Waco, TX: Baylor University Press).
Ruston, Roger. 2004. *Human Rights and the Image of God* (London: SCM).
Waldron, Jeremy. 2003. "Security and Liberty: The Image of Balance." *Journal of Political Philosophy*, Vol. 11, No. 2, pp. 191–210.
Westmoreland-White, Michael L. 1997. "Contributions to Human Rights in Dietrich Bonhoeffer's Ethics." *Journal of Church and State*, Vol. 39, No. 1, pp. 67–83.
Wolterstorff, Nicholas. 1984. *Reason within the Bounds of Religion* (Grand Rapids, MI: Eerdmans).
Wolterstorff, Nicholas. 2008. *Justice: Rights and Wrongs* (Princeton, NJ: Princeton University Press).
World Council of Churches (WCC) Eighth Assembly. 1999. *Together on the Way: 5.7 The Universal Declaration on Human Rights*. At: http://www.wcc-coe.org/wcc/assembly/hudec-e.html.
World Council of Churches (WCC). 2003. *A Church of All and for All – An Interim Statement*. At: http://www2.wcc-coe.org/ccdocuments2003.nsf/index/plen-1.1-en.html.

22
Confucianism and human rights

Justin Tiwald

One of the most accessible ways to wrap one's mind around the controversy over Confucianism and human rights is to consider what would happen to a well-functioning family if it instituted many of the same practices as rights-protecting societies. As many Confucians see rights-protecting societies, their members have certain obligations to others by virtue of the fact that they are fellow citizens or fellow human beings, not by virtue of being friends, cousins, neighbors, or siblings. People are free or even encouraged to lay claim to their rights when they are threatened, and when they do so there are formal and often informal mechanisms that help to protect them. When they invoke their rights, they typically invoke them *against* other citizens, creating a potentially adversarial relationship between them. And the rights that people claim tend to be fixed and non-negotiable, making them less inclined to look for ways to harmonize their interests with one another.

If families were to operate in these ways, most of what is distinctive (and distinctively valuable) about family life would be undermined. Within the family, members often act out of love or a sense of commitment to their role-specific responsibilities (as mothers, grandfathers, daughters, or brothers), not out of concern that other members wield the power to claim and thus enforce their rights against them. Family members are constantly renegotiating and revising the ways that they work to protect the interests of each member, which makes them reluctant to lay down hard-and-fast obligations and entitlements for any one of them. A family that behaved as people in rights-protecting societies often do would either be profoundly dysfunctional or no family at all. On the Confucian view, much of the dysfunctionality of the rights-protecting family is dysfunctional in rights-protecting societies as well. People should be encouraged to harmonize their interests. They should act out of affection or a sense of commitment to their responsibilities as neighbors, community elders, and colleagues, without the threat that others might use rights-enforcing mechanisms against them.

Among the worries that Confucians have about rights-protecting institutions, three of the most prominent can be drawn from the ways in which well-functioning societies should mirror well-functioning families. The first is that rights-protecting social institutions emphasize role-independent obligations and entitlements that we have as fellow human beings, at the expense of role-dependent concerns that we have as neighbors, coworkers, acquaintances, and so on. The second is that rights give rights-holders too many ways to undercut the hierarchical structure of Confucian institutions. The third and probably most pervasive concern is that the practice of invoking and enforcing rights introduces too much conflict and adversarial thinking. To give a preview of my argument, I aim to show that (1) the worry about role-dependent ethics underestimates the versatility of human rights principles, (2) the Confucian commitment to social hierarchy poses a more serious problem for the integration of Confucianism and human rights, which can be accommodated only by compromising the system of checks and balances that Confucians normally prefer, and (3) the worry about social conflict and disharmony poses the most fundamental challenge to those who wish to reconcile core Confucian doctrines with the practice of protecting rights. I will begin with a rough definition of human rights and then proceed to this three-part analysis. I will focus primarily on the two texts most widely considered to be the foundations of *orthodox* Confucian beliefs: the thought of Kongzi (Confucius) and Mengzi (Mencius), which the tradition respectively derives from the *Analects* and the *Mengzi*.[1]

What is a human right?

A "human right" in the sense that I will use here requires two things at minimum: something to which virtually all human beings are entitled, and some set of significant rules or norms that helps to guarantee the entitlement, should normal means fail. If Huang has a right to shelter, it is not enough that someone be obligated to provide her with shelter. There should be mechanisms in place to help guarantee that the right is protected. When people talk about human rights, they sometimes speak as though having something of fundamental worth to which all human beings are entitled is sufficient for it to be a right, whether or not there are significant mechanisms that help to protect it. But rights in this thin sense are not the primary object of contention in Confucian circles: it is uncontroversial that Confucians believe a decent government should provide its citizens with an array of basic goods. The primary Confucian worry is that the practice of claiming and enforcing these rights will undercut traditional social structures (Peerenboom 1998, pp. 248–251).

Rights and role-dependent ethics

One feature of the well-functioning family is that people generally treat one another in role-specific ways: children generally respect the wishes and instructions of their parents, parents attend to their children's education and development, and (perhaps) grandparents dote on their grandchildren. Ethics within families is thus largely *role-dependent:* the relevant ethical obligations (and corresponding entitlements) depend largely on the social relationship between the person who is obligated and the person to whom the obligation is owed. It is widely held that well-functioning Confucian communities should exhibit the same role-dependent ethical outlook on a larger scale, and some have cited this as a reason to think rights-protecting practices problematic for Confucians (Rosemont 1988; Ames 1988).

There are at least two versions of this claim at work here. One, which is most important for our purposes, is that Confucian ethics is role-dependent *in content*: the particular kinds of obligations and entitlements by which we live varies largely according to the social roles that one plays. Scholars often attribute this to the Confucian emphasis on the traditional "five relationships" (*wu lun*), and the importance of living according to traditional rituals and proprieties (*li*). The "Five Relationships" are father and son, husband and wife, elder brother and younger brother, ruler and ruled, and friend and friend. Confucians traditionally see these as playing the most important role in maintaining social harmony and cultivating moral virtue (Mengzi 1990,

3A4; Van Norden 2008, p. 71). The other version of this claim is that Confucian ethics is based in a role-dependent *conception of persons*: when we properly explain why a person has one entitlement rather than another, we do not appeal to characteristics or properties that confer moral standing regardless of her relationships to others (such as the properties that make her a human being); instead, we can only appeal to specific social roles that she has vis-à-vis particular others, as a colleague, daughter, sister, and so on. In the words of Henry Rosemont, Jr., speaking on behalf of the latter view, "For the early Confucians there can be no *me* in isolation, to be considered abstractly: I am the totality of roles I live in relation to specific others" (Rosemont 1988, p. 177; see also Rosemont 1991).

Let us look more closely at these two claims. Although the role-dependent conception of persons might point to something distinctive about Confucian ethics, it would be a stretch to conclude that Confucians see persons as constituted *entirely* by their roles. Among the ways that Confucians use to explain what is good or bad about a person, two are prominent: one, as Rosemont indicates, is to describe how well he performs his roles; the other and more prevalent one is to describe how closely the person's character approximates the chief Confucian virtues, which share certain behavioral and psychological features regardless of his role. For example, a humane or benevolent (*ren*) person exhibits love and concern, and a wise (*zhi*) person is a good judge of human character. If the pure role-based conception of persons were correct, then among these two patterns, the former would play the more fundamental explanatory role: that is, the Confucians would explain what is good or bad about a person's character in terms of how well he executes his role-specific responsibilities. But in the foundational Confucian texts, passages that could plausibly be construed as final appeals to role-based responsibilities are quite rare (*Analects* 12.11, pp. 130–131). Final appeals to the virtues are ubiquitous, and where Kongzi and Mengzi have opportunities to explain what is right or wrong about the way someone manages his or her role-specific obligations, they often do so by appealing to virtues that cut across roles, such as benevolence (*ren*), wisdom (*zhi*), or trustworthiness (*xin*) (Ivanhoe 2007). The two virtues whose prescriptions vary most according to one's relative status and position are righteousness (*yi*) and ritual propriety (*li*), but these too have universal features: the righteous are unbiased in their judgments and indifferent to personal benefit; the ritually proper are reverent and attentive (or "fully present") on the appropriate occasions (*Analects* 4.10, pp. 32–33; 4.16, p. 35; 3.12, pp. 21–22; 19.1, p. 221). Finally, the Confucian masters think these virtues are worth cultivating no matter what role one might assume – whether one finds oneself an outcast or in a position of power and influence, or whether one assumes the role of a child or a parent, cultivating and manifesting these virtues is necessary for all. While these problems may not be the end of the story for defenders of the purest version of the role-based conception of persons, they surely impose upon them a tremendous burden of proof. Another un-Confucian implication of the pure role-dependent conception is that there are no direct obligations to those who leave society altogether, as Ames appears to acknowledge (1988, pp. 210–211).

There is also a legitimate question about the implications of the role-dependent conception of persons for the actual content of Confucian ethical norms. The particular array of my obligations to Huang might be grounded in my relationship to her as a friend rather than brother or mere fellow citizen, but there might be some overlapping obligations that all people – whether friends, brothers, or mere fellow citizens – share. If I see a moral imperative to criticize a policy at the risk of imprisonment, some might be obligated to encourage me, some (such as my family) might be obligated to discourage me, but it is conceivable that all of them should at least permit me to speak. Less controversially, family members and mere acquaintances may be obligated to victims of abuse in different ways, but all share the minimal obligation to help stop the abuse. So long as we can find areas of significant overlap across types of role-based obligations, this will be enough to ground a system of entitlements that apply to all human beings, conceivably entitlements of many different types.

In spite of the controversy about role-independence in Confucianism more generally, there is a widespread consensus that Confucian peoples share a common obligation to attend to others' basic needs and interests. At the same time, most scholars believe Confucians prioritize needs and interests differently than do many liberal democracies. The *Analects* and the *Mengzi* do not particularly stress the value of autonomy or political participation, and instead emphasize the ruler's duty to provide for (a) the basic material needs of the people and (b) the conditions necessary to develop essentially social virtues – the virtues necessary to contribute properly to one's family and one's community (Xiao 1983, pp. 95–97). This emphasis is reflected today in scholars and other public figures who say that Confucian societies should give the highest priority to "subsistence rights" (*shengcun quan*) and the community-oriented rights necessary to become a full and virtuous member of society (Peerenboom 1993, p. 55; Rosemont 2004). However, Angle and Svensson point out that Mengzi gives the people no power to act against rulers who neglect their basic material needs, even though he thinks their misbehavior is often understandable and excusable (2001, pp. xix–xx).

The way that many contemporary Confucians defend these rights is by appeal to the chief Confucian virtue *ren,* most often translated as "humaneness" or "benevolence." Joseph Chan has made perhaps the most influential argument for this view:

> human persons are first and foremost moral agents capable of realizing *ren,* which means, among other things, a certain ability or disposition to care for and sympathize with others. Although the sites for the realization of *ren* are commonly found in personal relationships such as those of father – son and husband – wife, there are *nonrelational* occasions when moral actions are also required by *ren.*
>
> *(Chan 1999, pp. 217–218)*

Even strangers, Chan suggests, are owed a minimum level of dignity and humane treatment, for which our properly cultivated sensitivities to human suffering equip us. And Chan's evidence points to elements of Confucian doctrine widely regarded as central to the thought of Kongzi and Mengzi, including Kongzi's famous Golden Rule ("do not impose upon others what you yourself do not desire"), and Mengzi's suggestion that we can discern the roots of benevolence in our natural reaction to a presumably unknown child on the verge of falling into a well (*Analects* 12.2, p. 126; *Mengzi* 2A6, pp. 45–46; Chan 1999, p. 218). Chan here discusses the importance of *exercising* humaneness, but we could add another set of obligations having to do with developing or providing for the *cultivation* of it, which requires a steady supply of basic needs, a nurturing and relatively self-sustaining family, and arguably (when resources are sufficient) state-sponsored education (*Mengzi* 1A3, pp. 3–5). Kongzi and Mengzi both think that living a virtuous life among others is one of the most important constituents of human well-being, and undercutting a person's ability to become virtuous is tantamount to mutilation or robbery (*Mengzi* 1B8, p. 26; 2A6, p. 47).

Of course, just because Confucians should put the rights of subsistence and moral development first, it does not follow that they should reject entirely the usual slate of political rights and liberties. Scholars argue that there are still reasons for Confucians to guarantee freedom of expression, but these reasons would make the freedom more circumscribed and contingent. Chan argues convincingly that a Confucian right of free speech would not automatically extend to speech that inflames racial hatred or appeals to prurient interests (1999, p. 234). Tongdong Bai suggests that a right to criticize the government might only be justified when government corruption or mismanagement makes it necessary (2009, pp. 84–85). Daniel Bell suggests that Confucianism forbids the acquisition of property through "unrighteous means," construed much more broadly than theft or blatant deception to include such things as begging or neglecting the needs of elderly parents (2006, pp. 231–254). One popular way of explaining why such rights are more circumscribed and contingent is that Confucians see them as justified primarily on instrumental grounds. On the Confucian view, political participation and individual autonomy do not have tremendous intrinsic value, so Confucians will be more concerned with how property rights, liberties, and voting rights contribute to other ends, such as social harmony or moral development (Angle 2002, pp. 239–249; 2009, pp. 209–215; Peerenboom 1993, p. 55).

These assertions about political rights and liberties are controversial, but no matter what their plausibility and scope, there is sufficient evidence to conclude that the challenge of role-dependent ethics – by itself – only affects the shape that human rights might take in a Confucian society, not the fundamental viability of rights-protecting practices in Confucian societies.

Rights and social hierarchy

Rights provide their holders with ways of limiting the authority of their superiors. In the case of certain political rights (such as the right to choose one's leaders by election) the threat is obvious. We have seen that these political rights would be scaled back in a society that adheres to basic Confucian principles, but that other rights – such as rights to basic welfare and education – look to be more promising candidates for compatibility. For Confucians concerned about preserving traditional hierarchical structures, however, even non-political rights are cause for uneasiness. This is because a right in the sense we are using here gives the right-holder the power to *claim* it. That is, it gives the right-holder the power to alert others to the fact that her right is threatened or violated, and in so doing compel others to take action on behalf of her right. If this is a threat to Confucian hierarchy, however, the nature of the threat is not immediately apparent, and thus bears closer examination.

Let us say that a construction worker, Chun-yuen, has a mother who is diagnosed with a rapidly progressing terminal illness, and Chun-yuen has a right to receive a certain amount of paid leave when necessary to care for a dying parent. Chun-yuen has sisters who could also care for the mother, but their mother prefers to spend her final days with her son. However, Chun-yuen's supervisor refuses to grant Chun-yuen leave: the supervisor knows that Chun-yuen's sisters will be much better caretakers than Chun-yuen himself, and he is reluctant to lose Chun-yuen's help in the middle of the peak construction season. Chun-yuen tries to convince his supervisor that he is a more competent caretaker than his supervisor thinks, and that his absence will not unduly affect the company's productivity. His supervisor disagrees. With no better options, Chun-yuen declares that he will report his case to the relevant rights-protecting authority – perhaps a union or human resources officer – and his supervisor relents.

This is a threat to the company hierarchy, but it is not entirely clear what kind. Some might think Chun-yuen's ability to claim his right is threatening because it casts doubt on his supervisor's judgment, for it gives Chun-yuen the power to raise objections to his supervisor's decisions, often in a very public way. But on the strict Confucian view this too is perfectly acceptable – even encouraged. According to the classical Confucians, authority figures should welcome remonstrations (*jian*) and should not be afraid to change course in light of a persuasive case. The difference here is that in the Confucian case, the superior has the power of *final review:* even if he grants his subordinates some role in the decision-making process, he is free to act against their advice when he sees fit (*Mengzi* 1B7, pp. 24–26).

A better reason to think Chun-yuen's right undermines the company hierarchy is because it provides him with one area of life – the area of life concerning family leave – over which his immediate superior does *not* have the power of final review. This phenomenon does not seem to trouble most believers in the rights-compatibility of Confucianism. It is somewhat difficult to see why not. As Chan has noted, the most authoritative Confucian texts – such as the *Analects* – actually countenance rare acts of disobedience, even by sons against their fathers (1999, pp. 222–226). But this is somewhat beside the point here, since Chun-yuen's right consists not just in having a moral prerogative to disobey under rare circumstances, but in having institutional mechanisms that guarantee regular protection under well-defined circumstances. Rights in the sense that is most controversial for Confucians require a degree of social cooperation and reinforcement, and grant the right-holder considerable latitude in choosing when to claim them.

A more likely reason why rights-compatibilists are unmoved by rights like Chun-yuen's is because the power it grants him is *contained*. It does not give him any say over the supervisor's decisions regarding hiring and firing, the supervisor's assignment of tasks to employees, or any of the countless other routine decisions that fall under the supervisor's prerogative. Even if we add a number of other work-related rights – such as rights to breaks or overtime pay – the scope of Chun-yuen's decision-making sovereignty is relatively small.

There are a couple of responses one might have to the argument that rights only provide subordinates with contained powers of limited scope. One is to insist (in the manner of a slippery slope argument) that human psychology is such that, once subordinates are granted limited powers over their superiors, they will naturally incline to claiming more and more such powers for themselves, and perhaps society will grow increasingly tolerant of this expansion of power. But even if we reject this debatable empirical claim, many Confucians will find one thing troubling about the contained power to claim one's right to family leave or overtime pay: namely, that the right to these things is hard and fast and not usually susceptible to bending or breaking. Kongzi and Mengzi insist that conducting human affairs calls for much more nuance and discretion than hard-and-fast rules can provide, both because morality itself is better suited to flexible "rules of thumb" than invariant principles, and because the warmth of genuine care and concern is lost when one applies laws and regulations too rigidly (Ivanhoe 2008a).

A remaining move for the rights-compatibilist is to point out that even in the eyes of most rights-oriented thinkers, there will be special provisions for the suspension of rights in extraordinary circumstances. Presumably Chun-yuen's right to family leave could be suspended if his labor were necessary to cope with a national crisis (to build shelters for people made homeless by an earthquake, for example). Perhaps it would be acceptable to deny him his family leave if his company were teetering on the verge of bankruptcy. Nevertheless, a crucial difference between most rights-protecting social institutions and Confucianism is that the former often handle exceptions by appealing to a third party, such as a court or a board of arbitration. Most rights-protecting societies assume that properly guaranteeing people's rights – such that discretion to suspend them is not abused – requires a separation of powers. If Chun-yuen's right is to be suspended, therefore, it will likely be someone other than his immediate supervisor who suspends it. On the Confucian view, there is no compelling need to de-centralize power in this way, and doing so might in fact interfere with the more caring and cohesive administrative practices of a single political authority.

Rights-claiming and social conflict

One of the most pervasive worries about Confucianism is that the practice of claiming one's rights is conflictual. That is, it both reflects a breakdown in social harmony and is a cause of further social strain. Our hypothetical rights-protecting family is illustrative here. Rights-claiming within a family implies that there is a breakdown in trust. If the youngest brother in the family needs medicine which his well-paid older sister is best positioned to buy, and he relies on a right to compel her to pay for it, it would seem that he no longer trusts his sister to act in his best interest. Moreover, rights-claiming initiates a process that has the potential to lead to forced compliance, which casts a threatening shadow over what should be the sister's more spontaneous or affectionate motives to help her brother. And finally, the fact that the brother resorts to rights-claiming implies that he thinks his sister's cares and concerns conflict with his own, as though it would not particularly pain her to see her brother suffering from a debilitating illness. By Confucian lights, members of the same communities should have a similar sense of trust and care, and they should share the presupposition that their concerns will converge with the concerns of other community members, at least on matters of importance. Even if there are some instances where rights-claiming does not reflect a breakdown in trust and care, it is enough for Confucians that they frequently do, and that the divisive ways of thinking that rights-claiming evokes will tend to grow on those who do it.

On this issue most scholars of Confucianism take their cues from Confucian views about law and litigation. If we assume that rights come packaged with mechanisms of enforcement, then many (although perhaps not all) of the relevant mechanisms of enforcement might be enshrined in law and backed up with the coercive power of government. On this point there is widespread consensus that laws are at best a "fallback apparatus," to use Joseph Chan's phrase (1999, p. 221), to be utilized only when preferred ways of protecting people's interests have failed. For example, neighbors engaged in a land dispute should find ways that draw upon their mutual affection and commitment to neighborly cooperation. If these are insufficient the neighbors should try to arrive at some sort of mutual agreement. Invocation and enforcement of law is necessary only when consensus cannot be reached, as Kongzi maintains in a widely cited passage in the *Analects:* "When it comes to hearing civil litigation, I am as good as anyone else. What is necessary, though, is to bring it about that there is no civil litigation at all" (*Analects* 12.13, p. 132).

The view that Confucianism can make room for rights as a fallback apparatus is widespread. The problem is that both parties to the Confucian debate – rights-compatibilists and rights-incompatibilists – tend to cite this view and declare victory for their side. Rights-compatibilists think it shows that Confucian doctrines can make room for the essential features of human rights thought (Chan 1999, pp. 220–222). Rights-incompatibilists think that it shows that Confucian values – while not utterly opposed to rights – are nevertheless deeply averse to them (Ames 1988, p. 213; Ihara 2004). What, then, do the two sides disagree about? In what follows I will venture some answers and then show that they force both sides to think more precisely about the sort of fallback mechanism they have in mind.

At first blush, there might not seem to be anything particularly distinctive about the Confucian "fallback apparatus" view. Many liberal thinkers also regard rights-claiming as an inferior alternative to systems that protect interests by appealing to personal affection and other social bonds. To be sure, some liberal rights thinkers believe rights-claiming can have some intrinsic value for the claimant – as a source of dignity or self-esteem, for example (Feinberg 1970). But others see cases of rights-claiming as a necessary but unfortunate recourse for people who would be better served by affection and other social bonds (Waldron 1988). It would be surprising if they did not.

On my view, we cannot see what is truly distinctive about a Confucian version of the fallback apparatus account of rights until we think about more passive ways in which rights can influence the moral contours of human behavior. Much of the talk about fallback rights focuses on what happens once someone decides to claim her rights, but the mere existence of the right, even when unclaimed, has a remarkable effect on group dynamics as well. In fact, many of the worries about rights that are manifest in the analogy to the rights-protecting family are more concerned with the *power to claim* rights than rights-claiming itself. For the high-earning sister and her sick younger brother considering whether to acquire medicine for him, awareness of their claimable rights ("rights consciousness") might encourage them to think of their interests as competitive with one another. If the brother has a right to garnish his sister's wages, just knowing that he could potentially enforce this right would cast a shadow over their relationship, warping their feelings and motives in ways fundamentally at odds with family life.

There are other ways in which rights can alter the moral dimensions of relationships even when they go un-invoked. If I have a right to something that would significantly benefit someone else, then opting not to exercise the right affects the moral quality or praiseworthiness of my act. Let us say I am on a rural highway and come across someone who needs help changing a flat tire. I have a right to use my spare time as I wish, but I decide to help the unfortunate driver nonetheless. In rights-protecting societies, many would construe this as making my act supererogatory, and nobler than it would have been if there were no such right. Had there been good Samaritan laws that required me to provide aid to drivers with flat tires and thus no right to refrain from helping, it would have been less admirable of me to help (Meyer 1997). Confucians are arguably less comfortable with this way of thinking, particularly if the unfortunate driver is related to me as a member of my community or fellow citizen. To see why, consider again how this way of thinking might play out in the context of a family. Imagine that my younger brother is struggling in his Chinese history courses and needs my tutoring, and yet I have a right to use my spare time as I wish. If we apply the same principles here as we did in the case of the flat tire, there should be something nobler or more valuable about helping my brother. But this is a bizarre and disconcerting conclusion. Surely helping my brother is the least I could do.

This shows that rights – even in the form of a fallback apparatus – have both active and passive ways of influencing social dynamics and the moral quality of actions. Traditional Confucians would find even the passive forms troubling. This being the case, can Confucianism make room for rights as a fallback apparatus? On my view, much depends on how and under what circumstances the fallback mechanism would be set into motion. If the rules and procedures that help people to claim and enforce their rights are available at any time, should an oppressor's behavior become egregious enough, then they would figure prominently in the minds and calculations of community members. Were a land dispute to arise, each party would come to the dispute with an acute awareness of their legal and moral entitlements and an understanding that it would take relatively little trouble to secure them. Rights in this case are close to the foreground, so to speak. At the other end of the spectrum are rights-protecting rules and procedures that only get established when a social unit has reached the point of complete breakdown – perhaps when political authorities utterly neglect the interests of the larger community, or when most neighbors would sooner settle differences by violence. If this is how we conceive of the fallback apparatus, rights are sunk well into the background, being neither at the forefront of the potential rights-holders' minds nor a near-term threat to rights-abusers.

With a clearer understanding of the difference between a rights apparatus that is in the foreground and one that is in the background, we can now identify a set of issues about which rights-compatibilists and rights-incompatibilists truly disagree. In the most familiar rights-protecting societies, rights are clearly foregrounded. People are encouraged to "know your rights!" and society members are aware that should their rights be abused or endangered, the rules, procedures, and legal authorities are at the ready. If these practices can be integrated into traditional Confucian societies without significant cost to their core principles, then presumably the fallback apparatus should be near at hand for them as well. As we have seen, this seems highly implausible, for even passive forms of influence are cause for consternation among Confucians.

Although this poses a significant challenge for defenders of the rights-compatible reading of Confucianism, it also highlights an array of issues that rights-incompatibilists need to articulate more clearly. Some, such as Roger Ames, speak as though Confucians might already have rights-protecting laws that should nevertheless go un-invoked (1988, p. 213). There is in fact some textual evidence for this view: in the *Analects* and some less canonical sources, Kongzi and the sage kings are seen establishing laws without ever using them (Wang 1990, *Analects* 20.1, p. 233). But as we have seen, this position is not specific enough to identify what is distinctive about Confucianism, since many liberal rights thinkers also prefer that rights go un-invoked. Other rights-incompatibilists, such as Craig Ihara, seem to indicate that a proper Confucian society would institute rules and procedures only when the community is in complete disarray (2004, pp. 27–28). Without further clarification, however, this would appear to offer little recourse to small groups of oppressed peoples in otherwise functional communities. Moreover, it at least appears to tell against the aforementioned evidence that Confucians endorse the establishment of laws and procedures for litigation, so long as they find ways of not using them. If a viable position is to be found, it must fall somewhere between the view that rules and procedures "kick in" only at the point of complete social breakdown, and the view that oppressed individuals should be able to walk to the nearest police station and file an actionable report against other community members (however reluctantly). Intriguingly, the theorists who have been clearest about the extent to which rights-protecting mechanisms can be foregrounded are those who seek compromises between traditional (classical or canonical) Confucian values and contemporary liberalism (Angle 2009, pp. 216–222; Ivanhoe 2008b). As these positions are avowed innovations or modifications of traditional Confucianism, however, those who defend strong versions of rights-incompatibilism need to identify the ways in which a true Confucian fallback apparatus would stand even further in the background than these compromises suggest.

Conclusion

An important upshot of this analysis is that the debate about Confucianism and human rights turns greatly on how Confucians might structure the *power to claim* individual rights. Issues that do not bear directly on this structure – such as the role-dependent elements of Confucian ethics – are somewhat less important to those most concerned about justifying rights (particularly individual rights) on orthodox Confucian grounds. The threat that rights pose to social hierarchy turn out to have much to do with whether or not the power to entertain and enforce rights-claims can be separated from the authorities responsible for everyday decision-making. And in the debate about the conflictual aspects of rights-claiming, we cannot even distinguish the two sides until we look at the ways in which the mere power to claim rights (rather than the regular practice of claiming them) might or might not fit into a Confucian society. A crucial step forward, then, is to look closely at the many configurations that this sort of power can take. Should the rights-holder herself be the one that is encouraged to claim her rights, or would it be better to have people claiming rights on one another's behalf? How can rights be a fallback mechanism without figuring too largely in the thoughts and calculations of community members? Should traditional Confucians allow that certain minority groups have rights-claiming rules and procedures more readily available than others? These might appear to be nothing more than the finer points of the debate, but until they are sorted out it will be hard to identify the real tensions between orthodox Confucianism and most contemporary rights-based ideologies.

Note

1 Chinese editions and English translations of these texts are plentiful. I will use the traditional form of citation employed in most editions, which identifies each work by book and chapter number (e.g., *Analects* 2.4, *Mengzi* 6A1), and then cite the relevant page numbers in Slingerland 2003 (in the case of the *Analects*) and Van Norden 2008 (in the case of the *Mengzi*).

References

Ames, Roger T. 1988. "Rites as Rights: The Confucian Alternative," pp. 199–216 in Leroy S. Rouner, ed. *Human Rights and the World's Religions* (South Bend, IN: Notre Dame University Press).
Angle, Stephen C. 2002. *Human Rights and Chinese Thought* (Cambridge: Cambridge University Press).
Angle, Stephen C. 2009. *Sagehood: The Contemporary Significance of Neo-Confucian Philosophy* (Oxford: Oxford University Press).
Angle, Stephen C. and Marina Svensson, eds. 2001 *The Chinese Human Rights Reader: Documents and Commentary 1900–2000* (Armonk, NY: ME Sharpe).
Bai, Tongdong. 2009. *Jiu Bang Xin Ming: Gu Jin Zhong Xi Can Zhao Xia De Gu Dian Ru Jia Zheng Zhi Zhe Xue* (A New Mission for an Old State: Classical Confucian Political Philosophy in a Contemporary and Comparative Context) (Beijing: Peking University Press).
Bell, Daniel A. 2006. *Beyond Liberal Democracy: Political Thinking for an East Asian Context* (Princeton, NJ: Princeton University Press).
Chan, Joseph. 1999. "A Confucian Perspective on Human Rights for Contemporary China." In Joanne R. Bauer and Daniel A. Bell, eds., *The East Asian Challenge for Human Rights* (Cambridge: Cambridge University Press).
Feinberg, Joel. 1970. "The Nature and Value of Rights." *Journal of Value Inquiry*, Vol. 4, pp. 243–260.
Ihara, Craig K. 2004. "Are Individual Rights Necessary? A Confucian Perspective," pp. 11–30 in Kwong-loi Shun and David B. Wong, eds., *Confucian Ethics: A Comparative Study of Self, Autonomy, and Community* (Cambridge: Cambridge University Press).
Ivanhoe, Philip J. 2007. "The Shade of Confucius: Social Roles, Ethical Theory, and the Self," pp. 41–56 in Ronnie L. Littlejohn and Marthe Chandler, eds., *Polishing the Chinese Mirror: Essays in Honor of Henry Rosemont, Jr.* (New York: Global Scholarly Publications).
Ivanhoe, Philip J. 2008a. "The 'Golden Rule' in the Analects," pp. 81–108 in David Jones, ed., *Confucius Now: Contemporary Encounters with the Analects* (Peru, IL: Open Court Publishers).
Ivanhoe, Philip J. 2008b. "A Confucian Contribution to Justice, Gender, and the Family." *Jeremiah Lecture Series*, University of Oregon Center for Asian and Pacific Studies, Eugene, March 2.
Kongzi (Confucius). 1990. *Lun Yu Ji Jie* (The Collected Explanations of the Analects). Ed. Shude Cheng (Beijing: Zhong hua shu ju).
Mengzi (Mencius). 1990. *Mengzi*. Ed. and Trans. Bojun Yang (Beijing: Zhong hua shu ju).
Meyer, Michael J. 1997. "When Not to Claim Your Rights: The Abuse and the Virtuous Use of Rights." *Journal of Political Philosophy*, Vol. 5, No. 2, pp. 149–162.
Peerenboom, Randall. 1993. "What's Wrong with Chinese Rights? Toward a Theory of Rights with Chinese Characteristics." *Harvard Human Rights Journal*, Vol. 6, pp. 29–57.
Peerenboom, Randall. 1998. "Confucian Harmony and Freedom of Thought," pp. 234–236 in William Theodore de Bary and Weiming Tu, eds., *Confucianism and Human Rights* (New York: Columbia University Press).
Rosemont, Henry, Jr. 1988. "Why Take Rights Seriously? A Confucian Critique," pp. 167–182 in Leroy S. Rouner, ed., *Human Rights and the World's Religions* (South Bend, IN: Notre Dame University Press).
Rosemont, Henry, Jr. 1991. "Rights-bearing Individuals and Role-bearing Persons," pp. 71–101 in Mary I. Bockover, ed., *Rules, Rituals, and Responsibility: Essays Dedicated to Herbert Fingarette* (LaSalle, IL: Open Court Publishers).
Rosemont, Henry, Jr. 2004. "Whose Democracy? Which Rights? A Confucian Critique of Modern Western Liberalism," pp. 49–71 in Kwong-loi Shun and David B. Wong, eds., *Confucian Ethics: A Comparative Study of Self, Autonomy, and Community* (Cambridge: Cambridge University Press).

Slingerland, Edward, trans. 2003. *Confucius Analects: With Selections from Traditional Commentaries* (Indianapolis, IN: Hackett).

Van Norden, Bryan W., trans. 2008. *Mengzi: With Selections from Traditional Commentaries* (Indianapolis, IN: Hackett).

Waldron, Jeremy. 1988. "When Justice Replaces Affection: The Need for Rights." *Harvard Journal of Law and Public Policy*, Vol. 11, pp. 625–647.

Wang, Su, ed. 1990. *Kongzi Jia Yu* (Sayings of the School of Kongzi) (Shanghai: Shanghai gu ji chu ban she).

Xiao, Gongquan. 1983. *Zhong Guo Zheng Zhi Si Xiang Shi* (A History of Chinese Political Thought), Vol. 1 (Taipei: Lianjing).

23
Islamic conceptions of human rights

Irene Oh

Events following the September 11, 2001, terrorist attacks on the World Trade Center in the United States, including bombings in London and Madrid, contribute to negative Western perceptions of Islam as a religion of violent extremists who hold little respect for innocent human life. Militant attacks claimed by al-Qaeda, Muslim suicide bombers, and Islamic political groups such as Hamas lead many Westerners to understand Islam as a tradition incapable of promoting justice, peace, or human rights. Such acts of violence dominate Western perspectives of Islam. According to the 2005 Pew Global Attitudes Project, Islamic extremism concerns the majority of the public in Russia (84 percent very or somewhat concerned), India (82 percent), Germany (78 percent), Spain (77 percent), the Netherlands (76 percent), Great Britain (70 percent), the United States (70 percent), France (63 percent), and Canada (56 percent). Although the citizens of Muslim-majority nations are also worried about Islamic extremism, they understand Islam as a multidimensional tradition capable of both violating and supporting human rights.

The same Pew Global Attitudes Project (2005) survey revealed that in countries such as Morocco, Pakistan, Turkey, Indonesia, and Jordan, Muslim-majority publics shared concerns with Western publics over Islamic extremism. Yet, these Muslim-majority publics tend to welcome Islam in political life. How to explain this apparent discrepancy? Islam, like any other major world religion, is subject to various interpretations and practices. Certain basic tenets identify a person's beliefs and practices as "Islamic," but there are significant differences in the ways individual Muslims live their lives as Muslims. Literally translated as "submission," Islam requires that Muslims submit themselves to the will of God, but much variation exists with regard to what a life of submission requires. The ability to accept Islam as accommodating a range of such differences enables one to view Islam as the source of both violence and peace, injustice and justice. Although Islam, as interpreted by extremists such as the Taliban or al-Qaeda, violates human rights, Islam as interpreted by the majority of Muslims around the world is a religion synonymous with human rights.

The fact that most Muslims believe human rights and Islam are compatible begs the question of whether there exists a universally accepted definition of human rights. Just as Islam has evolved over centuries to accommodate a wide variety of interpretive beliefs and practices, the definition of human rights too has changed over time. The 1948 Universal Declaration of

Human Rights might be considered a normative description of human rights, but it has been both elaborated upon and criticized by different groups over the last five decades. Muslims have embraced the general concept of human rights, but have also expressed criticisms of Western-bias in human rights declarations. While Muslims might claim that Islam supports human rights, an Islamic concept of human rights likely differs at points from conceptions of human rights found in other religious communities. This is not to say that Islamic views of human rights betray a "true" notion of human rights, but rather to alert us to the shifting articulation of human rights (Glendon 2001; Waltz 2004).

An understanding of how Islam might be variously interpreted to violate and to promote human rights requires a basic understanding of the foundational history of Islam as well as common terms used within the religious tradition. Following this introduction to Islam will be a section that explores in greater depth the evolution of *shari'a* (commonly translated as Islamic law) and the relationship between *shari'a* and human rights. Finally, this chapter will address human rights from the perspective of major Islamic thinkers.

A brief overview of Islam

Familiarity with the basic history of Islam, its beliefs, and rituals is vital to understanding contemporary discussions of Islam and its compatibility with human rights. Much of Islamic ethics derives from the reverence of the first Muslims, and variations in interpretations of this paradigmatic era result in different responses to the concept of human rights. Present-day individuals and communities may, for example, claim that the practices of seventh-century Muslims constitute the purest expression of Islam, and so interpret and attempt to construct societies that they believe closely emulate this early era. Other Muslims accept the founding of Islam as existing within a particular historical context. Rather than view this history as requiring literal reproduction, they view it as a progressive model for change. Although Muslim extremists who violate human rights are commonly associated with "literalist" interpretations of Islam, many progressive Muslims understand themselves to be the more accurate interpreters of the early tradition. In any case, it is clear that one requires a familiarity with the historical outlines of Islam to comprehend contemporary human rights discussions concerning Islam.

Islam dates back to the seventh century CE when a well-respected merchant on the Arabian peninsula claimed to receive divine messages and shared them with members of his tribe (for more complete introductions to Islam, see Denny 2006; Lings 1983; Hodgson 1974). Muhammad, regarded by Muslims as the last prophet in the Abrahamic religions (Judaism and Christianity), grew up in the mountainous region known as the Hijaz, an area known both for trade and warfare. According to Muslim tradition, Muhammad (b. 570 CE) was born into the tribe of the Quraysh, orphaned at a young age, and raised by his extended family to become a successful merchant in the Arabian peninsula. The environment of Muhammad's youth imparted skills that would prove valuable to a future leader. As a Hijazi, Muhammad was an expert in long-distance trading, which required that he be able to fight to protect and raid caravans, as well as that he diplomatically forge alliances to broker safe trading routes and share profits. At the time of Muhammad's birth, very little political unity existed on the Arabian peninsula beyond these opportunistic partnerships. Most alliances were the result of trade agreements or of tribal associations. The peoples of the Arabian peninsula did, however, share a common Arabic language, were members of similarly structured tribes with familiar customs, and were familiar with the narrative of Abraham. These traits would later assist Muhammad in bringing together the first Muslim community.

Arabia prior to Muhammad has traditionally been characterized by Muslims as existing in a state *al-Jahiliyya*, commonly translated as "ignorance" or "barbarism." Arabians prior to Islam were considered ignorant of the knowledge of God, as well as of virtue, honor, and civility. Unchecked cycles of violence, barbarism, and idol worship were common to this period of *al-Jahiliyya*. Pilgrims traveled to Mecca, an important trading center in the Hijaz, to worship variations of Greek and Roman gods and deities of natural phenomenon (rocks, springs, groves), in addition to the Abrahamic god of Jews and Christians. Amid *al-Jahiliyya*, the art of poetry recitation stood out as a singular symbol of high culture. Extremely popular, poetry contests would honor poets who were believed to be literally inspired by *jinn* (spirits) who transmitted lyrical tales, historical events, and other narratives. When Muhammad would later claim to have been visited by the angel Gabriel, the highly poetic quality of his recitations would help to convince his companions that, indeed, he had been visited by a spirit. Such words and phrases, his companions would reason, could not have come from a merchant, but must have been transmitted by God.

When at the age of 40 Muhammad received the divine revelations that would eventually become the Qur'an, he was deeply disturbed. Although he regularly retreated into a cave to meditate, this was the first time that he experienced divine visions and messages. His wife, Khadija, comforted him and encouraged him to accept these unusual revelations. Khadija, the wealthy businesswoman and widower who fifteen years previously had proposed marriage to Muhammad, a man twenty-five years her junior, soon became the first convert to Islam. Her conversion was followed by close friends and members of his tribe, among whom would be Ali, Abu Bakr, and Uthman, future caliphs of the nascent Muslim community.

The Qur'an (literally, the recitations) contains the primary record of divine revelations sent by the Abrahamic God to Muhammad. The messages found in the Qur'an are varied, including typical prophetic warnings against idolatry and descriptions of a monotheistic God and God's creation, as well as guidance for moral living. The Qur'an also contains references to previous prophets in the Jewish and Christian traditions, such as Moses, David, and Jesus. These themes, while not unfamiliar to Muhammad's Meccan audience, were nonetheless considered a major betrayal to his own tribe's livelihood. In particular, Muhammad's incursions against idolatry jeopardized the Quraysh's vital commerce with polytheistic traders and pilgrims. The threat of persecution against Muhammad eventually became so great that in 622 CE he and a group of followers would travel northward to the city of Yathrib (Medina) for refuge. The year of this migration would become known as the Hijra and marks the start of the Muslim calendar.

Muhammad displayed strong leadership abilities in Medina by bringing relative peace to a city previously torn by tribal factions. He authored the Constitution of Medina, which united the tribes of Medina in case of external threat and encouraged the toleration of different religious groups within the city. From Medina, Muhammad also proved himself a capable military leader by defeating a Meccan army in the Battle of Badr (624 CE) and many others to follow. Throughout this period, Muhammad continued to receive divine revelations. Many Qur'anic verses that appear legalistic in nature, such as those dealing with inheritance or the treatment of slaves, derive from this period in Medina, when administrative concerns of the Muslim community, the *umma*, loomed large.

Muslims admire Muhammad for his political and military acumen, but the veneration of Muhammad ought not to be confused with the worship of him as a god. Many Muslims consider his life, both public and private, worthy of imitation. Muhammad's words and deeds, documented and complied in texts known as the *sunna* (traditions), which include *hadith* (reports about the Prophet), are studied alongside the Qur'an as guides for moral living. Four of the five "pillars" of Islam, which include ritual prayer, alms-giving, fasting, and the *hajj* (pilgrimage to Mecca) are directly related to the practices of Muhammad. The first pillar, a statement made by Muslims attesting to a monotheistic God and the prophethood of Muhammad, confirms the significance of Muhammad in Islam. Although Muhammad is understood as the most virtuous practitioner of God's message, he remains but a human prophet, while the Qur'an is traditionally understood as divine. Muhammad is a human transmitter of God's divine word. For all his importance to the tradition and generations of Muslims, Muhammad never claims to be the author of the Qur'an, but rather views himself as the vessel through which God's words emerge for the benefit of humanity.

By the time of his death in 632 CE, Muhammad had expanded Islam's reach to areas beyond the borders of Medina and Mecca. Despite the early successes of the Islamic empire, plans for its future were uncertain. Muhammad had not left clear plans for the leadership of the *umma* following his death. Those nearest to Muhammad, his companions and his kin, quarreled over the issue of succession. Disagreement over the leadership of the community would lead to the division of the Muslim community into Sunni and Shi'ite factions. The Sunni, so named for its insistence upon tradition, claimed that Muhammad's succession should be determined by a traditional caucus of elders, while the Shi'i of 'Ali, referring to the political party that supported 'Ali, claimed that Muhammad promised the leadership to his cousin 'Ali. The Sunni prevailed in their campaign for the first caliph, but 'Ali would eventually become recognized as the fourth and last of the caliphs to have known Muhammad while he was still alive.

The first half-century of Islam, from the time Muhammad received his initial revelations to the death of 'Ali in 661 CE, is remarkable for a number of reasons. In a few short decades, Islam became firmly established as a distinct religious tradition, a community of Muslims united as a religious and political entity, and the Islamic empire expanded territorially to reach northern Africa, the Anatolian peninsula, and Persia. The presence and growth of this third Abrahamic tradition would continue well into the present day. Today, well over one billion people throughout the world consider themselves Muslims, making Islam the second largest religion following Christianity. Not only in the Middle East, but also in South Asia, Africa, and increasingly, in North America, Europe, and South America, the impact of Islam as a religious and political force cannot be underestimated.

Shari'a: interpreting history and human rights

Many human rights concerns about Islam focus on *shari'a*. In certain Muslim communities *shari'a* is undeniably practiced in such a way that grossly violates the rights of women and minorities; however, the more profound struggle for human rights proponents involves not only these bad laws, but the creation and interpretation of *shari'a*. *Shari'a*, commonly referred to as Islamic law, refers literally to a road, street, or path. It encompasses not merely that which is legal or illegal, but more broadly outlines a way to direct one's entire being. The question of who gets to determine and challenge existing *shari'a* ought to be of equal, if not greater, concern than specific laws and practices. John Kelsay (2007) asserts that Islamic militants have dangerously managed to convince some Muslims that they are both worthy and competent interpreters of *shari'a*. The claim to be legitimate interpreters of *shari'a* must be challenged in order to stop human rights violations committed in the name of Islam.

Shari'a developed alongside the rise of the scholarly class in the eighth through ninth centuries. As the Islamic state continued its expansion, the need arose for legal experts who could facilitate the standardization of the law governing a vast and diversely constituted empire. The growth of Muslim communities geographically, culturally, and historically distant from the seventh-century Arabian context of the Qur'an meant that the interpretation and application of the Qur'an became increasingly important for the cohesiveness of the empire. Legal scholars, equipped with a standardized Qur'an (canonized by the third Caliph, Uthman) and increasingly reliable documentation of the words and practices of Muhammad, developed systems and tools of jurisprudence (*fiqh*) to determine laws compatible with the teachings found in the Qur'an and the *sunna* of Muhammad.

The sources of *shari'a* include the Qur'an, the *sunna*, and *hadith*, and of these three sources, the Qur'an is considered the most important. For Muslims, the Qur'an, unlike the *sunna* and *hadith*, is divine in nature, whereas the *sunna* and *hadith* understood as the work of humans. Although the content of the *sunna* addresses the life of the Prophet, the process by which various sayings and practices of the Prophet were verified is understood as a kind of library science refined by scholars. Hence, Muslims believe that there is only one true version of the Qur'an, but accept different compilations of *sunna* and *hadith*.

The Qur'an, which contains 114 chapters, or *suras*, contains some guidance on moral and legal matters, and is somewhat limited in scope. It is not only relatively short (about the length of the New Testament), but also reflects the concerns pertinent to seventh-century Arabia. The *sunna* of the Prophet Muhammad contributes to the body of law by providing details absent from the Qur'an. The Qur'an, for example, directs Muslims to purify themselves for prayer, but does not specify how prayers ought to be performed. The *sunna* provides this level of detail by describing eye-witness accounts of the physical movements and words performed by Muhammad during prayer. Eventually, five major approaches to understanding the Qur'an and *sunna* developed. These "schools" represent different ways of practicing Islam, and include the Jafari (Shi'ite), Hanafi (Sunni, found predominantly in Turkey, Central Asia, and the Indian subcontinent), Maliki (Sunni, found predominantly in Egypt, north and west Africa), Shafi'i (Sunni, found predominantly in Egypt, east Africa, southern Arabia, and Malaysia), and Hanabli (Sunni, found predominantly in Mesopotamia, Syria, and Palestine). In keeping with the notion that Islam can be variously interpreted, Muslims generally consider the differences among the schools wholly legitimate. Although the Sunni and Shi'ite schools both recognize the Qur'an and the *sunna* as the primary sources of *shari'a*, Shi'ite Muslims acknowledge the special authority of imams (religious leaders) and their ability to exercise independent interpretations (*ijtihad*) of the law.

Common to the approaches to *shari'a* among the different schools is their use of scales of permissibility with regard to specific behaviors. *Shari'a* describes whether certain acts are *wajib* (required), *mustahab* (rewarded, but not required), *mubah* (neutral), *makruh* (deserving of punishment), or *haram* (forbidden). If they disagree with each other concerning specific cases, most schools differ only slightly on degrees of permissibility. In the case of fasting, for example, all the schools require that Muslims fast during Ramadan, but will differ in degrees in response to the question of whether a Muslim who unintentionally breaks the fast needs to compensate for this. The schools may also differ slightly with regard to ritual performance. In the case of prayer, one school may say one part of a prayer more loudly or softly than another, the height of one's hands may be lower or higher depending upon the school, and whether or not to cross one's arms at specific moments during the prayer ritual may vary.

In order to determine the law in the case that the Qur'an and the *sunna* were unclear, Muslim jurists rely upon *fiqh*, which provides a number of legal tools appropriate for different situations. When a community has legal needs that are not discussed in the Qur'an or *sunna*, a Muslim jurist may exercise his personal opinion, or *ra'y*, to reflect upon how one might interpret the Qur'an and *sunna* to apply to the situation. *Al-ra'y*, the most flexible of the jurisprudential tools, is especially helpful for determining laws specific to a local community and which might not be applicable to others. A more restrictive and exacting version of *ra'y* is *qiyas*, or analogical reasoning. *Qiyas* produces a more limited number of legal possibilities compared to *ra'y* by limiting legal conclusions to analogous situations. For example, in order to determine if marijuana is a permitted substance in Islam, a jurist applying *qiyas* might compare marijuana to alcohol, and conclude that by analogy, Muslims are not permitted to use marijuana. The most restrictive form of legal reasoning, *ijma*, requires a consensus of Muslim jurists. Following a *hadith* in which Muhammad reportedly claimed that his community would never agree on an error, *ijma* is the most binding of *fiqh* approaches and trumps other forms of legal reasoning.

In the Sunni tradition, *ijma* has been an especially dominant form of jurisprudence and acknowledged for providing a stable source of authority. In the Shi'ite legal tradition, *ijtihad*, a form of independent reasoning performed by *mujtahids* (legal scholars), has played a prominent role. *Ijtihad*, more restrictive than *ra'y* but less restrictive than *qiyas*, connotes an intellectual struggle undertaken by a legal scholar who has attained the proper qualifications necessary for undertaking *ijtihad*. Trained in classical Arabic, considered virtuous by his community, and familiar with the Qur'an and *sunna*, the *mujtahid* carefully employs *ijtihad* to come to an original legal conclusion. The reliance upon *ijtihad* in Shi'ism, which emphasizes the power bestowed upon individual *mujtahids*, appears to reflect the authoritarian structure of Shi 'ism. In practice, however, *mujtahids* tend to respect the opinions of the great early jurists of their communities, thereby providing a relatively stable and continuous source of law.

Although some Sunni jurists maintain that the "gates of *ijtihad*" are closed and that no new innovations in law can be made, "*shari'a* reasoning" as Kelsay describes it, continues to the present day. Reasoning through *shari'a* in theory provides Muslim jurists structured ways to develop laws appropriate and responsive to contemporary life that responsibly draw upon traditional sources. It involves not merely the selective quotation of Qur'an or *hadith* to support one's opinion, but rather historically tested jurisprudential methods of coming to specific conclusions about the law. *Shari'a* demands deep knowledge of the early history of Islam, facility with a wealth of legal opinions, and intellectual precision. Moreover, participation in the community of Islamic laws requires that one welcome debate by other jurists. There is no "high court" of Islam that pronounces with some finality the appropriateness of a law. Even when a *mufti*, an authority in legal scholarship, pronounces a *fatwa* (formal legal opinion), it is considered but one opinion, and Muslims are free to seek out alternate opinions.

Many Muslim extremists who identify with Wahhabi approaches to the *shari'a* may fairly be criticized for the "intellectual laziness" of their opinions (Kelsay 2007, p. 185). Wahhabism, an Islamic movement inspired by Muhammad ibn 'Abd al-Wahhab (1703–1791), is an ultra-conservative Hanbali approach to Islam formally allied with the Saudi royal family. More recently, Wahhabism has been associated with the religious and political views of Islamic militants including Osama bin Laden and members of the Taliban. Characterized by the strict rejection of beliefs, practices, and rituals considered modifications from the original followers of Islam, Wahhabism has faced much opposition for their violent attempts to enforce their worldview upon other Muslims. Although Wahhabis claim the value of *ijtihad*, their intellectual intolerance renders the movement irresponsibly rigid and simplistic.

Scholars such as Kelsay and Khaled Abou el Fadl have found that Wahhabism's oppressive restrictiveness, especially with regard to the behavior of women, "rests less on a careful examination of sources, and more on longstanding prejudices" (Kelsay 2007, pp. 184–185). The Wahhabist interpretation of *shari'a* regards women as inherently guilty for seducing men and causing social unrest. Their false understanding of *shari'a* and poor application of *fiqh* enable Taliban men to justify the isolation of and violence against women so as to prevent and punish the sin of sexual temptation. Abou el Fadl argues that the Wahhabi's interpretation of *shari'a* is based on selective *hadith*, ignores the opinion of several prominent legal scholars, and fails to consider the changing context of women's (and men's) lives since the seventh century (Kelsay 2007, pp. 186–187; Abou el Fadl 2001). Even the controversial scholar Tariq Ramadan holds in agreement with Abou el Fadl that while the Qur'an and early sources may provide the inspiration for Muslims today, they must do so "without ever imposing a definitive model, a timeless code, or, more broadly, a dogma for action" (Ramadan 2004, p. 145). Ramadan, like Kelsay and Abou el Fadl, is critical of traditionalists and literalists who are incapable of reforming and reinterpreting *shari'a* to accommodate advances in human rights and to fit contemporary contexts.

In order to guarantee the human rights of women, as Amina Wadud reminds us, the very structure of *shari'a* needs to be reconsidered so as to accommodate women's voices. The "experiences of the majority of Muslim women," she writes, "with regard to their most intimate needs and concerns, remain silent and invisible in the process of the leading discourse of progressive Islamic transformation" (Wadud 2006, p. 52). Interpreting *shari'a* to honor human rights requires not only egalitarian laws, but also an egalitarian process that considers the perspectives of women and other marginalized groups.

Islamic thinkers on human rights

Major Islamic thinkers in the twentieth century have embraced the concept of human rights, but not without criticism. The range of Islamic scholars, from the most conservative and "fundamentalist" in worldview to the most progressive and reform-minded tends to agree upon the compatibility of Islam with human rights. They also agree that international human rights norms display a Western bias. They disagree, however, with regard to their hermeneutical and interpretive approaches to Islam. More specifically, they hold different opinions concerning the influence of Western ideas on Islam. The more conservative thinkers tend to perceive Western notions of human rights as corruptive to Islamic traditions, whereas the more reformist scholars tend to receive Western ideas as potential sources of insight.

Scholars such as Sayyid Qutb and Abul A'la Maududi (1977, p. 7), who are considered to be among the most conservative and anti-Western thinkers of the twentieth century, support the notion of human rights, despite its Western origins. In particular, they endorse the central concepts of governance by the people, toleration, and freedom of conscience. They argue that within Islam, one can not only find basic human rights, but the perfection of these rights. Maududi, for example, insists that Islam offers humankind an exemplary form of democracy. (The terms "conservative," "fundamentalist," "progressive," and "reform-minded" are used here with some caution. These terms are employed because of the convenience and familiarity of these terms for the general reader. For greater clarification of the complexity of these descriptors, see Safi 2003.) Qutb states that Islamic governance is superior to democratic governance. Not only do Islamic governments provide equality and freedom, but they also assume a holistic approach that cares for the spiritual and material needs of citizens (1970, pp. 8, 31, 69, 88). Qutb touts the value of toleration found in the Qur'an and the *sunna*. He cites leaders such as Salah al-Din, who stood out as a religiously tolerant Islamic leader during the Crusades. Qutb also compares Islamic governments to apartheid South Africa and the plight of Native Americans in the United States. With regard to the treatment of women, Qutb explains that Western societies discriminate against women by failing to provide them adequate financial protection, whereas women in Islamic societies have always been ensured of the right to their own property (1970, pp. 49–53). Both Maududi and Qutb claim that Islam has long protected the right to freedom of conscience (Qutb 1970, pp. 12, 167, 93, 94). Maududi cites the Qur'an: "There shall be no coercion in matters of faith," and explains that this applies to Jews, Christians, and followers of all other faith traditions (1977, p. 30). Islam and human rights, they assert, are not only compatible, but Islam epitomizes human rights.

The embrace of human rights by Qutb and Maududi ought not to be construed as an endorsement of a Western emphasis on rights. Rather, Qutb and Maududi argue for the commensurability of Islam with human rights as a way to assert the superiority of Islam to Western value systems. Their writings on human rights coincide with the official end of Western colonialism, and their strategy of upholding an idealized Islam as an antidote to undue Western influence is clear (Childs and Williams 1997, p. 55). During the previous century, Western European countries, including Great Britain, France, and the Netherlands, colonized territories ranging from the Indian subcontinent to portions of West Africa and forced radical changes upon Muslim communities. Forced instruction and use of Western languages, the imposition of Western-style dress codes, and the implementation of Western legal systems disrupted existing social, legal, and cultural norms. With the end of colonialism in the first half of the twentieth century, Islamic thinkers such as Qutb and Maududi viewed a revival of Islam as a means to empower demoralized Muslim communities.

The attempt to uphold Islam as an antidote to colonialism's harms challenges human rights norms commonly accepted in the West. While espousing Islam as a champion of human rights, Qutb and Maududi also express a willingness to curb freedom of speech and impinge upon the right to privacy when necessary to uphold Islamic values. Qutb, for example, believes that Muslims should avoid Western scholarship in the social sciences and the humanities, including the disciplines of philosophy, history (historiography in particular), psychology, ethics, and comparative religions (Qutb 2000, p. 201). He believes that exposing young Muslims to literature in these areas will contaminate their Islamic worldviews. Although he stops short of banning such literature altogether, the tendency to forbid or limit so extensively Western culture and ideas defies common Western conceptions of freedom of conscience and toleration. While Western nations do, in fact, ban certain types of publications, the reasons for such restrictions must generally prove overwhelmingly compelling. For example, bans against child pornography intend to protect children from unquestionable harm. In Germany, pro-Nazi literature is banned because of its history, but pro-Nazi literature in other countries such as the United States is not.

Western legal thought considers the right to free speech as both necessary for and an expression of the free conscience. From this perspective, Qutb's limitations upon free speech in order to protect impressionable Muslim minds pose barriers to the right to freedom of conscience. Similarly, Maududi supports the toleration of other religious traditions, but he also believes that Islamic governments must uphold the Qur'anic duty to promote the good and forbid the bad. His lack of specificity in determining the good and the bad would potentially enable an Islamic government to refuse to tolerate certain behaviors on the grounds that it violates a Qur'anic injunction. The tension between toleration and upholding Qur'anic virtue remains unresolved, with serious consequences for human rights (Maududi 1977, p. 28).

While Qutb and Maududi represent one end of an ideological spectrum, other thinkers such as 'Abdullahi Ahmed An-Na'im, Fatima Mernissi, and Abdol Karim Soroush are often described as liberal Islamic scholars (Kurzman 1998). They espouse views that tend to align with Western notions of free speech and women's rights, and they vigorously denounce Islamic extremism. For these thinkers, *shari'a* cannot be accepted without being tested against a variety of interpretive methods. Soroush, in stark contrast to Qutb, articulates an approach to *shari'a* that invites critique from a wide variety of sources, both from within and external to Islam. This approach requires not only the toleration of but also inquiry into non-Islamic literature and bodies of knowledge. Soroush (2000, p. 100) accepts the reality that freedom of speech will result at times in distasteful, even libelous literature, but accepts such abuses as necessary to the discovery of universal truths. In his view, democracies require a multiplicity of views, and guaranteed freedom of speech is necessary for the flourishing of democracies.

The consideration of plural perspectives as a legitimate way to question aspects of the Qur'an and *hadith* is a strategy employed by Mernissi to investigate the grounds of misogynistic texts. Mernissi, in her essay, "A Feminist Interpretation of Women's Rights in Islam (1998)," delves into the science of *hadith* to undermine the assumed legitimacy of *hadith* that discredits women. Using as an example a well-known *hadith*, which states, "Those who entrust their affairs to a woman will never know prosperity!" Mernissi argues that such teachings have a deleterious effect upon the rights and advancement of women. She systematically explores a number of sources to argue that this particular *hadith* was likely transmitted through an untrustworthy source, and therefore should not be included in the canon of legitimate *hadith* (Mernissi 1998). Mernissi combines feminist paradigms with classical jurisprudential techniques to subvert patriarchal religious texts. Her scholarship not only dismantles long-standing assumptions about the validity of certain *hadith*, but also demonstrates how feminist perspectives provide novel critiques of the use of *fiqh*.

Like Mernissi, An-Na'im offers original insights into the Qur'an and *sunna* using unorthodox hermeneutical methods. An-Na'im's mentor, Mahmoud Mohamed Taha, interpreted the Qur'an to distinguish between later sections of the text that should be understood in the historical context of seventh-century Arabia and earlier sections of the text that should be understood as universalistic and applicable throughout history (Taha 1987; Mahmoud 2008). This method, while resolving problematic aspects of the Qur'an, such as those that accept slavery and misogyny, is also criticized by many Muslim scholars as not merely progressive, but heretical. The earlier messages, which tend to be more general and theological in content, more easily justify major historical shifts such as women's rights and the abolishment of slavery. For example, these Qur'anic passages testify to God's nature and emphasize the shared lineage Muslims have with Jews and Christians: "Surely, those who believe and the Jews and the Christians and the Sabians who so believe in God and the Last Day, and do good deeds shall have their reward with their Lord, and no fear [shall come] upon them, nor shall they grieve" (Qur'an 2:62; Taha 1998, p. 273).

Later Qur'anic texts, which tend to be more legislative in nature, are difficult to reconcile with progressive movements. These later portions of the Qur'an often dealt with specific administrative details that arose as the Prophet Muhammad led the nascent Muslim community in Medina. Parts of the Qur'an that were revealed during this time might, for instance, legislate that women should receive a lesser inheritance than men (Qur'an 4:11, 176), or that a woman's testimony counts as only half that of a man's (Qur'an 2:282). For Islamic legal scholars who attempt to reconcile the Qur'an with human rights advances, negating or abrogating (*naksh*) these Qur'anic passages is one strategy that may be effective, albeit controversial. The process of abrogating certain Qur'anic passages as less applicable than others raises difficult questions about the omniscience and perfection of God, the author of the Qur'an. Taha and An-Na'im's hermeneutical approach to the Qur'an, more so than approaches employed by other scholars, is questionable on this account, but is also laudable for taking seriously the duty to engage in intellectual struggle with the word of God.

For Soroush, discussion and disagreement among Islamic scholars is the hallmark of genuine *fiqh*. To call reform-minded scholars like Mernissi or Taha "progressive" is a bit misleading because of the traditional expectation of the best legal scholars to master and question the *shari'a*. The history of *shari'a* can be characterized by debates among scholars who were not only contemporaries, but also by debates through time between generations of scholars. To exercise one's independent judgment (*ijtihad*) in determining *shari'a* for new situations as they arise is required not only of Shi'ite scholars like Soroush, but also among Sunni scholars. Although the emphasis upon *ijtihad* is dominant among Shi'ite legal schools, there is within Sunni legal schools the notion that when the law is uncertain or ambiguous, the practice of *ijtihad* is "a religious duty incumbent upon those in the community who are learned enough to be capable of performing it" (Hallaq 1997, p. 117). With the rise of human rights as a moral category in the mid-twentieth century, Muslim legal scholars have had to exercise *fiqh* to determine its applicability to Islam. Acknowledging human rights as compatible with Islam, although an important first step towards the universality of human rights, ultimately requires more than its rhetorical acceptance. Scholars such as Qutb who claim to endorse human rights while simultaneously refusing the legitimacy of non-Islamic insights into the human condition not only delegitimize their endorsement of human rights, but also weaken the intellectual tradition of *shari'a*.

Conclusion: situating Islamic extremism in the human rights debate

Although scholars such as Qutb and Maududi are often blamed for supplying Muslim extremists with their ideological bases, such associations fail to appreciate fully the complexity of Islamic history and *shari'a* (Berman 2003). The charismatic leadership of organizations like the Taliban and al-Qaeda has oversimplified and selectively sampled the scholarship of conservative Islamic scholars to support their campaigns. Their anti-Western stance falsely equates human rights with Western imperialism. The claim that human rights are tainted Western cultural colonialism – and therefore ought not to be supported – is not only inaccurate, but also ignores the fact that Qutb and Maududi endorsed basic notions of human rights. However problematic their specific arguments on human rights may be, neither denied rights to women and non-Muslims to the extent that the Taliban and al-Qaeda have. Certain articulations of human rights are arguably the product of Western influence, but the core concept of human rights has received remarkably universal support (Waltz 2004). Perhaps what is more glaringly inconsistent about the worldview of Islamic extremists is their attempt to destroy the fertile intellectual grounds that produced thinkers like Qutb and Maududi.

The injustices of Western hegemony are real, but the solution lies not in the oppression of fellow Muslims and the killing of non-Muslim civilians. Such actions not only indicate an ignorance of *shari'a* but a lack of respect for the religious tradition that grew out of the formative period of Islam. The majority of Muslims around the world who believe that an Islamic government can promise human rights are not unaware of the dangers of Muslim extremism. Rather, they are likely drawing upon their knowledge of the history of Islam that indicates the compatibility of democracy, toleration, freedom of conscience, and women's rights with their religious beliefs. Ensuring human rights in Muslim states will not emerge from the forced imposition of Western ideals, but from the recognition of shared values found across different religious, philosophical, and political traditions.

References

Abou el Fadl, Khaled. 2001. *Speaking in God's Name: Law, Authority, and Women* (Oxford: Oneworld).

Berman, Paul. 2003. "The Philosopher of Islamic Terror." *New York Times Magazine*, March 23.

Childs, Peter and R. J. Patrick Williams. 1997. *An Introduction to Post-Colonial Theory* (New York: Prentice Hall).

Denny, Frederick. 2006. *An Introduction to Islam* (Upper Saddle River, NJ: Pearson).

Glendon, Mary Ann. 2001. *A World Made New: Eleanor Roosevelt and the Universal Declaration of Human Rights* (New York: Random House).

Hallaq, Wael B. 1997. *A History of Islamic Legal Theories: An Introduction to Sunni Usul al-Fiqh* (New York: Cambridge University Press).

Hodgson, Marshall G. S. 1974. *The Venture of Islam: Conscience and History in a World Civilization Vol. 1* (Chicago: University of Chicago Press).
Kelsay, John. 2007. *Arguing the Just War in Islam* (Cambridge, MA: Harvard University Press).
Kurzman, Charles, ed. 1998. *Liberal Islam: A Sourcebook* (New York: Oxford University Press).
Lings, Martin. 1983. *Muhammad: His Life Based on the Earliest Sources* (Rochester, VT: Inner Traditions International).
Mahmoud, Mohamed. 2008. *A Quest for Divinity: A Critical Examination of the Thought of Mahmud Muhammad Taha* (Syracuse, NY: Syracuse University Press).
A 'la Maududi, Abul. 1977. *Human Rights in Islam* (Lahore, Pakistan: Islamic Publications).
Mernissi, Fatima. 1998. "A Feminist Interpretation of Women's Rights in Islam." In Charles Kurzman, ed., *Liberal Islam: A Sourcebook* (New York: Oxford University Press).
Pew Global Attitudes Project. 2005. "Islamic Extremism: Common Concern for Muslim and Western Publics." Pew Research Center. At: http://pewglobal.org/2005/07/14/islamic-extremism-common-concern-for-muslim-and-western-publics.
Qutb, Sayyid. 1970. *Social Justice in Islam*. Trans. John B. Hardie (New York: Octagon Books).
Qutb, Sayyid. 2000. "Islam as the Foundation of Knowledge." In Mansoor Moaddel and Kamran Talatoff, eds., *Contemporary Debates in Islam: An Anthology of Modernist and Fundamentalist Thought* (New York: St. Martin's Press).
Ramadan, Tariq. 2004. *Western Muslims and the Future of Islam* (Oxford: Oxford University Press).
Safi, Omid, ed. 2003. *Progressive Muslims: On Justice, Gender, and Pluralism* (Oxford: Oneworld).
Soroush, Abdol Karim. 2000. "Reason and Freedom." In *Reason, Freedom, and Democracy in Islam: Essential Writings of Abdolkarim Soroush*. Trans. Mahmoud Sadri and Ahmad Sadri (New York: Oxford).
Taha, Mahmoud Mohamed. 1987. *The Second Message of Islam* (Syracuse, NY: Syracuse University Press).
Taha, Mahmoud Mohamed. 1998. "The Second Message of Islam." In Charles Kurzmanm, ed., *Liberal Islam: A Sourcebook* (New York: Oxford University Press).
Wadud, Amina. 2006. *Inside the Gender Jihad: Women's Reform in Islam* (Oxford: Oneworld).
Waltz, Susan. 2004. "Universal Human Rights: The Contribution of Muslim States." *Human Rights Quarterly*, Vol. 26, No. 4, pp. 799–844.

24

A non-religious basis for the idea of human rights

The Universal Declaration of Human Rights as overlapping consensus

Ari Kohen

The argument that religion provides the only compelling foundation for human rights is both challenging and thought provoking, and answering it is of fundamental importance to the furthering of the human rights agenda. For if we are able to establish a compelling non-religious foundation for the idea of human rights that can stand alongside the religious one, we will have made it easier for an ever-widening group to reach a consensus on the manner in which they ought to treat one another, even if they are unable to reach any other agreement. I argue that the Universal Declaration of Human Rights provides us with all we need to defend human rights; in particular, I contend that the process by which it was drafted and the deliberations surrounding the subsequent human rights instruments represent the best possible proof of the universal applicability of the rights that they put forward.

This project is quite different from showing, for example, that someone such as Michael Perry (1996, 2006) is incorrect about religion providing a compelling grounding for human rights, and I do not think that he is. The language of human dignity, upon which the concept of human rights rests, can certainly find a solid foundation in many of the world's great religious texts, especially – as Perry notes – the Christian Gospels. The Christian language of love and respect for the other, as well as of the equality of persons, provides a strong justification for the belief that people ought to be treated with respect and compassion and that they ought not to be abused or otherwise harmed. That said, this appeal to Christian love will not necessarily be persuasive or compelling to those who do not share the Christian worldview, despite Perry's desire for his religious foundation for human rights to be persuasive to others. In *The Idea of Human Rights*, Perry writes, for example, "Imagine someone saying to a Bosnian Serb: 'The Bosnian Muslim, too, no less than you, is sacred. It is wrong for you to rape her.' If 'sacred' is meant in the subjective sense, the Bosnian Serb can reply: 'Sacred to you and yours, perhaps, but not to me and mine. In the scheme of things, we happen not to attach much value to her life'" (1996, p. 28). It seems to me, based on this example, that Perry is seeking a foundation for human rights that would enable us to persuade the Bosnian Serb that he is wrong about the Bosnian Muslim. As he writes later, "If every human being is sacred in the objective sense, then, in violating the Bosnian

Muslim, the Bosnian Serb does not merely violate what some of us attach great value to; he violates the very order of creation" (1996, p. 28).

Moreover, Perry's claim that religious worldviews provide the only intelligible foundation for the idea of human rights seems to fly in the face of ample evidence that such worldviews can also be compatible with beliefs and behavior completely antithetical to the idea of human rights. From this account of Perry's theory come two important facets of providing an adequate justification for the idea of human rights, which I believe he fails to provide. These are *inclusivity* and *persuasiveness*. In other words, a compelling foundation for the idea of human rights needs to speak to the largest possible number of people from the greatest number of different traditions and must also provide reasons for its account that are persuasive to those people. As Jürgen Habermas argues in *Between Facts and Norms*, "Only those action norms are valid to which all possibly affected persons could agree as participants in rational discourses" (1999, p. 107). Failing to satisfy these conditions leaves us with human rights that are partial and local, as opposed to universal; on my reading, this failure also prohibits me from making any claims that go beyond my own subjective understanding of how human beings ought to treat one another.

I also want to argue that, in an attempt to locate a non-religious grounding for human rights that fulfills these two conditions, we must be careful not to minimize or overlook entirely the indignity, injustice, and cruelty that are central to the human rights discourse. This is a common problem for theorists, as we sometimes get carried away with our abstractions. But any examination of human life that discusses only theoretical harms or abstracts away from abuses removes the discussion too far from the real world in which human rights are actually violated. And so my project turns from what is largely a metaphysical one to a more practical, political one. No longer are we concerned with providing an intelligible non-religious foundation for the idea of human rights *for its own sake*; instead, our goal has become to provide a foundation that can be said to speak to the problem of human rights as it exists in the world, to consider what Habermas (1999, p. 9) terms the "basic questions" of practical philosophy: "'What ought I do?' or 'What is good for us in the long run and on the whole?'" What follows, then, in this chapter, is what I take to be a non-religious foundation for human rights that goes a long way toward fulfilling the necessary justificatory conditions of inclusivity, persuasiveness, and practicality just outlined. In contrast to the many existing objectivist theories of human rights, I will argue that there might not actually be a feature or quality inherent in human beings from which our rights spring. Indeed, I believe that searching for rights-grounding aspects of human nature has led many non-religious rights theorists astray. Following Richard Rorty, I will contend that these features or qualities are not found so much as they are created.

And so, let us consider the particular episode of creation in question, in which people actually came together to argue for and agree upon the human rights norms of the post-World War II era. It is well known that the Universal Declaration of Human Rights (UDHR) is a product of one of the United Nations' earliest established committees, the Economic and Social Council's Commission on Human Rights. The Declaration was drafted and edited under the chairmanship of Eleanor Roosevelt, though she did not remain at the Commission's helm during the push for its passage by the General Assembly. That task fell to Charles Malik of Lebanon, who had served as the Commission's rapporteur and one of the Declaration's chief framers from the beginning. Members of the Commission came from eighteen different nations, thirteen of whom alternated at three-year intervals and five of whom – the United States, the Soviet Union, the United Kingdom, France, and China – were permanent. In addition to these permanent members, the first members of the Commission represented a diverse body of nations: Australia, Belgium, Byelorussia, Chile, Egypt, India, Iran, Lebanon, Panama, the Philippines,

Ukraine, Uruguay, and Yugoslavia (for more on the establishment and first session of the Human Rights Commission, see Glendon 2001, pp. 30–50).

Given this list of different countries, cultures, religious traditions, and political systems, there were heated debates about the wording of nearly every one of the thirty articles of the UDHR, as well as of the introductory clauses. Much of the trouble, however, was not cultural, coming instead in the form of a series of alternating Soviet representatives. They had been instructed to dig in their heels on what Moscow viewed as potential threats to the concept of national sovereignty: "the right to freedom of movement, the right to a nationality, a nation's right to accord asylum to political refugees, and protections against arbitrary expulsion from a country" (Glendon 2001, p. 59). Other arguments arose around the difficult question of how implementation of the rights in the UDHR would be achieved (Glendon 2001, pp. 84–86) and the charge, again from the Soviets, "that the United States wanted a Declaration that was as 'short and empty as possible'" (Glendon 2001, p. 88). From the beginning, though, the greatest point of contention centered on the idea of grounding the rights that the Declaration set out. After having arrived at what seemed to be some agreement on the various articles, the Commission revisited the draft as a whole and focused on the language of each article, spending a great deal of time on Article 1's general statement concerning the human person:

> [Carlos] Romulo [of the Philippines] had slightly revised the first article in the working group to read: "All men are brothers. They are endowed by nature with reason and conscience. They are born equal in dignity and rights." Malik ... now proposed substituting the words "by their Creator" for "by nature." He cited the American Declaration of Independence ... That amendment was opposed ... on the grounds that references to God would undermine the universality of the document. [The Soviet representative] moved to drop the entire article, saying that it made no sense to clutter up the document with vacuous assertions, whether they were drawn from eighteenth-century French philosophy or from the Bible.
>
> *(Glendon 2001, p. 89)*

This account demonstrates the challenge inherent in any cross-cultural attempt to ground the idea of human rights. Malik, for example, felt that it was important to assign the source of our rights to a Creator, while this sort of focus, for others, could damage the document's acceptability for a great many people.

Though the Commissioners were ultimately persuaded of the importance of leaving the document – and, in particular, its first article – free of any statements that might take away from its claim to universality, the question of grounding the Declaration's rights was far from settled. In the point-by-point discussion of each of the Universal Declaration's thirty articles that took place in committee before it could move to the General Assembly for a vote, the drafters were called upon to defend their decisions with respect both to the language used and the rights that were chosen. The first article remained one of the most contentious, not the least because it is a statement about human nature rather than an enumeration of a right. After this fire had been put out by Roosevelt, who explained that, "Article 1 did not refer to specific rights because it was meant to explain why human beings have rights to begin with" (Glendon 2001, p. 146), the discussion shifted to an amendment by the Brazilians to include the words, "all human beings are created in the image of and likeness of God" (Glendon 2001, p. 146). This proposal was ultimately defeated, but only after China's P. C. Chang stepped in to defend the universal applicability of the article as it stood:

> His own country, he pointed out, comprised a large proportion of humanity, and its people had ideals and traditions different from those of the Christian West. Chinese ideals included

> good manners, decorum, propriety, and consideration for others. Yet he, as the Chinese representative on the Human Rights Commission, had refrained from proposing those ideals for inclusion in the Declaration ... Article 1 as it stood, Chang said, struck just the right note by calling upon all men to act toward one another in a spirit of brotherhood. That was consistent with the Chinese belief in the importance of considerate treatment of others – and also with the ideals of eighteenth-century Western thought. The first line of the article, therefore, should refer neither to nature nor to God. Those who believed in God, he suggested, could still find the idea of God in the strong assertions that all human beings are born free and equal and endowed with reason and conscience.
>
> *(Glendon 2001, p. 146)*

Chang's argument is an important one, as it outlines how each culture might find its own particular vision within even the most controversial articles. This did not mean, as some were afraid, that one culture or another would have to compromise values or traditions; instead, it meant that the document had to represent what John Rawls would term, years later, an overlapping consensus (Rawls 1971; 1993, pp. 133–172; 2001).

And when Charles Malik introduced the Universal Declaration to the General Assembly, he recognized the unusual nature of the document before him: "Unlike previous declarations of rights that had sprung from particular cultures, he said, the Universal Declaration was something new in the world" (Glendon 2001, p. 164). Its uniqueness, clearly, stemmed from the agreement it represented between so many divergent cultures and traditions on an issue, the grounding of human rights, that was vastly contentious. And, indeed, Malik points out exactly this fact in his speech, highlighting "places in the Declaration where [each country] could either find its own contribution or the influence of the culture to which it belonged... Due to the immense variety of its sources, the Declaration had been constructed on [what he called] a 'firm international basis wherein no regional philosophy or way of life was permitted to prevail'" (Glendon 2001, p. 165).

But this quotation from Malik's speech begins to lead us down the wrong path through its assertion that no single philosophical or religious tradition, what Rawls calls a comprehensive doctrine, won out over any other. Instead, I argue that the Universal Declaration represents a much greater achievement. It is not simply that no single tradition was victorious in setting out the foundation of human rights that others could accept, though it is true that none was; instead, the Declaration's virtue is that everyone was able to agree upon and endorse a *common* foundation: the dignity of the human person. This is true of the General Assembly: in 1948 the Declaration was approved without a single vote cast against it and it holds true to an even greater extent more than fifty years later (see Glendon 2001, pp. 169–170 for a description of the details of this vote). And, as Forsythe (1998, p. 508) has noted, "No state has ever sought to join the United Nations but reserve against Articles 55 and 56 of the UN Charter, which mandate cooperation on human rights. Of the eight states that abstained from the General Assembly vote in 1948 approving the Universal Declaration, all but Saudi Arabia have publicly renounced their abstentions."

As Jack Donnelly points out, in an argument similar to mine, "The increasing political prominence of human rights over the past few decades has led more and more adherents of a growing range of comprehensive doctrines to endorse human rights but (only) as a political conception of justice" (2003, p. 41). This caveat, important for Donnelly's argument that there remain some comprehensive doctrines that are anathema to the idea of human rights, is noteworthy here for a different reason. The distinction between comprehensive doctrines and political conceptions of justice is a vitally important one for Rawls's argument about achieving an overlapping consensus. As Donnelly notes, "Because the latter address only the political structure of society, defined independent of any particular comprehensive doctrine, adherents of different comprehensive doctrines may reach an 'overlapping consensus' on a political conception of justice" (2003, p. 40). In other words, we may be unable to come to any agreement where our religious or philosophical traditions and beliefs are concerned, but this need not prevent us from coming to consensus on a political conception of justice. Indeed, we may find our comprehensive doctrines quite at odds, but this is precisely why Rawls counsels us to leave them out of our political deliberations. In his own words, "we do not put forward more of our comprehensive view than we think needed or useful for the political aim of consensus" (1993, p. 153).

I agree with Donnelly's assessment that

> Even where citizens do not have a particularly sophisticated sense of what a commitment to human rights means, they respond to the general idea that they and their fellow citizens are equally entitled to certain basic goods, services, protections, and opportunities. The Universal Declaration offers a good first approximation of the list that they would accept, largely irrespective of civilization, after considerable reflection.
>
> *(Donnelly 2003, p. 39)*

But I take the argument a step further, as I do not believe that Donnelly's conception of the overlapping consensus represented by the UDHR speaks to the problem posed throughout this chapter. In other words, Donnelly and I differ in the *substance* of that consensus, as he believes that it centers on the rights that the Commission enumerated rather than the foundation of those rights. On that question, Rawls recommends silence and Donnelly seems to be in agreement with him, noting only that the consensus has formed around "something very much like Ronald Dworkin's idea that the state is required to treat each citizen with equal concern and respect" (Donnelly 2003, p. 43). In my estimation, Donnelly is not saying much more, here, than the state is required to respect citizens' human rights, which – clearly – is the consensus established by the UDHR. More importantly, though, I want to argue that its drafters arrived at a consensus on the *reason* behind the requirement that the state respect human rights; this is the idea that human beings have dignity, and it is this consensus that makes the Declaration unique in comparison to all of the previous rights instruments that human beings have drafted.

And yet, I also think that it is more than this cross-cultural agreement about human dignity that grounds the contemporary human rights regime. For the notion that human beings possess dignity seems to open the door to yet another question; that is, one must wonder from where we have acquired this dignity. And, in so wondering, we are back at the problem first outlined by Michael Perry, namely whether the concept of dignity – like its religious coeval, sacredness – can be understood in the absence of a religious cosmology. This is the sort of problem that Rawls wants to help us avoid by telling us to keep quiet about our comprehensive doctrines when we enter into deliberations over political conceptions of justice. It seems to me, though, that we do not need to flinch from this sort of discussion because the international community has already agreed on the answer to Perry's questions; indeed, I want to argue that it is the experience of coming to consensus on the question of a foundation for human rights that provides the concept's grounding. Human dignity and the human rights that stem from it, on my reading, are socially constructed ideas in the way that, for example, the trees outside my office are not. But this, I think, is necessarily going to be true simply because dignity and rights are ideas rather than objects. As such, it seems to me that they must be constructed; ideas, after all, do not exist in the world independently of human experience in the way that trees do. I am confident that trees would exist in the absence of human beings; human dignity, however, would not. It might be the case, then, that human beings actually have inherent dignity, and it might not be; but, whether or not our dignity is something real, something that actually exists in the world, it is incumbent upon all of us to act as though it is, as though it does, because we have agreed to do so.

This entire discussion raises the interesting, controversial, and related problems of whether consensus itself can have morally justificatory force and whether agreement is a sufficient guide on questions of right action. As Habermas correctly points out, "Communicative reason ... does not itself supply any substantive orientation for managing practical tasks – it is neither informative nor immediately practical" (Habermas 1999, p. 5). While I have been implicitly arguing that the overlapping consensus on the idea of human rights has justificatory power and obligates us to act in accordance with the rights enshrined in the Universal Declaration, I must also note the powerful counterexamples presented by Nazi Germany and American slavery, both of which established a consensus that defenders of human rights consider obviously immoral and criminal. Although it is clear that Germans reached a consensus on (or at least majority support for) the anti-Semitic Nazi regime and the American South reached a consensus on slavery, those agreements are notably different from the one described in this chapter. In what sense, though, is this consensus different? How is it possible for one sort of consensus to have justificatory weight while others do not? There are, I maintain, a number of conditions that must be met for any given consensus to have justificatory power, and I argue that this particular consensus meets those conditions. Following Habermas, "the claim to legitimacy on the part of a legal order built on rights can be redeemed only through the socially integrative force of the 'concurring and united will of all' free and equal citizens" (Habermas 1999, p. 32). A chief difference, then, is that the consensus on human dignity and human rights – unlike those of Nazism or the antebellum American South – is the result of a highly participatory process, one that accepted input from a more diverse group than had ever been assembled. As we have seen, the Human Rights Commission included members of newly independent nations, representatives from socialist and capitalist countries, spokespersons from the powerful and the weaker states alike, and officials from both the East and West. Discussions on the foundations of human rights and on the content of the UDHR engaged a politically, culturally, religiously, economically, and geographically diverse group, one that was representative of the fledgling United Nations itself. By contrast, any potential consensus on genocide or slavery quite clearly fails to take into account the dissenting voices of the groups targeted by those policies and their allies. While the agreement on human dignity and human rights might not have been unanimous, it was certainly overwhelming. The same cannot be said of a less participatory consensus.

Of course, there were a great many groups not represented in these deliberations. Indeed, a wide array of the nations and groups recognized today were not acknowledged at the time of the UDHR's drafting. Examples are easy to come by and certainly include the myriad African states granted independence in the decades after World War II, indigenous peoples around the globe, and groups – like lesbians, gays, bisexuals, and transgender people – that are still unrecognized in some parts of the world today. That said, I want to argue that this seeming weakness actually helps to demonstrate a strength of this particular consensus. Once again following Habermas, I argue that a second necessary component of a legitimate consensus is that "the decisions ... are both contingent and revisable" (Habermas 1999, p. 33). In the case of this particular consensus, it is clear that the process did not end with the drafting and passage of the Universal Declaration. For although the UDHR itself has not been amended and has achieved, many argue, the status of customary international law, an entire group of increasingly inclusive institutions has arisen from this auspicious beginning. The process that began with the drafting of the Declaration has evolved to include such diverse entities as the United Nations Convention on the Elimination of all forms of Discrimination Against Women, the Declaration on the Rights of Indigenous Peoples, and the Convention on the Rights of the Child. In addition, it is notable that the newly independent states of the Organization of African Unity went on to draft their own declaration of rights – the African [Banjul] Charter on Human and Peoples' Rights – that recognizes their desire "to co-ordinate and intensify their co-operation and efforts to achieve a better life for the peoples of Africa and to promote international co-operation having due regard to the Charter of the United Nations and the Universal Declaration of Human Rights" (1997, p. 473). Although some critics suggest that the revisable nature of the Universal Declaration might leave it open to radical change or outright reversal, I argue instead that its revisability has directly contributed to a deeper, more lasting, and more legitimate set of institutions. As Habermas notes, "Without religious or metaphysical support, the coercive law tailored for the self-interested use of individual rights can preserve its socially integrating force only insofar as the addressees of legal norms may at the same time understand themselves, taken as a whole, as the rational *authors* of those norms" (Habermas 1999, p. 33). And, indeed, these various human rights conventions and declarations *have* achieved the force of law, as embodied in a variety of regional courts and the newly established International Criminal Court.

Finally, this quotation from Habermas brings us to a third important condition for consensus to achieve justificatory weight. In addition to its inclusive and participatory nature and its contingency and revisability, a consensus must also be achieved through a democratic and deliberative process. According to Habermas, "modern law lives off a solidarity concentrated in the value orientations of citizens and ultimately issuing from communicative action and deliberation" (Habermas 1999, p. 33). As discussed in detail in this chapter, the drafting and adoption of the Universal Declaration were quite clearly democratic and deliberative processes in which the participants carefully considered, discussed, and voted upon not only the language to employ in each of the Declaration's thirty articles but also on the philosophical underpinnings of the document itself. I want to argue, here, only that the process of drafting and adopting the Universal Declaration was a democratic one, rather than that those who participated in that process were somehow democratic themselves or were the representatives of democratic governments. As this chapter has demonstrated, many of the countries represented in these deliberations were not themselves democratic, and this could certainly constitute a challenge to the claim that the millions of people represented by these individuals at the United Nations participated in any meaningful way in the drafting and adoption of the UDHR. That said, the intervening years have seen the end of many of these non-democratic governments – the Soviet Union, for example – and the adoption, by the new and more democratic regimes, of the principles enshrined in the Universal Declaration.

As Habermas points out, "the binding energies of language can be mobilized to coordinate action plans only if the participants suspend the objectivating attitude of an observer, along with the immediate orientation to personal success, in favor of the performative attitude of a speaker who wants to *reach an understanding* with a second person about something in the world" (Habermas 1999, p. 18). And indeed, one of the truly unique features of the consensus arrived at by the Commission is the record of discussion and deliberation of such a diverse group on a wide range of opinion not only about the human good – about what enables us to flourish – but also about what brings us to grief. Dershowitz (2004) makes much of this point – indeed, he bases his entire argument on it – and, I believe, rightly so. Yet I see his conclusion as lacking the sort of specificity that I am attempting to reach, here, on the question of the foundation for human rights, which – contra Dershowitz – I take to be human dignity rather than human wrongs.

The opening clauses of the Universal Declaration speak to this point, especially in recognizing that "disregard and contempt for human rights have resulted in barbarous acts which have outraged the conscience of mankind, and the advent of a world in which human beings shall enjoy freedom of speech and belief and freedom from fear and want has been proclaimed as the highest aspiration of the common people" (United Nations 1997, p. 407).

To conclude, the Declaration's drafting process was (and continues to be) a highly inclusive one. It is also, in my estimation, persuasive, and its persuasiveness arises in no small part from its having met the conditions set out above for achieving justificatory force. Finally, the consensus on human rights and human dignity is sufficiently grounded in the real world to meet the condition of practicality; it is able to embrace many divergent viewpoints with the intention of involving the widest array of peoples in this vital discussion. And, indeed, Eleanor Roosevelt made this point herself about the substance of the consensus:

> Now, I happen to believe that we are born free and equal in dignity and rights because there is a divine Creator, and there is a divine spark in men. But, there were other people around the table who wanted it expressed in such a way that they could think in their particular way about this question, and finally, these words were agreed upon because they ... left it to each of us to put in our own reason, as we say, for that end.
>
> *(Glendon 2001, p. 147)*

The subtext of this statement also speaks to my point, for Roosevelt argues that this particular consensus, reached on such an important philosophical question as the nature of man, allows everyone to come to the table and discuss the idea of human rights regardless of *why* they hold this belief. Rawls makes the same point, noting that, "The idea of an overlapping consensus leaves this step to be taken by citizens individually in line with their own comprehensive views" (Rawls 1993, p. 153). The nations of the world may disagree on a great many things – philosophical as well as practical – but they have all agreed on this important point: every human being is entitled to the rights enshrined in the Universal Declaration by virtue of the inherent dignity that is common to us all. It is this agreement that serves as a plausible account of a non-religious grounding for human rights. It does not have the objective weight, for example, that Michael Perry's religious foundation might – for those who believe in the particular religious story he tells. But its strength lies in the space it opens up for an ever-widening group of diverse people to join in the conversation about rights. And I argue that *this* is a far greater virtue than simply being able to maintain our own beliefs about the transcendent origin of human rights.

References

"African [Banjul] Charter on Human and Peoples' Rights." 1997. In Micheline R. Ishay, ed., *The Human Rights Reader: Major Political Writings, Essays, Speeches, and Documents from the Bible to the Present* (New York: Routledge).

Dershowitz, Alan. 2004. *Rights from Wrongs: A Secular Theory of the Origins of Rights* (New York: Basic Books).

Donnelly, Jack. 2003. *Universal Human Rights in Theory and Practice* (Ithaca, NY: Cornell University Press).

Forsythe, David P. 1998. "Human Rights Fifty Years After the Universal Declaration: Reconciling American Political Science and the Study of Human Rights." *PS: Political Science and Politics*, Vol. 3.

Glendon, Mary Ann. 2001. *A World Made New: Eleanor Roosevelt and the Universal Declaration of Human Rights* (New York: Random House).

Habermas, Jürgen. 1999. *Between Facts and Norms: Contributions to a Discourse Theory of Law and Democracy*. Trans. William Rehg (Cambridge: MIT Press).

Perry, Michael J. 1996. *The Idea of Human Rights: Four Inquiries* (Oxford: Oxford University Press).
Perry, Michael J. 2006. *Toward a Theory of Human Rights* (Cambridge: Cambridge University Press).
Rawls, John. 1971. *A Theory of Justice* (Cambridge, MA: Harvard University Press).
Rawls, John. 1993. *Political Liberalism* (New York: Columbia University Press).
Rawls, John. 2001. *The Law of Peoples* (Cambridge, MA: Harvard University Press).
United Nations. 1997. "United Nations Universal Declaration of Human Rights." In Micheline R. Ishay, ed., *The Human Rights Reader: Major Political Writings, Essays, Speeches, and Documents from the Bible to the Present* (New York: Routledge).

Part IV

Social, economic, group, and collective rights

25

Group rights

A defense

David Ingram

Introduction

Human rights belong to individuals in virtue of their common humanity. Yet it is an important question whether human rights entail or comport with the possession of what I call group-specific rights (sometimes referred to as collective rights), or rights that individuals possess only because they belong to a particular group. The Universal Declaration of Human Rights (UDHR) says they do. Article 15 asserts the right to nationality, or citizenship. Unless one believes that the only citizenship compatible with a universal human rights regime is cosmopolitan citizenship in a world state – a conception of citizenship that is not countenanced by the UDHR – one must interpret the human right to citizenship as a universal right to a particular group right.

Other UN Conventions affirm the right of national minorities and indigenous people to cultural autonomy. These include the Convention Concerning Indigenous and Tribal Peoples in Independent Countries (1989) and the Declaration of Rights of Persons Belonging to National or Ethnic, Religious or Linguistic Minorities (1993). In these cases the right attributed to the group is understood as protecting an individually held human right to freedom of religion, association, or cultural expression. Because these individual rights are exercised collectively (as a social practice) and exclusively (by members of a particular group only), they ensure that individual members of a particular group have the freedom to act (worship, associate, express themselves culturally) unhindered by outsiders.

However, groups often view their right to freedom of religion, association, and cultural expression in an entirely different way. Not only do they wish that their individual members be free from outside interference (free in the negative sense) but they wish to be freely self-determining as a group (free in the positive sense). That is, they wish to collectively define their own identity, including the identity of their individual members, according to the dominant views of the majority. This right to *collective self-determination* entitles a group to limit the full exercise of its members' human right to act as they wish whenever the group determines that this exercise endangers the identity of the group. In these cases, the *internal* threat to the group's cultural identity posed by the heterodox practices of its own members appears to be indistinguishable from the *external* threat to the group's cultural autonomy posed by outsiders.

I shall argue that groups are sometimes morally entitled to limit (but not suspend) the exercise of their members' human rights under certain conditions. Following Thomas Pogge (2008), I regard human rights as claims that individuals raise against institutions that are supposed to guarantee them the conditions and resources necessary for leading a minimally decent human life (a standard that is sensitive to social progress and socio-cultural relativity). Because institutions are imperfect and fallible, assessing their compliance with (or fulfillment of) human rights involves weighing their overall success along a number of variables that normally preclude simple judgments that fall into the either/or of fully satisfying or fully violating a human right. An institution may perform reasonably well in insuring that almost all of the persons on whom it is imposed are relatively successful in enjoying human right X but not human right Y; likewise, it may insure that some persons on whom it is imposed have greater success in enjoying a human right than others.

In some respects the notion of limitation operant here is familiar to us from our own understanding of what liberal democratic societies legitimately demand of their citizens. No right – human or otherwise – is exercised unconditionally, since rights sometimes conflict with one another and their possession is contingent upon respecting the rights of others, which normally involves accepting some limitations on what may be said or done. Laws merely codify how the majority understands these limits. Also, many philosophers have argued that the meaning of human rights is far from settled, so that even a liberal democratic interpretation of rights of the sort that is contained in the first article of the UDHR is far from being universally accepted. Article 1 states that "All human beings are born free and equal in dignity and rights." This article can be given a distinctly liberal interpretation if "equal" is understood as "same" and "rights" are understood to include political rights to equal participation in government (Article 21.1) and "freedom to manifest his [*sic*] religion or belief in teaching practice, worship, and observance" "in public or private" (Article 18).

Leaving aside the possibility that human rights do not entail the extensive liberty associated with a liberal understanding of them, I shall argue that groups can sometimes be morally justified (and not merely legally entitled) to limit the expressive liberty of their individual members so long as they are both ontologically and morally legitimate and provide dissenters with reasonable opportunities for exit.

A brief history of group rights

Although the philosophical debate on group rights is relatively new, the concept itself is quite ancient. In pre-modern societies it was not unusual for persons to enjoy special privileges (freedoms) or carry special burdens depending on their membership in a particular class or group. Indeed, this was the norm rather than the exception: different standards of licit (or illicit) conduct applied to persons depending on their rank in society. Even crime and punishment was assessed in this way. The invention of citizenship rights in ancient Greece and Rome introduced uniform standards of conduct that applied across groups but these rights did not supplant prevailing privileges and burdens associated with the group rights and duties. "Natural law" conceptions of right developed by Stoic philosophers over two thousand years ago did indeed apply to individuals qua individuals, solely in virtue of their humanity. However, the tendency of these conceptions to level (or even eliminate) distinctions between master and slave, patrician and plebe, did not jeopardize the system of group rights as such until the advent of the European Enlightenment in the late seventeenth century. The birth of nationalism and the push for democratic liberal reform in the early nineteenth century lent further impetus to the decline of aristocratic privileges based on birth. However, the spread of European colonialism in Africa and Asia again required the diplomatic recognition (and protection) of different ethnic and religious groups, protections that in some cases had been in effect for many years under the aegis of native governments. Group rights continued to play an important role in the Ottoman and Austro-Hungarian empires until their dissolution at the conclusion of World War I. But the League of Nations' protection scheme for national minorities that was adopted in 1919 later presented Hitler with a pretext for militarily reincorporating territories occupied by irredentist (unassimilable) German nationals living in Czechoslovakia and Poland, a "protection" of national minorities that precipitated both World War II and the Holocaust.

Liberal democracies, of course, had their own problematic history of group-differentiated rights. The United States, the universally recognized leader of the "free world" at the end of World War II, was finally forced to confront its own legal form of racial segregation and discrimination during the Cold War. The civil rights movement that accompanied this confrontation presented itself as a struggle to extend universal human rights, now officially recognized by the United States and all signatory nations to the United Nations' ratification of the UDHR (1948), to blacks as individual placeholders of universal humanity rather than as members of a despised race. Since the movement made no distinction between racial and national (specifically indigenous) minorities, its equation of emancipation with integration and assimilation fully precluded any defense of group rights for the sake of preserving cultural groups.

Since the 1970s, however, liberals in the United States and Canada – not to mention liberals in France, Germany, Spain, and Italy – have been confronted with a number of recalcitrant indigenous, ethnic, and religious minorities who strongly reject the equation of emancipation and assimilation. Even the civil rights movement was forced to concede that race- and gender-blind anti-discrimination law was largely ineffectual apart from affirmative action and other group-based remedies. The resulting introduction of racial, ethnic, and gender classifications in statutory law was defended by its advocates as a departure from the old classifications that were intended to stigmatize women and minorities as inferiors; for here, differential treatment was justified as a temporary remedy for achieving the kind of integration and "sameness of treatment" that color- and gender-blind policies had failed to achieve (Dworkin 1986, pp. 394–396; Ingram 2006, pp. 37–40; Ingram 2000, p. 290n2).

Categories of group rights

In order to defend the use of special group protections, preferences, and exemptions within a liberal democracy that constitutionally upholds integration and equal treatment as the supreme law of the land, we must first examine the concept of group rights in more detail. Group rights come in many varieties. For the sake of simplicity we can distinguish between two broad categories of group rights: *instrumentalist* and *collectivist*. As noted above, some group-specific rights serve to protect more basic rights (human rights, constitutional rights, or statutory rights) that individuals possess *as individuals*. These instrumental group rights, which serve to protect individuals from discrimination, can be broken down into three categories. First, there are instrumental group rights, such as rights to bilingual education and affirmative action (see below), which enable members of disadvantaged or marginalized groups to *assimilate* into the mainstream. Although they function by granting differential entitlements, group rights of this nature are intended to be temporary and remedial and, most importantly, are oriented toward guaranteeing *sameness* of treatment for everyone, regardless of their individual or group-based differences. Second, there are instrumental rights, such as rights to exemptions and other *accommodations* based on religion or moral conscience, which enable members of religious groups to practice their faith freely. Unlike the first class of instrumental group rights, this class of instrumental group rights is not aimed at assimilating marginalized groups into the mainstream so that their members will be treated the same way as everyone else. Instead, this second class of instrumental group rights is intended to protect the right to be *different* from the mainstream. Third, rights to *political representation* that give special political entitlements and protections to minorities (e.g., by guaranteeing them a certain number of legislative seats, a power of veto over certain kinds of legislation, and so on) are supposed to ensure them an equal opportunity to elect candidates of their choice and influence legislation that significantly impacts their lives. This aim is neutral with respect to achieving assimilation or preserving difference and instead consists in providing a secondary political remedy for ensuring that discriminatory policies targeting minorities will not be enacted.

A collectivist group right, by contrast, preserves and protects the cultural identity of a group by permitting the group to limit the basic human, constitutional, or statutory rights of its own members to believe and behave as they individually think fit. These rights can be broken down into two categories. First, there are collectivist rights that directly limit the behavior of individual members. For instance, laws mandating that members of a cultural group speak a certain language or practice a certain religion enable the majority within that group to define the group's identity. Second, as in the case of instrumental group rights, rights to special political representation are often demanded as a way of securing these collectivist rights.

The above classification of group rights represents a cursory breakdown of the different aims and functions that group rights serve and so provides a glimpse of some of the complexities involved in discussing group rights. At the same time it oversimplifies these complexities and for that reason cannot be regarded as exhaustive. For instance, it might be thought that immigrant groups and racial minorities typically demand instrumental rights in order to assimilate while religious and ethnic minorities demand instrumental rights in order *not* to assimilate. Again, it might be thought that indigenous peoples and national minorities typically demand collectivist and representation rights. But this simple correspondence of group and group right is somewhat premature. Indigenous peoples, for example, often claim both instrumentalist and collectivist group rights. They seek anti-discrimination protections for their individual members (including affirmative action preferences) while also seeking special rights to political representation and rights to tribal self-determination. African-Americans, too, have fused support for Black Nationalist educational programs with support for affirmative action placement and hiring and forms of race-conscious political representation.

Preliminary questions about group rights

Philosophers have questioned the legitimacy, if not coherence, of both instrumental and collectivist group rights. Do groups possess well-defined boundaries that enable the identification of their members? What conditions, for example, must be met before one can claim to be an African-American who is eligible for preferential placement in law school? Do even well-defined groups possess the kind of unitary will or unitary interest base that would entitle them to claim a right? Assuming that these *ontological* questions are answered in the affirmative, one might ask whether there aren't additional requirements of a *moral* nature that a group must satisfy in order to be a candidate for a group right protection. Can groups that have not experienced oppression claim special rights? Can groups that are intolerant of other groups do so?

Again, one might question whether instrumental group rights that aim to protect individual rights are properly designated as group rights. Perhaps the only genuine group rights – as distinct from differential rights that compensate for individuals' group-related disadvantages – are collectivist rights that groups claim against their own members. The question then arises whether this limitation is morally defensible. Finally, one might question whether group rights must be legal rights rather than moral rights. Despite the fact that the most familiar group rights are legal rights – the group-based entitlements and duties of citizenship and of treaty-law, as well as the legal exemptions and preferences of civil rights law being cases in point – one might argue that certain groups have a moral right to preserve themselves which transcends and even limits the individual moral rights of their members. Beyond arguing that such preservation serves a higher-order moral good (in much the same way that preservation of the community or the state serves a higher-order moral good) one might argue that not protecting a particular group renders individual members of that group more politically vulnerable. This argument, however, contravenes a venerable principle that moral rights essentially aim to protect the dignity and integrity of individuals against the overweening interference of the group to which they belong. (For a recent version of this objection, see Habermas 2005.)

Three general attitudes towards group rights

Broadly speaking, we can distinguish three positions regarding the soundness of group-specific rights: formalism, instrumentalism, and collectivism. By formalism I mean the doctrine that law and morality must treat persons exactly the same way regardless of their particular differences. It therefore recognizes only individual rights. What I call instrumentalism, by contrast, holds that law and morality can sometimes treat persons differently, based on their personal, social, or group-based characteristics. Differential treatment is intended to compensate for handicaps that prevent persons from equally exercising their individual rights. The group-specific remedies instrumentalism recommends for protecting members of disadvantaged groups are therefore instrumental to securing their individual rights and so cannot limit them. Collectivism rejects this last condition. It argues that groups can sometimes legitimately claim rights against their own individual members.

Formalism captures our belief in the fundamental moral *equality* of all human beings; all people deserve equal – here, meaning the same – consideration and treatment, regardless of their concrete differences. This ideal of equality is especially exemplified in the concept of human rights and in criminal law, where justice is said to be "blind" to personal and social differences. However, what appears to be true in the abstract appears false in the concrete. This is obviously the case in social, family, and civil law, where persons are treated differently depending on their personal, social, and group-based differences. Even criminal law allows consideration of differences when it treats minors and mentally handicapped persons charged with crimes differently from normal functioning adults. Sentencing guidelines – especially when they permit victim impact statements as well as statements regarding mitigating factors favoring the defendant – allow particularities of social background to affect the jury's or judge's deliberations. Rape shield laws that specifically protect woman (but not men) as well as statutes criminalizing abortion may be said to have a group-specific "disproportionate impact" built into them.

A rigid defender of formalism might argue that the above instances of differential legal treatment are morally wrong because they violate the ideal of moral equality. Different treatment, it is argued, is preferential or discriminatory treatment, and so is incompatible with showing equal moral respect (or providing equal legal protection) for all. This is precisely the objection leveled against affirmative action programs in the United States. However, most formalists allow that under some circumstances different treatment is necessary in order to ensure equal treatment. Exempting conscientious objectors from military service protects their equal freedom of religion and conscience; entitling profoundly disabled persons to access special benefits protects their equal right to live and participate in the social life of the community; and targeting oppressed minorities in recruiting prospective employees for governmentally funded jobs and professional schools protects their equal right against discrimination. Furthermore, as I noted above, short of endorsing a cosmopolitan conception of citizenship under one world government, the moral equality of human beings qua human must be institutionally embodied at the level of the nation, in which the content of moral equality will be defined differently, from nation to nation (see, for instance, Rawls 1999).

The ontological objection to group rights

I will assume that instrumental group rights are not inherently morally objectionable. Before examining whether collectivist group rights also satisfy this condition, we must address two ontological objections to the general concept of group rights. First, it can be doubted whether there are any well-defined groups of individuals of the sort that an ascription of a group right presupposes. Second, it can be doubted whether groups as such possess the necessary ontological conditions that enable them to claim a right or possess a right by virtue of some common will or interest.

The first objection fails when we consider groups whose boundaries are defined by legal stipulation. Persons entitled to special rights in virtue of their membership in income- or age-groups fall within this category. However, the claim that the problem of group identity can be resolved by legal stipulation is still question-begging, since the question is whether such stipulated identities can be philosophically justifiable. This objection proves especially powerful when considering groups whose boundaries cannot be so stipulated. Racial groups are intransigent in this regard. The definition of race provided by the infamous "one drop" rule prevalent in the USA during the second half of the nineteenth and the first half of the twentieth centuries was based on bad science and could not in any case be applied since persons could "pass" as more than one racial type according to a competing phenotypical understanding of racial categories. Modern genetics provides some help in tracing genealogies of group descent but race and ethnic categories do not map onto genes and phenotypes. The widely accepted view that these categories are socially constructed and political would seem to exacerbate the problem of identification further. Even if such categories have real, objective purchase on the way in which people actually understand themselves and relate to others, the "underlying reality" may belie their real force and efficacy, as postmodernists and poststructuralists have argued. In short, it may be plausibly argued that these ethno-racial categories for delineating groups simply conceal the irreducible individuality, plurality, and heterogeneity of human forms of life behind the facade of fictive labels, thereby casting aspersions on the ontological identity of groups as such.

Unless the criteria stipulated for defining a group by ascription can be applied, membership in the group cannot be reliably determined. But many groups are not defined by third-person ascription but by first-person attachments and identifications, which would appear to simplify the assignment of group membership. To be sure, this apparent advantage in simplicity presumes that subjective (first-person) identifications are more reliable (accurate) and legitimate than third-person ascriptions. But why should a man who is judged by all commonly accepted criteria to be "white" but who nonetheless insists on being classified as "black" (and who, we shall assume, genuinely thinks he is black) be eligible for an affirmative action preference? Furthermore, even if we should accept first-person identifications as authoritative for determining membership in a group, it is hardly clear what this means. Should unreflected and otherwise socially constrained self-identifications be judged as reliable as identifications that are reflected and totally voluntary? A person can "identify" with a group into which he or she had little choice in joining, either because he or she was born into it or acquired it by way of customary ascription. Such is the case with groups associated with ethnicity, religion (often "inherited" from parents), gender, race, and perhaps sexual orientation. In these cases, first-person identification – often tacit, weak, and unexpressed – provides an unreliable basis for defining group membership.

The situation improves somewhat if the identification in question is entirely voluntary and explicitly expressed, as when a person expressly votes for a particular party that represents the interests of a particular group, or when a person voluntarily resides within a religious community or officially converts from one religion to another. Still, the voluntary nature of group ascription does not necessarily ease the problem of delimiting a group's boundaries. As the recent hubbub over the US census form shows, the tendency in today's liberal multicultural societies to treat ethno-racial identification as a matter of personal choice has not been favorably received by all ethno-racial minorities. Recent arrivals to the USA from South America who find themselves classified as "Hispanic" or "Latino/a" may come to accept these ascriptions as their own. But should they? "Hispanic" refers to an Iberian cultural legacy that many of these arrivals may not – voluntarily (upon reflection) identify with; likewise "Latino" refers to a mixed cultural legacy with its own counter-meanings (the term was introduced by the French in the mid-nineteenth century to designate a linguistic and religious [Catholic] affinity; more recently it has taken on national–political overtones in the struggle against US imperialism). While Linda Alcoff (2006) has defended the use of "Latino/a" as a valid term of group identity, Jorge Gracia (2004) has argued that "Hispanic" is the preferred identifying term.

The second ontological challenge to group rights questions whether groups – as distinct from individual persons – can be the sorts of entities to which one can meaningfully ascribe rights. For simplicity, let me clarify this problem by focusing on two major ways of thinking about rights. The first way, which descends from the social contract tradition, views rights as *claims* that arise, in the first place, by mutual agreement, as an outcome of will. The second way, which descends from utilitarianism, views rights as goods designating basic *interests* (Wellman 2001, pp. 18–20).

Both views have their advantages and disadvantages. The will-theory (contract-inspired) view of rights would appear to deny rights to animals, children, and mentally handicapped persons. At best, one might say that these "persons" hold their rights "virtually" insofar as their caretakers can claim these rights on their behalf. But this suggests that their right to claim them in this way must be based on some prior good, interest, or vital capability. In this case it would be possession of a basic good, interest, or capability that would be the basis for ascribing rights so that claiming a right would be subsequent to and supervenient upon this possession. Be that as it may, it seems equally incontestable that rights – whatever their grounds for attribution – also designate demands or claims that one agent can bring against another (despite the fact that, as the UDHR Preamble rightly notes, human rights also designate standards of progress and civilization that are continually evolving).

We need not resolve the debate over the ontology of rights in order to ask whether groups can be said to possess a "will" or a "common interest." Contrary to the formalist objection, some groups *are* capable of claiming rights. I am thinking, of course, of formally organized groups who possess a legal charter or constitution, such as corporations, that have a well-defined chain of command and decision-making. Leaving aside the fact that corporations often possess an organizational and volitional complexity that blurs the lines of corporate responsibility and so weakens the extent to which they exhibit will and personality – a complexity that is rendered all the more recalcitrant to reductive, unitary accounts of will and personality when the model of the corporation is extended to include stakeholding conceptions that bring to the fore divided wills that cannot always be legally harmonized – it can nonetheless be asserted that corporations possess considerably more cohesion than a mere "aggregate" or "collection" of strangers (Sartre's famous example of persons queuing up at a bus stop comes to mind).

But most groups that claim rights possess a middle range of volitional personality. The transition from an aggregate to an assertive group with personality – which roughly coincides with Marx's famous distinction (of Hegelian provenance) between a class existing "in itself" (a group of persons who have yet to consciously identify with one another as sharing politically salient interests) and a class existing "for itself" (the same group who has expressly recognized itself as possessing such interests) – is historically well documented. Sartre's famous example of an disorganized rabble of *sans culottes* spontaneously "fusing" into an army possessing leadership and will as they storm the Bastille illustrates how quickly groups can be infused with identity and purpose, become politically solidified through internal monitoring and enforcement, and then degenerate once again into bureaucratically ossified "series" of alienated units who no longer express their common will through anything resembling a process of voluntary consent (Sartre 1991).

The interesting question is whether members of *aggregate* groups that lack a sense of their own will and identity can claim group-specific rights. If we adopt the interest-conception theory of rights, we can scarcely deny that they can. Just how "common" such interests must be and how consciously those who ostensibly possess them must also assert them is disputable, however. Children are ascribed common interests that they would scarcely affirm as their own (such as the interest in education, healthy diet, and so on); these interests, in turn, are often the basis for assigning them group-specific rights to schooling, nutritional and health benefits denied to adults. Women and members of a racial minority who may not be unified in consciously affirming a common group interest may still merit certain group-based rights. Even when the only common interest that might be attributed to members of these groups is an interest in not being discriminated against, a special group right to so-called *descriptive* political representation can still be justified. For it can be argued that the mere symbolic (token) presence of a woman or minority government officer acts to diminish the harm in question, quite apart from his or her active representation of a common interest or policy (as distinct from a common perspective, say). Indeed, such rights to descriptive representation can be justified as a pre-emptive measure even after discrimination has abated and the group in question has reverted to a less politically organized, aggregate status (Young 2000).

Groups and rights: a response to the moral objection

Let us assume that objections to a group's ontological worthiness for possessing rights are met. If a group claims a moral right to preserve its identity against the changeable views and practices of its own members, then the objection immediately arises that no group obviously has that kind of right. However, one reason for thinking that it might is that the preservation of cultural identity is an intrinsic human good necessary for the enjoyment of other goods, including the robust exercise of free choice based on what Charles Taylor calls "strong evaluations," or evaluations based on an appeal to higher-order culturally defined conceptions of the good life.

One version of this argument – call it the socio-biological argument – holds that cultural groups have a right to preserve themselves because doing so advances cultural diversity, which is necessary for the flourishing (if not continued existence) of the human species. Because cultural groups pass down unique ways of adapting to the world that are analogous to the unique ways in which organisms adapt to their environment, cultural diversity, so it is argued, is just as essential to adaptation as is biodiversity.

Even if cultural diversity were essential to the flourishing (or preservation) of the human species – a fact that cannot be empirically demonstrated – it is far from obvious that it is best promoted by preserving the cultural identity of groups against changes provoked by interactions with other groups. Leaving aside the difficulty (not to mention moral dubiousness) of policing individuals' choices regarding which groups they choose to identify and interact with (Habermas 1994), it may actually be the case – counterintuitive though it may seem – that cultural diversity thrives only when such changes are allowed to occur. Cultural groups typically preserve themselves in the same way that organisms do: by changing themselves to meet environmental challenges. One such challenge occurs when native cultural traditions have fallen into a state of internal crisis. In this case, resolving the crisis may require the culture in question to learn from another culture (MacIntyre 1988).

Ideally it might seem that this learning process should be mutual and equal, so that no culture (or cultural group) comes to dominate any other culture (or cultural group). No cultural group, we might think, should assimilate all other cultural groups. However, even when such assimilation occurs the result is often dynamic and generative of new cultural forms. In any case the extinction of a cultural group by no means spells the end of its cultural ideas, as evidenced by the global dissemination of Christianity and other artifacts of Roman provenance.

Notwithstanding these facts, the waning of a cultural group undoubtedly poses political – and one might say, moral – risks to its members, especially if the process of assimilation or dissolution is sudden. Advocates of Deaf Culture who argue that widespread implantation of cochlear hearing aids amounts to cultural genocide may be chided for over-exaggeration, but there can be little doubt that the rapid advance of cochlear implantation techniques – followed by the rapid decline of persons identifying as members of the deaf community – will mean less political clout for that community and therefore less capacity to combat discrimination targeting the deaf. This moral vulnerability would still exist even if sign language survived as a "dead" language.

It is this kind of argument, which appeals to the moral harm that cultural disintegration poses to the individual members of a cultural group, that would have to be marshaled to support the right of the group in question to preserve itself. This argument, however, would only be necessary, but not sufficient, for establishing at best a *prima facie* (or qualified) case for such a right.

Before discussing what additional arguments would have to be made for establishing this right, let me briefly address the arguments that would have to be made for a less sweeping group right of the sort typically advanced on instrumentalist, rather than collectivist, grounds. Instrumentalist group rights aim to protect individuals against discrimination. Hence, in order to justify an instrumentalist group right for a particular group it must first be shown that its individual members are presently discriminated against on the basis of their group identity. Second, it must be shown that effectively mitigating such discrimination requires endowing these individuals with a special group right.

The history of civil rights law in the USA shows how these considerations come into play. During the 1960s and 1970s, the US federal government enacted civil rights laws designed to protect blacks, women, and other selected minorities from discrimination. These laws proved inadequate because they required that plaintiffs provide documentary evidence demonstrating the discriminatory intent of defendants. They also proved inadequate in dealing with institutional (or unintended) discrimination. In some cases, defendants did not intentionally discriminate for prejudicial reasons, but simply did what was most expedient – hiring, promoting, or placing people who were closest to them geographically, culturally, socially, physically and (presumably) psychologically. In these cases, under-representation of women and minorities was attributed to institutional and structural factors reflecting the legacy of past – but not necessarily present – discrimination.

Affirmative action was the name given to a set of policies – ranging from active recruitment to hiring and placement quotas – designed especially to combat unintended, institutional discrimination on the part of employers and institutions of higher education that received government money. By the late 1970s affirmative action preferences were being attacked (rightly or wrongly) for violating the rights of white males to equal treatment and for being ineffective. Finally, alternative remedies for combating institutional discrimination that were adopted in the 1990s suggested that affirmative action policies might not have been as necessary as their proponents had once claimed.

The use of race-conscious methods in redrawing congressional voting districts in the 1980s and 1990s displays the same set of considerations exemplified in affirmative action. The question was whether a pattern of racially polarized voting obtained that prevented racial minorities from electing representatives of their choice. The debate that ensued revolved around whether redrawing selected voting districts in order to ensure that minorities were the majority in these districts effectively enabled them to elect representatives of their choice, and did so, moreover, in a way that no race-blind remedy could.

The moral conditions mentioned above that attach to the instrumental use of group-specific protections and preferences correspond to the minimal legal conditions for granting instrumental group rights. Such protections and preferences must be shown to be necessary in light of the ineffectiveness of non-group-specific alternatives. Other moral conditions attach to the character of the group itself. In particular, groups whose members are intolerant of outsiders and espouse racist, sexist, and ethno-centrist views are less deserving of group rights protection.

Determining which groups merit a loss of preference or protection, however, is a political challenge that admits of no easy solution. Religious groups pose a special challenge to liberal democracies. Constitutionally, such regimes must not impair freedom of religious conscience by burdening religious groups with regulations that apply in a general way to all groups and individuals; yet exempting such groups from regulation appears to violate the very impartiality of the law. The tension is perhaps greatest when considering regimes that are founded on an opposition between national *esprit du corps* and religion, as witnessed by the recent turmoil over Muslim women wearing headscarves in public places in France. In constitutional regimes that have some entanglement, short of establishment, with religion (Germany, Canada, and the United States provide tax exemptions and some tax revenues to religious organizations), the tension is no less acute. Why should Bob Jones University in Greenville, South Carolina, lose its tax-exempt status as a religious institution of higher learning by prohibiting interracial dating while the Catholic Church, which bans women from becoming priests, retain it? That Bob Jones University was not complying with the spirit and intent of the Civil Rights Act, which equates racial separation with racist stigma, seems clear. Although the same could have been said of the Catholic Church's ban on women priests during the days when it officially endorsed the inferiority of women, it cannot be said of the Church today. Unfortunately, the neat logic underlying the law's different treatment of Bob Jones University and the Catholic Church is not available to us in dealing with a host of other issues, including gay rights. Should persons who find homosexuality abhorrent for religious reasons be compelled by law to rent to homosexuals, or should they be granted a group right exempting them from this provision?

Two additional questions arise when considering the moral worthiness of a group to merit a collectivist group right. First, one might object that no group whose very identity was constituted by another group, through acts of domination and coercion, deserves to be preserved. Because racial identity fits this description it might be thought that racial groups should not be preserved and that the proper policy in dealing with them is racial integration. Yet in the USA some blacks (above all black Muslims and black nationalists) oppose integration. They rightly argue that black racial identity has become a mark of pride and solidarity among many African-Americans rather than the stigma of inferiority blackness once invoked. They also argue (again rightly) that integration will spell the end of African-American communities and their distinctive, geographically bounded cultural institutions. Although members of these groups may want instrumental group rights (affirmative action) that enable them to overcome racial discrimination in education and employment, they may also want collectivist group rights aimed at preserving the group and guaranteeing political representation. (Among the collectivist group rights they might lobby for are rights to special schools providing Afro-centric education and rights to special school districts.)

The use of group rights to preserve racial groups is doubtless more problematic than the use of such rights to preserve ethnic or religious groups, if for no other reason than that race is a false biological ideology that was imposed on racial minorities by Europeans and their North American counterparts to ensure their domination, though some scholars defend racial groupings as the basis of identity (Outlaw 1995; Mills 1998; Ingram 2000, ch. 3; and Ingram 2004, ch. 2).

And it is largely racism that explains the continued existence of a segregated and marginalized African-American community, culture, and identity today. On the other hand, it can be argued that free acceptance – not imposition – best describes the attitude of most contemporary blacks to their racial identity. In any case, religious groups and ethnic sub-nationalities also had their identities forged through complex acts of imposition and exclusion and no one denies their legitimacy, so the mere fact of imposition and exclusion, it might be argued, ought not to count against the legitimacy of racial groups.

A second objection against collectivist group rights – that such rights permit the majority (or a dominant minority) within the group to impose a distinctive community, culture, and identity on the group's *own* members – is harder to dispel. Here, the moral legitimacy of the group hinges on the extent to which rank-and-file members exercise some (preferably democratic) influence in shaping it. Not only must each member have a real opportunity to contribute in this endeavor, but each must be capable of doing so with a modicum of reflection. In other words, it is not enough that individual members contribute by passively (habitually) imbibing and passing down the group's cultural ethos; they must also do so with the knowledge that other real possibilities for constituting this ethos exist. So, even if the members initially come to identify with the group unreflectively and unfreely in the course of socialization, they should later come to identify with it reflectively (Appiah 1994).

The right to exit

Connected to the above condition, which presumes that one's membership in and allegiance to a group that limits one's freedom is reflective rather than habitually constrained, is the condition that one be free to exit the group without suffering undue hardship. Freedom to exit depends on the group making this a viable option for its members. Several examples illustrate the importance of this condition. Denying cochlear implants to young congenitally deaf children – the position defended by advocates of Deaf Culture – preserves deaf community against the danger of assimilation at the expense of withdrawing an exit option for these children, who show poor rates of success in mastering written and spoken language. Allowing Amish parents to remove their children from school at the age of 14 so that they can fill their proper role within the Amish community preserves Amish community by denying their children exposure to different lifestyles as well as the technical and civic skills they would need to succeed in the outside world, thereby also denying them a robust exit option (Ingram 2000, ch. 4; 2004, chs. 3 and 6).

What makes these cases so difficult is that the right to exit, while not being denied outright – the Amish practice of forcing young adults to leave the community for one year so that they can decide "on their own" whether to return to the community as "permanent" residents expressly endorses this right – cannot be robustly exercised for lack of supporting conditions. Of course, being born into any group constrains our options to exit that group in the future. I may have to learn a new language and undergo re-acculturation if I choose to emigrate to a foreign country. I may have to undergo sex-change surgery and gender-reassignment training if I want to become a member of a different sex/gender group than the one nature and socialization imposed on me; I may have to undergo cosmetic surgery if I want to become (or "pass") as a member of a different race than the one my society currently ascribes to me. In general, however, it is easier (in terms of possessing the requisite competence, if not the psychological disposition) to alter one's physical appearance than it is to be "born again" into a new cultural identity; and it is easier to be re-socialized than to acquire a basic capability for choosing (or communicating).

Assessing the degree to which a group's practices cross the threshold from constraining a right to exit to effectively denying it will require looking carefully at the extent to which the practices in question deny the development of a basic competence requisite for freedom of choice. We may be inclined to think that the denial of cochlear implantation crosses that line by imposing a natural "disability" while socialization into a narrow culture whose power over the individual is reinforced by great social pressure does not.

Even when the preconditions for robustly exercising an exit option are present the psychological costs of doing so may be prohibitive. These costs limit the use of this option in resolving conflicts between groups and dissident minorities. Although the option seems to offer an attractive solution for resolving conflicts between minority dissidents and dominant majorities within confessional religious orders, the psychological costs of exiting a religious community can be extreme. Thus, while it might seem natural for evangelical Christian dissidents of traditional indigenous communities to leave these communities – thereby preserving both their right to proselytize and the right of the community to practice its traditional religion without interference – the costs associated with uprooting oneself from the community of one's ancestors may be prohibitive. In cases like this, the only workable solution seems to be mutual accommodation or compromise, where one or both sides voluntarily consent(s) to limit the exercise of their rights.

Conclusion

To summarize: I have argued that both instrumentalist as well as collectivist group rights may be morally justifiable. Instrumentalist group rights are easiest to defend because they do not necessarily conflict with the equal exercise of individual rights and, indeed, are expressly promoted for this very purpose. Collectivist group rights, by contrast, do conflict with the exercise of individual rights and so their defense is conditional on the satisfaction of additional ontological and moral factors. Since these rights aim to protect the beliefs, practices, and identities of groups against the subversive actions of their own individual members – which to the dominant majority within the group appear to be indistinguishable from intolerant acts undertaken by outsiders – we must first assume that these collective beliefs, practices, and identities are freely and reflectively endorsed by the majority and not merely imposed on them by a ruling elite (through techniques of brainwashing and other forms of coercive mind-control). Second, said beliefs, practices, and identities must meet a threshold of civility and tolerance with respect to the beliefs, practices, and identities of other groups that meet this same threshold. Groups do not merit moral or legal recognition that fail to meet this expectation.

In response to the question why groups merit collectivist group rights in the first place, the answer is that individuals suffer (avoidable) and considerable harm when the community in which they belong declines in numbers and diminishes in political influence. The harm in question need not take the form of invidious discrimination (or a civil rights violation) that might be remedied by individually tailored civil rights protection or instrumentalist group protection. It suffices that the harm in question seriously imperils the group members' sense of self by robbing them of a source of social recognition and self-determination. As communitarians rightly point out, our sense of security depends upon our belonging to particular groups of persons who care about us deeply and on whom we can rely – not as a stranger cares about (relies on) a stranger but as a kinsman cares about (relies on) a kinsman.

A more difficult question is whether this line of reasoning justifies the right of a dominant social group to preserve its demographic and political advantage against less dominant groups. The example of immigration is instructive in this regard. Can a dominant group of European-descended people in the United States seek to preserve its identity (if one can call it that) by controlling the flow of immigration from Latin America? Few would deny that it has a right to maintain the integrity of its political order by insisting that immigrants at least teach their children the dominant language of the land (English). Too much cultural fragmentation, especially along linguistic lines, can be – although as the example of Canada, China, India, Belgium, Switzerland, and South Africa amply attest, need not be – antagonistic to the political integrity of a nation. But the right to preserve the linguistic identity of one's country, whether defensible or not, falls considerably short of the right to preserve the identity of white, European (or Anglo-Saxon) culture. Liberal multicultural democracies that depend on immigration are morally committed by their very constitutions to be non-exclusionary in this respect. Furthermore, it goes without saying that they are committed to respecting the universal human rights of desperate foreigners to asylum and refuge, regardless of their racial and cultural identity.

By contrast, indigenous peoples and indeed any nation with a special identity as a sanctuary for an oppressed religious minority (as in the case of Israel) may indeed have a right to grant preferential treatment to just those immigrants who identify with the thick, cultural identity of the dominant group (or belong to that group, according to criteria determined by the majority). The notorious case involving the Black Seminoles of Oklahoma shows that any appeal to the "majority" within a group can be question-begging (that is, it can falsely presume that the question of who is already a member in good standing has been settled). The case involves a $52 million compensation being paid by the Federal government to members of the tribe, who have traditionally included descendants of former slaves who joined the tribe over 150 years ago. Although Black Seminoles were officially recognized as members of the tribe by an 1866 treaty, the dominant group of self-described "pure blood" Seminoles now wish to deny them this status so that they (the "pure bloods") alone can enjoy the benefits of government compensation. What makes this appeal to "blood quantum" so problematic is that it was never recognized as a criterion of tribal membership until the US government imposed it on indigenous peoples in the 1880s in order to diminish the number of landholdings that "mixed race" Indians would be entitled to (Ingram 2004, pp. 56–57; Ingram 2000, p. 113).

That said, collectivist group rights are more straightforwardly defensible when they are expressly tailored to protecting *minority* cultural groups from being assimilated into the mainstream within a larger society. Consocial states, such as Switzerland and Bosnia, and multination states, such as Canada, immediately come to mind as examples of polities that have accorded collectivist accommodation and representation rights to sub-groups.

References

Alcoff, L. 2006. *Visible Identities: Race, Gender, and the Self* (Oxford: Oxford University Press).

Appiah, A. 1994. "Identity, Authenticity, Survival: Multicultural Societies and Social Reproduction," pp. 149–163 in C. Taylor et al., *Multiculturalism: Examining the Politics of Recognition* (Princeton, NJ: Princeton University Press).

Dworkin, R. 1986. *Law's Empire* (Cambridge, MA: Harvard University Press).

Gracia, J. 2004. "Hispanic Identity." Pp. 289–311 in J. Gracia and E.-M. Zaibert, eds., *Latin American Philosophy for the Twenty-First Century* (Buffalo, NY: Prometheus).

Habermas, J. 1994. "Struggles for Recognition in the Democratic Constitutional State," pp. 107–148 in C. Taylor et al., *Multiculturalism: Examining the Politics of Recognition* (Princeton, NJ: Princeton University Press).

Habermas, J. 2005. "Equal Treatment of Cultures and the Limits of Postmodern Liberalism." *Journal of Political Philosophy*, Vol. 13, No. 1, pp. 1–28.

Ingram, D. 2000. *Group Rights: Reconciling Equality and Difference* (Lawrence: University Press of Kansas).

Ingram, D. 2004. *Rights, Democracy, and Fulfillment in the Era of Identity Politics* (Lanham: Rowman & Littlefield).

Ingram, D. 2006. *Law: Key Concepts in Philosophy* (London: Continuum).

MacIntyre, A. 1988. *Whose Justice? Which Rationality?* (South Bend, IN: University of Notre Dame Press).

Mills, C. 1998. *Blackness Visible: Essays on Philosophy and Race* (Ithaca, NY: Cornell University Press).

Outlaw, L. 1995. "On Race and Philosophy." *Graduate Faculty Philosophy Journal*, Vol. 18, No. 2, pp. 175–199.

Pogge, Thomas. 2008. *World Poverty and Human Rights* (London: Polity Press).

Rawls, J. 1999. *The Law of Peoples* (Cambridge, MA: Harvard University Press).

Sartre, J.-P. 1991. *Critique of Dialectical Reason*. Vol. 1 (London: Verso).

Wellman, C. 2001. "Alternatives to a Theory of Group Rights." In C. Sistare, L. May, and L. Francis, eds., *Groups and Group Rights* (Lawrence: University Press of Kansas).

Young, I. 2000. *Inclusion and Democracy* (Oxford: Oxford University Press).

26

Economic rights

Past, present, and future

Gerald J. Beyer

Over the course of history a diverse array of thinkers such as John Locke, Mary Wollstonecraft, Karl Marx, Martin Luther King, Jr., Amartya Sen, and Pope John Paul II have argued for the existence and fulfillment of economic rights. In addition, myriad public advocates, politicians, and practitioners have promoted the right to work, education, health care, housing, clean and sanitary living conditions, and other economic rights. Among them are Franklin Delano and Eleanor Roosevelt, Bangladeshi microlending pioneer Muhammad Yunus, musical luminaries Shakira and Bono, physician-activist Paul Farmer, and Iranian Nobel laureate Shirin Ebadi. Contemporary leaders from across the globe, such as China's Hu Jintao, Liberia's Ellen Johnson Sirleaf, Brazil's Luiz Inácio Lula da Silva, German Chancellor Angela Merkel, and US President Barack Obama have expressed their commitment to many economic rights. In 1948 the United Nations Universal Declaration of Human Rights (hereafter UDHR) officially recognized economic rights as equally legitimate to social, cultural, civil and political rights. In 1966, the UN Declaration sought to make these rights legally binding obligations in the International Covenant on Economic, Social, and Cultural Rights (hereafter ICESCR), which was created separately from the International Covenant on Civil and Political Rights (hereafter ICCPR). Among the economic rights enumerated in the UDHR and ICESCR are the right to an adequate standard of living, to sufficient nutrition, to work, the right to a fair wage, the right to unionize, to rest and leisure, to participation in cultural life, the right to health care, to social security, and the right to education.

In spite of these clear endorsements of economic rights, theorists and politicians have challenged their validity on numerous counts. More importantly, hundreds of millions of people have died and the vast majority of the world's population struggles to survive daily because they have been deprived of the economic rights enshrined in these international agreements. Although death and suffering wrought by the hands of terrorists or natural disasters rightfully elicit broad sympathy and swift responses, bigger killers such as poverty, malnutrition, and disease go largely unchecked. As Hertel and Minkler (2007, p. 1) point out, twenty thousand people died as a result of terrorism during the years 1998–2005, while twenty-two million people perished due to lack of resources in just one year. According to the latest available World Bank data, about 1.4 billion people live in extreme poverty, surviving on less than \$1.25 a day. Approximately 2.5 billion people, or 47 percent of the world's population, live below the \$2 a day poverty standard (Chen and Ravallion 2008, pp. 23–24). More than seventy million children are denied the right to education globally, while more than 700 million adults remain illiterate according to UNESCO. UNICEF reports that about 24,000 children die *each day* due to preventable diseases. Roughly 100 million women have died prematurely due primarily to the neglect of female health care and nutrition, especially during childhood (Sen 1999, pp. 104–107). Clearly the economic rights of vast swaths of the world's population remain empty promises. The debates about economic rights are not merely academic. The fate of billions of people rests on whether or not economic rights are accepted and implemented.

This chapter describes the emergence of the idea of economic rights and argues for its cogency and importance. First, a short historical sketch reveals the gradual evolution toward the contemporary view that all human beings possess economic rights. By no means exhaustive, it suffices to demonstrate that concern for economic rights is not exclusively Western, socialist, or modern. The second section of the chapter probes the contemporary theoretical debates concerning economic rights in order to provide greater conceptual clarity. It demonstrates that many of the opponents' criticisms can be refuted by explicating precisely what it means to say that someone possesses a right to an economic good. Finally, the conclusion examines present and future ways of promoting and implementing economic rights for all.

Economic rights: a brief historical sketch

The modern idea of economic rights ostensibly arose as a nineteenth-century response to the injustices experienced by workers during the Industrial Revolution and as a product of European socialist and Christian Democratic traditions (e.g., Donnelly 2003, p. 58; Glendon 2001, p. xvii). Although these factors did lead to greater prominence of economic rights, many historical antecedents at least exhibit the roots, if not the concept, of economic rights. Scholars rightfully caution against anachronistically reading the modern language of human rights into ancient traditions. The universality of human rights was not always accepted and practiced in the pre-modern world. Yet obligations to the poor and notions of economic justice in numerous ancient religions and schools of thought adumbrate later extensions of economic rights to all. Modern human rights talk is alien to, for example, the Hebrew Bible. Nonetheless, the Hebrew Scriptures, most prominently in the Decalogue, articulate the conditions for the flourishing of the community and its members. By observing the commandments, "the community is committed not only to the love of God and neighbor but to concrete kinds of conduct that its members pledge to one another they will not individually commit" (Harrelson 1997, p. 162), it appears that the commandments were meant to create the situation of freedom within which human beings can become who they are meant to be. In this vein, although the Bible speaks primarily of duties, it can be argued that the commandments, and other injunctions such as paying fair wages in Deuteronomy 24:14, Leviticus 19:13, Jeremiah 22:12–14, and James 5:4 in the New Testament, function analogously to the economic rights contained in the UDHR and ICESCR. Similar prescriptions for just economic relationships can be found throughout the ancient Near East, for example in the Code of Hammurabi (Lohfink 1995, pp. 13–21). Interestingly, the Bible seems to have explicitly influenced the thinking of Grotius, Kant, Locke, and others about human rights (Ishay 2004, p. 57).

Although some contend that duties and obligations do not necessarily imply rights (e.g., Hart 1984, p. 83), it is not a stretch to claim that if someone has a duty to another, it entails giving the other his or her due. In other words, duties give rise to a person's right to be treated in a certain way; duties imply corresponding rights and vice versa. Basil of Caesarea, a fourth-century CE bishop, goes as far as saying that superfluous possessions do not belong to their owner. Rather, they belong to those in need. It is a grave injustice not to satisfy the needs of the poor whenever possible (Basil 1959, p. 332). While not explicitly conferring rights to the poor, it moves in this direction. According to many early Christian authorities, the poor are owed what they need out of justice, not merely as a matter of charity. Some even claimed that denying those in need amounts to theft and sometimes homicide (Gonzalez 1990, p. 177).

Traditions outside of Judaism, Christianity, and the ancient Near East also exhibit the seeds of modern economic rights. The Quran, Hindu, and Buddhist texts all enjoin solicitude for the poor and show concern for the right to property and just relations between employers and employees (Ishay 2004, pp. 37–40). Both Confucius (5th c. BCE) and Mencius (3rd c. BCE) stressed the obligation of rulers to provide goods such as food and education, "which were seen as necessary for people's self-cultivation of their moral potential, and ... their human and cosmological destiny" (Twiss 2003, p. 284). In short, certain tenets of ancient religions and traditions foreshadow modern rights language, including economic rights (Ishay 2004, pp. 35–40; Kelsay and Twiss 1994, pp. 61–79) It is telling in this regard that the 1998 Universal Declaration of Human Rights by the World's Religions unequivocally endorse rights to education, just remuneration, food, health care, etc.

Whether or not philosophers prior to the modern period articulated a doctrine of human rights, let alone economic rights, is contentious (Tierney 2002). Donnelly, for example, argues that Aquinas, representative of the Scholastic period (9th to 16th c. CE), did not espouse human rights at all and was not a proponent of the right to private property. In his view, Aquinas's use of *ius* did not include the modern understanding of a subject possessing a right (Donnelly 2003, pp. 76–77). Finnis, however, contends that the subjective notion of rights was among Aquinas's usage of the term *ius* (Finnis 2002, pp. 407–408). Prescinding from this debate, Aquinas certainly comes close to positing the right of the poor to that which they need to survive. He states that in cases of real and manifest deprivation, a person may justifiably fulfill the need "by means of another's property, by taking it openly or secretly." Moreover, as a matter of "human right," this does not constitute stealing "because that which he takes for the support of his own life becomes his own property by reason of that need" (Thomas Aquinas, *Summa Theologica*, II. II. 66.7).

Only a few of the salient figures who expounded economic rights during the Enlightenment and Industrial era can be discussed here. John Locke's *Second Treatise of Government* (1690) postulated the right to private property. Locke seemingly qualified it by the right of others "to preservation" and necessary things for subsistence, although scholars dispute what he actually meant (Locke 1980, pp. 18–19; Tuckness 2008, pp. 474–476). In addition, some observers purport that Locke defended private property as a political right rather than an economic right, but this interpretation has been rightfully rejected (Donnelly 2003, p. 31; Shue 1996, p. 153). The American revolutionary Thomas Paine referred to the "rights to subsistence, to some form of social security, to education, and to employment" in the *Rights of Man* (Vincent 1986, p. 12). The *Declaration of Sentiments*, drafted by Elizabeth Cady Stanton and adopted at the 1848 Seneca Falls Convention, demanded women's rights to property, to remunerative work, equal education, and voting (Ishay 2004, p. 162).

In 1875 Karl Marx famously deemed civil and political rights abstractions because they did not take account of the unjust economic structures of capitalism. Marx envisioned the eventual abolishment of these "bourgeois" rights and the capitalist system, which systematically exploits workers. The ushering in of the highest phase of communism would actualize economic rights, captured in Marx's dictum "from each according to his ability, to each according to his need" (Marx 1978, pp. 530–531). Other socialists during the Industrial era, including the Welsh utopian thinker Robert Owen and German socialist feminist Clara Zetkin, echoed Marx on the right to education, subsistence, work, etc. (Ishay 2004, pp. 135–143, 160–161).

A staunch critic of socialism and *laissez-faire* capitalism, Pope Leo XIII argued that natural law and the protection of human dignity demands a number of worker's rights in his 1891 encyclical *Rerum Novarum*. He explicitly mentions the right to private property, a wage that ensures basic necessities and "reasonable and frugal comfort," and a family's right to all things necessary for its preservation. According to Leo, the poor have a special claim to such rights (Leo, §10, 29, 34). A few decades earlier "Social Catholics" in Europe such as Archbishop Ketteler of Mainz and the Fribourg Union pressed for the right to a just wage and the right to private property qualified by the "primordial" right to subsistence of others (Mich 2001, pp. 11–12). By the late eighteenth and early nineteenth centuries, a number of countries had formally adopted such economic rights, for example in Frederick the Great's Prussian General Code, the Norwegian Constitution of 1814, and the French Constitution (Glendon 2001, pp. 185–186). On the ground, labor movements asserted the rights of all workers to safer conditions and better wages in Great Britain and the USA Developments in the commitment to economic rights also occurred in non-Western contexts. For example, premodern Islamic jurists built upon the foundational norms of economic justice in the Quran and Sunna (Davis and Robinson 2006, pp. 172–173; El-Sheikh 2008, p. 120; Ishay 2004, pp. 39–40). They developed a discourse of rights and duties that insisted on property rights and the duty of subjects to obey their ruler with the expectation that the ruler provided for their material needs of subjects. In addition, they propounded the "public right" to limit property entitlements that threaten the well-being of others, with the provision of just compensation for property easements (Abou El Hadl 2003, pp. 333–338). The seventeenth-century neo-Confucian Huang-Tsung-hsi argued for laws protecting the welfare of the people (Twiss 2003, p. 287). Moreover, Huang's great emphasis on education was a "strong functional analogue to a human right" according to Sumner Twiss (2003, p. 290). It is no surprise, therefore, that the Chinese philosopher Peng-Chun Chang, one of the key drafters of the UDHR, reminded his colleagues that the guaranteeing of economic well-being was not a Western innovation (Glendon 2001, p. 180).

In the twentieth century Latin America emerged as the "forgotten crucible" of human rights (Glendon 2003). Mexico, for example, included far-reaching economic rights and protections in its 1917 Constitution (Carozza 2003, pp. 302–303). The Bogotá Declaration of 1948, signed by twenty Latin American countries and the United States, contained many of the economic rights later codified in the UDHR and served as a "major source" during its drafting, as did other Latin American human rights statements (Glendon 2001, pp. 58, 141; Glendon 2003, p. 38). The Latin American delegates, spearheaded by the Chilean judge Hernán Santa Cruz, vehemently advocated for according social and economic rights equal weight with civil and political rights in the UDHR (Glendon 2001, pp. xx, 185). Their singular contributions to the UDHR, which uniquely balanced the individual and the communal good, and rights and duties, were explicitly recognized on the floor of the UN General Assembly in 1948 (Glendon 2003, pp. 38–39). This "distinctive" Latin American approach to human rights has been traced back to Bartolome de Las Casas, the sixteenth-century defender of the rights of Amerindians (Carozza 2003, pp. 289–296).

The delegates from China, Europe, Australia, Lebanon, the Soviet bloc, Muslim countries, and Latin America all supported economic rights in the UDHR. In addition, Franklin Delano and Eleanor Roosevelt greatly contributed to their advancement. The social and economic rights of the UDHR "contained more than an echo" of FDR's "four freedoms" and his Economic Bill of Rights of 1944 (Glendon 2001, p. 186). Roosevelt elaborated rights to "useful" work, a living wage, decent housing, "a good education," and health care, among others. In his view, the link between these rights and human freedom had become "self-evident" (Roosevelt 1989, p. 313). Eleanor Roosevelt, who chaired the UN Human Rights Commission, won the Truman administration's support for economic rights and ensured their place in the UDHR (Glendon 1998, pp. 1166–1167; Glendon 2001, pp. 43, 45, 186).

The UDHR ushered in a new era for economic rights, but the Cold War years exacted a toll. The Soviet Union alleged that the USA denied its citizens' economic rights in order to legitimate its own regime. On the other hand, the USA decried the violation of civil and political rights in the Soviet Union, thus attempting to claim the moral high ground (Steiner and Alston 2000, p. 250; Vincent 1986, pp. 61–75). This led to the creation of the two separate covenants, the ICCPR and ICESCR, in 1966. In the political sphere, the United States has opposed the recognition of economic rights ever since. No US President has urged ratification of the ICESCR since President Carter's futile attempt to obtain the Senate's consent (Steiner and Alston 2000, p. 250; Koh 2001).

Despite these setbacks, progress has occurred since the UDHR. The European Social Charter of 1961 contains a much more expansive list of economic rights than the ICESCR, defines them more precisely, and establishes a more rigorous implementation verification scheme (Donnelly 2007, pp. 44–45). In 1981 the Organization of African Unity (OAU) promulgated the Banjul Charter, which posits a number of economic rights. It also states that "civil and political rights cannot be dissociated from economic, social and cultural rights in conception as well as universality" (Oloka-Onyango 1995). Several nations have inserted economic rights provisions in their constitutions, with South Africa making them equally enforceable rights (Osiatyński 2007, p. 61). According to international law expert Henry J. Richardson III, South Africa's Constitutional Court has "provided a model" for "effectively enforcing economic, social, and cultural rights as legal rights" (Richardson 2007, p. 72). More than 125 nations have adopted six major International Labor Organization (ILO) Conventions, which protect workers' rights and safety (UNDP 2000, p. 76).

In addition to these positive steps, the growth in popular movements championing economic rights represented one of the most hopeful signs of the twentieth century. For example, Cesar Chavez, inspired by Saul Alinsky and Catholic social teaching, mounted a successful farmworkers' rights movement in the United States (Mich 2001, pp. 166–173). Under Communism in Poland, *Solidarnos'c'* struggled for "bread and freedom." The first paragraph of the official Solidarity Program adopted in September 1981 demonstrated the commitment to the full panoply of human rights, including specific economic rights (Beyer 2010, pp. 19–20). For decades Aung San Suu Kyi has led a human rights campaign in Burma, arguing that civil, political, economic, social, and cultural rights are interconnected and equally crucial for the empowerment of the poor (Kyi 1995, p. 17). Many non-governmental organizations (NGOs) likewise came to recognize the need to strive for the rights of the marginalized contained in the ICCPR and the ICESCR (UNDP 2000, p. 76). Energized by feminists such as Simone de Beauvoir, women's movements sprung up throughout the world to fight for women's economic rights. Their activism lead to the 1979 UN Convention on the Elimination of All Forms of Discrimination Against Women (CEDAW), which contains provisions such as the right to work, equal remuneration, and paid maternity leave (Ishay 2004, pp. 296–298). Although the USA abstained, 131 countries signed on to CEDAW, which stimulated constitutional and legal changes favorable to women's economic rights in many nations (UNDP 2000, p. 117).

Of course, the aspirational statements of declarations and even laws have not always translated into the tangible realization of economic rights. While significant progress was made in some areas in the twentieth century, such as expanding access to basic education and the female economic activity rate, the statistics at the outset of this chapter reveal that much work remains to be done. At least some of the problem stems from continuing ideological resistance to economic rights theory. The following section will attempt to debunk the major theoretical challenges to economic rights.

Do economic rights exist? The contemporary debates

In the twentieth century many scholars, religions, and philosophical traditions deemed all human rights, including economic rights, equally rooted in and required by the dignity of the human person. Over time, however, Maurice Cranston's (1983) contention that economic rights are not real rights gained traction. Since then people have leveled several criticisms against the idea of economic rights.

Human dignity: the foundation of all human rights?

Many human rights theorists contend that all human beings possess certain "inalienable" rights by virtue of their dignity. According to David Hollenbach (1979, p. 68), "the thread which ties all these rights together is human dignity. Human dignity is not an abstract or ethereal reality but is realized in concrete conditions of personal, social, economic and political life." The Roman Catholic human rights tradition, for example, "has been a process of discovering and identifying these conditions of humanity. These conditions are called human rights" The UDHR's opening paragraph postulates the "recognition of the inherent dignity and of the equal and inalienable rights" of all people as the "foundation of freedom, justice and peace in the world." Jacques Maritain, who played a role in the drafting of the UDHR, explains that the phrase "dignity of the human person" signifies that the human person possesses certain rights "by virtue of the natural law" and is "owed" certain things simply because they are human (Maritain 1971, p. 65).

Some thinkers question the legitimacy of the "human dignity" paradigm itself, and its cogency as a foundation for economic rights. The critique starts with a definition of a right. According to Alan Gewirth (1982), the statement "A has a right to X against B by virtue of Y" captures the formal elements of a right. Thus, in the human dignity paradigm, I have a claim to something against (perhaps more aptly, from) someone or some group of persons simply because I possess human dignity. One kind of objection to this hinges on an apparently missing logical step:

1. Person A possesses human dignity.
2. Therefore, Person A has a right to economic good X from B; B owes and has a duty to provide A with X.

The missing intermediary step could be stated as follows:

2a. Human dignity requires recognition by others.

According to Ping-cheung Lo, "It is one thing to say that I have dignity, which refers to myself alone. But it is quite another thing to say that I can rightly demand that others provide me with basic economic goods as something they owe me. There is a logical gap between these two propositions" (1988, p. 707). Other types of criticisms have been raised. For example, the nexus between the "generic notion of dignity" and specific right remains "'intuitively fitting' or merely esoteric" according to John Coleman (1984, p. 351). In this case, another missing step would be: good X must be granted for the recognition of human dignity, accompanied by lucid argument as to why the recognition of human dignity requires this particular good. Another problem stems from the apparent tautological nature of appeals to human dignity as the basis of human rights. Gewirth contends if the statements "A has human rights" and "A has human dignity" appear to be equivalent, "the attribution of dignity adds nothing substantial to the attribution of rights and someone who is doubtful about the latter attribution will be equally doubtful about the former." As a result, Gewirth concludes that the argument does not meet the requirement of noncircularity (Gewirth in Coleman 1984, p. 351). In addition, Michael Novak fears that human dignity is undermined by a system that guarantees "desirable goods" to all its members. He presumes that economic rights will engender a lack of regard for the virtue of self-reliance, which is eminently necessary to human dignity (Novak 1985, p. 11).

Do these arguments render the human dignity paradigm irreparably debilitated? Is there a more compelling foundation for economic rights, such as Gewirth's "necessary conditions for human actions?" (1984, p. 93). Perhaps the foundational question is irrelevant. In preparation for the drafting of the UDHR, remarkable widespread agreement on concrete rights prevailed among the participants from all parts of the globe despite strong disagreement on their justifications (Maritain 1949, pp. 9–10). Henry Shue argues that people can claim to have rights without being able to appeal to overarching principles that "serve as their reasons for their demands" (Shue 1996, pp. 15–16). His attractive approach shows on a case-by-case basis why certain "basic" rights are required for the free exercise of all other rights. Nonetheless, a vital reason for the clarification of the foundation of human rights exists. The philosophical foundations of human rights affect the interpretation of rights and their practical applications. In other words, one's understanding of the foundation of a human right, such as the right to sustenance, will affect one's interpretation of what it means to possess that right. As a result, divergent conceptions of the foundations of human rights will hinder agreement concerning the implementation of rights and the adjudication of competing rights claims (see McKeon 1949, pp. 35–36; Maritain 1949, pp. 16–17).

As a result, it is worth answering the critics and clarifying the human dignity paradigm. Novak's admonition that economic rights foster a culture of dependency will be handled appropriately in a later section concerning the guarantor of human rights. Gewirth's conundrum regarding the noncircularity requirement can be dispensed with relatively easily. Although the UDHR formulation of "human dignity and human rights" obfuscates the matter, human rights and human dignity are not "equivalent." Human dignity "stands behind" human rights; it is the source of human rights. Human beings are endowed with dignity. This dignity should be affirmed by the community in which human beings live. Therefore, human beings possess rights to which correlative duties exist. These duties are ordered towards the affirmation of dignity. Human rights are necessary for the affirmation of dignity and in order to allow human beings to participate in the common good. To say this differs from stating that "A has human dignity" *and* "A has human rights." Succinctly stated, "A's human rights flow from A's human dignity." As Hollenbach maintains, human dignity "is more fundamental than any human right" (1979, p. 90). Human rights flow from and are necessary for the recognition of human dignity.

The charge that one cannot deduce from human dignity that human beings are "owed" certain economic goods by others holds only if one accepts an underlying atomistic anthropology. Human rights thinking is never devoid of an anthropological framework. Many human rights traditions are undergirded by social anthropologies, which stress both rights and duties. Most religious traditions maintain that humans exist to live with and for one another in community, as was intimated above. For example, many Islamic jurists have maintained "God created human beings weak and in need of cooperating with others" (Abou El Hadl 2003, p. 329). Judaism starts with the assumption that the all persons have duties to others (Dorff 2003, p. 215). The Reformed tradition stresses this point emphatically: "rights are grounded in responsibilities ... and responsibilities ... belong to the very essence of what it means to be human" (Wolterstorff 1983, p. 83). Philosophers from Aristotle to contemporaries like Michael Sandel also regard human nature as social. Sandel contends that, "justice requires an inter-subjective conception of the self ... a self communally-constituted" (1998, p. 70; see also p. 11). Human rights requires this notion of the self. The UDHR itself adopted "a fairly specific image of the human person," mirroring the social anthropology discussed here (Glendon 1998, p. 1172). Evolutionary theorists now point to the validity of a social anthropology while disproving exaggerated claims about the individualistic nature of the person that have dominated economics, political theory, and international relations over the past century (Wilson 2002; de Waal 2006).

Put another way, the criticism fails to see the connection between human rights, the common good, and the conceptions of the person, society, and state articulated in many rights frameworks. For example, Pope John XXIII's claim that "since men [*sic*] are social by nature they are meant to live with others and to work for another's welfare" (§31) fills in the "logical gap." It legitimates the move from "A has human dignity" to "person A has a right to economic good X from B," provided that we demonstrate that X is necessary for A's life worthy of dignity (an issue to be addressed below). Roman Catholicism, like Judaism, Islam, Confucianism, and other schools of thought, insists that society exists in order to aid individuals and groups to flourish. It follows that society, by its very nature, has obligations to its members. This obligation, however, functions dialectically; society exists to protect human rights while "human rights are the minimum conditions for life in the community" (USCCB 1992, §17). Human dignity is threatened when people cannot participate in society as a result of debilitating social, political, and economic conditions. In other words, the chief responsibility of a society is to ensure that individual rights are respected and "coordinated with other rights" so that each individual can fulfill her or his duties in society and promote the common good. Following Maritain, this understanding of human nature is aptly referred to as personalist communitarianism (Maritain 1966, p. 65). Given a rich social anthropology as a backdrop, it should be easy to apprehend why the move from human dignity to human rights is valid. The "Person A" of formal logic becomes a human person in the personalist, communitarian sense. In this vein, perhaps it would be more illuminating to say that the foundation of rights is the dignity of the human person *qua member of the human family*.

Hollenbach indicates an awareness of the potential problem raised by the second criticism. He writes: "human dignity is nearly empty of meaning. This is so because without further specification the notion of human dignity lacks all reference to particular needs, actions and relationships" (Hollenbach 1979, p. 90). However, the Roman Catholic tradition, for example, does explain the nexus between specific rights and human dignity (perhaps to greater or lesser degrees in regard to particular rights). If one looks at Roman Catholic rights thinking within the whole of its tradition, one will encounter these vital connections. In Hollenbach's words, the process of the "specification of the concrete conditions for the realization of dignity in action has been the continuing endeavor of the tradition since Leo XIII. It is this very process that has produced the Catholic human rights tradition" (Hollenbach 1979, p. 91). Hollenbach correctly stresses that the historical context reveals to us what is necessary for the protection of human dignity. For example, Pope Leo's cognizance of the "misery and wretchedness" of the poor and the "callousness of employers and the greed of unrestrained competition" prompted him to promote the right "to procure what is required to live" (§2). For the poor, this can only be achieved through work and just wages (§34). In short, I would submit that in some cases, such as the right to life, the relationship to human dignity may be obvious. In other cases, such as the right to basic medical care and basic education, the connection may be somewhat more nebulous. Nonetheless, this would call for greater clarification of the nexus between dignity and specific rights, rather than abandonment of the human dignity paradigm.

Further clarification can be gained from the exposition of a whole set of anthropological presuppositions that coincide with the belief that the "dignity-filled" nature of the human being commands the recognition of human rights (and duties). These claims flesh out what it means to say the human being possesses dignity. Many proponents of human rights, along with the UDHR, embrace the following:

1. the teleological nature of the human being (i.e., by nature human beings are meant to flourish, grow, and develop towards certain "ends");
2. human beings are endowed with unique rational, relational, moral, and spiritual capacities;
3. human beings have a transcendent dimension (i.e., what they do in the present lifetime points beyond their life, in some way);
4. the "ends" toward which human beings tend can only be achieved in community because humans are by nature social beings (see Article 29 of UDHR); Glendon (1998, p. 1172) demonstrates how most of these anthropological beliefs provided content to the dignity concept in the UDHR. It lacks, however, any reference to the transcendent dimension of the human person.

How the "ends" toward which human nature tends and how inherent human capacities must be protected and fostered determines the scope and content of human rights and thus the demands of human dignity. Of course, a full-blown theory of rights would need to elaborate on these "ends" and these capacities in order to demonstrate the relationship between them and corresponding human rights. If human rights represent that which enables us to become who we are destined to be, we must ascertain who it is we are destined to be, at least in some sense. Disagreement certainly exists concerning the overarching purpose of human life. Few, however, would disagree that human beings are not meant to be marginalized in any way, certainly not the adherents of civil and political rights who reject economic rights. If we accept this assumption about the purpose of human life, it follows that "minimum economic resources are due people by right, and not simply as a desirable part of the full common good. This is the case because persons can be just as effectively excluded or left out of the life of the community by long-term unemployment or homelessness as by the denial of the vote or freedom of speech" (Hollenbach 1988, p. 106). In other words, if human dignity requires the ability to avoid marginalization, and conversely the ability to participate in the common good, we must posit economic rights as vehicles towards that end.

Which economic rights? Expansive lists versus "basic rights"

Which economic rights are necessary for the recognition and protection of human dignity? Which economic goods are required in order for all human beings to participate in the common good? Two approaches tend to dominate economic rights thinking pertaining to this issue. The first approach contends that a broad array of economic rights should be guaranteed. Many of the international documents mentioned earlier fall into this category. Roman Catholic rights theory has also adopted this approach.

Various camps have attacked this "expansive list" approach. Jean Kirkpatrick, the US ambassador to the UN under Reagan, quipped that "[s]uch declarations of human 'rights' take on the character of 'a letter to Santa Claus' ... They can multiply indefinitely because no clear standard informs them, and no great reflection produced them" (Kirkpatrick 1989, p. 364). Cranston remarked that putative rights in the UDHR to "social security" and "holidays with pay" are "admirable," but not real rights. Denying real rights amounts to "a grave affront to justice." A lack of paid holidays hardly qualifies (Cranston 1983, p. 12). Coleman, who generally accepts economic rights, bemoans the lack of a theory of "basic rights" in the Roman Catholic tradition (1984, pp. 355–361).

The plethora of economic rights in documents like the ICESCR does beg the question of realistic implementation. Budgetary limitations may require difficult choices to be made in the event of conflicting, often expensive, claims to rights. Thus, a theory of basic rights has advantages. Some theorists who affirm a broad spectrum of economic rights do acknowledge rights conflicts given fiscal constraints. Hollenbach prioritizes the theories of justice and love in Roman Catholicism to indicate the ordering of certain rights claims, giving priority to the rights of the poor and marginalized (1979, pp. 141–178). Pope John Paul II and the US Catholic bishops, while affirming a wide array of economic rights, conclude that, "first among these rights are the rights to life, food, clothing, shelter, rest, medical care and basic education" (USCCB 1992, §80).

The ICESCR acknowledges that implementation of economic rights is "subject to the availability of resources ... and the obligation is one of progressive realization." Nonetheless, such acknowledgments provide little wisdom as to how to make tough choices that affect the lives of millions. In countries that struggle to pay off massive debts, policy decisions must be made that prioritize, for example, the right to basic, preventive health care over the right to adequate shelter or vice versa. Therefore, whole groups experience denials or "deferrals" (explication of the difference to follow) of their rights.

Basic rights theories, such as Shue's, must complement the greater goal of securing all of the economic rights enshrined in international agreements. A clearer understanding of basic rights can help discern which economic rights take priority in cases of conflict. Yet, even basic rights theories lack the kind of specificity required to adjudicate between policy decisions in the "tough cases" (when two basic rights genuinely conflict). Later sections of this chapter will employ Shue's theory because a basic rights theory can contribute to the adjudication of conflicting rights claims in many instances. First, the problem of correlative duties must be addressed.

Who must guarantee economic rights? The problem of correlative duties

A great deal of misunderstanding exists in the economic rights debate concerning the problem of correlative duties. On the one hand, critics of economic rights incorrectly assume that proponents are "statists" that believe that governments should supply the objects of economic rights in every situation. On the other hand, proponents sometimes do not clearly stress their acceptance of the principle of subsidiarity, which postulates the state should only assume roles and responsibilities that individuals and local civic organizations cannot perform themselves in order to sustain a society (Beyer 2010, pp. 93–94). A related problem in the debate stems from what might be called "the myth of self-reliance."

The possibility of exercising (and guaranteeing) economic rights never takes place in a social, economic, juridical, and political vacuum. Novak, for example, demands that individuals first and foremost are responsible for their own health, provision of shelter, nutrition, clothing, etc.

(1987, pp. 43, 45). This is a reasonable *prima facie* duty. However, individuals *always* act in social contexts that enable, hinder, or preclude the realization of self-reliance to varying degrees. In other words, self-reliance is always co-determined by the conditions that make it possible. Total self-reliance, completely divorced from some form of external aid, does not exist. Even the arguably most esteemed self-reliant individual, the entrepreneur, relies on a juridical, economic, and educational framework established and sustained by governmental structures. Yet, the anthropology of the "rugged individual," which is deeply embedded in American culture particularly (see Bellah et al. 1996, pp. 32–35, 144–147; Taylor 1976, p. 90), fails to acknowledge this. In contradistinction, French philosopher Gabriel Marcel trenchantly states that even "the most self-centered of us looks to others and only to others for his final investiture" (1978, p. 16; see also Maritain 1966).

Support networks inhering in families, religious entities, civic organizations, and the government itself always in some way contribute toward the ability to care for one's self. American critics of economic rights and their alleged link to a culture of dependency downplay that their immigrant grandparents and the following generation were beneficiaries of government aid in the form of the GI bill, public works programs, social security, which is state welfare after the first four years of benefits (Thurow 1996, p. 109), and numerous state and federal investments, such as public education. Novak, for example, admits this but adds this aid was graciously accepted; it was not exercised as a right. "Rights" foster dependency, but "desirable goods" do not (Novak 1987, p. 45). In addition, ethnic and religious organizations assisted many immigrants in finding jobs, homes, etc. In short, the "rugged individual" of the American collective memory possessed a great deal of "social capital," which many of our members of society appear not to have today. The social networks that aided our recent ancestors in attaining "human capital" have withered in recent decades (Putnam 2000, p. 283). Given this situation, they have a right to claim aid from the state *when necessary*.

In order to illustrate this point, take for example, the right to affordable housing. Members of society are first and foremost responsible for finding, securing, and maintaining their own homes. Yet, the government *and* other civil actors have a *duty* to create the necessary conditions within which individuals can exercise their right to housing; i.e., society must create policies and institutions that will make affordable housing available to all. In accordance with subsidiarity, if a person's family, religious entity, banks, or any other non-governmental organization does not create lending policies and investment in affordable housing, it becomes the government's obligation. This is what it means to say that all have a right to housing and that society and the state have correlative duties. In most cases, the government is not obligated to "distribute" houses to all members of society. It can fulfill its obligation by creating taxation policies, favorable zoning laws, and banking regulations favorable to the development of affordable housing. Hence, persons maintain their responsibility for themselves, while the state and society facilitate doing so. When the state and society together fail to meet their obligations, the state must compensate by taking full responsibility for the procuring of this right. Thus, when banks decided to "red-line" in the earlier part of the twentieth century, the government had an obligation to prohibit such unfair banking policies or directly provide low-interest loans to African-Americans, who were being discriminated against by banks.

John Paul II similarly understands economic rights and correlative duties. While the state bears the responsibility for "overseeing and directing the exercise of human rights in the economic sphere," individuals and various groups in society should primarily ensure these rights (John Paul II 1992, §48). Following Shue (1996, p. 119), an important proviso should be added: insofar as the individuals who bear the obligation need not sacrifice their own basic right in doing so. The Pope chooses the example of the right to work. He delineates a middle course between the ill-fated socialist alternative of all work provided by the state and the laissez-faire insistence on no governmental interference in the labor market. According to him, "the state has a duty to sustain business activities by creating conditions which will ensure job opportunities, by stimulating those activities where they are lacking or by supporting them in moments of crisis" (John Paul II 1992, §48).

Acknowledging that the realization of economic rights requires action by the government led Cranston to conclude that they do not exist because they are not practicable. Most governments simply do not have the resources to procure them. Civil and political rights, so-called negative rights, merely entitle people to be left alone. They require little resources. Cranston's claim, however, rests on a fallacy. Shue correctly contends rights to physical security require costly "social institutions" to secure them (1996, pp. 38–40). The same can be said for rights to privacy, free speech, a fair trial, etc. Moreover, "sometimes subsistence rights only require that individuals are protected from those who might harm them" (Shue 1996, p. 40). In addition, the aforementioned examples demonstrate that having economic rights is not always tantamount to the provision of the object of the right for all. Claiming that someone has a right to something, such as work, housing, or nutrition, says nothing about *how* that right is to be fulfilled. It does not convey that all those who so desire should receive "hand-outs." However, many people fear just this, particularly in the American context. In their view, the welfare state, or even worse, socialism, sucks the life out of our "Paul Bunyans" and "Benjamin Franklins" when discussion of economic rights take place.

To reiterate, two things must be accomplished in order to further understanding of economic rights. First, the "myth of self-reliance" must be abandoned in favor of accepting that all people are dependent on others. This is the case to an ever-increasing degree in our expanding global economy. Therefore, national and international society has an obligation to create the conditions within which individuals may exercise their right to sustenance. Second, specification of the actual content of formal economic rights needs to be undertaken. This would evince that sometimes economic rights mandate direct aid from the state. For example, the state or multinational agencies must protect the individual from rights violations brought about by transnational corporations (Shue 1996, pp. 52–53, afterword). However, many non-governmental duty-bearers often carry the greater share of obligations. Does this create an "indeterminate" bearer of the correlative duties attached to economic rights? Appealing to the Kantian notion of "imperfect duties," Amartya Sen argues that correlative duties are assigned to "anyone who can help." He admits that this may mean in some cases that rights may remain unfulfilled, at least temporarily (Sen 1999, pp. 229, 231). Shue helpfully augments the imperfect duties paradigm by positing different kinds of interrelated duties attached to each right: (1) duties to avoid depriving, (2) duties to protect from deprivation, and (3) duties to aid the deprived. Everyone bears *at least* the first kind of duty towards the fulfillment of another's rights (Shue 1996, pp. 52–53). The strength of a subsidiarity-based perspective resides in its insistence that anyone who can help must but also that in the event no single person or groups carry the capacity, the state must bear the ultimate obligation to make sure its weakest members do not slide into utter deprivation. When a state cannot legitimately fulfill these obligations, it should appeal to international agencies and foreign governments for help. Indeed, in today's highly interdependent world, economically disadvantaged countries cannot alone secure the full panoply of economic rights for their citizens. Weaker nations often cannot enforce rights violations by powerful countries and multinational corporations. Wealthy countries bear obligations toward the people of struggling nations, especially because some see them as partly responsible for their economic misery. Unfortunately, such international obligations often go unnoticed, even though human rights agreements since the UDHR underscore them (Skogly and Gibney 2007).

Although not a panacea, the emphasis on the broad spectrum of duties pertaining to each right and the multilevel groups of agents who are obliged by them serves an important purpose. It should place lesser burdens on the two agents who tend to bear the most in much thinking about human rights: the individual rights-bearer or the state. "Spreading the duties out" in this manner should lead to less frequent conflicts among competing rights. Logically, if we recognize the existence of more capacities to fulfill obligations, less difficulty should arise in performing those duties; i.e., more resources will be available for the fulfillment of rights. However, this does not imply that enough resources will be available at all times to recognize all claims to economic rights. Does this lead us to the necessary conclusion that economic rights cannot be considered universal? Conversely, acknowledging the distinction between possessing and exercising a right provides a key step in understanding the implementation of economic rights and attenuating rights conflicts (Maritain 1949, p. 15).

Economic rights: "provisional universals?"

Is it possible to assert that certain universal economic rights exist that are subject to conditions? Can they remain unfulfilled or perhaps forfeited in some situations, while retaining their universal nature? According to Novak, "welfare" rights are conditional. Echoing Cranston, he contends that any state that pledges economic rights to food, clothing, shelter, etc. to all its citizens would cease to be a limited state. Conversely, if it secures these rights for a smaller class of citizens, i.e., those "in need," these economic rights cease to be universal and inalienable, two necessary characteristics of human rights (Novak 1987, p. 48). Thus, it is better to view them as "desirable goods" that cannot be considered rights. Novak's argument is problematic, given the claims above that (1) all people obtain help from the government, and other societal groups, in some form; and (2) the procurement of economic rights can often be achieved without direct provision by the government. Nonetheless, in a sense, human rights should be seen as provisional, universal, and inalienable. More precisely, the fulfillment of a right may be provisional, but not the right itself.

In cases of conflicting economic rights (competing for resources), the fulfillment of some economic rights can be "deferred" until a future time. This only applies to real conflicts. For example, necessary spending on education might conflict with necessary spending on health care when local governments must choose due to scarcity of resources. However, the putative right to amass wealth without constraint cannot conflict with the right to sustenance (see Hollenbach 1979, pp. 141–178; Niebuhr 1960, p. 259). To use Shue's language, a mere preference can never trump a basic right (1996, pp. 104, 112, 118, 120–130). In the case of genuine conflict, the fulfillment of an economic right is subject to a proviso: the claimant must wait until resources are made available that will enable the fulfillment of the right. This view is compatible with the "progressive realization" strategy articulated in the ICESCR. The right does not vanish; its fulfillment is simply deferred. As Sen states, "we can surely distinguish between a right that a person has which has not been fulfilled and a right that a person does not have" (1999, pp. 230–231). It would seem that a liberal rights theorist would grant this. For example, a liberal would probably not concede that because citizens of Communist countries did not have the right to free enterprise the right did not exist. To say this would be tantamount to concluding the right to free enterprise is not universal. Because human rights are inherently universal, the only response is this right existed but was not recognized. The linchpin of this argument resides in that human rights are ontologically rooted; just as universal human dignity cannot be eradicated, that which flows from it, human rights, cannot be eviscerated despite invidious human efforts to do so. Human dignity can, of course, be affronted. This happens when humans cannot fully flourish and exercise their inherent capacities as a result of rights violations. Likewise, specific rights can be universal even though they are not always and everywhere realized.

Economic rights advocates may find the contention that economic rights can be deferred disconcerting. This stance is perhaps largely why the majority of the world's population experiences denials of economic rights. Such an abhorrent state of affairs demands that safeguards be incorporated into the progressive realization framework. First, as John Langan states, we must assign to "human rights a *prima facie* status which would put the burden of justification on those who propose to override these claims; and we would be affirming a corresponding *prima facie* obligation on other persons to satisfy these claims" (1982, p. 73). A corollary is that a right can only be deferred for a morally legitimate reason. Furthermore, steps must be taken to ensure the eventual procurement of the right; this precludes "moral lethargy" that might become satisfied with a less than optimal status quo. If this stipulation is not met, the right has been violated, not deferred. When a government violates basic rights absent a real conflict due to scarcity of resources, "its decrees would be wholly lacking in juridical force" (John XXIII 1992, §61). Second, the procurement of *basic rights* cannot be deferred justifiably: "a basic right may not be sacrificed in order to secure the enjoyment of a non-basic right" (Shue 1996, p. 19). Not fulfilling a basic right is always a human rights violation.

Among the three types of basic rights, Shue lists security rights, subsistence rights, and liberty rights. Security rights include the right not to be subjected to murder, torture, mayhem, rape, or assault. Subsistence rights include "unpolluted air, unpolluted water, adequate food, adequate clothing, adequate shelter and minimum preventative public health care." None of these basic rights can be sacrificed because "the enjoyment of them is essential to the enjoyment of all other rights ... if a right is basic, other, non-basic rights may be sacrificed, if necessary, in order to secure the basic right" (1996, p. 19). For example, if someone lacks adequate nutrition they cannot truly benefit from preventive medicine; the lack of a minimum caloric intake leads to diminished cognitive functioning and eventually to death. Nutrition, in turn, is of little value to someone who must endure the threat of physical violence. The precise meaning of each of these rights is open to debate. One may object that attaining completely unpolluted air or water is impossible. Thus, Shue prudently qualifies his argument; he later refers to "minimum cleanliness of air and water" (1996, pp. 20–25). Even such definitions need to be established by experts. Nonetheless, generally speaking, a person should have a right to that which enables her or him to live an average lifespan without the need for tragic interventions. Despite any ambiguities that persist (such as "average lifespan"), Shue's primary point remains valid. Would a person lacking food enjoy the benefits of shelter, or vice versa? Over time deprivation of any of these basic rights causes serious deficiencies, such as malnutrition or fever due to exposure, eventually leading to brain damage, other incapacities, or death (1996, p. 25). Fulfillment of rights to goods that protect against such possibilities cannot be deferred. The final section of this chapter will return to this. Prior to doing so, it must treat another aspect of the provisional nature of economic rights.

At first glance, it may appear fallacious or inhumane to argue that economic rights can be "forfeited." Yet, the non-exercise of some economic rights by the right-bearer may (excluding basic rights) forfeit the claim he or she has towards any relevant duty-bearers. The case becomes more complex when dealing with basic rights. Does the non-exercise of the right to preventive health care temporarily eliminate the corresponding duties? I think not. The difference is that in the case of basic rights, the duty-bearers must at all times be ready to fulfill their obligations to the best of their capacities. However, it would seem unjust to make the same claim in regard to non-basic rights while knowing that the futile efforts and wasted resources of the duty-bearers could be utilized towards the greater fulfillment of other basic rights. For example, it seems justified to claim that someone who has balked at accepting adequate work can temporarily forfeit the ability to demand the recognition of his or her right to work. The corresponding duties are suspended until the person exhibits a real commitment to working. The fulfillment of the right may be abrogated indefinitely if the person does not strive towards finding gainful employment. Once again, the right does not vanish. If rights are not exercised and the ability to claim corresponding obligations is forfeited temporarily, they do not cease to exist. Thus, the fulfillment of some economic rights, not the rights themselves, can be provisional.

Some conflicts of rights cannot be legitimately adjudicated based on the basic/nonbasic rights distinction and the "apparent versus real" conflict distinction. These distinctions may be useful to limiting the number of conflicts that take place in the practical realizations of economic rights. Unfortunately, not all rights conflicts fall within this rubric.

Real conflicts of economic rights: stretching the limits of the common good

This chapter has argued that the fulfillment of economic rights should not be as burdensome on the state as critics insist. Introducing flexibility into the economic rights agenda and allowing for deferment when necessary deflates Kirkpatrick's criticism. A necessary proviso to this acknowledgment stresses the importance of *who* decides *what* rights can and should be deferred. All citizens must be afforded the opportunity to participate in this decision-making process at some level. The absence of the necessary participatory structures creates a situation in which people do not truly enjoy the exercise of any rights. As Shue contends, "to enjoy something only at the discretion of someone else, especially someone powerful enough to deprive you of it at will, is precisely not to enjoy a right to it" (1996, p. 78).

Apparent rights conflicts often resemble real conflicts at first glance because all nations face competing budgetary constraints. For example, spending on education may have to be prioritized less in order to care for an aging population in certain countries. However, in order to distinguish real conflict from apparent conflict, national and local budgets must be subjected to careful scrutiny. What appears to be a morally legitimate deferral of a right's fulfillment may actually be a clear instance of an unjustifiable rights violation. A few examples should demonstrate the point.

Since the fall of Communism, the Polish government has decreased spending on education, while private schooling increased dramatically. More than 60 percent of all university students now pay tuition (Beyer 2010). In the 1980s, one out of every 14 high school graduates from rural areas attended institutions of higher learning. Today the ratio is one out of 140, approximately 2 percent. Children from rural areas also have less access to government-funded preschools and kindergartens. Their teachers are not nearly as qualified as urban teachers. Families from rural areas also have much less ability to pay for educational services.

In the 1990s Poland's government devoted a large percentage of its budget on social security spending. On the face of it, this seems to have given rise to a conflict between the right to social security for the elderly and the right to education, a right that is enshrined in the Polish constitution. Yet, the amount spent on social security seems disproportionate in this situation. The real income of retirees rose by 13.6 percent from 1990 to 1998. The ratio between the average retirement pension and the average salary grew from 53 percent to 73 percent, making it one of the highest in all of Europe. While it is true that some retired persons struggle to survive financially, far greater numbers of children live in poverty in Poland. Furthermore, those who made more under the Communist system, such as military generals, now reap generous pensions. It seems dubious that the rights of the elderly to a pension trump the rights of children from villages to obtain a good education, particularly those elderly whose pension affords them a very high standard of living. Furthermore, other areas of the state budget could be reduced to help achieve the right to education for all children. For example: (1) introduce a negatively graduated pension system, which would protect the elderly poor and transfer funds from those who do not need it and (2) introduce legislation to limit the salaries of politicians, who earn nine times more than the average Pole, and spend the savings on education.

Poland could also have spent less on military expenditures. All nations must take a hard look at defense spending given massive economic rights violations. For example, Burma, ranked among the world's poorest countries by the UNDP, spends roughly 40 percent of its national budget on defense. This is nearly 200 percent more than on education and health combined (Open Society Institute 2005). The USA has the highest poverty and infant mortality rates among industrialized nations. Yet, its budget officially earmarked $638 billion for defense in 2010. The actual spending will likely approach $1 trillion. The editors of *America* (2010, p. 2) calculate that thirty new jets alone will cost about $7 billion dollars, while ensuring a place for every at-risk American child in a quality pre-school would cost about $5.7 billion.

These kinds of trade-offs must be considered. A lack of political will does not constitute a morally legitimate reason for deferring economic rights. The politics of indifference rather than limited resources often causes human deprivation. As Sen points out, most famines occur due to a lack of political will, not economic scarcity (1999, pp. 16, 160–189). Succinctly stated, there are fewer real conflicts of economic rights than meets the eye. Sen rightly stresses the importance of political participation and political pressure in the face of lethargic governments who often clamor about budgetary constraints on their ability to fulfill economic rights. Because children do note vote, and tend to suffer from poverty disproportionately, someone must lobby for them. Perhaps more vigorous political advocacy might provoke some governments to realize that nuclear warheads and various other "necessary expenditures" should be placed on Santa Claus lists.

There are, of course, governments that face real conflicts. Rights of the needy can conflict with other rights of the needy. I merely advocate stripping away all of the false claims to conflicts before adjudicating the truly tragic and difficult choices concerning the prioritization of economic rights. In such cases, an approach such as Shue's basic rights theory appears indispensable. The right to education is extremely valuable and necessary to the thriving of today's economy, which is driven by investment in human capital. However, its fulfillment may have to be deferred, or given less priority, when doing otherwise would lead to widespread malnutrition or disease. Such cases may be rare, but if the right to basic health care and nutrition competes for resources with the right to education, the former must prevail. Admittedly primary education comes close to meeting the criteria of a basic right. Without literacy and numeracy skills, women have often suffered and even died because they were not cognizant of their basic rights (Sen 1999, pp. 185–209). Yet, the likelihood of securing other rights without education seems greater than the likelihood of securing them without nutrition or basic health care (Shue 1996, p. 20). Of course, when states genuinely must defer the realization of an important right, such as education, they can and should appeal to other nations and international bodies for assistance to fulfill that right. All nations must contribute to the successful construction of an international order that makes the recognition of all human rights possible (see Skogly and Gibney 2007). One might make the case that education should rank among the highest priorities in a just international order (Beyer 2010, pp. 152–156).

Looking toward the future of economic rights

The idea of economic rights continues to be hotly contested. Clearing up some of the conceptual issues might encourage its acceptance. In practical terms, economic rights proponents must convince critics that economic rights are not socialist, a fear that the recent debates about health care in the United States awakened. A strategic approach might start with an ethic of solidarity, and then elaborate economic rights as one of its requirements. The language of solidarity bridges the duties–rights and individual–communal divides better than rights language alone. An ethic of solidarity has the advantage of stressing the right to participation in the creation of just social structures as its basic requirement. Solidarity seeks to empower all people to fulfill their economic rights and, in turn, empower others to do the same (Beyer 2010).

Equally important are practical forms of advocacy that are making strides towards the realization of economic rights for as many people as possible. For example, the living wage movement has pushed many local US governments to adopt living wage ordinances and produced positive outcomes (Mich 2009). Economic rights advocacy should prioritize a living wage, because without just compensation for work, human beings cannot afford the basic goods needed to flourish. Moreover, a human rights framework based on subsidiarity and solidarity deems individuals procuring these goods for themselves and their families more appropriate *whenever possible* rather than the government or any other intermediary agency.

Examples of important activism abound. The Poor People's Campaign for Economic Rights has continued the work of Martin Luther King by appealing to articles 23, 25, and 26 of the UDHR to demand their rights to a decent livelihood. Similar movements have defended the economic rights of marginalized people in South Africa and the Philippines (Hertel and Minkler 2007, pp. 28–31). Workers' rights movements are on the rise in places like Bangladesh and Mexico, and transnational advocacy has increased thanks to communication technology and cheaper travel (Hertel 2006). Agencies like Médecins sans Frontières and Partners in Health have advanced the right to health care among the poor. Buoyed by the support of rock star Bono and other celebrities, large-scale campaigns such as "One" have successfully pressured wealthy nations to commit more resources to global economic rights. Colombian singer Shakira promotes the right to education with her foundation Pies Descalzos ("Bare Feet"), which defrays the cost of schooling for disadvantaged children.

Numerous NGOs have used the Grameen Bank model and achieved tremendous success empowering women and men to exercise their right to economic rights through microlending. Recently its founder Muhammad Yunus has touted the "social business" model, which harnesses profitable corporations towards social goals (Yunus 2007). Worldwide relief agencies such as Catholic Relief Services use microlending, fair trade, and ethical consumerism to help farmers live lives of dignity and self-sufficiency by ensuring just and sustainable incomes (Korgen 2007). Governments, courts, international bodies, and human rights advocates have developed more sophisticated ways to measure, monitor, and enforce economic rights (Hertel and Minkler 2007). In short, much has been accomplished to revitalize the economic rights agenda. However, much work remains to be done, and everyone has an obligation to play a role in it.

Acknowledgment

Sections of this chapter have been previously published in Beyer 2005. Reprinted here with permission.

References

Abou El Hadl, Khaled. 2003. "The Human Rights Commitment in Modern Islam." In J. Runzo, N. Martin, and A. Sharma, eds., *Human Rights and Responsibilities in the World Religions* (Oxford: Oneworld).

America Editors. 2010. "Weakened by Defense." *America*, Vol. 202, No. 2.
Basil of Caesarea. 1959. "I Will Pull Down My Barns." In *The Sunday Sermons of the Great Fathers*. Vol. III, Trans. M. F. Toal (Chicago, IL: Regnery).
Bellah, Robert, Richard Madsen, William M. Sullivan, Ann Swidler, and Steven M. Tipton. 1996. *Habits of the Heart: Individualism and Commitment in American Life* (Berkeley: University of California Press).
Beyer, Gerald J. 2005. "Beyond 'Nonsense on Stilts': Towards Conceptual Clarity and Resolution of Conflicting Economic Rights." *Human Rights Review*, Vol. 6, No. 4.
Beyer, Gerald J. 2010. *Recovering Solidarity: Lessons from Poland's Nonviolent Revolution* (South Bend, IN: University of Notre Dame Press).
Carozza, Paolo. 2003. "From Conquest to Constitutions: Retrieving a Latin American Tradition of the Idea of Human Rights." *Human Rights Quarterly*, Vol. 25, No. 2.
Chen, Shaohua and Martin Ravallion. 2008. "The Developing World Is Poorer Than We Thought, But No Less Successful in the Fight Against Poverty." *Policy Research Working Paper 4703* (Washington, DC: World Bank).
Coleman, John. 1984. "Catholic Human Rights Theory: Four Challenges to an Intellectual Tradition." *Journal of Law and Religion*, Vol. 2, No. 2.
Cranston, Maurice. 1983. "Are There Any Human Rights?" *Daedalus*, Vol. 112, No. 4.
Davis, Nancy J. and Robert V. Robinson. 2006. "The Egalitarian Face of Islamic Orthodoxy: Support for Islamic Law and Economic Justice in Seven Muslim Majority Nations." *American Sociological Review*, Vol. 71, No. 2.
Donnelly, Jack. 2003. *Universal Human Rights in Theory and Practice*. 2nd edn (Ithaca, NY: Cornell University Press).
Donnelly, Jack. 2007. "The West and Economic Rights." In S. Hertel and L. Minkler, eds., *Economic Rights: Conceptual, Measurement, and Policy Issues* (Cambridge: Cambridge University Press).
Dorff, Eliot. 2003. "A Jewish Perspective on Human Rights." In J. Runzo, N. Martin, and A. Sharma, eds. *Human Rights and Responsibilities in the World Religions* (Oxford: Oneworld).
El-Sheikh, Salah. 2008. "The Moral Economy of Classical Islam: A Fiqhiconomic Model." *Muslim World*, Vol. 98, No. 1.
Finnis, John. 2002. "Aquinas on Ius and Hart on Rights: A Response to Tierney." *Review of Politics*, Vol. 64, No. 3, pp. 407–410.
Gewirth, Alan. 1984. "Are There Any Absolute Rights?" In Jeremy Waldron, ed., *Theories of Rights* (Oxford: Oxford University Press).
Glendon, Mary Ann. 1998. "Knowing the Universal Declaration of Human Rights." *Notre Dame Law Review*, Vol. 73, No. 5.
Glendon, Mary Ann. 2001. *A World Made New: Eleanor Roosevelt and the Universal Declaration of Human Rights* (New York: Random House).
Glendon, Mary Ann. 2003. "The Forgotten Crucible: The Latin American Influence on the Universal Human Rights Idea." *Harvard Human Rights Journal*, Vol. 16.
Gonzalez, Justo. 1990. *Faith and Wealth: A History of Early Christian Ideas on the Origin, Significance, and Use of Money* (San Francisco, CA: Harper & Row).
Harrelson, Walter J. 1997. *The Ten Commandments and Human Rights* (Macon, GA: Mercer University Press).
Hart, H. L. A. 1984. "Are There Any Natural Rights?" In Jeremy Waldron, ed., *Theories of Rights* (Oxford: Oxford University Press).
Hertel, Shareen. 2006. "New Moves in Transnational Advocacy: Getting Labor and Economic Rights on the Agenda in Unexpected Ways." *Global Governance*, Vol. 12.
Hertel, Shareen and Lanse Minkler. 2007. "Economic Rights: The Terrain." In S. Hertel and L. Minkler, *Economic Rights: Conceptual, Measurement, and Policy Issues* (Cambridge: Cambridge University Press).
Hollenbach, David. 1979. *Claims in Conflict: Retrieving and Renewing the Catholic Human Rights Tradition* (New York: Paulist Press).
Hollenbach, David. 1988. *Justice, Peace, and Human Rights: American Catholic Social Ethics in a Pluralistic Context* (New York: Crossroads).
Ishay, Micheline. 2004. *The History of Human Rights: From Ancient Times to the Globalization Era* (Berkeley: University of California Press).
John XXIII. 1992. "*Pacem in Terris*." In David J. O'Brien and Thomas A. Shannon, eds., *Catholic Social Thought: The Documentary Heritage* (Maryknoll, NY: Orbis Books).

John Paul II. 1992. "*Centesimus Annus*." In David J. O'Brien and Thomas A. Shannon, eds., *Catholic Social Thought: The Documentary Heritage* (Maryknoll, NY: Orbis Books).
John Paul II. 1998. *Message of His Holiness Pope John Paul II for the Celebration of the World Day of Peace: "From the Justice of Each Comes Peace For All."* At: http://www.vatican.va/holy_father/john_paul_ii/messages/peace/documents/hf_jp-ii_mes_08121997_xxxi-world-day-for-peace_en.html.
Kelsay, John, and Sumner Twiss. 1994. *Religion and Human Rights* (New York: The Project on Religion and Human Rights).
Kirkpatrick, Jean. 1989. "Establishing a Viable Human Rights Policy." In Walter Lacquer and Barry Rubin, eds., *The Human Rights Reader* (New York: Meridian Press).
Koh, Harold Hongju. 2001. "A Wake-Up Call on Human Rights." *Washington Post*, May 8, Sec. A.
Korgen, Jeffrey Odell. 2007. *Solidarity Will Transform the World: Stories of Hope from Catholic Relief Services* (Maryknoll, NY: Orbis Books).
Kyi, Aung San Suu. 1995. "Freedom, Development, and Human Worth." *Journal of Democracy*, Vol. 6, No. 2.
Langan, John. 1982. "A Revision of the Liberal Tradition." In J. Langan and Alfred Hennessey, eds., *Human Rights in the Americas: The Struggle for Consensus* (Washington, DC: Georgetown University Press).
Lo, Ping-cheung. 1988. "Are There Economic Rights?" *Thomist*, Vol. 52, No. 2.
Locke, John. 1980. *Second Treatise of Government*. Ed. C. B. Macpherson (Indianapolis, IN: Hackett).
Lohfink, Norbert F. 1995. *Option for the Poor: The Basic Principle of Liberation Theology in the Light of the Bible* (N. Richland Hills, TX: Bibal Press).
McKeon, Richard. 1949. *The Philosophical Bases and Material Circumstances of the Rights of Man*. Ed. UNESCO (New York: Columbia University Press).
Marcel, Gabriel. 1978. *Homo Viator: Introduction to a Metaphysic of Hope*. Trans. Emma Craufurd (Gloucester, MA: Peter Smith).
Maritain, Jacques. 1949. "Introduction." In UNESCO, ed., *Human Rights: Comments and Interpretations* (New York: Columbia University Press).
Maritain, Jacques. 1966. *The Person and the Common Good*. Trans. John J. Fitzgerald (South Bend, IN: University of Notre Dame Press).
Maritain, Jacques. 1971. *The Rights of Man and the Natural Law*. Trans. Doris C. Anson (New York: Gordian Press).
Marx, Karl. 1978. "Critique of the Gotha Programme." In Robert C. Tucker, ed., *The Marx–Engels Reader*. 2nd edn (New York: W.W. Norton).
Mich, Marvin Krier. 2001. *Catholic Social Teaching and Movements* (Mystic, CT: Twenty Third Publications).
Mich, Marvin Krier. 2009. "Living Wage Movement and Catholic Social Teaching." *Journal of Catholic Social Thought*, Vol. 6, No. 1.
Niebuhr, Reinhold. 1960. *Moral Man and Immoral Society* (New York: Charles Scribner's).
Novak, Michael. 1985. "Economic Rights: The Servile State." *Catholicism in Crisis*, Vol. 10.
Novak, Michael. 1987. "The Rights and Wrongs of the 'Economic Rights': A Debate Continued." *This World*, Vol. 17.
Oloka-Onyango, J. 1995. "Beyond the Rhetoric: Reinvigorating the Struggle for Economic and Social Rights in Africa." *California Western International Law Journal*, Vol. 26, No. 1.
Open Society Institute. 2005. *Burma: Country in Crisis*. At: http://www.soros.org/initiatives/bpsai/articles_publications.
Osiatyński, Wiktor. 2007. "Needs-Based Approach to Social and Economic Rights." In S. Hertel and L. Minkler, eds., *Economic Rights: Conceptual, Measurement, and Policy Issues* (Cambridge: Cambridge University Press).
Pogge, Thomas. 2008. *World Poverty and Human Rights*. 2nd edn. (Cambridge: Polity Press).
Putnam, Robert. 2000. *Bowling Alone* (New York: Simon & Schuster).
Richardson, Henry J. 2007. "Patrolling the Resource Transfer Frontier: Economic Rights and the South African Constitutional Court's Contributions to International Justice." *African Studies Quarterly*, Vol. 9, No. 4.
Roosevelt, Franklin. 1989. "Economic Bill of Rights." In Walter Lacquer and Barry Rubin, eds., *The Human Rights Reader* (New York: Meridian Press).
Sandel, Michael. 1998. *Liberalism and the Limits of Justice*, 2nd edn (Cambridge: Cambridge University Press).

Sen, Amartya Kumar. 1999. *Development as Freedom* (New York: Knopf).
Shue, Henry. 1996. *Basic Rights: Subsistence, Affluence, and U.S. Foreign Policy*, 2nd edn (Princeton, NJ: Princeton University Press).
Skogly, Sigrin I. and Mark Gibney. 2007. "Economic Rights and Extraterritorial Obligations." In S. Hertel and L. Minkler, eds., *Economic Rights: Conceptual, Measurement, and Policy Issues* (Cambridge: Cambridge University Press).
Steiner, Henry J. and Philip Alston. 2000. *International Human Rights in Context: Law, Politics, Morality*. 2nd edn (Oxford: Oxford University Press).
Taylor, Joshua Charles. 1976. *America as Art* (New York: Harper & Row).
Thurow, Lester. 1996. *The Future of Capitalism: How Today's Economic Forces Shape Tomorrow's Economic World* (New York: Penguin Books).
Tierney, Brian. 2002. "Natural Law and Natural Rights: Old Problems and Recent Approaches." *Review of Politics*, Vol. 64, No. 3, pp. 389–406.
Tuckness, Alex. 2008. "Punishment, Property and the Limits of Altriusm: Locke's International Asymmetry." *American Political Science Review*, Vol. 102, No. 4.
Twiss, Sumner B. 2003. "Confucian Values and Human Rights." In J. Runzo, N. Martin, and A. Sharma, eds., *Human Rights and Responsibilities in the World Religions* (Oxford: Oneworld).
United Nations Development Program (UNDP). 2000. *Human Development Report 2000: Human Rights and Human Development* (New York: Oxford University Press).
UNICEF. 2009. *State of the World's Children: Special Edition*. At: http://www.unicef.org/rightsite/sowc/fullreport.php.
United States Catholic Conference of Bishops (USCCB). 1992. "Economic Justice for All: A Catholic Framework for Economic Life." In David J. O'Brien and Thomas A. Shannon, eds., *Catholic Social Thought: The Documentary Heritage* (Maryknoll, NY: Orbis Books).
Vincent, R. J. 1986. *Human Rights and International Relations* (Cambridge: Cambridge University Press).
de Waal, F. B. M. 2006. *Primates and Philosophers: How Morality Evolved*. Edited and introduced by Stephen Macedo and Josiah Ober (Princeton, NJ: Princeton University Press).
Wilson, David Sloan. 2002. *Darwin's Cathedral: Evolution, Religion, and the Nature of Society* (Chicago, IL: University of Chicago Press).
Wolterstorff, Nicholas. 1983. *Until Justice and Peace Embrace: The Kuyper Lectures for 1981 Delivered at the Free University of Amsterdam* (Grand Rapids, MI: W.B. Eerdmans).
Yunus, Muhammad. 2007. *Creating a World without Poverty: Social Business and the Future of Capitalism* (New York: Public Affairs).

27

Language rights

The forgotten dimension of human rights

Stephen May

Introduction

Over the past sixty years, the notion that language rights might be accorded the status of a fundamental human right and be recognized as such by nation-states and supranational organizations has been both highly contentious and widely contested. The key point of contention has not been on the general right of an individual to continue to speak a language (any language) unmolested in the private or familial domain, since this broadly accords with the protection of individual human rights that has developed in the post-Second World War era and is thus relatively uncontroversial. Of course, this does not mean that states have always adhered to even this general human rights principle. Franco's Spain is a clear historical example where such individual language rights were foreclosed for all other than Castilian speakers. The ongoing state-sanctioned proscription of Kurdish in Turkey and Tibetan in China are two contemporary examples of states that continue to flout this human rights' principle. Rather, the controversy has focused on whether speakers of minority languages have the right to maintain and use that particular language in the public, or civic realm – most often in, but not necessarily limited to, education.

The sociolinguist Heinz Kloss (1977) has encapsulated this key distinction via his notions of "tolerance-oriented" and "promotion-oriented" language rights. For Kloss, tolerance-oriented language rights ensure the right to preserve one's language in the private, non-governmental sphere of national life. These rights may be narrowly or broadly defined. They include the right of individuals to use their first language at home and in public, freedom of assembly and organization, the right to establish private cultural, economic, and social institutions wherein the first language may be used, and the right to foster one's first language in private schools. The key principle of such rights is that the state does "not interfere with efforts on the parts of the minority to make use of [their language] in the private domain" (Kloss 1977, p. 2).

In contrast, promotion-oriented rights regulate the extent to which language rights are recognized within the *public* domain, or civic realm of the nation-state. As such, they involve "public authorities [in] trying to promote a minority [language] by having it used in public institutions – legislative, administrative and educational, including the public schools"

(Kloss 1977, p. 2). Again, such rights may be narrowly or widely applied. At their narrowest, promotion-oriented rights might simply involve the publishing of public documents in minority languages. At their broadest, promotion-oriented rights could involve recognition of a minority language in all formal domains within the nation-state, thus allowing the minority language group "to care for its internal affairs through its own public organs, which amounts to the [state] allowing self government for the minority group" (Kloss 1977, p. 24).

It is this latter notion of promotion-oriented language rights that is the focus of this chapter. In what follows, I want to explore why this notion has been, and continues to be, so controversial. In addressing this issue, I will explore relevant debates in two key, interdisciplinary, areas – political theory and international law.

Language rights and political theory

I begin with political theory because its central concern with the rights attributable to citizens in modern nation-states would appear to be directly pertinent to the question of language rights. And yet, what is most striking is the relative absence of *any* sustained argument in political theory about language rights, beyond those that involve access to the state's majority language(s). Minority language rights, particularly promotion-oriented rights for those groups whose first languages differ from the state language(s), are seldom discussed directly. The notable, and still singular, exception to this is Kymlicka and Patten's (2003) edited collection, although even here the majority of the contributors, with the exception of May, Rubio-Marin, Grin, and Réaume, remain largely skeptical and/or opposed to the recognition/implementation of such rights.

A key reason for this lack of direct discussion of promotion-oriented language rights for minority groups, and a related skepticism towards their recognition and implementation, lies in the normative understanding, post-Second World War, of human rights as primarily, even exclusively, individual rights. In contrast, the right to the maintenance of a minority language has generally been articulated in the political arena – both well before the Second World War and since (Thornberry 1991a, 1991b; de Varennes 1996; see also below) – on the basis that the particular language in question constitutes a collective or communally shared good of a particular linguistic community. After all, if a language is to continue to be spoken it requires, by definition, someone else to talk with. On this basis, when a language ceases to be spoken by a community of speakers, it has already effectively perished. Little wonder then, that such claims have received scant sympathy and made even less progress in a political environment largely opposed to group-based rights claims.

The difficulties facing arguments in favor of group-based language rights are most clearly illustrated by the normative ascendancy in political theory of orthodox liberalism, which addresses the person *only* as a political being with rights and duties attached to their status as *citizens*. Such a position does not countenance private identity, including a person's communal membership, as something warranting similar recognition. These latter dimensions are excluded from the public realm because their inevitable diversity would lead to the complicated business of the state mediating between different conceptions of "the good life" (Rawls 1971, 1985; Dworkin 1978). On this basis, personal *autonomy* – based on the political rights attributable to citizenship – always takes precedence over personal (and collective) *identity* and the widely differing ways of life that constitute the latter. In effect, personal and political participation in liberal democracies, as it has come to be constructed in orthodox liberalism, ends up denying group difference and posits all persons as interchangeable from a moral and political point of view (Young 1993).

Communitarian critiques of liberalism point out that this strict separation of citizenship and identity in the modern polity understates, and at times disavows, the significance of wider communal affiliations, including one's language(s), to the construction of individual identity. As Sandel (1982) stresses the communitarian view, for example, there is no such thing as the "unencumbered self" – we are all, to some extent, *situated* within wider communities that shape and influence who we are. Likewise, Charles Taylor argues that identity "is who we are, 'where we're coming from.' As such, it is the background against which our tastes and desires and opinions and aspirations make sense" (1994, pp. 33–34). These arguments also highlight the obvious point that certain goods, such as language, culture, and sovereignty, cannot be experienced alone; they are, by definition, communally shared goods. A failure to account for these communal goods, however, has led to a view of rights within liberal democracy that is inherently individualistic and that cannot appreciate the pursuit of such goods other than derivatively (Van Dyke 1977; Taylor 1994; Coulombe 1995).

In short, individualistic conceptions of the good life may preclude shared community values that are central to one's identity (Kymlicka 1989, 1995, 2001), including language. Conversely, as Habermas has put it, "a correctly understood theory of [citizenship] rights requires a politics of recognition that protects the individual in the life contexts in which his or her identity is formed" (1994, p. 113). As Habermas observes:

> A "liberal" version of the system of rights that fails to take this connection into account will necessarily misunderstand the universalism of basic rights as an abstract leveling of distinctions, a leveling of both cultural and social differences. To the contrary, these differences must be seen in increasingly context-sensitive ways if the system of rights is to be actualized democratically.
>
> *(Habermas 1994, p. 116)*

Criticism of the inherent individualism of orthodox liberalism is not limited to communitarian critiques, however; an important point, since communitarian critiques have themselves been extensively criticized for both essentializing and homogenizing group identities (see Mouffe 1993; Ellison 1997; Carter and Stokes 1998).

The most prominent political theorist to chart a middle ground here has been Will Kymlicka (1989, 1995, 2001, 2009), who has argued consistently from a liberal perspective that the attempts of theorists like Rawls (1971) and Dworkin (1978) to separate citizenship from communal identity actually still retain an implicit recognition of cultural membership as a primary good. Following from this, Kymlicka has proffered his notion of "group-differentiated rights" – which, he acknowledges, can also include language rights – as a means of bridging the orthodox liberal–communitarian divide. A key to Kymlicka's position is his rejection of the assumption that group-differentiated rights are "collective" rights that, *ipso facto*, stand in opposition to "individual" rights. Group-differentiated rights are not necessarily "collective" in the sense that they privilege the group over the individual – they can in fact be accorded to individual members of a group, or to the group as a whole, or to a federal state/province within which the group forms a majority. For example, the group-differentiated right of francophones in Canada to use French in federal courts is an *individual* right that may be exercised at any time. Alternatively, the right of the Québécois to preserve and promote their distinct culture in the province of Québec highlights how a minority group in a federal system may exercise group-differentiated rights in a territory where they form the majority.

In short, there is no simple relationship between group-differentiated rights accorded on the basis of cultural membership and their subsequent application. As Kymlicka concludes, "most such rights are not about the primacy of communities over individuals. Rather, they are based on the idea that justice between groups requires that the members of different groups be accorded different rights" (1995, p. 47).

A related argument developed by Kymlicka in support of this position, and one that can also be usefully extended to language rights, is his distinction between what he terms "internal restrictions" and "external protections" (1995, pp. 35–44). Internal restrictions involve *intra*-group relations where an ethnic or national minority group seeks to restrict the individual liberty of its members on the basis of maintaining group solidarity. These rights are often associated with theocratic and patriarchal communities and, when excessive, may be regarded as illiberal. In contrast, external protections relate to *inter*group relations where an ethnic or national minority group seeks to protect its distinct identity (including a linguistic one) by limiting the impact of the decisions of the larger society. External protections are thus intended to ensure that individual members are able to maintain a distinctive way of life *if they so choose* and are not prevented from doing so by the decisions of members outside of their community (see Kymlicka 1995, p. 204 n.11). This too has its dangers, although not in relation to individual oppression in this case but rather the possible unfairness that might result between groups. The ex-apartheid system in South Africa provides a clear example of the latter scenario. However, as Kymlicka argues, external protections need not result in injustice: "Granting special representation rights, land claims, *or language rights* to a minority need not, and often does not, put it in a position to dominate other groups. On the contrary ... such rights can be seen as putting the various groups on a more equal footing, by reducing the extent to which the smaller group is vulnerable to the larger" (1995, pp. 36–37; my emphasis).

Kymlicka argues that, on this basis, liberals can endorse certain external protections where they promote fairness between groups while still contesting internal restrictions which unduly limit the individual rights of members to question, revise, or reject traditional authorities and practices (see also Kymlicka 2001, 2009). In relation to the various group-differentiated rights outlined earlier, Kymlicka argues that "most demands for group-specific rights made by ethnic and national groups in Western democracies are for external protections" (1995, p. 42). Even where internal restrictions are also present, these are usually seen as unavoidable by-products of external protections rather than as desirable ends in themselves. Given this, it is possible to argue that minority language rights constitute a legitimate external protection (May 2008a) since, as Kymlicka concludes, "leaving one's culture, while possible, is best seen as renouncing something to which one is reasonably entitled" (1995, p. 90). Relatedly, he argues:

> The freedom which liberals demand for individuals is not primarily the freedom to go beyond one's language and history, but rather the freedom to move within one's societal culture, to distance oneself from particular cultural roles, to choose which features of the culture are most worth developing, and which are without value.
>
> *(Kymlicka 1995, pp. 90–91)*

Adopting this more inclusive position on language rights for minority groups within modern nation-states accords closely with an earlier (pre-Second World War) understanding of political theory, as illustrated by Hobhouse (1928), who believed that "[t]he smaller nationality does not merely want equal rights with others. *It stands out for a certain life of its own*" (146; my emphasis). Accepting such a position in relation to human rights might also pragmatically address and ameliorate the many political conflicts where language has been, or remains, a key factor. Ongoing conflicts include here the Baltics, Belgium, Canada, Sri Lanka, Tibet, and Turkey, to name but a few (see Horowitz 1985; Safran 1999; May 2008a). Language has also been a key feature in many historical contexts, such as Franco's Spain with respect to the suppression of all languages other than Castilian during his regime, and in many colonial and postcolonial contexts in relation to the consistent derogation and exclusion of the languages of indigenous peoples (see May 2008a, chap. 8, for further discussion). Yet, as Weinstein (1983) observes, while political theorists and other commentators have had much to say about "the language of politics," very few have had anything to say about "the politics of language" (for similar observations, see also Grillo 1989; Kymlicka 1995; Blommaert 1996; Holborow 1999).

Language rights and international law

These ambivalences towards any recognition of group-based rights in political theory, including language rights, are also closely reflected in the domain of international law, particularly as it has come to be defined by the (1948) United Nations Universal Declaration of Human Rights. As is widely known, all references to ethnic and national minorities were deleted from the final version of the Declaration. Article 2 of the Declaration states: "Everyone is entitled to all the rights and freedoms set forth in this Declaration, without distinction of any kind, such as race [*sic*], colour, sex, religion, political or other opinion, national or social origin, property, birth or other status." Consequently, minorities, as such, do not enjoy rights in the Declaration. Various attempts at including a recognition of minorities in the text were strongly opposed at the draft stages, the consensus being that "the best solution of the problems of minorities was to encourage respect for human rights" (see Thornberry 1991b, pp. 11–12). This was, in turn, the result of an emerging widespread conviction at that time that minority group rights were somehow incompatible with national and international peace and stability. As Claude has observed of these developments:

> The leading assumption has been that members of national minorities do not need, are not entitled to, or cannot be granted rights of special character. The doctrine of human rights has been put forward as a substitute for the concept of minority rights, with the strong implication that minorities whose members enjoy individual equality of treatment cannot legitimately demand facilities for the maintenance of their ethnic particularism.
>
> *(Claude 1955, p. 211)*

Language rights are especially prone here to ongoing associations with the (unnecessary) promotion of ethnic particularism at the perceived expense of wider social and political cohesion. As the prominent sociolinguist Joshua Fishman ably summarizes this view:

> Unlike "human rights" which strike Western and Westernized intellectuals as fostering wider participation in general societal benefits and interactions, "language rights" still are widely interpreted as "regressive" since they would, most probably, prolong the existence of ethnolinguistic differences. The value of such differences and the right to value such differences have not yet generally been recognized by the modern Western sense of justice.
>
> *(Fishman 1991, p. 72)*

And yet, what this view conveniently ignores is a long history in international law of just such recognition of language rights, usually within a wider approach of specific cultural protection for minority groups. In the nineteenth century, for example, treaties were often employed for the protection of minority groups, initially on the basis of religion and later on the grounds of nationality (Thornberry 1991a). These practices culminated in the general organization of the League of Nations, established in the wake of the First World War. The League endorsed a range of bilateral treaties aimed at securing special political status for minority groups within Europe in what came to be known as the Minority Protection scheme (de Varennes 1996, pp. 26–27). These minority treaties – overseen by its Permanent Court of International Justice (PCIJ) – were primarily concerned with the protection of "displaced" minorities in other nation-states, the result in turn of the reorganization of European state boundaries after the First World War (Wolfrum 1993; Packer 1999). They included two principal types of measures: (1) individuals belonging to linguistic minorities, among others, would be placed on an equal footing with other nationals of the state; (2) the means of preserving the national characteristics of minorities, including their language(s), would be ensured.

In the most prominent legal ruling on these provisions – the (1935) Advisory Opinion on Minority Rights in Albania – the PCIJ stated that these two requirements were inseparable. It concluded that "there would be no true equality between a majority and a minority if the latter were deprived of its own institutions and were consequently compelled to renounce that which constitutes the very essence of its being a minority" (see Thornberry 1991a, pp. 399–403). On the basis of this judgment, linguistic minorities were confirmed in their right to establish private schools and institutions, a *minimum* tolerance-oriented right. However, where numbers warranted, another key principle in international law with respect to minority protection, public funding of minority language-medium schools, was also advanced, a more promotion-oriented right. In respect of this, and other similar decisions, linguistic minorities were defined purely on a numerical basis – that is, as constituting less that 50 percent of the population. That said, freedom of choice as to membership in a minority also seemed to permeate the treaties, a point to which I will return.

As we have seen, however, subsequent developments in international law were rapidly to supersede these treaties and the principles upon which they were based. Minority language and education rights were largely subsumed within the broader definition of human rights adopted by the United Nations since the Second World War. Human rights were thought, in themselves, to provide sufficient protection for minorities. Accordingly, no additional rights were deemed necessary for the members of specific ethnic or national minorities. Nonetheless, even within this more generalist framework of rights, there have been echoes, albeit weak ones, of the principles of minority protection with respect to language and education. The most notable of these has perhaps been Article 27 of the (1966) International Covenant on Civil and Political Rights (ICCPR), which imposes a *negative* duty on nation-states with respect to the protection of the languages and cultures of minority groups:

> In those states in which ethnic, religious or linguistic minorities exist, persons belonging to such minorities *shall not be denied* the right, in community with the other members of their group, to enjoy their own culture, to profess and practise their own religion, or *to use their own language*. (my emphasis)

Before proceeding to examine Article 27 in relation to its specific implications for language and education, I should first point out the problematic nature of the initial clause "In those states in which ethnic, religious or linguistic minorities exist." Like many other examples of supranational and/or international law (see below), their successful enactment depends in the end on the compliance of nation-states. But even more than this, nation-states have to agree in the first instance that the legislation is applicable to them. Thus, the initial tentative formulation in Article 27 has allowed some nation-states in the past simply to deny that any such minorities exist within their jurisdiction. France is one such example where this has occurred, but there are many others, including Malaysia, Thailand, Japan, Burma, Bangladesh, and many Latin American nation-states (see de Varennes 1996; Thornberry 1991a, 1991b). This pattern of avoidance has been addressed more recently by new guidelines in the General Comment of the Covenant, adopted in April 1994, which stipulate that the state can no longer solely determine whether a minority is said to exist or not within its territory. However, the "problem of compliance" remains an ongoing one.

Be that as it may, I want to explore here what the actual obligations entailed in Article 27 might involve – in particular, to what extent these reflect a tolerance- or promotion-orientation to minority language rights. Likewise, I am interested in exploring further the degree to which these rights attach to groups and/or to individual members of these groups. Dealing with the latter first, the process of agreeing the particular form of wording in Article 27 provides us with some important clues. As Patrick Thornberry explains, from an initial proposal that "linguistic minorities shall not be denied the right ... to use their own language" the final wording of Article 27 was arrived at as follows:

> The [UN] Sub-Commission preferred that "persons belonging to minorities" should replace "minorities" because minorities were not subjects of law and "persons belonging to minorities" could easily be defined in legal terms. On the other hand, it was decided to include "in community with other members of their group" after "shall not be denied" in order to recognise group identity in some form.
>
> *(Thornberry 1991a, p. 149)*

The tension evident here between individual and group ascription is reflected in the question of who exactly can claim rights under Article 27. This question has been tackled on two fronts. First, following the precedent set by the earlier minority treaties, "minorities" in Article 27 have come to be defined strictly in numerical terms. A minority is defined as a group who share in common a culture, a religion and/or a language and who constitute less than 50 percent of a *state's* population. Thus a minority may be numerically dominant in a particular province (as, for example, are the Québécois in Québec and the Catalans in Catalonia) but may still be classified as a minority within the nation-state. Second, any person may claim to be a member of a linguistic minority group on the basis of self-ascription. However, to benefit from Article 27 they must also demonstrate that some *concrete* tie exists between themselves and the minority group. In relation to a minority language, this would require a real and objective tie with that language. It would not be sufficient, for example, to be a member of a minority ethnic group that is known to speak a particular language if the individual does not speak that language. Nor are particular languages, and the rights associated with them, tied to specific ethnic groups since more than one ethnic group may speak the same language. Determining that an individual belongs to a particular linguistic minority is thus not an issue of establishing some type of legal or political category, it is principally an objective determination based on some concrete link between an individual and a linguistic community (de Varennes 1996).

The definition of what constitutes a linguistic minority for the purposes of Article 27 is important for another reason. It determines whether the rights to minority language and education are tolerance- or promotion-oriented rights. Two opposing schools of thought are clearly evident here. Following the influential review of the scope of Article 27 by Capotorti (1979), some commentators, including myself (see Thornberry 1991a, 1991b; Tollefson 1991; Skutnabb-Kangas 1998, 2000; May 1999, 2004), have argued that while the words "shall not be denied" could be read as imposing no obligation on a state to take positive action to protect those rights, an alternative and equally compelling view "is that to recognize a right to use a minority language implies an obligation that the right be made effective" (Hastings 1988, p. 19). On this basis, it has been argued that Article 27 can be said to encompass a promotion-orientation to language rights, with attendant state support, rather than the more limited tolerance-oriented right that a solely negative duty implies.

This promotion-oriented perspective on language rights can also be linked directly to education. For example, Article 2(b) of the (1960) Convention Against Discrimination in Education specifically provides for the establishment or maintenance, for linguistic reasons, of separate schools, provided attendance is optional and the education is up to national standards. Moreover, Article 5 of this Convention recognizes the *essential* right of minorities to carry on their own educational activities and, in so doing, to use *or teach in* their own language. It subsequently qualifies this right, somewhat contradictorily, by making it conditional on a state's existing educational policies, and by ensuring it does not prejudice national sovereignty and the ability of minorities to participate in national life. However, the right to minority language education can nevertheless be established (Hastings 1988).

The question remains though – to what extent should minority language and education be funded by the state, if at all? Promotion-oriented rights suggest they should but also necessarily impose limits on who is eligible. Capotorti's (1979) review, for example, was predicated on the understanding that Article 27 applied solely to national minorities – immigrants, migrant workers, refugees, and non-citizens were excluded. In contrast, tolerance-oriented rights imply no such obligation on the state. While necessarily more limited, such rights may at least have the advantage of being able to apply to a wider range of minority groups.

And this brings us to the opposing school of thought on Article 27. Fernand de Varennes (1996) argues that Capotorti's interpretation of a more active obligation by the state on behalf of national minorities, and the subsequent commentary which has endorsed this position, does not reflect the actual intentions of Article 27. Indeed, Capotorti admitted as much at the time of his review. In effect, he set aside what the drafters originally meant because of his concern that a negative duty was not sufficient to protect minority language and education rights. In hindsight, de Varennes suggests that Capotorti's pessimism may have been misplaced. After all, the minorities' treaties had already established the long-standing principle of *private* language and education for minorities, without any hindrance from the state. Indeed, where sufficient numbers warranted, there was also a recognition that some form of state-funded minority education could be established. As de Varennes concludes:

> Article 27 thus appears to be part of a long-established and continuous legal continuum that the rights of linguistic minorities to use their language amongst themselves must necessarily include the right to establish, manage and operate their own educational institutions where their language is used as the medium of instruction to the extent deemed to be appropriate by the minority itself.
>
> *(de Varennes 1996, p. 158)*

The debates on the merits of Article 27 as an instrument for promotion-oriented rights remain ongoing. Be that as it may, we can at the very least conclude that Article 27 sanctions a clear baseline for tolerance-oriented language and education rights. This level of protection for minority language and education rights applies to all minority groups on the basis of the strict numerical interpretation of minorities within international law. Indeed, where a minority has sufficient numbers, there remains some additional scope for state-funded language education, although given the emphases of Article 27 this decision remains at the discretion of the nation-states themselves. Which brings us to the central problem of Article 27 and, indeed, most international law in this area, including more recent developments (see below). In short, much of the implementation of such measures is still dependent on what nation-states *deem appropriate*. The result is thus left to the vicissitudes of internal national politics where the provision of minority rights is viewed principally as one of political largesse rather than a fundamental question of human rights. The consequence of this in turn is, more often than not, the adoption of the bare minimum level of rights required (and sometimes not even that).

Notwithstanding this difficulty, a more promotion-oriented view of minority language and education rights does appear to be gaining some ground, at least for national minorities – that is, those minority groups with an established historical association with a particular territory. In this respect, there have been a number of recent instruments in international law that, at least in theory, allow for a more promotion-oriented perspective on language and education rights. These instruments are, in turn, a product of a more accommodative approach to minorities in the post-Cold War era (Preece 1998).

One of the most significant of these is the United Nations Declaration on the Rights of Persons Belonging to National or Ethnic or Religious Minorities, adopted in December 1992. This UN Declaration recognizes that the promotion and protection of the rights of persons belonging to minorities actually contributes to the political and social stability of the states in which they live (Preamble). Consequently, the Declaration reformulates Article 27 of the ICCPR in the following way:

> Persons belonging to national or ethnic, religious and linguistic minorities ... have the right to enjoy their own culture, to profess and practise their own religion, and to use their own language, in private *and in public*, freely and without interference or any form of discrimination.
>
> *(Article 2.1; my emphasis)*

We can thus see here that the phrase "shall not be denied" in Article 27 has been replaced by the more active "have the right." In addition, and significantly, the formulation recognizes that minority languages may be spoken in the public as well as the private domain, without fear of discrimination. That said, the 1992 UN Declaration, unlike the ICCPR, remains a recommendation and not a binding covenant – in the end, it is up to nation-states to decide if they wish to comply with its precepts. In a similar vein, the actual article which deals with minority language education (Article 4.3) qualifies the more general positive intent of Article 2.1 considerably: "States *should* take *appropriate* measures so that, *wherever possible*, persons belonging to minorities have *adequate* opportunities to learn their mother tongue *or* to have instruction in their mother tongue" (Skutnabb-Kangas 2000, pp. 533–535).

Other developments in pan-European law also reflect these competing tensions between, on the one hand, a growing accommodation of promotion-oriented minority language and education rights and, on the other, an ongoing reticence of nation-states to accept such a view. The (1992) European Charter for Regional or Minority Languages is one such example. It provides a sliding scale of educational provision for national and regional minority languages (but not immigrant languages) which ranges from a minimal entitlement for smaller groups – pre-school provision only, for example – through to more generous rights for larger minority groups, such as primary and secondary language education. Again, however, nation-states have discretion in what they provide, on the basis of both local considerations and the size of the group concerned.

European nation-states also retain considerable scope and flexibility over which articles of the Charter they actually choose to accept in the first place. In this respect, they are only required to accede to 35 out of 68 articles, although 3 of the 35 articles must refer to education.

The process here is twofold. A state must first sign the Charter, symbolically recognizing its commitment to the Charter's values and principles. Following this, states can ratify the treaty – formally recognizing, in this case, which particular regional or minority languages within the state are to be recognized under the treaty's auspices. On this basis, 33 European states have since signed the Charter, although only 24 of these have actually ratified it (Grin 2003; Nic Craith 2006). As of 2009, 9 European states had signed the Charter but not ratified it: Azerbaijan, Bosnia and Herzegovina, France, Iceland, Italy, Malta, Moldova, Russia, and the Former Yugoslav Republic of Macedonia.

A similar pattern can be detected in the (1994) Framework Convention for the Protection of National Minorities, which was adopted by the Council of Europe in November 1994 and finally came into force in February 1998. The Framework Convention allows for a wide range of tolerance-based rights towards national minorities, including language and education rights. It also asserts at a more general level that contributing states should "promote the conditions necessary for persons belonging to national minorities to maintain and develop their culture, and to preserve the essential elements of their identity, namely their religion, language, traditions and cultural heritage" (Article 2.1). That said, the specific provisions for language and education remain sufficiently qualified for most states to avoid them if they so choose (Thornberry 1997, Troebst 1998; Grin 2003; Nic Craith 2006; Trenz 2007).

Developments in international law then are at once both encouraging and disappointing. The principle of separate minority recognition in language and education is legally enshrined at least as a minimal tolerance-oriented right – that is, when restricted to the private domain. However more liberal interpretations of tolerance-oriented rights (involving some state support where numbers warrant), and certainly more promotion-oriented rights, remain largely dependent on the largesse of individual nation-states in their interpretation of international (and national) law with respect to minorities. As a result, there are as yet no watertight legal guarantees for the recognition and funding of minority language and education rights.

However, there *is* an increasing recognition within international and national law that significant minorities within the nation-state have a *reasonable* expectation to some form of state support (de Varennes 1996; Carens 2000). In other words, while it would be unreasonable for nation-states to be required to fund language and education services for all minorities, it is increasingly accepted that, where a language is spoken by a significant number within the nation-state, it would also be unreasonable not to provide some level of state services and activity in that language.

These developments have also been expedited by growing pressure from many minority groups themselves, who are increasingly unwilling to accept the ongoing marginalization of their languages and cultures as the price for their inclusion in the civic realm. The cumulative result has seen the gradual expansion of separate language and education entitlements within modern nation-states. This is particularly so for national minority groups and is illustrated clearly by the successful re-instantiation in recent times of previously marginalized national minority languages in Wales (May 2000; Mann 2007; Williams 2007), Catalonia (Guibernau 1997; Costa 2003; Colino 2009), Québec (Keating 1996; Oakes 2004; Oakes and Warren 2007), and New Zealand (May 2004, 2008a, ch. 8).

Conclusion

The underlying premise of this chapter is that a group-differentiated approach to citizenship can significantly enhance the possibilities and prospects of language rights as a key human right.

This is particularly so for promotion-oriented rights, which allow for the use of minority languages in the public or civic realm, including within education.

However, the validity of promotion-oriented rights, as well as the basis on which they might be granted, remains controversial and contested. Ongoing opposition to promotion-oriented language rights in a range of national contexts is often couched in terms of individual rights – most usually, the right of majority language speakers to remain monolingual (May 2000, 2008a). Opposition is also regularly framed within a discourse of "illiberality" (Barry 2000) – that the establishment of promotion-oriented rights is somehow an illiberal imposition on majority language speakers. But this begs the key question: if majority language speakers can regard the formal recognition of their language, within their own historic territory, as an inalienable right (with no question of illiberality), why cannot national minority speakers as well?

A third oppositional theme relates to the perceived "fragmentation" of nation-states – that recognition of separate language and educational entitlements will inevitably undermine social cohesion and political stability (Barry 2000; Huntingdon 2005). However, contra to these claims, it can be argued that it is the *denial* of language rights rather than their *recognition* that is *most* likely to precipitate social and political instability, as seen in the genesis of numerous political conflicts in the modern age. As Fernand de Varennes observes, under these circumstances, "any policy favouring a single language to the exclusion of all others can be extremely risky ... because it is then a factor promoting division rather than unification. Instead of integration, an ill-advised and inappropriate state language policy may have the opposite effect and cause a levée de bouclier" (de Varennes 1996, p. 91).

A final criticism comes from another direction – namely, that the provision of promotion-oriented language rights in international law and in those regions or states where promotion-oriented language rights are recognized remains, as we have seen, largely limited to national minority group members. There is still little meaningful language rights provision for other ethnic (immigrant) minority groups. Indeed, given the active retrenchment, post-9/11, of the wider politics of multiculturalism, particularly in Europe (Modood 2007; May 2008b), even tolerance-oriented language rights for these latter groups are now under threat. This constitutes a considerable and ongoing human rights challenge in the current social and political climate.

And this returns us to a key theme that has permeated this chapter – that the provision, and/or extension, of language rights within (and across) nation-states remains fragile and easily undone. In an era where the notion of individual human rights so dominates, developing and implementing a group-differentiated understanding of language rights for minority groups is clearly neither easy nor fashionable. Ongoing opposition to such rights suggests as much. But it is crucial precisely because it is the key mechanism by which we can (and should) rethink social and political organization, at supranational, nation-state, and sub-state levels, in more linguistically plural, egalitarian, and inclusive ways.

References

Barry, B. 2000. *Culture and Equality: An Egalitarian Critique of Multiculturalism* (Cambridge, MA: Harvard University Press).

Blommaert, J. 1996. "Language and Nationalism: Comparing Flanders and Tanzania." *Nations and Nationalism*, Vol. 2, pp. 235–256.

Capotorti, F. 1979. *Study on the Rights of Persons Belonging to Ethnic, Religious and Linguistic Minorities* (New York: United Nations).

Carens, J. 2000. *Culture, Citizenship and Community: A Contextual Exploration of Justice as Evenhandedness* (Oxford: Oxford University Press).

Carter, A. and G. Stokes. 1998. *Liberal Democracy and Its Critics* (Cambridge: Polity Press).

Claude, I. 1955. *National Minorities: An International Problem* (Cambridge, MA: Harvard University Press).
Colino, C. 2009. "Constitutional Change Without Constitutional Reform: Spanish Federalism and the Revision of Catalonia's Statute of Autonomy." *Publius: The Journal of Federalism*, Vol. 39, pp. 262–288.
Costa, J. 2003. "Catalan Linguistic Policy: Liberal or Illiberal?" *Nations and Nationalism*, Vol. 9, pp. 413–432.
Coulombe, P. 1995. *Language Rights in French Canada* (New York: Peter Lang).
de Varennes, F. 1996. *Language, Minorities and Human Rights* (The Hague: Kluwer Law International).
Dworkin, R. 1978. "Liberalism," pp. 113–143 in S. Hampshire, ed., *Public and Private Morality* (Cambridge: Cambridge University Press).
Ellison, N. 1997. "Towards a New Social Politics: Citizenship and Reflexivity in Late Modernity." *Sociology*, Vol. 31, pp. 697–717.
Fishman, J. 1991. *Reversing Language Shift: Theoretical and Empirical Foundations of Assistance to Threatened Languages* (Clevedon, UK: Multilingual Matters).
Grillo, R. 1989. *Dominant Languages: Language and Hierarchy in Britain and France* (Cambridge: Cambridge University Press).
Grin, F. 2003. *Language Policy Evaluation and the European Charter for Regional or Minority Languages* (London: Palgrave-Macmillan).
Guibernau, M. 1997. "Images of Catalonia." *Nations and Nationalism*, Vol. 3, pp. 89–111.
Habermas, J. 1994. "Struggles for Recognition in the Democratic Constitutional State," pp. 107–148 in A. Gutmann, ed., *Multiculturalism: Examining the Politics of Recognition* (Princeton, NJ: Princeton University Press).
Hastings, W. 1988. *The Right to an Education in Māori: The Case from International Law* (Wellington, NZ: Victoria University Press).
Hobhouse, L. 1928. *Social Evolution and Political Theory* (New York: Columbia University Press).
Holborow, M. 1999. *The Politics of English: A Marxist View of Language* (London: Sage).
Horowitz, D. 1985. *Ethnic Groups in Conflict* (Berkeley: University of California Press).
Huntingdon, S. 2005. *Who Are We? America's Great Debate* (New York: Free Press).
Keating, M. 1996. *Nations Against the State: The New Politics of Nationalism in Québec, Catalonia and Scotland* (London: Macmillan).
Kloss, H. 1977. *The American Bilingual Tradition* (Rowley, MA: Newbury House).
Kymlicka, W. 1989. *Liberalism, Community and Culture* (Oxford: Clarendon Press).
Kymlicka, W. 1995. *Multicultural Citizenship: A Liberal Theory of Minority Rights* (Oxford: Clarendon Press).
Kymlicka, W. 2001. *Politics in the Vernacular: Nationalism, Multiculturalism, and Citizenship* (Oxford: Oxford University Press).
Kymlicka, W. 2009. *Multicultural Odysseys: Navigating the New International Politics of Diversity* (Oxford: Oxford University Press).
Kymlicka, W. and A. Patten, eds. 2003. *Language Rights and Political Theory* (Oxford: Oxford University Press).
Mann, R. 2007. "Negotiating the Politics of Language: Language Learning and Civic Identity in Wales." *Ethnicities*, Vol. 7, No. 2, pp. 208–224.
May, S. 1999. *Indigenous Community-Based Education* (Clevedon, UK: Multilingual Matters).
May, S. 2000. "Accommodating and Resisting Minority Language Policy: The Case of Wales." *International Journal of Bilingual Education and Bilingualism*, Vol. 3, No. 2, pp. 101–128.
May, S. 2004. "Medium of Instruction Policy in New Zealand," pp. 21–41 in J. Tollefson and A. Tsui, eds., *Medium of Instruction Policies: Which Agenda? Whose Agenda?* (Mahwah, NJ: Lawrence Erlbaum).
May, S. 2008a. *Language and Minority Rights: Ethnicity, Nationalism and the Politics of Language* (New York: Routledge).
May, S. 2008b. "Critical Multiculturalism and Education," pp. 33–48 in *Routledge International Companion to Multicultural Education* (New York: Routledge).
Modood, T. 2007. *Multiculturalism: A Civic Idea* (Cambridge: Polity Press).
Mouffe, C. 1993. *The Return of the Political* (London: Verso).
Nic Craith, M. 2006. *Europe and the Politics of Language: Citizens, Migrants, and Outsiders* (London: Palgrave-Macmillan).
Oakes, L. 2004. "French: A Language for Everyone in Québec?" *Nations and Nationalism*, Vol. 10, No. 4, pp. 539–558.
Oakes, L. and J. Warren. 2007. *Language, Citizenship and Identity in Quebec* (Basingstoke, UK: Palgrave-Macmillan).

Packer, J. 1999. "Problems in Defining Minorities," pp. 223–273 in D. Fottrell and B. Bowring, eds., *Minority and Group Rights in the New Millennium* (The Hague: Kluwer Law International).

Preece, J. 1998. *National Minorities and the European Nation-States System* (Oxford: Clarendon Press).

Rawls, J. 1971. *A Theory of Justice* (Oxford: Oxford University Press).

Rawls, J. 1985. "Justice as Fairness: Political Not Metaphysical." *Philosophy and Public Affairs*, Vol. 14, pp. 223–251.

Réaume, D. 1999. "Official Language Rights: Intrinsic Value and the Protection of Difference," pp. 245–72 in W. Kymlicka and W. Norman, *Citizenship in Diverse Societies* (Oxford: Oxford University Press).

Safran, W. 1999. "Nationalism," pp. 77–93 in J. Fishman, ed., *Handbook of Language and Ethnic Identity* (Oxford: Oxford University Press).

Sandel, M. 1982. *Liberalism and the Limits of Justice* (Cambridge: Cambridge University Press).

Skutnabb-Kangas, T. 1998. "Human Rights and Language Wrongs – A Future for Diversity?" *Language Sciences*, Vol. 20, pp. 5–27.

Skutnabb-Kangas, T. 2000. *Linguistic Genocide in Education – Or Worldwide Diversity and Human Rights?* (Mahwah, NJ: Lawrence Erlbaum).

Taylor, C. 1994. "The Politics of Recognition," pp. 25–73 in A. Gutmann, ed., *Multiculturalism: Examining the Politics of Recognition* (Princeton, NJ: Princeton University Press).

Thornberry, P. 1991a. *International Law and the Rights of Minorities* (Oxford: Clarendon Press).

Thornberry, P. 1991b. *Minorities and Human Rights Law* (London: Minority Rights Group).

Thornberry, P. 1997. "Minority Rights." pp. 307–390 in *Collected Courses of the Academy of European Law*. Vol. VI, Book 2 (The Hague: Kluwer Law International).

Tollefson, J. 1991. *Planning Language, Planning Inequality: Language Policy in the Community* (London: Longman).

Trenz, H. 2007. "Reconciling Diversity and Unity: Language Minorities and European Integration." *Ethnicities*, Vol. 7, No. 2, pp. 157–185.

Troebst, S. 1998. *The Council of Europe's Framework Convention for the Protection of National Minorities Revisited* (Flensburg, Germany: European Centre for Minority Issues).

Van Dyke, V. 1977. "The Individual, the State, and Ethnic Communities in Political Theory." *World Politics*, Vol. 29, pp. 343–369.

Weinstein, B. 1983. *The Civic Tongue: Political Consequences of Language Choices* (New York: Longman).

Williams, C. 2007. *Language and Governance* (Cardiff: University of Wales Press).

Wolfrum, R. 1993. "The Emergence of 'New Minorities' as a Result of Migration," pp. 153–166 in C. Brölmann, R. Lefeber, and M. Zieck, eds., *Peoples and Minorities in International Law* (Dordrecht, Netherlands: Martinus Nijhoff).

Young, I. 1993. "Together in Difference: Transforming the Logic of Group Political Conflict." pp. 121–150 in J. Squires, ed., *Principled Positions: Postmodernism and the Rediscovery of Value* (London: Lawrence & Wishart).

28

Children's rights

David Archard

United Nations Convention on the Rights of the Child

There has been extensive philosophical discussion, especially in recent years, of the idea of children's rights. Little if any of this work, however, makes reference to what must be seen as the inescapable starting point for any such discussion, namely the United Nations Convention on the Rights of the Child (UNCRC 1989). The importance of this Convention is to be explained as follows.

First, the CRC is the most widely ratified convention. Nearly two hundred states have ratified it, and only two – the United States of America and Somalia – have failed to do so. The Convention has in consequence a status not possessed by any other international legal instrument.

Second, the CRC has, in the twenty years since it was adopted by so many states, exercised a deep and pervasive influence on the way in which we think about the status of children. Those who frame laws, design institutions, and seek to mold practices that have anything to do with the interests and well-being of children cannot avoid making reference to what the CRC insists must be done.

Third, this influence is given particular bite by the following considerations. The CRC imposes clear and specific obligations upon state parties. A familiar criticism of universal rights is that, in the absence of institutional provision for their promotion and protection, they may amount to little more than statements of admirable aspirations. The CRC leaves parties to its ratification in little doubt as to what they must do. In some cases the imperative to give effect to the Convention has led states – the Netherlands and Norway are two examples – to incorporate it into domestic law.

More particularly, the Convention requires states to submit regular reports to the Committee on the Rights of the Child – which was set up by the Convention – on the measures they have adopted which give effect to the rights laid out in the Convention. The CRC has thus instituted institutional measures by which states make themselves accountable for their successes and failures judged by its standards.

Fourth, it is at least arguable that this practical influence has been good for children. Since its ratification the situation of children has, on the whole and in a number of critical respects, improved. Child mortality has decreased; children's educational opportunities have expanded and improved; there has been a reduction in the numbers of child soldiers and in the extent of child labor; measures to tackle child trafficking and exploitation have been developed; the criminalization of corporal punishment, as for instance in Nordic states, can be attributed to the influence on domestic law of the Convention; and, finally, there have been many initiatives, sponsored by the United Nations, to give children a voice and to increase their influence on the formation of policy, such as Children's Parliaments. All of these changes can be attributed in significant part to the Convention and its ratification.

Fifth, the CRC gets it generally right about what children are entitled to, and about the areas in which children's interests ought to be protected and promoted. The extent of its ratification reflects broad international agreement about the rights that children possess. The CRC codifies in the form of an extensive set of entitlements what most individuals everywhere believe to be due to children.

Sixth, the CRC is a document of global import. It lays out the rights possessed by all children wherever they happen to live. It has been ratified by all but two states. Moreover, although children face many of the same problems whatever their nationality, a significant number face problems that require addressing on a global or transnational level: children are trafficked for the ends of sexual exploitation; children can be stateless refugees; children may be sent abroad to be married or to be genitally mutilated.

The importance of the Convention should give anyone concerned with the welfare and interests of children strong reasons both to endorse it and to construct any argument for improving the condition of children within its terms. Someone, in consequence, might well be committed to supporting the CRC even though he holds that it is a fundamental mistake to believe either that children do have rights or that they have just those rights they are given in the Convention.

This is an instance of a familiar strategy that might be termed the "political" defense of a law or policy. Sometimes bad or imperfect laws ought to be supported because they are, for all of that, better than any other realistically available alternative. A political defense of a law starts from an appraisal of what needs to be achieved but is realistic about what can be achieved in the particular circumstances, ones that may well be less than ideal. An existing law, judged defective by the standards of an ideal law, may nevertheless be the best we can hope for in the current situation, and thus the optimal means of realizing those outcomes – or what is closest to those outcomes – which the ideal law aims to secure.

In short, philosophical skeptics about the idea of children's rights who nevertheless believe that the improvement of children's lives is a pressing practical imperative have a political reason to support the CRC. At the very least they have good reason to start any discussion of children's rights by making reference to the Convention, both as a putative statement of what rights children have and also as an instrument whereby the lives of children may be improved.

Philosophical skepticism about children's rights

Philosophical skepticism about children's rights may concede the existence of the CRC yet exploit a familiar distinction between moral and legal rights. Skeptics will point out that there are plentiful examples of people having rights in law that they should not morally have, as well as examples of people having moral rights that they lacked in law. Women in nineteenth-century England did not have the right in law to vote and to dispose of their own property. Men in nineteenth-century England had a right, or at least a legal permission, to rape their wives, since rape within marriage was not a criminal offense. Women ought morally to have the same rights as men. The fact that the law in nineteenth-century England gave men rights it did not give to women has little or no moral weight. It does not settle the moral question of whether women and men have the same rights.

So the fact that the CRC gives children rights still leaves it open as to whether children are indeed morally justified in having them. Should children have the rights given to them by the CRC? There are two kinds of philosophical skepticism about the rights that are given to children by the CRC. There is a view that children do have rights but not the rights that the CRC gives them. On this view the CRC gets it wrong not about the rights of children in general but about the particular rights which the Convention lists. One might, for instance, think that although children should have some rights, they should not be given a right "to freedom of association and to freedom of peaceful assembly."

According to the more general critical thesis children should not have any of the rights listed in the CRC because children are not morally entitled to any rights. This position has been defended by a number of philosophers. Before considering this view it is worth indicating the full range of positions it is possible to hold in respect of children's rights. There is the "liberationist" view that children should have all the rights that adults have inasmuch as an oppressive and mistaken ideology of "childishness" underpins the contrived separation of childhood incapacity from adult competence (Farson 1974; Holt 1974; Cohen 1980; discussed in Archard 2004, ch. 5). There is a view that children have some but not all of those rights that adults have. A further version of this view holds that children may have at least some rights that adults do not. Useful here is Joel Feinberg's distinction between A-rights, those that only adults possess, C-rights, those that only children possess, and A–C rights, those possessed by both adults and children (Feinberg 1980). A possible, if controversial, example of a C-right is the right of every child to be loved (Liao 2000). Finally there is the view that some children lack rights but that other children might be argued to have them. It is thus plausible to think both that infants clearly lack rights and that older children, young persons, do not (Griffin 2004).

The liberationist case represents the most explicit defense of the view that children are unjustly denied the rights that all other humans possess. Liberationists appealed to the intuitively attractive idea that children are a group unjustly disadvantaged by the denial of their proper status, just as in response to their oppression women and ethnic minorities had also previously had to lay claim to *their* rights. That view gained ground in the 1960s and the 1970s with the consequence that many now do find uncontroversial the idea that children have rights. This broad consensus – if not endorsed by all philosophers – has in turn been responsible for a wealth of published material as well as activism in respect of children's rights within the areas of education, citizenship, social and welfare services, and criminal justice (Franklin 2002).

The 1960s and the 1970s were also a time in which the legal status of the child was radically reassessed. The landmark America Supreme Court case of *In re Gault* (1967) formally recognized the equal entitlement of juveniles and adults to due process rights. In England the rise of children's rights in the 1980s was an observable legal phenomenon, and it coincided with a reassessment of the claims parents had over their children. It was not merely that parents could no longer be viewed as having some sort of ownership claim over their offspring. There was also recognition of what Lord Scarman, in the celebrated English law case *Gillick* (1986), called "the underlying principle of the law," namely that "parental right yields to the child's right to make his own decisions" when the child can be deemed to have such a right (*Gillick* [1986], p. 186). Thus in English law the "emergence of children's rights" was almost exactly contemporaneous with the "eclipse of parental rights" (Eekelaar 1986a, 1986b).

It is against that background that philosophical skepticism about children's rights can be better appreciated. Such skepticism may be rationally motivated either by considerations about children and what is owed to them (O'Neill 1988; Purdy 1992) or by the worry that rights should not apply in the context of adult–child relations. The family, according to this second worry, is not a proper domain of right-regulated activity (Schrag 1980; Schoeman 1980). According to such an account, familial relationships, if defined by rights and obligations, would lack, or would come to lack, the natural and spontaneous mutual affection that ought to characterize them.

The first source of skepticism about children's rights appeals to three sorts of reason, which may or may not be combined. First, in order to have rights, those who hold them must be possessed of certain basic qualifying capacities. These capacities are ones whose possession makes sense of the idea of there being a point to having rights or to exercising them. For instance, imagine you think that the ultimate point of human rights – what in the last analysis justifies them – is that they protect the exercise by human beings of their autonomy. Then it makes sense to believe that only those who have autonomy, who can exercise autonomous choices, should have rights. Children, certainly very young children, lack autonomy. They are deficient in certain cognitive abilities – those of making sense of themselves and of the world around them – and certain volitional capacities – those of independent decision-making – which are the foundation of autonomy. Adults have these capacities; children do not.

There is a second reason for denying rights to children, namely that doing so is damaging to the point and value of according rights. Rights are a very important way of marking out those who have them as entitled to certain kinds of treatment – treatment moreover that is fitting or appropriate to their moral status. If, so the argument continues, we extend the scope of rights – who have them and what rights they have – beyond their proper scope, then we devalue rights. In a much-quoted but very useful metaphor, "rights-inflation" (Sumner 1987) reduces the currency of rights. Rights do not and cannot amount to much when, for instance, they are the sorts of thing that certain sorts of things – such as trees and fleas – have; or when the human rights of human beings include an entitlement to paid holidays.

It is of course possible to ensure that children receive the protection that befits their nature without giving them rights and without thereby weakening the considerable and valuable power that the language of rights otherwise has.

Third, thinking of children as having rights does *them* no favors. In fact, so the argument goes, it is harmful to the interests of children that they should be given rights. For the exercise of rights implies the exercise of fundamental choices about matters of central importance to the rightsholder. Children are not equipped to make these choices, and, if granted the freedom to make them, they will make them in ways that are damaging to their own interests. Indeed they will harm not only their present selves but also their future selves. In other words, it is adults who are harmed by allowing their childhood selves to choose how to lead their lives. Imagine, for instance, that children were permitted a right to decide whether or not to be educated. Then children might choose not to go to school. This is bad for children but it is also – and probably to a great degree – bad for their later selves. Adults who have not had an education will lead worse lives than those who have had an education.

This basic thought is given admirable expression by the seventeenth-century English philosopher John Locke. Locke thought that human beings were born into a condition in which they were not yet able to exercise their reason and behave as that reason instructed them, namely as accountable moral agents. Locke thought that they would – and with the appropriate guidance from adults – eventually acquire this ability: "*Children*, I confess are not born in this full state of *Equality*, though they are born to it" (Locke 1698, II, chapter vi, § 55). To get to that state of reason that marks out human beings as different from, and above, animals (mere "brutes") required, Locke thought, a process of education and tutelage at the hands of adults. Children, left to their own devices, would fail to realize their potential as rational creatures.

They would end up no better off than animals: "To turn him loose to an unrestrain'd Liberty, before he has Reason, to guide him, is not the allowing him the priviledge of his Nature, to be free; but to thrust him out amongst Brutes, and abandon him to a state as wretched, and as much beneath that of a Man, as theirs" (Locke 1698, II, chapter vi, § 63).

Those who think that according rights to children does them no favors do not, of course, believe that we should not do everything that we can to safeguard their interests. There are ways we should behave toward children. We, as adults, owe duties to children that command us both to protect and to support children and to desist from harming or abusing them. However, we can be under duties to those who, nevertheless, do not have rights that can be claimed against us. Those who deny that animals have rights may nevertheless believe – and indeed one would hope that they do believe – that humans have duties towards animals: not to treat them cruelly for instance.

A typology of children's rights: the three Ps

It is standard to note that the CRC gives children different types of rights. According to a familiar and much cited division the typology is one of the three Ps: protection, provision, and participation rights (e.g., Lansdown 1994, p. 36). Provision rights ensure that children are supplied with what are viewed as important goods or benefits. For example there is "the right of the child to the enjoyment of the highest attainable standard of health and to facilities for the treatment of illness and rehabilitation of health" (Article 24); "the right of every child to a standard of living adequate for the child's physical, mental, spiritual, moral and social development" (Article 27); and "the right of the child to education" (Article 28).

Protection rights offer children safeguards against different kinds of unacceptable treatment: abuse, cruelty, neglect, exploitation. For example there is the right of the child to be protected "from all forms of physical or mental violence, injury or abuse, neglect or negligent treatment, maltreatment or exploitation, including sexual abuse, while in the care of parent(s), legal guardian(s) or any other person who has the care of the child" (Article 19); to be protected "from all forms of sexual exploitation and sexual abuse" (Article 34); and "to be protected from economic exploitation and from performing any work that is likely to be hazardous or to interfere with the child's education, or to be harmful to the child's health or physical, mental, spiritual, moral or social development" (Article 32).

Participation rights entitle children to play their part as independent agents in a range of important activities. For example, there are the rights to "freedom of expression" (Article 13); to "freedom of thought, conscience and religion" (Article 14); and "to freedom of association and to freedom of peaceful assembly" (Article 15).

In order to appreciate how these different types of rights for children are ultimately justified it helps to compare the case of children with that of adults. Adults can be given provision rights; they are also given participation rights. It is in respect of protection rights that the differences with children emerge. In the first place adults do of course have rights not be harmed. They have a right against physical assault, for instance. But adults, unlike children, have the fundamental power to waive such rights. An adult can consent to be treated in ways that, absent such consent, would count as assault. So adults can engage in physically harmful sporting events; they can be tattooed; they can voluntarily engage in sado-masochistic activities. Children, by contrast, need to be protected against harmful treatment *whatever* they might choose. Children cannot choose to be harmed.

In the second place some of the forms of ill-treatment against which the CRC protects children can only be understood by making reference to the peculiar vulnerabilities of childhood.

Children can be abused and neglected because they are dependent upon the care of adults. Children as a group, and by comparison with adults, are more vulnerable to the kinds of treatment against which they need to be protected and are less able to defend themselves against ill-use. Thus the Preamble to the CRC repeats the statement first made in the Preamble to the earlier Declaration of the Rights of the Child (1959) that "the child, by reason of his physical and mental immaturity, needs special safeguards and care, including appropriate legal protection, before as well as after birth."

In other words, and in brief, the existence of protection rights for children rests upon and is justified by a fundamental paternalism. This paternalistic attitude stands in direct and marked contrast with the justification of participation rights for children, which views them as agents capable of expressing their views, professing religious beliefs, and associating with others. Indeed participation rights are sometimes characterized as "empowerment" rights (LeBlanc 1995, ch. 6), which view those who hold and exercise them as "active, creative beings in charge of, or at least struggling to shape, their lives ... [who] must be empowered to act and to lead autonomous lives" (Donnelly and Howard 1988, pp. 234–235).

The central tension

This contrast between participation rights and protection rights for children finds notable and general expression between the two key rights of the CRC – those enshrined in Articles 3 and 12. These articles state, respectively, that in all matters affecting the child "the best interests of the child shall be a primary consideration" and that "the child who is capable of forming his or her own views" has "the right to express those views freely in all matters affecting the child, the views of the child being given due weight in accordance with the age and maturity of the child." Notably perhaps Article 3 does not use the word "right." The tension between a best interest principle and a child's right to express her own views on matters affecting her interests is not simply an abstract or theoretical conflict of attitudes toward the child. It is a tension that yields conflicting practical recommendations in those situations where we must decide what to do in respect of a child, and where what the child wants is at odds with what adults who must make that decision judge is best.

There are various ways to resolve the tension between protectionism and empowerment. One could discount the views of the child when these are at odds with the judgment of best interests. Or, on a modified version of this simple view, one might see the child's best interests as "paramount" and thus as trumping the child's views whenever there is disagreement between what the child wants and what adults think is best. On the modified account the child's views have *some* weight. It is not that when they conflict with best interest they have no weight and are simply discounted. The child's view, however, is never weighty enough to outweigh a judgment of best interest. It is always and in every circumstance outweighed by the determination of best interest. However, both views – the simple and the modified – appear to deny that Article 12 has any independent status. Nothing in the framing of the CRC suggests that this article should be regarded, in relation to the other articles, as of no or lesser importance. Indeed Article 2 of the CRC insists that "States Parties shall respect and ensure the rights set forth in the present Convention to each child without discrimination of any kind."

A second way to resolve the conflict between hearing the views of the child and a best interest principle is to see the views of the child as being important only *instrumentally* as a means of determining what is best for the child. Hearing what a child thinks or wants helps adults make a more informed judgment of the best outcome, all things considered. There are two ways in which this happens.

First, knowing what a child thinks improves our initial judgment of what is best for the child. We can be clearer about how things are for the child as matters currently stand; we gain insight into what makes her life go better or worse. The child's views function to inform an overall diagnosis of the child's condition. Second, knowing what a child wants to happen allows us to estimate the costs of implementing our judgment when this goes against the child's wishes. The child will resist or she will not cooperate; she will resent our acting as we do.

The problem with this instrumental approach to the hearing of a child's views is the way in which it arguably misrepresents the point of doing so. Imagine two possibilities. The first is the case in which we could work out what was best for the child without any need to hear the child's views. Hearing the child would have no instrumental value for us. The second is the case of children we can know in advance to be insufficiently mature for their views to count. Once again, hearing the child would carry little or no weight. In both cases there would be no imperative to hear the child.

Article 12 insists upon the right of the child to be heard even when there is apparently no point in doing so. For instance, in Norway there is a legal obligation upon adults to hear the views of any child over the age of 7. At this age a child is capable of forming and expressing a view but also almost certainly not mature enough to make her own decisions. Yet the child is seen, consistently with Article 12, as having a right to express her views.

The different understandings of the right enshrined in this article come down to a contrast between two views of the point of hearing the child. According to one, the child's voice is not the authoritative one of an adult and has consultative value. An adult's views as to what is in his or her interests are, subject to standard constraints, properly determinative of what should happen. A child's views are not determinative in this manner but can, and should, guide adults in their determination of what to do (Brighouse 2003). The contrasting view is that children have a fundamental right to be heard. It is the right of those who have their own views, and who are capable of forming them, to express those views, and thus to play some role in the deliberative procedures that determine outcomes affecting their interests. A child is a source of views in her own right, and this should be recognized, even if the content of those views is not determinative of the outcome and even if the content of those views is not given a great deal of weight (Archard and Skivenes 2009).

The moral and political status of the child

At the end of the day, disputes about children's rights come down to disagreements about the child's moral and political status. Within the currently dominant paradigm of English-speaking political philosophy, children have been accorded little or no status, and their moral claims have largely been overlooked or discounted. For instance, those individuals who contract the terms of social justice in John Rawls's famous "original position" are defined as mature and rational adults who have capacities that children lack (Rawls 1971). That neglect of children is changing (Archard and Macleod 2004).

However there are clearly unresolved ambiguities in the way that the status of the child is conceived. The most fundamental ambiguity is that encapsulated in a dyad that has been especially influential in recent sociology of childhood studies: "being" versus "becoming" (Qvortrup 1991). On one hand the child is seen as "not-yet" an adult, and is defined, privatively, in terms of what it is not. The child essentially lacks those properties that mark out the mature adult. On the other the child is seen as possessed of a nature which is different from that of the adult but not, for all of that, to be thought of as unworthy of consideration. Jean-Jacques Rousseau is enormously influential in this context with his insistence that it is wrong to "seek the man in the child without thinking of what is before being a man." "Childhood," he write, "has its (place) in the order of human life. The man must be considered in the man, and the child in the child" (Rousseau 1762 [1979], pp. 34 and 80).

Cutting across this fundamental ambiguity is a further dispute about whether or not the very idea of childhood as a distinct state or stage of human life is an invention or construction of modernity. Hugely influential in this regard has been the work of Philippe Ariès (1960).

Resolving the question of the moral and political status of children is fundamental if the whole issue of children's rights is properly to be addressed. Moreover resolving it is also important for the insights gained into the moral and political status of adults. The standard contemporary presumption – at the heart of Western liberal moral and political philosophy – is that adults should be treated as the authors of their own lives. This view received canonical expression in John Stuart Mill's *On Liberty* (1859), and informs much of the philosophical writing inspired by, and subsequent to, John Rawls's *A Theory of Justice* (1971). Of course Mill famously exempted children from the scope of his liberty principle, which "is meant to apply only to human beings in the maturity of their faculties" (Mill 1859 [1974], p. 69).

It may be proper to acknowledge that there is no clear bright line between childhood and adulthood. This allows us better to see why the children, as possessed of rights appropriate to their status, demand to be seen *both* as in need of protection *and* as capable of showing some but not all of the capacities of an adult decision-maker. Not to see the pull of both demands is to understate the complexity of the child's status. In many ways the CRC – which represents the proper starting point for any consideration of children's rights – admirably represents the pull of these demands.

References

Aiken William, and Hugh LaFollette, eds. 1980. *Whose Child? Parental Rights, Parental Authority and State Power* (Totowa, NJ: Rowman & Littlefield).

Alston Philip, S. Parker, and J. Seymour, eds. 1992. *Children, Rights and the Law* (Oxford: Oxford University Press).

Archard David. 2004. *Children, Rights and Childhood*, 2nd rev. edn (London: Routledge).

Archard David, and Colin M. Macleod, eds. 2004. *The Moral and Political Status of Children* (Oxford: Oxford University Press).

Archard David and Marit Skivenes. 2009. "Balancing a Child's Best Interests and a Child's Views." *International Journal of Children's Rights*, Vol. 17, pp. 1–21.

Ariès Philippe. 1960. *L'Enfant et la vie familiale sous l'ancien régime* (Paris: Libraire Plon). Trans. Robert Baldick as *Centuries of Childhood* (London: Jonathan Cape, 1962).

Brighouse Harry. 2003. "How Should Children Be Heard?" *Arizona Law Review*, Vol. 45, pp. 691–711.

Cohen Howard. 1980. *Equal Rights for Children* (Totowa, NJ: Littlefield, Adams).

Declaration of the Rights of the Child. 1959. At: http://www.cirp.org/library/ethics/UN-declaration/.

Donnelly J. and R. Howard. 1988. "Assessing National Human Rights Performance: A Theoretical Framework." *Human Rights Quarterly*, Vol. 10, pp. 214–248.

Eekelaar John. 1986a. "The Emergence of Children's Rights." *Oxford Journal of Legal Studies*, Vol. 6, No. 2, pp. 161–182.

Eekelaar John. 1986b. "The Eclipse of Parental Rights." *Law Quarterly Review*, Vol. 102, p. 4.

Farson Richard. 1974. *Birthrights* (London: Collier Macmillan).

Feinberg Joel. 1980. "The Child's Right to an Open Future." In W. Aiken and H. LaFollette, eds., *Having Children: Philosophical and Legal Reflections on Parenthood* (Oxford: Oxford University Press).

Bob Franklin ed. 2002. *The New Handbook of Children's Rights: Comparative Policy and Practice* (London: Routledge).

Gillick v. West Norfolk and Wisbech Area Health Authority. 1986. AC 112.

Griffin James. 2004. "Do Children Have Rights?" In D. Archard and C. Macleod, eds., *The Moral and Political Status of Children* (Oxford: Oxford University Press).

Holt John. 1974. *Escape from Childhood: The Needs and Rights of Children* (Harmondsworth: Penguin).
In re Gault.1967. 387 US 1.
Lansdown Gerison. 1994. "Children's Rights." In Berry Mayall, ed., *Children's Childhoods: Observed and Experienced* (London: Falmer Press).
LeBlanc Lawrence, J. Lawrence LeBlanc. 1995. *The Convention on the Rights of the Child: United Nations Lawmaking on Human Rights* (Lincoln: University of Nebraska Press).
Liao S. Matthew. 2000. "*The right of children to be loved*." D.Phil Thesis submitted to the University of Oxford.
Locke John. 1698 [1963]. *Two Treatises of Government*. Edited and with an introduction by Peter Laslett (Cambridge: Cambridge University Press).
Mill John Stuart. 1859 [1974]. *On Liberty*. Edited and with an introduction by Gertrude Himmelfarb (Harmondsworth: Penguin).
O'Neill Onora. 1988. "Children's Rights and Children's Lives." *Ethics*, Vol. 98, pp. 445–463. Reprinted in P. Alston, S. Parker, and J. Seymour, eds., *Children, Rights and the Law* (Oxford: Oxford University Press, 1992).
Purdy Laura M. 1992. *In Their Best Interests? Case Against Equal Rights for Children* (Ithaca, NY: Cornell University Press).
Qvortrup J. 1991. *Childhood as a Special Phenomenon: An Introduction to a Series of National Reports* (Vienna: European Centre).
Rawls John. 1971. *A Theory of Justice* (Cambridge, MA: Harvard University Press).
Rousseau Jean-Jacques. 1762 [1979]. *Emile, Or on Education*. Introduction, translation and notes by Allan Bloom (Harmondsworth: Penguin).
Schoeman Ferdinand. 1980. "Rights of Families: Rights of Parents, and the Moral Basis." *Ethics*, Vol. 91, pp. 6–19.
Schrag Francis. 1980. "Children: Their Rights and Needs." In W. Aiken and H. LaFollette, eds., *Whose Child? Parental Rights, Parental Authority and State Power* (Totowa, NJ: Rowman & Littlefield).
Sumner L.W. 1987. *The Moral Foundation of Rights* (Oxford: Clarendon Press).
UNCRC. 1989. The United Nations Convention on the Rights of the Child. At: http://www2.ohchr.org/english/law/crc.htm.

29

The development of international child law

The definition of "the child" and implementation mechanisms

Jenny Kuper

Introduction

Twenty-one years after the 1989 UN Convention on the Rights of the Child (CRC) entered into force, and largely due to its influence, the international landscape of child law and policy has changed beyond recognition and continues to change. The CRC is the most rapidly and widely ratified of all the international human rights treaties. It was adopted by the UN General Assembly without a vote on 20 November 1989, and less than a year later, on 2 September 1990, it entered into force having been ratified by the requisite twenty states. It now has 193 States Parties, leaving only two countries – the USA and Somalia – still to ratify. (However, the USA signed it on 16 February 1995 and Somalia signed on 9 May 2002. In November 2009 it was announced that Somalia was making plans to ratify, while the USA was undertaking a review of the CRC with a view to possible ratification.)

While far from perfect in either its content or its implementation, the CRC illustrates, among other things, the impact that international law can have and its capacity to evolve over time and in different contexts.

This chapter will briefly outline the background and history of the drafting of the CRC, including its definition of the "child," and then present an overview of its main features and its implementation mechanisms. Other international implementation mechanisms will then be considered, before discussing the only other general international (although regional) child law treaty currently in force: the 1999 African Charter on the Rights and Welfare of the Child (ACRWC).

Convention on the Rights of the Child: background, history, and definition of "child"

Background

A useful starting point is to consider the concept of "childhood" (meaning, in this context, that period of time in which a person is legally considered a child). This concept is important, as it is essential to the modern legal notion that children are persons in law, entitled to specific rights and subject to certain responsibilities.

There has been an ongoing controversy about the historical status of children. In the European context, some writers (e.g., the French writers Ariès [1962] and De Mause [1974]) argued that children were – until about the seventeenth or eighteenth centuries – treated in some ways as if scarcely distinguishable from adults. These writers questioned whether, in previous centuries, childhood was seen as a distinct period in a person's life, whether children were regarded as being vulnerable or having a special status, or entitled to special protection or rights. However, other writers (e.g., Orme 2003) maintain that there was a general recognition of a distinct period of childhood as early as the thirteenth century, or medieval times.

Yet others have argued that childhood is a relative concept, which changes according to the historic period, the geographic place, the particular culture, and socio-economic conditions. This approach, in acknowledging the danger of a Eurocentric focus, has much to recommend it.

Further, in looking at many traditions – including religious traditions such as Islam and the Judeo-Christian tradition – it is evident that there is a cross-cultural notion of childhood as a period of time with a distinct status attached to it. However, this distinct status does not necessarily imply better treatment, as exemplified by child marriage, child circumcision, and corporal punishment of children.

This raises the question of the tension between universal norms and cultural relativity, a fascinating topic that cannot be explored here in any depth but one that is worth bearing in mind when looking at the content and implementation of any international law, including child law. This topic has been tackled by various writers. As regards children, one writer has suggested strategies for bridging the gap between universal norms and particular cultures by encouraging discussion within individual states, using arguments that are internally valid in that society to find a common basis of values without being elitist or intrusive (An-Na'im 1994).

In any event, whatever the social underpinning of the notion of childhood, early in the last century international law began to grant a separate status to children, starting with treaties of the International Labour Organization (ILO) in 1919 regulating minimum ages and night work of children and young people in industry. The initial emphasis of this and other early law and policy was on child protection/child welfare, with children seen primarily as vulnerable. Over the decades, since the first international declaration specifically on the rights of the child in 1924 (see below), this emphasis has begun to shift to child empowerment, with the child being regarded as a more active participant in his or her own life and as a holder of rights.

Bearing in mind these debates about "childhood," the section below will consider the definition of "child" in international law.

Definition of child

To start with the definition of "child" in the CRC, Article 1 states that a child is "every human being below the age of eighteen years unless under the law applicable to the child, majority is attained earlier." What does this say, however, about the beginning and end of childhood? Neither of these is clearly defined.

To consider first the beginning of childhood, the general principle is that international legal protection starts at birth, but states can extend this to the pre-birth period, i.e., to start from conception. The key issue here, of course, is whether the particular state is pro- or anti-abortion, and this was indeed a contentious issue in the drafting of the CRC. Ultimately, the Working Group drafting the CRC dealt with this controversy by leaving the definition vague and therefore up to the discretion of individual states.

As regards the end of childhood, clearly again the CRC leaves room for state discretion, so that any particular country is thereby entitled to set the age of majority at, e.g., 16 or 17. However this practice is discouraged by the Committee on the Rights of the Child, which monitors implementation of the CRC, and there is an emerging norm of 18 being widely accepted as the age of majority. Of course individual states do, in their own domestic legislation, set different qualifying ages for children to engage in specific activities (e.g., to get married, vote, drink alcohol), and this can vary widely between states. Further, many international instruments do set age limits regarding specific issues (e.g., the 1980 Hague Convention on the Civil Aspects of International Child Abduction applies only to children under 16).

The question here as regards international law is whether this vague definition in the CRC is a problem. The simple answer is that it is not, in that at least there is a general understanding that the term "child" refers to a person from birth to about the age of 16. However, the not-so-simple answer is that it can cause problems, as some writers have argued (Grover 2004).

Certainly this issue becomes more complex when considered in the light of demographics. For example, in some countries the majority of the population is under 18, and the European Defense Agency (EDA) has recently estimated that by 2025 "the average African's age is projected to be twenty-two." On the other hand, the life expectancy of populations in the North is consistently increasing, and the EDA estimates that by 2025 "the average European will be forty-five years old." Thus the real meaning of childhood and youth in these two contexts will vary enormously. In some countries the norm will inevitably be that most "children" under 18 will be working, having children, running their own households, etc.

History of international child law

As regards the history of international child law and policy leading to the adoption of the CRC, this section will consider only the main relevant developments.

Other than ILO treaties already mentioned, the first major international document specifically focusing on children was the 1924 Declaration of the Rights of the Child (1924 Declaration). This simple document – a non-binding League of Nations resolution – consists of five points outlining key social, emotional, and economic requirements of children, couched in the "child welfare" language of the time. The Declaration coins the now well-known phrase "mankind owes the child the best it has to give," subsequently reiterated in various other documents regarding children. To modern ears some of its terminology sounds patronizing – e.g., "the child that is backward must be helped ... and the orphan and the waif must be sheltered and succored" (Principle 2). For its time, however, this Declaration was quite radical.

In the years following the adoption of this Declaration, there was a growing awareness in the international community regarding the situation of children, particularly in the aftermath of World War II. This ultimately found expression in the 1959 Declaration of the Rights of the Child (1959 Declaration), and in all the main general human rights treaties that began to proliferate in the postwar period.

As regards the 1959 Declaration, the initial impetus for this was a desire that the UN, as successor to the League of Nations, should confirm the 1924 Declaration. However, as the process gathered pace the 1924 Declaration was expanded from five to ten principles. The 1959 Declaration thus included various new provisions, concerning, for example, protection without discrimination (Principle 1) and the right to name and nationality (Principle 3). Further, the now fundamental concept of "the best interests of the child" was invoked (in Principles 2 and 7). Although still non-binding, this Declaration was adopted unanimously by the UN, which indicates a consensus at that time regarding certain basic principles on the treatment of children.

These two international Declarations specifically regarding children thus began to pave the way for other international law focusing on children, including the CRC.

As these developments were taking place, various key global international legal instruments – which were not child-specific – were being drafted, and it is worth briefly mentioning these in tracing the growth of legal norms regarding children. These global treaties apply as a whole to all human beings, including children, and also contain specific child-focused principles.

Most significant are the three main human rights instruments: (1) the 1948 Universal Declaration of Human Rights (UDHR) (again, a non-binding UN resolution, although one now so well accepted that is considered part of customary international law), (2) the 1966 International Covenant on Civil and Political Rights (ICCPR), and (3) the 1966 International Covenant on Economic, Social and Cultural Rights (ICESCR) – the latter two both widely ratified treaties. All of these contain key measures providing generally for children, as well as more specific provisions regarding particular aspects of their lives, such as education, labor, family issues, etc. Thus, e.g., Article 25 of the UDHR contains the general provision that "Motherhood and childhood are entitled to special care and protection." Similar measures are set out in the ICCPR (Article 24[1])and in the ICESCR (Article 10[3]).

Regional treaties also make special mention of children. In brief, these include measures set out in the 1948 American Declaration on the Rights and Duties of Man (Article 7); the 1969 American Convention on Human Rights (Article 19) and the 1981 African Charter on Human and Peoples' Rights (Article 18[3]). Interestingly, the 1950 European Convention on Human Rights is the weakest of these treaties, containing only a few provisions regarding children in specific circumstances (e.g., Articles 5[1][d] and 6[1]), although there are many child-related provisions in the 1961 European Social Charter, in particular its Article 7.

As regards the international law of armed conflict, the first measures specifically regarding children appear in the 1949 Geneva Conventions, particularly in Geneva Convention IV regarding the protection of the civilian population. However, it was only in the 1977 Geneva Protocols that the underlying principle was articulated providing for the special treatment of children generally in armed conflict.

Thus, all the main regional and global treaties contain measures for the special treatment of children. In addition there is a plethora of more specific international measures regarding children in particular circumstances, which cannot be outlined here.

Prior to the CRC therefore, there were these scattered provisions in international treaty law and other legal instruments, and there were the two non-binding Declarations specifically on children. This generated an impetus towards a binding treaty specifically on children, combining all the pertinent rules in one document – ultimately leading to the drafting of the CRC and, regionally, the ACRWC.

Drafting of the Convention on the Rights of the Child

The drafting of the CRC was initiated by a representative of the Polish government who tabled an initial version at the UN in 1978, expanding on the 1959 Declaration. This led to the creation of a Working Group to draft the proposed new treaty. The Working Group included UN member states, other international governmental organizations (such as the ILO and, later, UNICEF), and the International Committee of the Red Cross. It was unusual for its time in that it worked actively with many non-governmental organizations (NGOs). The first meeting was held in 1979, and the Working Group then generally met annually until 1988.

Certain features of the Working Group exerted a strong influence on the ultimate content of the CRC. First, the Working Group operated on consensus, with mixed results. Agreement was generally reached on the many contentious issues discussed, but in some instances this resulted in agreement only on the lowest common denominator. A particularly striking example here was Article 38 on children in armed conflict (see below). Further, the Working Group was initially quite small and dominated by countries of the North, although there was active participation by a few Southern countries. In later years there was an increase in numbers of countries from the South, but nonetheless the CRC has been open to the criticism of being too Eurocentric.

Dilemmas in the drafting process

During the ten years in which the Working Group was engaged in the drafting process a number of controversial issues had to be confronted, many of these reflecting clashes of cultural values. They included:

a) *Minimum age of childhood* (Article 1 – discussed above): the pro- and anti-abortion debate;
b) *Freedom of thought, conscience, and religion* (Article 14). The freedom to choose religion is apparently not a concept accepted in Islam. Reference to choice was therefore dropped, in "the spirit of compromise." The article now says simply: "states shall respect the right of the child to freedom of thought, conscience and religion";
c) *Adoption* (Article 21). Again, there is no right to adoption as such in Islam (although there is provision for "kafala," an alternative process), so a compromise was reached. Accordingly, Article 21 only applies to states "that recognize and/or permit the system of adoption," thus providing safeguards for children involved in adoption rather than facilitating adoption itself;
d) *Children in armed conflict* (Article 38). A number of contentious issues arose here, but the most heated debate centered on the age at which children could legitimately participate in armed conflict as combatants. Ultimately the Working Group reached an acrimonious consensus on the current standard at that time: i.e. the age of 15, rather than 18. This has now been superseded to some extent by recent developments (see below).

Overview of the Convention on the Rights of the Child

Innovative provisions

The final version of the CRC incorporated many articles that were new in international law regarding children. These included:

a) Article 3 – that "the best interests of the child shall be a primary consideration" in all actions concerning children;
b) Article 8 – states to respect "the right of the child to preserve his or her identity ... without unlawful interference";
c) Article 12 – that children capable of forming their own views should be able to express these views freely in matters affecting them, depending on their capacity to do so;
d) Article 19 – states to take measures to protect the child from intra-familial violence;
e) Article 24 – prohibiting harmful traditional practices;
f) Article 25 – periodic review of treatment of children placed by state authorities;
g) Article 28 – that school discipline "is administered in a manner consistent with the child's human dignity";

h) Article 37 – deprivation of liberty of child should be the last resort and for the shortest appropriate period of time;
i) Article 39 – states to promote the recovery and reintegration of child victim of, *inter alia*, armed conflict, neglect, abuse and torture.

Core articles

An underlying theme in the CRC is that certain categories of rights become more significant as the child progresses from infancy to the age of 18, so that the more protective rights increasingly give way to the participatory rights.

Within this framework, some rights are considered to be core principles that are to be read into all the other provisions of this treaty. These are generally accepted to be:

a) Article 2 – non-discrimination principle;
b) Article 3 – best interests principle;
c) Article 6 – right of children to life, development, and survival;
d) Article 12 – views of children to be given due weight.

Other fundamental norms stated in this and other key international treaties – such as the protection from torture and analogous treatment – of course remain central.

One of the most challenging of the core principles to apply is Article 3, the "best interests" principle (for critique see, e.g., Guggenheim 2006). Clearly, views of the "best interests" of a particular child are often subjective, and there have been many cases in which courts have been required to pass judgment on this issue, both in the domestic and international arena (*Minister of State for Immigration and Ethnic Affairs v Teoh* 1995; *Ye and Qui v Minister of Immigration* 2009; *AC and Others v Manitoba* 2009).

Overview of provisions

The CRC brings together civil, political, economic, social, and cultural rights in one treaty. It also incorporates both human rights law and the laws of armed conflict (the latter via Article 38). A number of these rights are already articulated in the global human rights treaties outlined above (e.g., the ICCPR) and apply to children as they apply to all persons, but the CRC makes clear beyond doubt that children are entitled to these global rights.

According to its Article 4, states must undertake appropriate measures to implement the rights set out in the CRC. However, as regards economic, social, and cultural rights, they are only obliged to take such measures to "the maximum extent of their available resources" (i.e., progressive realization). (Again, compare with the ACRWC, below.)

The rights articulated in the CRC can be classified in four categories, sometimes called the "four P's," which do overlap to some extent:

a) *Protection* from abuse and exploitation (e.g., Articles 11 [regarding illicit transfer and non-return – e.g., kidnapping by one parent]; 19 [protection from abuse]; 24[3] [traditional practices]; 32 [protection from economic exploitation/hazardous work]; 33 [narcotics]; 34 [sexual exploitation]; 35 [trafficking]; 36 [other forms of exploitation]; 37 [torture, etc.]; 38 [armed conflict]);
b) *Prevention* of harm (closely linked to protection) (e.g., Articles 6 [right to life, etc.]; 7 [entitlement to name, nationality, and care by parents]; 8 [right to identity]; 25 [right to review of care and treatment]);

c) *Provision* to meet basic needs – largely economic and social rights (e.g., Articles 3[3] [good standards in institutions, etc. for children]; 6 [right to life, etc.]; 23 [adequate care for the disabled]; 24 [right to health]; 26 [social security]; 27 [adequate standard of living]);
d) *Participation* in matters affecting the life of the child (e.g., Articles 12 [views of the child]; 13 [freedom of expression]; 14 [freedom of thought, etc.]; 15 [freedom of association]; 17 [access to information]).

Previous provisions in legal instruments regarding children focused on the first three categories above. The inclusion of participation rights, and especially Article 12, was quite a radical new departure.

One important provision worth mentioning is Article 41, which states that nothing in the CRC should affect provisions that are "more conducive to the realization of the rights of the child" contained in other national or international law applicable to any state – i.e., the highest standard of applicable law should always prevail.

Optional protocols

As time has passed, certain weaknesses in the CRC are being addressed via the creation of new laws, two of which have taken the form of Optional Protocols (additional treaties) linked to the CRC. These are the 2000 Optional Protocol on the Involvement of Children in Armed Conflict (OP Armed Conflict) (132 states were party to this as of 5 May 2010) and the 2000 Optional Protocol on the Sale of Children, Child Prostitution, and Child Pornography (OP Sale of Children) (137 states party as of 5 May 2010).

The OP Armed Conflict started life in response to the low standard set by the Working Group drafting the CRC, and basically aims to limit the participation and use of children under 18 in armed forces. In brief, it provides that no under 18s should be subject to compulsory recruitment into regular armed forces, and that states must raise the minimum age for voluntary recruitment to at least the age of 16. Further, if a country does have under-18-year-olds in its armed forces, they should not directly participate in conflict. Also, states are obliged to take "feasible measures" to prevent non-governmental forces under their jurisdiction from recruiting or using under 18s.

As regards the OP Sale of Children, states that are party to this are obliged to prohibit the sale of children, child prostitution, and child pornography and to enforce the prohibition through legal and administrative measures.

These two Optional Protocols – and perhaps particularly the former – are having a significant impact on child law and policy internationally, and compliance with them is monitored through the implementation mechanisms of the CRC. The UN has also recently agreed (in March 2010) to draft a new Optional Protocol on a communications procedure under the CRC (see below).

Convention on the Rights of the Child: implementation measures

The implementation measures in the CRC are set out in its Articles 42 to 45, although Article 4 (requiring legislative, administrative and other measures to be taken) is also relevant. The Committee on the Rights of the Child (the Committee), established under Article 43, has published useful guidelines for states on their implementation obligations (see General Comment No. 5 [2003]).

Under Article 42, states are to make the principles and provisions of the CRC widely known to both adults and children. The Committee is concerned here, e.g., to know whether the

CRC has been translated into all languages used in any particular state; what steps are taken by the state to promote knowledge of the CRC, and what training is provided for parents and professionals.

Article 43 established the Committee on Rights of the Child, initially as a group of ten experts, but the membership was expanded to eighteen from November 2002. These experts are selected according to geographical representation and are to serve in their personal capacity, not as government representatives. They serve for four-year terms and can be re-elected. The Committee meets for sessions of three weeks, three times per year.

The Committee is crucial to the successful implementation of the CRC and has various roles: e.g., it can issue General Comments, which are guidelines that assist states to interpret their obligations (such as General Comment No. 5 above). The first one, published in 2001, focused on the aims of education (Article 29 [1]). The Committee has now published twenty General Comments, covering issues such as adolescent health and the rights of children with disabilities and indigenous children. At the time of writing, its most recent General Comment (2009) concerned the rights of the child to be heard.

The Committee also holds general days of discussion once a year, when it invites NGOs, experts, and others to discuss issues of concern regarding children: for example, the economic exploitation of children and violence against children. In September 2008 the discussion focused on "the right of the child to education in emergency situations." Normally the Committee makes a recommendation as a result of these discussions, some of which (e.g., the 1992 day of discussion on children in armed conflict) have had far-reaching effects.

Probably the main role of the Committee, however, is in monitoring state reports. Under Article 44, states are to submit reports on the measures they have adopted to give effect to the CRC rights and on the progress made. These reports are to be submitted within two years of entry into force of the CRC in that state, and every five years after that. The Committee has set out guidelines for both initial reports and periodic reports, and for reports under the two Optional Protocols.

During the reporting process, one member of the Committee will then act as a rapporteur for each report and draw up questions to be put to the country representatives who appear before the Committee. There follows a public hearing, where the aim is to have a "constructive dialogue." After this, the Committee draws up its Concluding Observations on the state report, in which it can make strong and detailed recommendations. The country concerned should then act on these recommendations and summarize progress in its next report.

For example, the Committee's Concluding Observations of 20 October 2008 on the most recent report of the UK commended the UK for some progress achieved, for example, for the adoption of relevant new legislation. It went on to express concern regarding various issues, such as the general demonization of children, especially adolescents; the high numbers of children given custodial sentences; the use of physical restraint techniques on children deprived of their liberty; the fact that the UK had not (yet?) prohibited corporal punishment within the family; and the need for the UK to raise the age of criminal responsibility and improve provision for children with disabilities.

Finally, under Article 45 – an important provision which facilitates, e.g., funding for states with limited finances – the CRC provides that, for its effective implementation and to encourage international cooperation, "specialized agencies, UNICEF and other UN organs" can be represented and involved in the work of the Committee. These and "other competent bodies" (which include NGOs) are thereby invited to contribute advice, reports, and other support, including financial support, to particular countries. There is in fact a large and very active NGO Group for the CRC, which often provides alternative or supplementary reports.

The Committee must also report to the UN General Assembly every two years on its activities.

Reservations

Despite these implementation provisions and the undoubted impact that the CRC has had, one of the main factors that undermine the effectiveness of the CRC is the many reservations and similar statements that have been made by governments ratifying this treaty. By such statements, governments can exclude or modify the application of some treaty provisions in relation to themselves, although under Article 51 of the CRC this is prohibited if the particular statement is incompatible with the CRC's "object and purpose." However, this prohibition is not strictly observed, and the relatively liberal reservation regime under the CRC has allowed a large measure of "cultural relativism" and enabled many states to ratify, despite some sweeping reservations (e.g., from Saudi Arabia, Iran, and Qatar, to provisions in the CRC that were considered incompatible with the provisions of Islamic law).

The CRC is silent about the legal effect of reservations and has no mechanism to determine their validity, although the Committee has made known its critical view of these and has discussed this issue on a number of occasions both in general and in relation to specific states. Other states party to the CRC can object to a particular state's reservation, but this does not generally invalidate the reservation or that state's ratification of the treaty (Kuper 1997b).

Assessment of Convention on the Rights of the Child

Inevitably the CRC features both strengths and weaknesses. As regards the latter, in addition to the problem of reservations mentioned above there are a number of other problems. One is that the CRC does not contain a complaints mechanism whereby the Committee could hear cases brought by or on behalf of individual children. This is obviously a deliberate omission, no doubt motivated by a desire to encourage wide ratification of the treaty. However, there is now a strong campaign to allow individual complaints under the CRC (a principle which the Committee itself supports) in line with a number of other key human rights treaties. As already mentioned, the UN has agreed that an intergovernmental Working Group can begin drafting a new Optional Protocol to establish a communications procedure under the CRC. Its first meeting was scheduled for December 2010.

Another weakness in implementing the CRC is the fact that the CRC Committee is one of the few such Committees that does not have a formal procedure to follow up state compliance with its Concluding Observations, although moves are underway to address this. Also problematic is the vague wording of many articles, perhaps particularly those dealing with economic and social rights. Moreover, this treaty is surprisingly silent on various issues, including the particular requirements of the girl child.

A further big challenge is that the CRC has been to some extent a victim of its own success. The treaty was so widely and rapidly ratified that it soon fell behind in the reporting process, and at one point the Committee had a backlog amounting to two or three years. The addition of the two Optional Protocols has inevitably added to the workload. The backlog of reports was in fact one of the reasons for increasing the membership of Committee from ten to eighteen. This allowed the Committee, in 2006, to divide into two chambers (nine members in each) so that it could have parallel discussions with states, thus dealing with two reports simultaneously and reducing the backlog.

Despite these difficulties, the Committee has risen to the challenge posed by the rather weak implementation mechanism through its serious and increasingly outspoken approach in the reporting process, and the use of strategies such as the days of discussion to highlight issues of particular concern and take action on these.

Further, a recent UNICEF study titled "The Impact of the Implementation of the CRC" (UNICEF 2004) has indicated significant progress in international implementation of the CRC. The findings of this ongoing study, looking at sixty-two regionally representative countries, have included: (1) that there is a continuing process of child-related law reform – for example, the CRC is incorporated into domestic law in two-thirds of the countries studied, and nearly a third include child rights provisions in their constitutions; (2) moreover, independent national institutions focusing on child rights have been established in about thirty-eight of the countries studied, and (3) the majority of countries studied have adopted comprehensive national strategies based on the CRC.

Implementation more broadly

Before considering the ACRWC, it is important to note that the CRC and "child rights" generally are implemented in a variety of ways not limited to the implementation mechanisms in this treaty, or even to the legal arena.

World summit, national programs of action, etc.

One significant development reflects concern with, in particular, children's economic and social entitlements. This resulted in the 1990 World Summit on Children, attended by many heads of state, which aimed to formulate practical measures to achieve these entitlements via a Plan of Action that, among other things, called for international cooperation and for the creation of National Programs of Action. The Programs of Action set measurable goals and strategies for improving child survival and development in individual countries, e.g., goals regarding health, education, and protection of children in difficult circumstances.

There was a mid-decade review in 1996 regarding progress made, and further reviews have taken place, notably the UN Special Session on Children (May 2002) which aimed to make some of the relevant international standards more binding and measurable, and included about 400 child participants. The Special Session culminated in the official adoption, by some 180 nations, of its outcome document, "A World Fit for Children." The new agenda included twenty-one specific goals and targets for the next decade, focusing on four key priorities: promoting healthy lives; providing quality education for all; protecting children against abuse, exploitation, and violence; and combating HIV/AIDS. A further review at a UN gathering in December 2007 discussed progress made in implementing the "World Fit for Children" agenda, and the process is continuing.

Litigation

The human rights of children are frequently the subject of litigation in courts both internationally (e.g., regional courts in the Americas, Europe, and Africa, and the International Criminal Court [ICC]) and domestically. While a number of important "child rights" cases predate the CRC, increasingly many court hearings refer directly to CRC provisions. In this way court proceedings can to some extent remedy the lack of an individual complaints mechanism in the CRC (although court proceedings and treaty complaints mechanisms differ in various ways, e.g., treaties rely primarily on public embarrassment and international pressure, rather than enforcement mechanisms such as fines or imprisonment).

By way of example of the range of issues tackled and the various fora in which the hearings take place, a few interesting cases are briefly outlined below, in chronological order. These cases represent simply the "tip of the iceberg" of fascinating child-related cases in international fora (and many such cases are heard in countries not cited here, e.g., in India). (Domestic cases are not considered here.)

- *Villagran-Morales et al. v. Guatemala* – a 1999 case before the Inter-American Court of Human Rights, in which Guatemala was found guilty – in relation to the kidnapping, torture, and deaths of a group of street children – of a number of breaches of international law, including the right to life and failure to provide special child protection measures. In interpreting the latter, the Court referred to provisions in the CRC.
- *Roper v. Simmons* – a case decided in 2005 by the US Supreme Court in which it reversed its previous position and declared that it was unconstitutional to impose capital punishment for crimes committed while a person was under the age of 18. In reaching this decision, the court made reference to the test of "evolving standards of decency" and had regard to practices in other countries, noting that the USA and Somalia were the only non-ratifying countries to the CRC, including its Article 37 expressly prohibiting capital punishment for crimes committed by juveniles. (On a related issue, the US Supreme Court was, at the time of writing, considering whether it was a violation of the Eighth Amendment prohibition of "cruel and unusual punishments" to sentence a juvenile offender to a life sentence without parole for a crime in which no one died. The defendants in two separate cases were 13 and 16 at the time of their offense [see *Sullivan v Florida* and *Graham v Florida*]).
- *Provisional Measures regarding Brazil: Matter of Children Deprived of Liberty in the "Complexo do Tatuape" of FEBEM*, Order of the Inter-American Court of Human Rights – a 2007 Order regarding the treatment of hundreds of children (320 in April 2007) in a state-run penal institution in Brazil. Issues before the Court included the death of one inmate and allegations of torture or ill-treatment generally. Of particular interest here was the proactive role taken by the Court, which had, for example, requested that Brazil forward to the Court a list of all the inmates in the institution, with precise information regarding matters such as the release date of each inmate. The Court also required Brazil to keep informing the Court, every two months, of provisional measures taken.
- *DH and Others v. Czech Republic* – a 2007 case before the European Court of Human Rights, which found that the Czech Republic had discriminated against Roma children and violated their right to education, on the grounds that a disproportionate number of Roma children were being placed in special schools without adequate justification and hence were placed at a disadvantage.
- *Hadijatou Mani v. Niger* – a 2008 case heard before the Community Court of Justice of the Economic Community of West African States (ECOWAS) in which Niger was found to be in breach of its own laws and international obligations as regards protecting its citizens from slavery. The citizen here was Hadijatou Mani, sold into slavery in 1996 at the age of 12. The Court found violations of, among other things, the prohibition of slavery, discrimination, and arbitrary detention. This case is one of the few slavery cases heard before an international court and the first against Niger. Further, it was the first judgment of the ECOWAS court to address serious human rights violations. (In a further groundbreaking case in November 2009 ECOWAS declared that all Nigerians are entitled to education as a

legal and human right. See *Socio-Economic Rights and Accountability Project [SERAP] v. Federal Government and Universal Basic Education Commission [UBEC])*.

In this context it is worth noting that the ICC and the Special Court for Sierra Leone have prosecuted and heard a number of significant cases regarding children in armed conflict, for example, concerning the recruitment and use of child soldiers, and regarding "forced marriage." It is beyond the scope of this chapter to outline these cases here, but they are cited in the References.

The International Tribunal for the Former Yugoslavia and the International Criminal Tribunal for Rwanda have also passed relevant judgments.

African Charter on the Rights and Welfare of the Child

This chapter will conclude by looking quite briefly at the ACRWC, the only general regional child-focused treaty currently in force. It was preceded by the 1979 Declaration of Rights and Welfare of the African Child and, like the CRC, includes civil, political, economic, social, and cultural rights as well as human rights and humanitarian law provisions.

Forty-eight out of a possible fifty-three African states had, at the time of writing, ratified this treaty, which entered into force in November 1999. Unlike the CRC, it thus took nearly ten years to come into force, being adopted by the Organization of African Unity (now the African Union [AU]) in 1990.

This treaty is of interest as a regional instrument that is in some ways similar to but also quite different from the CRC. As regards differences between the ACRWC and the CRC, these include the following:

- first, a generalization, i.e., that in the ACRWC the more political–participation-oriented rights (e.g., regarding freedom of expression) tend to be weaker from a "child rights" perspective;
- linked to that is the fact that the parental/guardianship role is expressed more strongly in the ACRWC. Generally there is more emphasis throughout this treaty on the role of parents/guardians as regards, for example, freedom of thought, conscience, and religion, and restrictions on children's privacy rights.
- further, some economic and social rights – concerning access to information, social security, and rights of children of minorities – are not included at all. This could well be due to resource limitations anticipated by those drafting this treaty. Nonetheless, it is noteworthy that the ACRWC does not call for "progressive realization" of economic and social rights ("to the maximum extent of their available resources," as in Article 4 of the CRC). In that sense its advocacy of economic and social rights is potentially stronger.

As regards specific provisions, it is not surprising to find throughout this treaty an emphasis on the particular situation of children in Africa. Thus, for example, the Preamble states that the situation of most African children "remains critical due to the unique factors of their socio-economic, cultural, traditional and developmental circumstances" and recognizes "that the child occupies a unique and privileged position in the African society."

The substantive articles of the ACRWC also differ in some important respects from those in the CRC. One significant difference is the definition of "child," set out in Article 2 of the ACRWC: i.e., "a child means every human being below the age of eighteen years." The ACRWC thus leaves no room for reducing the age of majority below eighteen, as does the CRC.

Other differences between the two treaties include the following:

- Article 4 – the best interests of the child in the ACRWC are "the" paramount consideration, not "a" paramount consideration as in the CRC;
- Article 11(2) – emphasis on education to strengthen African morals and values, and Article 11(6) – specific provision for education of girls who become pregnant (child mothers);
- Article 18(3) – no child to be deprived of maintenance due to marital status of parents;
- Article 21 – an entire article on harmful social and cultural practices, including a prohibition on child marriage (under 18);
- Article 22 – as regards armed conflict, this prohibits the recruitment and use of children as defined in the ACRWC, thus setting the age at 18 rather than 15 as in the CRC. Further, this article specifically applies to internal armed conflict/civil war. However, the ACRWC has no equivalent to Article 39 CRC, regarding the duty to rehabilitate and reintegrate;
- Article 23 – refugee children – specifically refers to children who are "internally displaced";
- Article 29 – specific prohibition against use of children in begging;
- Article 31 – long and interesting article setting out various responsibilities of children to their parents, communities, and nation. The closest equivalent to this appears in Article 29(1) of the CRC, on the aims of education.

The ACRWC also omits certain further CRC provisions, e.g., it does not protect children from life imprisonment without the possibility of release (Article 37 CRC), or provide for alternatives in lieu of custodial measures (Article 40 CRC).

Implementation mechanisms

As regards its implementation mechanisms, the ACRWC again differs in some important respects from the CRC.

- Article 33 provides for an African Committee of Experts on the Rights and Welfare of the Child (ACRWC Committee). This consists of eleven members and is similar to the CRC in that members serve in their individual capacity, with only one national from any particular state. This Committee was formed in July 2001 and started work in March 2002, so its work is still in the relatively early stages compared to the CRC Committee. Its fifteenth session was held from 10 to15 March 2010.
- By Article 37, the ACRWC Committee members cannot be re-elected.
- Article 42 sets out the mandate of the ACRWC Committee, which is more proactive than that of the CRC Committee, including wide-ranging "protection and promotion" functions.
- As with the CRC, the ACRWC Committee monitors compliance via a reporting mechanism, although the requirement here is that countries submit reports every three years.
- A notable difference, however, is found in Article 44 of the ACRWC, which establishes a complaints mechanism allowing the ACRWC Committee to "receive communications, from any person, group or non-governmental organization recognized by the Organization of African Unity, by a Member State, or the United Nations relating to any matter covered by this Charter."

- In addition the ACRWC Committee is granted even greater freedom of action under Article 45, authorizing it to investigate on its own motion any matter falling within the ambit of the Charter. It is required to submit a report on its activities every two years to the AU.

In practice, the ACRWC Committee decided its initial priority was encouraging ratification through missions to countries, advocacy, and lobbying. In that context, it made a number of country visits. It has focused on three courses of action:

a) 16 June each year has been declared African Day of the Child – to raise consciousness on particular issues, for example, Africa's Orphans; Combat Child Trafficking;
b) hearings of the Committee – seen as opportunities to engage in dialogue with partners on key issues;
c) advocacy and investigative missions to member states such as Sudan and Uganda.

The ACRWC Committee works closely with NGOs and civil society organizations, and country reports from these organizations are accepted.

Assessment of the African Charter on the Rights and Welfare of the Child

On paper at least the ACRWC is in some ways more progressive than the CRC both in its content and implementation mechanisms. It also has the advantage of being more specific to the region. Time will tell whether indeed it can live up to its promise.

Various challenges have already arisen. There is a problem of resources and funding, which has been an ongoing issue and has undoubtedly contributed to the ACRWC Committee's somewhat slow start. The ACRWC Committee's rules provide that it should meet twice a year for not more than two weeks on each occasion. However, even this has been difficult to achieve as it has struggled to find funding for a Secretariat and therefore administrative matters have been problematic, including translation of documents into the various agreed languages (English, French, Portuguese, and Arabic). Although its first session was held in May 2002, this Committee only adopted Guidelines for Consideration of Initial Reports in 2004, so the two-year period for submission of reports was delayed and started in November 2004. At the time of writing, some reports had been submitted, the first four being from Egypt, Mauritius, Rwanda, and Nigeria. By November 2009 the ACRWC Committee had read and issued its first recommendations to Egypt and Nigeria. It had also received reports from at least seven other countries, and had received at least one communication (from a group in N. Uganda) but had not as yet had the procedures in place to act on this.

In 2009 an independent evaluation of the work of the ACRWC Committee was underway, commissioned by the AU with UNICEF support. It will assess the work of this Committee, including funding issues, and propose a draft Plan of Action for the next five years.

One particular challenge in implementing the ACRWC is the potential difficulty faced by both African states and the ACRWC Committee in balancing different principles, e.g., on one hand the principle that the African heritage should inspire an African concept of rights of the child, but on the other hand, that customs, etc., contrary to this Charter should be discouraged. There is also the vexed question of how to balance Article 31, on the responsibilities of the child, against the many child rights provisions in the Charter. Some of the latter – e.g., on child marriage – arguably set a higher standard than the CRC and also contravene customary practices in various African countries. It may be helpful here to have recourse to Article 1(2) of the ACRWC, which, like Article 41 of the CRC, provides that the highest standard ("more conducive to the realization of the rights" of the child) should always apply.

Nonetheless, it is worth emphasizing – as mentioned above in the context of cultural relativity – that the CRC faces similar dilemmas to some extent, since there is inevitably tension between the aspirational universal standards and individual state practice. Implementation of the human rights of children on the global, regional, and domestic levels is and will remain a complex and continuing process.

References

AC and Others v Manitoba (Director of Child and Family Services) 2009, SCC (Supreme Court, Canada) 30, 26 June.

An-Na'im, A. 1994. "Cultural Transformation and Normative Consensus on the Best Interests of the Child." In P. Alston, ed., *The Best Interests of the Child* (Oxford: Clarendon Press).

Ariès, P. 1962. *Centuries of Childhood* (New York: Vintage Books).

De Mause, L. 1974, *The History of Childhood* (London: Souvenir Press).

DH and Others v Czech Republic 2007, (App No 57325), 47 E.H.R.R. 3.

Graham v Florida 2009, Supreme Court of the United States, No. 08-7412, 9 November.

Grover, S. 2004. "On Recognising Children's Universal Rights: What Needs to Change in the Convention on the Rights of the Child." *International Journal of Children's Rights*, Vol. 12, pp. 259–271.

Guggenheim, M. 2006. "Ratify the Convention on the Rights of the Child But Don't Expect Any Miracles." *Emory International Law Review*, Vol. 20, pp. 43–67.

Hadijatou Mani v Niger 2008, Community Court of Justice of the Economic Community of West African States, 27 October.

Kuper, J. 1997a. *International Law Concerning Child Civilians in Armed Conflict* (Oxford: Clarendon Press).

Kuper, J. 1997b. "Reservations, Declarations and Objections to the 1989 Convention on the Rights of the Child," pp. 104–113 in *Human Rights As General Norms and a State's Right to Opt Out: Reservations and Objections to Human Rights Conventions* (London: British Institute of International and Comparative Law).

Minister of State for Immigration and Ethnic Affairs v Teoh 1995, High Court of Australia, 7 April.

Orme, N. 2003. *Medieval Children* (New Haven, CT: Yale University Press).

Prosecutor v Brima, Kamar and Kanu 2008, Sierra Leone Special Court, SCSL-2004-16-PT, Appeals Chamber Judgment 22 February.

Prosecutor v Charles Ghankay Taylor 2009, Sierra Leone Special Court, SCSL-03-0I-T, latest Trial Chamber decision 30 November, Appeals Chamber decision 8 December (ongoing).

Prosecutor v Germain Katanga and Mathieu Ngudjolo Chui 2009, International Criminal Court, ICC-01/04-01/07, commencement of trial 24 November (ongoing).

Prosecutor v Joseph Kony, Vincent Otti, Okot Odhiambo and Dominic Ongwen 2005, International Criminal Court, ICC-02/04-01/05, warrant of arrest unsealed 13 October.

Prosecutor v Moinina Fofana and Allieu Kondewa 2008, Sierra Leone Special Court, SCSL-04-14-T, Appeals Chamber Judgment 28 May.

Prosecutor v Sesay, Kallon, and Gbao 2009, Sierra Leone Special Court, SCSL-04-15-T, Trial Chamber Judgment 25 February.

Prosecutor v Thomas Lubango Dyilo 2009, International Criminal Court, ICC-01/04-01/06, commencement of trial 26 January (ongoing).

Provisional Measures regarding Brazil: Matter of Children Deprived of Liberty in the "Complexo do Tatuape" of FEBEM 2007, Inter-American Court of Human Rights, 3 July (also 10 June and 25 November 2008).

Roper v Simmons 2005, Supreme Court of the United States, No. 03-633, 1 March.

Socio-Economic Rights and Accountability Project (SERAP) v Federal Government and Universal Basic Education Commission (UBEC) 2009, Community Court of Justice of the Economic Community of West African States, (No. ECW/CCJ/APP/0808), 19 November.

Sullivan v Florida 2009, Supreme Court of the United States, No. 08-7621, 9 November.

Tysiac v Poland 2007, (App no. 5410/03), 45 E.H.R.R. 42.

UNICEF. 2004. *Summary Report of the Study on the Impact of the Implementation of the Convention on the Rights of the Child* (Florence: Innocenti Research Centre). At: http://www.unicef-irc.org/publications/pdf/CRC_Impact_summaryreport.pdf.
Villagran-Morales et al v Guatemala 1999, Inter-American Court of Human Rights, 19 November.
Vo v France 2005, (App no. 53924/00), 40 E.H.R.R. 12.
Ye and Qui v Minister of Immigration 2009, NZSC (New Zealand Supreme Court) 76, 20.

30
The right to food

Clair Apodaca

Chronic hunger and malnutrition affect the lives and futures of millions of people every year. Severe malnutrition is associated with increased physical deformities, skeletal growth retardation, blindness, morbidity, and even death. Furthermore, hunger results in restricted behavior whereby food-seeking activities become the sole focus of life. Food is needed for both human dignity and human development. A human rights approach to hunger calls on the binding obligation or duty of the states or other duty-bearers to fulfill the entitlement to food. The hungry individual is a rights claim-holder. A human right to food also allows the hungry to seek remedy and resolution for the violation of the right. The elimination of hunger, using a human rights approach, positions the individual as a subject of law with legitimate claims and entitlements to food against the state as primary duty-bearer. From this perspective, hungry people are legally entitled to adequate food nutrition as a matter of right.

Food as a human right

A human right can be understood as an interest so fundamentally important to human dignity that it imposes duties on others for its fulfillment. Due to the severely debilitating effects and suffering caused by the lack of food, the right to food is indispensable in securing human dignity. International human rights law clearly establishes such entitlements to food. In order to achieve the goals and aspirations of the United Nations, states have endorsed an international legal code that protects and enhances human dignity. The Charter of the United Nations, adopted in 1945, declares that one of the organization's primary purposes is to:

> achieve international co-operation in solving international problems of an economic, social, cultural, or humanitarian character and in promoting and encouraging respect for human rights and for fundamental freedoms for all without distinction as to race, sex, language, or religion.
>
> *(Article 1[3])*

The UN Declaration of Human Rights, which many legal theorists claim has reached the status of obligatory customary law, states that, "Everyone has the right to a standard of living adequate for the health and well-being of himself and his family, including food" (Article 25). The International Covenant on Economic, Social and Cultural Rights (ICESCR) is the principal source of legal obligations and provisions protecting economic and social rights. Article 11 of the ICESCR is the core provision in securing the "fundamental" right to food. Subsection 1 of Article 11 states: "The States Parties to the present Covenant recognize the right of everyone to an adequate standard of living for himself and his family, including adequate food ... " Subsection 2 further clarifies: "The States Parties to the present Covenant, recognizing the *fundamental* right of everyone to be free from hunger, shall take, individually and through international co-operation, the measures, including specific programmes, which are needed." The ICESCR creates legal obligations that had been accepted by 158 ratifying countries as of September 2008.

In 1999, the Committee on Economic, Social, and Cultural Rights (CESCR), the body created to oversee and monitor states' implementation of the ICESCR, issued General Comment No. 12, "The Right to Adequate Food." General Comment No. 12 reaffirmed the right to food as being fundamental to human dignity and crucial for the realization of all other human rights. It also recognized that the right to food requires availability and access. General Comment No. 12 states:

> The right to adequate food is realized when every man, woman and child, alone or in community with others, has physical and economic access at all times to adequate food or means for its procurement. The right to adequate food shall therefore not be interpreted in a narrow or restrictive sense which equates it with a minimum package of calories, proteins and other specific nutrients ... Every State is obligated to ensure for everyone under its jurisdiction access to the minimum essential food which is sufficient, nutritionally adequate and safe, to ensure their freedom from hunger.

A year later, the CESCR issued General Comment No. 14, "The Right to the Highest Attainable Standard of Health," which further expounded that the right to food is an integral component of the right to health. The Committee understands the right to health to include the "underlying determinants of health, such as access to safe and potable water and adequate sanitation, an adequate supply of safe food ... " General Comment No. 14 also recognizes the special protection given to children in the state's obligation to realize the right to health for all its citizens.

According to Alston and Tomasevski (1984), "hunger [is] by far the most flagrant and widespread of all serious human rights abuses," and children are undoubtedly the primary victims of this kind of abuse. The 1989 Convention on the Rights of the Child (CRC) was developed because the members of the international community agreed that children were (and still are) particularly vulnerable and needed special care and protection. The widespread support for children's rights is expressed by the fact that the CRC enjoys near universal acceptance, and it went into effect within a year of the treaty being opened for ratification. The CRC transformed children's moral claims to food into legal rights to food. Several articles of the CRC deal directly with the child's right to food and nutrition:

> Article 24: "State Parties recognize the right of the child to the enjoyment of the highest attainable standard of health ... State Parties shall pursue full implementation of this right

> and, in particular, shall take appropriate measures ... to combat disease and malnutrition, including ... through the provision of adequate, nutritious food."
>
> Article 27(3): "State Parties ... shall in case of need provide material assistance and support programs, particularly with regard to nutrition, clothing and housing."

Article 2(1) affirms that the primary obligation for ensuring the rights listed in the CRC falls on the state (when the child's family or caregivers cannot or will not adequately provide for the child). Second, Article 5 stipulates that international organizations along with the international state donors also bear responsibility to the hungry child. The need for international assistance and cooperation is seen as essential for the realization of the right to food, and it is also part of the original obligation of protection of economic, social, and cultural rights. The obligation to protect and provide for children has been accepted by 192 countries through the ratification of the CRC (with the notable exceptions of Somalia and the United States).

The international community of states has repeatedly affirmed that there are economic and social human rights standards, which include the right to food. Rights relating to an adequate standard of living, food and nutrition, and health care are included in a variety of morally and legally binding international documents demonstrating global acknowledgment and acceptance. Table 30.1 provides a brief summary of the long history of morally binding declarations and resolutions supporting the right to food and indicating global acceptance of this right.

Although these documents do not have the status in international law as do treaties, they do demonstrate evidence of an international agreement on the right to food as a human right. The right to food has been affirmed by documents, resolutions, and plans of action at numerous conferences and summits attended by the vast majority of the world's governments.

Human rights obligations

If individuals have a right to food, this right implies an obligation on the part of the duty-bearer. Critics claim a right is essentially meaningless unless some person or institution is identified as being responsible for the fulfillment of that right. However, rights are no less authentic simply because they are unrealized rights or that the correlative duties are imperfect. A perfect obligation is one where "a specific duty of a particular agent for the actual realization of that right" is clearly identified (Sen 2000, p. 495). A perfect obligation specifies who is due the right, how the right is to be satisfied, and who has the duty to fulfill the obligation. An imperfect obligation is one where, in the words of Sen, "no particular person or agency has been charged with bringing about the fulfillment of the rights" (2000, p. 497). Human rights do not depend on pinpointing precise duties, identifying particular victims, or even determining who has the specific obligation to fulfill the right. If you can feasibly help a nameless victim in some general way, you have the duty to help, particularly if the act, such as feeding starving children, requires relatively little personal cost. In the case of the human rights violation of the starving individual, the duties cannot easily be assigned to one particular duty-bearer or another. To quote Sen, "if others can help, then there is a responsibility that goes with it. Even if it is not specified who will have to do what in order to help the victimized person, there is a general need for a responsible consequence-evaluating agent to consider her general duty to help others (when reasonably feasible)" (2000, p. 494). The concept of imperfect obligations takes us beyond the moral duty of individuals to help feed starving people toward the idea of obligations derived from the consequence of unjust actions or policies deployed by structures and systems of powerful states and transnational organizations. International entities have an obligation to assist if they helped to create, maintain, or benefit from the injustice of hunger.

Table 30.1 Non-treaty documents, reports, expert opinions, global conferences, and resolutions acknowledging the right to food

1959	*UN Declaration on the Rights of the Child* (Article 4: "The child shall have the right to adequate nutrition, housing, recreation and medical services")
1974	United Nations General Assembly, Resolution 3348, *Universal Declaration on the Eradication of Hunger and Malnutrition*
1983	ESC Report on the *Right to Adequate Food as a Human Right*
1984	International Law Association formed Right to Food Committee/Netherlands Human Rights Institute held a conference on food
1986/1987	Limburg Principles/ UN HR Commission approved Limburg Principles
1990	World Summit for Children, *Plan of Action for Implementing the World Declaration on the Survival, Protection, and Development of Children*
1992	International Conference on Nutrition, *World Declaration on Nutrition*
	UN Conference on the Environment and Development, Rio de Janeiro
1993	World Conference on Human Rights, Vienna (WCHR), *Draft Guidelines: A Human Rights Approach to Poverty Reduction Strategies, Programs of Action*
1994	The International Conference on Population and Development, Cairo
1995	Fourth World Conference on Women, Beijing (FWCW), *Beijing Declaration and Platform for Action*
	World Summit for Social Development, Copenhagen (WSSD), *World Summit for Social Development Programme of Action*
1996	World Food Summit resulting in *Rome Declaration and Plan of Action*
1997	*Draft Code of Conduction on the Right to Adequate Food*
1999	CESCR *General Comment No. 12*
2000	Special Rapporteur on the Right to Food
	Millennium Summit of the United Nations: Goal 1 to eradicate extreme poverty and hunger
	Office of the High Commission for Human Rights: Commission on Human Rights Resolution 2000/10 The Right to Food
2001	Secretary General's Decade Review "We the Children"
2002	UN General Assembly Resolution 56/155 The Right to Food
	Declaration of the World Food Summit: Five Years Later
	UN General Assembly Special Session "A World Fit for Children"
2003	Office of the High Commission for Human Rights Commission on Human Rights Resolution 2003/25 The Right to Food
	UN General Assembly Resolution 57/226 The Right to Food
2004	UN General Assembly Resolution 58/186 The Right to Food
	Office of the High Commission for Human Rights Commission on Human Rights Resolution 2004/19 The Right to Food
2005	World Summit and Special Session on Children
	Office of the High Commission for Human Rights: Human Rights Resolution 2005/18 The Right to Food
	UN General Assembly Resolution 59/202 The Right to Food
2006	UN General Assembly Resolution 60/165 The Right to Food

State obligations

The human rights literature shares a common presumption that the state is the principal duty-bearer. A state's duties concerning human rights, according to Eide (1996), the first UN Special Rapporteur on the Right to Food, entail three forms of obligations: the obligation to respect human rights, the obligation to protect human rights, and the obligation to provide, that is to fulfill and facilitate in the attainment of the human rights to food. The obligation to respect human rights, in this case the right to food, requires the state to refrain from directly or indirectly interfering with the attainment of food or from doing anything that violates or infringes on procuring food.

A second mode of obligation is the obligation to protect human rights. The obligation to protect compels the state to prevent other individuals or business concerns from violating the right to food or otherwise interfering with people's enjoyment of their rights. The third level of state obligation is the duty to provide. The state has the obligation to fulfill the basic human need for food of all those persons living within its jurisdiction. The fulfillment of human rights covers both the actual provision of food and the legal and jurisdictional infrastructure necessary to enact laws, administer programs, litigate violations, etc. Facilitating opportunities means increasing access to resources and conditions for people to fulfill their own rights. Individuals, as agents and not as mere objects of the right to food, are responsible for providing for their own needs. Certain rights-holders, however, may depend more on entitlements, for example, children and the elderly.

States have accepted this responsibility by signing international treaties. By ratifying the human rights treaties the state has accepted the provisions within the treaty and agreed to become responsible for the domestic and international implementation of those provisions (unless the state made some specific reservation to the treaty provisions). The CESCR stated that "a State Party in which any significant number of individuals is deprived of essential foodstuffs, of essential primary health care, of basic shelter and housing, or of the most basic forms of educations is, prima facie, failing to discharge its obligations under the Covenant" (UN 1991, para. 10). States that are party to the ICESCR or CRC have the responsibility to respect, protect, provide, and facilitate, to the maximum of their resources, the right to food.

When a state is unable to meet its duty to its citizens to fulfill the human right to food, due to insufficient resources or other reasons, it has an incontrovertible obligation to appeal to the international community. The United Nations General Assembly (2001) affirmed the need for the impoverished state to appeal to the international community for humanitarian aid if the state is to meet its obligation to fulfill the human right to food for its citizens in accordance with its treaty commitments. States that fail to make an appeal or delay making the appeal are in violation of their treaty commitments. But, equally important, the recipient state has the obligation to use that aid for reducing poverty and feeding the hungry.

Extraterritorial obligations of foreign states

The contemporary ethical debate on an affluent state's obligation to provide food aid to foreign citizens can be traced to Peter Singer's well-known 1972 essay on famine relief. Singer argues that rich states have a moral obligation to assist starving people in poor countries "if it is in our power to prevent something bad from happening [and most people would agree that death and suffering due to lack of food is bad], without thereby sacrificing anything of comparable moral importance, we ought, morally, to do it" (Singer 1972; reprinted in Aiken and LaFollette 2002, p. 28). This obligation, according to Singer, is not dependent on proximity or distance. As one can imagine, Singer is not without his critics (Hardin 1974; Murphy 1993; Miller 1998; Cullity 2004). The debate on the obligation to aid hungry people becomes more contentious when one considers persistent unremitting hunger rather than the acute hunger associated with natural disasters and famines. The elimination of global chronic hunger would entail a boundless obligation, requiring a continual transfer of resources from the affluent to the destitute until the problem of hunger is resolved. Many resist this demanding view of obligation. Certainly, most Western states oppose either a moral or a legal binding obligation regarding the perpetual transfer of resources.

Although there is still a debate as to whether and to what extent international states and transnational organizations have obligations to foreign citizens, legal theorists, within the last decade, have generally noted that state parties to the ICESCR (Article 11 of the ICESCR twice acknowledges the importance of international cooperation for the realization of food, while no other specific right receives this recognition) and the CRC have accepted the concept of shared responsibility, that is, the obligation to provide international assistance and international cooperation. Marks explains: "The principle of shared responsibility means, at a minimum, that opportunities must exist to assess whether and to what extent each country's development policy – including its relations with donors, lenders and investors – is consistent with the shared objective of human development and human rights" (2007, p. 71). The phrase "through international assistance and co-operation" in Article 2 of the ICESCR implies that richer states have a moral duty to create a cooperative international order, to encourage and promote conditions that will facilitate the realization of rights, including economic assistance and technical aid. Nickel (1996) explains that, with the shared responsibility to satisfy the right to food, when one of the parties fails to live up to its responsibility, the other parties in the system will see their responsibilities increased. When the government, the primary duty-bearer, is unable or unwilling to fulfill its duty, the international community must then assume greater responsibility.

Beyond obligations assumed by foreign states through the ratification of international treaties, states can become obligated for the human rights effects of their "external activities, such as trade, development cooperation, participation in international organizations, and security activities" (Skogly and Gibney 2002, p. 781). Thus, there are two other ways states can become obligated to prevent hunger in foreign countries. First, it is generally assumed that people are morally obligated to assist those people they have harmed. Therefore, affluent states, particularly if they were colonial powers, can be seen as having created the conditions of hunger in developing countries. What is referred to as causal responsibility, through economic policies, unfair trade relations, resource extraction, foreign aid, or odious debt practices, makes those affluent countries morally duty-bound to assist those suffering from their foreign activities. States' activities in the international realm, either individually or in collaboration with other states, can and do affect the human rights of foreign populations.

Second, states are obligated because they have made promises, however vague, to help. LaFollette and May (1995) believe that affluent countries are morally and perhaps legally bound to help those they have explicitly agreed or promised to help. When a state signs an international treaty, such as the ICESCR or the CRC, it becomes bound to the provisions of the treaty (less reservations). Both the ICESCR and the CRC recognize the importance of international cooperation for the realization of the right to food. Thus, a state's legal obligation to cooperate would extend to international organizations where states work collectively with others to solve global problems, including the global scourge of hunger and malnutrition.

Transnational obligations of international financial institutions (IFIs)

The UN Charter (Article 1) states that one of the purposes of the United Nations Organization is to "achieve international co-operation in solving international problems of an economic, social, cultural, or humanitarian character, and in promoting and encouraging respect for human rights and for fundamental freedoms for all without distinction as to race, sex, language, or religion" (UN, n.d.). And according to the websites of both the International Monetary Fund (IMF) and the World Bank, their stated mission goals are to foster international cooperation in the reduction of poverty. The IMF website (n.d.) reports that "the IMF is an organization of 187 countries, working to foster global monetary cooperation, secure financial stability, facilitate international trade, promote high employment and sustainable economic growth, and reduce poverty." The World Bank (2004) proudly declares: "At the World Bank we have made the world's challenge – to reduce global poverty – our challenge."

As members of the UN family, specialized agencies such as the IMF and World Bank are required to engage in international cooperation and respect human rights. In fact, as Kracht reports, former UN Secretary General Kofi Annan (1997–2007) affirmed that "all UN funds, programs and specialized agencies should be guided by the international human rights framework" (2006).

Furthermore, international governmental organizations are bound indirectly since they are composed of states bound by the treaties. The specialized agencies of the UN are made up of states that are parties to international human rights treaties and, therefore, hold obligations to protect and provide economic rights of citizens. Therefore, international organizations have a minimum duty to respect the obligations of their constituent members. From a legal perspective, affiliated agencies of the UN are subject to human rights obligations on two fronts. International governmental organizations are obligated as members of the UN family and are also bound by the obligations of the member states (Skogly and Gibney 2002).

Philosophers, religious leaders, and the majority of humanity would agree that "people are morally responsible to those to whom they cause harm" (LaFollette and May 1995, p. 74). This belief is obvious if we are the direct cause of the harm. In addition, some hold a more controversial belief that we are morally responsible for the harm created by the institutions or organizations that we actively participate in or benefit from. For example, Pogge believes that "we are asked to be concerned about human rights violations not simply insofar as they exist at all, but only insofar as they are produced by social institutions [such as the World Bank or the IMF] in which we are significant participants" (1992, p. 52). Many claim that poverty is compounded by the implementation of austerity measures, sometimes known as structural adjustment policies (SAPs), imposed by the IMF and the World Bank. A major fault of the programs initiated by the IFIs, pro-poor activists claim, is that they focus on state economic growth rather than on alleviating the poverty of citizens. These economic reforms can include privatization of the economy, reductions in government spending on social welfare projects, elimination of subsidies (including food subsidies), and institution of user-fees for health and education services. Thus, Andreassen et al. (1992) found that international lending increased food insecurity and required poorer households to spend larger amounts of their meager budgets on food. Whether one believes that the international financial institutions associated with the UN have a shared responsibility to uphold the core mission of the UN or not, it is reasonable to expect that these specialized agencies ought to refrain from conducting themselves in a manner that breaches or hinders the UN's core objectives.

Transnational obligations of multinational corporations

Multinational corporations are not parties to international treaties. They neither signed nor ratified the UN Charter, the ICESCR, or the CRC. Yet, there is, according to George Kent (2005), a growing consensus that nonstate actors (such as multinational corporations) have the obligation to *respect* the human right to food and to refrain from violating people's attempt to acquire adequate levels of food. However, as Kent acknowledges, there is little agreement that nonstate actors have a duty to *protect*, *provide*, or *facilitate* the right to food. Multinational corporations (MNCs) have the moral duty to refrain from causing human rights violations through their policies and actions, but they do not have the moral obligation to prevent others from interfering with the right to food, nor do they have the responsibility to provide food to the hungry. Simply put, in contemporary international law, there are no binding legal ties to these moral obligations for multinational corporations.

How can private parties be held accountable for the violation of the right to food? Again, we return to the philosophical premise presented above that an entity is morally responsible for the harm it causes. If the MNC is the direct or indirect cause of the violation it should be responsible for the harm created. As an example of how multinational corporations may directly violate the right to food, the International Council on Human Rights speculates that "companies might hoard food to push up prices, or otherwise deliberately promote scarcity of an essential food production" (2002, p. 35). MNCs have a strong duty not to perform actions that cause harm. However, MNCs should also be held accountable for their indirect violations of the human right to food. If the actions or corporate policies of an MNC creates an environment that causes hunger, the MNC is responsible for the resulting hunger and malnutrition. For example, if an MNC engages in dumping low-level hazardous chemicals in the water used by local farmers to irrigate food crops, which in the long term destroys the fertility of the soil and thereby makes agriculture impossible, the MNC is morally responsible for the resulting hunger and malnutrition suffered by the local village folk.

There are some who believe that MNCs may have a moral obligation to protect and provide. Because MNCs do business in poverty stricken countries, they are in the best position to help – being both well placed and well heeled to aid hungry individuals. This position is best articulated by Thomas Scanlon's argument in *What We Owe to Each Other*. Scanlon states that "if you are presented with a situation in which you can prevent something very bad from happening, or alleviate someone's dire plight, by making only a slight (or even moderate) sacrifice, then it would be wrong not to do so" (1998, p. 224). Multinational corporations have considerable financial resources, technical expertise, and global presence, which put them in a position to "alleviate someone's dire plight." A failure to render assistance, if you can do so without placing yourself in harm's way, is morally wrong. Oftentimes, at least in the domestic situation, it is legally wrong also. Good Samaritan laws, found in the United States, Canada, and the EU, are legal standards that require bystanders to assist people in distress, unless doing so would put the bystander in harm's way.

In addition, MNCs are often used as tools of state power, and therefore carry a responsibility in tandem with the state (Stephens 2002). Ratner (2001) explains that because states "need to rely on businesses to supply them with material for various unacceptable activities, corporations may work in tandem with governments in abusing human rights." MNCs can be complicit in the wrongdoings undertaken by their partners. This is true even if the corporation only benefits from the policies or actions taken by the state that cause the harm inflicted on others and was not an active participant in the wrongdoing.

Conclusion

In sum, the human right to food can be located in the human rights framework of the Universal Declaration of Human Rights, the ICESCR, and the CRC. In addition to the economic protections provided by these treaties, children benefit from particular rights detailed in the CRC. Regardless of their age, nationality, or state of residence, every human being has rights, authentic and legitimate claims upon domestic and international society. The right to food is a human right. As a human right, the right to food entails a claim on both domestic and international resources, imposing duties on states and international actors. The obligation to feed the hungry is both a moral and legal duty accepted by the nation-state and international community. A moral duty is an imperative to do what is right and good while a legal obligation is action required by law. The international community of states and transnational actors were guided by their moral obligations to draft and ratify international treaties and other normative instruments recognizing the human rights of people to adequate levels of food and to be free from hunger. The ICESCR and the CRC transform moral duties to adequate food into legal obligations.

References

Aiken, William and Hugh LaFollette, eds. 2002. *World Hunger and Morality* (New York: Prentice-Hall).

Alderman, Harold. 1992. *Incomes and Food Security in Ghana*. Working Paper No. 26 (Washington, DC: Cornell Food and Nutrition Policy Program).

Alston, Philip and Katarina Tomasevski. 1984. *The Right to Food* (Leiden, Netherlands: Martinus Nijhoff).

Andreassen, Bard-Anders, Alan Smith, and Hugo Stokke. 1992. "Compliance with Economic and Social Human Rights: Realistic Evaluations and Monitoring in the Light of Immediate Obligations." In Asbjorn Eide and Bernt Hagtvet, eds., *Human Rights in Perspective: A Global Assessment* (Oxford: Blackwell Publishers).

Cullity, Garrett. 2004. *The Moral Demands of Affluence* (Oxford: Clarendon Press).

Eide, Asbjorn. 1996. "Human Rights Requirements to Social and Economic Development." *Food Policy*, Vol. 21, No. 1, pp. 23–39.

Hardin, Garrett. 2002. "Lifeboat Ethics: The Case Against Helping the Poor." In William Aiken and Hugh LaFollette, eds., *World Hunger and Morality* (New York: Prentice-Hall).

International Monetary Fund. N.d. *About the IMF*. Viewed 14 July 2010. At: <http://www.imf.org/external/about.htm>.

John Hoddinott. 1999. *Operationalizing Household Food Security in Development Projects: An Introduction* (Washington, DC: International Food Policy Research Institute).

International Council on Human Rights. 2002. *Beyond Voluntarism: Human Rights and the Developing International Legal Obligations of Companies* (Versoix, Switzerland: ICHRP).

Kennedy, Eileen and Howarth Bouis. 1993. *Agriculture/Nutrition Linkages: Implications for Policy and Research* (Washington, DC: International Food Policy Research Institute).

Kent, George. 2005. *Freedom From Want: The Human Right to Adequate Food* (Washington, DC: Georgetown University Press).

Kracht, Uwe. 2006. *Food is a Human Right*. Hunger Notes, World Hunger Education Service. At: <http://www.worldhunger.org/articles/global/foodashumrgt/kracht.htm>.

LaFollette, Hugh and Larry May. 1995. "Suffer the Little Children." In William Aiken and Hugh LaFollette, eds., *World Hunger and Morality* (New York: Prentice-Hall).

Marks, Stephen. 2007. 'Obligations to Implement the Right to Development: Philosophical, Political, and Legal Rationales," pp. 57–78 in Bard Anders Andreassen and Stephen Marks, eds., *Development as a Human Right* (Cambridge, MA: Harvard School of Public Health).

Miller, R. 1998. "Cosmopolitan Respect and Patriotic Concern," *Philosophy and Public Affairs*, Vol. 27, No. 3, pp. 202-224.

Murphy, Liam. 1993. "The Demands of Beneficence." *Philosophy & Public Affairs*, Vol. 22, No. 4, pp. 267-292.

Nickel, James. 1996. "A Human Rights Approach to World Hunger," pp. 171-185 n William Aiken and Hugh LaFollette, eds., *World Hunger and Morality* (New York: Prentice-Hall).

Office of the High Commission for Human Rights (OHCHR). 2002. *Draft Guidelines: A Human Rights Approach to Poverty Reduction Strategies*. At: <http://www1.umn.edu/humanrts/instree/povertyreductionguidelines.html>.

Pogge, Thomas. 1992. "Cosmopolitanism and Sovereignty." *Ethics*, Vol. 103, No. 1, pp. 48-75.

Ratner, S. 2001. "Corporations and Human Rights: A Theory of Legal Responsibility," *Yale Law Journal*, Vol. 111, No. 3, pp. 443-545.

Scanlon, T. 1998. *What We Owe to each Other* (Cambridge, MA: Harvard University Press).

Sen, Amartya. 1981. *Poverty and Famines: An Essay in Entitlement and Deprivation* (New York: Oxford University Press).

Sen, Amartya. 2000. "Consequential Evaluation and Practical Reason." *Journal of Philosophy*, Vol. 97, No. 9, pp. 477-502.

Singer, Peter. 1972. "Famine, Affluence, and Morality." *Philosophy and Public Affairs*, Vol. 1, No. 3.

Skogly, Sigrun and Mark Gibney. 2002. "Transnational Human Rights Obligations." *Human Rights Quarterly*, Vol. 24, No. 3, pp. 781-798.

Staatz, John. 2000. "Strategic Pathways and Interactions to Cutting Hunger in Half in Africa." At: <http://www.aec.msu.edu/agecon/fs2/africanhunger/strategicpaths.pdf>.

Stephens, Beth. 2002. "The Amorality of Profit: Transnational Corporations and Human Right." *Berkeley Journal of International Law*, Vol. 20, pp. 45-90.

United Nations. N.d. *Charter of the United Nations*. Viewed 14 July 2010. At: <http://www.un.org/en/documents/charter/chapter1.shtml>.

United Nations. 1991. Report on the Fifth Session. U.N. Doc. E/1991/23, Annex III.

United Nations General Assembly. 2001. 'The Right to Food." A/56/210, GA 56th session.

World Bank. 2004. *About Us*. Viewed 14 July 2010. At: <http://go.worldbank.org/DM4A38OWJ0>.

31
The rights of refugees

Hakan G. Sicakkan

Refugees are special kinds of foreigners who interact with states in a unique way. Their interactions with states are distinct from other state–individual relations that political and legal theories delineate because they are neither inter-state relations nor center–periphery, state–citizen or citizen–citizen relations. The postwar notion of state, which originates from the principles manifest in the Peace of Augsburg of 1555, Westphalia Treaty of 1648, and the Wilsonian principles of 1918, prescribes states' right to determine who to let in and who to exclude from their territories. On the other hand, through the 1951 Geneva Convention relating to the Status of Refugees and its related 1967 Protocol, the liberal element of the very same ideology renders the states responsible for protecting refugees. By granting refugee status to foreigners, a state abandons its right to decide on their movements across its territory as well as its own discretion about how to treat foreigners. The state is also obliged by the Geneva Convention to guarantee civil and social rights to refugees. Therefore, the notion of refugee as defined in international law today is the only known phenomenon whereby a sovereign state and a person of foreign nationality, representing only his or her own person, interact with each other, to advance their claims for, respectively, *sovereignty* and *protection*.

Development of the notion of refugee

"In everyday speech a refugee is someone who has been compelled to abandon his home" (Zolberg et al. 1989). This sociological feature of the refugee condition is crucial. However, throughout history, the meaning of the refugee concept has transformed as a corollary to the political realities. It is primarily the changing form and content of the association between the rulers and the ruled that has determined the meaning of the refugee concept. Empirically, the political dimension of the phenomenon is more characterizing than its sociological dimension.

Until the French Revolution, protection was given to *fugitives* on a private basis by those who were emphatic enough to identify with the persecuted. In ancient and medieval times, for instance, the utilization of temples and churches for protecting fugitives was known as sanctuary. Temples in Egypt, Greece, and Rome, for example, provided sanctuary. Sanctuaries served at that time as shelters for people escaping violence and states' penalties. Forcible removal of or violence to people in sanctuary was considered a sacrilege (Zolberg et al. 1989). In the European feudal states, refugees were royal family members and members of the landed aristocracy whose inherited "natural" rights were denied. As all rights were based on kin, slaves were excluded from protection, and nobles in trouble generally sought shelter in the lands of other nobles with whom they shared interests in terms of power relations, politics, or religious beliefs. Toward the end of the Middle Ages, estates began to replace the feudal organization, and serfs gradually gained mobility. Religious belonging started to become the new social stratification factor, and religious minorities' situation gradually worsened in Europe. Spain, for instance, expelled the Jews and the Moors in the fifteenth century.

After the Reformation, religion became the major association between the rulers and the ruled. The Peace of Augsburg in 1555 adopted the principle of *Cuius regio, eius religio*, which established each prince's right to determine whether Roman Catholicism or Lutheranism would be his subjects' religion. The situation of religious minorities during the Wars of Religion in France, known also as the Huguenot Wars (1562–1598), exemplifies as well the conception of the refugee as bearer of a certain religious belief that was "undesirable" in a state. Such people were helped through military interventions and provisions of asylum by states that had an interest in protecting the respective religion. Spain, for example, intervened in France (1589–1598) in order to ensure that a Catholic should take over the French throne. In the sixteenth and seventeenth centuries, there were further flights to America from religious persecutions in Europe. The Peace of Westphalia in 1648 made the territorial boundaries more relevant to the refugee condition. In the eighteenth century, the exodus of *émigrés* during the French Revolution expanded further the refugee concept. After the fall of the Bastille in 1789, those who fled the bourgeois persecution were royalists from *all classes* (Zolberg et al. 1989). The term *émigré* connoted the political refugee who was persecuted for his or her political status or opinion.

During the interwar period (1918–1939), the refugee was a Russian opponent of Bolshevism or a member of an ethnic minority. In addition to approximately 1.5 million people fleeing the Bolshevik Revolution in 1917, many people belonging to ethnic minorities left their homes after the new Wilsonian international order was established. The interwar period was characterized by mass exchanges of minority populations between the new nation-states, such as the Turkish–Greek population exchanges. In the League of Nations treaties and arrangements of 1926 and 1928, the refugee was a person who did not enjoy the protection of the government of the country of his or her origin. A refugee was defined in 1926 as "any person of Russian origin who does not enjoy or who no longer enjoys the protection of the Government of the Union of Socialist Soviet Republics and who has not acquired another nationality" (Goodwin-Gill 1985). During Japan's invasion of China in the 1930s and 1940s, internally displaced people in China were referred to as "refugees" in American official communications (Lee 1996). Later, Article 1 of the 1933 Convention relating to the International Status of Refugees defined the refugee similarly.

Similar definitions were adopted for Armenian, Turkish, Assyrian, Assyro-Chaldean, and assimilated (Syrian or Kurdish) refugees. The decisive criterion in determining the refugee status in all these definitions was the presence or the lack of "protection" by the governments concerned (Lee 1996).

Other significant political events in the interwar period were Hitler's accession to power in Germany in 1933, annexation of Austria in 1938 and Czechoslovakia in 1939, the Loyalist defeat in Spain in 1939, and anti-Semitic legislation in Eastern Europe. The refugees produced by these events, for example, Jews and Loyalists, were not sufficiently protected (slave labor, forced repatriation, etc.). After the Paris Conference held in 1938, with the participation of thirty-two countries, a permanent committee was established in London in order to achieve progress in protection of these refugees. During World War II, the refugee was a Jew, who had no getaway.

The end of World War II constitutes the historical context of today's refugee concept. In 1946, the International Refugee Organization (IRO) identified "persons of German ethnic origin" who were expelled, or were to be expelled, from their countries of birth into the post-war Germany, as persons who are "not the concern of the Organization," something which follows the aforementioned historical trend of defining a refugee in terms of interplays between states, politics, dominant ideologies, and normative conceptions of what the link between citizens and states ought to be. Also, for the first time in history, the 1946 Constitution of IRO used explicitly the phrase "being outside the country of nationality" in the legal definition of a refugee. The 1951 Geneva Convention adopted the same criterion.

Another important feature of the postwar change in the refugee concept is that the 1951 Convention supplemented the earlier criterion in the 1933 Convention of "lack of protection by a state" with the requirement of "persecution," in which the state as persecutor or endorser of non-state agents' persecution was implicit. Seen in a historical perspective, with its (implicit) requirements of "state persecution" instead of "lack of protection by a state" and "being outside the country of nationality," the 1951 Refugee Convention represents a restrictive conception of the refugee:

> Any person who, as a result of events occurring before 1 January 1951 and owing to well-founded fear of being persecuted for reasons of race, religion, nationality, membership of a particular social group or political opinion, is outside the country of his nationality and is unable or, owing to such fear, is unwilling to avail himself of the protection of that country; or who, not having a nationality and being outside the country of his former habitual residence as a result of such events, is unable, or owing to such fear, is unwilling to return to it.
>
> *(Art. 1A)*

The Geneva Convention was approved at a United Nations conference on 28 July 1951. There are now 147 signatories to either the Geneva Convention or the Protocol, or to both. Originally, the Convention aimed to protect the European refugees after World War II. Later, all regional and temporal limitations were removed by the 1967 Protocol in order to expand the Convention's scope. Indeed, the Geneva Convention, with the optional 1967 Protocol, is the basic international instrument of refugee law. The refugee law also comprises customary law, peremptory norms, some regional instruments, and some states' constitutional asylum laws, which in some cases define additional legal categories.

The regional instruments include the 1966 Bangkok Principles on Status and Treatment of Refugees adopted at the Asian-African Legal Consultative Committee in 1966, the 1969 OAU Convention Governing the Specific Aspects of Refugee Problems in Africa, the 1984 Cartagena Declaration on Refugees for Latin America, the 1976 Council of Europe's Recommendation 773 (1976) on the Situation of de facto Refugees, and the 2004 European Union's Council Directive on minimum standards for the qualification and status of third-country nationals and stateless persons as refugees or as persons who otherwise need international protection and content of the protection granted.

Concerning alternative legal categories, whereas France, Germany, Portugal, and Spain keep their constitutional protection scheme separate from their national refugee definitions, which are in principle copied from the 1951 Geneva Convention, Greece and Italy merge the refugee convention with their constitutional-protection rules examination. States' alternative legal categories are shaped by their own political histories (Sicakkan 2008): all European countries – i.e., France, Germany, Greece, Italy, and Portugal – that experienced liberation wars from authoritarian regimes during and after World War II have the category of "freedom fighters" in their constitutional asylum laws. Among the countries that have a constitutional asylum scheme, the only exception from this rule is Spain, which has itself had problems with ETA-based freedom fighters.

This depiction outlines the interplays between politics, state ideologies, and the refugee definition. The notion of refugee is premised upon the association between rulers and the ruled, just like the meaning of the citizen. As the diversity of associations between rulers and the ruled was augmented, the refugee concept extended. The 1951 Geneva Convention froze this historical process of extension, however, by defining the refugee as *the antonym of the postwar citizen*. As the associations between the ruler(s) and the ruled are apparently not a constant over time and space, any rigid definition of a refugee premised on a specific, singular association will be an incomplete descriptive category. Also across countries and regions, both historical and new formations of citizenship ideals represent different loyalty structures and a variety of associations between the state and the individual, and hence, different notions of refugee. Each state is, thus, likely to interpret the refugee concept based on its own historical or particular conception of the citizen.

The rights of refugees

Convention refugees are to enjoy all the rights mentioned in the 1951 Geneva Convention. The main principle in the Convention determining which rights should be accorded to refugees is mentioned in Article 7, paragraph 1: "Except where this Convention contains more favorable provisions, a Contracting State shall accord to refugees the same treatment as is accorded to aliens generally."

However, the Geneva Convention also lists a range of provisions that give more favorable rights to refugees than aliens; in some cases, the Geneva Convention even asks the states to grant the same rights to refugees as their own citizens. The first column of Table 31.1 gives a list of the aliens' rights that the Convention obliges the states to grant to refugees. The areas in which the Convention asks the states to treat refugees more favorably than other aliens are listed in the second column. It should be noted that the majority of the rights listed in column two relate to procedures of recognition of refugee status – with the exception of "naturalization rules." In some other areas, the Convention advises the states to grant the same rights as their own nationals, which are listed in the third column.

Various countries extend the rights mentioned in the Geneva Convention. Extended rights can be classified under four categories: (1) cultural rights (mother tongue training, family reunification), (2) welfare and economic rights (health services, employment, job seeking, vocational training), and (3) residence and accommodation rights. In principle, the extension of refugees' rights by states is a consequence of the rights that their own citizens are entitled to. Therefore, extended refugee rights vary from country to country. In any attempt to depict the rights of refugees, it is adequate to consider both the rights defined in the Geneva Convention and the countries' own rights categories (Sicakkan 2008). However, my focus in this chapter is on the basic rights of refugees that are not country specific.

In practice, the refugee rights in Table 31.1 are interpreted in the light of a wide range of other relevant international legal instruments of human rights (Table 31.2). Indeed, the UNHCR's Executive Committee affirmed that "the institution of asylum, which derives directly from the right to seek and enjoy asylum set out in Article 14(1) of the Universal

Table 31.1 Rights of refugees in the Geneva Convention

The same rights as aliens in general	*More favorable rights than aliens in general*	*The same rights as nationals*
Movable and immovable property (art. 13)	Exemption from reciprocity (art. 7)	Religious rights (art. 4)
Self-employment (art. 18)	Exemption from exceptional measures (art. 8)	Rationing – where applied to citizens (art. 20)
Exercise of liberal professions (art. 19)	Continuity of residence (art. 10)	Artistic rights and industrial property (art. 14)
Housing (art. 21)	Personal status, more particularly rights attaching to marriage (art. 12)	Rights of association, non-political and non-profit organizations and trade unions (art. 15)
Public education beyond elementary education (art. 22, par. 2)	Administrative assistance/ representation towards third countries (art. 25)	Access to courts (art. 16)
Freedom of movement (art. 26)	Identity papers and travel documents (art. 27, art 28)	Wage-earning employment (art. 17)
	Transfer of assets to another country (in case of resettlement) (art. 30)	Elementary public education (art. 22, par.1)
	Unlawful entry or presence in the country (no penalty or unnecessary detention) (art. 31)	Public relief and assistance (art. 23)
	No expulsion – except national security/public order grounds (art. 32)	Wages, salaries, labor, and social security rights (art. 24)
	Non-refoulement (art. 33)	Fiscal charges (art. 29)
	Naturalization (art. 34)	

Declaration of Human Rights, is among the most basic mechanisms for the international protection of refugees" (UNHCR ExCom Conclusion No. 82). However, states' strict entry requirements, carrier sanctions, border closures, detention of asylum seekers, and other measures to hamper access to asylum procedures render the right to seek and enjoy asylum hard to achieve in practice.

The list of legal instruments in Table 31.2 testifies to the fact that refugee rights are tightly connected with human rights in both normative and legal terms. These instruments aim to guarantee the right of seeking and enjoying asylum by defining the minimum objectives of asylum determination procedures and by identifying the exemptions from the general aliens' laws that apply only to refugees and asylum seekers. Most importantly, the 1951 Geneva Convention and its related protocol oblige the states to give a fair treatment to all asylum seekers. The general objective of these rules is to ensure that refugees and asylum seekers be clearly distinguished from other aliens and that their applications for protection be fairly evaluated. These include (1) general rules concerning non-criminalization of asylum seeking, (2) exemption from the rules on identity, travel and visa documents, (3) exemption from the rules on detention, return and expulsion of aliens, and (4) exemption from the immigration laws and rules that may be too restrictive in some receiving countries.

The right of *non-refoulement* has over the years proved to be one of the most important legal instruments. Article 33 of the 1951 Geneva Convention on prohibition of expulsion or return ("*refoulement*") states that: "No Contracting State shall expel or return ("*refouler*") a refugee in any manner whatsoever to the frontiers of territories where his life or freedom would be threatened on account of his race, religion, nationality, membership of a particular social group or

Table 31.2 Basic rights regarding protection of refugees in various international and regional legal instruments

	THE RIGHTS OF REFUGEES					
	Seeking and enjoying asylum from persecution	*Liberty and security of person (protection against detention and penalty for illegal entry)*	*Non-refoulement*	*Due process, including during refugee status determination*	*Freedom of move-ment, procedural rights in expulsion/ prohibition against collective expulsion*	*Legal identity, status and documentation*
Geneva Convention	Art. 33	Art. 31	Art. 33	Art. 16	Arts. 26, 31, 32	Arts. 27, 28
UNHCR Revised Guidelines on Applicable Criteria and Standards relating to the Detention of Asylum Seekers		All				
UNHCR Guidelines on Protection and Care of Refugee Children		All				
UNHCR ExCom Conclusions	Nos. 82, 93, 94, 97	Nos. 44, 72, 85	Nos. 6, 7, 22, 30, 85, 102	Nos. 8. 30, 87		Nos. 35, 49, 91
UNHCR ExCom Standing Committee on Detention of Asylum-seekers and Refugees: The Framework, the Problem and Recommended Practice		All				
UN Declaration on Territorial Asylum	UNGA Resolution 2312 (XXII)		UNGA Resolution 2312 (XXII)			
UN Rules for Juveniles Deprived of their Liberty		All				
UN Standard Rules for the Treatment of Prisoners		All				

UN Body of Principles for the Protection of All Persons under Any Form of Detention or Imprisonment		All				
Convention relating to the Status of Stateless Persons				Art. 16		Arts. 27, 28
Universal Declaration of Human Rights (UDHR)	Art. 14	Art. 9	Art. 5	Art. 11	Art. 13	
Human Rights Committee, General Comments		Nos. 8, 15, 21, 27	Nos. 20, 31		No. 27 (art. 12)	No. 17 (art. 24)
International Declaration on the Protection of All Persons from Enforced Disappearance			Art. 8			
International Convention for the Protection of All Persons from Enforced Disappearance			Art. 16			
Principles on the Effective Prevention and Investigation of Extra-Legal, Arbitrary and Summary Executions			Principle No. 5			
International Covenant on Civil and Political Rights (ICCPR)		Arts. 9, 10	Art. 7	Art. 14	Arts. 12, 13	Arts. 16, 24(2)

(*Continued*)

Table 31.2 (Contd.)

	THE RIGHTS OF REFUGEES					
	Seeking and enjoying asylum from persecution	*Liberty and security of person (protection against detention and penalty for illegal entry)*	*Non-refoulement*	*Due process, including during refugee status determination*	*Freedom of movement, procedural rights in expulsion/ prohibition against collective expulsion*	*Legal identity, status and documentation*
Convention against Torture and Other Cruel, Inhuman or Degrading Treatment or Punishment			Art. 3			
Convention on the Rights of the Child (CRC)	Art. 22	Art. 37			Art. 10	Arts. 7, 8
Convention on the Elimination of All Forms of Racial Discrimination (CERD)				Arts. 5, 6	Art. 5	
Convention on the Elimination of All Forms of Discrimination against Women (CEDAW)					Art. 15(4)	
Guiding Principles on Internal Displacement						Principle 20
African Charter on Human and People's Rights	Art. 12(3)	Arts. 5, 6; and Art. 24 of the Protocol		Arts. 7 and 12(3)	Art. 12	Art. 5
American Convention on Human Rights (ACHR)	Art. 22(7)	Arts. 5, 7	Art. 22(8)	Arts. 8, 25	Art. 22	Art. 18

American Declaration of the Rights and Duties of Man (ADHR)	Art. XXVII					
Bangkok Principles on the Status and Treatment of Refugees			Art. III			
Charter of Fundamental Rights of the European Union	Art. 18					
European Convention for the Protection of Human Rights and Fundamental Freedoms (ECHR)		Arts. 3, 5	Art. 3	Art. 6 of Protocol No. 7	Arts. 2, 3, 4 of Protocol No. 4; Art. 1 of Protocol No. 7	
OAU Convention Governing the Specific Aspects of Refugee Problems in Africa	Art. II		Art. II(3)			Art. VI

political opinion." In addition to persons whose claims are pending, this rule has also saved lives in cases where the status of a person as a refugee was not easy to prove or determine. However, although states' obligations of *non-refoulement* in human rights law are of absolute nature, article 33(2) of the Geneva Convention is stricter when stipulating that "a refugee for whom there are reasonable grounds for regarding as a danger for the country in which he is, or who ... constitutes a danger to the community of that country" may not claim the right of *non-refoulement*.

States and their responsibility to protect refugees

When they are outside their country of origin, asylum seekers are basically subject to two kinds of law: (1) the 1951 Geneva Refugee Convention and (2) the receiving states' immigration laws. The former defines states' responsibilities to protect the refugees, and the latter manifests states' sovereignty over their own territory. Whereas the former aims to oblige the states to allow entry and give protection to refugees, the latter functions as states' tool for distinguishing between citizens and aliens. Scholars of refugee studies agree that the latter law has now won over the former – i.e., more often than ever before, states downplay their international responsibility to protect refugees and asylum seekers. In the present context of states' frequent denial of refugee rights, recent research in refugee studies has shifted focus towards the problems of refugee protection, states' asylum procedures, and a reformation of the Geneva Convention.

Concerning states' asylum procedures, the majority of states *do* have asylum laws and institutions that conform to the 1951 Geneva Convention. One would therefore expect the outcomes of these national asylum laws and institutions to be similar. However, it has been shown that this is not the case (Holzer et al. 2000a, 2000b; Gibney and Hansen 2003; Gibney 2004; Neumayer 2005). How, then, is it possible for states to "lawfully" refuse a genuine refugee? The answer to this question lies in the relationship between states' asylum recognition rates and their national asylum determination frames; it is, among other things, the small nuances in states' asylum determination procedures – especially their procedures regarding asylum seekers' access to asylum determination – and how they deal institutionally with asylum applications, that explain the fact that states can deny protection to genuine refugees without violating the Geneva Convention provisions directly (Sicakkan 2008).

As to the reformation of the Geneva Convention, since the 1980s the problematic international political situation around the protection of refugees has divided refugee studies researchers into two camps. The first, *reformists,* assert that it is no longer possible to convince states to reassume full responsibility for refugees; one should therefore devise a new international refugee regime or reformulate the present refugee laws in order to make refugee protection possible again (Garvey 1985; Hathaway and Neve 1997; Schuck 1997; Harvey 1998; Juss 1998). However, there are two main groups with conflicting views on the reformist side: One group of researchers on the reformist side – *realists* – argue that states could only be made responsible through a reformed refugee convention that is more sensitive to states' interests (Hathaway and Neve 1997). Another group of reformists – *idealists* – envisaged a solution in an expansion of the refugee definition to include people fleeing new types of social and political conflicts (Loescher 2001).

The second camp, *conventionists*, on the other hand, argue that to reform the Geneva Convention in either direction will only dilute the original intentions behind it (Anker et al. 1998). They state that the present international refugee law and the refugee regime is a good enough protection tool, and that one should instead engage in efforts to convince states to reassume their responsibility for the refugees (Fitzpatrick 1996; Anker et al. 1998; Chimni 1998; Loescher 2001).

Roberts (1998) concludes in one of his essays that "Although the 1951 Convention as amended gives guidelines for good practice which remain valuable, there is not likely to be a standard concept of what refugees are and how they should be treated." Loescher argues that:

> If the Convention is to be reformed, changes should not aim to weaken the protection mechanism but rather to strengthen it. The priority should be to broaden the definition of refugee to recognize victims of civil wars, to ensure voluntary repatriation, and to formally recognize the right to seek asylum and obtain it. Since these developments are unlikely to occur – despite the professed human rights commitment of most Western states – it is essential to re-emphasize that the 1951 Convention properly applied, remains the essential underpinning of the refugee protection system.
>
> *(Loescher 2001, p. 366)*

The reformulation projects and their critics have important internal differences. Although they agree on the inefficiency of the current refugee regime and share the common goal of an effective protection system, their ethical points of departure and the means they propose for protection are different. In the absence of better alternatives, there is little reason to disagree with Loescher's view.

The citizen–alien paradigm and singular notions of refugee

Harvey asserts that "Any single vision of a monolithic law will simply not be subtle enough for the dynamism and complexity of the issue" (Harvey 1999). Indeed, singular definitions of a refugee fail to recognize certain human sufferings that constitute the refugee condition. The problem with singular approaches is that they derive from states' particular citizenship ideals, political visions, and images of person. This means that states' operative definitions are derivatives of their own ideals of citizenship. The predicament is that different citizenship ideals construe different couplings between citizenship and refugeehood.

Human sufferings that are recognized as the fundament of the refugee condition vary. Whereas the freedom to use one's mother tongue or the freedom of religion, for example, are considered as relevant criteria by some states based on their own historical citizenship ideals, these are not given emphasis in other states' dealings with refugee issues. Germany and Greece, for example, give special treatment to co-ethnic refugees while the liberal–individualist states treat co-ethnics and others equally. In brief, the absence of freedom to express one's belonging to an ethnic or religious group or to a nation or a culture is regarded as a real human suffering by some states, but this may not be equally meaningful in the context of the historical experiences of some other states (Sicakkan 2008). This is about what different states regard as worthy of protecting: autonomy of persons, cultures of communities, citizens and their civic belongings, or diasporic belonging of their co-ethnics.

The citizen–alien paradigm also introduces various sets of criteria for determining which refugee protection instruments are preferable. Some instruments are individual protection schemes (e.g. temporary or permanent political asylum), collective protection of groups (temporary or permanent), creation of safe zones in the regions close to conflict areas, efforts to eliminate the root causes of refugee flows, unilateral or multilateral preventive state actions, or diplomatic or military interventions in the conflict areas or countries that generate refugees. Citizenship ideals valorize these methods and tools of protection differently. While states with a liberal–individualist citizenship tradition usually prefer permanent individual asylum as the main protection tool, states with a communitarian–collectivist history of citizenship tend to prefer temporary collective protection of refugee groups, while putting less emphasis on individual protection (Sicakkan 2008).

When refugeehood and citizenship are conceptually tied thus to each other, human sufferings that constitute the refugee condition are conceived in terms of the receiving states' citizenship ideals rather than in terms of actual human sufferings. By tying the notion of refugee to a citizen ideal, one risks detaching it from human rights. The coupling between citizenship and refugeehood also substantiates aporetic questions such as whether states should prioritize their obligations to their citizens or assume their responsibility for refugees. Only when the refugee is defined in terms of a citizenship ideal and "as a function of the interstate system" (Sassen 1999) can such questions be vindicated. Such coupling between citizenship and refugeehood is a consequence of the current dominance of the citizen–alien paradigm in approaches to state–individual relations.

Towards a human-rights based notion of refugee

The alternative to the citizen–alien paradigm is a human rights-based notion of refugee. The question is not about states' having to choose between their citizens' and foreigners' claims; it is about choosing between *citizens' claims for a better life* and *refugees' claims for a life at all*. By conceptualizing the refugee in terms of citizenship, one trivializes this crucial point. When the question is put forth as a choice between *a better life* and *a life at all*, we are in the domain of human frailty (Buttle 2003; Elliot and Turner 2003), individuals' inalienable human rights, and the human sufferings that are caused by human rights violations.

The counter-argument is that this perspective misses the nuance between human rights and refugee rights. It has been argued that, although refugee rights derive from human rights, the Geneva Convention is only meant to cover a specific category of people and, in principle, it does not deal with all sorts of people whose human rights are violated. Also some pragmatic arguments have been advanced, claiming that a further extension of the refugee definition will paralyze the already inefficient refugee protection system (Hathaway and Neve 1997). Similar to the detachment in citizenship theories, also this analytical distinction between refugee rights and human rights further detaches the notion of refugee from human rights, but this time for the sake of efficiency and feasibility.

A notion of refugee that is entrenched in the idea of human rights makes *human suffering that cannot be avoided without another state's protection* the centre of the refugee definition, no matter what the reasons for persecution, discrimination, endangering, non-protection, or domination may be. Such a refugee definition should entail the following characteristics:

First, the consequence of giving *suffering* a central place is that not only race, ethnicity, religion, nationality, or political persuasion are relevant when deciding who the refugees are, but also other individual and collective factors such as sexuality, mobility, gender, generation, clan, family, and new forms of belonging.

Second, such a model emphasizes persons' real sufferings that can be avoided with another state's protection rather than the receiving or sending states' particularistic interpretations of the "reality." Therefore, this notion of refugee emphasizes the principle of non-protection or lack of protection by a state, which was more strongly integrated into the refugee concept before 1946, as strongly as the principle of persecution.

Third, the focus on *suffering* renders also the location of people irrelevant. People may suffer severely and subsist in the refugee condition wherever they are. The human-rights based notion of refugee tones down the emphasis in the 1951 Geneva Convention on the condition of "being outside of the country of origin," and seeks to open the possibility of applying for asylum independently of where people are.

Finally, the 1951 Geneva Convention places *fear* in the center of the refugee definition. Although fear may seem like a less socially constructed concept than suffering, it is not as universal a human feeling as assumed. The "universal" concept of *fear* increases the risk of excluding many context-dependent human sufferings that put people in refugee-like conditions. Instead of pretending to capture a universal feature of humans in a Hobbesian manner, the definition of refugee should be context sensitive. *Human suffering* should be emphasized as strongly as *fear* in the refugee definition.

Furthermore, protection principles such as collective versus individual protection or temporary versus permanent protection may each be useful in different situations. The human-rights based notion of refugee goes beyond the doctrinal protection regimes and opens the way to deploying a diversity of protection instruments that may be useful in different situations. Although each state considers some protection instruments as irrelevant, states also have their own repertoires of protection instruments that may be relevant in different refugee situations. A human-rights based approach requires merging the different tool-repertoires of the current states and deploying the available protection tools when they serve the goal of protection.

My above arguments invite a trip back to the spirit behind the 1951 Geneva Convention, which is based on humanitarian norms, human rights, and human frailty. The human-rights notion of refugee is based on an ontology which entails human suffering as the constitutive element of human frailty. This supports the ideals behind the Geneva Convention's definition of a refugee against states' particularistic (mis)interpretations of the refugee definition. This conception carries the notion of a refugee to where it really belongs – from a Westphalian discourse of state and citizenship, which is based on *the frailty of persons as "citizens,"* to a human rights discourse based on *the frailty of persons as "humans."*

References

Anker, D., J. Fitzpatrick, and A. Shacknove. 1998. "Crisis and Cure: A Reply to Hathaway/Neve and Schuck." *Harvard Human Rights Journal*, Vol. 11, pp. 295–310.

Buttle, N. 2003. "The Ethics of Human Frailty." *Journal of Human Rights*, Vol. 2, No. 2, pp. 227–233.

Chimni, B. S. 1998. "The Geopolitics of Refugee Studies: A View from the South." *Journal of Refugee Studies*, Vol. 11, pp. 350–374.

Elliott, A., and B. S. Turner. 2003. "Introduction: Towards an Ontology of Human Frailty." *Journal of Human Rights*, Vol. 2, No. 2, pp. 129–136.

Fitzpatrick, J. 1996. "Revitalizing the 1951 Refugee Convention." *Harvard Human Rights Journal*, Vol. 9, pp. 229–253.

Garvey, J. I. 1985. "Towards a Reformulation of International Refugee Law." *Harvard International Law Journal*, Vol. 26, pp. 483–500.

Gibney, M. J. 2004, *The Ethics and Politics of Asylum: Liberal Democracy and the Response to Refugees* (Cambridge: Cambridge University Press).

Gibney, M. J. and R. Hansen. 2003. "Asylum Policy in the West: Past Trends, Future Possibilities." *Discussion Paper No. 2003/68* (Helsinki: World Institute for Development Economics Research [WIDER]).

Goodwin-Gill, G. S. 1985. *The Refugee in International Law* (Oxford: Clarendon Press).

Harvey, C. J. 1998. "Taking Human Rights Seriously in the Asylum Context? A Perspective on the Development of Law and Policy." In F. Nicholson and P. Twomey, eds., *Current Aspects of UK Asylum Law and Policy* (Aldershot: Ashgate).

Harvey, C. J. 1999. "Talking about Refugee Law." *Journal of Refugee Studies*, Vol. 10, pp. 101–134.

Hathaway, J. C. 1997. *Reconceiving International Refugee Law* (The Hague: Martinus and Nijhoff Publishers).

Hathaway, J. C. and R. A. Neve. 1997. "Making International Refugee Law Relevant Again: A Proposal for Collectivized and Solution-Oriented Protection." *Harvard Human Rights Journal*, Vol. 10, pp. 115–211.

Holzer, T., G. Schneider, and T. Widmer. 2000a. "Discriminating Decentralization: Federalism and the Handling of Asylum Applications in Switzerland, 1988–1996." *Journal of Conflict Resolution*, Vol. 44, pp. 250–276.

Holzer, T., G. Schneider, and T. Widmer. 2000b. "The Impact of Legislative Deterrence Measures on the Number of Asylum Applications in Switzerland (1986–1995)." *International Migration Review*, Vol. 34, pp. 1182–1216.

Juss, S. 1998. "Toward a Morally Legitimate Reform of Refugee Law: The Uses of Cultural Jurisprudence." *Harvard Human Rights Journal*, Vol. 11, pp. 311–354.

Lee, L. T. 1996. "Internally Displaced Persons and Refugees: Towards a Legal Synthesis." *Journal of Refugee Studies*, Vol. 9, pp. 27–42.

Loescher, G. 2001. *The UNHCR and World Politics: A Perilous Path* (Oxford: Oxford University Press).

Neumayer, E. 2005. "Asylum Recognition Rates in Western Europe: Their Determinants, Variation, and Lack of Convergence." *Journal of Conflict Resolution*, Vol. 49, pp. 43–66.

Roberts, A. 1998. "More Refugees, Less Asylum: A Regime in Transformation." *Journal of Refugee Studies*, Vol. 11, pp. 375–395.

Sassen, S. 1999. *Guests and Aliens* (New York: The New Press).

Schuck, P. H. 1997. "Refugee Burden-Sharing: A Modest Proposal." *Yale Journal of International Law*, Vol. 22, pp. 243–297.

Sicakkan, H. G. 2008. *Do Our Citizenship Requirements Impede the Protection of Political Asylum Seekers? A Comparative Study of European Practices* (Lewiston, NY: The Edwin Mellen Press).

Zolberg, A, A. Suhrke, and S. Aguayo. 1989. *Escape from Violence: Conflict and the Refugee Crisis in the Developing World* (Oxford: Oxford University Press).

32

The rights of the disabled

Doris Zames Fleischer

The efforts of people with disabilities to achieve their civil rights in the United States have taken many forms, including demonstrations and sit-ins, lobbying, legislation, and judicial review. The disability rights movement – akin to civil rights movements by African Americans and other ethnicities, women, and the LGBT community (lesbian, gay, bisexual, and transgender) – sought to challenge the prevailing wisdom by redirecting the public mindset from the medical/charity model to the civil rights model. Disability rights activists argue that people with disabilities are not only the largest minority (over one in five Americans according to the definition in the Americans with Disabilities Act), but also that the number is continually growing as the total population ages. Counterintuitively, the greater the technological advances, the greater the numbers of people with disabilities, as more people survive disabling conditions that formerly would have been fatal. At the same time, those technological advances enable those with disabilities to live increasingly rewarding and productive lives.

President Franklin Roosevelt, disabled by polio eleven years before being elected President, has been appropriately credited for his political astuteness, as well as his founding of and devotion to the rehabilitation center for "polios," Warm Springs (so far ahead of its time in its anti-institutional character), as well as the drive that resulted in the development of a polio vaccine. Yet his approach to disability as a private challenge rather than a civil rights issue was understandable given the fact that, from the founding of this nation, people with disabilities were, as disability scholar and activist Frank Bowe observed, segregated and denigrated:

> Because popular perceptions equated disability with inability, existence of disability appeared reason enough to deny a person with a disability the right to participate in societal life. Within families, persons with disabilities were hidden, disowned, or even allowed to die through withholding of life-support services. Within disabled individuals, self-perception inevitably reflected prevailing social attitudes, keeping people from even attempting to become self-reliant.
>
> *(Bowe 1980, pp. 8–9)*

In fact, by the early twentieth century, eugenicists were advocating sterilization, even mercy killing, for people with a variety of disabilities.

Ironically, in 1935, while Roosevelt, a wheelchair user, was serving the first of four terms as President of the United States, a groundbreaking disability rights group, the League of the Physically Handicapped, was emerging in New York City as a result of an existing policy that prevented well-qualified potential workers from securing government employment because of their disabilities (F. Haskell, 1995, pers. comm.). What makes it unmistakable that this policy was a consequence of discrimination was the fact that so many of these job seekers had such minimal disabilities that they were, in some cases, scarcely discernible, let alone ever likely to interfere with their job performance. Though their organization was short-lived (four years) and their legacy almost forgotten, these determined activists – who occupied government offices and met in Washington, DC with one of the president's chief advisors, Harry Hopkins – made contributions that were paramount. First, by exposing the disability discrimination in government hiring, they significantly diminished such practices by government entities. Second, they demonstrated an unequivocally political approach to disability that countered the medical model and, instead, heralded the civil rights vision.

It is important to note, however, the issues specific to people with sensory disabilities: literacy for blind people and communication for deaf people. Louis Braille's embossed dot formulation provided blind people with a way to achieve the ability to read, using their fingers, and to write, using a stylus, thus allowing them to be literate and, hence, integrated in the wider society. There is convincing historical evidence that if the natural access to Sign language, from birth, for prelingually deaf children is fostered rather than impeded, then deafness does not interfere with the intellectual achievement of such individuals. For example, in *Everybody Here Spoke Sign Language: Heredity Deafness on Martha's Vineyard*, Nora Ellen Groce describes how in the mid-nineteenth century in this locale, where one-fourth of the population contracted hereditary deafness, the entire community learned Sign, which was treated as another language, not an accommodation for a disability (Groce 1985). Deaf people flourished as leading members of this community, for "there was free and complete intercourse between the hearing and the deaf. Indeed the deaf were scarcely seen as 'deaf,' and certainly not seen as at all 'handicapped'" (Sacks 1989, p. 32).

The problem was the effect of the well-intentioned, but unwise, efforts of hearing people to coerce deaf, especially prelingually deaf, people to deal with language as if they were not deaf, that is, to lip-read and speak, rather than Sign. As a consequence of the misguided eugenics movement, as well as educators who thought that they were encouraging integration of those who were deaf with the hearing world, the 1880 Congress of Milan banned the learning and using of American Sign Language (ASL) and substituted oralism. Although deaf teachers were barred from voting at this Congress, the endorsement of this decision by such leaders as Alexander Graham Bell, Samuel Gridley Howe, and Horace Mann resulted in limiting the intellectual maturation of generations of deaf children, especially those whose deafness preceded their acquisition of language (Sacks 1989, pp. 26–27).

Although the channel for communication for people who hear is mouth to ear, for people who are deaf the channel is hand and facial gesture to eye. Because, as linguistic scholar Steven Pinker pointed out, language is not a "cultural artifact," but a "biological birthright," an instinct comparable to web-spinning in a spider, discouraging the first language natural to the deaf child, Sign, is equivalent to interfering with the structure of the learner's brain (Pinker 1994, p. 237). After functioning in Sign, the deaf learner is then capable of acquiring facility in other languages. Since language learning occurs on a kind of developmental timepiece in which the years until age 6 are critical, the deaf child's failure initially to communicate in Sign is likely to induce significant cognitive impairment.

Having access to spoken language, as well as a Braille system that followed the logic of English grammar (unlike ASL, which, for historical reasons is close to French), blind people generally were integrated into American society well before deaf people. Though too often exploited by Sheltered Workshops – which were formed in the mid-nineteenth century by Samuel Gridley Howe, originally to provide blind workers with self-respect and self-reliance – blind people led their own organizations, such as the American Foundation for the Blind, as early as 1929. Later, Jacobus tenBroek, the blind labor activist who, in 1940, founded the National Federation of the Blind, argued for legislation that would amend the Civil Service Act of the United States so that discrimination because of blindness would be barred (Matson 1990, pp. 31–34). Advances in technology such as the Kurzweil reader, which turns print on paper to speech, the voice synthesizer, which changes print on the computer screen to speech, and the Braille keyboard have continued to move toward leveling the playing field for blind people.

On the other hand, as a result of roughly one hundred years of oral education for deaf children, a largely uneducated, alienated, and segregated deaf population – who had internalized the demeaning self-image imposed upon them – remained powerless to gain leadership roles in the organizations that served this population. Thus, it is not surprising that the first major uprising at Gallaudet University, founded in 1864 and dedicated to the higher education of the deaf or hard of hearing, did not occur until 1988. Students were protesting the failure of this institution, in its long history, ever to have a deaf president. A deaf Gallaudet professor rallied the demonstrators, proclaiming, "It's long past due that Gallaudet had a deaf president as testimony that deaf people are leading themselves" (Sacks 1989, p. 76). The students' achievement of their demand for a deaf president, I. King Jordan, was also a victory for Deafness as a culture based on ASL. Since 1988, the selection of the Gallaudet presidents has had to meet with the approval of the university's student body.

It was disability activist Edward Roberts who, beginning in the early 1960s, saw the importance of expanding the choices available for people with disabilities. Specifically, he used his advocacy skills to help secure the goal of self-determination and independent living for this population. Roberts understood that achieving the goal of independent living for people with disabilities involved a reconsideration of the idea of "rehabilitation," originally conceived of in a military context. "Rehabilitation" retains the vision of the medical model in its language and its purpose as people with disabilities, referred to as patients or clients, are helped to recuperate or recover so that they can fit into the mainstream. As disability researcher Gerben DeJong pointed out, "independent living" employs the language of civil rights, as those with disabilities – referred to as consumers choosing their own destiny – are encouraged to locate the supports that they need in order to use their own resourcefulness, not only to integrate into society, but also to reform it (DeJong 1984).

Roberts was so disabled by polio, which he contracted at age 14, that he had to teach himself glossopharyhngeal breathing, known as frog breathing (in which one swallows air into one's lungs), in order to spend time outside of an iron lung. By the time he sued the University of California at Berkeley in 1962 in order to gain admission – the same year that James Meredith sued the University of Mississippi to become the first African-American student to attend that institution – Roberts was, as described by disability activist and writer Cheryl Marie Wade (1994, p. 17), "armed with self-esteem and a portable respirator." Thus he was able not only to counter the administration's argument, as recalled by Roberts, that "we [administrators] tried cripples, and they don't work" (Roberts 1995, p. 3), but he also became one of the leaders of the Rolling Quads, as socially active quadriplegics followed him to the Berkeley campus. Imbued with the energy that permeated Berkeley as a result of civil rights battles and the Free Speech Movement in the early 1970s, Roberts founded the Center for Independent Living (CIL), governed *by* and *for* people with disabilities. Using people with disabilities as peer counselors, the CIL provided – and continues to provide – legal assistance, education and job development, training in independent living skills, health maintenance, and information regarding accessible housing and transportation, as well as attendant care.

In 1975 Roberts was appointed by California Governor Jerry Brown as director of the Department of Rehabilitation; in that capacity, Roberts used the CIL as the model for independent living centers in each of the twenty-eight California counties, as well as throughout the nation and even the world. In fact, joined by dedicated disability rights activists such as Judith E. Heumann, he founded the World Institute on Disability (WID) in 1983, an internationally recognized public policy center that focuses on issues and problems that directly affect the ability of people with disabilities to live full and independent lives. As required by all independent living centers, a majority of the Board and staff of WID are persons with disabilities.

As wheelchair-using polio survivor Justin Dart, a prime mover in the disability rights struggle, explained, "Our society puts people like Fred Fay [a major disability rights activist and wheelchair user] into nursing homes at far more cost than would be required to empower them" (Dart 1992, p. 8). Advocates for the concept of "independent living," including the National Council on Independent Living and local independent living centers such as California's Center for Independent Living, the Center for the Independence of the Disabled in New York, and Chicago's Access Living, have fought to permit people with disabilities to live in their own homes, in their own communities, rather than in nursing homes. While ADAPT – dating its origins back to 1975 and known as the shock troops for the disability rights movement – has used the courts to carry out its goals, it emphasizes street fighter tactics, demonstrations, and sit-ins to achieve its primary mission for the disability population: deinstitutionalization and independent living.

Despite the strong advocacy efforts of disability rights groups, especially ADAPT, which spearheaded major demonstrations (as well as the grave disappointment of disability rights activists over the failure of the inclusion of the Community Choice Act [CCA] in the proposed health care reform bill of 2010), efforts to secure passage of this Act are still ongoing. As the principal sponsor of the CCA, Senator Tom Harkin (D-Iowa) pointed out: "in [the 1999] *Olmstead v. L.C. decision* the Supreme Court recognized that needless institutionalization is a form of discrimination under the Americans with Disabilities Act." He added: "We in Congress have a responsibility to help States meet their obligations under the Community Choice Act, which is designed to do just that, and to make the promise of the ADA a reality. It will help rebalance the current Medicaid long term care system, which spends a disproportionate amount on institutional services" (Harkin 2009).

The CCA also requires services to be provided in the most integrated setting appropriate to the needs of the individual. In effect, the money can follow the individual to a community-based setting rather than an institution, as has been partially achieved in some states by means of Medicaid waivers (S. Gold, 2009, pers. comm.). As of this writing, the CCA has not yet been reported out of Congressional Committees, and its passage as federal legislation is most uncertain, at least in the short term.

The similar goal of expanding the opportunity of children with disabilities to be included in general classrooms, rather than isolated in separate educational environments, was ostensibly achieved with the 1975 passage of the Education for All Handicapped Children Act, later known as the Individuals with Disabilities Education Act (IDEA).

Statistics regarding education of students with disabilities, as late as the 1960s, were appalling. John Gliedman and William Roth pointed out that while one in eight such children received no education whatsoever, over half did not receive an appropriate education (Gliedman and Roth 1980, p.173). Disability rights advocates have consistently argued, however, that inclusion of students with disabilities, insofar as possible, in general classrooms, served not only these students, but also nondisabled students and the wider society.

The point was that educating students with disabilities in "the least restrictive environment," also known as "the most integrated setting," as defined in the IDEA, creates a learning experience that is a microcosm of the real world, in which nondisabled students appreciate that, despite the variety of ways of being in the world, including living with a disability, all people have a common humanity. At the same time, inclusion of students with disabilities significantly increases the probability that such students will become integrated and productive members of the community, who will live satisfying lives, securing self-fulfilling jobs, earning good salaries. Thus, not only will they be participating effectively in the social, economic, and political fabric of the society, but also they will be reforming that society by fostering social change and advancing diversity.

Responding to the negative outcomes with respect to the education of students with disabilities that have resulted from the fact that the IDEA has never been funded at the level that Congress intended, disability rights advocates continue to argue for that appropriate funding. Still, there is a the backlash against the IDEA that has taken two forms: first, fear that nondisabled children are being shortchanged to pay for the education of children with disabilities; second, reluctance to include such children in regular classrooms, especially when schools are being held to strict testing standards. So fervent is this backlash that proposals to dilute standards, or even exclude accountability, for educating children with disabilities have been seriously considered by Congress. Lawsuits under the IDEA by parents on behalf of their children with disabilities continue to be filed, with some courts ruling in favor of the parents, other courts siding with the school district.

Another issue critical to the disability rights movement involves the argument for so-called "death with dignity." This euphemism may have emotional appeal to some people, but other proponents of physician-assisted suicide have clear economic motives.

As Marilyn Golden, a policy analyst with Disability Rights Education and Defense Fund (DREDF), noted in 1999, in testifying against California's proposed "Death with Dignity Act (AB 1592):

> To cut costs and boost profits, HMO's and managed care bureaucrats are already overruling doctors' treatment decisions, sometimes hastening patients' deaths. AB 1592 would accelerate the decline of quality in California's health care system. The cost of the lethal medication under AB 1592 is approximately $35 to $50, far cheaper than the cost of treatment for most long-term medical conditions. The incentive to save money by denying treatment is already a significant danger; it would be far greater if this bill were passed.
>
> *(Golden 1999)*

Thanks to Golden and other opponents of physician-assisted suicide, such as Not Dead Yet, the proposed law failed to pass the California legislature, despite the continuing efforts of proponents of "death with dignity." In 1997, the Oregon Death with Dignity Act had passed, permitting physician-assisted suicide. In 2008, the state of Washington enacted comparable legislation permitting terminally ill adults seeking to end their life to request lethal doses of medication from medical and osteopathic physicians. In a 2009 decision, the Montana Supreme Court also legalized physician-assisted suicide. In contrast to the nondisabled population, the danger of such legislation and rulings is exponentially greater for people with disabilities, for they are often assumed by the general public, including many in the medical establishment, to have an "unacceptable" quality of life.

Federal civil rights protection for people with disabilities occurred in two stages: Section 504 of the Rehabilitation Act of 1973 and the 1990 Americans with Disabilities Act. The former covers the public sector, barring discrimination against people with disabilities in programs receiving federal financial assistance, even including those operated by major corporations. Unbeknownst to President Nixon, the Congress, or even disability rights activists, staff members on the Senate Committee on Labor and Public Welfare adapted and inserted the language of Title VI of the Civil Rights Act of 1964 in the final draft of the 1973 bill. Yet once disability rights activists became cognizant of this law, which finally allowed them to file legal complaints when they faced discriminatory practices, they galvanized the disability community and took action. In order for Section 504 to be effective, however, it was necessary for implementing regulations to be issued and promulgated because the law was succinctly stated in merely one sentence: "No otherwise qualified handicapped individual in the United States, shall, solely by reason of his handicap, be excluded from the participation in, be denied the benefits of, or be subjected to discrimination under any program or activity receiving federal financial assistance."

James Cherry, a white student with a significant disability, who was attending Howard University Law School – devoted to the education of African-American students and thus steeped in the civil rights tradition – successfully sued the Secretary of Health, Education, and Welfare (HEW), David Mathews, for his failure to issue the required Section 504 implementing regulations. Despite the July 1976 order by Judge John L. Smith of the U.S. District Court for the District of Columbia, that HEW develop and promulgate Section 504 regulations "with all deliberate speed," the task was still not accomplished when Joseph Califano became the HEW Secretary in the administration of the newly elected President Jimmy Carter. Since Carter had given his assurances, in a campaign speech on September 1976 at Warm Springs, that he would do what was necessary to enforce Section 504, the national disability rights movement responded vigorously when Carter, as president, did not honor his commitment to the disability community in a timely fashion. The focus of the demonstrations and sit-ins took place on April 5, 1977, in Washington, DC, as well as mainly in the locations of the ten regional offices of HEW: Atlanta, Boston, Chicago, Dallas, Denver, Kansas City, New York, Philadelphia, San Francisco, and Seattle. With this national campaign achieving its purpose, the April 28, 1977, signing by HEW Secretary Joseph Califano of the implementing regulations of Section 504 of the Rehabilitation Act of 1973, the disability rights movement had found its muscle.

With respect to the 1990 Americans with Disabilities Act (ADA), disability activists were the prime movers, from its inception, as they played a pivotal role in the genesis of the law, as well as in writing and lobbying for it. As chair of Texas Governor William Clements's Task Force for Long-Range Policy for People with Disabilities in the early 1980s, Justin Dart, later known as "the father of the ADA," began his struggle for what would ultimately become the ADA, a federal disability civil rights law that dealt with the private sector as well as the public sector. It became increasingly evident, not only to disability advocates, but also to a number of federal legislators, that a law was required that was more comprehensive than Section 504, which focused on the public sector. Since over 80 percent of the jobs are found in the private sector, one of the most persuasive arguments for the necessity of a new law was the need to increase the work opportunities for 75 percent of unemployed people with disabilities who have the qualifications and desire for employment (*Ragged Edge* 1998, pp. 5–6).

As one of the Reagan appointees to the National Council on Disability, the federal agency that proposed the ADA in 1986, Dart noted how disability issues transcend party identification. He conferred with former Democratic appointees to the Council, especially Judith E. Heumann, an influential wheelchair-using disability rights activist, whom he referred to as his mentor though she was roughly twenty years his junior. The original thirteen-page 1988 draft version of the ADA was an outline for the more specific, and more realistic, fifty-two page 1990 enacted bill. The cross-disability consolidation of forces focusing on passage of the ADA resulted in members of the disability community mailing out more than one million New Year's postcards (printed by the Epilepsy Foundation) for Congress, which read, "Don't weaken a law that will strengthen America" (Dart 1992, pp. 4–5). In addition, Congress received hundreds of thousands of other mailings and phone calls from disability advocates demanding no weakening amendments to the ADA. The point was made clear, repeatedly, by all these communications that any weakening amendments would be a vote against the then 43 (now 54) million Americans with disabilities.

Disability activists organized two marches of people with varied disabilities to muster support for the ADA, one march in which people in wheelchairs pulled themselves up the steps of the Capitol, and another in which the demonstrators waited at the Capitol for hours to get word that the bill had been passed. The overwhelming vote for the ADA, 377 to 28 in the House and 76 to 8 in the Senate, to a great degree has been credited by Dart to "A ragtag hodgepodge of advocates with disabilities, families, and service providers, who had never completely agreed on anything before" who joined "a few farsighted members of the older civil rights movement," and some business people, as well as some members of Congress and the Administration to defeat "the richest, most powerful lobbies in the nation" (Dart 1992, p. 5).

Dart added: "It's a fallacy that the ADA costs too much. It's the discrimination that costs too much. We can't afford not to get the disabled into the work force so they can lead independent and productive lives" (EEOC 1996, p. 8). Ally of Justin Dart, Betsy Ogle, pointed out the relevance of the ADA to all people in the nation, given the fact that no one is immune from disability: "The ADA can be viewed as an insurance policy against discrimination that every American in this society should cherish and protect as a matter of enlightened self interest" (EEOC 1996, p. 40).

The passage of the ADA, however, did not end discrimination against people with disabilities. In its July 2007 report, *The Impact of the Americans with Disabilities Act: Assessing the Progress toward Achieving the Goals of the ADA*, the National Council on Disability concluded that although much progress has been made, "Many Americans with disabilities remain frustrated that disability discrimination has not been eliminated ... People with disabilities reported [that] the ADA has not been fully enforced; the barriers [that] they face remain primarily attitudinal. Additionally, there is a growing backlash against disability rights and the ADA." That backlash is evident in the dismal employment statistics for people with disabilities. A February 2010 report by the Office of Disability Employment Policy of the US Department of Labor concluded that the percentage of people with disabilities in the labor force was only 21.9 percent.

Such a backlash was also apparent in major decisions by the US Supreme Court, which both narrowed the definition of disability and, by expanding the "sovereign immunity" provision of the US Constitution, limited the power of Congress to enact legislation protecting the rights of people with disabilities. Supreme Court decisions had practically eviscerated Title I, the employment title of the ADA, which was the primary reason that the law was enacted. More specifically, by invoking what has been labeled "the new federalism," the Court subverted the intent of Congress to expand employment of people with disabilities. For example, in a 5 to 4 decision, the Supreme Court held in 2001 in *University of Alabama v. Garrett* that suits in federal courts by state employees to recover money damages under Title I of the ADA are barred by the Eleventh Amendment provision of "sovereign immunity."

However, the Supreme Court did not have the last word here. Disability rights advocates kept the pressure on until the case was remanded to a lower federal court and, in 2003, the

US Court of Appeals for the Eleventh Circuit ruled that plaintiffs were indeed entitled to seek money damages under Section 504 of the Rehabilitation Act. The Circuit Court held that Congress conditioned states' receipt of federal funds constituted a waiver of their Eleventh Amendment immunity. Inasmuch as other federal appellate courts have come to different conclusions on this issue, it is possible that the Supreme Court will consider this matter once again.

Disability rights advocates effectively lobbied the US Congress to secure a significant victory with the passage of the ADA Amendments Act of 2008 (ADAAA). The Act, in effect, reverses Supreme Court decisions in several major employment cases (*Sutton et al. v. United Air Lines*; *Murphy v. United Parcel Service, Inc.*; and *Albertsons, Inc. v. Kirkingburg*) by expanding the interpretation of the definition of "disability." Earlier Court decisions created a "Catch-22" situation whereby individuals could be denied employment because of real or perceived disabilities, but they could not seek a remedy under the ADA because of "mitigating measures," such as preventive medication or eye glasses, which, according to the Court, rendered the employee non disabled. The ADAAA, in effect, rejected the Supreme Court's rulings regarding the use of mitigating measures and required employers to make reasonable accommodations to employees and job applicants with disabilities. Regulations implementing the Act, issued by the Equal Employment Opportunity Commission in 2009, are intended to, according to Acting EEOC Vice Chair Christine M. Griffin, "shift the focus of the courts from further narrowing the definition of disability and putting it back to where Congress intended when the ADA was enacted in 1990" (EEOC 2009).

Lack of preparedness is most disturbingly evident in the way that the G.W. Bush administration failed to deal effectively with the return of so many veterans from wars in Afghanistan and Iraq with physical and mental traumas. Thanks to some improvements in body armor and the immediate medical attention often available, the ratio of wounded soldiers to those killed in action far exceeds that for any other war in which the nation has been engaged. Because of these increased survival rates, however, the nature of the most common wounds are often dramatically more severe than those stemming from earlier conflicts. Also, the increased time and number of deployments, as well as the decreased time between deployments, has had a major impact on military personnel, leading to a rise in the number of disabled veterans, especially with respect to psychiatric disabilities, including post-traumatic stress disorder (PTSD) (Glantz 2009).

PTSD and traumatic brain injury (TBI) have been appropriately designated as the signature wounds of these wars. Other common devastating disabilities resulting from these conflicts have been multiple amputations and clinical depression. One consequence of the immense burden placed on this volunteer military force has been the unprecedented increase in suicides of returning veterans. A recent report by the Veterans Affairs Department revealed that the suicide rate among 18- to 29-year-old men went up 26 percent from 2005 to 2007. More recently, from January 2009 until September 2009, the number of US active troop suicides had already met the previous year's total count with 140 confirmed suicides. As of late November, in 2009 there were more suicides among military personnel who were, or had been, deployed in Iraq and Afghanistan than there were combat deaths (Donnelly 2009).

Although the existence of Gulf War syndrome, treated with skepticism and even hostility in the early 1990s, has been convincingly confirmed, an unacceptable number of newly disabled veterans of the wars in Iraq and Afghanistan have not received appropriate health care services and benefits upon their return to the United States (P. Sullivan, 2009, pers. comm.). The scandal at Walter Reed Hospital revealed how a tangled and uncaring bureaucracy prevented these veterans from receiving the medical and psychological treatment their military service warranted. Further exacerbating the plight of such disabled veterans is evidence that the Department of

Defense had been providing low disability ratings of veterans' wounds, thereby dramatically skewing downward the appropriate disability benefits that they could receive from the federal government for their battle-connected injuries. Such a practice is crucial because it helps determine whether soldiers will get annual disability payments and health care after they are discharged.

Despite media accounts of the plight of returning veterans, the American public may not fully understand that at least a trillion dollars will have to be spent for the continued health care of these veterans, many of whom are in their late teens and will be receiving government benefits for the remainder of their lives (Stiglitz and Bilmes 2008). Such advocacy organizations as Veterans for Common Sense, Iraq and Afghanistan Veterans of America, and Iraq Veterans Against the War have been aggressive in their continuing efforts to protect the rights of military personnel. Legislation did take effect, however, in the Obama administration in December 2009, providing for an increase in the rates of compensation for veterans with service-connected disabilities and the rates of dependency and indemnity compensation for the survivors of certain disabled veterans. It was also reported in the *New York Times* of July 8, 2010, that the federal government is preparing to issue new rules "that will make it substantially easier for veterans who have been found to have post-traumatic stress disorder to receive disability benefits, a change that could affect hundreds of thousands of veterans from the wars in Iraq, Afghanistan and Vietnam."

Disability rights activists have maintained the pressure to ensure that assistive devices and new communications technology have played an ever-growing role in enabling people with disabilities to increase their independence and become active participants in society. The "assistive technology" provisions in such federal laws as Section 508 of the amended Rehabilitation Act of 1973 dealing with electronic and information technologies, the 1990 ADA Title IV dealing with telecommunications, and the Telecommunications Act of 1996 have been instrumental in improving the quality of life for people with disabilities. Similarly, such activists also have stood firm in their demand for the accessibility of voting equipment. Although Congress enacted the Help America Vote Act (HAVA) in 2002 guaranteeing by law the opportunity for people with disabilities to privately and independently cast an accurate and secure ballot in every polling station throughout the country, the goals of such legislation are far from being reached.

The resistance to disability civil rights is not only evident in the unsatisfactory education and employment statistics for people with disabilities, but also in the failure to provide adequate health care for this population. The deleterious effects of a broken health care system on non-disabled Americans are greatly magnified in the population of those with disabilities unable to access the services that they require. In addition, disability rights advocates fear the emergence of a new eugenics, a consequence of the evolution in genetic research, resulting in diminishing diversity by weeding out so-called imperfect people. People with disabilities that are immediately discernible, characterized as "visible disabilities," often experience prejudice in a manner different from those with "invisible disabilities," that is, disabilities that are not easily perceptible. The former are too likely to encounter precipitous discrimination, especially, for example, in employment; the validity of the conditions included in the latter group too often is viewed with a contemptuous skepticism.

The question as to which group has the more severe disabilities can be answered only on an individual basis. For example, who is more disabled, a person with obvious mobility impairment, whipping around in an aerodynamic wheelchair, or another person with a serious heart ailment or a debilitating psychiatric condition, but no apparent disability? Still, any examination of the current situation regarding people with disabilities in the United States must take into account the recent economic recession, the unusually high unemployment rates, and the severe cuts in state and local budgets – all factors adversely affecting the disability population. In addition, uncertainty, at this writing, regarding proposed federal legislation affecting health care and education makes it difficult to forecast how people with disabilities will fare in the coming years.

Opponents of civil rights for people with disabilities presume that this population is seeking unwarranted considerations such as generous benefits, windfall legal settlements, and excessive accommodations, all of which allegedly burden the rest of society. The tendency of the mainstream media to treat disability as a strictly medical issue reinforces such a view. What those who are not supporters of disability civil rights disregard are the costly effects of disability discrimination, despite the persistent efforts of people with disabilities to dismantle the barriers preventing them from joining society as productive and contributing members, as well as to transform society by increasing diversity. The fact is that "visible" and "invisible" disabilities are part of the human condition to which all are susceptible.

In May 2008, President George W. Bush signed into law the Genetic Information Nondiscrimination Act (GINA), which will protect Americans against discrimination based on their genetic information when it comes to health insurance and employment. The bill passed both houses of Congress overwhelmingly. The long-awaited measure, which has been debated in Congress for thirteen years, will pave the way for people to take full advantage of the promise of personalized medicine without fear of discrimination. Such legislation underscores how no one is immune from such discrimination. No society that is equitable and enlightened can ignore this reality or fail to appreciate the primacy of civil rights for people with disabilities.

In July 2009, the United States finally signed the United Nations Convention on the Rights of Persons with Disabilities, becoming the 142nd country to sign this document, which actually came into force in 2008 (M. Bristo, 2009, pers. comm.). The critical role of the 1990 Americans with Disabilities Act as setting a standard for other countries should not be underestimated. For the United States to be a party to the Convention and bound by its provisions, however, the Senate must ratify it by a two-thirds vote. Inasmuch as the Convention and the ADA differ on a number of important issues, it is unclear how such ratification would impact American law. Nevertheless, ratification by the United States, even with reservations that alleviate concerns by conservative critics of the Convention, would still acknowledge the existence of an international standard for the more than 650 million people with disabilities worldwide. Furthermore, being a party to the Convention would ally the United States with other nations in underscoring the indivisibility of disability rights and human rights.

References

Bowe, F. 1980. "An Overview Paper on Civil Rights Issues of Handicapped Americans: Public Policy Implications." In *Civil Rights Issues of Handicapped Americans: Public Policy Implications* (Washington, DC: United States Commission on Civil Rights).

Dart, J. 1992. "The ADA: A Promise To Be Kept." Unpublished.

DeJong, G. 1984. "Independent Living: From Social Movement to Analytical Paradigm." In *The Psychological and Social Impact of Physical Disability* (New York: Springer).

Donnelly, J. 2009. *Rising Military Suicides*. At: http://www.congress.org/news/2009/11/25/rising_military_suicides.

Equal Opportunity Employment Commission (EEOC). 1996. *Proceedings*.

Equal Opportunity Employment Commission (EEOC). 2009. *Press Release*.

Glantz, A. 2009. *The War Comes Home: Washington's Battle Against America's Veterans* (Berkeley: University of California Press).

Gliedman, J. and W. Roth. 1980. *The Unexpected Minority: Handicapped Children in America* (New York: Harcourt Brace Jovanovich).
Golden, M. 1999. "Some Thoughts on AB 1592, 'Death With Dignity Act'" California Disability Alliance. At: http://disweb.org/cda.
Groce, N. 1985. *Everyone Here Spoke Sign Language: Hereditary Deafness on Martha's Vineyard* (Cambridge, MA: Harvard University Press).
Harkin, T. 2009. "Community Choice Act." Center for Independent Living Southwest Kansas. At: http://www.cilswks.org/docs/CCAsum08a.pdf.
Matson, F. 1990. *Walking Alone and Marching Together: A History of the Organized Blind Movement in the United States, 1940–1990* (Baltimore, MD: National Federation of the Blind).
Pinker, S. 1994. *The Language Instinct: How the Mind Creates Language* (New York: William Morrow and Company).
Ragged Edge. 1998. "Follow-up to 1994 Research." September/October (Louisville, KY: Avocado Press).
Roberts, E. 1995. "Highlights from Speeches by Ed Roberts." Unpublished.
Sacks, O. 1989. *Seeing Voices: A Journey into the World of the Deaf* (Berkeley: University of California Press).
Stiglitz, J. E. and L. J. Bilmes. 2008. *The Three Trillion Dollar War: The True Cost of the Iraq Conflict* (New York: W.W. Norton).
Wade, C. M. 1994. "Disability Culture Rap." In Barrett Shaw, ed., *Ragged Edge* (Louisville, KY: Avocado Press).

33
Fetal rights

Jonathan B. Imber

The origin of the term "fetal rights" can be attributed to a variety of developments in the history of law, science, and politics. Since 1973, following the United States Supreme Court's rulings in *Roe v. Wade* and *Doe v. Bolton*, politics has dominated debates over what such a right means, given the existence of the fetus within a woman's uterus. The question of when an abortion is and is not permitted has been for several decades inseparable from any definition of a fetus's rights. But whether and when a fetus has rights in the vernacular of "human" rights is contested in ways perhaps unique to the discourse on human rights generally. Unlike disability rights and other forms of rights (including animal rights) that acknowledge both a form of independence as well as varying degrees of dependence on others to assert and fulfill, fetal rights (until the much more recent controversy over stem cell research) presuppose a location (i.e., uterus) over which an individual woman's control is ascribed first to her alone, affording her the prerogative (in those nations where abortion is legal) to decide whether the fetus is deserving of the utmost protection or no protection whatsoever. In this respect, fetal rights can be opposed on any grounds that seek to deny a woman's own right of decision-making (e.g., her bodily integrity and assertion of self-determination) inherent to the conditions (some in her control and others not) under which the fetus either does or does not survive.

Some aspects of law, medicine, and science

No one contests the existence of the fetus as a distinct entity in its creation as a human being. From biblical times, the unborn child was said to "exist" at that stage when a mother began to "show" and certainly at the point in a pregnancy when a fetus moved (i.e., quickening). The moral implications of the developmental stages of pregnancy were for centuries a part of common law considerations in determining what kind of crime had been committed if a pregnant woman had been harmed in such a way as to end the life of her unborn child. The unborn child was always considered something less than autonomous and thus the meaning of its legal existence was mediated, as a matter of course, by what happened to the mother. It is important to note that the adjudication of particular cases of harms against mothers and their unborn children should also be considered in a broader demographic context that until nearly the end of the nineteenth century was defined by high rates of infant mortality. Among the very first commercially sold and displayed photographs at that time were memorial photographs of deceased infants and young children. By the end of the nineteenth century, such images signified the arrival of the age of the "priceless" child that came with a rapid decline in the rates of infant mortality.

The alliance of the medical profession in the United States with legal institutions that eventually guaranteed the profession's own self-policing for more than a century had profound implications for the emergence of fetal rights. First, quite apart from the medical profession's efforts throughout the nineteenth century to curb any role in the provision of abortion by those other than regular physicians, a broad consensus at that time existed that abortion was a sin. But the theological justifications for calling abortion a sin were less important to doctors than the medical justifications for preserving human life *in utero*. Second, during the course of the nineteenth century, with dramatic improvements in surgery, a debate over the preferred medical procedure, craniotomy (which resulted in the destruction of the unborn child) or Caesarian section, to save the life of a mother imperiled by her pregnancy, eventually turned on the belief that if *both* lives could be saved, then all the better from a medical standpoint. In other words, the simplest logic prevailed in the protection of unborn life, underwritten as it was by a firm commitment on the part of the medical profession to the belief that the interruption of pregnancy resulting in the intentional destruction of the fetus should only be resorted to for the gravest reasons. But, as one obstetrician, Dr. Samuel Clagett Busey (1828–1901) observed:

> If a pregnant woman possesses the natural and inalienable right to terminate the life of her child at term, she cannot be denied the right to terminate it at any period of gestation, and criminal abortion would then become an accomplishment of the highest significance. The early destruction of embryonic life would be the simplest and surest escape from the perils of utero-gestation and parturition; would effectually withdraw from further scientific pursuit the advances in obstetrics which seek the elimination of craniotomy; more certainly extinguish the instincts and attribute of maternity; nullify the laws of reproduction; and reduce woman to a level more degrading than any to which the most barbaric of primitive people consigned her.
>
> *(Busey 1889, pp. 288–289)*

Medical progress had the potential to undermine what Busey called the instincts and attributes of maternity, providing women with a historically unprecedented opportunity to decide for themselves whether or not to continue a pregnancy. Once the relative safety of continuing a pregnancy to term could be compared less favorably to interrupting it early on, the same logic that had in Busey's time led to the use of Caesarian section over craniotomy could no longer be supported by any kind of broader cultural consensus about the value of all human life. From that point on, such value would increasingly be placed in the heart and mind of the individual pregnant woman.

Medical progress was, in fact, the condition necessary to make individual choice and discretion a real possibility in the sense that the risk to a pregnant woman's life was reduced by medical oversight. At the same time, however inadvertently, this same progress also proceeded on the basis of protecting fetal life more directly and effectively. Throughout the first half of the twentieth century, pregnant women afflicted with various illnesses, in particular heart, lung, and kidney diseases, were offered the option to end a pregnancy for the sake of their health and potentially their lives. During this period, the term "therapeutic abortion" appeared in the medical literature, referring specifically to those cases where "medical indications" justified ending a pregnancy. By the mid-twentieth century, virtually no medical indications remained for such a justification as the management of pregnancy improved and the life and health of the mother could be assured. Medical progress, focused on the condition of pregnancy itself, also assured the life of the unborn.

Two parallel developments in medical progress in surgical and diagnostic techniques opened new possibilities in the management of pregnancy that should be directly linked to significant social movements in the second half of the twentieth century: second-wave feminism and the right-to-life movement. Because the cultural struggles that defined pro-life and pro-choice movements have been viewed primarily in political terms, the underlying medical developments without which neither movement could have gained as much public attention as each has, have been obscured and taken for granted. Surgical improvements in the performance of abortion, particularly in the early stages of pregnancy (9 to 12 weeks) were first accomplished in Eastern Europe following the end of the Second World War. By most accounts, the technical improvements alone were sufficient to counter the longstanding objections to abortion as a form of birth control, even though to this day in the United States abortion is still morally characterized as a last resort. Surgical techniques evolved to allow for the routine and relatively safe performance of abortions outside hospital settings. For decades following the legalization of abortion in the United States in 1973, the abortion clinic served as one of the most contested sites in the conflict over the rights of the fetus.

The most important development in the emergence of fetal rights in retrospect was not surgical but rather diagnostic. In an ironic sense, as the right of a woman to end a pregnancy became less and less a matter for medical oversight, consultation, and intervention, particularly before the end of the first trimester of pregnancy, the fetus became more and more defined as a "patient" under the designation of"prenatal care."The long-term health of human beings staked more in the first nine months of life than at any previous time. Consider a few examples in the past several decades: concerns about low birth weight; about the impact on fetal development of alcohol and certain illicit drugs; about exposure to environmental toxins; and about iatrogenic harms caused by licit medications, have combined with the use of prenatal diagnostic techniques (and improved understanding of genetics) to establish pregnancy as one of the most scrutinized stages in the development of human life. Much of the reaction against any definitive claim, legal or otherwise, of what fetal rights should consist is predicated on the explosion of knowledge about fetal development that has taken place in the past half-century. For those most opposed to any legal restrictions on a woman's right to determine whether or not she will carry a pregnancy to term, medical involvement is nevertheless greater today than ever before.

The first two major incidents that led to greater diagnostic scrutiny and surveillance happened in the 1960s. Pregnant women exposed to rubella (i.e., German measles) were faced with the difficult choice about whether to end their pregnancies at a time when no certain diagnosis of a fetus's health was available. Around the same time, the drug thalidomide was prescribed to pregnant women in Britain and Europe to relieve morning sickness in early pregnancy. Thousands of children whose mothers took the drug were born with a variety of birth defects. These two incidents were formative in ushering in a new level of scrutiny of pregnancy itself. Immunization against rubella (and other childhood diseases) and greater safeguards put in place to assure the safety of prescribed medicines served as symbols in a much larger public health campaign aimed at reducing morbidity and mortality. Tobacco and alcohol were defined as deleterious to pregnancy, with the growing awareness that a mother's health was deeply entwined with the health of her unborn child.

The increased burden of responsibility on pregnant women, in effect calling for a kind of medically prescribed asceticism, has had lasting consequences on public attitudes about the fetus. The culture wars, particularly in the United States, over abortion reflect only one aspect of a continuing bifurcation in the perceived status of the fetus in terms of human rights discourse. It would appear that one indelible quality of any human right is that it must be defined in some collective fashion underwritten by the rule of law. The contrast now apparent between a woman's right to choose (the conventional assertion in the United States of a woman's right regarding the disposition of her fetus) and the elaborate surveillance of fetal health (including surgery *in utero*) raises anew the implications for human rights discourse generally about the fundamental meaning *not* of "right" but of "human." In the United States, at least, the fetus has less protection from the state than a dog does. This is not to draw any specific moral conclusion – although what may appear morally obvious to some is fiercely contested by others – but rather to point to the less controversial idea that the welfare of animals rests largely in concerns about cruelty toward them, even as the definition of cruelty expands to include the scientific use of animals for experimentation. That expansion suggests an analogy to the welfare of the fetus, including various legal cases that have addressed whether a woman can be forced to undergo medical treatment for the sake of her fetus; whether companies can unilaterally exclude fertile women from certain kinds of work that would expose them and their unborn children to harm; and what the legal ramifications are for pregnant women who expose their unborn children to harm due to substance abuse. In all such cases, some commentators have argued that the law has created over time a greater adversarial relationship between a pregnant woman and her unborn child, diminishing, in effect, the sovereignty of motherhood and expanding the individual fetus's separate existence as a rights-bearing human being.

Claims about the growing adversarial nature of pregnancy, which pits the interests of the mother against her unborn child, have been made in the context of an unprecedented growth in medical surveillance which has resulted in a kind of benign eugenics whose aim remains the optimizing of health in all children brought into the world. From the standpoint of human rights, little in this trend would strike many as problematic. On occasion accusations have been made against those who advocate middleclass values about family planning insofar as such values put pressure on poorer women to limit their childbearing, including the use of abortion. "Choice" in such cases has rhetorical implications that serve political values embraced by certain social strata more than others.

The future of fetal rights

The debate over fetal rights has been most prominent in the United States in large part because of the intimate role that the United States Supreme Court has played in the abortion controversy over the past four decades. When the Court found a constitutional basis for permitting a woman to exercise only minimally circumscribed control over her reproduction, it relied a great deal on the medical knowledge of the time. In what is perhaps the most enduring insight of this litigation, Justice Sandra Day O'Connor, in 1983, writing only a decade after *Roe v. Wade*, defined in a memorable dissent the predicament that would face lawmakers in the future:

> The Roe framework, then, is clearly on a collision course with itself. As the medical risks of various abortion procedures decrease, the point at which the State may regulate for reasons of maternal health is moved further forward to actual childbirth. As medical science becomes better able to provide for the separate existence of the fetus, the point of viability is moved further back toward conception. Moreover, it is clear that the trimester approach violates the fundamental aspiration of judicial decisionmaking through the application of neutral principles "sufficiently absolute to give them roots throughout the community and continuity over significant periods of time ..." A. Cox, The Role of the Supreme Court in

> American Government 114 (1976). The Roe framework is inherently tied to the state of medical technology that exists whenever particular litigation ensues. Although legislatures are better suited to make the necessary factual judgments in this area, the Court's framework forces legislatures, as a matter of constitutional law, to speculate about what constitutes "accepted medical practice" at any given time. Without the necessary expertise or ability, courts must then pretend to act as science review boards and examine those legislative judgments.
>
> (City of Akron v. Akron Center for Reproductive Health, Inc., *et al., 462 U.S. 416 [1983]*)

O'Connor's principal concern was with the application of what she termed the "Roe framework" with continued challenges to its relevance in a world of changing medical knowledge and technology. The "collision course" has given rise to two quite different kinds of controversies, each one the result of this framework.

First is O'Connor's observation that State regulation of abortion procedures for the sake of maternal health would be less and less applicable as the medical risks of such procedures decreased. Yet in the intervening years, the controversy over "partial-birth" abortions, that is abortions accomplished by procedures guaranteed to assure the destruction of the fetus *in utero*, replaced any initial concerns about the safety of the procedures themselves *to maternal health*. It was O'Connor's second observation that "As medical science becomes better able to provide for the separate existence of the fetus, the point of viability is moved further back toward conception" that serves as the foundational claim for the existence of "fetal rights." These can hardly be described as natural rights in the conventional sense without taking into account the role that medicine and medical technology play in their protection. At the present time, with sophisticated neonatal intensive care available, "viability" may exist as early as 22 weeks in pregnancy. The prospect of even less developed fetuses surviving with the assistance of medical technology continues to appear remote, but the illusion here is to imagine that there may never be a demand for gestational technologies that eliminate the need for female parturition completely. This may be the scenario of *Brave New World*, but its possibility can hardly be denied any longer on technical grounds.

The claims for women's rights have been in nearly every respect part of the central foundation for all human rights. This makes the interests of the fetus all the more problematic, since such interests are by definition subordinated to the interests of women's rights which obviously include reproductive rights. Nevertheless, the challenge that any universal theory of human rights must confront is how to reconcile competing interests when clear principles are neither available nor forthcoming. The case of fetal rights poses such an enduring challenge.

References

Busey, Samuel C. 1889. *The Wrong of Craniotomy upon the Living Fetus: Sixth Annual Address of the President, Delivered before the Washington Obstetrical and Gynecological Society, October 19th, 1888* (New York: William Wood & Company).

Imber, Jonathan B. 1986. *Abortion and the Private Practice of Medicine* (New Haven, CT: Yale University Press).

Imber, Jonathan B. 2008. *Trusting Doctors: The Decline of Moral Authority in American Medicine* (Princeton, NJ: Princeton University Press).

34

The human rights of the elderly

Frédéric Mégret

The human rights of the elderly is a topic that is somewhat neglected. Domestically, it is a dimension that is increasingly taken into account in at least some countries, but often in a haphazard way. Internationally, the debate on the predicament of senior citizens in terms of rights is only beginning (Rodriguez-Pinzon and Martin 2002). This is not to say that the elderly are not a concern, but that the issue is typically debated through registers, analytical or normative, other than that of human rights: medical, welfare, philosophical, political, economic, etc. The principal universal international human rights instruments do not contain any elderly-specific provisions, except perhaps for the International Covenant on Economic and Social Rights' reference to a right to "social insurance," which is sometimes understood to cover pension rights. Most international elderly-specific instruments, such as the 1982Vienna International Plan of Action on Ageing or the 1991 UN Principles for Older Persons are not comprehensive human rights instruments.

Yet arguably the elderly raise specific issues in terms of human rights and can be said to have distinct "human rights experiences." In other words, although the elderly certainly have the same rights as all human beings, what these rights mean is dependent on certain fundamental characteristics of one's human condition. Being at the end of the life cycle counts as a very distinctive feature of the human experience, and the failure to recognize specific elderly needs in terms of human rights is arguably part of a problematic construction of old age (Williams 2003).

Not only that, but the elderly are the fastest growing population worldwide, and one that raises major societal and political challenges. Even though they remain a relatively small minority (around 7 percent of the global population), it is a very significant one that is expected to be bigger than the number of children under 5 within a decade and to double by 2040. Nor is this only a first world phenomenon: the rate of growth of the elderly population in the Global South is double the rate of that of the North (62 percent of the world's seniors live in the developing world). Within the elderly, the very old (above 80) are also the fastest growing population, creating new challenges.

This phenomenon is beginning to be recognized, and international instruments such as the Madrid International Plan of Action on Ageing increasingly give credence to the idea that the problem of the old cannot be dealt with in a just way without relying at least in part on a rights framework. This chapter will seek to provide an introduction to the rights challenges raised by older persons. Developing a human rights regime that is adapted to the needs of the elderly should be seen as part of a larger fragmentation of the human rights project (Mégret 2008a). Like women, persons with disabilities, or children before them, specialized treatment would be a recognition that "the elderly have distinct human rights, which were not addressed specifically in the 1948 Universal Declaration of Human Rights or other relevant human rights instruments."

This chapter will begin by giving a broad presentation of the elderly population as a distinct group in society and one that raises specific dilemmas in terms of rights. It will then show how this distinctness raises important conceptual and legal issues for the human rights project.

The specificity of the elderly as a distinct population

The status of the elderly is constructed by a series of continuously evolving social representations. In some societies the elderly may be viewed as the repositories of certain wisdom and guardians of social continuity; in others they may be seen as symbols of conservatism and privilege. These perceptions, in turn, shape the rights debate as it seeks to come to terms with the distinctiveness of the old as a population.

Definitional issues

Although there is always a tendency to define "old age" in non-biological, subjective terms (an "old" person can be "young," and vice versa), there are some dangers to defining the quality of being "old" on the basis of certain qualities or characteristics commonly (but possibly wrongly) associated with the old. One may end up "essentializing" old age when the category is arguably very diverse and elastic (indeed, "the existence of definitions may feed society's rampant ageism" [Williams 2003, p. 105]). If anything, the quality of being old from a rights point of view should be associated with the particular life experience of being toward the end of the life cycle (possibly starting around 60), although finding a cut-off date for "old age" will be difficult. The best view is probably that old age as a category lies at the intersection of certain objective and subjective criteria.

The elderly are arguably a population that is merely distinguished from the rest of the population by their age. In that, they are not unlike children, who are already the object of many specific legal regimes and their own international human rights instrument. The elderly as a population may be harder to define than children, but even with children some definitional issues have arisen at the margin (when does one exit childhood?). It should also be remarked that the quality of being "elderly" (as that of being a "child") may be culturally and geographically relative, dependent on average life expectancy, lifestyle, etc. This is true of most groups that have been the object of specific human rights attention (e.g., racial groups, indigenous peoples, gender, etc.), and certainly no impediment to specific treatment. However, the idea of the elderly as a socially constructed category also brings some difficulties if it is used to determine individuals' belonging to that category, rather than the category itself (in that some may not define themselves as "elderly," something which may deserve recognition).

It is also worth pointing out that the elderly are more a category of population than a constituted group within it, although they may to a degree act or be perceived as acting as a group through socialization and an at least objective community of interests. Seniors are an internally varied population with occasionally contrasting and even conflicting priorities. The experience of old age, even of something such as elder abuse, can be very different depending on "gender, race and class"(Stoller and Gibson 1999). Older citizens may want specific rights attention, or on the contrary insist that their rights should be construed strictly identically to those of the rest of the population. Legitimate fears about "ageist" discrimination may arise even when the issue is defining a distinct elderly group to better protect its human rights. There is a risk, for example, that in investing the elderly with certain characteristics one will end up reifying them as a group.

The power–vulnerability paradox

As a population, the elderly raise a number of issues. In some ways, they can appear as a particularly powerful group in society. They may be wealthier on average than the rest of the population and concentrate a relatively high portion of capital as a result of lifelong accumulation. They may be very well integrated in society – benefiting in their old age from support from their descendants. They may also benefit from a culture and traditions that emphasize their accomplishments and the inherent respect in which they should be treated. The image of the elderly population, moreover, is one that is increasingly framed at least in the West in terms of independence, prosperity, and leisure. Senior citizens may also concentrate a larger share of political power, which may occasionally fuel critiques that the elderly are in a position to perpetuate certain of their advantages (Meyer et al. 1994). Gerontocracy has been described as government by the elderly, and there is some truth to the notion that many societies are governed by their most senior members. However, government by the elderly obviously does not necessarily mean government *for* the elderly. Recent research suggests that the elderly are also prime supporters of education expenses and not simplistically prone to support programs that benefit them at the expense of others (Street and Cossman 2006).

In other ways, the elderly can be seen as a particularly vulnerable segment of the population. Indeed, studies show that in many societies this is true of a majority of the population. Old age renders them more vulnerable not only to disease, senescence, and death, but also to various forms of abuse and exploitation. The elderly may be in disproportionate need of support, care, and services, whether provided by the state or their family. They have been shown to be particularly vulnerable in times of economic recession and restructuring, armed conflict, episodes of mass violence, major disasters, or even seasonal variation. They may be particularly vulnerable to certain forms of crime, including scams to deprive them of their assets. In the developing world, migration of the young has weakened the family as the traditional structure of support of the aged. The old will often be a prime target for poverty, exclusion, and marginalization and may suffer from negative stereotyping. This contrast between the elderly as relatively affluent and powerful and the elderly as isolated and vulnerable is one of the elements that arguably sets apart this group from others (i.e., unlike children, who are more naturally seen as mostly vulnerable).

Inter-generational justice

Finally, the elderly may find themselves at the heart of increasingly strong debates about inter-generational justice. Although "deep" inter-generational justice will occasionally involve debates about the duties of the living vis-à-vis the yet to be born, the debate is more commonly about the duties of the old towards the young and vice versa. The relationship between elderly policy and inter-generational justice has been particularly recognized by the European Union.

The growing relative number of elderly and their increasing overall needs, combined with the shrinking of the young, is putting social protection systems under strain and encouraging the perception that the elderly benefit disproportionately from the state's resources. It may prompt demands to reduce benefits afforded to the elderly, that they give up jobs badly needed by the young (or paradoxically, that they work longer), that they pay more taxes, that they be disenfranchised, or even that some health resources be diverted away from them to the young. Such debates have an old history. Some utilitarian and economic views seem to militate strongly against full respect for the rights of the elderly. For example, Christopher Callahan has argued that older people should be excluded from social citizenship, and that society's resources should be targeted towards the young who can benefit from them comparatively more (Callahan 1987; Jecker 1988). The elderly would lose the full rights associated with citizenship, although they would still be morally entitled to care from younger members of society.

This sort of reasoning has been attacked on a variety of grounds, especially in the health sector (Hunt 1993). Apart from the fact that it may not yield the economic advantages anticipated, it seems to fail to take elderly rights seriously, to rely on a reduction of the contribution of the elderly to society (assessed in terms of its economic impact), and to be ageist and discriminatory in essence. It may involve unacceptable forms of compulsion and arbitrariness. However, the argument remains a lively one in both health and philosophical circles, and distributive justice issues arise that cannot be dismissed out of hand by rights rhetoric, especially in conditions of scarcity that mandate that certain choices (dialysis, organ transplant, etc.) be made (Veatch 2006). Conversely, a major concern in some societies may be the treatment of the elderly by the young, and indeed the vulnerability of the former to the latter. Apart from the oft-heard complaint that the young have "lost respect" for the old, there is no doubt that, confronted with an aging population creating a greater economic and social burden on the relatively younger, tensions will arise. This relational element between the elderly and the rest of the population constitutes a particularly dynamic aspect of their status.

Some cross-cutting issues raised by elderly rights: adapting rights to old age

The challenge when it comes to a population as relatively distinct as the elderly is to try and determine what is specific about the way in which their rights can be protected/violated. Certain rights will inevitably carry a different resonance in the context of the life experience of the old. For example, the right to life may be particularly sensitive for those reaching the end of the life cycle. There have long been particular concerns about the possibility of the death penalty in relation to the elderly. More generally, there is a suspicion that the elderly are vulnerable to particular forms of killings, including through neglect or "health care rationing." Although the euthanasia debate is not limited to the elderly, old patients may either be vulnerable to decisions to withdraw care from them, or may actually seek to refuse life-sustaining treatment. In both cases, crucial human rights issues arise.

The right to be free from torture and cruel or inhumane treatment might also help frame issues of elderly abuse, including some of the more discreet forms of neglect (e.g., malnutrition, insufficient medical care), harm of a predominantly psychological nature (intimidation, humiliation), or sexual abuse. The right to be free from arbitrary detention may turn out to be a powerful way to challenge detention in care institutions in circumstances where older persons' will has insufficiently been taken into account. Already, many cases have alleged violations of the right to a fair and expeditious judicial determination in the assessment of pension rights but also more generally in the adjudication of a number of significant legal disputes. The argument is that older citizens cannot afford to wait years to know the outcome of cases that are crucial to the quality of their old-age life experience. The right to family life may also be challenged in new and unexpected ways in the case of the old. For example, it has increasingly been invoked by elderly couples who risked being separated (or being separated from their children and grandchildren) by decisions to place them in separate care homes. Political rights may also be at risk, in a context where proposals that the elderly be disenfranchised are not unheard of (Stewart 1970) and where creeping threats on the right to vote may exist in relation to older citizens with mobility impairments.

Finally, economic and social rights will also be crucial to older persons, and is often at risk of being neglected. The UN Committee on Economic, Social, and Cultural Rights (CESCR) authored a General Comment emphasizing the need to "pay particular attention to promoting and protecting the economic, social and cultural rights of older persons." The "right to social security" is often presented as particularly significant and understood as involving some right to old-age support. For example, the ILO social security conventions indicate that states parties should "establish general regimes of compulsory old-age insurance," and there is an international push for instituting old-age benefits even for persons who have not contributed to social-insurance schemes, particularly women. The right to an "adequate standard of living" has been understood in relation to the elderly as being strongly correlated to the principle of autonomy. Housing, health, even education are all rights that may assume a particular importance in old age.

Discrimination and the problem of ageism

Although the right to equality is a distinct right, the problem of discrimination against the aged is also a much broader conceptual and social problem that deserves to be analyzed from multiple angles. Discrimination against the elderly is typically associated with certain "ageist" trends in society that may portray the elderly in a negative light. Ageism has been defined as the view that "people cease to be people, cease to be the same people or become people of a distinct and inferior kind, by virtue of having lived a specified number of years" (Johnson and Bytheway 1993, p. 28). Although it has been compared to sexism and racism, it is also a more subtle form of discrimination, age involving as it does the passage through a transitional status in the life cycle by potentially all human beings (one, in addition, to which most aspire).

Ageism can be quite evident in popular culture and a certain glorification of youth. It is a phenomenon arguably accentuated by industrialization, modernization, and globalization, which corrode traditional respect for the elderly, even as they lead to social and family dislocation. Ageism may be accentuated by societies' prevalent individualism and consumerism and a tendency to discount the value that its older members can make to communal life given their perceived non-productive status. Finally, it is a set of attitudes that may have been made worse in the last decades by the extremely rapid development of technologies and the difficulty of some among the senior population to keep up with changes (e.g., the increasing digital divide between generations). One of the results may be a consequent devaluation of older persons' know-how, which had traditionally provided them with a strong sense of social relevance.

Ageism may make the old particularly vulnerable to abuse. As a result of discrimination, the elderly may be denied access to health care, voting, work, education, etc., on the basis of their age. The labor market is one area where older persons face significant obstacles, and where mandatory retirement laws have put issues of inter-generational justice in sharp focus. Old age is also a condition that must be seen in relation to a number of other causes for discrimination with which it intersects, particularly gender (older women outnumber older men) or indigenous origin. For example, the CESCR considers that "States parties should pay particular attention to older women who, because they have spent all or part of their lives caring for their families without engaging in a remunerated activity entitling them to an old-age pension, and who are also not entitled to a widow's pension, are often in critical situations."

The main international human rights instruments typically do not mention age per se as a ground of discrimination. However, as the CESCR put it, "Rather than being seen as an intentional exclusion, this omission is probably best explained by the fact that, when these instruments were adopted, the problem of demographic ageing was not as evident or as pressing as it is now." This is confirmed by the fact that the main human rights instruments are in reality quite open-ended about discrimination and mention the possibility of discrimination on the grounds of "other status." Moreover, the Convention on the Rights of Persons with Disability, one that may be of relevance to many within the elderly population, expresses concern in its Preamble about the fate of elderly persons with disabilities and urges states to adopt measures to combat prejudices, including those based on age (article 8). Article 13 of the European Communities Treaty had also expressly prohibited discrimination in relation to age, as does article 21 of the Charter on Fundamental Rights of the European Union.

In dealing with the problem of discrimination against the elderly, one paradox is that the very creation of a category of elderly human rights might reinforce some of the problems it is supposed to alleviate. In this respect, just as some among persons with disabilities do not want to be seen as members of that category, some older persons may understandably resist being defined, even marginally, in relation to their age. The challenge is to ensure that the need to take into account the specific needs of the elderly in terms of rights does not lead to the creation of a sort of "rights ghetto" that artificially reinforces the distinctiveness of the elderly. For the cure not to be worse than the ill, it needs to be established clearly that any elderly-specific approach is a complement to the normal full enjoyment of their rights.

Especially in advanced economies, many of the cases that have been litigated by the elderly on human rights grounds involved claims challenging mandatory retirement ages as being discriminatory. This is one area where considerations of inter-generational justice can be strong: mandatory retirement is presented as a way of making employment available for the young. The assumption, which is a deeply ingrained one, is that work is scarce and that retirement will sooner or later free up positions. Of course, some elderly may be very happy with mandatory retirement and see it as a way of protecting them from a never-ending life of work, especially when mandatory retirement is accompanied by a pensions system. On the one hand, it is generally understood that work is a defining element of the human condition and that only strong arguments will militate against denying someone the opportunity to work merely on the basis of their age (although the argument that there is no obligation by the state to provide work beyond a certain age may be easier to make). There is evidence that retirement can be a traumatizing life experience, one that is sometimes linked to feelings of uselessness and loss of control among the ageing population.

Some have criticized the basic economic reasoning behind mandatory retirement (i.e., that it frees up employment for the young). In circumstances where life expectancy increases constantly, one judge has pointed out that "an 'elite' group of people can afford to retire, but the adverse effects of mandatory retirement are most painfully felt by the poor. Women are particularly affected as they are less likely to have adequate pensions" (L'Heureux-Dubé 1990). Others insist that, especially given that only a minority will want to continue to work in old age, to deny them that possibility altogether is incompatible with basic freedoms. Gradually, some states have at least moderated mandatory retirement laws, partly for economic reasons, but also on the basis of civil rights arguments that "put simply, it is discriminatory to forcibly retire people who do not wish to retire"(McCallum 1990, p. 197; MacGregor 2006). This remains a contentious issue in some countries, especially in Europe, although a leading British elder rights NGO has brought a partly successful challenge of such laws before the European Court of Justice (CJEC 2009).

However, differential treatment (in the employment field or any other) is only discriminatory to the extent that it cannot be justified by a legitimate policy goal to which the practice is rationally and proportionally related. Some policies, in this respect, have been faulted for relying on generalizations about the elderly when individual assessments would have been possible (the dissenting opinions of L'Heureux-Dubé and McLachlin in *Dickason v. University of Alberta* can be found in [1992] 2 S.C.R. 1103).

Certainly the correlation that is often implicitly made between aging and declining working efficiency is highly questionable if it is not accompanied by individualized assessment. The situation is different if the age limit is justifiable on account of certain characteristics of a profession, although some courts have been criticized for considering too willingly that some elderly workers would be unfit for certain jobs (Klassen and Gillin 1999). The question as it has been raised before a number of domestic jurisdictions, therefore, is whether a mandatory retirement age is really a necessary and proportional measure (i.e., given that most people will be quite happy to retire anyhow). Generally, courts have refused to strike out mandatory retirement policies that seemed to be justified by the need to manage worker mass, preserve labor market flexibility, or renew staff, especially in areas such as universities where younger members may bring new perspectives. (See, for example, in Canada, *McKinney v. University of Guelph* [1990] 3 S.C.R. 229; *Dickason v. University of Alberta* [1992] 2 S.C.R. 1103.)

It is also worth emphasizing that, as with all equality jurisprudence, equality may mean quite different things in different circumstances: equal treatment when there is no particular valid reason to differentiate, but also possibly different treatment to offset the effect of de facto disparities. Certainly, the elderly will at times be in strong need of economic and medical support, along with specialized forms of care to respond to the particular changes they confront. At a certain level, a rights policy for the elderly may require group specific rights and instruments, and even some forms of positive discrimination (for example, subsidized or free social services for certain categories of retirees). Furthermore, as with other issues of rights discrimination, states have a duty to combat "ageist" prejudices and discrimination. The Convention on the Elimination of Discrimination against Women (CEDAW) was the first treaty to impose such a broad obligation, which has a societal and proactive dimension that goes beyond ensuring that discrimination does not occur in specific cases. States are asked to promote a certain image of the equal value and even positive contributions that the elderly can make to society.

Changing the focus: care institutions, the private sector, and the family

One of the consequences of taking into account the specific challenges of the elderly in terms of rights is a refocusing on a range of intermediary bodies. The role of collective bargaining by trade unions in relation to potentially discriminatory mandatory retirement ages, for example, has been explored. In Germany, for instance, mandatory retirement has been considered legal precisely because it is part of collective bargaining (Simitis 1993). Although the elderly may be at risk of abuse from the state, they are also quite likely to be under the care of public and private institutions, some steps removed from the state itself. As far as public institutions are concerned, one trend has seen states adopt specific human rights instruments in nursing homes (e.g., the US Residents' Bill of Rights, the California Welfare and Institutions Code). As part of their "obligation to protect," states should also ensure that individuals within their jurisdiction do not experience rights violations from third parties. This is particularly important in the case of the elderly, especially in the face of attempts to exclude the liability of private care institutions. For example, the British government has intervened to stress that private providers of care on behalf of a local authority should be considered "public authorities" for the purposes of the

Human Rights Act. Moreover, it has made it clear that it will extend the Human Rights Act to individuals placed in privately run nursing homes.

Attention to the plight of the elderly may also help reassess the scope of the state's human rights obligations and the responsibilities of the family. One reason for failing to take elderly rights sufficiently seriously is a tendency to see the old as often withdrawing into "private" life towards the end of their existence, and an assumption that they will be taken care of by their relatives. The term "abuse" itself is richly connoted with the implication that "abuse" is something fundamentally different from "public" cruel and inhuman treatment (or even semi-public criminal behavior). In that respect, the elderly may not be in that different a position conceptually than feminists' critique of women's traditional social, political, and economic "invisibility"(Sullivan 1995). Some forms of abuse – for example by grandchildren against their grandparents – may be so intensely "private" as to being typically ignored by public authorities.

Laws that penalize abuse directly at the hands of relatives may make sense of part of the state's duty to protect individuals from violations by third parties, including in the private. However, laws may typically be more reluctant to impose positive obligations on such relatives (e.g., children) to take care of the old. Some states have clearer laws imposing a number of filial obligations of care on children (i.e., an obligation not to abuse "by neglect"), but such laws may be difficult to enforce in a context of evaporating solidarities, mobility, and care outsourcing. Moreover, it does not deal with the fact that the elderly may not have relatives, or that the state may be liable for elderly abuse and neglect whether or not they have such relatives. Subject to a standard of reasonableness (for example, protecting the elderly cannot justify groundless invasions of privacy), the state is to make sure that the elderly should be protected. In some cases, this might extend to protecting the elderly against forms of self-neglect.

Conclusion

Although elderly issues are increasingly framed in terms of human rights, it is far from obvious that the natural trajectory of rights-informed approaches will necessarily simply involve a translation of all existing medical, social, and welfare registers into rights language. In fact, this might constitute an impoverishment of the overall approach used to tackle elderly challenges. Rather, even as human rights language intensifies some of the claims made by the elderly, it will hybridize with other normative languages.

Human rights discourse is uniquely suited to "de-naturalizing" certain issues, and "re-politicizing" them. For example, contra a certain vision of the difficulties of old age as an inevitability, it might help to point out that the experience of the elderly is at least as much constructed by social, economic, and political factors as it is by the mere fact of biological old age. In other words, it is not old age that renders certain rights hard to enjoy, but a particular conception of old age that would deny the full enjoyment of their rights to the ageing. Human rights might also help politicize certain issues. For example, in countering a vision of their needs as mostly involving "state-sponsored medical care and old age pensions … most elderly rights groups might object to such a limited concept of societies' duties to them, preferring instead that greater attention be given to issues of autonomy and personal liberty" (Fagan 2002, p. 336). Furthermore, contra a powerful medical lobby that would reduce the problem of old age to its health dimension understood in a narrow biological sense, as physical decline (Estes and Binney 1989), human rights discourse can emphasize that the older persons' health is at least as much constructed by certain political choices that can be challenged. It is, for example, the fact that society has *chosen* not to assign sufficient staff to certain institutions that makes them unable to treat the elderly with all the dignity they deserve.

At the same time, some of the limitations of human rights language are well known. Human rights set certain goals that often require extensive further interpretation to translate into state obligations; they tend to address states parties rather than the whole range of actors that might conceivably violate/promote rights; they are quite indeterminate in terms of required policies, even as policies may be crucial to protect rights. This is why treaties like the UN Disabilities Convention now include a much more richly textured mix of rights, goals, standards, best practices, and the like, and they profoundly restructure rights language in the process (Mégret 2008b). Elderly focused instruments may come, for example, to emphasize duties as well as rights, including the duties not only of the state but also of society and family members towards the elderly. Themes that have acquired prominence in the UN Disabilities Convention – such as autonomy, independence, or "reasonable accommodation" – may assume a significant role in assessing elderly rights.

Adopting a truly rich human rights approach will also involve reassessing the positive contributions of the elderly to society in positive, non-ageist terms. The Madrid International Plan of Action (para. 10) for example, emphasizes the need for "changes in attitudes, policies and practices at all levels in all sectors so that the enormous potential of ageing in the twenty-first century may be fulfilled." The elderly can be repositories of knowledge, particularly traditional knowledge, and a bridge with the past. In AIDS-ridden societies, they have often emerged as principal providers for their grandchildren after the death of parents. There are many examples not only of elderly associations working on issues of specific concern to the elderly, but also of specific forms of elderly activism with more general social transformative goals. A better understanding of these contributions may go a long way toward remedying some of the problem of discrimination. Finally, a global discussion on the rights of the elderly will inevitably comport a significant North–South dimension, as attitudes to the elderly are compared and challenged.

References

Callahan, D. 1987. "Terminating Treatment: Age as a Standard." *The Hastings Center Report*, Vol. 17, No. 5, pp. 21–25.

CJEC. 2009. Judgment of the court, in Case C-388/07, *The Incorporated Trustees of the National Council on Ageing (Age Concern England) v. Secretary of State for Business, Enterprise, and Regulatory Reform*, 5 March.

Estes, C. L. and E. A. Binney. 1989. "The Biomedicalization of Aging: Dangers and Dilemmas." *Gerontologist*, Vol. 29, No. 5, p. 587.

Fagan, A. R. 2002. "An Analysis of the Convention on the International Protection of Adults." *Elder Law Journal*, Vol. 10, p. 334.

Hunt, R. W. 1993. "A Critique of Using Age to Ration Health Care." *British Medical Journal*, Vol. 19, No. 1, p. 19.

Jecker, N. S. 1988. "Disenfranchising the Elderly from Life-Extending Medical Care." *Public Affairs Quarterly*, Vol. 2, No. 3, p. 51.

Johnson, J. and B. Bytheway. 1993. "Ageism: Concept and Definition." In J. Johnson and R. Slater, eds., *Ageing and Later Life* (London: Sage).

Klassen, T. R. and C. T. Gillin. 1999. "The Heavy Hand of the Law: The Canadian Supreme Court and Mandatory Retirement." *Canadian Journal on Aging*, Vol. 18, No. 2, pp. 259–276.

L'Heureux-Dubé, J. 1990. In *McKinney v. University of Guelph*, 3 S.C.R. 229.

McCallum, J. 1990. "Australian Mandatory Retirement Challenged." *Journal of Aging & Social Policy*, Vol. 2, No. 3, pp. 183–200.

MacGregor, D. 2006. "Neglecting Elders in the Workplace: Civil Society Organizations, Ageism, and Mandatory Retirement." *Canadian Journal on Aging*, Vol. 25, No. 3, pp. 243–246.

Mégret, F. 2008a. "The Disabilities Convention: Human Rights of Persons With Disabilities or Disability Rights?" *Human Rights Quarterly*, Vol. 30, No. 2, p. 494.

Mégret, F. 2008b. "The Disabilities Convention: Towards a Holistic Concept Of Rights." *International Journal of Human Rights*, Vol. 12, p. 261.

Meyer, M. H., D. Street, and J. Quadagno. 1994. "The Impact of Family Status on Income Security and Health Care in Old Age: A Comparison of Western Nations." *International Journal of Sociology and Social Policy*, Vol. 14, Nos. 1/2, pp. 53–83.

Rodriguez-Pinzon, D. and C. Martin. 2002. "The International Human Rights Status of Elderly Persons." *American University International Law Review*, Vol. 18, p. 915.

Simitis, S. 1993. "Denationalizing Labour Law: The Case of Age Discrimination." *Comparative Labour Law Journal*, Vol. 15, p. 321.

Stewart, D. J. 1970. "Disenfranchise the Old." *New Republic*, Vol. 163, Nos. 8–9, pp. 22–29.

Stoller, E. P. and R. C. Gibson. 1999. *Worlds of Difference: Inequality in the Aging Experience* (Thousand Oaks, CA: Pine Forge Press).

Street, D. and J. Cossman. 2006. "Greatest Generation or Greedy Geezers? Social Spending Preferences and the Elderly." *Social Problems*, Vol. 53, No. 1, pp. 75–96.

Sullivan, D. 1995. "The Public/Private Distinction in International Human Rights Law." In Julie Peters and Andrea Wolper, eds., *Women's Rights, Human Rights: International Feminist Perspectives* (London: Routledge).

Veatch, R. M. 2006. "How Age Should Matter: Justice as the Basis for Limiting Care to the Elderly." In Helga Kuhse and Peter Singer, eds., *Bioethics: An Anthology* (Oxford: Blackwell).

Williams, J. 2003. "When I'm Sixty-Four: Lawyers, Law and Old Age." *Cambrian Law Review*, Vol. 34, p. 103.

35

Environmental human rights

Richard P. Hiskes

Introduction

The prospect of human rights relating to the environment currently enjoys, somewhat ironically, more standing in human rights treaties, many national constitutions, and international agreements than it does among human rights theorists. Among scholars the whole concept of environmental human rights remains fraught, considered a third-generation right that crosses too many conceptual boundaries and requires resolutions of too many philosophical disputes before it can be acknowledged. Several scholars have presented arguments for environmental human rights, including Hancock (2003), Hayward (2005), Hiskes (2005, 2009), Nickel (1993), Picoloti and Tallant (2003), and Weiss (1989). Nevertheless, because environmental human rights – if they do exist – presume duties that cross borders both temporally and geographically, the philosophical and legal cases for their reality remain unpersuasive for many, and in practice their promise remains unfulfilled.

Despite this scholarly ambivalence as well as practical difficulties in implementation, since 1981 several international accords have named environmental rights as rights duly held by all persons. In international documents beginning with the African National Charter (1981) and in scholarly literature these rights are sometimes listed singly, especially and most recently as in the human right to water; sometimes they are simply referred to collectively as "rights to a safe environment" (Nickel 1993), or evocatively as "planetary rights" (Weiss 1989); occasionally they are enumerated as the rights to clean air, water, and soil (Hiskes 2005). In international circles environmental issues are increasingly framed in terms of human rights, especially in relation to – or as part of – other rights such as to health, national development, or cultural self-determination. It is this convergence of environmental human rights with other second- or third-generation rights that both accounts for their appeal in international conventions and encourages the epistemological suspicion in academic or legal argument.

To appreciate the impact of environmental human rights in contemporary human rights theory and politics it is essential to account for both sides of their emergence in international agreements and in scholarly debate. In what follows I will begin by exploring how environmental human rights have been incorporated into recent international conventions and agreements over the past thirty years. It can also be noted in passing that during that time several newly written national constitutions have also incorporated various versions of environmental rights. By 1998 over fifty national constitutions included language referring to either expressly stated environmental rights or to state obligations to protect the environmental heritage of present and future generations (Anton 1998). Though the United States Constitution does not include environmental rights in its Bill of Rights, five state constitutions – Hawaii, Illinois, Massachusetts, Montana, and Pennsylvania – explicitly name the right to a healthy environment.

Following this canvas of the current applications of environmental rights within national and international documents and agreements I will explore the conceptual background of environmental rights. This area of discussion is rife with disagreement concerning the ontological status of environmental human rights *qua* rights, since if they are indeed rights their addressees are somewhat unconventional within human rights politics. Furthermore, environmental rights appear as *emergent* rights, both in the sense of being new and because they invoke collective phenomena and group rights in controversial new ways. Finally, environmental human rights imply a unique relationship with future generations in which both the rights of future persons and justice across generations (itself a debatable concept traditionally rejected by philosophers) must be accepted as concrete realities for environmental human rights to follow logically.

International agreements and environmental human rights

For at least thirty years, many nations have, through a series of agreements, moved closer to a legal recognition of the human right to a safe environment. Legal scholar Richard Herz (2000, p. 58) counts 350 multinational treaties and 1,000 bilateral treaties, in addition to numerous resolutions between intergovernmental organizations that assert a duty within international law to protect the environment. This does not necessarily mean that environmental human rights are currently incorporated into international law, since the responses of nations regarding their environmental obligations are variable and often denied, as the case of the Kyoto Protocols and the later (2009) Copenhagen Accords make evident. Nevertheless, the sheer number of international documents over the past several decades carrying invocations to recognize environmental obligations and even employing the language of human rights in doing so is impressive.

Beginning with the UN Conference called in Stockholm in 1972, international obligations to protect the environment first became formulated within the language of human rights. The Stockholm Declaration averred in its first principle that:

> [M]an has the fundamental right to freedom, equality, and adequate conditions of life, in an environment of a quality that permits a life of dignity, and well-being, and he bears a solemn responsibility to protect and improve the environment for present and future generations.

By employing both concepts of dignity and future generations the Stockholm Declaration, though itself non-binding on its 114 signatory nations, clearly paved the way for a variety of subsequent declarations proclaiming both individual environmental human rights (especially the right to water) and national obligations for protecting those rights of present and future generations.

As an example of the legacy of Stockholm, Article 24 of the African Charter of Human and People's Rights (also called the "Banjul Charter") (1981) declares: "All peoples shall have the right to a general satisfactory environment favourable to their development." The Charter's invocation of "people's rights" initiated within the human rights community discussion of the idea of "group rights," is a concept also relevant to the idea of environmental rights as will be discussed later.

In 1987 the UN World Commission on Environment and Development (WCED) issued its report, called "Our Common Future" but better known by the name of its chair, Gro Harlem Brundtland. Coining the term "sustainable development" and characterizing it as "development that meets the needs of the present without compromising the ability of future generations to meet their own needs," the Brundtland Report did more than firmly establish environmental protection as essentially an issue of inter-generational justice, though it certainly did that. It also "presented the basic goals of environmentalism as an extension of the existing human rights discourse" (Hayward 2005, p. 55). The Report states, "All human beings have the fundamental right to an environment adequate for their health and well-being" (WCED 1987, p. 348).

Also of note, Article 24 of the UN Convention on the Rights of the Child (UNCRC), a treaty ratified by most of the world's nations with a few notable exceptions, such as the USA, stipulates a child's right "to the enjoyment of the highest attainable standard of health." In paragraph c, the Article admonishes signatories that this right requires that they "combat disease and malnutrition, including within the framework of primary health care, through, inter alia, the application of readily available technology and through the provision of adequate nutritious foods and clean drinking water, *taking into consideration the dangers and risks of environmental pollution*" (emphasis added). Like the Brundtland Report, by focusing on the rights of children the UNCRC brings to the idea of environmental human rights a clear focus on future generations, thereby linking the idea of environmental human rights with the goal of inter-generational justice.

Extension of the focus on the environmental human rights of groups or peoples continued in the report of the UN Sub-Commission on the Prevention of Discrimination and Protection of Minorities (1994). It reaffirmed "a conception of human rights and the environment which captures the spirit of the Principle 1 of the 1972 Stockholm Declaration" (Hayward 2005, p. 56). The Report of the Sub-Commission, known as the Ksentini Report, included a set of "Draft Principles on Human Rights and the Environment," in which its first principle declares, "human rights, an ecologically sound environment, sustainable development and peace are interdependent and indivisible." Though such postulated interdependence and indivisibility might be said to ignore myriad potential conflicts between human rights in general and economic development, in its second principle the Declaration asserts, "all persons have the right to a secure, healthy and ecologically sound environment." Furthermore, this right is indistinguishable from other human rights in terms of force or coverage: "This right and other human rights, including civil, cultural, economic, political and social rights, are universal, interdependent, and indivisible" (p. 75).

The Sub-Commission's Draft Principles highlight the group's focus on environmental rights, since it is primarily a report on the rights of minorities. Still, in its enumeration of environmental human rights it relies mostly on the more traditional language of individual "persons" rather than of groups or "peoples." Representative statements are the following from Part I:

- All persons have the right to a secure, healthy and ecologically sound environment.
- All persons have the right to freedom from pollution, environmental degradation and activities that adversely affect the environment ...
- All persons have the right to safe and healthy food and water adequate to their well-being.
- Everyone has the right to benefit equitably from the conservation and sustainable use of nature and natural resources ...

The Ksentini Report also expanded environmental human rights by declaring that included among them were procedural guarantees relating to the process of making environmental legislation in the furtherance of those rights. Its Draft Principles also included an entire section (Part III) given over to listing the procedural rights citizens possess in the making of new environmental regulations to protect against climate change. In so doing the Report also incorporated an important distinction into the discussion of environmental human rights that so far has set these rights off from most other human rights. That distinction denotes both a substantive and procedural side to environmental rights. It is the procedural environmental rights invoked in Part III of the Draft Principles that signal a theoretical innovation in human rights thinking heralded by this new convergence between environmentalism and human rights:

15. All persons have the right to information concerning the environment. This includes information, howsoever compiled, on actions or courses of conduct that may affect the environment and information necessary to enable effective public participation in environmental decision-making. The information shall be timely, clear, understandable and available without undue financial burden to the applicant.
16. All persons have the right to hold and express opinions and to disseminate ideas and information regarding the environment.
17. All persons have the right to environmental and human rights education.
18. All persons have the right to active, free and meaningful participation in planning and decision-making activities and processes that may have an impact on the environment and development. This includes the right to a prior assessment of the environmental, developmental and human rights consequences of proposed actions.
19. All persons have the right to associate freely and peacefully with others for purposes of protecting the environment or the rights of persons affected by environmental harms.
20. All persons have the rights to effective remedies and redress in administrative or judicial proceedings for environmental harm or the threat of such harm.

These procedural human rights relating to environmental policy making were given a substantial legal boost in 2001 by the United Nations Economic Commission for Europe (UNECE) Convention on Access to Information, Public Participation in Decision-making, and Access to Justice in Environmental Matters. Usually referred to as the Aarhus Convention after the Danish city in which it was signed, this treaty focused on democratizing interactions between citizens and their governments on environmental matters and included a unique compliance provision. The Compliance Review Mechanism allowed citizens to communicate concerns about any state party's compliance (including their own government's) directly to a UN committee empowered to explore the merits of the complaint. Two years later the Kiev Protocol was addended to the Aarhus Convention in order to guarantee citizens' access and reporting rights in the specific environmental policy area of pollutant release and transfer registers (RTRs) (UNECE 2007).

One final development within international agreements concerning environmental rights relates specifically to the human right to water. This right is usually included in any list of environmental rights, though it also appears in the context of discussions of other human rights, including those to health, national development, or self-determination (Gleick 1999; Russell 2009). As strictly an environmental right, it was defined in 2003 by the UN Committee on Economic, Social, and Cultural Rights (CESCR) in its General Comment 15 as: "indispensable for leading a life in human dignity … [I]t entitles everyone to sufficient, safe, acceptable, physically accessible and affordable water for personal and domestic uses" (pp. 1, 2.) The human right to water is also explicitly named in the Convention on the Elimination of All Forms of Discrimination against Women (CEDAW 1980), specifically as a protection implied by the right to development. In addition, the Convention on the Rights of the Child (UNCRC 1990) names the right to water as part of the human right to health.

Even viewed strictly as an environmental right, the right to water can be interpreted variously, as part of the general environmental right to clean air, water, and soil, as a specific right regarding access, or as a claim against governmental privatization of water supplies or delivery. The latter is frequently an issue of economic development within Third World countries, in the form of water privatization policies adopted by debtor governments in order to meet loan requirements from the World Bank.

From this brief summary it is clear that environmental human rights have become persistent topics of agreement on the international stage and even within major international documents and conventions. Nevertheless, they pose several challenges to accepted human rights theory and practice, and at this stage their acceptance by international commissions and bodies far exceeds that by human rights scholars. It is worth exploring this reluctance to accept environmental human rights as legitimate constraints on governmental, corporate, or even individual behavior. Environmental human rights as a concept (and/or as a set of practices or guarantees) raises interesting possibilities concerning how human rights can alter ethical or political discussions. Indeed, the success of environmentalism as a movement or political mandate might depend on the muscularity of the "rights language" surrounding international and national issues of sustainability and environmental justice.

Environment and the reconceptualization of human rights

In its Draft Principles concerning environmental rights, the Ksentini Report from the UN Sub-Commission on the Prevention of Discrimination and Protection of Minorities (1994) revealed a conceptual paradox concerning human rights that illuminates how environmental human rights generate foundational issues for human rights as a whole. Though this was a report specifically identifying "groups" to be protected and elsewhere in the document referring to those groups' "collective rights," the Draft Principles themselves rely on the same individualistic language of "persons" and their "individual rights" that echoes the wording of most human rights documents back to the Universal Declaration of Human Rights (UDHR).

Environmental rights seem especially prone to being viewed as group rights, since by the very nature of what is being protected (air, water, soil) they call attention to group impacts. That is, they invoke "emergent" effects of group behavior that are difficult to reduce to the behavior of individuals acting alone. Furthermore, environmental protection based on rights seems to require that the addressee of the rights be a supranational one, since the natural world that requires protection does not recognize political borders – nor do the threatened waterways, air masses, or soil groups. Finally, environmental rights seem to invoke the rights of future generations as well, since environmental impacts both detrimental and restorative can take generations to be fully revealed. If future generations can be said to have rights, however, they can only be viewed as group rights – the rights of the group of future persons that function as restrictions on our actions today. Finally, because of their unique relationship to time, environmental rights invoke notions of justice across generations, a possibility usually denied by philosophers, given that justice usually requires reciprocity of some sort and reciprocal relations with persons who do not yet exist simply seems illogical.

To summarize, three foundational issues regarding human rights are highlighted by environmental rights:

1. Can there be group rights, especially of "emergent" groups like future persons, and what does it mean to accept the idea of emergent rights?
2. If there are environmental rights, who is their addressee, since no nation-state by itself can affect the global environment?
3. If environmental rights presume justice across generations in the protection of future persons' environmental rights, how can they provide for the reciprocity with future persons that justice relations traditionally require?

In the remainder of this chapter I will briefly comment on each of these contributions to human rights theory posed by environmental human rights.

Environmental rights and emergent group rights

By its very nature the environment calls attention to the interconnectedness of all human life and the impacts it has as a whole on natural systems. Ecology as a science teaches this lesson of interconnectivity more than any other; one of its corollaries is that impacts on the environment such as pollution are ontologically emergent. That means that for practical purposes it is unproductive to try to separate out each individual contribution to the phenomenon of air or water pollution. In other words, pollution is an "emergent" phenomenon, a harm for which we are essentially all to blame as contributors. But if rights in general are responses to the existence of harms against which we deserve the protections of rights, and if the harms are themselves emergent, then so must be the rights to which they give rise.

Environmental rights are emergent then in at least two ways. First, they are new rights and the products of recent events, namely various modern forms of environmental degradation. They are also the products of new knowledge about the environment and how interconnected processes and impacts characterize it. This means obviously that part of the claim of environmental rights is that it is possible for "new" human rights to emerge. Some might find this controversial, citing Maurice Cranston's (1967) famed characterization of human rights "real and supposed." Yet to deny this is to doom human rights to a static, even moribund, domain, one that increased human experience and innovation would quickly exceed.

Second, environmental human rights are emergent in that, as responses to emergent harms, they arise from human relationships and their impacts on the natural world. The depredations visited upon the environment are the product of collective behavior of individuals *in relations*. These can be legal relations like corporate, societal, or even familial relationships. The point here is that as a species our impacts on the environment emerge from behavior patterns generated by the relationships by which we act jointly in ways that affect the environment. Societal norms and patterns of consumption, corporate decisions about resource usage or production, and family decisions about property use or purchasing all carry effects for the surrounding environment.

In their emergence from human relationships environmental harms raise the possibility that their corresponding environmental rights might also be grounded in the human capacity for having relationships rather than on the more traditional foundation of human reason or dignity. This interesting theoretical direction is explored in several contributions to human rights theory such as Donnelly (1989), Hiskes (2009), and Metz (2010). If environmental rights do indeed lead to a reformulation of human rights as grounded not in human reason as traditionally claimed since Kant, but in (and emergent from) the human capacity for relationships, this would supply an important link between rights theory and communitarianism (Sandel 1982; Taylor 1989), as well as between human rights and feminist theory (Benhabib 2002; Gould 2004).

At the very least, in their emergent character environmental rights make a strong case for the notion of group rights. Some of this arises from the concomitant group harms to which they respond, but more than that, groups qua groups in a variety of contexts claim environmental rights. Examples include community or tribal claims over water supplies, traditional hunting grounds, burial grounds, and the like. Additionally, whole nations, or in the USA whole states, make rights claims specifically over water impoundments or rivers, and also claim group sovereignty based on rights over natural resources or even habitats like the Everglades or tropical rain forests. In fact, societies often include as part of their cultural identity the claims they presume over important natural features of their territory and what they have meant in defining their national character. Examples of such environmental characterizations of cultural identity include the American frontier, the Egyptian Nile, or the Tibetan Himalayas.

When environmental human rights become group claims, as often happens in international law, two questions immediately arise which form the substance of the next two sections. First, who (or what) is the addressee of environmental rights claims, and how does this question impact the overall efficacy of environmental human rights? Second, since the group most often invoked in environmental rights claims is the set of all future persons, what is the relationship of environmental rights to the prospect of environmental justice across generations? In responding to these two issues the legal and conceptual influence of environmental human rights on the whole human rights regime becomes apparent.

The addressee of environmental human rights

Beginning with the UDHR, the "addressees" of human rights have always been considered both legally and logically to be nation-states and their governments. This has meant first that rights are "addressed" to those governments in that they are individually obligated to protect rights and to further their full realization among all their citizens. Realistically, national governments are the addressees of human rights for two other reasons: first, because governments are most likely to be the greatest threat to their citizens' human rights; and second, because in the international system power is distributed along national lines. Thus national governments are "charged" with protecting rights rather than postulating some supranational agency with considerably more power than, for instance, the United Nations. In this way human rights have been delivered into modern international politics without actually challenging its most basic presumption: national sovereignty.

Environmental human rights pose something of a dilemma for this understanding of the addressee of human rights. Though the international community has on occasion intervened into domestic politics in the name of other human rights (invocations of rights against genocide provide the best examples), environmental rights would seem to provide an almost endless supply of pretexts for violations of state sovereignty. All nations negatively affect their natural environments to varying degrees, and those effects impact their neighboring states and the global environment as well. By its very nature the "environment" as such recognizes few national boundaries, and environmental impacts are almost never contained within particular nations. The currently most discussed environmental impact is termed "*global* warming" for a reason (even if "climate change" is more accurate) – the environment is global. How then can the politics of environmental human rights remain *national*, that is, tied to national governments as the addressee of those rights?

Within present international politics as discussed in the first half of this chapter, the addressee dilemma is mostly avoided by international accords ranging from the Stockholm Declaration to the Kyoto Protocols simply by binding signatory nations to *aspire* to the goals established by the recognized environmental rights put in jeopardy by each nation's contribution to climate change. Such a resolution maintains state sovereignty and addressee status certainly, but does some violence to the whole idea of a right as a legitimate claim that can be enforced, not merely hoped for. The exception of course was the Aarhus Convention, which in its unique Compliance Mechanism made it possible for citizens of any state to make claims to an international review panel. But here, too, the actual coercive power of the UN panel withers when confronted by a state unwilling to amend its practices.

The dilemma appears somewhat irresolvable: if states remain the addressees of human rights, then environmental rights will exercise at best a vague power to persuade or to make appeals to the morality of environmental stewardship. On the other hand, when international organizations or states have come together to set joint policy protecting the environment, enforcement has been lacking and the muscular power of "rights" claims is diminished not only for environmental rights but also potentially for all human rights.

A more optimistic assessment is provided by Hayward (2005) and Hiskes (2009). Both see environmental rights as posing this dilemma for human rights enforcement generally, but suggest that environmental rights might act as a bridge between the original, nation-state address of human rights and a potentially more global one based on international consensus of national constitutions. Both argue for environmental human rights provisions to be incorporated within all national constitutions. Though this obviously maintains the state at least on the surface as the addressee of environmental rights, if all nations incorporated such provisions into their constitutions this would manifest a dramatic moment of international consensus on the authority of environmental rights. In any case, such a step would dramatically witness how environmental rights have altered the conceptual and legal terrain of human rights generally.

Environmental rights and inter-generational justice

Just as environmental human rights expand the geographical borders of the domain of human rights, they also transgress temporal boundaries as well. Most arguments for environmental protection, whether founded on rights or not, invoke the needs and plight of future generations who will live with the legacy of our environmental impact. When future generations are invoked it is usually in the midst of a moral argument stressing the virtue of conservation or of caring about our children's children. Such arguments do carry some persuasive power, but usually not enough to sustain a conservation effort in the face of the sacrifices demanded of the living. And the future has little legal standing or real political power to force the living to conserve – future generations are always in the minority in the eyes of those who currently wield power. As a result, even in democracies, environmental concerns, especially those that invoke inter-generational justice, languish near the bottom of the political agenda.

Environmental human rights carry the potential to change the relationship between present and future generations, and are unique in this regard compared to all other rights. Thus, conservation or sustainability policies written in the language of environmental human rights supply new power to the claims of future generations, potentially enough to balance the scales between present and future. It is worth briefly exploring further this efficacious aspect of environmental human rights.

Environmental human rights differ from other rights in the relationship they presume with future generations of rights holders. Because policies meant to protect or sustain the environment by necessity extend far into the future, they invoke the living conditions of future persons as part of the argument for changing current practices. If those policies were to be grounded on the idea of environmental human rights, what would be invoked are the environmental rights of those future persons, perceived as a group. In other words, current policies would be enacted on the grounds of protecting the environmental rights of future generations. In a moment we will see how this has a reciprocal benefit to living persons sufficient to call this a relationship of justice across generations; first, we should note the uniqueness of environmental human rights from all other rights because of this relationship.

All other rights, including basic human rights to free speech, to life, or to be free from torture, do not logically require that those rights be sustained in the future in order to protect them in the present. If free speech ended after my death, that eventuality would not have affected my enjoyment of this right during my lifetime; the same would be true for the right to be free from torture, to vote, to own property, or any other right. What happens to rights after living rights holders die does not affect either them or their own personal rights.

Environmental rights, however, can only be protected in the present if they extend into the future, since, for example, cleaning a polluted river may take generations. Therefore, a concern only with the rights of living persons will not guarantee that the river will eventually become potable; that result can only be achieved if the rights of future persons are protected *as fully* as current persons. The realization of my environmental human rights, in other words, lies precisely in the protection of future generations' environmental human rights. This is, then, a benefit felt by the living that comes from the future – a reciprocation of a kind. It is a giving back or return on investment that rebounds reflexively from my protection of the future's rights.

Such reciprocal benefit is what philosophers since Aristotle have argued is necessary for justice to pertain between people, and it is the reason why inter-generational justice has always been considered illogical (see Ball 1985 and Barry 1999 for current forms of this argument). But if environmentalism grounded in environmental human rights can deliver such a reciprocal effect, then inter-generational justice at least in environmental terms is indeed not only possible, but also essential for the fate of the planet.

A final point to be made concerning inter-generational justice based upon environmental human rights is that no matter how reciprocal a relationship is, it can only be *just* if, as John Rawls (1971) would say, it is also *fair*. At this point it would seem that respecting the future's environmental rights delivers a great benefit for future persons but only sacrifice for those living now. This is certainly not an equal relationship it would seem, and also not fair. However, the fairness requirement is the reasoning behind the legal insistence that environmental rights also include procedural rights of various kinds, including rights to access to information and to participation in the decision process for environmental policy. Nickel (1993) argues for these, and, as noted earlier, these procedural human rights are included in major international documents like the Ksentini Report and in the agreements at Aarhus and the Kiev Protocol. Procedural environmental rights balance the scales between present and future generations. The future is assured of the substantive human rights of a clean environment; present citizens receive some of these benefits too as their environment improves, but also claim the procedural rights of participation in the policy process.

Conclusion: the contribution of environmental human rights

The substantive–procedural distinction that squares the environmental contract between present and future generations and renders it just ironically mirrors the overall impact of environmental human rights as a conceptual and legal innovation in human rights theory and practice.

The first half of this chapter explored how environmental human rights have entered the vocabulary, practices, and politics of the human rights regime through a variety of international agreements and conventions. Environmental human rights have become part of the procedural guarantees that international adherence to human rights is aimed at delivering. But so far the benefits have mostly been only procedural; that is, without sufficient enforcement environmental human rights remain mostly aspirational, not substantive. Such aspirations should not be dismissed however; they represent innovative ideas and passions serving the process of establishing a more just world.

But substantively, environmental human rights can have a major effect on the way human rights as a whole are understood. The second half of this chapter has explored the substantial impact the theory of environmental human rights has on traditional concepts of rights, justice, and human identity. Environmental human rights fundamentally alter the substance of human rights in terms of what they portend for our understanding of the foundation of human rights, who the bearers of human rights are, and the nature of obligations to which human rights give rise. In their emergence both in human rights theory and in international politics, environmental rights testify that the dynamism of human rights as a concept, a human aspiration, and as a political force for justice in the world, flourishes both now and in the future.

References

African [Banjul] Charter on Human and Peoples' Rights, adopted 27 June 1981, OAU Doc. CAB/LEG/67/3 rev. 5, 21 I.L.M. 58 (1982).

Anton, Ronald K. 1998. "Comparative Constitutional Language for Environmental Amendments to the Australian Constitution." At: http://www.elaw.org/resources/text.asp?ID=1082.

Ball, Terrence. 1985. "The Incoherence of Intergenerational Justice." *Inquiry*, Vol. 28, pp. 321–337.

Barry, Brian. 1999. "Sustainability and Intergenerational Justice." In Andrew Dobson, ed., *Fairness and Futurity* (New York: Oxford University Press).

Benhabib, Seyla. 2002. *The Claims of Culture* (Princeton, NJ: Princeton University Press).

Convention on the Rights of the Child (UNCRC), adopted 20 Nov. 1989, G.A. Res. 44/25, UN GAOR, 44th Sess., art. 24, UN Doc A/44/49 (1989), 1577 UNTS 3.

Cranston, Maurice. 1967. "Human Rights, Real and Supposed." In D. D. Raphael, ed., *Political Theory and the Rights of Man* (Bloomington: Indiana University Press).

Donnelly, Jack. 1989. *Universal Human Rights in Theory and Practice* (Ithaca, NY: Cornell University Press).

Gleick, Peter H. 1999. "The Human Right to Water." *Water Policy*, Vol. 1, pp. 487–503.

Gould, Carol C. 1988. *Rethinking Democracy* (New York: Cambridge University Press).

Gould, Carol C. 2004. *Globalizing Democracy and Human Rights* (New York: Cambridge University Press).

Hancock, Jan. 2003. *Environmental Human Rights* (Farnham, UK: Ashgate).

Hayward, Tim. 2005. *Constitutional Environmental Rights* (Oxford: Oxford University Press).

Herz, Richard. 2000. "Litigating Environmental Abuses Under the Alien Tort Claims Act: A Practical Assessment." *Virginia Journal of International Law*, Vol. 40, pp. 545–632.

Hiskes, Richard P. 2005. "The Right to a Green Future: Human Rights, Environmentalism, and Intergenerational Justice." *Human Rights Quarterly*, Vol. 247, pp. 346–367.

Hiskes, Richard P. 2009. *The Human Right to a Green Future: Environmental Rights and Intergenerational Justice* (New York: Cambridge University Press).

Metz, Thaddius. 2010. "Human Dignity, African Morality and Capital Punishment: A New Philosophy of Human Rights." *Journal of Human Rights*, Vol. 9, No. 1.

Nickel, James W. 1993. "The Human Right to a Safe Environment: Philosophical Perspectives on its Scope and Justification." *Yale Journal of International Law*, Vol. 18, pp. 281–285.

Picoloti, Romina and Jorge Daniel Tallant. 2003. *Linking Human Rights and Environment* (Tucson: University of Arizona Press).

Rawls, John. 1971. *A Theory of Justice* (Cambridge, MA: Harvard University Press).

Russell, Anna F. S. 2009. "International Organizations and Human Rights: Realizing, Resisting or Repackaging the Right to Water?" *Journal of Human Rights*, Vol. 9, No. 1.

Sandel, Michael J. 1982. *Liberalism and the Limits of Justice* (Cambridge: Cambridge University Press).
Taylor, Charles. 1989. *Sources of the Self* (Cambridge, MA: Harvard University Press).
United Nations Committee on Economic, Social, and Cultural Rights (CESCR). 2003. General Comment No. 15, Comm. On Econ., Soc. & Cult. RTS., 29th Sess., Par. 1, Un Doc. E/c12/2002/11.
United Nations Convention on the Elimination of Discrimination against Women (CEDAW). 1980. Adopted 18 Dec. 1979, G.A. Res. 34/180, U.N. GAOR 34th Sess., art. 14, U.N. Doc. A/34/46, 1249 U.N.T.S. 13.
United Nations Convention on the Rights of the Child (CRC). 1990. Adopted 20 Nov. 1989, G.A. Res. 44/25, U.N. GAOR, 44th Sess., art. 24, U.N. Doc A/44/49, 1577 U.N.T.S. 3.
United Nations Economic Commission for Europe (UNECE). 2007. (Kiev Protocol). At: www.UNECE.org/env/pp/prtr.htm.
United Nations Sub-Commission on the Prevention of Discrimination and Protection of Minorities. 1994. UN Doc. (Ksentini Report) E/CN.4/Sub.2/1994/9.
Weiss, Edith Brown. 1989. *In Fairness to Future Generations* (Irvington-on-Hudson, NY: Transnational).
World Commission on Environment and Development (WCED). 1987. "The 'Brundtland Report'." In *Our Common Future* (Oxford: Oxford University Press).

36

Climate change and human rights

Nancy Tuana

Global climate change is arguably one of the most challenging ethical and political issues facing humankind. Potential impacts of climate change include changes in precipitation patterns leading to more and longer droughts in some areas and increased rainfall in others, as well as more intense weather events such as sea surges and hurricanes, glacial melting, and sea-level rise. Impacts also include deterioration of water resources in some areas, as well as changes in the vectors of disease-borne illnesses and biodiversity loss (Parry et al. 2007). Given the wide-ranging effects of climate change, it is seen by many as one of the greatest threats to human well-being and development, with adverse impacts expected on human health, water and food security, economic activity, natural resources, physical infrastructure, and the environment.

An international political response to climate change emerged in the 1990s, leading to the adoption in 1992 of the United Nations Framework Convention on Climate Change treaty (UNFCCC). The UNFCCC, which sets out a framework for action aimed at stabilizing atmospheric concentrations of greenhouse gases in order to avoid "dangerous anthropogenic interference" with the climate system, entered into force in March 1994 with over 160 signatories.

The ultimate objective of the UNFCCC is "to achieve stabilization of atmospheric concentrations of greenhouse gases at levels that would prevent dangerous anthropogenic interference with the climate system ... within a time-frame sufficient to allow ecosystems to adapt naturally to climate change, to ensure that food production is not threatened, and to enable economic development to proceed in a sustainable manner" (1992, Article 2).

The UNFCCC also establishes a series of principles, many of which recognize that issues of justice are at the heart of efforts to respond to global climate change. The first principle, for example, the principle of common but differentiated responsibilities and capabilities, emerges from the normative values of justice and fairness. This principle is based on the fact that the current and historical greenhouse gas emissions of industrialized countries have contributed more to global climate change than those of developing countries, as well as recognizing that industrialized countries have more resource capacity to devote to climate change mitigation and adaptation. Hence, the UNFCCC recognizes that although all nations have a common interest in stabilizing emissions and reducing the impact of climate change, a fair division of the costs of doing so must include consideration of responsibility, need, and ability. Although issues of justice were at the heart of the UNFCCC, it has only been in recent years that the connection between climate change and human rights has been explicitly recognized.

Linking climate change and human rights

The first formal petition explicitly linking climate change and human rights was filed in December of 2005. Sheila Watt-Cloutier, the elected Chair of the Inuit Circumpolar Conference, submitted a petition to the Inter-American Commission on Human Rights (IACHR) on behalf of the Inuit of the Arctic regions of the United States of America and Canada. The petition requested IACHR's assistance in obtaining relief from human rights violations resulting from climate change impacts caused by acts and omissions of the United States.

Citing evidence from both traditional knowledge of hunters and elders as well as peer reviewed science, including the 2001 Third Assessment Report of the Intergovernmental Panel on Climate Change (IPCC) and the 2004 Arctic Climate Impact Assessment, the petition documented current impacts on the Arctic environment and cited scientific evidence of projected future impacts. According to the petition:

> The impacts of climate change, caused by acts and omissions by the United States, violate the Inuit's fundamental human rights protected by the American Declaration of the Rights and Duties of Man and other international instruments. These include their rights to the benefits of culture, to property, to the preservation of health, life, physical integrity, security, and a means of subsistence, and to residence, movement, and inviolability of the home.
>
> *(Petition to the IACHR 2005, p. 5)*

It is not surprising that the first human rights-related challenge regarding the impacts of climate change emerged from the Inuit. Although there are documented impacts of climate change being recorded across the globe, the Arctic and Antarctic have experienced the most rapid rates of warming. According to the most recent IPCC report, "The impacts of this climate change in the polar regions over the next 100 years will exceed the impacts forecast for many other regions and will produce feedbacks that will have globally significant consequences" (Anisimov et al. 2007, p. 655). IACHR, however, refused to process the petition.

The Inuit petition was followed in November of 2007 by the Malé Declaration on the Human Dimension of Global Climate Change. Representatives of the Small Island Developing States, in a meeting convened by the Maldives, signed an international agreement that concurred with the Inuit linkage of climate change and human rights violations: "climate change has clear and immediate implications for the full enjoyment of human rights including *inter alia* the right to life, the right to take part in cultural life, the right to use and enjoy property, the right to an adequate standard of living, the right to food, and the right to the highest attainable standard of physical and mental health" (2007, p. 2).

Like the Arctic and Antarctic regions, the Small Island Developing States are highly vulnerable to the impacts of climate change. These countries are very susceptible to sea-level rise and extreme weather events such as sea surges, both of which would lead to loss of often densely populated coastal lands and salinity of coastal water supplies and farming land. The impacts of climate change are in fact already adversely affecting coral reefs and other marine ecosystems that sustain island fisheries (Mimura et al. 2007).

The leadership of the Maldives and the collaboration of the Small Island Developing States are a reflection in part of the severity of the impact of unmitigated climate change upon these low-lying island states. To cite just one example included in the report submitted by the Maldives to the United Nations Office of the High Commissioner for Human Rights (OHCHR), the current frequency of sea surges of 0.7 meters, which temporarily flood the majority of the islands in the Maldives, is once a century. Climate change impacts could raise the occurrence of such sea surges to an annual event. This would have a disastrous impact in that almost half of the population lives within one hundred meters of the coastline (2008, p. 20). Sea-level rise and extreme weather events could result in the Maldives literally losing their statehood and becoming what many refer to as "climate exiles."

While agreeing with the Inuit position linking climate change and human rights, the approach of the Small Island Developing States was not to litigate, but rather to attempt to influence the process of international climate negotiations through the UNFCCC processes. To help initiate this process, the Malé Declaration urged the Conference of the Parties (COP) of the UNFCCC, scheduled to meet one month later in Bali, to work with the OHCHR and the United Nations Human Rights Council to assess the human rights implications of climate change. The idea was to provide a new vision for imbedding a human rights framework into the negotiating process.

The argument for the link between climate change and human rights received support from the 2007/2008 Human Development Report, *Fighting Climate Change: Human Solidarity in a Divided World*, issued by the United Nations Development Programme. The report lists climate change as *the* defining development issue of our generation, claiming that it threatens to be the cause of "major human development reversal in our lifetime," and argues that the impacts of global climate change constitute "an immense, long-term and global challenge that raises difficult questions about justice and human rights, both within and across generations" (Watkins 2007, pp. 1, 111).

The report's position on climate change as a violation of universal human rights is unequivocal. "The real choice facing political leaders and people today is between universal human values, on the one side, and participating in the widespread and systematic violation of human rights on the other." Its authors concurred that allowing climate change to evolve would "represent a systematic violation of the human rights of the world's poor and future generations and a step back from universal values" (Watkins 2007, p. 4). Referencing Article 3 of the Universal Declaration of Human Rights, "everyone has a right to life, liberty, and personal security" (1948), the report concludes that "inaction in the face of the threat posed by climate change would represent a very immediate violation of that universal right" (Watkins 2007, p. 60).

The coupling of human rights and climate change received its strongest support when the OHCHR agreed in March 2008 to accept resolution 7/23 of the Human Rights Council. This resolution requested that the OHCHR:

> in consultation with and taking into account the views of States, other relevant international organizations and intergovernmental bodies, including the Intergovernmental Panel on Climate Change, the secretariat of the United Nations Framework Convention on Climate Change and other stakeholders, to conduct, within existing resources, a detailed analytical study of the relationship between climate change and human rights, to be submitted to the Council prior to its tenth session.
>
> *(Human Rights Council 2008, para. 1)*

The OHCHR study on the relationship between climate change and human rights was published in January 2009 (A/HRC/10/61) and subsequently submitted to the tenth session of the Human Rights Council held in March 2009. The purpose of the study was defined as identifying "how observed and projected impacts of climate change have implications for the enjoyment of human rights and for the obligations of States under international human rights law" (OHCHR 2009, p. 1).

A large portion of the OHCHR study is focused on the impacts of climate change, acknowledging that "global warming will potentially have implications for the full range of human rights" (2009, p. 8). The report lists six human rights which they deemed as being most directly related to climate change impacts: the right to life; the right to adequate food; the right to water; the right to health; the right to adequate housing; and the right to self determination (2009, pp. 8–15). The report underscores the greater burden of climate-related impacts on the most vulnerable groups: "The effects of climate change will be felt most acutely by those segments of the population who are already in vulnerable situations due to factors such as poverty, gender, age, minority status, and disability." The report pays particular attention to detailing the disparate impact on the rights of women, children, and indigenous peoples, stressing that "under international human rights law, States are legally bound to address such vulnerabilities in accordance with the principle of equality and non-discrimination" (2009, p. 15).

The aim of the Malé Declaration on the Human Dimension of Global Climate Change (2007) was to forge a link between climate change and human rights that would serve as a basis for impacting the UNFCCC negotiation process. The ultimate goal was to infuse a human rights framework into the emerging successor treaty to the original Kyoto Protocol, which expires in 2012. Some may interpret the OHCHR report as only partially successful in this respect. For while the OHCHR report provided a basis for seeing the clear links between climate change impacts and the full enjoyment of human rights, it denied that climate change could be seen as constituting a violation of human rights "in a strict legal sense" (2009, p. 23). This decision against framing climate change impacts as a violation of human rights rested on three concerns.

First, it is virtually impossible to disentangle the complex causal relationships linking historical greenhouse gas emissions of a particular country with a specific climate change-related effect, let alone with the range of direct and indirect implications for human rights. Second, global warming is often one of several contributing factors to climate change-related effects, such as hurricanes, environmental degradation, and water stress. Accordingly, it is often impossible to establish the extent to which a concrete climate change-related event with implications for human rights is attributable to global warming. Third, adverse effects of global warming are often projections about future impacts, whereas human rights violations are normally established after the harm has occurred (2009 ¶ 70, p. 23).

Although the OHCHR Report did not interpret climate change harms as human rights violations, it did underscore a strong link between human rights and climate impacts that could be seen as a basis for influencing the UNFCCC negotiation process. Stressing that "human rights obligations provide important protection to the individuals whose rights are affected by climate change or by measures taken to respond to climate change" (2009 ¶ 71, p. 24), the report emphasized that States must take "deliberate, concrete and targeted measures" in the face of climate impacts "towards the full realization of economic, social and cultural rights to the maximum extent of their available resources" (2009 ¶ 75, ¶ 76, p. 25).

The OHCHR Report concludes with the claims that "human rights standards and principles should inform and strengthen policymaking in the area of climate change" (2009 ¶ 80, p. 26) and that international human rights law complements the UNFCCC by "underlining that international cooperation is not only expedient but also a human rights obligation and that its central objective is the realization of human rights" (2009 ¶ 99, p. 30).

Based on the OHCHR Report, the Human Rights Council adopted resolution 10/4 in March 2009. This resolution reaffirmed the human rights dimensions of climate change as well as upholding "that human rights obligations and commitments have the potential to inform and strengthen international and national policy-making in the area of climate change, promoting policy coherence, legitimacy and sustainable outcomes" (2009b, p. 2) and encouraged exchange of information on this topic between the OHCHR and the secretariat of the UNFCCC.

Resolution 10/4 included a decision to hold a panel discussion in June in Geneva on the relationship between climate change and human rights. The summary of those discussions as well as the resolution were made available to the COP at the UNFCCC meetings in Copenhagen in December (COP15). Arguably one of the most recent links between human rights concerns and climate change was identified during that panel, namely the issue of climate-related forced migrations. A number of the delegates at the meeting in Geneva called attention "to the projected dramatic increase in population movements over the next decades as a consequence of climate change-related effects" (HRC, 2009b, ¶ 93, p. 14). There was general agreement that a host of legal questions were emerging from this phenomenon, from the need to identify an agreed legal definition of the concept of "environmental refugees," to the potential loss of statehood for those nations where the majority of their landmass will be rendered uninhabitable due to climate change impacts. While efforts to integrate human rights protections into the UNFCCC agreements were robust during the COP15 meetings in December 2009 in Copenhagen, the Copenhagen Accord that resulted from the meetings does not mention human rights. The Accord, while not legally binding, reaffirms the objective of keeping the maximum temperature rise to below 2 degrees Celsius; the commitment to list developed country emission reduction targets and mitigation action by developing countries for 2020; as well as funding commitments to enable and support enhanced action on mitigation, including substantial finance to reduce emissions from deforestation and forest degradation (REDD-plus), adaptation, technology development and transfer and capacity-building (UN 2009). However, while not reflected in the language of the Accord, efforts by various non-governmental organizations to integrate human rights protections into the final agreement are very likely to continue as the UNFCCC prepares for COP16 and the rounds of talks leading up to it.

What justice requires: the role of human rights in climate change policy

As human rights concerns begin to take a more prominent role in the context of international policy to address climate change, the goal is not to reframe climate change policy as a human rights issue, but rather to explore how attention to human rights concerns can help improve policy development in the areas of adaptation (adjustment in natural or human systems in response to unavoidable and unavoided impacts of climate change, both actual and/or expected) and mitigation (reducing greenhouse gas [GHG] emissions to eliminate or reduce the long-term impacts of climate change).

One common theme in the recent literature on human rights and climate change is the contention that shifting from an "emission rights" framework to a human rights framework will result in better climate policy (see e.g., International Council on Human Rights Policy 2008 and Hayward 2007). Market-based policy mechanisms embedded in the Kyoto Protocol (UN 1998), in particular Emissions Trading and the Clean Development Mechanism (CDM), treat emissions as property that can be traded and acquired. The CDMs, for example, allow developed countries to invest in emission reduction or removal projects in developing countries as a way to earn certified emission reduction credits (CER). The CERs can then be traded or sold, and used by industrialized countries to a meet a part of their emission reduction targets.

There are many criticisms of the effectiveness of carbon trading schemes, but there are also serious concerns regarding the equity of these mechanisms. Some, for example, argue that they will entrench and even worsen current economic inequities by enabling developed countries to own the emission reductions arising from the easier and least expensive abatement options, resulting in greater costs to the developing country when they pursue their own abatement programs (Banuri and Gupta 2000). There is also concern that such mechanisms focus on emission reductions that are efficient in the short run rather than the long run.

Arguments have begun to emerge that a human rights perspective will move the discussion away from economic solutions or property rights and focus attention on the effects of climate change on the satisfaction of people's basic needs and call attention to potential human rights threats. It is also believed that a human rights perspective will shift the emphasis to our mutual responsibilities to one another rather than to debates about emission rights. As stated by Abdulla Shahid, the Maldives Minister of Foreign Affairs, in the conclusion of his opening speech at the Small Island States Conference on the Human Dimensions of Climate Change:

> The aim of the human approach to climate change is to remind all peoples of the bonds and mutual dependency that tie us all together. By highlighting the ultimate human impact of climate change, and by emphasising the web of rights and responsibility that link us all together, we hope that the Human Dimension of Climate Change initiative will provide an added spur or catalyst to drive the world towards a mutually beneficial solution to the problem of climate change and, in-so-doing, ensure that all the peoples of the United Nations, whether in large countries or small, can move together towards a prosperous, environmentally sustainable, and peaceful future.
>
> *(Shahid 2007)*

Marc Limon, in his survey of the literature on human rights and climate change, identifies five themes emerging from arguments for the benefits of a human rights perspective in the context of climate change.

1. It helps to "shift the focus of international debate on climate change more directly onto individuals and the effects of climate change on their lives";
2. It amplifies "the voices of those who are disproportionately affected by climate change";
3. It has the potential to "'level the playing field' in international negotiations";
4. It could "contribute, qualitatively, to the construction of better policy responses at both the national and international level";
5. It can facilitate a viable global solution by "emphasizing international cooperation."

(Limon 2009, pp. 450–452)

A report titled "Climate Change and Human Rights" prepared by the International Council on Human Rights Policy (ICHRP) deploys the concept of a "human rights threshold" as a basis to improve the knowledge base upon which climate change predictions arise and to improve policy responses. Human rights thresholds are defined as "levels of protection for individual rights which can be regarded as the minimum acceptable outcome under a given policy scenario" (2008, p. 18). The ICHRP report advocates using human rights thresholds and threats as analytic tools for refocusing policy on likely human costs. They argue that this approach would have the benefit of identifying "future dutybearers" as well as "the adequacy of response institutions and redress mechanisms" (2008, p. 18).

One key claim of the ICHRP report is that a transition from emission rights to human rights thresholds will call attention to a series of issues that have been elided by the current approach. They give as example the question of what constitutes "dangerous climate change."

Many scientists have argued that the most serious impacts of climate change would likely be avoided if global average temperatures rise by no more than 2 degrees Celsius above pre-industrial levels. The ICHRP report notes that although this claim may appear reasonable from an aggregate perspective, it "will appear much less so for whom such an increase involves irretrievable losses to livelihood and culture, or those living in places likely to experience warming at higher levels than average." They continue that "while a cost–benefit analysis might conclude that hardships in one place can be set off against benefits in another, such calculations are impermissible for human rights, which views each individual harm on its own terms" (2008, pp. 19–20).

A human rights perspective, in moving away from an aggregate perspective, will also shift the lens of policy by calling attention to the fact that policy that addresses human costs will require that those costs be both spatially and temporally disaggregated. In other words, human rights thresholds would not only require attention to human costs, but would also require examination of those costs not only in different spatial locations, e.g., Small Island Developing States, least developed nations, etc., but also to such costs across time, thus bringing issues of inter-generational justice to bear on policy.

As a third example, some have argued that a human rights perspective forms the foundation for an inter-generational justice position regarding climate change (e.g., Nickel 1993; Thorme 1991). Theorists and activists alike are advocating for what they call a "right to a safe environment," namely, the right to an environment that has not been so degraded as to put the basic needs of future generations at risk. Advocates for this position argue that in defending the right to a safe environment for future generations, the present generations will also benefit in that the only way to accomplish the former is to protect the right to a safe environment of current generations.

Concerns about adaptation to climate change have begun to play a much greater role at the UNFCCC. Although the main aim of the Convention was to stabilize greenhouse gas concentrations to prevent dangerous anthropogenic interference with the climate system, a number of articles recognized the need for adaptation. For example, the Convention commits countries to prepare for and facilitate adaptation, including the commitment that developed countries assist developing countries in meeting the costs of adaptation to the adverse effects of climate change (1992, Articles 4.1 and 4.4). However, although always a part of the Convention, the fact that mitigation efforts have been slower than expected, combined with some impacts, such as Arctic sea ice melt, being more rapid than projected, has moved the issue of adaptation and funding for adaptation in the least developed, and often most vulnerable, countries to center stage in the last two COPs.

Human rights issues have been strongly linked to the call for attention to adaptation needs. Climate change threatens to undermine development goals, including the UN Millennium Development Goals (MDGs) for the poorest people in the world, who are also often those most burdened by the impacts of climate change. For vulnerable countries, adaptation to climate change will be an essential element of preparing for and responding to climate change. Adaptation, however, requires significant resources beyond what are already needed to ensure that basic needs are satisfied and to achieve development objectives such as the MDGs of ending extreme poverty and hunger, reducing child mortality and improving maternal health, and providing universal primary education (UN 2000).

The Kyoto Protocol includes provisions for an Adaptation Fund to assist developing country Parties to the Protocol that are particularly vulnerable to the adverse impacts of climate change meet the costs of adaptation (UN 1998). The first steps were taken to set up this fund in 2001 during the COP7 meetings of the UNFCCC in Marrakesh. The fund is financed with proceeds from the Certified Emission Reduction Units issued for Clean Development Mechanism projects as well as other sources. Although the governance structure for the fund has been put in place, at the time of COP15, the Board was not yet ready to invite Parties to submit proposals.

As the mechanisms for the Adaptation Fund are being finalized, there is a lot of pressure from human rights advocates to include a human rights framework within these mechanisms to both set funding priorities and measure the effectiveness of investments from the fund. The ICHRP Report, for example, contends that there are three benefits of incorporating a human rights perspective within the context of adaptation. First, "a human rights optic can help make the case for swift, substantial and directed adaptation funding." Second, it would "help to orient future research, set priorities, assist in evaluation and galvanise support." Third, "adequate fulfillment of human rights within vulnerable states would itself provide a solid basis for autonomous adaptation" (2008, p. 25).

Although advocates for incorporating the link between human rights and climate change within the UNFCCC mechanisms stress the value of this link for adaptation, the human rights impacts of mitigation strategies also remain a priority. There are multiple paths towards carbon stabilization, and it is argued that a human rights lens is needed to identify the human rights consequences of different mitigation strategies and choose between them. "Human rights standards and thresholds offer one way to manage the dilemma ... because they provide benchmarks of acceptable outcomes based on widely-agreed principles and, indeed, on legal stricture" (ICHRP 2008, p. 30). From the most recently proposed program, Reduced Emissions from Deforestation and Degradation (REDD) to Emissions Trading to biofuel substitution programs, mitigation efforts have the potential to impact human rights, both positively and negatively. Including a human rights lens in the context of mitigation strategies is arguably the best way to secure human rights protections.

Conclusion

Although a human rights framework was not incorporated into the United Framework Convention on Climate Change or the Kyoto Protocol, there are good reasons for including a human rights perspective to ensure that these regimes are both more just and more effective. Increased attention to the human dimensions of climate change can help to ensure that measures to respond to climate-related impacts will at a minimum respect, and perhaps even promote, human rights.

References

Anisimov, O. A., D. G. Vaughan, T. V. Callaghan, C. Furgal, H. Marchant, T. D. Prowse, et al. 2007. "Polar Regions (Arctic and Antarctic)," pp. 653–675 in M. L. Parry, O. F. Canziani, J. P. Palutikof, P. J. van der Linden, and C. E. Hanson, eds., *Climate Change 2007: Impacts, Adaptation and Vulnerability: Contribution of Working Group II to the Fourth Assessment Report of the Intergovernmental Panel on Climate Change* (Cambridge: Cambridge University Press).

Banuri, T. and S. Gupta. 2000. "The Clean Development Mechanism and Sustainable Development: An Economic Analysis." In P. Ghosh, *Implementation of the Kyoto Protocol* (Manila: Asian Development Bank).

Hayward, T. 2007. "Human Rights Versus Emissions Rights: Climate Justice and the Equitable Distribution of Ecological Space." *Ethics and International Affairs*, Vol. 21, No. 4, pp. 431–450.

Human Rights Council. 2008. *Resolution 7/23, Human Rights and Climate Change*. At: http://ap.ohchr.org/documents/E/HRC/resolutions/A_HRC_RES_7_23.pdf.

Human Rights Council. 2009a. *Panel Discussion on the Relationship Between Climate Change and Human Rights*. At: http://www2.ohchr.org/english/issues/climatechange/docs/SummaryPanelDiscussion.doc.

Human Rights Council. 2009b. *Resolution 10/4, Human Rights and Climate Change*. At: http://ap.ohchr.org/documents/E/HRC/resolutions/A_HRC_RES_10_4.pdf.

Intergovernmental Panel on Climate Change (IPCC). 2001. *Climate Change 2001*, IPCC Third Assessment Report. At: http://www.ipcc.ch/ipccreports/tar/.

International Council on Human Rights Policy (ICHRP). 2008. *Climate Change and Human Rights: A Rough Guide* (Versoix, Switzerland: ICHRP).

Limon, M. 2009. "Human Rights and Climate Change: Constructing a Case for Political Action." *Harvard Environmental Law Review*, Vol. 33, pp. 439–476.

Maldives. 2008. *Maldives Submission under Resolution HRC 7/23(25 September)*, Submission of the Maldives to the Office of the High Commissioner for Human Rights. At: http://www2.ohchr.org/english/issues/climatechange/docs/submissions/Maldives_Submission.pdf.

Malé. 2007. *Malé Declaration on the Human Dimension of Global Climate Change*. At: http://www.ciel.org/Publications/Male_Declaration_Nov07.pdf.

Mimura, N., L. Nurse, R. F. McLean, J. Agard, L. Briguglio, P. Lefale *et al.* 2007. "Small Islands," pp. 687–716 in M. L. Parry, O. F. Canziani, J. P. Palutikof, P. F. van der Linden, and C. E. Hanson, eds., *Climate Change 2007: Impacts, Adaptation and Vulnerability: Contribution of Working Group II to the Fourth Assessment Report of the Intergovernmental Panel on Climate Change* (Cambridge: Cambridge University Press).

Nickel, J. 1993. "The Human Right to a Safe Environment: Philosophical Perspectives on its Scope and Justification." *Yale Journal of International Law*, Vol. 18, pp. 281–285.

Office of the High Commissioner for Human Rights (OHCHR). 2009. *Report on the Relationship Between Climate Change and Human Rights A/HRC/10/61 (15 January)*. At: http://daccess-dds-ny.un.org/doc/UNDOC/GEN/G09/103/44/PDF/G0910344.pdf?OpenElement.

Parry, M. L., O. F. Canziani, J. P. Palutikof, P. J. van der Linden, and C. D. Hanson, eds. 2007. *Contribution of Working Group II to the Fourth Assessment Report of the Intergovernmental Panel on Climate Change* (Cambridge: Cambridge University Press).

Petition to the Inter-American Commission on Human Rights Seeking Relief from Violations Resulting from Global Warming Caused by Acts and Omissions of the United States. 2005. At: http://www.inuitcircumpolar.com/files/uploads/icc-files/FINALPetitionSummary.pdf.

Shahid, A. 2007. *Opening Statement at the Inauguration of the Small Island States Conference on "The Human Dimension of Global Climate Change," Malé*. At: http://www.foreign.gov.mv/v2/speech.php?speech=24&page=3.

Thorme, M. 1991. "Establishing Environment as a Human Right." *Denver Journal of International Law and Policy*, Vol. 19, No. 301, pp. 303–305.

United Nations. 1948. *The Universal Declaration of Human Rights* (UDHR). At: http://www.un.org/en/documents/udhr/.

United Nations. 1992. *Framework Convention on Climate Change* (UNFCCC). At: http://unfccc.int/resource/docs/convkp/conveng.pdf.

United Nations. 1998. *Kyoto Protocol to the United Nations Framework Convention on Climate Change*. At: http://unfccc.int/resource/docs/convkp/kpeng.pdf.

United Nations. 2000. *Millennium Declaration*. At: http://www.un.org/millennium/declaration/ares552e.htm.

United Nations. 2009. *Framework Convention on Climate Change, Copenhagen Accord*. At: http://unfccc.int/resource/docs/2009/cop15/eng/l07.pdf.

Watkins, K. 2007. *Fighting Climate Change: Human Solidarity in a Divided World*, Human Development Report 2007/08. At: http://hdr.undp.org/en/media/HDR_20072008_EN_Complete.pdf.

Part V

Critical perspectives on human rights organizations, institutions, and practices

37

The tension between peace and justice in the age of peace-building

Henry F. Carey

A long-established formula holds that there cannot be peace without justice, and no justice without peace. Kenneth Boulding argued that a stable peace is one where the idea of war hardly enters into consciousness, having considered their conceptions of justice (Boulding 1978). In most of the world, where neither peace nor justice is stable, the relationship itself is the subject of politics. The choice of pursuing peace or justice, however really meant by its articulator, will occur in post-conflict situations. Opposition and government leaders, such as former Haitian President Jean Bertrand Aristide, make it a mantra of: "No peace–no justice. No justice–no peace." He may have meant revenge, in addition to prosecutions and a decent chance for the downtrodden. Judge Richard Goldstone (1995) insisted, "The only way that there can be reconciliation in Rwanda is if there is justice." He may have meant prosecutions, but also a customary legal system of *gacaca* that is legitimate in Rwandan terms. One of the most renowned legal genocide scholars, M. Cherif Bassiouni, has insisted that peace depends upon justice, particularly in the duty to prosecute genocide in any challenge of transitional justice (Bassiouni 2002).

Of course, it is also possible that insisting on justice is perceived as a threat that might also lead to violent reactions. Pauline Baker (1996) has concluded that those interested in justice fit a different paradigm from those who favor peace, who pragmatically accept that those responsible for violent human rights violations would never agree to stop a conflict if threatened afterwards with prosecution. This is what Huntington called the "torturer's problem" (Huntington 1992). Justice can be suggested in a variety of ways, from prosecution, which is viewed by some as impractical in some developing countries without institutions or funds. Paul van Zyl appears to have amended an earlier critical position taken against universal prosecutions, at least on a mass basis, which he made in light of his own experience as Executive Director of the South African Truth and Reconciliation Commission. More recently, he commented that prosecution of high-ranking defendants is preferable, in light of the experience extraditing Charles Taylor for trial (Van Zyl 2009). Mark Drumbl (2007) convincingly argues that prosecution is inappropriate given customary law alternatives in traditional societies (including "holistic" approaches).

One alternative formula to reconciling peace and justice is that of Abraham Lincoln, at least in his Second Inaugural Address, where he declared, "With Malice toward none and Charity toward all, we will bind our nation's wounds." His was an effort to reconcile the Confederacy to the Union, in what was only a month before his assassination. He implicitly offered amnesty and reintegration, so long as the Southerners also accepted liberty and equality for all. Lincoln's formulation emphasized and reintroduced into American discourse the philosophy of the preamble to the US Declaration of Independence, as the text was read – as opposed to how it was intended – to join the commitment to union in the Constitution's Preamble. Lincoln's approach balanced union with liberty and forgiveness with justice. Instead of prosecutions for the Southern secession or for war crimes by combatants of both sides, Lincoln insisted on freedom for slaves. He substituted an absolute priority for the constitution in suspending the rule of law, insisting that the country return to its founding principles, which also include the protection of liberty through legal and political means. The way to the rule of law is hardly a neat formula and one whose complexity is founded as much on foundational principles as on strict adherence to procedure. It is a dilemma as well, because attempting to promote the rule of law as part of any peace-building project is not going to be easy to formulate or define, let alone realize. One may not remember that the Versailles Treaty called for prosecutions, but none were seriously undertaken, and the rest, as they say, was history.

Progress remains not only necessary, but also possible, and the great struggles must continue: or so we believe on faith, given the lack of alternatives. This includes our faith in Churchill's dictum that democracy is the worst system, except for all the others that have been tried. Yet, humans and human institutions being fallible, and war inevitable, the struggle for peace and/or justice requires that elites and masses alike overcome fear to practice what they preach, or perhaps think that they have a hope or a theory. Acting is easier said than done. When some of the greatest writers of a generation, Günter Grass and Milan Kundera, informed for the Nazis and the Communists, however innocently, acting out of obligation, fear, and desperation, how much more challenging is it for risk-averse, ordinary people and elites with interests to courageously take chances for peace and justice? Before she joined the George W. Bush administration as National Security Advisor, Condoleezza Rice advocated reading or listening to the views of those with whom you disagree. One can indeed learn from the research and commentary of those of different views. Negotiated peace may not be possible unless the other sides' views are taken seriously. Otherwise, one will be prone to groupthink or stuck in a Kuhnian paradigm, where everyone thinks and talks alike, as everyone goes along in order to get along. Most elites, masses, and non-governmental organizations (NGOs) are as likely to "stick to their own kind" ideologically and technically as government leaders and interest groups.

Resistance to perceived and actual tyranny can be violent and non-violent. Whenever it is violent, the targeted state asserts that the violence is illegal and illegitimate. Philosophers might argue, based on Locke or Marx, that the violent resistance is justified, assuming it is aptly targeted against the illegitimate state and proportionate. However, endorsing resistance to tyranny, even if implied by advocating peace *cum* justice, may not be possible non-violently against warlike regimes and without extraordinary elite and mass courage and vision.

Demands for justice can create conflict that in theory should not be violent, but in practice results in instability. Huntington pointed to the lack of institutions as the culprit (Huntington 1968). Revolutionary theorists blame the structures of injustice. Rational choice theorists look for costs and benefits. Relative deprivation theorists point to rising expectations. Demands for peace, by the same token, range from those who organize pacifist social movements to those who seek conflict situations that are ripe for peaceful negotiation. In spite of instability from the fault lines of civilizations, weak and failing states, natural resource scarcities, zones of ideological, ethnic, and religious extremism, the desire for peace and justice is a permanent feature of contemporary politics. Peace and justice have always been large concerns of the great religions, yet consensus among these religions seems impossible to achieve. Indeed, the very effort to understand peace and justice seems to be a cause of conflict that in theory should be non-violent, but might, in the case of Huntington's well-circulated "clash of civilizations," prove to be a self-fulfilling prophecy (Huntington 1993).

Pursuing peace and justice may involve dealing with inconsistent logics. These include such things as democratization and nation building and peace through amnesty and accountability. Does the revelation of secret atrocities in Yugoslavia, Northern Ireland, South Africa, and Spain, for example, correlate with reconciliation and peace? Part of the answer would depend on how peace is defined. One would assume so since all have had a limited negative peace. Are the NGO reports, truth commissions, forensic investigations, and judicial investigations the cause? Or have they helped make positive peace less likely? Spain's successful transition from the intense hatred of the civil war did precede the more recent investigations into past Franco era atrocities, such as at the women's prison. Judge Baltazar Garzon, a worldwide human rights hero for his extradition request and indictment of Pinochet, was unable to continue investigations into Franco's crimes against humanity because of another platitude, "Time heals all wounds," which many in Spain did not want reopened in 2008–2009.

Alternative conceptions of peace

Peace is a relatively modern invention of societies. It is based on the structures, laws, and institutions that manage inevitable *conflict*, and these usually must be developed into a comprehensive "positive peace" over many years (Howard 2001). The greater complexity and relative success of multilateral, peacekeeping missions, along with NGO mediation in Zimbabwe, Nicaragua, Zambia, and South Africa, for example, have given new impetus to political and scholarly efforts to institutionalize peace-building. However, the science of forging a positive peace is not always so clear.

Many opposing ideologues, at least in the era of Obama in the USA, claim the mantle of the president's "favorite" theologian, Christian realist and ex-pacifist Reinhold Niebhur. Realists and neo-conservatives admire him because he supported US entry into World War II, was a staunch anti-communist, and ultimately embraced the need for US military power. American liberals admire his opposition to the Vietnam War and his warning against the hubris and risks of asserting US power. He initially argued, in the vein of Roman idealists, that efforts to seek peace and justice go together, though he warned that the protagonists should be charitable and forgiving (Niebhur 1932). Perhaps charity and forgiveness are contraindicated if justice is defined as prosecuting war criminals. However, torturers and murderers, who are potential peace-makers, have also been prosecuted, leading to more durable peace in some cases. Niebhur (2008) also argued that the USA, in adapting the Machiavellian view of a set of separate public ethics opposed to private ethics, must emerge as corrupt in making it necessary to use power and force against evil in international affairs. Even the democratic socialist, Michael Walzer, in accepting a version of Weber's "Problem of the Dirty Hands," concedes that exceptional situations might require exceptions to either prosecuting or punishing official criminality, where the lives of many can be saved, or at least would be morally justified, even if punishment might be issued (Walzer 2004).

Both the left and the right often adopt self-serving, "ends-justifying the means" rationalizations of overreaching policies that fail to achieve the stated ends and resorting to means that are unethical and illegal, that resort to exceptionalism to conventional public ethics for official actions. Machiavelli might have justified such exceptions, but only if they achieve the bona fide public interest. However, ineffective, unethical, or illegal actions are often undertaken on behalf of both liberal and conservative forms of idealism, leading to myths, denials, and delusions to justify unsustainable policies. No matter how harmful, cultural exceptionalism in the USA is called "American Exceptionalism" and excuses or ignores inconsistencies with international law and liberal ethics, or even enlightened self-interest. However, versions of peace and justice are immensely complex and contested and the goals and means remain clouded or unexamined in public debates.

Debates within the discipline of peace studies among those generally embracing the concept of the *positive peace* reflect the view that peace without justice, which includes an economic dimension, in addition to human rights and prosecutions, is not a sufficient condition for sustainable or stable peace. Johan Galtung argued that all these conditions are required. Even if peace were defined as a negative peace in the absence of war, it requires that both direct violence and structural violence be absent. The latter is "reproduced in the agricultural, industrial, commercial and administrative sectors of society." Among these structures are Galtung's neo-Marxist view that the "way that surplus is extracted from the lower levels and transferred upwards, making the higher levels richer at the expense of the lower levels, producing the famous 'gaps' in development (and) often highly differential morbidity and mortality rates between rich and poor nations" (quoted in Claude and Weston 2006, p. 282). Kenneth Boulding, by contrast, argued that justice and development were separate analytic categories. He argued that peace reflected economic factors, which could respond to selfish motives, but also needed to be tempered through altruistic ones. In the three main systems that he analyzed – exchange, threat, and integrative systems – the latter was based on love and courage and needed to overshadow the self-interest and fear that characterize the first two systems. Boulding's attention to economic realities also led some to view his work as coldly rational while he sought to avoid *naïveté* (Boulding 1963). Galtung, as well as Boulding's pacifist wife, Elise Boulding, appear to have felt this disagreement profoundly, arguing that peace and justice cannot be segregated.

As *normative* advice, pacifism poses a dilemma because there are no options in the face of violent repressors except resistance and martyrdom. Pacifism only works when the repressing state is unwilling or unable to repress because the reputational costs or the perceptions of legitimacy no longer allow it. It is indeed true that pacifism would be the ideal solution if all key actors could be convinced to cooperate and stop competing for power. Unfortunately, the more likely route to the dilemmas of international or domestic anarchy would be a form of world government achieved not through integration but through conquest and domination by one state. Pacifism is an explanation, but not an answer to the dilemmas of peace-building – at least not until a bottom-up process can change minds and create a culture of peace, if not a culture of justice and human rights as well.

The emergence of peace-building

The contemporary theory of peace-building, by contrast, holds out the theory of positive peace, where pursuing peace requires justice, whether defined institutionally as due process prosecutions of criminals or human rights protection as the overall pattern of state–society relations. The notion that human rights were necessary for the maintenance of international peace was a fundamental principle behind the founding of the United Nations. The connection of peace to justice, based on human rights, is also at the heart of theory of peace-building over the long run. This foundation is rooted as much in civil and political rights as in economic, social, and cultural rights. Peace-building fundamentally presumes and attempts the positive peace: the attempt to build systems, both international and domestic, to protect human rights. It assumes that peace comes through justice, largely defined as minimum protection of civil liberties and political democratic rights, if not basic economic, social, and cultural rights. The peace-building project attempts to assert especially negative rights immediately, since all a state has to do is to halt repression, while building positive rights is a process that occurs over time. The human rights revolution was fundamentally built by NGOs, which began to emerge strongly in the 1970s. Relatively small groups with relatively small amounts of financial resources could document abuses and contradict government denial of human rights abuses. The problem is that in many cases, NGO monitoring of human rights does not lead to peace over the short run. Sometimes, though the evidence is somewhat ambiguous, peace can be fostered, such as in the notorious phrase of former Senator Daniel Patrick Moynihan, by "benign neglect" (Clymer 2003). In the case of the East Asian newly industrialized countries (NICs) and most recently in China, there is a correlation between repression, economic growth, and long-term improvement of human rights. Of course, there are many other examples of repression of human rights correlated with economic stagnation or decline and further deterioration of human rights. By the same token, Andrew Moravcsik (2005) and others have argued that regime liberalization, which is intended to reduce human rights violations by opening space for civil society and the market, is paradoxically likely to increase the number of human rights violations. This increase results either because reform is inherently destabilizing to an established order or because more liberal regimes in transition commit more violations to repress opposition. Whether or not these empirical relationships hold in peace-building situations, in the interests of simplicity and justice, peace-building rightly focuses on human rights improvement, even where states regard the NGO efforts as dangerous or subversive.

The UN developed Secretary General Boutros-Ghali's 1993 *Agenda for Peace*, a plan for reconciling peace and justice, as well as working to reduce the frequency and severity of war. Based on earlier concepts of peacekeeping, peace-making, and preventive diplomacy, the *Agenda for Peace* argued for policies, structures, and programs of *post-conflict peace-building* (with the hyphen initially spelled in both words), as "action to identify and support structures which will tend to strengthen and solidify peace in order to avoid a relapse into conflict." Peace-building is efforts among two or more states, the then Secretary General declared, that are mutually beneficial, designed to prevent the recurrence of crises, through sustained cooperation to address economic, social, cultural, and humanitarian problems (Boutros-Ghali 1993, Section II, para.21 and para.VI, paras. 55–59). It is noteworthy that the Secretary General envisioned peace-making and peacekeeping to address primarily political projects, such as election monitoring, government institutional reform, and human rights protection. While this sequencing made theoretical sense, it became clear that political problems could not possibly be resolved during peace-making and peacekeeping stages any more than economic, social, cultural, and humanitarian problems could be delayed until the end of peace-making and peacekeeping.

Defining peace-building

What type of peace is a part of peace-building? Peace studies assume that peace is a paradigm that has been achieved in the past and therefore is achievable in the future, and have developed the notion of a positive peace. A negative peace is simply the absence of war and violence and may include things like non-armed conflict and instabilities; a positive peace is the notion that to have sustainable peace you need sustainable democratization, economic development, rule of law, and a process of accountability for national memory, which would include some sort of truth and reconciliation commission or other institutions to address the past. Positive peace as a goal implies coincidental multitasking among the aforementioned processes. The positive peace approach in practice means you need to try and accomplish as many of these things as necessary at once because it is difficult to secure agreement on the sequence of these processes and with a number of NGOs involved to prioritize or decide on a sequence of events.

When one thinks of the peace-building rhetoric, the aphorisms all ring true. "One must never stop trying." "Everyone has a peace-building task." "We had thought that the debate over tradeoffs between peace and justice was finally over since it has been used by the culprits to blackmail perpetrators." "The threats of prosecution bring peace-makers to the table rather than chase them away." Such statements are empirically testable. It is possible to argue that one does not lose by trying to engage an enemy in a post-accord peace-building effort (Barnes 2005, pp. 7–27). After all, there are precedents for negotiating with the devil or enemy, despite the political heat that Barack Obama received in the summer of 2007 for asserting such. Yet, the USA has negotiated with Arafat, Kaddafi, the Soviets, and even Saddam; because there was a mutual interest in moving out of trouble to make a peace, on which peace could be built. It is difficult to know when such efforts are born of necessity with the possibility that both partners will want to dance with each other, and when such overtures amount to fantasy, and a dangerous fantasy at that. Yet, even when dealing with diamond- or oil-smuggling bandits who are leading rogue regimes, it may be possible to make peace. The wealth that they obtain through artificially inflated prices is caused by shortages born of war and cartels enforced at gunpoint. It is sometimes abetted by embargoes with the perverse incentives of making the rogue leaders even wealthier. Yet, such rogue leaders might, for example, want to take their money and run, rather than eventually face armed intervention to overthrow and punish them.

In UN parlance, peace-building refers to formal peace missions. The academic definitions tend to be broader, referring not only to formal and informal efforts to sustain peace, but also to efforts by parties to facilitate conditions that indirectly make peace more likely. The first, more narrow definition, places the focus on what the UN, states, and NGOs do to form and consolidate peace agreements over time. The second, broader definition also examines structural conditions in justice and the economy, as well as the interactions of societies that were formally at war. The difficulty with the first definition is its concern with peace as the absence of war. The difficulty with the second definition is that it considers so many factors that are often beyond the control or efforts of the participants. In terms of significance, the direct conditions in the first concept would appear to be more salient, if incomplete. Yet, even here, shortcomings in formal institutions may not depict the whole story.

Democracy, as the essence of the peace-building project, combines what Sartori called "peace-like politics"(Sartori 1987) with the protection of human rights. In other words, democracy combines the rule of law with limited majority rule, checked by anti-majoritarian (i.e., anti-democratic) checks like judicial protection of rights, separation of powers with checks and balances, and bicameralism. Several books have warned against democracy promotion in unready regimes. Fareed Zakaria (2007) has warned that democracy instituted by elections puts the cart before the horse of checks and balances in democratic governance. Instead of democracy leading to freedom, freedom is reduced unless democracy is defined as including the checks and balances being established before regimes are declared as democracies. Even more problematic, argues Amy Chua, is the export of globalized markets based on majority rule, which leads to extreme violence against economically dominant minorities (Chua 2003). Of course, the greatest danger from democratic-capitalism promotion is terrorism, a low-probability, catastrophic event. The more probable scenario from peace-building is likely to continue to be that too much democracy too soon proves to be anti-democratic in practice.

Alternative interpretations of peace and justice in democratic transitions abound. Some scholars such as Huntington argue that the most stable transitions – i.e., those that achieve peace, even if the regime is not peace-like or law-like – are top-down transitions controlled by the military or former elites, where space for opposition, press reporting, and NGO mobilization expand at a reasonable pace over time (Huntington 1992, ch.1). Critics like Stepan note that such a transition protects the military's interest in surviving as an institution, defeating all guerrilla, terrorist, and radical ideas, preserving its military prerogatives and creating new ones in intelligence agencies, limiting human rights accountability (Stepan 1989). Still others maintain that the evil military dictatorship, which began the wave of authoritarian regime changes in Latin America, was only overcome by an awakening of civil society that effectively conquered the authoritarian state (Stepan 1987), which saw that the costs of repression exceeded the benefits (Dahl 1971). It is clear that the paths to democratization and peace can be many, and it is quite difficult, just thinking of democratization, to think of many generalizable policies fitting the different contexts. The question is whether NGOs can adjust to the particular tasks that vary from societal takeover of a state on the one hand versus a top-down transition led by authoritarian forces in the military, intelligence agencies, and/or business or populist elites on the other.

Democracy alone cannot ensure a sustainable peace. Economic considerations must be addressed simultaneously with the democratization process. Resources must be available, most likely provided by donors through NGOs, to assist in the overall transition period with the provision of goods and services and in order to stimulate the economy (Hamre and Sullivan 2002, pp. 85–96). The provision of food is essential in preventing resurgence of violence. As de Montclos explains, "war and famine are related in two ways: as war provokes famine, famine also incites conflict" (De Montclos 2001, pp. 95–100). Resources are also important in helping aid the transition from combatants to civilian workers, which is crucial for security purposes (Rotberg and Albaugh 1999, p. 87). Economic progress, or lack thereof, can hinder the democratization process greatly. As Ho-Won explains, economic instability is one of the main obstacles to democracy. In particular, peace would not be durable without equitable development that benefits the majority of people in the society combined with income-creating opportunities for the poor. Thus, development activities need to be geared toward mitigating economic hardships and reintegrating the society across ethnic, racial, religious, and other divisions (Ho-Won 2005, p. 124). In order to ensure democratic achievements, economic considerations must be included in the peace-building process. These processes must all be implemented simultaneously in order for a peace agreement to succeed, and in order to prevent governments and rebels from manipulating NGOs.

The record in peace-building

The record of a few cases exemplifies the limitations of peace-building. El Salvador is characterized by a situation of *negative peace*, though some functional parliamentary institutions and reformed military institutions were generated. Bosnia is a *negative peace* ensured by the presence of initially NATO and the UN forces, and now EU police as peacekeeping forces. Bosnia has received far more resources, some of which were stolen by armed forces in certain parts of the country. Then there is Haiti, which has had two peace missions, beginning in 1994 and then in 2004. In recent years, since the election of René Préval and the demobilization of many gangs, there has been a negative peace, reliant on the UN Stabilization Mission in Haiti (MINUSTAH). Despite devastating tropical storms and the unprecedented earthquake on January 12, 2010, persistent poverty, poorly trained troops, electoral fraud, and corruption, Haiti is moving forward, even though insecurity and economic problems would likely worsen quickly when and if the UN withdraws. Even if one spends enough money and puts enough troops on the ground, one may not have self-sustaining institutions and NGOs, which are the rudimentary requirements for a positive peace. Clearly, Haiti has a parallel state of NGOs that feed the population but have not led to self-sustaining institutions and economic growth. NGOs from abroad or financed from abroad will achieve certain tasks, but what has been proven is that outsiders can "stage" or at least affect the activities that normally would be coordinated by a domestic government.

There are many failing or failed states in the world, but few get significant attention and the resources that the theory of a positive peace would require. It is clear that US attention to peace-building, or support for a UN mission to do the same, occurs most often and in largest measure in those states where the USA has concerns and interests. In contemporary terms, those states with terrorist threats, such as Haiti, Afghanistan, Pakistan, and Yemen, are those cited as failed states that require significant support from donor conferences and peace missions. Countries such as Somalia and Sudan also receive attention, but less of a rhetorical or financial commitment. Failed states in Central Asia and most of Africa rarely are singled out for efforts to build a positive peace, and in many cases, even an explicit effort to establish and maintain a negative peace. Furthermore, in those states that do receive UN, US, or Western attention for peace-building, the entire domain of activities managed by the USA, largely on its own terms, include law enforcement, diplomatic, military, and economic efforts, as well as covert actions that become part of orchestrated efforts in positive peace-building.

Transitional justice and peace

Post-conflict or transitional justice present ubiquitous and continuous dilemmas for democra tization. Democratization requires the need to reconcile the desire for justice and peace, which are arguably contradictory, and closure and the need to maintain memory of atrocity, which are also contradictory. Some alternatives to prosecution, particularly truth commissions or traditional justice systems, could also offer roles for NGOs to adduce evidence of wrongdoing. However, advocating these options, or even advocating amnesties, pardons, or inaction, may incite opposition from international NGOs asserting that crimes against humanity must be prosecuted as international crimes with universal jurisdiction and without any statute of limitations. The dilemma is whether to disrupt the pursuit of peace by insisting on the prosecution of injustices.

Just because there is a supposed tradeoff between peace and justice or human rights does not always make it so. For example, it had been predicted that the International Criminal Tribunal for the former Yugoslavia (ICTY) and indictments of key leaders would make it impossible to establish peace on the ground in Bosnia. However, only months after that ad hoc tribunal was operating, a peace agreement was negotiated at Dayton in November 1995. Clearly, the power situation on the ground was much more important than the effects of an international tribunal. On that footing, Human Rights Watch has argued vociferously on behalf of the arrest warrant to promote the rule of law, human rights, and justice, and the ultimate indictment and prosecution of the President and other officials in Sudan. When the International Criminal Court (ICC) Prosecutor Luis Moreno O'Campo issued an arrest warrant on July 14, 2008, there were many fears that the dilemma of peace versus justice would arise. The threat is that extremists will take over from both sides. Many also feared that government security forces would threaten those who might celebrate the decision, such as refugees, whether or not the decision was actually carried out. The peace negotiations on Darfur have been led by the United States and the UN Security Council. As a legal matter, these issues are also determined by these foreign actors, as well as those elites on the ground. NGOs are merely advocates for positions.

Perceptions that reform is desirable are sometimes based on inappropriate Western constructs or ideals. While African NGOs have certainly called attention to legal and other human rights abuses, they do not yet have the capability to press for prosecutions in regimes that do not prosecute themselves. Patrimonialism inhibits the autonomous development of such institutions. South Africa is quite different, enjoying NGOs that helped establish and implement its Truth and Reconciliation Commission. Its civil society is developed enough to examine its past and has begun prosecuting those, such as the architect of biological warfare against civilians, Wouter Basson, who refused to testify about their crimes. Weaker African NGOs, such as in Rwanda (and others of the poorest countries), have had no truth commissions.

The belief that there is "no reconciliation without penitence," that the "truth will set you free," that sanctions must be placed on all violent regimes (even if the poor society is victimized and the ruling elites exploit scarcities), or there can be "no peace without justice" (as opposed to those who see a tradeoff between peace and justice) are all conventional platitudes based on the assumption that peace-building cannot proceed without confronting a painful past. It is politically incorrect, but the reality, based on simple empirical evaluation, suggests a more conflicted and complicated picture. Demanding apologies, asserting the truth, and pressing for prosecution can all have unintended consequences, often the opposite of those intended.

The desire for peace can be quixotic, where states, NGOs, and intergovernmental organizations (IGOs) cannot agree on what kind of peace is appropriate. Moreover, the means of effecting, maintaining, and building peace is fraught with conflicting incentives, interests, and definitions. While pursuing one version of peace and justice can be the basis for consensus, the means can reduce the chances for peace, indeed, may require, in the absence of other alternatives, that oxymoron, peace enforcement, by paradoxically "bombing for peace." If the "nature of the beast" is perceived as a choice between utopias and dystopias, which produce contradictory interpretations of reality and alternative realities, then peace-building is doomed to fail. These competing realities increase the perceived stakes because alternative governing visions and administrations often seek to change everything that the other side advocates and believes.

The choice between justice and peace is a false one. Many societies are simply unable to protect human rights or prosecute violations of human rights. The best solution that has emerged is truth commissions, with all of their imperfections (Hayner 2002). They may not achieve the truth, or when they approach it, they may open, rather than heal, old wounds. Forgiving the unforgivable is often too much for those who live in post-conflict societies. For peace-building to optimize peace and justice, in their multitudinous manifestations, the struggle to build the rule of law, substantively based on human rights, must be allowed to evolve over the life cycle of institution-building. This will require patience, but also an eye toward identifying and eliminating the worst forms of human rights abuse. There will be disagreements, often profound, on what those institutions should look like and how different values can be compromised.

Where a consensus is needed is that human rights NGOs continue improving the objectivity and sophistication of their analysis. While the challenges are broader than can be discussed in this chapter, maintaining quality standards in documenting human rights violations remains the single most important way to reconcile the tensions between peace and justice. Neither value is sacrosanct, but getting the facts right is the best place to start to increase the pressure on a humane order. Aside from the difficulty in maintaining credibility, reliability, and truthfulness, the presentation of findings must be relevant and simple enough to understand. Often, the authors of violations are known or suspected with very high degrees of confidence. The temptation is to make accusations that cannot be proven with documentation. Cases against suspected criminals are often circumstantial, which is necessarily complex and often subjective. It is very difficult to explain why it is often believed that someone with the motive for killing or torturing someone also ordered the acts. The standards of suspicion are rarely acceptable as sufficient to corroborate an assertion of guilt. Beyond specific actions, systematic patterns of gross human rights violations should be documented where possible and presented in systematic fashion. Statistics on victims alone might suffice in deterring or at least identifying repeated patterns of unlawful decisions and actions of one side against another. Comparisons over time and space can be made about victims, classified by age, gender, ethnicity, region, and timing. Alas, the more complex the interpretation, the more the conclusions can be deliberately or accidentally misinterpreted or be contested as spurious or biased. This will be a muddling-through process toward decent reporting of the indecent. In the end, the effort to reconcile peace and justice can be ultimately achieved, but not solved, at least not without some structural changes that lower the stakes involved in the post-conflict pursuit of justice. The best structural solution is to think that enemies are no longer enemies. Pursuing justice is one way to transform the "other." The dilemma is that it can also lead to the unanticipated consequences which serve neither peace nor justice. Smaller steps where consensus appears possible are most likely to be effective in mitigating conflict.

References

Baker, Pauline H. 1996. "Conflict Resolution Versus Democratic Governance: Divergent Paths to Peace." Pp. 563–572 in Chester A. Crocker and Fen Osler Hampson with Panela Aall, eds., *Managing Global Chaos: Sources and Response to International Conflict* (Washington, DC: US Institute of Peace Press).

Barnes, Catherine. 2005. "Weaving the Web: Civil Society Roles in Working with Conflict and Building Peace." In *People Building Peace II: Successful Stories of Civil Society* (Boulder, CO: Lynne Rienner).

Bassiouni, M. Cherif, ed. 2002. *Post-Conflict Justice* (Ardley, UK: Transnational Publishers).

Boulding, Kenneth. 1963. *Conflict and Defense: A General Theory* (New York: Harper).

Boulding, Kenneth. 1978. *Stable Peace* (Austin: University of Texas Press).

Boutros-Ghali, Boutros. 1993. *An Agenda for Peace*. UN Document A/47/277-S/24111 (New York: UN Press).

Chua, Amy. 2003. *World on Fire: How Exploring Democracy Breeds Ethnic Hatred and Global Insecurity* (New York: Random House).

Claude, Richard Pierre and Burns H. Weston. 2006. "Questions for Reflection and Discussion." *Human Rights in the World Community* (Philadelphia: University of Pennsylvania Press).

Clymer, Adam. 2003. "Former Senator Daniel Patrick Moynihan Dead at 76." (Obituary) *New York Times*, March 26. Accessed 28 December 2010. At: http://www.nytimes.com/2003/03/26/obituaries/26CNDMOYNIHAN.html?ex=1094875200&en=382d07780ef51612&ei=5070&pagewanted=1.

Dahl, Robert. 1971. *Polyarchy: Participation and Opposition* (New Haven, CT: Yale University Press).

De Montclos, Marc-Antoine Perous. 2001. "A Crisis of Humanitarianism." *Forum for Applied Research and Public Policy*, Vol. 16, No. 2, pp. 95–100.

Drumbl, Mark. 2007. *Atrocity, Punishment, and International Law* (Cambridge: Cambridge University Press).

Galtung, Johann. 2006, Quoted in Hamre, John J. and Gordon R. Sullivan. 2002. "Toward Postconflict Reconstruction." *Washington Quarterly*, Vol. 25, No. 4, pp. 85–96.

Goldstone, Richard. 1995. "Exposing Human Rights Abuses – A Help or Hindrance to Reconciliation?" Matthew O. Tobriner Memorial Lecture. *Constitutional Law Quarterly*, Vol. 22, No. 3, University of California, Hastings College of Law, pp. 607–622.

Hamre, John J. and Gordon Sullivan. 2002. "Toward Postconflict Reconstruction." *Washington Quarterly*, Vol. 25, No. 4, pp. 85–96.

Hayner, Priscilla B. 2002. *Unspeakable Truths: Facing the Challenges of Truth Commissions* (London: Routledge).

Howard, Michael. 2001. *The Invention of Peace* (New Haven, CT: Yale University Press).

Ho-Won, Jeong. 2005. *Peacebuilding in Postconflict Societies: Strategy and Process* (Boulder, CO: Lynne Rienner).

Huntington, Samuel P. 1968. *Political Order in Changing Societies* (New Haven, CT: Yale University Press).

Huntington, Samuel P. 1992. *The Third Wave: Democratization in the Late Twentieth Century* (Norman: University of Oklahoma Press).

Huntington, Samuel P. 1993. "The Clash of Civilizations." *Foreign Affairs*, Vol. 72, pp. 22–49.

Moravcsik, Andrew. 2005. *Human Rights, Sovereignty, and American Unilateralism: American Exceptionalism and Human Rights* (Princeton, NJ: Princeton University Press).

Niebuhr, Reinhold. 1932. *Moral Man and Immoral Society: A Study in Ethics and Politics* (New York: Charles Scribner).

Niebuhr, Reinhold. 2008. *The Irony of American History* (Chicago, IL: University of Chicago Press).

Rotberg, Robert I. and Ericka A. Albaugh. 1999. *Preventing Conflict in Africa: Possibilities of Peace Enforcement* (Cambridge: World Peace Foundation).
Sartori, Giovanni. 1987. *Theory of Democracy Revisited* (London: Chatham House).
Stepan, Alfred, ed. 1987. *Democratizing Brazil* (Princeton, NJ: Princeton University Press).
Stepan, Alfred. 1989. *Rethinking Military Politics: Brazil and the Southern Cone* (Princeton, NJ: Princeton University Press).
Van Zyl, Paul. 2009. "Defining Transitional Justice." At: http://its.law.nyu.edu/faculty/coursepages/data/DEFINING%TRANSITIONAL%20JUSTICE%20March%202005.pdf.
Walzer, Michael. 2004. "Political Action: The Problem of the Dirty Hands." In Sanford Levinson, ed., *Torture: A Collection* (Oxford: Oxford University Press).
Zakaria, Fareed. 2007. *The Future of Freedom: Illiberal Democracy at Home and Abroad* (New York: W.W. Norton).

38
Social responsibility and human rights

Morton Winston

During the latter half of the twentieth century, international human rights became the dominant form of moral and legal discourse. However, at the beginning of the twenty-first century, there is increasing emphasis on the notion that individuals and organizations also have certain social responsibilities with respect to human rights for which they may be held accountable. Governments have traditionally been viewed as the primary bearers of the moral and legal responsibilities entailed by human rights, and continue to be so regarded. However, the new discourse of social responsibility for human rights modifies the state-centric approach by proposing that many kinds of private non-state actors, such as multinational corporations, intergovernmental institutions, and even individuals and civil society organizations, also have responsibilities for observing, promoting, and fulfilling human rights. The concept of social responsibility should be understood as encompassing more than just duties related to human rights, and is often invoked as a way of describing duties to protect environment quality, prevent unnecessary harm to animals, and promote other important social goods. However, the present discussion will be restricted to those kinds of social responsibilities that are derived from or are related to human rights, an important subclass of the wider concept.

The question of the relationship between rights and duties has a long history in moral and legal philosophy. Most people believe that human moral agents have certain responsibilities to society, at least some of which flow from other people's rights. Rights and responsibilities are often seen as correlative, so that if someone is a right-holder who has a right to something, then someone else must be a duty-bearer who has a responsibility to observe, protect, and fulfill that right. If we are talking about human rights, which belong to all human persons despite differences in race, gender, nationality, religion, property, and other characteristics, and are held to be universal, indivisible, and inherent, then it is plausible to suppose that the duties and responsibilities that derive from human rights must also be universal, indivisible, and inherent.

However, this is not entirely accurate: with respect to the "duty-side" of human rights there is a division of moral labor in which different individuals and different organs of society have different kinds of duties regarding human rights. The social responsibilities associated with human rights, while common, are also differentiated, particularly with respect to positive duties; they can be ascribed both to human persons and to certain kinds of organizations; they are ascribed separately to particular moral agents but are also shared; the right-holders who are the objects of these responsibilities include both fellow citizens and noncitizens; and the scope of these responsibilities potentially encompasses the full range of human rights recognized under contemporary international human rights law. While many of the duties and responsibilities that are correlated with human rights are *prima facie*, in that there may be valid ethical considerations that excuse or justifiably limit some actors' responsibilities with respect to human rights, fulfilling these responsibilities is not optional, and duty-bearers may be held accountable to society for their enactment of them.

The goal of this chapter will be first, to indicate more precisely the ways in which social responsibilities are linked to human rights. Second, the chapter will explain the concept of corporate social responsibility and describe how it is being used in moral and political discourse. Third, the chapter will conclude with a brief discussion of the relationship between the acceptance and enactment of social responsibilities and the development of the human moral personality.

Duties to the community

The Universal Declaration of Human Rights (1948), which is the template for the entire canon of Post-World War II human rights declarations, treaties, covenants, and conventions, has often been criticized for failing to prominently mention the notions of duties and responsibilities. The only place in the UDHR where duties to the community are explicitly mentioned comes towards the end of the document in the first clause of Article 29, which reads, "Everyone has duties to the community in which alone the free and full development of his personality is possible." This statement is elliptical and rather mysterious. What are these duties? How does one define community? What do these duties have to do with the development of human personality? And why does it say "alone"?

The drafting history of the UDHR provides important insights into the meaning of this text. According to Johannes Morsink, earlier drafts of the UDHR placed the concept of duties prominently at the beginning of the document, but through a series of decisions and compromises it was whittled down and finally moved to the end (1999, pp. 241–248). The first article of John Humphrey's draft stated: "Every one owes a duty to his State and to the (international society) United Nations. He must accept his just share of responsibility for the performance of such social duties and his share of such common sacrifices as may contribute to the common good" (Morsink 1999, p. 241). After several delegates objected to the emphasis on duties to the State, as opposed to society or the community, particularly because it could be interpreted as endorsing a duty of loyalty to unjust or undemocratic states, Humphrey's text was rejected in favor of an alternate draft prepared by the French delegate, René Cassin, which had as Article 2: "The object of society is to afford each of its members equal opportunity for the full development of his spirit, mind and body"; and as Article 3: "Man is essentially social and has fundamental duties to his fellow-men. The rights of each are therefore limited by the rights of others" (Morsink 1999, p. 243). Cassin's text was then condensed to read, "Everyone has duties to the community which enables him freely to develop his personality," and once this was done, it was recommended by the Chinese delegate P. C. Chang that the statement be moved to the end for stylistic reasons, so as not to discuss limitations of human rights before announcing those same rights. The Australian delegate, Alan Watt, then proposed inserting the word "alone" into the statement in order to emphasize that there was "an organic connection between the individual and the community" which made it impossible for individuals to develop their humanity apart from the societies to which they belong (Morsink 1999, p. 246). As Morsink notes, "This word 'alone' may well be the most important single word in the entire document, for it helps us answer the charge that the rights set forth in the Declaration create egoistic individuals who are not closely tied to their respective communities," thereby recognizing the "communitarian dimension" of human rights (1999, p. 248).

But the interdependence of rights and responsibilities has been largely overlooked in the subsequent development of the human rights canon where the dominant focus is on the rights of individual persons and on the legal obligations of governments toward them, rather than social responsibilities of private individuals and non-state actors with respect to human rights. The idea of the individual's duties to the community is explicitly mentioned in the African Charter on Human and People's Rights (1981), where there is a brief list of eight specific enumerated duties including: to one's family, to society, to work and pay taxes, not to "compromise the security of the State," and to "preserve and strengthen African cultural values." But some commentators object to this kind of enumeration of duties; another commentary on UDHR Article 29 notes that, although there are now many authoritative enumerations of human rights, there is no authorized international catalogue of the individual's duties to his/her community and argues that this is because "there is no such thing as fundamental or 'human' duties in the same sense as there are rights. Any catalogue of duties to the community – as one finds in some constitutions – would therefore be to some extent arbitrary or a matter for domestic law and politics" (Opsahl and Dimitrijevic 1999, p. 634). They also note that many legal scholars of human rights hold that "Duties to the community belong wholly to the moral and political sphere and can hardly be translated into law" (Opsahl and Dimitrijevic 1999, p. 641). The view that the "duties to the community" referred to in Article 29 belong wholly to the ethical or moral sphere is also consonant with a statement in the Preamble of the American Declaration of the Rights and Duties of Man (1948), which states, "Duties of a juridical nature presuppose others of a moral nature which support them in principle and constitute their basis." This statement provides an important clue to the nature of the duties to the community being invoked by UDHR Article 29; they are to be understood primarily, but not exclusively, as *moral duties or ethical responsibilities* one owes to other members of society.

Moral duties and ethical responsibilities differ from legal obligations in that they are not issued by a sovereign law-making authority, are not codified in "black letter law," are not enforced by the police powers of states, and are not normally justiciable in the way in which legal obligations to conform to statutes, contractual obligations, and case law are enforceable by courts. Moral duties are informal and are commonly enforced only by social sanctions such as moral disapprobation. Ethical responsibilities are also notoriously difficult to define and are subject to variable interpretations depending on one's background philosophical and religious beliefs, one's culture, and the particular social expectations that are associated with particular roles and stations in society. But it does not follow from this that such ethical responsibilities do not exist, or that they are unimportant. As the statement from the American Declaration recognizes, legal obligations must be based upon moral duties, for to answer the question, "Why ought one obey the law?" by saying that it is one's legal obligation to do so, begs the question.

So then, it seems clear that the phrase "duties to the community" in Article 29 must mainly refer to *moral* duties and responsibilities that individuals, and some kinds of non-state actors, have toward society or their communities, not primarily to legal duties they have towards the state, nor to legally enforceable obligations they might have towards other non-state actors. This is the sense of "social responsibility" that is most frequently used nowadays. However, it is important to recognize that individuals and corporate non-state actors also have certain strict legal obligations that derive from human rights. Governments are the primary addressees of human rights claims, and under international human rights law, they have the obligations to observe human rights, protect their own citizens against violations of human rights, and provide remedies, and in some cases reparations, to individuals whose human rights have been violated. However, individuals and corporate non-state actors also have strict legal obligations to respect the human rights of others, both those of their fellow citizens and also those of non-nationals. Human rights have multiple addresses, and there is a division of moral labor among these different classes of duty-bearers. For example, everyone has a strict moral and legal obligation not to torture or enslave human beings, to observe these rights, but it is mainly governments that have the responsibility to protect people against violations of these rights. As James Nickel explains it, "The right to protection against torture can be universal without all of the corresponding duties being against everyone, or against a single world-wide agency. What is required is that there be for every right-holder at least one agency with duties to protect that person against torture" (Nickel 2007, p. 41). This agency will usually be the government of the country in which the right-holder has citizenship or resides, but in cases in which the state fails to adequately fulfill its responsibilities, the duty to protect individuals against serious forms of human rights abuse may devolve onto others, who can be considered secondary addresses of these rights. The notion of devolution of the responsibility to protect human rights has been particularly prominent in discussions of the "responsibility to protect" individuals and peoples against genocide and other forms of mass violence and has led to a re-examination of the international norms concerning humanitarian intervention (Evans and Sahnoun 2001).

The term "responsibility" is now often used instead of "duty" to designate the particular kinds of moral obligations that individuals and non-state corporate entities have toward their communities and to society in general. The word "responsibility" is used in at least two distinct senses in moral discourse. One way this term is used is to assign liability, culpability, or blame for an actor's past actions. This "backward-looking" sense of "liability responsibility" is not generally what is meant when people speak of the social responsibilities of individuals and corporations. Liability responsibility is backward-looking and aims to assign blame for harm caused by an agent's own actions. Social responsibilities, in the moral sense, are forward-looking and are directed at preventing or correcting large-scale or systematic forms of oppression or injustice or avoiding harms that result from the participation of many moral agents in unjust social and economic institutions. When we speak of a person's duties, we generally mean specific demands for action that are placed upon their wills by others. Duty has come to suggest action in which the agent merely complies or in which he or she acts heteronomously in accordance with the will of another. Social responsibilities, on the other hand, when understood in the moral sense, describe moral obligations that are self-assumed and are often discretionary. The responsible moral agent is someone who "responds" to the existence of injustice or oppression in morally appropriate ways through their own autonomous decisions and actions without any external authority or sanction compelling him or her to do so.

Robert Goodin has noted, "Responsibilities are to consequentialistic ethics what duties are to deontological ones. Duties dictate actions. Responsibilities dictate results" (Goodin 1986, p. 50). As he explains, "Both duties and responsibilities are prescriptions of the general form: A ought to see to it that X, where A is some agent and X some state of affairs." However, in the case of duties, the state of affairs, X, is the result of some action of A's own doing, while in the case of responsibilities the X clause need not refer to specific actions on the part of A because the agent can delegate his or her responsibilities to others. For example, a captain of a ship has the responsibility to see to it that the ship does not hit an iceberg (or anything else), that is to ensure that particular states of affairs are avoided. But he can fulfill his responsibility not to bring about these states of affairs by delegating the actual steering to others. When he does so, the captain retains overall responsibility in that he must see to it that those to whom he delegates his responsibility act in the appropriate ways, and he will be held accountable for mishaps if they occur. But what matters for responsibilities is that a certain outcome or state of affairs be obtained, not who is performing the specific actions needed in order to obtain them.

This feature of the concept of responsibility makes it particularly apt for describing the kinds of institutionally mediated social responsibilities that individuals and organizations have with respect to their positive duties to protect and fulfill human rights. Moral philosophers distinguish between negative duties, which require that moral agents forgo certain types of actions, or simply refrain from interfering with others, and positive duties, which require that one act in certain ways to bring about states of affairs that may involve giving up resources or privileges that one already possesses. The negative duties correlated with human rights, such as the duty not to torture or enslave others, because they involve omissions, are universal and can be ascribed to everyone. However, as Henry Shue has argued, with respect to the positive duties entailed by human rights there is a division of moral labor in which "the positive duties need to be divided up and assigned among bearers in some reasonable way" (Shue 1988, p. 690). The ways in which these positive duties and responsibilities are assigned must, moreover, provide for differing degrees of responsibility deriving from the limitations and capacities of different agents and the positional relationship between the duty-bearers and the right-holders who are the ultimate beneficiaries of their responsibilities.

In order to fulfill their positive social responsibilities with respect to human rights, individuals commonly delegate them to mediating institutions. For instance, by paying taxes we support police forces, courts, public schools, and other governmental institutions that function as the institutional means by which we discharge our social responsibilities to protect and fulfill our own human rights to security, justice, and education as well as those of our fellow citizens. Thomas Pogge has argued that in discussing the positive duties associated with human rights, we should employ an "institutional understanding" that recognizes that, "By postulating a person P's right to X as a human right we are asserting that P's society ought to be (re)organized in such a way that P has secure access to X and, in particular, so that P is secure against being denied X or deprived of X officially: by the government or its agents or officials" (Pogge 1995, p. 114). Under the institutional understanding, individuals and corporate non-state actors do not have direct responsibilities for protecting and fulfilling all human rights; rather they have the responsibility to ensure that appropriate mediating institutions fulfill these obligations.

In cases where there exist well-functioning public institutions that effectively protect and efficiently fulfill human rights, the individual's positive responsibility to his or her community consists in accepting a fair share of the burdens and costs associated with maintaining them, usually through the payment of taxes. It is often the case, however, that important human rights are not adequately protected by existing public institutions, for instance, with respect to social and economic rights, as evidenced by the plight of homeless and hungry people in many countries. In such cases, the individual's social responsibilities to his or her community can be discharged by means of donations to voluntary civil society organizations and non-governmental organizations whose missions are directed to the fulfillment of various human rights. In some cases, individuals may wish to discharge their social responsibilities with respect to human rights by advocating that governments and corporations do more to fulfill their own social responsibilities with respect to neglected and unfulfilled human rights, while in other cases, individuals may become "social entrepreneurs" and create new private institutions that directly address the task of fulfilling human rights and securing their universal effective enjoyment.

Social responsibilities for human rights must thus be understood to include some legal obligations, for instance, to respect the rights of others and to pay one's fair share of taxes to support just and effective mediating institutions. But they also call upon individuals and corporate non-state actors to utilize the powers and capacities at their disposal in a voluntary but conscientious fashion in order to prevent and correct injustices due to inadequate human rights implementation and protection mechanisms. In some cases this may require supporting voluntary organizations dedicated to improving human rights protection and implementation, or creating new institutions that will function to fulfill human rights more effectively.

Corporate social responsibility

Although governments are the primary addressees of human rights claims and are held to bear legal responsibilities to observe human rights, protect their citizen's enjoyment of human rights from various kinds of threats, and provide remedies and reparations to those whose human rights have been violated, there has been an increasing awareness that many of the threats to human rights come not from government but rather from powerful non-state actors (Alston 2005; Clapham 2006). In recent years there has been a growing interest in the topic of the responsibilities of non-state actors, particularly multinational corporations, with respect to human rights, which has been led by a global corporate social responsibility (CSR) movement. The emerging social expectations that corporations should be accountable to society for their social and environmental performance has spurred a variety of initiatives by governments, NGOs, and business associations designed to define the specific responsibilities of multinational companies (MNCs) with respect to human rights, including the Sullivan Principles (1977), the OECD Guidelines for Multinational Corporations (1976), the UN Global Compact (2000), and the UN "Norms on the Responsibilities of Transnational Corporations and other Business Enterprises with Regard to Human Rights" (2003). Most recently, the topic has been the subject of a series of consultations and reports mandated by the UN Human Rights Council by Professor John Ruggie (2008), who is the Secretary General's Special Representative for Business and Human Rights.

The traditional view of the social responsibilities of corporations held by laissez-faire economists, such as Milton Friedman, is that the sole responsibility of business is to generate wealth for its owners (Friedman 1970). While the goal of maximizing shareholder value still describes the primary legal obligation of public corporations, the idea that corporations also have significant *social* and *environmental* responsibilities has gained significant traction in recent years. A major theoretical innovation in business theory that helped propel this shift was the development of "stakeholder theory" (Freeman 1984). According to this view, corporations have social responsibilities to a variety of stakeholders, for instance, to their employees, their customers, their suppliers and business partners, residents of their host communities, and society at large, as well as their owners and investors. While from a legal point of view a corporation may be described as a "legal person" or a "nexus of contracts," from a social point of view, corporations sit at the center of networks of social relations and their activities impact various groups of stakeholders. John Elkington (1998) coined the term "triple-bottom line" to describe ethical business practices that take social and environmental impacts on all stakeholders into account. The elements of the triple bottom line (TBL) are: "people" or social capital, "planet" or natural capital, and, of course, financial capital or "profit."

The main focus of the CSR movement to date has been on the "negative externalities" of corporate business activity, that is the costs and harms to society and to the environment that do not typically show up in the audited financial reports. These can include, for instance, complicity in human rights abuses committed by governments, use of forced labor and child labor, endangering the health and safety of employees, denying their employees rights of freedom of association and collective bargaining, discrimination, excessive working hours, inadequate compensation, environmental pollution and degradation including carbon emissions, threats to public health, damage to fragile ecosystems, inappropriate waste disposal, bribery and corruption, unfair or fraudulent marketing, inadequate consumer data and privacy protection, and other problems that are directly or indirectly due to business activity. While some of these matters can be tied directly to particular company's practices, in other cases the problems are structural and systematic and are due to the interaction of market forces.

For example, it is very likely that many of the consumer goods purchased by shoppers in the developed countries can trace their origins to abusive or exploitative factory conditions in the poor countries where these goods are now generally made. Consumers are not responsible for these poor labor conditions in the causal or the liability senses of that term. But consumers do nevertheless have certain ethical duties regarding these systematic economic injustices. The philosopher Iris Marion Young, who calls these kinds of duties *political responsibilities*, notes that they are often international in scope because, "the social relations that connect us to others are not restricted to nation-state borders" (Young 2004, p. 371). The supply chains that end at the point of purchase in our big-box discount stores typically begin in some factory in China or Bangladesh or another developing country. By purchasing that pair of sneakers made in China, we are interacting with a complex set of economic and political institutions that make it possible for workers halfway around the globe to be producing goods that end up in our stores, and eventually on our feet and in our closets. Our consumer behavior assumes the existence of these transnational market institutions, and so by participating through them in a global system of production, distribution, and marketing, our consumer decisions indirectly affect the distant workers who produced these goods. While these extended forms of social relations are mutual – the same complex supply chain that connects us with Chinese factory workers connects them with us – the character of the relationship between the parties is morally asymmetrical due to factors that Young calls *positional power* and *vulnerability*.

She argues that, "While everyone in the system of structural and institutional relations stands in circumstances of justice that give them obligations with respect to all the others, those institutionally and materially situated to be able to do more to affect the conditions of vulnerability have greater obligations" (Young 2004, p. 371). This would seem to imply that the retail corporations that source their merchandise from developing countries, and are in part responsible, in the liability sense, for encouraging or exploiting unjust labor conditions, should bear a greater degree of social responsibility for correcting them. She also argues that since the power relationships that give rise to this kind of asymmetrical moral responsibility are objective, the assignment of such responsibilities to moral agents does not depend on their recognition or consent. The fact that many other people also participate in the economic relations found within global supply chains does not absolve or diminish any one person's or company's responsibility for protecting vulnerable workers from exploitation and abuse. It is a shared social responsibility borne by all those who participate in the global market economy, but especially those who, because of their greater power or capability, are in a position to ameliorate or prevent injustice from being visited upon the more vulnerable participants in the process of production.

But the point of assigning social responsibility to consumers and corporations is not to blame them for participating in economic institutions that produce injustice, but instead to urge them to "take responsibility for altering the processes to avoid or reduce injustice" (Young 2004, p. 379). Unlike the negative duties and responsibilities derived from human rights, these positive, forward-looking social responsibilities allow for considerable discretion on the part of agents as to how their responsibilities are discharged. Social responsibilities are also shared; my having a social responsibility to address a global injustice does not remove or diminish your similar social responsibility to do so. Social responsibilities address morally unacceptable outcomes that are produced by the interaction of many persons with unjust institutions, where each person "is personally responsible for the outcome in a partial way," even though, "the specific part that each plays in producing the outcome cannot be isolated and identified" (Young 2004, p. 380). The global CSR movement, then, has been calling upon individuals – but particularly multinational corporations – and other powerful non-state actors, such as the World Bank, not only to avoid direct violations of human rights, but also to accept a fair share of the social responsibility for correcting social and economic injustices and preventing future abuses of human rights.

While there is no commonly accepted definition of CSR, this term is widely understood, particularly within the business community, to refer only to voluntary moral responsibilities, distinct from any legal obligations that corporations may have. Standard accounts of CSR portray corporate responsibilities as a pyramid. Legal obligations, such as the fiduciary duties of corporate directors and regulatory requirements imposed by either an MNC's home or host country, are the base. Social responsibilities, for instance concerning human rights and environmental protection, are the middle. Corporate philanthropy, such as gifts to causes that are unrelated to the core activities of the business enterprise, are at the top, these last being optional, but praiseworthy (Leisinger 2006). Setting the boundary between those corporate responsibilities that should be legal obligations and those that should remain moral social responsibilities has generated a great deal of controversy. Corporations generally prefer voluntary self-regulation to government-imposed legal requirements, while non-governmental organizations generally prefer the opposite. But, as Jennifer Zerk (2006) has argued, "the debate as to whether CSR should be 'voluntary' or 'mandatory' is misguided for several reasons." In most jurisdictions there are legal requirements grounded upon human rights norms, for instance, that prohibit companies from discriminating on the basis of race, sex, or religion in the hiring of employees, that protect worker safety in the workplace, or that legally prohibit the use of child labor and forced labor and other unjust and abusive labor practices. However, in many countries in which MNCs operate, these sorts of requirements are not well enforced. So, if a particular multinational corporation that operates both in Denmark and Bangladesh adopts a policy prohibiting the use of child labor worldwide, is that policy the result of a legal obligation or a moral responsibility? Obviously, it is both. The boundaries between what is legally required, morally expected, and merely beneficial for companies to do are fluid and subject to political bargaining. But corporations do have legal obligations to observe human rights, as well as certain moral responsibilities to address forms of oppression and injustice produced by inadequate fulfillment or implementation of human rights, just as human moral agents do.

In the current global debate, there is a spectrum of opinion as to whether mandatory legal regulation or voluntary self-regulation is the better strategy for advancing the CSR agenda. A broad definition of CSR that includes both legal obligations and moral responsibilities is neutral on this debate by assuming that in the foreseeable future there will be a mixture of normative regimes, including national and international laws, emerging social expectations, "soft-law" approaches, contractual obligations, and voluntary self-regulation through enlightened self-interest, which in combination will regulate the ways in which MNCs operate in the global economy of the twenty-first century. This is essentially the view being promoted by the UN's Special Representative for Business and Human Rights, who has proposed that States have the primary duty to *protect* persons residing in their territories against human right abuses by non-state actors, including corporations, while corporations have responsibilities to *respect* human rights and to exercise "due diligence" to ensure that they do not harm human rights. Due diligence is considered to be "a process whereby companies not only ensure compliance with national laws but also manage the risk of human rights harm with a view to avoiding it" (Ruggie 2008, p. 25). The exercise of due diligence requires both negative duties of avoidance and omission and positive duties of commission, which may involve the expenditure of resources to proactively prevent human rights abuses from occurring. A third element of this framework, providing better access to remedies for persons whose human rights have been abused, is proposed as a shared social responsibility of states, business enterprises, and civil society organizations, which should cooperate in creating effective judicial and non-judicial grievance mechanisms through which individual claims can be adjudicated and resolved.

Social responsibility as a virtue

Some might object to the concept of social responsibility I have described because they believe that the positive duties involved in human rights fulfillment and enjoyment are imperfect duties of charity, which, while praiseworthy, are not required. The term "supererogation" is used by moral philosophers to describe a class of moral actions that are familiar to most people. Etymologically it means, "the act of paying out more than is required or demanded." As David Heyd writes, superogatory acts are "optional or non-obligatory, that is – distinguished from those acts which fall under the heading of duty … they are beyond duty, fulfill more than is required, over and above what the agent is supposed or expected to do" (Heyd 1982, p. 1). Acts of supererogation may be defined as follows:

> An act is supererogatory if and only if:
> 1. it is neither obligatory nor forbidden,
> 2. its omission is not wrong, and does not deserve sanction or criticism – either formal or informal,
> 3. it is morally good, both by virtue of its (intended) consequences and by virtue of its intrinsic value (being beyond duty),
> 4. it is done voluntarily for the sake of someone else's good, and is thus meritorious.
>
> *(Heyd 1982, p. 115)*

Examples of supererogation include saintly and heroic acts; acts of charity, generosity and philanthropy; acts of kindness and consideration; acts of mercy and forgiveness; and other voluntary acts which, while praiseworthy, are not required. Performing such acts is generally considered a mark of moral virtue, but society does not demand that everyone be virtuous.

However, the social responsibilities that derive from human rights do not seem to precisely fit this description of supererogatory actions, in that they sometimes involve acts or omissions the commission of which would expose the agent to informal sanctions or moral disapprobation. Social responsibilities for human rights seem to occupy an intermediate position between legal obligations, which are non-optional and peremptory, and acts of supererogation, which are purely voluntary and whose non-performance does not expose the agent to moral criticism or demands for accountability.

So, for example, it would be a purely supererogatory act to donate money so that a local little league baseball team can buy new uniforms; that is, it would be praiseworthy, but cannot be demanded, and omitting doing so would not subject one to moral blame or criticism. But suppose there is a natural disaster such as a flood or earthquake, or that there is genocide or a campaign of ethnic cleansing, and tens of thousands of people are homeless and in dire need of emergency relief assistance. In this case, the decision to omit donating to a competent humanitarian relief organization when one is easily capable of doing so could be regarded as blameworthy, even though one would be within one's rights not to do so. Some people may be excused from fulfilling this social responsibility for various reasons, for instance, because they have other more compelling responsibilities that conflict with their doing anything to aid the victims of the natural disaster, or because the costs and sacrifices they would incur by doing so are too great. But individuals who can do something to help the victims, and have no good excuse for not doing it, but choose not to, are morally blameworthy for they have failed to fulfill one of their social responsibilities. Donating to humanitarian relief efforts, on this view, is a non-optional yet non-peremptory social responsibility. In other words, it is something we can criticize others for not doing, although we cannot legitimately demand that they do so or punish them for failing to do so. The social responsibilities that derive from humanitarian needs and human rights differ from purely supererogatory acts that merely provide some benefits to the community but are not required to fulfill anyone's human rights.

The distinction between the performance of purely supererogatory acts and the fulfillment of one's social responsibilities with respect to human rights is not always clear in the way in which we use these terms in ordinary language, partly because both kinds of actions are highly discretionary. Persons have many options about how they can direct their donations to fulfill their social responsibility to provide humanitarian relief and advance other forms of human rights protection and fulfillment, and it is important to inquire carefully about such matters as cost-effectiveness and whether some forms of aid do create a culture of dependency or fuel corruption when choosing which agencies to support. However, none of these sorts of concerns and issues serve to excuse competent and capable moral agents from donating something to some voluntary mediating institutions or others involved in the fulfillment of inadequately protected or implemented human rights. Doing so is a non-optional moral obligation that can be understood as fulfilling a social responsibility that moral agents have toward other members of the international community with respect to their human rights.

Social responsibilities are discretionary, and their specific contents, that is, what they require one to do or not do, will vary depending on contextual and situational variables, as well as personal capacities, opportunities, and talents. If one happens to be a wealthy, world-famous rock star, like Bono, then maybe a good way to discharge your social responsibilities is to organize a global fund for HIV/AIDS and get a lot of companies to sell "Red" branded merchandise, some profits from which go to provide medical treatment for persons afflicted with this disease. But if you are a third-grade teacher in a rural school, this model probably will not work for you. But there are still lots of other things people of ordinary means can do to try to address structural injustice and improve human rights implementation. If you occupy an elected government office, you probably have access to information and powers that would enable you to do more on certain issues than other people. If so, then you ought to be doing those things, but it would be absurd to suggest that everyone should do the same things you are doing, because other people do not occupy your office or role. Because social responsibilities are discretionary they require that moral agents make a judgment about what it is they themselves can do with the talents and resources at their disposal, to improve the way society is organized for the protection and enjoyment of human rights.

Moreover, the content of one's social responsibilities depends on the current social, economic, and cultural problems that need to be addressed. There is a sense in which social responsibilities are not *prescriptive* in the same way as ordinary moral norms. By ordinary moral norms I mean things like "Do not lie," "Do not steal," "Keep your promises," and so forth. Ordinary moral norms embody specific rules of conduct that attempt to mark out those actions that are morally permissible from those that are not. Following such normative ethical guidance is rather like using a cookbook; one simply follows the directions. But in thinking about one's social responsibilities, this kind of approach will not do. Instead the moral agent is required to consult his or her conscience, and to survey the particular situational variables together with his or her positional and relational capacities and then creatively figure out what it is they ought to do to discharge their social responsibilities. The process is dynamic and creative, and one in which the moral agent is actively "taking responsibility" rather than passively accepting duties laid upon them by others. The root of the word "responsibility" is "respond"; social responsibilities are those moral responsibilities that prompt us to *respond* to the "big problems of the world" – social injustice, human rights abuse, poverty, disease – and within the limits of our own capabilities, to do our part to "repair the world."

For those who are religiously inclined, this idea of social responsibility can be understood as implying that because humans have free will we are co-creators, along with God, of the moral order and that by performing our moral duties and freely discharging our social responsibilities we are actively fulfilling God's will. The ability to guide one's own moral behavior and to exercise the particular powers and capabilities at one's disposal in order to contribute to upholding and repairing the moral order is also a way of thinking about what Article 29 means when it speaks of "the free and full development of [the human] personality." To become a fully mature moral agent, one who has reached the highest stage of moral development, it is necessary that one voluntarily accept and effectively discharge one's social responsibilities. The ability to autonomously accept and bear moral responsibilities that benefit others is a uniquely human capacity and may be the true ground of human dignity. Aristotle, the great Greek philosopher, thought that the supreme purpose of human life, its *telos*, was something he called *eudaimonia*. This term is often translated as "happiness" or sometimes as "flourishing," but what Aristotle is really trying to express is the idea that we fulfill ourselves as human beings by acquiring the capacity and the disposition to act in the "best way we can, at the things we do best, for the good of others." Only by taking responsibility for helping to repair the large-scale problems of society can each of us, through the active engagement of our own creative moral agency with the world, realize the "free and full development" of the human moral personality.

References

Alston, P., ed. 2005. *Non-State Actors and Human Rights* (Oxford: Oxford University Press).

Clapham, A. 2006. *Human Rights Obligations of Non-State Actors* (Oxford: Oxford University Press).

Elkington, J. 1998. *Cannibals with Forks: The Triple-Bottom Line for 21st Century Business* (Gabriola Island, BC: New Society Publishers).

Evans, G. and M. Sahnoun. 2001. *The Responsibility to Protect* (Ottawa: International Commission on Intervention and State Sovereignty).

Freeman, R. E. 1984. *Strategic Management: A Stakeholder Approach* (Boston: Pitman).

Friedman, M. 1970. "The Social Responsibility of Business Is to Increase Its Profits." *New York Times Magazine*, 13 September.

Goodin, R. E. 1986. "Responsibilities." *Philosophical Quarterly*, Vol. 36, No. 142, pp. 50–56.

Heyd, D. 1982. *Supererogation: Its Status in Ethical Theory* (Cambridge: Cambridge University Press).

Leisinger, K. M. 2006. *On Corporate Responsibility for Human Rights* (Basel Novartis Foundation for Sustainable Development).

Morsink, J. 1999. *The Universal Declaration of Human Rights: Origins, Drafting and Intent* (Philadelphia: University of Pennsylvania Press).

Nickel, J. W. 2007. *Making Sense of Human Rights* (Malden, MA: Blackwell).

Opsahl, T. and V. Dimitrijevic. 1999. Articles 29 and 30, pp. 633–652 in G. Alfredsson and A. Eide, eds., *The Universal Declaration of Human Rights: A Common Standard of Achievement* (The Hague: Kluwer Law International).

Pogge, T. W. 1995. "How Should Human Rights Be Conceived?" *Jahrebuch für Recht und Ethik*, Vol. 3, pp. 103–120.

Ruggie, J. G. 2008. *Protect, Respect and Remedy: A Framework for Business and Human Rights* (Geneva: Human Rights Council).
Shue, H. 1988. "Mediating Duties." *Ethics*, Vol. 98, No. 4, pp. 687–704.
Young, I. M. 2004. "Responsibility and Global Labor Justice." *Journal of Political Philosophy*, Vol. 12, No. 4, pp. 365–388.
Zerk, J. A. 2006. *Multinationals and Corporate Social Responsibilities: Limitations and Opportunities in International Law* (Cambridge: Cambridge University Press).

39

The ethics of international human rights non-governmental organizations

Daniel A. Bell

International human rights and humanitarian non-governmental organizations (INGOs) are major players on the world stage. An INGO is defined here as an organization with substantial autonomy to decide upon and carry out human rights and/or humanitarian projects in different regions around the world. According to this definition, the Danish Institute for Human Rights, for example, is an INGO because it has substantial autonomy to decide upon and carry out projects in Asia, Africa, and elsewhere (though its funds come largely from the Danish Ministry of Foreign Affairs and most of its staff is Danish). The core mission of a human rights INGO is to criticize human rights violations and/or promote human rights in various ways (in contrast, say, to religious organizations that may promote human rights as a by-product of missionary work). Humanitarian organizations may employ the normative language of human rights, but they are distinguished by what they do, that is providing immediate assistance to those whose rights (especially the rights to food and decent health care) are being violated. These missions often overlap in practice, and some organizations, such as OXFAM, do both. INGOs fund human rights projects, actively participate in human rights and humanitarian work, and criticize human rights violations in foreign lands. They work in cooperative networks with each other, with local NGOs, and with international organizations. They consult and lobby governments and international organizations, sometimes participating in high-level negotiations and diplomacy for global policy development. They cooperate and negotiate with economic and political organizations in the field for the implementation of their projects, whether this be monitoring or assistance. In short, they are generating a new type of political power, the purpose of which is to secure the vital interests of human beings on an international scale, regardless of state boundaries.

Needless to say, good intentions are not always sufficient to produce desirable results. In an imperfect and unpredictable world, human rights INGOs often face ethical dilemmas that constrain their efforts to do good in foreign lands. How do people who want to do good behave when they meet obstacles? Is it justifiable to sacrifice some good in the short term for more good in the long term? And which human rights concerns should have priority? Like other organizations, INGOs are constrained by scarce time and resources and must choose between competing goods. Human rights practitioners experience hard choices, compromises, and prioritizing as ongoing features of their moral world. In such cases, long lists of fairly abstract desiderata such as the Universal Declaration of Human Rights that do not take into account real-world constraints do not help much. So how do human rights INGOs set their moral priorities? On what basis do they choose how to do good, and where to do it? How should their decisions be critically evaluated? Can their choices be improved? What role, if any, can theorizing about human rights contribute to these questions?

In this chapter, I will discuss the ethical challenges encountered by human rights INGOs as they attempt to do good at home and abroad and to refine thinking on the relative merits and demerits of ways of dealing with those challenges. These organizations are often viewed as "good" counterweights to authoritarian state power and exploitative multinationals or "bad" agents of liberal capitalism and Western values. A more nuanced evaluation of human rights INGOs needs to delineate the typical constraints and dilemmas they face in their attempts to achieve their aims. The idea is to see what kinds of questions and problems emerge when one thinks of human rights from the perspective of people or organizations who have to make choices about how best to promote rights in concrete contexts, rather than simply from the perspective of abstract theory or even general policy recommendations. Such knowledge is essential for minimizing the harm unintentionally done by lack of knowledge of how the world actually works. On the other hand, the conceptual resources, normative frameworks, and historical knowledge provided by academic theorists might help to guide moral prioritizing of human rights INGOs as they choose between different possible ways of doing good. Moral theorizing that is sensitive to actual constraints of practitioners can perhaps provide a sounder basis for decision-making than ad hoc adaptation to less-than-ideal circumstances.

This chapter is divided into three sections that correspond roughly to themes that have generated the most debate in the aforementioned dialogues: the ethical challenges associated with interaction between relatively rich and powerful Western-based human rights INGOs and recipients of their aid in the South; whether and how to collaborate with governments that place severe restrictions on the activities of human rights INGOs; and the tension between expanding the organization's mandate to address more fundamental social and economic problems and restricting it for the sake of focusing on more immediate and clearly identifiable violations of civil and political rights.

Northern INGOs and Southern aid recipients: the challenge of unequal power

Most human rights and humanitarian INGOs are based in the West. With their executives and offices centralized in key Western cities, program officers and coordinators are then sent in the field. As Alex de Waal (2001, p. 15) notes, "[i]n its basic structure, the ethics business is like many global businesses [with] its headquarters in a handful of Western centers, notably New York, Washington and London." From a practical point of view, this may create a special challenge in foreign lands where detailed knowledge of different linguistic, social, cultural, and economic circumstances is more likely to ensure success. The history of aid projects in the developing world is littered with blunders that could have been avoided with more detailed local knowledge (Edwards 1999). It is not merely a strategic matter of understanding and using "the other" for the purpose of promoting one's fixed moral agenda, however. INGO representatives must also grapple with ethical dilemmas that arise when they are trying to help people in poor Southern countries.

The need to raise funds has generated ethical questions within human rights INGOs. International non-governmental organizations reliant on public support must choose between dubious but effective fund-raising tactics that enhance their capacity to do work on behalf of human rights and "appropriate" methods that limit fund-raising success and constrain its ability to do good. Betty Plewes and Rieky Stuart of Oxfam Canada condemn the "pornography of poverty," vivid images of helpless, passive poor and starving Third World peoples that are used by Northern-based INGOs to raise money from the public for their development work. Emotional appeals of this sort based on notions of guilt and charity have been relatively effective at raising funds:

> [In 2004] in Canada the five largest NGOs (mainly child sponsorship organizations) raised over $300 million from private donations ... [Child sponsorship organizations] tell us that these images of misery and passive victimization generate much more in donations than alternatives they have tested, and that it is vital to raise large amounts of money in order to be able to carry out relief and development work.

Such images, however, convey other more destructive images.

Messages like these can undermine INGOs' efforts to create a broader understanding of the underlying structures causing poverty and injustice. These images portray people as helpless victims, dependent and unable to take action, and convey a sense that development problems can only be solved by Northern charity. They ignore Northern complicity in creating inequality. At the very least they convey a limited picture of life in Southern countries. At their worse they reinforce racist stereotypes.

In view of the drawbacks associated with charity-based approaches, Oxfam Canada rejects pornography of poverty images and instead uses positive images of poor people improving their lives and clever or ironic images, such as its award-winning ad during the O. J. Simpson trial that used only text to compare the amount of media coverage of that event with the much smaller coverage of the Rwanda genocide taking place at the same time. The problem, however, is that "good" NGOs may get penalized because other NGOs may not have such scruples regarding fund-raising practices. As Keith Horton and Chris Roche (2007a, p. 8) note, "the obvious way to tackle such problems is by binding agreements not to engage in practices that are harmful at the collective level."

Human rights INGOs also disburse aid to relatively poor Southern hemisphere countries, and this gives rise to another source of tension. On the one hand, INGO grantmakers need to set clear mandates and do their best to secure successful outcomes. On the other hand, human rights aid is often most effective if grantees play an important role in articulating and pursuing what they perceive to be the most pressing problems in their local (Southern) communities. These conflicting desiderata are discussed by Mona Younis, formerly program officer for the Mertz Gilmore Foundation.

The Mertz Gilmore Foundation (MGF), one of the leading US human rights funders, is known in the philanthropic community for its readiness to fund controversial issues that most grantmakers are reluctant to support. It prides itself on being field-driven, with program staff members taking their cues regarding needs and opportunities from the respective fields with which they are engaged. MGF also provides direct funding to grantees so that they could be more autonomous and responsive to local concerns, as well as open-ended renewable funding that affords grantees a certain amount of security.

Taking its cues from local human rights groups in the South, MGF recognized the focus on economic and social rights (ESR) as well as the interconnection between ESR and civil and political rights (CPR). In the beginning of 2003, it decided to focus grantmaking on economic rights where even a small amount of resources can make a substantial difference in poor countries, in contrast to the traditional focus on civil and political liberties by US human rights groups. The problem, however, is that it is difficult to monitor the success of grants scattered abroad to organizations without Western-style standards of due diligence. As Younis notes:

> few U.S. foundations are willing to support grassroots groups abroad because of the costs involved in administering such grants and concerns regarding due diligence. Faced with a chicken–egg predicament – local groups require funding to establish institutions capable of meeting the standards of due diligence that funders require of groups they fund – U.S. funders and foreign grantseekers may not meet and grantmakers may continue to prefer funding Northern intermediaries.

In the case of the Mertz Gilmore Foundation, its initial foray into ESC rights-focused funding and direct support for NGOs in poor countries came to an abrupt end, partly because the foundation's board doubted the effectiveness of scattered grants around the world. Instead, MGF decided to focus entirely on social and economic justice issues inside the USA.

Larger foundations, such as Ford and the Open Society Institute, do continue to disburse human rights aid to grantees in the South. But these grantees often need to change their organizational structure and conceptions of priorities in order to obtain funding and support from wealthy Northern INGOs. This pressure to "institutionalize" and "professionalize" means that local NGOs can lose vital linkages to their constituencies, which ultimately limits their capacity to effect social change. As Younis puts it:

> Emulating human rights NGOs in the North, where for decades human rights work has been treated as the preserve of lawyers and legal experts, would discourage participation – a vital resource in the global South. Given that even U.S.-based human rights groups now lament their limited reach into and engagement with the U.S. public and the resulting failure to establish solid constituency-based support for human rights, is it wise for U.S. funders to promote the same professional model for groups in the South?

Such dilemmas are further explored by Steven Weir, the Asia and Pacific Director of Habitat for Humanity (HFH). HFH is an INGO founded in the USA in 1976 with the goal of helping people acquire adequate housing, which the organization sees as a basic human right and a prerequisite for the effective enjoyment of many other rights. Its mission is to secure the right to housing without discriminating against any ethnic group, religion, or sex. In practice, however, trade-offs must be made. Weir notes that "[t]he contextual reality for NGOs is characterized by tradeoffs between competing human rights and more frequently, between human rights and cultural norms that stand in opposition to human rights as they are defined in various UN texts." The drawbacks of imposing human rights norms on reluctant "benefactors" is illustrated with HFH's experience in Fiji and Papua New Guinea. HFH insisted that its projects be structured according to Western-style democratically elected rotating local boards, but this conflicted with the chiefly system that overseas local matters. Because HFH's methodology insulted the local chief and was anathema to the villagers, its projects were relatively ineffective. In response to such experiences, HFH has developed different ways of dealing with the conflict between human rights and local cultural norms.

One response is to distinguish between short-term and long-term ways of challenging local cultural norms that conflict with human rights norms, with immediate focus on "errors of commission" and "errors of omission" being challenged later: "For example, affiliates who discriminate in favor of the relatives of local committee members or fellow church members are immediately put on probation while an uneven distribution of homeowner ethnicity and religion is corrected in the long run by improving systems development and continued monitoring for conformance." Another strategy is to compromise on the human rights norm itself, on the assumption that some change is better than none. For example, HFH favors gender equity on local boards, but it compromises with local patriarchal norms by not insisting on more than 30 percent representation by women. A demand for full equality would not only be impractical, Weir notes, it would also conflict with HFH's commitment to local participation and control over the process. Perhaps the most culturally sensitive response is to allow for institutional learning in response to input from non-Western cultures. In the case of Fiji and Papua New Guinea, HFH created a broader regional organizational structure with a network of sub-committees or satellite branches that respect the local chiefly tradition, a strategy that seems to be resulting in increased cooperation and sustainability.

Bonny Ibhawoh draws on these dilemmas of North–South interaction and aims to provide constructive guidance to understanding and addressing them. Ibhawoh argues that the main problem does not lie in the geographical imbalance of the organizational structures of most human rights INGOs. Although based in the North, many INGOs have developed strong representations and networks in the South that keep them well connected with local situations. Moreover, Southern NGOs do not always welcome more INGO presence in their communities. In post-authoritarian African states such as South Africa and Nigeria, the influx of better-funded INGOs in the late 1990s was seen as undermining the local human rights NGOs and hampering their capacity-building efforts. In the competition for scarce donor funds, there was concern that the more influential INGOs would get funds for local projects that would otherwise have gone to them. Ibhawoh suggests a division of labor, with the larger and more established INGOs working with local NGOs to pursue domestic objectives.

The main challenge to the legitimacy of Northern-based INGOs lies in the ideological framework that underpins much of their work: "The first component is the hapless victim in distress; the second is the non-Western government whose action or inaction caused the violation; and the third component is the rescuer – the human rights INGO, the external aid agency, the international institution or even the journalist covering the story – whose interest is seen as inseparable from that of the victim." This framework is problematic because it assumes that the primary responsibility for human rights abuses lie with Southern governments and, consequently, pays insufficient attention to how the structures of globalization negatively affect human rights conditions in the South. This tendency is linked to another problematic feature of INGO work, namely, the disproportionate concern with civil and political rights at the expense of social and economic rights. Ibhawoh points to studies that draw links between the operations of international financial institutions and transnational corporations and human rights abuses in Third World countries, and he argues that Northern INGOs should pay more attention to the negative impact of economic globalization on economic rights in the South.

Another challenge for Northern INGOs lies in the conflict between human rights norms and local cultural norms. "Culture talk" has been (mis)used by privileged elites in the Asian and African values debates for the purpose of holding on to power, but Ibhawoh notes that in some cases the deployment of culture talk to challenge the work of INGOs has deeper social roots. Ndubisi Obiorah raised the example of human rights workers in Nigeria who welcome the work of INGOs in the country but state that it would be very difficult, given local cultural and religious beliefs, to press for gay and lesbian rights. In such cases, Ibhawoh suggests that the INGO need not alter its normative vision, but it can either opt for a gradualist approach to promote the contested right in the long term or it can confront the injustice head-on, similar to the uncompromising US civil rights movement. Neither approach is ideal, however.

The gradualist approach carries the cost of sending the message that the interests of vulnerable and marginalized minorities do not rank high as a priority, and the confrontational approach risks alienating local communities and partners in the South and undermining the rest of the work of the human rights INGO.

INGOs and governments: the challenge of dealing with states that restrict the activities of INGOs

Human rights INGOs often need to grapple with the question of whether or not to deal with governments to help remedy human rights violations. One important area of controversy is the issue of government funding for INGOs. Many INGOs do accept government funds, and the main advantage, of course, is that they can carry out their projects without wasting too much time and money on fund-raising efforts. This raises questions about their independence, however: "Many of the largest and most respectable INGOs of today (such as Save the Children and Oxfam) were born and raised in opposition to government policy and vested interests at the time. But can this role continue when Northern NGOs are becoming more and more dependent on government support?" (Hulme and Edwards 1997, p. 280).

The dilemmas of dependence on government funds are vividly illustrated by Lyal Sunga of the University of the Raoul Wallenberg Institute of Human Rights and Humanitarian Law. Sunga discusses the acute dilemmas forced upon INGOs working in coalition-occupied Iraq. Prior to the war, most INGOs vociferously denounced the Bush/Blair arguments for invading and occupying Iraq. Some representatives of INGOs did meet with US government officials to clarify the extent to which they could operate freely inside Iraq, but US government officials offered funds on the condition of a formation of a clear chain of command between US authorities and INGOs.

The demise of the Saddam government flung the door wide open for INGOs to enter the country and set up their own operations, and the pre-war fears over the independence, neutrality, and impartiality of INGOs proved to be well founded. In effect, the Bush administration forced NGOs either to disagree publicly with the US government's policies or to quietly accept USAID funding for Iraq-related programs and surrender their prerogative to criticize US policy, even if they felt that the use of military force worsened the humanitarian situation. Several INGOs, including the International Rescue Committee, CARE, and World Vision, made the difficult decision not to seek USAID funding under these conditions.

The independence of INGOs that chose to work in Coalition-occupied Iraq was further curbed by being forced to rely on Coalition authorities for security. The US government linked the presence of INGOs in Iraq as an indicator of the Coalition's success, "thereby identifying NGOs with US policy and politicizing NGO work throughout the country." Moreover, the White House policy to bring humanitarian aid to Iraq through the Department of Defense meant that soldiers were assigned to carry out humanitarian tasks in addition to their usual military duties, a policy that led to the erroneous impression among ordinary Iraqis that NGOs cooperating with Coalition forces supported the Coalition's invasion and occupation of Iraq. Many INGOs were concerned that their personnel would be indistinguishable from soldiers and thus be made the targets of attack, and they decided to leave the country.

Sunga draws implications for INGOs working in conflict zones. He argues that accepting funding from a belligerent in an armed conflict should not necessarily undermine an INGO's independence from government, because not all governments have adopted the hardline approach of USAID and the Bush administration. But when a government forces INGOs to toe the line, the kinds of dilemmas experienced in Iraq are inevitable. Sunga therefore favors a division of labor between human rights INGOs, whose calling is to draw attention in the most effective manner to human rights violations, and humanitarian INGOs, whose mission is to relieve suffering by extending assistance on a neutral basis and to refrain from political commentary.

But humanitarian INGOs may also face ethical challenges in cases where their individual actions in themselves may be good but the combination of actions may be to buttress evil governments and military groups. For example, the collective presence and action of INGOs in the Great Lakes region of Africa in the 1990s may have allowed the perpetrators of genocide to regroup and manipulate relief supplies and other refugees (Horton and Roche 2007b, p. 6; Bell and Carens 2004). An appropriate response might be cooperation among humanitarian agencies to resist the manipulation of aid by ill-intentioned authorities, but this is easier said than done (Cullity 2007).

Another important area of controversy regards the pros and cons of collaborating with less-than-democratic governments, such as that of China. INGOs such as the Ford Foundation and the Danish Center for Human Rights focus on the necessity of collaborating with such governments in order to achieve any improvement in human rights or any success in pursuing humanitarian goals. It is obvious that such governments do not welcome critical perspectives from outside forces (not to mention inside forces), which puts human rights and humanitarian INGOs in a difficult position. Nonetheless, the INGO "engagers" argue that the advantages of collaboration outweigh the disadvantages.

The Danish Institute for Human Rights (DIHR) adopts a collaborative approach. The DIHR has been funding and supporting various human rights projects in China, including a program concerned with the prevention and use of torture and ill-treatment by police in the pre-trial phase, another program designed to train Chinese legal scholars and practitioners in European law and practice, a human rights center in a provincial capital, a project providing legal aid to women, and a death penalty study. These activities require active collaboration with the government sector: "In authoritarian states, where the local NGOs might be few or non-existent within certain sectors, cooperation with governments might be the only option." It would be a mistake, the DIHR implies, to always view less-than-democratic governments as evil perpetrators of human rights abuses. Sometimes, government officials are sincerely committed to improving the rights situation in selected areas. Where human rights violations do occur, this may be due to institutional inertia rather than to active state-willed perpetration of violations. It could also be due to lack of technical skills and know-how, and the government might welcome INGO aid in this respect. In sum, "the successful cases demonstrate that it is indeed possible to obtain very good results even in authoritarian regimes."

The DIHR recognizes that there is an obvious drawback associated with this partnership with less-than-democratic governments approach: INGOs working in China often choose to "avoid politically sensitive issues" such as labor rights, press freedom, and the political rights of dissidents and "avoid politically sensitive places" such as Tibet and Xinjiang. Thus the DIHR argues for an international division of labor, with organizations such as Human Rights Watch adopting a confrontational approach while engagers such as DIHR cooperate with governments on long-term projects.

INGOs and economic rights: the challenge of dealing with global poverty

The two largest human rights INGOs – Amnesty International (AI) and Human Rights Watch (HRW) – traditionally focused exclusively on civil and political rights (CP) rights, but both organizations have decided to expand their concerns to include work in the area of economic, social, and cultural (ESC) rights. In the case of HRW, however, the organization has reason to limit its work on ESC rights, according to Kenneth Roth, Executive Director of HRW.

Effectiveness is the key here. In Roth's view, human rights INGOs such as HRW (as distinct from national and local ones) tend to be most effective when they employ the methodology he calls "shaming": investigating, documenting, and publicizing behavior by states (and some non-state actors) that conflicts with international human rights norms. For the shaming methodology to work, Roth writes, "clarity is needed about three issues: violation, violator, and remedy. That is, we must be able to show persuasively that a particular state of affairs amounts to a violation of human rights standards, that a particular violator is principally or significantly responsible, and that there is a widely accepted remedy for the violation." Roth argues that these requirements can often be met, even when dealing with ESC rights.

Roth argues that these three conditions for effective shaming usually coincide in the realm of civil and political rights, but that they tend to operate independently in the realm of ESC rights. He suggests that the nature of the violation, violator, and remedy is clearest when it is possible to identify arbitrary or discriminatory governmental conduct that causes or substantially contributes to an ESC violation, but that these three dimensions are less clear when the ESC shortcoming is largely a problem of distributive justice. In those circumstances, human rights INGOs that employ a shaming methodology should refrain from intervention because they will not be able to have any significant impact on the problem. Roth is careful to point out that his argument applies only to INGOs working in countries away from their organizational base, not to local and national NGOs which often employ methodologies besides shaming and have clearer standing to speak out about the proper direction of politically contested national policies in their own states. He also specifies that his argument does not apply to INGOs addressing the domestic or foreign policy of their "home" governments, where they have standing comparable to that of a local human rights group.

Roth's critics do not accept Roth's view that there is such a tight link between the effectiveness of human rights INGOs and the methodology of shaming. What Roth sees as pragmatic, they see as unduly cautious and conservative. Ibhawoh, for example, recognizes that INGOs will have difficulty promoting some economic rights using the "naming and shaming" method that has been employed for the promotion of civil and political rights, but he argues that INGOs should learn from organizations in the South that have successfully used new methodologies for advocacy of economic rights, such as education and mass mobilization: "rather than argue that ESC rights are 'not doable' the focus should be on fashioning new tools for the task ahead." A related argument is that the focus on effectiveness might draw attention away from what is really important. If the most severe and extensive violations of human rights stem not from the misbehavior of authoritarian rulers but from the global maldistribution of wealth and power and from structural features of the international political and economic systems, then to limit the activities of the international human rights organizations to problems where there are clear standards, a clear culprit, and a clear remedy may render the organizations irrelevant to the most important struggles for justice today.

Like HRW, Amnesty International recently expanded its mission to include ESC rights. This decision followed lengthy internal debate, as noted by Curt Goering, Deputy Executive Director of Amnesty International USA. AI members raised a number of objections to the change, many of which were tied to the impact of change on the effectiveness of the organization. Some feared that expanding the mandate to include ESC rights would cause the organization to lose its clear focus and make its work too diffuse. They pointed out that there was still a lot of work to be done in existing areas of concern. Some worried that the inclusion of ESC rights in AI's mandate would blur what had been a clear organizational identity and jeopardize AI's hard-won reputation for consistency, credibility, and impartiality. Also, there was worry it could undermine the unity and cohesion of the movement because they felt that there was not the same degree of consensus within the membership of AI and within the wider public about the moral status of ESC rights as there was about the moral status of CP rights, in part because it is often much harder to establish standards for ESC rights or to determine what constitutes a violation of them. Still another concern was that the organization did not have the expertise to address issues of ESC rights and that, if AI attempted to acquire the necessary expertise, it would lead to an undesirable shift in power away from the membership toward the professional staff.

Despite these powerful objections, AI decided to expand its mission to include ESC rights within its ambit of concern. According to Goering, three lines of argument played a particularly important role in identifying the advantages of an expanded mandate and in overcoming the objections to change. First, the focus on CP rights had sometimes led to misguided priorities that implicitly downplayed or ignored the sometimes more serious areas of human suffering. One example frequently cited in internal debates was Sudan, "where in 1994 the government engaged in massive displacement of local populations and destruction of their crops and food reserves, and it was difficult to explain why AI treated the shooting and torture of a few victims as human rights violations and the manufactured starvation of thousands as background." Second, there was strong support for an expansion of AI's mandate among its branches in the South: "importantly to an organization that strived to be truly international, the CP focus was also seen as a barrier to development of AI's structure and membership in the South." Third, AI responded to the argument that its CP focus was biased towards male concerns: "Some noted that women's experience of human rights is often different to men's: property rights and reproductive rights, and the rights to health, education and nutrition were some of these areas." In the end, the vast majority of AI members found the arguments for expanding the formal mission of the organization more persuasive than the arguments for the status quo.

As the world's largest human rights INGO with substantial grassroots support in the South and extensive cooperative links with Southern human rights NGOs, AI may have less of a need to prioritize rights and methodologies compared to smaller Western-based organizations. Still, it is worth asking if AI is spreading itself out too thin. The problem may not be that it has incorporated ESC rights but rather that it does not prioritize them relative to other rights. Thomas Pogge of Yale University argues that human rights INGOs should focus first and foremost on the elimination of severe poverty and they should concentrate their resources in places that offer the most favorable environments for the cost-effective reduction of severe poverty, rather than seek to spread their projects out in many different countries.

Relying on quantitative methods as well as the arguments of contemporary philosophers, Pogge puts forward the following moral principle governing INGO conduct: "Other things being equal, an INGO should choose among candidate projects on the basis of the cost effectiveness of each project, defined as its moral value divided by its cost. Here a project's moral value is the harm protection it achieves, that is, the sum of the moral values of the harm reductions (and increases) this project would bring about for the individual persons it affects." On this basis, he argues that INGOs have an obligation to concentrate their limited funds in places that allow for the cost-effective reduction of severe poverty. Since efficiency tends to be higher in countries with better government policies and/or a higher incidence of poverty, this would mean concentrating funds in a few countries: Pogge names Ethiopia, Uganda, India, and Bangladesh as likely worthy candidates of INGO aid.

One problem with Pogge's view is that he may be underestimating the difficulty of measuring the effectiveness of aid designed to relieve poverty. Joseph Carens articulates other objections to Pogge's view. He notes that few INGOs would disagree with Pogge's argument that INGOs have responsibilities to both the poor and oppressed abroad and to the contributors on whose behalf they set priorities. The problem is, "[w]hat if the contributors' own views of their moral responsibilities – the ones they want the INGOs to carry out – lead to different priorities from the ones that flow from Pogge's principle? Should the INGOs adopt Pogge's priorities or those of their contributors?" Carens responds that even if we assume that the INGOs are convinced by Pogge's argument, they could not (justifiably) override the views of contributors that cannot be so convinced. One reason is practical: "if an INGO were to persist in a course that its contributors regarded as morally wrong and the contributors learned this, the INGO would lose its contributors and so soon would have no funds to spend." The second reason is moral: "The people running the INGOs are not morally free to follow their own moral views (by hypothesis here, Pogge's principle) and to disregard those of their contributors, precisely because of the trustee relationship between INGOs and contributors to which Pogge has drawn our attention."

As Keith Horton and Chris Roche (2007b) note, however, the view of INGOs as purely voluntary associations that owe obligations first and foremost to contributors can be challenged from two directions. If those living in developed countries are in fact obliged to assist those living in extreme poverty, human rights INGOs could be seen as executors of those obligations. Second, the recipients of aid may also have an important role in determining the practices of INGOs. So the original will of the contributors may be only one factor among several that ought to influence the priorities of NGOs.

One common theme that emerges from dialogues between theorists and practitioners is that human rights INGOs always have to compromise to some extent. As William Pace of the World Federalist Movement put it, NGOs make constant priority calculations in order to be most effective in their actions. But normative values often conflict in practice and the NGOs face ethical challenges as they make priority calculations. By shedding light on the ethical challenges typically encountered by those trying to do good in the international arena and putting forward suggestions for better ways of dealing with those challenges, it is hoped that mistakes can be avoided, moral outlooks improved, and human rights more effectively implemented.

Acknowledgments

This chapter is a condensed and updated version of the introduction to Daniel A. Bell and Jean-Marc Coicaud, eds., *Ethics in Action: The Ethical Challenges of International Non-governmental Organizations* (New York: Cambridge University Press/United Nations University Press, 2007). Unless otherwise indicated, I have quoted from the introduction to that book. The introduction draws on the multiyear dialogues on human rights between high-level representatives of human rights INGOs and prominent academics from various backgrounds and disciplines that work on the subject of human rights and I am grateful to the participants in those dialogues. The unattributed quotes in this entry are drawn from these dialogues and have been checked with the participants and published in the introduction to *Ethics in Action*. I would also like to thank Keith Horton who forwarded some papers presented at a dialogue between human rights practitioners and theorists on the theme "Ethical Questions for Non-Governmental Organizations," 18–20 July 2007 in Melbourne.

References

Bell, Daniel A. and Joseph H. Carens. 2004. "The Ethical Dilemmas of International Human Rights and Humanitarian NGOs: Reflections on a Dialogue Between Practitioners and Theorists." *Human Rights Quarterly*, Vol. 26, No. 2, pp. 317–320.

Cullity, Gareth. 2007. "Compromised Humanitarianism." Paper presented at conference on Ethical Questions for Non-Governmental Organizations, Melbourne, 18–20 July.

de Waal, Alex. 2001. "The Moral Solipsism of Global Ethics Inc." *London Review of Books*, Vol. 23, No. 16, p. 15.

Edwards, Michael. 1999. *Future Positive: International Cooperation in the 21st Century* (London: Earthscan).

Horton, Keith and Chris Roche. 2007a. "Introduction to Project on Ethical Questions for Non-Governmental Organizations." Melbourne, 18–20 July.

Horton, Keith and Chris Roche. 2007b. "Afterword to Project on Ethical Questions for Non-Governmental Organizations." Melbourne, 18–20 July.

Hulme, David and Michael Edwards. 1997. "Too Close to the Powerful, Too Far from the Powerless." In *NGOs, States and Donors: Too Close For Comfort?* (New York: Palgrave Macmillan).

40

International financial institutions and their impacts on human rights

Current and prospective research

M. Rodwan Abouharb

Introduction

Recent protests in Seattle, Washington DC, Prague, Turin, and Buenos Aires have deluged meetings of the World Trade Organization (WTO), International Monetary Fund (IMF), and World Bank, as well as the summits of the Group of 8 (G8) industrialized countries and Summit of the Americas. The common theme across all these protests was the protestors' conviction that these institutions have negative effects in the developing world. Protestors have questioned the motives and criticized the impacts of these institutions on the economies and societies of liberalizing countries. The popular press has reported upon the activities of these institutions extensively. There has been considerable criticism of the austerity measures used by the IMF and World Bank, especially their key tool, structural adjustment agreements, and the harsh human rights consequences of these agreements in developing countries.

Stepping back and taking a deep breath we might want to ask, is all this criticism warranted? How can we be sure that the effects of World Bank and IMF structural adjustment worsen the human rights of citizens in developing countries? Another way of asking this question might be: would these countries have worsened their human rights record even if the World Bank and IMF had not become involved? Similar critical questions might be: don't these institutions help countries in crisis, which may also be those countries most likely to have a bad human rights record anyway? All these questions indicate that there may be something particular about the countries that go under these programs in the first place, what has been described as a "selection issue" in the literature. Indeed, it may be that these countries already had bad human rights records and that one should not blame the World Bank and IMF for helping countries most in need. Defenders of these institutions and the structural adjustment process (Rogoff 2003) make a number of compelling arguments. Most important is the argument that these institutions assist those countries that are in economic difficulties. In fact, they argue that if these international financial institutions had not entered the fray, the consequences would have been much worse. Thus, any negative human rights consequences are not because of the IMF or World Bank but rather the underlying difficult situation that these countries faced in the first place. Moreover, why should structural adjustment programs (SAPs) have any consequences for human rights violations? Has the academic community generated any answers when trying to assess the impact of these institutions?

In short, yes, the conclusions of recent studies, which have controlled for what have become known as "issues of selection," have concluded that SAPs promoted by the World Bank and IMF have worsened government respect for a variety of human rights (Abouharb and Cingranelli 2006, 2007, 2009). They examined the effects of World Bank and IMF SAPs in 131 developing countries between 1981 and 2003, and found after controlling for the effects of selection that the effects of SAPs have been to worsen government respect for physical integrity rights that include the right not to be murdered, politically imprisoned, or extra-judicially killed. The consequences of these SAPs have also worsened government respect for economic and social rights, as well as workers' rights (Abouharb and Cingranelli 2007).

The most recent round of quantitative research has provided considerable support for earlier qualitative and quantitative research that did not account for these underlying selection issues. The negative consequences of these programs on both the economic and physical integrity rights of citizens in the developing world have been documented in much of the qualitative literature (Buchmann 1996; Chipeta 1993; Commonwealth Secretariat 1989; Daddieh 1995; Elson 1990; Fields 2003; Friedman 2000; Handa and King 1997; Meyer 1998; Munck 1994; Sadasivam 1997; Structural Adjustment Participatory Review International Network (SAPRIN) 2004; Sowa 1993; World Bank 1992; Zack-Williams 2000). In comparison the quantitative literature examining the economic consequences of SAPs has been far more divided on its effects. Early quantitative research described the furor in the qualitative research about the negative effects of structural adjustment agreements as "much ado about nothing" (Killick 1995). More recent quantitative research has found that countries under SAPs have lower rates of economic growth and higher levels of income inequality than those that never went under these programs in the first place, even controlling for what have been described as issues of selection. These issues of selection mean that already poorly performing countries participating in these programs might have worsened economic outcomes regardless of intervention from international financial institutions (Przeworski and Vreeland 2000; Vreeland 2002, 2003). In the context of this research, issues of selection would mean that countries undergoing these programs might have worse government levels of human rights regardless of involvement with the World Bank and IMF. While there seems to be a great deal of evidence linking SAPs to worsened physical integrity rights as well as economic and social rights outcomes, we may wish to ask, why should SAPs be linked to human rights violations in the first place?

This chapter will review the theoretical arguments that link SAPs to human rights repression and consider some of the research examining the effects of these institutions on human rights. The chapter will then examine the different approaches that have been used to assess the effects of international financial institutions (IFIs) and point the reader toward useful research strategies for trying to understand the effects of these institutions. Finally the chapter will indicate areas of future research.

Theoretical linkages between structural adjustment and repression

There are three routes that link SAPs to worsened human rights outcomes in developing countries. Each theoretical linkage stems from what has been described as the threat-repression nexus (Most and Starr 1989; Simon and Starr 1996; Starr 1994). The key argument of the threat repression nexus was that political leaders who believe their regime to be strong and secure will be less likely to violate the human rights of their citizens as a means to maintain political control.

The likelihood of repression increases if they believe that the strength of domestic threats or international threats or both combined is equal or greater than the strength of the regime they wish to protect. They may use repression of human rights as one of the strategies to redress an undesirable imbalance in the strength–threat ratio (Poe 2004). To be sure, testing the theory is complicated, because the regime has multiple strategies or tools available to reach a more desirable ratio of strength to threat. Still, research has shown that domestic threats, especially violent domestic threats, are associated with subsequent increases in the level of repression of civil and political rights (Davenport 1995, 1996; Gurr 1986; Poe 2004; Poe and Tate 1994; Poe et al. 1999). The findings have not been quite as strong and consistent, but many studies also have shown that involvement in international war is associated with increased repression (Poe 2004; Poe and Tate 1994; Poe et al. 1999). The theory of Most and Starr has not yet been explicitly tested, however, because no one has measured the ratio of strength to threat and connected that ratio to repression of various types.

The first route I have described as the "IFI implementation effects," which link IFIs to worsened human rights outcomes and stems from the impact of implementing SAPs that often lower levels of economic growth. The IFI implementation effects argument links the negative economic consequences of SAPs to increased levels of threat regimes face. This increased level of threat is followed by greater repression. This route emphasizes the fact that these programs have worsened an already bad situation. Most of the qualitative research examining the impacts of SAPs has demonstrated the deleterious consequences for many groups within society. In general, structural adjustment agreements (SAAs) require loan recipient states to reduce government spending for social programs (Chipeta 1993; Fields 2003; Handa and King 1997; Sowa 1993; Meyer 1998; World Bank 1992; Zack-Williams 2000). Some studies have emphasized the disproportionate negative economic human rights consequences for women (Buchmann 1996; Commonwealth Secretariat 1989; Elson 1990; Sadasivam 1997), for public sector employees, and for low-wage workers (Daddieh 1995; SAPRIN 2004). The poor and those in the public sector have seen their wages fall in real terms (Daddieh 1995; Munck 1994; SAPRIN 2004; Vreeland 2002), while at the same time they have faced increased living costs due to the removal of price controls and subsidies for essential commodities (Zack-Williams 2000). The implementation of SAAs also has worsened the relative position of the poorest by increasing income inequality (Daddieh 1995; Friedman 2000; Handa and King 1997). Moreover, efforts by developing countries to make their economies more business friendly have resulted in the adoption of policies hostile to worker rights (SAPRIN 2004). Examples demonstrating how the common provisions in SAAs often lead to worsened economic and social outcomes for a broad spectrum of society are numerous and compelling. Recent quantitative research has also found that countries under SAPs have lower rates of economic growth and higher levels of income inequality than those which never went under these programs in the first place, even controlling for issues of selection (Przeworski and Vreeland 2000; Vreeland 2002, 2003).

The consequences of these agreements have lowered levels of economic growth (Przeworski and Vreeland 2000; Vreeland 2003); worsened the human rights situation in many countries (Abouharb and Cingranelli 2007; Franklin 1997; Keith and Poe 2000; Pion-Berlin 1984; McLaren 1998) and also increased probability of civil conflict (Abouharb and Cingranelli 2007; Stiglitz 2002). Political entrepreneurs persuade groups that have lost out to demand a redistribution of power and wealth for that group's benefit. Indeed, one important variant of the threat-repression linkage emphasizes that the main source of domestic conflict within developing countries is the hardship experienced by some segments of their populations. Hardships may be the basis for social movements that threaten elites, who respond with increased repression (Arat 1991;

Blomberg and Hess 2002; Fearon and Laitin 2003; Gurr 2000; Lindstrom and Moore 1995). To the extent that SAPs increase hardships for segments of society, the threat-repression nexus links these hardships to greater protest against the government, which responds with greater repression to maintain control. To be sure there is debate about the extent to which governments undertake all of the policy changes mandated by SAPs (Killick 1995; Van de Walle 2001). The second and third routes of my argument do not rely upon governments implementing the conditions associated with these loans, rather they point to how the very interaction of governments with these IFIs can generate political unrest leading to more repression as governments seek to maintain political control.

The second route described as the "IFI negotiation effects" details how the negotiation of a structural adjustment agreement with these international financial institutions constitutes a marker of government weakness. The negotiation of SAPs often generates a nationalistic backlash against the government for collaborating with "Western Institutions." Opposition groups sensing governmental weakness sanction collective action. This action often includes the use of violence against the government as these groups try to take advantage of this situation for their own political gain. Two examples, the first from Egypt: the government's willingness to negotiate with the IMF was portrayed by the Muslim Brotherhood, which has used violence to further its cause, as further evidence that the government was too friendly with the West (Kienle 2001). In many cases the Egyptian government has responded to such protests with repression of its citizens. In Nigeria, the Shagari administration had assiduously avoided entering into an IMF agreement despite great need because the general public's view toward the IMF was one of "vehement popular antipathy" (Callaghy 1990, p. 269). The government avoided entering into negotiations with the IMF until winning re-election. Having been safely re-elected, the administration decided to enter into structural adjustment negotiations with the IMF. Subsequently, a military coup toppled the civilian administration (Vreeland 2003). Authoritarian regimes such as the one imposed upon the Nigerian population also have worsened human rights records than their democratic counterparts.

The third route described as the "IFI relative deprivation effects" links SAPs to increased levels of domestic unrest by increasing peoples' levels of relative deprivation. Governments that go under IMF SAPs may generate higher expectations from their citizens about the future of the nation's economy. If these expectations are not satisfied, their citizens may feel relatively deprived. Relative deprivation describes the differences between what an individual expects and whether these expectations are satisfied. When their expectations are not satisfied the reaction is often violent (Davies 1969; Feierabend and Feierabend 1966; Gurr 1970). I argue that these programs fail to improve most peoples' socio-economic circumstances. In some cases these programs will actually worsens citizens' conditions. In either case, according to the relative deprivation framework, the failure to improve citizens' socio-economic circumstances or the worsening of them will increase the likelihood that these people respond with violence against their government. In the case of Sierra Leone, there was evidence that the government was implementing many of the conditions associated with the IMF SAP (Keen 2005). However, the socio-economic circumstances of most citizens were made worse by these changes. Keen (2005) notes that civil servants who lent assistance to the rebels in the civil war that took place were most concerned about improving their future economic outcomes. These civil servants were apprehensive about the potential loss of their jobs as the government reduced the size of its bureaucracy under SAP mandates from the IMF. The civil war in Sierra Leone saw some of the worst atrocities by government against its own population in recent times (Berkeley 2001).

Approaches taken to assess the consequences of structural adjustment programs

Previous research has utilized a variety of approaches to assess the macroeconomic consequences of these programs. Understanding the weaknesses of the various approaches is important for those who wish to assess the impacts of SAPS on other areas including human rights. What has become important in the debate about whether these programs have been beneficial or detrimental in the countries that have undertaken them is how one actually assesses their consequences. This discussion is relevant to the broader topic of how one wishes to assess the consequences of any public policy (Collier 1991). The application of a social science framework is critical to understanding the consequences of any policy choice that is made. As our understanding and application of social science frameworks to the topic of public policy outcomes becomes more sophisticated, it is important to examine the validity of previous research given our new knowledge of best practice in these situations. The approaches taken by previous research examining the consequences of structural adjustment fell into four broad categories: planned target method, before and after, with and without, and controlling for issues of selection.

Planned target method

This method was an early approach used by the World Bank and IMF to assess the effectiveness of their programs. The "planned target" method compares what was expected to happen during the period and what actually happened (Mosley et al. 1991, p. 189). This method, however, suffers from a number of limitations. Some have argued that World Bank targets are "optimistic guesses ... and cannot predict exogenous events bearing on the economic outcomes" (Mosley et al. 1991, p. 189). Thus, if a country under-performs economically this may be erroneously attributed to a fault in the design of the program or in its implementation. In fact an under-performing economy may have nothing to do with the design of the program or its implementation. It may be that the indicators examined do not reflect the effects of the program but instead some exogenous factor (Mosley et al. 1991, p. 189).

Before and after approach

This approach compares the situation in a loan recipient state before and after they enter into an agreement. Any change in outcomes of interest is attributed to the loan agreement. Much of the previous research, both qualitative and quantitative, that has examined the consequences of structural adjustment agreements has taken this approach (e.g., Chipeta 1993; Commonwealth Secretariat 1989; Handa and King 1997; Kane 1993; Pastor 1987a, 1987b; Sadasivam 1997; Sklånes 1993; Sowa 1993; Vuorela 1991). The findings across these approaches have been uniformly negative, indicating that the consequences of structural adjustment have had a variety of negative economic affects lowering economic growth, lowering government spending in areas of health and education, lowering personal income, increasing income inequality, reducing protections for workers, and having detrimental economic and social effects on women.

While this approach is intuitive it cannot control for the counterfactual, what would have happened if the country had not gone under a program? A number of authors have noted that a key problem with this approach is that other factors outside of the program that also affect, for example, economic growth, may change over the period under examination (Vreeland 2003; Mosley et al. 1991). Thus, if the situation has improved or worsened in comparison to the time before the countries implemented these programs then one may conclude (incorrectly) that the change in situation is simply due to the imposition of structural adjustment agreements (Mosley et al. 1995). However, this is an inappropriate conclusion because there may well be a myriad of other factors that effect this change (Harrigan and Mosley 1991). Each of these critiques calls for an approach that includes a counterfactual, a counter example of what would have happened had a country not undertaken a structural adjustment agreement from these institutions.

The "with and without" approach

A third approach that is also intuitive is to use a counterfactual method, which explicitly attempts to assess what would have happened in these countries had they not entered into structural adjustment agreements. A number of different procedures have been undertaken utilizing counterfactual econometric simulations and most similar system designs, which paired similar countries that did and did not enter into these agreements and then compared the levels of economic growth across them (Dorosh et al. 1996; Frausum and Sahn 1996; Gylfason 1987; Harrigan and Mosley 1991; Mosley et al. 1995; Sahn 1996). The findings of this approach have varied from indicating that structural adjustment programs have had no macroeconomic effects to marginal effects. In many cases, the findings are sensitive to small changes in the samples of cases used.

The most similar systems design has attracted concern (King et al. 1994; Przeworski and Tuene 1970) because of the difficulty in being able to control for all factors that may have a subsequent impact on economic growth or, in the case of this research, human rights. Nevertheless, the idea of controlling for other factors associated with economic growth as an attempt to tease out the impact of structural adjustment agreements by comparing cases where similar countries did and did not enter into them does control for the impacts of the world economy. The limitation to this approach is that there may be systematic differences between countries that enter into these programs and others that do not. Many of the factors that make countries good candidates for structural adjustment such as economic difficulty are also likely to have an effect on the subsequent success of any agreement. For example, it is possible that a country's economic growth would have declined regardless of a structural adjustment agreement because it was already in economic difficulty. Indeed, a structural adjustment package may actually have made that drop in growth smaller than it would have otherwise been. The problem of course is that without controlling for the factors that affect whether countries enter into these agreements it is difficult to conclude whether the consequences witnessed were a function of structural adjustment or would have taken place anyway.

Controlling for issues of selection

Most of the research that has tried to discern the consequences of SAPs controlling for issues of selection (Achen 1986; Heckman 1988; Przeworski and Vreeland 2000; Vreeland 2002, 2003) has been interested in their economic effects (e.g., Conway 1994; Khan et al. 1990; Przeworksi and Vreeland 2000). More recently research has examined the effects on economic rights (Vreeland 2002; Abouharb and Cingranelli 2007). The concept of selection refers to the idea that the variety of factors that make countries candidates for structural adjustment agreements, such as being in economic difficulty, especially issues such as shortfalls in foreign currency reserves, are also important factors in affecting the macroeconomic conditions conducive to economic growth. The findings of this research have described the consequences of these programs on economic growth as negative. There is also good reason to believe that a number of issues that make countries more likely to need SAPs also make them more likely to violate the human rights of their citizens.

In the context of the present research, one must be able to distinguish whether the negative effects on the human rights practices of governments found by previous research (Franklin 1997; Keith and Poe 2000; McLaren 1988) were the result of the economic difficulties that made the loan recipient country a good candidate for a structural adjustment agreement in the first place or were the consequence of the SAA itself. Single-stage models cannot provide an answer to that question.

Research exists about when countries enter into agreements with the World Bank and IMF (Abouharb and Cingranelli 2004, 2005, 2006, 2007; Joyce 1992; Stone 2004; Przeworski and Vreeland 2000; Vreeland 2003). This literature has found that poor countries, those in economic difficulty, and those with little trade, tend to enter into these programs. Since only certain types of countries enter into these agreements, there may be a "selection effects" bias. Empirical tests that do not account for these selection effects may erroneously blame the World Bank and IMF for making things worse when they were simply trying to help countries in difficulty. The important question here is whether these factors mean that the World Bank and IMF tend to become involved with governments that have lower levels of respect for human rights. If so, then one needs to account for these issues in any subsequent analysis. Empirically one can resolve the selection effects issue by modeling the factors that increase the probability of countries entering into structural adjustment agreements. Inverse Mills ratios from the equation describing which countries enter into structural adjustment agreements can then be included in subsequent models estimating the dependent variable of interest. In this research, inclusion of these ratios allows one to test the effects of SAPs, controlling for the effects of selection on human rights. Existing work has sought to account for these underlying selection effects when estimating the impact of World Bank and IMF structural adjustment agreements on government respect for physical integrity rights (Abouharb and Cingranelli 2006, 2007) and the impact of the IMF on economic growth (Przeworski and Vreeland 2000; Vreeland 2003). To be sure, using ratios would also require the use of a bootstrapping procedure to make sure that standard errors produced are correct (Mooney and Duval 1993). The second point is that while I argue that most of the effects on human rights take place because of the economic consequences of these SAPs, there are additional routes, already noted, that do not rely upon implementation of SAPs to worsened human rights outcomes.

Conclusions: assessing the effects of IFIs on human rights, avoiding the pitfalls

This chapter has indicated the state of best practice for those wishing to conduct theory-driven empirical work assessing the human rights effects of international financial institutions. Two recommendations are offered: the first stresses the importance of using approaches that allow the researcher to understand the effect of a policy change. The second examines the joint effects of these institutions.

The first recommendation concerns trying to understand the effect of any policy change. When trying to understand the consequences of any policy prescription it is critical to be able to distinguish between what would have happened if the policy had not changed. In most empirical work the first step in this process is by collecting data where the structural adjustment was and was not undertaken. The underlying assumption in the first step is that when collected this data will provide a representative sample of the potential range of cases. As we have seen, this approach is not sufficient when governments as well as IFIs have choices about whether or not to undertake these agreements. Thus, one needs to account for the fact that the group of countries undertaking these agreements may constitute a non-random sample of all the countries that could have potentially undertaken these structural adjustment programs. In order to assess the effects of these SAPS one needs to account for the underlying criteria that led governments and institutions to agree to them in the first place in order to assess the effects of these policies on government respect for human rights.

The second recommendation is to emphasize the study of the joint effects of these programs. If one is interested in the consequences of structural adjustment, then one should study the agreement rather than the institutions themselves, since the aims of both the World Bank and IMF are very similar with respect to the purposes of structural adjustment agreements. While this may seem obvious almost all the research to date (with the exception of Abouharb and Cingranelli 2007) has concentrated on one institution or the other rather than on the programs themselves. The focus on either institution, I argue, leads one to underestimate the effects of SAPs.

Areas of future research

There are a variety of areas for future research. Our understanding of what constitutes best practice means that many of the areas examined by earlier research should be revisited. Furthermore the availability of new datasets, such as the Cingranelli and Richards (2004) human rights dataset that examines governments' respect for a wide variety of human rights including physical integrity, economic and social, workers', and women's rights, has also made large sample cross-national time series work examining the consequences of IFIs over a variety of human rights much easier. Many questions remain to be answered, including the effects of IFIs on many economic rights and the rights of children and women. Other issues remain very much in their infancy, such as questions examining the effects of IFIs on democratic rights. There is also much to be done for a better understanding of how the effects of IFIs on government respect may change overtime. All these possibilities mean there is a broad and exciting future research agenda that will not only provide rich theoretical knowledge about how transnational organizations can have significant effects on government respect for human rights, but also provide important policy-relevant information concerning one of the most hotly contested current issues: the impacts of international financial institutions on human thriving.

References

Abouharb, M. R. and D. Cingranelli. 2004. "Human Rights and Structural Adjustment: The Importance of Selection," pp. 127–146 in S. C. Carey and S. C. Poe, eds., *Understanding Human Rights Violations: New Systematic Studies* (Aldershot, UK: Ashgate).

Abouharb, M. R. and D. Cingranelli. 2005. "When the World Bank Says Yes: Determinants of Structural Adjustment Lending," pp. 204–230 in G. Rani, J. R. Vreeland, and S. Kosack, eds., *Globalization and the Nation State: The Impact of the IMF and the World Bank* (London: Routledge).

Abouharb, M. R. and D. Cingranelli. 2006. "The Human Rights Effects of World Bank Structural Adjustment Lending, 1981–2000." *International Studies Quarterly*, Vol. 50, No. 2, pp. 233–262.

Abouharb, M. R. and D. Cingranelli. 2007. *Human Rights and Structural Adjustment* (Cambridge: Cambridge University Press).

Abouharb, M. R. and D. Cingranelli. 2009. "IMF Programs and Human Rights, 1981–2003." *Review of International Organizations*, Vol. 4, No. 1, pp. 47–72.

Achen, Christopher H. 1986. *The Statistical Analysis of Quasi-Experiments* (Berkeley: University of California Press).

Arat, Zehra. 1991. *Democracy and Human Rights in Developing Countries* (Boulder, CO: Lynne Rienner).

Berkeley, Bill. 2001. *The Graves Are Not Yet Full: Race, Tribe and Power in the Heart of Africa* (New York: Basic Books).

Blackmon, P. 2008. "Rethinking Poverty through the Eyes of the International Monetary Fund and the World Bank." *International Studies Review*, Vol. 10, pp. 179–202.
Blomberg, S. B. and G. D. Hess. 2002. "The Temporal Links Between Conflict and Economic Activity." *Journal of Conflict Resolution*, Vol. 46, No. 1, pp. 74–90.
Buchmann, C. 1996. "The Debt Crisis, Structural Adjustment and Women's Education: Implication for Status and Social Development." *International Journal of Comparative Sociology*, vol. 37, pp. 5–30.
Callaghy, T. 1990. "Lost Between State and Market: The Politics of Economic Adjustment in Ghana, Zambia, and Nigeria," pp. 257–319 in J. Nelson, ed., *Economic Crisis and Policy Choice: The Politics of Adjustment in the Third World* (Princeton, NJ: Princeton University Press).
Chipeta, C. 1993. "Malawi," pp. 105–188 in A. Adepoju, ed., *The Impact of Structural Adjustment on the Population of Africa: The Implications for Education, Health, and Employment* (New York: United Nations Population Fund).
Cingranelli, D. L. and D. L. Richards. 2004. The Cingranelli and Richards (CIRI) Human Rights Data Project. At: www.humanrightsdata.org.
Collier, D. 1991. "The Comparative Method: Two Decades of Change," pp. 7–31 in D. Rustow and K. Erickson, eds., *Comparative Political Dynamics: Global Research Perspectives* (New York: HarperCollins).
Commonwealth Secretariat. 1989. *Engendering Adjustment for the 1990s: Report of a Commonwealth Expert Group on Women and Structural Adjustment* (London: Commonwealth Secretariat).
Conway, P. 1994. "IMF Lending Programs: Participation and Impact." *Journal of Development Economics*, Vol. 45, pp. 365–391.
Daddieh, C. 1995. "Structural Adjustment Programs and Regional Integration: Compatible or Mutually Exclusive," pp. 243–271 in K. Mengisteab and B.I. Logan, eds., *Beyond Economic Liberalization in Africa: Structural Adjustments and the Alternatives* (Cape Town: SAPES).
Davenport, C. 1995. "Multi-Dimensional Threat Perception and State Repression: An Inquiry Into Why States Apply Negative Sanctions." *American Journal of Political Science*, Vol. 39, No. 3, pp. 683–713.
Davenport, C. 1996. "Constitutional Promises and Repressive Reality: A Cross National Time Series Investigation of Why Political and Civil Liberties Are Suppressed." *Journal of Politics*, Vol. 58, pp. 627–654.
Davies, J. C. 1969. "The J-Curve of Rising and Declining Satisfactions as Cause of Some Great Revolutions and a Contained Rebellion," pp. 547–576 in H. D. Graham and T. R. Gurr, eds., *Violence in America: Historical and Comparative Perspectives* (Washington, DC: US Government Printing Office).
Dorosh, P., B. Essama-Nssah, and O. Samba-Manadou. 1996. "Terms of Trade and the Real Exchange Rate in the CFA Zone: Implication for Income and Distribution in Niger," pp. 147–182 in D. E. Sahn, ed., *Economic Reform and the Poor in Africa* (Oxford: Oxford University Press).
Elson, D. 1990. "Male Bias in Macro-Economics: The Case of Structural Adjustment," pp. 1–28 in D. Elson, ed., *Male Bias in the Developmental Process* (Manchester: Manchester University Press).
Fearon, J. D. and D. Laitin. 2003. "Ethnicity, Insurgency, and Civil War." *American Political Science Review*, Vol. 97, No. 1, pp. 75–90.
Feierabend, I. K. and R. I. Feierabend. 1966. "Aggressive Behavior Within Polities, 1948–1962: A Cross-National Study." *Journal of Conflict Resolution*, Vol. 10, pp. 249–271.
Fields, A. Belden. 2003. *Rethinking Human Rights for the New Millennium* (New York: Palgrave Macmillan).
Franklin, J. 1997. "IMF Conditionality, Threat Perception, and Political Repression: A Cross-National Analysis." *Comparative Political Studies*, Vol. 30, pp. 576–606.
Frausum, Y. V. and D. E. Sahn. 1996. "Perpetuating Poverty for Malawi's Smallholders: External Shocks and Policy Distortions." pp. 115–141 in D. E. Sahn, ed., *Economic Reform and the Poor in Africa* (Oxford: Oxford University Press).
Friedman, Thomas L. 2000. *The Lexus and the Olive Tree* (New York: Anchor Books).
Gurr, Ted Robert. 1970. *Why Men Rebel* (Princeton, NJ: Princeton University Press).
Gurr, Ted Robert. 1986. "The Political Origins of State Violence and Terror: A Theoretical Analysis," pp. 45–71 in Michael Stohl and George Lopez, eds., *Government Violence and Repression: An Agenda for Research* (Westport, CT: Greenwood Press).
Gurr, Ted Robert. 2000. *People versus States: Minorities at Risk in the New Century* (Washington, DC: United Institutes of Peace).
Gylfason, Thorvaldur. 1987. *Credit Policy and Economic Activity in Developing Countries with IMF Stabilization Programs* (Princeton, NJ: Princeton Studies in International Economics).
Handa, S. and D. King. 1997. "Structural Adjustment Policies, Income Distribution and Poverty: A Review of the Jamaican Experience." *World Development*, Vol. 25, No. 6, pp. 915–930.

Harrigan, J. and P. Mosley. 1991. "Assessing the Impact of World Bank Structural Development Lending, 1980–1987." *Journal of Development Studies*, Vol. 27, No. 3, pp. 63–94.
Heckman, J. J. 1988. "The Microeconomic Evaluation of Social Programs and Economic Institutions." In *Chung-Hua Series of Lectures by Invited Eminent Economists, Number 14* (Taipei: Institute of Economics Academia Sinica).
Joyce, J. P. 1992. "The Economic Characteristics of IMF Program Countries." *Economics Letters*, Vol. 38, pp. 237–242.
Kane, K. 1993. "Senegal," pp. 60–68 in A. Adepoju, ed., *The Impact of Structural Adjustment on the Population of Africa: The Implications for Education, Health, and Employment* (Portsmouth, NH: Heinemann).
Keen, D. 2005. "Liberalization and Conflict." *International Political Science Review*, Vol. 26, No. 1, pp. 73–89.
Keith, L. and S. C. Poe. 2000. "The United States, the IMF, and Human Rights," pp. 273–299 in D. F. Forsythe, ed., *The United States and Human Rights* (Lincoln: University of Nebraska Press).
Khan, M., I. P. Montie, and H. Haque. 1990. "Adjustment with Growth." *Journal of Development Economics*, Vol. 32, pp. 155–179.
Kienle, Eberhard. 2001. *A Grand Delusion: Democracy and Economic Reform in Egypt* (London: I.B. Tauris).
Killick, Tony. 1995. *IMF Programmes in Developing Countries: Design and Impact* (London: Overseas Development Institute).
King, G., R. O. Keohane, and S. Verba. 1994. *Designing Social Inquiry: Scientific Inference in Qualitative Research* (Princeton, NJ: Princeton University Press).
Lindstrom, R. and W. H. Moore. 1995. "Deprived, Rational or Both? 'Why Minorities Rebel' Revisited." *Journal of Political and Military Sociology*, Vol. 23, No. 2, pp.167–190.
McLaren, Lauren M. 1998. "The Effect of IMF Austerity Programs on Human Rights Violations: An Exploratory Analysis of Peru, Argentina, and Brazil." *Annual Meeting,* Midwest Political Science Association.
Meyer, William H. 1998. *Human Rights and International Political Economy in Third World Nations* (Westport, CT: Praeger).
Mooney, Christopher Z. and Robert D. Duval. 1993. *Bootstrapping: A Nonparametric Approach to Statistical Inference* (Newbury Park, CA: Sage).
Mosley, P., J. Harrigan, and J. Toye. 1995. *Aid and Power: The World Bank and Policy Based Lending, Volume 1: Analysis and Policy Proposals* (London: Routledge).
Most, B.A. and H. Starr. 1989. *Inquiry, Logic and International Politics* (Columbia: University of South Carolina Press).
Munck, R. 1994. "Workers, Structural Adjustment, and Concertacion-Social in Latin-America." *Latin American Perspectives*, Vol. 21, No. 3, pp. 90–103.
Pastor, Manuel. 1987a. *The International Monetary Fund and Latin America: Economic Stabilization and Class Conflict* (Boulder, CO: Westview Press).
Pastor, M. 1987b. "The Effects of IMF Programs in the Third World: Debate and Evidence from Latin America." *World Development*, Vol. 15, No. 2, pp. 365–391.
Pion-Berlin, D. 1984. "The Political Economy of State Repression in Argentina," pp. 99–123 in M. Stohl and G. A. Lopez, eds., *The State as Terrorist: The Dynamics of Governmental Violence and Repression* (Westport, CT: Greenwood Press).
Poe, S. C. 2004. "The Decision to Repress: An Integrative Theoretical Approach to the Research on Human Rights and Repression," pp. 16–38 in S. C. Cary and S. C. Poe, eds., *Understanding Human Rights Violations* (Burlington, VT: Ashgate).
Poe, S. C. and C. N. Tate. 1994. "Repression of Physical Integrity in the 1980s: A Global Analysis." *American Political Science Review*, Vol. 88, No. 4, pp. 853–872.
Poe, S. C., C. N. Tate, and L. Keith. 1999. "Repression of the Human Right to Physical Integrity Revisited: A Global Cross-National Study Covering the Years 1976–1993." *International Studies Quarterly*, Vol. 43, pp. 291–313.
Przeworski, Adam and Henry Teune. 1970. *The Logic of Comparative Social Inquiry* (Malaba, FL: Krieger).
Przeworski, A. and J. R. Vreeland. 2000. "The Effects of IMF Programs on Economic Growth." *Journal of Development Economics*, Vol. 62, pp. 385–421.
Rogoff, K. 2003. "The IMF Strikes Back." *Foreign Policy*, Vol. 134, pp. 39–46.
Sadasivam, B. 1997. "The Impact of Structural Adjustment on Women: A Governance and Human Rights Agenda." *Human Rights Quarterly*, Vol. 19, No. 3, pp. 630–655.
Sahn, D. E. 1996. "Economic Reform and Poverty: An Overview," pp. 3–28 in D. E. Sahn, ed., *Economic Reform and the Poor in Africa* (Oxford: Oxford University Press).

Simon, M.V. and H. Starr. 1996. "Extraction, Allocation, and the Rise and Decline of States." *Journal of Conflict Resolution*, Vol. 40, No. 2, pp. 272–297.
Sklånes, Tor. 1993. "The State, Interest Groups and Structural Adjustment in Zimbabwe." *Journal of Development Studies*, Vol. 29, No. 3, pp. 401–428.
Sowa, N. K. 1993. "Ghana," pp. 7–24 in A. Adepoju, ed., *The Impact of Structural Adjustment on the Population of Africa: The Implications for Education, Health, and Employment* (Portsmouth, NH: Heinemann).
Starr, H. 1994. "Revolution and War: Rethinking the Linkage Between Internal and External Conflict." *Political Research Quarterly*, Vol. 47, No. 2, pp. 481–507.
Stiglitz, Joseph E. 2002. *Liberalization and Its Discontents* (New York: W.W. Norton).
Stone, R. 2004. "The Political Economy of IMF Lending in Africa." *American Political Science Review*, Vol. 98, No. 4, pp. 577–592.
Structural Adjustment Participatory Review International Network (SAPRIN). 2004. *Structural Adjustment: The Saprin Report: The Policy Roots of Economic Crisis, Poverty, and Inequality* (London: Zed Books).
Van de Walle, Nicolas. 2001. *African Economies and the Politics of Permanent Crisis, 1979–1999* (Cambridge: Cambridge University Press).
Vreeland, J. R. 2002. "The Effect of IMF Programs on Labor." *World Development*, Vol. 30, No. 1, pp. 21–39.
Vreeland, J. R. 2003. *The IMF and Economic Development* (Cambridge: Cambridge University Press).
Vuorela, Ulla. 1991. "The Informal Sector: Social Reproduction and the Impact of Economic Crisis on Women," pp. 109–124 in H. Campbell and H. Stein, eds., *Tanzania and the IMF: Dynamics of Liberalization* (Harare, Zimbabwe: Southern Africa Political Economy Series Trust).
World Bank. 1992. *The World Bank Operational Manual: Operational Directive Adjustment Lending Policy (OD 8.60)*. At: http://wbln0018.worldbank.org/institutional/manuals/opmanual.nsf.
Zack-Williams, A. B. 2000. "Social Consequences of Structural Adjustment," pp. 59–74 in E. Brown, G. Mohan, R. Milward, and A. B. Zack-Williams, eds., *Structural Adjustment: Theory, Practice and Impacts* (London: Routledge).

41

Transnational corporations and human rights

Elena Pariotti

Globalization, transnational corporations and changes in the structure of law

One of the most relevant effects of globalization on the law concerns the role played by private actors operating in the economic field (Clapham 2006). In particular, transnational corporations (hereinafter TNCs) have acquired not only increasing freedom of movement among legal orders, but also the ability to influence the lawmaking process within the transnational law sphere, as it has been shown by the diffusion of the "new lex mercatoria" (Carbonneau 1990). More generally, it has been widely recognized that corporations play a pervasive role in public national and international policy-making (Addo 1999, p. 3). This awareness has led to the examination of how TNCs can be made responsible and accountable. That is why increasing attention has been given in the literature to situations in which private actors like TNCs may violate or even, as I will show later on, promote human rights. Speaking of the internationalization of human rights in the globalization age means considering the way in which international law addresses non-state actors in order to regulate their conduct and to compel such actors to respect principles, rules, and good practices.

In this chapter, the term "transnational corporations" refers to corporations operating in several countries in multiple jurisdictions. Implicit in TNCs is their capacity to transcend national boundaries and the fact that they are usually limited liability companies. These features seem to be better expressed by the term "transnational corporation" than by the term "multinational enterprise," which often occurs in legal documents on the topic. Corporations becoming transnational can be relevant for human rights when their activity is able to affect individuals, communities, and the environment not only in their home country but also in the host countries, and when their economic and organizational size make them interact with governments.

One of the most recent and innovative trends in the field of human rights and international law is how to properly regulate and deal with the challenges posed by the conduct of private actors such as TNCs (Clapham 2006, 2001, pp. 513–516). Such attention can be justified in two ways. On the one hand, the state has an obligation to protect human rights and to prevent actors subject to state control from infringing the rights of others. On the other hand, according to a more recent perspective, there is a need for TNCs to be directly responsible for human rights violations that they may bring about (Clapham 2001, p. 513). Two main theoretical, doctrinal, and practical problems must be addressed in order to ground and strengthen the new status of TNCs under international law. Such issues deal with, first, the possibility of ascribing legal personality to TNCs under international law and, second, the existence of the horizontal effect of human rights.

Do TNCs have a legal personality under international law?

What is the legal status of TNCs? It is obvious that "the question of responsibility and accountability on the international plane is part of a broader question regarding the legal personality of the MNC" (Jägers 1999, p. 261). Provided that entities owe responsibility under international law if they can be regarded as subjects of international law, i.e., when they have an international legal responsibility, establishing whether TNCs can be held legally responsible under international law requires us to first address the notion of legal personality (Jägers 1999, pp. 261–267). According to the mainstream doctrine, the conditions for being recognized as a legal subject are: (i) being direct addressees of norms containing rights and duties; and (ii) having the *jus standi* (and *locus standi*), or procedural competencies before international tribunals, on the basis of these norms. According to different doctrines, both of them or only one of them are required.

Of course, the lack of an explicit recognition of legal personality to TNCs may prevent the construction of effective enforcement mechanisms for human rights when they are violated by TNCs. However, there is not complete agreement on the question of the relationship between the legal basis for TNCs' human rights responsibilities or on the possibility of ascribing legal personality and legal subjectivity to TNCs. A trend has emerged that is willing to ascribe legal personality to TNCs in a weaker sense than that of the state's legal personality. Some positions maintain that there is a close nexus between legal personality and legal responsibility; other positions deny such a nexus.

The latter perspective rests on a view of international law whereby the multiplication of relevant actors is taken seriously, regardless of their formal legal status, giving more weight to their role as *participants* (Friedmann 1964, pp. 70–71; Higgins 1994, p. 50; Jägers 2002, p. 23). In this sense, recognition of the role played by all participants in international law would allow international law to be approached in a realistic rather than a formalistic manner. The necessary character of the nexus between legal personality, on the one hand, and the possibility of being a holder of rights and duties, on the other hand, is denied (Jägers 2002, p. 23). Nor does the notion of legal personality turn out to be completely clear from a judicial perspective either. In the workings of the International Court of Justice, legal personality comprises three elements: international legal subjectivity, international legal capacity, and international *jus standi*. But the International Court of Justice does not say anything about the relationship among these elements, such as whether, for example, all of them or only one or two of them are required. In spite of this uncertain definition, this perspective argues that TNCs have a legal personality, though to a limited degree (Jägers 2002, pp. 27–34; Kinley and Tadaki 2003, pp. 945–946), to the extent that they are addressees of rights and duties, that in some cases they also have *jus standi* and are subject at least to international jurisdiction, i.e., the jurisdiction of the European Court of Human Rights (ECHR). From this perspective, the role to be given to the notion of legal personality is weakened on the premise that "legal personality is a theoretical concept construed for practical purposes" (Jägers 1999, p. 266), that "the whole notion of subjects and objects has no credible reality and ... no functional purpose" (Higgins 1994, pp. 49–50) and that it would be better to speak of "participants instead of subjects" (Jägers 1999, p. 267). Therefore, the dominant position in the contemporary structure of international order and relations "requires that MNCs are included in the system of international law" (Jägers 1999, p. 267).

TNCs and human rights horizontal effect

Partly regardless of issues surrounding the notion of legal personality, international treaty law concerning human rights does not directly place obligations on TNCs: "Binding international duties of MNCs have to be deduced from instruments that were originally directed at States" (Jägers 1999, p. 265; see also Jägers 2002; Clapham 1993). That is why the topic of the TNCs' responsibility for human rights requires clarification regarding whether at least a partial horizontal effect of human rights exists or not (Clapham 2006, p. 59; Chinkin 1999).

The debate on the existence of a horizontal effect for human rights began after the preparatory work for the International Covenant on Civil and Political Rights (ICCPR) in 1966. In this context, "horizontal effect" means the applicability of norms containing human rights to relationships among private subjects, and the justiciability of such norms among private subjects (Clapham 2006, pp. 516–521). In the Universal Declaration of Human Rights (UDHR) Article 30 states that: "Nothing in this Declaration may be interpreted as implying for any State, group or person any right to engage in any activity or to perform any act aimed at the destruction of any of the rights and freedoms set forth herein." Article 2(3)(a) of the International Covenant for Civil and Political Rights states that: "Each State Party to the present Covenant undertakes: (a) To ensure that any person whose rights or freedoms as herein recognized are violated shall have an effective remedy, notwithstanding that the violation has been committed by persons acting in an official capacity." And the European Convention for the Protection of Human Rights and Fundamental Freedom (ECHR) in Article 13 states that: "Everyone whose rights and freedoms as set forth in this Convention are violated shall have an effective remedy before a national authority notwithstanding that the violation has been committed by persons acting in an official capacity." All of these articles imply the possibility of applying the human rights that they set forth to the relationships among non-state subjects.

The main human rights international sources seem to accept the idea that human rights can be violated not only by governments but also by private actors, and they establish private duties at four different levels. According to Knox (2008, p. 18), at the lowest level human rights law "contemplates that states have general duties to restrict private actions that interfere with the enjoyment of human rights, but leaves to governments the task of specifying the resulting private duties." This is the case for the ICCPR in Article 2, the ECHR in Article 1, the African Charter in Article 1, the Convention of Elimination of Racial Discrimination (CERD), the Convention of the Rights of the Child, and the Convention of Elimination of Discrimination against Women (CEDAW). In all these sources, private duties are indirectly imposed because governments have obligations to *ensure* rights. Ensuring a right involves securing the rights at stake from interference deriving from private actions. At a higher level, human rights law "specifies the private duties that governments are obliged to impose" (Knox 2008, p. 18). Examples can be found within the domain of labor rights, such as in CERD, Article 5(f), in CEDAW, Article 13(b), and within the International Labor Organization Conventions (N. 98, 1949; N. 105, 1957; N. 138, 1973; N. 155, 1981, N. 182, 1999). The idea is that "to be meaningful, labor protections must address not only governments, but also private employers" (Knox 2008, p. 24). At a third level, "human rights law directly places duties on private actors but continues to leave enforcement of those duties to domestic law" (Knox 2008, p. 18). At the highest level, human rights law places duties directly on private actors, and specifies and "enforces such duties at the international level, through international tribunals or other institutions" (Knox 2008, p. 18). International criminal law lies in between the third and fourth level of duties, depending on the existence, the jurisdiction, and the preconditions for the exercise of the jurisdiction of international courts. Since 2001, the relevant court is the International Criminal Court (ICC) (Clapham 2000, 2008; Knox 2008, pp. 27–30). In summary, private duties are therefore graduated and imposed either indirectly or directly. Moreover, when imposed directly, the enforcement may be, in different cases, either domestic or international.

Whether private duties (relevant for TNCs) are specified or not, directly or indirectly, it can be concluded that a horizontal effect for human rights does exist, but that it concerns only human rights that imply negative correlative duties, mainly concerning the rights to life, fundamental freedoms, and non-discrimination (Clapham 1993, pp. 94–107). Social rights can be included among the rights for which international law contemplates private correlative duties, but only insofar as they imply negative duties (i.e., duties not to interfere).

Indirect state responsibility for human rights violations by TNCs

Another relevant dimension concerning the state's responsibility for human rights violations by TNCs should be considered. This principle is, without doubt, set by the international law on human rights. For example, paragraph 18 of the *Maastricht Guidelines on Violations of Economic, Social and Cultural Rights* provides:

> The obligation to protect includes the State's responsibility to ensure that private entities or individuals, including transnational corporations over which they exercise jurisdiction, do not deprive individuals of their economic, social and cultural rights. States are responsible for violations of economic, social and cultural rights that result from their failure to exercise due diligence in controlling the behavior of such non-State actors.

Nevertheless, further problems arise since home states are often developing countries, where in many cases the government may not be interested in guaranteeing human rights, or may take advantage of complicity with the conduct of TNC, and, of course, vice versa (Jungk 2006). So, host states may be willing to apply domestic rules when the legal norms of the home states of TNCs are based on higher standards (Muchlinski 1999, p. 110). This is why it is relevant to establish whether indirect state responsibility can reach out to the overseas activity of TNCs. Up to now, the only effective system for transnational human rights claims against TNCs (before US courts) is internal to the US legal order and is provided by the application of the Alien Tort Claims Act (ACTA) to the activities of TNCs abroad (Clapham 2006, pp. 252–261; Jones 2004, pp. 21–63).

Specific problems relating to the attribution of liability arise in the case of firms that form part of a large group structure with a holding company and subsidiaries, all of which may be characterized by limited liability. It can be difficult to identify and ascribe responsibilities among the parent firm and the subsidiaries. Each firm of the group is, in front of third parties, a separate legal entity, and this maximizes the advantages (for the firm) of limited liability. In this context, limited liability not only limits the liability of the shareholder to the value of their shared capital, but also limits the responsibility of a parent firm for the conduct of its subsidiaries. As it has been pointed out, "Each legally distinct entity is subject to the laws of the countries in which it operates, but the transnational corporate group or network as a whole is not governed directly by international law" (Ruggie 2007, p. 824). There is, therefore, a specific and high risk that the ostensibly illegal actions of TNCs that form part of a corporate group may go unpunished, since the principle of limited liability also makes it very difficult, if not in some cases impossible, to sanction a firm's conduct both at domestic and at international level (De Schutter 2005, pp. 227, 276–281). For that reason, the principle of the legal separation between the parent firm and its subsidiaries tends to be weakened by the notion and doctrine of "enterprise entity," which aims at "piercing" the corporate veil (Meeran 1999) stemming from limited liability, or at establishing norms shaping corporate responsibility. From this perspective, responsibility is derived from the *fact* of economic integration and subsidiarity (Muchlinski 1999, pp. 328–330). The principle according to which a parent firm may be charged for a subsidiary's conduct when they make an "economic unit" has been set forth in an EU legal order, especially as part of the European Court of Justice (ECJ) case law. In other terms, the formal separation of firms due to their distinct legal personality under the domestic legal orders of their home states may not rule out the unity of their conduct on the market, or holding the parent company liable for the subsidiary's conduct, if (i) the latter lacks autonomy of action, and (ii) its conduct is the consequence of the parent's commands. Using this principle, the ECJ applied anti-trust EU law in an extra-territorial way to corporations whose home states were not member states of the EU, but which worked within the EU common market and were controlled by EU companies (Adinolfi 1990, p. 500).

Teubner (1990), in a critique of the "enterprise entity doctrine," argues that its limit lies in the fact that it is grounded in a hierarchic view of a company. According to Teubner's perspective, it may be better to embrace a network view of an organization, which is summed up by the notion of a "polycorporative network" (Teubner 1990, p. 80). The main consequence of this view is that responsibilities are decentralized along three levels: the level of each company belonging to the group, the parent company level, and the corporate group level (Teubner 1990, pp. 87–92). It seems, however, that this critique does not necessitate the rejection of piercing the corporate veil, which remains the major problem in ascribing responsibility to corporations.

Corporate obligations for human rights between law and ethics: the soft law pathway

Given the theoretical and practical difficulties in ascribing legal responsibilities to TNCs, international law has developed alternative tools in order to prevent violations of and foster compliance with human rights norms. Such instruments belong to the domain of soft law: they are not formally binding, and mainly serve to diffuse sensitivity and regard for human rights, as well as to promote the voluntary allegiance of influential actors in the relevant fields. Soft law tools are mainly of three kinds.

The first kind is the guidelines and standard-setting tools of inter-governmental organizations, such as the *Guidelines for Multinational Enterprises* promoted by the Organization for Economic Cooperation and Development (OECD), as an add-on to the *Declaration on International Investment and Multinational Enterprises* (Working Party 2001). The *Guidelines* are addressed to TNCs operating in, or from, the adhering states of the OECD with regard to worldwide business operations. This "globalization" of the OECD guidelines rests on the idea that, when firms operate in states that do not give sufficient regard to human rights, the firms themselves more than the states have the interest, first of all for reasons of their reputation, to avoid being implicated in complaints procedures. OECD guidelines are implemented through National Contact Points that are in charge of handling inquiries within the adhering countries as well as of promoting discussions and initiatives among governments, businesses, and non-governmental organizations on the matter covered by the guidelines. A further specific monitoring body (OECD Watch) has been created.

The second kind of soft law tool comprises the declarations of international organizations and non-governmental organizations, such as the International Labor Organization (ILO)

Tripartite Declaration (International Labor Organization 2006), which is aimed at TNCs, but also to governments and employers' and workers' organizations. The implementation of the Declaration is managed, through periodic surveys, by the Sub-Committee on Multinational Enterprises; the UN *Norms on Responsibilities of Transnational Corporations and Other Business Enterprises with Regard to Human Rights* (United Nations Commission on Human Rights 2003), adopted by the Sub-Commission on the Promotion and Protection of Human Rights in 2003. The *Global Compact* (United Nations n.d.) may be included in this group of tools, even if it is, strictly speaking, a personal initiative of the former UN Secretary-General, Kofi Annan. These tools put obligations on TNCs regarding obligations both to ensure equality of opportunity and treatment, to protect the environment, and to protect specific human rights, such as freedom of association, the right to collective bargaining, the elimination of all forms of forced or compulsory labor, the effective abolition of child labor, and the elimination of discrimination with respect to employment and occupation. Other tools may be mentioned, such as the *Business Charter for Sustainable Development* promoted by the International Chamber of Commerce (ICC) and the International Finance Corporation's (IFC) *Environmental and Social Standards* (2006). They aim to prevent TNCs themselves from infringing human rights and to prevent their direct, beneficial or silent, complicity in violations. Direct complicity "occurs when a company knowingly assists a state in violating human rights" (Clapham 2006, p. 221). Beneficial complicity "suggests that a company benefits directly from human rights abuses committed by someone else" (Clapham 2006, p. 221). Silent complicity "describes the way human rights advocates see the failure by a company to raise the question of systematic or continuous human rights violations in its interaction with the appropriate authorities" (Clapham 2006, p. 222).

The third kind of soft law instruments belong to the domain of self-regulation and are mainly multi-stakeholder in form, with mechanisms based on certification systems or that involve partial legislation, often specific for particular economic sectors. There are many such tools, which are broad-based according to the various domestic, regional, or sector-linked initiatives. For example, the *Voluntary Principles on Security and Human Rights* (2000) tends to diffuse respect for human rights by permeating the relationships between companies and host governments (e.g., the *Principles* are often incorporated into legal agreements between such parties). We may also mention the *Global Reporting Initiative* (n.d.), the *Extractive Industries Transparency Initiative* (2007) (for the extractive sector), the *Kimberle Process Certification Scheme* (n.d.) (which is devoted to diamond extraction activity), and *Social Accountability 8000* (Social Accountability International 2008) as the main example of third-party certified process. Certification systems are voluntary at the outset but, once embraced and implemented, they constrain a firm's conduct through (domestic) legislative tools, and make their relationship with governments more transparent.

All of these tools directly address corporations and seem to be the outcome of a convergence between the international law of human rights and the corporate social responsibility (hereinafter CSR) paradigm. Thus, there seems to be a convergence between the legal and ethical approaches to corporate responsibility. The CSR paradigm is based on the idea that firms should not only maximize profit and shareholders' interests, and control (and account for) their negative externalities and obey the law, but also contribute to social development and the common welfare. In other words, firms are required to take on an idea of responsibility that goes beyond their strict legal duties, and take into account the wider and broader interests of various stakeholders. Stakeholders (i.e., those who are in some sense affected by a firm's activity [Langtry 1994, pp. 432–433; Lozano 2005; Phillips 2003]) may be internal (i.e., employees, suppliers, sub-contractors, clients, etc.) or external (e.g., environment, community, members of the public, etc.). Social impact indicators are embedded, according to this view, in the very idea of profit.

Obligations are stretched so that firms turn out to have economic, legal, and moral duties at the same time.

The main convergence ground between the international law of human rights and the CSR paradigm is the will to lead firms to respect and promote principles of justice that in substance overlap with human rights, when understood according to a broad view, or with principles which human rights are an expression of.

Soft law tools embracing this view set down not only negative obligations to respect human rights, but also positive obligations concerning human rights protection (e.g., involving duties on firms to control the conduct of their subsidiaries as well as suppliers and sub-contractors) and promotion, even in the absence of a legal framework or governmental input. The means selected to pursue these aims and to implement principles of international law are codes of conduct, social accountability systems, cause-related marketing, the promotion of social impact projects, certification systems, and auditing processes. Such means aim at putting (transnational) corporations under the control of international agencies and public opinion, and to ensure their compliance with points such as freedom of association and the right to collective bargaining, the elimination of any form of forced and child labor, anti-discriminatory conduct in access to work, the protection of the environment, anti-corruption conduct, and so on. As MacBarnet (2009, p. 62) notes: "What is emerging in the arena of CSR is a complex interaction between government, business and civil society, private law, state regulation and self-regulation, at national and international levels."

It is obvious that the aims of the CSR paradigm change depending on whether corporations operate in states where human rights are supported by legal norms, or whether they operate where such support does not exist. In the first case, economic activities have a limit in legal norms, and CSR can function as a valuable input for TNCs to go beyond the law. In the second case, since the host state may not be capable of, or interested in, ensuring compliance with human rights, CSR tools seemingly take on the function of superseding the law. Therefore, a set of means which originally should have led TNCs to go beyond the law are brought in instead of the law or to support it. As we have seen above, home states may also have problems in exercising extra-territorial control over TNCs and in making human rights justiciable. This is why convergence between the CSR paradigm and international law can play a strategic role for the internationalization of human rights (Sullivan and Hogan 2002, p. 70). The voluntary character of CSR tools makes them suitable regardless of state borders, something that is very important in the age of globalization, a main feature of which is the weakening of governments' ability to control economic activities. So, what could be a weakness for CSR tools – their non-binding character – may in fact become an advantage.

Moreover, the reference to CSR seems to be synergic with a reformulation of human rights taxonomy that is not based on the traditional distinction (and sometimes tension) between civil rights and social rights. According to such a new view, human rights are comprised of three kinds of correlative duties: (i) the duty to respect, (ii) the duty to protect; (iii) and the duty to fulfill. Shue (1996, pp. 51–55) discusses "duties to avoid depriving," "duties to protect from deprivation," and "duties to aid the deprived." Such a view on the correlative duties of human rights has been widely taken into consideration and discussed specifically with regard to the definition of TNCs by Donaldson (1989, ch. 5).

With reference to the conduct of corporations, *respect* means that firms have an obligation not to interfere with the enjoyment of the rights at stake; *protection* involves a commitment by firms to control their partners, suppliers, or sub-contractors to ensure that they respect human rights; and (iii) *fulfillment* requires that firms promote rights, that is take proactive measures to provide goods and services and to improve the social justice in the communities in which they operate (Jägers 2002, pp. 75–95).

It is worth noting that negative and positive obligations in soft law tools are given the same emphasis, and that duties to respect, protect, and promote are regarded as having the same weight. This may be troublesome to the extent that negative and positive human rights obligations, when they are referred to private actors, have a different status in international law (Pariotti 2009, pp. 146–153). Negative obligations are supported by hard laws, which seem to have a horizontal effect and tend to be increasingly binding for both state and non-state actors. Norms expressing positive obligations, on the contrary, do not have any horizontal effect, and cannot be directly binding on non-state actors. So, insofar as rights implying negative obligations are concerned, the incorporation of CSR view and tools makes soft law over-inclusive (Knox 2008, p. 41) and negatively interfere with the internationalization process, which already aims at making rights binding for both state and private actors. On the contrary, as far as rights implying positive obligations are concerned, the overlap between (soft) law and CSR tools seems to be a meaningful pathway for framing a diffuse sensibility for social justice and for stimulating those who are in power to do something, regardless of their legal status, to contribute to its fulfillment. The open-endedness typical of positive correlative duties concerning social rights and that has been often regarded as the main cause for the ineffectiveness of such rights, is not actually a problem in itself, since it may be corrected by applying the notion of a minimum core of rights, which cannot be renounced and on the basis of which, in absence of compliance, one may speak of a consensually agreed upon human rights *violation*.

Self-regulation tools, moreover, may be thought of as having the peculiar potential, among soft law means, to foster involvement in human rights from below. Nevertheless, it has been pointed out that they have to improve their accountability mechanisms (Ruggie 2007, pp. 836–837). Furthermore, special attention must be given within them to their coherence with hard law instruments and mechanisms, since they are often mixed up with legislative measures. Generally speaking, soft law regarding TNCs and human rights seems to be important, much more for shaping new *methods* encouraging the compliance with human rights than for its *content*. Such methods may be appreciated, and can be fruitful in the transnational sphere insofar as they can foster participation from civil society and give concrete expression to the idea – set down by hard law sources on human rights and widely accepted by scholars – that, regardless of their formal legal status, those who have the power to do something to protect and promote human rights should properly exercise such power.

References

Addo, M. K. 1999. "Introduction," pp. 3–37 in M. K. Addo, ed., *Human Rights Standards and the Responsibility of Transnational Corporations* (The Hague: Kluwer).

Adinolfi, A. 1990. "The Legal Notion of the Group Enterprise: The EC Approach." In D. Sugarman and G. Teubner, *Regulating Corporate Groups in Europe* (Baden-Baden: Nomos).

Carbonneau, F., ed. 1990, *Lex Mercatoria and Arbitration: A Discussion of the New Law Merchant* (Dobbs Ferry, NY: Transnational Juris Publications).

Chinkin, C. 1999. "A Critique of the Public/Private Dimension." *European Journal of International Law*, Vol. 10, No. 2, pp. 387–395.

Clapham, A. 1993. *Human Rights in the Private Sphere* (Oxford: Clarendon Press).

Clapham, A. 2000. "The Question of Jurisdiction Under International Criminal Law over Legal Persons: Lessons from the Rome Conference on an International Criminal Court," pp. 193–195 in M. Kamminga and S. Zia-Zarifa, eds., *Liability of Multinational Corporations Under International Law* (The Hague: Kluwer).

Clapham, A. 2001. "Revisiting Human Rights in the Private Sphere: Using the European Convention on Human Rights to Protect the Right of Access to the Civil Courts," pp. 513–535 in C. Scott, ed., *Torture as Tort: Comparative Perspectives on the Development of Transnational Human Rights Litigation* (Oxford: Hart).

Clapham, A. 2006. *Human Rights Obligations of Non-State Actors* (Oxford: Oxford University Press).

Clapham, A. 2008. "Extending International Criminal Law Beyond the Individual to Corporations and Armed Opposition Groups." *International Journal of Criminal Justice*, Vol. 6, pp. 899–926.

De Schutter, O. 2005. "The Accountability of Multinationals for Human Rights Violations in European Law," pp. 227–314 in P. Alston, ed., *Non-State Actors and Human Rights* (Oxford: Oxford University Press).

Donaldson, T. 1989. *The Ethics of International Business* (Oxford: Oxford University Press).

Extractive Industries Transparency Initiative. 2007. *The EITI Principles and Criteria*. At: http://eitransparency.org/eiti/principles.

Friedmann, W. 1964. *The Changing Structure of International Law* (London: Stevens & Sons).

Global Reporting Initiative. n.d. *The Global Reporting Initiative*. At: http://www.globalreporting.org/Home.

Higgins, R. 1994. *Problems and Process: International Law and How We Use It* (Oxford: Clarendon Press).

International Chamber of Commerce. n.d. *The Business Charter for Sustainable Development*. At: http://www.iccwbo.org/policy/environment/id1309/index.html.

International Finance Corporation. 2006. *Environmental and Social Standards*. At: http://www.ifc.org/ifcext/sustainability.nsf/Content/EnvSocStandards.

International Labor Organization. 2006. *Tripartite Declaration of Principles Concerning Multinational Enterprises and Social Policy*. At: http://www.ilo.org/wcmsp5/groups/public/—ed_emp/—emp_ent/documents/publication/wcms_094386.pdf.

Jägers, N. 1999. "The Legal Status of the Multinational Corporation under International Law." pp. 259–270 in M. K. Addo, ed., *Human Rights Standards and the Responsibility of Transnational Corporations* (The Hague: Kluwer).

Jägers, N. 2002. *Corporate Human Rights Obligations: In Search of Accountability* (Antwerp: Intersentia).

Jones, S. 2004. *Corporations and Transnational Human Rights Litigation* (Oxford: Hart Publishing).

Jungk, M. 2006. *Complicity in Human Rights Violations: A Responsible Business Approach to Suppliers* (Copenhagen: Danish Institute for Human Rights).

Kimberley Process. N.d. *The Kimberley Process*. At: http://www.kimberleyprocess.com.

Kinley, D. and J. Tadaki. 2003. "From Talk to Walk: The Emergence of Human Rights Responsibilities for Corporations at International Law." *Virginia Journal of International Law*, Vol. 44, No. 1, pp. 931–1023.

Knox, J. H. 2008. "Horizontal Human Rights Law." *American Journal of International Law*, Vol. 102, No. 1, pp. 1–47.

Langtry, B. 1994. "Stakeholders and the Moral Responsibilities of Business." *Business Ethics Quarterly*, Vol. 4, No. 4, pp. 431–443.

Lozano, J. M. 2005. "Towards the Relational Corporation: From Managing Stakeholder Relationships to Building Stakeholder Relationships (Waiting for Copernicus)." *Corporate Governance*, Vol. 5, No. 2, pp. 60–77.

MacBarnet, D. 2009. *Corporate Social Responsibility Beyond Law, Through Law, For Law*. Edinburgh School of Law Working papers Series 2009/03. At: http://papers.ssrn.com/sol3/papers.cfm?abstract_id=1369305&rec=1&srcabs=1459548.

Meeran, R. 1999. "The Unveiling of Transnational Corporations: A Direct Approach," pp. 161–170 in M. K. Addo, ed., *Human Rights Standards and the Responsibility of Transnational Corporations* (The Hague: Kluwer).

Muchlinski, P. 1999. *Multinational Enterprises and the Law* (Oxford: Blackwell).

Pariotti, E. 2009. "International Soft Law, Human Rights and Non-State Actors: Towards the Accountability of Transnational Corporations?" *Human Rights Review*, Vol. 10, No. 2, pp. 139–155.

Phillips, R. 2003. "Stakeholder Legitimacy." *Business Ethics Quarterly*, Vol. 13, No. 1, pp. 25–41.

Ruggie, J. G. 2007. "Business and Human Rights: The Evolving International Agenda." *American Journal of International Law*, Vol. 101, No. 4, pp. 819–840.

Shue, H. 1996. *Basic Rights. Subsistence, Affluence, and US Foreign Policy*. 2nd edn (Princeton, NJ: Princeton University Press).

Social Accountability International. 2008. *Social Accountability 8000*. At: http://www.sa-intl.org/_data/n_0001/resources/live/2008StdEnglishFinal.pdf.

Sullivan, R. and D. Hogan. 2002. "The Business Case for Human Rights: The Amnesty International Perspective," pp. 69–87 in S. Bottomley and D. Kinley, eds., *Commercial Law and Human Rights* (Dartmouth: Ashgate).

Teubner, G. 1990. "Unitas Multiplex: Corporate Governance in Group Enterprises," pp. 67–104 in D. Sugarman and G. Teubner, eds., *Regulating Corporate Groups in Europe* (Baden-Baden: Nomos).

United Nations. n.d. *The Ten Principles*. At: http://www.unglobalcompact.org/AbouttheGC/TheTENPrinciples/index.html.

United Nations Commission on Human Rights. 2003. *Economic, Social and Cultural Rights*, UN Doc E/CN.4/Sub.2/2003/12/Rev.2. At: http://www.unhchr.ch/huridocda/huridoca.nsf/(Symbol)/E.CN.4.Sub.2.2003.12.Rev.2.En.

Voluntary Principles on Security and Human Rights. 2000. *The Voluntary Principles on Security and Human Rights*. At: http://www.voluntaryprinciples.org.

Working Party on the OECD Guidelines for Multinational Enterprises. 2001. *The OECD Guidelines for Multinational Enterprises*. Organization for Economic Cooperation and Development. At: http://www.oecd.org/officialdocuments/displaydocument.pdf.

42

Reparations for human rights abuses

Ereshnee Naidu and John Torpey

This chapter focuses on the role of reparations in contributing to justice, recognition, and healing for survivors of gross human rights violations. Thus far, the activities associated with reparations have by and large been confined to the legal realm. By focusing on the role of reparations in addressing human rights violations in the international context, the meaning of the term, and the complexity of the process of obtaining reparations, we show that the notion of reparations encompasses measures far beyond the legal system and that it has far-reaching political and social implications for societies seeking to make amends for prior misdeeds and oppression. Second, by drawing on the cases of the South African Truth and Reconciliation Commission (TRC) and of the controversy over reparations for slavery in the United States, the chapter highlights the contested nature of reparations claims-making and argues that reparations efforts have as much potential for positive social transformation as they do for division.

Reparations in the international context

The right to a remedy for victims of gross violations of their human rights is asserted in a variety of the regional and international human rights documents that have emerged during the post-World War II period. But it was the compensation to the survivors of atrocities committed by the Nazis during World War II that set the major precedent for the reparations programs that followed. With the burgeoning of the transitional justice field since the 1990s, the issue of reparations for victims of gross human rights violations took center stage in national and international law and politics. The term reparations refers to efforts to make amends for an injustice by restoring victims of gross human rights violations to their position prior to those violations. The notion of reparations implies a structured and procedurally just way of redressing human rights violations (Hamber 2006).

In mapping the sources and types of reparations claims, Torpey (2006) notes that there have been three basic sources of claims. The first set of claims arises from violations perpetrated during World War II and includes those arising from state-sponsored mass killings, forced labor, sexual exploitation, and related misdeeds perpetrated by the Axis powers. The second source of reparations claims arises in the aftermath of a transition to democracy and has frequently focused more on clarifying the circumstances of previous repression than on repairing the damage done, as in post-Communist Eastern Europe and in Latin America after the military's departure from power. The third source of reparations claims arises from European colonialism and its depredations, although one might see the case of the Korean "comfort women" – sexual slaves dragooned by the Japanese army during World War II – as a mixed case, given that the Japanese had colonized Korea beginning in 1910 and were thus drawing on colonial subjects in this instance. A sub-category of "post-colonial" claims involves cases of "internal colonialism," such as American slavery, Jim Crow, and South African apartheid.

As distinct from these three *sources* of reparations claims-making, there are two basic *types* of claims. The first type is one that seeks to compensate the *direct* victims of human rights violations who continue to bear the burden of these harms. Many of the Holocaust claims fall into this category. Such claims are rooted in *commemorative* forms of reparations. They are mainly *backward-looking* in the sense that they are not chiefly intended to rectify current economic or social disadvantage; rather, they are meant to right the wrongs of yesterday, if only symbolically. The second type of claim, by contrast, is one that attempts to redress the wrongs arising from a system of domination whose consequences persist into the present. As in the cases of American slavery and South African apartheid, these may take the form of both *symbolic* and *economic* calls for reparations. These are more *forward-looking* in the sense that they aim at transforming current social conditions that are legacies of the earlier system of domination (Torpey 2006).

The Basic Principles and Guidelines on the Right to a Remedy and Reparation for Victims of Gross Violations of International Human Rights Law and Serious Violations of International Humanitarian Law (hereafter "the Guidelines": the Guidelines are also sometimes referred to as the Bassiouni Principles; in an earlier incarnation, they were colloquially known as the van Boven principles – in each case after the prominent international human rights lawyers who were chiefly responsible for drafting and shepherding them through UN channels toward their ultimate adoption) outline remedies for victims of gross human rights violations, drawing on international instruments such as the UN Charter, the Universal Declaration of Human Rights, and the international covenants on human rights (the International Covenant on Civil and Political Rights, etc.) in framing the right to reparation. More specifically, Article 5 of the Guidelines provides a definition of "victims" and stresses the victims' right of access to justice, and the relevant state's responsibility to undertake reparations efforts that meet the economic, social, psychological, and political needs of victims. According to the Guidelines, reparations can take the following forms:

- *Restitution* includes measures that aim to restore the victim to the original situation before the violation occurred, and may include restoration of liberty; enjoyment of human rights, identity, and family life; restoration of employment; and restitution of property.
- *Compensation* involves measures that take mainly material forms and aim to compensate for wrongs such as physical or mental harm, lost education or employment opportunities, and moral injustice.
- *Rehabilitation* includes measures to provide and make available medical and social services for victims.
- *Satisfaction* involves a range of measures including the establishment and public announcement of the facts behind the injustices, clearing the names of those unjustly victimized, apologies, and the commemoration of victims. Truth commissions – those much-heralded vehicles for coming to terms with the past – would thus generally fall under the rubric of "satisfaction."

- *Guarantees of non-repetition* include measures related to policy, practice, and institutional reform, such as civilian control of the military and security forces; independence of the judiciary; and an overall respect for and promotion of a "culture of human rights."

As outlined in the Guidelines, reparations are diverse in form and can range from financial measures to symbolic actions, taking both individual and collective forms. Many truth commissions, such as those held in Argentina, Chile, Guatemala, South Africa, Sierra Leone, and, most recently, Liberia, have recommended a wide range of reparations measures. Yet the understanding of the concept of reparations varies somewhat in each case and its interpretation depends upon the political, social, and economic context prevailing in each country. Common to all the cases, however, is that reparations are viewed as a mechanism to institute or restore the rule of law, recognize the suffering of victims, rebuild social relations, and promote processes of reconciliation, justice, and truth-seeking. They also aim to instill the moral imperative, "never again."

A growing literature assesses overall strategies for nations to address their violent pasts (Chapman and van der Merwe 2007; Hayner 2001; Kritz 1997), some of it assessing the impact of truth commissions and even the ways in which different transitional justice processes (such as reparations) work together to achieve the overall goals (de Greiff 2006). More recent literature, however, has shown greater skepticism about the impact of truth commissions and whether they do, in fact, assist in reconciliation and preventing future conflict (Borer 2006; Brahm 2007; Hamber 2009; Mendeloff 2004; van der Merwe et al. 2009). Despite a growing consensus among international human rights lawyers that victims of gross human rights violations are entitled to reparations, and the fact that reparations are based on the legal principle of proportionality (de Greiff 2006), many reparations programs have been viewed as unsuccessful. Given the almost impossible task of truly making up for the wrongs suffered by victims of gross human rights violations, no program of reparations is likely to achieve the standard of compensating victims fully in proportion to the harm that they suffered. As Maier (2003, p. 297) argues, reparations can only really move the loss from the realm of the irrecoverable to a space of political negotiation. Furthermore, a standard of proportionality is problematic in its very attempt to quantify the harm, as harm becomes relative and thus creates hierarchies of victimhood (de Greiff 2006; Chaumont 1997). Additionally, as a political project that focuses on righting the wrongs of the past, reparations claims-making runs the risk of supplanting a progressive vision for the future (Torpey 2006; for an attempt to provide such a vision, see Judt 2010).

In contrast to the more critical analyses of the consequences of reparations, de Greiff's (2006) analysis of reparations as a social and political project that can contribute to goals of recognition, civic trust, and social solidarity in transitional societies is useful in understanding the positive role that reparations can play for individual victims and the broader society. These features can, he argues, give the project of reparations a more forward-looking character. Since reparations are inherently linked to justice, one of its primary purposes is recognizing the intrinsic worth or dignity of the individual as a human being and a citizen. In constitutional democracies, citizenship involves reciprocal recognition of equality and human dignity. On an individual level, reparations facilitate an understanding of the effects of the socio-political milieu upon the individual; they recall that the individual has indeed been violated through the unjust actions of others and that the violation deserves recompense to ensure the re-establishment of equal conditions among all citizens (de Greiff 2006). Similarly, in her study of the role of apology for past injustices, Nobles (2008) notes that apology (as a form of reparations) can change the meaning and terms of citizenship for survivors or their descendents. Apologies provide a mechanism with which to advance the rights and obligations of citizenship as well as to change the boundaries of membership in a more inclusive direction. Furthermore, apologies serve to acknowledge the injustice of past wrongs and thus may serve as an impetus for programs that seek to ameliorate the social and political disadvantages and inequalities that flowed from those wrongs (Nobles 2008).

On a political level, reparations have the potential to restore civic trust. While the legal system may be able to address law-breaking behavior, it is through the individual's interaction with fellow citizens and with the state that civic trust is more likely be developed. The granting of reparations to victims of human rights violations highlights the political will of the state and citizens to re-establish equality and respect among themselves. As de Greiff (2006) argues, the failure to provide reparations to victims often sends a message that democracy is being constructed on the atrocities that they have suffered, without adequate attention to their justified claims. Conferral of reparations, however, can facilitate a process of political inclusivity, as all citizens become equal participants in a shared political project.

"Social solidarity is the type of empathy characteristic of those who have the disposition and willingness to put themselves in the place of other" (de Greiff 2006, p. 464). In stratified societies, reparations can thus be a part of a new social contract that enables victims once again to become active members of society. While a reparations project alone cannot foster social solidarity, it can serve as a catalyst for renewed social bonds. Furthermore, reparations projects are often based on the assumption that victims and perpetrators (and society at large) are able to resume political dialogue; as such, reparations can facilitate a process of renewed social interaction.

The South African Truth and Reconciliation Commission

For many years before its first democratic election in 1994, South Africa was a pariah in the international community, the last bastion of legally sanctioned white supremacy. A country that was notorious for its apartheid policies of racial segregation and discrimination, South Africa was lauded for its comparatively "peaceful" transition to democracy. However, the transition to democracy brought with it a variety of expectations and challenges. A major challenge faced by the post-apartheid government of Nelson Mandela concerned how to address the legacies of the apartheid past while still ensuring that the myth of the "rainbow nation" remained a plausible vision for the future. The Promotion of National Unity and Reconciliation Act No. 34 of 1995 (Act) was the enabling legislation that mandated the establishment of a Truth and Reconciliation Commission.

With its inception in 1996, the TRC constituted for many a beacon of hope for reconciliation and healing in its attempt to uncover the hidden past of apartheid-era conflicts. At the core of the TRC project was the aim to develop a new national narrative that both accounted for the country's ugly past and promised forgiveness and a new beginning for those who acknowledged past wrongdoing. While the South African TRC has been celebrated as a model of post-conflict transitional justice efforts and has since been replicated in post-conflict countries such as Liberia and Sierra Leone, the fact that the TRC prioritized reconciliation over matters of truth and justice has by and large resulted in a failure to live up to the expectations of survivors. The shortcomings of the TRC essentially fall into two categories. The first relates directly to the interpretation of the Act and the narrowly defined mandate that the TRC undertook, and the second concerns the unfinished business of the TRC regarding reparations and prosecutions.

Apartheid: a failed political project

The apartheid system was based on a racist ideology that aimed to marginalize blacks and other non-whites in favor of white privilege and domination. However, given ideological constructs regarding reconciliation and forgiveness, the practical constraints related to the lifespan of the

TRC, as well as financial and human resource constraints, the TRC made an implicit distinction between race and racism, on the one hand, and politics on the other. The TRC's terms of reference paid specific attention only to "gross human rights violations," which related mainly to physical violations as a result of political affiliation or ideology, but excluded the economic disparities that arose from apartheid. In contrast, Fullard (2004) argues that the permeation of racial domination into everyday life, and its impact on different social structures, was itself a human rights violation and was therefore declared a crime against humanity by the United Nations.

Although the TRC as a process sidestepped issues of economic inequality, the Reparation and Rehabilitation Committee (RRC) of the TRC attempted to address the structural legacies of racism by providing a holistic reparations framework in its final recommendations. The RRC recommended that reparations were necessary to "restore human and civil dignity" and to enable victims of gross violations of human rights to come to terms with the past. The RRC (TRC 2003) acknowledged the public debate around reparations and the tendency to focus on individual financial grants, noting that the reparation policy proposed by the RRC was much broader in intent. In other words, it did not focus simply on financial compensation. The recommended reparations policy was shaped by the Guidelines' principles of redress, restitution, rehabilitation, restoration of dignity, and guarantees of non-repetition. In keeping with these principles, urgent interim reparations, individual reparations, symbolic reparations, community rehabilitation programs, and institutional reform were recommended as the most significant forms of reparations.

Furthermore, the RRC recognized the complexity of the TRC process itself and the fact that "virtually every Black South African can be said to be a victim of human rights abuse" (TRC 2003). It thus highlighted the need for the various forms of reparations to complement each other. Some argued that the various forms of reparations should aim to improve the socio-economic conditions of victims and their communities, thereby acknowledging both those victims that testified before the Commission and those who comprise the broader South African citizenry (TRC 2003). Overall the recommendations for reparations sought to frame the individual experiences of victimization within a broader national context.

Despite recommendations for a holistic reparations policy, the RRC was viewed as one of the weakest of the three TRC committees in terms of promoting and fulfilling the goals of reconciliation. According to Wilson (2001), the limited powers of the RRC – its inability to grant urgent reparations, its lack of power to develop a reparations policy, and its reliance on the President's Fund rather than a fund of its own to fulfill its recommendations – led to the perception that the RRC had failed survivors. However, the TRC itself seemed to understand its limited power and its reliance on political will to take forward the process that it had only just begun. The TRC continually reminded victims (many of whom were in dire material need) that they should limit their expectations for financial reparations as they would most likely get only a fraction of the amount that they expected.

Overall those groups who had a stake in the work of the TRC, such as survivors, scholars, government officials, and field workers, supported the recommendation for a holistic reparations strategy. However, the broader South African public has been more skeptical about the idea of reparations. In his survey of the attitudes of the South African public towards the TRC, Gibson (2005) found that while black South Africans responded more positively to the work of the TRC than did white South Africans, overall the majority of respondents were satisfied with that body's work. There was most consensus about the TRC's success in its truth-seeking function and its ability to provide families of victims with more information about their loved ones. The policy regarding reparations, however, was viewed most negatively by all respondents as compared to the evaluation of other areas of the TRC's work, such as prosecutions and guaranteeing non-repetition of the past. Here again, however, the results were divided along racial lines, with more blacks than whites supporting compensation (Gibson 2005).

Apart from the varying public and civil society views regarding the TRC's recommendations on reparations, former victims and their NGO advocates have accused the South African government of having little will to press forward on the matter of reparations. Thus far there has been no attempt by the government to offer a coordinated, integrated approach to reparations. In 2003, then-President Thabo Mbeki announced a one-off payment of Rand 30,000 (approx. US$4,000) to 18,000 victims who had testified before the TRC. He also announced that "community reparations" would be implemented as a broader socio-economic strategy that would benefit all South Africans rather than only individual victims. According to Hamber (2006) community reparations can be defined as a strategy that seeks to provide access to a form of collective service for a large but select group of individuals that have jointly suffered in some way.

Although Mbeki did not define the concept of community reparations, it was clear that this notion had a broader meaning than simply targeting a section of the victimized population. Mbeki also agreed that a variety of symbolic reparations would be undertaken, in the form of renaming public facilities and of national commemorative ceremonies and in keeping with the recommendations outlined in the TRC report. According to Hamber (2006), no reparations program has thus far been granted in this way, or has been officially called "reparations." Hamber argues that community reparations, if not undertaken as a part of a broader reparations strategy, are problematic in the sense that violence is experienced individually and personally. Such a collective strategy alone does not fulfill the needs of individual victims. As an exclusively forward-looking strategy, it does not publicly acknowledge the moral wrong of the violation or shame those that were responsible for the violation. Furthermore, in the case of South Africa, access to and improvement of social services was the campaign pledge of the African National Congress (ANC), and was considered a right rather than a part of reparations.

The South African government's attitude toward reparations was further highlighted by its unwillingness to address the TRC's recommendations on the role of the business sector during apartheid and the recommendations for reparations to be made by business. Following the business and labor hearings, the TRC acknowledged in no uncertain terms that "business was central to the economy that sustained the South Africa state during the apartheid years" (TRC 2003). Accordingly, the TRC outlined a variety of recommendations such as a wealth tax and a one-time levy on private and corporate income to supplement funding for reparations programs. However, the South African government rejected these recommendations as well as the corresponding advocacy efforts by such prominent figures as Archbishop Desmond Tutu.

Following the government's unwillingness to address the role of the corporate sector as both a beneficiary of apartheid and a key player in perpetuating human rights violations, in 2002 a group of South Africans represented by the Khulumani Support Group sued twenty international banks and corporations in the US federal courts under the Alien Tort Claims Act for undertaking business in South Africa during apartheid. The Khulumani Support Group is one of the largest survivor support groups in South Africa. It was formed in 1995 by survivors and families of victims of human rights violations and was set up in response to the pending TRC (Colvin 2006). While the case is still underway, it is worth noting that the Mbeki government of the time filed documentation with the district court and appeals court outlining its opposition to the case on the grounds that it would discourage foreign investment in the country. In September 2009, however, the new South African president, Jacob Zuma, announced his support of the Khulumani Support Group lawsuit and has rescinded the government's previous opposition to the case.

The South African government's reluctance to hold big business accountable points to a key question faced by all reparations programs: Who should bear the costs? In the South African case, the logical answer might seem to be that the beneficiaries of apartheid's political and economic domination should be held to account, as these were the institutions that were responsible for and benefited from most of the violations inflicted upon victims. As in post-war (West) Germany, however, the successor government is as a practical matter the only one that can assume the obligations incurred by the misdeeds of its predecessor. The burdens created by the injustices of the past must be dealt with by those seeking to create a more democratic present.

As noted above, the matter of reparations in South Africa remains fraught with controversy and remains part of the unfinished business of the TRC. Apart from the fact that its implementation and support are largely dependent on political forces, the lack of a comprehensive strategy thus far has resulted from a shortage of political will on the part of the South African government. As Nkosinathi Biko of the Steve Biko Foundation argues, "There is a general lack of understanding and insensitivity around the purpose of reparations, where reparations are equated with enrichment and financial benefits" (Naidu 2004). Despite an innovative set of recommendations from the TRC, reparations have failed to be adequately implemented in post-apartheid South Africa. While the government's stance toward the lawsuit initiated by Khulumani Support Group indicates a new position on the reparations question, the record thus far is one of very limited compensation at best.

The myth of the rainbow nation

> There is transformation; we are free and you can move around without fear. (Kulumani Survivor Support Group grandchild, 2005)
>
> We are still divided. (Herzlia High School learner, 2005)
>
> Yes, things have changed, but in South Africa black people stay in shacks, whereas white counterparts have a good lifestyle. That should change. (Kulani High School learner, 2005)
>
> *(Excerpts taken from Naidu and Adonis 2007)*

As previously noted, the TRC's failure to address legacies rooted in race has helped shape race relations in post-apartheid South Africa. While Theissen and Hamber (1998) optimistically highlighted the potential for reconciliation and the respect for a culture of human rights among younger South Africans, recent studies show that the socio-economic legacies of discrimination continue to affect current generations. A study by Naidu and Adonis (2007) concerning the cross-generational transfer of memory shows that there were generally mixed feelings among South African youth regarding levels of reconciliation. Although most young people felt that there was positive change that related directly to political freedoms, most black youngsters argued that there was limited attitudinal change. Both black and white youth admitted that racial segregation was still a reality for many of them and that they have had limited social interaction with people of other races. Bonilla-Silva (2003) refers to this as the naturalization frame of racism, which is often used by whites to explain certain racial phenomena as natural. For example, the preference to socialize with one's own race is rationalized as non-racial since minorities (or majorities in the South African case) also do it. Furthermore, many black youth expressed concerns about the continued economic deprivation experienced by mainly black South Africans, citing high unemployment rates, lack of service delivery, and the perception that the Black Economic Empowerment (BEE) scheme (analogous to affirmative action in the United States) continued to benefit only a limited number of middle-class black South Africans.

The very nature of the apartheid system ensured that the quality of life for black South Africans was drastically diminished by policies that denied to blacks educational opportunities, access to housing and health, free speech, cultural expression, freedom of association, etc. These structural forms of unequal treatment permeated various aspects of life (Naidu and Adonis 2007). Despite fifteen years of democracy, three democratic elections, and various attempts to extinguish the laws and policies that perpetuated systems of discrimination, systematic structural inequality persists and informs the daily experiences of black South Africans.

In 2008, the South African Human Rights Commission (SAHRC) acknowledged that "racism is alive and well in South Africa." In a statement to the Johannesburg Press Club in 2008, chairperson of SAHRC Jody Kollapen discussed the shortcomings of the TRC process in dealing with issues of race. He argued that the reconciliation process was undertaken at the expense of real transformation, noting that "hardly anything was asked of white South Africans." Additionally, the TRC process itself focused on the "excesses" of apartheid rather than engaging ordinary South Africans more broadly with regard to the meaning of apartheid and its impact on the lived experiences of ordinary South Africans (*Mail and Guardian* 2008). It is significant to note that Kollapen's view of the lack of accountability of white South Africans in the TRC process is a perspective widely held among scholars and human rights practitioners. As Mamdani (1998) argues, the TRC's focus on political violence diverted attention from the advantages that accrued to white South Africans, focusing on a limited number of "direct" perpetrators rather than on the wrongs done to the vast majority of non-white South Africans who were disadvantaged by the apartheid system.

In sum, the South African TRC process was politically and ideologically problematic and did not fully address the needs of those who had endured its indignities and deprivations. However, the process was largely symbolic in nature and valuable for South Africa's transition to democracy in the sense that it helped create a new national narrative that marked the change of political regimes. While the RRC proposed a progressive and holistic reparations strategy, the interpretation of those recommendations and the general lack of political will to implement them have left survivors disappointed. Still, the process was successful in bringing to the fore the "hidden" truths about the past, enabling the re-telling of a more comprehensive, multilayered history that acknowledged a racist past. If nothing else, the TRC has enabled South Africans to challenge unapologetically the apartheid legacy and to continue a dialogue concerning some of the practical and moral dilemmas involved in overcoming the legacies of the white minority regime and creating an equitable, democratic society.

Reparations for slavery in the USA

> The answer to the slavery question was already embedded in our Constitution – a Constitution that had at its very core the ideal of equal citizenship under the law … and yet the words on a parchment would not be enough to deliver slaves from bondage … What would be needed is Americans in successive generations who were willing to do their part.
>
> *(Obama 2008)*

In his Philadelphia address on race and racism during the 2008 election campaign, Barack Obama cited the US Constitution as a marker of justice, liberty, and equal citizenship for all people in the United States. The US Constitution is perhaps the most celebrated such document among the liberal democracies, despite the fact that the Constitution was itself tainted by racist ideology. Critics such as Feagin (2000) argue that the 1787 Constitutional Convention was as much about protecting the racial and economic interests of wealthy men who made their living through slavery as it was about forming a democratic government. There was of course considerable debate among the framers of the Constitution over the future of slavery in the new republic. Among other issues, there was the question of whether slaves would count as persons or as property for purposes of determining congressional representation and tax liabilities. The matter was ultimately resolved by giving the states representation based on a formula counting its free population plus three-fifths of "all other persons"; in a sign of the delicacy of the issue, "slavery" was not mentioned. Congress would also have the power to ban the slave trade, but not until at least twenty years had passed. The slave trade then came to be outlawed in 1808, but slavery itself was not eliminated until 1865. Officially sanctioned slavery eventually came to be replaced by a system of "Jim Crow" segregation – enshrined in the 1896 Supreme Court decision in *Plessy v. Ferguson*, upholding the constitutionality of the "separate but equal" doctrine – that held black people down for another seventy years. Despite persistent legacies of racism and discrimination, however, substantial strides have been made in overcoming racial prejudice and enlarging the black middle class in the United States since the "civil rights revolution" of the mid-1960s (see, e.g., Patterson 1997). It is against this complex background of enduring inequality and major social change – a change symbolized in part by the election of Barack Obama as the country's first black president – that the contemporary movement for reparations for American blacks pursues its aims.

"Forty acres and a mule"

Claims for reparations for slavery date at least as far back as 1865, when General William Tecumseh Sherman announced, in Special Field Order No.15, a plan for settlement of free blacks in which each family would receive forty acres of land. While this plan saw at least 40,000 families settled on some 400,000 acres of land, the plan was soon revoked by President Andrew Johnson, who restored Confederate owners to their land, leaving black families in a state of impoverished betrayal.

The call for different types of reparations has since seen many ebbs and flows. While on a trip to Africa in 1998, former president Bill Clinton denounced slavery, but did not make an official apology. In June 2009, the US Senate passed a resolution acknowledging and apologizing for slavery. Against this background, one might be inclined to conclude that the USA is not a nation quick to apologize (see, e.g., Savelsberg and King 2005). While the 2009 Senate resolution could be attributed to a variety of factors, including intensified international trends toward apologies for past injustices (see Gibney et al. 2008), apology alone may not be enough to address centuries of inequality and oppression. Further, as Brophy (2006a) demonstrates, the US Congress and state legislatures do in fact have a long history of paying reparations to different groups. As far back as 1864, pursuant to a clause in the Emancipation Proclamation, the US Congress paid approximately $5 million as compensation to slave *owners* in the District of Columbia. In 1971, under the Alaskan Native Claims Act, the US Congress paid an indemnity of $962.5 million and deeded 40 million acres of land to Native American tribes. In accordance with the terms of the Civil Liberties Act of 1988, some $1.65 billion was paid to Japanese-Americans interned during World War II. Various academic institutions and corporations have lately admitted their role as beneficiaries of slavery and undertaken reparations programs that have included studies of the institutions' role in slavery, apologies, and financial compensation.

Yet the US federal government has remained reluctant to apologize for slavery, and Congress has so far refused to approve a bill to study whether reparations are warranted – John Conyers's symbolically named (and, for twenty years, annually ignored) H. R. 40. Furthermore, it was only in 2003 that former President George W. Bush signed a bill approving the establishment of a National Museum of African-American History and Culture in Washington, DC. Why, then, has there been so much official reluctance to deal with the slave past in the country with a major Holocaust Memorial Museum, commemorating events that took place far from our shores? What are the barriers to repairing the damage of the slave and segregated past, which continues to permeate American life?

There is little doubt that the history of race-based slavery which was unique to the United States, coupled with the segregation laws and practices of the Jim Crow era, not only entrenched the oppression of blacks but had far-reaching socio-economic consequences. Legislation such as the Fair Labor Standards Act (FSLA) (Katznelson 2005) and practices such as "red-lining" (Massey and Denton 1993) have prevented blacks from accumulating wealth, resulting in a black–white wealth ratio of perhaps 10 to 1 (Oliver and Shapiro 1997). The disadvantages faced by blacks in terms of wealth are reflected in and reinforced by patterns of intense residential segregation by race and class, higher rates of unemployment relative to whites, lower relative educational attainment, higher mortality, vastly disproportionate rates of incarceration, and corresponding difficulties in building cohesive family units. There is a *cumulative* quality to black disadvantage in the United States that makes it difficult to escape, as its dimensions ramify throughout the lives of poor blacks and continue to complicate efforts to attain middle-class status (Katznelson 2005).

While these inequalities alone might seem compelling grounds for reparations, there is also an array of arguments against reparations. While some stress the practical challenges of undertaking a reparations program for slavery (e.g., Posner and Vermeule 2003), there are others that question the very morality of reparations programs. Many studies concerning reparations for slavery argue that the actual costs of the damages inflicted by slavery and its sequelae cannot be calculated, rendering the question of reparations moot. However, as de Greiff (2006) argues, for any reparations program to advance political and social change, the discussion must shift away from the principle of strict proportionality to broader socio-political goals related to recognition and the rebuilding of civic trust and social solidarity. It is also important to note that, as a result of the lobbying efforts from reparations advocates, especially those associated with Holocaust-related wrongs, the notion of reparations in the USA has come to be associated primarily with individual payments (Torpey 2006).

Still, as we have seen, there is a significant difference between straightforward monetary compensation and reparations more broadly understood. While the former does not necessarily require any declaration of responsibility on the part of the offending party (as often happens when corporations settle cases), the idea of reparations is based on the notion that injustices must be recognized for what they are, and accordingly a specific group or individual must be held responsible for that injustice. In the case of the USA, even during slavery days, slaveholding was far from a universal phenomenon, and of course no one has legally owned slaves for a century and a half. There have also been many beneficiaries of black oppression who are themselves non-white and who have sometimes suffered for who they are as well. How then can today's non-black Americans – say, the Vietnamese boat person who is now a US citizen as an indirect consequence of our war in Vietnam – be expected to pay for an injustice in which they were not directly involved? Brophy (2006b) argues that culpability can be imputed to the state for imposing the harm of slavery and establishing the legal framework that enabled it. The state is a representative of the taxpayers, and taxpayers are responsible for outstanding public debts. Furthermore, one might argue that, in addition to blacks, there are various other racial and ethnic groups that continue to experience social and economic marginalization. Yet as noted earlier, Brooks (2006) argues that chattel slavery was different from other forms of slavery in that it was essentially race-based and specifically targeted African-Americans. In this view, the moral enormity and the arguable long-term social and economic consequences of slavery justify singling out blacks for special treatment.

While the concept of reparations in the USA is by and large focused on monetary transfers, as previously noted reparations can take on diverse and complementary forms to fulfill the purpose they are meant to achieve. To be sure, if the logistical and legal challenge of identifying contemporary victims of slavery can be overcome (since there are no actual survivors of slavery), cash payouts would serve to improve the lives of many black families. Yet given the profound economic and other needs of many poor blacks, such payments would likely be largely symbolic in nature and in any case they would have only a limited impact on the inequalities associated with race in American life. Accordingly, Torpey (2006) argues that legalistic approaches cannot resolve the problems associated with America's history of racial oppression. He argues that it is only by moving the debate outside of the courtrooms that the demand for reparations is likely to gain credence, if not ultimately to succeed. Similarly, Brooks (2007) argues that a forward-looking atonement model characterized by apology, reparations, and justice, rather than a tort model that may include public or private lawsuits, will be more successful in actually addressing the moral and social legacies of slavery.

The politics of reparations for black Americans became more complicated with the rise of Barack Obama on the American political scene. When asked about his views on reparations, President Obama responded that while an apology might be appropriate, it would not greatly improve the lives of black Americans. He noted that, in lieu of reparations, social service programs focusing on improved health care and access to education should be implemented. While such programs would be targeted at the population at large, these would especially benefit and "disproportionately affect people of color" (Wills 2008). Obama's view of the matter, though not employing the term "collective reparations," echoes the aforementioned position regarding community reparations that was articulated by Thabo Mbeki. Yet such measures in themselves may not be regarded as adequate by some because they fail to fulfill the moral imperative of *recognizing* that an injustice has been done and that it is necessary for that injustice to be corrected in some way. To such critics, a program that does not address these concerns therefore cannot fully address the moral, psychological, and social dimensions of racial oppression in the same way a more complete reparations program might do.

Finally, some scholars addressing the matter of reparations argue that since demands for reparations are based on identity politics, they may not only be divisive but may also entrench among reparations-seeking groups a self-conception rooted in victimhood (Torpey 2006; Brophy 2006a). Similarly, Barkan (2000) argues that there has been no restitution program that has lifted the burden of victimization; instead, most have simply routinized that burden. Still, the very discussion of restitution for slavery validates black experiences of victimization (Barkan 2000). As Brophy (2006a) argues, the debate over reparations is part of a broader debate concerning race and equality in the contemporary United States. As Yamamoto (2007) notes, however, similar to the Japanese–American redress campaign that set the stage for other reparations claims-making, the African-American reparations campaign may also provide broader impetus to the pursuit of racial and social justice.

The impact that reparations have on individuals and society depends to a substantial degree on the process whereby they are agreed upon. In his examination of the impact of reparations programs for Japanese-Americans and Japanese-Canadians who were interned during World War II, Torpey (2006) shows that the process of undertaking any reparations program is not only a politically fraught and contested process, but also that it may or may not meet the needs of victims. While the formerly "interned" were divided over the value of monetary reparations as against symbolic reparations in the form of an apology, it was ultimately the process of claiming reparations itself, and the treatment of victims in the course of that process, that resulted in its relative success in the eyes of those previously wronged. Through different forms of redress, different levels of reconciliation were achieved. Thus, while many victims of the internment may not feel fully integrated into society, many now occupy "a space between vengeance and forgiveness" (Minow 1998).

For the United States, reparations would be more about bringing underlying tensions and divisions to the fore and directly addressing the issues of racism, privilege, and power that continue to play themselves out in the lived realities of all Americans. Such a discourse would highlight the legacy of racial injustice in the United States. As Brophy (2006a) notes, there is at present no definitive conclusion about the matter of reparations, but it is only in identifying the key arguments for and against reparations that the debate can become more focused and the utility of the argument better assessed.

Patterson (1997) argues that African-Americans may share experiences of exploitation similar to those of people of other races, such as the white working class, yet it is the cumulative "Acts of History" that are specific to African-Americans. The fact that only African-Americans can make a claim that their ancestors lived under a system of slavery; that only African-Americans were systematically shut out of the industrial revolution of the late nineteenth century; and that only African-Americans suffered the humiliation and legal discrimination of Jim Crow laws makes this a history that is unique in American experience – legacies of which continue to affect African-American life in the USA today (Patterson 1997). In order to get beyond glib claims that Americans now find themselves in a "post-racial" context, greater efforts must be devoted to highlighting these legacies and how they have shaped the fate of blacks in the United States.

It has been argued throughout this chapter that reparations involve a moral recognition of injustice. In recognizing the injustices of the past, even in a backward-looking way, reparations seek to repair the past by laying the foundation for a newly defined future. Not only will such a process validate the experiences of discrimination experienced by blacks by acknowledging the history of racial oppression; it will also serve to heighten awareness of the patterns of privilege and discrimination for future generations. Acknowledgment of the pervasive impact of racism and discrimination on social life in the USA is likely to be a crucial precondition for substantial transformation of racial inequalities. The adoption of a reparations policy alone would not overcome the structural inequalities or the socio-cultural prevalence of racism. Yet debates over such a policy would serve to stimulate public dialogue around the issue and lay to rest any denial of the actual legacies of racism and inequality.

Conclusions

There is no doubt that demands for reparations are controversial in any context and can lead to divisions within society. By their very nature, no reparations program is going to fully satisfy all parties. It is necessary, however, to understand the multiple meanings that reparations may have and the varied forms they may take. In South Africa, despite an innovative set of recommendations from the TRC, the lack of a political will to promote reparations policies, and the absence of a process that focuses on the needs of survivors, reparations have come to be viewed as failing the broader objectives set forth by the TRC. In the United States, meanwhile, monetary reparations to blacks – the ones that advocates mainly have in mind – are likely to do relatively little to address the socio-economic conditions of blacks and in any case have so far faced strong political opposition, a situation that shows no signs of changing significantly.

Furthermore, while many survivors of conflict and historical injustices may indeed be in serious material need, cases such as those from South Africa and Argentina suggest that some survivors may actually prefer other forms of reparations that are more symbolic in nature – measures that are linked to truth-telling and acknowledgment of the suffering that they have undergone. While we are by no means advocating that one form of reparation replace another, it is important to note that survivors and victims cannot be reduced to a unified group. Survivors have diverse experiences, and as such their needs vary from one individual to another. So rather than reducing the notion to checks, reparations – viewed as a holistic, inclusive strategy to come to terms with the past – can serve a variety of purposes for the state, the survivors, and the broader society.

More broadly, it is important to note that "reparations are laden with value judgments for victims" and for many victims it is the very denial of their victim status and the social and political silence around the violations and discrimination that they have undergone that is most distressing (Hamber and Palmary 2009). If conceived within a framework of recognition, the restoration of dignity, and positive social transformation, reparations can be an important catalyst for renewed civic engagement as well as strengthen the ties of democratic citizenship where all citizens can participate in the re-imagining of a future based on social justice and equality.

References

Barkan, E. 2000. *The Guilt of Nations: Restitution and Negotiating Historical Injustice* (Baltimore, MD: John Hopkins University Press).

Bonilla-Silva, E. 2003. *Racism Without Racists* (New York: Rowman and Littlefield).

Borer, T. A., ed. 2006. *Telling the Truths: Truth Telling and Peace Building in Post-conflict Societies* (Notre Dame, IN: University of Notre Dame Press).

Brahm, E. 2007. "Uncovering the Truth: Examining Truth Commission Success and Impact." *International Studies Perspectives*, Vol. 8, No. 1, pp. 16–35.

Brooks, R. 2006. "The New Patriotism and Apology for Slavery." In E. Barkan and A. Karn, eds., *Taking Wrongs Seriously: Apology and Reconciliation* (Stanford, CA: Stanford University Press).

Brooks, R. 2007. "Redress for Slavery: The African American Struggle." In M. Du Plessis and S. Pete, eds., *International Perspectives on Reparations for Gross Human Rights Violations* (Oxford: Intersentia).

Brophy, A. L. 2006a. *Reparations: Pros and Cons* (Oxford: Oxford University Press).

Brophy, A. L. 2006b. "Reconsidering Reparations." *Indiana Law Review*, No. 811, pp. 811–849.

Chapman, A. and H. van der Merwe, eds. 2007. *Truth and Reconciliation in South Africa: Did the TRC Deliver?* (Philadelphia: University of Pennsylvania Press).

Chaumont, Jean-Michel. 1997. *La Concurrence des Victimes: Genocide, Identite, Reconnaissance* (Paris: Editions La Decouverte).

Colvin, C. 2006. "Reparations Program in South Africa." In P. de Greiff, ed., *Handbook of Reparations* (Oxford: Oxford University Press).

de Greiff, P., ed. 2006. *The Handbook of Reparations* (Oxford: Oxford University Press).

Feagin, J. R. 2000. *Racist America: Roots, Current Realities and Future Reparations* (New York: Routledge).

Fullard, M. 2004. *Displacing Race: The South African TRC and Interpretation of Violence*. Research Report, Centre for the Study of Violence and Reconciliation. At: http://www.csvr.org.za/docs/racism/displacingrace.pdf.

Gibney, M., R. E. Howard-Hassmann, J.-M. Coicaud, and N. Steiner, eds. 2008. *The Age of Apology: Facing up to the Past* (Philadelphia: University of Pennsylvania Press).

Gibson, J. L. 2005. "The Truth about Truth and Reconciliation in South Africa." *International Political Science Review*, Vol. 26, No. 4, pp. 341–361.

Hamber, B. 2006. "Narrowing the Micro and the Macro: A Psychological Perspective on Reparations in Societies in Transition." In P. de Greiff, ed., *Handbook of Reparations* (Oxford: Oxford University Press).

Hamber, B. 2009. *Transforming Societies After Political Violence: Truth, Reconciliation and Mental Health* (New York: Springer).
Hamber, B. and I. Palmary. 2009. "Gender, Memorialization and Symbolic Reparations." In R. Rubio-Marin, ed., *The Gender of Reparations: Unsettling Sexual Hierachies While Redressing Human Rights Violations* (Cambridge: Cambridge University Press).
Hayner, P. 2001. *Unspeakable Truths: Confronting State Terror and Atrocity* (New York: Routledge).
Judt, T. 2010. *Ill Fares the Land* (New York: Penguin).
Katznelson, I. 2005. *When Affirmative Action Was White: An Untold Story of Racial Inequality in Twentieth-Century America* (New York: W.W. Norton).
Kritz, N., ed. 1997. *Transitional Justice: How Emerging Democracies Reckon with Former Regimes* (Washington, DC: US Institute of Peace Press).
Maier, Charles S. 2003. "Overcoming the Past? Narrative and Negotiation, Remembering and Reparation: Issues at the Interface of History and the Law." In J. Torpey, *Politics and the Past: On Repairing Historical Injustices* (Lanham, MD: Rowman and Littlefield).
Mail and Guardian. 2008. "Racism Alive and Well in South Africa." At: http://www.mg.co.za/article/2008-03-11-racism-alive-and-well-in-south-africa.
Mamdani, M. 1998. "A Diminished Truth." *Siyaya*, Issue 3.
Marrus, M. R. 2006. *Official Apology and the Quest for Historical Injustices*. At: http://webapp.mcis.utoronto.ca/resources/MCIS_Controversies/2006_CGPS3_Marrus_Official_Apologies.pdf.
Massey D. S. and N. A. Denton. 1993. *Segregation and the Making of the Underclass* (Cambridge, MA: Harvard University Press).
Mendeloff, D. 2004. "Truth-Seeking, Truth-Telling, and Postconflict Peacebuilding: Curb the Enthusiasm?" *International Studies Review*, Vol. 6, No. 3, pp. 355–380.
van der Merwe, H., V. Baxter, and A. R. Chapman. 2009. *Assessing the Impact of Transitional Justice: Challenges for Empirical Research* (Washington, DC: US Institute of Peace).
Minow, M. 1998. *Between Vengeance and Forgiveness: Facing History After Genocide and Mass Violence* (Boston: Beacon Press).
Naidu, E. 2004. *Symbolic Reparations: A Fractured Opportunity*. Research Report, Centre for the Study of Violence and Reconciliation. At: http://www.csvr.org.za/docs/livingmemory/symbolicreparations.pdf.
Naidu, E. and C. Adonis. 2007. *History on Their Own Terms: Relevance of the Past*. Research Report, Centre for the Study of Violence and Reconciliation. At: http://www.csvr.org.za/docs/livingmemory/history.pdf.
Nobles, M. 2008. *The Politics of Official Apologies* (Cambridge: Cambridge University Press).
Obama, B. 2008. *Obama Race Text*. At: http://www.huffingtonpost.com/2008/03/18/obama-race-speech-read-th_n_92077.html.
Oliver, M. and T. M. Shapiro. 1997. *Black Wealth/White Wealth: A New Perspective on Racial Inequality* (New York: Routledge).
Patterson, O. 1997. *The Ordeal of Integration: Progress and Resentment in America's "Racial" Crisis* (New York: Basis Civitas).
Posner, Eric A. and A. Vermeule. 2003. "Reparations for Slavery and Other Historical Injustices." *Columbia Law Review*, Vol. 103, No. 3, pp. 689–748.
Savelsberg, Joachim and Ryan King. 2005. "Institutionalizing Collective Memories of Hate: Law and Law Enforcement in Germany and the United States." *American Journal of Sociology*, Vol. 111, No. 2, pp. 579–616.
Theissen, G. and B. Hamber. 1998. *A State of Denial: White South African's Attitudes to the Truth and Reconciliation Commission*. Research Report, Centre for the Study of Violence and Reconciliation.
Torpey, J. 2001. "Making Whole What Has Been Smashed: Reflections on Reparations." *Journal of Modern History*, Vol. 73, No. 2, pp. 333–358.
Torpey, J. 2006. *Making Whole What Has Been Smashed: On Reparations Politics* (Cambridge, MA: Harvard University Press).
Truth and Reconciliation Commission. 2003. *Introduction*. Report of the Rehabilitation and Reparation Committee, South Africa Department of Justice. At: http://www.info.gov.za/otherdocs/2003/trc.
United Nations. 2006. *Basic Principles and Guidelines on the Right to a Remedy and Reparation for Victims of Gross Violations of International Human Rights Law and Serious Violations of International Humanitarian Law*. At: http://www2.ohchr.org/english/law/remedy.htm.

Wills, C. 2008. "Obama Opposes Slavery Reparations." *Huffington Post*, 2 August. At: http://www.huffingtonpost.com/2008/08/02/obama-opposes-slavery-rep_n_116506.html.

Wilson, R. 2001. *Politics of Truth and Reconciliation in South Africa* (Cape Town: Cambridge University Press).

Yamamoto, E. K. 2007. "Japanese American Redress and African American Reparations." In T. M. Martin and M. Yaqinto, eds., *Redress for Historical Injustice in the United States: On Reparations for Slavery, Jim Crow and Their Legacies* (Durham, NC: Duke University Press).

43

Memory and human rights

Daniel Levy and Natan Sznaider

Human rights discourse has become an omnipresent feature of international politics. Images of human rights abuses and the attendant political rhetoric seeking to assuage mass atrocities suffuse the global media. However, many obstacles remain toward the fulfillment of human rights ideals – first and foremost, the legally sanctioned and normatively embedded sovereignty of nation states. Yet human rights declarations, formulated as a set of rules, regulations, and norms, do constitute a challenge to one of the central tenets of sovereignty, namely the principle of non-interference in so-called internal affairs. When it comes to certain types of abuses, human rights are about humans and not about members of specific states. The end of the Cold War in 1989 and the emergence of global interdependencies have highlighted the tensions between the imperatives of a Human Rights Regime, the unbounded universal "we" and the prerogatives of sovereignty, the political community, the bounded "we." The notion of a "human rights regime" refers to a system that is "defined as principles, norms, rules and decision-making procedures around which actor expectations converge in a given issue-area" (Krasner 1982, p. 185).

While this dichotomous view certainly has relevance, it is our contention that the consolidation of the Human Rights Regime has not so much led to the erosion of state sovereignty but rather to its transformation. More specifically, human rights themselves have become a principle of political legitimacy, inaugurating a new kind of politics (Levy and Sznaider 2006b). Although the rights revolution of the last two decades has not always deterred human rights abuses, it has created strong normative and institutional foundations able to penetrate the shield of sovereign impunity. Increasingly, compliance with a set of human rights norms – such as dignity and rights for all – is circumscribing the legitimacy of unacceptable state actions. Adherence to a minimal set of human rights ideals has become a significant, albeit uneven factor in global politics and a prerequisite to preserving legitimate sovereignty.

One factor that has contributed to a rapprochement between particular (national) identifications and universal (human rights) orientations in many countries is the decoupling of nationhood and state. Here the state is increasingly considered a neutral institution that regulates the affairs of its citizens without necessarily providing an exclusionary sense of belonging. Clearly states have retained most of their sovereign functions, but the basis for their legitimacy is no longer primarily conditioned by a contract with a bounded nation. It is also determined by a state's adherence to a set of nation-transcending human rights ideals. Thus legitimacy is mediated by the extent to which states engage with (or commit to) an emerging human rights regime, blurring the boundaries of internal and external affairs.

We examine the link between human rights and sovereignty through the analytic prism of historical memories. Historical memories refer to shared understandings of and responsibilities for the significance the past has for the present concerns of a community. Through memory, a political community validates challenges and reproduces itself. More specifically, we argue that historical memories of past failures to prevent human rights abuses have become a primary mechanism through which the institutionalization of human rights idioms and their legal inscription during the last two decades have transformed sovereignty. The global proliferation of human rights norms is driven by the public and frequently ritualistic attention to memories of their persistent violations. The emergence of this global "memory imperative" finds its expression in a set of political and normative expectations to engage with past injustices (Levy and Sznaider 2010).

Historically, it is a European phenomenon that emerged against the backdrop of memories of World War II and the Holocaust (Levy and Sznaider 2005). These memories also formed the backdrop against which the United Nations formulated various human rights conventions, thus establishing a global context. War atrocities themselves had not previously led to the triumph of human rights. They were not part of international relations prior to World War II: the Covenant of the League of Nations did not even contain explicit references to human rights. In contrast, human rights have a central place in the preamble and Article 1 of the UN Charter. The link between the Holocaust and the emergence of a moral consensus about human rights is particularly evident in the genesis and the consolidation of the Universal Declaration of Human Rights that was adopted by the General Assembly of the newly formed United Nations on December 10, 1948. The Declaration, as well as the UN charter itself, must be understood as direct responses to the shared moral revulsion of the delegates to the Holocaust – a sentiment that was also reflected in the direct connection between the Declaration and some of the legal principles established in the Nuremberg war crime trials.

This link was also manifested in the close working relationship between the United Nations War Crimes Commission and the Human Rights Division of the nascent United Nations (Morsink 1999). In both cases, concerns about the illegality of retroactive jurisprudence were overcome by replacing conventional (i.e., national) legal principles with the broader notion of international law and its implicit appeal to a civilized consciousness, now viewed as a safeguard against the barbarous potential of national sovereignty. Together they were decisive in shaping the way contemporary human rights norms limit state sovereignty by providing international standards for how states can treat their own citizens. Human rights are therefore less a matter of philosophical or religious worldviews, but based on historical experiences and concomitant memories of catastrophes. Memories of the Holocaust have evolved into a universal code that is now synonymous with an imperative to address past injustices (both legally as well as in commemorative terms). Although the "memory imperative" originated with the centrality of Holocaust memories during the 1990s, it has become a de-contextualized code for human rights abuses as such.

Most opposition to injustice is now articulated through the categorical denial and remedial efforts of rights violations. The victims of the present can no longer find salvation in the future but must be redeemed by connecting their experience to an iconographic past of human rights violations. Nation states engage (or are expected to) with their own history in a skeptical fashion. This dynamic explains both the importance of human rights norms as a globally available repertoire of legitimate claim-making and the particular appropriation of this universal script. Rather than presupposing an abstract notion of political interests (grounded, for instance, in power or capital), we probe how, once institutionalized, human rights idioms themselves constitute political interests shaping power balances and by extension the contours of sovereignty. Memory politics of human rights have become a new form of political rationality and a normative requirement for state legitimacy. Sovereign rhetoric is increasingly evaluated by the extent to which it is related to the legal recognition of human rights. To be sure, memory clashes abound, providing ample evidence that the prominence of human rights does not imply the end of the national and at times even raises the specter of re-nationalization or re-tribalization. However, the prevalence of human rights, the mediated proliferation of memories of human rights abuses and their association with particularistic politics does signify the diminishing normative return of nationalism in international politics.

Memory imperatives: human rights and the transformation of sovereignty

How exactly does memory work contribute to these fundamental changes and the growing salience of human rights? Contrary to conventional approaches that associate memory with national identifications, we propose a cosmopolitan conception of memory focusing on the simultaneity of universal and particular outlooks. We do not treat universalism and particularism as superior or inferior moral choices, but rather look at them as modes of existence that can change over time. We historicize these notions, thereby de-moralizing them, while retaining them as valuable sociological tools. This has consequences for the study of memory. The cosmopolitanization of memories refers to practices that shift attention away from the territorialized nation state and the ethnically bound frameworks commonly associated with the notion of collective memory (Levy and Sznaider 2005). Rather than presuppose the congruity of nation, territory, and polity, cosmopolitanized memories are based on and contribute to nation-transcending idioms, spanning territorial and national borders.

Accordingly we consider the recent proliferation of human rights ideals as a new form of cosmopolitanism, exemplifying a dynamic through which global concerns become part of local experiences. The choice of cosmopolitanism as a new moral and political idiom in this connection is not arbitrary. It relates to political and intellectual forms predating the era of the nation state. Crucially, it has resurfaced at a time when the basic premises of the nation state have been challenged and the shape of its sovereignty is being transformed. Cosmopolitanized memories capture the social modalities dealing with difference, such as universalism, relativism, ethnicity, nationalism, and multiculturalism. Universalist versions of cosmopolitanism (e.g., Nussbaum 2002) oblige us to respect others as equals as a matter of principle, yet for that very reason it does not involve any requirement that would arouse curiosity or respect for what makes others different. Even more, the particularity of others is sacrificed to a postulate of universal equality that denies its own context of emergence and interests. In contrast, cosmopolitan memories presuppose a "universalistic minimum" involving a number of substantive norms that must be upheld at all costs. These substantive norms include the sanctity of the body (Turner 2006) and the avoidance of unnecessary cruelty (Sznaider 2001). We use the term "cosmopolitan common sense" when we have good reasons to assume that most individuals would be willing to defend this minimum (Beck and Sznaider 2006, p. 19).

In the following we highlight two dimensions of memory politics that are particularly important for theorizing the prominence of human rights and the transformation of sovereignty: the fragmentation of memories reflective of and contributing to the decoupling of nation and state; and the de-contextualization of memories, compelling the abstraction of concrete historical suffering, thereby facilitating nation-transcending identifications with others. The fact that memories are no longer exclusively beholden to the idea of the nation state is of central importance. Today there is a pervasive trend toward national and global introspection that has prompted numerous countries around the world to "come to terms with their past" (Levy and Sznaider 2005). "Inventions of Nationhood" during the nineteenth century were based on heroic conceptions and formative myths that were transmitted by "traditional" and "exemplary" forms of narrativity. In contrast, the history of Western European nation states during the last quarter of the twentieth century was characterized by a self-critical narrative of their national pasts. While traditional and exemplary narratives deploy historical events to promote foundational myth, skeptical narratives also incorporate events that focus on past injustices committed by one's own nation. Cosmopolitanized memories thus evolve in the context of remembered continuities that view the past of the nation through its willingness to come to terms with injustices committed in its name.

This focus on memories of past injustices is accompanied by another tendency; namely, the transition from *history politics*, which is characterized by a state-centric dynamic (through official commemorations, textbooks, etc.) to *memory history*, which corresponds to the fragmentation of memories and their privatization (Diner 2003). This transformation manifests itself in the changing relationship of memory and history. The difference between memory history and conventional historical narratives is instructive. History is a particularized idea of temporal sequences articulating some form of (national) development. Memory, on the other hand, represents a coexistence of simultaneous phenomena and a multitude of pasts. (National) history politics corresponds to the *telos* of modernity (as a kind of secularized religion or civic religion). Memory can dissolve this sequence, which is a constitutive part of history. Memory history is a particular mnemonic mode which moves away from state-supported (and state-supporting) national history.

The previous (attempted) monopoly by the state to shape collective pasts has given way to a fragmentation of memories borne by private, individual, scientific, ethnic, religious, and other mnemonic agents. Although the state continues to exercise an important role in how we remember its history, it now shares the field of meaning production with a host of other players. Modes of collective memory are being cosmopolitanized and also exist on supra- and sub-national levels. The formation of cosmopolitan human rights memories does not eliminate the national perspective, but makes nationhood one of several options of collective self-understanding. As the state loses its privileged command over the production of collective values (e.g., nationalism), human rights memories become politically and culturally more consequential.

In both the national and global case, the success of identification with distant others is predicated on the ability to produce shared memories that at once generate concrete references (to heroic deeds of the nation or particular human rights atrocities) and the possibility to draw abstract identifications from them (the need to forget the misdeeds of the nation as Ernest Renan put it, and remember selectively as the uneven pursuit of human rights appears to indicate). It is a delicate balance, which has come under increased pressure with the aforementioned proliferation and fragmentation of memories. The claim that the nation state is an unproblematic container for solidarity is profoundly ahistorical. Ironically, when national cultures were invented, they were open to the same criticisms as those directed at global culture today. They were dismissed as superficial and inauthentic substitutes for local cultures that were once rich in tradition, and they were taken to task for being much too large and alienating. Surely, it was argued, nobody would ever identify with the impersonal image of the nation. As history has shown, this prediction was wrong. In his seminal 1983 treatise on the origins of nationalism, Benedict Anderson quips about the limits of solidarity when he poses the rhetorical question "Who would be willing to die for the European Community?" This comes as somewhat of a surprise, given Anderson's constructivist approach, which stipulates that all communities, and especially nations, are entities that are fundamentally imagined. The very belief that there is something fundamental at their root is the result of a conscious myth-building process. To come into existence, the nation state at the *fin de siècle* depended on a process by which existing societies used representations to turn themselves into new wholes that would act immediately on people's feelings and on which they could base their identities; in short, making them into groups with which individuals could identify. The essential point of Anderson's thesis, which is often overlooked, is that a new system of values requiring self-sacrifice and willingness to live together is necessary in the transition to nationhood. In the pre-modern era, solidarity was based primarily on direct contact with those who were close (ethical boundaries corresponded to village boundaries); with the "nationalization of the masses," it became necessary to identify with many other people via an "imagined community" whom one could not possibly get to know personally. We do not know each other, and yet we feel united as citizens of the same country.

This distant quality also permeates the salience of universal (human) or particular (national) rights as they are mediated, among other things, by the extent to which memories of past human rights abuses are transmitted as concrete or abstract forms. The latter are proliferating with the cosmopolitanization of memories. Human rights matter only to the extent that their universality is recognized. This recognition, in turn, is predicated on a process of de-contextualization by which memories of concrete (particular) atrocities are transformed into abstract (universal) violations of humanity. Without this de-contextualization it is difficult to re-contextualize memories of human rights as abstract categories and thus ensure their recognition as universal lessons for humanity. This process of abstraction is also necessary in order to re-inscribe memories of past atrocities into particular experiences. At the same time, this process of abstraction does little to change the fact that communities transmit different memories of the past, based largely on the extent to which memories of past abuses are a concrete part of shared experiences or whether they lack the kind of proximity (or distance) that allow them to become abstract principles. Accordingly, the strength of human rights principles in a given national context is the product of the tenuous balance of particular (concrete) and universal (de-contextualized) memories. The latter are in essence a form of forgetting. The relationship between memory and forgetting has received significant attention in the literature (Ricoeur 1999). However, contrary to most views, we do not treat memory as an antidote to forgetting. Instead we suggest that institutionalized memories of human rights abuses imply forgetting. The institutionalization of such memories and thus their ability to mobilize legitimate political claims is largely based on the process of de-contextualization, which in turn requires a shift from concrete memories to abstract remembrance. In other words, there is a move away from the concrete (i.e., particular) experience toward a more abstract (i.e., universal) message in order to reappropriate and recast one's own memories of past abuses in the contours of a globalized human rights discourse. As a result, we are frequently witnessing the institutionalization of the remembrance of barbarous acts at the expense of memories of the barbarity of these acts.

The distinction between memory and remembrance is not incidental. Nor can it be reduced to the so-called instrumentalization of memories. Memory vacillating between the concrete and the abstract, and its implied de-contextualization, can be related to three dimensions. It inheres in the course of action that gives memories their ritualistic strength. Ritualization depends on mediation, which by definition requires a certain form of abstraction. Considering the various channels through which memories of past human abuses are communicated, we consider this as a process of mediated forgetting. Failure to remember is also implied insofar as proximity to that which is remembered can shape the relative political–cultural significance it has for a community. Put differently, the universality of human rights necessitates a certain distance from the actual events being remembered. Lastly, the immanence of this dynamic is not just the product of historical and geographic proximity but also the result of temporal distance from the events that are being remembered.

One way of looking at this phenomenon empirically is to focus on the de-contextualization of memories of human rights abuses, which function as a precondition for the spread of human rights as a universally recognized idiom. The de-contextualization of particular memories of human rights abuses and their universal re-appropriation can be addressed by distinguishing between who is remembering and what is remembered. Moreover, cosmopolitan memories of human rights abuses are circumscribed by the historical occurrence of a forgiveness narrative that has further contributed to the shift from memory to remembrance and a corresponding transition from concrete individual to more abstract collective dimensions (Levy and Sznaider 2006a). Memories of human rights violations have become a subject of public negotiations and been subjected to the imperatives of forgiveness and reconciliation (Olick 2007).

By historicizing human rights, we thus propose a political sociology of human rights that is not based on some universalized metaphysical appeal but primarily transmitted through the proliferation of globally produced memories of failures to address human rights abuses. These mnemonic practices are firmly embodied in historical references (e.g., Holocaust, Balkan Wars, Rwanda) and institutional manifestations (e.g., International War Crime Tribunals). The main difference between the universalistic origins of human rights and their recent cosmopolitan manifestations is that the latter unfold on the background of a globalized imagination. This does not imply convergence or homogenization, but rather the emergence of a locally situated recognition that sees humanity as a meaningful category of membership, not in a normative but a political, cultural, and legally consequential terminology in line with de-nationalized conceptions of membership. Exclusion from the nation is no longer synonymous with exclusion from the protection of the state. The continuous transposition of cosmopolitan memories about failures to prevent human rights abuses has changed the conditions of membership. The surplus of legitimacy that human rights conceptions currently enjoy is neither an irreversible nor an evenly distributed process. Memories of human rights abuses, as well as failures to address them in time, are thus facets of a conflictual conception of collective memory. Memory is diverse and plural. It tells more than one story. Often these stories are contradictory and do not recount one single narrative. And they do not need to. Witnesses in trials make this point quite clearly. This is particularly relevant to contemporary debates in liberal democracies where national cultures and their homogeneous conceptions of the collectivity are challenged by the multicultural compositions of their societies.

The cosmopolitan turn and the concomitant proliferation of human rights and recognition are closely related to the aforementioned changes in moral sentiments since 1945. Memories of the great wars have transformed human rights sensibilities, at least in Western liberal democracies. Can there be a cosmopolitan reaction to the ever so present spectacle of human rights violations? Are "we" responsible for the suffering of remote others? How should people respond when confronted with pictures of the beaten, tortured, and murdered? With compassion? What does compassion mean in the context of a globalized human rights politics? Compassion involves an active moral impetus to address others' suffering.

There is a strong relationship between human rights consciousness and the emergence of a globalized cosmopolitan and liberal society, with its distinctive features of an expanded global awareness of the presence of others and the equal worth of human beings driven by memories of past human rights violations. Through these memories and their institutionalization in international conventions, the nature and sentiments of compassion have changed. Cruelty is now understood as the infliction of unwarranted suffering, and compassion is an organized, public response to this evil, as in human rights politics. With the lessening of profoundly categorical and corporate social distinctions triggered by the memories of barbarism, compassion can become more extensive and set a politics of human rights into motion. The capacity to identify with others, and in particular with others' pain, is promoted by the profound belief that others are similar to us. This identification is based on ontological equality.

Global media memories and human rights

However, both the "memory imperative" and the recognition of the other require recurrent forms of mediation in order to sustain the Human Rights Regime. Here the globalization of media images plays a crucial role (Tester 2001). Developments in the field of communications go hand in hand with new forms of memory. According to Hutton (1993), oral cultures rely on memories of lived experiences. In cultures of literacy, however, we "read" to retrieve forgotten wisdom from the past. The invention of the printing press to produce books and newspapers was crucial in this process of reconstructing the past. How do the new global media transform memory cultures? The technological revolution that introduced the printing press textualized culture. The printed text led to an externalization of knowledge and laid the foundation for references to shared knowledge. The global media have led to yet another revolution in the reception of knowledge, values, and memories by promoting a visual culture. We now remember things with the aid of images, which helps to explain why exhibitions, films, memorials, and other media are becoming so important.

Compassion enters into current debates on the universal and contextual foundations of ethics as depicted in the global media. Globalization transforms cultures and its meaning-making vocabularies. This transformation becomes most evident when the particularities that make up a culture are divorced from their original spatial (i.e., local and national) contexts. Culture can no longer be understood as a closed national space, because it now competes constantly with other spaces. Transnational media and mass culture such as film and music loosen the national framework without abandoning it entirely. The globalization of communication technologies challenges national identities by confronting the viewer with the presence of others. In the process, conceptions and ideas about the world come into conflict with exclusivist notions of national self-understanding. Even television viewers who never leave their hometown must integrate global value systems that are produced elsewhere into their national frame of reference. The rise of rapid, electronically based communication has led to an interlocked system without national borders. The immediate speed and imagery of the new global communications facilitate a shared consciousness and cosmopolitan memories that span territorial and linguistic borders.

Many of these global developments are possible only because of technological breakthroughs in electronic media. One feature particularly salient for the globalization of the human rights discourse is the rise of media events, where a live and concentrated local action can be shared by the world (Dayan and Katz 1992). This is how the world is transported into the local. Distant others can be part of, and engender, emotions of everyday life. Human rights politics is put into action when the sight of suffering leads to political action intended to lessen the suffering of others. This is only possible with a shared language that makes the suffering of others understandable. For the current suffering of others to be made comprehensible it must be integrated into a cognitive structure that is connected to the memory of other people's suffering. In this way, earlier catastrophes become relevant in the present and can determine a future that is articulated outside the parameters of the nation state. However, there are communal boundaries to this globalized compassion. What has changed, spurred on by globalized imaginations, is the emergence of cultural and legal recognitions perceiving of humanity as a meaningful category of membership. Not merely in a normative sense but in a political, cultural, and legally consequential terminology in line with de-nationalized concepts of membership. Exclusion from the nation is no longer synonymous with exclusion from the protection of the state.

Memories of atrocities and memories of fear

As much as the end of the Cold War constituted an important juncture for the consolidation of the human rights regime, the terrorist attacks of September 11, 2001, and their geo-political aftermath have added a new urgency to debates about the political status of human rights and sovereign prerogatives. Terrorism challenges the political salience of human rights principles and frequently causes the state to revert to one of its founding imperatives: the provision of security for its citizens (Sznaider 2006). When people feel insecure they will appreciate the security the state can provide. If they fear nothing more than violent death they will accept the state as ultimate protector. Anti-terrorist measures and expanding executive powers frequently infringe upon civic and human rights and have led some to demand that sovereignty be less conditional (Ignatieff 2004). Terrorism shifts attention away from state abuse and redirects national memories to failures of the state to protect its citizens.

However, despite these challenges, or perhaps precisely because of them, even the national interest rhetoric through which anti-terrorist measures are justified continues to be articulated in the global context of a human rights discourse. The recurrence of strong executive powers and national interest politics weaken international legitimacy and require extensive justifications vis-à-vis human rights standards. Current suspensions of human rights are not taking place in the middle of political crises but rather in the context of ongoing political reconfigurations. International terrorism is occurring at a historical moment when the classic nation state, which monopolized the means of violence and whose task it was to neutralize the fear of violent death into civilized channels, is being transformed. As soon as the state is recognized as the only source of legitimate violence, people internalize the state's authority as the "mortal god," to employ Hobbes's metaphor of the Leviathan. This means that the state needs to be worshipped as the new legitimate god, introducing a modern sovereignty in which God's sovereignty was transferred to the state.

Since the terror attacks on September 11, international politics have left the realm of calculability, and the rules of warfare must be renegotiated. The Westphalian Order, grounded on the notion that a stable and peaceful political order can only be maintained by mutually supportive vows of non-intervention between political entities, no longer holds. The modern human rights regime is premised on the notion that the prevention of human suffering takes precedence over the principle of sovereignty. This is the opposite of Hobbes and runs counter to the state's claim to provide security. The perceived suffering of strangers and the impulse to alleviate that suffering is one of the unintended consequences of the global process. The strength of human rights consists not only in their institutionalization but also in the realization, perpetuated by continuous reminders of past failures, of their fragility. Every time gross human rights violations are committed, they are not perceived as evil but as a (our) political failure, carrying the seeds, at least potentially, of real action. Memories of past abuses, which by definition remind us of a breakdown of the regime, have been driving human rights remedies and have further raised the political costs of committing such abuses.

References

Anderson, Benedict. 1983. *Imagined Communities: Reflections on the Origins and Spread of Nationalism* (London: Verso).

Beck, Ulrich and Natan Sznaider. 2006. "Unpacking Cosmopolitanism for the Social Sciences: A Research Agenda." *British Journal of Sociology*, Vol. 57, No. 1, pp. 1–23.

Dayan, Daniel and Eliahu Katz. 1992. *Media Events: The Live Broadcasting of History* (Cambridge, MA: Harvard University Press).

Diner, Dan. 2003. *Gedächtniszeiten: Uber Jüdische und Andere Geschichten* (Munich: C.H. Beck).

Hutton, Patrick. 1993. *History as an Art of Memory* (Hanover, NH: University Press of New England).

Ignatieff, Michael. 2004. *Lesser Evil: Political Ethics in an Age of Terror* (Princeton, NJ: Princeton University Press).

Krasner, Stephen. 1982. "Structural Causes and Regime Consequences: Regimes as Intervening Variables." *International Organization*, Vol. 36, pp. 185–205.

Levy, Daniel and Natan Sznaider. 2005. *Memory and the Holocaust in the Global Age* (Philadelphia, PA: Temple University Press).

Levy, Daniel and Natan Sznaider. 2006a. "Forgive and Not Forget: Reconciliation Between Forgiveness and Resentment," pp. 83–100 in Elazar Barkan and Alexander Karn, eds., *Taking Wrongs Seriously: Apologies and Reconciliation* (Palo Alto, CA: Stanford University Press).

Levy, Daniel and Natan Sznaider. 2006b. "Sovereignty Transformed: A Sociology of Human Rights." *British Journal of Sociology*, Vol. 57, No. 4, pp. 657–676.

Levy, Daniel and Natan Sznaider. 2010. *Human Rights and Memory* (University Park, PA: Penn State University Press).

Morsink, Johannes. 1999. *The Universal Declaration of Human Rights: Origins, Drafting, and Intent* (Philadelphia: University of Pennsylvania Press).

Nussbaum, Martha. 2002. *For Love of Country?* (Boston: Beacon Press).

Olick, Jeffrey K. 2007. *The Politics of Regret: On Collective Memory and Historical Responsibility* (London: Routledge).

Ricoeur, Paul. 1999. "Memory and Forgetting," pp. 5–12 in Richard Kearney and Mark Dooley, eds., *Questioning Ethics* (London: Routledge).

Sznaider, Natan. 2001. *The Compassionate Temperament: Care and Cruelty in Modern Society* (Lanham, MD: Rowman & Littlefield).

Sznaider, Natan. 2006. "Terrorism and the Social Contract." *Irish Journal of Sociology*, Vol. 15, No. 1, pp. 7–23.

Tester, Keith. 2001. *Compassion, Morality and the Media* (Maidenhead, UK: Open University Press).

Turner, Bryan S. 2006. *Vulnerability and Human Rights* (University Park, PA: Penn State University Press).

44

Truth commissions and human rights

Margaret Urban Walker

Truth commissions are the institution most emblematic of the emerging principle that individual victims of political violence and mistreatment, and societies in which serious human rights violations obtain, are entitled to an investigation and disclosure of facts concerning these abuses (on the emerging principle, see Méndez 1997 and 2006). In the aftermath of armed conflict or severe political repression, truth commissions are temporary institutions charged with discovering, and disseminating in a final report, a truthful record of events, causes, patterns, and individual or institutional responsibilities pertaining to specified human rights violations during a particular period of time (Minow 1998; Rotberg and Thompson 2000; Hayner 2001; Freeman 2006; Borer 2006). Other means of uncovering, documenting, and disseminating the truth about human rights abuses include the authoritative findings of criminal judicial proceedings or of "truth trials"; reports by human rights organizations and national, intergovernmental, and international bodies and organizations; the opening of previously secret state files; the excavation and forensic study of human remains; the revision of history texts for use in schools; and research, educational, archival, or memorial projects by governmental or non-governmental entities. Yet truth commissions have rapidly become a standard transitional justice measure following violence, repression, or conflict, refined over the past three decades by accumulated experience, the articulation of international norms prescribing truth recovery, and the technical support of international organizations (see United Nations High Commission on Human Rights 2006). Widespread and rapid proliferation of truth commissions and ambitious claims made for what truth commissions might do has prompted closer scrutiny of these claims, research on the efficacy of truth commissions, and consideration of the limitations and tensions inherent in truth commission proceedings and aims. In this chapter the first section looks at the evolution of a human right to the truth about human rights violations in international instruments. The next section overviews diverse claims made for what truth commissions aim at or accomplish. The third and final section registers some critical concerns about truth commissions or the claims made about their effects.

A right to the truth

A 2005 draft resolution by the United Nations Commission on Human Rights requested that a study by the Office of the United Nations High Commissioner on Human Rights define the basis, scope, and content of a "right to the truth," and best practices and recommendations for the implementation of this right in the aftermath of conflict or of massive or systematic human rights violations (United Nations Commission on Human Rights 2005b). The resolution mentions both judicial and non-judicial truth-seeking mechanisms "such as truth and reconciliation commissions." The "Study on the Right to the Truth" (hereafter, "the Study"), submitted in 2006, traces the legal and historical basis for the right, finding recognition of the right in international treaties and instruments; national, regional, and international jurisprudence; and resolutions of universal and regional intergovernmental bodies (United Nations Commission on Human Rights 2006). The right to the truth is "both an individual and a collective right" (paragraph 36) held by victims of gross human rights violations, their families and relatives, and also "society" (paragraph 58). The truth in question encompasses causes leading to the individual victim's victimization; causes and conditions pertaining to the violation of international human rights and humanitarian law; progress and results of investigations of violations; circumstances and reasons for the perpetration of the violations; the circumstances in which violations took place; the fate and whereabouts of victims if dead or missing; and the identity of perpetrators (subject to appropriate safeguards) (paragraphs 38–40). The 2006 Study acknowledges multiple mechanisms that can implement the right to the truth, including international and national criminal tribunals, truth trials (judicial proceedings limited to investigations and the compilation of case files, without prosecution), truth commissions, national human rights institutions, archives, administrative and civil proceedings, and historical projects (paragraphs 47–54). It concludes that the "the right to the truth about gross human rights violations and serious violations of human rights law is an inalienable and autonomous right," (paragraph 55) and a "non-derogable right" not subject to limitations (paragraph 60). A follow-up report by the Office of the High Commissioner on Human Rights in 2007 surveys responses to the Study by 16 countries and several non-governmental organizations (United Nations Human Rights Council 2007). It describes the right to the truth as "evolving steadily" (paragraph 87) and recommends further in-depth study of the contribution of criminal justice systems, the protection of records and archives concerning human rights violations, and the institutional means, procedures, and mechanisms for implementing the right to the truth (paragraph 92).

What aims of the right to the truth do these documents identify? The 2006 Study notes that legal acts establishing truth commissions in particular "ground themselves in the need of the victims, their relatives and the general society to know the truth about what has taken place; to facilitate the reconciliation process; to contribute to the fight against impunity; and to reinstall or to strengthen democracy and the rule of law," a fairly sweeping agenda (United Nations Commission on Human Rights 2006, paragraph 14). The Study adds the objective for truth commissions of "making a credible historical record and thereby to prevent the recurrence of such events," and notes that some truth commissions provide "a cathartic forum for victims, perpetrators and the broader society to publicly discuss violations, often with the ultimate aim of reconciliation and sometimes to achieve a measure of justice" (paragraph 15). While the individual's right to the truth functions instrumentally to the fulfillment of other rights, such as individual victims' (and families' and relatives') rights to investigation and information, to access justice, to an effective remedy, to reparation, and so forth, the Study links individual access to truth to "a basic human need" and to addressing the "anguish and sorrow" of, for example, families of the disappeared. The societal aspect of a right to truth centers on creating a credible historical record with intent to prevent repetition of documented violations. The 2007 response reports that some states hold that the "purpose" of the right to the truth is "to restore to the victims of manifest violations of human rights their dignity and to ensure that such misdeeds do not recur" (United Nations Human Rights Council 2007, paragraph 13). Recent conceptualization of the right to the truth thus encompasses both victim-centered and society-centered aims.

The path to recent recognition of the right to the truth as an inalienable and autonomous right passes through other international instruments, especially those concerning principles for combating impunity and principles and guidelines concerning the victim's rights to a remedy and reparation in the wake of gross human rights violations and serious violations of humanitarian law. (Also relevant are guidelines on internal displacement and on enforced disappearance). The Updated Set of Principles (hereafter, "Set of Principles") to combat impunity puts "the right to know" of victims and of "a people" among the three categories of principles for combating impunity, alongside the right to justice and the right to reparation (United Nations Commission on Human Rights 2005a). The Set of Principles lists first the inalienable right of "every people" to know "the truth about past events concerning perpetration of heinous crimes" as a "vital safeguard against the recurrence of violations" (Principle 2), and gives separate place to the duty to "preserve the collective memory from extinction and, in particular, at guarding against the development of revisionist and negationist arguments" (Principle 3). Finally and separately, the Set of Principles asserts the "imprescriptable right to know the truth" of victims and their families about violations they have suffered (Principle 4). The Set of Principles gives special attention to the establishment and role of truth commissions (Principles 6–13) and to the preservation of archives and public access to them (Principles 14–18), although not to the exclusion of judicial investigation and criminal prosecution as other truth recovery paths. The Set of Principles thus gives a somewhat fuller emphasis to the societal dimensions of a right to truth, stressing the aims of preventing both future reoccurrence of violations and the denial of past violations. While preventing denial may be seen as serving to prevent repetition, the Set of Principles seems to underscore the independent claim a society or people has to accurate collective memory, saying, "A people's knowledge of the history of its oppression is part of its heritage and, as such, must be ensured" (Principle 3). This emphasis on a collective right of a people to know its history and on the idea of truth as the heritage of a people was present in the original articulation of principles to combat impunity (sometimes called the Joinet principles) that speaks in the plural of "the main objectives of the right to know as a collective right," mentioning prevention of violations by drawing on history and guarding against the "perversions" of history through revisionism and negationism (United Nations Commission on Human Rights 1997).

The Basic Principles and Guidelines on the Right to a Remedy and Reparation (United Nations General Assembly 2006b; hereafter "Basic Principles") specifies three categories of remedies to which victims of gross human rights violations have a right: access to justice; reparation; and relevant information concerning violations and reparations mechanisms. The right to the truth concerning violations appears in a dual role. There is an entitlement of victims and their representatives to "learn the truth" about the causes of their victimization and on causes and conditions pertaining to the gross violations of human rights (Section X). In addition, among the reparations measures to which victims are entitled are forms of "satisfaction," including the right to "verification of the facts and full and public disclosure of the truth" (consistent with the well-being of the victim and others involved); to a search for the whereabouts of the disappeared, the identities of abducted children, and the remains of those killed; and to the inclusion of "an accurate account of the violation that occurred in international human rights law and international humanitarian law training and in educational material at all levels" (Section IX, 22, b, c, and h). The Basic Principles recognizes that groups of victims may be targeted collectively and that groups should be able to claim reparation (Section VIII, 13). "Society" or "a people" do not figure in these guidelines for the rights of individuals, except insofar as it is considered a form of satisfaction, and hence a kind of reparations to individual victims, for the truth about violations to be embodied in legal training and educational materials, presumably to insure that the reality and their experience of violation is preserved and given authoritative status. Unlike the

Study and the Set of Principles, the Basic Principles do not explicitly link the entitlement of victims to a truthful accounting to guarantees of non-repetition. Guarantees of non-repetition are treated as a distinct kind of reparations, and entitlements to truth are not directly associated with the aim of preventing future violence. The Preamble to the Basic Principles does, however, mention not only the plight of and benefits to the victim and survivors, but also "future human generations" as a concern (Preamble).

In summary, the central understandings embodied in international instruments through which an autonomous right to the truth has evolved appeal both to interests and needs of victims and families, as well as to societal interests and needs. Needs and interests of victims and families include psychological needs to be relieved of suffering and needs for the reaffirmation of dignity. The societal interests include knowledge that leads to effective prevention of abuses, but also interests in truthful collective memory as a people's heritage.

The aims of truth commissions

A truth commission is a temporary body constituted to gather information and testimony relevant to determining, and delivering in a final report, a true and authoritative record of human rights abuses during a specified period of violence, repression, or conflict. Truth commissions and the international instruments that affirm the rights of victims and societies to know the truth about episodes of violence and repression have developed in tandem in recent decades. There have been over forty truth commissions. Truth commissions have become an accepted, and often expected, way of addressing victims' and societies' rights to the truth. All truth commissions share the core task of investigating, clarifying, and disseminating certain truths about episodes or eras of human rights abuse. Yet truth commissions differ considerably in their origins, constitution, mandates, powers, legitimacy, and resources. Truth commissions can be charged to examine relatively compressed periods or decades of abuse (a three-year period in Haiti; a thirty-six-year armed conflict in Guatemala; decades of removal of mixed-race Aboriginal children in Australia). They can be established by executive order (Argentina; Chile), legislative action (South Africa), or through internationally brokered agreements (El Salvador; Timor-Leste); some prominent truth recovery reports have been generated unofficially, by extra-governmental entities (Brazil).

There can be many truth commissioners or few, who are appointed through different processes (three non-Salvadorans appointed by the Secretary-General of the United Nations to El Salvador's Commission; in Argentina, twelve nationals, and in Chile eight Chileans, named by the President; in Guatemala, two Guatemalans named from within and one non-Guatemalan United Nations representative; in South Africa, seventeen South Africans, representing varied constituencies, selected through a highly consultative process within the country). Resources vary greatly (a \$10 million Guatemalan budget; over \$30 million in South Africa). Officially empowered truth commissions may enjoy more or fewer investigative powers, such as those of search and subpoena (South Africa's TRC enjoyed significant subpoena, search, and seizure powers it rarely used; Timor-Leste's commission could impose criminal penalties on individuals for failures to cooperate or for intimidating witnesses; earlier Latin American commissions had no such powers). The mandates of truth commissions can leave more or less room for interpretation of their investigative mission. Truth commissions are not tasked to tell simply "the truth" or "the whole truth;" rather, their mandates provide terms of reference that indicate with varying degrees of precision which kinds of violations are to be investigated and the period of conflict or repression to be examined. The violations under investigation are usually those that qualify as grave or gross abuses of human rights, in particular, such crimes "on the body" as disappearance, extra-judicial execution, torture, arbitrary detention, and, more recently, rape and other sexual violence and forced recruitment. East Timor's Commission for Reception, Truth, and Reconciliation, however, developed an innovative system of Community Reconciliation Procedures to deal with restitution by perpetrators for lesser harms such as theft, assault, or damages to property. Truth commissions are not usually charged to examine socio-economic or social–structural issues, although these may play a role in a commission's explanatory task. Recommendations for the reform of institutions (especially judicial, military, penal, and security ones) are always among a truth commission's recommendations.

Resources and time constraints determine how much a commission can do. Some commissions have focused on illustrative or "window" cases to illuminate broader patterns of violence (El Salvador), while others have tried to make determinations in as many individual cases as they can (around 3,400 individual cases in Chile's National Commission on Truth and Reconciliation; more than 7,500 cases in Guatemala's Commission for Historical Clarification). In either approach, it is inevitable that many cases will go unreported, and of those reported, many will receive no additional investigation. While the global fame of South Africa's Truth and Reconciliation Commission made public testimonies of (a minority of) victims a new standard to which later commissions conformed (Peru, Timor-Leste), significant earlier commissions (Chile, Haiti, Argentina) proceeded in private, making their findings known only through a final report. While the TRC's perpetrator testimony in amnesty hearings was often riveting, the TRC's controversial procedure of trading truth for information has not been repeated. Some truth commissions have identified perpetrators by name in their final reports (Chad, El Salvador, South Africa), while others have not (Chile, Guatemala), and some have referred the names of individuals confidentially to other authorities (Chile, Argentina, Timor-Leste). Organizations such as the International Center for Transitional Justice offer information, support, and training for truth commissions, and there are both technical challenges (for example, ways to obtain, organize, and assess data) and human concerns (for example, how to protect the safety and deal with the material and psychological needs of victims and witnesses) about which much has been learned. Local circumstances and resources, however, leave many choices open for the design, authority, and operation of truth commissions in their particular political, social, and cultural context.

The mandates that establish the scope and powers of truth commissions, and the final reports that truth commissions are always charged to return, identify a variety of aims that justify and guide their work. (Discussions that enumerate aims include Hayner 2001, p. 24; Méndez 2006, p. 144; Borer 2006, p. 26). The most fundamental task of a truth commission is to tell the truth – about individual cases, overall patterns, or both – it is charged to tell; this aim, while obvious, is not in fact simple (see next section). All truth commission mandates and reports, however, claim that the commission should or can serve a variety of other important goals for victims of violence and their society, and these goals are diverse (see United States Institute of Peace Truth Commissions Digital Collection (n.d.) for many mandates and truth commission reports). Two of the most commonly stated goals of truth commissions are to "restore the dignity" of victims of severe abuses and to establish the truth so as to prevent a reoccurrence of the violations documented. Other goals stated either by commissions or by the surrounding literature include: recognizing the suffering of victims and of families; promoting the healing of victims and providing a cathartic experience; preserving the memory of victims; creating public accountability for individual perpetrators, institutions, or society at large; combating impunity of perpetrators of gross abuses; rehabilitating and reintegrating perpetrators; recommending institutional reforms to prevent repetition; recommending appropriate reparations for victims; recommending prosecutions; preventing denial and revisionist histories; confronting public ignorance of abuses and their consequences; creating a new national narrative and a shared collective memory; contributing to national reconciliation; promoting a culture of respect and human rights; strengthening democracy and the rule of law.

Many aspirations of truth commissions clearly depend on factors that lie beyond what a commission itself can accomplish or control (for example, strengthening democracy or fostering national reconciliation), while others fall within the tasks that are a constitutive part of a commission's assigned work (producing a credible record or recommending reforms and reparations). The aim of restoring or affirming the dignity of victims, avowed by all truth commissions, seems to lie between. When a commission hears victims' stories, it validates victims' sense of injustice by confirming their experience of abuse and, in recent commissions, gives some victims a public stage to speak out against their abusers. Yet whether victims will feel that they have been adequately recognized, their suffering addressed, and their claims to justice honored can depend as well on actions the truth commission itself cannot take (for example, criminal trials or other incapacitation of perpetrators, reparations, memorials, or widespread public acceptance of the findings a commission offers). It is clear that only some effects of a truth commission process or its products may be distinguished and assessed in the short term. Longer-term contributions to personal well-being, or to social and political developments, are not easily assessed (but see de Greiff 2006 and Brahm 2007).

Critical responses to truth commissions

How well do truth commissions serve the individual and collective human right to the truth? Many claims have been made for the salutary effects of victim participation in truth commissions, the societal acknowledgment they represent, or the longer-term preventive impact of an accurate history of human rights abuse. A recent wave of research on the effects of truth commissions promotes closer scrutiny, and some skepticism, about what truth commissions have been shown to do, or can be expected to do.

There is not yet a large body of evidence concerning truth commissions' impacts, and most research has focused on the South African Truth and Reconciliation Commission (Chapman and van de Merwe 2008). Although victims uniformly strongly support and value truth-telling, evidence for the therapeutic value of truth commissions for victims is ambivalent and does not support strong claims of individual psychological benefit (Mendeloff 2009). Therapeutic effects are unlikely in any case, as most victims who give a statement to a truth commission have a brief encounter with a statement taker, and even the minority of victims who testify publicly do not thereby receive sustained therapeutic attention. Moral and political recognition of victims' dignity achieved through public acknowledgment and giving voice to victims is not reducible to psychological effects, but may remain largely (if meaningfully) symbolic without other measures to ensure justice and material and social support (Walker 2010). Deeply individual issues of mourning and reparation cannot be expected to coincide with social and political imperatives to "move on" in the transition; at the same time, victims seek truth, justice, and accountability, which are deeply linked to their sense of individual reparation (Hamber 2009).

The contribution of truth commissions to a society's reckoning with its own past is highly dependent on the record the truth commission establishes, a commission's own legitimacy and authority, the credibility and wide dissemination of its findings, and a significant impact on public understandings and attitudes. Any unilateral direct effect of a truth commission on the prevention of future violence or repression is unlikely, although implementation of recommendations made by a commission on the basis of its findings might have important preventive functions. Whatever the contribution, short or long term, to the resolution of conflict, the rule of law, and future stability a truth commission might make, it is likely that other factors, particularly structural changes (legal, economic, and political), a political environment that supports dissemination and discussion of truth commission findings, and action on the commission's most urgent recommendations will play a decisive role (Fletcher and Weinstein 2009). Still, publicity of truth commission proceedings and wide dissemination efforts, as in South Africa, have been found to produce some notable effects, such as recognition by a large majority there that the system of apartheid was a crime against humanity and some apparent impact of the TRC process and findings on reconciliation, as defined by several measures (Gibson 2004). If these outcomes are valid for South Africa, however, it does not follow that a truth commission process will produce similar results elsewhere. Even in a given setting, it is possible that not all truth commission goals are compatible; pressing issues of accountability may not, for example, be conducive to stability or reconciliation (Leebaw 2008).

At its core, every truth commission is charged to accomplish one task, whatever hoped-for effects eventuate or not. A truth commission is supposed to produce a truthful accounting of actions and events within its mandate, as well as the circumstances and patterns that provide context and explanation of what has occurred, including the actions or failures to act of individuals (whether identified or not), groups, and institutions. Scrutiny of truth commission operations of gathering, assessing, and organizing evidence and testimony has produced mixed verdicts on, and some skepticism about, the completeness, accuracy, and relevance of the truth that actual truth commissions have told. There are tensions between the desires of individuals to have their testimonies heard and respected, and to find out more information about their specific cases or the fate of the loved ones they have lost, and the role of truth commissions in determining a larger comprehensive narrative of causes and patterns of violence and repression. The micro-level truths of individual cases and the macro-level truth of patterns and trends pose different demands on data-gathering and analysis, and truth commission methodologies may fail to meet either or both of these tasks adequately (Chapman and Ball 2001). Truth commissions, starting with South Africa's TRC, have taken an increasingly sophisticated view of the multiple kinds of truth (factual, narrative, dialogical, restorative) that a commission must confront. Nonetheless, tensions between a legalistic model of establishing facts relevant to particular abuses of domestic, international human rights, and international humanitarian law; giving voice and a dignifying role to victims through individual, and sometimes public, testimonies of victims, relatives, and witnesses; and engaging in systematic data collection to establish empirically sound generalizations, are not easily overcome in the context of time-limited and resource-constrained truth commissions. It may be that disaggregation of truth commissions' truth-recovery functions, and longer-term projects of ongoing collection and analysis of data beyond the time and scope of a truth commission, are ways to address these tensions. A truth commission, however, is not a research project in pursuit of a disinterested truth. It is an institution structured by moral and political purposes meant to capture some particular truths urgently needed in specific political contexts, and in doing so to announce commitments to human dignity and responsibility that are embedded in the framework of human rights.

References

Borer, Tristan Anne, ed. 2006. *Telling the Truths: Truth Telling and Peace Building in Post-Conflict Societies* (South Bend, IN: University of Notre Dame Press).

Brahm, Eric. 2007. "Uncovering the Truth: Examining Truth Commission Success and Impact." *International Studies Perspectives*, Vol. 8, pp. 16–35.

Chapman, Audrey R. and Patrick Ball. 2001. "The Truth of Truth Commissions: Comparative Lessons from Haiti, South Africa, and Guatemala." *Human Rights Quarterly*, Vol. 23, pp. 1–43.
Chapman, Audrey R. and Hugo van der Merwe. 2008. *Truth and Reconciliation in South Africa: Did the TRC Deliver?* (Philadelphia: University of Pennsylvania Press).
de Greiff, Pablo. 2006. "Truth-Telling and the Rule of Law." In Tristan Anne Borer, ed., *Telling the Truths: Truth Telling and Peace Building in Post-Conflict Societies* (South Bend, IN: University of Notre Dame Press).
Fletcher, Laurel E. and Harvey M. Weinstein. 2009. "Context, Timing and the Dynamics of Transitional Justice: A Historical Perspective." *Human Rights Quarterly*, Vol. 31, pp. 163–220.
Freeman, Mark. 2006, *Truth Commissions and Procedural Fairness* (Cambridge: Cambridge University Press).
Gibson, James L. 2004. *Overcoming Apartheid: Can Truth Reconcile a Divided Nation?* (New York: Russell Sage Foundation).
Hamber, Brandon. 2009. *Transforming Societies after Political Violence: Truth, Reconciliation, and Mental Health* (Dordrecht: Springer).
Hayner, Priscilla. 2001. *Unspeakable Truths: Confronting State Terror and Atrocity* (New York: Routledge).
Leebaw, Bronwyn Anne. 2008. "The Irreconcilable Goals of Transitional Justice." *Human Rights Quarterly*, Vol. 30, pp. 95–118.
Mendeloff, David. 2009. "Trauma and Vengeance: Assessing the Psychological and Emotional Effects of Post-Conflict Justice." *Human Rights Quarterly*, Vol. 31, pp. 592–623.
Méndez, Juan E. 1997. "Accountability for Past Abuses." *Human Rights Quarterly*, Vol. 19, pp. 255–282.
Méndez, Juan E. 2006. "The Human Right to Truth: Lessons Learned from Latin American Experiences with Truth Telling." In Tristan Anne Borer, ed., *Telling the Truths: Truth Telling and Peace Building in Post-Conflict Societies* (South Bend, IN: University of Notre Dame Press).
Minow, Martha. 1998. *Between Vengeance and Forgiveness: Facing History After Genocide and Mass Violence* (Boston: Beacon Press).
Rotberg, Robert I. and Dennis Thompson, eds. 2000. *Truth v. Justice: The Morality of Truth Commissions* (Princeton, NJ: Princeton University Press).
United Nations Commission on Human Rights. 1997. *Question of the Impunity of Perpetrators of Human Rights Violations (Civil and Political).* Revised final report prepared by Mr. Joinet pursuant to Sub-Commission decision 1996/119, United Nations Document E/CN.4/Sub.2/1997/20/Rev.1, 2 October.
United Nations Commission on Human Rights. 2005a. *Impunity: Report of the Independent Expert to Update the Set of Principles to Combat Impunity, Addendum, Updated Set of Principles for the Protection and Promotion of Human Rights Through Action to Combat Impunity.* United Nations Document E/CN.4/2005/102/ Add. 1, 8 February.
United Nations Commission on Human Rights. 2005b. *Regulation on the Right to Truth.* United Nations Document E/CN.4/2005/L.84, 15 April.
United Nations Commission on Human Rights. 2006. *Study on the Right to the Truth: Report of the Office of the United Nations High Commissioner on Human Rights.* United Nations Document E/CN.4/2006/91, 8 February.
United Nations General Assembly. 2006b. *Basic Principles and Guidelines on the Right to a Remedy and Reparation for Victims of Gross Violations of International Human Rights Law and Serious Violations of International Humanitarian Law.* United Nations Document A/RES/60/147, 21 March.
United Nations Human Rights Council. 2007. *Rights to the Truth: Report of the Office of the Higher Commissioner for Human Rights.* United Nations Document A/HRC/5/7, 7 June.
United Nations High Commissioner on Human Rights. 2006. *Rule-of-Law Tools for Post-Conflict States: Truth Commissions.* New York: United Nations.
United States Institute of Peace. N.d., *Truth Commissions Digital Collection.* At: http://www.usip.org/library/truth.html#tc.
Walker, Margaret Urban. 2010. "Truth Telling as Reparations." *Metaphilosophy*, Vol. 41, Issue 4, pp. 525–545.

45
The international rights of migrants

Raquel Aldana

The following chapter introduces key international legal protections available to migrants in their journey from their countries of origin to escape repression or in search of a better life, during their residence as foreign nationals in their host nations, and when confronting the enforcement of domestic immigration laws against them. This chapter does not address the rights available to stateless persons or victims of human trafficking, nor does it discuss the norms governing the rights of migrants treated as "enemy aliens" in foreign lands.

A right to migrate?

International human rights law does not establish a right of persons to migrate from their country of nationality to a third country. Several human rights treaties create a right for persons to leave any country, including their own (e.g., article 13 of the Universal Declaration on Human Rights (UDHR)) but there is no reciprocal obligation on the part of third nations to receive non-nationals into their territory. To the contrary, a nation's right to control the entry of non-nationals into their territory is a well-established principle of international law, which is subject only to that state's treaty or customary law obligations.

The rights of forced international migrants

Since World War II, nations have recognized through treaty and practice certain rights for persons who have been forced to leave their homes and who cross an international border. Sometimes, people become internally displaced persons and remain in their country; however, they do not have the same legal and institutional support as those who have managed to cross an international border.

The most important legal instruments that protect forced international migrants are the 1951 Convention relating to the Status of Refugees and its 1967 Protocol. Nearly sixty years after adoption, 165 of the world's 200 or so nations are either parties or signatories to the treaty and the Protocol. Article 1 of the 1951 Convention legally defines refugees as persons residing outside of their country of nationality who are unable or unwilling to return because of a "persecution or a well-founded fear of persecution on account of race, religion, nationality, and membership of a particular social group or political opinion." Asylum seekers are persons who have moved across international borders in search of protection under the 1951 Convention but whose claim to refugee status has not yet been determined. The 1967 Protocol applied the 1951 refugee definition universally which until then had protected only persons leaving their homes because of events occurring before 1951 and coming principally from Europe.

The 1951 Convention did not define the term "persecution" and its meaning has been the subject of great debate. Generally, persecution implicates some type of identifiable grave harm or suffering that is caused by the actions or failures of a state to protect a person's fundamental human rights. Thus, persecution generally implicates harms caused directly by state actors but it can also implicate the acts of third parties who act in collusion with the state or with impunity. Examples of persecution include torture or forced sterilization or coerced abortion but not economic or employment discrimination. Persecution can either refer to persecution in the past or to future persecution. Past persecution can be the sole basis for the granting of refuge, even in the absence of future persecution, because it creates a presumption of a "well-founded fear" of persecution in the future, unless there are fundamentally changed circumstances. Further, the requirement that persecution be "on account of" connects the persecution to one of the protected five grounds such that a central reason for the persecution must be because of race, religion, nationality, or membership in a political party or social group. Some of these grounds have raised definitional challenges, such as when asylum seekers base their claim on neutrality rather than on express political choices or when the persecutor imputes a political opinion on the victims, regardless of their actual beliefs. Another complexity pertains to the term "social group," which has generally required that groups share "immutable" characteristics, such as sex, color, gender, or kinship ties or some shared experience such as former military leadership. The term has also evolved to include sexual orientation (Martin et al. 2007).

Later regional bodies have sought to expand the universal legal definition of refugee. The advent of violent strife in Africa following decolonization led the Organization of African Unity (OAU) in 1969 to adopt the Convention Governing the Specific Aspects of Refugee Problems in Africa (OAU Refugee Convention), which expanded in article I(2) the refugee definition to apply also to persons fleeing from "external aggression, occupation, foreign domination or events seriously disturbing public order." Similarly, in 1985, the General Assembly of the Organization of American States (OAS) adopted a formal resolution, AG/RES 774/XV-0/85 (Dec. 9, 1985), resolving to underscore the importance of the Cartagena Declaration on Refugees, a document adopted by experts with close parallels to the OAU Refugee Convention.

An ongoing debate is whether persons who meet the legal definition of refugee possess a right to both seek and to be granted asylum. The conflict became apparent during the drafting of the UDHR in 1947 when a number of states successfully changed the language of article 14, paragraph 1 from "Everyone has the right to seek and to be granted asylum" to its final version "Everyone has the right to seek and to enjoy in other countries asylum from persecution." The 1951 Convention did not resolve this ambiguity. The treaty specifies standards for the legal status, rights, and treatment of persons who are refugees and who are present in the territory of a treaty party. However, meeting the refugee status definition does not entitle the refugee to legal residence, much less admission. Even the OAU Refugee Convention simply contains a pledge that member states shall use their "best endeavors consistent with their respective legislations to receive refugees and to secure [their] settlement" (article 2).

Some of the specific rights listed in the 1951 Convention are limited solely to those "lawfully in" the host country. Lawfully admitted refugees are guaranteed equal treatment in exercising enumerated civil and political rights, such as the right to engage in employment and access to public assistance or social security. In addition, all refugees physically present in the territory of a treaty party enjoy certain basic rights, the most important of which is the *nonrefoulment* provision of article 33. Under this provision, states cannot return refugees to territories where their life or freedom would be threatened. Subsequently, other human rights treaties, most notably, article 3 of the Convention Against Torture and Other Cruel, Inhuman or Degrading Treatment or Punishment (CAT), which bars expulsion, return, or extradition of a person to another state "where there are substantial grounds for believing that he would be in danger of being subjected to torture," have also provided a special *nonrefoulment* protection. Unlike the 1951 Convention, the torture *nonrefoulment* protection applies no matter the motivation for the torture or the inhuman or degrading treatment.

In practice, the *nonrefoulment* protection has virtually been transformed into a de facto right of asylum, at least for those who manage to establish physical presence in the territory of another. However, this hinges on the human rights traditions of the host country who might find it politically unthinkable to keep asylum seekers in perpetual limbo or indefinite detention. Some nations, including the United States, however, are moving toward a harsh mandatory detention practice for asylum seekers precisely to encourage these individuals to abandon their legal claims and return to their countries (Martin et al. 2007). These detention practices raise human rights concerns discussed below.

Another significant problem of asylum seekers today is a state's refusal to admit into their territory persons who are seeking refuge. When ships carrying asylum seekers suffer peril at sea, nations do have a duty to rescue those in danger at sea as part of an ancient international maritime obligation. Once the initial rescue has occurred, however, international maritime law is silent as to any ongoing obligation owed by the shipmaster. Nations generally refuse admittance and some interdict asylum seekers at sea in order to avoid the *nonrefoulment* obligation. The USA has maintained, for example, that the *nonrefoulment* protection has no application in the high seas, a position at odds with the international bodies' interpretation of the 1951 Refugee Convention (*Sale v. Haitian Ctrs. Council, Inc.* 1993; *Haitian Ctrs. For Human Rights v. United States* 1997). Moreover, interdiction practices have not been found to violate the right of nationals to leave their country (*Xhavara and Others v. Italy and Albania* 2001). European Union nations are also entering into repatriation or readmission agreements with African nations as a precondition to development aid and are collaborating with African nations to forcibly restrict the emigration of its nationals, including with criminal sanctions (Nessel 2009). These practices amount to aiding and abetting African nations to breach the right of their nationals to leave the country and run contrary to the 1951 Refugee Convention prohibition against *refoulment* in "any manner whatsoever."

Regional agreements and freedom of movement

Some nations have entered into treaties that allow free movement for members within their economic integration territories. The most well known example is that of the European Union (EU), although to a lesser extent regions have adopted similar measures. This trend to increase the right to migrate for members within an economic region, however, has developed alongside the goals of greater immigration restriction against non-members.

European Union

The European Union introduced the concept of European Citizenship in article 17 of the Treaty of Maastricht of 1992. Article 18 creates the most important identifiable right of a citizen of the Union: "the right to move and reside freely within the territory of the Member States," subject to any conditions set elsewhere in the Treaty or implementing legislation. This right to free movement had developed over fifty years, applying initially solely to those who qualified as workers and then expanding to non-workers but still retaining fundamental distinctions between the rights attaching to each. The Maastricht Treaty became less categorical with regards to the application of rights to all EU citizens.

Of course, only nationals of an EU state have EU citizenship (article 17) and EU states retain the right to limit the accession of states into the union and the admission of immigrants from the outside into their territories. Also, some EU states have suspended some of the rights of EU citizenship for the nationals of countries who only recently joined the union (Bermann 2009). Furthermore, under Declaration 2 of the Treaty of the European Union, EU states largely retain the legal right to decide domestically who is a "national" of a member state and, consequently, who then become citizens of the Union. Given that EU citizenship is derivative of EU state nationality, EU nations exert political peer pressure to influence the domestic choice of law and practices on issues of nationality (Bermann 2009). As dictated by the European Court of Justice (ECJ), EU member decisions on nationality conferral, however, should be taken with "due regard to Community law," which imposes some legal limits on domestic sovereignty over nationality determinations when such conflict with the freedom of movement guarantee (see *Micheletti v. Delegacion del Gobierno* 1992). These limits could apply, for example, when EU nations deny EU citizenship to nationals who reside or have prolonged stays outside of EU territories, or deny nationality to the children of these nationals (see, e.g., *Zhu v. Sec'y of State for the Home Dep't* 2004).

Most rights of EU citizenship are generated by reciprocity between member states and are activated only when a citizen of one member state takes up residence in another member state (known as second-country nationals [SCNs]). Two directives from 2000 on anti-discrimination policies provide general protection against discrimination in the member states independent of nationality, as does a 2004 directive, which codified and expanded the rights of SCNs (Council Directive 2000/43, 2000; Council Directive 2000/78, 2000; Council Directive 2004/58, 2004). EU citizenship grants SCNs access to employment and self-employment and to equal treatment with the nationals of that country in matters of social security and public welfare benefits. Employment-related discrimination is defined extensively, while prohibited grounds of discrimination in access to goods and services are limited to racial and ethnic origin. SCNs also enjoy special political rights since they can vote and be elected in their country of current residence, in the European Parliament, and in local elections.

Despite the comprehensive prohibition of discrimination against SCNs, there is no perfect equality of rights between SCNs and nationals of the host country (known as first-country nationals or FCNs) (Kochenov 2009). Foremost, the conditions referenced in article 18 of the Treaty of Maastricht on freedom of movement preserve the public policy, public security, and public health limitation on free movement of workers in article 39(3) and the parallel limitation on the free movement of the self-employed in article 46 and 55. Thus, this right becomes dependent on the secondary legislation; i.e., Council Direction 2004/38, aimed to give it practical effect. Under this directive the right of free movement depends very much on the particular class of those wishing to use it – worker's free movement is, for example, far easier to exercise than persons without independent means. Currently, the latter's right to enter and reside in another EU state is not unconditional after three months; rather, they must then establish sufficient financial means and health insurance to stay. Additionally, EU states are not obligated to provide social assistance during the first three months of residence of any SCN. Furthermore, any SCN who poses a threat of becoming an unreasonable burden on the social assistance system of the host society may lose his right of residence.

The introduction of EU citizenship has in some cases improved the rights of EU nationals legally residing in EU states in which they are not nationals, as well as the rights of certain long-term residents of person from non-EU states. Council Directive 2003/109/EC, governing the legal status of long-term residents of persons from non-EU states (known as third-country nationals [TCNs]), for example, grants the right to TCNs (after five years of residence in one member state and after passing integration tests) to move to another member state and take up employment there without being subjected to regulations that apply to newly arriving TCNs. Also, the ECJ has prohibited the automatic deportation of EU citizens who fail to provide documents necessary to obtain residence and has also treated EU nationals already in possession of a residence permit as legal residents even when they fail to meet the residency requirements at the time the case is decided (see, e.g., *Georgios Orfanopoulos and Raffaele Oliveri v. Land Baden-Wurttenberg* 2004; see also *Comm'n v. Belgium* 1981).

African Union

For at least half a century, African nations pursued regional economic integration through the creation of subregional institutions, which ultimately paved the way for the establishment of the African Economic Community (AEC) in 1991. With the adoption of the Treaty Establishing the African Economic Community, member states undertook to progressively secure for their nationals the rights of free movement, residence, and establishment within the Community (Art. 43).

More than a decade earlier, the right to free movement had already been adopted by the Economic Community of West African States (ECOWAS) with the adoption of the 1979 Protocol on Free Movement of Persons, Rights of Residence and Establishment. (ECOWAS is made up of fifteen African states, including Benin, Burkina Faso, Côte D'Ivoire, Gambia, Ghana, Guinea, Guinea Bissau, Liberia, Mali, Niger, Nigeria, Senegal, Sierra Leone, and Togo.) This Protocol was designed to function in three phases, each having a transition time frame of five years starting in 1980, the date the Protocol entered into force. Phase 1 rights, Protocol A/P1/5/79, included the right to entry into member states without a visa, followed by the right to stay in the territory for a period of 90 days without the need for a residence permit. Phase 2 rights, Protocol A/P3/5/82, gave member states authority to determine who shall qualify as citizens of their respective states, and thus, gain ECOWAS citizenship. That same year, Protocol A/Sp.2/7/82 was ratified to protect citizen's right of residence, as well as to safeguard fundamental human rights for unauthorized migrants, including a right to benefits for performed labor, removal procedures that protect human rights, and an obligation to facilitate documents for persons seeking to regularize their status. Subsequently, Protocol A/SP.1/7/86 guaranteed nationals of ECOWAS states the right to work in the territory of member states and included special protections concerning border areas, as well as for seasonal or itinerant migrant workers. Finally, Protocol A/SP2/5/90 protected ECOWAS citizen rights to property and asset ownership and the creation and management of enterprise and companies without discrimination.

The AEC Treaty made the right of free movement possible for the entire region. The AEC Treaty has been in operation since May 1994 and is being established in six stages of variable duration over a transition period not exceeding thirty-four years from the date of entry into force of the Treaty. Each of the stages consists of specific activities to be implemented concurrently. The free movement of peoples and factors of production is contemplated in the sixth stage. As part of this commitment, AEC members agreed to conclude a Protocol on the Free Movement of Persons, Right of Residence and Right of Establishment. In November 2009, the East African Community (EAC) signed a landmark Protocol for a common market, the Protocol on the Establishment of the East African Community (EAC) Common Market, which came into force in July 2010. Under the Protocol, member states are obligated to guarantee free movement of persons who are citizens of other member states as well as to ensure non-discrimination of the citizens of the partner states (articles 76 and 104). (The EAC members are Kenya, Uganda, Tanzania, Rwanda, and Burundi.) East Africans shall also enjoy the freedom of employment. National governments, however, may limit the free movement of persons for public policy, public security, or health reasons.

The Americas

The Americas have entered into a series of subregional agreements to achieve economic integration that contain provisions for the free movement of people. Some notable exceptions are trade agreements between the United States or Canada and other Latin American or Caribbean nations, such as the North American Free Trade Agreement or the Central American Free Trade Agreement-Dominican Republic. Such treaties contemplate solely the temporary movement of "business persons" for economic activities or professionals to engage in business activities at the professional level but retain strict immigration constraints for permanent immigration or other types of temporary travel. In contrast, trade agreements among Latin American or Caribbean nations treat the freedom of movement of its peoples across nations as an integral part of economic integration for the region. These include the Central American Integration System (SICA), the Caribbean Community (CARICOM), the Common Market of the South (Mercosur), the Andean Community of Nations (CAN), and the Union of South American Nations (UNASUR).

- In 1993, five Central American nations (Guatemala, El Salvador, Nicaragua, Costa Rica, and Honduras) plus Panama signed the Central American Economic Integration Protocol to the 1960 General Treaty on Central American Economic Integration. This Protocol of Guatemala included article 18 which encouraged its members to establish the free movement of labor and capital among the members.
- In 1989 with the adoption of the Grand Anse Declaration, CARICOM (Antigua and Barbuda, Barbados, Belize, Dominica, Grenada, Jamaica, Guyana, Suriname, St. Kitts and Nevis, St. Lucia, St. Vincent and the Grenadines, and Trinidad and Tobago) formally promoted the free movement of skills, which entailed the right of CARICOM nationals to seek employment in any member state without the need for work permits and permits of stay. Then, in 2001, the Revised Treaty of Chaguaramas establishing the CARICOM Single Market and Economy included article 45, which committed member states "to the goal of the free movement of their nationals within the Community." This right is being implemented in phases and has begun primarily by focusing on highly skilled migrants, including graduates, media persons, artists, musicians, sportspersons, and university graduates. In 1990, CARICOM states also agreed that all CARICOM nationals should be free to travel within the community more freely and since 2005, CARICOM states began issuing CARICOM passports as a measure to promote a hassle-free travel policy in the region. To date, about 12 CARICOM states issue CARICOM passports.
- In 2002, Mercosur members (Argentina, Brazil, Paraguay, and Uruguay) and associated nations Chile and Bolivia signed an Agreement on the Residence for Nationals of the Member States of Mercosur, and established between them a zone of free residence with other rights for their nationals, subject only to a requirement of good conduct or no criminal history. Included in the Agreement were the rights to stay beyond the 90 days for purposes of tourism, to study and to work without restrictions, the free transfer of capital,

including from wages, and the right to similar social security benefits as those enjoyed by the nationals of the host country. Then in 2008, Mercosur nations, joined by six associated nations, (Bolivia, Chile, Colombia, Ecuador, Peru, and Venezuela) signed the Agreement on Travel Documents between the Mercosur and Associated Member States (Mercosur/CMC/Dec. no. 18/08) which allows nationals to travel solely with their respective national identification cards.

- Especially in the last decade, the Andean Community (Bolivia, Colombia, Ecuador, and Peru) has adopted norms and regulations to govern Andean migrant workers. In 2000, for example, the Andean Community adopted Decision 545, titled Andean Instrument of Migrant Workers, which sought the gradual creation of a right of free movement for workers and the immediate imposition of certain fundamental rights for authorized migrant workers, including the right against discrimination and the right to free association and family unification. Decision 583 also granted migrant workers certain social security rights, including access to medical care and pension benefits.
- In May 2008, the Mercosur and the Andean Community of Nations, as part of a continuing process of South American integration, signed the treaty setting up UNASUR, an intergovernmental union integrating the Mercosur and the Andean Community of Nations. Modeled after the EU, UNASUR seeks, among other goals, to create a South American citizenship. As of the date of this writing, the UNASUR constitutional treaty has not yet entered into force.

Asia-Pacific

Regional economic integration in Asia is lagging far behind other regions of the world. While there is talk about region-wide economic integration, Asia is currently principally a "noodle bowl" of "trade-lite" agreements that are not as robust or as comprehensive as compared to those in the rest of the world. Bilateral cooperation even within Association of Southeast Asian Nations (ASEAN) or the Asian-Pacific Economic Cooperation has failed to address a growing problem in the region of vulnerable migrant workers. Since 2006, for example, the International Labor Organization/Japan Managing Cross-Border Movement of Labor in Southeast Asia program has worked to promote more open labor migration policies in the region. Despite these efforts, so far no ASEAN country has agreed to pioneer an experiment with the free movement of labor across its borders.

One notable exception is the framework built up between Australia and New Zealand. Free movement of people between Australia and New Zealand is guaranteed under a series of ministerial agreements known as the Trans-Tasman Travel Arrangements (TTTA). These arrangements apply to all movements, including those for labor market and non-labor market reasons, such as retirement or study. They hold for all citizens of the two countries and also for citizens of other Commonwealth countries who have been granted permanent residence in either Australia or New Zealand. For these residents, no prior permission is required to enter the other country but, since 1981, a passport has been required. New Zealand and Australia have also entered into bilateral social security agreements designed to share the burden of social security payments to residents of one country who have moved to the other country. The benefits concerned are old-age pensions, superannuation, and payment for people with severe disabilities. Under these arrangements, residents of one country moving to the other are entitled to receive the social security benefits of the country in which they take up residence. Under the shared responsibility principle, Australia and New Zealand each contribute to benefit payments in proportion to the working life the recipient has spent in each country.

A right to family reunification for migrants?

Certain authorized migrants who are staying lawfully in the country have been granted a right to family reunification under a few international human rights treaties that could obligate a state to grant entry to a limited class of protected peoples. A general right to migrate for purposes of family unification is not found in human rights treaties, however, because the right to family unification is generally conditioned on a state's right to protect its borders.

Even so, minor children may come closest to being recognized as having a fundamental right to trans-border family reunification. In the Convention on the Rights of the Child, which has near universal ratification, article 10(1) creates an obligation on states parties to deal with "applications by a child or his or parents to enter or leave a States Party for the purposes of family unification ... in a positive, humane and expeditious manner." While this may be highly positive, a closer reading of article 10(2) suggests it falls short of codifying a right to family reunification as such. Under article 10(2), "State Parties shall respect the right of the child and his or her parents to leave any country, including their own, and to enter their own country." This phrase limits the right of entry to one's own country. Moreover, countries have imposed a declaration or reservation to article 10, subjecting this right to the nation's domestic immigration policy when ratifying the treaty.

Refugees, once granted status, generally are also accorded a right to family. The refugee's right to family unity or reunification is not included in the 1951 Refugee Convention itself. Rather, it is found in Recommendation B of the Final Act of the 1951 United Nations Conference of Plenipotentiaries on the Status of Refugees and Stateless Persons. Generally, states have heeded the recommendation to grant a right to family reunification upon granting refugee status; a similar right is not conferred, however, upon persons protected under the Torture Convention *nonrefoulment* principle.

In the context of migrant laborers, the International Labor Organization (ILO) has principally urged states to adopt measures to recognize a right to family reunification for migrant workers, although falling short of codifying it as a fundamental right. The first example of this is the ILO's Recommendation No. 86 concerning Migration for Employment (Revised), paragraph 15(1) of which reads: "Provisions should be made by agreement for authorization to be granted for a migrant for employment introduced on a permanent basis to be accompanied or joined by the members of his family." Article 13(1) of the Convention Concerning Migrations in Abusive Conditions and the Promotion of Equality of Opportunity and Treatment of Migrant Workers (C 143) has a broader scope yet still leaves states a very wide discretion, stating that: "A Member *may* take all necessary measures which fall within its competence and collaborate with other Member States to facilitate the reunification of the families of all migrant workers legally residing in its territory." Paragraph 13(1) of Recommendation No. 151 Migrant Workers Recommendation 1975 (R151) takes a more forceful view on family reunification, stating that "All possible measures should be taken both by countries of employment and by countries of origin to facilitate the reunification of families of migrant workers as rapidly as possible." More recently, the UN finally codified a right to family reunification for migrant workers in article 44 of the International Convention on the Protection of Rights of All Migrant Workers and Members of Their Families (CRMWF), which provides that states "shall take appropriate measures to ensure the protection of the unity of the families of migrant workers." The treaty has not been ratified, however, by many nations with net immigrant populations.

Under EU Community law, Directive 2003/86/EC recognizes the right of TCNs lawfully residing in the territory of the members states to be joined by their nuclear family members, subject to certain conditions. A more limited right to family unification also attaches whenever

EU citizens exercise their right to freedom of movement by relocating to another EU member state. The ECJ interpreted Directive 2004/38, subject to public policy, security, and health conditions, to guarantee EU citizens the right to be accompanied or joined by their spouses, partners, and minor or adult children (the latter if dependency is established) who are non-EU citizens in the host member state because a different outcome would unduly restrict their freedom of movement guaranteed under EU Community law (see *Metlock and Others* 2008). Only EU citizens who cross a border into another EU state, however, may exercise these rights, as family reunification is not similarly recognized for EU citizens in a purely "internal situation" (see *Morson and Jhanjan case* 1982).

The European Court of Human Rights (ECtHR) has rejected familial unity-based claims, at least when the family member is not already in the country (see *Abdulaziz, Cabales and Balkandali v. United Kingdom* 1985). The ECtHR has, however, at least in cases involving minor children and their parents, recognized a right to family reunification, even after long years of separation, so long as family ties have been maintained (see *Tuquabo-Teke v. The Netherlands* 2003 and *Sen v. the Netherlands* 2001). A state's interest in controlling immigration can nonetheless supersede a right to family reunification for minor children when the parents are not permanent residents or when family reunification is possible in a third alternative country (see *Gul v. Switzerland* 1996).

A right to stay?

Generally, a nation's sovereignty over their borders extends to the expulsion of non-nationals from their territory. This power is at its highest when immigrants have made an unauthorized entry into the nation that seeks to expel them, although countries can also condition the right to stay even for lawful permanent residents.

The UN Human Rights Committee (UNHRC), the monitoring body of the International Covenant on Civil and Political Rights (ICCPR), has a growing body of cases interpreting the right to family unification in the context of expulsion under article 17 of the ICCPR. The UNHRC adopts a balancing test and weighs the state's interest in promoting public safety and enforcing immigration laws with the petitioner's interests to stay in the country, as measured by the length of stay in the host country, the age, and the family's financial and emotional independence (see, e.g., *Winata v. Australia* 2001and *Canepa v. Canada* 1997).

The application of the "best interest of the child" standard when family unification involves a child has also limited the expulsion power. The "best interest of the child" standard is codified in the Convention on the Rights of the Child (CRC) (article 3) and it is part of most nations' laws on child welfare. The Committee on the Rights of the Child, the CRC's monitoring body, has stated that states must conform their domestic immigration laws to ensure family reunification (UN Comm. on the Rights of the Child, Concluding Observations on Norway 2000). The "best interest of the child" standard has also been relevant in interpretation of other human rights treaties that contain provisions on children. For example, the ECHR held that splitting up a family through deportation "must be supported by sufficiently sound and weighty considerations in the interest of the child" (*Olsson v. Sweden* 1988 and *Scozzari v. Giunta v. Italy* 2000). Similarly, the Inter-American Commission on Human Rights (ICHR) held that the "absence of any procedural opportunity for [consideration of the best interest of the child] in proceedings involving removal of a parent ... raised serious concerns" given that the state's right to immigration control must be balanced against the harm to the individual (Inter-Am. Comm'n on Human Rights, Report on the Situation of Human Rights of Asylum Seekers Within the Canadian Refugee Determination System 2000).

As well, the ECtHR has received a growing number of complaints against EU nations' expulsion decisions based on a right to family protected under article 8 of the ECHR. In cases involving immigrants who have lived in the host country since childhood and had only tenuous ties to their country of origin, the ECtHR has considered expulsion a violation of article 8, even when the applicant has a criminal record (see, e.g., *Berrehab v. the Netherlands* 1988; *Moustaquim v. Belgium* 1991; and *Slivenko and Others v. Latvia* 2003). Additionally, the European Court of Justice (ECJ) has extended an indefinite right to residence to third-party parents who birth EU citizen children as long as these parents served as caretaker to the dependent citizen family member, considering that expulsion would contravene the right to family under article 8 of the ECHR (*Zhu v. Sc'y of State for the Home Dep't* 2004). The ECJ has not extended a similar right to short-term temporary visitors who are not either married to a EU citizen, such as parents, unless they qualify as "dependent" family member under Directive 73/148/ECC (*Jia v. Migrationsverket* 2007).

The everyday rights of migrants

The fundamental rights codified in human rights treaties apply to all persons present and residing in the territory of states, irrespective of immigration status. Moreover, the non-discrimination principle protects immigrants against distinctions drawn on the basis of alienage in their everyday lives. In fact, even the nondiscrimination principle articulated in the International Covenant on Economic, Social and Cultural Rights (CESCR) allows for no distinctions between nationals and immigrants (article 2(2)), save for the distribution of economic rights by developing nations (article 2(3)). As such, as a general matter, immigrants should be treated equally and enjoy the same benefits and guarantees as the nationals of their host country. Treaties specifically governing the rights of immigrants, however, allow states to distinguish between the types of rights accorded to legal immigrants and to those who entered the territory without authorization. This is especially true in the distribution of certain social and economic rights. This creates a potential conflict between the general human rights treaties which states are required to resolve in favor of immigrants.

The ILO was the first international organization to provide human rights protections to migrant workers in the host territory. In 1939, the ILO adopted Convention 66, the Migration for Employment Convention and others that followed (C 97 in 1949), that governed the orderly recruitment of migrant workers and provided for equal treatment with national workers with respect to working conditions, trade union membership, and enjoyment of the benefits of collective bargaining, accommodations, social security, employment, taxes, and legal proceedings, but limited these benefits to legal immigrants. In 1975, the ILO, through Convention 143, devoted a whole section to the phenomenon of irregular migration and to interstate collaboration towards prevention and codified the right to equal treatment in employment practices and work-related benefits for legal migrants. Article 9 of C 143 also entitled unauthorized workers to equal rights with respect to those arising from past employment, including remuneration, social security, and other benefits. C 143, however, has been ratified by very few nations, in contrast to the comparable treaties that create rights solely for legal migrants.

Then in 1985, the UN General Assembly adopted the Declaration on the Human Rights of Individuals Who Are Not Nationals of the Country in Which They Live. The Declaration affirmed that all immigrants should enjoy a multitude of rights simply by virtue of their presence in the territory of a state, including to life and security of person; freedom from arbitrary arrests and torture; equality before the courts and due process, including the right to an interpreter and to consular communication; the choice of spouse and the ability to marry and found a family;

freedom of thought and religion; and to retain their own language and culture. Subject to national security and public health and morals restrictions, the Declaration also codified the rights to freedom of expression and peaceful assembly and to property. Under the Declaration, however, only legal residents enjoy the right to freedom of movement within the borders of their state, as well as a host of economic rights such as to health protection, medical care, social security, social services, education, and rest and leisure, but only if "undue strain is not placed on the resources of the state" (article 8(c)). In addition, worker rights, including to safe and healthy working conditions, to fair wages, and to union representation, are reserved for legal immigrants.

In 1990, the UN opened for signature the Committee on the Rights of Migrant Workers and Their Families (CRMWF), which came into force in 2003. To date, only 42 nations have ratified it, none of which are significant net recipients of immigration. Like the Declaration, the UN Migrant Convention recognizes rights for all migrants but also reserves some rights only for legal migrants. The CRMWF expands on the same fundamental rights as the Declaration for migrants but also adds a few important additional rights such as ex post facto prohibition, protection of identity documents, and a right to a basic education and to a name, registration, and nationality for immigrant children. The additional rights for legal migrants under the CRMWF include broader rights to unionization; political participation, including voting; freedom of movement within the territory; equality to nationals with respect to social rights, including education, housing, and health, family reunification; equality of taxation with nationals; and other workplace rights, including unemployment and protection from dismissal. In contrast, unauthorized workers are only recognized a right to urgent medical care.

In addition, the CRMWF contains workplace protections for all migrants, irrespective of status. These include protection against slavery and all forms of forced labor; equal remuneration conditions and terms of employment, unless waived through contract; a right to reimbursement of any collected social security benefits even for unauthorized workers not entitled to social security under domestic law; and the right to participate in unions conditioned upon national interests of public security and order. The Inter-American Court and the ILO affirmed that international norms guarantee the right to equal treatment regarding freedom of association and the right to organize trade unions in two decisions that criticized the US Supreme Court's *Hoffman Plastic* decision that denied backpay remedies to undocumented workers who were dismissed by their employer in retaliation for their union activities (Juridical Condition and the Rights of the Undocumented Migrants 2003; Comm. on Freedom of Ass'n 2002; *Hoffman Plastic Compounds, Inc. v. National Labor Relations Board* 2002). A more recent ILO case against Spain also declared that the right of association of unauthorized workers is on par with that of other workers (Case No. 2121, Definitive Report, Complaint Against the Government of Spain presented by the General Union of Workers of Spain (UGT) 2002). Similarly, the UN Committee on the Elimination of Racial Discrimination interpreted the International Convention on the Elimination of All Forms of Racial Discrimination in 2004 to entitle unauthorized workers "to the enjoyment of labour and employment rights, including the freedom of assembly and association" (General Recommendation No. 30, Discrimination Against Non Citizens 2004).

In 1999, the UN Commission on Human Rights appointed a Special Rapporteur for the human rights of migrants with a mandate to examine "ways and means to overcome the obstacles existing to the full and effective protection of the human rights of [migrants]." The Special Rapporteur acts on information submitted to him regarding alleged violations of the human rights of migrants by sending urgent appeals and communications to concerned governments to clarify and/or bring to their attention these cases. The Special Rapporteur also conducts country visits upon the invitation of states, in order to examine the state of protection of the human rights of migrants in the given country. The Special Rapporteur submits a report of the visit to the Human Rights Council, presenting his findings, conclusions, and recommendations. Additionally, the Special Rapporteur annually reports to the Human Rights Council about the global state of protection of migrants' human rights, his main concerns, as well as the good practices he has observed. In his report, the Special Rapporteur informs the Council of all the communications he has sent and the replies received from governments. Furthermore, the Special Rapporteur formulates specific recommendations with a view to enhancing the protection of the human rights of migrants. Upon request of the Human Rights Council, the Special Rapporteur may also send reports to the General Assembly. Also, since 2004, in response to the low ratification of binding treaties governing the rights of immigrants, the ILO has adopted a Multilateral Framework on Labour Migration which is working with social partners and other international organizations to develop a non-binding multilateral framework of rights-based approach to labor migration.

Regionally, the European Convention on the Legal Status of Migrant Workers, ratified to date only by 11 nations, confers a number of civil and economic rights, including in the workplace, although restricted to authorized immigrants. In addition, the Council of Europe has adopted numerous non-binding standards aimed at protecting immigrants, including the Parliamentary Assembly Resolution and Recommendation on the Human Rights of Irregular Migrants (Resolution on the Human Rights of Irregular Migrants, EUR.Parl.Doc. 2006; Recommendations on the Human Rights of Irregular Migrants 2006). These documents contain a number of minimum civil and political, as well as social, economic, and cultural rights that should apply to unauthorized immigrants. Other regional bodies have not adopted binding treaties but have resorted to enforcement mechanisms or soft-law to improve the rights of migrants. The Inter-American Commission established a Special Rapporteur on Migrant Workers and Members of Their Families in 1997 to promote the human rights of migrant workers in the region, with many of the same functions as the UN Rapporteur. Finally, the Association of Southeast Asian Nations (ASEAN) adopted a 2007 Declaration on the Protection and Promotion of the Rights of Migrant Workers. The document has significant limitations, however, including that it is phrased in terms of state obligations and not individual rights and conditions certain obligations to the domestic laws.

Immigration enforcement and rights

Due process rights in immigration proceedings

Generally, due process rights for immigrants apply only to those who have entered the territory of another nation and are facing expulsion, as opposed to exclusion. For asylum seekers, the *nonrefoulment* principle, however, may require states to implement procedures to ensure against rejection of asylum seekers who have not yet reached the frontier, such as those applying at a nation's consulate or who are interdicted at sea. Article 3 of the 1967 UN Declaration on Territorial Asylum, for example, states that "[n]o person … shall be subjected to measures such as rejection at the frontier," although it recognizes an exception for reasons of national security or in cases of mass influx.

The right to be free from arbitrary expulsion is recognized in several human rights treaties. Article 13 of the International Covenant on Civil Political Rights (ICCPR), for example, generally requires an individualized review by a competent authority before a state may expel a person legally present in its territory. The Human Rights Committee has found a violation of article 13 when persons have not been given an opportunity to submit their reasons against expulsion (see *Hamel v. Madagascar* 1987 and *Giry v. Dominican Republic* 1990). A recent European Council Committee of Minister's Twenty Guidelines on Forced Return affirm and has expanded on some of the norms that govern expulsion, including the promotion of voluntary over forced return; a prohibition against forced return to persecution, torture, or mistreatment; a prohibition against collective expulsion; the right to be notified of a removal order; and the right to an effective remedy against removal before a competent authority (Council of Europe 2005).

Immigrants' due process rights in expulsion proceedings, however, are not equivalent to those accorded to defendants in criminal trials. Most states treat immigration proceedings as civil, not criminal. As such, fewer rights, including the right to counsel or the right against self-incrimination, are guaranteed in immigrant proceedings. Although not specifically in the context of immigration proceedings, a right to free counsel in civil proceedings is an emerging norm in international law, however. In particular, in 1984, the UN Human Rights Committee issued General Comment No. 13, stating that article 14 of the ICCPR applies to civil as well as criminal proceedings. Then in 2007, the HRC issued new General Comment No. 32, which replaced General Comment No. 13, and notes that that "[s]tates are encouraged to provide free legal aid in [noncriminal cases], for individuals who do not have sufficient means to pay for it. In some cases, they may even be obliged to do so" (United Nations, Human Rights Committee, General Comment No. 32 [90th sess. 2007]). Moreover, the Convention on the Elimination of All Forms of Racial Discrimination (CERD) has been construed by United Nations monitoring bodies to encompass rights to civil counsel (International Convention on the Elimination of All Forms of Racial Discrimination 2008). Regionally as well, the European Court on Human Rights has considered a right to counsel in civil proceedings a fundamental part of due process protected under article 6 of the European Human Rights Convention (see *Airey v. Ireland* 1979 and *Morris v. United Kingdom* 2005). Similarly, in an advisory opinion involving the rights of migrant workers, the Inter-American Court on Human Rights recognized that due process for immigrants in labor disputes required a guarantee of free legal aid representation (Mexico Case 2003).

Detention

Several human rights instruments govern the treatment of asylum seekers and other immigrants in detention for purposes of immigration control. As a general matter, detention of migrants for immigration control is not prohibited under international law but it is subject to certain limitations and conditions.

First, the Refugee Convention establishes two restrictions under article 31 on the detention of asylum seekers. First, states cannot impose penalties for the illegal entry of persons who are escaping repression, provided they present themselves without delay to the authorities and show good cause for their illegal entry or presence. Second, detention is permissible only when necessary and only until their status in the country is regularized or until they obtain admission into another country. The growing practice of mandatory detention of asylum seekers raises significant questions of legality under article 31. The first is that mandatory detention of all asylum seekers violates the necessary detention requirement. The Executive Committee of the UN Commission for Refugees (UNHCR) has concluded (Conclusion 44) that detention of asylum seekers should normally be avoided in view of the hardship it represents (UNHCR Executive Committee Conclusion on International Protections 1986). Thus, it has restricted the conditions for detention to include those necessary to verify identity, to determine the basis of the asylum claim, to deal with cases where refugees have destroyed or possess fraudulent documents, or to protect national security or public order.

A second challenge is that mandatory detention of asylum seekers constitutes a proscribed penalty under article 31. No consensus on this issue exists among legal experts, even when nations resort to mandatory detention practices as a means to discourage asylum seekers from seeking asylum in their territories. The UNHCR has also called for judicial review of detention decisions, as well as humane detention conditions, including housing asylum seekers separately from criminals and avoiding prolonged detention (UNHCR Revised Guidelines on Applicable Criteria and Standards Relating to the Detention of Asylum Seekers, Guideline 10 1999).

Human rights treaties also generally impose certain due process guarantees for a person in detention. Article 9 of the ICCPR, for example, requires not only that arrested individuals receive prompt notice of the charges against them but also to challenge the legality of their detention without delay. In addition, the proscription against arbitrary detention found in several human rights treaties of general application also imposes substantive limits on immigration detention. The Human Rights Committee when interpreting this requirement in article 9 of the ICCPR, for example, has found that arbitrariness is not just when detention is against the law but incorporates elements of inappropriateness, injustice, and lack of predictability. As such, detention must not only be lawful but also reasonable in all circumstances, such as to prevent flight, interference of evidence, or to protect the public from danger. The authority to detain children is included in article 37(b) of the CRC but it must be a measure of last resort and for the shortest appropriate period of time.

In contrast, the European Court on Human Rights has not required that immigration detention be reasonably necessary to prevent the commission of an offense or to prevent a person from fleeing, but it has held that detention must be taken with the intent to deport and be required only when deportation proceedings are in progress and pursued with due diligence (*Chahadl v. the United Kingdom* 1996 and *Quinn v. France* 1995). This may be because the European Court on Human Rights specifically refers to "migrant in detention" and provides that detention is permissible in cases of "the lawful arrest or detention of a person to prevent his effecting an unauthorized entry into the country or a person against whom action is being taken with a view to deportation or extradition." This is also consistent with the Twenty Guidelines on Forced Return adopted by the Council of Europe (2005), although detainees must also be guaranteed a judicial remedy to determine the legality of their detention.

With regard to conditions of detention, article 10 of the ICCPR requires that all persons deprived of liberty "be treated with humanity and with respect for the inherent dignity of the human person." Incommunicado detention is an example of inhuman treatment within the meaning of article 10 (see *Penarrieta, Pura de Toro et al. v. Bolivia* 1987). In 1955, the Standard Minimum Rules for the Treatment of Prisoners were adopted to interpret article 10 of the ICCPR. The Standard Minimum Rules specify what material needs and services must be provided to detainees and requires different categories of detainees be kept in separate institutions. The 1988 Principles for the Protection of All Persons under Any Form of Detention or Imprisonment, which also interpret article 10 of the ICCPR, further provide that detainees must have access to the outside world and independent supervision of detention conditions, and access to educational and cultural materials. Similarly, article 17 of the CRMWF requires that all immigrants be separated from convicted persons, save in exceptional circumstances; equality of treatment with nationals in state prisons; equal rights to family visitation as nationals and for states to pay attention to the problems posed to immigrant families due to incarceration. Similar standards for the basic rights of children in detention are found in the 1990 Rules for Juveniles Deprived of Their Liberty, while the 1999 UNHCR Revised Guidelines on Applicable Criteria and Standards Relating to the Detention of Asylum Seekers governs the detention of asylum seekers. At the regional level, the Council of Europe (2005) Twenty Guidelines on Forced Return also govern detention conditions and provide similar protections to those found in the universal documents.

References

Abdulaziz, Cabales and Balkandali v. United Kingdom. 1985. Eur. Ct. H. R. 7.

Airey v. Ireland. 1979. 32 Eur. Ct. H.R. (ser. A) at para. 21.

Bermann, George A. 2009. "European Citizenship at Center-State," *Columbia Journal of European Law*, Vol. 15, pp. 165–168.

Berrehab v. the Netherlands. 1988. Eur. Ct. H.R. 3/1987/126/177; 10730/84, Council of Europe, 28 May.

Canepa v. Canada. 1997. U.NHCR, U.N. Doc. CCPR C/59/D/558/1993.

Case No. 2121, Definitive Report, Complaint Against the Government of Spain presented by the General Union of Workers of Spain (UGT). 2002. In 327th Report of the Committee on Freedom of Association, International Labor Officer Governing Body, GB 283/8, 283rd Session.

Chahadl v. the United Kingdom. 1996. ECHR, 1996-V.

Comm. on Freedom of Ass'n, *Complaints Against the Government of the United States Presented by the American Federation of Labor and the Congress of Industrial Organizations (AFL-CIO) and the Confederation of Mexican Workers (CTM).* 2002. Report no. 332, Case No. 2227, Vol. LXXXVI, 2003, Series B, No. 3.

Comm'n v. Belgium. 1981. Case C-149/79, E.C.R. 3881.

Council Directive 2000/43. 2000. O.J. (L 180) 22 (EC).

Council Directive 2000/78. 2000. O.J. (L 303) 16 (EC).

Council Directive 2004/58. 2004. O.J. (L2 99) 35 (EC).

Council of Europe. 2005. Forced Return: Twenty Guidelines, adopted by the Committee of Ministers, Strasbourg, 4.V.2005.

General Recommendation No. 30, Discrimination Against Non Citizens. 2004.

Georgios Orfanopoulos and Raffaele Oliveri v. Land Baden-Wurttenberg. 2004. Joined Cases C-482 & C-493/01, E.C.R. I-5257.

Giry v. Dominican Republic. 1990. Comm'n No. 193/1985, U.N. Doc. CCPR/C/39/D/193/1985.

Gul v. Switzerland. 1996. Eur. Ct. H. R. 5.

Haitian Ctrs. For Human Rights v. United States. 1997. Case 10.675, Inter-Am. C.H.R., Report No. 51/96, OEA/ser.L/V./II.95 doc. 7 rev. at 550.

Hamel v. Madagascar. 1987. Comm'n No. 155/1983, U.N. Doc. CCPR/C/29/D/155/1983.

Hoffman Plastic Compounds, Inc. v. National Labor Relations Board. 2002. 535 U.S. 137.

Inter-Am. Comm'n on Human Rights, Report on the Situation of Human Rights of Asylum Seekers Within the Canadian Refugee Determination System. 2000. OEA/Ser.L./V/II.106.

International Convention on the Elimination of All Forms of Racial Discrimination: Consideration of Reports Submitted by States Parties Under Article 9 of the Convention. 2008. CERD/C/USA/CO/6 ¶ 22.

Jia v. Migrationsverket. 2007. Case C-105, 7 E.C.R. 545.

Juridical Condition and the Rights of the Undocumented Migrants. 2003. Inter-Am. Ct. H.R. Advisory Op. OC-18/03.

Kochenov, Dimitry. 2009. "IUS Tractum of Many Faces: European Citizenship and the Difficult Relationship Between Status and Rights," *Columbia Journal of European Law*, Vol. 15, pp. 169–237.

Martin, David A., T. Alexander Aleinikoff, Hiroshi Motomura, and Maryellen, Fullerton. 2007. *Forced Migration Law and Policy* (St. Paul, MN: Thomson West).

Metlock and Others. 2008. 3 C.M.L.R. 39.

Mexico Case. 2003. Inter-Am. Ct. H.R. (ser. A) No. 18, at 1 Sept. 17 (advisory opinion).

Micheletti v. Delegacion del Gobierno. 1992. Case C-369/90, ECR 1-4223.

Morris v. United Kingdom. 2005. 41 E.H.R.R. 22.

Morson and Jhanjan case. 1982. E.C.R. 3723.

Moustaquim v. Belgium. 1991. 193 Eur. Ct. H. R. (ser. A).

Nessel, Lori A. 2009. "Externalized Borders and the Invisible Refugee," *Columbia Human Rights Law Review*, Vol. 40, pp. 625–699.

Olsson v. Sweden. 1988. 130 Eur. Ct. H. r. (ser. A) 33–34.

Penarrieta, Pura de Toro et al. v. Bolivia. 1987. Communication No. 176/1984, UN Doc. CCPR/C/31/D/176/198.

Quinn v. France. 1995. ECHR, 1995-A 311.
Recommendations on the Human Rights of Irregular Migrants. 2006. Eur. Parl. Doc. 1755.
Resolution on the Human Rights of Irregular Migrants. 2006. Eur. Parl. Doc. 1509.
Sale v. Haitian Ctrs. Council, Inc. 1993. 509 US 155.
Scozzari v. Giunta v. Italy. 2000. 2000-VIII Eur. Ct. H. R. 471.
Sen v. the Netherlands. 2001. Eu. Ct. H.R. App. No. 31465/96.
Slivenko and Others v. Latvia. 2003. (App no. 48321/99) (GC) Eur. Ct. H.R. 2002-II.
Tuquabo-Teke v. The Netherlands. 2003. Eu. Ct. H. R., App. No. 60665/00.
UN Comm. on the Rights of the Child, Concluding Observations on Norway. 2000. Para. 196, UN Doc. CRC/C/15/Add.126.
UNHCR Executive Committee Conclusion on International Protection. 1986. No. 44 (XXXVII). Detention of Refugees and Asylum Seekers.
UNHCR Revised Guidelines on Applicable Criteria and Standards Relating to the Detention of Asylum Seekers, Guideline 10. 1999.
United Nations, Human Rights Committee, General Comment No. 32 (90th sess. 2007). CCPR/C/GC/32, para. 10.
Winata v. Australia. 2001. UNHCR, U.N. Doc. CCPR/C/72/D/930/2000.
Xhavara and Others v. Italy and Albania. 2001. Eur. Ct. H. R. 39473/98.
Zhu v. Sec'y of State for the Home Dep't. 2004. Case C-200/02, European Court of Justice.

46

The humanitarian–human rights nexus

A global culture perspective

Joshua J. Yates

The paradox of humanitarianism's crisis

It is no secret that humanitarianism is in crisis. At least it is no secret among humanitarians themselves. "How can so many well-educated, cosmopolitan, and to a fair degree well-intentioned people," asks a leading practitioner (de Waal 1997, p. 66), "work within institutions with such noble goals to such little effect?" Yet what troubles humanitarians goes deeper than the specter of ineffectiveness. A more disturbing issue is how humanitarian action itself actually becomes part of the problem it is supposed to remedy. In spite of their most solemn of principles, *Primum Non Nocere* – "First, do no harm" – humanitarians confront the unforeseen ways in which in crisis after crisis their saving work aids and abets violent conflict, famine, and human rights abuse (Anderson 1996). Few episodes demonstrated this more traumatically than the Rwandan refugee camps, where humanitarian assistance intended for victims actually strengthened the power of *genocidaires*. Though an extreme case, Rwanda is not unique. It is but a horrific incidence of a recurrent dilemma. Yet many practitioners contend that the so-called "paradox of humanitarian action" goes deeper still (Terry 2002; Tirman 2003). In some places – most famously Darfur – it functions as a substitute for direct international political action, while in other places – most notably Iraq – it is increasingly indistinguishable from the strategic aims of an occupying force. According to Samantha Power (2008), the 2003 bombing of the UN headquarters in Baghdad, which killed twenty-one diplomatic and humanitarian personnel, "made it clear that the United Nations and humanitarian groups had moved from the 1990s, when their flags no longer offered protection, to a phase in which their affiliations made them outright targets of Al Qaeda and other violent extremists."

As a consequence, many humanitarians see their organizations as pawns in the contradictory post-Cold War, post-9/11 geopolitical strategies of evasion and intervention. Either way, it is hard to disagree with disaster journalist David Rieff's (2002) evaluation that humanitarianism is "an emblem of political failure."

This severe self-criticism is not without irony: the crisis of conscience among humanitarians has come during what can only be described as a humanitarian boom. The numbers tell the story. Since 1863, with the founding of the International Committee of the Red Cross, the number of international non-governmental humanitarian organizations has grown to over 1,500, and many are among the most well-known "brands" in the world. With combined financial resources in the billions of dollars annually, it is estimated that the philanthropic work of private aid agencies affected the lives of 250 million people between 1985 and 1995 alone. According to the OECD/DAC Development Cooperation 2000 Report, flows of emergency and distress relief increased from $766 million in 1989 to $4.3 billion in 1999 (of total official development assistance in those years of $43.4 billion and $56.37 billion, respectively) (Charlton and May 1995, p. 240).

In terms of manpower, one observer reports that, "At any given moment as many as 75,000 civilian professionals work full-time in the middle of crises on various humanitarian tasks, whether protection, relief, post-conflict reconciliation, or rehabilitation. They receive headquarter support from at least an equal number of administrative, legal, and logistical officials, making a total of perhaps 150,000 or more full-time civilian humanitarians" (Smyser 2003, p. 7). Smyser underscores the point: "The number of 74,000 civilian professionals working in humanitarian crisis zones may not seem large in a world population of billions, but it represents the equivalent of what four to six U.S. Army divisions could put on the line at any given moment in a ground operation. Few national armies can match it with their forces" (Smyser, 2003, p. 7). Add to these numbers tens of thousands of peacekeeping soldiers who now routinely support humanitarian operations, plus thousands of advocacy and human rights activists and lawyers who champion the cause of the voiceless and oppressed in the name of international law, and you have a profound world-historical development.

Hand-in-hand with this growth in numbers and resources has come greater organizational influence, legitimacy, and power at a world level. From the United States' Agency for International Development, to the World Bank, to NATO, nearly all national governments and major international institutions recognize humanitarian organizations as principle sources of credible information, as primary deliverers of social services, and as frontline advocates. Even the UN Security Council now includes humanitarian INGOs in decision-making processes concerned with complex emergencies around the world. In 1997, the Security Council held its first-ever meeting with NGOs, who briefed the Council on complex emergencies in Africa (Lindberg and Bryant 2001, pp. 197–198). How, then, do we explain the pervasive sense of crisis? The fact that humanitarians are no longer peripheral actors on the world stage is certainly part of a larger answer. For better or for worse, humanitarians have become leading characters in tragic dramas of human suffering that play out daily across the planet. Beyond this common-sense assessment, most conventional accounts limit explanation to the external constraints placed on humanitarian action by political and economic circumstance. As we have seen, many humanitarians feel forced into a role as the "designated conscience" of fickle Western publics, or worse, the handmaiden of neo-liberal imperialism. (Rieff 2002; Tirman 2003). In yet another popular rendering, humanitarian organizations are more culprit than victim; they are "greedy" institutions preoccupied with self-preservation and thus captive to the mad scramble for aid dollars and photo opportunities in the latest world emergency (Cooley and Ron 2002).

As useful as these explanations are in detailing the external social, political, and economic crises that shape humanitarian action, by themselves they leave an impoverished picture of what this crisis of conscience represents. *They fail to account for the sources of the crisis that are internal to the humanitarian project itself.* We catch a glimpse of this dimension in the fact that it is the humanitarian practitioners themselves who utter the most serious critiques. They judge the validity of their own practices, moreover, from some putative moral high ground. By exposing the violation of some norm or principle, these practitioners appeal to a standard of moral judgment they fully expect will be shared by their colleagues within the field as well as without. This belies a cultural reality that resists reductions to self-interested choices of rational actors or the ideological component of neo-liberal political economy. Crucially, conventional accounts fail to consider how humanitarian action is not merely shaped by its environs, but is also constitutive of it: the humanitarian project is one of the most fundamental legitimating rationales of Western modernity and its governing institutions – and today, Western modernity and its governing institutions constitute a rudimentary global culture.

The crisis of humanitarianism takes on a very distinctive shape and significance in light of this global culture. It represents a struggle over the very meaning and purpose of humanitarianism, animated by the fateful merger of two imperatives reflecting developments in global culture itself: *the humanitarian imperative*, formalized in the Geneva Conventions as the legal right to assistance, and *the human rights imperative*, enshrined in the Universal Declaration of Human Rights as the duty to protect, and increasingly, as the controversial right to intervene.

Global culture and moral order

Arising primarily out of the West, a world-level cultural order (not to be confused with a universal culture) has been developing in fits and starts over the past few centuries (Thomas et al. 1987; Boli and Thomas 1999). While not internally monolithic, it is institutionally ubiquitous and in crucial respects hegemonic. Since World War II, it has come to underwrite the moral purposes, and thus the legitimacy, of democratic governments, the United Nations and other international organizations, major world financial institutions like the World Trade Organization (WTO) and the International Monetary Fund (IMF), a constellation of scientific and technological infrastructure, and expert knowledge that makes world-level organization possible, not to mention the panoply of INGOs, multinational firms, and transnational activism that today encompass the globe. Taken as a whole, the organizational structure of this global culture amounts to an "imagined community" of institutional forms – a social ontology. The moral order inherent in this world-level community is premised on the consent of rational, autonomous, capable, and responsible agents, of which the individual and the nation-state are foundational. To borrow from philosopher Charles Taylor (2004, p. 10), moral order is, in this way, "more than just a set of norms; it also contains what we might call an 'ontic' component, identifying features of the world that make the norms realizable."

Like all world-cultural organizational forms, humanitarian INGOs implement a certain normative "accounting." They do so in three senses: first, they embody *accounts of reality* by which they posit not only "what is," but also "what ought to be" and "what ought *not* to be;" second, they embody *accounts of value* whereby we can determine "what counts as genuine human progress or regress;" and finally, they embody *accounts of obligation* by which we can know "what should be done" to generate progress toward world-cultural goals and "who is responsible for such action." Their specific world-cultural mandate concerns progression (or lack thereof) of all world-cultural actors toward upholding the moral order to which these accounts speak. The world-cultural purpose of the nation-state, for instance, is to secure for its citizens progress, symbolized by national GDP; equality, symbolized in the language of political rights; and security, symbolized in terms of troops and tanks, and increasingly by international law. Wherever the principal structure and underlying moral order of the imagined community has broken down, such as when a state fails to fulfill is world-cultural purposes, there, at the limits of law and order and at the forfeiture or annulment of the social contract, the humanitarian imperative activates. Of particular note is how, in the *absence* of a world state, humanitarian INGOs become the last resort, or the rearguard of this moral order at the periphery, while at the same time, they are the first resort, or the vanguard, at its center.

To put it provocatively, humanitarian INGOs may or may not be saving the world from natural disaster, poverty, disease, famine, or violent conflict, but they are "saving" people and places at the peripheries of power from total disintegration with international order. And while INGOs may or may not be instigating virtue or altruism in policy makers, multinational corporations, or armed forces, they are making them more mindful of the moral order that grounds their legitimacy. Seen from the perspective of global culture, humanitarian INGOs are recognized as the principal moral arbiters of the "good" international society and the bearers of the tacit moral order from which the present world order derives much of its shape and plausibility.

Yet for as much integration and coherence as this picture of global culture suggests, the reality is much more complicated – global culture is neither static, nor uncontested. The sheer diversity and inequality of social relations that exists around the world ensures severe limitations and opposition. The processes of cultural enactment are prone to imperfection and idiosyncrasy, and strikingly vulnerable to manipulation. In light of such challenges, it is not surprising the present global culture has deep internal tensions. It is to these we now turn.

The fateful merger and its consequences

One of the most significant hallmarks of world-cultural development is the emergence of human rights as a globally pervasive, if not always compelling, political and legal discourse. Few have embraced human rights more fervently, more thoroughly, or with more effect than the humanitarian. The merger of humanitarian and human rights imperatives has splintered the humanitarian project into rival camps along a continuum: from "strict," classic humanitarianism embodied by the Red Cross at one end, to "expansive" humanitarianism epitomized by the cross-borderism of Médecins Sans Frontières, and, further still, by the solidarist-interventionism championed by groups such as CARE. Over the last two decades, this continuum has also been a trend line.

Three key developments mark this trend from strict to expansive humanitarianism, each observable within the accounts of reality, value, and obligation to which world-cultural organizations ritually give expression. The first development involves the evolving conception of the individual person – the cornerstone of world-cultural ontology – not simply as a passive recipient of aid, but increasingly as a "stakeholder" and "rights bearer." The second concerns the shift away from "mere charity" and meeting immediate needs, to a holistic focus on "root causes." The third, extending the logic of holism, is the controversial push for intervention. We take each in turn.

The victim as rights bearer

The modern humanitarian endeavor begins and ends on two key presuppositions about reality: first, the irreducible building block of all human society is the individual person, and second, this essential fact holds true everywhere on earth. Humanitarianism is thus founded on a patently obvious idea: by virtue of a common humanity, all people possess the same fundamental needs and desires, regardless of geography, ethnicity, religion, class, or race. Therefore, every human person is a potential victim in need of humanitarian services. Humanitarian action is universally applicable because it makes sense of (and thus orders) an otherwise anomic world with its ready-made ontology; identities may change from crisis to crisis, but the basic stock of actors, litany of problems, catalogue of behaviors and interests, and possible outcomes remain constant the world over. What at first seem to be unique problems unfold as part of our universal human condition.

While the immediate goals of all humanitarian action are to relieve human suffering and save lives, the ultimate goal is to empower people to care for themselves, to determine their life purposes, and to take the actions necessary to attain those purposes. At work is a conceptualization of the individual as an autonomous empowered self. The individual is stripped down to a unified, agentic core, doing away with arbitrary, ascripted attributes which compromise the "blind" benevolence of humanitarian impartiality. By stripping the individual to its most irreducible aspect – its "choosing self" – we can arrive at what is both universal and sacred: agency.

Anything that overrides, undermines, or corrupts individual agency is seen as a violation of human dignity. Every tyranny overrides it; extreme material deprivation undermines it; even the well-intentioned paternalism of humanitarians corrupts it by fostering dependency. Consider this excerpt from *The Oxfam Handbook of Development and Relief*:

> Strengthening people's capacity to determine their own values and priorities, and to organize themselves to act on these, is the basis of development. Development is about women and men becoming empowered to bring about positive changes in the their lives; about personal growth and public action; about both the process and the outcome of challenging poverty, oppression, and discrimination; and about the realization of human potential through social and economic justice. Above all, it is about the process of transforming lives, and transforming societies.
>
> *(Eade and Williams 1995, p. 9)*

In other words, beyond restoration of human dignity, humanitarian individualism includes empowering people to realize their full potential and to achieve a sufficient level of material well-being while making independent choices on matters which affect them, ultimately affecting their environments for the better. Victims become the ideal change agents. A vision of progress is embedded in the language of empowerment and change. It is hoped that empowerment will bring about macro-change; collectively, fully realized capable selves *can* change the world. The empowered individual becomes the bedrock upon which the scaffolding of humanitarian action is built.

The scaffolding, however, is constructed with the language and legal proscriptions of human rights. Human rights restore fundamental dignity by establishing parameters about the necessary conditions for individual potential and collective progress. With the gradual shift to human rights over the past few decades, the moral register of humanitarian action changes from empowerment to entitlement and from benevolence to justice. The salience of this change is seen in the widespread (and now prevailing) change in the language of INGO mission statements where victims are routinely described as "stakeholders" and "rights bearers." Against the pragmatics of classic humanitarianism, which sought to aid victims in episodes of acute crisis *when permitted to do so*, today's humanitarianism advocates a more categorical approach, where duties are owed no matter the circumstances, regardless of permission.

"The [fundamental] imperative to assist," observes a prominent scholar of humanitarianism (Minear 2002, p. 40), "framed in isolation from the concomitant commitment to protect, is now understood to produce threadbare humanitarian action." In the words of the president of the French *Action Contre La Faim*, a leading anti-hunger organization: "The problem with the traditional idea of humanitarianism is that it demands access for workers to reach victims who then become objects of 'our' compassion. What I support is the victim's access to their rights – that is, a construction that makes them subjects, not objects" (quoted in Rieff 2002, p. 310). This is the sentiment of the majority of practitioners, as many increasingly favor a full spectrum of rights, including social, cultural, and economic rights. Today's victim of natural disaster or violent conflict is no longer considered *lucky* to be a recipient of foreign aid and the charity of strangers; today's victim is *entitled* to the protection of his or her rights, ideally by the state, but by humanitarians in the breach.

To put it this way greatly oversimplifies the fateful merger between humanitarianism and human rights. The evolution in global culture to which this merger gives paradigmatic expression was neither inevitable nor smooth. Yet, once rooted, its impact on humanitarianism has been profound.

The call for holistic action

"Holistic change is the kind of change we should be looking at," contends a public health specialist and veteran of a number of leading humanitarian INGOs. "That involves looking at the whole community from the physical to the developmental to the mental to the emotional to the spiritual. You are looking at changing people's lives, not just how many vegetables they eat" (J. Yates, 2010, pers. comm.). Beginning in the late 1960s and crystallizing in the early 1990s, half a century of failure in formerly distinct enterprises culminated in a push for a more holistic and integrated approach among relief, development, and human rights groups. The goal was both ethical and practical refinement – a fuller and more consistent affirmation of human dignity and increased effectiveness. This push is most evident in the effort to develop metrics that account for the "root causes" of humanitarian problems.

Although a long-time practitioner at Oxfam-UK (Stockton 2004, p. 3) admits, "measures of crude mortality, infant mortality, malnutrition (acute and chronic) have fairly widely recognized validity," he maintains that, "they do not give us any insight into the quality of 'dignity,' nor do they typically provide any indications of vulnerability to political violence." The president of CARE (O'Brien 2004, p. 32) is more forceful: "What is the point of applying Band-Aids to a festering sore, of providing a bed for the night in a crumbling edifice? Agencies that save lives are obliged also to address the root causes of conflict, which are political at the core."

The most influential and institutionalized effort to develop such holistic measures has come from the United Nations Development Program (UNDP). Starting in 1990, the UNDP has published the *Human Development Report,* which has developed several composite indices to measure different aspects of human development beyond the conventional metrics of GDP and crude mortality rates. The centerpiece of this work is the Human Development Index (HDI). The HDI is a uniquely interdisciplinary index, drawing from demography, epidemiology, nutritional science, public health, education, and economics, and intentionally aligning them within the frame of both negative and positive human rights. Lest there be doubt about the centrality of human rights, the introduction to the 2000 *Report* was emphatic: "In short, human development is essential for realizing human rights, and human rights are essential for full human development." In the axiology of expansive humanitarianism, human development and human rights are now understood not merely as complementary, but as mutually constitutive.

The same logic pushing humanitarians to go beyond "strict" humanitarianism to address "root causes" also pushes them toward an expansive account of obligation.

"Above all nations – is Humanity." These early watchwords of the International Red Cross reveal the aspiring universalism that has been at the heart of modern humanitarianism since its inception. All humanitarian INGOs, strict and expansive, begin from the tacit premise and priority of world citizenship, and from this premise "the humanitarian imperative comes first" – people in crisis have a right to receive humanitarian assistance, and INGOs have the right to offer it.

However, with the ratification of the Universal Declaration of Human Rights, the polarity of humanitarian law begins to be reversed. Indeed, the most striking feature of an entire body of subsequent international law is how, paying dutiful homage to national sovereignty, it has steadily elevated the individual to the same level of inviolability as the state. The human rights imperative that animates this trajectory signals a major turning point in the evolution of global culture. While we must never confuse the establishment and proliferation of international human rights norms and conventions with their enforcement in practice, we are witnessing, in the words of former UN Secretary-General Javier Perez de Cuellar, "what is probably an irresistible shift in public attitudes toward the belief that the defense of the oppressed in the name of morality should prevail over frontiers and legal documents" (quoted in François 1995, p. 3).

With this switching polarity, the structure of obligation changes. Every individual is now a bearer of fundamental rights and is owed the protection of those rights merely by virtue of his or her humanity. The primary guarantor of this is the state – and when the state fails, whether in willful disregard of its obligations or not, then, writes long-time humanitarian analyst Hugo Slim (2002, p. 118), "that duty automatically falls to others. As a categorical imperative, humanitarian duty is boundless. We all ought to do it." In principle, the ethical implication is clear enough: "we" means everyone who can; in practice, however, the political implications and distribution of obligation are far from clear. Not surprisingly, on this point strict and expansive humanitarians differ vehemently.

Sadako Ogata, the former UN High Commissioner for Refugees, has provided the rallying cry for the expansive position: "There are no humanitarian solutions to humanitarian problems." The implications could not be clearer for humanitarians of this ilk: the right to provide assistance on behalf of victims and the duty to protect their basic human rights must now be understood in light of the *ultimate obligation to intervene*. Leading the charge has been expansive humanitarian's most controversial figure, Bernard Kouchner. One of the founders of Médecins Sans Frontières, Kouchner notoriously broke from MSF to form Médecins Du Monde. "Classic humanitarianism," argues Kouchner, "protects the victims and accepts [massacres] as reality. Modern [expansive] humanitarianism accepts no such thing. Its ambition is to prevent the massacres" (quoted in Rieff 2002, p. 288). In the innovative parlance of Kouchner, the watchword of expansive humanitarianism is *ingerence humanitaire*. What is essential for Kouchner and others like him is that we finally complete the push toward holism. The push to address "root causes" through the entire continuum of humanitarian action, from immediate relief to development to human rights advocacy, concludes with enforcement and protection – if necessary by military force, as necessary with humanitarians leading the way. With humanitarian intervention, the fateful merger of humanitarian and human rights imperatives finds its fullest and most fateful expression. It has led to what once would have been considered, and for a minority of humanitarians remains, a clear and straightforward contradiction in terms: In its extreme form, humanitarian intervention is justification for making aid conditional and, paradoxically, even for waging war.

Significantly, this new humanitarianism has also enjoyed legitimacy in the halls of power – in the UN Security Council, WTO, and in bilateral agencies such as USAID, the UK's DIFD, and the EU's European Commission Humanitarian Aid Office (Macrae and Leader 2000). Confidence in the extreme version of this expansive project has faltered in the face of America's war in Iraq and in the push not only by US coalition forces but also by the UN and other European states toward a policy of "coherence" between civil, humanitarian, and military objectives. The implications of intervention and the coherence agenda, it turns out, follow an agonizingly paradoxical logic: (1) INGOs, frustrated with decades of failed development and recurring humanitarian crises, push for an expansive human rights-based humanitarianism that addresses "root causes"; (2) expansive humanitarians recognize that "root causes" are inherently political and begin to advocate for political action as the only solution to humanitarian problems, which typically translates to UN or state intervention in the name of humanitarian ideals and human rights enforcement; (3) and yet, as the UN and powerful states begin to pay heed and act, humanitarians find their fundamental principles jeopardized – there is role confusion between military, civil, and humanitarian practitioners; humanitarian neutrality and impartiality are questioned as aid seems to take sides; and this, in turn, jeopardizes the security and access of humanitarian practitioners in the field. At the end of this cycle, expansive humanitarians again confront the problem of *Primum Non Nocere,* of whether they have become complicit in the very suffering and human misery they try to ameliorate. Summarizing the predicament of expansive, human rights-based humanitarian action is the former Director of MSF-Holland (Milliano, quoted in Macrae and Leader 2000): "The relationship between humanitarian aid and political action has always been ambiguous. The moment that political forces are absent or not coherent we ask for political action. The moment they get involved, we ask them to stop."

Global culture's paradox of expectations

Where does this leave us? The evolution of global culture, embodied in the fateful merger of the benevolence of the humanitarian imperative and the justice of the human rights imperative, has produced an unavoidable dilemma. Benevolence and justice are among the most powerful moral imperatives of global culture, and combining them is bound to resonate at both individual and collective levels. Without question their merger inspires us to extend our moral commitments to greater categories of people and across greater geographical and social distances. It also makes us vulnerable to the acute disillusionment that comes with promising more than can be delivered. Does humanitarianism tempt us, as human rights lawyer David Kennedy (2004, p. xviii) contends, "to hubris ... to the conviction that we know more than we do about what justice can be"? Though we claim certain advancement in our humanitarian efforts, we must acknowledge it has come at the price of a tortured conscience. *Because we believe the causes of suffering are knowable, we expect they can be overcome.* The world-cultural imperative to rid the world of suffering, to end hunger, and to ensure justice stumbles consistently against our repeated failures to live up to it. This is the crux of humanitarianism's crisis, a pronounced antinomy at the heart of global culture itself. Between the transformational optimism of expansive humanitarianism and strict humanitarianism's "humanism of bad news," between the undying dreams of perpetual peace and the haunting echoes of "never again," the paradox of expectations is among the defining moral quandaries of our time.

References

Anderson, Mary. 1996. *Do No Harm: How Aid Can Support Peace – Or War* (Boulder, CO: Lynne Rienner).

Boli, John and George Thomas. 1999. *Constructing World Culture: International Non-governmental Organization since 1875* (Stanford, CA: Stanford University Press).

Charlton, Roger and Roy May. 1995. "NGOs, Politics, Projects, Probity: A Policy Implementation Perspective." *Third World Quarterly*, Vol. 16, No. 2.

Cooley, Alexander and James Ron. 2002. "The NGO Scramble: Organizational Insecurity and the Political Economy of Transnational Action." *International Security*, Vol. 27, No. 1, pp. 5–39.

de Waal, Alex. 1997. *Famine Crimes: Politics and the Disaster Relief Industry in Africa* (Bloomington: Indiana University Press).

Eade, Deborah and Suzanne Williams. 1995. *The Oxfam Handbook of Development and Relief.* Vol. 1 (Oxford: Oxfam).

François, Jean. 1995. *Populations in Danger* (London: Médecins Sans Frontières).

Kennedy, David. 2004. *The Dark Side of Virtue: Reassessing International Humanitarianism* (Princeton, NJ: Princeton University Press).

Lindberg, Marc and Coralie Bryant. 2001. *Going Global: Transforming Relief and Development NGOs* (Bloomfield, CT: Kumarian Press).

Macrae, Joanna and Nicholas Leader. 2000. "Shifting Sands: The Search For 'Coherence' Between Political and Humanitarian Response to Complex Emergencies." *Humanitarian Policy Group Report*, Overseas Development Institute, no. 8.

Minear, Larry. 2002. *The Humanitarian Enterprise: Dilemmas and Discoveries* (Bloomfield, CT: Kumarian Press).

O'Brien, Paul. 2004. "Politicized Humanitarianism: A Response to Nicholas de Torrente." *Harvard Human Rights Journal*, Vol. 17.

Power, Samantha. 2008. "For Terrorists, a War on Aid Groups." *New York Times*, 19 August.

Rieff, David. 2002. *A Bed for the Night* (New York: Simon & Schuster).

Slim, Hugo. 2002. "Claiming our Humanitarian Imperative: NGOs and the Cultivation of Humanitarian Duty." *Refugee Survey Quarterly*, Vol. 21, No. 3.

Smyser, W. R. 2003. *The Humanitarian Conscience: Caring for Others in the Age of Terror* (New York: Palgrave Macmillan).

Stockton, Nicholas. 2004. "Measuring Humanitarian Impact: Why We Must Begin By Measuring Morbidity." Lecture to the Fritz Institute, Washington, DC, June.

Taylor, Charles. 2004. *Modern Social Imaginaries* (Durham, NC: Duke University Press).

Terry, Fiona. 2002. *Condemned to Repeat? The Paradox of Humanitarian Action* (Ithaca, NY: Cornell University Press).

Thomas, George, John W. Meyer, Francisco Ramirez, and John Boli. 1987. *Institutional Structure: Constituting State, Society, and the Individual* (London: Sage).

Tirman, John. 2003. "The New Humanitarianism: How Military Intervention Became the Norm." *Boston Review*, December/January.

47

Bystanders to human rights abuses

A psychosocial perspective

Irene Bruna Seu

While much has been written about perpetrators of mass atrocities and victims of human rights abuses, literature and research on the bystander – the third corner in any atrocity triangle (Cohen 2001; Staub 2003) – is still sparse and fragmented. Establishing a coherent line of inquiry into bystander behavior has proved difficult due to issues of definition and the conceptual and disciplinary boundaries of the term. Social psychologists began to study the passive bystander phenomenon in the 1970s, as a reaction to the murder of Kitty Genovese. The "passive bystander phenomenon" has, strictly speaking, pertained since then, to lack of intervention in emergency situations. However, this line of inquiry has subsequently expanded into the wider field of pro-social behavior, which investigates what prompts people to help in general.

Sociologists have also been interested in the topic, particularly in relation to bystanders to mass atrocities. They have concentrated on ordinary people witnessing crimes against humanity over a prolonged period of time, as in Nazi Germany (e.g., Geras 1999; Cohen 2001) rather than studying bystander behavior in sudden emergency situations.

Some sociological debates have focused on the "Politics of Pity." Boltanski's (1999) formulation, which draws on Arendt (1990), defines it as politics inherently based on spectacle; it is essentially about creating a relationship between the self and a distant stranger. This also relates to media and communication studies of political, ideological, and cultural meanings underpinning the processes through which distant suffering is "mediated," and how a humanitarian crisis is portrayed might affect the responses of audiences (e.g., Adams 1986; Cartwright 2008, Chouliaraki 2006).

The common denominator in all these debates is the inquiry into what happens in the gap between knowledge and action (Cohen 2001). This characterizes all discussions on bystander passivity, whether technically called the "passive bystander phenomenon" by psychologists, or the more general definition of any ordinary person witnessing human suffering and not intervening. Hence, the definition of passive bystander used in this chapter is partly borrowed from Staub: "The individual or collection of individuals, including nations, who witness what is happening" (2003, p. 4) and decide not to act in response to that knowledge.

The work reported in this chapter addresses the gap between knowledge and action from an empirical point of view, discussing data from bystanders explaining their passivity to the suffering of distant strangers. In the specific, the participants were asked to reflect on and discuss instances when human rights abuses had been committed. They were given two Amnesty International appeals (one on human rights abuses in Afghanistan and one on torture) and an article from the liberal British newspaper *The Guardian* on the West's collusion with human rights abuses in Saudi Arabia. However, the participants' comments covered the much wider field of humanitarian aid, charity donations, and helping and giving in general. This suggests that the reactions discussed in this chapter are of relevance to the "passive bystander phenomenon" in general. The data was generated through a series of focus groups, carried out over a period of four years, with an ethnically, socio-economic, gender, and age diverse group of participants (twelve in the UK and six in the Basque country, Spain).

Active and passive bystanders

Mainstream psychology has focused recently on psychological factors that may facilitate or interfere with audiences' pro-social responses in general and, more specifically, to charity and humanitarian appeals. Some have suggested that differences in responses are due to donors' decision-making styles (Supphellen and Nelson 2001). Some have argued that humanitarian appeals provoke "psychophysical numbing" where the human ability to appreciate loss of life reduces as the losses increase (Slovic 2007).

Other psychologists have focused on "identifiable victim effect" theory. This is where a response is more likely when the appeal identifies an individual victim (Kogut and Ritov 2005) or specific family (Small and Loewenstein 2003; Warren and Walker 1991). There is some debate as to whether this could be attributed to smaller numbers evoking more compassion (Kogut and Ritov 2005) or because it enabled the respondents to feel more competent (Warren and Walker 1991).

There have been mixed results when the "theory of planned behavior" (Smith and McSweeney 2007) or the "dual processing theory" (Epstein 1994) have been applied to audience apathy. Slovic (2007) and Epstein (1994) have blamed the failure of System 2 (rational, normative analysis) to inform and direct System 1's processing of information (experiential, intuitive, and affect-based response). Loewenstein and Small (2007) have focused on the interaction between "sympathy" and "deliberation" and how the two are affected by proximity, similarity, vividness, and individual past and vicarious experiences. Others have perceived audiences as active agents who might be motivated to actively avoid feelings of empathy for those in need, lest they be motivated to help them (Shaw et al. 1994).

Some psychologists have explored audiences' (un)responsiveness in terms of immediacy of or identification with the victim. Contrary to generally held beliefs, Eckel et al. (2007) found that those who were nearer to areas worst hit by Hurricane Katrina were less responsive to related appeals due to "Katrina overload." Levine and Thompson (2004) found that social category relations, rather than geographical proximity or emotional reactions, were the most important factors in increasing responsiveness to humanitarian appeals.

Ervin Staub has studied psychosocial factors that prompt perpetrators to commit crimes against humanity, but also the continuum that can lead bystanders to either support the crimes – whether directly by turning into perpetrators themselves or by indirectly supporting the perpetrators through their passivity and lack of opposition – or turn into rescuers (Staub 1989a, 1989b, 1999, 2002, 2003). He claims that when humans harm or witness somebody harming another, they need to "justify their actions and create reasons for their actions in the form of ideas, beliefs, and ideologies ... that justifies what they are doing" (1989b, p. 41). In this sense, they share the same "societal tilt" of the perpetrators.

Staub (1989b) claims that bystanders are locked in the same continuum as the perpetrators so need to progressively defend themselves from the victim's suffering and reduce their own empathy and identification with the victim. They can participate in the cultural devaluation of the victim. They can reason that the victims deserve their fate. They may avoid processing available information about the actions of the perpetrators; in short, they may progressively deny reality.

Cohen (2001) and van Dijk (1992) have argued that denial comes in many forms, each with its own cognitive, emotional, social, political, and cultural functions. Van Dijk has claimed that denial is part of a strategy of defense, presupposing implicit or explicit accusations and may be pre-emptive (1992, p. 91). Similarly, Cohen (2001) draws attention to the culturally available accounts of justifications and excuses that form the vocabulary of moral passivity within our society. He argues that we use a "multitude of vocabularies – justifications, rationalizations, evasions – to deal with our awareness of so many images of unmitigated suffering" (2001, p. 8).

These vocabularies are increasing and becoming more convoluted as they are used in an attempt to bridge the moral and psychic gap between "what you know and what you do." Cohen states that the techniques of evasion, avoidance, deflection and rationalizations should draw on good – that is, believable – stories. He draws on C. Wright Mills's work (1940), according to which accounts of denial are not mysterious internal states, but typical vocabularies with clear functions in particular social situations: "Accounts are learnt by ordinary cultural transmission, and are drawn from a well established, collectively available pool. An account is adopted because of its public acceptability. Socialization teaches us which motives are acceptable for which action" (Cohen 2001, p. 59). Hence, a denial account does not simply give a plausible, acceptable story about an action (e.g., "this is what I do"), but also provides crucial moral accountability for the speaker ("this is why what I do is all right").

Cohen's theory of denial starts from a psychological perspective, but firmly positions bystanders in the social dimension and makes them reliant on socially available "good stories" to justify their inaction. This also implies that, once a culture of passivity is established, passive bystanders are unlikely to challenge that societal tilt. This lends support to claims made by trait psychologists that bystanders are essentially conformists. Drawing on several studies on bystanders, Baum (2008) defines personality of the passive bystander as "conventional," "conforming," and fundamentally motivated by "safety and social status."

This brief review highlights the role played by both social and psychological factors in bystander passivity, hence the need for a theoretically multifaceted and multidisciplinary approach to bystander behavior. A psychosocial model is required to take into account both the social and the psychological in terms of what audiences are equipped to understand, make sense of, and deal with when confronted with information about human rights abuses. We need a conceptual model able to account for the multiple ways in which all the dimensions – cultural, biographical, psychosocial, and normative – intersect with each other, to determine active or passive responses.

This chapter begins to integrate these dimensions, by moving back and forth between three levels of interpretation, as shown in Figure 47.1. Looking at how members of the public describe their personal experience to begin with and taking what they are saying at face value as a description of their reactions, thoughts, and emotions results in a simple mapping of audiences' responses.

As we need to know how and through what resources bystanders produce "good stories" that are convincing and easily accepted, moving away from understanding these statements as straightforward expressions of individuals' experiences and reactions, what audiences say should also be read as socially constructive accounting to justify passivity. Therefore, at the social/ideological level, "thicker" meanings are attributed to what audiences say, and attention is paid to the social and ideological action performed by their statements. In Dean's words (2004), these are "highly

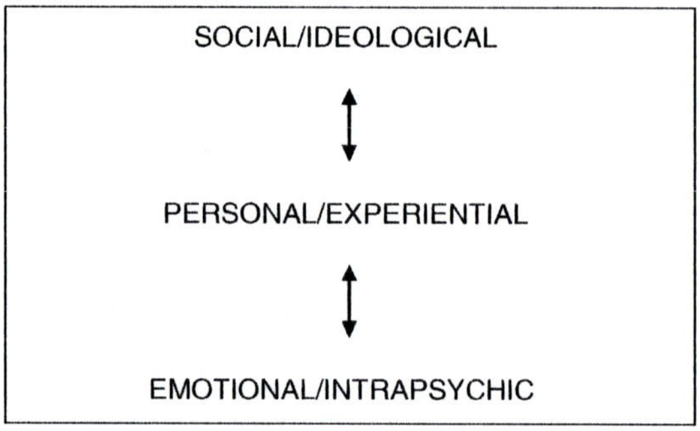

Figure 47.1 Bystander phenomena; a psychosocial model

self-conscious narratives about the collective construction of moral availability," or what Cohen (2001) defines as "implicatory denial."

The third level is the most tentative, as it implies unconscious or at least subconscious operations such as emotional conflicts, defenses, and reaction formations. Psychosocial analysis posits that the real events of the external, social world are defensively, as well as discursively, appropriated. Without claiming direct access to the bystander's internal worlds, a psychosocial approach looks at the emotions and emotional conflicts provoked by the information about human rights abuses and what can be intuited about the underlying intrapsychic dynamics.

The arrows in the box do not signify that these three dimensions are in a linear relationship with each other, but that our only access to all three levels is through personal experiences described by bystanders. This shows that, ultimately, there are words, spoken at a particular time and context, but also present are intrapsychic, emotional, and social dynamics that are an essential part of the "personal experience." In short, all three levels are essential components of the "bystander phenomenon."

This chapter discusses three themes: "the web of passivity," "complex emotions," and "denial and humanitarian appeals." They will be discussed in terms of how they are personally and emotionally experienced, and psychosocially determined. A belief in the possibility of change and progress requires faith in the idea of fluidity, rather than viewing the positions taken by bystanders as static and immovable.

Most participants elected to participate in the discussion because they were openly supportive of human rights. This is partly what makes the data so intriguing; these individuals cannot, by any stretch of the imagination, be described as "uncaring," or as holding extreme or openly reactionary views. The gap between knowing, caring, and doing is fascinating in that it does not lend itself to simple, single-dimensional interpretations. Yet, what this chapter asks is, in a way, rather simple: "What does the ordinary person think, feel, and, crucially, do as a result of knowing about human rights abuse when the knowledge comes from appeals designed to provoke active response and engagement?"

The web of passivity

Figure 47.2 summarizes the main excuses and justifications recurring in all the focus groups and forms a powerful vocabulary of inaction, which includes a wide range of explanations and justifications. Stan Cohen (2001, p. 59) makes an important distinction between justifications and excuses. Justifications are "accounts in which one accepts responsibility for the act in question,

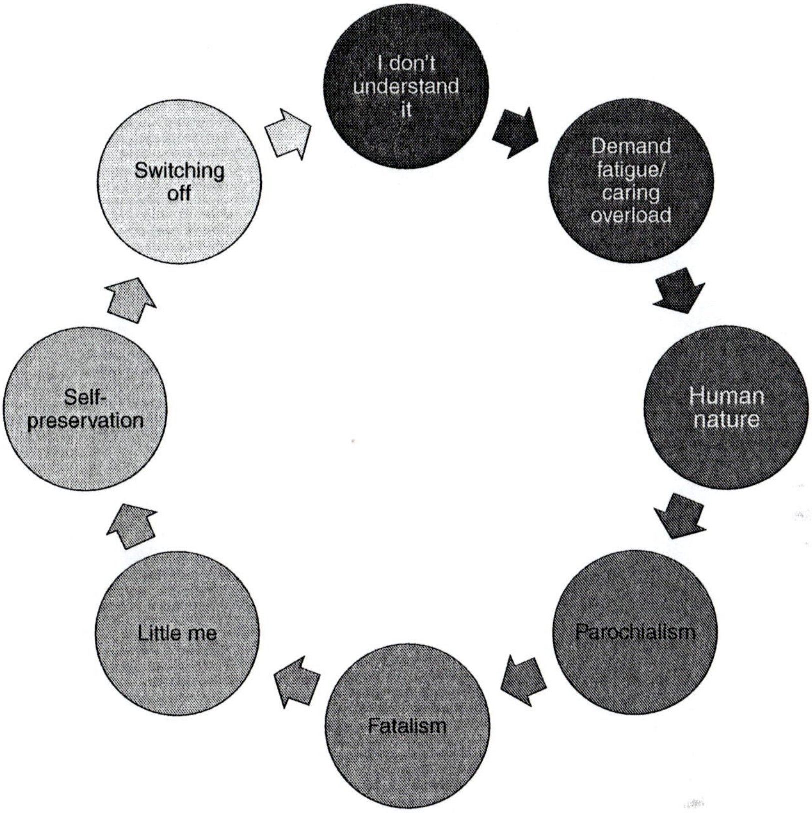

Figure 47.2 Excuses and justifications; the vocabulary of passivity

but denies the pejorative quality associated with it," whereas excuses are "accounts in which one admits that the act in question is bad, wrong or inappropriate, but denies full responsibility." These are everyday, familiar accounts, hence easy to recognize and therefore to normalize. The very existence of such accounts suggests that passive bystanding is not due to lack of internalization of moral normativity. All participants felt the need to justify themselves, implying their unspoken agreement with the social responsibility imperative. The extent to which the passive bystanders are actually conflicted about not doing more is not known. They are perhaps simply paying lip service to what is recognized as a social expectation in order to warrant their moral standing.

In any event, what the participants say is crucial information in itself, both in terms of its origins and in terms of how these excuses and justifications could be counteracted by educational programs and more sophisticated campaigns. Hence, Figure 47.3 represents the rich, convoluted, and ever-increasing vocabulary for bridging the moral and psychic gap between the sense of who you are and how your action (or inaction) looks (Cohen and Seu 2002).

The diagrams convey the content of this vocabulary and, graphically, how it operates as a web. They identify eight themes or key explanations used by the audiences when talking about human rights abuses and their own reactions to the knowledge of such abuses. Some links seem stronger than others – possibly for biographical reasons that make certain attitudes entrenched and hard to change, or because some narratives may have a particularly strong social currency at

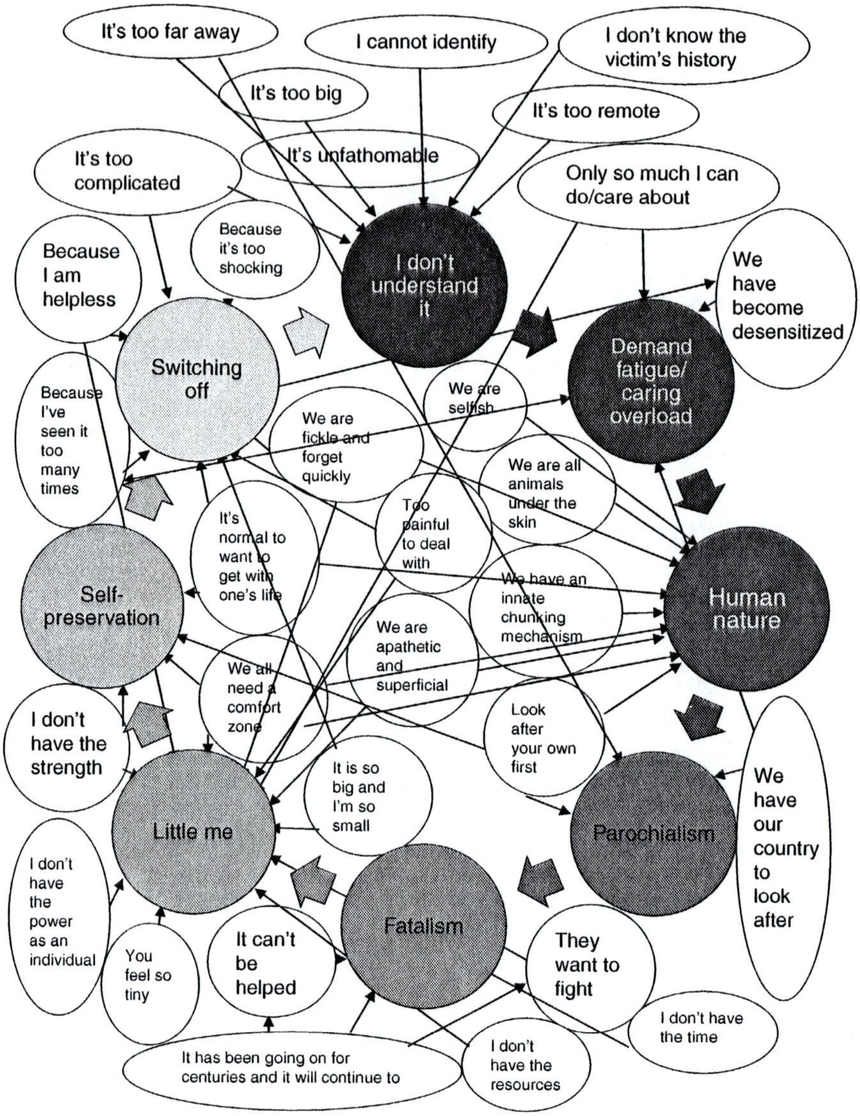

Figure 47.3 The web of passivity

a particular time (e.g., "I don't have the time"; "the information is shocking") while others are repeated absentmindedly.

Although the individual explanations can be grouped thematically under one of these justifications, taken in isolation they might appear as weak and banal. Yet, by linking to others, they lend support to each other and contribute to an ostensibly robust and more convincing narrative. Each individual strand deserves much more research and discussion than there is the space for here. It is the intersections of distinctive strands and their knitting together that ultimately makes the web strong and keeps individuals locked in their passivity. Current knowledge of the individual strands is patchy, despite the plethora of untested assumptions about them. The findings we do have are the result of linear and single-dimensional lines of investigation. Information is thus only available about one particular factor, looked at in isolation, for example diffusion of responsibility or identifiable victim effect.

The pictured "web of passivity" takes a holistic and relational approach to passive bystanding and aims to show graphically how people defend from knowledge of the suffering of distant others, while at the same time becoming entangled in the web. It is easy to imagine how bystanders might find it easier to add more and more strands in order to justify their passivity, getting more entangled and thus, as Staub suggests, increasingly conforming to the societal tilt and becoming progressively more passive. The diagram in Figure 47.3 illustrates the circular and cumulative operation of sets of justifications, rather than suggesting a linear or logical progression from one dimension to the next. These types of excuses and justifications overlap with one another and can be used to explain different types of accounts. The common statement "I don't understand it" was often part of narratives describing incomprehension at the horrors of what one human being could do to another. Fred (pseudonyms are used throughout) stated, "It's too painful to deal with and you can't, it doesn't relate, you can't see any way which it relates to your own experience, so it's like, it could be happening on another planet."

There was also bewilderment at the complexity of the social and political situation of the country where abuses were taking place. These two usages show that participants were involved in what they were told and that they were emotionally or cognitively out of their depth, and ill-equipped for dealing with the information. At other times, "I don't understand" implied a distancing move through lack of identification with "them," as victims and perpetrators were often not differentiated. This kind of explanation did not simply express a sense of disjunction from one's ordinary and well-known world, but was used to create an "Us and Them" division, whereby people doing horrible things were simply different, with all the pejorative implications. Carol, from Kenya, said "If this is happening to a white person, a Muslim, another tribe it's no big deal. It's no big deal really for me because it's them, you know that, it's not me and it's not the people who, it's not the people what I belong to. So, it's easy to disassociate myself and not really feel."

Many of the key building blocks in the web have been discussed elsewhere (Seu 2003, 2007; Cohen and Seu 2002) particularly in relation to how psychological discourses and psychobabble have become an integral part of the vocabulary of everyday excuses put forward by the passive bystander. For example, human nature is repeatedly, directly or indirectly, referred to as an explanatory concept. It permits people to express opinions or make descriptive comments about human behavior and motivation as if they were immutable facts. This is a very powerful rhetorical move, used sometimes to talk about the inevitability of human rights abuses, thus essentializing them and removing them from their specific social and historical context. Joel stated, "we are all animals under the skin, aren't we … it's just a very thin veneer of civilization." Emma alleged, "the story has happened already and after the Second World War they said 'no more' but and again, it must be something in human nature." Talking of human rights in this way feeds bystanders' fatalism – another block in the chain – and implicitly exonerates them from doing anything. What can anybody do when it is human nature? Human nature is also used by bystanders to explain their passivity: "We are apathetic and superficial"; "We are fickle and forget after two days"; "We have an innate chunking mechanism (to divide what we care about into manageable chunks)"; "Isn't it our human nature that if there is something going around on the other end of the country … we will feel sorry for an hour or two and then forget about it." These statements symbolically draw a line in the sand – this is how it is and cannot be changed – and contribute to the sense that a bystander's passivity is impenetrable, intractable, and immutable.

If psychological theories can support all sorts of beliefs and recommend rather differing behaviors, we need to look at the ideological climate that supports them and the rhetorical function that they perform. In this instance lay-psychological accounts of human nature and evolution are used to depoliticize, de-contextualize, individualize, and essentialize human choice and atrocities. Kagan (2002) astutely points out that "Humans are selfish and generous, aloof and empathic, hateful and loving, dishonest and honest, disloyal and loyal, cruel and kind, arrogant and humble; ... I suspect that some people feel better when they learn that their less social urges are natural consequences of their phylogenetic history" (Kagan 2002, p. 49). He argues that in a society in which a large number of strangers must compete for a small number of positions of dignity, status, and economic security, it is adaptive to be self-interested and disadvantageous to be too cooperative, too loyal, too altruistic, or too reluctant to protest against unjust advantage taken by another. He states, "rather than acknowledge that the structure of our society has forced each of us to adopt self-interest as the first rule, many Americans find it more attractive to believe that this mood is an inevitable remnant of our animal heritage and, therefore, one must learn to accept it" (Kagan 2002, pp. 48–49). The potential use of lay-psychology to justify bystanders' passivity is particularly relevant to the next section, which discusses bystanders' emotional reactions.

The emotional bystander

Information about horrific human rights abuses stirs up complex emotional reactions, but are these the reactions that humanitarian organizations would like to provoke with their appeals? Are these emotions leading to the kind of action – the immediate response of donating to the appeal and the more long-term response of increased sensitization and active engagement with the issues – hoped for by human rights campaigners and appeal makers? There are two sets of issues here: the first relates to whether audiences have the "right" responses – anger, shock, outrage, shame, guilt, compassion; the second is whether these lead directly to action.

Psychology has offered some explanations of the role played by emotions in driving audiences to act or not. Slovic (2007) has explained "psychophysical numbing," which he defines as the inability to act or have an emotional reaction to mass human tragedy, as resulting from humanity's incapacity to comprehend large numbers of losses and sufferers. Epstein (1994) has explained that inaction is the result of a disconnection between emotional and normative appreciation of the appeal leading to short-lived strong emotional reactions, not followed by action. Others (Shaw et al. 1994) have looked at conscious emotional resistance as the cause of inaction. They found that people actively avoid empathy when they become aware of the potential cost of their help. Unfortunately, there is hardly any empirically based knowledge about bystanders' emotional reactions to human rights abuses. In its absence, some key untested assumptions seem to prevail. For example, there seems to be a widespread expectation that, when informed about human rights abuses, audiences' primary emotional responses will/should be concerned with the suffering of others.

In the focus groups I carried out with bystanders, there were only seventeen discernible instances when participants referred to emotional reactions in thirty hours of discussions. These emotional reactions expressed overwhelmingly a primary preoccupation with self. Responses moved from generalities and stereotypical discussions about social and political conditions "over there" to complete self-absorption with "how does this advert make *me* feel." Worryingly, the "other," victim of torture and atrocities, suffering and needing was absent overall. It is therefore questionable whether the shocking and potentially numbing effect of the images is the key issue behind bystander passivity, or if it is bystanders' reflexive reaction to their own emotional response. Provoking intense emotions of this kind appears to backfire on campaigners. Most focus group participants resented the moral nagging and guilt-inducing tone of these messages. They seem to have the opposite effect, fueling a more active resistance to the message rather than spurring them into action, as discussed in more detail later.

Three groups of emotions were identified on the basis of whether they moved people sympathetically toward the victim, away from the victim, or briefly to the victim and then back to themselves. Of the "Self → Other" group, anger, empathy, and sympathy were the most prominent emotions. All these emotions were completely other-oriented and altruistic, thus moving sympathetically the subject towards the other. This often involved identification. Carol said, "It's just like I'm angry because for me all the time I keep thinking, I mean, what if it was to happen in my country? And I was there, is this the kind of fear I would have to live with?" The second group of emotions covering "Self ← Other" includes the shocked reactions such as "upset and disturbed"; "emotionally destroying"; "sick and appalled"; "horror." As audiences find the information traumatic, they tend to disconnect from it. In this sense these emotions repel the self away from other and turn the bystander passive. The third group "Self → Other → Self" refers to the emotional loop between first experiencing empathy and compassion and the coming back to the self through self-reflexive assessment of one's emotional reaction and the ensuing emotional reaction provoked by such self-awareness.

The first group of emotions is the most straightforward and, crucially, exactly what humanitarian agencies seek to evoke in the public. There was some acknowledgment that this type of emotions could even provoke action. Amy reported, "I think guilt and compassion make you want to do something"; Lily said, "[I feel] guilty especially when you know there's something you can do." Guilt will be covered later, as it is not a straightforward emotion. Empathy unquestionably links audiences to the suffering of others and, as the quotes above testify, can potentially prompt a bystander to take action. The other two groups of emotions are much more complicated and their role in influencing the active or passive response of the bystander is unclear. I have discussed in detail elsewhere (Seu 2003) how the narratives around shock tactics, psychic numbing, and desensitization need to be understood not only to discover how this type of traumatic emotional experiences end up being defended against, thus increasing passivity, but also how, equally, they can be read as a sophisticated self-conscious rhetoric of denial.

Feeling "desensitized" and "numb" was one of the main explanations given by bystanders for their passivity. Jack says: "There is, there is, I mean, one of the first words that were mentioned was desensitization, you see, you're hearing everyday about something of horror happening in this country, whether it be a child disappearing, somebody being raped, somebody being knifed at the side of the road, or whatever, it does happen in this country, the more people watch tele, the more people read newspapers, it's constantly being shuffled at you and it's becoming almost more acceptable to hear about these things." As Dean (2004, p. 1) argues, it is now commonsensical and generally accepted that, contrary to modernity's expectations that images of suffering would stimulate sensitivity to that suffering, the effect of those images is to brutalize spectators and normalize atrocities, turning the likeness of these events into a form of brutality in themselves. Dean questions the ease with which this is accepted and turned into an explanation for "psychic numbing."

Compassion fatigue has been defined as "becoming so used to the spectacle of dreadful events, misery or suffering that we stop noticing them" (Tester 2001, p. 13). As Cohen (2001) points out, the populist psychology thesis of "compassion fatigue" is a composite of several psychological concepts. One is the cognitive concept of information overload denoting a quantity and intensity of stimuli that exceed our mental capacity to pay attention; i.e., we reach "audience saturation." "An audience watches a TV documentary showing children with legs blown off by land-mines; by the sixth child, they feel themselves running out of psychic diskette space; their mind can't cope anymore; they change to another channel" (Cohen 2001, p. 188). Normalization is another related concept. Images once seen as intolerable eventually become accepted as normal. Hence the potential impact of an image is lost because of its familiarity. Elsewhere (Seu 2007) I have explored how such terms might acquire their power and currency in everyday language, not necessarily because of their explanatory potential, but because of the current discursive power of psychological disciplines.

Here, I will briefly reflect on how the "desensitized bystander" should be understood as a psychological subject as well as a moral agent. Hence psychology and psychoanalysis are simultaneously explanatory paradigms and rhetorical resources for morally acceptable justifications of apathy. Furthermore psychoanalysis, through the concepts of defense mechanisms, reaction formation, and the ideal Self, can also be used to theorize about the nature of the threat from which participants defend themselves.

In the first case the fact that knowledge of human rights abuses is traumatic is taken at face value. The shutting off, closing down, turning away, not wanting to know are considered as defense mechanisms. People end up in a state of self-defensive desensitization either because audiences find the shock tactics used to disseminate the information and the content of the information itself traumatic, or because audiences have become indifferent due to overexposure to horrific news. Bob states:

> Well you tend to shut yourself off from it because it's so, um, appalling. And, um, you sort of feel sick; your stomach makes you feel that it's really, you don't want to know anything about it. Um, so, it's like, if you see a lot of it you then becomes, it doesn't become anything, ... You desensitize yourself. And if you only see little bits of it, you get the opposite effect, where it's repulsion, all right, so, you see these sort of posters, and a lot of the time they're just, you know, make you repulse against it and you just want to run away from it. You don't want to look at it.

Here two types of causation are offered for desensitization. The "shutting down" is a self-protective operation to shocking information – what in classical psychoanalysis would be called a defense mechanism (see Seu 2003 for a more detailed discussion). Steiner (1999) claims that as a result of simply knowing of so many atrocities in the twentieth century "the mind sickens and grows numb." In this case, the information is conceived as traumatic in itself and the bystander's passivity is an understandable form of self-protection. The second explanation claims that desensitization is the result of what mainstream psychologists call "habituation": the repeated exposure to the same stimulus increasingly dims the reaction to it, finally leading to complete lack of response. In sociological terms, something originally exceptional and traumatic becomes normalized. However, these explanations can also simultaneously be understood as the incorporation of psychological terms into the vocabulary of denial.

The third group of emotions, which are hoped for by campaigners, also has a complicated relationship to bystander behavior, but for different reasons. Pressing the guilt button does not always provoke the desired reaction, as can be inferred from Leila's words. Leila said: "Let's shock you a bit and say that if you don't wanna read this what more can I say? How wicked must you be if you're not moved by these stories then give us the money we'll just, you know, accept that you're a you know, you're cold-hearted or something."

Virtually all focus group participants resented the moral nagging and guilt-inducing tone of these messages. They fuelled a more active resistance to the message. Neil felt judged and his moral stance unfairly questioned: "In some ways I'd like to give to Amnesty. The main reason why I don't actually is I'm not going to sit here and read through an advert with something which I agree is completely wrong and shouldn't go on, and then being made to feel that guilty, then all I want to do is pick it up and throw it away." Stuart and Kath agree: they don't actually throw away the information, but they have never read an entire text till the end. They have detected the meta-message coming up: "read this or be a bad person." This is "quite trapping," or "it puts me off."

These people have their own guilt "going around" in their minds and daily lives. The fact that these appeals provoke more guilt does not make them successful. Jane conveys a depressing and almost visceral sense of endless circuits of guilt: "We all felt uncomfortable reading it. And so if we send more money then we're going to have to read more of it and, and feel more guilty and going through the whole thing again and again. It's just, paying fifteen pounds isn't going to stop the guilt next time you read it." Participants concentrated far more on the *technique* (the "tricks") by which their guilt was induced than to the guilt-inducing *content* of the message. Ian complains: "I felt I was being programmed. I was being fed, manipulated. They were trying to make you feel guilty to fill in their form, you know ... the first one said, if you can't think of anything to write then please fill in this coupon with a few blank lines ... I felt absolutely insulted by that point."

There is a worrying disconnection between guilt and the information. Claim-makers and their critics agonize over how much guilt-evoking information and context is required to spur people into action. This misses the point in that the undenied and undeniable truths of the message become irrelevant and its moral appeal undermined as soon as the audience feels that the information has been selected to emotionally blackmail them into giving money. At the extreme, this may delegitimize the message and the sender. Any shifting of focus from the content of the information to its imputed manipulative function subtly turns the relationship between organization and audience into a buffer zone, an extra layer to distance oneself from the horrors of the information.

Neil even takes the all-purpose floating signifier "human rights" to insist that organizations such as Amnesty be kept away from his door. He has a "right" not to have his Sunday morning contentment disturbed: "you're being told that if you're not doing anything ... I'm feeling guilty for this, and now that's affecting my human rights. I shouldn't have to feel like that when I'm reading something in a newspaper."

Denial and humanitarian appeals

This section explores some of the complexities of the relationship between mediation of suffering through appeal-making and audiences' reactions. It is important to look at audience feedback on how appeals are received, as well as operations of denial to gain insights into bystander passivity.

Things are certainly not going according to plan if humanitarian agencies' expectations are for some kind of linear chain of empathy from the information, through the emotional reaction, to action. Audiences seem to bypass most of the content of the message as a communication of distant suffering, focusing instead on how the message is told. They appear to be preoccupied with a critical evaluation of the message per se, the campaigners, and the recommended action i.e., giving a donation (see Seu 2010 for a more detailed discussion). What bystanders lack in pro-social action, they compensate for with the sophisticated rhetorical and discursive moves they use to effectively neutralize appeals.

There are generally three targets on which denial is focused: the message regarding human rights abuses, the messenger (mainly Amnesty International), and the action recommended by the appeal. The common strand, when talking about these three factors, is always a justification for passivity, while preserving the moral credentials of the passive bystander. Human rights agencies' mandates are twofold, as campaigners for human rights and makers of appeals. As campaigners, they strive to inform the public and to raise awareness of human rights abuses. They aim to raise funds using their appeals, by focusing attention on specific current issues that they are working on. In both instances they address audiences as moral agents. Yet, there seems to a striking mismatch between campaigners' intentions and audiences' reception of appeals. Participants positioned themselves as critical and discerning consumers rather than as moral agents. Passive bystanders disregarded the function of the message as a plea for emphatic, moral responsiveness to the information at the heart of any kind of campaign and focused instead on the message itself, which was scrutinized closely for its style, function, and truthfulness.

Trudy said: "It's a very clever campaign; I mean it does actually do what it's supposed to do ... And when you read that, the first thing you want to do is put your hand in your pocket and send them a cheque. That's what it's supposed to do and it will. It does do that because you get so moved by it, you think, well I'll do anything to help and then it's got this thing about donations at the bottom of it and after reading that you would ..." Trudy introduces a theme, echoed by other participants in various ways, that the message is "doing some kind of work," well beyond informing the reader about suffering in a distant place, which hardly gets mentioned. Thus, according to Trudy, this is a "clever" and successful piece of text: it operates by moving audiences into giving a donation. It first tells a moving story, which gets the reader to think and feel s/he "would do anything to help." Then the reader finds a strategically located box asking for a donation. Not all participants were as appreciative as Trudy. On the contrary, as briefly mentioned earlier, the vast majority felt manipulated and resentful. Neil said:

> Again even, even with this article, even with this article from Amnesty International. It is a rhetoric in a way, because when Amnesty give us this they give it to us in this formula. We always read that we're about to give you a horror story, we give you the horror story; now give us your money. It's always every single time you read anything from a charity it comes with that formula. And that in a way is a rhetoric. I think in a way you feel responsible but then you start questioning then you don't have time and then you stop. Your responsibility fades.

The chain of events described by Neil appears to be quite different from the one hoped for by humanitarian organizations. According to Neil, the attempt to emotionally arouse the audience provokes the opposite reaction, making them resentful and passive. This resentment is then channeled into undermining agencies and charities that get bundled together. Joel said: "It's meant to tear your heart strings and then twice at the beginning and at the end, there's a little form for you to fill in and start giving money." The sense that "all they want is my money" quickly turns into a deeper questioning of agencies with asking whether the information is truthful. Mandy stated:

> As I was going through some of it I was thinking oh, I know somebody who actually works in Afghanistan and I'll check with him. You know, what it's like. I know somebody who lives in the Middle East and was married to a Middle Eastern man, I'll check with them. And then I began to think, I wonder how many of these are actually true. I know it probably sounds terrible to say it because Amnesty wouldn't pick a story up, wouldn't create a story, but there is such a thing as marketing, and you sort of wonder. A lot of these charities the money, just, just goes in people's pockets unfortunately, so many cases with, people start up a charity 'cause you can do that easily. You don't have to have a permit, by law and the

> money can go straight into some guy's pocket. And I, I'd dread to say that happens with Amnesty. I would think probably they, like bona-fide, I don't know. Makes you cynical that you see all these different cases and things.

The inevitable *sequitur* is, "Can we trust them?" Roy is succinct and to the point: "In money terms I don't trust them."

There is also a questioning of the action proposed by the appeal as it is claimed that "money won't help as it addresses the symptom not the cause," "money will be wasted by the agencies," and "money will go into the wrong pockets." Joel argues:

> No it goes to the leaders more often than not, people like Mobutu who was the third richest man in the world at some point with the money that was being given to them by ordinary people in the street mostly. And just to make this ghastlier he got richer and richer stuffing his way in, in vaults in Switzerland, it's ludicrous; if anything we should decide not to give.

This depressing picture is very informative about the nature of bystander passivity. First, it shows how effectively bystanders shift the moral gaze from themselves to the agencies, the ones who, in audiences' eyes, have to justify their behavior. The storyline is not one of social responsibility and empathy, but one of assessment of trustworthiness of campaigners. The resulting moral imperative is the legitimation and normalization of suspicion and skepticism. Second, it positions audiences as the victim, which might partly explain why the actual victim of atrocities hardly gets mentioned. Third, it provides a compelling justification for bystander passivity.

Conclusions

This chapter has illustrated the necessity for a psychosocial conceptual model of bystander passivity that takes into account bystanders' stated personal experience, their vocabulary of denial, and the emotional complexity of their responses. First of all, the expression of bystanders' experience should be taken at face value as important information of how knowing about human rights abuses affects them. Bystanders reiterate how they feel constantly under demand by humanitarian agencies and charities and how this puts them on the defensive. Audiences are very experienced in being addressed as consumers; as such they are highly sophisticated and capable of self-reflection and self-protection. Together with the shocking nature of the information, what is experienced as over-demand contributes to feeling overwhelmed and not having enough resources to respond. This immediately presents humanitarian agencies with a difficulty: how to convey the urgency and intensity of need without overwhelming audiences. The competition for resources among agencies does not help. In this scenario, it seems crucial that appeals and campaigners make the information and the demands manageable for the public. I expect confirmation and appreciation of the value and effectiveness of their helpful actions would go a long way towards empowering bystanders and that it would support those bystanders already leaning towards action.

This seems important even when what bystanders say is understood as vocabulary of denial. If we take Baum's (2008) view that bystanders are essentially conformists, it is crucial to know more about the vocabulary of denial to provide citizens with alternative discourses for social responsibility and success stories of active bystanders. For example, success and empowerment stories could counteract narratives of powerlessness and the consequent switching off. This might also help with the emotional resistance caused by the unavoidable shocking component of the information and the related conflictual feelings.

Yet, although this might have an effect on individuals who are already leaning toward action, it is unlikely that it will make much difference as a singular factor. It seems that only a stronger culture of social responsibility could begin to chip away at the web of passivity. The confluence of conformity and socially acceptable narratives of passivity with a resistance caused by the informational trauma makes the bystander unlikely to become active. It clearly still happens for a section of the population, what Stan Cohen (2001) calls "'the conscience constituency': Well educated, high socio-economic status, more liberal politically," but, unfortunately, this is still a relatively small number of people.

References

Adams, W. C. 1986. "Whose Lives Count? TV Coverage of Natural Disasters." *Journal of Communication*, Vol. 36, No. 2, pp. 113–122.

Arendt, H. 1990. *On Revolution* (Harmondsworth, UK: Penguin Books).

Baum, S. K. 2008. *The Psychology of Genocide: Perpetrators, Bystanders, and Rescuers* (Cambridge: Cambridge University Press).

Boltanski, L. 1999. *Distant Suffering: Morality, Media and Politics* (Cambridge: Cambridge University Press).

Cartwright, L. 2008. *Moral Spectatorship* (Durham, NC: Duke University Press).

Chouliaraki, L. 2006. *The Spectatorship of Suffering* (London: Sage).

Cohen, S. 2001. *States of Denial: Knowing About Atrocities and Suffering* (Cambridge: Polity Press).

Cohen, S. and I. B. Seu. 2002. "Knowing Enough Not To Feel Much: Emotional Thinking About Human Rights Appeals." In M. Bradley and P. Pedro, eds., *Truth Claims: Representation and Human Rights* (London: Rutgers University Press).

Dean, C. J. 2004. *The Fragility of Empathy After the Holocaust* (Ithaca, NY: Cornell University Press).

Eckel, C., P. Grossman, and A. Milano. 2007. "Is More Information Always Better? An Experimental Study of Charitable Giving and Hurricane Katrina." *Southern Economic Journal*, Vol. 74, No. 2, pp. 388–411.

Epstein, S. 1994. "Integration of the Cognitive and the Psychodynamic Unconscious." *American Psychologist*, Vol. 49, pp. 709–724.

Geras, N. 1999. *The Contract of Mutual Indifference: Political Philosophy After the Holocaust* (London: Verso).

Kagan, J. 2002. "Morality, Altruism, and Love." In S. G. Post, L. G. Underwood, J. P. Schloss, and W. B. Hurlbut, eds., *Altruism and Altruistic Love. Science, Philosophy and Religion in Dialogue* (Oxford: Oxford University Press).

Kogut, T. and I. Ritov. 2005. "The 'Identified Victim' Effect: An Identified Group, Or Just a Single Individual?" *Journal of Behavioral Decision Making*, Vol. 18, pp. 157–167.

Levine, M. and K. Thompson. 2004, "Identity, Place, and Bystander Intervention: Social Categories and Helping After Natural Disasters." *Journal of Social Psychology*, Vol. 144, No. 3, pp. 229–245.

Loewestein, G. and D. A. Small. 2007. "The Scarecrow and the Tin Man: The Vicissitudes of Human Sympathy and Caring." *Review of General Psychology*, Vol. 11, No. 2, pp. 112–126.

Mills, C. Wright. 1940. "Situated Actions and Vocabularies of Motive." *American Sociological Review*, Vol. 5, No. 6 (December), pp. 904–913.

Seu, I. B. 2003. "'Your Stomach Makes You Feel that You Don't Want to Know Anything About It': Desensitization, Defence Mechanisms and Rhetoric in Response to Human Rights Abuses." *Journal of Human Rights*, Vol. 2, No. 2, pp. 183–196.

Seu, I. B. 2007. "Psychology's Contribution to Bystander Non-Intervention." *Social Practice/Psychological Theorising* Article 6. At: http://sppt-gulerce.boun.edu.tr.html.

Seu, I. B. 2010. "Doing Denial; Audience Reaction to Human Rights Appeals." *Discourse and Society*, Vol. 21, No. 4, pp. 438–457.

Shaw, L. L., C. D. Batson, and R. M. Todd. 1994. "Empathy Avoidance: Forestalling Feeling for Another in Order to Escape the Motivational Consequences." *Journal of Personality and Social Psychology*, Vol. 67, No. 5, pp. 879–887.

Slovic, P. 2007. "'If I Look at the Mass I Will Never Act': Psychic Numbing and Genocide." *Judgement and Decision Making*, Vol. 2, No. 2, pp. 79–95.

Small, D. A. and G. Loewenstein. 2003. "Helping a Victim or Helping the Victim: Altruism and Identifiability." *Journal of Risk and Uncertainty*, Vol. 26, p. 5.

Smith, J. R. and A. McSweeney. 2007. "Charitable Giving: The Effectiveness of a Revised Theory of Planned Behavior Model in Predicting Donating Intentions and Behaviour." *Journal of Community and Applied Social Psychology*, Vol. 17, pp. 363–386.
Staub, E. 1989a. *The Roots of Evil: The Origins of Genocide and Other Group Violence* (Cambridge: Cambridge University Press).
Staub, E. 1989b. "The Evolution of Bystanders, German Psychoanalysts, and Lessons for Today." *Political Psychology*, Vol. 10, No. 1, pp. 39–52.
Staub, E. 1999. "The Origins and Prevention of Genocide, Mass Killing and Other Collective Violence." *Peace and Conflict: Journal of Peace Psychology*, Vol. 5, pp. 303–337.
Staub, E. 2002. "The Psychology of Bystanders, Perpetrators and Heroic Helpers." In L. S. Newman and R. Erber, eds., *Understanding Genocide: The Social Psychology of the Holocaust* (Oxford: Oxford University Press).
Staub, E. 2003. *The Psychology of Good and Evil: Why Children, Adults and Groups Help and Harm Others* (Cambridge: Cambridge University Press).
Steiner, G. 1999. *Portage to San Cristobal of A.H.* (Chicago: University of Chicago Press).
Supphellen, M. and M. R. Nelson. 2001. "Developing, Exploring, and Validating a Typology of Private Philanthropic Decision Making." *Journal of Economic Psychology*, Vol. 22, No. 5, pp. 573–603.
Tester, K. 2001. *Compassion, Morality and the Media* (Berkshire, UK: Open University Press).
van Dijk, T. A. 1992. "Discourse and the Denial of Racism." *Discourse and Society*, Vol. 3, No. 1, pp. 87–118.
Warren, P. E. and I. Walker. 1991. "Empathy, Effectiveness and Donations to Charity: Social Psychology's Contribution." *British Journal of Social Psychology*, Vol. 30, pp. 325–337.

48

The proportionality problem and human rights NGOs

Don A. Habibi

Introduction

The human rights revolution

Since the newly formed United Nations ratified the Universal Declaration of Human Rights in 1948, there has been a dramatic revolution in human rights (HR). There are now many more detailed human rights conventions as well as an expansion of the details and jurisdiction of international law. The international human rights movement (IHRM) has inspired numerous organizations and individuals to play major roles in promoting human rights. It has helped to inspire civil rights movements and social welfare programs around the world. Women, the poor, ethnic and religious groups, persecuted minorities, and nonconformists have overcome marginalization in many parts of the world. Colonialism and overt racism have retreated, and self-determination, equality, respect, and tolerance have advanced. The revolutions of technology, information, communications, and globalization have helped to spread a human rights consciousness around the world, and even dedicated individuals can be a force for quite drastic change. The movement has helped to restrain and bring down tyrannical regimes, free captives, and change how wars are fought. The HR revolution has invigorated and informed the debate over Just War Theory and universal moral law. The reach of international courts has put war criminals on notice that they can be brought to justice. The force of international humanitarian law (IHL) will continue to grow as the IHRM steadily proceeds to build it up and increase our reliance on law for setting standards and resolving disputes. HR and IHL have gone from strength to strength, and the world is the better for it. More and more people, including policymakers, are coming to understand that these provide better ways to resolve differences than war, terror, force, destruction, and other forms of violence. The movement still has a lot of work to do and a long way to go. Success is hardly assured. To reach what John Rawls (1993) and others (Martin and Reidy 2006; Arnsperger 2006; Brown 2006) refer to as a "realistic utopia" will require something that has been sorely lacking: skillful navigation with a moral compass.

The moral foundations

Central to the mass popularity of human rights is its moral simplicity. HR values commit us to appreciating the humanity of all, acting morally and treating others with fairness and respect. HR are "primarily ethical demands" (Sen 2004, p. 319) that transcend legal commands, for they are justified with or without governmental approval. People intuitively associate HR with the right and the good. We certainly differ on the details, but there is widespread agreement that some things are so bad they should never be done to anyone (e.g., murder, torture, slavery, wanton cruelty), and that there are some things basic to living a minimally decent life that should be promoted for everyone (e.g., access to health care, education, fair governance, equal protection under the rule of law). The unifying "idea of a shared humanity" connects us and entitles us to help others (Sen 1997). The universal appeal of HR comes from its moral foundations. As Amartya Sen (2004, p. 315) puts it: "There is something deeply attractive in the idea that every person anywhere in the world, irrespective of citizenship or territorial legislation, has some basic rights, which others should respect. The moral appeal of human rights has been used for a variety of purposes, from resisting torture and arbitrary incarceration to demanding the end of hunger and of medical neglect." Some of these purposes have more appeal than others. To figure out which, Sen appeals to the marketplace of ideas. "The universality of human rights relates to the idea of survivability in unobstructed discussion." We need to submit our ideas to ethical scrutiny through a process of global public reasoning (Sen 2004, pp. 315, 320; see also Rawls 1996, pp. 119–125 and Etzioni 2010). In this chapter, I examine the intense focus on Israel and the role of the IHRM. I contend that there exists a proportionality problem that is a dominant factor in the global debate. This skews the open moral dialogue and constitutes a deeply unattractive misuse of the moral appeal of HR.

Unfortunately, the rise of HR consciousness and IHL are not sufficient conditions to bring us to utopia. Nor can we count on the triumph of reason in public debate. The marketplace of ideas is often unfair, imbalanced, and dishonest rather than free in J. S. Mill's conception. The public – even a majority – is not always objective and impartial. Well-informed, rational people need to reflect and deliberate on how best to evaluate and balance competing claims, interests, and values. In an ideal world, they provide moral leadership in guiding our understanding and application of HR values – especially as the movement gains power. In this world, it is the loudest and strongest who lead the IHRM. Of course, there is no official, centralized administration of the IHRM, nor should there be. The de facto leader, however, is a major part of the problem. The United Nations devotes far more of its time and resources to vilifying Israel and supporting Palestinians than to any other conflict. Elsewhere, I have argued that this obsessive focus harnesses the means of production of the extensive UN system and amounts to institutionalized racism (Habibi 2007, pp. 7–10). In addition, many HR NGOs also focus obsessively against Israel. The most energetic, creative, well-financed, and well-publicized activism is directed against the Jewish state.

There is an institutionalized bias tarnishing the IHRM. Yet there remain organizations and individuals who care about HR and the future of the movement. This chapter is a rational appeal to all those who believe that HR must be a moral force, rather than an economic, politicized, commercialized, or racist force. When it comes to Israel and her neighbors, vast disparities of attention cannot be explained in terms of HR: they are based on power politics and constitute a manipulation of HR. As I will explain, the scrutiny focused on Israel is so disproportionate that it is quantitatively and qualitatively unique. The standards and terminology are different and the frequency and tone of criticism is particularly harsh. The perspectives are one-sided, and the unique context of Israel's predicament is dismissed as irrelevant. This would make sense if Israel were among the worst HR offenders. However, by any objective measure, this is not the case. The reasons for this imbalance are many and complicated. I will explore some of these reasons and argue that they undermine the moral foundations of HR.

My focus in this chapter will be on the failure of the major non-governmental organizations (NGOs) to play their crucial role as a moral check and balance to the politicized nation states. This breakdown is most evident in the obsessive focus on Israel and the corresponding disproportionate lack of focus on the world's most deadly and egregious HR violations. The following section provides background on the role of NGOs as major players in the IHRM. The third section likens the proportionality problem to the malady of attention deficit disorder. I describe this problem as a combination of "hyperfocus" and "malign neglect." The fourth section argues that the IHRM is guilty of bias and offers relevant context to put Israel's actions into a more accurate perspective. The proportionality problem undermines not only the credibility of NGOs large and small, but also the integrity, legitimacy, and moral authority of the IHRM. The final section concludes by arguing for the need to address this problem, correct it, and repair the reputations of the movement by returning to the moral foundations of HR.

The rise of the non-governmental organizations

The status of the NGOs was marginal back in 1948. Since then, their influence and power have skyrocketed. Among them are highly significant players in the international arena. They have managed to get a seat at the diplomatic table alongside the nation states. The great advantage the human rights NGOs bring to the table is that they can do their good work without subverting their values to political and economic interests. Indeed, a major reason why they have achieved a seat at the table and not been shooed away as interlopers is that they are uniquely qualified to play an essential moral role that nations do not. While governments often present their policies in moral terms, they ultimately follow what they regard as their national interests. Money, power, and partisan interests tend to corrupt moral values. Policymakers know that *realpolitik* and *raison d'état* trump moral considerations of the right and good. It is therefore vital that *independent* international HR organizations not lack courage in speaking truth to power and that they use their unique moral position to provide a corrective balance. They can go where nations, partisan organizations, and self-interested corporations do not: they can use their bully pulpit to name and shame powerful and protected offenders. Their soft power affects hard power. Mass communication can gain mass appeal, with which political leaders must contend. Local and international legal systems are now increasingly available as a means of publicity and enforcement. Soft power can set forces into motion that demoralize and weaken support for an offending regime and even launch internationally recognized armies to intervene. The NGOs' special role and power is now a force to reckon with.

NGOs perform a variety of activities. Local, regional, international, and specialized NGOs can be crucial for gathering information and educating at the grassroots level. Their commitment to human rights values makes them more credible than governments. They presumably have a moral standing that gives them a high level of authority to monitor, document, bear witness to, referee, educate, lobby, and expand the understanding and applications of human rights. It also gives them a special moral authority to embarrass human rights offenders; mobilize media campaigns; file lawsuits; and support sanctions, boycotts, and divestment – all in the name of HR and IHL. They appeal to an international audience running the gamut from politicians, academics, artists, and labor unions, to the masses.

In general, the people who comprise the IHRM are dedicated to a noble endeavor. Their high ideals serve a cause that is good and right. In terms of their popular image, they deserve halos for their contributions. The beneficence of HR notwithstanding, it is worth asking: is power wielded carefully, responsibly, wisely, prudently, fairly, justly, and ethically? The proportionality problem makes clear that the answer is "no" on all counts.

Attention deficit disorder and the phenomenon of hyperfocus: the proportionality problem

Many dedicated HR advocates believe that the stronger the IHRM becomes, the better the world will be. I dissent from this view on moral grounds. The NGOs' role as a moral check on state power and other forms of power is often dysfunctional where it is most needed. The crucial responsibility of the major independent international NGOs to set their priorities in line with HR values has often been forfeited and forgotten. Instead, they contribute to the problem.

The proportionality problem is an imbalance brought on by what I call "hyperfocus" and "malign neglect." It resembles the human condition of attention deficit disorder (ADD) in that it entails sustained and sometimes obsessive, biased concentration on particular points of fascination, along with a dysfunctional distraction from matters of vital importance.

The tragic Arab–Israeli conflict involves a variety of human rights issues that should not be ignored. To be sure, Israel should be held accountable for its HR failings, just like any other nation. Nonetheless, Israel's violations are not worthier of attention than numerous other HR violations in the Arab world and beyond. Yet, the historical record demonstrates that Israel has garnered far more critical scrutiny from the IHRM than those committing the far more egregious offenses that are overlooked and underreported. I call this phenomenon "hyperfocus."

As I have already mentioned, over the years, the UN has spent more of its time and resources on the Arab–Israeli conflict than on any other world problem. The problem does not end with the openly partisan UN. In my own research (Habibi 2007, pp. 11, 16), I noted that for several years, the International Committee for the Red Cross (ICRC) spent more money, maintained more offices and clinics, and committed more personnel to aiding Palestinians than it did for *all* of North Africa and East Asia *combined* or *all* of South America and the Caribbean *combined.* According to its archives, Amnesty International (AI) has produced more documents critical of Israel than for Algeria, Bahrain, Comoros, Djibouti, Kuwait, Mauritania, Morocco/Western Sahara, UAE, and Yemen *combined.* Similarly, Human Rights Watch (HRW) has published far more documents critical of Israel than it has for Algeria, Jordan, Mauritania, Morocco, Syria, and Yemen *combined.* By any objective measure, the severity, scale, frequency, and extent of the HR violations of these Arab countries are much greater than Israel's offenses. Note, the slavery, routine use of torture and cruel punishment, brutal methods of warfare, terrorism, mass expulsions, and oppression of women and minorities endemic in the Arab world constitute far more serious violations.

The intensity of hyperfocus is magnified when one considers differences in population and area size. Seen in this physical context, the concentration of resources dedicated to the Israeli–Palestinian conflict is extraordinary. Consistently over time, more human rights workers operate in this small arena than anywhere else, and Israel receives more critical scrutiny than any other country. In a 2006 study, the Capital Research Center factored in population size and found that AI scrutinizes Israel far more than any other country. Similarly, the Israeli–Palestinian conflict is covered by the highest concentration of international media, which ensures constant news coverage. Both Israeli and Palestinian organizations receive generous amounts of international financial aid, which buys influence and creates vested interests. The Palestinian people have the distinction of being the largest per capita recipients of international financial aid in the world since the end of World War II (Sharp 2006; Habibi 2007, p. 28). Taken together, these factors ensure that ethical scrutiny informed by free and open discussion is overwhelmed by an imbalanced global perspective. This situation is unique. Hyperfocus distorts how the world perceives HR and conflicts from Afghanistan to Zimbabwe.

I can understand why – for reasons of *realpolitik* – the UN serves the Arab League by obsessing against Israel, lavishing attention, money, and support on the Palestinians, and downplaying or denying the egregious HR violations of Arab states. After all, 1.3 billion people worldwide, fifty-seven Muslim states (including 300 million people in twenty-two Arab states), and fabulous oil wealth translate into massive diplomatic support and economic clout. Just as no nation has the courage to challenge China over its ruthless and genocidal occupation of Tibet, nation states shy away from seriously challenging Arab and Muslim regimes over their considerable HR failures. There are exceptions that prove the rule. In the few cases where the liberal democracies took strong stands over HR issues (e.g., Saddam's invasion of Kuwait, Sudan's genocidal campaign against Darfur) it is worth noting that it took decades for them to stop supporting those regimes. But why – in the name of human rights – should AI, HRW, and the ICRC take such a lopsided approach to the Middle East? Does paying considerably less attention to the violations of Arabs serve the cause in some way? Is AI worried that Algeria or Syria will not let its researchers or monitors in to investigate? Is HRW worried that the rich and powerful of Saudi Arabia will cut off their funding? Is the ICRC concerned that Hamas and Hezbollah will break off relations if their exploitation of civilians as human shields is publicized and made into a major issue? Is the liberal HR community still hoping that by energetically teaming up with the UN, the Arab League, the Organization of the Islamic Conference, and the non-aligned bloc, it will win over the Ummah and the dictatorships to the cause of universal HR and IHL? If so, these once noble organizations are not only wasting their time, they are squandering their moral capital.

The problem goes beyond deciding priorities and self-censorship. Hyperfocus goes against HR values. It exposes double standards in whom the HR community holds accountable for violating universal rights. Holding one side less responsible may imply sympathy and understanding, but it also implies a lack of agency. This patronizing condescension reveals a bigotry of lower expectations. It is also counterproductive for the cause of improving HR, IHL, and the laws of armed conflict (LOAC). By downplaying or denying consistent violations of the principle of noncombatant immunity (PNI), it encourages a form of asymmetric warfare that thoroughly obscures the distinction between civilians and combatants. When considered alongside the institutionalized racism of the UN; the openly stated genocidal aims of Iran, its Arab proxies, the Palestine Liberation Organization (the latter's goal of eliminating the Zionist entity was reaffirmed at the Fatah Conference in August, 2009 [Begin 2010]), and the Jihadists; the propaganda campaigns of dictatorships (which utilize state-controlled media and educational institutions and entail open incitement to hatred); and the NGOs' Durban Strategy to use the language of HR and IHL to demonize and delegitimize Israel, those who take HR seriously need to ask themselves whom they wish to serve. The vast disparities of attention and treatment pervert HR and turn them into politicized weapons.

In order to reclaim their mantle as the staunchest advocates and guardians of universal human rights, the major NGOs must rectify their ADD problem by recalling their unique responsibility to act justly and uphold their professed universal values. They are supposed to speak up for the forgotten victims, rather than join with those who benefit from having the IHRM distracted, redirected, and compromised.

Malign neglect and its costs

The development of technology and communications make it difficult for perpetrators to hide their crimes, such that most large-scale violations no longer go unnoticed. As Michael Walzer (2007, p. 237) puts it, "It may be possible to kill people on a very large scale more efficiently than ever before, but it is much harder to kill them in secret ... Perhaps horrific crimes are still committed in dark places, but not many; contemporary horrors are well-lit." With the dramatic availability or information and international awareness of human rights, people of good conscience recognize that the excuse of "We didn't know" no longer applies. Large-scale violations cannot be kept secret, but authoritarian regimes and local powers are still able to protect their images by controlling access and intimidating reporters and HR activists. This makes it much more difficult to gather hard evidence and documentable proof, especially when compared to working in open societies committed to civil liberties (Fletcher 2008).

Yet for all the progress of the past generation, the most horrific violations of human rights still occur on a massive scale with relatively little notice. The biggest, bloodiest atrocities, such as genocide, slavery, torture, and barbaric warfare remain commonplace in many parts of the world. Tragically, examples are numerous. By far the worst offenses take place in authoritarian regimes and failed states. Nonetheless, the international NGOs are interested in looking where it is easier and comfortable.

In the Arab world, ruthless regimes, such as Syria, Libya, and Saudi Arabia, manage to crush potential domestic opposition with such severe violence that surviving dissidents can only exist underground or in exile. Genocidal civil wars in Lebanon and Yemen resulted in hundreds of thousands killed. The civil war in Algeria cost 200,000 lives (Baldwin 2008). In Sudan, the death toll from the government's jihadist war against non-Muslims is estimated to be two million. The total destruction of hundreds of villages, rape, and race-based slavery were the tactics of choice. None of the Arab League member states has a free press, artistic or academic freedom, or an independent judiciary. The equal rights of women, ethnic minorities, and even ethnic majorities are routinely trampled upon. Migrant workers, homosexuals, and nonconformists are routinely abused, and refugees escaping oppression in neighboring states are often killed by soldiers and police near the borders. Detainees (be they criminals, dissidents, refugees, or unlucky victims of arbitrary police states) face the real possibility of torture. The Arab world's abysmal human rights record notwithstanding, Israel gets more attention and harsher treatment from the IHRM. Even with the harshest view of Israeli policies and actions, this is difficult to justify in terms of human rights. The irony is that the Arab nations and their HR organizations are the most vociferous critics of Israel's HR record. When one considers the Arab nations' records (including their own cruel treatment of Palestinians), a rational person might assume that the Arab dictatorships would rather avoid the language of HR and lie low. However their selective outrage has proven to be highly effective for shifting the spotlight to their despised enemy. It is an irony of ironies that they give hypocrisy a bad name and get rewarded for it. Irony is compounded into travesty when the supposedly neutral ICRC and the well-funded, well-informed, and supposedly independent AI and HRW aid and abet this perversion of HR.

The Islamic world is also a HR disaster that is largely neglected. The Indonesian government has conducted genocidal campaigns against its own citizens, be they ethnic Chinese, Acehnese, Moluccans, or Timorese, with a death toll over one million. Despite the intensity and severity of the many religious, ethnic, tribal wars in the former Soviet Union, these conflicts have not held the serious attention of the UN, the media, or for that matter, the IHRM leadership. The war in Chechnya has received only sporadic attention, and the bloodier war in Tajikistan has somehow been overlooked. These two genocidal wars have entailed indiscriminate bombardment of civilians, led to approximately two million refugees, and killed over one hundred thousand people. The Russian invasion of Georgia in August 2008 briefly caught the attention of nation states, NGOs, and the general public. But in sharp contrast, the more horrific ethnic-cleansing wars involving Georgia and the regions of Ossetia and Abkhazia in the early 1990s were ignored. Similarly, the wars and ethnic cleansing in Nagorno Karabakh, Azerbaijan and Armenia, Transnistria and Moldova, and between Kyrghiz and Uzbeks failed to attract the attention or commitment of resources from the IHRM remotely comparable to the Israeli–Palestinian conflict. Even though these entail more blatant violations of HR, IHL, and LOAC, much higher death tolls, greater destruction of property, and large refugee flows, the IHRM has taken less interest in these conflicts than in Israel's conflicts with Hezbollah, Hamas, and the Palestinian Authority. Even when wars directly impact the flow of oil and the global economy (as in the former Soviet Union, the Algerian Civil War, and the Iran–Iraq War), they do not attract a fraction of the attention piled on Israel. And let us not forget the millions of victims in Africa. Tribal wars in Sierra Leone, Liberia, Burundi, Somalia, Uganda, Mozambique, and even Rwanda all received less attention than the Israeli–Palestinian conflict. The war in the Congo has cost over four million lives and counting – at the rate of approximately 45,000 people dying each month. It is bad enough that the UN and the international media avoid these conflicts for political reasons, commercial interests, or out of convenience, intimidation, fear, and racism. But there is no valid excuse for the independent, international NGOs to neglect these most terrible human rights atrocities in favor of a hyperfocus on Israel.

There is no question that the IHRM could have done far more to educate, name and shame, and use their bully pulpits to scream truth to power and move the international community to address these most urgent violations of HR, IHL, and LOAC. These horrors could have been greatly diminished or even prevented. Soft power could have raised the price not only for evil dictators but also for those who support them militarily, diplomatically, and economically. In dialogue with defenders of the IHRM, some note that they have no influence over rogue regimes, thus, naming and shaming North Korea, Burma, or Sudan will not have any impact. Hyperfocus is thus explained in terms of Israel's openness, pliability, and vulnerability to pressure. But there is still plenty the IHRM can do with its "soft power" without putting their monitors in harm's way. For example, AI and HRW, in the case of Sudan, can name and shame those who support and enable Sudan's genocidal campaigns against its own citizens. Murderous dictators, generals, militias, and rebels could not have operated as freely if they had half the scrutiny that Israel receives. The IHRM did not even begin to use the tools at their disposal satisfactorily. For all intents and purposes, the great distraction enabled the criminal perpetrators of the worst HR offenses to use extreme violence to deal with their problems. AI and HRW have been clearly aware of the massive extent of HR violations in the aforementioned places, much of which they dutifully documented. But they have been distracted from following up and doing their job.

The decline and fall of the NGOs: a tale of two contexts

Much of the high-profile NGO activism is indistinguishable from the activities of the politicized UN. Israel's HR violations, real and alleged, are high on the international agenda, and many NGOs enthusiastically cast Israel as an international pariah. In some instances, the vilification so unfairly dominates the agenda that even UN officials or AI and HRW notice, but they nonetheless participate in the obsessive, one-sided focus on Israel, and contribute to the "Durban Strategy" of delegitimizing and isolating Israel through such measures as boycotts, embargoes, sanctions, divestment, and "lawfare." For prominent instances, the excessive hyperfocus of the UN Human

Rights Council (as well as its predecessor, the UNCHR) or the farce of the Durban World Conference on Racism in September 2001 are examples. The NGO Forum at Durban openly adopted the "Durban Strategy," seeking to delegitimize and demoralize Israel as "a racist, apartheid regime" and harnessing the rhetoric as well as the power of the IHRM to serve the Palestinian cause. "Lawfare" denotes the use of the law as a weapon of war, or more specifically, the abuse of the law and legal systems for strategic political or military ends. It exploits court systems in democratic countries by filing lawsuits to gain publicity or using universal jurisdiction to harass political and military leaders for war crimes, crimes against humanity, or other grave violations of international law (Lawfare Project n.d.). Israeli leaders have been the primary targets of this strategy. The justification is that these measures are ostensibly moral and supposedly strengthen the HR regime. But for the sake of consistency, it is worth asking HR activists who are pushing these efforts why they do not support boycotts of Algeria, Syria, Saudi Arabia, or for that matter, China, Colombia, or Sri Lanka. Indeed, only Israel is in the docket, and universities, churches, consumer groups, artists, and labor unions are increasingly joining with the longstanding Arab boycott of Israel. The use of Israeli, Belgian, British, Greek, Spanish, and American courts to challenge Israel's policies is also part of the Durban strategy supported by the major HR NGOs. Whether these strategies will demoralize Israelis or bring political changes remains to be seen. Already, they are achieving a propaganda victory by dominating the debate with repetitive negative branding. By force of numbers, persistent repetition, conviction and certainty, and the institutional advantages of power politics, passionate activists have mobilized the IHRM in their hypocritical campaign. With the special strength of the shameless, they have obscured the greatest HR violations and millions of victims have fallen off the radar.

If the activities of the IHRM are an indication, Israel is a serial HR violator and international outlaw beyond the pale, deserving to be in the bad company of Sudan, Iran, North Korea, and Burma. In the rhetoric of high-profile people such as Noam Chomsky, Desmond Tutu, and Jimmy Carter, Israel behaves like Nazi Germany and is worse than apartheid South Africa. Such opinions are widely held but unsustainable in open moral debate. They reflect the severe distortions of the proportionality problem and hold Israel to unique standards. They require control over terminology, novel interpretations, and selective applications of IHL. This raises issues of fairness, equality, and justice and ignores the very relevant context of Israel's predicament as a nation threatened with an existential war on multiple fronts.

For those who believe in the necessity and utility of international law, it is problematic to apply it inconsistently and to make Israel the test case for our understanding of such terms as "military occupation," "excessive force," "indiscriminate force," "disproportionate use of force," and "collective punishment." The IHRM seldom uses these terms outside the context of Israel. For example, the blatant cases of belligerent military occupation and forced population transfers, such as Turkey's occupation of Northern Cyprus, are not regarded as an occupation by the ICRC, AI, or HRW. China's occupation of Tibet and parts of Assam and Sikkim taken from India; Morocco's occupation of territory from Western Sahara; Western Sahara's occupation of Mauritanian territory; Russia's occupation of Japan's Kuril Islands and Finland's Karelia are not defined as occupations. All other things equal, Israel is deemed guilty of occupying territory. And given some pertinent facts, Israel makes a poor test case. The territories were captured in a defensive war, and were seized from previous "occupiers." There had never in history been a sovereign state of Palestine. The Jewish connection to the land dating back to ancient times and Israel's legitimate self-defense needs also make this a highly contentious territorial dispute. Moreover, the definition of "occupied territory" requires a stretch, as the Gaza Strip (controlled by Hamas) and a large portion of the West Bank (controlled by the Palestinian Authority) are not controlled by the Israel Defense Forces (IDF). (Under international law, "occupied territory" is defined in Section III, Article 42 of the Fourth Geneva Convention: "Territory is considered occupied when it is actually placed under the authority of the hostile army. The occupation extends only to the territory where such authority has been established and can be exercised." The only Israeli soldier in Gaza is Gilad Shalit, who was kidnapped by Hamas in a cross-border raid.) Nonetheless, it has become the paradigm case, and these facts are deemed irrelevant. AI, HRW, and the ICRC all have settled the matter and refer to the "Occupied *Palestinian* Territories." By endorsing "resistance to occupation" by various means, "including armed struggle," the UN and EU have legitimized Palestinian terror tactics. Never mind that indiscriminate attacks on Israeli and Jewish civilians preceded the occupation that began in 1967 or even 1948. Now, many of the same tactics such as suicide bombings, jet hijackings, hostage taking, attacks on worshippers, tourists, and schools have become a scourge throughout the world. As we see in Afghanistan, Pakistan, Iraq, and elsewhere, Muslims are often the victims.

There is much relevant context that is shut out of the debate by the guardians of HR. Charges of excessive, disproportionate use of force are often highly subjective. And no military that must fight wars recognizes an obligation to limit the use of force to a level that HR activists might define as proportionate. Instead, militaries recognize the necessity to use superior and overwhelming force when needed for self-defense, to deter aggression, or to ensure victory. Tactics designed to "shock and awe," or the Powell Doctrine are cases in point.

Among Israel's adversaries, the intentional blurring of the distinction between combatants and noncombatants both for offensive and defensive purposes is widely overlooked, and at times, excused. Illegal, perfidious tactics such as combatants dressing as civilians and purposely embedding themselves among noncombatants; using children as combatants; storing military equipment in, and firing from, schools, mosques, churches, residential apartment buildings, and hospitals; and commandeering ambulances and UN vehicles to ferry troops and supplies, endanger civilians and greatly increase the number of casualties. Instead of blaming the perpetrators of these tactics, HRW and AI protest Israel's tactics amidst such conditions. For all the concern over IHL, the Israeli government and military receive far more criticism and opprobrium than Hezbollah, Hamas, and Fatah, which use such perfidy routinely. In April 2002, Fatah gunmen fleeing arrest shot their way into the Church of the Nativity, barricaded themselves, and turned it into a battle zone. The Vatican blamed Israel for the thirty-eight-day standoff. Palestinian militants have little incentive to change their illegal tactics – which can be characterized as terrorism. Israel must fight under asymmetrical conditions. IHL does not allow for reciprocity, so whatever tactics are used against Israelis are no excuse for Israeli misbehavior – it is irrelevant. Israeli actions that result in civilian casualties are roundly condemned, assumed to be intentional, and often denounced as war crimes.

The essential context of how combat operations are conducted elsewhere in the world is also kept out of the equation. From a comparative perspective, the IDF has a notable record for restraint and caution to avoid harming civilians – especially considering the perfidious tactics it is up against. For all its errors – and there are many – the IDF has the lowest ratio of noncombatants killed to combatants killed of the actively engaged militaries in the world. Its record is better than NATO in Afghanistan or against Serbia, and better than the USA and Britain in Iraq (Kemp 2009; Harold 2008).

Yet it is the IDF that gets far more and far harsher criticism than any other military. The proportionality problem is even more glaring when one considers the comparative inattention on extreme violators of PNI, such as the Russian, Algerian, Pakistani, Indonesian, Filipino, and Sri Lankan militaries, which like Hezbollah and Hamas intentionally target civilians and inflict collective punishment, but on a far more efficient, deadlier scale. Sri Lanka's defeat of the Tamil Tigers resulted in a death toll thirty times greater than Operation Cast Lead in Gaza.

The UN, China, and Burma were very supportive of Sri Lanka's crushing victory over terrorism. AI and HRW called for investigations, but devoted (on my estimate) thirty times less attention to making this an international priority as compared with Gaza.

Major HR offenders such as Sri Lanka do not get equal treatment in comparison with Israel. Israel is held to unique standards, but not China, Indonesia, Russia, Syria, Libya, or Saudi Arabia. Their political, diplomatic, and economic power protects them. But the independent NGOs forgot that the greater, more extensive persecution and suffering of Tamils, Tibetans, Uigurs, Acehnese, South Moluccans, Chechens, Georgians, Uzbecks, Arab Christians, Kurds, Berbers, and Shia Muslims should not matter less. When examined in the global context, the singular treatment of Israel is manifestly unfair. The extensive naming and shaming of Israel is better described as condemning and humiliating. It does harm and discredits the IHRM. Even though overt racism has subsided worldwide, it is still with us in many forms, including institutionalized racism. Anti-Semitism has made an impressive comeback. The proportionality problem is a contributing factor, and the IHRM has played an active role in this regression (Habibi 2007, pp. 20–22). The Jewish people still have valid grounds to protest that they are held to higher standards and singled out for harsher treatment.

This raises serious moral issues of equal treatment, fairness, and accountability. It reflects a failure to understand that claims of inalienable, indefeasible, indefatigable universal rights and applications of international law are grounded in principles of equality and justice. They apply to us all as beings of worth and dignity. They preclude double standards and glaring inconsistencies. Yet double standards and inconsistencies are abundantly evident in the case against Israel. The problem is worsened and the consequences are compounded when the independent NGOs say little and do nothing to expose this bad faith manipulation of HR. They play along.

The politicized NGOs may be lacking in credibility to those who recognize this corrupted state of affairs, but they are often influential in shaping public opinion. However, they are overplaying their hand and their victories will be Pyrrhic. They can no longer assume that people are not paying attention and that the intuitive appeal of HR will prevail. The revolution in information technology that has brought a leap in human rights consciousness also shines light on the NGOs' performance. This underscores the need to bring changes in how they operate. Their very success – their importance and power – calls for professionalism and accountability. Their future status and effectiveness depends on having credible moral voices. They must be honest about the facts and be fair, impartial, and consistent in their application of universal HR. This commitment to basic principles of justice is what gives them access and believability. But when the leading NGOs are constantly distracted from (and even protect) the greatest human rights abusers, they squander their reputations and become propaganda organs.

The failure of leadership and its consequences

In a recent *Foreign Affairs* article, Haugen and Boutrous (2010) argue that international law meant to protect HR is ineffective in the developing world because it is rarely enforced. It is therefore imperative for the HR community to build up the political will and capacity among law enforcement bodies and to help construct functioning public justice systems where they are needed the most. As much as I agree with their call for this to become the mandate of the IHRM in the twenty-first century, I hesitate to support their position given the current disposition of HR activism. Extending the power of international law is far less likely to help the forgotten victims than it is to be applied prejudicially. Why should rational people wish to strengthen a human rights regime that is increasingly corrupted? At present, the activism of the IHRM is not directed toward helping those who need it most. It is driven by a politicized agenda that enables brutal dictatorships to exploit HR and IHL to damage the reputation of an open, liberal democracy facing war on multiple fronts. There is something morally amiss when those who comply the least can successfully wield HR as a harpoon to weaken, outmaneuver, and persecute their enemy, while deflecting attention from their own severe violations. The independent HR NGOs ought to reconsider what happened to their objectivity and where they are leading the movement.

I contend that it is inappropriate for the NGOs to join the mobbing of a diplomatically weak and isolated nation. It may be tempting to target Israel because it is "like low-hanging fruit" but this bullying is an abuse of power (Birnbaum 2010). By concentrating their critical scrutiny on Israel, by favoring one side in a highly complex conflict and dismissing the relevant context, the guardians of HR have turned their bully pulpits into bullying platforms. By neglecting the undeniably greater HR emergencies, they have failed those who need them most. By supporting a racist campaign rather than speaking out against it, they have failed as moral leaders and undermined the cause of HR. Unless the double standards are addressed, the selective and hypocritical misuse will continue – to the detriment of HR and IHL as means for bringing justice to the world. For where there is no equality of treatment, impartiality, balance, consistency, and fairness, there is injustice, and the IHRM should have no part in it.

Human rights NGOs are entitled to make their own decisions and allocate their resources however they wish. But they must not forget their moral calling. If other major players, such as nation states (characterized by politicized voting blocs) and the international media (motivated by competition for ratings and revenue) are obsessing on a popular, comfortable, well-marketed, and well-financed conflict, then this is *all the more reason* for leaders of the international HR NGOs to provide some measure of balance. There is no danger that Israel's many HR violations will fall into obscurity. But serious damage occurs when the NGOs neglect to play their designated unique role in the international arena. The leaders ought to remember their mission statements and focus their considerable resources where they can do the most good and reduce the greatest harms. They should not serve the agendas and interests of the partisan, self-interested nation states, organized religion, corporations, the mass media, and propagandized mobs. They certainly must not permit their noble cause to be hijacked to serve the propaganda interests of the worst offenders. They should be educating, mobilizing, speaking truth to power, and make efforts to offset the proportionality problem. Even better, they should bring attention to this problem in order to expose the hypocrisy and restore equality of treatment, impartiality, and fairness. Instead, the leadership of the IHRM has, in effect, aided and abetted those who are most contemptuous of HR.

There needs to be a serious debate on the problems of proportionality, hyperfocus, and malign neglect. I am not optimistic that the human rights leadership will submit to ethical scrutiny, concede my points, commit to corrective and distributive justice, reassess their priorities, and reallocate their resources. Their policies are entrenched and they are not moral guardians who can handle constructive criticism. Birnbaum (2010) quotes Robert James (a member of HRW's Middle East and North Africa advisory committee) saying that HRW is chronically incapable of introspection and "they cannot take criticism." The irony is that HRW dishes out criticism and demands transparency, but it is immature and poor at taking criticism. However, even if they do not address my arguments, the debate can and will proceed without them.

There are enough people of good will who: believe in equal treatment and fairness; appreciate the difference between democracies and dictatorships and how this affects access and the flow of information; understand the contextual differences between rights during wartime and peacetime; perceive where the greater HR problems lie; recognize the failures of the IHRM; and appreciate the unprecedented potential to improve the world. The future of the

IHRM is at stake. There is much work to be done in order to realize this potential. Bringing these shortcomings to the attention of the sincere public is a necessary first step to move the HR NGOs to live up to their principles and become part of the solution.

References

Arnsperger, Christian. 2006. "What Is Utopian About the Realistic Utopia?" *Revue Internationale de Philosophie*, Vol. 3, No. 237.

Baldwin, Shawn. 2008. "In Algeria, A Tug of War for Young Minds." *New York Times*, 23 June. At: http://www.nytimes.com/2008/06/23/world/africa/23algeria.html.

Begin, Benny. 2010. "Constructive Clarity in Israeli–Palestinian Negotiations." *Jerusalem Center for Public Affairs*, Vol. 10, No. 3.

Birnbaum, Benjamin. 2010. "Minority Report: Human Rights Watch Fights a Civil War over Israel." *New Republic*, 27 April.

Brown, Chris. 2006. "The Construction of a 'Realistic Utopia': John Rawls and International Political Theory." *Review of International Studies*, Vol. 28, No. 1, pp. 5–21.

Capital Research Center. 2006. "Moynihan's Law." *Organization Trends*.

Etzioni, Amitai. 2010. "The Normativity of Human Rights Is Self-Evident." *Human Rights Quarterly*, Vol. 32, No. 1, pp. 187–197.

Fletcher, Martin. 2008. *Breaking News* (New York: Macmillan).

Habibi, Don. 2007. "Human Rights and Politicized Human Rights: A Utilitarian Critique." *Journal of Human Rights*, Vol. 6, No. 1.

Harold, Marc. 2008. "Truth as Collateral Damage." *The Guardian*, 22 October. At: http://www.guardian.co.uk/commentisfree/2008/oct/22/afghanistan-nato.

Haugen, Gary and Victor Boutros. 2010. "And Justice for All: Enforcing Human Rights for the World's Poor." *Foreign Affairs*, Vol. 89, No. 3.

Kemp, Richard. 2009. Testimony before the UNHRC, 16 October. At: http://vodpod.com/watch/2353770-col-richard-kemp-on-the-goldstone-report.

The Lawfare Project. N.d. *What Is Lawfare?* At: http://www.thelawfareproject.org.

Martin, Rex and David Reidy, eds. 2006. *Rawls's Law of Peoples: A Realistic Utopia?* (Hoboken, NJ: Wiley-Blackwell).

Rawls, John. 1993. "The Law of Peoples." *Critical Inquiry*, Vol. 20, No. 1, pp. 36–68.

Rawls, John. 1996. *Political Liberalism* (New York: Columbia University Press).

Sen, Amartya. 1997. "Human Rights and Asian Values: What Lee Kuan Yew and Le Peng Don't Understand About Asia." *The New Republic*, Vol. 217, Nos. 2–3, pp. 16–17.

Sen, Amartya. 2004. "Elements of a Theory of Human Rights." *Philosophy & Public Affairs*, Vol. 32, No. 4, pp. 315–356.

Sharp, Jeremy M. 2006. "U.S. Aid to the Palestinians." CRS Report for Congress, 2 February.

Walzer, Michael. 2007. "The Argument About Humanitarian Intervention." In David Miller, ed., *Thinking Politically: Essays in Political Theory* (New Haven, CT: Yale University Press).

49

Jewish non-governmental organizations

Michael Galchinsky

Human rights history and Jewish history have been inextricably intertwined. The history of Jews' persecution as an ethnic and religious minority, especially the Nazis' systematic deprivation of Jews' rights, became a standard reference for postwar activists after 1945 who argued for a global system limiting states' power over their citizens. Many Jewish activists saw a commitment to international human rights as the natural outgrowth of traditional Jewish values. Jews could be especially active in advocating for universal rights protections not only because their suffering conferred moral standing on their cause but also because they could plumb a rich religious and philosophical tradition to find support for a cosmopolitan worldview and because they nurtured generations of experienced organizers.

Jews did not always seek, find, or emphasize the universalism in their tradition. For example, although human rights activists interpreted the phrase "Never Again," associated with the Holocaust, as an imperative to work on behalf of the rights of all people, Zionists often interpreted the phrase as a clarion cry to enable Jews to defend their own rights by building up a Jewish state. Most activists found themselves living in the contact zone among commitments to international human rights, Jewish nationalism, and domestic pluralism.

Jewish human rights activists made significant early contributions to the formation of the new human rights system. In 1945 the American Jewish Committee (AJC), a civil and human rights organization formed in the United States in 1906, led a coalition of civic, labor, and church organizations that succeeded in convincing states' representatives at the San Francisco Conference that human rights should become one of the central components of the United Nations Charter. Raphael Lemkin, an international lawyer who was also a Polish Jew, coined the term "genocide" and with his lobbying efforts almost single-handedly achieved the UN General Assembly's adoption of the Genocide Convention in 1948. He received substantial monetary and organizational support in his effort from Jewish non-governmental organizations. René Cassin, who had been president of the Alliance Israélite Universelle, another Jewish NGO, played a key role in the drafting of the Universal Declaration of Human Rights. For two generations after the Holocaust, Jewish activists contributed to standard-setting, monitoring, advocacy, coalition-building, and establishing and serving on international tribunals to create a global safety net for Jews and other minorities.

Human rights activism and Jewish religious and political thought

Jewish human rights activism bears comparison with the activism of other groups, whether defined as ethnic, religious, immigrant, diasporic, or national. Jews have approached the question of human rights through all of these lenses depending on the political and social conditions in their specific contexts. Different groups of Jews have addressed human rights through reference to two continuously evolving bodies of historical texts: their religious tradition and their political thought. They have also understood their human rights work as part of a history of Jewish activism dating to the early nineteenth century.

These traditions do not speak with a single voice on the question of human rights, either individually or together. In all three arenas, Jews have navigated a difficult course between forms of universalism and particularism.

Religious tradition

Ever since human rights law began to be codified by the League of Nations in the 1920s, and especially since the establishment of the United Nations, Jews have engaged in a spirited debate among themselves over the extent to which the Hebrew Bible, the Mishnah, the Talmud, and subsequent additions to the religious canon have served as foundations for modern rights talk. Claims that Judaism is the source of human rights have sprung from two different inclinations: (1) the desire to justify one's own activism within traditional sources; and (2) the prophetic desire to use the rights endorsed by the tradition as a way to criticize current international, Jewish, or Israeli practices.

The term "human rights" appears nowhere in the Hebrew Bible or in other Jewish sacred texts. The covenant between the Israelites and God assumes that the authority to give and take away all privileges rests with God; whereas, modern political theory assumes that the rights are inalienable entitlements of all human beings. The Mishnah and Talmud, the other core sacred texts in the tradition, do not generally theorize human rights because they are concerned with how to preserve Jews' distinct communal identity in Diaspora rather than to merge Jews with non-Jews into what would to them have seemed a nonsensical political category called humanity.

Nonetheless, Jewish religious universalists have argued that one can "tease out" from the ancient sources certain dispositions – unevenly expressed – toward pluralist tolerance, protection of certain disfavored classes (e.g., widows, orphans, and strangers), and respect for the dignity of the human person. These dispositions can serve as human rights resources in the Jewish tradition (Haas 2005).

Irwin Cotler, formerly a professor of international law at McGill University and head of the Canadian Ministry of Justice, has written that "If human rights has emerged as the new 'secular religion' of our time, then the Jewish religion is at the core of this new secular religion of human rights – the whole symbolized by the normative exhortation in the Jewish religion of *Tikkun Olam* – the responsibility to 'repair the world.'" Cotler also cites the Genesis concept of *b'tselem elohim*, that all humans are made "in the image of God," which he says is "the essence of a religion organized around the inherent dignity of the human person and the equal dignity of all persons" (Cotler 1998). Arik Ascherman, director of Rabbis for Human Rights, an Israeli human rights NGO, has similarly articulated a Jewish liberation theology, asserting that Jews must merge "the Torah of Jewish Law with the Torah of International Law."

A systematic attempt to merge these two legal systems was made by the former Israeli Supreme Court Justice Haim Cohn, who found in the tradition's ethical commandments the basis for the vast majority of human rights in the UDHR. Writing in 1989 in response to the first Palestinian intifada, Cohn sought to lay an intellectual foundation for the burgeoning human rights network in Israel. Although he made no mention of the Israeli–Palestinian conflict, he did invoke the biblical injunction not to oppress the stranger in order to criticize his country's treatment of Israeli Arabs (Cohn 1989). It is no surprise that Justice Cohn helped found the earliest Israeli human rights organization, the Association for Civil Rights in Israel.

As this example indicates, a thorough knowledge of selected resources within the tradition has helped Jewish activists, members of the judiciary, rabbis, and policymakers articulate what made their mission distinct within the human rights field and has attracted other Jews to their cause.

Yet the universalist commandment to "let justice well up like water, righteousness like an unfailing stream" sometimes rubs up against a particularist strain of Jewish religious thought. Proponents of this view – including René Cassin himself – emphasize that the Torah and Talmud are exemplified by the Ten Commandments and by Talmudic law. Torah demands duties; it does not confer rights. It outlines what a Jew must do, not what a human being is entitled to expect. Religious particularists do not necessarily reject human rights, only the contention that such rights are founded on divine authority. Most of the more religiously observant Jewish sects, from modern Othodoxy to Chabad, have rejected the human rights discourse as a rationalist outgrowth of modernity and Enlightenment rather than a discourse well grounded in Torah. In its extreme form, however, religious particularism can become exclusive and hierarchical. The religious nationalism of some West Bank settlers, for example, is founded on the biblical promise to Abraham that he and his descendants would possess the territory on the west bank of the Jordan River. Biblical texts demanding that the Israelites tear down the Canaanites' altars could not be the source for the international right to religious freedom. The book of Joshua, in which God commands the Israelites to put thirty-one Canaanite kings, with all their people and possessions, to the sword, could not serve as the source for the Genocide Convention.

As is the case with every ancient theological corpus, Judaism is comprised of sources separated by hundreds or thousands of years. Jewish activists have sometimes had to grapple with the fact that not all of this material can be assimilated to a contemporary human rights perspective. In their encounter with human rights, religious Jews have had to begin by selecting a usable past.

Modern Jewish political thought

The tradition of religious thought has exerted a shaping pressure on many, but by no means all, Jewish activists. Most of the Jewish human rights organizations have been of the secular-liberal type, driven less by religious concepts than by the concepts promoted by post-Enlightenment Jewish political thought. At the same time, political thinkers also exhibit the particularism–universalism dialectic with regard to rights (see Walzer et al. 2000).

Post-Enlightenment Jewish thought includes Enlightenment rationalism, emancipationism, political Zionism, internationalism, and cosmopolitanism. In any given instance, Jewish thought is not merely a meditation on timeless problems, but a context-specific response to the thinker's contingent understandings of Jewishness, in all its ethnic, religious, linguistic, national, and diasporic complexity.

In his *Theologico-Political Treatise*, Baruch Spinoza (1632–1677), who was excommunicated from the Amsterdam Jewish community for heresy, began to move political philosophy from its basis in divine law to a human-centered foundation on what is "universal or common to all men, for we have deduced it from universal human nature" – specifically from humans' capacity for reason (Spinoza 2005). As a rationalist critic of religious authority, Spinoza has sometimes been seen as a founder of the political thought driving contemporary Jewish human rights work.

Moses Mendelssohn's emancipationist classic, *Jerusalem: Or On Religious Power and Judaism* (1789), written during the ferment of the French Revolution, took Jewish political thought a step closer to modern rights advocacy. Mendelssohn undertook to balance the powers of religion and state and to argue for freedom of conscience, religion, or belief. Mendelssohn carried forward Spinoza's rationalist project, but did not go as far as Spinoza, arguing that the divine law is merely a particular expression of "the universal religion of mankind" (Mendelssohn 1983). Mendelssohn participated in an increasingly intricate dance between advocating Jews' civil and political rights and maintaining their cultural and religious traditions. He wanted to be able to have his Goethe and eat his Talmud, too.

The rise of modern political Zionism in the late nineteenth century should be seen as a reaction against the perceived failure of the emancipation efforts, in addition to being the Jewish version of European nationalism. Theodor Herzl (1860–1904) was convinced that European states could not live up to the promises of the Declaration of the Rights of Man and Citizen. In *The Jewish State* (1896), he suggested that "Universal brotherhood is not even a beautiful dream" because conflict among peoples is "essential to man's highest efforts" (Hertzberg 1997). Max Nordau (1849–1923), Herzl's close associate, told the First Zionist Congress in Basel in 1897 that human rights appealed to logic rather than sentiment, where anti-Semitism still reigned, and hence they would never be extended to Jews (Hertzberg 1997). Conditioned by ongoing czarist pogroms, Zionists thought it was the moment for self-preservation, not for worrying too much about the rights of others. Zionist thinkers have been wading through the thicket of relations between ethno-nationalism and pluralist toleration ever since.

If in the modern period particularism often took the form of nationalism, universalism manifested itself most often as internationalism, in both its socialist and liberal varieties. Although Jews played a disproportionate role in the development of socialist theory, they did so largely as workers rather than Jews. Marx set the pattern in his essay "On the Jewish Question" (1843), in which he declared that "the *political* emancipation of the Jew ... is the *emancipation of the state* from Judaism" (Ishay 2007); that is individual Jews deserved their rights as long as they were willing to give up their collective identity. Similarly, Rosa Luxemburg wrote in 1916 that she felt that she had no greater feeling for "Jewish sorrows" than for "the wretched victims of the rubber plantations in Putumayo, or to the Negroes in Africa with whose bodies the Europeans are playing catch-ball ... I have no separate corner in my heart for the [Jewish] ghetto" (quoted in Mendes-Flohr and Reinharz 1995).

It was in liberal internationalism that European and American Jews made their most lasting mark on human rights thought. As early as the Congress of Berlin (1878), Jewish NGOs were making important contributions to the establishment of human rights principles, not just to protect Jews in Europe, but other minority groups as well (Fink 2004). A common theme was that of American Jewish thinkers like Judah L. Magnes and Supreme Court Justice Louis Brandeis who associated American ideals of equality and freedom with Jewish ideals (Mendes-Flohr and Reinharz 1995). In the 1920s, the Committee of Jewish Delegations asserted at the founding of the League of Nations that the League should establish a body for monitoring abuses of the rights of minorities in the Eastern European countries that had lost World War I. Their idea became codified in the Minorities Treaties (Fink 2004). In 1950, Jacob Blaustein, the president of the American Jewish Committee, wrote that the fortunes of Jews in the Diaspora were "tied to the fate of liberal democracy ... under which all citizens, irrespective of creed or race, can live on terms of equality" (quoted in Mendes-Flohr and Reinharz 1995).

Newer forms of Jewish political thinking have developed since the 1990s, and they, too, have exhibited a dialectic between the particular and the universal. Globalization has brought Jewish political communities from around the world – in both Israel and the Diaspora – in closer, transnational contact. Global Jewish political communities have expressed cosmopolitan views on some issues – e.g., with regard to genocide in Darfur. On other issues, such as the question of human rights practices in Israel, they have exhibited conflicts over the meaning of citizenship rights in a Zionist state. The belief that Jews in Israel and the Diaspora share, or can share, public policy orientations is implicit in the names of organizations like the Jewish People Public Policy Institute, the World Jewish Congress, the Consultative Council of Jewish Organizations, and Jewish World Watch. Whether that unity of purpose extends to cosmopolitanism, and whether it exists as ideal or reality, have to be tested case by case.

Formation of Jewish human rights NGOs

Ever since Jews were first invited to make the transition from aliens to citizens, the basic condition of Jewish life in liberal democracies has been that participation in the Jewish community is voluntary. Although Jews are bound together by familial, communal, ethnic, religious, and national ties, they are no longer bound by state law to remain Jews. Exit always looms as an option. The fundamentally voluntary nature of Jews' association has profoundly influenced the form of their political behavior. Since the nineteenth century, Jews have organized their politics through a globally dispersed set of NGOs, none of which represents the whole, and each of which brings its own constituency and mission to the table. This complex, multipolar structure has had important effects on the development of Jewish human rights activism.

Four different kinds of modern Jewish rights NGOs have emerged. The first group has consisted of those originally established to protect Jews' citizenship rights in their home countries. In time, these NGOs expanded their scope to work on behalf of vulnerable Jews abroad. Since the 1940s, Jews have worked with the United Nations and in regional forums such as the Organization for Security and Cooperation in Europe. They include: Board of Deputies of British Jews (est. 1815); B'nai B'rith International (est. 1847); Alliance Israélite Universelle (est. 1840); American Jewish Committee (est. 1906); South African Board of Jewish Deputies (est. 1912); and International Association of Jewish Lawyers and Jurists (est. 1969). Each of these organizations gained consultative status in UN human rights bodies, either independently or by integration into one of two international Jewish NGOs, the Consultative Council of Jewish Organizations (est. 1947) and the Co-ordinating Board of Jewish Organizations (est. 1947). All of these groups were secular–liberal in orientation.

A second group consisted of NGOs that were denominational or interdenominational in character. These included: Agudas Israel World Organization, the political arm of Eastern European Orthodoxy (est. 1912); the International Council of Jewish Women (est. 1923); and the World Jewish Congress (est. 1936). Each of these organizations began as federations of national organizations reacting to crises in world Jewry – Czarist attacks on religious freedoms, the Ukrainian pogroms of 1919, and Nazi anti-Semitism, respectively. Each of these groups gained independent consultative status at the UN. They were sometimes joined by the World Union of Progressive Judaism, the political arm of Reform and Reconstructionist Jews, particularly in their work on behalf of religious freedoms.

In some cases, a state's domestic NGOs were able to contribute to international monitoring and legislation. This third group included, for example, the American Association of Ethiopian Jewry, which played a key role in organizing Operation Solomon, the Israeli airlift of 14,310 Ethiopian Jews in May of 1991. The most important organizations of this type were those that worked on behalf of Soviet Jews' rights to emigration and religious and cultural freedom in the 1970s and 1980s, such as the National Council of Soviet Jewry and the Union of Councils of Soviet Jews, both based in the United States, or members of various Jewish "refusenik" groups in the USSR. Working with – and sometimes against – the Soviet, American, Israeli, and Dutch governments, these NGOs were instrumental in keeping the public aware of the need to secure the refuseniks' right to emigrate and of Soviet people's need for greater religious freedom and protected cultural rights. Their work with American lawmakers to pass the Jackson–Vanik Amendment to the Trade Act (1974), linking Soviet acquisition of Most Favored Nation trade status to Jewish emigration levels, had an impact on US–Soviet Cold War relations.

Finally, a fourth group of NGOs consisted of those established in Israel beginning in the mid-1970s. These organizations have, in many cases, adopted international human rights standards to monitor, protest, and publicize violations inside and outside the Green Line, bringing litigation on behalf of victims of abuse and providing caseworker services. In addition, some of them – especially the Association for Civil Rights in Israel and B'Tselem – have formally interacted with international human rights bodies, giving oral and written submissions to treaty bodies, for example to the Committee Against Torture or the Human Rights Committee.

NGOs in the Israeli group were formed in two waves. The first wave arose in reaction against the occupation in the early 1970s, the Lebanon war of 1982, and the first Palestinian intifada in 1987–1989. These NGOs include: Association for Civil Rights in Israel, B'Tselem, HaMoked: Centre for Defence of the Individual, Rabbis for Human Rights, Physicians for Human Rights (Israel), Public Committee against Torture in Israel, and Israel Coalition against House Demolitions.

A second wave emerged in the wake of the failure of the Oslo peace accords of the late 1990s and the subsequent onset of the second intifada, which occurred in 2000–2005. Machsom (meaning "checkpoint") Watch was founded in 2001 as a women's organization monitoring treatment of Palestinians at checkpoints in the West Bank. In 2004 a group of Jews and Arabs formed Ta'ayush (Arabic for "life in common") as an antiracist organization. Gisha (meaning "access") focuses on Palestinians' freedom of movement. Yesh Din (meaning "there is judgment") works on a broad range of issues in the territories. Israeli human rights NGOs were often joined by peace activists, reservists, and demobilized military personnel.

Jewish NGOs' broad approach

Although Jewish NGOs' human rights activism has often focused on protecting vulnerable Jewish communities, it has also extended beyond the boundaries of the Jewish community into the infrastructure of the human rights system. Jewish NGOs also contributed to UN standard-setting (Korey 1988). Many of their submissions in the drafting stages of human rights treaties were summarily incorporated into the treaties – e.g., the World Jewish Congress's submissions of language on the rights to self-determination, asylum, and prevention of discrimination and protection of minorities in the International Covenant on Civil and Political Rights (ICCPR). The International Council of Jewish Women played a prominent role among NGOs in the drafting of the Convention on the Rights of the Child. The American Jewish Committee's Sydney Liskofsky was the principal drafter of the Declaration on the Elimination of All Forms of Religious Intolerance. Morris Abram, a one-time AJC president and ambassador to the US Human Rights Delegation, drafted the Convention on the Elimination of All Forms of Racism and Related Intolerance. Felice Gaer, director of AJC's Jacob Blaustein Institute for the Advancement of Human Rights, was the first woman and first American to sit on the Committee against Torture, was appointed and became chair of the US Commission on International

Religious Freedom, and was a principal force at the Beijing conference that established that "women's rights are human rights." Jewish NGOs' pervasive concerns have included:

- civilian and refugee protections;
- protection of minorities and prevention of discrimination;
- religious freedoms;
- the rights of women, children, and families;
- the prohibition of apartheid;
- prohibition, prevention, and termination of genocides and mass killing.

Jewish NGOs have also worked to ensure that the human rights norms codified in the UDHR, the Covenants, and later treaties could be implemented: they advocated the rights of individual and group petition and made significant contributions to creating the position of high commissioner for human rights. Jews continued to struggle for the position until 1994 when it was finally established, and they constituted a key activist constituency (along with, among others, Amnesty International and the Carter Center) in working to make the office as effective as possible (Gaer 1997).

Jewish NGOs have often joined coalitions of the larger NGOs to cement alliances, magnify their influence, and wrap their particular Jewish concerns in a more universal framework. AJC's Felice Gaer helped craft an influential joint statement signed by twenty women leaders and activists regarding "Women and the Bosnian Peace Process: Preliminary Questions on Ten Issues of Concern," which was circulated by Secretary of State Madeleine Albright and influenced the NATO commander in Sarajevo. The statement argued that rape and other gender-specific crimes must be treated as war crimes by international tribunals. The statement helped guide the preparation of the relative articles of the Rome Statute of the International Criminal Court. The Save Darfur Coalition, the umbrella organization of over 170 NGOs working to stop the genocide in Sudan, bears an even more direct imprint from Jewish NGOs. It was founded by the American Jewish World Service's director, Ruth Messinger, as an outgrowth of her humanitarian aid work in Africa: work explicitly underpinned by Torah-based conceptions of universal social justice. Holocaust survivor and Nobel laureate Elie Wiesel helped oversee the creation of the US Holocaust Memorial Museum's Committee on Conscience, which alerts the administration and the public to genocides in progress.

Internal dynamics

Jewish NGOs' collaborations were rarely formal or contractual, which enabled them the flexibility to go their own ways when their organization's mission warranted. Jewish NGOs have created a kaleidoscopic range of interrelations among themselves, resembling, by turns, independent action, coordination, competition, and conflict. In their interactions about rights, Jews have produced a system of dynamic relations.

In Israel, there has been extensive, albeit ad hoc, coordination among NGOs, specifically on the issues of torture, house demolitions, and freedom of movement restrictions in the occupied territories. NGOs specializing in litigation (for example the Association for Civil Rights in Israel [ACRI]) would take specific cases to the Israel Supreme Court sitting as the High Court of Justice: HaMoked specializes in casework, B'Tselem in monitoring and information-gathering, Physicians for Human Rights in documenting the medical impact of violations, and Rabbis for Human Rights in grassroots actions and education. The most successful collaboration resulted in the Supreme Court's ruling in 1999 that all forms of torture, including "moderate physical pressure," were prohibited. The court's president, Aharon Barak, stated from the bench before his ruling that the human rights NGOs had provided the key documentation on which the ruling was based.

On the other hand, Israeli NGOs have not always agreed on goals, tactics, or legal sources. Some NGOs have refrained from working with peace activists, fearing that the latter's political agenda would compromise their own status as nonpartisan human rights observers. When the delays at Israel's system of checkpoints in the West Bank resulted in a Palestinian woman giving birth in her car, the ACRI argued that the human rights network should work to ameliorate conditions at the checkpoints. The more maverick NGOs, however, protested that the checkpoints themselves were illegal, and hence the NGOs had to stand for their complete removal rather than amelioration. The disagreement had a constructive effect. Policymakers and the public began to distinguish between "radical" and "mainstream" options, which in turn enabled the "mainstream" group's amelioration proposals to seem like a compromise. Thus the split among NGOs worked to establish a continuum of possible action that resulted in some movement to prevent future violations.

Productive tensions have also emerged with regard to the proper source of authority to which an NGO should appeal – Israeli law, Jewish law, or international law. Most NGOs have been founded as secular organizations that combine appeals to Israeli and international norms. Some, however, like the Israel Religious Action Center, the political arm of the Reform movement in Israel, have developed an ideology based in a particular interpretation of biblical and Rabbinic sources.

At the global level, too, a fluid coalition politics has reigned. Perhaps the most prominent cases of Jewish internal cooperation and conflict have developed in instances where human rights activists coalesced to protect vulnerable Jewish communities. The most well known such effort was the movement to gain the right of emigration for Soviet Jews denied exit visas. A largely non-contractual network developed that included Soviet Jewish activists, international and state-based NGOs, the Israeli, Dutch, and US governments, and high-powered individuals. Each of these actors brought its own strengths and mission to the network.

Israel sought to assert control, maintaining that the state was the centerpiece of the global Jewish political process. The Israeli Liaison Bureau, the government agency tasked with working on the Soviet Jewry question, frequently collaborated with the various Diaspora NGOs. The Bureau became concerned that after an initial period in the mid-1960s to mid-1970s in which the Jewish emigration movement was led by Zionists seeking to go to Israel, Soviet Jews in the 1980s were now opting to go to other places besides Israel (primarily the United States and Germany) by a ratio of 2:1. In keeping with the Zionist ideology of encouraging Jewish exiles to be "ingathered" into the homeland, Israeli governments under Golda Meir, Yitzhak Rabin, and Menachem Begin sought to compel those who opted for other destinations to land first in Tel Aviv, seeking, not the international human right to emigrate, but the right to emigrate to *Israel*.

But many Diaspora Jews believed that Soviet Jews should have "freedom of choice" to immigrate to any state they desired. American and European Jews tended to interpret the case as one of applying a universal right to a particular situation. Diaspora Jews also protested Israel's attempt to control how information was gathered and distributed. So while the network succeeded in helping to bring two million Soviet Jews out of the country, its success could not be credited to its internal cohesion (Lazin 2005).

The existence of both collaboration and conflict among Jewish political actors amounts to an *unsystematic system* that, because of and not in spite of its adversarial qualities, has often worked for Jews' overall benefit. The fluid structure of Jews' relations on rights issues provides a modus operandi by which bodies with diverse authority structures, missions, and capacities in a multipolar world can find their way to mutual projects.

Reactions to criticisms of Israel

Although Diaspora activists embraced international human rights during the 1950s and 1960s, their enthusiasm began to cool in the mid-1960s. The primary reason was that many members of the new UN majority – including the Communist bloc, Arab states, and newly independent African and Asian states – began to use the human rights system not just to criticize Israel for particular violations but to ostracize it from the community of nations. The General Assembly's resolution of 10 Nov. 1975 (A/RES/3379 [XXX]) equated Zionism with racism and initiated decades of condemnations of Israeli rights practices by various UN bodies. The Commission on Human Rights adopted more resolutions condemning Israel than it did for any other state, including states practicing genocide. The General Assembly entertained two resolutions to expel Israel from the organization. Until May of 2000, when it was admitted to the Western European and Others group, Israel was denied access to a UN regional group, which prevented it from being assigned to UN committees. Israel was the subject of two emergency special sessions of the General Assembly, a rarely invoked forum that has not been used in cases of genocide. Until June 2006, when the International Committee of the Red Cross (ICRC) changed its rules, Israel's national emergency medical and disaster aid service, Magen David Adom (meaning "Red Star of David") was denied affiliate status. At the World Conference against Racism, Racial Discrimination, Xenophobia, and Other Forms of Related Intolerance in Durban, South Africa, in August of 2001, the draft Declaration and Programme of Action included numerous mentions of Israel, although by rule no specific country was to be singled out.

Beginning in the 1970s Jewish NGOs began to identify such behavior as a "New Anti-Semitism," designed to turn Israel into a pariah and deny the Jewish people their right to self-determination. In some cases, the tension produced by commitments to international human rights and Jewish nationalism caused activists to withdraw their support from the human rights system. More often, NGOs continued their work with various human rights bodies while expending a greater and greater proportion of their resources defending Israel from its critics and pushing for reforms in the UN system. For example, UN Watch, a UN reform organization, was a spin-off of the AJC.

What they perceived as politically motivated allegations of Israeli violations caused many activists to experience ambivalence about international human rights. For example, in the late 1970s, activists in the American Jewish Committee responded to the Zionism=Racism resolution in seemingly contradictory ways. In public, they mounted a substantial public defense of Israel's rights record. Privately, however, the director of AJC's human rights arm, Sidney Liskofsky, discussed with his staff "the Jewish ambivalence re: the Israel–human rights question." The staffers wrung their hands over whether there was any substance to the charges of abuse, and worried that such abuses might cause a negative backlash against Diaspora Jews. On 18 October 1977, Abraham Karlikow, AJC's European director in Paris, sent a letter marked "Confidential" to Liskofsky and other staffers frankly discussing this ambivalence. Recognizing "the special difficulties Israel faces," he nonetheless called for AJC to help build "a human rights-impartial body inside Israel." The result was that for the first time AJC intervened in Israeli human rights politics. It worked confidentially with Haim Cohn and a group of non-governmental Israelis to establish the Association for Civil Rights in Israel. The split between AJC's public and private responses illustrates in stark terms the difficulties of balancing commitments to international human rights and Jewish nationalism.

The difficulties have continued through the present. Although Israel helped draft the Rome statute of the International Criminal Court, the state nonetheless declined to ratify the treaty. The sticking point was a clause criminalizing a state's resettlement of its own civilians in territory it occupies. Israel interpreted this clause as the world community's attempt to restrain the West Bank settlement enterprise. Hence it decided not to join a court designed, among other things, to punish the perpetrators of genocide.

Although Jewish activists resented what they perceived as the political manipulation of the human rights system to excoriate Israel, many continued working for a fairer and more effective human rights system. These activists did so because they believed it was better to struggle for human rights than to revert to a world of unquestionable state power; because they carried deep historical memories and had witnessed recent instances of Jewish suffering; because they sought to answer their tradition's call for universal justice; because they hoped to strengthen Israel's democracy; and because they believed that genocide should never be allowed to occur again.

References

Cohn, H. 1989. *Human Rights in the Bible and Talmud* (Tel Aviv: MOD Books).

Cotler, I. 1998. "Jewish NGOs and Religious Human Rights: A Case Study." In Michael J. Broyde and John Witte, Jr., eds., *Human Rights in Judaism: Cultural, Religious, and Political Perspectives* (Northvale, NJ: Jason Aronson).

Fink, C. 2004. *Defending the Rights of Others: The Great Powers, the Jews, and International Minority Protection, 1878–1938* (Cambridge: Cambridge University Press).

Gaer, F. 1997. "NGOs and the UN High Commissioner for Human Rights." Carter Center, Atlanta, pp. 81–96.

Galchinsky, Michael. 2007. *Jews and Human Rights: Dancing at Three Weddings* (Lanham, MD: Rowman & Littlefield).

Haas, P. 2005. *Human Rights and the World's Major Religions, Volume 1: The Jewish Tradition* (Westport, CT: Praeger).

Hertzberg, A. 1990. *The French Enlightenment and the Jews* (New York: Columbia University Press).

Hertzberg, A., ed. 1997. *The Zionist Idea* (Philadelphia, PA: Jewish Publication Society).

Ishay, M., ed. 2007. *The Human Rights Reader*. 2nd edn (New York: Routledge).

Korey, W. 1988. *NGOs and the Universal Declaration of Human Rights: "A Curious Grapevine."* (New York: St. Martin's Press).

Lazin, F. 2005. *The Struggle for Soviet Jewry in American Politics: Israel Versus the American Jewish Establishment* (Lanham, MD: Lexington Books).

Mendelssohn, M. 1983. *Jerusalem: Or On Religious Power and Judaism*. Trans. Allan Arkush (Waltham, MA: Brandeis University Press).

Mendes-Flohr, P. and J. Reinharz, eds. 1995. *The Jew in the Modern World: A Documentary History*. 2nd edn (New York: Oxford University Press).

Spinoza, B. 2005. *A Theologico-Political Treatise*. Trans. R. H. M. Elwes (New York: Cosimo).

Walzer, M., M. Lorberbaum, and N. Zohar. 2000. *The Jewish Political Tradition*. Vol. 1 (New Haven, CT: Yale University Press).

50

Have human rights failed humans?

The discord between human prosperity and human rights

Mirko Bagaric

Introduction

Human rights as the orthodox moral currency

The human rights crusade has trumped all other moral dialogue and is the standard way to express moral claims and many legal entitlements. Yet existence remains harsh for those members of half the world's population who struggle to live on less than $2.50 per day – their experience of human rights is mainly at the conversational and aspirational level. This is not because of a lack of resources. There is enough grain alone to make every person on the planet fat. There is a disturbing paradox behind the mantra that is the human rights industry: human rights have not fostered a demonstrable improvement to human prosperity.

The concept of human rights is alluring. As individuals we are attracted to rights, especially of the so-called human variety. Human rights promise to provide us with a moral shield and confer entitlements upon us. As a community we therefore collectively embrace human rights. The rights wave seems unstoppable. Socially, morally, and politically it is the manner in which we now most commonly assert claims against others and the state. Intellectually, it is almost heresy to criticize rights. Countless institutions, centers, and departments have spawned against the backdrop of paying homage to human rights. Whole journals are devoted to rights. Hundreds of books have dogmatically preached rights. There are more than a hundred instruments at the international law level sprouting human rights. Most countries at the domestic level have a charter or bill of rights that gives legal status to human rights.

Human rights are probably overrated

Yet the currency that is human rights is probably overvalued. A human rights ethic is inward looking – focusing on "me." But humans are not atoms. We live in communities. Human rights encourage individualism, when reality compels community. The focus on the individual is self-defeating. It is a reason that we are inhibited as a world community from implementing measures that would lift global and individual prosperity to a level that is commensurate with world resources. In this chapter, I argue that the concept of human rights is undesirable. To advance human prosperity we should be thinking and projecting not in terms of rights but in terms of flourishing. We should recalibrate the universal moral psyche and our social and economic imperatives to improving the living conditions of all humans.

Aim and scope of this chapter

The arguments I offer in support of my hypothesis are three-fold. First, there is no empirical evidence to show a link between human rights and an increase in human flourishing. Studies of human living standards reveal billions of people presently living in appalling conditions. Second, countries that wholeheartedly embrace human rights continue to wholeheartedly embrace massive discrepancies in national living standards. Finally, human rights-embracing nations are generally the strictest nations when it comes to refusing to share their opulent rights-enhancing shores with the hungry and destitute.

In this chapter, I do not purport to conclusively rebut the theory that human rights promote human flourishing. There are many social, economic, political, and moral factors that contribute to overall human prosperity. It is not tenable to keep these conditions static and isolate the impact of a human rights moral ethic on human flourishing. My aim is less modest: to encourage readers to stop sheepishly championing human rights and inquire as to whether there is a more prosperity-enhancing ethic that as a worldwide community we should be embracing and promoting.

Human rights – the standard moral currency

Post-World War II growth of human rights ideology

Human rights discourse is the most widespread and popular moral currency. It permeates the value and belief system of most contemporary societies. This is a relatively new phenomenon. Human rights as moral trumps emerged from the ashes of the atrocities of World War II. "Never again" was the theme to emerge from this carnage. Human rights were the most obvious moral choice to give grounding to this commitment. As Tom Campbell points out: "The human rights movement is based on the need for a counter-ideology to combat the abuses and misuses of political authority by those who invoke, as a justification for their activities, the need to subordinate the particular interests of individuals to the general good" (Campbell 1996b, pp. 1, 13). Human rights by their very nature drill down to the individual level. They promise protections and entitlements to people. They thus confer invisible barriers that can be erected against tyrants, governments, and other individuals. They also promise minimum entitlements that can be asserted against the broader community. If human rights are observed, then, so theory runs, humans will be accorded fundamental necessities and will never again be wantonly killed and violated.

There is now, more than ever, a strong tendency to advance moral claims and arguments in terms of rights (Sumner 1987, p. 1). Assertion of rights has become the customary means to express our moral sentiments. As Sumner notes: "there is virtually no area of public controversy in which rights are not to be found on at least one side of the question – and generally on both" (Sumner 1987, p. 1). The domination of rights talk is such that human rights have at least temporarily replaced maximizing utility as the leading philosophical inspiration for political and social reform (Hart 1983, pp. 196–197).

The atrocities in World War II were the catalyst for the United Nations, which in turn was the driving force behind a number of international documents, variously called bills, charters, or resolutions, which enshrine catalogues of rights. The UN Charter has as one of its main aims to protect human rights. Its preamble states that:

> WE THE PEOPLES OF THE UNITED NATIONS DETERMINED to save succeeding generations from the scourge of war, which twice in our lifetime has brought untold sorrow to mankind, and to reaffirm faith in *fundamental human rights, in the dignity and worth of the human person, in the equal rights of men and women and of nations large and small*, and to establish conditions under which justice and respect for the obligations arising from treaties and other sources of international law can be maintained, and *to promote social progress and better standards of life in larger freedom*.
>
> AND FOR THESE ENDS to practice tolerance and live together in peace with one another as good neighbours, and to unite our strength to maintain international peace and security, and to ensure, by the acceptance of principles and the institution of methods, that armed force shall not be used, save in the common interest, and *to employ international machinery for the promotion of the economic and social advancement of all peoples*. (emphasis added)

The human rights objectives of the UN Charter have been promoted by a number of defining rights documents. The Universal Declaration of Human Rights was adopted by the UN Resolution 217(III) of 10 December 1948. It is the single most important human rights instrument in the world. The main splendor of the document is that it purports to transcend all cultures and traditions. In effect the rights catalogue in the UDHR was split into two separate documents: the International Covenant on Economic, Social, and Cultural Rights 1966 (the ICESCR) and the International Covenant on Civil and Political Rights 1966 (the ICCPR). These UN Covenants are designed to elaborate on rights in the UDHR and to provide a legal mechanism for the recognition of these rights.

The widespread acceptance of the covenants is underlined by the fact that over 150 states have ratified each of these documents. Rights contained in these documents have been further particularized in more than one hundred other international law human rights documents that now exist (several dozen of the key ones are catalogued at: http://www2.ohchr.org/english/law). The UDHR and the Covenants (especially the ICCPR) have been the template for the domestic bills of rights that now exist as part of the domestic law of most countries. Australia is the only Western country without a constitutional or legal bill of rights. However, two jurisdictions have recently enacted their own rights charters: Charter of Human Rights and Responsibilities 2006 (Vic) and the Human Rights Act 2004 (ACT).

Rights are intellectually questionable

The rights culture has taken hold despite shaky intellectual underpinnings for rights. For centuries philosophers have failed to find credible answers to the most basic questions regarding the foundation and provenance of human rights, such as: What are rights? Where do they come from? How can you tell the difference between real and pretend rights? Which right wins when there is a clash (Bagaric 2006)?

Such difficulties resulted in Jeremy Bentham declaring that there is no such thing as natural rights. To him they were "nonsense on stilts" (1962, pp. 489, 523–524). Two hundred years after Bentham, one of the most eminent legal philosophers of the twentieth century, H. L. A. Hart reached the same conclusion: "It cannot be said that we have had ... a sufficiently detailed or adequately articulated theory showing the foundation for such rights and how they are related to other values. Indeed the revived doctrines of basic rights are ... in spite of much brilliance, still unconvincing" (Hart 1983, p. 195).

Still it is feasible at least to identify the minimum aspects of a right. McCloskey (1976, pp. 99, 115) believes rights to be simply entitlements, while in Sprigge's view "the best way of understanding ... that someone has a right to something seems to be to take it as the claim that there are grounds for complaint on their behalf if they do not have it" (1997, pp. 216–217). Still further, rights have been variously defined as follows: "claims and entitlements to benefit from the performance of obligations" (Marshall 1973, pp. 228, 241); "those minimum conditions under which human beings can flourish [as moral agents] and which ought to be secured for them, if necessary, by force" (Kleinig 1978, p. 36); and the "liberties each man hath, to use his own power, as he will himself, for the preservation of his own nature" (Hobbes 1946, pp. 84–85). Galligan (1988, pp. 69, 88) defines a right as a "justified claim that an interest should be protected by the imposition of correlative duties"; while Campbell notes that "the standard view is that rights are moral entitlements and human rights are those moral entitlements which are the possession of all persons everywhere" (1996a, p. 164).

There are numerous concepts that are adverted to in the above definitions. Drawing a line through the definitions, the most pervasive definition of a "right" is that a right is a presumptive benefit or protection one can assert against others. This is a somewhat minimalist definition and some commentators will offer more fulsome accounts. However, this is not important for the purposes of this chapter. What is relevant to note about the above definition is that rights are innately individualist in character. They can either take the form of benefits or protections. By the term "benefit," I mean a positive entitlement such as the right to a fair trial. As for the term "protection," I mean a negative entitlement, such as the right to be free from a particular violation.

There are no settled limits regarding the content of rights. This is evident from the UDHR, which includes some important rights such as the right to life, liberty, and property. Less obvious, but still desirable, are the rights to freedom of movement and expression. But, wholly contentious are the rights to privacy and rest and leisure, as proclaimed in articles 12 and 25 of the UDHR. The term "presumptive" is used because no right is indefeasible or absolute.

As discussed below, it is the inward-looking and non-absolute features of rights that to some extent undermine rights effectiveness.

Human rights for all, so then why are so many living in abject destitution

If most of the world, and especially the disproportional resource-rich first-world wholeheartedly embraces human rights, then one would expect that most humans, to the extent that it is humanly possible, would find themselves living in conditions where they have access to at least the necessities of life. Yet, the reality is the contrary. Recent data show that three billion people, almost half the world's population, live on less than $2.50 per day and more than 80 percent of humanity lives on less than $10 per day (Chen and Ravallion 2008). UNICEF estimates that 25,000 children die per day of poverty – the equivalent of one child dying every 3.5 seconds. The main killers are hunger and readily preventable illness (Shah 2010b). The gap between the rich and the poor remains at striking levels. In 2005, the wealthiest 20 percent of people used 76.6 percent of total private resources, while the poorest 20 percent used 1.5 percent (Shah 2010a).

It is important to note that although these figures are jarring, there have been some improvements over the past few years in the living standards of the third world generally. The World Bank reports that the portion of the developing world's population living in extreme economic poverty, which is defined as less $1.25 per day, has dropped to 26 percent in 2005, from 52 percent in 1981 (World Bank n.d.). However, the rate of poverty reduction is slowing due to the 2008–2009 global financial crisis (UN News Service 2009).

The main response by the first world to address third-world destitution is to commit 0.7 percent of their gross national income to the United Nations Official Development Assistance. This was pledged nearly forty years ago in a resolution to the General Assembly. To date only five countries have met or surpassed this target: Luxembourg, Denmark, Norway, Sweden, and the Netherlands (Millennium Project 2006). Australia commits about 0.25 percent of its GDP, the United States 0.22 percent, and the United Kingdom 0.48 percent.

Human rights proponents could argue that poverty rates are improving, albeit slowly, and that this shows that human rights dialogue is proving to be an effective catalyst for enhancing prosperity. It is impossible to totally rebut this argument – this would require two parallel worlds, one with and one without a commitment to the human rights ideology and a comparison of global prosperity in both worlds.

The best that can be done is to remove the speculation from the inquiry and ask whether the current levels of global destitution, against the backdrop of the human rights ideology in which we live, are acceptable. The answer is definitive: no. This raises concerns about the efficacy of human rights as a means for improving human prosperity.

Lack of actual commitment to human rights even in human rights-embracing countries

The betrayal of human rights at the pragmatic level is evident not only at the global level but also at the domestic level. This undermines the possible counter that continued third-world destitution results from the inability of the first-world nations to adequately alter living conditions beyond their borders, as opposed to a flaw with a human rights ethic. The wealth disparity even in many of the world's richest countries remains at alarming levels. In the United States the percentage distribution of total income received by the poorest fifth of the population fell from 3.8 percent to 3.4 percent during the period 1990 to 2006; while for the top 5 percent during the same period it increased from 18.5 percent to 22.3 percent (US Census Bureau 2010).

A recent report by the U.S. Agriculture Department has indicated that the number of American families struggling to feed their members is growing (Nord et al. 2009). The annual *Household Food Security* report showed that in 2008, 14.6 percent of American families encountered problems providing adequate food. This is an increase of 11 percent from 2007. This is the highest level since the survey commenced in 1995. The gap between the rich and poor is growing in most wealthy nations. In a twenty-year study of its thirty member countries (all of which have a charter or bill of human rights, except for Australia) published in 2008, the Organization for Economic Cooperation and Development (OECD) noted that wealth inequality had increased in twenty-seven nations. The inequalities were starkest in Mexico and Turkey, followed by the United States. The study noted that in the United States the richest 10 percent earn an average of $93,000, while the poorest 10 percent earn an average of $5,800 (OECD 2008).

Human rights for all, so then why do we reject desperate foreigners?

The starkest repudiation of an actual commitment to human rights comes in the form of the growing fortresses that are first-world national borders. A universal and irreducible principle of human rights discourse is the prohibition against discrimination. Individuals should be permitted to immigrate to the country and region of their choosing unless there is a relevant moral reason for restricting their entry and stay. Certainly, the best way to fix third-world poverty is by massively increasing migration to the West. Left to their own devices many people would gravitate to life-sustaining resources, leading to a rough equilibrium between the world's resources and its population.

That is not to suggest that Africa would empty overnight into the Western world. Some of its citizens are too destitute to hobble to a more plentiful border. Some will not want to come, in any event. But huge numbers will follow the yellow brick road to prosperity in the West. There is one fundamental obstacle to Western nations relaxing border controls: racism. Discrimination on the basis of race is the lynchpin of the whole of Western migration policy.

Nationhood and the practice of excluding others from our shores is so embedded in the Western psyche that many readers will find it jarring to contemplate that this practice is morally objectionable. Yet, there is no reason in principle that migration controls could not be radically reduced worldwide, to something akin to that currently in place for citizens of European Union countries travelling throughout the EU.

For most of human history there have been few migration limits. Now we are moving to an age of "anti-migration," with advanced (Western) economies tightening immigration intakes during the latter part of the twenty-first century (Bagaric *et al.* 2007, ch. 1). Restrictive immigration policies are racist unless there is a morally relevant basis for tightly limiting the number of people we permit to join our privileged society. A relevant reason cannot be a person's birthplace. This is merely a happy or unhappy accident. Much of what is important to a person's flourishing should not turn on so little – morality requires that to the maximum extent possible luck be taken out of the benefits and burdens equation.

National security is commonly used to justify a tight migration policy. While nations have a legitimate right to security, this only justifies a policy of strict security checks. This is tacitly accepted by Western governments, all of which accept massively more tourists than permanent arrivals. Western nations are relaxed about tourists because they derive a net positive economic advantage from them. This gain, however, is not a moral justification for consigning much of the world to a life of destitution, merely a Western expedient. It has also been claimed that too many foreigners would diminish our material prosperity. Research is equivocal about this. Some models suggest the opposite – that immigrants have a net positive effect on the economy (Bagaric *et al.* 2007, ch. 1).

In any event, a slight diminution in the living standard of Western countries is a small price to pay to reduce global destitution. To determine whether a more relaxed approach to migration is justifiable, one cannot look at the situation only from the perspective of the locals. There is no ethical basis for ranking the interests of one person higher than another.

Arguments that open migration would lead to cultural dilution are unsound. What for one person represents cultural dilution, for another amounts to cultural enrichment. There is no objective point of reference from which these positions can be set off. They are by definition culturally relevant. Morality, on the other hand, consists of universal principles, which apply to all people equally. This vision represents a vastly different world. People ought to be able to travel and settle in any country of their choice so long as they do not present a security threat and the nation has the resources to sustain them.

Is this likely to happen in the foreseeable future? No. Patriotism and materialism are such powerful forces that no amount of moral persuasion is likely to quickly reverse existing Western migration policies. The Western world must at least start seriously debating the notion of the free movement of people, otherwise forever be forced to accept the racists within their borders. For present purposes it is important to note that human rights discourse is applied in a manner more akin to a local etiquette as opposed to a universal principle in relation to acknowledging the interests of humans not from Western shores.

Possible explanation for rights failure

There are two main reasons for the impotence of human rights so far as human prosperity is concerned. The most important relates to the core fabric – the DNA – of human rights. They are inward-looking. Human rights innately encourage us to focus on how we as individuals are faring. Human rights do not prompt, invite, or suggest any sense of responsibility or obligation to others. There is nothing inherent in the human rights ethic to suggest that individuals who are utterly self-regarding in their actions are not morally complete. The only caveat to this is that it is unacceptable to violate the rights of others, but there is nothing requiring or urging us to advance the human rights of others. This induces an individualist and selfish mindset. The focus is on the "me," not on others. This occurs at the individual level and also at the group and national country level. It is not surprising that prosperous nations care little for the lot of individuals living in poorer countries.

Second, there is no coherent manner in which to prioritize rights. The need to rank and prioritize rights stems from the fact that no rights are absolute. The non-absolute nature of rights has even been acknowledged by leading non-consequentialist rights proponents. Ronald Dworkin accepts that it is correct for a government to infringe on a right when it is necessary to protect a more important right, or to ward off "some great threat to society" (Dworkin 1977, pp. 199–202). In a like manner, Robert Nozick (1981, p. 95) states that consequential considerations would take over to "avert moral catastrophe." Rights often conflict with other rights. They can also conflict with the wider community good. When either of these scenarios occurs, difficult balancing processes need to be undertaken. These are made more difficult by the fact that there is no coherent guidance regarding the relative importance of rights and the weight that should be given to broader community interests.

For example, while the right to property is desirable, it not clear that this right (in the form of keeping profits from their drugs) extends to justifying multinational pharmaceutical companies continuing to deny life-saving medicines to millions of people who cannot afford the price of medication. It is also unclear as to what extent the freedom of association and movement can be invoked to disrupt city streets in order to agitate for political or social change. It is easy to multiply such examples. The lack of a rights hierarchy permits profoundly obscene rights distortions and priorities to occur. For example, the Western world's increasing fascination with the right to privacy must seem incomprehensible to the third-world citizens struggling for the necessities of life – and indeed for the 14.6 percent of American families struggling to put adequate food on the table. The jurisprudence governing the circumstances in which rights should be limited is akin to randomness, and in such a vacuum there can only be one winner – the person that yells the loudest and has the most resources.

Potential shortcomings with my critique of human rights

My critique of rights-based discourse is obviously not conclusive. As noted at the outset the number of variables that contribute to human flourishing is almost infinite, and hence it is not feasible to identify with certainty the actual roadblocks that currently apply to wide-ranging human flourishing. However, it is clear that the widespread endorsement of human rights has not resulted in anything approaching a world where most people enjoy human rights at anything other than the conversational level. This should at least prompt a degree of suspicion regarding the efficacy of human rights.

Second, it could be argued that human rights are not meant to enhance human flourishing. If not, then there is no better reason to ignore them – principles might sound important, but only a focus on consequences can put food into empty stomachs. If it was established that human rights cause net suffering (for example, because rights such as free speech prompt violence and rebellion), then they would have few proponents – although every society has its fanatics and masochists.

A preferable approach – develop an ethic aimed at enhancing global prosperity

In the end, what matters most to people is their flourishing. The prevailing moral ethic should promote this aim. Humans have a need for the necessities of life: food, shelter, and clothing. Beyond that, it could be argued that the things that are important for prosperity (i.e., which make people happy) are too divergent for meaningful generalizations to be made. Hence, understandably moral and legal reformers and commentators have largely bypassed empirical data in framing moral standards and legal prescriptions.

Relatively new research suggests, however, that each of us are similar in terms of the things that are conducive or inimical to well-being. Despite superficial differences in terms of the lifestyles that we choose to lead and the manner in which we express and project ourselves, at the base we are all built relatively similarly. Social and brain scientists have been making considerable headway into the issue of human well-being. With a large degree of accuracy they have identified the things that make us happy. These are not just vague guesses based on a few new common-sense observations about the sort of things that make us tick. Using brain-imaging sensors they are able to ascertain the patterns of behavior conducive to happiness.

Dr Richard Davidson from the University of Wisconsin has identified an index for the brain's set point for moods. The images show that when we are distressed (anxious or depressed), the most active parts of the brain are the amygdala and the right prefrontal cortex. When we are in positive moods those brain areas are quiet and there is increased activity in the left prefrontal cortex. A person's normal mood range can be ascertained by noting the baseline level of activity in right and left prefrontal areas. The further the ratio tilts to the left, the happier we are. It appears that the Buddhists monks who for centuries have been preaching the art of happiness have actually mastered the art. When their brains were imaged, their baseline points were most to the left.

Wide-ranging studies of thousands of people across many countries confirm the matters that promote well-being. One important finding relates to the connection between happiness and money. It emerges that once we are above the poverty line money makes only a small contribution to our level of happiness and once we reach about the average level of income it makes virtually no difference to our level of contentment. In fact people who focus on the accumulation of wealth are actually more likely to be unhappy. Materialistic values are counter-productive, as over time they heighten insecurity, which is one of the primary causes of unhappiness.

In a nutshell, the things that seem to be conducive to happiness are fit and healthy bodies, self-esteem, optimism, a sense of control, close relationships, challenging work and active leisure, punctuated by adequate rest and a faith that entails communal support, purpose, and acceptance. The interests central to the attainment of these goals include high-quality medical care; access to education; liberty; protection of the family; freedom of religion; the right to welfare (so that all people can afford adequate food and clothing); and publicly funded education – at least to the end of secondary level. Research of this nature has resulted in a number of institutions creating human indexes of well-being, which stipulate the matters that are supposedly cardinal to human flourishing. The Legatum Prosperity Index, which measures prosperity across the globe notes that in developed countries the most important components of well-being are: continued high levels of income; good health; political rights and civil liberties; freedom of choice; charitable giving; family life; equality of opportunity; pleasant natural environment; community life; religious freedom. Australia ranked the highest of 104 surveyed countries in the prosperity index, followed by Austria and Finland, which tied for second place. Next were Germany, Singapore, and the United States.

Interests that are popularly termed rights, but seem to have little bearing on well-being, include the right to privacy and reputation. The current state of evidence does not suggest that these interests in fact are important to well-being. The commonalities of the human species provide a strong basis for confidence that it is possible to make accurate predictions regarding the protections and benefits that best promote human flourishing. Future research should be directed to ascertaining with more particularity and certainty which interests are most central to human flourishing.

But in light of the current evidence, there is a sure basis for rejecting the slavish endorsement of abstract norms and moving toward the pursuit of concrete standards. Governments and individuals should be judged principally by the extent to which they advance these ideals – locally and abroad. Moral thinking needs to be directed to our obligation to ensure that each person, no matter where situated, has the opportunity to enjoy these ideals.

Conclusion

A regrettable aspect of social and moral discourse is that it lacks the same rigor as scientific analysis. Moral imperatives continue to be trumpeted, as opposed to proven. The louder and more appealing the trumpet the more likely that consensus will be reached. Often consensus is reached despite any intellectual analysis or empirical inquiry. Such is the case with the current embrace of human rights. This is despite the lack of testing or evidence that human rights are positive ideals.

Before we go down the path of reflexively championing human rights discourse, we should inquire into the evidence linking human rights to human flourishing. There is no such evidence. In fact the weight of evidence is to the contrary. Instead of promoting human rights, we should map out the interests that are important for human prosperity. The universal and irreducible goal should be to confer these interests to each individual. The degree to which we as individuals and collectively as countries assist in securing these goals for all of humanity should be the ultimate standard upon which we are evaluated.

References

Bagaric, M. 2006. *How to Live: Being Happy and Dealing with Moral Dilemmas* (Lanham, MD: University Press of America).

Bagaric, M., K. Boyd, P. Dimopoulos, S. Tongue, and J. Vrachnas. 2007. *Migration and Refugee Law in Australia* (Cambridge: Cambridge University Press).

Bentham, J. 1962. "Anarchical Fallacies: Being an Examination of the Declaration of Rights Issued during the French Revolution." In J. Bowring, ed., *The Works of Jeremy Bentham*. Vol. 2 (New York: Russell & Russell).

Campbell, T. 1996a. *The Legal Theory of Ethical Positivism* (Aldershot, UK: Dartmouth Publishing).

Campbell, T. 1996b. "Realizing Human Rights." In T. Campbell, D. Goldberg, S. McLean, and T. Mullen, eds., *Human Rights: From Rhetoric to Reality* (London: Blackwell).

Chen, S. and M. Ravallion. 2008. *The Developing World Is Poorer than We Thought, But No Less Successful in the Fight Against Poverty* (Washington, DC: World Bank).

Dworkin, R. 1977. *Taking Rights Seriously*. 4th edn (Cambridge, MA: Harvard University Press).

Galligan, D. J. 1988. "The Right to Silence Reconsidered." *Current Legal Problems*, Vol. 41.

Hart, H. L. A. 1983. *Essays in Jurisprudence and Philosophy* (New York: Oxford University Press).
Hobbes, T. 1946. *Leviathan* (London: Blackwell).
Kleinig, J. 1978. "Human Rights, Legal Rights and Social Change." In E. Kamenka and A. E. Tay, eds., *Human Rights* (London: Hodder & Stoughton).
McCloskey, H. J. 1976. "Rights: Some Conceptual Issues." *Australian Journal of Philosophy*, Vol. 54.
Marshall, G. 1973. "Rights, Options and Entitlements." In A. W. B. Simpson, ed., *Oxford Essays in Jurisprudence* (Oxford: Clarendon Press).
Millennium Project. 2006. "The 0.7% Target: An In-Depth Look." At: http://www.unmillenniumproject.org/press/07.htm.
Nord, M., M. Andrews, and S. Carlson. 2009. "Household Food Scarcity in the United States, 2008." Economic Research Report No. (ERR-83), United States Department of Agriculture Economic Research Service. At: http://www.ers.usda.gov/Publications/err83/dbgen.htm.
Nozick, R. 1981. *Philosophical Explanations* (Cambridge: Harvard University Press).
Organization for Economic Co-operation and Development. 2008. "Growing Unequal? Income Distribution and Poverty in OECD Countries." At: www.oecd.org/els/social/inequality/GU.
Shah, A. 2010a. "Poverty Facts and Stats." *Global Issues*. At: http://www.globalissues.org/article/26/poverty-facts-and-stats#src3.
Shah, A. 2010b. "Today, Over 24,000 Children Died Around the World." *Global Issues*. At: http://www.globalissues.org/article/715/today-over-25000-children-died-around-the-world.
Sprigge, T. L. S. 1987. *The Rational Foundation of Ethics* (London: Routledge).
Sumner, L. W. 1987. *The Moral Foundation of Rights* (New York: Oxford University Press).
UN News Service. 2009. "Financial Crisis to Deepen Extreme Poverty, Increase Child Mortality Rates." UN News Centre. At: http://www.un.org/apps/news/story.asp?NewsID=30070.
US Census Bureau. 2010. "Income, Expenditures, Poverty, and Wealth." *The 2010 Statistical Abstract*. At: http://www.census.gov/compendia/statab/cats/income_expenditures_poverty_wealth.html.
World Bank. N.d. *Overview: Understanding, Measuring and Overcoming Poverty*. Poverty Reduction and Equity. At: http://go.worldbank.org/RQBDCTUXW0.

Part VI

Law and human rights

51

International law and human rights

Brian D. Lepard

Introduction

The protection of fundamental human rights by international law is one of the great legal achievements of the twentieth century. (For an overview, see Steiner *et al.* 2008.) Prior to 1945, the idea of universal human rights found only embryonic expression in international treaties and customary international law. These expressions built on earlier conceptions of human dignity that appeared in revered religious texts such as the Hebrew Scriptures, the New Testament, and the Qur'an. The Enlightenment conception of at least some human beings as deserving of equal rights also was a progenitor of the modern human rights idea (Ishay 1997, pp. 1–173).

The adoption of the text of the United Nations Charter by the delegates assembled at the San Francisco Conference in October 1945, quickly followed by the approval by the UN General Assembly of the Universal Declaration of Human Rights (UDHR) on December 10, 1948, propelled the subject of human rights to the forefront of international legal dialogue, alongside such traditional topics as regulation of the use of force and interstate economic relations. These two seminal documents laid the foundation for the modern-day human rights movement, which has transcended the legal realm and entered the mainstream of moral and political discourse.

The sources of international human rights law

International human rights law, like international law generally, derives from three well-established "sources": treaties, customary international law, and general principles of law. All three of these sources are recognized in the Statute of the International Court of Justice (ICJ). (See ICJ Statute, art. 38[1].) In addition, some scholars believe that UN human rights declarations and resolutions such as the UDHR may constitute a fourth source, however inchoate, of international norms. These latter norms, which are typically not fully binding, are sometimes referred to as "soft law" (Shelton 2006, pp. 180–183).

Turning to the first three sources, modern-day international law traces its roots to the Peace of Westphalia of 1648, which finally ended the horrifically bloody Thirty Years War in

Europe by recognizing the idea of independent sovereign states. International law emerged as the product of explicit or implicit agreements among these states on rules to govern their relations with one another. Explicit agreements normally take the form of treaties, which are essentially written contracts between two or more states. They can range from bilateral agreements between two states to broad multilateral treaties like the UN Charter. Through treaties, states undertake binding legal obligations toward one another (Vienna Convention, arts. 2[1][a], 26).

In addition, many norms have also evolved, through time, into customary international law. Customary law is recognized in the Statute of the ICJ, which refers to "international custom, as evidence of a general practice accepted as law" (ICJ Statute, art. 38[1][b]). As suggested by this brief reference, customary international law has traditionally been defined as a less formal law among two or more states that arises from their behavior and beliefs. In particular, a norm attains the status of customary international law when (1) there is a consistent practice among states that is engaged in over some unspecified period of time, and (2) states believe that this practice is legally required. The second requirement is often referred to as "*opinio juris sive necessitatis*," or, more briefly, "*opinio juris*." These are considered objective and subjective requirements, respectively, for the formation of customary international law (Lepard 2010, p. 6).

Customary legal norms bind all states, except those that have persistently objected to a particular norm. The "persistent objector" doctrine is well established in international law, although actual examples of its invocation are very difficult to identify (see Lepard 2010, pp. 7, 36–37, 229–242).

The Statute of the ICJ also acknowledges a third source of international law, which it refers to as "general principles of law recognized by civilized nations" (ICJ Statute, art. 38[1][c]). This source has a shorter pedigree than that of treaties and customary law. It is widely recognized to encompass general principles that appear in the national legal systems of most nations, such as principles of estoppel and *res judicata* (Lammers 1980, pp. 59–66). However, other authorities, including the ICJ itself, affirm that it also includes general principles of international law (Lammers 1980, pp. 57–59, 66–69). And some scholars have argued that "general principles of moral law" fall within its reach (Lepard 2010, p. 165). Certain commentators believe that UN declarations and resolutions are potent evidence of general principles of law (Simma and Alston 1988–1989, pp. 102–108).

Customary norms or general principles of law that are regarded as particularly important may rise to the level of "peremptory" norms, or "*jus cogens*." According to traditional doctrine a state can never lawfully avoid its obligations under a *jus cogens* norm. Importantly, under customary rules now reflected in the Vienna Convention on the Law of Treaties, a treaty that conflicts with a preexisting peremptory norm is entirely void (Vienna Convention, art. 53). It is generally accepted that *jus cogens* norms bind even those states that have persistently objected to their formation (Lepard 2010, pp. 250–251).

The ICJ has recognized a related but distinct category of international legal obligations, which it has referred to as "*erga omnes*" obligations. It first explained this category in the *Barcelona Traction Case*, decided in 1970. It defined *erga omnes* obligations as "obligations of a State towards the international community as a whole," which can be distinguished from typical obligations of a state that arise "vis-à-vis another State" (*Barcelona Traction Case* 1970, p. 32, para. 33). The Court declared that "by their very nature" *erga omnes* obligations are "the concern of all States. In view of the importance of the rights involved, all States can be held to have a legal interest in their protection" (*Barcelona Traction Case* 1970, p. 32, para. 33). As discussed below, the Court identified a number of human rights norms as ones that create *erga omnes* obligations.

International human rights and treaties

The idea that persons of all nationalities have an inherent dignity, even if not rights, found tentative expression in some early multilateral treaties dealing with specific threats to human dignity, such as slavery and war, including the Final Act of the 1815 Congress of Berlin, which condemned the slave trade, the Geneva Convention of 1864, which laid down protections for the wounded on the battlefield, and the Hague Conventions of 1899 and 1907, which regulated the conduct of warfare. Delegates at the Paris Peace Conference of 1919 declined to provide general human rights protections in the League of Nations Covenant, rejecting proposals by President Woodrow Wilson of the USA to protect religious freedom and by the Japanese government to prohibit discrimination on the basis of race or nationality (Thornberry 1991, pp. 38–40). However, the Covenant did establish a system of international mandates, and those states responsible for these territories (referred to as "mandatories") were obligated under the Covenant to ensure certain minimal standards of just treatment to native inhabitants of these territories. The Covenant also required member states to endeavor to secure fair and humane labor conditions (see League of Nations Covenant, arts. 22–23).

During the lifetime of the League of Nations, the victorious states in World War I entered into various treaties with newly recognized states, requiring them to grant a wide variety of protections to racial, national, religious, and linguistic minorities within their jurisdiction. The legal effect of these treaties is generally understood to have lapsed with the demise of the League of Nations itself and the inauguration of a new legal order under the UN Charter (Thornberry 1991, pp. 38–54). At the same time, the League pioneered the use of individual petition procedures for members of minority groups, created the post of High Commissioner for Refugees, and oversaw adoption of a number of treaties granting legal protections to refugees (see Thornberry 1991, pp. 44–46; Jaeger 2001, pp. 727–732).

The UN Charter was the first multilateral treaty explicitly to articulate the concept of *universal* human rights enjoyed by every single human being, regardless of his or her particular status, for example, as an inhabitant of a League of Nations mandate or as a member of a particular minority group. Human rights protections found expression in a number of key Charter provisions. In particular, the Charter affirms that one of its primary purposes is to "reaffirm faith in fundamental human rights, in the dignity and worth of the human person, [and] in the equal rights of men and women" (UN Charter, preamble). It further requires member states to take joint and separate action in cooperation with the UN to help it promote "universal respect for, and observance of, human rights and fundamental freedoms for all without distinction as to race, sex, language, or religion" (UN Charter, arts. 55[c], 56).

The drafters of the Charter understood that these rudimentary provisions would be expanded upon by an "international bill of rights," which would include a nonbinding declaration, a treaty, and measures of implementation. The Commission on Human Rights established by the Charter, and acting under the leadership of Eleanor Roosevelt of the USA, soon embarked on the task of drafting the envisioned declaration, which became the UDHR (Morsink 1999). The UN General Assembly adopted the UDHR on December 10, 1948.

Formally, like all General Assembly resolutions, the UDHR is only a "recommendation" pursuant to Article 13 of the Charter (see UN Charter, art. 13, para. 1[b]), and, unlike the Charter, it is not a treaty. However, as discussed below, it is widely accepted that many provisions of the UDHR are now part of customary international law. Some scholars contend that all of the operative standards in the UDHR have become customary law. Moreover, certain commentators believe the UDHR expresses general principles of law and may even constitute part of the "soft law" described above, a fourth source of international law. Others argue that the

UDHR may be regarded as an authoritative interpretation of the human rights provisions of the UN Charter.

The drafters of the UDHR referred to it as a "common standard of achievement for all peoples and all nations" (UDHR, preamble). It affirms in Article 1 that, "all human beings are born free and equal in dignity and rights. They are endowed with reason and conscience and should act towards one another in a spirit of brotherhood" (UDHR, art. 1). It then lists many particular human rights. Conventionally, these are considered to fall into two main categories: (1) "civil and political" rights and (2) "economic, social, and cultural" rights.

Civil and political rights protected by the UDHR include freedom from discrimination on the grounds of race, color, sex, language, religion, political opinion, nationality, property, birth, or other status; the rights to life, liberty, and security of person; freedom from slavery or servitude; freedom from torture and other cruel, inhuman, or degrading treatment or punishment; the right to recognition before and equal protection of the law; the right to an effective remedy for human rights violations; freedom from arbitrary arrest, detention, or exile; the right to a fair and public hearing by an independent and impartial tribunal; the right to be presumed innocent until proven guilty; the right to privacy; freedom of movement and residence; the right to seek and enjoy asylum from persecution; the right to a nationality; the right to marry; the right to own property; freedom of thought, conscience, and religion; freedom of opinion and expression; freedom of peaceful assembly and association; and the right to take part in government, directly or through elected representatives (see UDHR, arts. 2–21).

Economic, social, and cultural rights recognized in the UDHR encompass, among others, the right to social security; the right to work and to just and favorable conditions of work and to protection against unemployment; the right to rest and leisure; the right to a standard of living adequate for one's health and well-being and that of one's family, including food, clothing, housing, medical care, and necessary social services; the right to education; and the right to participate in the cultural life of one's community (see UDHR, arts. 22–27).

The original plan to draft a single binding human rights treaty was soon revised and agreement was reached to establish two separate treaties, one on civil and political rights, and the other on economic, social, and cultural rights. Many years of arduous negotiations were required for the UN General Assembly to reach agreement on the text of these treaties in 1966, which became known as the International Covenant on Civil and Political Rights (ICCPR), and the International Covenant on Economic, Social and Cultural Rights (ICESCR). As of December 31, 2010, there were 167 and 160 states parties to these two treaties, respectively (http://treaties.un.org). The ICCPR is now the foremost treaty on civil and political rights generally, and is frequently cited in national court decisions.

In addition to the ICCPR and the ICESCR, the UN General Assembly has adopted the text of numerous more specialized human rights treaties, beginning with the Convention on the Prevention and Punishment of the Crime of Genocide ("Genocide Convention"), approved a day before the UDHR, on December 9, 1948. Under Article 1 of the Convention parties recognize that genocide is a crime under international law and undertake to prevent and punish it (Genocide Convention, art. 1). In 1965, a year before approval of the ICCPR, the General Assembly adopted the International Convention on the Elimination of All Forms of Racial Discrimination. The General Assembly adopted the Convention on the Elimination of All Forms of Discrimination Against Women in 1979, the Convention Against Torture in 1984, the Convention on the Rights of the Child in 1989, and the Convention on the Rights of Persons with Disabilities in 2006. These treaties bind those states that have ratified them. The Convention on the Rights of the Child has attracted the most ratifications of any global human rights treaty, with 193 states parties as of December 31, 2010 (http://treaties.un.org). Other important human rights-related treaties concluded under UN auspices are the 1951 Convention Relating to the Status of Refugees and the 1967 Protocol Relating to the Status of Refugees. (See ibid.)

This proliferation of human rights treaties in the last sixty years was accompanied by the further development of international humanitarian law. In 1949, four new Geneva Conventions were adopted under the auspices of the International Committee of the Red Cross, providing, respectively, protections for the wounded and sick in the field; the wounded, sick, and shipwrecked at sea; the treatment of prisoners of war; and the protection of civilian persons. Article 3 of each of these Conventions protects certain fundamental human rights of noncombatants in non-international armed conflicts, for example by prohibiting violence to life and person, and in particular, murder, mutilation, cruel treatment, and torture (Geneva Convention IV, art. 3, para [1]). The 1949 Conventions were supplemented by two additional protocols in 1977, dealing respectively with international and non-international armed conflicts, and by a third additional protocol in 2005, dealing with the adoption of an additional distinctive neutral emblem.

While the law of war and international humanitarian law, which focus on armed conflict, developed historically along lines distinct from that of international human rights law, the two bodies of law are increasingly converging. A challenging issue facing various international bodies and tribunals is how to coordinate them when both may appear to govern a particular situation. The legality of responses to terrorism is one of the issues that brings into play both strands of law.

Although the UN has served as the focal point for the negotiation and adoption of many important human rights treaties, regional organizations have also, since the mid-twentieth century, sponsored the negotiation and adoption of regional human rights agreements. These treaties have in turn provided the foundation for sophisticated human rights monitoring systems.

Most notably, the Council of Europe in 1950 adopted the Convention for the Protection of Human Rights and Fundamental Freedoms (European Convention on Human Rights). That treaty establishes a European Court of Human Rights. Over the last six decades, the Convention and the Court have come to exercise significant influence in Europe. The Court's caseload has expanded immensely and it has become, in effect, the court of last resort for European citizens who believe their rights have been violated. The Convention had forty-seven parties as of December 2010 (http://conventions.coe.int). Furthermore, the European Union, in order to make human rights a greater focus of its own activities, adopted in 2000 the Charter of Fundamental Rights of the European Union, which became binding European Union law under the Treaty of Lisbon, which entered into force in 2009.

The Organization of American States (OAS) also established a human rights system in the post-war years, founded on the 1948 Declaration on the Rights and Duties of Man, adopted the same year as the UDHR. That system includes an Inter-American Commission on Human Rights. In 1969 the OAS adopted the American Convention on Human Rights, which as of December 2010 had been ratified (without subsequent denunciation) by twenty-four states (www.oas.org/juridico/english/ sigs/b-32.html). The Convention established an Inter-American Court of Human Rights, whose influence is growing, but still does not rival that of the European Court of Human Rights (American Convention on Human Rights, arts. 33, 52–69). Furthermore, in 1981 the African Union adopted the African (Banjul) Charter on Human and Peoples' Rights. A 1998 Protocol to the Charter established an African Court on Human and Peoples' Rights, whose judges were first elected in 2006 (see generally http://www.african-court.org/en/).

International human rights and customary international law

Many human rights norms have become part of customary international law, and thus bind all states, except, in the case of some norms, states that persistently have objected to them. In certain cases norms have first crystallized as customary law and then been incorporated into the above-mentioned treaties; in other cases treaty standards themselves, over time, have evolved into universal customary norms (Lepard 2010, pp. 191–207).

A number of early twentieth-century national judicial opinions recognized an emerging customary law relating to certain human rights norms. For example, in 1900, the US Supreme Court declared in *The Paquete Habana* that a customary norm had arisen prohibiting the seizure of civilian fishing vessels in wartime – a norm based in part on humanitarian considerations (*The Paquete Habana* 1900, p. 708). From early, infrequent, precedents such as this, references in judicial opinions to particular human rights rules as customary norms began to proliferate hand in hand with the emergence and growth of international human rights declarations and treaties.

Despite the indisputable existence of customary human rights law, the status of particular human rights norms as customary norms has engendered much controversy. Some commentators maintain that all of the substantive rights recognized in the UDHR are now part of the corpus of customary law, primarily because of the repetition of state support for the UDHR in the sixty-odd years since its adoption, including references to it in numerous state constitutions (Humphrey 1979, p. 29). Most scholars, however, adopt a more cautious approach under which particular rights are analyzed individually, and evidence is compiled and examined with respect to state practice and *opinio juris* relating to that right (Lillich 1985, p. 407).

Scholars have recognized a number of particular rights as customary law. The *Restatement (Third) of the Foreign Relations Law of the United States* affirms that modern-day customary international law prohibits states from practicing, encouraging, or condoning genocide, slavery or the slave trade, the murder or causing the disappearance of individuals, torture or other cruel, inhuman, or degrading treatment or punishment, prolonged arbitrary detention, systematic racial discrimination, or "a consistent pattern of gross violations of internationally recognized human rights" (*Restatement (Third)*, vol. 2, §702). Various commentators have asserted that a number of additional rights have entered the corpus of customary law (Meron 1989, pp. 79–135).

International and national court decisions have held that many rights are now protected by customary international law. Thus, the ICJ has declared in a number of decisions that customary international law prohibits genocide (*2006 Armed Activities Case (DRC v. Rwanda)* 2006, pp. 31–32, para. 64; *2007 Genocide Convention Case* 2007, para. 161). National court decisions have reached the same holding regarding genocide. Furthermore, various national judicial decisions affirm that state-sponsored torture is a violation of customary international law (*Filartiga v. Pena-Irala* 1980, p. 882 [US]; *Suresh v. Canada* 2002, paras. 61–64 [Canada]).

Despite these broad areas of consensus among scholars and courts regarding the customary law status of a well-defined set of core human rights, disagreement persists about whether other rights, and even some of these most basic ones, actually meet the criteria for classification as customary law. Some scholars are concerned that the state practice requirement is not met because most states actually violate the right in question, rather than protect it.

With respect to torture, for example, certain commentators have called into question whether it is prohibited by customary law because so many countries torture their citizens and noncitizens (Simma and Alston 1988–1989, pp. 86–87). Other scholars, however, take the position that inconsistent state practice does not prevent a norm that expresses universally held moral convictions, such as the prohibition of torture, from forming part of customary law (Schachter 1991, p. 90). In the 1980 US case of *Filartiga v. Pena-Irala*, the court affirmed that the "fact that the prohibition of torture is often honored in the breach does not diminish its binding effect as a norm of international law," especially because no government, according to the US Department of State, had claimed a right to torture its own nationals (*Filartiga v. Pena-Irala* 1980, pp. 884, 884 n.15).

Similar debates persist about the customary law status of freedom of religion and belief. Again, some commentators, pointing to restrictions on religious belief imposed in the Muslim world and also imposed by states adopting other religious as well as ideological belief systems, maintain that the consistent state practice requirement is failed (International Law Association 1994, p. 548). Others scholars who emphasize the primacy of the *opinio juris* requirement and the relevance of ethical principles in determining customary law argue that freedom of religion and belief is indeed now protected by customary law (Lepard 2010, pp. 346–367).

In short, debates continue about the customary law status of particular human rights. Some of these disagreements arise because of more theoretical controversies concerning the relative role of the *opinio juris* and state practice requirements; others persist because of debates about whether or not a sufficient quantity of evidence exists to conclude that either or both of these requirements are met.

International human rights and general principles of law

Courts and scholars have recognized that a number of human rights norms, because of their recurrence in national legal systems, constitute general principles of national law that can apply by analogy on the international plane. Under traditional doctrine, these norms can thus be binding law even if they do not also fulfill the criteria for customary law, and in particular, the consistent state practice requirement (Simma and Alston 1988–1989, pp. 102–108; Meron 1989, pp. 88–89). For example, most scholars maintain that the prohibition of torture is a general principle of national law (*Restatement [Third]*, vol. 2, §702, Reporters' Notes, para. 5).

The ICJ and its predecessor the Permanent Court of International Justice have ruled that certain procedural norms, which have human rights implications, are general principles of national law. For example, the ICJ has affirmed that there "is a generally recognized principle of procedural law" that "questions of immunity are ... preliminary issues which must be expeditiously decided *in limine litis*" (*Immunity of Special Rapporteur Advisory Opinion* 1999, p. 88, para. 63).

There are few international court decisions specifically holding that a human rights norm is a general principle of international law. However, many of the norms that have been classified as customary international law might also be considered general principles of international law (Lepard 2010, pp. 166–167). Moreover, certain norms that the ICJ has characterized as general principles of international law, such as "the fundamental principle of international law that international law prevails over domestic law," have important implications for the application of international human rights law (*Applicability of the Obligation to Arbitrate Advisory Opinion* 1988, p. 34, para. 57).

Finally, there is authority for recognizing general principles of moral law (Lepard 2002, pp. 106–111). These are important ethical principles having some foundation in international legal texts and that ought therefore to bind all states, regardless of whether there is sufficient state practice supporting them or whether a particular state has ratified a treaty incorporating them. An example of such a general principle is the prohibition of genocide. Support for treating this prohibition as a general principle of moral law may be found in the ICJ's 1951 *Reservations to the Genocide Convention Advisory Opinion*, in which the ICJ stated that the prohibition was a principle "recognized by civilized nations as binding on States, even without any conventional obligation" (see *Reservations to the Genocide Convention Advisory Opinion* 1951, p. 23).

In short, while general principles of law have exercised less influence in international legal decisions on human rights than treaties or customary international law, they may have a potent role to play in the future of international human rights law.

International human rights declarations and resolutions

As noted above, some scholars have maintained that UN declarations and resolutions constitute an emerging fourth category of international law norms (for a discussion of the legal status of these declarations and resolutions, see Schachter 1991, pp. 84–105). Many UN General Assembly declarations and resolutions have exercised significant influence in global political and legal discourse. In the human rights area, these obviously include the 1948 UDHR.

Numerous other human rights declarations have been adopted by the General Assembly in the decades since 1948, including, for example, the 1981 Declaration on the Elimination of All Forms of Intolerance and of Discrimination Based on Religion or Belief and the 2007 Declaration on the Rights of Indigenous Peoples. These declarations may give rise to a form of "soft law" that is not fully binding but may have at least persuasive legal authority. (On the concept of persuasive authority and the persuasive legal authority of the UDHR, see Lepard 2010, pp. 54–57, 318–327.) Moreover, some of them, such as the Declaration on the Rights of Indigenous Peoples, recognize rights enjoyed by groups as well as individuals, which certain scholars characterize as "third generation" rights as distinguished from "first generation" civil and political rights and "second generation" economic, social, and cultural rights (Lepard 2002, p. 121).

Human rights norms recognized as *jus cogens* or *erga omnes*

Many human rights norms codified in treaties or treated as customary legal rules or general principles of law may have the further distinction of being peremptory (*jus cogens*) norms. These norms prevail in the case of a conflict with treaty provisions (Vienna Convention, arts. 53, 64), and, as noted above, it is also generally accepted that states may not excuse themselves from the obligation to observe these norms even if they persistently object to them.

According to some scholars, human rights norms that have attained this elevated status include the prohibitions of genocide, racial discrimination, torture, crimes against humanity, and slavery (*Restatement [Third]*, vol. 2, §702, Comment n.). Moreover, scholars have argued that particular norms of international humanitarian law are *jus cogens* (Meron 1986, p. 15). Some have taken the position that the freedom to change one's religion or belief is a *jus cogens* norm (Lepard 2010, pp. 364–367).

With respect to genocide, the ICJ has declared that it is "assuredly the case" that the prohibition of genocide is a norm of *jus cogens* (*2006 Armed Activities Case [DRC v. Rwanda]* 2006, 32, para. 64). It has also implied that the right of peoples to self-determination is a peremptory norm (*East Timor Case* 1995, p. 102, para. 29).

Numerous national cases have ruled that the prohibition of torture is not only a norm of customary law and a general principle of law, but also a peremptory norm (*Suresh v. Canada* 2002, paras. 61–64 [Canada]). The International Criminal Tribunal for the former Yugoslavia (ICTY) has reached a similar conclusion (*Prosecutor v. Furundžija* 1998, para. 153), as has the Human Rights Committee established under the ICCPR (UN Human Rights Committee 1994, para. 10).

A distinct minority of scholars have maintained that all the rights listed in the UDHR are peremptory norms (McDougal *et al.* 1980, p. 274). However, most commentators take the position that a right-by-right analysis is required that takes into account the relative importance of the right.

Even using such a more restrictive approach, many contemporary scholars have developed lists of *jus cogens* human rights norms that are far more expansive than the limited set of agreed *jus cogens* rights listed earlier (Martin 2002, pp. 346–347). The Human Rights Committee has also articulated a rather lengthy list, expressing the view that

> to subject persons to cruel, inhuman or degrading treatment or punishment, to arbitrarily deprive persons of their lives, to arbitrarily arrest and detain persons, to deny freedom of thought, conscience and religion, to presume a person guilty unless he proves his innocence, to execute pregnant women or children, to permit the advocacy of national, racial or religious hatred, to deny to persons of marriageable age the right to marry, or to deny to minorities the right to enjoy their own culture, profess their own religion, or use their own language

is to engage in a violation of a customary law norm that may also be a *jus cogens* norm (UN Human Rights Committee 1994, para. 8). A number of scholars have expressed concerns that state practice does not support this proliferation of asserted *jus cogens* norms (Shelton 2006, p. 173).

The ICJ has identified a number of weighty human rights norms as establishing *erga omnes* obligations. Indeed, in the *Barcelona Traction Case*, in which the Court first elaborated on the concept of these obligations, it offered a number of examples of them, many of which are human rights obligations. It referred to those obligations springing from

> the outlawing ... of genocide, as also from the principles and rules concerning the basic rights of the human person, including protection from slavery and racial discrimination. Some of the corresponding rights of protection have entered into the body of general international law (citing the *Reservations to the Genocide Convention Advisory Opinion*); others are conferred by international instruments of a universal or quasi-universal character.
>
> (*Barcelona Traction Case 1970, p. 32, para. 34*)

The Court has, in more recent cases, affirmed that, "the rights and obligations enshrined by the [Genocide] Convention are rights and obligations *erga omnes*" (*1996 Genocide Convention Case*, Preliminary Objections 1996, p. 616, para. 31). It has furthermore asserted that "the right of peoples to self-determination ... has an *erga omnes* character" (*East Timor Case* 1995, p. 102, para. 29). It has also declared that many rules of international humanitarian law incorporate *erga omnes* obligations (*Wall Advisory Opinion* 2004, p. 199, para. 157). A number of scholars have attempted to lay down criteria for determining which human rights norms establish *erga omnes* obligations (Lepard 2010, pp. 342–345).

There is a close relationship between *jus cogens* norms and *erga omnes* obligations. Indeed, most if not all *jus cogens* norms should qualify as *erga omnes* obligations (Lepard 2010, pp. 267–269).

International procedures for standard-setting and implementation

The implementation of international human rights legal norms – whether arising from treaty law, customary law, general principles of law, or "soft law" declarations and resolutions – has posed major challenges for the international community (Symonides 2003). With respect to treaties, implementation of treaty obligations remains problematic. Most contemporary UN human rights treaties establish a supervisory body composed of independent experts, such as the eighteen-member Human Rights Committee under the ICCPR, that can review reports by states on the measures they have taken to implement their obligations, and sometimes hear complaints of violations by individuals (ICCPR, arts. 28–45; ICCPR, First Optional Protocol).

However, these bodies can only make recommendations and not issue binding decisions (ICCPR, art. 40, para. 4; ICCPR, First Optional Protocol, art. 5, para. 4). Only the regional human rights treaties establish true human rights courts, and these have varied greatly in their powers and effectiveness, with the African Court of Human and Peoples' Rights being the most fledgling institution and the European Court of Human Rights the most senior and influential.

Various other international bodies play an important role in establishing human rights standards, drafting treaties that incorporate them, monitoring implementation of the standards, and occasionally sanctioning violations of them. The UN Charter created an intergovernmental Commission on Human Rights under the supervision of the UN Economic and Social Council. However, over the years the Commission's work became controversial due to its perceived politicization and marginal place in the UN system.

The Commission on Human Rights was replaced in 2006 by a new Human Rights Council elected by and reporting directly to the General Assembly, a move intended to give human rights greater prominence in the work of the UN. In addition, the resolution establishing the Council inaugurated a "universal periodic review" mechanism under which all UN member states would undergo regular scrutiny of their human rights record (G.A. Res. 60/251 2006, paras. 5[e], 9). However, the Council's work has also been criticized as being politically biased, and doubts have been expressed about the rigor of the universal periodic review process. Nevertheless, the Council each year adopts a number of resolutions, some of which call specific governments to account for violations of their international human rights obligations.

There are also individuals and bodies that operate under the Council's supervision, including special rapporteurs, special representatives, independent experts, and working groups. These mechanisms are referred to as "special procedures." The holders of these mandates examine, monitor, report on, and make recommendations with respect to human rights situations generally relating to a particular theme, such as religious freedom, or on human rights situations in particular countries or regions (http://www2.ohchr.org/english/bodies/chr/special/index.htm). Mandate holders act in their personal and independent capacities rather than serving as government representatives. In addition, the Council has an Advisory Committee composed of eighteen independent experts that can give it advice upon its request.

In 1993, the United Nations established the post of UN High Commissioner for Human Rights (see GA Res. 48/141 (1993)). This position was intended to be a high-level focal point for diplomatic efforts to improve member states' observance of their international human rights obligations. Holders of this post have faced the challenge of reconciling their responsibility to call governments to account for human rights violations with the need to garner support from UN member states for their human rights promotion activities.

The ICJ can hear complaints by one state that another state has violated its legal obligations, including its obligations under international human rights law. For example, Bosnia successfully brought an action against Serbia and Montenegro alleging violations of obligations under the Genocide Convention, which resulted in a 2007 judgment in the *2007 Genocide Convention Case* (see *2007 Genocide Convention Case* 2007). Importantly, however, the ICJ, unlike regional human rights courts, has no authority to hear complaints brought by individual human rights victims, and unlike the criminal tribunals discussed below, it has no jurisdiction to consider criminal charges against individuals (ICJ Statute, art. 36).

As a last resort, the Security Council has the power under Chapter VII of the U.N. Charter to order economic or even military sanctions against a state if it determines that the state has engaged in conduct amounting to a threat to the peace, breach of the peace, or act of aggression. Certain violations of international human rights obligations might be treated as a "threat to the peace" or even a "breach of the peace" warranting these sanctions (Lepard 2002, pp. 149–178).

Indeed, over the last fifty years the Council has declared that a number of situations including human rights violations posed a threat to the peace, including the situations in South Africa, Southern Rhodesia, Somalia, and Darfur (SC Res. 1593 2005 [referring the situation in Darfur to the Prosecutor of the International Criminal Court, discussed below]).

Beginning in the early 1990s and continuing in the 2000s, the Security Council authorized a number of UN peacekeeping and peace-building operations, as well as multinational coalitions, to use nondefensive force to achieve human rights objectives, such as in Somalia, Haiti, Bosnia, Rwanda, the Central African Republic, and the Democratic Republic of the Congo. These uses of force have ranged along a wide continuum, from minimal nondefensive force employed by troops in UN peace operations, to large-scale military interventions conducted by multinational coalitions. More expansive military ventures for human rights purposes are often referred to as "humanitarian intervention" (Lepard 2002). Building on these precedents, in the first decade of the twenty-first century the UN endorsed on paper the concept of a "responsibility to protect" victims of mass atrocity crimes, including, if necessary, through the use of globally sanctioned force as a last resort (Evans 2008).

The 1990s and early 2000s have also witnessed the establishment of international tribunals and courts to try individuals suspected of having committed serious crimes under international law and prevent impunity for the perpetrators of these grave crimes. Many of these crimes constitute violations of international human rights law, such as genocide. These tribunals and courts include the ICTY and the International Criminal Tribunal for Rwanda (ICTR), established in 1993 and 1994 respectively by the UN Security Council using its Chapter VII powers. They also include the International Criminal Court (ICC), created by the 1998 Rome Statute of the ICC (Ratner *et al.* 2009, pp. 209–255).

The ICC has the power to try individuals accused of genocide, crimes against humanity, or serious war crimes, if national authorities are unwilling or unable to investigate or prosecute them (Rome Statute, arts. 5–8, 17). Proceedings before the ICC may be initiated by the state party, the Prosecutor, or the UN Security Council (Rome Statute, arts. 13–15). As of December 2010 the Prosecutor had begun investigating cases involving the Democratic Republic of the Congo, the Republic of Uganda, the Central African Republic, Darfur, the Sudan, and Kenya. The situation in the Sudan was referred by the Security Council, and the ICC in 2009 and 2010 issued arrest warrants for President Omar Hassan Ahmad Al Bashir on charges of crimes against humanity, war crimes, and genocide (http://www.icc-cpi.int).

All of these tribunals represent an important step towards the more reliable enforcement of at least some elements of international human rights and humanitarian law. However, they only have the power to punish individuals rather than states. Some observers believe that respect for global human rights and humanitarian norms can best be achieved by these efforts to sanction individual perpetrators, while others emphasize that states must be held to account for their human rights violations. In any event, the work of the ICC in particular has sparked controversy in some countries, including the USA, because of its perceived infringement upon state autonomy regarding criminal prosecutions of nationals.

Outside the UN system, numerous regional organizations and looser affiliations of states have human rights agencies that engage in a multitude of activities aimed at encouraging observance of human rights standards, including those that constitute legal obligations. These encompass, to give one example, election monitoring and other human rights promotion activities of the Organization for Security and Co-operation in Europe. Non-governmental organizations also play a critical role in bringing to public attention violations of international human rights law and in making proposals for revising it and promoting its implementation and enforcement.

International human rights law and national law

Under international law, international human rights obligations prevail over conflicting national laws (*Applicability of the Obligation to Arbitrate Advisory Opinion* 1988, p. 34, para. 57). However, national legal systems vary in the role they accord to international law. Under some constitutional orders, treaty obligations, including those under international human rights treaties, are directly incorporated in national law, albeit often subject to certain qualifications (Janis 2003, pp. 100–101 offers Article 55 of the French Constitution of 1958 as an example). In these systems treaties may be referred to as "self-executing." Other countries' legal systems require that human rights treaty obligations be incorporated through a specific act of the national parliament or legislature in order to be binding within the domestic legal order (Janis 2003, pp. 98–100). In these systems treaties may be called "non-self-executing."

The US Supreme Court has determined, based on Article VI of the US Constitution, that some US treaty provisions are self-executing while others are not (see, e.g., *Foster v. Nielson*, 1829, p. 314). The US Senate, in giving its advice and consent to the ratification of human rights treaties, has adopted the practice of declaring that human rights treaties are non-self-executing and thus are not binding in US courts without a specific act of Congress. US courts have largely respected these declarations, but they have engendered much controversy among other states parties to these treaties and supervisory bodies, many of which believe that the USA, by failing in most cases to adopt implementing legislation, is thereby seeking to evade its obligations under the treaties. (For critiques of reservations and declarations of this nature, see UN Human Rights Committee 1994, especially para. 12.)

Furthermore, many human rights treaties allow states to make "reservations" to them, and indeed, the default rule under customary international law is that in the absence of a specific provision prohibiting reservations, states may make reservations upon ratification of a treaty, so long as the reservations are not incompatible with the "object and purpose" of the treaty (Vienna Convention, art. 19). Reservations effectively carve out exceptions to the treaty. The effectiveness of the international human rights treaty regime has been significantly weakened by the prevalence of many reservations (these concerns were expressed by the Human Rights Committee in UN Human Rights Committee 1994).

For example, Islamic states have frequently lodged reservations to treaty provisions protecting women's rights, indicating they will only be binding to the extent they do not conflict with the provisions of Islamic Shari'a law. And the USA has made a number of reservations to the ICCPR and other human rights treaties, having the effect of ensuring that the treaties will not provide human right protections greater than those granted under current Supreme Court interpretations of the US Constitution. The USA also expressed various "understandings" and made additional declarations upon ratification. (For treaty texts, as well as the text of reservations, understandings, and declarations, see generally http://treaties.un.org.)

Countries furthermore differ in their approach to the incorporation of customary international human rights law into domestic law. At least some countries consider human rights obligations to be "directly" incorporated in national law, so long as they do not conflict with national law. These include Canada, India, Israel, South Africa, and the United States, among others (see the examples given in Lepard 2010, pp. 177–178 n.22). The USA also has a unique statute, the Alien Tort Statute, which allows foreign citizens to bring a lawsuit in US federal court for civil torts committed in violation of the "law of nations" (28 USC §1350). US federal courts have applied customary international law in this context (see *Sosa v. Alvarez-Machain* 2004; *Filartiga v. Pena-Irala* 1980).

Moreover, various national governments have engaged in prosecutions of non-nationals for crimes under international law based on provisions of certain treaties, such as the Convention Against Torture, the Genocide Convention, and the 1949 Geneva Conventions, or based on the customary law concept of universal jurisdiction for serious international crimes. The late 1990s and 2000s witnessed a growing number of these national prosecutions, as exemplified by proceedings brought against General Augusto Pinochet of Chile in Spain and the United Kingdom in 1998 and 1999. However, in many countries these prosecutions were politically contentious.

The future of international human rights law

At the opening of the second decade of the twenty-first century, the future of international human rights law is uncertain. On the one hand, there are encouraging developments. The establishment of the ICC and other international criminal tribunals to try suspected perpetrators of the most egregious crimes is a positive innovation, as are national prosecutions of individuals for these crimes. Regional human rights courts continue to gain in influence. Another welcome development is the greater prominence accorded to international human rights law in global political discourse, exemplified by widely disseminated allegations that the USA and other states engaged in torture and additional violations of their international human rights law obligations as part of pursuing a "war against terrorism." The USA and other countries have modified their policies in response to these allegations. Many important human rights problems are now addressed in international legal documents, including multinational treaties and UN declarations and resolutions.

At the same time, human rights observers perceive some worrisome trends, including the rise of challenges from the developing world to the notion of truly "universal" human rights norms (see, e.g., some of the essays in Sajó 2004); increasing claims by governments to limit human rights in the interest of protecting state security or combating terrorism; attempts to weaken the UN's human rights supervisory machinery, by, for example, failing to give any body of independent experts the authority to investigate human rights situations without explicit authorization from the UN Human Rights Council; the failure of the Human Rights Council to act in a way universally perceived as unbiased and sufficiently proactive in its human rights monitoring activities; the continued absence of any global human rights court to which human rights victims can turn; the persistent limitations placed by many states on the incorporation of their international human rights obligations into domestic law; the absence of any coordinated system of sanctions against states that engage in gross human rights violations; and the impunity still enjoyed by many individual perpetrators of the most serious international crimes.

The effectiveness of international human rights law ultimately depends on the determination of governments to strengthen and uphold it. While non-governmental organizations have played an indispensable role in holding governments accountable for their human rights violations and pressuring them to take their obligations seriously, in the end governments themselves bear this vital responsibility.

References

American Convention on Human Rights. 1969. 1144 UNTS 123.

American Law Institute. 1987. *Restatement of the Law Third: The American Law Institute: Restatement of the Law: The Foreign Relations Law of the United States*. Vols. 1–2 (St. Paul, MN: American Law Institute Publishers) (Cited as *Restatement [Third]*).

Applicability of the Obligation to Arbitrate Under Section 21 of the United Nations Headquarters Agreement of 26 June 1947, Advisory Opinion of 26 April 1988, 1988 ICJ Rep. 12 (Cited as *Applicability of the Obligation to Arbitrate Advisory Opinion*).
Application of the Convention on the Prevention and Punishment of the Crime of Genocide (Bosnia and Herzegovina v. Yugoslavia), Preliminary Objections, Judgment of 11 July 1996, 1996 ICJ Rep. 595 (Cited as *1996 Genocide Convention Case*, Preliminary Objections).
Application of the Convention on the Prevention and Punishment of the Crime of Genocide (Bosnia and Herzegovina v. Serbia and Montenegro), Judgment of 26 February 2007 (Cited as *2007 Genocide Convention Case*).
Armed Activities on the Territory of the Congo (new application: 2002) (Democratic Republic of the Congo v. Rwanda), Jurisdiction and Admissibility, Judgment of 3 February 2006, 2006 ICJ Rep. 6 (Cited as *2006 Armed Activities Case [DRC v. Rwanda]*).
Barcelona Traction, Light and Power Company, Limited (new application: 1962) (Belgium v. Spain), Second Phase, Judgment of 5 February 1970, 1970 ICJ Rep. 3 (Cited as *Barcelona Traction Case*).
Charter of the United Nations. 1945 (Cited as UN Charter).
Convention for the Protection of Human Rights and Fundamental Freedoms. 1950. 213 U.N.T.S. 222 (Cited as European Convention).
Convention on the Prevention and Punishment of the Crime of Genocide. 1948. 78 U.N.T.S. 277 (Cited as Geneva Convention IV).
Convention Relative to the Protection of Civilian Persons in Time of War. 1949. 75 U.N.T.S. 287 (Cited as Geneva Convention IV).
Covenant of the League of Nations. 1919. (Cited as League of Nations Covenant).
Difference Relating to Immunity from Legal Process of a Special Rapporteur of the Commission on Human Rights. Advisory Opinion of 29 April 1999, 1999 ICJ Rep. 62 (Cited as *Immunity of Special Rapporteur Advisory Opinion*).
East Timor (Portugal v. Australia). Judgment of 30 June 1995, 1995 ICJ Rep. 90 (Cited as *East Timor Case*).
Evans, Gareth. 2008. *The Responsibility to Protect: Ending Mass Atrocity Crimes Once and for All* (Washington, DC: Brookings Institution Press).
Filartiga v. Pena-Irala, 630 F.2d 876 (2d Cir. 1980).
Foster v. Nielson, 27 U.S. (2 Pet.) 253 (1829).
Humphrey, John P. 1979. "The Universal Declaration of Human Rights: Its History, Impact and Juridical Character." pp. 21–37 in B. G. Ramcharan, ed., *Human Rights: Thirty Years after the Universal Declaration: Commemorative Volume on the Occasion of the Thirtieth Anniversary of the Universal Declaration of Human Rights* (The Hague: Martinus Nijhoff).
International Convention on the Elimination of All Forms of Racial Discrimination. 1966. 660 UNTS. 195.
International Covenant on Civil and Political Rights. 1966. 999 U.N.T.S. 171 (Cited as ICCPR).
International Law Association. 1994. Committee on the Enforcement of Human Rights Law. "Final Report on the Status of the Universal Declaration of Human Rights in National and International Law." Buenos Aires Conference.
Ishay, Micheline R., ed. 1997. *The Human Rights Reader: Major Political Writings, Essays, Speeches, and Documents from the Bible to the Present* (New York: Routledge).
Jaeger, Gilbert. 2001. "On the History of the International Protection of Refugees." *International Review of the Red Cross*, Vol. 83, pp. 727–737.
Janis, Mark W. 2003. *An Introduction to International Law*. 4th edn (New York: Aspen).
Lammers, Johan G. 1980. "General Principles of Law Recognized by Civilized Nations," pp. 53–75 in Frits Kalshoven, Pieter Jan Kuyper, and Johan G. Lammers, eds., *Essays on the Development of the International Legal Order in Memory of Haro F. Van Panhuys* (Alphen aan den Rijn, the Netherlands: Sijthoff & Noordhoff).
Legal Consequences of the Construction of a Wall in the Occupied Palestinian Territory. 2004. Advisory Opinion of 9 July 2004, 2004 ICJ Rep. 136 (Cited as *Wall Advisory Opinion*).
Lepard, Brian D. 2002. *Rethinking Humanitarian Intervention: A Fresh Legal Approach Based on Fundamental Ethical Principles in International Law and World Religions* (University Park: Pennsylvania State University Press).
Lepard, Brian D. 2010. *Customary International Law: A New Theory with Practical Applications* (Cambridge: Cambridge University Press).
Lillich, Richard B. 1985. "Invoking International Human Rights Law in Domestic Courts." *Cincinnati Law Review*, Vol. 54, pp. 367–415.

Martin, Francisco Forrest. 2002. "Delineating a Hierarchical Outline of International Law Sources and Norms." *Saskatchewan Law Review*, Vol. 65, pp. 333–368.

McDougal, Myres S., Harold D. Lasswell, and Lung-chu Chen. 1980. *Human Rights and World Public Order: The Basic Policies of an International Law of Human Dignity* (New Haven, CT: Yale University Press).

Meron, Theodor. 1986. "On a Hierarchy of International Human Rights." *American Journal of International Law*, Vol. 80, pp. 1–23.

Meron, Theodor. 1989. *Human Rights and Humanitarian Norms as Customary Law* (Oxford: Clarendon Press).

Morsink, Johannes. 1999. *The Universal Declaration of Human Rights: Origins, Drafting, and Intent* (Philadelphia: University of Pennsylvania Press).

Optional Protocol to the International Covenant on Civil and Political Rights. 1966. 999 U.N.T.S. 171 (Cited as ICCPR, First Optional Protocol).

The Paquete Habana. 1900. 175 US 677.

Prosecutor v. Furundžija. 1998. Judgment, Case No. IT-95-17/1-T, Trial Chamber, International Criminal Tribunal for the Former Yugoslavia, Judgment, 10 December.

Ratner, Steven R., Jason S. Abrams, and James L. Bischoff. 2009. *Accountability for Human Rights Atrocities in International Law: Beyond the Nuremberg Legacy*. 3rd edn (Oxford: Oxford University Press).

Reservations to the Convention on the Prevention and Punishment of the Crime of Genocide. 1951. Advisory Opinion of 28 May, 1951 ICJ Rep. 15 (Cited as *Reservations to the Genocide Convention Advisory Opinion*).

Rome Statute of the International Criminal Court. 1998. UN Doc. A/CONF.183/9* (Cited as Rome Statute).

Sajó, András, ed. 2004. *Human Rights with Modesty: The Problem of Universalism* (Leiden: Martinus Nijhoff).

Schachter, Oscar. 1991. *International Law in Theory and Practice* (Dordrecht: Martinus Nijhoff).

Shelton, Dinah. 2006. "International Law and 'Relative Normativity,'" pp. 159–185 in Malcolm D. Evans, ed., *International Law*. 2nd edn (Oxford: Oxford University Press).

Simma, Bruno, and Philip Alston. 1988–1989. "The Sources of Human Rights Law: Custom, *Jus Cogens*, and General Principles." *Australian Yearbook of International Law*, Vol. 12, pp. 82–108.

Sosa v. Alvarez-Machain. 2004. 542 U.S. 692.

Statute of the International Court of Justice. 1945. (Cited as I.C.J. Statute).

Steiner, Henry J., Philip Alston, and Ryan Goodman. 2008. *International Human Rights in Context: Law, Politics, Morals: Text and Materials*. 3rd edn (Oxford: Oxford University Press).

Suresh v. Canada (Minister of Citizenship and Immigration). 2002. 1 S.C.R. 3, 2002 SCC 1, 11 January.

Symonides, Janusz, ed. 2003. *Human Rights: International Protection, Monitoring, Enforcement* (Farnham, UK: Ashgate).

Thornberry, Patrick. 1991. *International Law and the Rights of Minorities* (Oxford: Clarendon Press).

United Nations. 1994. Human Rights Committee. General Comment No. 24. "Issues Relating to Reservations Made upon Ratification or Accession to the Covenant or the Optional Protocols Thereto, or in Relation to Declarations Under Article 41 of the Covenant." UN Doc. CCPR/C/21/Rev.1/Add.6.

Universal Declaration of Human Rights. 1948. G.A. Res. 217A (III) (Cited as UDHR).

Vienna Convention on the Law of Treaties. 1969. 1155 U.N.T.S. 331 (Cited as Vienna Convention).

52

The prosecution of human rights abuses

Dan Saxon

Civilization without justice would be a paradox.

(Opening Statement of the Prosecution, International Military Tribunal for the Far East, May 3, 1946)

Introduction

This chapter describes efforts made in national and international jurisdictions to prosecute persons responsible for gross violations of international human rights. The chapter begins with a review of the legal basis for such prosecutions, including a summary of the concept known as "universal jurisdiction." After a discussion of prosecutions that occur in national jurisdictions, the author reviews efforts to prosecute violators of fundamental human rights in international courts. Domestic and international efforts to prosecute perpetrators, while often incomplete and imperfect, are an important tool for the protection of fundamental human rights. Nevertheless, it is necessary to look beyond formal concepts of justice to find more comprehensive and sustainable ways to redress systematic human rights abuses.

The legal basis for the prosecution of persons responsible for violations of fundamental human rights

The concept known as the "the rule of law" retains a cherished place in democracies around the world. Without a system of laws and institutions that protect the rights of citizens against abuse and mistreatment, victimizers act with impunity, and nations experience widespread violations of fundamental human rights. For example, today in the eastern Democratic Republic of Congo a state of near impunity exists for perpetrators of gross violations of human rights, and only a handful are prosecuted by national Congolese courts or the International Criminal Court (Human Rights Center 2009, p. 5).

The creation and maintenance of the rule of law in any society, however, remains a complex, difficult, and sometimes violent process. The United States and other democracies have enjoyed functioning, albeit imperfect, legal systems for centuries. But countries emerging from the oppression of totalitarian regimes, civil war, or both often require generations of political, social, and economic development to create legal institutions that fairly and effectively protect the rights and interests of citizens.

A crucial pillar of the rule of law is the framework of police and judicial organs that investigate crimes and prosecute criminal offenders. These organs provide victims of crimes with an avenue for redress and protect communities from those who might endanger them. If these institutions are ineffective or corrupt, laws and constitutions lose their value and social cohesion breaks down, leading to widespread human suffering. Thus, states must prosecute those responsible for human rights violations, not only to redress wrongs done to victims, but also to combat impunity and deter future crimes and to maintain the legitimacy of the rights that were violated, as well as the state itself (Orentlicher 2009, pp. 2542–2550; Seibert-Fohr 2009, p. 285; "Selling" 2009, pp. 4–6).

Treaties, conventions, and statutes and violations of fundamental human rights

To support the development of the rule of law and the negation of impunity, a number of international treaties addressing particular kinds of egregious conduct require states to investigate and prosecute persons responsible for serious abuses of human rights. The Convention on the Prevention and Punishment of the Crime of Genocide (the Genocide Convention) obligates contracting parties to enact legislation to provide effective penalties for persons responsible for genocide. The Convention Against Torture and other Cruel, Inhuman or Degrading Treatment or Punishment (the Torture Convention) does the same. Under the International Convention on the Suppression and Punishment of the Crime of Apartheid, both national and international criminal responsibility shall apply to persons who commit, incite, abet, or cooperate in the commission of the crime of apartheid.

Furthermore, while they do not provide specifically for an obligation to punish human rights abuses, several international human rights conventions, arguably, contain implicit requirements of prosecution. For example, Article 2 of the International Covenant on Civil and Political Rights obligates states to ensure that persons whose rights or freedoms are violated have the opportunity to seek a remedy before competent authorities, even when the violation was committed by persons acting on behalf of the state. Article 13 of the European Convention on Human Rights and Fundamental Freedoms provides for the same remedy. In Latin America, Article 18 of the American Declaration of the Rights and Duties of Man requires that states make available "a simple, brief procedure" whereby courts will protect citizens from acts of authority that violate their fundamental constitutional rights. Finally, Article 5 of the African Charter on Human and Peoples' Rights demands that African states prohibit "all forms of exploitation and degradation of man." Obviously the level of protection of such rights and the effective implementation of these remedies varies from country to country. Nevertheless, these treaties and conventions provide a body of international legal norms dedicated to the protection of human rights including the obligation to prosecute.

Today, a great proportion of serious human rights abuses occur, tragically, during armed conflict. Historically, the use of more rudimentary weapons and more traditional, symmetrical forms of warfare concentrated the violence of war on soldiers. During the past century, however, the nature of warfare dramatically changed. More recently, the modern use of air power, propaganda, more and more powerful weapons, and asymmetrical forms of warfare has led to the death of countless civilians and prisoners of war and the massive destruction of civilian property.

Consequently, for many years, in an attempt to use law to reduce the suffering caused by war, states have promulgated numerous international declarations, conventions, protocols, and statutes that comprise the body of law known as "international humanitarian law" (IHL). For example, the signatories to the 1899 Hague Declaration Concerning Asphyxiating Gases pledged to abstain from the use of projectiles whose sole object was the diffusion of asphyxiating or toxic gases. In 1907, in The Hague Convention IV Respecting the Laws and Customs of War on Land, state parties pledged that prisoners of war "must be humanely treated." In 1949, the Third Geneva Convention Relative to the Treatment of Prisoners of War enlarged the protections previously accorded to prisoners by The Hague Conventions. In the same year, the Fourth Geneva Convention Relative to the Protection of Civilian Persons in Time of War became the first treaty directed exclusively to the protection of civilians in time of war (Roberts and Guelff 2000, pp. 60, 243, 299). Presciently, the 1949 Geneva Conventions contained a common provision (often described as "common Article 3") which applied protections to prisoners of war and civilians affected by non-international armed conflicts, such as situations of guerrilla warfare and wars of national liberation.

Importantly for the purposes of this chapter, the 1949 Geneva Conventions obliged all state parties to enact special legislation providing for the arrest and prosecution of persons responsible for grave breaches of the conventions. Such legislation should apply to all persons present on the territory of the state party who are suspected of grave breaches, whether or not those persons are nationals of the state party (ICRC 1958, p. 592).

In 1977, two additional protocols to the 1949 Geneva Conventions expanded on the protections described in common Article 3. These protocols extensively supplemented the protections of civilians during armed conflict proscribed in Convention IV of 1949. In particular, Additional Protocol I, which applies to international armed conflicts, emphasized two fundamental principles of international humanitarian law: "distinction" and "proportionality." "Distinction" requires parties to an armed conflict to distinguish between the civilian population and combatants and between civilian objects and military objectives. The parties must direct their military operations only against military objectives of the opposing party (Protocol Additional 1977a, Article 48). "Proportionality" obliges parties to take constant care during the conduct of military operations to "spare the civilian population, civilians and civilian objects" (Protocol Additional 1977a, Article 57). Planners and commanders of military attacks must take all feasible precautions to avoid and minimize any incidental injury to civilians and damage to civilian objects. Additional Protocol II, applicable to non-international armed conflicts, also contained provisions directed to the protection of civilians, but in far less detail than Additional Protocol I.

Significantly, Article 86 to Additional Protocol I codified the principle of "superior responsibility." This provision imposes criminal responsibility on military commanders and civilian superiors who knew, or should have known, that their subordinates committed or were about to commit grave breaches of the Geneva Conventions and failed to prevent or punish the crimes. After World War II, several Allied courts convicted German officers under this theory of liability (ICRC 1958, p. 591). Article 86 recognizes a superior's unique authority and ability to stop serious violations of international humanitarian law and defines the superior's legal duty to take measures within his or her power to avoid such violations.

The Rome Statute of the Permanent International Criminal Court (the Rome Statute) was adopted at a United Nations Diplomatic Conference in 1998. The jurisdiction of the International Criminal Court (the ICC) encompasses persons responsible for the "most serious crimes of concern to the international community," that is genocide, crimes against humanity, war crimes, and the crime of aggression. The Rome Statute defines "genocide" as certain actions, such as the killing of persons, performed with the intent to destroy, in whole or in part, a national, ethnical, racial, or religious group, as such. "Crimes against humanity" refers to acts such as murder, torture, rape, and deportation when committed as part of a widespread or systematic attack directed against any civilian population, with knowledge of the attack. "War crimes" encompass grave breaches of the 1949 Geneva Conventions such as willful killing and torture and other serious violations of the laws and customs of war such as intentionally directing attacks against civilians and/or civilian objects (International Criminal Court 1998, Articles 6–8).

The ICC may find criminally responsible those persons who directly participate in such crimes by commission, ordering, aiding and abetting, or acting pursuant to a common criminal purpose. The ICC may also prosecute military commanders and other superiors for their failure to prevent or punish the commission of such serious crimes by their subordinates (International Criminal Court 1998, Article 28).

The jurisdiction of the ICC, however, is complementary to national criminal jurisdictions. Therefore, in situations where a state genuinely investigates or prosecutes a case falling within the scope of the Rome Statute, the ICC will not assert its jurisdiction. The ICC may take jurisdiction over an event in cases where a national judicial system has collapsed or where state proceedings operate to shield a person from criminal responsibility are not conducted independently or impartially or are subject to undue delay (International Criminal Court 1998, Article 17).

When reviewed together, significant conceptual overlap exists between international treaties concerning the protection of fundamental human rights and the conventions, statutes, and other documents concerning IHL. Both bodies of law attempt to safeguard persons from unlawful conduct and redress wrongs that occur. The primary focus of international human rights law is the protection of individuals and groups from abuses committed by states or their agents. IHL tries to reduce the suffering of combatants and non-combatants affected by war and, therefore, prevent many violations of fundamental human rights. Thus, the practices of states and military forces during armed conflicts are often viewed through the prism of human rights law (Henckaerts and Doswald-Beck 2005, p. xxxi). Attempts to use these bodies of law to prosecute persons in national and international courts are discussed below.

Customary international law

Customary international law refers to the general practice of states that is accepted as law. In the context of war, custom has been a source of law since medieval times when codes of chivalry determined the conduct of knights and nobility (Meron 1998, pp. 3–7). In modern times, a rule of customary international law must contain two components: consistent state practice and a belief that such practice is required, prohibited, or allowed, depending on the nature of the rule, as a matter of law. Customary international law may encompass practices addressed by treaty law, such as the protection of non-combatants during armed conflicts accorded by the Geneva Conventions. The recognition that an IHL treaty promulgates customary law bolsters the moral claim of the international community for its observance by emphasizing its moral character and deep roots in community values (Meron 1999, p. 113). Significantly, however, customary international law may extend the legal responsibilities of states beyond those defined by treaties and conventions. Both national and international courts may invoke customary international law as a basis for the prosecution of persons responsible for serious human rights abuses and/or violations of IHL (Henckaerts and Doswald-Beck 2005, pp. xxix–xxxii).

Universal jurisdiction

Universal jurisdiction refers to the assertion of judicial authority over crimes regardless of the place where the crimes occurred or the nationality of the criminals or victims. It applies to the most egregious crimes under international law such as piracy, torture, war crimes, crimes against humanity, and slavery. For example, the Geneva Conventions implicitly provide for universal jurisdiction, and, as such, they are among the earliest examples of universal jurisdiction in treaty law. Thus, dozens of states have enacted domestic legislation requiring punishment for grave breaches of the Geneva Conventions and Additional Protocol I on the basis of universal jurisdiction (Segall 2001, pp. 40–41). With respect to human rights treaties, the Torture Convention obligates all state parties to ensure universal jurisdiction over "all acts of torture." Under customary international law, states have the right to exercise universal jurisdiction over war crimes, crimes against humanity and genocide (Segall 2001, p.68).

Universal jurisdiction "holds the promise of a system of global accountability – justice without borders" administered by national courts (Macedo 2004, p. 4). Indeed, the Rome Statute – which describes the duty of every state to exercise its criminal jurisdiction over those responsible for international crimes – has led many states to improve their legislation concerning universal jurisdiction (Hays Butler 2004, p. 70). For example, in 2009, the Netherlands and the United Kingdom considered legislation to broaden their jurisdiction over the crimes of genocide, crimes against humanity, and war crimes (Trial Watch 2010). Since World War II, more that fifteen states have exercised universal jurisdiction to investigate or prosecute international crimes. Other countries have extradited accused to states for prosecution based on universal jurisdiction (Amnesty International 2009).

Several exercises of universal jurisdiction in recent years demonstrate the breadth of its reach over time and space. In 1989, the British House of Lords found that former Chilean dictator Augusto Pinochet did not enjoy immunity from prosecution or extradition for a limited number of acts of torture that occurred in Chile (Falk 2006, pp. 97–120). In a Spanish court in 2008, Judge Santiago Pedraz began hearing evidence in a case from Guatemala brought by survivors of the Guatemalan army's counterinsurgency campaign in 1982. The victims allege that former army General Efrain Rios Mont and seven other military and civilian officials are responsible for the crimes of genocide and crimes against humanity for their roles in the campaign that resulted in the deaths of thousands of Mayan civilians (National Security Archive 2009). In December 2009, a Belgian court convicted Rwandan citizen Efram Nkezabera, a former Interahamwe militia leader, of war crimes committed during the 1994 Rwandan genocide (Trial Watch 2010). Universal jurisdiction, therefore, has become a viable prosecution tool against persons who previously enjoyed impunity from responsibility for gross violations of international human rights.

Domestic prosecutions

Of course, the exercise of universal jurisdiction would be unnecessary if the governments where the crimes occurred had investigated and prosecuted those who were responsible for them. During the last decades of the twentieth century, many nations, from Central and South America to Africa and southeastern Europe, suffered widespread and horrific human rights violations. Simultaneously, their government institutions often lacked the means and the will to prosecute the individuals responsible for these crimes.

One jurist observes that "crime is, by its definition, an offense against the society in which it occurs" (Kirby 2006, p. 246). Successful domestic prosecutions reflect the state's interest and ability to protect the fundamental rights of its citizens and maintain a society controlled by the rule of law. Thus, the efforts to strengthen the ability of *national* jurisdictions to prosecute persons responsible for gross violations of human rights occurring within their territories is, ironically, probably the most important factor in the *international* movement to curtail and redress human rights abuses.

Recently, several states that previously suffered widespread human rights violations have begun to redress these injustices. For example, in November 2009, a Colombian court convicted a retired army general, Jaime Humberto Uscategui, of murder and sentenced him to forty years in prison for his role in a 1997 massacre by far-right militias. This was the most severe sentence imposed on a senior Colombian official in a case of collusion with right-wing death squads ("Retired General" 2009, p. 3). Also in 2009, a Guatemalan court ruled that cases of "forced disappearance" from Guatemala's long-running armed conflict (which ran from 1961 to 1996) were not subject to a statute of limitations. That ruling opened the door to the prosecution and conviction of Felipe Cusanero, a former army collaborator, for the disappearance of six members of a rural Mayan community between 1982 and 1984. It was Guatemala's first conviction for the crime of forced disappearance (Latham 2009). In the former Yugoslavia, for several years the international community has assisted Serbia, Croatia, and Bosnia and Herzegovina to establish War Crimes Courts that prosecute crimes committed in the region between 1991 and 1995 and during the Kosovo conflict in 1999 (ICTY 2010, pp. 3–5).

In Rwanda, following the 1994 genocide of hundreds of thousands of ethnic Tutsi by Hutu gangs and militia, Rwanda's jails and prisons were overwhelmed with Hutu men and women suspected of participation in the murder of Tutsi. During the ten years after the genocide the national courts conducted approximately ten thousand trials of alleged perpetrators. But even that impressive figure left nearly ninety thousand persons still incarcerated in overcrowded conditions, awaiting trial. To expand the scope of the prosecutions, the government of Rwanda turned to a traditional form of justice called "*gacaca*," referring to the grassy lawns on which village elders often made decisions about disputes within the community. Rwanda's use of this traditional system of transitional justice, made up of members of local communities who are not legal professionals, suggests that prosecutors can look beyond formalistic notions of justice when other methods may provide greater benefits to communities struggling to recover from mass atrocities (Schabas 2005, pp. 880–895).

Strategies that move beyond formal judicial procedures and even beyond justice itself may provide new frameworks and mechanisms for redressing gross violations of human rights. Recently, a group of international justice experts opined that even when prosecutions are viable:

> neither criminal trials nor alternative forms of justice, such as truth commissions, reparations, lustration or indigenous models, were sufficient in and of themselves to address the commission of mass atrocities. Rather, it was acknowledged that each of these mechanisms was useful and often several were needed for a particular conflict to maximize peace and restore justice.
>
> *(Crimes Against Humanity Initiative 2009, para. 15)*

This reality demonstrates that the search for redress for gross violations of human rights must find new and more effective forms of expression that may include non-legal initiatives. "Justice," viewed more broadly, demands broad reforms of the structures of power that create systematic human rights abuses. Thus, efforts in economic development and expanded education opportunities may have to replace retributive justice in order for societies to move beyond the suffering caused by war and repression.

International prosecutions of persons responsible for gross violations of human rights

As described above, gross human rights violations commonly occur during situations of armed conflict. International law requires, however, that during wartime, belligerent parties must treat civilians and other non-combatants humanely. In one of the first international efforts to hold accountable persons who violated this principle, after World War II, the allied powers prosecuted many of the leading Nazi war criminals at Nuremburg and Japanese war criminals in Tokyo (*Trial of the Major War Criminals Before the International Military Tribunal* 1948, pp. 27–92, 171–367; *International Military Tribunal for the Far East* 1948, pp. 1137–1211). Today, in an effort to build on the precedents established at Nuremberg and Tokyo, persons responsible for violations of international humanitarian law are prosecuted at the ad-hoc International Criminal Tribunal for the Former Yugoslavia (ICTY) and the International Criminal Tribunal for Rwanda (ICTR), the Special Court for Sierra Leone (SCSL), the Extraordinary Chambers in the Courts of Cambodia (ECCC) and the permanent ICC.

Establishment of the ad-hoc tribunals: victors' justice?

Some accused and commentators have argued that ad-hoc tribunals such as the ICTY (where I am a prosecutor) are illegal institutions, that the trials there have no basis in law and represent no more than "victors' justice" (*Prosecutor v. Slobodan Milošević* 2001, Initial Hearing, pp. 2–4). When similar criticisms were made about the Nuremburg trials, however, Justice Robert Jackson, the Chief United States Prosecutor, said: "Either the victors must judge the vanquished or we must leave the defeated to judge themselves" (Arendt 1963, p. 274).

Few people today would argue seriously that it was wrong for the USA, the UK, France and the former Soviet Union to prosecute the major German war criminals at Nuremburg shortly after the close of World War II. As discussed above, adequate conditions must exist in national jurisdictions before domestic courts can prosecute individuals responsible for serious violations of international human rights and humanitarian law that occurred *within* those jurisdictions. This reality created the need for ad-hoc international criminal tribunals and, more recently, for the ICC.

With respect to the ICTY, the United Nations Security Council (UNSC) created the tribunal as an instrument of its legal powers under Chapter VII of the United Nations Charter. Article 52 of Chapter VII accords the UNSC with powers to take necessary action to secure international peace and security.

In 1995, during an interlocutory appeal in the first ICTY prosecution, the Appeals Chamber of the ICTY examined whether the Tribunal had been established under law. In ruling that the ICTY was lawfully established, the Appeals Chamber found that the UNSC properly created the ICTY under the Security Council's mandate to address *transnational* issues affecting international peace and security, and that the crimes considered by the ICTY are *universal*. The UNSC established the ICTY to prosecute massive crimes, crimes that by their scope and ferocity attacked the very nature of humankind. These are crimes that transcend the interests and security of any individual victim and any state (*Prosecutor v. Dusko Tadić* 1995, paras. 57–59). And if the crimes committed in the former Yugoslavia were committed not only against individuals but also against all humankind, then only a court representing humankind, an international court, would be the appropriate forum for these trials. Since the ICTY began its work in The Hague, ethnic Serbs, Croats, Bosnian Muslims, Macedonians, and Kosovo Albanians have been indicted, tried, convicted, and (in some cases) acquitted. These results belie the argument that the Tribunal was established only to hold accountable members of the "losing" side of the Yugoslav wars for violations of international humanitarian law.

Very practical problems led to the creation of the ICTY in The Hague. When the UNSC established the ICTY in 1993, the war still raged in the former Yugoslavia and egregious violations of international human rights and humanitarian law continued. Under those conditions, it was not realistic to expect that one or more of the states involved in the fighting would carry out fair and open prosecutions.

Similarly, after the 1994 genocide decimated Rwanda, the UNSC established an international tribunal, located in Tanzania, to prosecute those responsible for serious violations of international humanitarian law during the genocide. Concurrently, the UNSC called for international cooperation to strengthen the courts and judicial system of Rwanda (United Nations Security Council 1995).

In the case of Cambodia, a group of experts initially determined in 1999 that the Cambodian judicial system, weakened by neglect and corruption, was unable to conduct fair prosecutions of those most responsible for the genocide that occurred during the Khmer Rouge regime (Ratner 2009, pp. 350–353). This conclusion eventually led to the establishment of a hybrid Tribunal, the Extraordinary Chambers in the Courts of Cambodia (ECCC), composed of Cambodian and international judges and prosecutors, which completed its first trial in late 2009.

The question of whether the "victors" of a conflict should prosecute members of the "losing" side, however, is actually a tangent from more fundamental issues concerning international criminal tribunals. The important questions to address are: In the context of prosecutions of such massive crimes, what does it mean to have a "fair" trial? And are these trials fair?

The tensions of fairness

The conduct of trials at international tribunals often requires daily balancing tests between different legal principles, and between the rights and interests of different parties. For example, during the early years of the ICTY's work, common law principles and procedures dominated the ICTY Rules and Procedures of Evidence. Under the common law, decisions about guilt or innocence of accused are made by juries of laypersons who often have no legal training or experience. The rules about the admission of evidence during trials are highly technical and strict to ensure that lay jurors do not consider unreliable or otherwise inappropriate material in their determination of guilt or innocence. When rules about the admission of evidence are highly technical, however, trials will last longer because more time is required to determine whether evidence should be admitted.

Courts in domestic jurisdictions would rarely address the massive crimes that are the focus of the international criminal tribunals. These crimes often involve many hundreds, if not thousands, of victims and require extraordinary amounts of evidence to prove. Indeed, in a few short months in Rwanda in 1994 and in Kosovo in 1999, there were hundreds of thousands of victims. The prosecution of persons responsible for such mass atrocities often requires enormous resources and specialized knowledge. For example, the exhumation of mass graves, often in remote locations, involves forensic pathologists, archaeologists, anthropologists, interpreters, and security personnel, as well as logistics officers. Moreover, demographers – important to demonstrate irregular population fluctuations – and military officers and scholars who understand the military, historical, and political context of an armed conflict are also invaluable assets.

Not surprisingly, the combination of massive crimes, huge quantities of evidence, and technical common law evidentiary rules resulted in slow moving and protracted trials at the ICTY, fostering criticism that the proceedings undermined the rights of accused to an expeditious trial and the interests of victims in seeing that justice is done (Ratner 2009, p. 252).

By contrast, in the civil law or "continental" legal tradition, decisions about guilt or innocence are made by judges who are trained to evaluate and weigh evidence before reaching their conclusions. Consequently, civil law rules concerning the use of evidence are much less technical and facilitate the admission of evidence at a much faster speed. In an effort to expedite trials at the ICTY, the Tribunal adopted certain civil law mechanisms, such as the admission of witness testimony in writing under certain conditions and a more liberal approach toward the admission of documentary evidence. The new hybrid system of common law and civil law rules helped speed up the pace of trials.

It is easy for jurists from the common law tradition to argue that these civil law procedures lack the evidentiary protections found in the common law. These safeguards, however, should be less important if fact-finders are professional judges – trained to evaluate whether evidence is relevant and probative – rather than juries of laypersons. Furthermore, the admission of witness evidence in writing brings other advantages. When courts receive written witness testimony, traumatized victims do not have to appear at trials and suffer the trauma of reliving the violence they endured during the conflict.

The use of large amounts of written witness evidence, however, may vitiate the principle that trials must be public and transparent; that for justice to be done, it must be seen to be done, to maintain the legitimacy of the process. This principle is a cornerstone of the work of any judicial system. For example, Article 67 of the Rome Statute, entitled "Rights of the Accused," begins "[i]n the determination of any charge, the accused shall be entitled to a public hearing." Admission of written testimony undermines that principle, as the victims and other members of the public will not know the content of that written testimony.

In addition, by accepting the testimony of witnesses in writing, courts may undermine the interests of victims to face those allegedly responsible for their suffering and describe their experiences in a public court. The statutes of the ICTY and the ICTR, as well as the Rome Statute, direct that the tribunals must protect the interests of victims and witnesses in matters such as physical and psychological well-being, safety, dignity, and privacy. Many victims and witnesses feel a profound moral duty as well as a powerful psychological need to testify about the crimes perpetrated against them. The admission of large amounts of witness evidence in writing means that opportunities to testify are reduced.

Other conflicts arise between the obligation to protect the interests of victims and witnesses at international criminal tribunals, the duty to ensure that accused can prepare their defense properly, and the importance of transparent proceedings. International criminal tribunals lack any police powers and must rely on (often hostile) governments to protect the security of witnesses upon their return home. Yet, victims and witnesses often continue to live in the same communities where many of the perpetrators of the crimes committed against them also reside and may continue to hold positions of power. In addition to these vulnerabilities, the same witnesses are frequently poor and sick, and they have suffered or witnessed highly sensitive and traumatic crimes such as sexual assaults. Not surprisingly, the same victims and witnesses will be concerned about the possible consequences of their testimony on their family members.

In an effort to protect such vulnerable victims and witnesses, international criminal tribunals have devised a series of protective measures to shield a witness's identity from the public during trial proceedings. In the most serious cases, judges may order that testimony be heard in closed proceedings whereby the public will never learn the identity of the witness or have access to his or her evidence.

Of course, the use of protective measures cuts against the grain of public judicial proceedings. Therefore, prior to directing the use of witness protective measures, a party to a trial must convince the judges that objective facts exist to demonstrate that the witness faces a real threat to his or her safety or security (*Prosecutor v. Ljube Boškoski and Johan Tarčulovski* 2007, para. 4). For example, evidence of direct threats or attacks against a witness or his or her family, if related to the criminal proceedings, often constitute grounds for the use of protective measures.

But the full scope of the proper use of witness protective measures is difficult to measure. For example, under certain circumstances, a witness's fear, if well founded, that he/she will lose employment or that his/her children will suffer harassment in school in retaliation for the witness's testimony, might warrant the use of protective measures to shield the witness's identity. More speculative security concerns, however, such as the possible consequences for witnesses should certain political sectors come to power in the witness's home country, are less credible grounds for the use of protective measures. International judges must carefully weigh restrictions on the public nature of trials against possible dangers to witnesses should the fact of their testimony become available to the public.

Witness protective measures may also be imposed prior to the start of a trial and, in exceptional cases, Trial Chambers will permit the prosecution to delay the disclosure of the identity of witnesses to the defense. By shortening the time available for a defendant to prepare to cross-examine his or her witnesses, however, these measures abridge the (pre-eminent) fair trial rights of accused (*Prosecutor v. Radoslav Brdanin and Momir Talic* 2000, paras. 20 and 31).

These examples illustrate the frequent tensions in international criminal prosecutions between legal principles underlying the fair trial rights of accused, the need to protect the integrity of the proceedings, and the rights and interests of other members of the international community. Judges, prosecutors, and defense counsel often debate these issues in efforts to strike the proper balance between competing rights and interests and to maintain the overall fairness of the proceedings.

Unfortunately, these efforts do not always succeed. For example, the application of a defendant's right to self-representation at the ICTY has led to delays, inefficiencies, and frequent misbehavior and obstructionism on the part of self-represented accused (Wald 2009, pp. 51–54). One commentator describes ICTY jurisprudence about the application of this right as "a dark cloud" hanging over ICTY trials due to "serious flaws" in the legal analysis (Sluiter 2008). More critical thinking on the scope and application of the right to self-representation is necessary, and, indeed, in November 2009, the Trial Chamber presiding over the trial of Radovan Karadžić, who sought to represent himself, imposed defense counsel on Mr. Karadžić (*Prosecutor v. Radovan Karadžić* 2009).

Conclusion

In large and complex prosecutions for violations of human rights and humanitarian law, concerns about fairness to accused must be carefully balanced against other stakeholders in these trials. All those with interests in trials concerning crimes so grave that they "shock the conscience" of humankind, in particular the victims and the international community, also deserve a fair and expeditious trial free of misconduct and unnecessary delays. It may be impossible to strike a perfect balance, but, in the words of one commentator describing the Extraordinary Chambers for Cambodia, "An imperfect tribunal is far better than no tribunal at all" (Bernstein 2009, p. 42). In the long run, consistent and creative efforts, both at the national and international level, to bring some semblance of justice to societies that suffered from such crimes, will be an important guarantor of fundamental human rights.

References

Amnesty International. 2009. *Universal Jurisdiction.* At: http://www.amnesty.org/en/international-justice/issues/universal-jurisdiction.

Arendt, H. 1963. *Eichmann in Jerusalem: A Report on the Banality of Evil* (New York: Penguin Books).

Bernstein, R. 2009. "At Last Justice for Monsters." *New York Review of Books*, April 9.

Crimes Against Humanity Initiative. 2009. *Report on Phases I and II*, September 30 (St. Louis: Washington University School of Law).

Falk, R. 2006. "Assessing the Pinochet Litigation: Whither Universal Jurisdiction?" In Stephen Macedo, ed., *Universal Courts and Jurisdiction: National Courts and the Prosecution of Serious Crimes Under International Law* (Philadelphia: University of Pennsylvania Press).

Hays Butler, A. 2004. "The Growing Support for Universal Jurisdiction in National Legislation." In Stephen Macedo, ed., *Universal Jurisdiction: National Courts and the Prosecution of Serious Crimes Under International Law* (Philadelphia: University of Pennsylvania Press).

Henckaerts, J. and L. Doswald-Beck. 2005. *Customary International Humanitarian Law.* Vol. I (Cambridge: Cambridge University Press).

Human Rights Center. 2009. *Annual Report* (Berkeley: University of California).

International Committee of the Red Cross (ICRC). 1958. *Commentary to the Geneva Conventions of 12 August 1949.* IV Geneva Convention Relative to the Protection of Civilian Persons in Time of War (Geneva: ICRC).

International Criminal Court. 1998. *Rome Statute.* At: http://untreaty.un.org/cod/icc/statute/romefra.htm.

International Criminal Tribunal for the Former Yugoslavia (ICTY). 2010. "Assessing the Legacy of the ICTY." Background Paper, Conference of the International Criminal Tribunal for the Former Yugoslavia. The Hague, 23–24 February.

International Military Tribunal for the Far East. 1948. *Judgment*, 1 November, pp. 1137–1211.

Kirby, M. 2006. "Universal Jurisdiction and Judicial Reluctance." In Stephen Macedo, ed., *Universal Courts and Jurisdiction: National Courts and the Prosecution of Serious Crimes Under International Law* (Philadelphia: University of Pennsylvania Press).

Latham, B. 2009. "Human Rights Advocates Hail Guatemalan Court Ruling on Disappearances." *Voice of America News*, 15 September.

Macedo, S., ed. 2004. *Universal Jurisdiction: National Courts and the Prosecution of Serious Crimes Under International Law* (Philadelphia: University of Pennsylvania Press).

Meron, T. 1998. *Bloody Constraint: War and Chivalry in Shakespeare* (Oxford: Oxford University Press).

Meron, T. 1999. "Customary Law." In Roy Gutman and David Rieff, eds., *Crimes of War: What the Public Should Know* (New York: W.W. Norton).

National Security Archive. 2009. *Operation Sofia: Documenting Genocide in Guatemala.* Electronic Briefing Book No. 297. At: http://www.gwu.edu/~nsarchiv/NSAEBB/NSAEBB297/index.htm.

Orentlicher, D. 2009. "Settling Accounts: The Duty to Prosecute Human Rights Violations of a Prior Regime." *Yale Law Journal*, Vol. 100, No. 2537, pp. 2542–2550.

Prosecutor v. Dusko Tadić a/k/a "Dule." 1995. Decision on the Defence Motion for Interlocutory Appeal on Jurisdiction, Case No. IT-94-1-AR72, 2 October.

Prosecutor v. Ljube Boškoski and Johan Tarčulovski. 2007. Partly Confidential Decision on Prosecution's Motion for Protective Measures, Case No. IT-04-82-PT, 30 March.

Prosecutor v. Radoslav Brdanin and Momir Talic. 2000. Decision on Motion by Prosecution for Protective Measures, Case No. IT-99-36-PT, 3 July.

Prosecutor v. Radovan Karadžić. 2009. Decision on Appointment of Counsel and Order on Further Trial Proceedings, Case No. IT-95-5/18/T, 5 November.

Prosecutor v. Slobodan Milošević. 2001. Initial Appearance, Case No. IT-99-37-I.

Protocol Additional to the Geneva Conventions of August 12, 1949, and Relating to the Protection of Victims of International Armed Conflicts. 1977a. 16 I.L.M. 1391. At: http://www.icrc.org/Web/Eng/siteeng0.nsf/htmlall/genevaconventions.

Protocol Additional to the Geneva Conventions of August 12, 1949, and Relating to the Protection of Victims of Non-International Armed Conflicts. 1977b. 16 I.L.M. 1442. At: http://www.icrc.org/Web/Eng/siteeng0.nsf/htmlall/genevaconventions.

Ratner, S. 2009. *Accountability for Human Rights Atrocities in International Law* (Oxford: Oxford University Press).

"Retired General Sentenced to Forty Years." 2009. *International Herald Tribune*, 27 November.

Roberts, A. and R. Guelff. 2000. *Documents on the Laws of War*. 3rd edn (Oxford: Oxford University Press).
Schabas, W. 2005. "Genocide Trials and Gacaca Courts." *Journal of International Criminal Justice*, Vol. 3, pp. 879–895.
Segall, Anna. 2001, *Punishing Violations of International Humanitarian Law: A Guide for Common Law States* (Geneva: ICRC).
Seibert-Fohr, A. 2009. *Prosecuting Serious Human Rights Violations* (Oxford: Oxford University Press).
"Selling Justice Short: Why Accountability Matters." 2009. *Human Rights Watch*, July, pp. 4–6.
Sluiter, G. Karadzic. 2008. "On Trial: Two Procedural Problems." *The Hague Justice Portal*, 2 August.
Trial of the Major War Criminals Before the International Military Tribunal. 1948. International Military Tribunal, Nuremberg. IMTFE.
Trial Watch. 2010. "Ephrem Nkezabera." At: http://www.trial-ch.org/index.php?id=801&L=5&tx_jbtrial_pi2[tab]=facts&tx_jbtrial_pi2[profile]=ephrem_nkezabera_627&cHash=df24c15e6c.
United Nations. 1984. *Convention Against Torture and Other Cruel, Inhuman or Degrading Treatment or Punishment*.
United Nations Security Council. 1995. Resolution 955, S/RES/955 (1994).
Wald, Patricia. 2009. *Tyrants on Trial: Keeping Order in the Courtroom* (New York: Open Society Institute).

53

International human rights law and the war on terror

Robert J. Delahunty and John Yoo

Our starting point is that the rules of international law regulating armed conflicts (LOAC) govern the "war on terror." By war on terror, we refer to the conflict between the United States and the al Qaeda terrorist organization. On one side sits the United States Congress, the United States Supreme Court, the United Nations Security Council, and the North Atlantic Treaty Organization, which have all found that the September 11, 2001 terrorist attacks on New York City and Washington, DC initiated an armed conflict for purposes of the LOAC (NATO 2001; UN 2001a, 2001b; US Congress 2001). On the other sit prominent scholars and international organizations, among others, who have raised doubts about the applicability of the LOAC to this conflict.

It should be recognized that the war on terror does not fit easily within the main categories of armed conflict recognized by LOAC. It is not an international armed conflict between two signatories to the Geneva Conventions, as defined in common Article 2 of the treaties (Geneva Convention 1949, art. 2). It is not a "war of national liberation" under Additional Protocol I to the Conventions (Protocol Additional 1977a, art. I[4]). Nor is it a civil war or other internal armed conflict to which Additional Protocol II to the Geneva Conventions applies (Protocol Additional 1977b). Nonetheless, under the Supreme Court's ruling in *Hamdan v. Rumsfeld*, it is an armed conflict "not of an international character," within common Article 3 of the Geneva Conventions, to which at least some elements of the LOAC apply. We believe that the conflict is best described as a "transnational" one between a nation state and a terrorist group.

Defining the status of the conflict, however, does not settle whether, over and above the LOAC, the international law of human rights (IHRL) also applies to it. Our chapter addresses this critical issue. We shall focus specifically on the applicability of the International Covenant on Civil and Political Rights (ICCPR) to the conduct of hostilities in the war on terror (International Covenant 1966). In particular, we will consider the applicability of ICCPR art. 6(1)'s guarantee that "[n]o one shall be arbitrarily deprived of his life" to combat operations by the US Armed Forces outside the United States.

We do not argue that there is a clean separation between LOAC and IHRL. Some international human rights treaties, such as the Genocide Convention, clearly apply during armed conflict (Convention on the Prevention 1948, art. I), while some parts of the LOAC, like common Article 3 of the Geneva Conventions, can "constitute a kind of human rights provision"

(Schindler 1999, p. 715). Nevertheless, we contend, there are fundamental differences between the LOAC and IHRL as applied to the war on terror. We believe that these differences will become salient when considering the United States' use of unmanned Predator drones to kill suspected al Qaeda targets. One such incident occurred on November 3, 2002, in which Qaed Salim Sinan al-Harethi, a senior al Qaeda operative, was attacked while traveling with five companions in a car in Yemen. Citing the ICCPR, a UN Special Rapporteur took the position that the attack constituted a clear case of extrajudicial killing. The United States maintained that the ICCPR had no application to the incident, on the grounds that "[t]he conduct of a government in legitimate military operations, whether against Al Qaida operatives or any other legitimate military target, would be governed by the LOAC rather than by IHRL" (Report of the Special Rapporteur 2004).

In Section I, we survey the origins and growth of the LOAC and IHRL, and discuss the beginnings of their asserted convergence. In Section II, we restate and defend the traditional view that the LOAC and IHRL differ fundamentally in their scope, purposes, and protective concerns. We then argue that the ICCPR, in particular, should not be understood to regulate the conduct of armed conflicts otherwise governed by the LOAC. In Section III, we address objections that have been raised against this construction of the ICCPR. Finally, in Section IV, we apply the results we have reached to the controversy over the al-Harethi incident.

I.

The relationship between the LOAC and IHRL, though much studied, remains unsettled. Whether or not, as is sometimes asserted, they are rooted in a common principle of respect for humanity, they grew up independently, and only in recent decades have some argued that they are converging. Traditionally, the LOAC was the law that applied to the wartime conduct of one nation toward the citizens of another, while IHRL primarily regulated the peacetime relationship between a government and its citizens. According to Jean Pictet, the LOAC "is valid only in the case of armed conflict while human rights are essentially applicable in peacetime" (Pictet 1975, p. 15).

The LOAC is a centuries-old body of law, whose origins can be traced back to the ancient world, including the societies of Israel, Greece, and Rome, to classical Islam and medieval Christian Europe. Beginning in the second half of the nineteenth century, *jus in bello* came to be codified in such landmark instruments as the 1863 Lieber Code for the use of the Union Army in the American Civil War (Instructions 1863), which is regarded as the origin of "Hague Law," the 1864 Geneva Convention for the Amelioration of the Condition of the Wounded in Armies in the Field (Geneva Convention 1864), from which later "Geneva Law" derives, and the 1868 Declaration of St. Petersburg (Declaration 1868), which first introduced restrictions on the use of certain types of weapons in war. The Hague Conferences of 1899 and 1907 issued important conventions regulating the conduct of warfare and the use of weaponry, including the 1907 Convention (IV) with Respect to the Laws and Customs of War on Land (Convention 1907). The four Geneva Conventions of 1949, replacing the two Geneva Conventions of 1929 (Convention 1929) introduced new and more extensive protections for the victims of armed conflicts, including especially non-combatants in enemy or occupied territory. Owing largely to the demands of Third World and Communist bloc nations, the 1949 Conventions were significantly modified by two "Additional Protocols" from 1977. The LOAC continues to undergo active development, as for instance in the recent draft convention regulating the use of cluster bombs, to which 110 nations agreed in May 2008 (Convention on Cluster Munitions 2008).

IHRL also has a long and distinguished pedigree, although in an internationalized form it can be said to have originated as recently as the 1948 Universal Declaration on Human Rights. The UDHR was the first international instrument to provide for a common and comprehensive standard of human rights. The drafting history of the UDHR shows that the delegates understood that the UDHR would apply only in time of peace. For the first two decades of the post-war period, IHRL had little or no discernible relationship to the LOAC.

It was understood from the early stages of the drafting of the UDHR that it would not be self-executing, but rather would be implemented later. The implementing treaties – the 1966 ICCPR and its companion, the 1966 International Covenant on Economic, Social, and Cultural Rights (ICESCR 1966) took nearly two decades to prepare, and entered into force only in 1976. Not long after their submission, parts of the international community sought to introduce their norms into the LOAC. This process began with the United Nations International Conference on Human Rights in 1968 in Teheran (Proclamation of Teheran 1968). In a series of periodical resolutions from the same period, the General Assembly began to thread together the humanitarian requirements of the LOAC and the doctrines of IHRL. Advocates may have believed that the ICCPR and ICESCR might ameliorate contemporary armed conflicts such as the 1965 Indo-Pakistan war or the 1967–1970 Nigerian civil war. They also may have wanted to constrain or embarrass militarily powerful nations such as the United States, then at war in Vietnam, or Israel, whose regional dominance had just been demonstrated by its decisive victory in the 1967 Six-Day War.

The United Nations Human Rights Committee (UNHRC) – the organ charged with monitoring compliance with the ICCPR – followed up with an extraordinary campaign to alter the LOAC. In 1982, the UNHRC declared the "supreme duty to prevent wars" to be the "most important condition and guarantee for the safeguarding of the right to life" protected by the ICCPR (Nowak 2005, pp. 1092–1093). The leading commentator on the ICCPR has noted that this position entails that any killings in a war that was impermissible under the UN Charter would be a violation of Article 6(1) (Nowak 2005, pp. 125–126). Then in 1984, the UNHRC opined that the "designing, testing, manufacturing, possession and deployment of nuclear weapons are among the greatest threats to life which confront mankind," and therefore that "[t]he production, testing, possession, deployment and use of nuclear weapons should be prohibited and recognized as crimes against humanity" (Nowak 2005, pp. 1102–1103). On this view, the ICCPR would thus subsume the law of arms, which has been a core element of the LOAC, hammered out in difficult and protracted negotiations among states, their militaries, and non-governmental organizations. Setting apart the UNHRC's policy claims about the effects of nuclear weapons, it is a far cry from the ICCPR's original purposes for it to regulate nuclear weapons.

II.

Contrary to the views of the UNHRC, there are powerful reasons to conclude that the ICCPR does not apply to the relations between a state party and the nationals of an enemy state during armed conflict. The ICCPR, after all, was designed to implement the UDHR, which was intended to apply in peacetime. Human rights treaties are primarily addressed to protecting *a state's own nationals* (and others, like resident aliens, in its territory and under its jurisdiction) *from that state*, rather than with protecting the nationals *of a state with which it is or has been at war*. The underlying conceptions of the state in the two bodies of law differ fundamentally. In IHRL, the state exists principally to further the objectives and well-being of its subjects. By contrast, the LOAC characteristically imposes few or no duties on a state with respect to its own subjects.

Instead, the law regulates the unnecessary harms it may inflict *on foreign enemies*. As Col. G. I. A. D. Draper once said, IHRL "seeks to reflect the cohesion and harmony in human society and must, from the nature of things, be a different and opposed law to that which seeks to regulate the conduct of hostile relationships between states or other armed groups, and in internal rebellions" (Draper 1979, pp. 193, 199).

These underlying differences between the two bodies of law explain divergences between them that have puzzled some. IHRL norms, for example, are "derogable" in time of armed conflict or other public emergency, while those of the LOAC are not. In proper circumstances, the former's derogations can be considered to be in the interest of the affected population, which is the state's *own*. By contrast, LOAC generally may *not* be suspended, however grave the emergency, because the affected parties (normally, enemy combatants or civilians) would assumedly *not* be benefited by a hostile power's derogation. Moreover, even when a LOAC requirement may be abridged or suspended by a hostile power, the law typically places severe restrictions on the breadth and duration of that action.

Another important difference arises with the concept of "proportionality." Both bodies of law require a proportionality (or cost/benefit) analysis with respect to the use of lethal force. Within IHRL, as in American constitutional law (*Tennessee v. Garner* 1985), the interests of the target and unintended victims must be weighed against the attacker's use of force. Within the LOAC, however, only the interests of (civilian) third parties can be weighed, while the interests of the military target do not enter into the calculus at all. While the proportionality analysis requires a commander to appraise the "collateral damage" that his use of lethal force may impose on unintended victims of the attack, he does not need to give any weight to the (legitimate) target's interests in remaining alive or unwounded. As Col. Kenneth Watkin rightly puts it, "[a]n important distinction between [IHRL] and [the LOAC] in terms of controlling the use of force is that the former seeks review of every use of lethal force by agents of the state, while the latter is based on the premise that force will be used and humans intentionally killed" (Watkin 2004, p. 32).

These general differences between IHRL and the LOAC are reflected in the text of the ICCPR. Under Article 2, each state party undertakes "to respect and to ensure to all individuals *within its territory and subject to its jurisdiction* the rights recognized in the present Covenant." Some argue that, notwithstanding this language, the treaty applies, not only to a nation's activities on its territory, but, in addition, to its activities outside its territory, including war and belligerent occupation. But the conjunction of "territory" and "jurisdiction" plainly implies that the treaty does *not* apply extraterritorially. It therefore does not regulate the state's dealings with the nationals of another power with which it is in armed conflict outside its territory. Given that the ICCPR in express terms "applies only to individuals within the territory of a state that is a party to it," it follows directly that the treaty "is not applicable to acts of armed forces executed outside the national territory of a party state" (Schindler 1982, pp. 935, 939). This conclusion is buttressed by the interpretative rule that even a human rights treaty "cannot impose uncontemplated extraterritorial obligations on those who ratify it through no more than its general humanitarian intent" (*Sale v. Haitian Centers Council* 1993).

The *travaux préparatoires* to the ICCPR confirm this reading. In our view and that of others, "[t]he preparatory work cited by the [ICJ] actually establishes that the reference to 'within its territory' was included in Article 2(1) of the Covenant in part to make clear that states were not obligated to ensure the rights therein in territories under military occupation" (Dennis 2005, pp. 119, 123). Eleanor Roosevelt, the US representative and (at the time) the chair of the Commission on Human Rights (the body drafting the ICCPR), sought to add the language "within its territory" to the draft of the article, stating that the United States was "particularly anxious" not to assume "an obligation to ensure the rights recognized in [the draft ICCPR] to the citizens of countries under United States occupation," which then included Germany, Austria, and Japan (quoted in Dennis 2005, p. 124). Despite opposition, the American view prevailed, and later attempts to delete "within its territory" were defeated.

In its Advisory Opinion, *Legal Consequences of the Construction of a Wall in Occupied Palestinian Territory*, the ICJ adopted the view of UNHRC and some legal scholars that the ICCPR extended extraterritorially to foreign wars and occupations (Human Rights Committee 2004, §10). Despite the fact that it has received the ICJ's blessing, we find that interpretation wholly unpersuasive. In effect, these arguments read the territorial restriction out of Article 2 altogether, violating the general rule of construction that no word or phrase of a treaty should be considered to be meaningless or idle.

Even a cursory comparison of the language of ICCPR Article 2 with the jurisdictional clauses of comparable human rights instruments indicates that the reference to "territory" is not mere surplusage. Article 1 of the 1967 Optional Protocol to the ICCPR refers only to allegations of violations from "individuals subject to [a State party's] jurisdiction," thus eliminating any territorial element (999 U.N.T.S. 171, 6 I.L.M. 383 [1967]). That omission seems clearly purposeful. Likewise, Article 1 of the 1953 European Convention for the Protection of Human Rights and Fundamental Freedoms, the key jurisdictional provision of that human rights treaty, binds the states parties to "secure to everyone *within their jurisdiction* the rights and freedoms" defined in that treaty (213 U.N.T.S. 221, E.T.S. 5 [1953]). Yet even though Article 1 lacks any express territorial limitation, the European Court of Human Rights' case law "is quite plain that liability for acts taking effect or taking place outside the territory of a member state is exceptional and requires special justification" (*Al-Skeini et al. v. Secretary of State for Defence* 2008, opinion of Baroness Hale of Richmond). Again, Article 1 of the 1989 Convention on the Rights of the Child (1577 U.N.T.S. 3 [1990]) refers to the protection of children "within [the States parties'] *jurisdiction*," also omitting any reference to "territory." The intent to give these treaties a broader field of application than the ICCPR is manifest.

Moreover, applying the ICCPR to the extraterritorial military actions during armed conflict would create obvious and unsolvable anomalies. Article 6 lays down the nonderogable norm that "[n]o one shall be arbitrarily deprived of his life." Armed forces engaged in combat, of course, regularly target members of the enemy, as permitted by the LOAC – indeed, that license is the essence of such law. In *Le Contrat Social* (1762), Jean-Jacques Rousseau stated the generally accepted doctrine that "[t]he object of the war being the destruction of the hostile State, the other side has the right to kill its defenders while they are bearing arms" (Rousseau 1762, Book I, Part 4). Likewise, the Lieber Code states: "Military necessity admits of all direct destruction of life or limb of armed enemies, and of other persons whose destruction is incidentally unavoidable in the armed contests of the war." Or in the formulation of contemporary LOAC, combatants "have the right to participate directly in hostilities" (Protocol 1977a, Article 43). Of course, the ICCPR's prohibition on the "arbitrary" deprivation of life could be read to allow the intentional killing of legitimate targets by forces licensed under the LOAC to do so. But to concede that is tantamount to saying that the LOAC, rather than the ICCPR, regulates such uses of lethal force.

Other important provisions of the LOAC would also appear to be inapplicable if the ICCPR governed extraterritorial military activities. Consider belligerent occupation. If the ICCPR governed, then presumably the Occupying Power would have to ensure to the population of the occupied territory "the rights recognized in the [ICCPR], without distinction of any kind, such as race, colour, sex, language, religion, political or other opinion, national or social origin, property, birth or other status" (ICCPR 1966, Art. 2). Derogation would be only "[i]n time of public emergency which threatens the life of the nation and the existence of which is officially proclaimed" (ICCPR 1966, Art. 4[1]). However, the LOAC generally requires the Occupying Power to maintain the pre-occupation legal regime. Thus, Article 43 of the Annex to the 1907 Hague Convention (No. IV) Respecting the Laws and Customs of War on Land provides that the Occupying Power "shall ... respect, unless absolutely prevented, the laws in force in the country" (T.S. No. 539, 1 Bevans 631 [1907]). But an Occupying Power would be hard put to comply with both the nondiscrimination norm of the ICCPR and the LOAC norm of maintaining the occupied territory's prior legal system intact when the ousted government's laws had discriminated on the basis of race, sex, language, religion, or some other forbidden characteristic. As Lord Brown pointed out in his opinion in the House of Lords' 2007 decision in *Al-Skeini,* it was mistaken to argue that the UK, as a belligerent occupier of Iraq, was bound to apply the European Human Rights Convention throughout the areas it occupied. On the contrary, "the occupants' obligation is to respect 'the laws in force', not to introduce laws and the means to enforce them (for example, courts and a justice system) such as to satisfy the requirements of the Convention" (*Al-Skeini et al. v. Secretary of State for Defence* 2008).

Starting from the premise that the ICCPR applies to the extraterritorial activities of a state party's military in situations of armed conflict or belligerent occupation, therefore, one is driven to a choice between two equally implausible alternatives. One is that the ICCPR displaces the LOAC altogether. Few if any would go that far. The other is that the international legal regime governing armed conflict is a *pastiche.* Selected provisions of the ICCPR will be held to be applicable to situations of armed conflict, but no intelligible principle is offered for determining which provisions are incorporated and which are not, and no evidence seems to exist that the state parties to the ICCPR intended some, but not others, of its provisions to apply in those circumstances. The ICJ's *Wall* opinion illustrates the difficulties of the pick-and-choose approach. In holding the ICCPR to be applicable along with the LOAC in Palestinian territory under Israel's belligerent occupation, the ICJ stated that "some rights may be exclusively matters of international humanitarian law; others may be exclusively matters of human rights law; yet others may be matters of both these branches of international law." Yet the ICJ failed to identify any principles to determine when IHRL rules applied in a situation of armed conflict (or post-conflict occupation) instead of, or in addition to, LOAC rules (Dennis 2005, pp. 119, 133).

The older understanding of the relationship of the LOAC and the ICCPR thus seems to us far more coherent. The LOAC constitutes the legal regime governing situations of armed conflict. IHRL establishes a territorial legal regime applicable to the relations between a state party and (broadly) its own population, except when certain of its provisions are expressly (or by ineluctable inference) applicable to armed conflict.

Again, however, we must stress that we are *not* speaking here of "internal" armed conflicts. It may well be that IHRL is applicable, at least to some degree, in such conflicts. A civil war may occur entirely within the territory of a state party, and those involved in it may all (or nearly all) be subject to its jurisdiction. Absent a valid derogation, the ICCPR might continue to apply. Furthermore, the conventional LOAC governing "internal" armed conflicts is rather meager. In these circumstances, it has seemed sensible to assume that the IHRL applies. The difficulty is, however, that the obligations of IHRL are asymmetrical: the state party to the internal conflict will be bound by the ICCPR, but its opponents will not be. Even if an insurgent group were able to enter into a "special agreement" of the kind contemplated by common Article 3, and were thus in a position to bind itself to ICCPR-type norms, what *incentives* would it have to do so? Thus, even if IHRL can be said to extend to internal armed conflicts, it is hard to see how it could reach *all* of the parties to such a conflict.

III.

Two scholarly works in particular have made the claim followed by the ICJ in the *Wall* case. In a highly influential 1981 essay, Professor (now ICJ Judge) Thomas Buergenthal argued that ICCPR Art. 2(1)'s phrase "within its territory and subject to its jurisdiction" is "clearly" [*sic*] disjunctive rather than conjunctive (Buergenthal 1981, p. 74). The conjunctive reading, he asserts, "is specious and would produce results that were clearly not intended" (Buergenthal 1981, p. 74). He reasons that it would allow states to easily evade the ICCPR by conducting activities against its own citizens, such as the right to travel or to a fair trial, outside its own territory (Buergenthal 1981, p. 74).

We agree, of course, that such a result is absurd. And it is a well-established canon of construction that "[g]eneral terms should be so limited in their application as not to lead to ... an absurd consequence ... The common sense of man approves the judgment mentioned by Puffendorf, that the Bolognian law which enacted, 'that whoever drew blood in the streets should be punished with the utmost severity,' did not extend to the surgeon who opened the vein of a person that fell down in the street in a fit" (*US v. Kirby* 1868). But it is a fallacy to conclude that the ICCPR *in its entirety* must be given extraterritorial application. The absurdity that arises when *particular* clauses are not applied extraterritorially (in some or all instances) does not entail that *every* clause in the ICCPR is (or is presumptively) extraterritorial in scope. Buergenthal's argument would enable the exceptions to swallow the rule. The fact that it would be absurd to apply the Bolognian law prohibiting the drawing of blood on the street to a surgeon performing an emergency, life-saving operation does not mean that that statute could not be applied to a duelist.

Buergenthal also argued that "[t]he terms 'territory' and 'jurisdiction' as used in Article 2(1) may take on special meaning in special situations." He provided the example "where a state party is in actual control of all or a part of the territory of another state and is alleged to be violating the rights of individuals in that territory" (Buergenthal 1981, p. 76). He cited in support the 1975 decision of the European Commission on Human Rights in *Cyprus v. Turkey,* which interpreted Article 1 of the European Convention on Human Rights (Buergenthal 1981, p. 1977). As discussed above, that jurisdictional article provides that state parties (which included both Cyprus and Turkey) "shall secure to everyone within their jurisdiction the rights and freedoms defined in section I of this Convention." Turkey contended that although it had invaded Cyprus, it had neither annexed it nor established a military or civil government there, and that it could be held liable only for violations of the Convention within its own territory. The Commission rejected Turkey's argument, interpreting the term "jurisdiction" functionally, so as to include all persons under Turkey's "actual authority and responsibility, whether [its] authority is exercised within [its] own territory or abroad." Buergenthal deduced that "just as a sound test for determining 'jurisdiction' is actual authority, the test for determining what is a state party's 'territory' should also take into account the reality of 'authority' or 'control'" (Buergenthal 1981, p. 77).

If Buergenthal's analysis were correct, the ICCPR would have applied to belligerent occupations such as the American occupations of Germany, Japan, and Austria. As we have seen, however, the ICCPR's *travaux* make perfectly clear that the US delegation proposed the addition of "within its territory" into Article 2(1) precisely to *avoid* the possibility of being held liable for ICCPR violations in occupied territory. The United States' position prevailed.

Furthermore, Buergenthal over-read the *Cyprus* case. The Commission held Turkey liable for any Convention violations it committed in the parts of Cyprus that the Turkish military was occupying – reasonably so, given that the Convention would have applied to *the whole* of Cyprus in the absence of Turkey's occupation of part of it, and that Turkey was a party to the Convention (Bello et al. 1996, pp. 98, 101). It would have been incongruous to hold that Turkey's invasion and occupation of northern Cyprus *relieved* Turkey from observing the obligations of the Convention there. As the European Court of Human Rights has subsequently recognized, the extension of the jurisdictional provision of the European Convention to the situation in Cyprus was intended "to avoid a 'vacuum in human rights' protection" when the territory "would normally be covered by the Convention" (*Al-Skeini et al. v. Secretary of State for Defence* 2008, opinion of Lord Brown). The original *Cyprus* case therefore has been sharply limited by later "Strasbourg" case law and cannot be used to defend Buergenthal's revisionary interpretation of ICCPR Article 2(1).

In another revealing scholarly work, Professor Louise Doswald-Beck raises the question of "whether human rights law adds extra conditions to the [LOAC] prohibitions on attack" (Doswald-Beck 2006, p. 900). Assuming that the answer is "clearly" *Yes* in the cases of belligerent occupation and non-international armed conflicts, she argues that there is no reason why the same would not true of *international* armed conflicts. She concedes that "the [LOAC] treaties do not provide a rule that … a combatant may not be attacked if he or she may be arrested." But, she urges, "the reason for this absence should be looked at more carefully, in particular in the light of the old rule concerning the prohibition of assassination, in order to see whether the human rights rule is so very different from the original rules and philosophy of [the LOAC]" (Doswald-Beck 2006, p. 900). Reviewing the traditional LOAC prohibitions on assassinations, Doswald-Beck argues that the basis for the ban lay in the fact that the hostilities were normally carried out by close fighting between combatants in land battles or by sieges. Arrest was not a realistic option in those circumstances, because unless an enemy combatant was killed or severely incapacitated by wounding, he might well continue fighting. The ban on assassinations arose insofar as it involved *treachery.* In contemporary international armed conflict, however, "hostilities now occur not only during battles on the ground but also from a distance by aircraft and missiles" (Doswald-Beck 2006, p. 902). Consequently, she appears to say, the ban on assassination no longer survives in international armed conflict. It appears (although she does not spell this out) that the reason for its disappearance must be that aerial warfare, unlike land warfare, precludes the possibility of treachery.

Doswald-Beck also appears to argue, however, that the reasons for the traditional LOAC ban on assassinations continue to hold good in the contexts of non-international war and belligerent occupation. Her chief reason appears to be that in those circumstances, government forces can arrest suspected insurgents or other enemy combatants with no greater risk to themselves than the police normally encounter in arresting dangerous persons. She concludes: "under the traditional law of war, killing combatants in such situations [i.e., where arresting them was possible] would have been considered an assassination. Is human rights law therefore so incompatible, at least with the original rules and philosophy of the law of war?" In her view, "the specific rules of human rights law as they apply to the right to life, and as these have been interpreted in practice, are not incompatible" (Doswald-Beck 2006, p. 902).

We find Doswald-Beck's arguments unconvincing. To begin with, the LOAC simply does not forbid the use of lethal force against even an unsuspecting enemy combatant if he is not actively participating in hostilities and poses no immediate danger (Dinstein 2002, pp. 139, 153–154). Consider sniping. Sniping has long been a lawful method of warfare, even though it can contain an element of surprise. It is not prohibited by the LOAC's ban on assassination (Parks 1992, p. 3). Moreover, a sniper may lawfully take an enemy combatant's life without even affording him the opportunity to surrender; and sniper fire is allowed even when the target is not present in the zone of hostilities. But if snipers may be used lawfully in international armed conflict to kill an unsuspecting soldier behind the front, why may they not be used to kill an al Qaeda leader in the mountains of Afghanistan? And if snipers may be used, why not drones armed with Predator missiles?

We see no reason why these LOAC rules should vary depending on the nature of the armed conflict. Thus, while we agree with Doswald-Beck that the contemporary LOAC relating to *international* conflicts plainly does not ban (what might be seen as) the "assassination" of enemy combatants, we see no reason to distinguish that situation from *non-international* (including transnational) armed conflict. In all these types of conflict, it may sometimes be possible to arrest an enemy combatant rather than killing or wounding him. But the LOAC governing international conflicts does not prohibit the use of lethal force against such an enemy even then. Why then should the LOAC for non-international conflicts do so? Moreover, the fact that an armed conflict is "internal," or that it is occurring during a military occupation, hardly entails that it will be easier to arrest enemy combatants than it usually is in international conflicts (*Adalah v. GOC Central Command* 2005, ¶ 16).

IV.

In light of the preceding analysis, we now turn to the United States' use of unmanned drones to kill suspected al Qaeda terrorists. We shall consider here the recent article by Professor Philip Alston, the United Nations Special Rapporteur on extrajudicial, summary, or arbitrary executions, and his co-authors, dealing with that subject (Alston et al. 2008, p. 183). Our prior analysis has defended many of the core claims we make in response to Alston. Alston's argument also hinges on the ICJ's jurisprudence, most especially its construction of the ICCPR in the *Nuclear Weapons* case. If the ICJ's reasoning there fails, then the centerpiece of the Special Rapporteur's argument fails as well.

Alston argues that the United States has been mistaken in reading the *Nuclear Weapons* Opinion to stand for the idea that the LOAC is the applicable *lex specialis* that governs the conduct of hostilities. He quotes the opinion's language that "the protection of the [ICCPR] does not cease in times of war," except by derogation, and that derogation does not apply to the "respect for the right to life." The ICJ, Alston notes, observed that "[i]n principle, the right not arbitrarily to be deprived of one's life applies also in hostilities." Thus, according to Alston, the ICJ "asserts in its opening sentence the overriding principle that in fact the Covenant does continue to apply during armed conflict," specifically the right not to be arbitrarily deprived of life. The *lex specialis* of LOAC, concludes Alston, does not displace IHRL. It only appears when interpreting a specific right's application to armed conflict (Alston et al. 2008, p. 193).

Thus, the Special Rapporteur assumes the question of the legality of the United States' action in killing al-Harethi reduces to a dispute over the construction of the ICJ Advisory Opinion in *Nuclear Weapons.* He further assumes to be both correct on the law and controlling in its application. But even if the Special Rapporteur's interpretation is sound, the question whether the ICJ's ruling *is legally correct* must be considered. We believe that the understanding of the ICCPR that the Special Rapporteur takes the ICJ to have adopted is plainly erroneous.

Nuclear Weapons' proposition that the protection of the ICCPR "does not cease in times of war," except when a proper derogation is made, is uncontroversial. We, of course, concur. The ICCPR covers the relations between a state and those in its territory and subject to its jurisdiction even in wartime, and the possibility of derogation would make little sense if this were not so. The ICJ next observes, again uncontroversially, that the ICCPR's prohibition on the arbitrary killing of those whom it protects is nonderogable, even in wartime. Again, we of course agree. But from those unexceptionable premises, the ICJ (as the Special Rapporteur reads *Nuclear Weapons*) then affirms that the ICCPR's prohibition on arbitrary killing extends to conditions *in combat,* traditionally regulated by the LOAC. That conclusion is a flat and obvious *non sequitur.* Moreover, the ICJ (on the Special Rapporteur's account) makes that wholly unwarranted inference with no reference whatsoever to the jurisdictional language of Article 2 of the ICCPR; to the intent of the state parties that ratified that clause of the ICCPR or to the decisions of the General Assembly with respect to it; to any ensuing state practice, including derogations (*Al-Jedda v. Sect'y of State for Defence* 2007, ¶ 38, opinion of Lord Bingham); to the general purposes of the ICCPR, as distinct from those of the LOAC; to the traditional understanding of the fundamental divergences between the ICCPR and the LOAC; to the language of the jurisdictional provisions of other comparable IHRL instruments; or to any legal scholarship. In short, the ICJ has superimposed the ICCPR on all cases of armed conflict by the merest judicial fiat.

The practical applications of the ICCPR to the combat situations that the United States faces in the conflict with al Qaeda – so far as the ICJ can be understood to give any intelligible instruction on those matters at all – are absurd. It would seem, for example, that the US military would have an obligation to have arrested al-Harethi, even at some risk to its own personnel, had that been feasible, rather than to have fired on him. As we have seen, the LOAC has never laid down such a rule; on the contrary, enemy combatants may lawfully be attacked, whatever the circumstances in which they are found. If the Special Rapporteur is right, however, IHRL would apparently forbid the United States to kill even Osama bin Laden while he was asleep or at breakfast, if by some undefined standard there was some chance of capturing him alive.

The United States might well prefer to capture high-value al Qaeda targets alive, rather than killing them. For one thing, such captives could well yield intelligence information of extraordinary importance; for another, their capture would prevent them from being considered "martyrs;" for a third, if they were killed rather than captured, doubts might well arise whether the United States had identified them correctly. But in the remote regions of Yemen and Pakistan where these targets are likely to be found, capture rather than killing is likely to be a practical impossibility. The circumstances of combat operations may force a choice between the alternatives of killing these targets in a very brief window of opportunity, or letting them escape. In our view, it is a perversion of IHRL to fault the United States for choosing, in those circumstances, to kill them.

Conclusion

Fundamental to both the LOAC and IHRL is the regulation and restraint of state violence. In the case of the LOAC, the law seeks to abate the violence and hardship of armed conflict and to prevent unnecessary suffering, even on the part of the combatants. In the case of IHRL, the law seeks to prevent violence, injustice, and oppression on the part of a state, especially when inflicted on those under its domination and control.

But the state is not the only source of violence. As political theorists have often reminded us, the state exists primarily to *prevent* violence at the hands of foreign enemies and local criminals. Consequently, even constraints on state violence must have their limits, or the state would be unable to perform its indispensable protective functions.

The LOAC and IHRL differ essentially in the nature of the considerations that they recognize as counterweights to the interest in restricting state violence. As a general matter, the LOAC represents an effort to achieve a realistic and sustainable balance between the humanitarian imperatives to avoid or mitigate the hardships, suffering, and death caused by armed conflict and the countervailing imperatives of "military necessity." By contrast, IHRL seeks to equilibrate the state's need to provide security against crime, maintain public order, and administer legal justice to the individual's interests in life, liberty, and property.

The chief error committed by those who seek to merge the LOAC into IHRL is to collapse the balance that the LOAC seeks to achieve into the different kind of balance whose attainment is IHRL's chief objective. As a consequence, the proponents of this idea minimize the extent to which the state may deploy violence as a matter of "military necessity," and maximize the extent to which the state must undertake precautionary legal processes before using force. The conditions of armed conflict (especially, of course, when the life of the nation is at stake) permit and indeed require the state to use force on a scale, of a lethality, and with an intentionality that make it wholly different from the violence that the state may inflict in performing its common policing functions. The failure to acknowledge this fact condemns the project of assimilating the LOAC to IHRL to futility.

The extension of IHRL to armed conflict has also set human rights doctrine on a collision course with itself. On the one hand, there is an emerging IHRL-based doctrine of *jus ad bellum*, called "humanitarian intervention." Under this doctrine, states may or must intervene in the internal affairs of other countries – with or without authorization from the UN Security Council – in order to correct and prevent human rights abuses within those countries. The doctrine of humanitarian intervention underlay Western involvement in several recent armed conflicts, including those in Kosovo (1999) and Somalia (1992), and it played some part (if an incidental or *post hoc* one) in the Second Gulf War (2003). On the other hand, we have seen throughout this chapter that there is an emerging IHRL-based *jus in bello* that would, for instance, make the lethal targeting of enemy combatants far more problematic than it is under the ordinary rules of the law of war. To put the matter starkly, then, the conflict between the two emerging branches of IHRL is this: on the one hand, it drives nations into wars to vindicate human rights; on the other hand, it makes it harder to fight and win those wars.

Finally, the extension of IHRL to armed conflict may have significant consequences for the success of international law in advancing global welfare. Rules of the LOAC represent the delicate balancing between the imperatives of combat and humanitarian goals in wartime. The LOAC has been remarkably successful in achieving compliance from nations at war in obeying these rules. This is most likely due to the reciprocal nature of the obligations involved. Nations treat prisoners of war well in order to guarantee that their own captive soldiers will be treated well by the enemy; nations will refrain from using weapons of mass destruction because they are deterred by their enemy's possession of the same weapons. It has been one of the triumphs of international law to increase the restrictions on the use of unnecessarily destructive and cruel weapons, and to advance the norms of distinction and the humane treatment of combatants and civilians in wartime.

IHRL norms, on the other hand, may suffer from much lower rates of compliance. This may be due, in part, to the non-reciprocal nature of the obligations. One nation's refusal to observe freedom of speech, for example, will not cause another country to respond by depriving its own citizens of their rights. If IHRL norms, which were developed without much, if any, consideration of the imperatives of combat, merge into the LOAC, it will be likely that compliance with international law will decline. If nations must balance their security needs against ever more restrictive and out-of-place international rules supplied by IHRL, we hazard the guess that the latter will give way. Rather than attempt to superimpose rules for peacetime civilian affairs onto the unique circumstances of the war on terror, a better strategy for encouraging compliance with international law would be to adapt the legal system already specifically designed for armed conflict.

References

Adalah v. GOC Central Command IDF. 2005. At: http://www.icrc.org/ihl-nat.nsf/0/7FFDDA5378172C9CC12573870052330F.

Al-Jedda v. Sect'y of State for Defence. 2007. UKHL 58. At: http://www.parliament.the-stationery-office.co.uk/pa/ld200708/ldjudgmt/jd071212/jedda-1.htm.

Al-Skeini et al. v. Sect'y of State for Defence. 2008. 1 A.C. 153, 204 [2007] UKHL 26, U.K. House of Lords 2007.

Alston, Phillip, Jason Morgan-Foster, and William Abresch. 2008. "The Competence of the UN Human Rights Council and Its Special Procedures in Relation to Armed Conflicts: Extrajudicial Executions in the 'War on Terror.'" *European Journal of International Law*, Vol. 19.

Bello, Judith Hippler, Juliane Kokott, and Beate Rudolf. 1996. *"Loizidou v. Turkey." American Journal of International Law*, Vol. 90.

Buergenthal, Thomas. 1981. "To Respect and to Ensure: State Obligations and Permissible Derogations." In Louis Henkin, ed., *The International Bill of Rights: The Covenant on Civil and Political Rights* (New York: Columbia University Press).

Convention on Cluster Munitions. 2008. At: http://www.icrc.org/web/eng/siteeng0.nsf/html/cluster-munitions-news-290508!OpenDocument.

Convention on the Prevention and Punishment of the Crime of Genocide. 1948. 78 U.N.T.S. 277, 9 December.

Convention Relative to the Treatment of Prisoners of War. 1929. At: http://www.icrc.org/ihl.nsf/FULL/305?OpenDocument.

Convention (IV) Respecting the Laws and Customs of War on Land and its Annex: Regulations Concerning the Laws and Customs of War on Land. 1907. At: http://www.icrc.org/ihl.nsf/385ec082b509e76c4125 6739003e636d/1d1726425f6955aec125641e0038bfd6.

Declaration Renouncing the Use, in Time of War, of Explosive Projectiles Under 400 Grammes Weight. 1868. At: http://www.icrc.org/ihl.nsf/FULL/130?OpenDocument.

Dennis, Michael J. 2005. "Application of Human Rights Treaties Extraterritorially in Times of Armed Conflict and Military Occupation." *American Journal of International Law*, Vol. 99.

Dinstein, Yoram. 2002. "Legitimate Military Objectives Under the Current *jus in bello." International Legal Studies*, Vol. 78.

Doswald-Beck, Louise. 2006. "The Right to Life in Armed Conflict: Does International Humanitarian Law Provide All the Answers?" *International Review of the Red Cross*, Vol. 88, No. 864.

Draper, G. I. A. D. 1979. *Humanitarian Law and Human Rights*. Acta Juridica.

Geneva Convention for the Amelioration of the Condition of the Sick and Wounded of Armies in the Field. 1864. At: http://www.jstor.org/pss/2212368.

Geneva Convention Relative to the Treatment of Prisoners of War. 1949. 6 U.N.T.S. 3316, T.I.A.S. No. 3364. At: http://www.icrc.org/Web/Eng/siteeng0.nsf/htmlall/genevaconventions.

Human Rights Committee. 2004. *Nature of the General Legal Obligation on States Parties to the Covenant*. U.N. Doc. CCPR/C/21/Rev.1/Add.13. At: http://www1.umn.edu/humanrts/gencomm/hrcom31.html.

Instructions for the Government of Armies of the United States in the Field (Lieber Code). 1863. At: http://www.icrc.org/ihl.nsf/FULL/110?OpenDocument.

International Covenant on Civil and Political Rights. 1966. 999 U.N.T.S. 171, 16 December.

International Covenant on Economic, Social and Cultural Rights. 1966. United Nations, Treaty Series, vol. 993, p. 3. At: http://www.unhcr.org/refworld/docid/3ae6b36c0.html.

NATO. 2001. "Statement by the North Atlantic Council on Collective Defense," 12 September.

Nowak, Manfred. 2005. *U.N. Covenant on Civil and Political Rights: CCPR Commentary*. 2nd edn (Kehl am Rhein, Germany: Engel).

Parks, W. Hays. 1992. *Memorandum of Law: The Legality of Snipers*. Dept. of the Army Pamphlet 27-50-241, 1992-DECD Army Law.

Pictet, Jean. 1975. *Humanitarian Law and the Protection of War Victims* (Geneva: Henry Dunant Institute).

Proclamation of Teheran, Final Act of the International Conference on Human Rights. 1968. Teheran, U.N. Doc. A/CONF.32/41.

Protocol Additional to the Geneva Conventions of August 12, 1949, and Relating to the Protection of Victims of International Armed Conflicts. 1977a. 16 I.L.M. 1391. At: http://www.icrc.org/Web/Eng/siteeng0.nsf/htmlall/genevaconventions.

Protocol Additional to the Geneva Conventions of August 12, 1949, and Relating to the Protection of Victims of Non-International Armed Conflicts. 1977b. 16 I.L.M. 1442. At: http://www.icrc.org/Web/Eng/siteeng0.nsf/htmlall/genevaconventions.

Report of the Special Rapporteur, on Extrajudicial, Summary or Arbitrary Executions. 2004. United Nations Economic and Social Council, Commission on Human Rights, E/CN.4/2004/7/Add.1, 24 March.

Rousseau, Jean-Jacques. 1762. *The Social Contract.* Trans. G. D. H. Cole. N.p.
Sale v. Haitian Centers Council, Inc. 1993. 509 U.S. 155, 183.
Schindler, Dietrich. 1982. "Human Rights and Humanitarian Law: Interrelationship of the Laws." *American University Law Review*, Vol. 31.
Schindler, Dietrich. 1999. *Significance of the Geneva Conventions for the Contemporary World.* 1999. Int'l Rev. Red Cross no. 836. 31 December.
Tennessee v. Garner. 1985. 471 U.S. 1.
United States v. Kirby. 1868. 74 U.S. 482, 486–487.
UN Security Council. 2001a. *Res. 1368*, 12 September.
UN Security Council. 2001b. *Res. 1373*, 28 September.
US Congress. 2001. *Authorization for the Use of Military Force*, Pub. L. No. 107–40, 115 Stat. 224.
Watkin, Kenneth. 2004. "Controlling the Use of Force: A Role for Human Rights Norms in Contemporary Armed Conflict." *American Journal of International Law*, Vol. 98, No. 1.

Part VII
Narrative and aesthetic dimensions of human rights

54

Cultures of rescue and the global transit in human rights narratives

Sidonie Smith

> The social fields in which human rights are violated are complex beyond the understanding of any one view or discipline.
>
> *(Farmer 2003, p. 12)*

> The human rights narrative arrives pre-encoded as a conduit into history – through its relay of the invisible or the unthinkable, through mourning, through the ordeal of its very enunciation and inscription. Thus it functions as a medium for historicity, but a medium that interposes itself between the witness, reader, auditor, adjudicator, and anamnesis. The testimony has a double density and *gravitas* due to its historiographical vocation and artifactual status; it is a window of historical visualization and also a historical object, midwifed from materialities of pain and suffering.
>
> *(Feldman 2004, p. 164)*

> I knew just one Little School, but throughout our continent there are many 'schools' whose professors use the lessons of torture and humiliation to teach us to lose the memories of ourselves. Beware: in little schools the boundaries between story and history are so subtle that even I can hardly find them.
>
> *(Partnoy 1986, p. 18)*

Conduits of inquiry

How do we enter a discussion of "human rights narratives"? Cautiously and respectfully, acknowledging Paul Farmer's observation about the complexity of "the social fields in which human rights are violated" and, I would add, in which that violation is witnessed and made public. Do we start with an emphasis on "human rights" as a contemporary regime for addressing radical suffering and injustice? Witness testimony provides an evidentiary ground for recording, naming, and intervening in conditions that are framed and presented as human rights violations by survivors, activists, and institutional players in the United Nations and member states. To approach human rights narratives from this perspective is to apply a narrow definition: they are narratives told by first-person witnesses enduring the aftereffects of terror and trauma who explicitly invoke human rights discourse. Produced and circulated within human rights institutions and contexts of activism, they include field reports, testimony transcribed from truth and reconciliation hearings, child soldier narratives, and the journals of political prisoners smuggled out during or published after incarceration. As sites/scenes of witnessing to radical injury and harm, they can be organized, informally orchestrated, or feral. Some narratives may gain global attention, as did Rigoberta Menchú's *I, Rigoberta Menchú* (1984); others may remain relatively obscure, tucked away in commission reports. They may also be incorporated into collective genres, such as web-based archives and recuperative arts projects (Schaffer and Smith 2004, ch. 2). Reading or listening to these human rights narratives, we might attend to the material conditions of witnessing to injury and harm; or to the structural conditions of giving testimony within networks of human rights activisms; or to the conventions of story forms emerging from particular histories of violation, the Holocaust, apartheid in South Africa, the cultural revolution in China, the Tiananmen resistance movement in China, or the Rwandan genocide.

Or do we place emphasis on "narratives," enlarging our catchment to encompass heterogeneous genres engaging histories and personal experiences of violence and suffering? In this case, we could define "narrative" expansively to incorporate multiple media – novels, plays, memoirs, and testimony, but also documentary film, graphic memoir, experimental cinema, performance art, photography, installations, blogs, and so on. As Elizabeth Goldberg observes, such literary, filmic, graphic, performance, and virtual narratives may be produced and/or performed by first-person witnesses but are often produced and/or performed by second-person witnesses, artists/writers/film makers who are removed in time and location from conditions and events of rights violations and who thus produce what Goldberg terms "distanced-observer witness" narratives (2007, p. 153). In focusing on heterogeneous genres and media of human rights narratives, we confront vexing questions raised by the different work genres do in addressing the "crisis in representation" hovering over and permeating sites of radical violence – what Allen Feldman above terms the "relay of the invisible or the unthinkable" and Alicia Partnoy describes as a confusion of memory and loss of both story and history. We can parse the relation of genres to particular histories of violence, torture, or rape, for instance. We can parse the distinct circuits of address various genres direct toward readers/viewers in their effort to enlist empathetic identification or active engagement with struggles for justice. We can track the effects of remediation as representations and stories take shape across different media. We can probe the ethics of aestheticizing suffering and survival.

Do we enter by placing emphasis on the "narrative" told by human rights instruments, documents, and discourses? In this case, we could produce a narrative about the debates circulating around human rights politics, producing close readings of such theorists as Mahatma Ghandi, Hannah Arendt, Judith Butler, or Pheng Cheah, among others. In this vein, Joseph Slaughter tells a wonderful story of that conjunction, explicating to great effect the discussion of Daniel Defoe's *Robinson Crusoe* that took place in debates about the human personality as delegates hammered out the founding documents of the contemporary human rights regime in the decade after World War II (Slaughter 2007, ch. 1). We could stretch our timeline further back, taking an expansive view of genres and an expansive view of temporality. We might turn to Michel de Montaigne's "Des cannibals," which engages questions of the status of the human in the contact zones of global exploration and conquest, or Álvar Núñez Cabeza de Vaca's *La Relación*, first published in 1542, a narrative of exploration that both accounted for the indigenous communities in the "New World" and critiqued the degradation, dehumanization, and aggression conquistadores visited on native peoples (The Cabeza de Vaca Relación Digitization and Access Project).

Coming forward in time, we might ponder the ways in which forms of the literary projected the relationship of persons to "the human" and "the state" as a post-Enlightenment project. In which case we might go back to the French and American revolutionary periods and the European *Bildungsroman*, as Slaughter does when he reads the *Bildungsroman* as "a sort of novelistic wing of human rights" (2007, p. 25). Approaching human rights law and the *Bildungsroman* as "mutually enabling fictions," Slaughter tracks "the conceptual vocabulary, deep narrative grammar, and humanist social vision that human rights law shares with the *Bildungsroman* in their cooperative efforts to imagine, normalize, and realize what the UDHR and early theorists of the novel call 'the free and full development of the human personality'" (2007, p. 4). Barbara Harlow had remarked on the politics of the *Bildungsroman* form and its projection of the normalization of a particular form of individualized subjectivity. Slaughter uses Harlow's argument as a starting point to elaborate this relationship by bringing the same kind of close reading to the discourses of human rights as he does to the postcolonial novels he puts in dialogue with that discourse. We learn how to be subjects of rights through such activities as reading realist novels of incorporation for the "realist" novel form of *Bildungsroman* itself narrates the story of incorporation of the individual into the social sphere of the nation-state. In other words, "the *Bildungsroman* and human rights are cooperative technologies of incorporation whose historic social work was to patriate the once politically marginal bourgeois subject as national citizen" (Slaughter 2007, p. 166). The legacies of this mutually sustaining relationship can be seen in the contemporary postcolonial novel and its projection of the politics of reading. Writing and reading the *Bildungsroman* written since the 1940s, within Europe and North America and within dispersed global locations around the world undergoing uneven processes of decolonization and globalization, becomes part of the process by which contemporary subjects imagine themselves incorporated into a global imaginary of universal rights and responsibilities. For Slaughter, contemporary postcolonial iterations of the *Bildungsroman* form, emerging from dispersed global locations (e.g., South Africa, Canada–Sri Lanka, Zimbabwe, and Chile), invoke, reinterpret, and expose the paradoxes at the heart of the form in confronting state violence and the geopolitics of colonialism's afterlives. This is to put contemporary novel forms in intimate conversation with human rights discourse and its long history.

The long view on human rights narratives can be understood as a project of re-archivization. Narratives from an earlier moment are reread as rights narratives after subsequent events and cultural forms focus attention on particular histories, subject positions, conditions of enunciation, and the politics of claiming a voice and the authority to write counter-history. In the United States, eighteenth- and nineteenth-century slave narratives and twentieth-century prison memoirs of black activists from the 1960s and 1970s have been rehistoricized as episodes of rights narration. In Australia, Sally Morgan's widely read narrative of discovering and recuperating the story of her mother's and grandmother's indigenous identity and heritage, *My Place* (1987), was rearchived as a story of the "Stolen Generation" after the special 1997 Human Rights Commission Inquiry into the Stolen Generation. Emerging from the activism mobilized during the United Nations Decade of Indigenous Peoples, that inquiry brought broad public attention to the hidden history of the Australian government's policy of forced removal of mixed-race children from their families and communities. This expansive definition of human rights narratives renders the past elastic, as scholar/activists put the past under a new definition.

In addition to larger questions of definition and framing, human rights narratives present us with a proliferation of questions. Do we approach human rights narratives as story scripts? Or do we see them as social action, critical for the function they serve as opposed to the form they take? Do we see them as sites of agency, of telling otherwise, thus offering alternative jurisdictions, in Leigh Gilmore's (2003) phrasing, to official juridical scenes of adjudication?

Or do we see them as organized, tamed, reframed, and constrained within the institutions and protocols of contemporary human rights witnessing? Do we see them as one story form in the larger, global traffic in narratives? Or as complicit vehicles of Western hegemony and neoliberal ideology?

Having entered a particular narrative, whether as genre or act, where do we direct attention? To the witnessing subject? Do we explore the conditions of witnessing, including who becomes a witness and how witnessing to radical injury and harm is related to identity statuses (gender, ethnicity, sexuality, race, religion, etc.), their lived realities and their discursive construction? Or do we hone in on the narrator and the rhetoric of his or her rights claims? Or the psychic mechanisms of giving an account? Or the intersubjectivity of sites of witness binding first- and proximate or distant second-person witnesses? Do we think of the witness as part of an ensemble of participants in multiple locations of activity? In this case, we might ponder the relationship of the witness to the proximate interlocutor. Or to the addressee (or reader/listener) of the narrative projects. Or the paratextual apparatuses that situate and authenticate the narrative. Or the agents, publishers, marketers, and pundits who commodify the narrative, aid in its circulation, and proffer initial readings for the public. Or the distant reader, sitting alone with a material book or listening on a podcast. Or the reading communities to which texts are directed and marketed and through which narrative meanings and calls to action are activated.

Do we shift our term of reference to "discourse," which would be to explore how narratives deploy, reference, represent, and circulate the languages of rights, the human, and the state? To do so would shift focus to discourses of human rights inflecting acts of narration and the subject positions those discourses instantiate – victim, perpetrator, and more recently beneficiary, and to differentiated figures of victimage: "the refugee," "the child," the "child soldier," the "comfort woman."

Do we begin our discussion with issues of forgetting and remembering (or amnesia and anamnesis)? Here the focus turns to the afterlife of events in the past on survivors – leading to the formulation of theories of traumatic remembering (e.g., Caruth 1995; Felman and Laub 1992). Or to "textual traumata," to use Deborah Staines's (2008) term, those textual gaps or disjunctions or stutters that signal eruptions of some uncontained, unprocessed past? Or to the psychic processes associated with shaping and telling, to forms of what Suzette Henke (1998) calls "scriptotherapy"? Or, stepping back from the neuroscience or psychoanalysis of remembering and from the text and from the act of telling as impossible in the face of the crisis of representation, do we probe the limits of the reparative project of therapeusis as the primary pathway to survival in the wake of traumatic suffering and loss? With this move to put pressure on Western theories and practices of therapeusis, we might register that potential violence of the terms of cure themselves, as Alan Feldman (2004) does in his exploration of the trauma aesthetic he observed at work in the Truth and Reconciliation Commission hearings in South Africa. In those compelling scenes of witness, Feldman problematized the restaging of the scene of asymmetrical power that joins victim and perpetrator. Or we might consider what the project of therapeusis occludes of the other ways through which individuals and communities cope with the afterlife of violence and harm, alternative forms of memorializing and recovery. Which would prompt inquiries into overlapping, disjunctive, and heterogeneous kinds of memory – individual, collective, generational, national, impersonal.

What is our methodology? Is our project one of deep reading? Is our analysis psychoanalytically focused on psychic processes as and in narrative? Is it a project of rhetorical analysis? Or materialist analysis of the book or performance, the production, and the circulation of human rights narratives? Is our approach one of cultural studies, exploring how it is that human rights narratives intersect with the global traffic in stereotypes or the global traffic in rights literacies?

Does our methodology involve qualitative research into the lived experiences of surviving and writing about violence or qualitative research into how readers respond to human rights narratives? And what theoretical terms or concepts organize and nuance our explorations of human rights narratives? Traumatic rupture. Spectacles of witnessing. The ethics of empathetic identification. The ethics of fictionalizing (Goldberg 2007). Metrics of authenticity (Hua Hsu 2009). Rhetorics of unsettlement (Hesford 2004). Opacity and the conditions of accountability (Butler 2005). Fables of incorporation (Slaughter 2007). Remediation as afterlife. Sober truth. The sentimental hinge (Howard 2007; Berlant 2008). Psychic wounds and jurisdictions (Gilmore 2003). The scandal of the hoax. The trauma aesthetic (Feldman 2004). Truth claims and truth effects. The alterity industry; the traffic in stereotypes; soft weapons (Whitlock 2006). Idioms of agency (Butler 2005). Sedimented history and contingent agency (Agrawal n.d.). Cultures of rescue.

I have extended this series of questions as a way of surveying for readers from diverse disciplines the definitional, generic, textual, theoretical, and methodological foci characterizing current approaches to "human rights narration." The field of human rights and literature roils with these confounding questions, evidenced in the work of the last decade, the books, special journal issues, and articles directing scholarly and activist attention to narratives of radical injury and harm and their afterlives in the contemporary regime of human rights. Among noteworthy books are the following: Judith Butler, *Giving an Account of Oneself* (2005); Anne Cubilié, *Women Witnessing Terror* (2005); James Dawes, *That the World May Know* (2007); Elizabeth Swanson Goldberg, *Beyond Terror: Gender, Narrative, Human Rights* (2007); Kay Schaffer and Sidonie Smith, *Human Rights and Narrated Lives: The Ethics of Recognition* (2004); Joseph Slaughter, *Human Rights, Inc.: The World Novel, Narrative Form, and International Law* (2007); Gillian Whitlock, *Soft Weapons* (2006); and edited collections, among them Wendy S. Hesford and Wendy Kozol's *Just Advocacy* (2005) and Mark Philip Bradley and Patrice Petro's *Truth Claims: Representation and Human Rights* (2002).

As a way to move from the level of generative questions motivating studies of human rights narratives to a more focused discussion, I turn now to one of the theoretical phrases introduced above – cultures of rescue – as a productive phrase for thinking about questions of agency and commodification that trouble our understanding of the affect, efficacy, and ethics of narration in the context of the global regime of human rights.

Reading and rescue

The contemporary regime of human rights, as Farmer (2003) observes, operates to address and manage injustice, the violence and discrimination directed at the marginalized and disempowered around the world by states and their agents. This arena of rights management sustains and is supported by the cultures of the four Rs – rescue, repair, redress, and reconciliation. Rescue is the operative term for my purposes here. The rescue agenda takes shape and unfolds through official UN and member state bodies and through organized networks and less-hierarchical meshworks of non-governmental organizations (NGOs). Official bodies and NGOs seek to mobilize international outrage and pressure political actors to intervene. To gain traction for a cause in the wider public, advocates try to mobilize people as activists, and they depend upon people to imagine themselves as world citizens and potential rescuers of those suffering elsewhere. Human rights narratives, narrowly and broadly defined, aid in this project. But, we might ask, what is the object of rescue, for the project of rescue is multilayered? Victims certainly: men, women, and children suffering the everyday injustices of repressive regimes, political dissidents within states, victims of horrific events such a genocide or extended eruptions of violence.

But what else is being rescued: memory, history, childhood, life itself? And the foundational tenets of human rights, the concept of "the free and full development of the human personality," the human community. And who is doing the rescue? An ensemble of actors (real, rhetorical, virtual): the witness, the imagined addressee, real listeners and readers (primarily in developed nations), publishers, state agents, NGO personnel, United Nations personnel and entities. All of these actors can be positioned as rescuers through the processes and products of human rights narration and its circulation.

Consideration of two human rights narratives, one written and published first in the former Bosnia, the other written and first published in Uttar Pradesh, India, prompt us to rethink cultures of rescue. The first returns us to the war in Bosnia in the early and mid-1990s and the publication of Zlata Filopević's diary. I have written elsewhere on "*Zlata's Diary* and the Circulation of Stories of Suffering Ethnicity" (Smith 2006); in that essay I was particularly interested in thinking about how genres of the witnessing are implicated in the management of salient ethnicities as circulated through the sentimental politics of the human rights regime. Here I want to focus briefly on the politics of rescue played out in the diary and with the diary.

Zlata Filopović began keeping a diary of everyday life in Sarajevo in September of 1991 and continued her diary writing for two years as the siege gained a stranglehold on the inhabitants of the formerly cosmopolitan and multiethnic city. Filopević's diary chronicles the daily experiences and thoughts of a middle-class teenager conversant in global teen culture and anxious about the survival of her family as they are inexorably impacted by the conditions of life under siege. In the summer of 1993, the teenager submitted her diary to one of her teachers who then sought and found sponsorship for its publication through the International Centre for Peace. Upon publication, journalists covering the war attached the aura of celebrity to the young girl, labeling her the "Anne Frank of Sarajevo." Features of the diary itself suggest that even before publication Filopević had modeled herself as a kind of latter-day Anne Frank under duress: the diarist/narrator refers directly to Frank, and the diary reproduces a rhetorical address of diarist to interlocutor/friend similar to Frank's rhetorical address (in this case "Mimi" to Frank's "Kitty"). Within months, just before Christmas 1993, Filopević and her parents were flown from Sarajevo to Paris. That flight out of the war zone was facilitated by a French photographer and funded by the French publisher of the diary, Le Robert Laffont-Fixot. In France the diary appeared in early 1994 as *Journal de Zlata*. From France the diary traveled to the United States, where it was published by Viking (after a bid of $560,000) and appeared as *Zlata's Diary: A Child's Life in Sarajevo*. The introduction by journalist Janine di Giovanni produces an interpretation of the diary for the reader.

Packaged and marketed for a global audience (with intimate photographs of Zlata in wartime and facsimiles of pages from the original handwritten diary), the "Zlata" of the published book becomes the quintessential sentimental witness, commodified as a figure of middle-class adolescence, an innocent victim whose childhood is stolen from her by anonymous adult politicians. Here as elsewhere, "the child" becomes the witness par excellence of rights abuses because the child is positioned as a truly needy and innocent victim and because the child's act of witnessing appears uncontaminatedly transparent. This apparent innocence and transparency function as (almost) unassailable "metrics of authenticity" (Hsu and Lincoln 2009) in the project of documenting harm. The child, childhood, and this child "Zlata" are all in need of rescue. A series of rescues thus characterizes this scene of human rights witnessing. The diary is rescued from obscurity by its publication (three times). But it is also rescued from obscurity by its attachment to the predecessor diary, that of Anne Frank. The teenager and her parents are literally rescued from the war zone. In her introduction, di Giovanni shames the reader for his/her inattention to the events in Bosnia, exhorting Westerners to demand rescue – of childhood and Bosnia.

Filopević's flight from Sarajevo in December 1993 makes rescuers of a teacher, photographer, and publishers in France and the United States, and eventually of hundreds of thousands of students in the United States who subsequently read the story of "Zlata" in the 1990s because of its incorporation into secondary school lesson plans. Teachers thus educated young Americans about "human rights" through a reading praxis encouraging affective identification across transnational difference. Critically, the Croatian-Bosnian "Zlata," situated as a modern-day Anne Frank, is read through the projection of "sameness" in a diaristic record of globalized adolescence interrupted. The diary's projection of the abstract universality of cosmopolitan adolescence under attack – in the US edition Filopević's ethnicity goes unremarked – facilitates empathetic identification and makes childhood rescuers of hundreds of thousands of school children. The sentimental rescue of Zlata Filopović through thousands of readings, with assurances that unlike Anne Frank this girl survived with her diary, plays out and obscures the realpolitik of rescue involved in the commodification of sentimentalized suffering within the transnational "alterity industry" (Whitlock 2006). Ultimately at these scenes of adolescent reading, sentimentalized rescue unfolds as singularity and invites what Hsuan L. Hsu and Martha Lincoln (2009) refer to as "individual altruistic action" on the part of readers.

How might personal witnessing within the culture of rescue evade asymmetrical power relations joining rescued to rescuer, avoid the singularizing of suffering in pursuit of structural analysis, and short-circuit the feel-good sentimentality of rescue reading? Let me turn to a collective human rights narrative that performs the hard labor of self-rescue, the 2004 book, published by the University of Minnesota Press in 2006 as *Playing with Fire: Feminist Thought and Activism through Seven Lives in India* by the Sangtin Writers and Richa Nagar. The Sangtin Yatra (parsed as "a term of solidarity, of reciprocity, of enduring friendship among women") comprises a group of seven women who at the time of composition were employed as rural field workers for an NGO in Uttar Pradesh, India, addressing domestic violence and the human rights of women in local communities. Over the course of several years, they came together outside the workplace to explore their personal histories and develop a fuller analysis of the intersection of various kinds of violence, not only sexism but also caste-ism, class antagonism, and religious antagonism.

As an intervention in contemporary human rights politics, the Sangtin project of self-rescue is to produce knowledge about rural women activists working for an NGO and to constitute the women as knowledge makers claiming their authority to "talk back" to the elite women running the NGO. The seven Sangtin women act to resist becoming exemplary or evidentiary subjects, victims in need of rescue by the more privileged leaders in the NGO. To remain in that position is to be dispossessed of their stories, to be consigned to the subject position of the "raw" subject, uninformed, incapable of producing usable analysis (see Watson 2008). To shift from "victim" position to position of agent, the seven Sangtin authors begin with diary writing. But the individual diaristic record of their experiences as field workers is not the end of the writing process; it is the starting point. Their process brings them together to share their writing and revise their understanding of experience as a result of collective analysis. Richa Singh, one of the elite women of the NGO, joins the women in their discussions of their diary entries and the analysis those entries prompt. Sociologist Richa Nagar serves as a compiler, drafting a version of the conversations and revising them after review by the women. She also does the labor of situating the experiences the women analyze in the contexts of global formations, such as neoliberal economics. Through this extended engagement with diary writing and rewriting, the Sangtin women produce structural analysis of the experience of being a woman in the family, community, and nation by analyzing the making of "woman" as disempowered, unvalued, and suspect. They also produce intersectional analysis that links gender with other experiential axes, such as economics, politics, sexuality, religion, class, and caste, and links women relationally to others.

Ultimately, the "book" that we hold in our hands resists sentimentalized rescue-reading. For one, it incorporates multiple texts, thereby destabilizing the prioritizing of an original, authentic victim narrative. These layers include traces of the original diaries that are present as epigraphs to some of the chapters and in quotes within various sections; the edited transcript of the oral engagement of the group with the diaries; the drafts of the group discussions; the overlay of redrafting, as in the additions made when the women decide they need to remember happy moments of childhood; the first completed version of the Sangtin Yatra published in Hindi in India; the translated *Playing with Fire* published in English by a university press in the USA, which includes an introduction and postscript by Nagar, the former presenting the project and the latter describing the controversy that erupted after the book's publication in India. The effect of this multiplicity of sites and levels of narration is to render this human rights narrative anything but transparent: it does not emanate from any one place; its immediacy is constantly mediated by successive overlays; its "truth to experience" continually renegotiated.

Second, the referent of the text produced is not an intimate "I" of a victim, the common figure of attachment in rescue-reading. Throughout *Playing with Fire*, the characterization of the individual women remains minimal; what is narrated is women writing and analyzing in relation – the situating of the person in the context of social strictures, norms, and identities. Throughout the "authors" introduce phrases in quotes attributed to "the community" – so that the individual can be understood as a social subject of communal norms. And the text performs this relationality through its "blended but fractured we" (Sangtin Writers 2006, p. xxxiv): sometimes the "we" of the seven diary writers, sometimes the "we" of the eight activists in the NGO, sometimes the "we" of those eight activists and the sociologist Richa Nagar, the nine members of the Sangtin. Julia Watson observes that "*Playing with Fire* centers on the telling of life stories as a process not just of meaning-making but of creating an unstable and dialogic 'we' defined by both its blending and its fissures" (2008). As this unstable "we" owns the narrative of its members and produces collective knowledge, a gap opens between the "we" of narration in the finished text and the prior diary writing of the individual Sangtin members, which is re-scripted through third person narration. "I," "she," and "we" shift continually as the "text" speaks its collective knowledge through three disjunctive yet overlapping discursive modes: the narrative, informational, and analytical. The individual life provides the evidentiary ground of the analysis but is not the end. The goal is methodological, the pursuit of structural analysis grounded in the experiential. Both the privileging of method and the hybridity of the product unsettle the culture of rescue by forestalling empathy and identification. There is no singular narrative center of victimization to which readers can affectively bind. The "fractured we," with its slippery personal pronouns, textual layers, and discursive disjunctions, unsettles this identification.

Third, this hybrid autoethnography often routes self-rescue through sentimentality, but does so in such a way as to extend the distance between the "fractured we" and the reader. Throughout a corporate project reaching toward structural analysis, sentimental metaphors and clichés are woven into the seven field workers' descriptions of their lives and those of their co-writers. In part, these tropes and clichés reference oral forms of communication and communal norms of exchange. Yet it becomes clear that sentimental tropes and clichés become a way of sharing emotion, valuing the affective dimension of the experience being narrated, and communicating the feeling of the past. Moreover, the collective invocation of sentimental metaphors and clichés binds the women as a collective "we," a "we" sharing the densities of common affect as well as critical analysis of differences. Indeed, *Playing with Fire* affirms an important role for sentimentality in projects aiming beyond the individual story of victimization to structural analysis. The text at once circulates a discourse of sentimentality and displaces sentimentality through structural analysis, and in this way severs the reader from too easy access to an unproblematic identification across difference.

"Conceiv[ing] life writing as a practice sharable among the marginally literate and across levels of literacy and social access" (Watson 2008), *Playing with Fire* as project and product ultimately disentangles the women from the subject position of victim without agency. In this way both project and product make an intervention in the field of human rights activism by rerouting human rights narration from the logic of rescue. Indeed, *Playing with Fire* mounts a sustained critique of the ways in which a culture of rescue informs the human rights regime and feminist NGOs active in rights work. The Sangtin writers have taken the knowledge they produced through their collective ethnography to the field as organizers of improverished, illiterate, and marginalized men and women. In a subsequent essay written with Richa Nagar, several of the Sangtin writers call for rights work to eschew identitarian rights politics:

> When women's issues are collapsed into a pre-designated gender and a pre-marked body, and "feminist activism" is gathered and piled into a predetermined list of issues, and when a complex political and cultural economy at local and global scales becomes associated with such a classification, feminism becomes an institutionalized structure, a bureaucracy, and a commerce that feeds the status quo. A compartmentalization of poverty and violence along the lines of gender helps sustain the existing caste- and class-based structures of privilege and deprivation.
>
> *(Sangtin Writers 2010, p. 26)*

In Uttar Pradesh the Sangtin writers continue to participate in debates about the management practices of rescue "feminism." Elsewhere the published book circulates this local project to metropolitan centers and to classrooms in developed countries exporting the culture of rescue. There its project may well unsettle the affective yoking of sentimental attachment and victim storytelling by raising vexing questions about how to participate in cultures of justice-making ethically, without reproducing the justificatory tropes of neediness and victimization.

Conclusion: structure, agency, narrative

One could imagine eschewing the commodification of witness testimony as a way to challenge the stranglehold of sentimental politics in the culture of rescue. Indeed, new technologies of rescue may well be working in this direction. They now include remote sensing technologies, increasingly used in documenting massive rights violations and the movements of populations fleeing from the destruction of homes and communities. As Andrew Hersher (2009) observes, the technology of remote sensing has turned satellites into "prostheses" in the "human sensorium," promising greater capacity to "detect" and respond to human rights violations. With global positioning technology everyone at a computer terminal linked to the Internet can turn surveillance techniques into tools for the advancement of justice and for intervention in sites of violence. But, Hersher cautions, such technology of documentation has the paradoxical effect of throwing into question the fundamental belief in the authority of the human being on the ground to make claims of violation. Indeed, Hersher cautions that what is new to human rights advocacy, the utilization of remote sensing and satellite photography, is its "depletion" – rhetorically and materially – of the authority of human beings to witness to traumatic violence. Remote sensing, used to confirm evidence on the ground, ends up calling that on-the-ground evidence of witnessing into question. "Its existence," he concludes, "renders the evidence unprovable on its own terms." Its status as "proof-positive" thus remakes testimony as "inadequate proof." This turn to the prosthetic of remote sensing shifts notions of objectivity: the truth of the witness is replaced by the truth of the satellite.

On the ground, of course, the work of witnessing remains a messy affair. Human rights narratives ground rights activism. But they also draw charges of false witnessing, for, as Anne Cubilié notes: "the practice of testimony will [n]ever be free of controversies over questions of historical veracity and ideological motivation" (2004, p. 8). Scandals erupt periodically, calling into question the authenticity and veracity of best-selling human rights narratives circulating in the developed world. Rigoberta Menchú's *I, Rigoberta Menchú* (1984) and Ishmael Beah's *A Long Way Gone* (2008) are just two of the most publicized instances of challenge. On the ground, too, the arenas of rescue subject survivors of violence and rights abuses of all kinds to scenes of re-victimization – before those responsible for carrying out violence, through repeated activist requests for testimonials of degradation, through suspicions directed at survivors by parties invested in continued silence about conditions of abuse. On the ground, too, human rights narratives become "soft weapons" (Whitlock 2006) serving Western interests and abetting the traffic in stereotypes. Whitlock elaborates how the memoirs by Iranian women exiles published in the West circulate versions of beset womanhood under Islam to readers ready to condemn the backwardness and barbarity of Middle Eastern cultures and peoples. The cultures of rescue ensure that certain forms of victimization – child soldier narratives, narratives of beset womanhood – become and/or remain salable to a broad public.

Yet, however problematic the contexts of narration, the politics of circulation, and the unpredictability of reception, human rights narratives contribute to an archive, as Feldman (2004) observes. As human rights narratives travel from one audience/reader to another, from one medium to another, from one global location to another, they become at once crisis demand, generic formation, performative act, intersubjective exchange, cultural capital, and transnational traffic. In their complexity, they not only reproduce the sentimental politics of the culture of rescue, they also stage critiques and produce theory about the politics of human rights narration – of the subject, the state, the effects of globalization. They make sustained interventions in the cultures of rescue, as do the Sangtin writers in *Playing with Fire*, by exposing a surfeit of rescue sentiment. Global positioning technologies may help us to see where people are going, how they are displaced, how they wander. The homes and communities they have left behind. But human rights narratives complicate our registers of objectivity. They reveal different metrics of authenticity, integrity, and sincerity; circulate different logics of personhood and different languages of rescue; enter or exit the global traffic in stereotypes unpredictably; expose asymmetrical distributions of power across actors and institutions; travel at different velocities across multiple publics; carry different packaging; and converge in different media. They educate us about the cultures of rescue and the limits of our management of injustice through the human rights regime.

References

Agrawal, Arun. N.d. "Indigenous Knowledge/Power." Unpublished paper.

Beah, Ishmael. 2008. *A Long Way Gone: Memoirs of a Boy Soldier* (New York: Farrar, Straus and Giroux).

Berlant, Lauren. 2008. *The Female Complaint: The Unfinished Business of Sentimentality in American Culture* (Durham, NC: Duke University Press).

Bradley, Mark Philip and Patrice Petro, eds. 2002. *Truth Claims: Representation and Human Rights* (New Brunswick, NJ: Rutgers University Press).

Butler, Judith. 2005. *Giving an Account of Oneself* (New York: Fordham University Press).

Cabeza de Vaca, Álvar Núñez. 1993. *The Account: Álvar Núñez Cabeza de Vaca's Relación*. Trans. Martin A. Favata and José B. Fernández (El Paso, TX: Arte Publico Press).

The Cabeza de Vaca Relación Digitization and Access Project. At: http://alkek.library.txstate.edu/swwc/cdv/project.html.

Caruth, Cathy, ed. 1995. *Trauma: Explorations in Memory*. Baltimore, MD: Johns Hopkins University Press.

Cubilié, Anne. 2004. "Introduction: The Future of Testimony." *Discourse*, Vol. 25, Nos. 1 and 2, pp. 4–18.

Cubilié, Anne. 2005. *Women Witnessing Terror: Testimony and the Cultural Politics of Human Rights* (New York: Fordham University Press).

Dawes, James. 2007. *That the World May Know: Bearing Witness to Atrocity* (Cambridge, MA: Harvard University Press).

Di Giovanni, Janine. 1994. "Introduction," pp. v–xiv in *Zlata's Diary: A Child's Life in Sarajevo* (New York: Penguin).

Farmer, Paul. 2003. *Pathologies of Power: Health, Human Rights, and the New War on the Poor* (Berkeley: University of California Press).

Feldman, Allen. 2004. "Memory Theaters, Virtual Witnessing and the Trauma-Aesthetic." *Biography*, Vol. 27, No. 1, pp. 163–202.

Felman, Shoshana and Dori Laub. 1992. *Testimony: Crises of Witnessing in Literature, Psychoanalysis, and History* (New York: Routledge).

Filopević, Zlata. 1994. *Zlata's Diary: A Child's Life in Sarajevo* (New York: Penguin).

Gilmore, Leigh. 2003. "Jurisdictions: I, Rigoberta Menchú, The Kiss, and Scandalous Self-Representation in the Age of Memoir and Trauma." *Signs*, Vol. 28, No. 2, pp. 695–718.

Goldberg, Elizabeth S. 2007. *Beyond Terror: Gender, Narrative, Human Rights* (New Brunswick, NJ: Rutgers University Press).

Henke, Suzette. 1998. *Shattered Subjects: Trauma and Testimony in Women's Life-Writing* (New York: St. Martin's Press).

Hersher, Andrew. 2009. Paper delivered at the symposium "Translating Testimony: Negotiating Rights across Languages." University of Michigan, November 9.

Hesford, Wendy. 2004. "Documenting Violations: Rhetorical Witnessing and the Spectacle of Distant Suffering." *Biography*, Vol. 27, No. 1, pp. 104–144.

Hesford, Wendy S. and Wendy Kozol, eds. 2005. *Just Advocacy?: Women's Human Rights, Transnational Feminism, and the Politics of Representation* (New Brunswick, NJ: Rutgers University Press).

Howard, June. 2007. "Sentiment," pp. 213–217 in Bruce Burgett and Glenn Hendler, eds., *Keywords for American Cultural Studies* (New York: New York University Press).

Hsu, Hsuan L. and Martha Lincoln. 2009. "Health Media and Global Inequalities." *Daedalus*, spring.

Hua Hsu. 2009. "The Fraud Squad." *Bookforum*, February/March, p. 42.

Menchú, Rigoberta 1984. *I, Rigoberta Menchú: An Indian Woman in Guatemala*. Ed. Elisabeth Burgos-Debray. Trans. Ann Wright (London: Verso).

Montaigne, Michel de. 1958. "Des cannibals." In *The Complete Essays of Montaigne*. Trans. Donald M. Frame (Stanford, CA: Stanford University Press).

Morgan, Sally. 1987. *My Place* (Freemantle: Freemantle Art Museum).

Partnoy, Alicia. 1986. *The Little School: Tales of Disappearance and Survival in Argentina* (San Francisco, CA: Cleis Press).

Sangtin Writers and Richa Nagar. 2006. *Playing with Fire: Feminist Thought and Activism through Seven Lives in India* (Minneapolis: University of Minnesota Press).

Sangtin Writers: Reena, Richa Nagar, Richa Singh, Surbala. 2010. "Still Playing with Fire: Intersectionality, Activism, and NGO-ized Feminism." In *Critical Transnational Feminist Praxis* (Albany: State University of New York Press).

Schaffer, Kay and Sidonie Smith. 2004. *Human Rights and Narrated Lives: The Ethics of Recognition* (New York: Palgrave Macmillan).

Slaughter, Joseph. 2007. *Human Rights, Inc.: The World Novel, Narrative Form, and International Law* (New York: Fordham University Press).

Smith, Sidonie. 2006. "*Zlata's Diary* and the Circulation of Stories of Suffering Ethnicity." *WSQ: Women's Studies Quarterly*. Special issue titled "The Intimate and the Global,"Vol. 34, Nos. 1/2.
Staines, Deborah. 2008. "Textual Traumata: Letters to Lindy Chamberlain." *Life Writing*,Vol. 5, No. 1.
Watson, Julia. 2008. Unpublished paper delivered at the International Auto/Biography Association meeting, University of Hawaii-Manao, June.
Whitlock, Gillian. 2006. *Soft Weapons: Autobiography in Transit* (Chicago: University of Chicago Press).

55

Literature and human rights

Kerry Bystrom

We have on the one hand literature – an expansive category by which we might mean anything from autobiography to literary fiction, poetry, and drama or the acts of reading and storytelling. On the other hand we have human rights, itself a diverse set of legal instruments and political practices as well as an internally variegated social and cultural discourse. What is the relationship between them?

One way to begin to unpack this question is by turning to a frequently cited example. In 1859, Swiss reformer Henry Dunant happened upon the massive destruction caused during the Battle of Solferino in the second Italian War of Independence. This experience prompted him to write *A Memory of Solferino* (1862), a tract that describes from the eyewitness perspective both the scene of the battle and the ensuing attempts made by various parties to care for its sick and dying victims. Calling for the establishment of "relief societies" to aid wounded soldiers and an "international principle" that would support these societies, Dunant's memoir laid the foundation for the establishment of the International Committee of the Red Cross and the adoption of the First Geneva Convention for the Amelioration of the Condition of the Wounded in Armies in the Field (HA UG 1986, 30–31). The Red Cross and the Geneva Conventions, expanded in many ways since their early formation at Dunant's instigation, are often cited today as the respective models for human rights and humanitarian aid work and for international law.

Certainly, one can question the directness of the causal link between the writing of *A Memory of Solferino* and the formation of the Red Cross or the adoption of the First Geneva Convention. Was Dunant's book the *only* reason that these things happened? How did the writing of the book inform, and to what extent was it informed by, Dunant's other activism? How did it intersect with the actions of many others who supported his crusade? Further, one might question the ability of human rights legislation to translate back into political practice. As the policies of extraordinary rendition and torture developed by the US government under the Bush administration show, the social imaginary underlying the Red Cross and the Geneva Accords is not necessarily hegemonic. Nevertheless, Dunant's *A Memory of Solferino* provides "one of the most objectively successful" examples of the power that texts and stories have to influence political imaginations and actions (Slaughter 2009, p. 90). The challenge for human rights activists as well as for students and critics of literature engaged with human rights is to pin down more precisely what that power is, how and why it functions in particular circumstances, and how and why it fails in others.

Instead of providing one overarching theory that resolves this problem, this chapter maps a series of approaches taken by writers, scholars, activists, and writer-scholar-activists. Taking its cue from Dunant, it begins with analyses of the relation between narratives of witness or testimony, international law, and human rights advocacy. The following section examines the telling of personal narratives and the way in which activists shape the stories of others in order to help these "others" claim rights, posing both as potentially helpful acts in human rights campaigns. The chapter then turns to literary fiction. It focuses on fiction rather than drama or poetry in order to supplement other chapters in this collection and because fiction has been the most thoroughly linked to human rights in recent scholarship. Specific prose forms such as the novel historically structured social imaginaries, shaping the way people envisioned their identities, their relation to others, and the boundaries of their communities. Contemporary novels, such as non-fictional narratives of witness, build on this tradition to generate, disseminate, and naturalize new visions of connection and distance between people – tasks intimately bound up with the project of advancing human rights. More frequently than non-fictional narratives of witness, contemporary novels also expose problems with the human rights project including the formal conventions or plot lines typically associated with it. Finally, the chapter turns from literary works to the broader question of reading. This section explores arguments about close reading, critique, and the ethics of the textual encounter, as they relate to the discourses, practices, and legal foundations of human rights.

Narratives of witness

Freedom of speech, including the ability to bear witness to one's own experience, is one of the fundamental guarantees of human rights. Indeed, in a pioneering article entitled "A Question of Narration: The Voice in International Human Rights Law," Joseph R. Slaughter (1997) makes the argument that human rights law as developed from the French Declaration of the Rights of Man and Citizen (DRMC, 1789) and outlined in documents such as the Universal Declaration of Human Rights (UDHR, 1948) can essentially be understood as "a commitment to the voice, as a tool to guarantee recourse to individual narration" (Slaughter 1997, p. 429). If as Slaughter argues international law has at its epicenter the protection of the individual's right to give voice to her own story, then it is also true that these stories – once given voice – play a key role in strengthening and expanding the jurisdiction of human rights laws and norms. Personal testimonies and eyewitness reports about the suffering of others were historically foundational to building an international consensus for human rights. Such narratives of witness remain central to projects of raising awareness of human rights abuses, mobilizing empathy and action to stop them, and obtaining redress for them once they have occurred.

In *Human Rights and Narrated Lives: The Ethics of Recognition*, Kay Schaffer and Sidonie Smith (2004) comprehensively chart the historical and contemporary points of intersection between human rights and personal testimony or what they term "life narrative" (2004, pp. 13–34). They argue that especially "over the last twenty years, life narratives have become one of the most potent vehicles for advancing human rights claims" (2004, p. 1). Stories involved in this work, Schaffer and Smith assert, tend to take a particular form. They are "strong, emotive stories often chronicling degradation, brutalization, exploitation, and physical violence; stories that testify to the denial of subjectivity and loss of group identities" (2004, p. 4). As they depict histories of pain and suffering, these narratives "invite an ethical response" from a community of readers or listeners, and they have a "strong affective dimension" which can have both positive and negative impacts on readers or listeners (2004, p. 4). Their desired outcome is "recognition" by others of the narrator and his or her claims (2004, p. 5). Simplifying a bit, one could describe these as narratives of victimhood and suffering that claim identification and empathy from the reader, in the hopes that these might lead to action.

Testimonies from the Holocaust, itself one of the primary spurs for drafting the UDHR, often exemplify the pattern that Schaffer and Smith describe above. Such testimonies have at their heart representations of suffering. Primo Levi's *Survival in Auschwitz* (1996 [1958]), for instance, describes in detail the author's own experience in a German death camp. It exposes the strategies of dehumanization used by the Nazis to destroy the Jewish people as it documents their lasting effects on survivors. Levi draws attention to the difficulty of bearing witness to catastrophe, showing the failures of both individual memory and shared language. Yet he simultaneously insists on the need for his story to be told. He begins his memoir with an appeal to the reader to actively engage with his narrative. The urgency of this appeal becomes apparent in the memoir's startling epigraph, a poem ending with the lines: "Meditate that this came about:/ I commend these words to you./ Carve them in your hearts/ At home, in the street,/ Going to bed, rising;/ Repeat them to your children,/ Or may your house fall apart,/ May illness impede you,/ May your children turn their faces from you." (1996 [1958], p. 9). This curse is warranted because Levi sees paying attention to stories such as his as the only way to stop similar abuses from happening to new victims in new circumstances.

Related appeals for attention and engagement, based on the narration of individual and collective experiences of suffering, are made in *testimonios* of state terrorism in Latin America. Such appeals may have been even more urgent because the abuses that the texts depict were still happening at the time of publication (Cubilié 2005, p. xv). The most famous example is that of Rigoberta Menchú, author (with Elisabeth Burgos-Debray) of *I, Rigoberta Menchú: An Indian Woman in Guatemala* (1984). This book outlines the struggles of Menchú, her family, and her wider Quiché Mayan community with both poverty and the violence waged against them by the state during Guatemala's civil war. It was published at the height of the Guatemalan government's genocide of the indigenous Mayan population. Menchú's *testimonio* brought global attention to the plight of her community, especially when she was awarded the 1992 Nobel Peace Prize, and was an important contributing factor to the signing of the Peace Accords that ended the civil war in 1996. At the same time, the book's success in creating international solidarity prompted a backlash by conservative academics in the United States, who felt that students should not be required to read the text, as well as by skeptics who accused Menchú of fabricating experiences for publicity. This controversy, as Schaffer and Smith note, points to authors' inability to control the effects of their own stories, and shows how testimonies can achieve results quite different from what the authors intended (2004, p. 31).

If texts such as Menchú's have played a visible role in ending human rights abuses, personal narratives can also aid transitions from authoritarian governments to democratic regimes that will supposedly respect human rights and rule of law more generally. In *The Little School* (1986), Alicia Partnoy describes her own "disappearance" and torture by the military juntas who perpetrated Argentina's "Dirty War" (1976–1983). Published only two years following the end of the dictatorship, one year after the release of the *Never Again* report on the "disappeared," and during the legal trials of the juntas, her testimony forms part of a wider social movement to commemorate the dead and to embrace democracy. As the reference to the *Never Again* report reminds us, governments have recognized the power of victim's narratives to strengthen support for democratic governments and indeed have harnessed this power in institutions like truth commissions. While Argentina was one of the earliest countries to create such a body, the most spectacular example to date is that of the South African Truth and Reconciliation Commission

(TRC, 1996–1998). After the end of apartheid in 1994, the South African government collected over 21,000 stories from victims of gross human rights abuses perpetrated during the apartheid era. A percentage were staged in public hearings open to the community, recorded on video, broadcast on national and international radio and television, and included in the Commission's final report. According to TRC officials, this massive outpouring of personal narrative was meant to have two beneficial ends. First, giving testimony was understood to support the healing process of victims by validating and restoring the dignity of these individuals (Coundouritis 2006, p. 847). Second, testimonies were positioned as a site for forging a new democratic national community founded on respect for human rights and rule of law. Victims' stories became *the* ground of a new national narrative (Schaffer and Smith 2004, p. 11).

Using testimony or life narrative in this manner to achieve specific political goals raises ethical questions. Is it possible to attend to the needs of people giving testimony in the context of legal or quasi-legal hearings? What happens when memory stressed to its limits by traumatic experiences does not hold up to demands of legal accountability? Might not the process of bearing witness re-traumatize individuals rather than lead to healing? Whose stories get left out when testimonies are aggregated together and forced to follow a particular plot line? Will these collective stories inspire identification, empathy, and the acceptance of accountability among those who are not part of the victim group, or rather will they lead to backlash against victims and/or the new governments? Such questions have been extensively debated by the scholars cited above as well as Minow (1998) and Wilson (2002).

A related set of questions arises when we turn from examples of self-disclosure, where victims of human rights abuses choose to share their story with a wider community and maintain at least some agency in the process of doing so, to the act of shaping and telling the stories of others, ostensibly in order to help these "others" gain their rights. Perhaps even more than listening to the stories told *by* victims, the activity of communicating the stories *of* victims forms the core of human rights activism. James Dawes underscores this point in *That the World May Know: Bearing Witness to Atrocity* (2007), when he quotes a delegate from the International Commission of the Red Cross who claims: "most of the work that we do is just talking. Really, what is at the heart of the ICRC is to make representations" (2007, p. 78). This work of "mak[ing] representations," which Dawes labels the task of "document[ing] harms," surely describes the actions of Henry Dunant as he bore witness to the fallen Franco-Sardinian and Austrian soldiers at Solferino. It continues to comprise the work of individuals ranging from volunteers in organizations such as Turkey's Human Rights Association to photojournalists representing crises around the world (Dawes 2007, p. 78). Elaine Scarry likewise argues that the paradigmatic human rights group Amnesty International (AI) is fundamentally concerned with communicating individual pain and suffering to a wider public. AI letters must "record the passage of pain into speech" on behalf of an absent other, one who can only be the recipient rather than the agent of agitation done on his or her behalf (1985, p. 9).

Such representations offer possibilities similar to first-person victim testimony, like the potential to stir emotions that can in turn create a sense of ethical solidarity and motivate action. There is of course no guarantee that such beneficial ends will result. As the case of Menchú demonstrates, the results of representing suffering can be unpredictable. People can fail to move beyond empathy to action or even slide from empathy to indifference through "compassion fatigue" (Rieff 2002, pp. 33–34). Further, as Dawes argues, the act of shaping others' stories can become an ethical minefield: What happens when attempts to "help" victims of human rights abuses actually harm those victims, either by reducing them to their suffering or by forcing them to relive their victimization? Should one refuse to disseminate stories that may help on the grounds that they may also harm? (See Dawes 2007, pp. 166–177.) There are no easy answers, but the act of posing these questions may encourage more considered uses of personal testimony and related narratives of witness as they continue to circulate as tools of human rights advocacy.

Novels, sentimental and otherwise

Sophia A. McClennen argues that "culture and the narratives that sustain it are an essential force in shaping visions of shared humanity, or of threatening them" (2007, p. 15). Non-fictional narratives of witness, while highly visible in human rights work, are only one of many different types or genres of literature that together inform our social imaginaries in the way McClennen describes, providing the deep structures through which specific human rights claims are made and contested. Other genres may have more historically formative – if less immediately obvious – relations to human rights. One such genre that played a key role in configuring imaginaries of "shared humanity" in particular (and often less than universal) ways is the novel. Benedict Anderson (2006 [1983]) influentially defined the nation as an "imagined community" constructed as people read novels and other forms of print media and imagine their relation to other readers. The nation is important because, as Hannah Arendt (1973 [1951]) reminds us, human rights developed within the framework of Western nation states, and the nation state has traditionally been the guarantor of human rights. However, the concept of an imagined community of readers can easily extend to other scales of belonging. Margaret Cohen suggests that the communities created by novel reading were in fact originally transnational, forged in eighteenth-century exchanges between France and England. These early "sentimental communities" can be viewed as a kind of prototype for what we today term the international human rights community (2002, p. 107).

In part because of the historical importance of the novel, scholars of human rights from a variety of fields have focused on novelistic genres and subgenres. In Inventing Human Rights, Lynn Hunt (2007) positions the eighteenth-century epistolary or sentimental novel as the ground of possibility for human rights. She argues that the sentimental novel helped readers learn to feel empathy for people who did not, on the face of it, seem to be "like them." By reading the first-person letters that make up Richardson's *Pamela* (1740) or *Clarissa* (1747–1748) and Rousseau's *Julie* (1761), eighteenth-century Europeans came to understand that servants and women – two categories of people not historically seen to possess humanity to the same degree as the upper classes – had inner lives. As they experienced the rich inner life of Pamela or Clarissa, readers also came to sympathize with the suffering of these characters. Intellectually and, most crucially, emotionally engaging with these novels, readers ultimately came to accept both the protagonists and people like them as potential equals. As Hunt puts it, "[h]uman rights could only flourish when people learned to think of others as their equals, as like them in some fundamental fashion. They learned this equality, at least in part, by experiencing identification with ordinary characters who seemed dramatically present and familiar, even if ultimately fictional" (2007, p. 58).

The sentimental tradition carried on beyond the eighteenth century through massively popular novels like Harriet Beecher Stowe's *Uncle Tom's Cabin* (1852), often credited with helping bring an end to slavery in the United States. Famous scenes like the death of little Eva not only sold Stowe's novel but also the cause of abolition. After being transformed into melodrama, sentimentalism continues to animate middlebrow fiction (Cohen 2002, pp. 106–107). Many recent popular novels tap into this tradition to encourage readers to empathize with victims of human rights abuses and therefore to see them as part of the community of "shared humanity" that should possess human rights. Such an approach is compatible with and often suggestively mirrors the structure of narratives of witness described in the previous section, where the exposure of trauma or suffering informs readers about human rights abuses and opens the door to an empathetic engagement with victims. One example is Edwidge Danticat's *Breath, Eyes, Memory* (1994). This novel presents the story of Sophie Caco, a young Haitian girl who escapes from the violence of the Duvalier dictatorship to the United States, only to find herself subjected by her own mother to humiliating traditional "tests" of her virginity. Her struggles to move beyond the traumas prescribed to her by her nationality and her gender and to make a new life for herself call for recognition from the community of readers even as they reaffirm the strength of the main character. On a different register, Khaled Hosseini's bestseller *The Kite Runner* (2003) can be seen to bring Western audiences closer to the suffering of the Afghani people under the Taliban, which may itself potentially muster support for the troubled US involvement in the region.

The novel–empathy paradigm developed through the sentimental novel is appealing. However, as scholars have shown by exploring other genres, it is neither a full explanation of the relationship between literature and human rights nor an unambiguously desirable model. As Sarah Winter (2009) suggests, writers are often suspicious of passion as a political force. Pointing to books such as Jane Austen's *Emma* (1815), Mark Twain's *Adventures of Huckleberry Finn* (1884) and Chinua Achebe's *Arrow of God* (1964), Winter outlines a subgenre that she calls the "novel of prejudice" that trains readers not in sympathy but in reasoned engagement capable of breaking down the historically contingent but socially naturalized values that stop people from treating others with dignity. From a different perspective, in *Human Rights, Inc: The World Novel, Narrative Form, and International Law* (2007), Slaughter reveals how genres meant to extend human rights can lock individuals into specific and not always productive forms of rights claims. He focuses on the *Bildungsroman*, or the novel of development. This genre provides what he argues is the key plot line used by individuals outside the community of rights holders to claim inclusion in this community (2007, pp. 26–27, 95–105). If at the time of Goethe's *Wilhelm Meister* (1795–1796), this individual was the bourgeois male, then in the nineteenth and twentieth centuries, the *Bildungsroman* came to be used by women and former colonial subjects. These new authors used the form that originally sanctioned their exclusion from human rights in order to claim them, but in doing so they also altered the form. This can be seen in books like the Zimbabwean Tsitsi Dangarembga's *Nervous Conditions* (1988), a *Bildungsroman* that narrates the story of a young African girl achieving entrance to elite Rhodesian society even as it exposes the profound racism and sexism structuring both the society and the form – the *Bildungsroman* – used to gain entrance to it (Slaughter 2007, pp. 228–245).

The fact that genres can be, in Slaughter's phrase, "suspicious vehicles" of liberation – vehicles that perpetuate and disseminate a narrow, Eurocentric vision of human rights and the human even as they allow for the incorporation of new groups of people within this vision – points to the need to explore how literature can impede the full implementation of human rights even as it seeks to advance this project (2007, p. 33). As Dawes argues, authors using traditional, sentimentally inflected, and linear plot lines may negatively impact movements to stop human rights abuses or aid people in crisis situations by facilitating emotional catharsis in the reader. This can make action less likely for two reasons. First, readers may feel that they have already responded to a victim's pain simply by sharing it. Second, narratives that depict individual "successes" may lead readers to think that the crisis is over instead of recognizing that one battle does not win the war. These narrative strategies may also objectify and commodify the people who suffer from the human rights violations that they mean to remedy, "reducing" the humans suffering from abuses to victims and constraining their political agency (Dawes 2007, pp. 192–199, 208). Elizabeth Swanson Goldberg further warns against common narrative strategies such as "traditional chronological time, linear plot structures and omniscient or totalizing first person narrative points of view," because of their tendency to "reproduce fixed – predictable, and often thereby intractable – identity positions of victim and oppressor" (2007, p. 16). She shows how popular representations encourage individuals to claim rights on the basis of victimhood, thus perpetuating their "victim" status at the same time as people labeled "oppressors" are dehumanized and the reader's position of distance or "safety" is reinforced.

Against these tendencies, Dawes points to a contemporary genre that he calls the "human rights novel." Texts from this genre do not celebrate emotional connection or empathy, but rather use post-modern tactics to encourage readers to move beyond facile ideas of identification, to foreground the difficulty of communicating traumatic experiences, and to question the prospect of achieving resolution or closure (2007, pp. 190–229). Dawes indicates books such as J. M. Coetzee's *Waiting for the Barbarians* (1980) and Michael Ondaatje's *Anil's Ghost* (2000) as prototypical examples. Coetzee's exploration of an imperial bureaucrat struggling to come to terms with the brutal modes of warfare used by his superiors, and Ondaatje's representation of an archeologist and a forensic anthropologist attempting to prove the existence of state-sponsored murder in Sri Lanka, divert attention away from the victim to secondary witnesses of violence. These secondary witnesses struggle with but never actually gain access to the "truth" of the victim's experience, and instead are left to confront a violence that remains forever indecipherable. On the structural level, the novels use non-linear and open-ended narrative forms to represent the failure of their protagonists' attempts to communicate and alleviate suffering. Such structures refuse narrative closure or resolution, thus undercutting more traditional plot lines where the story of human rights abuses culminates in a happy ending or the success of the individual can be substituted for the ongoing trials of the community (Dawes 2007, pp. 196–197, 218–219).

Especially given the power of narrative to shape our social imaginaries, the work done by novelists and critics to promote reflection on the way literary forms endanger as well as promote human rights, and narrow as well as broaden the vision of human rights that activists struggle to implement, is a crucial addition to human rights studies. They provide a key corrective to the novel–empathy paradigm presented above. Yet, we should not deny the power of the straightforward story of suffering told in a linear fashion. As we have seen, narratives with this structure can be powerful tools of activism, while texts with high levels of mediation may forfeit the sense of immediacy and urgency less complex narratives can create. Instead of aligning post-modern narrative form with ethical responsibility, one might argue that form by itself does not have this political property. Rather, what emerges from the critiques above is a need to pair texts that call for an immediate emotional response with those that model critical engagement. We can hone our reading skills through the latter to interpret the former. It is by bringing identification and empathy into dialogue with skepticism in this way that literature can be what Judith Butler describes as a "critical" and an "effective" advocate for human rights (2006, p. 1661).

Reading

This chapter has suggested that, like non-fictional narratives of witness, novels engaged in advancing human rights claim empathy and therefore inclusion in the community of "shared humanity" of rights holders for those left outside this community. They also – and just as importantly – reveal the limitations of the typical empathy-inducing narratives, thus exposing the paradoxes involved in human rights work and teaching us to read more attentively and ethically. This turn to reading calls to mind a suggestion made some years ago by Thomas Keenan. In his book *Fables of Responsibility*, Keenan points to a need to unsettle literature from its common association with a text or "a given body of work" and instead to theorize it as "the act of reading itself" (1997, p. 1). Such a redefinition has a number of important implications for the relationship between literature and human rights. Dawes, Slaughter, Schaffer and Smith, and others have argued that the work of human rights is as much a matter of representation – the shaping of stories – as a matter of law. If an ethics of representation has emerged in the context of the discussions above, then Keenan's suggestion means that an ethics of representation must be paired with an ethics of reading.

At the heart of an ethics of reading lies the practice of critical analysis, understood in an expansive way to include an interrogation of the written and spoken word in general as well as of specific literary artifacts. This kind of critical analysis threads through the above sections but can be moved even more firmly to the center of discussion. Doing so may undo the division between non-fictional narratives and literary fiction seen in much scholarship on literature and human rights and re-inscribed here, opening up this system of categorization for question. Why do this work of separation? Is this the most productive way to think about the relation between literature and human rights? Should we be moving away from the definition of form as sufficient for articulating how literature interacts with human rights?

In the spirit of this expansive vision of critical analysis, Gayatri Chakravorty Spivak underscores the importance of "close reading." On one level, close reading techniques form the heart of a politics of accountability. By tracking the words people use and comparing them with their deeds, the gap between stated commitments to human rights principles and actual actions can be exposed. Even more importantly, however, close reading becomes a mode of constructive criticism meant to recognize the closures as well as the potential of the concepts undergirding the human rights enterprise and to refigure these concepts in ways that support a fuller human rights project (2006, p. 1609). Spivak's example, approached through a consideration of the question of translating the UDHR, is the concept of universality. She argues that the idea of universality underpinning and enshrined in the UDHR should not be jettisoned, but rather understood to form a complicated double bind with particularity in which neither concept can be sufficient on its own (2006, p. 1616).

The same kind of work is done by scholars like the contributors to Ian Balfour and Eduardo Cadava's *South Atlantic Quarterly* special edition "The Claims of Human Rights" (2004), who unpack the concepts of humanity, citizenship, and rights developed during the French Revolution and structuring the DRMC, by Slaughter (2007) in his analysis of the narrative trajectory informing the UDHR, and by Anne Cubilié (2005) in her exploration of the gendered foundation of this same document. Pointing to a more recent phenomenon, Mark Sanders (2007) rereads the South African TRC to move from the victim–empathy paradigm to that of translation, and poses the translation politics put in place during the TRC's public hearings as a vehicle for a radical revision of the meaning of shared humanity. It is through such attentive reading that the core concepts and current issues of human rights discourse can remain open to a continual critical analysis whose end goal is, as Balfour and Cadava proclaim, not to debunk the idea of human rights but to open it towards its transformative potential. This means striving for "a humanitarianism and democracy that would correspond to other, more just forms of humanitarianism and democracy than those we have with us today" (2004, p. 293).

Keenan sets out what is perhaps the culmination of this position. Following his redefinition of literature from a "given body of work" to "the act of reading" itself, he continues:

> By "reading" I mean our exposure to the singularity of the text, something that cannot be organized in advance, whose complexities cannot be settled out or decided by "theories" or the application of more or less mechanical programs. Reading, in this sense, is what happens when we cannot apply the rules. This means that reading is an experience of responsibility, but that responsibility is not a moment of security or of cognitive certainty.

> Quite the contrary: the only responsibility worthy of the name comes with the removal of grounds, the withdrawal of rules or the knowledge on which we might rely to make our decisions for us. No grounds means no alibis, no elsewhere to which we might refer the instance of our decision.
>
> *(Keenan 1997, p. 1)*

Keenan here poses reading as a model for an ethical political practice. The core of this ethics is absolute openness to the singular encounter, whether this means the encounter with the text or with another human being. When there are no rules or accepted theories that guide us in our reading or in our relations with others, each encounter must be forged through careful attention to the needs of the beings and texts with whom we interact and through an interrogation of our own position in this interaction; and it requires us, in the face of the irreducible complexity generated in this process, to come to a singular decision about how to act. Only through this kind of negotiation, Keenan argues, is real responsibility to a text or for another human being possible. Of course, this powerful vision faces various challenges. What would it mean – on the basis of this deconstructive ethics – to think of the project of human rights as something more than a matter of extending the rights outlined in the UDHR and various related Covenants ("applying the rules") to as many individuals as possible? Must we do this? How?

Conclusion

This chapter has traced three overlapping lines of inquiry into the relation between literature and human rights. The first focuses on the way non-fictional stories of victims – told by themselves or told by others – can become useful tools for human rights advocacy. It foregrounds the capacity of narratives of witness to spark an emotional or empathetic response that may, in particular conditions of circulation and reception, translate into action. It also tries to explain why these narratives can fail to translate into action. The second thinks more broadly about the historical work of literary fiction in shaping the imagined communities that determine access to the protection of human rights laws and the denial of this protection. It also opens up for analysis the forms or genres of storytelling through which those historically excluded from the regime of rights narrate their entrance, pointing to their possibilities as well as their closures. The final approach takes the widest angle, looking not at particular forms of literature but at the act of reading. It poses close reading as a critical intervention into human rights work, not only as a form of watchdog politics – exposing the hypocrisy and failures of specific uses of human rights instruments and rhetoric – but more crucially and fundamentally as a mode of keeping the human rights project accountable to a radical universal mission.

These lines of inquiry clearly do not exhaust the relationship between literature, broadly conceived, and human rights. They do however reveal a set of rich and varied intersections between the things that fall into these categories, thus illuminating a dense network of relations that calls for further research.

References

Anderson, B. 2006 [1983]. *Imagined Communities: Reflections on the Origins and Spread of Nationalism* (New York: Verso).

Arendt, H. 1973 [1951]. *Origins of Totalitarianism* (New York: Harcourt Brace Jovanovich).

Balfour, I. and E. Cadava, eds. 2004. "And Justice for All? The Claims of Human Rights." *South Atlantic Quarterly*, Vol. 103, Nos. 2–3.

Butler, J. 2006. "Afterword." *PMLA: Publication of the Modern Language Association of America*, Vol. 125, No. 5, pp. 1658–1661.

Cohen, M. 2002. "Sentimental Communities." In M. Cohen and C. Denver, eds., *The Literary Channel: The Inter-National Invention of the Novel* (Princeton, NJ: Princeton University Press).

Coundouritis, E. 2006. "The Dignity of the Unfittest: Victims' Stories in South Africa." *Human Rights Quarterly*, Vol. 28, pp. 842–867.

Cubilié, A. 2005. *Women Witnessing Terror: Testimony and the Cultural Production of Human Rights* (New York: Fordham University Press).

Danticat, E. 1994. *Breath, Eyes, Memory* (New York: Soho Press).

Dawes, J. 2007. *That the World May Know: Bearing Witness to Atrocity* (Cambridge, MA: Harvard University Press).

Goldberg, E. S. 2007. *Beyond Terror: Gender, Narrative, Human Rights* (New Brunswick, NJ: Rutgers University Press).

HA UG, H. 1986. "Dunant's Ideas – The Test of Time." In H. Dunant, 1986 [1862], *A Memory of Solferino*, International Committee of the Red Cross. At: http://www.icrc.org/Web/Eng/siteeng0.nsf/htmlall/p0361/$File/ICRC_002_0361_MEMORY_OF_SOLFERINO.PDF.

Hosseini, K. 2003. *The Kite Runner* (New York: Riverhead Books).

Hunt, L. 2007. *Inventing Human Rights: A History* (New York: W.W. Norton).

Keenan, T. 1997. *Fables of Responsibility: Aberrations and Predicaments in Ethics and Politics* (Stanford, CA: Stanford University Press).

Levi, P. 1996 [1958]. *Survival in Auschwitz: The Nazi Assault on Humanity*. Trans. Stuart Woolf (New York: Touchstone).

McClennen, S. A. 2007. "The Humanities, Human Rights and the Comparative Imagination." *CLCWeb: Comparative Literature and Culture*, Vol. 9, No. 1. At: http://docs.lb.purdue/clcweb/vol9/iss1/13.

Menchú, Rigoberta. 1984. *I, Rigoberta Menchú: An Indian Woman in Guatemala*. Ed. Elisabeth Burgos-Debray. Trans. Ann Wright (London: Verso).

Minow, M. 1998. *Between Vengeance and Forgiveness: Facing History after Genocide and Violence* (Boston: Beacon Press).

Partnoy, Alicia. 1986. *The Little School: Tales of Disappearance and Survival in Argentina* (San Francisco, CA: Cleis Press).

Rieff, D. 2002. *A Bed for the Night: Humanitarianism in Crisis* (New York: Simon and Schuster).

Sanders, M. 2007. *Ambiguities of Witnessing: Law and Literature in the Time of a Truth Commission* (Stanford, CA: Stanford University Press).

Scarry, E. 1985. *The Body in Pain: The Making and Unmaking of the World* (New York: Oxford University Press).

Schaffer, K. and S. Smith 2004. *Human Rights and Narrated Lives: The Ethics of Recognition* (New York: Palgrave Macmillan).

Slaughter, J. R. 1997. "A Question of Narration: The Voice in International Human Rights Law." *Human Rights Quarterly*, Vol. 19, No. 2, pp. 406–430.

Slaughter J. R. 2007. *Human Rights, Inc: The World Novel, Narrative Form, and International Law* (New York: Fordham University Press).

Slaughter, J. R. 2009. "Humanitarian Reading." In R. A. Wilson and R. D. Brown, eds., *Humanitarianism and Suffering: The Mobilization of Empathy* (New York: Cambridge University Press).

Spivak, G. 2006. "Close Reading." *PMLA: Publication of the Modern Language Association of America*, Vol. 121, No. 5, pp. 1608–1619.

Wilson, R. A. 2002, *The Politics of Truth and Reconciliation in South Africa: Legitimising the Post-Apartheid State* (Cambridge: Cambridge University Press).

Wilson, R. A. and R. D. Brown. 2009. "Introduction." In R. A. Wilson and R. D. Brown, eds., *Humanitarianism and Suffering: The Mobilization of Empathy* (New York: Cambridge University Press).

Winter, S. 2009. "The Novel and Prejudice." *Comparative Literature Studies*, Vol. 46, No. 1, pp. 76–102.

56

Theater and human rights

Florian Becker and Brenda Werth

More than any other artistic practice, and in part because of its concretely public character, theater has been subject to the demand that it be of political or social use. The relation of theater to human rights is no exception. Discussions of this relation often proceed from the assumption that the theater is or should be an instrument for promoting the cause of human rights, or at least for bringing to light specific violations of human rights. As we shall see, the second half of the twentieth century did indeed produce many dramatic works and theatrical practices that pursue these aims – often with considerable power. Nonetheless, and as Paul Rae (2009) and others argue, the relationship between theater and human rights is more complex than this. Even if one limits one's purview to the period following the adoption of the Universal Declaration of Human Rights (UDHR) in 1948, it is evident that what one might call the theater of human rights has done more than attempt to draw attention to incidents or practices regarded as abuses of human rights. It has sought to reveal the functioning of large-scale institutional structures of power that contribute to the violation of human rights or that prevent such violations from being addressed. It has explored the concept of human rights, helping us understand their content, character, and status. Just as importantly, it has criticized aspects of human-rights discourse and even attacked the very idea of a human right.

To account for the multiplicity of theatrical approaches to the causes and problems of human rights, and to provide a handle on the question of how one might begin to make sense of it, we will proceed by examining two key moments in the development of both theater and human rights. First we will trace the entangled histories of the invention of modern drama and the invention of the concept of human rights in eighteenth-century Europe. Then we will give an overview of some of the most prominent works of drama and theatrical projects that have addressed human rights since the promulgation of the UDHR, a period which can be referred to as the era of global human rights.

Drama and theater are deeply implicated in the invention of human rights. The theory and practice of drama in eighteenth-century Britain, France, and Germany is centered on the same concept as the emergent theory and practice of human rights: the universally or purely "human." If much has been written on the role of the novel in shaping and disseminating the conceptions of individual subjectivity and autonomy subtending the visions of human rights found in the American Declaration of Independence of 1776 and the French Declaration of the Rights of Man and Citizen of 1789, drama has been relatively neglected. Yet this should not make us overlook the fact that the theater, as Peter Holland and Michael Patterson (1997, p. 255) point out, assumes a greater function in society in the eighteenth century than it had at any time since fifth-century Athens. Drama can be shown to contribute significantly to the process that transformed the long tradition of natural *law* theory, revitalized in the previous two centuries by Grotius, Pufendorf, and Locke, into the idiom of natural *rights*, by making the individual subject the center of moral concern.

The shift from natural law to natural rights overlaps with the history of European theater in the development of eighteenth-century "bourgeois drama." For a cultural phenomenon that spans more than a century and several major European languages, the bourgeois drama has a remarkable degree of coherence. Most significant Western drama of the period is bourgeois both in the sense of being produced by middle-class practitioners for an emerging middle-class audience, and also because its concerns and perspectives are distinctively middle class. This stands in contrast to the dominant theater of the sixteenth and seventeenth centuries, where it was taken for granted that serious drama was tragedy, and that the protagonists of tragedy were of aristocratic social rank. When the rise of Calvinist Protestantism and capitalism dissolved the previous feudal order, it also dissolved the ethical evaluations bound up with it. As Alasdair MacIntyre (1966, pp. 166–167; 1980, pp. 57–59) has argued, to be a *human being* in traditional European societies was to fulfill a set of roles, each of which had its purpose in an orderly universe. To be a good man might mean simply to be a good father, husband, blacksmith, town citizen, and servant of God. As soon as the hierarchical system was no longer accepted without question, the term "human being" ceased to be a composite of such functional concepts, and ethical judgments lost any clear meaning (1966, pp. 172–174; 1980, p. 60). Eighteenth-century Western moral and political philosophy can be understood in large part as a series of attempts to invest the category of the purely or *naturally* human being with inherent ethical significance. The bourgeois drama participates in this effort alongside the century's reformulations of social contract theory, its theories of moral sense and sentiment, and its sentimental novel. All of these cultural forms at once express and engage in the construction of what Jürgen Habermas (1991 [1962]) calls the "bourgeois public sphere."

Of direct relevance to the beginnings of bourgeois drama in England is a general characteristic of Puritanism emphasized by Charles Taylor (1992, pp. 211–233), namely its revaluation of ordinary life. Puritanism shifts the locus of the good life from some special range of higher activities, such as participation in the *polis*, philosophy, heroic warfare, or sacred ritual, to the activities of everyday life, especially labor, marriage, and family life. The "innerworldly asceticism" of Puritanism, to use Max Weber's phrase, demanded utter dedication to whatever tasks in life one was allotted (2002 [1905]). By the early eighteenth century, this ethos of a disciplined productive life had widened into a broad appreciation of the virtues of commerce as a universally constructive and civilizing force. George Lillo's *The London Merchant* (1731), a play that exerted an incalculable influence upon the development of continental European drama, is the expression of a rising merchant bourgeoisie that is aware of its own achievements and worth. In the play, the merchants of London avert a possible invasion by the armada by preventing the Spanish king from obtaining a large loan from the bank of Genoa, thereby demonstrating not only their political clout but also their usefulness for the common good. The world of the play is one in which one can come to grief only by failing to heed the call of reason. As Peter Szondi (1973, pp. 53–54) observes, the play's continental admirers saw that, in pointing to the Puritan – bourgeois virtues of a life rationally organized for the orderly accumulation of wealth and to their harmony with the universal interest of humankind and the natural order, the play challenged the remaining privileges of the aristocracy.

The features of the play that would make such an impression on German and French playwrights in decades to come – the facts that it presented the "private woe" of its bourgeois protagonists in a more or less contemporary setting, in "artless" prose, and for the benefit of an audience that was predominantly bourgeois – caused little stir among a London audience that had been prepared for them by the existence, since the late seventeenth century, of a functioning *political* bourgeois public sphere that encompassed not only the famous coffeehouses and journals of the day but extended into the theater as well. Before the reinstatement of censorship by the Licensing Act of 1737 the London stages premiered biting political satires such as John Gay's *The Beggar's Opera* (1728) and Henry Fielding's *The Historical Register for the Year 1736* (1737). On the Continent, though, and as Habermas contends, the bourgeois public sphere constituted itself in the realm of literature and arts such as theater before serving the political emancipation of the bourgeoisie more directly, by challenging state policy and aristocratic privilege. In the salons of France and Germany, members of the educated bourgeoisie first engaged with members of noble court society on an equal footing in the common discussion of literature and the arts; only if the interlocutors faced each other as "mere human beings" could the "force of the better argument" be expected to assert itself over the social hierarchy (Habermas 1991 [1962], pp. 33–36). Debates about the arts thus laid the ground for the doctrine that public opinion was the expression of reason and that it alone had insight into the natural order.

The conception of a pure humanity that emerged at the time was not limited to the idea of a community of intellect or reason. As Habermas also stresses, the bourgeois public was also a community of emotion or sentiment. The bourgeois individuals who interacted as equals in the public sphere understood themselves to express there a subjectivity that had its source in the intimate sphere of the family, where the individual could cultivate and unfold an inner realm free from any extrinsic purpose (1991 [1962], pp. 46–47). The bourgeois patriarchal family and the subjectivity that was shaped within it – not least through letter-writing and the consumption of novels such as Samuel Richardson's *Pamela* (1740) and *Clarissa* (1747–1748) and Jean-Jacques Rousseau's *Julie* (1761) – were not at the time regarded as a part or product of a historically specific social formation but rather as the expression of authentic, natural, and universal humanity.

Denis Diderot, by far the most important theorist of the "serious genre" or "domestic drama" in France, believed that the "artificial" and corrupting institutions of the *ancien régime* stood in the way of a state of human affairs that was both reasonable and "natural." Like Rousseau, Diderot never doubted that "natural man" is good: "It is the bad conventions that have perverted man, and not human nature which we must blame" (1965 [1758], p. 195). The intrinsically good core of humanity was accessible in the one realm that lay beyond the corrupting influence of contemporary social institutions: the family. For Diderot, it is in their relations to other family members that persons of any social station manifest their universal human nature. Clytemnestra in Racine's *Iphigénie* (1674) discloses her purely human core when she "fill[s] her palace with cries" in despair over her daughter's impending sacrifice (1965 [1757], p. 91) and the tears of a woman at her murdered husband's feet will move the observer no less if she is a peasant than if she is a queen (p. 99). Diderot's own "domestic and bourgeois dramas," *The Natural Son* (1757) and *The Head of the Family* (1758), do not merely stage the sentimental community of the family on stage but also aim to generate such a community in the auditorium. From this objective arise all the main features of his "serious genre": its domestic setting, the rejection of meter and rhyme, the representation of "everyday experience," the use of the stage to paint a detailed image ("tableau") of the characters' emotions and their relations to each other, and the demand to rely less on language and more on the manifold nonverbal resources of acting.

As a supposedly natural human response, the tears that the domestic drama aims to elicit from the spectator are an apt "synecdoche," as Margaret Cohen (2002, p. 112) has put it, of the principally universal membership of the community of shared sentiment and mutual sympathy that the theater sought to construct. Yet in spite of this naturalization, Diderot's theater was not merely a refuge from a fallen social world. It was also the concrete space in which actual human beings could gather to imagine the more solidaric life they might be able to live in a different social order: "It is in going to the theater that they will save themselves from the company of the evil persons by whom they are surrounded, it is there that they will find those with whom they would like to live, it is there that they will see humankind as it is, and that they will reconcile themselves with it" (1965 [1758], pp. 192–193).

In German-speaking Europe, the theater played an even larger role in constituting a bourgeois public sphere. In the absence of any central institution for public debate, the theater became the decisive forum in which a politically powerless educated middle class shaped its self-conception as the representative of a universal human nature. Here as in France, the bourgeois community of tears was first invoked in the novel and in "serious comedy." Gotthold Ephraim Lessing, who was to become the century's preeminent theoretician and practitioner of bourgeois tragedy, praised the "comedy of tears" as "capable of winning universal applause and of bestowing a universal benefit" (1890 [1754], p. 52). Lessing's neo-Aristotelian concept of tragedy was premised on the conviction that "the human being who has the greatest capacity for pity is the best human being, the most prone to all social virtues and to all kinds of generosity." His own model tragedy *Miss Sara Sampson* (1755), which bears clear traces of *Clarissa* and *The London Merchant*, was to "enlarge our capacity to feel pity." In keeping with the ideas of the Scottish Enlightenment human improvement here takes the form of educating a sensibility centered on a capacity for a universal sympathy "in which humanity comes to experience itself" (1890 [1756], p. 68). Cultivated by drama, the spectator will be moved by "any person in misfortune, at any time and in any form."

In Lessing's *Emilia Galotti* (1772), as in Schiller's *Intrigue and Love* (1784), the bourgeois family is violated by absolutist power, in ways that would qualify today as breaches of human rights. In fact, the UDHR uncritically preserves the historical link between the family and human rights: "The family is the natural and fundamental group unit of society and is entitled to protection by society and the State" (Article 16). Lessing does not broach the question of how the bourgeoisie should respond to aristocratic abuses of power. In contrast, the Parisian Louis-Sébastien Mercier explicitly argues that the creation of pity in the theater should activate the bourgeois spectators to overcome their egoism and aid those wronged by the absolutist system. Calling on the playwright to act as the "public defender of the oppressed," Mercier formulated a conception of the politically engaged dramatist that is influential even today. His *New Essay on the Dramatic Art* (1773) crucially impacted the nascent German "Storm and Stress movement." Jakob Michael Reinhold Lenz, the movement's greatest dramatist, portrayed the family as a realm of oppression. In his "tragic comedies" *The Tutor* (1774) and *The Soldiers* (1776), the social structures of absolutism are not merely external barriers that prevent the political expression of an otherwise fully formed autonomous subjectivity. Internalized by the subject, they result in a stunted humanity and in the bourgeoisie's complicity in its own misery. Portraying the objectification of human beings, Lenz's drama comes close to exposing the bourgeois conception of universal humanity as an ideology. His dramaturgy relies on the hope that the theater might put spectators in touch with their natural selves by breaking through the rigidly conventional sensibilities encrusting them. In this respect, the drama of Storm and Stress is a forerunner of the poetics of shock that underlies twentieth-century Futurism, Dada, Surrealism, and Artaud's "theatre of cruelty."

While such insights would be taken up in the twentieth century, the main trajectory of European drama at the turn of the nineteenth century focused on an essential aspect of theater embedded in Lessing's work. The essential tension between spectator empathy and detachment seen in Lessing's *Nathan the Wise* (1779) remains the pivotal preoccupation of German drama from here on – most clearly in Johann Wolfgang von Goethe's *Iphigenia in Tauris* (1786), Friedrich Schiller's *Mary Stuart* (1800), and the dramas of Heinrich von Kleist (1777–1811). (Indeed, this constitutive dynamic continues to be exploited in much late twentieth and early twenty-first century theater.) In the classical German drama, as Benjamin Bennett argues, the dynamic of empathy and detachment enables the theater to function as a model of human self-consciousness. Just as the spectator is necessarily involved with and yet detached from the represented world, so too is the self-conscious being necessarily involved with her own states and yet detached from them. The self cannot be identical with its own states since it must at the same time be conscious of its own continuity throughout them. Drama, Bennett concludes, is therefore no "less 'inward' a form than the novel" (1986, p. 94). The theater's capacity to model self-consciousness connects it closely to the concept of human rights, since self-consciousness is a necessary condition of autonomous agency – the characteristically human capacity that human rights protect.

This post-Kantian turn to the problem of self-consciousness and autonomy is nowhere more evident than in the development of Schiller. If Schiller is confident in the efficacy of theater as an instrument of moral improvement and political liberation in *The Theater as a Moral Institution* (1784), he later argues in *On the Aesthetic Education of Humankind* (1795) that a fully human political society can only be constituted by internally free subjects. Art now provides the only space in which human beings can develop into such subjects, precisely because it does not serve any immediate economic or social purpose. Schiller's dramatic output, from *Fiesco* (1783) to *William Tell* (1804), is dedicated to exploring the problem of autonomy within a relentlessly instrumentalizing social world. In contrast, Georg Büchner roundly rejects the Schillerian conviction that social improvement could come about through the cultivation of the individual subject. In *Danton's Death* (1835) Robespierre's cult of virtue and Danton's liberal universalism equally fail to address the continuing material destitution of the Parisian masses. *Woyzeck* (1837) dissects the emptiness of a bourgeois discourse of human progress and contractual rights in the face of the utter dehumanization of the poor. Woyzeck's desperate poverty forces him to volunteer for a medical experiment, and his economic exploitation and constant humiliation at the hands of his social superiors never allow him to develop a sense of autonomous agency. Büchner himself had no doubt that the poor had the "right" to use violence against their late feudal oppressors.

Ironically, the twentieth-century playwright who has had the greatest impact on the theater of human rights in the post-UHDR era had no sympathy for the notion. In works such as *The Measures Taken* (1930) and *The Good Person of Szechwan* (1940), Bertolt Brecht presents universalist ethical thought as inescapably ideological. With Marx, Brecht believed that in the discourse of universal human rights the emerging bourgeoisie posited its interest in its own political emancipation as universally human. The abuses liberals condemned as violations of rights could in fact cease only when capitalism as a whole was abolished. In the meantime, the discourse and practice of human rights hinders genuine human emancipation. For playwrights and theater practitioners who do not share this point of view, Brecht's method has been useful for one main reason. Brecht believed that theater could and should generate knowledge about social reality. To this end, and building on the practices of Erwin Piscator (whose conception of political theater encompassed what came to be known as "documentary theater" after World War II), Brecht developed a plethora of theatrical techniques for representing the workings of large-scale economic structures and social institutions. These techniques have proven invaluable to those who believe that many of the contemporary economic, political, and supranational institutional structures in which the citizens of Western countries are imbricated contribute to the continuing violation of human rights or prevent them from being redressed.

Three post-Brechtian theater practitioners whose work has been consequential for the contemporary theater of human rights, as we will see below, are Samuel Beckett, Peter Weiss, and Augusto Boal. As is well known, Beckett forced audiences to confront the apparent collapse of Enlightenment humanism in works including *Waiting for Godot* (1949) and *Endgame* (1957). Weiss's *Marat/Sade* (1964) juxtaposes the individualist and radical strains of Enlightenment morality and investigates the possible contribution of theater to projects of social liberation. *The Investigation* (1965) uses the testimony of witnesses and defendants in the Frankfurt Auschwitz trial of 1963–1965 to demonstrate the implication of capitalist enterprise in the National Socialist concentration camp system, while *Viet-Nam Discourse* (1968) turns the resources of documentary theater onto the war in Vietnam. Beginning in the early 1970s, Boal adapted Brechtian strategies to combat poverty, protest military dictatorship, and expose the lasting effects of colonialism in Argentina, Peru, Ecuador, and his native Brazil. His manifesto *The Theater of the Oppressed* (1974) proved globally influential.

In short, theater contributed significantly to the emergence of human rights in eighteenth-century Europe and to their consolidation and critique up through the nineteenth and early twentieth centuries. It mobilized the dynamics of identification to construct an imagined community that extends to all humankind, deepened the sense that all humans have the potential for autonomous agency, highlighted the social conditions that prevent this potential's realization, and helped separate the concept of human rights from its metaphysical foundations. At the risk of leaving many gaps in our coverage, we turn now to a series of theatrical projects from the post-UDHR period, to outline the diverse roles played by theater in our current era, informed both by human rights and global capitalism. Specifically, in addition to the historical roles mentioned above, we will suggest that theater and performance not only assist in implementing "first generation" rights, but also help audiences become cognizant of, critically assess, and potentially implement "newer" rights such as economic and cultural rights or "the right to know." Further, they seek to address the consequences of what is currently understood as mass trauma. They do this by uncovering truths and documenting violence; by creating forums for active discussion about rights and ways to overcome social injustice, whether through performance aligned with truth commissions or in community theater; and by constructing sites of witness, mourning, and commemoration. All of these become threads in the discussion below.

The term "genocide," coined in 1943 by Raphael Lemkin in response to the Holocaust, and the UDHR, adopted in 1948, appeared within years of each other as attempts to develop a language to address the atrocities of war and to safeguard against future crimes by enumerating the universal rights to which all humans were entitled. Mass violence has continued to punctuate the post-World War II era on a global scale, creating a newfound consciousness of how trauma affects and interconnects our lives, and producing what Andreas Huyssen calls the "hypertrophy of memory" (2003, p. 3). The figure of Antigone has emerged as an icon for this culture, personifying resistance to the violence and repression of World War II in adaptations by Jean Anouilh (1943) and Bertolt Brecht (1948); to the South African system of apartheid in Athol Fugard's *The Island* (1973); to the Argentine dictatorship (1976–1983) in Griselda Gambaro's *Antígona furiosa* (Furious Antigone 1986), and to Peru's civil war during the 1980s and 1990s in Yuyachkani's *Antígona* (2000). These are just an emblematic few of the countless global permutations of the Sophoclean myth in contemporary culture since World War II.

Beyond Antigone, artists have responded to the mass traumas of the twentieth and twenty-first centuries with the aim of inventing language to expose, document, and denounce human rights violations. Theater practitioners construct sites of resistance and reflection; frame testimony, media, and visual technologies; and combine both textual narrative and embodiment in the formulation and transmission of this response. In her analysis of the transmission of cultural memory, Diana Taylor urges a turn from written to embodied culture, from "the archive" to "the repertoire." To engage this shift, she proposes "scenarios," which provide a productive paradigm for examining the relationships between human rights and theater (2003, pp. 16–19). Other performance theories such as "restored behavior," "surrogation," and "ghosting," put forth by Richard Schechner (1988), Joseph Roach (1996), and Marvin Carlson (2001), respectively, attest to the repetition inherent in performative practice and allude to the passage of time separating event and performance. In representing trauma, theater draws attention to its repetitive nature, as a conscious and potentially empowering reinterpretation of events.

One particularly powerful role of theater is to create a space for commemoration and mourning. For example, in her work with the Sistren Theater Collective, playwright Honor Ford Smith captures the strength of commemorative theater in *Letters from the Dead* (2009), a performance drawing on ritual procession and audience participation to remember and mourn the victims of urban violence in Kingston, Jamaica. Equally important, and linked to the process of commemoration, is the relationship between theater and witnessing. Building on the *testimonio*, the narrative genre of witnessing *par excellence*, theater transposes the act of witnessing to the theatrical space, turning actors into what Freddie Rokem calls "hyper-historians" (2000, p. 13). Catherine Filloux's *Eyes of the Heart* (Eugene O'Neill Theater Center, Connecticut, 1996) exemplifies the personal, political, and cross-cultural dimensions of witnessing through the portrayal of a character experiencing psychosomatic blindness from observing the mass executions carried out by the Khmer Rouge (1975–1979) in Cambodia.

Nowhere is this connection to witnessing stronger than in theater's involvement in post-conflict truth commissions and community tribunals. Truth commissions often express the goal of strengthening national unity even as international law steadily appropriates jurisdictional power from sovereign states, thus in some ways seizing the nation's role as guarantor and protector of rights. Most prominently, in South Africa, a number of plays produced in the decade following the Truth and Reconciliation Commission (1996–1998) have debated national reconciliation, justice, and accountability. Written by Jane Taylor and produced by William Kentridge and the Handspring Puppet Company, *Ubu and the Truth Commission* (Market Theater, Johannesburg, 1997) adapts elements from Alfred Jarry's *Ubu Roi* (1896) and introduces puppetry in a multimedia exploration of the theatricality of the hearings. In the play *Molora* (Barbican, London, 2008), Yael Farber likewise employs intertextuality in her adaptation of Aeschylus's *Oresteia* to portray South Africa's TRC. Other plays deconstruct the binary the TRC established between victimizer and victim (and white and black). Michael Lessac's *Truth in Translation* (Baxter Theatre, Cape Town, 2007) focuses on the role of the interpreters during the hearings, and John Kani's *Nothing But the Truth* (Market Theatre, Johannesburg, 2002) examines how one South African family deals with loss and internal conflict in a post-apartheid framework of stage-sanctioned national reconciliation.

Performed at the World Conference against Racism Summit in Durban in August 2003, *The Story I Am About to Tell* evolved through the work of survivors participating in the Khulumani support group, established in order to facilitate victims' access to the TRC. Ensuring community access was also a primary concern for the theater collective Yuyachkani in their collaboration with Peru's TRC (2002) in their performances of *Adios Ayacucho*, *Antigone*, and *Rosa Cuchillo*.

In creating the character Rosa Cuchillo, a mother who comes back from the dead to search for her disappeared son, Yuyachkani makes a direct appeal to women to come forward and offer their testimony in the TRC hearings. Theater's complementary role to the tribunals can also be appreciated in the Rwandan performing arts company *Mashirika* (1998), directed by Hope Azeda, whose plays carry on the work of the *gacaca*, a court system derived from a traditional form of community justice and refashioned to address the crimes of genocide and the possibility of national reconstruction.

The impressive body of theater to develop around truth commissions worldwide provides a significant function in both complementing the work of the hearings through enactments of dramatic justice and lending a critical eye to the limitations of the commissions. The inherent theatricality of the proceedings makes spectatorship a key discourse in relation to the commissions, raising the question of who, exactly, might benefit from the spectacle of justice. The South African TRC, in particular, has been subject to scrutiny for devising confessionary scenarios in which perpetrators receive amnesty for admission to their crimes in the presence of the victims, which, according to skeptics, turns the pursuit of justice into a political transaction and smoothes over unresolved complexities through forced implementation of a cathartic discourse. While some plays have promoted the objectives of truth commissions, others pointed to their shortcomings. In Ariel Dorfman's *Death and the Maiden* (Santiago, 1991), for example, the protagonist, a torture victim who survived the Chilean dictatorship, ultimately takes justice into her own hands, demanding that her torturer confess while holding him at gunpoint in her home. Her character illustrates a critical case of omission in the country's Truth Commission (The Rettig Report, 1991), which only addressed those murdered or disappeared and failed to take into account the survivors of torture.

Dorfman's play shows how theater can serve as a vehicle for uncovering truths and reassessing injustices that are not captured by official political or historical narrative. Like Dorfman, who has dedicated his life to human rights advocacy and literature, playwright and ex-president of Czechoslovakia (1989–1992) and the Czech Republic (1993–2003) Václav Havel has combined life roles as human rights activist, political dissident, statesman, and artist. His play, *The Memorandum* (1965), delivers an absurd satire of bureaucracy, portraying it nonetheless as an oppressive force in a critique of everyday life under Czech communism. Finding diverse ways of contesting and resisting dominant narratives also motivates Richard Norton-Taylor's "tribunal plays," including works like *Nuremberg* (1996) and *Justifying War* (2003), staged at London's Tricycle Theatre. In a revival of 1960s documentary theater, and similar to Weiss's *The Investigation*, Norton-Taylor's work dramatizes inquiries inspired by witness testimony from legal cases in order to expose the hypocrisy of war rhetoric and to examine discourses of truth and accountability.

Plays such as *My Name is Rachel Corrie* (Royal Court Theatre, London, 2005), by Alan Rickman and Katherine Viner, *The Laramie Project* (Ricketson Theatre, Denver, 2000), by Moisés Kaufman and the Tectonic Theater Project, and *Via Dolorosa* (Royal Court Theatre, 1998), by David Hare, signal renewed interest in documentary theater in the late twentieth and early twenty-first centuries. These plays can be linked to a range of human rights issues reflecting an imperative to showcase evidence and make information public and available to audiences in order to document and reassess the past. One example is *My Neck is Thinner than a Hair* (2004), produced by the Atlas Group in collaboration with Walid Raad, which incorporates multimedia performance and different forms of physical evidence to reconstruct the history of a car bombing that took place in Beirut in 1986. Another, produced by the Singapore based company TheatreWorks and directed by Ong Keng Sen, *The Continuum: Beyond the Killing Fields* (2001), blends traditional dance practice, puppetry, and documentary video to reveal personal accounts of the mass murder committed under Pol Pot's regime.

Through integration of video footage, eyewitness testimony, and excerpts from the press, these plays recall earlier styles in documentary theater pioneered by Piscator. However, one novelty in recent documentary theater lies in its relationship to the heightened preoccupation with transparency generated by the global explosion in mass media technologies and the means of disseminating and accessing information. Article 19 of the UDHR already makes reference to the mediation of information as a part of the right to freedom of expression, which includes the right "to seek, receive and impart information and ideas through any media and regardless of frontiers." Joseph Stiglitz shifts the focus to "the right to know," as a fundamental condition of democratic society and citizen participation in public discourse (2003, p. 115). A number of documentary plays have appeared to interrogate this "right to know," using recent US military interventions as case studies for an examination of the intersection of media, politics, and the production and reception of the war. In response to the 1991 Gulf War, Trevor Griffith's *The Gulf Between Us* (West Yorkshire Playhouse, Leeds, 1992) introduces media images from the war to resensitize audiences and unmask the US's manipulation of war discourse. Relying heavily on transcripts and interviews, David Hare's *Stuff Happens* (Olivier National Theatre, London, 2004) and Victoria Brittain and Gillian Slovo's *Guantanamo: Honour Bound to Defend Freedom* (Tricycle Theater, London, 2004), juxtapose the construction and distortion of political discourse surrounding the "war on terror," against the devastating human dimension of the military intervention. A related theme is that of surveillance. The performance *Dolores from 10–10*, by Coco Fusco and Ricardo Domínguez, in collaboration with the Electronic Disturbance Theater (Kiasma, Helsinki, 2001) reconstructs the story of a Mexican *maquiladora* worker who is detained by her boss and interrogated for twelve hours for trying to foster solidarity among workers. The performance was filmed on surveillance cameras and transmitted live on the Internet.

Especially since the 1960s, the city has itself become a stage for the production of a rich repertoire of street theater striving to raise awareness of social justice and political issues, exemplified, for example, by Boal's "invisible theater." Contemporary dramatists and performance artists have adapted this city stage in order to expose and denounce the effects of neoliberalism and explore the intersection of global economics with the politics of bodies and space. Many of these performances respond directly to the human rights declared in the UN Covenant of Economic, Social, and Cultural Rights (1966), which recognizes "the right of everyone to an adequate standard of living for himself and his family, including adequate food, clothing and housing, and to the continuous improvement of living conditions." In 2002 the Argentine artist Emilio García Wehbi designed the urban intervention *Proyecto Filoctetes*, using hyperreal mannequins strategically placed on the sidewalks of Buenos Aires to draw attention to the sharp increase in poverty and the sudden visibility of homelessness in the city. In another intervention, the Colombian company Mapa Teatro documented the demolition and eviction of the residents of the neighborhood of Santa Inés de Bogotá-El Cartucho. Directed by Heidi and Rolf Abdershalden, the project bore witness to the destruction of the historic neighborhood, which had long provided refuge to those uprooted and marginalized by violence and poverty. Performing urban intervention as a means of expressing solidarity with exploited groups is central to the longstanding left-wing theater company Janam (Jana Natya Manch), whose play *Machine* (New Delhi, 1978) took to the streets to declare support for the rights of workers and to protest their oppression in a capitalist system. Since the premiere of *Machine*, Janam has expanded its repertoire to include plays that address the effects of globalization, education, and women's rights. Grass-roots intervention and local participation are also key characteristics of community theater, a global phenomenon whose aim is to empower community residents through collective creation and performance (Van Erven 2001).

The transnational movement of bodies across borders has generated plays that highlight pressing rights issues surrounding the experiences of refugees and immigrants. Though the UDHR recognized everyone's right to leave one's country and return (Article 13), and to seek asylum from persecution in other countries (Article 14), reference to these rights is eliminated in almost all subsequent international rights documents. Writing in the aftermath of the World Wars, Hannah Arendt observed that the inalienable rights recognized in the Declaration of the Rights of Man revealed themselves to apply only to citizens of the nation state (1962, p. 292). Since World War II national and international NGOs have formed to work for the legal and political protection and recognition of refugee status. Theater has collaborated in this initiative. Founded in 2003, the project In Place of War, affiliated with the University of Manchester, seeks to study theater and performance practices that develop out of conflict and humanitarian crises. The project works in conjunction with several theater and arts initiatives involving refugees, such as Banner Theatre, Exodus, Ice and Fire, and Virtual Migrants.

A striking feature of many plays depicting the experience of mass trauma and human rights violations is that they are often staged far away from the regions where the violence occurs. For example, Lynn Nottage's *Ruined* (2008), a Pulitzer Prize-winning play inspired by Brecht's *Mother Courage* and set in the war-torn Democratic Republic of Congo, premiered at the Chicago Goodman Theater. Lessac's *Truth in Translation* has been staged in other post-conflict sites around the world, including Northern Ireland, Rwanda, Zimbabwe, and the Western Balkans. Argentina's Theater for Identity (Teatro por la identidad) festival was first established in 2001 by theater practitioners working with the Grandmothers of Plaza de Mayo (Abuelas de Plaza de Mayo), an organization aiming to raise awareness of the existence of children who were illegally appropriated and adopted during the country's military dictatorship (1976–1983). Starting in 2004 the festival also took place in Spain, adapting the mission of the festival to include themes related to memory of the Spanish Civil War. These global initiatives raise questions about the representation of conflict and how it is staged, perceived, and understood in different contexts. To what extent do these transnational performances promote knowledge of and engagement with rights violations in other areas of the world? How can the consolidation of a global audience promote cross-cultural networks of knowledge and empathy without homogenizing and commodifying contextually specific experiences of violence?

Article 2 of the UDHR recognizes rights without "distinction of any kind," specifically identifying "race, colour, sex, language, religion, political or other opinion, national or social origin, property, birth or other status" in this claim. Taking this definition into account, any play that focuses on one of these "distinctions" also engages human rights concerns, making the scope of the study of human rights and theater potentially infinite. One particularly ambivalent area in the consideration of human rights equality, as predicated upon freedom from discrimination, is cultural rights. Article 22 of the UDHR affirms, "Everyone has the right freely to participate in the cultural life of the community," thus framing cultural rights under the protection of freedom of expression. Conversely, the International Covenant on Civil and Political Rights (1966) makes explicit reference to cultural rights belonging to members of minority groups: "In those States in which ethnic, religious or linguistic minorities exist, persons belonging to such minorities shall not be denied the right, in community with the other members of their group, to enjoy their own culture, to profess and practice their own religion, or to use their own language." Theater intersects with both of these visions of cultural rights, as an artistic genre that both embodies the right to freedom of expression and transmits culturally specific perspectives, histories, traditions, and critiques of colonization. A large number of postcolonial plays take up the assertion of cultural rights amidst the legacy of imperialism. Wole Soyinka's *Death and the*

King's Horsemen (Nigeria, 1975) provides an emblematic case study of the clash between local cultural and colonial values. The performance artist Guillermo Gómez Peña presents his piece *Border Brujo* (1988–1989) to explore the hybridity of the US–Mexican border, described by Gómez Peña as a wound left by colonization. And Daniel David Moses's *Almighty Voice and his Wife* (Great Canadian Theatre Company, 1991) parodies the attempts of non-natives to construct "authentic" representations of indigeneity.

As noted, this chapter does not pretend to offer a comprehensive account across continents, cultures, and centuries, particularly since definitions of what constitutes human rights and performance are constantly in flux. Rather, we trace the interconnected development of Western drama and human rights in the eighteenth century, to highlight the ways in which modern drama and an emerging human rights discourse in Europe jointly transformed conceptions of subjectivity and spectatorship. We then turn to plays and performances in the second half of the twentieth and early twenty-first centuries that respond to mass trauma by offering a forum for mourning, commemoration, and testimony; exposing and denouncing human rights abuses; and introducing documentary evidence. Others complement the law in transitional contexts and point to the limits of reconciliation. Yet others explore "the self-perception of transnationality" (Beck 2000, p. 12) that informs the globalized age and captures, especially, the experience of dislocation produced by migration and exile. In our discussion of drama and human rights, we emphasize that theater, often functioning as a critical response to events, may also transform the discourses and overarching structures, conceptions, and institutions that establish the conditions for both human rights and their violation. We hope this historical and conceptual overview provides a point of departure for thinking about the interactions of theater and human rights as they evolve in the twenty-first century.

References

Arendt, H. 1962. *The Origins of Totalitarianism* (New York: Meridian Books).

Beck, U. 2000. *What is Globalization?* (Cambridge: Polity Press).

Bennett, B. 1986. *Modern Drama and German Classicism: Renaissance from Lessing to Brecht* (Ithaca, NY: Cornell University Press).

Carlson, M. 2001. *The Haunted Stage* (Ann Arbor: University of Michigan Press).

Cohen, M. 2002. "Sentimental Communities," pp. 106–132 in M. Cohen and C. Dever, eds., *The Literary Channel: The Inter-National Invention of the Novel* (Princeton, NJ: Princeton University Press).

Diderot, D. 1965 [1757]. "Entretiens sur le fils naturel," pp. 80–175 in P. Vernière, ed. *Denis Diderot: Œuvres esthéthiques* (Paris: Classiques Garnier).

Diderot, D. 1965 [1758]. "Discours de la poésie dramatique," pp. 189–287 in P. Vernière, ed. *Denis Diderot: Œuvres esthéthiques* (Paris: Classiques Garnier).

Habermas, J. 1991 [1962]. *The Structural Transformation of the Public Sphere: An Inquiry into a Category of Bourgeois Society* (Cambridge, MA: MIT Press).

Holland, P. and M. Patterson. 1997. "Eighteenth-Century Theatre," pp. 255–298 in J. R. Brown, ed. *The Oxford Illustrated History of Theatre* (Oxford: Oxford University Press).

Huyssen, A. 2003. *Present Pasts: Urban Palimpsests and the Politics of Memory (Cultural Memory in the Present)* (Stanford, CA: Stanford University Press).

Lessing, G.E. 1890 [1754]. "Abhandlungen von dem weinerlichen oder rührenden Lustspiele." pp. 6–53 in K. Lachmann and F. Muncker, eds. *Gotthold Ephraim Lessing: Sämtliche Schriften.* Volume 6 (Stuttgart: Göschen'sche Verlagshandlung).

Lessing, G. E. 1890 [1756]. "Des Herrn Jakob Thomson sämtliche Trauerspiele: Vorrede," pp. 66–71 in K. Lachmann and F. Muncker, eds. *Gotthold Ephraim Lessing: Sämtliche Schriften.* Vol. 7 (Stuttgart: Göschen'sche Verlagshandlung).

MacIntyre, A. 1966. *A Short History of Ethics: A History of Moral Philosophy from the Homeric Age to the Twentieth Century* (New York: Macmillan).

MacIntyre, A. 1980. *After Virtue: A Study in Moral Theory* (South Bend, IN: University of Notre Dame Press).
Rae, P. 2009. *Theatre and Human Rights* (Houndmills, Basingstoke: Palgrave Macmillan).
Roach, J. 1996. *Cities of the Dead: Circum-Atlantic Performance* (New York: Columbia University Press).
Rokem, F. 2000. *Performing History: Theatrical Representations of the Past in Contemporary Theatre* (Iowa City: University of Iowa Press).
Schechner, R. 1988. *Performance Theory* (New York: Routledge).
Stiglitz, J. 2003. "On Liberty, the Right to Know, and Public Discourse: The Role of Transparency in Public Life." In M.J. Gibney, ed. *Globalizing Rights* (Oxford: Oxford University Press).
Szondi, P. 1973. *Die Theorie des bürgerlichen Trauerspiels im 18. Jahrhundert* (Frankfurt: Suhrkamp).
Taylor, C. 1992. *Sources of the Self: The Making of the Modern Identity* (Cambridge, MA: Harvard University Press).
Taylor, D. 2003. *The Archive and the Repertoire: Performing Cultural Memory in the Americas* (Durham, NC: Duke University Press).
Van Erven, E. 2001. *Community Theatre: Global Perspectives* (London: Routledge).
Weber, M. 2002 [1905]. *The Protestant Ethic and the Spirit of Capitalism* (London: Penguin).

57

Architecture and human rights

Graeme Bristol

"Architecture" and "human rights" are terms we do not see together with any regularity. The reaction of architects to that particular combination of words is testament to the rarity with which these words are seen in the same sentence. What does architecture have to do with human rights? My purpose here is to answer that question briefly and to provide some background to the relationship between the work that architects do and the effect of that work on human rights.

To do that the first priority here is the definition of terms. One of the reasons for the surprise attending this combination of words lies in the definition of architecture itself.

Terms

The question, "What does architecture have to do with human rights?" is based on a relatively narrow definition of both architecture and human rights. The question implies that architecture is seen as a technical enterprise. Architects are hired by clients to marshal financial and material resources around the requirements of the client's particular needs for some kind of building. Part of that process involves dealing with laws and regulations governing land use (usually zoning bylaws) and buildings (building codes), the laws of gravity, and the nature of materials. These are all organized in a pleasing manner in keeping with the Vitruvian definition of architecture as "*firmitas, utilitas, venustas*" – "firmness, commodity, and delight" (Vitruvius, a Roman architect at the time of Augustus, wrote the Ten Books of Architecture. "Firmness, Commodity, and Delight" (Book I, Ch. 3) were from Henry Wotton's translation in his 1624 treatise, *The Elements of Architecture*. The Ten Books are available online at http://penelope.uchicago.edu/Thayer/E/Roman/Texts/Vitruvius/1*.html). Architecture, then, is seen as a product exhibiting these features. There is nothing in any of these three qualities of architecture that suggests anything about human rights. The durability of a building is a function of the materials and how they are brought together – a technical issue. The utility of a building is a function of the requirements of the client and, most of the time, the users. This can be relegated to a physical issue about efficiencies and ergonomics. Delight or beauty is a very subjective issue and related to the cultural context in which the building is built. The beauty of some buildings endures while that of others is, at best, fleeting. The Portland Building by Michael Graves is an example. At the time of the award of the design commission in 1982, Graves was lauded for bringing postmodernism into the mainstream of architecture. In October 2009, a mere twenty-seven years later, the building was featured in an article in *Travel & Leisure* as one of "The World's Ugliest Buildings" (http://www.travelandleisure.com/articles/the-worlds-ugliest-buildings/1). None of these three qualities appear to have much to do with human rights.

My use of the term "architecture" is defined by more than those Vitruvian elements. In this context the term refers to all design activities related to the development of the built environment. This would include planning and engineering as well as architecture. It involves our regulations governing land use as well as those governing buildings themselves. It involves civil engineering projects such as dams and highways as well as urban design and planning. As such, the term "development and human rights" might be more accurate except that "development" is such a broad term – including everything from curriculum development to infrastructure development – that it leads to more confusion that clarity, particularly with a wide variety of aid agencies.

In this context, the term "human rights" also requires clarification, particularly for the design professions. In the modern incarnation of human rights since the UN Universal Declaration of Human Rights (UDHR) in 1948, rights have been viewed in three basic categories:

- civil rights and liberties, such as speech, publication, association, religion movement;
- political rights, such as the ability to influence government and choose representatives;
- economic, social, and cultural rights, such as the right to work, the right to social security during illness and old age, the right to an income consistent with human dignity, the right to leisure, and the right to an education.

The first of these categories of rights can be considered to be generally negative, in that it provides freedom from the restrictions of others. The obligations of others that correspond to my civil rights are to leave me alone, to refrain from actions that restrict my liberties.

The second and third categories tend to be positive rights in that the obligations of others in realizing these rights require action and, frequently, money. Although there are costs associated with our right to influence our governments, we have come to accept these costs as a legitimate price for our ability to exercise those rights. It is the third category of rights that remains contentious. Unlike the right to be left alone, the right to housing entails some obligation on the part of society to fulfill that right through the provision of services, the transfer of wealth, and the investment of resources.

Karel Vasak, the Czech-born jurist and former legal advisor to UNESCO, had a different set of categories based on the French tripartite motto, "*Liberté, égalité, fraternité*" (Chauffour 2009, p. 32). These were the "three generations" of rights – civil and political rights (*liberté*) arising out of the French and American revolutions in the eighteenth century; economic, social, and cultural rights (*égalité*) arising after World War I; and, more recently, solidarity rights (*fraternité*), which would include collective rights, the right to self-determination, and the right to development, as well as rights related to sustainability – intergenerational equity and the right to resources – and those related to cultural heritage.

Historically, particularly in the West, the focus was on political and civil rights. Even in the drafting of the UDHR, conflicts arose concerning the emphasis on political and civil rights by the US and UK delegates and the emphasis on economic and social rights on the part of the Russian delegates. The perplexed response of architects is understandable, then, when the term "human rights" is joined with architecture. The assumption is that human rights mean civil and political rights. What does architecture have to do with voting or discrimination or the right to a fair trial? Architects, engineers, and planners are involved with development. All these issues of civil and political rights are the domain of lawyers, not architects.

And therein rests one of the basic problems of connecting rights to architecture. In the post-World War II evolution of human rights, there has been a compartmentalization of rights and development – a compartmentalization that led James Wolfensohn, the former president of the World Bank, to say in 2004:

> to some of our shareholders the very mention of the words human rights is inflammatory language. It's getting into areas of politics, and into areas about which they are very concerned. We decided just to go around it and we talk the language of economics and social development.
>
> *(Wolfensohn 2005, p. 21)*

On the one hand, then, we have engineers, economists, and social scientists and on the other lawyers and philosophers, each with their own strategies and actions – the former focusing on economic policy and infrastructure development and the latter focusing on political and legal reform (Robinson 2005, p. 27). As Wolfensohn's statement implies, those in the development sector tend to view their actions as apolitical, objective, scientific, technical, and value-neutral. The development sector continues to view the world of rights as one of abstraction, constantly shifting political positions, subjective, relative, and value-laden – a world to be avoided if work is to be completed on time and on budget.

This compartmentalization was pronounced enough even within the UN system; in the reform of the UN in 1997 the Secretary-General, Kofi Annan, called for reforms in the approach taken to the mainstreaming of rights in development practice. This was the rights-based approach to development (RBA). In his Annual Report, he said:

> The rights-based approach to development describes situations not simply in terms of human needs, or of developmental requirements, but in terms of society's obligation to respond to the inalienable rights of individuals. It empowers people to demand justice as a right, not as charity, and gives communities a moral basis from which to claim international assistance where needed.
>
> One of the key points of the RBA is the clear recognition of duties on the one hand and rights on the other. A needs-based approach, can be met out of charitable intentions, but rights are based on legal obligations (and in some cases ethical obligations that have a strong foundation in human dignity even though they are only in the process of being solidified into legal obligations).
>
> *(quoted in Nyamu-Musembi and Cornwall 2004, p. 3)*

Despite the United Nations Development Programme (UNDP) policy report in 1998, "Integrating human rights with sustainable human development," making that integrative shift in the field proved difficult, particularly in infrastructure development. It is no wonder, then, that architects and engineers practicing outside the UN system might find it difficult to make the connection between human rights and design. I intend here to give a few examples of how that connection can be made and what it can imply for practice.

Background

These connections were slow to develop. They started with the UN Universal Declaration of Human Rights and, in particular, Article 25:

> (1) Everyone has the right to a standard of living adequate for the health and well-being of himself and of his family, including food, clothing, housing and medical care and necessary social services, and the right to security in the event of unemployment, sickness, disability, widowhood, old age or other lack of livelihood in circumstances beyond his control.

It was just that one word, "housing." Housing is a right. Architects design housing. It was a weak connection but there was something there. The problem with the connection is in the implementation. Architects are typically at least one step removed from the duty to protect or provide for that right. This duty is borne by different levels of government through landlord–tenant legislation, through housing/tax subsidies, and so on. Architects and engineers may provide design services to a government client who is funding a housing project but under those circumstances they are providing technical support to the "duty-bearer" (the government authority) in providing for that right. As a connection, then, it is hardly enough.

There are two examples, though, that make this connection somewhat more firm.

Fair Housing Act

The Fair Housing Act (Title VIII of the Civil Rights Act of 1968) added to the prohibitions against discrimination by prohibiting discrimination in the sale, rental, or financing of housing based on race, color, religion, and national origin. In 1988 this Act was amended (Fair Housing Amendments Act of 1988) by expanding non-discrimination provisions to include disabled people and families with children. If the design of the housing unit is such that it restricts its use by the handicapped, the building owner is as much as saying, "You can't live here because you're handicapped (or black, or Jewish, or Asian, or female, single, etc.)." This kind of discrimination is outlawed because it infringes on the civil rights of people. In the case of the handicapped, it infringes on those rights by acts of design. Architects, then, have the opportunity to act for or against equity in the design of housing. Their knowledge and the use of it can dramatically affect people's access to civil rights. This marked one of the first instances where design was governed not only by building codes and land-use regulations but also by civil rights law.

While we would expect that building code regulations would cover any design requirements for the disabled, this was not quite the case, as SLCE Architects of New York learned when a complaint was filed against them and the developer of Avalon Chrystie Place, a residential apartment complex in Manhattan (see http://www.justice.gov/crt/housing/documents/avaloncomp.pdf for the text of the complaint). The US District Court, Southern District of New York, claimed that the kitchens and bathrooms were not useable for individuals using a wheelchair, that there was no reinforcement for later installation of grab bars, that the circulation (doors and hallways) into and through the dwelling unit was not accessible, and that the public areas of the building were not useable by people with disabilities. As such, they "[f]ailed to design and construct dwellings in compliance with the accessibility and adaptability features mandated by 42 U.S.C. § 3604 (f)(3)(C)" (available at http://www.law.cornell.edu/uscode/42/usc_sec_42_00003604----000-.html). The architects and developer, "[a]long with city officials, ... assert that compliance with what is known as Local Law 58 satisfies the standards set by the Fair Housing Act" (Bagli 2008). A spokesperson for one of the advocacy groups, Kleo King of United Spinal Association, made the key point: "The real point that the Department of Justice is trying to make is that people building these buildings have to look at both laws to make sure that they're in compliance" (Bagli 2008).

Architects will familiarize themselves with contract law, environmental law, insurance law, labor law, and a host of other legislation in addition to building codes and land-use regulations. Given the advice of Kleo King, it would seem prudent for architects to become more aware of the implications of human rights on their work.

Community level: the Pom Mahakan story

In 2001 the Bangkok Metropolitan Administration (BMA) ratified the Rattanakosin Master Plan for the old historic part of the city where the Grand Palace and many historic temples were located. The plan was largely driven by the desire to capture more tourist dollars in the city rather than just the beach resorts outside of Bangkok. To do this, the BMA intended to "beautify" the area by making the main ceremonial street – Ratchadamnoern – into what they described as the "Champs-Élysées of the East." In addition to reusing old office buildings for art galleries and museums, they also intended to create more park land around existing monuments such as *Wat Saket* (the Golden Mount).

Across the canal (*klong*) from the Golden Mount was an existing community which had been there for around 150 years – the Pom Mahakan community. They occupied a piece of land between the klong and the last remaining piece of the old wall of the city. It was about 50 meters wide and 150 meters long. At the north end was an old fort (*Pom*) which formed part of the original battlements of Rattanakosin. It was home to about three hundred people who, in January 2003, were faced with eviction notices from BMA as part of the first phase of this beautification imposed by the Master Plan.

Two months before this eviction notice, architecture students of King Mongkut's University of Technology Thonburi (KMUTT) began working with this community as part of a design studio. These yearly studios began as a response to a student competition by the International Union of Architects (UIA) to implement the Habitat Agenda in the students' home city. For this studio, then, it involved working with vulnerable communities on issues of culture, history, development, sustainability, and tenure as well as, in this context, parks. The BMA, as part of the Master Plan, was determined to remove this community in order to replace it with a park from which tourists could view the Golden Mount.

The students had been working with the community for two and a half months and were nearing the end of the semester in early March 2003. A presentation to the community had been prepared for Saturday, 25 January 2003, at which the students were to review with the community all that had been talked about and agreed upon over the last two months. It was a surprise to both the community and the students that the BMA had posted eviction notices on all the doors of the community. While the students were aware of the Rattanakosin Master Plan, no one was expecting it to be implemented any time soon. However, the BMA was giving them thirty days to vacate the land before the houses were to be torn down. Some of these houses were old traditional teak houses that were as old as the settlement itself. One of these old houses had been turned into a community museum.

With that notice, the students and the community had to rethink the program for improvement in the community. Why invest in building anything when they only had thirty days to move? At the same time, we could not abandon the project. Instead the students took what they had learned and compiled it all into a report that provided an argument about why this community should stay. Part of that argument was about history and culture – the community had amassed a great deal of information about the settlement, the people, the buildings, and trees on the land. Another part of the argument, though, was an alternative plan which included a park but kept the housing as well.

This document was presented to the community leaders in mid-February. They immediately took it to the BMA planning department and declared that they had an alternative plan for the development of this land and the proposed park. The BMA reaction really came as no surprise. "We're the planners here. Not you. We already have a plan and it's not this."

In many instances, this would have marked the end of their story, but this community and its leadership had been fighting BMA for years already and they were not ready to give up. They took the report to the National Human Rights Commission (NHRC) with the claim that their housing rights were being abridged. A hearing was scheduled for the first week in March.

Along with the community leaders, the architecture students attended this meeting. In addition to the students and the community – sitting in the back row – there were representatives from the BMA planning department, the office of the Governor of Bangkok, and the National Housing Authority, all of whom were there to fight the community's contention about this alleged human rights violation. At one point in the proceedings the NHRC chairman requested that one of the architecture students present this alternative plan. For a very brief five minutes she explained that they had worked with the community in developing alternatives that would meet the needs of the BMA for a park and would also meet the needs of the community. She talked about the community history and how the plan intended to preserve it and she talked about the proposed community economic development plan that had been devised by the community. At the end of that presentation, the NHRC chairman said that he saw nothing wrong with this plan and did not know why the BMA planning department was so opposed to it. He asked the authorities to hold off on their eviction order and to review the plan and come to some amicable decision about how the rights of the community could be asserted while still allowing the Master Plan to be implemented. The penny dropped. This alternative plan proved to be an effective tool in the argument for human rights. This was not just about legal arguments; it was about design as well. Design can be used as a tool to support human rights.

The Pom Mahakan experience was not just about using design as part of an argument for continued tenure. In such documents as the UDHR, the Right to Development (DRD), Convention on the Rights of the Child (CRC), and many other international and national documents, we can see a number of rights that relate directly to development and to the Pom Mahakan experience. For example:

- Participation (DRD 2.3, 8.2) – "free and meaningful participation in development and in the fair distribution of the benefits resulting therefrom." A significant part of the design studio was related to participatory methodologies. In addition to its importance to determining a practical and relevant program for design, it is also good preparation for future work in the profession where, increasingly, participation in planning is required by legislation going as far back at the Environmental Protection Agency in 1972 (http://www.epa.gov/history/topics/fwpca/04.htm).
- Expression (UDHR 19, CRC 13.1, 31.2) – freedom of expression in any media. In the context of Pom Mahakan, this was particularly related to the Convention on the Rights of the Child and ensuring that children played a role in the design and development of the community in which they lived. Further, though, a case should be made that part of the expression of a community is in the way it creates its environment. In some cases the ancestors of the residents had planted the trees that the BMA considered to be part of the city's heritage. The residents were very protective and possessive of the old teak houses on the land. All of this could be considered to be part of a cultural expression at the community level.

- Information (UDHR 19, CRC 17) – cooperation in the production and exchange of information. Increasingly Freedom of Information Acts have been a cornerstone of transparency in government. With Pom Mahakan and so many other examples, information on planning and development proposals are rarely common knowledge for most city residents, particularly the poor. It is here that designers can use their "insider" knowledge of development to provide better access to communities in which they are working. Alternative planning is better done with information than without it. The Urban Resource Center in Pakistan, founded by a group of architects led by Arif Hasan, is a good example of how the design professions can actively support and promote this right.
- Education (UDHR 26, CRC 28, 29) – "directed to the full development of the human personality." This must occur with all participants – both adults and children in the community as well as students and faculty working with the community. In the Pom Mahakan example, the community leaders were teaching the local history, the students were providing the technical support and gathering data about the Rattanakosin Master Plan, and the children were learning about their built environment.
- Standard of living (UDHR 25.1) – "right to a standard of living adequate for the health and well-being of himself and of his family, including food, clothing, housing, and medical care and necessary social services." Again, the focus here is on housing and, with Pom Mahakan, the development of the alternative plan provided an argument for keeping the community where it was.

Much of what we see above here relates directly to citizenship and democracy, but it can, should, and sometimes must by law (participation) relate to the way we practice architecture.

Three focal points

It was out of the Pom Mahakan experience that the Centre for Architecture and Human Rights was founded. It was motivated by a basic question: What other connections might there be between human rights and architecture?

In addressing that question, there were three broad areas in which I saw possibilities: architecture itself, the urban context in which much of architecture exists, and finally the environment as a whole. With such an expansive set of domains, it was obvious that this was not just about architecture but about the process and products of development – about dams and roads, about urban planning and land use, about environmental justice and the right to the city. Here are just two examples in the field of architecture where that relationship between design and rights can be exercised to benefit both.

In addition to the human rights implications of universal design and participation in the design process, there is the relationship between building codes and housing rights. In developing countries where codes have often been imported from their colonizers, the weight of these codes is unbearable for the poor and, as a consequence, much of a city's housing stock is illegal (Hardoy and Satterthwaite 1989, p. 132). Western cities are not immune from the growth of illegal housing. Often this is a result of urban land economics. Where the cost of housing is beyond the reach of the middle class and the poor, the only options are either very long commutes into the city or subdividing existing housing into illegal suites. In one recent report out of New York City where city officials were clamping down on illegal suites, housing advocates reminded the officials that "illegal housing units will continue to exist so long as city building codes and zoning regulations prevent the construction of affordable housing" (Belsha 2010).

This is not a call to make buildings less safe in order to make them more affordable. Rather, it is an indication of the relationship between codes (part of our expertise as design professionals) and human rights. The design professions tend to focus on the technical aspects of these codes but there are broader implications that dramatically affect the rights of individuals and communities (Marcuse 1986).

Another area where architects and engineers can act in support of human rights is in construction contracts. A number of organizations including the International Labour Organization and the Building and Wood Workers' International are looking at the standard international construction contract from the perspective of enforcement of labor standards on site. If this is done through contractual obligation as well as legislation it might be more possible to establish and improve standards. This has already happened with environmental standards. Some architects and engineers will far exceed existing environmental regulations of the jurisdiction in which they are working by setting additional standards in the contract itself. If such additional requirements are possible and enforceable in order to raise environmental standards, they can certainly be enacted for human rights standards. This is a particularly important issue where there is very weak enforcement of labor laws on site and the extensive use of migrant labor, which often leads to the presence of children on construction sites – not as child labor but as toddlers who come with their working parents because there is nowhere else for them to go. Where there is no protection by unions or government agencies such as the Occupational Safety and Health Administration (OSHA), the problem of labor on construction sites is a significant human rights issue. Some protections are already happening through the use of "social clauses" being added to municipal and national government procurement contracts and construction contracts. However this still seems to be confined to Western countries where there are already other forms of protection and enforcement. It is where there are no other protections that international architects and engineers can use their persuasion to enforce not only important environmental standards but also human rights standards in their contracts.

There are many other areas where architects, engineers, and planners can use their skills to promote and protect human rights. In urban development, for example, these design professions can be involved in fighting exclusionary zoning, the privatization of public space, and, related to that, supporting the right to the city.

In the field of environmental protection, architecture has been active, particularly since the publication of the Brundtland Report, in supporting and advancing improved energy efficiency and better use of the material resources that make up the built environment. Where architects and engineers work on issues of sustainability, though, they focus very heavily on the technical aspects of energy and materials and very little on the equity aspects of sustainability. Toward what are the resources being directed? In another context this question was raised by the Architects, Designers and Planners for Social Responsibility (ADPSR) when they initiated their boycott of the design of prisons. It is their belief that following the 700 percent increase in the prison population since the mid-1980s, there must be a more productive way of using our skills as well as our financial and material resources. We could also start asking what the point might be of making more and more shopping malls that, while they may meet Leadership in Energy and Environmental Design (LEED) standards, are still temples to conspicuous consumption. Should architects and engineers leave all those decisions to their clients and simply provide technical support to getting the job done, whatever that job may be? As professions governed by legislation giving them a monopoly on the provision of these services, their first duty must be toward the public good and they are in a position to add their voices to the way in which the "public good" is defined.

Beyond that, as with the Chrystie Place example above where architects were caught short by following local regulations rather than the civil rights legislation of the Fair Housing Act, environmental law is moving beyond the technical. In an implementation of what has been called "Wild Law" (Cullinan 2003), the Community Environmental Legal Defense Fund (CELDF) has developed municipal legislation, now in use in a number of jurisdictions beginning with the Tamaqua Borough Council in Pennsylvania, which "recognizes that ecosystems in Tamaqua possess enforceable rights against corporations." With that we are no longer talking about "human" rights but the rights of ecosystems themselves. This argument was presented first in the early 1970s with Christopher Stone's essay "Should Trees Have Standing? Toward Legal Rights for Natural Objects" (Stone 1972). This was followed shortly thereafter by the Supreme Court judgment on *Sierra Club v. Morton* in which Justice Douglas, in his dissenting opinion, wrote:

> The critical question of "standing" would be simplified and also put neatly in focus if we fashioned a federal rule that allowed environmental issues to be litigated before federal agencies or federal courts in the name of the inanimate object about to be despoiled, defaced, or invaded by roads and bulldozers and where injury is the subject of public outrage.
>
> (Sierra Club v. Morton *1972)*

With the help of CELDF, the Sierra Club and many other environmental organizations, such laws are being enacted in many local and regional jurisdictions. The implications on the practice of architecture and engineering have yet to be examined.

Conclusion

There are many ways for architects, engineers, and planners to be blind-sided by rapidly evolving law. Under such circumstances it is important for the design professions to be much more aware of the implications of human rights on their work. More importantly, though, our built environment would be vastly improved by the inclusion of a rights-based approach to its design. That would include a much more engaged approach to participation of communities in the design of their buildings and public spaces.

In order for that to happen, there are a number of steps the Centre for Architecture and Human Rights is taking through:

- Education – for children, professional programs, continuing education for practicing professionals, training programs for field workers and community leaders.
- Action research – in particular, engaging students in research on current issues involving vulnerable communities. In 2008–10 at KMUTT this was focused on migrant construction workers in Bangkok.
- Demonstration projects – it is important to be able to show practicing professionals, students, and the general public how this can work. The first demonstration project was a daycare/school/community center for undocumented migrant construction workers.
- Monitoring – this would involve the monitoring of urban regulations governing land use and the built environment.
- Advocacy – like the Pom Mahakan community or a number of communities facing eviction after the tsunami in December 2004, there are situations where vulnerable communities need support to be able to provide alternatives to existing development proposals.

> They also need access to information about development proposals that is typically not forthcoming from any other source; students and professionals working with communities can help find and distribute that information.

From the construction of major dam projects to urban regeneration and expressways through cities – all of these developments have a profound but typically unrecognized effect on human rights. They certainly have an effect on environmental rights and, often, environmental justice. The more that relationship is recognized, the better the built environment will be.

References

Bagli, Charles V. 2008. "U.S. Says Many Apartments Violate Law on Disabled." *New York Times*, 18 August. At: http://www.nytimes.com/2008/08/19/nyregion/19disabled.html.

Belsha, Kalyn. 2010. "Battle Plan vs Illegal Housing." CityLimits.org. 13 April. At: http://www.citylimits.org/news/article.cfm?article_id=3930.

Chauffour, Jean-Pierre. 2009. *The Power of Freedom: Uniting Human Rights and Development* (Washington, DC: Cato Institute).

Cullinan, Cormac. 2003. *Wild Law: A Manifesto for Earth Justice* (Totnes, Devon: Green Books).

Hardoy, Jorge and David Satterthwaite. 1989. *Squatter Citizen: Life in the Urban Third World* (London: Earthscan).

Marcuse, Peter. 1986. "Housing Policy and the Myth of the Benevolent State." In Rachel Bratt, Chester Hartman, and Ann Meyerson, *Critical Perspectives on Housing* (Philadelphia, PA: Temple University Press).

Nyamu-Musembi, Celestine and Andrea Cornwall. 2004. "What is the 'Rights-Based Approach' All About? Perspectives from International Development Agencies." Institute of Development Studies, Sussex, *IDS Working Paper* 234.

Robinson, Mary. 2005. "What Rights Can Add to Good Development Practice," pp. 25–41 in Philip Alston and Mary Robinson, eds. *Human Rights and Development: Towards Mutual Reinforcement* (Oxford: Oxford University Press).

Sierra Club v. Morton. 1972. 405 U.S. 727.

Stone, Christopher D. 1972. "Should Trees Have Standing? Toward Legal Rights for Natural Objects." *Southern California Law Review*, Vol. 45, pp. 450–501.

Wolfensohn, James. 2005. "Some Reflections on Human Rights and Development," pp. 19–24 in Philip Alston and Mary Robinson, eds. *Human Rights and Development: Towards Mutual Reinforcement* (Oxford: Oxford University Press).

58

Photography without borders

Ariella Azoulay

Since the time they were conquered, and increasingly over the past two decades, the Occupied Territories have become an extended photography studio that can spread at any given moment to more and more areas, including private homes. The presence of Palestinians in those homes does not constitute an obstacle for the photographers milling about the studio; it affords the grounds and opportunity for their being there. There are countless more photographers roaming the studio than "ordinary" areas, and the local inhabitants are far more exposed to their activity than is the average citizen a few kilometers away.[1]

This is a flexible, modular, temporary studio that keeps pace with military operational activity and settlers' movements. It sets up in places that have been invaded for varying durations, sometimes for relatively lengthy periods, but mostly temporarily, for a limited and fleeting time, until the phenomenon that prompted it to be set up fades or disappears, interest in it is lost, the army packs up and leaves, or else the photographer is simply ousted from the area. The disbandment of the photographers who had been staying in one corner of the studio is always transitory, and is not evidence that this studio without borders has been closed forever. The studio continues to exist in this fashion so long as the separation between private and public space in the Occupied Territories is violently transgressed. The existence of a photography studio across an entire territory attests to the flawed civil status of the population residing in that territory. This flawed status is illustrated by the fact that Palestinians can be regularly photographed, at different hours of the day, in various life situations, within the boundaries of public space and no less so within the boundaries of their private space, which likewise becomes accessible to any cameras that happen to be around.

In recent decades, a substantial and ongoing presence of cameras in a particular region can serve to indicate an area where a disaster is occurring. However, a multiplicity and prevalence of cameras is merely the visible tip of an area prone to disaster. The relatively unhampered mobility of cameras between private and public spaces is the sign of a flawed spatial organization, and one to which the ruled population of that area has not consented. This spatial organization, whose tracks can be read in many photographs produced from this area, is an expression of what I term regime disaster.

It is very easy to strip this photograph (Figure 58.2) by Rina Castelnuovo of the details that identify it as regime disaster and see in it "a demolished house," *yet another* demolished house.

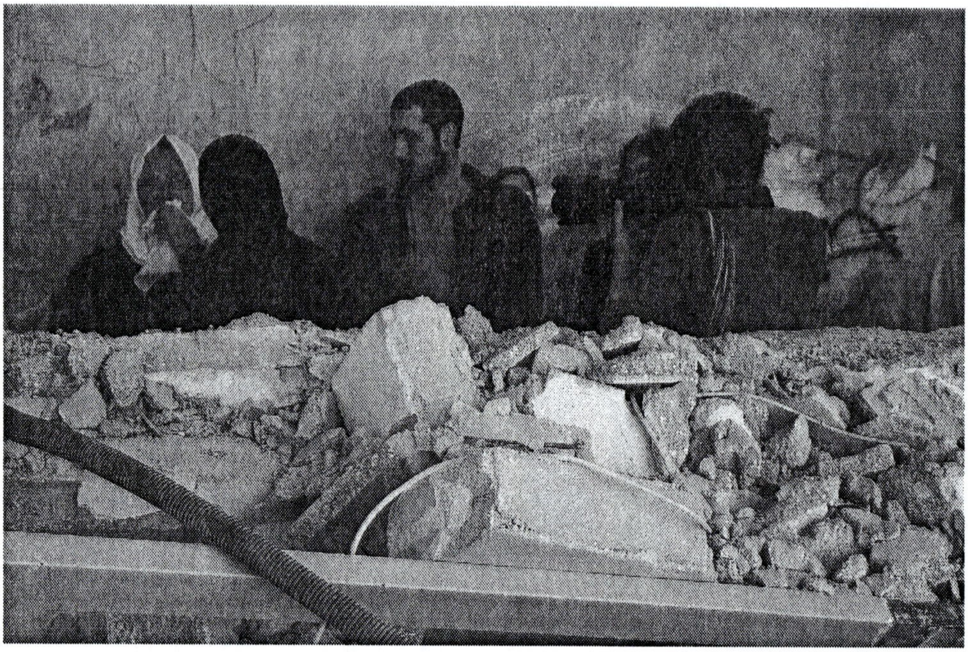

Figure 58.1 Anne Paq, Activestills.org, Jerusalem, Dec. 2007

We can also readily imagine the tent set up close to the house by one of the aid organizations, with the girl seated on the bed and facing the camera. Israel's last major operation in Gaza (December 2008–January 2009) turned tens of thousands of Palestinians into tent dwellers in a matter of weeks. The massive and concentrated devastation, which included damage to vital infrastructure, necessitated a "solution" of a different kind than the sort proffered when the destruction takes place in individual units. The "solution" that was provided for the problem that had been created is as old as the State of Israel – setting up a tent camp. This new tent campsite articulates the unbearable ease with which the violence of pillaging the home and destroying it is imprinted and presented as justified, and the Palestinian continues to be presented as a tent dweller by nature. The tent is a solution – temporary, permanent, or temporary-permanent – that is provided to Palestinians, for whom an exposed space such as this becomes home (see B'Tselem video clip). Sixty years of photographs like these have paved the awareness of Israel's Jewish citizens, as well as that of the citizens of the world, and have showed them that the Palestinian living environment comprises walls with holes or plain canvas tarps, as though it were second nature for Palestinians to live in tents. Reading a photograph such as the one by Rina Castelnuovo as a historic document can rescue it from the abstraction and naturalization of the visible, by cross-referencing the information that is registered in it with extra-photographic information. Thus the rendering of the house exposed can consistently be traced to an attack by a state violence, beginning with the disastrous loss of the home that belonged to the girl's grandparents, which happened when they were expelled from their homes in Palestine in the late 1940s, and became temporary residents of the Khan Yunis refugee camp. The military force accompanies its activity with cameras, or with photographers who are embedded with the unit or who maneuver independently along the roads the army has opened up. From the photograph it is possible to characterize and identify the type of destruction. We have before us "targeted" destruction that is

Figure 58.2 Rina Castelnuovo, Balata refugee camp, 2002

designed to hit a single housing unit in an apartment building. Destruction of this type pinpoints objectives and is executed out of an effort to focus the strike and limit the spread of damage to adjacent apartments in a way that would not appear to contradict the Supreme Court's rulings on the use of force in the Occupied Territories. The price of attaining the objective – destruction of an adjacent apartment, which the army deemed justified – was paid this time by the family whose home we are now looking at by mediation of the photograph. The demolished house in the picture *is not* the one the army wanted to destroy. Viewing the photograph as a historic document enables us to read in it not a one-time violation of a human right, but rather a regime template of the past 60 years wherein a house in which Palestinians reside is not protected, and its penetration is largely a matter of time and circumstances.

Regime disaster is prone to occur when one population group is ruled, over a lengthy period, in a different and distinct manner from other ruled groups. From a political standpoint, the dividing line between the two ruled populations, and their respective exposure to disaster for which the regime is responsible, usually lies between one being a population of citizens and the other a population of flawed citizens or non-citizens. When dealing with disaster areas, this dividing line assumes two additional features: the first has to do with photography, and takes the form of a division between those who are constantly exposed to being photographed and those who are not; and the second relates to space, and takes the form of a division between those who can retreat to a private space of their own and set a boundary to the regime and those who cannot.

My discussion is based on the Israeli–Palestinian case, but I draw from it a general perspective for rethinking human rights and photography in contexts where a violation or abrogation of rights occurs as part of a regime that thus treats a populace it rules. The State of Israel conquered the West Bank and Gaza Strip in 1967, ever since which it has governed their inhabitants as non-citizens. Politically, legally, and culturally speaking, the regime in Israel does not recognize the Palestinians in the Gaza Strip as ruled people who are subject to its authority and responsibility, and defines its rule over the Palestinians in the West Bank as a temporary matter. However, this fact does not alter the subjugation of Palestinians in the Occupied Territories to the ruling apparatus of the Israeli regime. Such a regime is a categorical example of differential rule of populations, which creates continual disaster or life on the verge of disaster, which provides a breeding ground for ongoing violation of human rights.

From the United Nations Partition Plan for Palestine of 1947 until today, the Israeli regime has destroyed some 300,000 Palestinian homes, and it is not done yet. It is impossible to go on interpreting such a massive destruction of homes as merely destruction of individual housing units that add up statistically. A phenomenon on such a scale as this generates new circumstances for mobility, a new ratio between private and public space, and a new political division between two ruled populations – those whose homes are safe and are worthy of protection, and those whose homes are susceptible to intervention by the regime and to the movement of cameras. In her 1949 article, "'The Rights of Man': What Are They?" Hannah Arendt established the loss of a home as the paradigm for loss of rights: "The first loss which the rightless suffered was the loss of their homes, and this meant the loss of the entire social texture into which they were born and in which they established for themselves a distinct place in the world" (Arendt 1949, p. 26). However, she very quickly abandoned the spatial context of her argument and made do with emphasizing what she maintained was unprecedented: "not the loss of a home but the impossibility of finding a new one" (ibid.). This matter characterizes only one part of the phenomenon. The other part, which is no less unprecedented, is ruled people whose homes become open to the intervention and movement of a military force. In order to begin tracing this destruction, one can and ought to make use of photographs – but these are not enough. It is necessary to reconstruct the method of spatial arrangement that makes it possible to produce photographs of the sort familiar from the Occupied Territories, which have no counterpart in the archives of photographs produced in regions where protected citizens live.

The studio without borders is not a private space over which the photographers operating in it have ownership and the power or authority to delimit it and differentiate it from the outside. Nor is it a public space in which everyone can participate in the same manner. The house that the photographers rush to when they accompany a detachment of combat soldiers, or reach ahead of, or in its wake, or the house that they enter at the behest of the Palestinians living there, or at the invitation of the commanding officer in charge of the incursion, or contrary to his orders, or the defenseless circumference of a house around which the photographer loiters together with other people who live in the area, provide photographers with new partitions with which to delineate a temporary corner for themselves in the studio and complete their work. Sometimes she shoots quickly, in a flash, the way one takes a snapshot in an unsafe area; sometimes the photographer benefits from the idleness that has been imposed on the inmates of the house, and photographs them with the walls of their home – or whatever is left of them – as the backdrop for his pictures.

This studio without therefore spans the length and breadth of the Occupied Territories, between private spaces that have become public, and between public spaces that have become private. "Its" dividers are erected and dismantled not according to orderly and well-known distinctions between private and public space or ownership, and with the consent of the private space's owners and the public space's users, but rather according to regime and military plans that are imposed on the residents and that inflict their shifting rules on the space. The space of this studio is organized and divided by partitions that are fixed and changing, stable and temporary, constructed of indurate and insubstantial materials. Most of the time the Palestinians stumble upon this studio as extras, with it frequently being located in their very own home.

Figure 58.3 Keren Manor, Activestills.org, Jayyus, 2009

Figure 58.4 Miki Kratsman

Figure 58.5 Miki Kratsman, Ein Beit Ilama refugee camp, Nablus, 2007

Even when they resist the passivity foisted on them, and act as active agents, they are revealed to be unprotected ruled people, because they cannot retreat to a private space and remain there safely, and they are not free to go out into public space and participate in it like all citizens.

These spatial circumstances, which naturally leave their mark on photographs, are the most categorical visual expression of a regime that deprives a particular ruled population of rights that it reserves for another ruled population. The method of ruling these signifies a systematic violation of human rights, and the growing presence over the years of human rights organizations in the Occupied Territories is a testament to that. Since the late 1980s, when the first Palestinian uprising – the intifada – broke out, the number of local and international human rights groups and humanitarian organizations in the Occupied Territories has multiplied. These began then to photograph and gather photographs in an extensive and systematic manner. They evinced a growing interest in photography as a work tool, and now those organizations have the largest archives in the field of human rights violations (in other archives, photographs attesting to such violations are scattered or kept under various categories). The photographs in their possession are natural candidates for any discussion that seeks to ascertain the place of photography in the human rights discourse and in the practices it entails. However, a critical discussion of the question of photography and human rights cannot be limited by the institutional boundaries that the organizations set in regard both to photographs and to the human rights concept itself. Nevertheless, tracing these institutional boundaries and the restrictions they impose is useful and perhaps even necessary for thinking beyond the limits of the judicial activism discourse. It enables recognizing the assertion that a human rights violation is whatever the human rights organizations portray as a human rights violation – through photographs, among other means – as a tautological assertion from which we should depart. This tautology is one of the main reasons why photographs that testify to regime disasters have been perceived in recent decades as photographs of human rights violations; see for example the numerous photographs that have been kept in government archives from 1948 onward, in which deportees or prisoners were photographed at the moment of receiving drinking water from the hands of those who were deporting or arresting them. Several examples like these from different periods can be seen in the two archival exhibitions I curated, *Constituting Violence* (2009) and *Act of State 1967–2007*.

There is something tempting about the notion that photographs that human rights organizations generate and collect have a common denominator, or at least specific qualities. However the sheer fact that precisely the same photographs and ones like them are collected by other entities as well – where they fulfill other needs and serve to obtain other goals – makes it impossible to substantiate such a claim. This is neither a random fact, nor a particularity of the human rights discourse, but rather a reflection of the ontological nature of the photograph as a document, the information registered therein always exceeds the specific intentions and interests that those involved in the act of photography wish to register in it: photographer, subjects, and spectators. When you treat the ontological nature of the photograph seriously, you realize that the photograph never seals the photographic event, but rather continues to exist as a heterogeneous arena of relationships. These relationships may involve violence, oppression, seduction, desire, power, and knowledge, and these may exist among all of those who took part in the act of photographing, and thereafter continue to take part in it through the mediation of the photograph. The multiplicity of people involved in the act of photographing is maintained by dint of the fact that at any given moment, another spectator who is interested in what appears in the photograph could materialize. This open-ended multiplicity prevents what is registered in the photograph from becoming fixed once and for all as stable content, and keeps the spectator from pointing to the photograph and saying what is in it or what it represents – for example, "This is a refugee," "This is a terror attack," or "This is a collaborator" – as though abstract categories such as these are what reflects the light registered in the photograph. A future spectator could always appear and argue, with regard to that selfsame photograph or on the basis of that photograph, that the photographed subjects became refugees only several months later, that the terror attack was a controlled explosion initiated by the security forces, that the female collaborator was in fact a victim of rape and blackmail. She could further show that filing photographs under "refugee photos" was part of a regime effort to make the transformation of citizens into refugees self-apparent.

Based on this same ontological assumption, I further argue that any classification of a photograph as "human rights discourse" or "by the state," or as an "approbatory" or "critical" photograph, does not characterize the photograph, but rather the manner in which whatever is visible in it gets shaped by a particular discourse at a given time. Labels such as "critical" or "approbatory" that are attached to a photograph and presume to typify it are not indicative of the photograph itself, but rather of the manner in which it is incorporated and utilized in a particular discourse. This could be the human rights discourse, which is limited to reporting the demolition of homes only when the outer walls of a house have been destroyed, while ignoring the circumstances that this destruction creates for the photographer or photographic act; by the same token, it might be the art discourse that identifies what is visible in a photograph with the photographer's intention, while completely ignoring the subjects' participation in the photographic act.

Nonetheless, when one browses the photograph collections belonging to human rights organizations, it seems the photographs have something in common. Based on the argument I presented briefly concerning the ontology of photography, I contend that what these pictures share is not the characteristics of the photos themselves, but rather the general usage to which these organizations put the photographs. The presentation of general indicators does not serve to erase the differences between the various organizations, nor the difference in the specific usages that each organization fashions, and by which means it sets itself apart;[2] it is the product of an effort to outline in the most general terms a portrait of an institutional photograph of human rights, from which I will deviate further on.

To that end, I will present three characteristics of the prevailing use of photography in human rights organizations.

The first characteristic pertains to the type of function that is ordinarily ascribed to photography: justifying an organization's activity. The *justifying photograph* comes as a result of the instrumental attitude of human rights organizations to photography (my use here of the term *instrumental* is not judgmental but rather descriptive): the organizations' interest in photography is limited to *photographs* and to their possibilities of serving the organization in its activity. The organizations generate and collect photographs when they contain evidence of that which prompts them to take action, i.e., when they contain traces of a human rights violation that justifies their intervention. In other words, the photograph is meant to provide a visual expression of the organizations' grounds for intervening, and using it makes it possible to justify their objectives and their work. Inherent to the justifying-photograph concept is the assumption that the photograph documents a phenomenon or a situation outside the photographic event, and is independent of it.

However, the photograph is usually presented by the organization as speaking for itself, and the justification appears from within it. But photographs do not speak, and justification of any sort is never present within a photograph. Extracting it requires framing the photograph in a particular way that will enable using what appears in it for the purpose of justifying. The prevailing method of framing that makes this possible is the second aspect that characterizes the use of photographs by human rights groups. The framing simultaneously wishes to demonstrate and to represent. A *representative demonstration* or *demonstrative representation* is achieved by linking a photograph of a concrete event to an abstract category that describes what appears in the photograph. The photograph, which always renders a multiplicity of details noticeable, is abstracted by means of some category from the human rights discourse, whereas the classifying, abstract category becomes tangible by means of the photograph. General search terms such as "refugees," "violence," and "home demolition" recur on the home pages of the various organizations' websites. These search categories are generally accompanied by a photograph.

The affiliation that is created between the photograph and the category is meant to be readable and immediate, as though words are superfluous; the photograph itself can stand for the category, and vice versa. The mode of framing is supposed to allow the photograph to manifest a concrete situation that justifies intervention and yet suspend the characteristics that are *too* concrete. What appears to the gaze is supposed to represent a familiar category and not a singular situation regarding which we must now start from scratch, come up with a suitable category for it, and explain why an intervention is necessary at all in such a situation as this. The demonstration and the representation are two similar yet inverse actions that move in contradictory directions: The demonstration is designed to transform the general into the concrete; to illustrate by means of an example that which is presented in the abstract, whereas the representation is designed to abstract and generalize the concrete, so as to overcome the multiplicity of instances and generate from them a general representation.

The third and final characteristic resides in the effect that is achieved as a result of the hybridization between representation and demonstration. This hybridization serves the organizations for presenting the human rights violation *"in itself."* The photograph must present it in an unambiguous manner so there can be no doubt that what is seen in the photograph is the violation of a human right. The violation in itself is a reduction of the violation to the way in which it is registered in its victims. Its identification as a human rights violation does not depend on the violators and is disconnected from the complex deployment responsible for it. This equation of the violation with the violated places the violation as demarcated and delimited to a certain location – for example, the body – where its explicit signs may be found. The violated, who are primarily the subjects photographed, appear in these photographs as carriers of a violation of a clear-cut category of human rights. By force of this fact, they can be portrayed as objects for intervention by organizations that represent the human rights discourse. In the event that it is possible to reconstruct – from the photographs, among other things – those directly responsible for the violation, they are identified, and certain human rights organizations are even involved in bringing them to justice. But the regime responsible for the violation, as well as the rest of the ruled – citizens for the most part – who support the regime directly or indirectly, and who perceive the violation of particular ruled individuals as self-evident, remain outside the photograph's *readability framework* that the organization fashions.

Again, these three characteristics do not characterize the photographs *themselves*, but rather the way in which the photographs are imbedded in the existing *institutional* discourse of human rights. The assumption that the violation of human rights is a delimited area that can be located at the polar ends of the violated, the violation, or the violator – and which the photographs only serve to document – goes hand in hand with a limited grasp of the photograph as documentation, which is ingrained in the attitude of human rights groups toward photography. The perception of photography as documentation of something that preceded it and is external to it, which is common in the human rights discourse, also finds expression in the prevailing debate on the matter, which confines itself to what is visible in the photographs, and asks about the modes of representation of human rights that are tailored therein (see for example Bradley and Petro 2002; Doise 2002; Hesford and Kozol 2005).

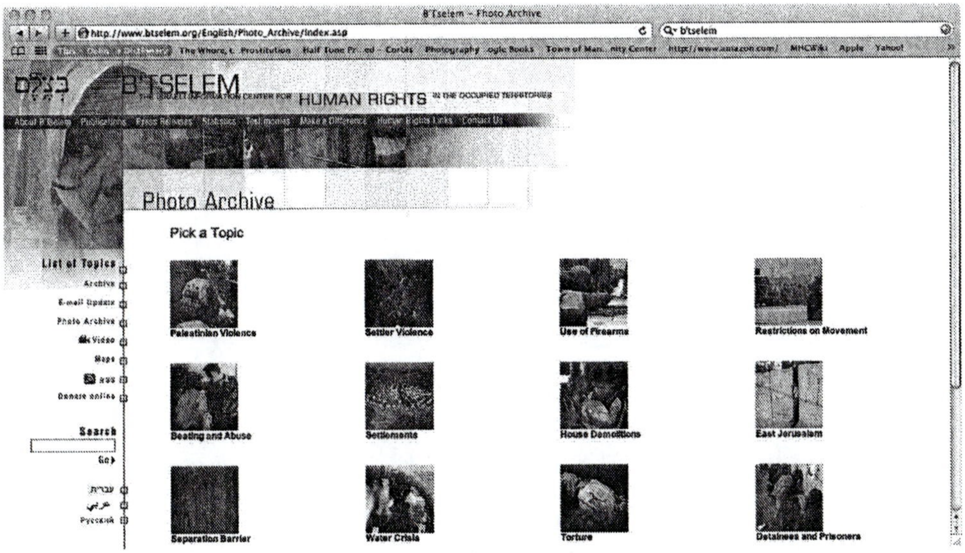

Figure 58.6 Website home page of the organization B'Tselem

Conceiving of photography as documentation enables the institutional discourse of human rights to be expressed through the photographs, and by means of the context that it generates for the gaze, it leads them to express the concept of human rights it is advocating. Priority is granted solely or mainly to what is registered in the frame, whereas that which leaves only traces in the photograph, whose existence can be surmised from what is registered in the frame – is irrelevant. In other words, the photographed event becomes an object of debate only after it has been abstracted and placed under a legal category, while the photographer and the act of photography – the photographing event as distinguished from the photographed event – are left outside the discussion. Thus, in the human rights discourse photography is transformed from a complex practice of relations that takes place *between* people into a manufacturing practice that is measured by its products – the photographs, and these according to whatever object whoever photographed them has framed for the gaze.

Breaking out of this cyclical relationship requires treating a photograph that was taken in a disaster zone as the basis for reconstructing the photographic situation, whose boundaries never correspond to the borders of the photograph's frame. In order to think beyond the limits laid down by the institutional human rights discourse, I propose returning to one of the emphatic origins of the human rights discourse – the French Revolution and the *Declaration of the Rights of Man and of the Citizen* that was formulated in its early months. In that historic context, the rights discourse was part of shaping a governed body politic that sought to protect itself against the regime. Only later, as Hannah Arendt showed in her book *The Origins of Totalitarianism* (1951/2009), the rights discourse became external to the regime, establishing itself as unbiased regarding the regime, and as interested only in the population that it has come to help. As part of this disjunction, categories that are employed to classify a population and rule it by differential means – "uprooted," "domestic uprooted," "refugees," or "stateless" – are no longer taken to be what they are: twisted categories that distinguish between ruled citizens and ruled non-citizens; and the citizens, who are ruled along with those populations, do not see those populations for what they are: populations that were violently transformed by the regime they continue to recognize as legal and agreed upon into the "remains" of the body politic to which they continue to belong. In certain cases they are removed altogether from the body politic of the ruled, as in the expulsion of 750,000 Palestinians from the territorial area in which the regime that founded the State of Israel in 1948 arose. This "non-ruled" population should also be tied to the regime that expelled it in order to learn about the nature of the regime (for more on the category of the "non-ruled," see Azoulay [2008b]).

Returning to these historic origins allows us to imagine a *new* – or renewed – human rights discourse, which besides the traditional assistance to a population designated as violated, would also provide help to the citizens who are ruled along with that population. The new intervention would help the privileged civilian population to identify and acknowledge the inherent flaw in their citizenship, a flaw that makes them accomplices to a regime crime that the regime does everything to keep from seeming a crime. A renewed look at the photographs (and at the photographic situation registered in them), not from the perspective that recognizes only those who were violated directly as objects for intervention by human rights discourse, allows us to read in the photographs not an individual portrait of this or that person, which is framed under the category of human rights violation, but rather traces of a differential regime under which a particular ruled population systematically suffers from a loss of rights, while another is protected from such a loss. These regime traces are evident, first and foremost, in circumstances where a given population is regularly susceptible to being photographed, usually not at its own initiative. But they are no less evident in the manner whereby the population of citizens is conscripted, often without its knowledge, to perceive the differential regime to which it is subject as an egalitarian regime – an egalitarianism that occurs among the citizenry as a whole, but which is violated on a structural basis when examined in relation to the ruled as a whole. Thus, as a result of a blatant policy of withholding civil information, the citizenry does not see the photographed subjects as part of the body politic, which is made up of ruled persons who share the same regime to which all are subject. Instead, it sees them as "Palestinians" – i.e., as non-citizens who forfeited one of the four basic human rights: the right to *resist oppression*. Hence the Palestinians appear as harbingers of their fate – objects for intervention by a human rights discourse that focuses on the tip that is the violation, and disconnects it from the context of the regime. A human rights discourse redesigned from a regime perspective, will let us see the very recruitment of citizens to take part in the creation of regime disasters – of which a particular ruled population is the main victim – as another type of human rights violation.

There have yet to arise international human rights groups that will rehabilitate this historic legacy of the human rights discourse that originated with the French Revolution. But budding signs in this direction can already be seen locally in an organization like Breaking the Silence, whose members, former soldiers – in other words, citizens who were drafted for army service as adolescents straight out of high school – became disillusioned with the actions they had perpetrated, and now wish to break the silence around them, which conceals their criminality.

At the time the photographs were taken, those holding the camera used it to manufacture souvenirs for themselves. In time, when they looked at the photographs, they came to realize what they had witnessed, what they had participated in:

> It was during the time of the soccer World Cup, and we were sweeping a certain village and had to go into one of the houses. Now, you've got an awesome platoon leader, he's also an Argentina fan, he also wants to see the game, so you tell him: "Listen, bro ... here and there ... this house and that house, it's the same thing, but here there's a television bro." So we went into the house with the television, just like that we cleared a family out of the house so we could watch the Argentina–Nigeria game.
>
> *(from testimonies collected by Breaking the Silence)*

The invasion of the soldiers in the picture into a Palestinian home, and the expulsion of its inhabitants, was not an unprecedented or exceptional act. This was not the first time that the invaders, as well as those whose home they invaded, had participated, whether actively or indirectly, in the flimsiness of the Palestinian house walls in the face of the Israeli might. By sharing the photograph with others, the soldiers were able to see, as well as to show, the crime in which they were complicit. The way the soldiers reframe photos taken during their military service under the title "breaking the silence," should be read as a first step toward rehabilitating their civil fitness and regaining the rights of which they had been robbed by the regime. I suggest that we read their act as a call for assistance addressed to the human rights community. Without taking anything from the victims of their atrocities, i.e., the Palestinians, and without creating any symmetry between perpetrators and victims, the soldiers are seeking recognition as victims too, victims of their own regime and their own government. The photographs contributed to the awakening of their consciousness and made them understand the "acts of state" they had performed to be crimes. This awakening has been belated not due to a personal blindness or defect but because the soldiers were made impaired citizens by their own regime; their military service has been both an effect of a civil malfunction orchestrated by the regime and an instrument in its reproduction. Without knowing or understanding it, their right to enjoy full, unimpaired citizenship has been violated. The discourse of human and civil rights should include this kind of violation within its frame and as part of its mission. To protect human rights means also to

Figure 58.7 Breaking the Silence, refugee camp near Ramallah, 2002

protect the right of the citizens not to be perpetrators and not to assist perpetrators of crimes. And this includes, as the case of breaking the silence makes plainly manifest, the right of citizens to criminalize the regime that has made them criminals.

Acknowledgment

This chapter has been translated from the Hebrew by Evie Goldfarb.

Notes

1 This phenomenon may be traced from its beginning in my book *Act of State* (2008a), which brings together more than 700 photographs spanning 40 years of occupation.

2 For a discussion of the specific uses made of one photograph by three local human rights organizations (B'Ttselem, Physicians for Human Rights, and Machsom Watch), see Ruth Ginsberg's doctoral dissertation (2010).

References

Arendt, H. 1949. "'The Rights of Man': What Are They?" *Modern Review*, Vol. 3, No. 1, pp. 24–37.

Arendt, H. 1951/2009. *The Origins of Totalitarianism* (in Hebrew), trans. Idit Zartal, Kav Adom (Tel Aviv: Hakibbutz Hameuchad).

Azoulay, A. 2008a. *Act of State: A Photographed History of the Occupation, 1967–2007* (in Hebrew) (Tel Aviv: Etgar).

Azoulay, A. 2008b. *The Civil Contract of Photography*, trans. from Hebrew by Rela Mazali and Ruvik Danieli (New York: Zone Books).

Bradley, M. P. and P. Petro, eds. 2002. *Truth Claims: Representation and Human Rights* (New Brunswick, NJ: Rutgers University Press).

B'Tselem – The Israeli Information Center for Human Rights in the Occupied Territories, *Uprooted Gazans in New Refugee Camps* [online video], 21 May 2009. At: http://www.btselem.org/hebrew/Video/20090521_CDP_Uprooted_Gazans_in_new_refugee_camps.asp.

Doise, W. 2002. *Human Rights as Social Representations* (London: Routledge).

Ginsburg, R. 2010. "With open eyes: a critical inquiry into the monitoring by Israeli human rights organizations in the Occupied Territories through interpretative readings of their reports," Ph.D. thesis, Bar-Ilan University, Ramat Gan.

Hesford, W. S. and W, Kozol. eds. 2005. *Just Advocacy? Women's Human Rights, Transnational Feminism, and the Politics of Representation* (New Brunswick, NJ: Rutgers University Press).

Part VIII

Geographies of rights

59

Human rights in China as an interdisciplinary field

History, current debates, and new approaches

Marina Svensson

The impact of 1989 and the beginning of a field

The aim of this chapter is to provide an overview of research on human rights in China thus far and identify and address some of the "white spots" in the field. I also want to discuss some recent debates as well as point out promising new approaches and work. I will argue for the adoption of new and more diverse frameworks and conceptual tools, and for the necessity of more interdisciplinary work, as I believe that this will both help us to identify new topics and trends as well as better explore how human rights are embedded and contested in Chinese society. The study of human rights in China is a relatively new field of research. Before 1989 there was only a handful of academic works in English (see for example Edwards *et al.* 1986). There had been a rich pre-1949 debate on human rights in China but later the topic became more or less taboo in China itself, and these earlier debates also remained unknown and under-studied by Western scholars until the 1990s (Svensson 1996, 2002). Furthermore, until 1989, few Western human rights organizations and foreign governments paid much attention to human rights violations in China, although organizations such as Amnesty International did publish reports on the country beginning in 1979. China's incorporation in the global human rights regime had furthermore been weak and half-hearted well into the late 1980s. The year 1989 and the crushing of the democracy movement changed all this. Thus 1989 is a watershed in many respects, and since then human rights issues in China have been on the international agenda and addressed by governments, non-governmental organizations (NGOs), international bodies, and the academic community alike.

Since 1989 the study of human rights in China has elicited strong interest from Western scholars. Different disciplines have taken somewhat different approaches, focused on different topics, and made different contributions to our understanding of the concept and history of human rights in China, and the role it has played in political and legal debates as well as in foreign relations. The early works mostly focused on topics such as Chinese culture and human rights, Chinese law and human rights, China's compliance with the international human rights regime, and the role of human rights in foreign relations more generally. The academic interest has undergone some significant shifts and turns over the years, to be further discussed below, that is both a result of more academic developments and the fact that the Chinese empirical reality itself has changed.

A striking feature of the post-1989 period is not only the growing interest of foreign scholars but also the birth of a domestic research community. A very crucial fact explaining this development is that human rights now is an officially sanctioned concept, in theory if not always in practice, culminating with the incorporation of human rights in the Chinese Constitution of 2004. Because of this official endorsement, and a closer official engagement with the international human rights regime, Chinese scholars and citizens are today more familiar with the idea of human rights than was the case in the past. Whereas before 1989 human rights was regarded as a foreign and sensitive topic, addressed, if at all, by marginalized dissidents, it is today a language understood and evoked in many everyday social and legal practices and struggles by diverse groups of people, including peasants, petitioners, and lawyers. This is a remarkable development, particularly in such a short span of time, the impact of which is yet difficult to assess.

In light of the fact that the Chinese empirical reality itself has changed with the embedment of a rights discourse in law and official ideology, thus giving rise to new possible topics and processes for study, so too have our focus and methods changed and developed to adjust to and make sense of these developments. Although not all the scholars discussed in the following would necessarily regard themselves as actually doing human rights research, or frame their research in explicit human rights terms, I would nonetheless regard much research on issues such as legal changes and concepts of justice, protests, citizens' engagement with different legal and political institutions, and the role of the Internet in public debate, as part of human rights research broadly defined. These scholars come from other disciplines than those previously, including sociology, political science, and anthropology, and they make use of more bottom-up, empirical and ethnographic approaches. This is a promising development that shows that the China human rights field has matured since the late 1980s as to both topics covered as well as methods and approaches used. However, there is need for more research that pays closer attention to the experiences and practices of ordinary citizens, including their notions of justice and engagement with legal institutions. Human rights provide a very useful framework for studying many different and pressing issues in contemporary Chinese society, including social, legal, and economic inequalities and struggles.

I am also calling for and want to draw attention to the fact that human rights and rights talk today also are part of more diverse cultural manifestations and forms of everyday resistance. Rights talk is framed in many subtle and different ways in art and film, and these forms of expression are helped by and spread through new information and communication technologies. The production and consumption of these mediated cultural forms are a more important part of many people's everyday imaginations and discussions on rights than readings of more philosophical treaties, legal actions, or more overt political activities. If we just look at theoretical discussions on human rights, the invocation of rights in legal processes, or more direct calls for human rights and open challenges to the regime, we risk missing an important aspect of how human rights are imagined, invoked, and embedded in today's more global and mediated Chinese society.

It should be acknowledged that there exist many conceptual, normative, and methodological challenges when it comes to research on human rights (Cesarini and Hertel 2005). Due to complex and long-standing political and ideological reasons, the meaning and scope of human rights continue to give rise to heated debates in China. However, it is important to remember that the dividing line is not only or simply between official and non-official views, or between China and the so-called West. Like elsewhere in the world we find divergent views within the academic community, between different disciplines, and in society itself. Despite the official recognition of human rights the issue remains highly sensitive, and the ability to get access to reliable data and do serious fieldwork continues to be very circumscribed, although the situation has much improved and there today exists a wealth of information on the Internet. For many interested in and working on human rights issues, both Chinese and foreigners, another challenge is how and whether it is possible to reconcile, for example, critical and independent academic research with more policy-oriented research, participation in legal aid projects, work as lawyers, or within the official administration. Due to issues of sensitivity and self-censorship, the relationship between groups such as scholars, officials, NGOs, and lawyers, although more fluid that in the past, remains highly fraught and problematic, and this also affects and inhibits human rights research in different ways.

Beyond Confucianism: culture and the vernacularization of human rights

Like human rights research elsewhere, philosophers, historians, students of intellectual history, and legal scholars dominated much of the first wave of research on human rights in the post-1989 period. It was thus not surprising that the issue of human rights and culture was one of the first topics to catch the attention of many scholars. Scholars coming from the field of philosophy (Angle 2002; de Bary 1998; Bauer and Bell 1999; Bell 2000; Xia 1995) in particular tried to tease out the impact of Confucianism on the Chinese human rights discourse and also attempted to identify notions supportive to human rights within the Chinese tradition. Some argued for a Confucian-inspired or -based human rights discourse. Other scholars (for example Svensson 1996, 2002; Weatherley 1999, 2008) took a different position and tried to uncover the political context of human rights debates in China since the late Qing dynasty. Svensson and Weatherley aimed to deconstruct and problematize Chinese culture and intellectual debates. In this process they brought attention to a previously neglected rich domestic debate on human rights as well as identified divergent strands and trends of thought within the Chinese culture and society itself. By exposing the power structures behind cultural arguments they raised some serious doubts about the need to seek support in the Confucian tradition in order to make human rights ideas more acceptable in Chinese society, thereby strongly refuting cultural–relativistic arguments (Svensson 2002). Other issues of contention in this debate concerned the impact of traditional culture versus that of socialism on the official Chinese human rights discourse, with Svensson and Weatherley tending to emphasize the importance of the latter.

This first wave of works on human rights was very much influenced by the events of 1989. Many works that appeared in the immediate post-1989 period that focused on the democracy movement itself (for example Calhoun 1997; Wasserstrom and Perry 1997) also tried to make sense of and explain the movement and crackdown in human rights terms. These works showed some divergent views on the movement, its members' understanding of concepts such as democracy and human rights, and the future of democracy more generally in China. In the aftermath of 1989 another hot topic closely related to these discussions was how, or indeed if at all, one could talk about civil society in the Chinese context (Wakeman 1993; Brook 1997). While these discussions have not been laid to rest, research on social and political developments since then have resulted in more mature and complex discussions on state–society relations and prospects for political reform and democracy (see for example Goldman and MacFarquhar 1999; Perry and Selden 2010).

The first wave of works on human rights were also inspired and challenged by the Asian values debate that culminated in the build up to the Vienna conference on human rights in 1993 (de Bary 1998; Bauer and Bell 1999; Bruun and Jacobsen 2000). The proponents of Asian values not only raised charges of Western cultural imperialism that drew attention, yet again, to issues of cultural relativism and universalism, but also to the issue of whether there was a specific Asian conception of human rights. The problem with the whole concept of Asian values was that it treated culture in a homogenous way and did not fully acknowledge or account for the existence of different views within the Asian societies themselves. Furthermore, the Asian values discourse did not pay careful attention to how global or non-local ideas are spread and made sense of in different local and cultural contexts. The Asian values debate, although not completely gone, lost much of its political momentum with the Asian financial crisis of 1997. Since then few proponents have been vocal on the issue, and academic articles on the topic have also virtually disappeared (Kingsbury and Avonius 2008).

In China the issue of Confucian or traditional culture and human rights once more became an issue after 2006 when President Hu Jintao launched his concept of "harmonious society." Concerns about stability and the overriding aim to solve simmering conflicts in society however lent this concept a distinct political bias towards control and repression of individual rights for the sake of the collective. It was not long before Chinese scholars close to the regime launched the idea of "harmonious rights" (Pils 2009). It is difficult to take the idea of harmonious rights very seriously given its political ramifications, weak theoretical basis, and constraining character, as well as limited circulation and acceptance in Chinese society where it was refuted and criticised by many Chinese netizens. Whereas some Western scholars have dismantled and criticised the idea (Pils 2009), others coming from a philosophical background and relating it to other Confucian ideas (Angle 2008) has taken it more seriously than seems warranted and necessary.

Scholars such as Angle, de Bary, and Bell have in general focused more on textual and abstract analyses of Confucian classics and neo-Confucian works, with relatively little attention paid to either official discourse and policy or the actual human rights situation on the ground. None of them have furthermore showed much interest in the views and activities of dissidents and ordinary citizens. It is instructive to note that Charter 08, the most recent manifesto by Chinese dissidents, signed by 300 people and later gathering some 8,000 signatories (Link 2009; Cha 2009), built on international human rights language and documents without any references to Confucianism or harmonious rights. I would argue that many Western scholars have overestimated the role and importance of the Confucian tradition for the contemporary Chinese human rights discourse and practice, as well as ignored how dissemination and vernacularization of human rights ideas actually take place in and are shaped by specific local and cultural contexts, including institutional and political factors.

Many of these works are thus stuck in very abstract discussions of philosophical concepts without exploring if and how they have a bearing or relevance to everyday life and struggles. It would be important to uncover to what extent and how Confucian, or traditional ideas more generally, influence ordinary citizens' discussions on and claims for rights and justice. Judging from more ethnographic research on rural and urban protests, as well as surveys of concepts of justice, the picture is quite complex and in a flux (O'Brien 1996, 2009; O'Brien and Li 2006; Michelson 2007b, 2008). Chinese citizens often frame their calls for justice in traditional terms such as *gongdao* (justice) and *yuan* (wrongs) but they do not hesitate to also refer to more contemporary rights language (Pils 2011). Traditional concepts and forms of protests quite naturally continue to influence people as they conceptualize notions of justice, talk about rights, or speak out against injustices, but these are intermingled with socialist notions of justice and increasingly also with contemporary and more global notions of human rights. A recent documentary film that focuses on the life and struggle of different petitioners, *Petition* directed by Zhao Liang, offers some revealing insights into how petitioners refer to both legal rights and human rights while also making use of traditional notions of justice and forms of protest. Before turning to a discussion of research on concepts of justice and the *weiquan* (rights protection) movement, let me first return to the issue of culture and the vernacularization of human rights ideas.

Works in other regional contexts have provided useful theoretical discussions and empirical examples of how human rights norms are internalized and localized in different societies (Risse *et al.* 1999; Goodale and Engle Merry 2007). In order to understand this process one has to acknowledge and take account of how processes of globalization impact on the human rights field. Human rights ideas are today spread through many different processes, institutions, and actors, including international law, the work of different international bodies such as the UN, NGOs and other transnational networks, and universities, as well as through the media. In a recent project Levitt and Merry (2009) have made a fruitful conceptualization of this process of dissemination and localization, a process they call vernacularization, that they then apply in a study on governmental bodies and NGOs working on gender and human rights issues in Peru, India, China, and the USA. Their approach draws attention to a number of aspects often neglected or simplified in discussions on the way culture and traditional ideas influence the understanding and implementation of human rights. Their main finding is that there indeed are many differences in the vernacularization process, and different attempts to adapt what they call a "global rights package" to local conditions and traditions of justice, but that there are equally big differences within societies themselves and between different types of organizations and institutions. These differences are due to organizational differences, different power bases and capital, diverse allegiances and ideologies, access to global networks, and level and type of education among actors themselves. In the case of China, for example, the human rights language, although sometimes muted, was more notable in the activities and views of NGO staff than in the government institutions (Liu *et al.* 2009).

> The Chinese case illustrates the importance of the organizational trajectories through which global discourses travel. Two of the three organizations we studied had strong ties to the government. The first, an actual government organization (GO), could only promote new notions of women's rights to the extent that they were consistent with government ideas of women's rights and interests. The GO supported women's rights inasmuch as they contributed to social stability. The GONGO, or government-supported NGO, went a bit further. It promoted a notion of rights in line with the government's position but also pushed for a more expansive, internationally informed notion of women's rights if and when it could be argued that it would contribute to the good of Chinese society as a whole. In contrast, the NGO, which receives much international support and funding, disseminated a notion of rights more in line with international treaties and documents.
>
> *(Levitt and Merry 2009, p. 456)*

But they also found that many actually "do women's rights" without calling it that because "framing human rights claims in local terms and adapting them to existing ideas of justice may mean abandoning explicit references to human rights language altogether" (Levitt and Merry 2009, p. 448).

The study is revealing because it shows the complex way human rights ideas are taken up and voiced in different societies and among different actors even in one particular society. How human rights are discussed depend on a mixture of cultural, organizational, and strategic factors and considerations at both the micro- and macro-level. By focusing on a variety of organizations in each society this study was able to show that the vernacularization process is fragmented and diverse, and that a complex interplay takes place between state-level actors and processes (ratification of human rights documents, legalization, implementation) and activities among actors at the micro-level such as individual officials and activists, NGOs, and so on. This approach is helpful for exploring how cultural and structural factors intertwine, as well as for explaining differences over time. In short, this approach is quite dynamic and grounded in its discussions of processes of internalization of human rights norms among various actors. It furthermore helps us better understand and conceptualize how culture, with all its different trappings, interpretations, and contemporary manifestations, influences human rights debates and practices. I believe that further analyses in this vein, dealing with other institutions, actors, and types of rights, would be highly useful as they would shed light on how and to what extent human rights have been embedded in Chinese society, and by which actors and processes.

New trends and research on domestic human rights debates and activism: officials, academics, and activists

Until the late 1980s official China usually dismissed human rights as a bourgeois idea without any relevance in a socialist society (Svensson 2002). But in the 1980s China also started to cautiously address the idea and in this process align itself with other socialist and developing states, emphasizing social and economic rights and the collective right to development, as well as the supremacy of sovereignty rights over individual rights. Although China became a member of the UN Human Rights Commission in 1981 and ratified the Convention on the Elimination of Discrimination against Women (CEDAW) in 1980, Convention on the Elimination of Racial Discrimination (CERD) in 1981, and the Convention Against Torture (CAT) in 1988, its involvement in international human rights work was very limited throughout the 1980s, while at home human rights was still a sensitive topic that permitted no serious research. After 1989, the Chinese state provided both resources and encouragement to different institutions, including the State Council and academic research institutes, to develop a more proactive Chinese human rights conception and policy to fend off Western human rights critique. As part of this work, China in 1991 began to issue so-called white papers on human rights. These white papers, published since then on an almost annual basis, outline human rights protection measures in China in general, as well as discuss special topics, including women's rights, freedom of religion, minority rights, etc. Centers for human rights research were also established in the early 1990s at academic institutes and universities. Later human rights education also began to be offered at several universities, often with support from Western human rights institutions (Oud 2006; Yeh 2009; Bjornstol 2009). Numerous articles and books on human rights have been published since the early 1990s, and today one can even find special sections with books on human rights in many bookstores. Several Western works on human rights have also been translated into Chinese. Many conferences on human rights have been held, and human rights training provided for police, prosecutors, and others under both domestic, foreign, and UN auspices (Woodman 2004).

Many of the more academic works published in the early 1990s were highly political or more philosophical and theoretical in character and did not deal with concrete domestic issues. Most Chinese human rights research is still confined within an officially sanctioned paradigm and directed toward specific political goals. One of the more interesting and path-breaking works to appear in China in the mid-1990s was an edited volume by Xia Yong (1995). The book differed from much other work at the time because it provided several case studies about perceptions of rights among different groups of people. But Chinese research on human rights is generally confined within the field of law, in particular international law, resulting in studies on international human rights treaties and the incorporation of human rights into domestic laws rather than more ethnographic studies. A few studies on more sensitive human rights topics such as torture and the death penalty have also appeared. Scholars and activists working in the field of gender studies have since the mid-1990s made important breakthroughs on issues related to gender and human rights. The UN conference on women's human rights held in Beijing in 1995 was very instrumental in opening up a new space and also gave Chinese women access to the human rights discourse. Since then Chinese scholars and activists have discussed many new topics related to women's rights such as domestic violence, HIV/AIDS, trafficking, the situation for migrant women, and gender and rights issues in domestic legislations more generally (see Bu and Milwertz 2007; Lee and Regan 2009; Stoltz *et al.* 2010). Scholars working on labor and rural issues also address the issue of rights in different ways, and the concept of *weiquan* (rights protection), to be discussed below, has now found its way into academic research as well. One of the more interesting scholars in this context is the sociologist Yu Jianrong who has written extensively on issues related to unrest and protests, and on how workers and peasants try to protect their rights and interests (see for example Yu 2005).

In the West an important strand of work in the early 1990s focused on dissidents and the democracy movements of 1978 and 1989 from both a human rights perspective and the perspective of social movements and civil society (see for example Calhoun 1997). These studies analyzed the writings and activities of the participants, the background to the protests, links to other groups and forms of protests in society, as well as the socio-political context of these protests more generally. Despite the lack of political reforms and the crushing of the democracy movement, Chinese citizens' possibilities to engage in public debate through the media and in semi-independent organizations have increased tremendously throughout the 1990s. As a result of this development the focus of Western scholars has shifted to a study of the growth of NGOs and other types of social movements and protests, as well as citizen activism online (see for example Tai 2006; Ho and Edmonds 2007; Ma 2009; Yang 2009). Another important set of work has focused on migrants and issues related to citizenship rights more broadly (Solinger 1999; Goldman and Perry 2002; Fong and Murphy 2006; Goldman 2007).

Reforms and a strengthening of the legal system have led to a growing rights or legal consciousness, and attempts by Chinese citizens to use the legal system to obtain justice and solve various conflicts. These calls for rights, although referring more to rights in national laws than to human rights per se, are part and parcel of what has become known as a *weiquan* (rights defense) movement. This is not a movement in the sense of a unified or organized movement with leaders and common goals. Instead it refers to the development of diverse calls and struggles for the protection of rights that engage different groups in society, including peasants, workers, migrants, petitioners, and lawyers (see Benney 2007; Fu and Cullen 2008, 2009; Lee 2007; Pils 2010). This development is a result of the adoption of different sets of laws confirming the legal rights of citizens, including consumer rights, labor rights, and property rights, as well as the growth of a professional group of lawyers and other supportive legal institutions, such as legal aid clinics, that help people protect their rights (Woo *et al.* 2007; Lee and Regan 2009). The *weiquan* movement differs from earlier dissident or democracy movements when it comes to the socio-economic status of the participants themselves, their views and understanding of rights, as well as the type and range of activities they are engaged in. The movement is not confined to intellectuals, which used to be the case with previous democracy movements, but attracts broader groups in society, including more established lawyers and journalists, as well as marginalized petitioners. There are furthermore stronger linkages and networks between different groups, although mostly on an informal and loose basis, that is much facilitated by the use of the Internet. A number of scholars have studied how groups such as peasants and workers engage with the law or are involved in protests (see further below), whereas others focus on the views and activities of the lawyers and legal activists in this *weiquan* movement (Fu and Cullen 2008, 2009; Pils 2010). The concerns of the movement are wide-ranging, including civil or political rights, such as freedom of speech, as well as socio-economic rights such as labor rights, land rights, and the rights of those living with HIV/AIDS, etc. In contrast to the democracy movements of 1978 and 1989, lawyers and activists in the *weiquan* movement see law as a useful and legitimate tool to protect people's rights. They thus work within the system at the same time as they also push for legal reforms and try to strengthen rights protection in society. The most successful and influential struggle to date led to the abolition of a special regulation directed at vagrants and people without identity papers. The abolition came about after the discovery that a young computer expert, Sun Zhigang, had been taken into custody and beaten to death by other inmates (Hand 2006). The success of this effort was to a great extent due to a unique collaboration between ordinary citizens, journalists, legal scholars, and lawyers. The Sun case is an early example of the importance of the Internet for public debate, and there is in general a strong link between the emergence of a rights defense movement and the growth of the Internet in China (Benney 2007; Yang 2009). Although some recent works focus on how individual lawyers, legal aid clinics, and journalists operate and push rights issues, there is a need for more work on how formal and informal linkages are forged and what the impact is on legal institutions and policy-makers. It is also useful to explore to what extent individual rights defenders in China are connected with a global rights movement. But it is equally important to know more about the official thinking behind recent repressive methods directed against lawyers, petitioners, and other rights defenders, and its long-term impact on social stability and trust in the legal and political system.

Human rights and international relations: internalization of human rights norms and the human rights implications of China's growing superpower status

A second hot topic brought to the fore in the immediate post-1989 period was the issue of the impact of foreign critique on the human rights situation in China, and whether it was possible to also talk about an internalization of human rights norms through China's participation in the international human rights regime. Related to this was the larger issue of the role of human rights in foreign relations. The fact that human rights in China now became a central issue in the UN as well as in bilateral relations provoked the interest of international relations scholars and others. Scholars such as Kent (1993, 1999, 2007) and Foot (2000) have studied how the human rights issue has unfolded in bilateral and multilateral relations, and analyzed differences over time, their causes, and implications. Of special concern in the early 1990s was the issue of whether, to what extent, and how foreign critique could lead to improvements, or whether engagement and legal aid would be more productive. This concern provoked discussions of how human rights norms are internalized in society, including in domestic laws, institutions, and among legal professionals and other groups of people.

International relations scholars focused more on official institutions, including governments and other policy- and lawmaking bodies, and to a more limited extent on the role of NGOs. Much of the work focused on official policies and activities in different international bodies, the ratification and reporting under international law, as well as the internalization of human rights norms in domestic laws. There is still however a lack of more in-depth ethnographic studies or surveys on whether or how human rights norms actually have been embedded in different institutions and bodies and through which processes. One of the more interesting studies is that led by Levitt and Merry (2009) discussed above. It is obvious that incorporation in the international human rights regime, academic exchanges, and foreign aid have had an impact, but exactly how and to what extent human rights are internalized and put into practice needs to be further explored. The whole issue of the impact of foreign aid in the human rights field is complex and highly debated but few comprehensive studies exist (Woodman 2004, 2007). A recent study of students having studied human rights at the university found considerable changes in attitudes among the students but concluded that the institutional context provided few opportunities for them to implement this knowledge in professional life upon their graduation (Yeh 2009). It would be interesting to compare the attitude and knowledge on human rights among this group of students with other students, or indeed with other groups in society, including people working in legal aid clinics and activists in the *weiquan* movement. Levitt and Merry's findings lead one to postulate that the internalization of some human rights norms probably have been smoother than others, and among some actors or institutions more than others. It is highly probable that since Chinese NGOs today are more active participants in a global network of human rights activism they embrace human rights norms to a higher extent than do governmental and legal institutions such as the police for example.

After so many years of various human rights exchanges and dialogues, different types of legal aid projects, human rights courses for different legal professionals, and proliferation of NGOs with international support and contacts, research in this field could yield some very interesting results. This kind of research would not only further our understanding of the extent and nature of the embedment of human rights norms in Chinese society, but would also have the potential to raise more general questions on the dissemination of human rights norms in authoritarian societies under the impact of globalization.

Human rights and international relations will remain a central topic as China's importance in world affairs continues to grow. China's growing geopolitical role, involvement in different international bodies, and foreign investments and business interests in different parts of the world, give the issue of human rights in foreign relations a totally new dimension and importance whose implications need to be carefully examined. China's economic influence and power sets it apart from earlier authoritarian countries such as the USSR and poses new challenges to both international human rights work and human rights research. China's involvement in Burma and Sudan has already come under scrutiny for its human rights implications (Kleine-Ahlbrandt and Small 2008). The deeper implications for human rights in these countries as well as the possible impact on Chinese domestic human rights policy, however, awaits further study. The economic and political importance and consequences of Chinese investments and involvements in Africa and Latin America is a new hot topic. Some scholars (Lee 2009) have already also begun to pay attention to its human rights consequences such as in the field of labor rights in Africa.

Human rights and domestic laws: legal reforms, rights-based law, and empowerment of marginalized groups

China's legal reforms have been closely followed and studied by Western scholars since the early 1980s (for good overviews see Peerenboom 2002; Clarke 2008). Early studies on law predominantly consisted of more textual and descriptive analyses of different laws and legal institutions. Since 1989 human rights violations have led to studies of specific issues and problems within the legal system. Many academic works have focused on issues related to the weak defense system in criminal prosecution, torture, the use of the death penalty, re-education through labor and the prison system more generally, as well as persecution of religious and minority groups. A number of works have dealt with new topics in the context of human rights, such as how the psychiatric system is used against dissidents (Munro 2006), and how the legal system in general is used against divergent and marginalized groups or abused during anti-crime campaigns (Tanner 2000; Keith and Lin 2006; Trevaskes 2010). The issue of minority rights has been very problematic throughout the PRC history but it has been difficult to conduct serious ethnographic studies on this sensitive topic. Although some academic works have been published in this field (Gladney 2004), the contribution of NGOs has been more significant to date (see for example Human Rights in China and Minority Rights Group 2007). Much more needs to be done as the issue of ethnic tensions has become acute in the last two years with unrest in both Tibet and Xinjiang. Many other topics, such as, for example, the death penalty continue to be difficult to probe in any great detail due to lack of statistics on the actual number of people sentenced to death, the nature of their crime, social background, and access to and quality of legal services provided, as well as the distribution of the death penalty geographically (see however Lu 2009).

How to assess and measure the situation for human rights with respect to specific rights and over time is a difficult issue. Peerenboom (2007 and Peerenboom *et al.* 2006) has argued that China is not doing so badly when it comes to human rights protection compared to other Asian countries or countries on the same level of economic development, and in particular given China's short history of legal reforms. Although it may be difficult to envision and establish clear measurement, it is obvious that further research on different types of rights and the rights of various groups, including migrants, women, minorities, and criminals, is much needed to understand the situation for human rights in China twenty years after Tiananmen.

With the deepening of the legal reforms and the growing impact on law on ordinary people's lives throughout the 1990s, specialized studies on commercial and financial law, administrative law, environmental law, gender and law, labor law, and so forth have mushroomed. With the maturing of legal institutions and the growth of the legal professions, several scholars have provided more in-depth studies of the work of lawyers (Michelson 2006, 2007a; Fu and Cullen 2008, 2009), the police (Dutton 2005), and judges (Trevaskes 2007). With respect to focus and methodologies we could talk about a socio-political turn in law studies in recent years. There is today a growing interest among both sociologists and political scientists to try to understand how, when, and to whom the law matters, and for what purposes it is used (see for example contributors to Diamant *et al.* 2005). Several recent studies address and discuss notions of justice and struggles for rights among different groups of people (Michelson 2007b, 2008; Michelson and Read forthcoming). The legal empowerment of the poor (LEP) approach developed by the Commission on Legal Empowerment of the Poor (Golub 2003) that has been put forward as an alternative to the prevalent rule of law orthodoxy is also an example of attempts to link studies of law, empowerment, and poverty reduction. The LEP refutes the earlier more top-down focus on formal legal institutions and pays more attention to whether and how different groups of citizens have access to and use legal institutions, whether they get justice, and whether they are empowered as a result. This approach could also usefully be explored in the Chinese context (for one preliminary example see Brandstädter 2008).

From philosophy to the everyday: a socio-political turn in human rights studies

Since the mid-1990s, many interesting studies on state–society relations and their implications for regime stability have appeared. Scholars have looked at different aspects, including forms of political participation and citizens' views and trust in the political leadership at various levels, as well as different forms of social unrest and rural and urban protests. Scholars studying village elections for example have raised the issue of whether villagers' sense of citizenship and empowerment has increased as a result of these elections. Workers, peasants, homeowners, and other groups make use of different language and different strategies, including litigation and petitioning, as well as resort to more open and sometimes violent protests when their rights are violated and their demands for justice ignored. A number of scholars (Gallagher 2005; Lee 2007) have studied workers who struggle to get better working conditions, obtain due payments, or receive compensation in cases of work injuries, in this struggle making varying use of different legal institutions and processes, whereas others have focused on the rural population (O'Brien and Li 2006). The growing social unrest in Chinese society, its causes, different forms, and state responses have received a lot of attention in recent years (for a useful collection see O'Brien 2009).

Two of the most influential scholars addressing both the issue of unrest and growing rights demands are the political scientists Kevin O'Brien and Lianjiang Li. In 1996 O'Brien wrote an article where for the first time he discussed the concept of "rightful resistance." In 2006 he and Li further elaborated on this issue in a book. Their research takes as its starting point the increase in and shifting forms of protests in the Chinese countryside. O'Brien's and Li's work has been quite central in what I would call a social-political turn in the study of rights in China. This turn is also evident in the increasing number of works by sociologists, more sociologically inclined legal scholars, and political scientists who study concepts of justice and legal struggles and their implications for state–society relations.

O'Brien and Li (2006) argue that new notions of entitlement, citizenship, and rights underpin emerging forms of resistance in contemporary China. They also make a point in drawing attention to the shifting relationship between central and local authorities, and how citizens can make use of the existence of fragmented and divergent interests within the state administration to their own benefit. In short they define rightful resistance as

> a form of popular contention that operates near the boundary of authorised channels, employs the rhetoric and commitments of the powerful to curb the exercise of power, hinges on locating and exploiting divisions within the state, and relies on mobilising support from the wider public. In particular, rightful resistance entails the innovative use of laws, policies, and other officially promoted values to defy disloyal political and economic elites.
>
> *(O'Brien and Li 2006, p. 2)*

Their work reveals an increasingly rights-conscious citizenry who while claiming their rights find useful support from and align themselves with certain officials, lawyers, and journalists. Although O'Brien's and Li's work mainly focuses on developments in the countryside, their insights and conceptual approach is also applicable for studying developments in urban China.

The idea of "rightful resistance" has, however, also been challenged and disputed. In several recent articles Elizabeth Perry (2007, 2008, 2009) has questioned O'Brien's and Li's work. She argues that Chinese citizens exhibit more of a "rules consciousness" with influences from old socialist rhetoric rather than a rights consciousness. She bases her view on several arguments. On the one hand she argues that Chinese citizens are not striving for rights against the regime but are more concerned to make the regime abide by its own rules and laws. This seems to miss the point that rights are now acknowledged in Chinese laws so what Chinese citizens actually are doing is calling for respect of their legitimate rights. Furthermore, since they are not always satisfied with current laws they also sometimes seek support in international law and human rights proclamations. Perry sees a strong continuity from Menicus, over Mao, to today's protests, in the similar concerns for socio-economic security, which she contrasts with the American civil rights movement and its focus on civil and political rights. Such a comparison is a bit halting because it overlooks struggles for social and economic rights in other Western societies as well as the linkage between civil and socio-economic rights in both the West and China. It furthermore overlooks past and contemporary Chinese struggles for civil rights such as freedom of speech, freedom not to be tortured, etc., as manifested in the work of *weiquan* lawyers, whom she does not mention at all. Her focus on selected examples of rural and urban protests is also far from comprehensive or convincing. She also focuses on more open protests per se, and not other types of resistance, such as petitioning, litigation, or written protests on the Internet that may have more invocations of civil rights. Works by Fu and Cullen (2008, 2009), Brandstädter (2008), Gallagher (2005), Lee (2007), O'Brien and Li (2006), and Pils (2010, 2011) clearly show that struggles for socio-economic security, including labor rights, property rights, and land rights, often are framed in terms of rights, albeit intermingled with more traditional notions. I would, however, agree with Perry that many rural protests often are framed in a traditional language of protest and socialist rhetoric but that does not preclude an awareness of and simultaneous invocation of legal rights of various kinds. It is obvious that not all Chinese would make use of the same concepts or employ the same language or tactics in all situations. Ethnographic work shows ample examples of the bewildering combination of tactics and rhetoric used.

Art, irony, and new media: playful cultural contentions, everyday resistance, and rights talk

It is important to remember that resistance and rights language can manifest itself in different ways in society. In China there is a long tradition of popular sayings (*shunkouliu*), satirical couplets and poems, and political jokes that criticize different forms of power abuse (Thornton 2002a, 2002b). This form of everyday resistance has long been circulated among broad groups of people in society both orally and in written form. The political and ideological potential of art was early on also realised by the Chinese Communist Party (CCP) itself. Revolutionary songs, plays, and opera were put into good use by the CCP both in its struggle for power and after 1949. But there have also been counter movements and attempts to use culture to challenge the ruling ideology. Many critical individuals resorted to poems, short stories, and art to criticize the prevalent ideology of class struggle and advocate more humanistic beliefs during the Cultural Revolution and later democracy movements. This independent and potentially subversive aspect of art has continued and become part of the struggling independent art scene (Barmé 2000). The topics and forms of critical, anti-establishment, or "subversive" manifestations of art are many. Whereas some are more overtly political, others are more playful and satirical and refrain from making direct political statements. The boundary between art and the political is furthermore fluid and people can easily be pushed into more political acts through certain events. One good example is that of the artist Ai Weiwei who has become an outspoken activist and filmmaker through his involvement in the struggle to get justice for the victims of the Sichuan earthquake (Osnos 2010).

The Internet has become a useful site for ordinary citizens to voice grievances and for journalists who cannot publish more critical reports in their own newspapers. There are many examples of how legal cases, arrests, and beatings of innocent people, and harassment of journalists have been taken up by netizens and lead to heated debates on the Internet, eventually forcing the authorities to back down and make thorough investigations. The Internet provides an immensely important and productive arena for publishing and circulating playful and satirical contentious writings (Yang 2009), including rights talks, writing in blogs, in the forms of political jokes, and the invention of new characters that poke fun at official slogans. In recent years the phenomenon of *e'gao*, "e" meaning "evil," and "gao" meaning "to make fun of" have appeared on the Internet (Wilson 2010). It refers to how mostly young people make use of different types of multimedia, such as music videos and films, to make fun of or subvert the meaning of original art works. While some scholars (such as Pils 2009) regard this development as a result of an increased repression, and thus a forced migration and dislocation of human rights work from legal institutions into artistic forms and virtual space, I rather interpret it as a widening of the human rights circle to include new groups in society that might be adverse to more overt legal and political struggles and prefer to use irony and satire to express their discontent, and I see it as a telling example of how the embedding of human rights talk in Chinese society is taking place in multiple ways in both artistic and everyday life.

An important aspect of this development, one that reflects that we live in an increasingly visual and mediated global society, is that human rights talk and other critiques today take more visual forms. A strong and lively independent documentary film movement has developed in China since the late 1980s, and many filmmakers take on hot and contested social issues and problems (Berry *et al.* 2010). In recent years Chinese documentary filmmakers have taken on issues such as HIV/AIDS, the Three Gorges Dam, land evictions and corruption, the petition system, and the killings of school children during the 2008 Sichuan earthquake. Contention on the Internet has also become increasingly visual as new multimedia and cheap technology enable broader groups of people to record and upload their videos on the Internet. There is today a broad range of people engaged in what one could call video activism, ranging from young people who make more satirical music videos and film clips, to more professional documentary filmmakers who take on social issues such as HIV/AIDS, to activists and ordinary citizens who join forces with lawyers to consciously document human rights violations and circulate their videos on- and off-line. Despite all the control and censorship of the Internet, Chinese people are becoming skilled in jumping the Great Firewall, and the Internet thus provides an important space for the circulation of contentious material and human rights documentation. The production, dissemination, and consumption of written and visual materials on the Internet have rapidly become a very fruitful and growing area for research. How different groups of people use and access media and new information and communication technologies is rapidly becoming an important topic for human rights research. Migrant workers for example make good use of cheap mobile phones to link up with each other and exchange information (Qiu 2009).

Concluding remarks: challenges and puzzles for human rights research

Human rights literature on China is still very much dominated by legal and international relations scholars, but scholars coming from other disciplines, such as sociology, anthropology, political science, and media and communication, although not always expressly framing their research in human rights terms, are increasingly addressing issues related to rights and justice in everyday life. Many issues and puzzles await scholars interested to further probe human rights research in China. Apart from those already listed in this chapter, others concern the role of the Chinese central state vis-à-vis other actors such as local governments, companies, and multinational corporations, when it comes to human rights violations. Human rights violations are today also committed by local thugs and businesses outside the reach of the state or with its tacit compliance. This development requires that we expand our scope of attention to investigate non-state actors as well. Another important issue is how to reconcile growing nationalism with growing calls for human rights. How will nationalism play out in China as the country becomes an even stronger power, and what are the implications for protection of minorities and other marginalized groups in society?

References

Angle, Stephen. 2002. *Human Rights and Chinese Thought: A Cross-Cultural Inquiry* (Cambridge: Cambridge University Press).

Angle, Stephen. 2008. "Human Rights and Harmony." *Human Rights Quarterly*, Vol. 30, No. 1, pp. 76–94.

Angle, Stephen and Marina Svensson. 2001. *The Chinese Human Rights Reader* (Armonk, NY: M.E. Sharpe).

Barmé, Geremie. 2000. *In the Red* (New York: Columbia University Press).

de Bary, Wm. Theodore. 1998. *Asian Values and Human Rights: A Confucian Communitarian Perspective* (Cambridge, MA: Harvard University Press).

de Bary, Wm. Theodore and Tu Weiming. 1999. *Confucianism and Human Rights* (New York: Columbia University Press).

Bauer, Joanne and Daniel A. Bell, eds. 1999. *The East Asian Challenge for Human Rights* (Cambridge: Cambridge University Press).

Bell, Daniel A. 2000. *East Meets West: Human Rights and Democracy in East Asia* (Princeton, NJ: Princeton University Press).

Benney, Jonathan. 2007. "Rights Defence and the Virtual China." *Asian Studies Review*, Vol. 31, No. 4, pp. 435–446.

Berry, Chris, Lu Xinyu, and Lisa Roefl. 2010. *The New Chinese Documentary Film Movement: For the Public Record* (Hong Kong: Hong Kong University Press).

Bjornstol, Elisabeth P. 2009. "Human Rights Law Education in China." *Web Journal of Current Legal Issues*, Vol. 1. At: http://webjcli.ncl.ac.uk/2009/issue1/bjornstol1.html.

Brandtstädter, Susanne. 2008. "Poverty, Legal Activism and Development in Rural China," pp. 97–108 in Dan Banik, ed. *Rights and Legal Empowerment in Eradicating Poverty* (Farnham, Surrey: Ashgate).

Brook, Timothy. 1997. *Civil Society in China* (Armonk, NY: M.E. Sharpe).

Bruun, Ole and Michael Jacobsen. 2000. *Human Rights and Asian Values: Contesting National Identities and Cultural Representations in Asia* (London: RoutledgeCurzon).

Bu Wei and Cecilia Milwertz. 2007. "Non-Governmental Organising for Gender Equality in China: Joining a Global Emancipatory Epistemic Community." *International Journal of Human Rights*, Vol. 11, Nos. 1–2, pp. 131–149.

Calhoun, Craig. 1997. *Neither Gods Nor Emperors: Students and the Struggle for Democracy in China* (Berkeley: University of California Press).

Cesarini, Paola and Shareen Hertel. 2005. "Interdisciplinary Approaches to Human Rights Scholarship in Latin America," *Journal of Latin American Studies*, Vol. 37, pp. 793–809.

Cha, Ariana Eunjung. 2009, "In China, a Grass-Roots Rebellion: Rights Manifesto Slowly Gains Ground Despite Government Efforts to Quash It." *Washington Post*, January 29. At: http://www.washington-post.com/wp-dyn/content/article/2009/01/28/AR2009012803886.html?sid=ST2009012900102.

Clarke, Donald C., ed. 2008. *China's Legal System: New Developments, New Challenges* (Cambridge: Cambridge University Press).

Diamant, Neil J., Stanley B. Lubman, and Kevin J. O'Brien, eds. 2005. *Engaging the Law in China* (Stanford, CA: Stanford University Press).

Dutton, Michael. 2005. *Policing Chinese Politics: A History* (Durham, NC: Duke University Press).

Edwards, Randle R., Louis Henkin, and Andrew J. Nathan. 1986. *Human Rights in Contemporary China* (New York: Columbia University Press).

Fong, Vanessa and Rachel Murphy, eds. 2006. *Chinese Citizenship: Views from the Margins* (London: Routledge).

Foot, Rosemary. 2000. *Rights Beyond Borders: The Global Community and the Struggle over Human Rights in China* (Oxford: Oxford University Press).

Fu, Hualing and Richard Cullen. 2008. "Weiquan (Rights Protection) Lawyering in an Authoritarian State: Building a Culture of Public Interest Lawyering." *China Journal*, No. 59, pp. 111–127.

Fu, Hualing and Richard Cullen. 2009. "Climbing the Weiquan Ladder: A Radicalizing Process for Weiquan Lawyers." October 11. At: http://ssrn.com/abstract=1487367.

Gallagher, Mary. 2005. *Contagious Capitalism: Globalization and the Politics of Labor in China* (Princeton, NJ: Princeton University Press).

Gladney, Dru C. 2004. *Dislocating China: Muslims, Minorities, and Other Subaltern Subjects* (Chicago, IL: University of Chicago Press).

Goldman, Merle. 2007. *From Comrade to Citizen: The Struggle for Political Rights in China* (Cambridge, MA: Harvard University Press).

Goldman, Merle and Roderick MacFarquhar, eds. 1999. *The Paradox of China's Post-Mao Reforms* (Cambridge, MA: Harvard University Press).
Goldman, Merle and Elisabeth Perry, eds. 2002. *Changing Meanings of Citizenship in Modern China* (Cambridge, MA: Harvard University Press).
Golub, Stephen. 2003. *Beyond Rule of Law Orthodoxy. The Legal Empowerment Alternative*, Carnegie Endowment, Rule of Law Series, No. 41, October.
Goodale, Mark and Sally Engle Merry, eds. 2007. *The Practice of Human Rights: Tracking Law Between the Global and the Local* (Cambridge: Cambridge University Press).
Hand, Keith. 2006. "Using Law for a Righteous Purpose: The Sun Zhigang Incident and Evolving Forms of Citizen Action in the People's Republic of China." *Columbia Journal of Transnational Law*, Vol. 45.
Ho, Peter and Richard Edmonds. 2007. *China's Embedded Activism: Opportunities and Constraints of a Social Movement* (London: Routledge).
Human Rights in China and Minority Rights Group. 2007. *China: Minority Exclusion, Marginalization and Rising Tensions*. At: http://www.minorityrights.org/686/press-releases/chinas-development-strategy-fails-to-benefit-critical-ethnic-minorities-and-masks-repression.html.
Keith, Ronald C. and Zhiqiu Lin. 2006. *New Crime in China: Public Order and Human Rights* (Abingdon: Routledge).
Kent, Ann. 1993. *Between Freedom and Subsistence: China and Human Rights* (Hong Kong: Oxford University Press).
Kent, Ann. 1999. *China, the United Nations and Human Rights: The Limits of Compliance* (Philadelphia: University of Pennsylvania Press).
Kent, Ann. 2007. *Beyond Compliance: China, International Organizations and Global Security* (Stanford, CA: Stanford University Press).
Kingsbury, Damien and Leena Avonius. 2008. *Human Rights in Asia: A Reassessment of the Asian Values Debate* (London: Palgrave Macmillan).
Kleine-Ahlbrandt, Stephanie and Andrew Small. 2008. "China's New Dictatorship Diplomacy: Is Beijing Parting With Pariahs?" *Foreign Affairs*, Vol. 87, No. 1, pp. 38–56.
Lee, Ching Kwan. 2007. *Against the Law: Labor Protests in China's Rustbelt and Sunbelt* (Berkeley: University of California Press).
Lee, Ching Kwan. 2009. "Raw Encounters: Chinese Managers, African Workers and the Politics of Causalization in Africa's Chinese Enclaves." *China Quarterly*, No. 199, pp. 647–666.
Lee, Tang Lay and Francis Regan. 2009. "Why Develop and Support Women's Organizations in Providing Legal Aid in China? Women's Rights, Women's Organizations and Legal Aid in China." *Journal of Contemporary China*, Vol. 18, No. 61, pp. 541–565.
Levitt, Peggy and Sally Merry. 2009. "Vernacularization on the Ground: Local Uses of Global Women's Rights in Peru, China, India and the United States." *Global Networks*, Vol. 9, No. 4, pp. 441–461.
Link, Perry. 2009. "China's Charter 08." *New York Review of Books*, 15 January. At: http://www.nybooks.com/articles/22210.
Liu, Meng, Yanhong Hu, and Minli Liao. 2009. "Travelling Theory in China: Contextualization, Compromise and Combination." *Global Networks*, Vol. 9, No. 4, pp. 529–554.
Lu, Hong. 2009. *China's Death Penalty: History, Law and Contemporary Practices* (London: Routledge).
Lubman, Stanley. 1999. *Bird in a Cage: Legal Reforms in China after Mao* (Stanford, CA: Stanford University Press).
Ma Qiusha. 2009. *Non-Governmental Organizations in Contemporary China: Paving the Way to Civil Society?* (London: Routledge).
Michelson, Ethan. 2006. "The Practice of Law as an Obstacle to Justice: Chinese Lawyers at Work." *Law and Society Review*, Vol. 40, No. 1, pp. 1–38.
Michelson, Ethan. 2007a. "Lawyers, Political Embeddedness, and Institutional Continuity in China's Transition from Socialism." *American Journal of Sociology*, Vol. 113, No. 2, pp. 352–414.
Michelson, Ethan. 2007b. "Climbing the Dispute Pagoda: Grievances and Appeals to Official Justice System in Rural China." *American Sociological Review*, Vol. 72, pp. 459–485.
Michelson, Ethan. 2008. "Justice from Above or Justice from Below? Popular Strategies for Resolving Grievances in Rural China." *China Quarterly*, Vol. 193, pp. 43–64.
Michelson, Ethan, and Benjamin L. Read (forthcoming). "Public Attitudes toward Official Justice in Beijing and Rural China." In Margaret Y. K. Woo, Mary E. Gallagher, and Merle Goldman, eds., *Chinese Justice: Civil Dispute Resolution in Contemporary China* (Cambridge, MA: Harvard University Press).
Munro, Robin. 2006. *China's Psychiatric Inquisition: Dissent, Psychiatry and the Law in Post-1949 China* (London: Wildly, Simmonds and Hill).

O'Brien, Kevin J. 1996. "Rightful Resistance." *World Politics*, Vol. 49, No. 1, pp. 31–55
O'Brien, Kevin J., ed. 2009. *Popular Protests in China* (Cambridge, MA: Harvard University Press).
O'Brien, Kevin J. and Lianjiang Li. 2006. *Rightful Resistance in Rural China* (Cambridge: Cambridge University Press).
Osnos, Evan. 2010. "It's Not Beautiful. An Artist Takes on the System." *New Yorker*, May 24.
Oud, Malin. 2006. "Creative Tensions and the Legitimacy of Human Rights Education: A Discussion on Moral, Legal and Human Rights Education in China." *Journal of Social Science Education*, No. 1. At: http://www.jsse.org/2006/2006-1/oud-china.htm/?searchterm=malin%20oud.
Peerenboom, Randall. 2002. *China's Long March Toward Rule of Law* (New York: Cambridge University Press).
Peerenboom, Randall. 2007. *China Modernizes: Threat to the West or Model for the Rest?* (Oxford: Oxford University Press).
Peerenboom, Randall, Carole J. Petersen, and Albert H. Y. Chen, eds. 2006. *Human Rights in Asia: A Comparative Legal Study of Twelve Asian Jurisdictions, France and the USA* (London: Routledge).
Perry, Elizabeth J. 2007. "Studying Chinese Politics: Farewell to Revolution?" *China Journal*, Vol. 57, pp. 1–22.
Perry, Elizabeth J. 2008. "Chinese Conceptions of 'Rights': From Mencius to Mao – and Now." *Perspectives on Politics*, Vol. 6, No. 1, pp. 37–50.
Perry, Elizabeth J. 2009. "A New Rights Consciousness?" *Journal of Democracy*, Vol. 20, No. 3, pp. 17–20.
Perry, Elizabeth J. and Mark Selden. 2010. *Chinese Society: Change, Conflict and Resistance*, 3rd edn (London: Routledge).
Pils, Eva. 2009. "The Dislocation of the Chinese Human Rights Movement," pp. 141–159 in Stacy Mosher and Patrick Poon, eds., *A Sword and a Shield. China's Human Rights Lawyers* (Hong Kong: China Human Rights Lawyers Concern Group).
Pils, Eva. 2010. "The Practice of Law as Conscientious Resistance: Chinese *Weiquan* Lawyers' Experience." In Jean-Philippe Béja, ed., *The Impact of China's 1989 Tiananmen Massacre* (London: Routledge).
Pils, Eva. 2011. "Taking *Yuan* Seriously in Beijing: Chinese Citizen Complaints against Injustice." *Temple International and Comparative Law Journal* (forthcoming spring).
Qiu, Jack Linchuan. 2009. *Working-Class Network Society: Communication Technology and the Information Have-Less in China* (Cambridge, MA: MIT Press).
Risse, Thomas, Stephen S. Ropp, and Kathryn Sikkink, eds. 1999. *The Power of Human Rights: International Norms and Domestic Change* (Cambridge: Cambridge University Press).
Solinger, Dorothy. 1999. *Contesting Citizenship in Urban China. Peasant Migrants, the State, and the Logic of the Market* (Berkeley, CA: University of California Press).
Stoltz, Pauline, Marina Svensson, Sun Zhongxin, and Qi Wang, eds. 2010. *Gender Equality, Citizenship and Human Rights: Controversies and Challenges in China and the Nordic Countries* (London: Routledge).
Svensson, Marina. 1996. "The Chinese Conception of Human Rights: The Debate on Human Rights in China, 1898–1949," PhD thesis, Lund University.
Svensson, Marina. 2002. *Debating Human Rights in China: A Conceptual and Political History* (Lanham, MD: Rowman and Littlefield).
Tai, Zixue. 2006. *The Internet in China: Cyberspace and Civil Society* (New York: Routledge).
Tanner, Harold. 2000. *Strike Hard! Anti-Crime Campaigns and Chinese Criminal Justice* (Ithaca, NY: Cornell University Press).
Thornton, Patricia. 2002a. "Framing Dissent in Contemporary China: Irony, Ambiguity and Metonymy." *China Quarterly*, Vol. 171, pp. 661–681.
Thornton, Patricia. 2002b. "Insinuation, Insult, and Invective: The Threshold of Power and Protest in Modern China." *Comparative Studies in Society and History*, Vol. 44, No. 3, pp. 597–619.
Trevaskes, Susan. 2007. *Courts and Criminal Justice in Contemporary China* (Lanham, MD: Lexington Press).
Trevaskes, Susan. 2010. *Serious Crime in China* (London: Routledge).
Wakeman, Frederic. 1993. "Civil Society and Public Sphere Debate, Western Reflections on Chinese Political Culture." *Modern China*, Vol. 19, No. 2, pp. 108–138.
Wasserstrom, Jeffrey and Elisabeth Perry, eds. 1997. *Popular Protests and Political Culture in China*, 2nd edn (Boulder, CO: Westview Press).
Weatherley, Robert. 1999. *The Discourse of Human Rights in China: Historical and Ideological Perspectives* (London: Macmillan).
Weatherley, Robert. 2008. "Defending the Nation: The Role of Nationalism in Chinese Thinking on Human Rights." *Democratization*, Vol. 15, No. 2, pp. 342–362.

Wilson, Magnus. 2010. "China's Cultural Evolution: Canon-mockery, E'gao, and Red Dining." *Telos*, Vol. 151, pp. 151–172.

Woo, Margaret Y. K., Christopher Day, and Joel Hugenberger. 2007. "Migrant Access to Civil Justice in Beijing." *Loyola University Chicago International Law Review*, Vol. 4, No. 2, pp. 101–146.

Woodman, Sophia. 2004. "Bilateral Aid to Improve Human Rights: Donors Need to Adopt a More Coherent and Thoughtful Strategy." *China Perspectives*, January–February.

Woodman, Sophia. 2007. "Driving without a Map: Implementing Legal Projects in China Aimed at Improving Human Rights," pp. 132–150 in Daniel A. Bell and Jean-Marc Coicaud, eds., *Ethics in Action: The Ethical Challenges of International Human Rights Nongovernmental Organizations* (Cambridge: Cambridge University Press).

Xia Yong, ed. 1995. *Zou xiang quanli de shidai: Zhongguo gongmin quanli fazhan yanjiu* [Toward an Age of Rights: Research on the Development of Chinese Citizen Rights] (Beijing: Zhongguo zhengfa daxue chubanshe).

Yang Guobin. 2009. *The Power of the Internet in China: Citizen Activism Online* (New York: Columbia University Press).

Yeh, Jessica I. 2009. "Promoting Human Rights in China Through Education: An Empirical Impact Evaluation of the Swedish Approach from a Student Perspective." *Asian-Pacific Law and Policy Journal*, Vol. 10, No. 1.

Yu Jianrong. 2005. "Social Conflict in Rural China Today: Observations and Analysis on Farmers' Struggles to Safeguard Their Rights." *Social Sciences in China*, pp. 125–136.

60

Human rights and human rights violations in the Southern Cone

Luis Roniger and Mario Sznajder

The societies of Argentina, Chile, and Uruguay – known as the core Southern Cone nations – share a history of Spanish colonization, political independence in the early nineteenth century, mass European immigration (more prominent in Argentina and Uruguay than in Chile) since the late nineteenth century, and a basic modeling according to Western institutions and ideas of development. These societies share a dual cultural dynamic. On the one hand, there is a substratum of respect for hierarchy, authority, and order, of Hispanic and Roman Catholic origins, with corporatist leanings. On the other hand, from an early stage, elites have looked to the centers of world development, absorbing from the latter secular Western ideas and ideologies, adapting them as part of their models of nation-building, as befitted their local structures and realities.

With the adoption of formal models of constitutional liberal democracy, elites interpreted the models in ways that stressed their authority and allowed the implementation of formal equality before the law in a manner that did not affect the hierarchical structure of society. Thus, while they responded to popular pressures by widening the scope of suffrage laws, elites organized the electoral processes in ways tainted by fraud, patronage, clientelistic manipulation, and vote buying, in order to keep control over the polity, its institutions and resources. Later on, Anarchist, Fascist, and Socialist orientations of European inspiration were re-elaborated and incorporated into local politics, and populist movements also developed, competing in their capacity to mobilize the middle and lower classes.

In the twentieth century Argentina, Chile, and Uruguay lived through intensive processes of social change, rural–urban migration, and modernization. After World War II, the three countries experienced increasing socioeconomic and political pressures. While in Chile and Uruguay the normative framework of formal democracy managed to contain these pressures until the 1970s, in Argentina it was biased towards a framework of populist symbolic and effective incorporation created by Peronism and shattered by the dislocation of social and political order. These trends produced in Argentina an intermittent pattern of civilian and military rule and, finally, the military coup in 1976. All three societies were marked by a basic dissonance between formal institutional frameworks shared with Western countries, on the one hand, and the "real" workings of social life, which contained strong elements of violence, authoritarianism, clientelism, and repression, on the other. The latter constantly modified and sometimes threatened to shatter the existing institutional format of these societies.

The Southern Cone countries underwent periods of civil unrest, repression, and human rights violations from the 1960s to the 1980s. The forms and extent of repression varied among them, with illegal abductions, torture, and disappearances figuring prominently in Argentina, political killings being salient in Chile, and long-term imprisonment of citizens being the rule in Uruguay. During authoritarian rule by military and civil–military dictatorships, the full extent of repression was difficult to assess as policies of disinformation played a major role in silencing the atrocities and massive human rights violations, and as many in society at large felt some relief with the policies of "order" that promised to end the previous stage of anarchical revolutionary and counter-revolutionary violence, which brought democracies to the verge of systemic breakdown. Eventually, democracies indeed were broken down throughout the region and the military assumed power by either joining a civilian president – as in Uruguay in 1973 – or by deposing the heads of state, as in Chile (11 September 1973) and Argentina (24 March 1976). Once in power, the military rulers imposed policies of ruthless repression of the left within their borders while they cooperated across borders with the intelligence and security networks of other countries in the region, in the framework of what became known as the Condor Operation. They thus decimated an entire generation of political and social activists and created legacies of massive human rights violations that would leave their imprint on these societies for years to come. At the same time, many of the persecuted left for political exile, mostly in the Americas and Europe.

The transitions to democracy took place in the 1980s, in various forms: in a precipitous manner in Argentina (1983), resulting from the military rulers' discredit in managing the economy and the calamitous defeat in the Malvinas/Falklands war; in a negotiated form in Uruguay (1985), resulting from a secret agreement between the major political forces and the command of the armed forces; and in Chile as the result of General Augusto Pinochet's defeat in a 1988 referendum over the regime's continuity, which opened the way to the restoration of democracy (in 1990).

In spite of these differences, which conditioned in part the terms of confrontation with past human rights violations once democracy was restored, all three societies faced a long-lasting process of confrontation with the results of past authoritarianism. The civilian rulers and the different sectors of society were caught between contrasted and sometimes polar versions of the past, between normative expectations and the constraints of political contingency, and between their will to consolidate democratic rule and at the same time grappling with the past legacy of human rights violations.

Such confrontation implied a tortuous process of coming to terms with the legacy of past atrocities, as they attempted to ascertain and confront the knowledge of what happened, and how to generate a more or less agreed version of events; whether and how to make those responsible accountable for their past deeds and bring them to justice; whether to ask forgiveness from the victims and expect expiation from the perpetrators; the enforcement of policies of compensations and reparations; how to honor the memory of the dead and perhaps reach a stage of reconciliation.

Likewise, they also had to address reshaping the domain of human rights in areas ranging from institutionalizing democratic patterns of public accountability to legal reforms, and from educational policies to the institutional treatment of human rights violations perpetrated after the return of democracy.

The simultaneity and urgency of these issues and the trade-off between their attainment and the pragmatic needs of post-conflict and post-authoritarian institutional stability have been the focus of intense inquiry and analysis in the literature on transitional justice (e.g., Crocker 1999; Hayner 1994; Skaar 1999; Falk 2000, pp. 199–216; Barahona de Brito 2009). It is important to realize, however, that these common challenges were confronted by specific institutional mechanisms adopted by the political leaders in each case; in ways that were specific to each state and society and according to the balance of forces between the different social and political actors; namely, the government, the military, the Church, intellectuals, and political actors who opposed the military rule and took over government after the transition to democracy, and diverse non-governmental organizations.

The major problems on the processes of political change were of accommodation between the old and the new forces during and after the transition; and the political problems generated by the experience of repression under the military. In this context, one needs to analyze the struggles, debates and crises, and institutional formations that took place in these societies following re-democratization in the 1980s and 1990s; the concrete policies adopted by the elites in dealing with these problems and the impact of these policies on the processes of reconciliation between the different sectors of these societies; and the tensions between the new normative expectations that crystallized with the establishment of the democratic regimes and the political constraints as they developed during this period. Political elites and social actors engaged in strategic interactions made choices in critical junctures while confronting the past experience in ways that shaped the legacy of human rights violations for years to come.

In this comparative framework, we identify a series of parameters of special importance in shaping the variations in institutional patterns and in patterns of interpretation in these societies. The most important among these parameters are the social, political, and legal traditions of each country; the constellation of social and political forces within it; the timing of the transition and the sequence of choices following it; the way in which each society reacted to the experience of the neighboring countries; the patterns of public mobilization and debate; and the symbolic involvement and collective catharsis of the different sectors of population in the recurring crises.

The thesis advanced here is that, once initial policies were adopted and installed in addressing all the various issues raised by the legacy of human rights violations, different visions of the past were also projected in symbolic struggles and actions and through a politics of memory and oblivion, in which each sector tried to gain public recognition and turn its vision of the recent past into the prevalent account of the past. The sectors that were most involved, namely the victims and the military, related to the issue of human rights in contrasting ways, with the victims trying to centralize it in the public sphere, and the military attempting to marginalize and project some relativism. Opinions were strongly divided on whether it was fundamental to remember the past as the basis of the democratization process, against forgetting the past or accepting its inclusion into history as necessary deeds done to save the country. Bystanders and members of the political classes participated in fraught debates as well, according to their own different agendas. The resulting policies thus became involved in a series of meaning-producing forms of projecting contrasting historical narratives and were refracted in a multiplicity of angles, creating a pluralistic public agenda, yet full of tension. Rather than disappear with the outcome of the first policies adopted, the issue of human rights violations acquired renewed validity as time passed, interplaying with the transformation of historical memory and the reshaping of collective identity in these societies time and again in the subsequent decades. That is, the partial addressing and resolution of the legacy of human rights violations immediately after democratization continued to underpin the issue on the political agenda, affecting the public spheres of the Southern Cone countries, and promoting a dynamics of recurrent crises, advances, and setbacks in the area of human rights.

The extent of repression and the discourse of human rights

Repression of political opponents and of co-nationals characterized much of the history of the countries of the Southern Cone. Nonetheless, two factors singled out the impact of the last wave of military rule in Argentina (1976–1983), Uruguay (1973–1985), and Chile (1973–1990) on the reshaping of the domain of human rights. These factors that singled out this phase in these societies' institutional and cultural development were, first, the magnitude of repression, which affected all sectors of society including the middle and upper classes; and, second, the interpretation of state violence in terms of the recently incorporated discourse of concern for human rights. As repression seemed to have affected societies at large and came to be interpreted through the internationally projected prism and discourse of human rights, accountability, and justice, the experiences of the last wave of repression emerged as having a distinctive impact on these societies' self-understanding, reconstruction of public spheres, and politics of reconciliation, oblivion, and memory.

The military governments systematically violated human rights within the framework of a National Security Doctrine (DSN) in its various national permutations but interpreted in terms of the bipolarity of the Cold War (Roniger 2009). According to this vision, shared by the military establishments of these nations, the basic parameters for defining policies were external and internal security needs and the defense of national interests and values. Such values had to be those of Western Christian civilization, the defense of private property and initiative, and the opposition to Communism and Marxism. Because of their historical and functional role, their formation and their professional training, the military saw themselves as guardians of the nation's values and traditions, especially in times of crisis such as these societies underwent in the last stages of the Cold War. At such times, they considered themselves entitled to assume power in order to carry out what they perceived as "national objectives." According to their views, military rule would channel the nation's real spirit through the state's machinery.

The armed forces were following an organic conception of the nation, which implied eliminating the enemy, since no "organs" or "cells" should be allowed to deviate from the basic parameters of the national values and traditions. If necessary, the armed forces would extirpate the threat, following the ideological visions they incorporated from the French theorists of counter-insurgence developed in the Algerian war and ideas of a total war with a Nazi pedigree, and reinforced by the strong anti-Communist visions taught in the School of the Americas and other US training centers of anti-guerrilla warfare attended by Latin American officers. The local idioms of organicism gave further credence to the DSN view of the primacy of the national well-being over individual rights and needs. According to this logic, individual rights, including the most basic human rights of life and physical integrity, could be subordinated to national aims whenever necessary. Repression of the leftist political and armed groups ensued, translated into illegal abductions, imprisonment, and torture in official and clandestine detention centers, assassinations and disappearances of adults and newborns, and an entire range of other atrocities and violations of individual rights.

A generalized and decentralized pattern of repression was typical of Argentina. This pattern was related to the previous history of violence of that country and, in particular, to the infighting of leftist and rightist sectors within Peronism and to the activity of paramilitary groups that acted against the left in coordination with the military already prior to the 1976 coup. During military rule, the decentralized character of violence persisted, albeit with some changes. The decentralization and lack of coordination, which in military terms could be related to the direct responsibility of area commanders following general orders concerning the "destruction of the subversion" and "the liquidation of the enemy," produced a widespread and uneven pattern of repression, which affected both politically mobilized forces as well as individuals tangentially involved in politics or not related at all. In hunting their enemies, the armed forces divided the country into five military areas, using the organizational design prepared for an international war. Within each area command, there was a further subdivision into operational brigades and battalions located near almost two hundred urban areas. Concurrently, and in coordination with the federal and provincial police forces, more than one hundred clandestine centers of detention were established. The chain of command in charge of the repression was parallel to the formal chain of command of the armed forces. The operations against the enemy were conducted by "task forces" (*grupos de tareas*) composed of different members of the armed and security forces. A pattern of rotation was established by the high commands, which resulted in the delegation of responsibilities and in the diffusion and displacement of guilt. This created a relatively long-lasting "pact of silence" among the security forces and heightened the levels of fear and lack of personal security of the civilian population. The vague character of the formal directives, coupled with the operational subdivision of the forces and the placing of direct responsibilities on the local commanding officers, generated a pattern of uncoordinated autonomy in the implementation of the military strategy. This, in turn, produced various levels of relatively undiscriminating and violent repression, which affected both activists and random individuals, resulting among other things in the illegal abduction and secret assassinations of between 10,000 and 30,000 individuals known as the *desaparecidos*, i.e., those who vanished and whose remains remain unknown. The profile of the Argentinean victims indicates that the sectors most severely affected were the working class and wide sectors of the middle class, especially students, professionals, and white collar employees. Both social activists and professionals suspected of belonging to a radical discipline, such as psychiatry, psychology, sociology, or political science, were especially targeted. Nearly a third of the victims were women, with a representation of housewives greatly exceeding the percentages of such victims in Chile and Uruguay.

Uruguay, too, had experienced a previous wave of violence between the left-wing urban guerrilla of the MLN (Tupamaros) and the security forces. The Tupamaros had been severely attacked and defeated during the last phase of President Bordaberry's civilian government, before the actual military assumption of power. Following the latter, the country witnessed massive arrests conducted mostly in the open; long-term reclusion of convicted prisoners; torture, albeit more controlled and limited than in Argentina; and assassinations of political opponents, though in smaller numbers than in the other countries of the area, and mostly with clearly targeted victims. At least 157 nationals "disappeared" and 95 political prisoners were killed, died from illness, or committed suicide in detention centers between 1972 and 1985. On average, for every 10,000 Uruguayans, thirty-one were detained for political reasons (many were abducted in Argentina), and most of them were subjected to torture. There are sources that place this rate at even higher levels. Many believe that Uruguay had in this period the highest record of political prisoners per capita in Latin America. The majority of the victims of repression were political militants; many of them were professionals and white collar employees. Most of the victims were males, while a fifth of them were women. In Uruguay, the urban nature of repression was pronounced, according to the demographic concentration of the population and the urban pattern of political mobilization. In contrast with Argentina, the lower ranks of the armed forces and the police were subjected in Uruguay to more precise orders concerning the methods and focus of repression.

The Chilean case can be considered closer to Uruguay in terms of the number of arrests, while similar to Argentina in the scope of repression and the pattern of torture, killing, and disappearances. The structure of the Chilean armed forces was highly vertical, which implied that in each corps and branch a complete subordination to the higher commands was the rule.

Compared with Argentina, the Chilean repressive apparatus was accordingly more hierarchically coordinated. Some 2,920 cases of killing as a result of human rights violations and political violence were examined by the Rettig Commission of Truth and Reconciliation; another 508 cases were presented but were considered beyond the mandate of the commission and, in another 449 cases, only the name of the person was known and the commission did not make further inquiries. The successor to the Rettig Commission, the National Corporation for Compensation and Reconciliation (CNRR), published a final report in August 1996, which confirmed 899 cases in addition to those documented by the Rettig Commission, bringing the total number of victims of killing and disappearance to 3,197. In the case of Chile, the murdered were mainly people belonging to clearly targeted sectors: political leaders and militants, individuals active in the labor movement, both urban and rural, students and intellectuals. These were mostly the sectors targeted also in Uruguay, although in Uruguay many of these managed to survive in prison. The number of people tortured is calculated by the human rights organizations to be in the tens of thousands. In Chile, for example, a National Commission on Political Imprisonment and Torture (known as the Valech Commission) carried out its investigation in 2004–2005, accepting more than 28,000 cases of torture as valid, while in January 2010, President Bachelet ordered a reopening of the registration procedures, a move that may result in the recognition of many new cases of proven torture.

Repression in the three countries led to hundreds of thousands of individuals fleeing into exile. Estimates put the numbers of Argentineans at around 300,000 and the number of Chileans on at least 200,000 and probably close to half a million, and that of Uruguayans at half a million; these estimates, however, conflate forced political and economic migrants. Exiles escaping repression in the Southern Cone were dispersed around the globe, finding refuge in dozens of countries worldwide (Sznajder and Roniger 2009). Repression extended abroad, targeting prominent members of the opposition in exile. Outstanding in such operations was the Chilean National Directorate of Intelligence (DINA), the security organ in charge of coordinating and implementing repression. General Augusto Pinochet delegated operational autonomy to the DINA with its commanding officer, Colonel Manuel Contreras, which was directly subordinated to the President of the Junta. It acted, similarly to the Argentinean and Uruguayan intelligence agencies, in the neighboring countries, but also in the USA and Europe. The DINA's most notorious actions abroad were the assassination of General Carlos Prats and his wife in Buenos Aires; the attempted murder of Bernardo Leighton, former vice-president of Chile, in Rome; and the killing of the former minister of Foreign Affairs, Orlando Letelier, and his American assistant, Ronni Moffit, in Washington, DC.

During the last wave of military rule in the Southern Cone, the repressive policies were legitimated on the basis of organicist nationalist ideas. According to these ideas, what was perceived as protecting the collective well-being of the "nation," in a context of internal struggle, justified the infringement of individual rights. In contrast, the international discourse of human rights – developed in the aftermath of the crimes against humanity and genocide committed in World War II – provided a new vision in which individual rights were given primacy as the basis for reshaping civilized and democratic public life, as sanctioned by international legislation and treaties.

The discourse of human rights violations in the context of the Southern Cone

The extent of repression, and the international publicity achieved through the work of local NGOs such as the *Madres of Plaza de Mayo*; the work of exiles connected with networks of solidarity, advocacy groups, and parliamentary representatives in Europe and the USA; and the efforts of international organizations such as Amnesty International and the UN Commission for Human Rights brought the discourse of human rights violations to the center of the public spheres of the Southern Cone polities even during military rule.

In this period, when censorship and political controls were fully in place, the governments reacted to this discourse mostly by denouncing it as part of a policy of defamation inspired by their leftist political enemies at home and abroad. The military governments rejected the discourse of human rights on two grounds. First, according to their views, situations of crisis allowed for the exceptional derogation of civil rights as envisaged by the human rights treaties (e.g., article 27 of the Inter-American Convention on Human Rights). From their perspective, coercive violence had been used, if at all, to the same extent as during previous civilian governments, in order to guarantee social order. In a principled line, they justified using violence in order to save their societies from a greater evil, namely the annihilation of all civil and political rights as part of a Marxist totalitarian takeover. Second, international pressures concerning the human rights issue were perceived by the military rulers and presented to the public as a blatant violation of sovereignty. The supporters of the military government rejected the absolute criteria advanced through the discourse of human rights and favored a relativist "national" vision that suggested the need to contextualize actions to understand their significance. Accordingly, they claimed that what the opposition to the military presented as human rights violations should have been put in perspective and interpreted as measures taken to prevent the disintegration of these societies, in the context of anarchy.

While certain minorities progressively adopted human rights as their banner for opposing military rule, wide sectors of the demobilized societies of the Southern Cone (those who can be seen as "bystanders") accepted the official versions and others reacted with apathy. Part of that "acceptance" was related to the lack of a "rights consciousness," thus allowing violations to be contextualized, thereby making the official positions easier to push on public consciousness. Dialectically, the work of advocacy groups at the international and transnational arena will progressively create what Keck and Sikkink (1998) have called a boomerang effect, i.e., the rulers and their supporters would be forced progressively to confront the accusations by phrasing their counter-arguments in terms of the same discourse of human rights (see also Risse *et al.* 1999). It was, however, during the transitions to democracy and following democratization that the discourse of human rights became the central idiom for dealing with the legacy of authoritarianism and for reshaping the identity of these societies, in terms of individual rights.

In the Southern Cone, the discourse of human rights exploded as the language that, anchored in internal experiences and international principles, served to express the need to reshape or rather construct anew the institutions and the collective identity of society, as monist military rule was replaced by pluralist democracy. Such construction or change was to be elaborated around two factors: first, the tacit or explicit condemnation of authoritarian rule; and second, the commitment to a basic normative of human rights, which was presented as antithetical to the principles followed by the military governments. This trend projected a new dimension of public life, which went beyond the formal and traditional understanding of democracy in the Southern Cone toward a vision of it as the framework in which the individual can expect full protection of human rights. In Argentina, for example, Raúl Alfonsín, as candidate of the Unión Cívica Radical party in the presidential elections of December 1982, was able to interpret such collective expectations. Alfonsín raised the banner of accountability and justice for the victims of repression in his electoral campaign, a factor that many saw enabling the UCR to defeat Peronism for the first time in Argentine history in an open presidential election.

In Argentina, Uruguay, and Chile, the main problem in incorporating the discourse of human rights did not stem from the formal adoption of principles but from the state's capacity to implement them. Implementation hinged upon many factors: the agency of social and political actors in shaping the public agenda and the relationship between the state in its various functional branches and those social and political actors, elites, and organizations interacting in the public spheres reopened by re-democratization. Still, the ways of adoption of the discourse of human rights and human rights violations, closely connected with a political project and its ethical message, also implied the fragility of the discourse. The changes operated in society during authoritarian rule prompted only a partial endorsement of the discourse of human rights by the citizens of the Southern Cone countries. Whereas parts of these societies fundamentally accepted a commitment to human rights, for others the discourse of human rights was politically tainted with adversarial intent and as such was polarizing and unacceptable. For many observers, human rights had to be balanced with more general needs and constraints at the center of the public agenda.

Human rights policies after the restoration of democracy

Following the demise of the military governments in Argentina, Uruguay, and Chile, the possibility arose to restructure the public sphere in democratic terms. Doing so involved recognizing the centrality of legal principles, of basic human and civil rights, and of the possibility of autonomous action by citizens, even when such action is opposed to those in power. But, in tandem with the prospects of reshaping the basic parameters of public life, all the issues submerged during military rule, including human rights violations, came to the fore. The full extent of massive human rights violations was made public. The disclosure did not carry with it an acknowledgment of past deeds by the societal sectors involved in repression. It triggered a debate and confrontation around the legacy of human rights violations and around issues of justice, accountability, and attainment of public knowledge and acknowledgment. The confrontation with these issues opened a wide range of policy alternatives and created serious problems for the new democracies, as the public agenda was dominated by matters of principle that demanded political solutions, in which elements of contingency weighed heavily.

The experience of massive human rights violations was a critical issue at the center of the public agenda in the reconstituted democracies, as it remained a source of conflict and polarization. The political leaderships adopted policies aimed to overcome the contradictory pressures and made constant calls to national reconciliation, a rhetorical device used as a constructive political formula geared to move on in an orderly democratic life. The terrible lessons of past polarization had taught that democratic life requires consensual methods of conflict resolution, and by calibrating ethical demands with contingent pressures, the new democratic governments attempted to address yet also close the book on past human rights violations, in ways that varied from country to country.

Argentina had the broadest range of policy options, as the transition to democracy occurred following the defeat in the Malvinas/Falklands war. Alfonsín's government (1983–1989) adopted a sweeping policy for treating the country's legacy of human rights violations. This policy was carried out through parallel channels. First, an impunity law of self-amnesty issued by the armed forces before leaving power was revoked by a resolution of the Argentine Congress. Second, a "truth commission," the Comisión Nacional sobre la Desaparición de Personas (CONADEP; the National Commission on the Disappearance of Persons), was charged officially with clarifying the fate of the thousands of *desaparecidos*. Part of the Commission's report, published under the name of *Nunca más* (Never Again), adopted the version of the victims as an authoritative account.

Third, the government demanded that the Supreme Council of the armed forces put on trial members of the governing Juntas and other high-ranking officers responsible for conducting the "Dirty War" against the radicalized and mobilized sectors of society. As this mechanism failed, civilian courts took over the cases, judged them, and convicted the former rulers (albeit in a differentiated manner), in a legal procedure that was unprecedented worldwide and in a sense was even bolder than the Nuremberg trials, since in this case former heads of state and powerful actors were put on trial by fellow citizens. Fourth, a special governmental agency was created for dealing with human rights issues, and mechanisms were established to provide material compensation for the victims of repression.

The effect of these mechanisms of truth and justice, especially the trials, was diminished following a series of partial military upheavals. As a result of military pressure, a series of laws were adopted (the Full Stop Law of December 1986 and the law of Due Obedience of April 1987), that diluted the government's policy of exemplary trial and punishment. The process came full circle when in 1990 the following president Carlos Menem issued pardons for the convicted and, confronting hyperinflation and a difficult economic situation that redirected public interest away from human rights, declared the issue closed.

In Uruguay, the negotiated character of the democratic transition and its timing close to the start of the regressive phase in Argentina conditioned the policies adopted, which were designed to close the issue of past human rights violations completely. In December 1986 a Law of Expiry of the Punitive Pretension of the State was promulgated that basically stopped the possibility of bringing former repressors to justice, with some exceptions such as in cases of personal illegal profiting or the abduction of victims' newborn children. Following this legislation, different sectors of civil society used a provision in the Constitution to request a national referendum on that legislation. A two-and-a-half-year-long process of collecting signatures and campaigning for the ratification or the annulment of the law produced much mobilization on both sides. It also generated a prolonged discussion on the dilemmas of normative principles versus the constraints created by political contingency. In the referendum, conducted in April 1989, the forces interested in annulling the law were defeated by a very narrow margin. The results of the referendum were widely interpreted as signaling the end of the debate and the definitive closure of the issue, a situation that would be maintained until the mid-1990s.

In Chile, a transition controlled by the military limited the possibilities of treating the legacy of human rights violations comprehensively. The institutional authoritarian enclaves that the military retained through the 1978 Amnesty Law, the 1980 Constitution, and the organic laws of the 1980s, posed restrictions on such treatment after democratization. Witnessing the daring policies of Argentina that completed a regressive cycle and the policies of Uruguay, whose civilian administration's attempt to close the book without addressing the legacy of repression was widely contested by civil society, the new civilian president Patricio Aylwin (1990–1994) and his advisors adopted a middle ground policy. That policy involved obtaining "all the truth and as much justice as possible" within the legal constraints inherited from Pinochet's regime. Governmental policies comprised a series of parallel mechanisms: an official commission of inquiry to reveal the general and individual circumstances that produced loss of thousands of lives (the Commission of Truth and Reconciliation); symbolic actions to vindicate the victims and provide material reparations to their families; and trials in those cases not covered by the military amnesty. By revealing the truth that had been secluded until then, and by transferring whenever possible individual cases for the judiciary to prosecute, the public sphere remained open to pending institutional crises. Although trials were focused on individual responsibility, without demanding general accountability from the branches of the armed forces, their prosecution generated the closing of ranks around the accused according to the patterns of loyalty, internal cohesion, and discipline discussed above. The possibility also existed of individual trials raising the question of commanders' responsibility in a way that would eventually implicate the higher ranks (for detailed analyses see Barahona de Brito 1997; Loveman 1998; Roniger and Sznajder 1999, pp. 51–108). The seeds of future crises were thus imprinted in the pattern of addressing the legacy of human rights violations in Chile, just as in the other Southern Cone countries.

Crises and new confrontations with the past

The efforts of the political leaderships in Argentina, Chile, and Uruguay to move on did not preclude a series of consecutive repercussions centered on the legacy of human rights violations resonating again in the public sphere. The repercussions were of different weights, and, although in none of the cases did they shatter democracy, they reopened the debate and brought the issue of the authoritarian legacy once more to the center of the public agenda. The political leaderships could not easily brush aside these triggers by using rhetorical figures or by adopting measures of little substantive content. In each case, the developments pointed to the inconclusiveness of the previous institutional mechanisms for dealing with the human rights violations legacy. They reflected as well how the issue of human rights violations was compounded following democratization with the question of whether it was possible to change the format of relationships between the armed forces, on the one hand, and the state and civil society sectors, on the other.

The legacy of human rights violations erupted once more in the center of the public agenda in Argentina, Uruguay, and Chile more or less simultaneously, in 1995–1996. One such crisis erupted when retired Captain Adolfo Francisco Scilingo, an Argentine ex-Navy officer, made a series of public appearances and confessed in March 1995 to having participated in the operations leading to the "disappearance" of political prisoners in the years 1976–1977. According to Scilingo, the victims were sedated, flown in Navy planes to mid-ocean, and thrown alive into the sea with heavy burdens so that their bodies would not be recovered and brought ashore. The revelations reproduced in media interviews and numerous press reports and articles, precipitated an agitated debate, acts of remembrance and public demonstrations over the legacy of human rights violations, the fate of the *desaparecidos,* the nature of civil–military relations, and the significance of democracy. The debate involved wide circles of participants, from the political class, the military, and concerned NGOs, to intellectuals, the Church, and the public in general, leading to reviews of conscience and various assessments of institutional responsibility. A new generation, mostly unconcerned about the legacy of the military period until then, heard for the first time about that experience and was shocked as the previous generation had been shocked a decade earlier. Although the case did not change the development of the ongoing presidential electoral campaign, which was conducted mainly around the concern for macroeconomic stability, it threatened to recreate the confrontation and polarization over the legacy of human rights violations in the public sphere. The 1995 revelations also served as a prelude to the acts commemorating the twentieth anniversary of the military coup, which produced a wave of condemnation of the security forces' past policies. Concurrently, violent attacks were carried out against some of the former members of the security forces, known for their involvement in the repression.

The case resonated regionally, in Chile and Uruguay. In Uruguay, Jorge Néstor Tróccoli, a retired Navy captain and student of anthropology at the time, recognized that although he had not participated in the worst acts of torture and assassination, he had fought a war in which the armed forces "treated their enemies inhumanely," alluding to the torture, disappearance, and murder of many of them. The case renewed demands of accountability around the case of the assassination in Buenos Aires of Colorado Senator Zelmar Michelini, Speaker of the Chamber of Deputies Héctor Gutiérrez Ruiz, Rosario Barredo, and William Whitelaw, in 1976. Annual massive marches of protest demanding full justice in this case started in 1996, on the twentieth anniversary of the killings.

A feeling of unfinished business was becoming apparent. Indications of the regional character of the problem abounded through the revelations of the Letelier case and through other revelations on the DINA's activities outside Chile; the detention and trial of Enrique Arancibia, an ex-member of the DINA, detained in Buenos Aires for his implication in the assassination of General Prats and his wife in 1974 in that city; revelations in 1996 about the assassination in Buenos Aires of Michelini and Gutiérrez Ruíz; the disappearance – and probable assassination – of more than one hundred members of the Uruguayan opposition to the military as well as nearly eighty Chilean nationals in Argentina in the 1970s; the disappearance and assassination of Argentine members of the opposition to the Argentine military, in Uruguay. The authoritarian states had annihilated their enemies without regard for national borders or areas of jurisdiction, and thus whenever the issue of disappearances, torture, or assassination became critical in one country in the region after democratization, strong echoes resounded in the others. Against the background of partial knowledge of the truth and restricted acknowledgment of the process's implications, the revelations of former members of the security forces rekindled wide claims for justice, spearheaded by the NGOs and the families of the victims. The complexity of civil–military relations explains the extreme sensitivity to this issue on the side of the military. At that time, the armed and security forces rejected the possibility of opening their records or of providing the testimonies of those who were involved in acts against civilians, i.e., of those who know the fate of the *desaparecidos*. The high commands of the armed forces systematically declined having any information about the missing individuals.

Likewise, the international dimensions of repression have brought third countries outside the Southern Cone to play an active role in determining the fate of their own disappeared citizens or the character of acts of terrorism committed in their territory by security forces sent by the Southern Cone countries. The difficulties inherent in the Southern Cone at that time for suing military personnel implicated in serious human rights abuses (amnesty and impunity laws and pardons) reinforced by the late 1990s the symbolic and institutional import of judicial actions initiated in such countries as the USA, Spain, Sweden, Italy, or France. Illustrative were the trial held in France against Argentinian Navy captain Alfredo Astiz for his involvement in the disappearance and murder of two French nuns, Leonie Duquet and Alice Domon, in which he was found guilty and sentenced *in absentia* to life in prison; and the trial which opened in Spain in 1996 to determine the whereabouts of 320 missing Spanish citizens in Argentina during the dictatorship (Sznajder and Roniger 1999). But perhaps the most important event in this direction was the arrest of Pinochet in London in October 1998, in connection with a request of extradition issued by Judge Baltasar Garzón. While Pinochet was ultimately released to return and possibly be judged in Chile, the detention and the proceedings pending the decision by the British authorities established an international precedent that broke the rule of impunity and exposed the tensions between the principles of national sovereignty and of universal justice and accountability. While in the short term, the former prevailed in the Pinochet case, in an international dimension, the case and the commitment taken by Chilean authorities to hear the case within Chile opened the way to boost many investigations, and trials involving the former dictator or other officers opened in the following years.

The regional and transnational character of repression carried with it the possibility of an international treatment under democracy. Thus, the subject was publicly reopened time and again not only by developments within each country but also by developments taking place in other countries. Even though states resisted foreign judicial action by resorting to arguments about the defense of national sovereignty, the issue resurged in the Southern Cone, not necessarily triggered from within.

Since then, progress has been made in several areas. First, advances have been made toward a more comprehensive truth in the cases in which only partial truth had been accomplished in the past. Thus, in Uruguay, where no official commission of truth was established following re-democratization and only a NGO, El Servicio Paz y Justicia (SERPAJ), published an unofficial account based on partial data, President Jorge Batlle undertook in August 2000 to establish a Commission for Peace, aimed at clarifying the whereabouts of the disappeared and dispelling the increasing tension and incremental public debate. Under its limited mandate, the Commission could not require information from the armed forces or proceed to identify those guilty of human rights violations. Instead, when it drafted its final report in August 2003, the Commission had managed to gather up full or partial information on those Uruguayans who had been kidnapped, tortured, and killed in the clandestine centers in Uruguay and Argentina from 1971–1981. In its report, the Commission confirmed the abductions and publicly acknowledged that the Uruguayans who died under those conditions has been murdered after being tortured in military barracks, which then provided the justification for digging in military installations. The Commission's final report also included recommendations to the government, such as the need for full reparations to the families of the disappeared, the amendment of the Criminal Code to criminalize torture and enforced disappearances, and the establishment of an official body to continue the work on the forced disappearances. The government responded to the report of the Commission in April 2003, approving the conclusions of the Commission and creating an agency to continue its work. Furthermore, the government announced it would pay compensation to the families of the victims who died in detention centers during the military regime and to the victims of guerrilla violence, a move that still has not materialized. However, the impact of the Commission was partial. In public polls, one-third of those surveyed were unaware that the Commission had given its final report in 2003.

A second domain is that of legal accountability for past human rights violations. Even before the cancellation of restrictive laws, legal proceedings accelerated in Argentina and Chile against former senior officers in the armed and security forces accused of human rights violations. The proceedings involved cases of death, disappearance, and the kidnapping of children born in captivity or kidnapped along with their parents, as well as prosecutions for illicit enrichment related to disappearances and abuses of the repressive apparatus. In parallel, some Argentinean courts adopted an innovative mechanism, the so-called Trials for Truth, geared to find out the fate and remains of *desaparecidos*. Given the framework of laws of impunity in the 1990s, relatives of the victims and human rights organizations claimed their right to truth regarding the circumstances of the death of their relatives, as anchored in ancient traditions in the law of nations. On this basis, truth trials were opened in the city of La Plata and other parts of the country. In them, the testimonies of survivors of clandestine detention camps provided data on the fate of fellow prisoners murdered and disappeared and whose deaths were not registered either by Justice or in the CONADEP report. These trials also allowed for "memory leaks" of ecclesiastical figures, civil servants of the dictatorship, and members of the armed forces and police, on what they knew about the political prisoners, their detention, where they were housed, and how they met their death. The trials for truth enabled a new approach to elucidate the fate of the detained–disappeared and illegally executed during the military dictatorship, opening new ground on truth finding. Needless to say, all this created consternation in some sections of the armed forces and the police.

Legal proceedings were supplemented in the case of Argentina by subsequent legal changes, which resulted in the annulment of the laws of Final Point and Due Obedience in mid-2003, being one of the first issues addressed under President Néstor Kirchner, a move further sanctioned later on by Supreme Court decisions. In 2007, the Supreme Court also declared the non-constitutional status of the pardons issued by Menem in 1990. All this opened the ground for a large numbers of trials against former repressors. By January 2010, close to six hundred former members of the security forces were under judicial process and forty-four had been convicted. Attempts are currently being made to try to bundle cases in order to speed up the judicial proceedings. In neighboring Chile, judicial processes advanced within legal limitations, but led to over one hundred convictions by 2009, yet there were also cases of annulment of sentences by higher courts. In August 2000, the armed and security forces – who had participated in a Dialogue roundtable with the victims, an initiative of the Minister of Defense under President Lagos – formally made a commitment to provide information that would shed light on the cases of the disappeared. As the Chilean Congress approved legislation to protect the identity of persons who provide information about the disappeared, retired generals agreed to collaborate in the search. Some legal and social sectors supported the compromise, others refused. Anyway, jurisprudence led by the mid-2000s to accepting that systematic torture is a crime against humanity. The protracted character of the trials has led to debate, e.g., following expressions of uneasiness with the lengthy process by the then presidential candidate Sebastián Piñera in November 2009.

A third domain is that of human rights in the educational programs of these countries. Until the mid-1990s the trends of decentralization and privatization of the educational system affected this area, since it was left to each school to decide how to address the issue, thus leaving room for a replication of the polarized visions of the past that lingered widely in these societies. Moreover, a trend could be identified that disengaged the study of human rights – usually undertaken in these countries in terms of the legal normative, within the framework of civic studies – from the study of past human rights violations, addressed in history studies. This uncorrelated approach affected the feasibility of students learning from past atrocities and perceiving the centrality of human rights for safeguarding individual life and basic freedoms. Finally, outstanding publications such as those produced by the Service of Peace and Justice of Uruguay had very reduced distribution, once again reflecting the apathy that surrounded the topic until then.

This started to change in recent years. Once the laws of Final Point and Due Obedience were abrogated, the Argentine government decreed in 2003 that in the educational system March 24 – the day of the coup of 1976 – would be a day devoted to critical historical analysis of the coup and its aftermath and to honoring the memory of the victims of political violence and state repression. Also in the educational system, September 16 has been dedicated to the memory of the infamous "Night of the Pencils," when high-school students who had mobilized in the 1970s to have subsidized bus tickets were detained and disappeared in the city of La Plata; in August 2003 President Kirchner signed a resolution extending the subsidized school ticket to the first years of secondary education. By 2007 a collection of CDs was made available for schools, addressing issues such as children's rights and the right to identity in the context of human rights and recent Argentine history (educ.ar). At the university level, graduate programs of study have been launched, such as a Master's degree in History and Memory at the National University of La Plata, and several programs in Contemporary History at various universities, which have addressed the legacy of human rights violations academically. In Buenos Aires there is a research program on Collective Memory and Repression, under the leadership of Elizabeth Jelin and sponsored by the Social Science Research Council in New York, which has trained many young researchers (e.g., Jelin 2003). In Uruguay, SERPAJ has been publishing booklets and an e-magazine on Education and Human Rights for teachers, continuing the very important educational work it started with democratization.

A report by the Inter-American Institute of Human Rights (2005) on "Human Rights Education," which examines nineteen countries of Latin America that have subscribed to or ratified the Additional Protocol to the American Convention on Human Rights in the Area of Economic, Social, and Cultural Rights, known as the Protocol of San Salvador, notes a number of differences between the countries of the Southern Cone, but notes that in the 1990s there was great progress in the general laws of education as well as in the formulation of programs in human rights that went beyond schools to cover also the judiciary, the police and the armed forces, and the officials of various ministries.

Another crucial area is related to deepening the collective memory of society by recovering testimonies, through the establishment of sites of memory, the issuing of publications, holding of seminars and press interviews, celebrating anniversaries, launching exhibitions of plastic arts and photography, and launching media events, including film festivals on human rights. Thus, for instance, there has been a flourishing of publications of printed testimonies and establishment of sites by associations of former prisoners, relatives of victims, and human rights organizations. Outstanding has been the work of an Argentine network of several such organizations, which established an umbrella association, called *Memoria abierta* (Open Memory) aimed at presenting testimonies to the wider public, and in Uruguay, the work of a group of former female prisoners known as *Memoria para armar* (Memory to be Constructed), who in 2001–2004 organized workshops to elicit such testimonies, later to be published partially in book format. This was a part of a larger series to be deposited at the Center for Interdisciplinary Uruguayan Studies of the University of the Republic, as patrimony of the cultural and political analyses of the experience of repression (e.g., *Editorial Trilce* in Uruguay; *Editora al Margen* in Argentina; and *LOM Ediciones* in Chile). Likewise, international seminars have been conducted in various Southern Cone cities since the late 1990s, with the participation of local and foreign academics and activists, which have done much to disseminate the consciousness of human rights.

Equally important has been the renewed effort to construct monuments and sites enshrining and honoring the memory of the victims, and museums aimed at capturing historical lessons from the grim legacy of the past. Chile was the first country to construct a public monument in memory of the detained–disappeared victims and those executed for political reasons, with contributions from private and public sources. The monument, inaugurated in February 1994 near the main entrance in the General Cemetery of Santiago, consists of a thirty-meter-long, four-meter-high marble wall, in which the names of more than four thousand victims of repression are engraved, and surrounded by four huge heads in marble, intended to represent the absent dead. Both Uruguay and Argentina erected sites of memory later, in the 2000s, either for budgetary reasons or, as in the case of Argentina, since the leadership of a prominent NGO such as the Madres de Plaza de Mayo refused to accept the idea, seeing in it an attempt to confine the memory of their children, a memory they were trying to disseminate in society at large. Accordingly, in these two countries, there was a constant parallel struggle over safeguarding for public memory some of the sites that had served as centers of repression and torture during the dictatorship. Finally, in the 2000s there was quite an explosive expansion in sites of memory. Most salient perhaps in Argentina was the site of the former School of Mechanics of the Navy (ESMA), one of the most gruesome centers of repression. Located in a central avenue in the capital city, it was dedicated as a Museum of Memory in 2004, after much struggle and debate about its use both with the state and among human rights organizations. Since then it has been partially opened and is to be fully opened in 2010. A monument in memory of the victims of state terrorism was opened in 2007 in the Park of Memory by the River Plata, into the waters of which many of the victims were thrown from the air to die. A Museum of Memory is also to be launched in the city of Rosario. Likewise, Uruguayan civil society challenged official decisions about the use of locales that had served as detention centers during the dictatorship and, once democracy was restored, were reassigned according to the new government's priorities. Perhaps most notable is the case of the Detention Center Penal de Punta de Rieles, the principal detention center for women under the dictatorship, and later on headquarters of the School of the Uruguayan Army. The state authorized a project to use the property as a penitentiary in order to ease the overcrowding in prisons. Opposing such a move, residents of the area and the association of former female political prisoners were mobilized, receiving support from SERPAJ, writing and sending petitions to the President and suggesting alternative uses for the property: to create a lieu de memoire, a Museum of Memories engaged in the pursuit of peace, etc. That project, first suggested in 2003 and reactivated following the state's initiative, could be largely funded by the government of Barcelona, which considered it of great value in the recovery of historical memory. In parallel, the mayor of Montevideo inaugurated in November 2007 the Museum of Memory of Uruguay. Among its objectives is to bring in the new generations so that they learn the recent history of their country, in order to strengthen the sense of Uruguayan national identity. In Chile too, only recently such sites were established. Villa Grimaldi, a notorious torture center in Santiago, now hosts a museum dedicated to human rights, and in late 2009 a "Route of Memory – Santiago 1973–1989" was opened in the capital.

In September 2003, Chile commemorated the thirtieth anniversary of the military coup and widely deployed acts, reports, publications, and television programs, which presented to the public, especially the younger generations, a shocking and painful reality that largely had been kept outside the public realm. This stimulated discussion on the awareness of Chilean society to the legacy of authoritarianism thirty years after the coup. Moreover, in 2007 Chilean and Argentinean files on human rights violations were incorporated as part of the "Memory of the World" archives of UNESCO, highlighting their importance and reassuring their existence and accessibility for future generations.

However, the struggle over collective memory has not been the preserve of the groups defending human rights. Thus, for example, retired General Manuel Contreras, the former commander of the DINA, in 2001 published a book entitled *The Historical Truth – La Verdad Histórica. El Ejército Guerrillero* – emulating his commander-in-chief who had been publishing a series of books since coming to power. He also gave interviews to the print and electronic media and launched a website where he not only presented his version of historical events but also criticized judges conducting trials against members of the armed forces and security. However, none of this prevented General Contreras's conviction for decades-long prison terms, in various cases in which he was implicated for human rights violations.

As we move in time away from the events themselves, debate opens about the structuring of the memory of repression. This occurs along various analytical axes. One of note has been identified by Ludmila da Silva Catela (2001) in a work on testimonies of relatives of missing persons, which highlights the tension between the evidence and the concern of those interviewed to selectively present the facts as they are conscious of their role in externalizing and materializing a certain "historical truth." Another axis refers to the fundamental question of leadership in the recovery of collective memory, which reveals tensions and varied strategies around the fundamental question of the degree of legitimacy of those who reconstruct the past based on personal experience of the repression, as direct victims, and the "others." A third analytical axis refers to the growing debate about the discursive and interpretive relationship created by the background of violence before the repression and its construction in terms of collective memory and truth, which involves a projection into the field of human rights violations.

Linked to all this, there are several practical and discursive axes of debate that have threatened to fracture the human rights movement. One is the issue of reparations to the victims and relatives of the victims. Just as for years the topic broke the common front of human rights associations in Argentina, the rupture was reproduced in Chile in the 2000s, when the association of relatives of the First Region, established in Iquique – a place full of historical symbolism in the history of the popular struggles of the twentieth century – publicly expressed disagreement with the official actions that ignored the issue of reparations. Tired of a state policy that centralized the symbolic reparation and neglected the practical needs of the victims and their families, the association broke with the Socialist Party and joined the opposition forces, specifically the UDI, in spite of the fact that this party had been one of the political pillars of the regime during the dictatorship. The change in position of the UDI, proposing a political compromise to the issue of the missing persons, responded to the advances made in the courts, which raised a serious threat to the military. The fact that this question became important for one of the main political allies of Pinochet and the military was seen as a positive development that enabled them to open the impasse created by the failure to repeal the amnesty law of 1978.

Also neglected was the long-delayed treatment of those who suffered torture under the military governments, in Chile and elsewhere. Having been outside the mandate of the Rettig Commission, nothing was done until the 2000s in terms of medical and psychological treatment for the victims, thus becoming another axis that required public and governmental attention. A third axis opened to new political and public debate concerns exiles and their children born abroad, whether they should enjoy citizenship rights. Chile has granted such rights already. Finally, there is an analytical axis directed at placing the military repression in the political logic of genocide, highlighting the systematic nature of violations of human rights and the common features shared by the repressive apparatuses operated by these dictatorships, comparing them to the policies of collective extermination of the Nazis in the Holocaust.

Around these lines sharp debates have been generated with important consequences for the structuring of various claims and political projects, projecting anew onto the public agenda the collective memory of the brutal repression suffered under the Southern Cone military governments in the 1970s and 1980s.

New issues and concerns with human rights violations also emerged under democracy, as in other societies. The rights of indigenous peoples and the integrity of their activists were specially singled out for protection in Chile, while the annual human rights reports prepared by the Universidad Diego Portales in the late 2000s also point out problematic abuses of power by police forces dealing with other minorities, with prison inmates and immigrants. A case of forced disappearance took place in Argentina in September 2006, when Jorge Julio López, a former survivor of the concentration camps of the 1970s who had just given testimony in a criminal trial against a former chief of police implicated in past human rights violations, was forcibly abducted and vanished without a trace again, probably assassinated. In all the Southern Cone countries marginal sectors continue to be criminalized by both society at large and the police, the latter reflecting the expectations of a strong hand voiced by all social sectors threatened by a sense of rising or widespread criminality. In addition, the justice system has still to address efficiently past and more recent cases, particularly in Argentina, where the public keeps demanding justice in cases such as that of the unsolved investigation into the bombing of the Jewish community building of AMIA in July 1994, which left eighty-five citizens dead and many more wounded. Investigative journalists, intellectuals, and activists may still be targeted by individuals in positions of power, whom they criticize. Among the best known cases is that of writer and journalist Alejandra Matus, whose book *El Libro Negro de la Justicia Chilena* was taken off shelves and led the president of the Supreme Court of Chile to charge her with a "criminal act against public order" on the basis of a Law of State Security of Pinochet's time. This forced Matus, who in the 1980s had been threatened with death, to flee the country in 1999 and seek refuge in the USA, where she stayed until a new press law was promulgated in 2001. On the other hand, in recent years, human rights organizations have gained confidence, strength, and voice and, in parallel to official human rights agencies created by the states, continue to monitor the human rights situation in the Southern Cone countries in highly professional ways.

The partial resolution of the human rights violations legacy in the Southern Cone has generated a situation in which the issue is still alive more than two decades after the respective transitions to democracy. Although most sectors of society and a great part of the military and security establishments recognize the negative legacies and their impact, resolution and reconciliation have not been attained, especially in the case of direct victims and perpetrators. Further elaboration of the legacies in terms of history, memory, reparations, and justice still goes on, although the intensity of the reverberations of the past seems to be fading away.

References

Barahona de Brito, Alexandra. 1997. *Human Rights and Democratization in Latin America* (Oxford: Oxford University Press).

Barahona de Brito, Alexandra. 2009. "Integrating Perspectives: Transitional Justice and Memory Cycles." Paper delivered at the IPSA World Congress, Santiago de Chile, July.

Crocker, D. A. 1999. "Reckoning with Past Wrongs: A Normative Framework." *Ethics and International Affairs*, Vol. 13, pp. 43–64.

Falk, Richard. 2000. *Human Rights Horizons* (New York: Routledge).

Hayner, Priscilla B. 1994. "Fifteen Truth Commissions, 1974–1994: A Comparative Study." *Human Rights Quarterly*, Vol. 16, pp. 597–655.

Inter-American Institute of Human Rights. 2005. *Inter-American Report on Human Rights Education. A Study of 19 Countries*. San José de Costa Rica: Inter-American Institute of Human Rights. At: www.hrusa.org/workshops/HREWorkshops/usa/FullReportChile.pdf.

Jelin, Elizabeth. 2003. *State Repression and the Labors of Memory* (Minneapolis: University of Minnesota Press).

Keck, Margaret and Kathryn Sikkink. 1998. *Activists Beyond Borders: Transnational Advocacy Networks in International Politics* (Ithaca, NY: Cornell University Press).

Loveman, Mara. 1998. "High-Risk Collective Action: Defending Human Rights in Chile, Uruguay and Argentina." *American Journal of Sociology*, Vol. 104, No. 2, pp. 477–525.

Risse, Thomas, Stephen Ropp, and Kathryn Sikkink, eds. 1999. *The Power of Human Rights: International Norms and Domestic Change* (Cambridge: Cambridge University Press).

Roniger, Luis. 2009. "U.S. Hemispheric Hegemony and the Descent into Genocidal Practices in Latin America," pp. 23–43 in Marcia Esparza, Daniel Feierstein, and Henry Huttenbach, eds., *State Violence and Genocide in Latin America: The Cold War Years* (New York: Routledge).

Roniger, Luis, and Mario Sznajder. 1999. *The Legacy of Human Rights Violations in the Southern Cone* (Oxford: Oxford University Press).

Silva Catela, Ludmila da. 2001. *No Habrá Flores en la Tumba del Pasado* (La Plata, Argentina: EdAl Margen).

Skaar, Elin. 1999. "Truth Commissions, Trials: Or Nothing? Policy Options in Democratic Transitions." *Third World Quarterly*, Vol. 20, No. 6, pp. 1109–1128.

Sznajder, Mario and Luis Roniger. 1999. "The Crises Beyond Past Crisis: The Unsolved Legacy of Human Rights Violations in the Southern Cone." *Human Rights Review*, Vol. 1, No. 1, pp. 45–64.

Sznajder, Mario and Luis Roniger. 2009. *The Politics of Exile in Latin America* (Cambridge: Cambridge University Press).

61

Human rights in the African state

Bonny Ibhawoh

The modern African state is in many ways a product of the post-Second World War universal human rights movement. The end of the war in 1945 marked the beginning of an era of renewed international emphasis on the themes of freedom, democracy, and fundamental human rights. These ideas had direct impacts on independence struggles throughout the continent. Although nationalist demands for independence had been mounting in many parts of the colonized world for several years, the Second World War made self-determination a living principle for many in the non-European world. The Allied Powers led by Britain and the United States proclaimed self-determination and other fundamental rights as universally applicable and the guiding principles of Allied policy. The war was presented as a struggle for the ideals of freedom, democracy, and self-determination against the oppression and tyranny of Nazism and Fascism. The Atlantic Charter issued by Prime Minister Winston Churchill and President Franklin Roosevelt in 1941 famously declared that both leaders "respect the right of all peoples to choose the form of government under which they will live" and that they wished to "see sovereign rights and self-government restored to those who have been forcibly deprived of them" (Atlantic Charter, 1941). In Africa as elsewhere in the colonized world, nationalists demanded that these ideals of freedom and self-determination used to justify Allied war campaigns in Europe be also extended to them.

After the war, this discourse of universal human rights anchored on political self-determination was reinforced with the establishment of the United Nations and, specifically, the provisions of the UN Charter and the Universal Declaration of Human Rights. The UN Charter endorsed the right of self-determination of peoples while the UDHR articulated common human rights standards which all nations and peoples were to strive to promote and respect. Heralded as "a magna carta for all humanity," the adoption of the UDHR by the UN General Assembly in 1948 marked the international recognition of certain fundamental rights and freedoms as inalienable universal values to which all individuals are entitled simply by virtue of their humanity (UN 1997; Glendon 2002, p. 214).

The UDHR was significant in the global anti-colonial movements of the post-war period and, specifically, the emergence of independent states in Africa because it reinforced the right of self-determination. With its emphasis on political and civil rights and its affirmation that government should be based on the will of the people, the UDHR helped to legitimize long-standing struggles against colonial domination. Anti-colonial nationalist movements across Africa drew on an emergent language of universal human rights and took advantage of the new international emphasis on the political right to self-determination to demand independence from European colonial rule.

Balancing individual and collective rights

The dominant theme in anti-colonial nationalist discourse was the right to national self-determination which was seen as the starting point and indispensable condition for all other human rights and freedoms. Collective rights expressed in terms of the right of peoples to national self-determination took precedence over individual rights. The discourse on the collective right to self-determination which was instrumental to the nationalist struggle was less relevant to articulating individual rights within the context of the post-colonial state.

The assumption was that individual rights can only be fully achieved when the collective rights of nationhood and self-determination are attained. Nationalist movements in Africa as elsewhere in the colonized world tended to emphasize the collective rights of nations, ethnicities, and communities rather than individual human rights. In nationalist discourse, collective rights were often expressed in political rather than social or economic terms. Responding to critics who questioned his emphasis on political independence over economic and social development, Kwame Nkrumah the Ghanaian nationalist who became prime minister of the country urged his countrymen: "seek ye first the political kingdom and all other things shall be added unto you" (Nkrumah 1957, p. 146). The clear emphasis in anti-colonial nationalist politics was on collective political rights.

With independence in the 1950s and 1960s, however, the emphasis in human rights discussions in Africa began to shift from collective political rights to collective social and cultural rights. Once independence was attained, nationalists who became political leaders sought to articulate and practice both the collective rights of national peoples and the individual rights of citizens. However, many new governments stressed the collective right of the states and communities at the expense of individual political, social, and economic rights.

In practical terms, the central challenge was how to balance individual rights enshrined in international human rights regimes which these new countries had signed on to, and the collective rights of peoples which was considered crucial to nation building. There was recognition that national human rights standards had to be founded on universal human rights principles. But there was also awareness that in order to be relevant to the unique circumstances of new nations, universal human rights principles had to bear what one writer describes as the "African cultural fingerprint" (Mutua 2002, p. 2). An African cultural fingerprint would soften the rigid individualism of the international human rights regime by emphasizing the group, duties, social cohesion, and communal solidarity.

The quest for congruence or a common meeting point between cultural traditions and modern national and international legal standards has been a central question in legitimizing and enforcing human rights in the African state. In 1963, African leaders under the auspices of the Organization of African Unity (OAU) expressly affirmed their adherence to the UDHR in the OAU charter (OAU Charter, art. 2) and subsequently in the African Charter on Human and People's Rights. But in affirming this commitment, the African Charter also stresses the "duty" of the individual to serve his national community and "to preserve and strengthen positive African cultural values" (African Charter 1963, art. 29). This approach, which stresses both individual and collective rights and duties, is also evident in the legal and constitutional frameworks for human rights protection adopted by many African states.

Human rights in the post-colonial state

In the quest for congruence between universal human rights and local cultures, one goal of the national constitutions and applicable human rights laws in many African countries has been the establishment of a regime of minimal universal human rights standards founded on the diverse cultural and religious orientations of the people. Questions remain, however, as to how best to strike the delicate balance between the individual human rights standards guaranteed by the state and the collective cultural rights claimed by groups. Implicit in this is the tension and, sometimes, contradictions between the national human rights standards of state law and policies on one hand and the objective sociocultural traditions of peoples on the other. One instance of this is the conflict between the constitutional guarantees of gender equality in national constitutions and the traditional status of women in many African cultures. Another is the conflict between the constitutional guarantees of children's rights and pervasive cultural attitudes which condone early marriages, forced marriages, and child labor. Yet, a complementarity, if not an absolute congruence, of state laws and cultural norms is required if national human rights regimes are to gain grassroots acceptance.

There is an assumption that insofar as national human rights standards enshrined in national constitutions reflect the collective national conscience, they present a higher order of human aspirations with a more effective mechanism for promotion and enforcement. They also provide a higher set of standards by which the various cultural traditions can be judged. For this reason it is understandable that national human rights laws take precedence over customary or cultural practices, at least in theory. The principle of the supremacy of national constitutions ensures that in legal interpretation national human rights guarantees take precedence over any other laws or customary practices. This position is made clear in the South African Constitution, which provides expressly that "no law, whether as a rule of common law, customary law or legislation, shall limit any right entrenched in [the Constitution]" (South African Constitution, ch. 2, sec. 36.) Similar provisions of constitutional supremacy exist in other African constitutions.

The reality, however, is not quite as simple. Sometimes the constitution gives no indication whether fundamental rights supersede customary law or vice versa. For instance, previous or current versions of the Constitutions of Zimbabwe, Swaziland, and Botswana provide that the application of African customary law is not subject to the prohibition on discrimination contained in the constitution (Bennett 1995, p. 28). Thus, ambiguities remain over how to uphold national human rights standards in practice against the background of the prevalence and dominance of customary practices which conflict with these standards. It may be possible to talk about the complementarities between universal human rights standards and local cultural traditions where there are no direct conflicts between them. However, in cases where local cultures explicitly and fundamentally contradict universal human rights standards, the quest for congruence or complementarities becomes problematic.

National human rights provisions have not had full effect in many African states partly because cultural practices persist that have great limitations on constitutional human rights guarantees. Constitutional and legal forms for recognizing and protecting human rights manifest shortcomings that result from the continuing conflicts with "traditional" cultural definitions and practices. One possible explanation for this may be that the development of national human rights regimes in Africa has not often been grounded on cultural traditions. Therefore, we must seek further explanations in the continent's history.

To understand the social and political dynamics of the human rights experience in the post-colonial African state, it is necessary to begin in the colonial setting. It is within the colonial setting that the contemporary idea of legal rights as entitlement, which individuals hold in relation to the state, first emerged. In his study of human rights in Africa, Claude Welch argues that a number of political constraints on the exercise of human rights, which currently manifest in African states, can be attributed directly to the imposition of external rule. He identifies three main features of colonial rule that tended to hinder human rights (Welch 1984, p. 13).

First, the basic shapes of the states themselves were the consequence of European administrative convenience or imperial competition. Colonialism created states in which the promotion of self-government was, at most, a minor priority for the ruling powers until the last years of the colonial interlude. Little opportunity existed even after independence for redrawing the boundaries, helping to set the stage for political conflicts, ethnic tensions, and later attempts at secession. Second, an authoritarian framework for local administration was installed, reducing most indigenous rulers to relatively minor cogs in the administrative machinery and leaving until the terminal days of colonialism the creation of a veneer of democratization. Colonial administrative apparatus failed to foster the kind of inclusive and consultative governance that is the foundation for sustainable democracies. Third, European law codes were introduced and widely applied, notably in the urban areas, while traditional legal precepts were incompletely codified, relegated to an inferior position in civil law, and applied particularly in the rural areas. The result was a bifurcated state cut along the lines of urban-based, rights-bearing "citizens" on one hand and custom-bearing rural "subjects" on the other (Mamdani 1996, p. 19).

Legal recognition and protection of rights in the colonial states of Africa was belated and inadequate, with constitutions hastily created at independence being in many cases the first significant expression of them. Specific provisions dealing with human rights tended more or less to be importations of Western European models with scant attention paid to the need to focus on local initiative and input. In many African states, initial constitutional provisions were drawn overwhelmingly from patterns familiar to the departing colonial power, hence reflecting assumptions far more common in the metropoles of Europe than in particular African societies. Being externally imposed, some of these constitutions lacked popular support and legitimacy.

Based on all these factors, some writers have suggested that the roots of the dismal human rights records of contemporary African states, particularly at the formal public level, should be sought partly in their colonial experiences. Critics argue that the imposition of colonial rule and the authoritarianism that characterized it distorted the recognition and protection of human rights in traditional African societies (Adegbite 1968, p. 69; Wai 1980, pp. 115ff.). Their cultural traditions, they contend, remain relevant to the quest for a viable human rights regime in the continent. On the other hand, some have also suggested that the European colonial powers introduced new and more appropriate human rights norms, which suited the transition from the old feudal order to modern multi-ethnic nation states. While these contentions remain open to debate, it is helpful to note that the framework of law and rights brought by colonialism reflected Western liberal assumptions that often conflicted with traditional cultural orientations, such as those about the responsibilities of chiefs and the nature of judicial settlement. In many cases, these conflicts between colonial standards and local expectations were further amplified by the sheer diversity of the cultural orientations of the constituent ethnic nationalities being lumped together under single administrative units.

Since independence, many African countries have attempted to reverse these trends. Old colonial-engineered constitutions have been revised and, in some cases, entirely new ones drawn up to meet new national realities. Particular attention has been given to human rights. The human rights provisions in these new constitutions are often a reflection of the UDHR, the African Charter on Human and Peoples' Rights, and other international human rights covenants. In some cases, as in Burundi, the constitution goes as far as to declare that the rights and duties proclaimed and guaranteed by the UDHR, the international pacts relative to human rights and the African Charter are an integral part of the Constitution (Burundi Constitution 2005, art. 12).

However, the broadening of the scope of constitutional human rights guarantees has not adequately addressed the continuing tensions and conflict between these guarantees and prevalent customary practices that are inconsistent with them. On the one hand we have national human rights ideals eloquently articulated in national constitutions – sometimes in exactly the same words as the UDHR and other international human rights instruments. On the other hand we are confronted with cultural practices and notions of rights that reflect local world views (or at least those of the dominant groups within the society), which in turn conflict with national human rights standards.

National constitutions versus cultural traditions

In addressing the apparent tension between cultural traditions and state human rights aspirations, one approach adopted in many African countries' constitutions has been to make express provisions guaranteeing collective cultural and family rights alongside basic individual rights. The African Charter for Human and People's Rights exemplifies this trend. Apart from its provisions for individual duties, one of the unique features of this Charter is its articulation of the right of peoples to their cultural development. The Charter proclaims that individuals have a duty to preserve and strengthen African cultural values in their relations with other members of the society (African Charter, art. 15). Similar provisions exist in several African countries' constitutions. The Ethiopian Constitution, for example, declares that the state has a responsibility to preserve the nation's cultural legacies and to support "cultures and traditions that are compatible with ... democratic norms" (Ethiopia Constitution 1995, art. 41[9]). In Ghana and Uganda, the constitutions guarantee that every person is entitled to enjoy, practice, profess, maintain, and promote any culture *subject to the provisions of the Constitution* (Ghana Constitution 1992 ch. 5, sec. 26[1]; Uganda Constitution 1995, ch. 4, sec 37). In some cases, as in Ghana and Nigeria, the constitutions further spell out the cultural objectives of the state under the ambiguous heading of "Directive Principles of State Policy" (Nigeria Constitution 1999, ch. 2).

Besides guaranteeing cultural rights and duties, a related feature of many African constitutions adopted since independence is that they also seek to expressly prohibit cultural practices that conflict with national or applicable international human rights standards. The Ghanaian Constitution makes a proviso, under the same section that guarantees the right of individuals to profess and promote their culture, that "all customary practices which dehumanize or are injurious to the physical and mental well-being of a person are prohibited" (Ghana Constitution 1992, ch. 5). This is a reflection of the ways in which some African nations have attempted to grapple with the challenge of finding a balance between protecting collective cultural rights while still upholding national human rights standards. However, the articulation of cultural rights in national constitutions and the prohibition of some customary practices that conflict with national human rights standards has had only limited effect in actually resolving the inherent conflicts between national human rights aspirations and some dominant cultural traditions.

The conflict continues in the practice of forced marriages and child marriages, despite national legislation that guarantee children's rights and the right to freedom of association. It manifests in the dominant cultural notions of gender roles. In particular, it appears in the different forms of cultural prejudices against women, in spite of national constitutional guarantees of gender equality and state ratifications of the Convention on the Elimination of All Forms of Discrimination against Women (CEDAW) and the UN Declaration on Minorities.

Those often at the center of this conflict are women and children, the most vulnerable groups in any society. Indeed, as the African preparatory meeting for the Beijing Women's Conference concluded in its report on the conditions of women's rights, "constitutional rights [in Africa] are abrogated by customary and/or religious laws and practices" (UN 1994). Perhaps the most prominent manifestation of this is the practice of "female genital mutilation (FGM)" or "female circumcision," which remains quite prevalent in many new African nations despite extensive national and international legislation against the practice.

Differing paradigms of cultural legitimacy

Social anthropologists have long identified the ambivalence of cultural norms and their susceptibility to different interpretation as one of the defining features of culture. In his conflict theory of culture, Ralf Dahrendorf posits the existence of more than one consensus or value system in a culture. Dissent, conflict, and change are as much a part of the essence of culture as are integration and consensus; either set of characteristics becomes dominant or more evident under certain historical conditions (Dahrendorf 1959, p. 235). Typically, dominant groups or classes within a society seek to maintain perceptions and interpretations of cultural values and norms that are supportive of their own interests and reinforce their positions, proclaiming them to be the only valid view of that culture. Such powerful groups and individuals tend to monopolize the interpretation of cultural norms and are able to manipulate them to their advantage. In contrast, dominated groups or classes may hold, or at least be open to, different perceptions and interpretations of culture that are helpful to their struggles for control for justice and improvements for themselves. This type of internal struggle for control over cultural sources and symbols can be said to underscore contemporary discussions about the cultural legitimacy of human rights in Africa.

The process of lawmaking in most African states has been characterized by varied and contrasting positions on how best to uphold minimum universally accepted human rights standards while at the same time taking into consideration the cultural orientations of local peoples. In other words, this process concerns what appropriate steps should be taken in the effort to ground new national and applicable universal human rights standards on the cultural traditions of local peoples without adversely compromising either. Two contrasting perspectives to this process can be identified and each demands some elaboration. On one hand, there are male-dominated, urban-based elites whose perception of "cultural legitimacy" focuses on the idealized African traditions of collectivism, definitive gender roles, and conservative male dominance and interpretation of moral values. Their views of culture and tradition are often patriarchal. While they may be well disposed to the institution of the core humanistic ideals of the universal human rights regime within the state, these groups argue for the retention of more cultural initiative on issues of private social relations such as those concerning religion, the family, and morality. This may be termed the "conservative paradigm" of cultural legitimacy.

On the other hand, however, there are emerging and increasingly vocal groups, represented mainly by local women's groups and non-governmental organizations (NGOs) working for women and minority rights, who argue the implicit individualism of human rights and whose ideas of cultural legitimacy exclude the perpetuation of culture-based patriarchies and gender inequalities. They focus instead on themes such as traditional methods of conflict resolution, the centrality of the family in social life, and the reciprocal relationship between rights and duties. While they subscribe to the view that universal rights be given some form of cultural interpretation, they use universal human rights language with its emphasis on individual rights to critique present cultural practices that infringe human rights. This reflects a "dynamic paradigm" of cultural legitimacy.

The discourse on the cultural legitimacy of human rights in Africa has tended to focus more on the conservative paradigm of cultural legitimacy than on the dynamic paradigm. It has, for the most part, involved debates among the dominant male elites in African states over how to ground constitutional rights on prevailing cultural traditions. Until very recently, little had been heard from advocates of the dynamic paradigm. The reasons for this are not far-fetched. For one, human rights discourse in Africa has generally focused more on human rights violations at the male-dominated formal public sphere than at the informal private sphere. Second, marginalized and submerged groups such as rural women and minority groups lack the means, organization, and power to articulate their positions in national human rights discourse. One example of the dominance of the discourse on the cultural legitimacy of human rights at the level of the conservative paradigm comes from the constitutional debates in Nigeria in 1979.

As part of the process of drafting a new constitution to replace the old independence constitution in 1978, the fifty "wise men" who made up the Constitutional Drafting Committee (hereinafter CDC) were confronted with the problem of what to do with section 28 of the old Nigerian Constitution which dealt with the rights (or absence of them) of so-called "illegitimate children." By exempting from its human rights guarantees against discrimination "any customary practice in force," section 28 of the old Constitution exempted from the prohibition against discrimination in the bill of rights any law imposing disability or restriction on any person "having regard to the *special circumstances* pertaining to the persons to whom it is applied" (Nigeria Constitution 1966, sec. 28, cl. 2[d]). This provision effectively meant (and was interpreted by the courts to mean) Constitutional approval, or at least condonement, of pervasive cultural traditions across the country that discriminated against children born out of wedlock, particularly with regards to inheritance rights. This was clearly in conflict with the universal principle that "all human beings are born free and equal in dignity and rights" (UDHR 1948, art. 1).

After heated deliberations, the CDC succeeded in changing this legal position. In its report, it recommended omitting the old Constitutional proviso that allowed for discrimination under certain circumstances of birth from the new bill of rights. To avoid any ambiguities, the new Constitution expressly provided that "No citizen of Nigeria shall be subjected to any disability or deprivation merely by reason of the circumstances of his birth" (Nigeria Constitution, chap. 4, sec. 42). What is interesting, however, is the difficulty it took the CDC to reach this seemingly obvious and long overdue Constitutional amendment. Explaining the rationale for its decision, the Committee stated:

> Our decision was based on the grounds that it is unjust to accord an inferior status to persons who were not in any way responsible for the situation in which they found themselves. Some members were highly critical of this decision ... They pointed out that under Islamic law, a *bastard* [*sic*] has no right to the estate of his deceased putative father. They argued that the present draft contains a provision which is *repugnant to morality and that nothing of the sort can be found in the laws or constitution of any other state.* The majority of members however did not agree that Section 35(3) is in anyway immoral and they were satisfied that it is in accordance with equity and natural justice.
>
> *(CDR 1966, p. xvii)*

Twenty years later, discrimination against children on the basis of the circumstance of their birth and prevailing cultural and religious traditions persists across the country – a testimony to the fact that the objections made by some of the "wise men," hard as they are to justify, were not misplaced. For them, the cultural legitimacy of constitutional rights clearly means the perpetuation of traditional conservative communal notions of morality even if, as in this case, it compromises individual rights.

This kind of conservative and male-dominated paradigm of cultural legitimacy is also evident in the position of some African states in relation to the CEDAW, which has the dishonor of being the convention with the greatest number of reservations by state signatories. In the African context, the reservations are intimately linked with compromises and accommodation made by ruling elites regarding cultural traditions on the one hand and women's sexual rights on the other. Article 5 of the Convention provides that state parties shall take all appropriate measures to "modify the social and cultural patterns of the conduct of men and women, with a view to achieving the elimination of prejudices and customary and all other practices which are based on the idea of the inferiority or the superiority of either of the sexes or on stereotyped roles for men and women" (CEDAW 1979). Although several African countries have ratified the CEDAW, many have done so with extensive reservations and rejected some of its requirements. Malawi, for example, rejected some provisions with the explanation that:

> Owing to the deep-rooted nature of some traditional customs and practices of Malawians, the Government of the Republic of Malawi shall not, for the time being, consider itself bound by such of the provisions of the Convention as require immediate eradication of such traditional customs and practices.
>
> *(Jensen and Poulsen, 1993, p. 6)*

This conservative paradigm of cultural legitimacy stands in contrast to the more dynamic paradigm of cultural legitimacy, a situation that is itself a reflection of the fundamental conflict between the implicit individualism of human rights and the importance of collectivism and definitive gender roles in most African cultures. However, for the marginalized groups at the receiving end of culture-based inequalities (as are many African women), cultural legitimacy is conceived in a different sense. Women's groups in Africa, while campaigning against such cultural practices as "female genital mutilation," degrading widowhood rites, and discriminatory customary rules of inheritance, have emphasized the need for human rights work to focus more attention on traditional systems of support for women in the family. Additionally, they assert that human rights work should consider the reciprocal relationship between rights and social responsibilities and traditional methods of conflict resolution that emphasize more of reconciliation than retribution.

Across Africa, many women's NGOs seem to have arisen primarily from this need to respond more effectively to the new demands caused by the breakdown or unresponsiveness of traditional structures to new social realities. NGOs working for women's rights – whether in the form of church councils as in Swaziland, Kenya, and Namibia, or as groups of women lawyers in Ghana, Uganda, and Nigeria – have focused on a dynamic, critical, and selective interpretation of cultural legitimacy. In Ghana, for example, the national federation of women lawyers (FIDA) has consistently argued that customary legislation and practices in areas such as inheritance and maintenance of children no longer safeguard women in present-day urbanized African societies. In its view, change is urgently needed in this culture-based legislation. Yet in its counseling and advocacy FIDA-Ghana canvasses the employment of traditional methods of conflict resolution based on securing consensus.

In Swaziland, one of the dominant women's rights NGOs, the Council of Swaziland Churches (CSC), pushes for critical debate and uses the global human rights debate to criticize cultural practices that no longer safeguard women. However, the organization is always "careful to avoid bias against traditional systems" (Jensen and Poulsen 1993, p. 6).

For these groups, cultural legitimacy of human rights is conceived more in terms of providing traditional economic security and support for women and families rather than recognizing culture-based gender roles in national human rights legislation.

Indeed, at the core of this apparent conflict between the paradigms of cultural legitimacy is the fact that the realities of present-day African societies, particularly in the urban areas, are characterized by the destabilization and breakdown (without effective alternatives) of traditional models of rights and support in the family. While traditional notions and institutions survive in appearance and prestige, and thus provide a basis for the continued calls for African states to ground human rights on them, they are largely emptied of their former economic and social content. The dilemma of the African state today is that the community and extended family are no longer able to play their social welfare roles, while the state is not yet able to replace them in doing this. Put differently, cultures are no longer able and constitutions are not yet able. Under such circumstances of social change and need, groups and individuals are beginning to apply different interpretations and strategies of cultural legitimacy depending on their interests and relative power. Thus while cultural relativists and the male-dominated groups of African elites have sought to maintain cultural legitimacy by tempering the modern content of human rights (as enshrined in national constitutions with a broad range of cultural norms and values), other less-prominent groups have been more critical and selective.

Making compromises: reconciling culture and constitution

Dominant groups or classes within society will continue to maintain perceptions and interpretations of cultural values and norms that are supportive of their own interests, proclaiming them to be the only valid view of that culture. Dominated groups, on the other hand, may hold, or at least be more open to, different perceptions and interpretations that are helpful to their struggle to achieve justice for themselves. This is typical of the internal struggle for control over the cultural sources and symbols of power within any society (An-Na`im and Deng, 1990, p. 20).

In spite of these realities, there is a real and urgent need to seek acceptable ways of ensuring the cultural sensitivity and legitimacy of national human rights regimes. In so doing, it is important to secure the agreement and cooperation of the proponents of cultural legitimacy's counter position in choosing and implementing national human rights standards. To harness the power of cultural legitimacy in support of national human rights standards, African states need to develop techniques for internal cultural discourse and cross-cultural dialogue. In addition, they must work toward establishing general conditions conducive to constructive discourse and dialogue. This approach assumes and relies on the existence of internal struggles for cultural power within society. Further, it encompasses the realization that certain dominant classes or groups would normally hold the cultural advantage and proclaim their view of culture as valid, while others will challenge this view, or at least desire to do so.

Thus, it is important to create space for a dialogue between weaker and stronger groups within the cultural community and society at large. Legitimizing national human rights standards requires recognition and cultivation of this dialogue. Women and minority groups must be able to dialogue over interpretations of cultural values with politicians, officials, traditional leaders, and family heads in both the rural and urban areas. If respect for human rights is to be achieved and made sustainable, human rights must reside not only in law but in the living and practiced culture of the people. There is a need, therefore, for dialogue among groups with different paradigms of cultural legitimacy on what role culture should play in legitimizing national human rights regimes within African states. What is advocated is some form of "cross-paradigmatic" approach to the quest for national consensus on the ways to enhance cultural legitimacy. Ideally, the object of such internal cross-paradigmatic dialogue would be to agree on a range of cultural support for national human rights, in spite of disagreements on the justification of those beliefs. While total agreement on cultural interpretation and application to human rights may not always be achieved, it is essential to keep the avenues for dialogue open.

In addressing the conflicts between national human rights standards and dominant cultural orientations, it is useful to bear in mind that national constitutional human rights provisions are not meant to regulate every aspect of human action within the society. They do not mandate specific social attitudes. Rather, they represent broad standards, ideally arrived at by consensus on which rights are considered fundamental within the state. Thus, national human rights provisions should still give room for cultural expression. In some cases, cultural communities within the state should still retain some latitude over how to implement these rights. For example, the constitutional right to freedom from discrimination on the grounds of gender may be a fundamental right, but there remains a margin of cultural interpretation as to what constitutes gender discrimination. Here, social and cultural contexts are crucial. The tradition in many African societies that stipulates that women may not hold certain traditional titles and offices or chieftaincy positions is no more an expression of gender discrimination than the rule among Catholic Christians which bars women from becoming priests. Such traditions become problematic when extended beyond the realms of culture and religion to imply the exclusion of women from public offices.

The point here is that to be effective, national human rights guarantees must allow for some form of cultural expression and initiative. Indeed, the same analogy can be made between national human rights provisions and international agreements. International human rights agreements are not meant to resolve controversial clashes over rights within individual societies nor do they mandate specific social policies. They are merely widespread agreements about what rights are fundamental, and countries retain great latitude over how to put these rights into practice.

In the same way, rather than seeking to prescribe new rules for social relations within cultural communities, national human rights laws should aim at successfully promoting human rights within the prevailing cultural attitudes and institutions. The challenge is to seek ways in which cultural practices through change, adaptation, and modification can be made to serve as a complement rather than a constraint to specific national human rights aspirations. In doing this, it is not enough to identify the cultural barriers and limitations to modern domestic and international human rights standards and to reject them wholesale. It is also not enough to attempt to uphold national human rights standards over these cultural traditions merely by legislative or executive fiats. It is more important to adopt a holistic and sensitive approach that seeks to understand the social basis of these cultural traditions and how cultural attitudes may be changed and modified to complement or at least conform to basic human rights standards. Such change and integration must be done with local initiative and involvement in a way that does not compromise the cultural integrity of the people. Local people and cultural communities must feel a sense of ownership of the process of change and adaptation.

Unfortunately, such processes of cultural change through local initiatives have not been common. In many African nations, human rights have merely been decreed from above through constitutional and other legal provisions, while cultural orientations and practices have been expected to conform by legislative fiat with these new human rights standards. Culture evolves, however, rather than transforms and the process of evolution is painstakingly gradual and complex. Cultural practices, being a reflection of collective social strength, acts as a framework by which self-interest is defined and realized within each community. Therefore, the cultural legitimacy of rights cannot be deduced or assumed from the mere fact that existing formal documents officially recognize the claim as a human right.

Beyond law: cultural reinvention

Many African states have demonstrated a willingness to introduce legislation holding national human rights above customs and cultural traditions where conflicts arise. However, their experiences show that formal legislative enactments alone cannot change pervasive cultural attitudes. Moreover, formal legislation alone cannot resolve the conflict between cultural traditions and national human rights standards. In the case of FGM, legislation has proven effective only where it has been integrated into other aspects of a comprehensive eradication strategy.

In several African countries where FGM legislation exists, it is not enforced for fear of alienating certain power bases or exacerbating tensions between practicing and non-practicing communities. No African country that has banned FGM, including Senegal, Egypt, Ghana, and Burkina Faso, dares enforce the law. Law by itself has not and cannot eliminate the influence of harmful customs nor remedy harmful traditional practices. The major constraint remains limited enforcement capacity particularly at local levels. In Guinea, FGM carries the death penalty but it has never been applied (*Economist* 1999, p. 45). Early attempts to enforce legislation against FGM in Sudan caused such popular outcries that enforcement was subsequently abandoned. In Burkina Faso, which incorporated a prohibition of FGM into its Constitution and prosecuted practitioners in connection with the deaths of young girls during female circumcision ceremonies, it soon became clear that criminalizing practitioners and families only succeeded in driving the practice underground and creating an obstacle to outreach and education (Jones *et al.* 1999, p. 219).

These experiences and others elsewhere have shown that in order for legislation to be effective it must be accompanied by a broad and inclusive strategy for community-based education and awareness-raising. Conflicts between cultural practices and national human rights standards as exemplified in the case of FGM need to be addressed from a holistic and coherent standpoint, which locates the problem within three interrelated frameworks – public health, cultural reorientation, and human rights. To be effective, such programs must necessarily involve local communities as changes in cultural attitudes and orientations can only be meaningful and sustainable if they come from within these local communities.

This approach to the problem of FGM would appear to have worked quite well in Kenya where some local communities have successfully introduced "alternative circumcision rites" to replace old traditions. Under the new procedure arrived at through communal dialogue and consensus, the people within these communities agreed to do away with the physical mutilation of the woman's body during the traditional female circumcision rites while retaining other harmless aspects of the circumcision rites (Mwakisha 1991). It responds to concerns by local peoples for whom such circumcision rites are central to socialization. For them, blanket abolition of the practice means losing important celebrations that endorse their identity and value.

The "alternative circumcision rites" initiative was the result of meetings among some Kenyan mothers seeking alternative ways to usher their daughters into womanhood without subjecting them to the ordeal and hazards of "facing the knife." The new rite of passage known as *Ntanira na Mugambo*, or "circumcision through words," uses a week-long program of counseling capped by community celebration and affirmation in place of the former practice. During the celebrations, which still include the traditional period of seclusion, the adolescent girls are taught the basic concepts of sexual and reproductive health and are counseled on gender issues and other customary norms. The modified rite includes all the meaningful aspects of the traditional ritual but "leaves the cut out" (Eliah 1999, p. 31). As a way of legitimizing the new procedure, the girls receive certificates certifying that they have undergone the traditional rites into womanhood (Reaves 1997). These innovations have produced hopeful results where previous efforts have failed. In one of the communities where the alternative circumcision rites were introduced and where about 95 percent of the girls previously had to undergo circumcision, the rate of FGM is estimated to have gone down to 70 percent (Achieng 1998).

A similar ritual by which the girl is declared a woman without being maimed is now carried out in parts of Uganda. The case of Uganda is particularly interesting because the new ritual was promoted not only by the women themselves but also by male elders in the clan who formed an Elders Association for the purpose of discussing changes to this and other cultural traditions (Chelala 1998, p. A23). This is an example of the "cross-paradigmatic" consensus of both the conservative and dynamic paradigms of cultural legitimacy being used to resolve the conflicts between cultural traditions and national human rights standards. Such cross-paradigmatic consensuses can be further explored in addressing other culture-based human rights violations in traditional widowhood rites and mourning taboos, child betrothals, and forced marriages.

Although the alternative circumcision rites initiative in Kenya and Uganda still faces some opposition, it is an example of the process of community involvement in advocacy, information, education, legislation, and policy formulation. This community involvement offers the best prospects for a culturally sensitive solution to resolving the conflict between national human rights and cultural traditions. Such initiatives may not always offer concrete results or guarantees of success, but they represent a creative and promising approach to resolving real and serious human rights issues.

These debates about modifying cultural practices to conform with modern rights standards are not exclusive to Africa or the "traditional" developing world. In Spain, a similar debate has raged in the past decade about modifying the centuries-old blood sport of bullfighting to conform with modern animal rights standards. As with the FGM debate, some advocates for reform have argued for a "reinvention" of the sport rather an outright ban. As one Spanish official put it, such cultural reinventions that reflect "more advanced values" are necessary to achieve a "dignified and respectable society" (Minder 2010). Indeed, in an age of rights, societies must continually seek to reinvent traditions through debates and dialogues to meet changing expectations. The model of cross-paradigmatic dialogue that this chapter advocates offers some directions on how societies can best undertake cultural reinventions to meet modern rights standards.

Conclusion

The efforts at ensuring the cultural legitimacy of human rights in the African state must begin with a proper understanding of both the general nature of the tension between national human rights regimes and cultural traditions and the internal tensions between contending paradigms of cultural legitimacy. Every cultural tradition contains some norms and institutions that are supportive of some human rights, as well as norms and institutions that are antithetical or problematic in relation to other human rights. Because respect for human rights is fostered by reason as well as by experience, a constructive approach to promoting human rights is to seek ways of enhancing the supportive elements of culture while redressing the antithetical or problematic elements in ways that are consistent with the cultural integrity of the tradition in question and the contending groups within it. It is counterproductive to attempt to enhance the awareness of human rights within any culture in ways that are unlikely to be accepted as legitimate by that culture or significant groups within it.

The promotion of national human rights standards against the background of the dominant cultural and social traditions in the state should be done with due respect to meritorious cultural values and traditions of local communities. The interplay between national human rights standards on one hand and local cultural orientations on the other should be a dynamic process of give and take, ideally through persuasion and dialogue, with legislation serving only to complement this process. What is advocated here is a two-way system of cross-fertilization in which cultural systems continually fertilize, and are fertilized by, national and universal social and legal standards. In this way, the gap between national human rights provisions and cultural orientations can be narrowed and constitutional rights can derive their legitimacy not only from state authority but also from the force of cultural traditions.

References

Achieng, Judith. 1998. "Ending the Nightmare Passage to Womanhood." At: http://www.woza.co.za/africa/womano.htm.

Adegbite, Latif O. 1968. "African Attitudes to the International Protection of Human Rights." In Asbjørn Eide and August Schou, eds., *International Protection of Human Rights: Proceedings of the Seventh Nobel Symposium*, Oslo, 1967 (New York: Interscience Publishers).

African Charter on Human and People's Rights. 1981. At: http://www.achpr.org.

An-Na`im, Abdullahi Ahmed and Francis M. Deng, eds. 1990. *Human Rights in Africa: Cross-Cultural Perspectives* (Washington, DC: Brookings Institution).

Atlantic Charter. 1941. At: http://www.nato.int.

Bennett, T. W. 1995. *Human Rights and African Customary Law under the South African Constitution* (Cape Town: Juta).

Burundi Constitution. 2005. At: http://unpan1.un.org/intradoc/groups/public/documents/CAFRAD/UNPAN004624.pdf.

CDR. 1976. *Report of the Constitution Drafting Committee* (Lagos: Nigerian Federal Ministry of Information).

CEDAW. 1979. United Nations Convention on the Elimination of All Forms of Discrimination against Women. Adopted 18 Dec. 1979, G.A. Res. 34/180, U.N. GAOR, 34th Sess., Supp. No. 46, U.N. Doc. A/34/46 (1980).

Chelala, Ceser. 1998. "New Rite is Alternative to Female Circumcision." *San Francisco Chronicle*, 16 Sept.

Dahrendorf, Ralf. 1959. *Class and Class Conflict in Industrial Society* (Stanford, CA: Stanford University Press).

Economist. 1999. "Female Genital Mutilation – Is it Crime or Culture?" Feb. 13.

Eliah, Elaine. 1999. "In Uganda, Elders Work with the UN to Safeguard Women's Health." *UN Chronicle*, Vol. 36, No. 1, pp. 31–33.

Ethiopia Constitution. 1995. At: http://www.africa.upenn.edu/Hornet/Ethiopian_Constitution.html.

Ghana Constitution. 1992. At: http://www.parliament.gh/constitution_republic_ghana.html.

Glendon, Mary Ann. 2002. *A World Made New: Eleanor Roosevelt and the Universal Declaration of Human Rights* (New York: Random House).

Jensen, Marianne and Karin Poulsen. 1993. *Human Rights and Cultural Change: Women in Africa* (Copenhagen: Danish Institute for Human Rights).

Jones, Heidi, N. Diop, I. Askew, and I. Kaboré. 1999. "Female Genital Cutting Practices in Burkina Faso and Mali and Their Negative Health Outcomes." *Studies in Family Planning*, Vol. 30, No. 3, pp. 219–230.

Mamdani, Mahmood. 1996. *Citizen and Subject: Contemporary Africa and the Legacy of Late Colonialism* (Princeton, NJ: Princeton University Press).

Minder, Raphael. 2010. "Looking for Wedge from Spain, Catalonia Bans Bullfighting." *New York Times*, 28 July. At: http://www.nytimes.com/2010/07/29/world/europe/29spain.html.

Mutua, Makau. 2002. *Human Rights: A Political and Cultural Critique* (Philadelphia: University of Pennsylvania Press).

Mwakisha, Jemimah. 1991. "Alternatives to FGM that Are Working." *Daily Nation* (*Kenya*), 14 April.

Nigeria Constitution. 1966 (Lagos: Federal Ministry of Information).

Nigeria Constitution. 1999 At: http://www.nigeria-law.org/ConstitutionOfTheFederalRepublicOfNigeria.htm.

Nkrumah, Kwame. 1957. *Ghana: The Autobiography of Kwame Nkrumah* (New York: Nelson).
OAU Charter. 1963. At: http://www.africa-union.org.
Reaves, Malik Stan. 1997. "Alternative Rite to Female Circumcision Spreading in Kenya." *Africa News Service*. At: http://www.hartford-hwp.com/archives/36/041.html.
South African Constitution. 1996. At: http://www.info.gov.za.
UDHR. 1948. Universal Declaration of Human Rights. Adopted 10 Dec. 1948, G.A. Res. 217A (III), U.N. GAOR, 3d Sess. At: http://www.un.org/en/documents/udhr/index.shtml.
Uganda Constitution. 1995. At: http://www.ugandaonlinelawlibrary.com/lawlib/constitution.asp.
United Nations. 1994. Draft African Platform for Action, Fifth African Regional Conference on Women, Dakar Senegal, 16–23 Nov., Doc. E/ECA/ACW.V/EXP/WP.6/Rev.4.
United Nations. 1997. Press Release GA/SHC/3421. "Legislation Not Enough to Overcome Cultural Attitudes, Practices Inhibiting Equal Treatment for Women, Third Committee Told." At: http://www.un.org/News/Press/docs/1997/19971023.GASH3421.htm.
Wai, Dunstan M. 1980. "Human Rights in Sub-Saharan Africa." In Adamantia Pollis and Peter Schwab, eds., *Human Rights: Cultural and Ideological Perspectives* (New York: Praeger).
Welch, Claude, E. Jr. 1984. "Human Rights as a Problem in Contemporary Africa." In Claude Welch and Ronald Meltzer, eds., *Human Rights and Development in Africa* (Albany: State University of New York Press).

Index

Page numbers in *Italics* represent tables; page numbers in **Bold** represent figures.